Ranking the '70s

Ranking the '70s

A Complete Compilation of the Chart Songs and Acts from Pop's Eclectic Decade

Dann Isbell & Bill Carroll

From the pages of
Cash Box

Ranking the '70s:
A Complete Compilation of the Chart Songs and Acts from Pop's Eclectic Decade
Copyright © 2015 Dann Isbell & Bill Carroll

Published by Jefrian Books, LLC
Dallas, TX

All rights reserved. No part of this book may be reproduced (except for inclusion in reviews), disseminated or utilized in any form or by any means, electronic or mechanical, including photocopying, recording, or in any information storage and retrieval system, or the Internet/World Wide Web without written permission from the authors or publisher.

Chart, chart positions and Cash Box logo copyright © 1970/79 by Cash Box magazine used by permission of Cashbox Magazine, Inc., 82 McFadden Lane, Ridgeway SC 29130

To contact the authors, please visit their website at
www.ranking-the-70s.com

Cover design by Arbor Books, Inc. and Lighthouse24

Printed in the United States of America

Ranking the '70s: A Complete Compilation of the Chart Songs and Acts from Pop's Eclectic Decade
Dann Isbell & Bill Carroll

1. Title   2. Author   3. Popular Music/History

Library of Congress Control Number: 2015949910

ISBN 10: 0692517790
ISBN 13: 978-0692517796

Praise for Ranking the '60s and Ranking the '70s

"Dann Isbell captured a true representation of every records' chart performance with his first book, *Ranking the '60s*. Now he and Bill Carroll have done it for the '70's. Our memories may fade…and radio has certainly done its part to bias history by limited selection for airplay…but the facts don't lie…every record that made the *Cash Box* charts from 1970–1979 is accounted for here, based on its actual chart performance at the time. It simply doesn't get more accurate than that."
--Kent Kotal / ForgottenHits.com

"The 70s was a great time of coming together in popular music. It was Eagles…and Al Green…and Elton and Barry and Cher…the Jackson 5…James Taylor…all happening at once. It was an honor to play it all on my radio show…and, now, it's a treat to sit back and read about how it all stacked up. Thanx Cousins Dann and Bill. I really appreciate your numbers. Well Done."
--"Cousin" Bruce Morrow / Host of *Cousin Brucie's Saturday Night Party* and *Cruisin' with Cousin Brucie* on SiriusXM Satellite Radio and author of *Rock & Roll…And the Beat Goes On*.

"Isbell takes a fresh look at the charts and ranks every song with precision…from the ones you missed to the ones you can't forget. Isbell's exhaustive research shines new light on this rich facet of '60s culture for fans and music scholars alike. This is very well done."
--Dave McAleer / Music consultant, (UK) Official Chart Company

"Dann Isbell has created an excellent ranking of '60s hit records and their performers based on a logical, well-thought-out point totaling system that puts all the widely varying years of the '60s decade on a more level playing field. It's interesting to compare this to the non-biased favorite song countdowns done in more recent times to see how some songs gain in popularity over the years while others just simply fall off the radar screen. I can't wait to dig in to *Ranking the '70s* to see how the favorites and the forgottens from that decade rank. These books are the perfect references and playlists for my internet show."
--Bob Radil, / Host, *The 60s/70s Show*, Rewound Radio

"The research is meticulous. The presentation is outstanding. Dann Isbell has placed the '60s under a microscope and exposed the obvious and obscure with equal precision. To those of us who grew up in this decade, he has encapsulated our musical lives perfectly."
--Ron Smith / Radio programmer and author of *Chicago Top 40 Charts*

To Casey Kasem

And now...on with the ranking....

CONTENTS

Foreword xi
Preface: Yes We Can Can..xiii
Introduction: Them Changes xv

Section 1
Ranking the Songs 1
An ordered listing based on chart performance of every song title to have peaked on *Cash Box*® magazine's Top 100 singles charts in the 1970s, along with its act, peak week and record label.

Section 2
Ranking the Acts 137
An ordered listing for the decade of every act to have peaked with one or more songs on *Cash Box* magazine's Top 100 singles charts in the 1970s, arranged according to total points for all songs for each act.

Section 3
Act Index 172
An alphabetical listing of all 1,698 acts whose songs peaked on the *Cash Box* magazine Top 100 singles charts during the 1970s, organized by configuration--soloists, duos and groups--along with their Top 100 entries ranked by order of chart performance.

Section 4
Song Title Index 273
An alphabetical listing of all 5,350 song titles that peaked on the *Cash Box* magazine Top 100 singles charts during the 1970s, together with their ranking for the decade.

Section 5
Appendix 313
The Scoring System Explained 314
Top 300 Songs of Each Year 321
300 High Intensity Singles 353
Records Charting Only on the Cash Box Top 100 357
The No. 1s 360
Fastest and Slowest Records to No. 1 364
Chart Singles of 25 Weeks or More 365
Records in Top 1000 by Natural Score Charting Fewer Than 14 Weeks 366
Highest Entries 368
Highest Exits 369
The Top 150 One-Hit Wonders 371
The Act Intensity Index 373
Acts Appearing on 50 or More Weekly Charts 377
Acts with 50 or More Consecutive Chart Weeks 379
No. 1s by Act 380
Two-Sided Winners 382
Record Labels of the '70s 385
About the Authors 386

Foreword

I am honored that Dann chose me to write this foreword, but honestly, it makes a lot of sense because Dann and I have so many things in common, including a passion for music, collecting charts, and a fascination for the process of how songs become hits. In essence, Dann and I are doppelgangers living completely different lives--Dann as a university linguistics teacher living in Taiwan and me working for iHeartMedia living here in Massachusetts, with lives both consumed by music and charts.

I first met Dann after my Top 1000 songs of all time for Los Angeles was printed in Warner Bros.' *Circular* magazine in 1972 and a national top hits list was printed in *Rolling Stone* in 1973. I contacted Dann back in 1973 after I read an article about his American Top 1300 in the Riverside *Press–Enterprise*. I was truly amazed that there was anyone else who loved music charts as much as I did and who was passionate enough to create a listing of the all-time biggest pop hits. Amazingly, both of us were driven to our passion for music and charts because we were both living in the Los Angeles area and had both discovered a new radio station that took our interest and turned it into a love affair of music and radio in the same year, 1965.

That station was 93 KHJ "Boss Radio"-Los Angeles which became the #1 hit music station in LA within a year and is considered by many experts to be the greatest radio station of all time.

KHJ was launched by two radio legends-to-be: consultant Bill Drake and Program Director Ron Jacobs. KHJ inspired the two of us to create lists of the biggest hits as Ron Jacobs and Betty Breneman, KHJ's music director, created the Top 93 of 1965 and, in 1966, the Top 300 of all time. Entranced by these countdowns, we became inspired to begin exploring the hit music process through music charts.

In response to a letter, Ron explained to me how their year-end charts were created and based on an inverse aggregate--or reverse rank--scoring system for the Boss 30 weekly hits. KHJ basically awarded 30 points for #1, 29 for #2, etc, then summed the points for each week to calculate a song's "chart life" score. Songs were then ranked.

That algorithm also formed the basis of calculating which songs were the biggest hits of any year and decade and, of course, the biggest hits of all time for the charts that Dann and I built. Now this method has been refined with a vastly improved algorithm.

The aforementioned Betty Breneman helped me get my first radio job at KRTH back in 1973 and I have been in radio for 42 years. My passion for the hit music process continued as a programmer and radio consultant, and that passion led me to write yearly articles about the Music Cycles and its three phases: Birth (Pop phase), Extremes and Doldrums.

Basically, the biggest hits change as the taste pendulum swings back and forth to reflect the cyclical growth and decay in popularity of Rock and Pop and R&B. It's a phenomenon with those phases in the same order that has repeated every ten years since the dawn of rock & roll. The genres and subgenres of the '70s, as described in the Introduction to *Ranking the '70s*, and as shown in the truly unusual graph in the endnote illustrate that theory nicely.

Dann stayed focused on his love affair with the music charts and continued pursuing his dream to create better and more accurate rankings of the hits. This tireless dedication has resulted in two fascinating books, *Ranking the '60s* and in collaboration with accomplished technician, Bill Carroll, this, his newest book, *Ranking the '70s*.

These amazing books provide a complete ranking of every single charting record of the decade. Also, Dann uses his highly accurate algorithms to rank all of the acts of each decade.

Both books are a must read for any fan of music, any chart collector, or anyone in any walk of life who loves pop culture and pop music from those decades.

Guy Zapoleon
SVP Programming Research and Strategy
iHeartMedia

Preface

Yes We Can Can

It is not at all uncommon for collaborations to be the product of a fortuitous meeting. Paul McCartney's introduction to John Lennon at the Woolton Parish Church Garden Fete may be the most famous example among writers. But it is quite exceptional for such collaborations to occur over a span of 7,700 miles as this one did.

In 2013, Bill decided to finally start a project that had been on his mind for nearly 20 years--how to use the data reduction methods he learned as a physical scientist to evaluate and compare records and acts. To get there, he would need to construct a charts database. He began a manual transcription of the *Billboard* "Hot 100" for the 1960s and 1970s.

One day around the time he had just started his database, Bill was listening to Lou Simon's "60s Satellite Survey" July 4 special on SiriusXM Satellite Radio. Lou mentioned that the research work for that show was done by Dann Isbell, author of *Ranking the '60s*. He also credited Kent Kotal, proprietor of the unbelievable blog, *Forgotten Hits*. In his enthusiasm to network into the world of chartologists, Bill contacted both Kent and Dann, talking about his ideas, and purchasing an electronic version of *Ranking the '60s* in the process.

Dann responded, "Good luck with your project. Let me know how it goes." By February of 2014, the database was done and Bill had started experimenting with published ranking methodologies, including Dann's, and developing some new techniques. A number of technical conversations ensued. In April, Bill finished an academic paper about those techniques based on the *Billboard* database and had assembled an analogous database for comparison purposes from the online *Cash Box* "Top 100" charts.

At that same time, Lou Simon asked Dann if a *Ranking the '70s* was in the offing. By coincidence, Rich Appel, *Billboard* editor/writer and host of the syndicated radio show, "That Thing with Rich Appel," did as well, and offered his support. In the past, Dann's response to this question had always been the same: "Only if I have a co-author." But by this time, with respected personalities in radio urging him on and his having knowledge of Bill's approach to the charts, Dann invited Bill to collaborate on such a book. Bill jumped at the chance, and when *Cash Box* gave permission to use its charts, the pieces were in place and the project was underway.

Doing a book of this kind is challenging in many ways. The total process took fifteen months from start to finish. "Countless hours" is not hyperbole in this case. Obviously, assembling all the information and coercing Microsoft Word to format it in the way you see was a major part of the work. But before any of that could be done, the underlying calculation engine had to be designed and agreed to.

The methodology as described in the appendix is new, made necessary by changes in the chart world over the decade. It was the subject of much debate between us, and many gigabytes of Microsoft Excel files to get it right. Surprisingly, the least challenging part was working totally by e-mail separated by thirteen time zones.

As authors, we have different points of emphasis. Bill is primarily a quant, and rigorous about the calculations. Dann is primarily an aesthete who cares that the comparisons be mathematically correct but also artistically correct. He is also a meticulous editor. For this kind of work, both approaches are necessary and so is a love of the music, a drive to catalog it and a passion for getting it right.

Ranking the '70s is the kind of book some enthusiasts will read cover to cover. On the other hand, it would particularly please us if you jumped to any page and saw something that surprised you enough to exclaim, "Wow, would you look at that!" Because that's what *Ranking the '70s* is all about.

Both the authors gratefully acknowledge the Cashbox brain trust: Bruce Elrod, Christopher Elrod and Doug Stroud for granting permission to slice and dice the "Top 100" charts in this fashion. Kudos also go to Randy Price, a master chartologist in his own right, who adapted them for the web. The owners of the charts encourage enthusiasts to use their lists, and we encourage readers to refer to them to put our rankings in context. We applaud Cashbox for its open access approach to its charts, which are available to all at http://cashboxmagazine.com/Archives.html.

Other resources were helpful as well. We acknowledge *Discogs* (http://www.discogs.com/) and *45cat* (http://www.45cat.com/)--two websites with voluminous discographies, including images of record labels that helped us get our facts correct.

More from Dann: I would like to thank all those who helped make *Ranking the '60s* a success, convincing me that this latter project was even possible: Kent Kotal of *Forgotten Hits*, Lou Simon at Sirius/XM, Rich Appel and his weekly webcast over Rewound Radio, That Thing with Rich Appel, Doug Heatherly of Lighthouse24 who reprised his role as our editing trouble-shooter and cover designer, also Larry Leichman and the fine folks at Arbor Books and at CreateSpace, and certainly all those who purchased the book.

I would also like to thank my wife Jessica for her extreme patience throughout this project, and to sons Jeffrey and Ian for their open ears whenever I wanted to share the progress of this book with them.

And from Bill: I want to thank my wife Mary who listens patiently to analytical chart discussions even when her husband uses them to monopolize and ruin dinner party conversation. During the preparation of this book she has seen way more of the back of my head than of my face.

Also, thanks to my son Will who developed a useful Excel macro for formatting one line in two different fonts, and to my daughter Allison and son Quin for critical reading and uncritical support.

Special professional thanks go to Flint Lewis, Dave Smorodin, Eric Slater and Brian Crawford, legal and publications colleagues at the American Chemical Society for pointers on the publishing business.

And finally thanks in absentia to my late brother Jim whose set of Joel Whitburn's Record Research books of *Billboard* chart reproductions started me on this adventure for real.

Dann Isbell
Bill Carroll
August 2015

Introduction

Them Changes

The history of pop music since 1955 holds one constant: a constant state of stylistic change. These changes, of course, do not occur in a vacuum; nor are they abrupt. They ascend and descend in popularity, overlapping for a time. (See endnote) They are culturally driven: art imitates life, particularly in music. As such, those changes regularly provide the basis of research for music hobbyists and historians, sociologists and others who trace pop music's evolution and attempt to explain it in the context of the times.

To that point, the decade of the '70s had its fair share of differing musical styles and at least its fair share of cultural change. SiriusXM's Lou Simon, who lives the era professionally every day, says, "The '60s saw the growth of rock bands, the power of political lyric, the freedom of youth. The '70s built on this with rock festivals, the birth of the singer-songwriter, the baby-boomers heading to discos." Think of the '70s as the eclectic decade in pop music history.

Suspend the present and take flight back to the 1960s-1970s transition. Having done so, you arrive at January 1, 1970. You tune in to your local AM Top 40 radio station and soon enough you hear the top songs for that week from '60s favorites Diana Ross & the Supremes, B.J. Thomas and Peter, Paul & Mary and breakout hits from two new groups you know next to nothing about, Led Zeppelin and the Jackson 5.

Then advance in time to December 31, 1979 and look back at how these five acts fared during the '70s. Two--Diana Ross & the Supremes and Peter, Paul & Mary--never charted again as groups. Their musical styles, pop-soul and folk, had fallen out of favor during the early '70s. Another--B.J. Thomas--switched from pop to country-pop to stay relevant (joining Country Grammy winners Olivia Newton-John and John Denver among other country-pop performers of the mid '70s).

The new arrivals of whom you had barely heard are now regarded as two of the decade's bigger acts. Led Zeppelin introduced hard rock to the national singles charts and this style stayed popular throughout the '70s while the Jackson 5 faded after tremendous success with pop-soul in the early '70s only to re-emerge with the beats of funk and disco (as The Jacksons for the latter).

The change in the fortunes of these five acts over the course of the decade provides a snapshot of what happened in general to the vast majority of acts who charted during the 1970s--the evolution of musical styles required acts to adapt. Those that did not were replaced by other acts considered more musically up to date.

The two most common genres in the history of pop music since 1955 have been R&B and Pop/Rock. Each has given us a continuous stream of subgenres or styles. Guy Zapoleon goes further and characterizes each decade--starting in the mid-50s--into three "phases": Rebirth, Extremes and Doldrums. Because his cycle decades are out of sync with the calendar decade, in his view, the '70s start with the Doldrums phase of the '60s, but become revitalized, particularly with the advent of disco as an "extreme." Let's test that more specifically.

In R&B, as the '70s dawned, soul was alive and well with branches both ascending and descending in popularity. The carry-overs from the '60s, Motown pop-soul, southern soul (Stax and Muscle Shoals) and Chicago soul (Impressions), were in decline while psychedelic soul (Temptations), funk (James Brown, Isley Brothers), Philly soul (O'Jays, Spinners) and smooth soul (Marvin Gaye, Roberta Flack) had yet to peak. Of all these branches, only funk maintained a strong presence into the late '70s.

By the mid '70s, disco, a style that could not be categorized as either R&B or Pop/Rock, had stormed the music scene--an example of a classic Zapoleon extreme. Disco (Donna Summer, Bee Gees) dominated the charts until the end of the decade. It became such a force that it seemed that nearly everyone had to "turn the beat around" and reinvent their work in the disco style. Consider Barbra Streisand of "People" fame doing "The Main Event/Fight" or even Rod Stewart's metamorphosis from "Maggie May" to "Do Ya Think I'm Sexy." In Pop/Rock at the beginning of the decade, just as in R&B, popular late '60s forms were in retreat; in this instance it was psychedelic pop, sunshine pop and bubblegum, pushed aside by the '70s' most dominant form, pop/soft rock (Elton John, Carpenters), with help from the music of the singer-songwriters (Carole King, James Taylor, Don McLean), heavy metal/hard rock (Led Zeppelin, Alice Cooper) and jazz-rock (Blood, Sweat & Tears).

After only a few years into the new decade, it was clear that Pop/Rock was evolving as new forms glam rock (David Bowie), blues rock (Eric Clapton), Southern rock (Allman Brothers Band, Lynyrd Skynyrd) and progressive/art rock (Moody Blues, Yes) were sending singles up the charts.

During the mid '70s, several of these forms were into or beginning their retreat while newer arrivals country-pop (Olivia Newton-John, Linda Ronstadt) and arena rock (Foreigner, Styx) gained chart status, followed by punk rock (Blondie) closer to the end of the decade.

It might seem counterintuitive that a decade with such a smorgasbord of styles should yield any consensus hits across the listening population, and yet, at times, that consensus emerged. Consider 1978, wherein only 19 songs topped the charts all year. "Night Fever," "Le Freak" and "Shadow Dancing" comprised 21 of the 52 weeks at #1. Disco was consensus in 1978.

More often than not, however, the years were closer to mimicking 1974--perhaps the dullest of the doldrum years. In that year, 48 different songs topped the charts and, for the year, no song or subgenre distinguished itself in terms of relative chart strength: the top three songs by natural score were "I Honestly Love You," (pop/soft rock) "Show And Tell," (smooth soul) and "The Streak" (novelty).

The '70s in pop music history has often been characterized as shallow with years of irrelevant songs and throwaway singles. But a look at its multitude of subgenres and styles should give one pause before coming to such a conclusion. In this sense, the '70s was as vibrant a decade as any before or after it.

Ranking the '70s: A Complete Compilation of the Chart Songs and Acts from Pop's Eclectic Decade is a listing of not only that decade's biggest hits and performers but of *all* songs and acts that appeared on the "Top 100" pop charts of *Cash Box* magazine.

This volume presents a single, comprehensive list of the songs in Section 1, ranking perennial favorites like "Bridge Over Troubled Water" and "Baker Street" with once-popular tunes such as "Gypsy Man" (War) and "Gypsy Woman" (Brian Hyland) and minor or regional gems like "13 Questions" (Seatrain) and "Lies" (J.J. Cale)

A similarly all-inclusive list of the acts is offered in Section 2 as all-but-forgotten performers like Joy of Cooking and Spaghetti Head can be found together with top acts like Cher and Chicago.

Sections 3 and 4 index the acts and song titles respectively. Section 3 categorizes acts as soloists, duos or groups alphabetically and with their song titles ordered based on chart performance while Section 4 indexes the song titles with decadal rankings provided for cross-reference.

Finally, there are a number of appendices that have "special purpose" lists. These lists include the top 300 records of each year, the top one-hit wonders, high intensity hits, records charting the most weeks, fastest and slowest records to #1, the top labels, and still more confections.

The first one, "The Scoring System Explained," deserves a bit more comment. There were profound changes in the economy and the industry in the '70s. Singles were in decline and albums ascendant, both for sales and airplay. A recession and two oil shocks impacted industry production and profitability. The number of records entering the charts declined by 35% between 1970 and 1979 and the number of scoring acts declined by 15% in the same period. Records tended to stay on the charts longer making it difficult to compare popularity on an apples-to-apples basis.

As with *Ranking the '60s*, our scoring system values the top echelons of the chart relatively higher than the lower echelons. In addition, to take into account the reduced competition for space on the chart in the late '70s, we developed a system to gauge the strongest charting records regardless of the surrounding competitive environment. We think this avoids a bias of the scoring system to the late '70s. The details are fully revealed in "The Scoring System Explained."

Endnote

The data from a study of the evolution of pop music in the US 1960-2010[1], can be used to generate a graph of overlapping genres in the 1970s. Here are shown Motown (in decline), Funk (a constant presence) and Disco (peaking at the end) as a percent of the records with identified genres for a 52-week moving period,

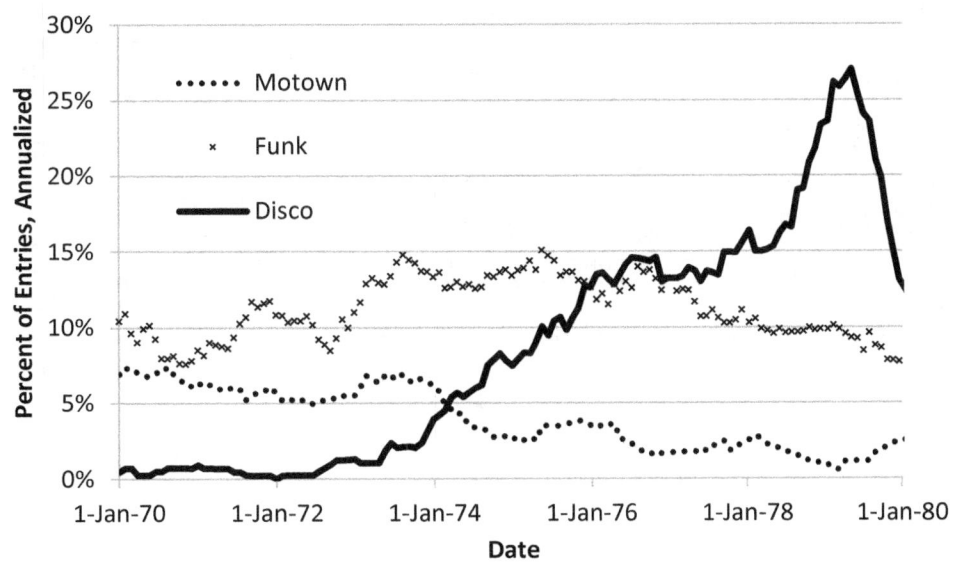

---

[1] Mauch, M., MacCallum, R. M., Levy, M., Leroi, A. M., "The evolution of popular music: USA 1960–2010" Royal Society Open Science, http://dx.doi.org/10.1098/rsos.150081. Mauch's research uses genre tags from LastFM (www.last.fm).

CASH BOX TOP 100 SINGLES

September 3, 1977

#	Title / Artist (Label) Publisher	8/27	8/20	Weeks On Chart
1	**BEST OF MY LOVE** EMOTIONS (Columbia 3-10544) WB	1	1	12
2	**YOUR LOVE HAS LIFTED ME (HIGHER AND HIGHER)** RITA COOLIDGE (A&M 1922) WB	3	4	17
3	**HANDY MAN** JAMES TAYLOR (Columbia 8-10557) B-3	5	6	13
4	**EASY** COMMODORES (Motown M 1418) CPP	4	5	15
5	**FLOAT ON** THE FLOATERS (ABC 12284) CPP	6	11	11
6	**I JUST WANT TO BE YOUR EVERYTHING** ANDY GIBBS (RSO 872) WB	2	2	20
7	**DON'T STOP** FLEETWOOD MAC (WB WBS 8413) CPP	9	12	9
8	**JUST A SONG BEFORE I GO** CROSBY, STILLS & NASH (Atlantic 3401) WB	8	9	15
9	**TELEPHONE LINE** ELECTRIC LIGHT ORCHESTRA (United Artists/Jet 1000) B-3	11	16	12
10	**HOW MUCH LOVE** LEO SAYER (WB WBS 8319) CPP/ALM	12	13	9
11	**YOU MADE ME BELIEVE IN MAGIC** BAY CITY ROLLERS (Arista AS0256) ALM	7	7	13
12	**GIVE A LITTLE BIT** SUPERTRAMP (A&M 1938) ALM	13	15	17
13	**ON AND ON** STEPHEN BISHOP (ABC 12260) ALM	15	20	17
14	**SMOKE FROM A DISTANT FIRE** THE SANFORD-TOWNSEND BAND (Warner Bros. WBS 8370) CH	16	18	11
15	**STRAWBERRY LETTER 23** BROTHERS JOHNSON (A&M 1949) ALM	17	22	8
16	**BLACK BETTY** RAM JAM (Epic 8-50357)	14	14	14
17	**SWAYIN' TO THE MUSIC** JOHNNY RIVERS (Big Tree/Atl. 16094) WB	19	24	11
18	**COLD AS ICE** FOREIGNER (Atlantic 3410) WB	22	26	7
19	**KEEP IT COMIN' LOVE** KC & THE SUNSHINE BAND (TK 1023) CPP	25	31	7
20	**STAR WARS THEME** MECO (Millennium/Casablanca 604) CPP	27	35	6
21	**STAR WARS** LONDON SYMPHONY ORCHESTRA (20th Century TC 2345) CPP	24	29	21
22	**BARRACUDA** HEART (Portrait/CBS 6-70004) WB	10	10	11
23	**DON'T WORRY BABY** B.J. THOMAS (MCA 40735) ALM	26	32	9
24	**CHRISTINE SIXTEEN** KISS (Casablanca NB 889) ALM	20	21	8
25	**NOBODY DOES IT BETTER** CARLY SIMON (Elektra 45413) B-3	31	37	7
26	**JUNGLE LOVE** STEVE MILLER BAND (Capitol 4466) WB	32	38	5
27	**EDGE OF THE UNIVERSE** BEE GEES (RSO 880) WB	29	34	7
28	**YOU AND ME** ALICE COOPER (Warner Bros. WBS 8349) WB	18	8	20
29	**THAT'S ROCK 'N' ROLL** SHAUN CASSIDY (WB/Curb 8423) WB	36	42	6
30	**HARD ROCK CAFE** CAROLE KING (Capitol 4455) CPP	35	39	7
31	**WHATCHA GONNA DO?** PABLO CRUISE (A&M 1920-S) ALM	21	3	22
32	**YOU'RE MY WORLD** HELEN REDDY (Capitol 4418) CH/B-3	23	19	19
33	**BOOGIE NIGHTS** HEATWAVE (Epic 8-50370) ALM	45	51	9
34	**I FEEL LOVE** DONNA SUMMER (Casablanca NB 884) ALM	52	62	5
35	**CAT SCRATCH FEVER** TED NUGENT (Epic 8-50425) WB	46	53	7
36	**I'M IN YOU** PETER FRAMPTON (A&M 1941) ALM	30	25	15
37	**SLIDE** SLAVE (Cotillion/Atlantic 44218)	33	27	12
38	**IT WAS ALMOST LIKE A SONG** RONNIE MILSAP (RCA PB-10976) ALM/CPP	40	43	11
39	**SUNFLOWER** GLEN CAMPBELL (Capitol 4445) WB	39	41	10
40	**ARIEL** DEAN FRIEDMAN (Lifesong 45022) B-3	38	33	2
41	**WAY DOWN** ELVIS PRESLEY (RCA 10998) ALM	54	48	12
42	**A REAL MOTHER** JOHNNY GUITAR WATSON (DJM/Amherst DJUS 1024)	43	44	10
43	**THE GREATEST LOVE OF ALL** GEORGE BENSON (Arista 251) CPP	51	54	6
44	**SIGNED SEALED DELIVERED** PETER FRAMPTON (A&M 972) ALM	61	—	2
45	**LITTLE DARLING (I NEED YOU)** THE DOOBIE BROTHERS (WB 8408) CPP	47	49	7
46	**DA DO RON RON** SHAUN CASSIDY (Curb/WB WBS 8365) CPP	34	42	6
47	**MY HEART BELONGS TO ME** BARBRA STREISAND (Columbia 3-10555) B-3	37	23	16
48	**SO YOU WIN AGAIN** HOT CHOCOLATE (Big Tree/Atlantic BT 16096) WB	49	52	9
49	**DAYTIME FRIENDS** KENNY ROGERS (United Artists UA XW 1027) B-3	57	64	5
50	**DO YOU WANNA MAKE LOVE** PETER McCANN (20th Century 2335) CPP	41	30	20
51	**UNDERCOVER ANGEL** ALAN O'DAY (Pacific/Atlantic PC 001) WB	28	17	23
52	**LOOKS LIKE WE MADE IT** BARRY MANILOW (Arista 244) ALM	42	40	18
53	**I WOULDN'T WANT TO BE LIKE YOU** ALAN PARSONS (Arista AS 0260) ALM	63	71	4
54	**HEAVEN IS ON THE SEVENTH FLOOR** PAUL NICHOLAS (RSO RS 878) CH	62	72	4
55	**TELEPHONE MAN** MERI WILSON (GRT 127) CPP	44	36	14
56	**IT'S SAD TO BELONG** ENGLAND DAN & JOHN FORD COLEY (Big Tree/Atlantic BT-16088) HAN	48	45	18
57	**SHE DID IT** ERIC CARMEN (Arista AS0266) WB	74	—	2
58	**ROCK AND ROLL NEVER FORGETS** BOB SEGER (Capitol 4449) CPP	55	50	9
59	**ANOTHER STAR** STEVIE WONDER (Tamla S4287) CPP	75	—	2
60	**HELP IS ON THE WAY** LITTLE RIVER BAND (Capitol 4428) WB	66	69	6
61	**I BELIEVE YOU** DOROTHY MOORE (Malaco/TK 1042) CPP/ALM	69	74	8
62	**L.A. SUNSHINE** WAR (Blue Note/UA BN-XW 1009) ALM	64	65	6
63	**I BELIEVE IN LOVE** KENNY LOGGINS (Columbia 10569) WB	68	73	8
64	**MARTIAN BOOGIE** BROWNSVILLE STATION (Private Stock PS 45149)	70	76	3
65	**I'M DREAMING** JENNIFER WARNES (Arista 252) ALM	67	70	7
66	**BRICK HOUSE** COMMODORES (Motown M1425)	77	—	2
67	**KNOWING ME, KNOWING YOU** ABBA (Atlantic 3387) ALM	50	46	17
68	**YOU LIGHT UP MY LIFE** DEBBY BOONE (Curb/WB 8446)	79	—	2
69	**DON'T IT MAKE MY BROWN EYES BLUE** CRYSTAL GAYLE (United Artists UA XW 1016) B-3	78	80	5
70	**MARGARITAVILLE** JIMMY BUFFETT (ABC AB 12254) WB	56	55	24
71	**LOOK WHAT YOU'VE DONE TO MY HEART** McCOO & DAVIS (ABC 1026) CPP	80	85	3
72	**HOUND DOG MAN** LENNY Le BLANC (Atlantic BT 16062)	—	—	1
73	**INDIAN SUMMER** POCO (ABC AB 12295) WB	81	83	7
74	**JUST REMEMBER I LOVE YOU** FIREFALL (Atlantic 3420) WB	82	91	4
75	**ANGEL IN YOUR ARMS** HOT (Big Tree/Atlantic BT 16085) CPP	59	57	30
76	**I GO CRAZY** PAUL DAVIS (Bang B-733)	84	—	2
77	**CAN'T YOU SEE** MARSHALL TUCKER BAND (Capricorn 0278) WB	87	99	3
78	**SURFIN' USA** LEIF GARRETT (Atlantic A 3423)	88	—	2
79	**DOG DAYS** ATLANTA RHYTHM SECTION (Polydor 144H) CPP	86	89	3
80	**IT'S A CRAZY WORLD** MAC McANALLY (Ariola America/Capitol P7665) CPP	71	58	11
81	**HOLD ON** WILD CHERRY (Epic 8-50365)	89	—	2
82	**GOOD MORNING JUDGE** 10CC (Mercury 73943) WB	85	90	4
83	**HEAVEN IS ON THE SEVENTH FLOOR** MIGHTY POPE (Private Stock 157) CH	83	86	4
84	**MY FAIR SHARE** SEALS & CROFTS (Warner Bros. WBS 8405)	—	—	1
85	**LOVE GONE BY** DAN FOGELBERG (Full Moon/Epic 50412)	76	75	8
86	**I JUST WANT TO MAKE LOVE TO YOU** FOGHAT (Bearsville WB 0319)	—	—	1
87	**IT'S ECSTASY WHEN YOU LAY DOWN NEXT TO ME** BARRY WHITE (20th Century 2350)	—	—	1
88	**DOES SHE DO IT LIKE SHE DANCES** ADDRISI BROTHERS (Buddah BDA 579) CCP	92	—	2
89	**DUSIC** Brick (Bang 734)	—	—	1
90	**(I'VE BEEN LOOKIN' FOR) A NEW WAY TO SAY I LOVE YOU** DRIVER (A&M 1966) ALM	94	95	5
91	**IF I HAVE TO GO AWAY** JIGSAW (20th Century 2347)	—	—	1
92	**SOMETHING BETTER** CHILLIWACK (Mushroom 7025)	—	—	1
93	**WE JUST DISAGREE** DAVE MASON (Columbia 3-10575)	—	—	1
94	**IT'S TOO HOT TO HANDLE** UFO (Chrysalis CHS 2157)	97	—	2
95	**SOME ENCHANTED EVENING** JANE OLIVER (Columbia 3-10527)	—	—	1
96	**LOVE ME ONE MORE TIME (JUST FOR OLD TIME SAKE)** KAREN NELSON AND BILLY T (Amherst 724)	98	98	4
97	**IN THE MIDDLE** TIM MOORE (Asylum 45394) CH	73	68	9
98	**C'EST LA VIE** GREG LAKE (Atlantic 3405) WB	99	—	2
99	**O-H-I-O** OHIO PLAYERS (Mercury 73932) CH	95	97	4
100	**FOR A WHILE** MARY MacGREGOR (Ariola America/Capitol 7667)	93	94	5

ALPHABETIZED TOP 100 SINGLES (INCLUDING PUBLISHERS AND LICENSEES)

Angel In Your (Song Tailors — BMI/ I've Got The Music — ASCAP) ... 75
Another Star (Jobete — ASCAP) ... 59
A Real Mother (Vir-Jon — BMI) ... 42
Ariel (Blendingwell — ASCAP) ... 40
Barracuda (Wilsongs/Know Mue/Play My Music — ASCAP) ... 22
Best Of My (Saggifire — BMI/Steelchest — ASCAP) 1
Black Betty (Folkways — BMI) ... 16
Boogie Nights (Rondor/Almo — ASCAP) ... 33
Brick House (Jobete — ASCAP) ... 66
Can't You See (No Exit — BMI) ... 77
Cat Scratch Fever (Magic Land — ASCAP) ... 98
C'est la vie (Palm Beach Int'l. Rec. Ltd. — ASCAP) 35
Christine Sixteen (Kiss — ASCAP) ... 24
Cold As Ice (Somerset/Evensong/WB — ASCAP) . 18
Da Do Ron (Trio/Mother Bertha — BMI) ... 46
Daytime Friends (Ben Peters — BMI) ... 49
Does She Do It (American Broadcasting — ASCAP) 88
Dog Days (Low-Sal — BMI) ... 79
Don't It Make (United Artists — ASCAP) ... 69
Don't Stop (Gen Too — BMI) ... 7
Don't Worry (Irving — BMI) ... 23
Do You Wanna (Amer. Broadcasting — ASCAP) .. 50
Dusic (Caliber/Good High— ASUP) ... 89
Easy (Jobete/Commodores Ent. — ASCAP) ... 4
Edge Of (Casserole/Flamm/Unichappell — BMI) .. 27
Float On (ABC-Dunhill/Wood Songs — BMI) ... 5
For A While (Silver Down — ASCAP) ... 100
Give A Little Bit (Almo — ASCAP) ... 12
Good Morning Judge (Man-Ken — BMI) ... 82
Handy Man (Unart — BMI) ... 3
Hard Rock Cafe (Colgems-EMI — ASCAP) ... 30
Heaven Is On (Keyboard Pendulum/Chappell — ASCAP) ... 54,83
Help Is On The (Australian Tumblewood — BMI) .. 60
Hey Hound Dog Man (Chrysalis/ Fancy That — ASCAP) ... 72
Hold On (Bema Music — ASCAP) ... 81
How Much (Screen Gems-EMI/Summerhill — BMI/ Chrysalis — ASCAP) ... 10
I Believe In Love (First Artists/Emanual/Gnossos/ Threesome — ASCAP) ... 63
I Believe You (Music Ways/Flying Addrisi — BMI) . 61
I Feel Love (Ricks — BMI) ... 34
If I Have To Go (Bell Size Music Inc. — ASCAP) ... 91
I Go Crazy (Web IV Music — BMI) ... 76
I Just Want (Stigwood/Unichappell — BMI) ... 6
I Just Want To Make Love (Arc Music Corp. — BMI) 86
I'm Dreaming (Almo — ASCAP/Irving — BMI) ... 65
I'm In You (Almo/Fram-Dee — ASCAP) ... 36
Indian Summer (Gold — ASCAP) ... 73
In The Middle (Michael Jackson/Ackee/ Andustin — ASCAP) ... 97
It's A Crazy (I've Got The Music — ASCAP) ... 80
It's Ecstasy When You Lay Down Next To Me (Sa-Vette Music Co. — BMI) ... 87
It's Sad To (Famous/Ironside — ASCAP) ... 56
Its To Hot (Intersong Music — ASCAP) ... 94
I've Been Looking (Irving — BMI) ... 90
It Was (Chess/Case David — ASCAP) ... 38
I Wouldn't Want (Wolfsongs — BMI) ... 53
Jungle Love (Sailor — ASCAP) ... 26
Just A Song (Thin Ice — ASCAP) ... 8
Just Remember (Stephen Stills — BMI) ... 74
Keep It Comin' Love (Sherlyn — BMI) ... 19
Knowing Me (Countless Songs — BMI) ... 67
L.A. Sunshine (Far Out — BMI) ... 62
Little Darling (Stone Agate — BMI) ... 45
Look What You've (Screen Gems — BMI) ... 71
Looks Like We Made It (Irving — BMI) ... 52
Love Gone By (Hickory Grove — ASCAP) ... 85
Love Me One (Time Square Music — BMI) ... 96
Margaritaville (Coral Reefer — BMI) ... 70
Martian Boogie(Ainal — BMI) ... 64
My Fair Share (Warner Bros. Music Corp. — ASCAP) 84
My Heart (Koppelman/Bandier/Music of Emanuel — BMI) ... 47
Nobody Does It (United Artists — ASCAP/ Unart — BMI) ... 25
O-H-I-O (Play One/Unichappell — BMI) ... 99
On And On (Stephen Bishop — BMI) ... 13
Rock And Roll Never (Gear — ASCAP) ... 58
She Did It (G.A.M. — BMI) ... 57
Signed Sealed (Jobete — ASCAP) ... 44
Slide (Spurbree — BMI) ... 37
Smoke From (Salmon/Mulhan/Unichappell/ Turkey Tunes — BMI) ... 14
So You Win (Island — BMI) ... 48
Some Enchanted Evening (Columbia) ... 95
Something Better (Mushroom) ... 92
Star Wars (Fox Fanfare — BMI) ... 20,21
Strawberry (Kidada/Off The Wall — BMI) ... 15
Sunflower (Stonebridge — ASCAP) ... 39
Surfin' USA (ARC Music — BMI) ... 78
Swayin' To (WB — ASCAP) ... 17
Telephone Line (Unart/Jet — BMI) ... 9
Telephone Man (Castleridge — BMI) ... 55
That's Rock 'N' Roll (C.A.M./USA — BMI) ... 29
The Greatest Love (Columbia Pictures — BMI) ... 43
Undercover Angel (WB — ASCAP) ... 51
Way Down (Leon/Ahab — BMI) ... 41
We Just Disagree (Columbia) ... 93
Whatcha Gonna (Irving/Pablo Cruise — BMI) ... 31
You And Me (Warner Bros. WBS) ... 28
You Light Up (Big Hill — ASCAP) ... 68
You Made Me (Chrysalis — ASCAP) ... 11
You're My World (Intersong — ASCAP/Gruppo Editoriale Ariston — BMI) ... 32
Your Love Has (Chevis/Warner-Tamerlane/ BRC — BMI) ... 2

Publishers Code

ALM-Almo BB-Big Bells B-3-Big Three CH-Chappell CPP-Columbia Pictures Publications Han-Hansen PS-Peer Southern WB-Warner Brothers

Section 1

Ranking the Songs

Over 5,300 songs appeared on a *Cash Box* Top 100 chart during the 1970s.[1] The titles have all been ranked and can be found somewhere within this list. Exactly where is determined by the application of the following methodology to their chart performance.

First, points were assigned by reverse rank order to a title's chart rank for every week it appeared on the Top 100. This means that a song at #100 received one point while another at #99 was given two points and onward up the chart until #1, with its one hundred points. The weekly numbers were added to give the record's score. Reissues, when they occurred, were summed to give a total score.

Then, for entries appearing in the weekly Top 30, additional points were assigned for that week up to the total as shown by this table:

Rank	Points	Rank	Points	Rank	Points
1	1000	11	190	21	100
2	824	12	184	22	97
3	658	13	178	23	94
4	529	14	172	24	91
5	434	15	166	25	88
6	345	16	145	26	85
7	310	17	140	27	82
8	277	18	135	28	79
9	246	19	130	29	76
10	217	20	125	30	73

---

[1] There are 5,368 unique combinations of titles and acts. Some are B-sides that charted as part of a two-sided winner (TSW) but not independently; some are 1970s intradecade reissues that have been combined into one entry (although both are shown in that entry); thus, there is a minor difference between the word "record" and "song." In the end, there are 5,350 rankings.

This weighting factor was applied to the Top 30 hits, first, to mirror the fact that song popularity is not proportional to the rank itself; it increases at a greater rate as the record climbs the chart. This is something the Top 100 was not intended to measure.

Assigning additional weight to the higher echelons is, in the first place, intuitive. Advancing from #2 to #1 seems like a bigger leap than advancing from #100 to #99. Moreover, if you follow the charts, much greater movement is seen in lower echelons than larger; once again, intuitively, higher echelons should carry higher values.

Additionally, any system rewards two qualities in varying measure: rank and time on the charts. A system like the one shown above gives more weight to rank; the reverse rank system preferentially rewards longevity. For example, the number 1 song for the '70s as measured by *Cash Box* and calculated by the reverse rank system is "I Go Crazy" by Paul Davis, largely on the basis of 36 weeks on the chart, but peaking at #7. Intuitively, "You Light Up My Life" is a more logical choice with only (!) 27 weeks on the chart, but 8 at #1.

The values chosen for these thirty ranks are empirical. However, there are at least eight published methodologies, most of which that take a similar approach, overweighting the upper echelons[2].

To compare records over time, a stable unchanging chart methodology is preferred to allow for comparison of equals to equals. Unfortunately, that was not the case in the 1970s. The number of records entering the charts declined by one-third over the ten years. Records moved more slowly up and down in the latter part of the decade than in the beginning of the decade. Consequently, records stayed on the charts longer, and scored higher. Similar to "grade inflation" it was clear that comparison of raw scores in different times did not produce a fair comparison.

As a result, we developed a process called normalization that allows us to find the strong performers versus their peers at the time they charted, and compare those superior results to develop the rankings. As a result of these calculations, there were very few ties. When ties occurred, they were broken by comparing peak positions, then weeks at that peak position. A full discussion of the total system can be found in the appendix, "The Scoring System Explained."

The consequent ordering of song titles resulted in some whimsical pairings: "Reunited" and "Without You" at No. 52 and No. 53, "Let's Do It Again" and "You Haven't Done Nothin'" at No. 300 and No. 299, "Movin' Out" and "Already Gone" at No. 1354 and No. 1353, "Way Down" and "Deeper and Deeper" at No. 1474 and No. 1475. No doubt you will discover other serendipitous couplings as you advance through the rankings on your own.

---

[2] A fuller reference to these methodologies appears in "The Scoring System Explained" as well as in Carroll, 2014, referenced in that appendix.

'70s Rank	TITLE	ACT	Peak Date	Label & No.
1	You Light Up My Life	Debby Boone	8-Oct-77	Warner/Curb 8455
2	Joy To The World	Three Dog Night	17-Apr-71	Dunhill 4272
3	American Pie	Don McLean	8-Jan-72	United Artists 50856
4	Shadow Dancing	Andy Gibb	3-Jun-78	RSO 893
5	Le Freak	Chic	16-Dec-78	Atlantic 3519
6	I'll Be There	The Jackson 5	24-Oct-70	Motown 1171
7	Raindrops Keep Fallin' On My Head	B.J. Thomas	10-Jan-70	Scepter 12265
8	Maggie May	Rod Stewart	9-Oct-71	Mercury 73224
9	Night Fever	Bee Gees	18-Mar-78	RSO 889
10	ABC	The Jackson 5	25-Apr-70	Motown 1163
11	Alone Again (Naturally)	Gilbert O'Sullivan	12-Aug-72	MAM 3619
12	I Think I Love You	The Partridge Family	21-Nov-70	Bell 910
13	Knock Three Times	Dawn	16-Jan-71	Bell 938
14	My Sweet Lord	George Harrison	19-Dec-70	Apple 2995
15	Venus	Shocking Blue	31-Jan-70	Colossus 108
16	Afternoon Delight	Starland Vocal Band	26-Jun-76	Windsong 10588
17	My Sharona	The Knack	18-Aug-79	Capitol 4731
18	Kiss You All Over	Exile	7-Oct-78	Warner/Curb 8589
19	Stayin' Alive	Bee Gees	4-Feb-78	RSO 885
20	Tie A Yellow Ribbon Round The Ole Oak Tree	Dawn Featuring Tony Orlando	28-Apr-73	Bell 45,318
21	Da Ya Think I'm Sexy?	Rod Stewart	3-Feb-79	Warner Bros. 8724
22	How Deep Is Your Love	Bee Gees	17-Dec-77	RSO 882
23	The First Time Ever I Saw Your Face	Roberta Flack	22-Apr-72	Atlantic 2864
24	Let's Stay Together	Al Green	12-Feb-72	Hi 2202
25	Spirit In The Sky	Norman Greenbaum	2-May-70	Reprise 0885
26	Brand New Key	Melanie	25-Dec-71	Neighborhood 4201
27	Bridge Over Troubled Water	Simon & Garfunkel	28-Feb-70	Columbia 45079
28	Let It Be	The Beatles	28-Mar-70	Apple 2764
29	I Write The Songs	Barry Manilow	3-Jan-76	Arista 0157
30	Family Affair	Sly & The Family Stone	27-Nov-71	Epic 10805
31	It's Too Late	Carole King	26-Jun-71	Ode 66015
32	Theme From Shaft	Isaac Hayes	13-Nov-71	Enterprise 9038
33	My Love	Paul McCartney & Wings	2-Jun-73	Apple 1861
34	Silly Love Songs	Wings	29-May-76	Capitol 4256
35	One Bad Apple	The Osmonds	13-Feb-71	MGM 14193
36	Crocodile Rock	Elton John	3-Feb-73	MCA 40000
37	Torn Between Two Lovers	Mary MacGregor	12-Feb-77	Ariola America 7638
38	I Want You Back	The Jackson 5	24-Jan-70	Motown 1157
39	The Tears Of A Clown	Smokey Robinson & The Miracles	12-Dec-70	Tamla 54199
40	Hot Child In The City	Nick Gilder	21-Oct-78	Chrysalis 2226
41	Never Can Say Goodbye	The Jackson 5	29-May-71	Motown 1179

'70s Rank	TITLE	ACT	Peak Date	Label & No.
42	How Can You Mend A Broken Heart	Bee Gees	14-Aug-71	Atco 6824
43	Bad Girls	Donna Summer	21-Jul-79	Casablanca 988
44	Rockin' Robin	Michael Jackson	15-Apr-72	Motown 1197
45	Baker Street	Gerry Rafferty	15-Jul-78	United Artists 1192
46	Tonight's The Night (Gonna Be Alright)	Rod Stewart	20-Nov-76	Warner Bros. 8262
47	American Woman	The Guess Who	16-May-70	RCA Victor 74-0325
48	Three Times A Lady	Commodores	12-Aug-78	Motown 1443
49	Indian Reservation (The Lament Of The Cherokee)	Raiders	24-Jul-71	Columbia 45332
50	War	Edwin Starr	5-Sep-70	Gordy 7101
51	Gypsys, Tramps & Thieves	Cher	30-Oct-71	Kapp 2146
52	Reunited	Peaches & Herb	5-May-79	Polydor/MVP 14547
53	Without You	Nilsson	4-Mar-72	RCA Victor 74-0604
54	I Just Want To Be Your Everything	Andy Gibb	30-Jul-77	RSO 872
55	Me And Mrs. Jones	Billy Paul	23-Dec-72	Phila. Int'l 3521
56	Rose Garden	Lynn Anderson	6-Feb-71	Columbia 45252
57	Ring My Bell	Anita Ward	30-Jun-79	Juana 3422
58	You're So Vain	Carly Simon	6-Jan-73	Elektra 45824
59	Emotion	Samantha Sang	11-Mar-78	Private Stk 45,178
60	(They Long To Be) Close To You	Carpenters	1-Aug-70	A&M 1183
61	One Less Bell To Answer	The 5th Dimension	26-Dec-70	Bell 940
62	Brandy (You're A Fine Girl)	Looking Glass	2-Sep-72	Epic 10874
63	Boogie Oogie Oogie	A Taste Of Honey	16-Sep-78	Capitol 4565
64	Jive Talkin'	Bee Gees	9-Aug-75	RSO 510
65	Convoy	C.W. McCall	17-Jan-76	MGM 14839
66	Grease	Frankie Valli	9-Sep-78	RSO 897
67	Let's Get It On	Marvin Gaye	1-Sep-73	Tamla 54234
68	Rhinestone Cowboy	Glen Campbell	13-Sep-75	Capitol 4095
69	Undercover Angel	Alan O'Day	2-Jul-77	Pacific 001
70	Baby Come Back	Player	14-Jan-78	RSO 879
71	She's A Lady	Tom Jones	27-Mar-71	Parrot 40058
72	Go Away Little Girl	Donny Osmond	2-Oct-71	MGM 14285
73	Escape (The Pina Colada Song)	Rupert Holmes	22-Dec-79	Infinity 50,035
74	Kiss And Say Goodbye	The Manhattans	17-Jul-76	Columbia 10310
75	A Horse With No Name	America	25-Mar-72	Warner Bros. 7555
76	Love Train	The O'Jays	31-Mar-73	Phila. Int'l 3524
77	Mr. Big Stuff	Jean Knight	31-Jul-71	Stax 0088
78	Nobody Does It Better	Carly Simon	22-Oct-77	Elektra 45413
79	Just My Imagination (Running Away With Me)	The Temptations	20-Mar-71	Gordy 7105
80	Thank You (Falettinme Be Mice Elf Agin)	Sly & The Family Stone	21-Feb-70	Epic 10555
81	You Don't Bring Me Flowers	Barbra & Neil	25-Nov-78	Columbia 10840

'70s Rank	TITLE	ACT	Peak Date	Label & No.
82	Philadelphia Freedom	The Elton John Band	12-Apr-75	MCA 40364
83	Miss You	The Rolling Stones	29-Jul-78	Rolling Stones 19307
84	A Fifth Of Beethoven	Walter Murphy & The Big Apple Band	9-Oct-76	Private Stk 45,073
85	Good Times	Chic	11-Aug-79	Atlantic 3584
86	What A Fool Believes	The Doobie Brothers	7-Apr-79	Warner Bros. 8725
87	Heart Of Gold	Neil Young	18-Mar-72	Reprise 1065
88	Too Much Heaven	Bee Gees	30-Dec-78	RSO 913
89	Make It With You	Bread	15-Aug-70	Elektra 45686
90	Killing Me Softly With His Song	Roberta Flack	10-Mar-73	Atlantic 2940
91	50 Ways To Leave Your Lover	Paul Simon	7-Feb-76	Columbia 10270
92	Half-Breed	Cher	6-Oct-73	MCA 40102
93	Mama Told Me (Not To Come)	Three Dog Night	11-Jul-70	Dunhill 4239
94	That's The Way (I Like It)	K.C. & The Sunshine Band	29-Nov-75	T.K. 1015
95	Sad Eyes	Robert John	29-Sep-79	EMI America 8015
96	Disco Duck (Part 1)	Rick Dees & His Cast Of Idiots	16-Oct-76	RSO 857
97	Fly, Robin, Fly	Silver Convention	22-Nov-75	Midland Int'l 10339
98	Hot Stuff	Donna Summer	2-Jun-79	Casablanca 978
99	We've Only Just Begun	Carpenters	7-Nov-70	A&M 1217
100	Take Me Home, Country Roads	John Denver	4-Sep-71	RCA Victor 74-0445
101	Don't It Make My Brown Eyes Blue	Crystal Gayle	3-Dec-77	United Artists 1016
102	I Honestly Love You	Olivia Newton-John	21-Sep-74 17-Dec-77	MCA 40280
103	Ain't No Mountain High Enough	Diana Ross	26-Sep-70	Motown 1169
104	Instant Karma (We All Shine On)	John Ono Lennon	28-Mar-70	Apple 1818
105	Want Ads	The Honey Cone	5-Jun-71	Hot Wax 7011
106	Draggin' The Line	Tommy James	14-Aug-71	Roulette 7103
107	My Ding-A-Ling	Chuck Berry	21-Oct-72	Chess 2131
108	Superstition	Stevie Wonder	20-Jan-73	Tamla 54226
109	Put Your Hand In The Hand	Ocean	24-Apr-71	Kama Sutra 519
110	Have You Never Been Mellow	Olivia Newton-John	8-Mar-75	MCA 40349
111	Lonely Night (Angel Face)	Captain & Tennille	3-Apr-76	A&M 1782
112	Welcome Back	John Sebastian	15-May-76	Reprise 1349
113	You've Got A Friend	James Taylor	7-Aug-71	Warner Bros. 7498
114	Doesn't Somebody Want To Be Wanted	The Partridge Family	3-Apr-71	Bell 963
115	Got To Be There	Michael Jackson	1-Jan-72	Motown 1191
116	Don't Pull Your Love	Hamilton, Joe Frank & Reynolds	31-Jul-71	Dunhill 4276
117	Heart Of Glass	Blondie	28-Apr-79	Chrysalis 2295
118	Spill The Wine	Eric Burdon And War	29-Aug-70	MGM 14118
119	Ball Of Confusion (That's What The World Is Today)	The Temptations	25-Jul-70	Gordy 7099
120	Show And Tell	Al Wilson	26-Jan-74	Rocky Road 30073
121	Island Girl	Elton John	8-Nov-75	MCA 40461

'70s Rank	TITLE	ACT	Peak Date	Label & No.
122	Delta Dawn	Helen Reddy	8-Sep-73	Capitol 3645
123	Star Wars Theme/Cantina Band	Meco	24-Sep-77	Millennium 604
124	The Night The Lights Went Out In Georgia	Vicki Lawrence	21-Apr-73	Bell 45,303
125	Lovin' You	Minnie Riperton	29-Mar-75	Epic 50057
126	Whole Lotta Love	Led Zeppelin	10-Jan-70	Atlantic 2690
127	We Are Family	Sister Sledge	23-Jun-79	Cotillion 44251
128	Mac Arthur Park	Donna Summer	11-Nov-78	Casablanca 939
129	The Long And Winding Road	The Beatles	13-Jun-70	Apple 2832
130	Pick Up The Pieces	AWB	1-Mar-75	Atlantic 3229
131	Daddy Don't You Walk So Fast	Wayne Newton	5-Aug-72	Chelsea 0100
132	I Am Woman	Helen Reddy	16-Dec-72	Capitol 3350
133	Bad Blood	Neil Sedaka	25-Oct-75	Rocket/MCA 40460
134	Lady Marmalade	Labelle	22-Mar-75	Epic 50048
135	The Love You Save	The Jackson 5	27-Jun-70	Motown 1166
136	You're The One That I Want	John Travolta And Olivia Newton-John	27-May-78	RSO 891
137	Love Will Keep Us Together	The Captain & Tennille	28-Jun-75	A&M 1672
138	Lean On Me	Bill Withers	15-Jul-72	Sussex 235
139	Love Theme From "A Star Is Born" (Evergreen)	Barbra Streisand	5-Mar-77	Columbia 10450
140	Don't Go Breaking My Heart	Elton John And Kiki Dee	7-Aug-76	Rocket/MCA 40585
141	The Streak	Ray Stevens	25-May-74	Barnaby 600
142	Superstar	Carpenters	9-Oct-71	A&M 1289
143	Disco Lady	Johnnie Taylor	10-Apr-76	Columbia 10281
144	Hey There Lonely Girl	Eddie Holman	21-Feb-70	ABC 11240
145	Signed, Sealed, Delivered I'm Yours	Stevie Wonder	22-Aug-70	Tamla 54196
146	My Eyes Adored You	Frankie Valli	15-Mar-75	Private Stk 45,003
147	Boogie Fever	The Sylvers	8-May-76	Capitol 4179
148	Short People	Randy Newman	28-Jan-78	Warner Bros. 8492
149	Oh Girl	The Chi-Lites	3-Jun-72	Brunswick 55471
150	Y.M.C.A.	Village People	27-Jan-79	Casablanca 945
151	Play That Funky Music	Wild Cherry	11-Sep-76	Epic 50225
152	Cracklin' Rosie	Neil Diamond	17-Oct-70	Uni 55250
153	(If Loving You Is Wrong) I Don't Want To Be Right	Luther Ingram	12-Aug-72	KoKo 2111
154	Can't Smile Without You	Barry Manilow	1-Apr-78	Arista 0305
155	The Candy Man	Sammy Davis, Jr.	10-Jun-72	MGM 14320
156	Dream Weaver	Gary Wright	27-Mar-76	Warner Bros. 8167
157	I Will Survive	Gloria Gaynor	10-Mar-79	Polydor 14508
158	Long Cool Woman (In A Black Dress)	The Hollies	16-Sep-72	Epic 10871
159	You Don't Have To Be A Star (To Be In My Show)	Marilyn McCoo & Billy Davis Jr.	1-Jan-77	ABC 12208
160	Tragedy	Bee Gees	17-Mar-79	RSO 918

'70s Rank	TITLE	ACT	Peak Date	Label & No.
161	Seasons In The Sun	Terry Jacks	2-Mar-74	Bell 45,432
162	The Way We Were	Barbra Streisand	9-Feb-74	Columbia 45944
163	Lookin' Out My Back Door	Creedence Clearwater Revival	3-Oct-70	Fantasy 645
164	Best Of My Love	The Emotions	20-Aug-77	Columbia 10544
165	Muskrat Love	Captain & Tennille	13-Nov-76	A&M 1870
166	Photograph	Ringo Starr	24-Nov-73	Apple 1865
167	Brother Louie	Stories	25-Aug-73	Kama Sutra 577
168	Midnight Train To Georgia	Gladys Knight & The Pips	10-Nov-73	Buddah 383
169	The Joker	Steve Miller Band	19-Jan-74	Capitol 3732
170	Nice To Be With You	Gallery	24-Jun-72	Sussex 232
171	Band Of Gold	Freda Payne	1-Aug-70	Invictus 9075
172	Frankenstein	The Edgar Winter Group	26-May-73	Epic 10967
173	Burning Love	Elvis Presley	11-Nov-72	RCA Victor 74-0769
174	Top Of The World	Carpenters	1-Dec-73	A&M 1468
175	TSOP (The Sound Of Philadelphia)	MFSB Featuring The Three Degrees	20-Apr-74	Phila. Int'l 3540
176	Mandy	Barry Manilow	18-Jan-75	Bell 45,613
177	(Your Love Has Lifted Me) Higher And Higher	Rita Coolidge	10-Sep-77	A&M 1922
178	Kung Fu Fighting	Carl Douglas	14-Dec-74	20th Century 2140
179	Mama's Pearl	The Jackson 5	6-Mar-71	Motown 1177
180	Love Machine (Part 1)	The Miracles	6-Mar-76	Tamla 54262
181	Shining Star	Earth, Wind & Fire	24-May-75	Columbia 10090
182	The Hustle	Van Mc Coy	19-Jul-75	Avco 4653
183	(You're) Having My Baby	Paul Anka	24-Aug-74	United Artists 454
184	You Make Me Feel Like Dancing	Leo Sayer	25-Dec-76	Warner Bros. 8283
185	All By Myself	Eric Carmen	13-Mar-76	Arista 0165
186	One Of These Nights	Eagles	26-Jul-75	Asylum 45257
187	Indiana Wants Me	R. Dean Taylor	14-Nov-70	Rare Earth 5013
188	Jackie Blue	The Ozark Mountain Daredevils	10-May-75	A&M 1654
189	Let Your Love Flow	Bellamy Brothers	1-May-76	Warner/Curb 8169
190	They Just Can't Stop It the (Games People Play)	The Spinners	25-Oct-75	Atlantic 3284
191	Too Late To Turn Back Now	Cornelius Brothers & Sister Rose	29-Jul-72	United Artists 50910
192	Bad, Bad Leroy Brown	Jim Croce	28-Jul-73	ABC 11359
193	Patches	Clarence Carter	19-Sep-70	Atlantic 2748
194	Right Back Where We Started From	Maxine Nightingale	24-Apr-76	United Artists 752
195	(Love Is) Thicker Than Water	Andy Gibb	4-Mar-78	RSO 883
196	I'll Take You There	The Staple Singers	20-May-72	Stax 0125
197	Fame	David Bowie	27-Sep-75	RCA Victor 10320
198	Rich Girl	Daryl Hall & John Oates	26-Mar-77	RCA 10860
199	I Can See Clearly Now	Johnny Nash	18-Nov-72	Epic 10902
200	You Sexy Thing	Hot Chocolate	14-Feb-76	Big Tree 16047

'70s Rank	TITLE	ACT	Peak Date	Label & No.
201	Precious And Few	Climax	26-Feb-72	Rocky Road 30055
202	I Gotcha	Joe Tex	29-Apr-72	Dial 1010
203	Get Up And Boogie (That's Right)	Silver Convention	19-Jun-76	Midland Int'l 10571
204	Rise	Herb Alpert	27-Oct-79	A&M 2151
205	Saturday Night	Bay City Rollers	27-Dec-75	Arista 0149
206	Smiling Faces Sometimes	Undisputed Truth	18-Sep-71	Gordy 7108
207	I'm Still In Love With You	Al Green	9-Sep-72	Hi 2216
208	The Entertainer	Marvin Hamlisch	1-Jun-74	MCA 40174
209	Bennie And The Jets	Elton John	13-Apr-74	MCA 40198
210	Knock On Wood	Amii Stewart	21-Apr-79	Ariola/Hansa 7736
211	The Loco-Motion	Grand Funk	4-May-74	Capitol 3840
212	Heartbeat - It's A Lovebeat	The DeFranco Family	17-Nov-73	20th Century 2030
213	Will It Go Round In Circles	Billy Preston	14-Jul-73	A&M 1411
214	Yo-Yo	The Osmonds	23-Oct-71	MGM 14295
215	Annie's Song	John Denver	27-Jul-74	RCA Victor 0295
216	Babe	Styx	24-Nov-79	A&M 2188
217	Laughter In The Rain	Neil Sedaka	1-Feb-75	Rocket/MCA 40313
218	It Don't Come Easy	Ringo Starr	19-Jun-71	Apple 1831
219	The Most Beautiful Girl	Charlie Rich	22-Dec-73	Epic 11040
220	No More Tears (Enough Is Enough)	Barbra Streisand/Donna Summer	15-Dec-79	Columbia 11125
221	You Make Me Feel Brand New	The Stylistics	22-Jun-74	Avco 4634
222	Get Ready	Rare Earth	27-Jun-70	Rare Earth 5012
223	Baby Don't Get Hooked On Me	Mac Davis	7-Oct-72	Columbia 45618
224	Love's Theme	Love Unlimited Orchestra	23-Feb-74	20th Century 2069
225	Everybody Plays The Fool	The Main Ingredient	14-Oct-72	RCA Victor 74-0731
226	Keep On Truckin' (Part 1)	Eddie Kendricks	3-Nov-73	Tamla 54238
227	Thank God I'm A Country Boy	John Denver	14-Jun-75	RCA Victor 10239
228	Please Mr. Postman	Carpenters	25-Jan-75	A&M 1646
229	Southern Nights	Glen Campbell	30-Apr-77	Capitol 4376
230	Don't Stop 'til You Get Enough	Michael Jackson	13-Oct-79	Epic 50742
231	Boogie Nights	Heatwave	19-Nov-77	Epic 50370
232	Boogie On Reggae Woman	Stevie Wonder	8-Feb-75	Tamla 54254
233	Boogie Down	Eddie Kendricks	16-Mar-74	Tamla 54243
234	Brown Sugar	The Rolling Stones	5-Jun-71	Rolling Stones 19100
235	If You Leave Me Now	Chicago	23-Oct-76	Columbia 10390
236	Sail On	Commodores	20-Oct-79	Motown 1466
237	Which Way You Goin' Billy?	The Poppy Family	13-Jun-70	London 129
238	Back Stabbers	The O'Jays	23-Sep-72	Phila. Int'l 3517
239	Song Sung Blue	Neil Diamond	1-Jul-72	Uni 55326
240	Rock Me Gently	Andy Kim	28-Sep-74	Capitol 3895
241	Uncle Albert/Admiral Halsey	Paul & Linda McCartney	25-Sep-71	Apple 1837

'70s Rank	TITLE	ACT	Peak Date	Label & No.
242	Candida	Dawn	10-Oct-70	Bell 903
243	We're An American Band	Grand Funk	22-Sep-73	Capitol 3660
244	Lowdown	Boz Scaggs	2-Oct-76	Columbia 10367
245	(Shake, Shake, Shake) Shake Your Booty	KC & The Sunshine Band	25-Sep-76	T.K. 1019
246	Sundown	Gordon Lightfoot	29-Jun-74	Reprise 1194
247	Misty Blue	Dorothy Moore	19-Jun-76	Malaco 1029
248	I Shot The Sheriff	Eric Clapton	7-Sep-74	RSO 409
249	At Seventeen	Janis Ian	20-Sep-75	Columbia 10154
250	The Lion Sleeps Tonight	Robert John	18-Mar-72	Atlantic 2846
251	I'll Be Around	The Spinners	25-Nov-72	Atlantic 2904
252	Give Me Love (Give Me Peace On Earth)	George Harrison	30-Jun-73	Apple 1862
253	Angie	The Rolling Stones	27-Oct-73	Rolling Stones 19105
254	Rock The Boat	The Hues Corporation	13-Jul-74	RCA Victor 0232
255	Treat Her Like A Lady	Cornelius Brothers & Sister Rose	3-Jul-71	United Artists 50721
256	Shambala	Three Dog Night	21-Jul-73	Dunhill 4352
257	Sunshine On My Shoulders	John Denver	30-Mar-74	RCA Victor 0213
258	Billy, Don't Be A Hero	Bo Donaldson And The Heywoods	6-Jul-74	ABC 11435
259	Live And Let Die	Wings	18-Aug-73	Apple 1863
260	The Night Chicago Died	Paper Lace	10-Aug-74	Mercury 73492
261	Too Much, Too Little, Too Late	Johnny Mathis/Deniece Williams	27-May-78	Columbia 10693
262	Dueling Banjos	"Deliverance" Soundtrack	3-Mar-73	Warner Bros. 7659
263	Hurting Each Other	Carpenters	4-Mar-72	A&M 1322
264	You Ought To Be With Me	Al Green	23-Dec-72	Hi 2227
265	Leave Me Alone (Ruby Red Dress)	Helen Reddy	5-Jan-74	Capitol 3768
266	Fire	Pointer Sisters	17-Feb-79	Planet 45901
267	Black And White	Three Dog Night	30-Sep-72	Dunhill 4317
268	Time In A Bottle	Jim Croce	12-Jan-74	ABC 11405
269	Loves Me Like A Rock	Paul Simon	29-Sep-73	Columbia 45907
270	How Long	Ace	31-May-75	Anchor 21000
271	If I Can't Have You	Yvonne Elliman	13-May-78	RSO 884
272	Please Mr. Please	Olivia Newton-John	2-Aug-75	MCA 40418
273	With A Little Luck	Wings	20-May-78	Capitol 4559
274	Touch Me In The Morning	Diana Ross	11-Aug-73	Motown 1239
275	In The Summertime	Mungo Jerry	5-Sep-70	Janus 125
276	Rainy Night In Georgia	Brook Benton	14-Mar-70	Cotillion 44057
277	Theme From S.W.A.T.	Rhythm Heritage	28-Feb-76	ABC 12135
278	Please Don't Go	KC & The Sunshine Band	8-Dec-79	T.K. 1035
279	Just The Way You Are	Billy Joel	18-Feb-78	Columbia 10646
280	Band On The Run	Paul McCartney & Wings	8-Jun-74	Apple 1873
281	Cherish	David Cassidy	8-Jan-72	Bell 45,150

'70s Rank	TITLE	ACT	Peak Date	Label & No.
282	Bridge Over Troubled Water	Aretha Franklin	29-May-71	Atlantic 2796
283	When I Need You	Leo Sayer	7-May-77	Warner Bros. 8332
284	You Ain't Seen Nothing Yet	Bachman-Turner Overdrive	23-Nov-74	Mercury 73622
285	I'm Your Boogie Man	KC & The Sunshine Band	4-Jun-77	T.K. 1022
286	Before The Next Teardrop Falls	Freddy Fender	7-Jun-75	ABC/Dot 17540
287	I'd Love You To Want Me	Lobo	2-Dec-72	Big Tree 147
288	Playground In My Mind	Clint Holmes	30-Jun-73	Epic 10891
289	Goodbye Yellow Brick Road	Elton John	8-Dec-73	MCA 40148
290	You're Sixteen	Ringo Starr	2-Feb-74	Apple 1870
291	Love Rollercoaster	Ohio Players	17-Jan-76	Mercury 73734
292	You Should Be Dancing	Bee Gees	4-Sep-76	RSO 853
293	Cat's In The Cradle	Harry Chapin	28-Dec-74	Elektra 45203
294	You're The First, The Last, My Everything	Barry White	11-Jan-75	20th Century 2133
295	Don't Give Up On Us	David Soul	16-Apr-77	Private Stk 45,129
296	I Wish	Stevie Wonder	29-Jan-77	Tamla 54274
297	More, More, More (Pt. 1)	Andrea True Connection	3-Jul-76	Buddah 515
298	I'm Sorry	John Denver	11-Oct-75	RCA Victor 10353
299	You Haven't Done Nothin'	Stevie Wonder	2-Nov-74	Tamla 54252
300	Let's Do It Again	The Staple Singers	20-Dec-75	Curtom 0109
301	Pillow Talk	Sylvia	23-Jun-73	Vibration 521
302	December, 1963 (Oh, What A Night)	The Four Seasons	20-Mar-76	Warner/Curb 8168
303	Last Song	Edward Bear	17-Mar-73	Capitol 3452
304	Love Hangover	Diana Ross	12-Jun-76	Motown 1392
305	Listen To What The Man Said	Wings	12-Jul-75	Apple 4091
306	Blue Bayou	Linda Ronstadt	24-Dec-77	Asylum 45431
307	Rock'n Me	Steve Miller	6-Nov-76	Capitol 4323
308	Nothing From Nothing	Billy Preston	12-Oct-74	A&M 1544
309	Up Around The Bend	Creedence Clearwater Revival	30-May-70	Fantasy 641
310	Get Down Tonight	K.C. & The Sunshine Band	23-Aug-75	T.K. 1009
311	What's Going On	Marvin Gaye	10-Apr-71	Tamla 54201
312	Lucy In The Sky With Diamonds	Elton John	4-Jan-75	MCA 40344
313	Neither One Of Us (Wants To Be The First To Say Goodbye)	Gladys Knight & The Pips	7-Apr-73	Soul 35098
314	Dark Lady	Cher	30-Mar-74	MCA 40161
315	Dancing Queen	Abba	2-Apr-77	Atlantic 3372
316	Hooked On A Feeling	Blue Swede	6-Apr-74	EMI 3627
317	Outa-Space	Billy Preston	8-Jul-72	A&M 1320
318	Imagine	John Lennon Plastic Ono Band	20-Nov-71	Apple 1840
319	Lonely Days	Bee Gees	30-Jan-71	Atco 6795
320	I Can Help	Billy Swan	30-Nov-74	Monument 8621
321	Could It Be I'm Falling In Love	The Spinners	24-Feb-73	Atlantic 2927

'70s Rank	TITLE	ACT	Peak Date	Label & No.
322	Don't Stop	Fleetwood Mac	17-Sep-77	Warner Bros. 8413
323	Down By The Lazy River	The Osmonds	4-Mar-72	MGM 14324
324	Look What You Done For Me	Al Green	20-May-72	Hi 2211
325	The Night They Drove Old Dixie Down	Joan Baez	2-Oct-71	Vanguard 35138
326	Why Can't We Live Together	Timmy Thomas	10-Feb-73	Glades 1703
327	The Closer I Get To You	Roberta Flack with Donny Hathaway	20-May-78	Atlantic 3463
328	Jazzman	Carole King	9-Nov-74	Ode 66101
329	Yesterday Once More	Carpenters	4-Aug-73	A&M 1446
330	Rainy Days And Mondays	Carpenters	26-Jun-71	A&M 1260
331	Don't Let The Sun Go Down On Me	Elton John	3-Aug-74	MCA 40259
332	Fire	Ohio Players	22-Feb-75	Mercury 73643
333	Groove Me	King Floyd	16-Jan-71	Chimneyville 435
334	Rock On	David Essex	23-Mar-74	Columbia 45940
335	Fallin' In Love	Hamilton, Joe Frank & Reynolds	6-Sep-75	Playboy 6024
336	Still	Commodores	17-Nov-79	Motown 1474
337	Dreams	Fleetwood Mac	11-Jun-77	Warner Bros. 8371
338	Oh, Babe, What Would You Say?	Hurricane Smith	17-Feb-73	Capitol 3383
339	When Will I Be Loved	Linda Ronstadt	21-Jun-75	Capitol 4050
340	He Don't Love You (Like I Love You)	Tony Orlando And Dawn	3-May-75	Elektra 45240
341	Everything Is Beautiful	Ray Stevens	6-Jun-70	Barnaby 2011
342	It's A Heartache	Bonnie Tyler	24-Jun-78	RCA 11249
343	Ladies Night	Kool & The Gang	22-Dec-79	De-Lite 801
344	Theme From Mahogany (Do You Know Where You're Going To)	Diana Ross	10-Jan-76	Motown 1377
345	Gypsy Woman	Brian Hyland	5-Dec-70	Uni 55240
346	Someone Saved My Life Tonight	Elton John	16-Aug-75	MCA 40421
347	Nights In White Satin	The Moody Blues	4-Nov-72	Deram 85023
348	Papa Was A Rollin' Stone	The Temptations	9-Dec-72	Gordy 7121
349	Angie Baby	Helen Reddy	21-Dec-74	Capitol 3972
350	Love Grows (Where My Rosemary Goes)	Edison Lighthouse	4-Apr-70	Bell 858
351	You're No Good	Linda Ronstadt	15-Feb-75	Capitol 3990
352	Cecilia	Simon & Garfunkel	30-May-70	Columbia 45133
353	Clair	Gilbert O'Sullivan	6-Jan-73	MAM 3626
354	Heartache Tonight	Eagles	10-Nov-79	Asylum 46545
355	Black Water	The Doobie Brothers	22-Feb-75	Warner Bros. 8062
356	All Right Now	Free	31-Oct-70	A&M 1206
357	The Wreck Of The Edmund Fitzgerald	Gordon Lightfoot	13-Nov-76	Reprise 1369
358	Ain't No Sunshine	Bill Withers	2-Oct-71	Sussex 219
359	Pop Muzik	M	27-Oct-79	Sire 49033
360	Ain't No Woman (Like The One I've Got)	Four Tops	14-Apr-73	Dunhill 4339
361	Da Doo Ron Ron	Shaun Cassidy	9-Jul-77	Warner/Curb 8365

'70s Rank	TITLE	ACT	Peak Date	Label & No.
362	(Hey Won't You Play) Another Somebody Done Somebody Wrong Song	B.J. Thomas	26-Apr-75	ABC 12054
363	The Cisco Kid	War	12-May-73	United Artists 163
364	Ramblin' Man	The Allman Brothers Band	20-Oct-73	Capricorn 0027
365	The Rapper	The Jaggerz	21-Mar-70	Kama Sutra 502
366	Dancing Machine	The Jackson 5	18-May-74	Motown 1286
367	Rock Your Baby	George McCrae	20-Jul-74	T.K. 1004
368	I'm Not In Love	10cc	9-Aug-75	Mercury 73678
369	Fire And Rain	James Taylor	7-Nov-70	Warner Bros. 7423
370	Got To Give It Up Pt. I	Marvin Gaye	18-Jun-77	Tamla 54280
371	Spanish Harlem	Aretha Franklin	11-Sep-71	Atlantic 2817
372	Love Won't Let Me Wait	Major Harris	21-Jun-75	Atlantic 3248
373	Lay Down (Candles In The Rain)	Melanie	11-Jul-70	Buddah 167
374	Whatever Gets You Thru The Night	John Lennon	16-Nov-74	Apple 1874
375	Higher Ground	Stevie Wonder	13-Oct-73	Tamla 54235
376	Let 'Em In	Wings	28-Aug-76	Capitol 4293
377	It Never Rains In Southern California	Albert Hammond	30-Dec-72	Mums 6011
378	Hotel California	Eagles	23-Apr-77	Asylum 45386
379	Hello It's Me	Todd Rundgren	22-Dec-73	Bearsville 0009
380	Sylvia's Mother	Dr. Hook And The Medicine Show	17-Jun-72	Columbia 45562
381	Keep It Comin' Love	KC & The Sunshine Band	8-Oct-77	T.K. 1023
382	Daniel	Elton John	9-Jun-73	MCA 40046
383	We Are The Champions	Queen	21-Jan-78	Elektra 45441
384	Troglodyte (Cave Man)	The Jimmy Castor Bunch	15-Jul-72	RCA Victor 48-1029
385	Lay Down Sally	Eric Clapton	1-Apr-78	RSO 886
386	Car Wash	Rose Royce	15-Jan-77	MCA 40615
387	You're In My Heart (The Final Acclaim)	Rod Stewart	14-Jan-78	Warner Bros. 8475
388	Just You 'N' Me	Chicago	15-Dec-73	Columbia 45933
389	Can't Get Enough	Bad Company	26-Oct-74	Swan Song 70015
390	Americans	Byron Mac Gregor	16-Feb-74	Westbound 222
391	Ben	Michael Jackson	21-Oct-72	Motown 1207
392	Sharing The Night Together	Dr. Hook	9-Dec-78	Capitol 4621
393	No No Song	Ringo Starr	5-Apr-75	Apple 1880
394	You Needed Me	Anne Murray	21-Oct-78	Capitol 4574
395	Wildfire	Michael Murphey	28-Jun-75	Epic 50084
396	Rikki Don't Lose That Number	Steely Dan	27-Jul-74	ABC 11439
397	Love So Right	Bee Gees	4-Dec-76	RSO 859
398	I Like Dreamin'	Kenny Nolan	12-Mar-77	20th Century 2287
399	How Much I Feel	Ambrosia	18-Nov-78	Warner Bros. 8640
400	Then Came You	Dionne Warwicke & Spinners	5-Oct-74	Atlantic 3029
401	Day After Day	Badfinger	29-Jan-72	Apple 1841
402	Holly Holy	Neil Diamond	3-Jan-70	Uni 55175

'70s Rank	TITLE	ACT	Peak Date	Label & No.
403	Hopelessly Devoted To You	Olivia Newton-John	23-Sep-78	RSO 903
404	Can't Get Enough Of Your Love, Babe	Barry White	14-Sep-74	20th Century 2120
405	Sometimes When We Touch	Dan Hill	18-Feb-78	20th Century 2355
406	My Life	Billy Joel	13-Jan-79	Columbia 10853
407	Turn Back The Hands Of Time	Tyrone Davis	16-May-70	Dakar 616
408	Dim All The Lights	Donna Summer	10-Nov-79	Casablanca 2201
409	Me And Bobby McGee	Janis Joplin	20-Mar-71	Columbia 45314
410	Lonely Boy	Andrew Gold	25-Jun-77	Asylum 45384
411	Run Joey Run	David Geddes	4-Oct-75	Big Tree 16044
412	Mr. Jaws	Dickie Goodman	18-Oct-75	Cash 451
413	Moonlight Feels Right	Starbuck	31-Jul-76	Private Stk 45,039
414	Blinded By The Light	Manfred Mann's Earth Band	5-Feb-77	Warner Bros. 8252
415	My Melody Of Love	Bobby Vinton	23-Nov-74	ABC 12022
416	Music Box Dancer	Frank Mills	14-Apr-79	Polydor 14517
417	Puppy Love	Donny Osmond	25-Mar-72	MGM 14367
418	Spiders And Snakes	Jim Stafford	2-Mar-74	MGM 14648
419	New Kid In Town	Eagles	19-Feb-77	Asylum 45373
420	Scorpio	Dennis Coffey And The Detroit Guitar Band	22-Jan-72	Sussex 226
421	Love To Love You Baby	Donna Summer	14-Feb-76	Oasis 401
422	Best Of My Love	Eagles	15-Feb-75	Asylum 45218
423	Stuck In The Middle With You	Stealers Wheel	26-May-73	A&M 1416
424	A Little More Love	Olivia Newton-John	17-Feb-79	MCA 40975
425	I Just Wanna Stop	Gino Vannelli	9-Dec-78	A&M 2072
426	Little Willy	Sweet	21-Apr-73	Bell 45,251
427	Sunshine	Jonathan Edwards	22-Jan-72	Capricorn 8021
428	Smokin' In The Boy's Room	Brownsville Station	26-Jan-74	Big Tree 16,011
429	Sister Golden Hair	America	14-Jun-75	Warner Bros. 8086
430	Hitchin' A Ride	Vanity Fare	27-Jun-70	Page One 21,029
431	Lyin' Eyes	Eagles	25-Oct-75	Asylum 45279
432	Baby I'm-A Want You	Bread	4-Dec-71	Elektra 45751
433	Tell Me Something Good	Rufus	31-Aug-74	ABC 11427
434	In The Rain	The Dramatics	22-Apr-72	Volt 4075
435	Ride Captain Ride	Blues Image	4-Jul-70	Atco 6746
436	Don't Leave Me This Way	Thelma Houston	9-Apr-77	Tamla 54278
437	I'm In You	Peter Frampton	23-Jul-77	A&M 1941
438	Gonna Fly Now (Theme From "Rocky")	Bill Conti	25-Jun-77	United Artists 940
439	You Are The Sunshine Of My Life	Stevie Wonder	19-May-73	Tamla 54232
440	Black Magic Woman	Santana	2-Jan-71	Columbia 45270
441	When Will I See You Again	The Three Degrees	7-Dec-74	Phila. Int'l 3550
442	Chuck E.'s In Love	Rickie Lee Jones	30-Jun-79	Warner Bros. 8825
443	Say, Has Anybody Seen My Sweet Gypsy Rose	Dawn Featuring Tony Orlando	22-Sep-73	Bell 45,374

'70s Rank	TITLE	ACT	Peak Date	Label & No.
444	Garden Party	Rick Nelson And The Stone Canyon Band	11-Nov-72	Decca 32980
445	Julie, Do Ya Love Me	Bobby Sherman	26-Sep-70	Metromedia 194
446	If You Don't Know Me By Now	Harold Melvin And The Blue Notes	2-Dec-72	Phila. Int'l 3520
447	No Time	The Guess Who	21-Feb-70	RCA Victor 74-0300
448	Hot Blooded	Foreigner	19-Aug-78	Atlantic 3488
449	Kodachrome	Paul Simon	14-Jul-73	Columbia 45859
450	Best Thing That Ever Happened To Me	Gladys Knight & The Pips	20-Apr-74	Buddah 403
451	Sweet Thing	Rufus Featuring Chaka Khan	27-Mar-76	ABC 12149
452	Reminiscing	Little River Band	14-Oct-78	Harvest 4605
453	Mockingbird	Carly Simon & James Taylor	30-Mar-74	Elektra 45880
454	Have You Ever Seen The Rain	Creedence Clearwater Revival	6-Mar-71	Fantasy 655
455	Feel Like Makin' Love	Roberta Flack	17-Aug-74	Atlantic 3025
456	Mercy Mercy Me (The Ecology)	Marvin Gaye	28-Aug-71	Tamla 54207
457	Handy Man	James Taylor	10-Sep-77	Columbia 10557
458	I Got A Name	Jim Croce	24-Nov-73	ABC 11389
459	Jam Up Jelly Tight	Tommy Roe	10-Jan-70	ABC 11247
460	Why Can't We Be Friends?	War	16-Aug-75	United Artists 629
461	Come And Get Your Love	Redbone	27-Apr-74	Epic 11035
462	I'd Really Love To See You Tonight	England Dan & John Ford Coley	11-Sep-76	Big Tree 16069
463	The Things We Do For Love	10 CC	9-Apr-77	Mercury 73875
464	Also Sprach Zarathustra (2001)	Deodato	24-Mar-73	CTI 12
465	Sir Duke	Stevie Wonder	28-May-77	Tamla 54281
466	The Rubberband Man	The Spinners	18-Dec-76	Atlantic 3355
467	Sing	Carpenters	14-Apr-73	A&M 1413
468	The Show Must Go On	Three Dog Night	11-May-74	Dunhill 4382
469	Love Is Alive	Gary Wright	24-Jul-76	Warner Bros. 8143
470	Mother And Child Reunion	Paul Simon	25-Mar-72	Columbia 45547
471	Fooled Around And Fell In Love	Elvin Bishop	22-May-76	Capricorn 0252
472	Smoke On The Water	Deep Purple	28-Jul-73	Warner Bros. 7710
473	I've Got Love On My Mind	Natalie Cole	30-Apr-77	Capitol 4360
474	Whatcha Gonna Do?	Pablo Cruise	13-Aug-77	A&M 1920
475	Get Down	Gilbert O'Sullivan	11-Aug-73	MAM 3629
476	Float On	The Floaters	17-Sep-77	ABC 12284
477	Show Me The Way	Peter Frampton	8-May-76	A&M 1693/1795
478	If I Were Your Woman	Gladys Knight & The Pips	30-Jan-71	Soul 35078
479	Be Thankful For What You Got	William DeVaughn	29-Jun-74	Roxbury 0236
480	Got To Get You Into My Life	The Beatles	7-Aug-76	Capitol 4274
481	Miracles	Jefferson Starship	25-Oct-75	Grunt 10367
482	In The Navy	Village People	19-May-79	Casablanca 973
483	Nights On Broadway	Bee Gees	6-Dec-75	RSO 515
484	I Want You To Want Me	Cheap Trick	28-Jul-79	Epic 50680

'70s Rank	TITLE	ACT	Peak Date	Label & No.
485	Have You Seen Her	The Chi-Lites	20-Nov-71	Brunswick 55462
486	Bohemian Rhapsody	Queen	24-Apr-76	Elektra 45297
487	Rockin' Pneumonia - Boogie Woogie Flu	Johnny Rivers	6-Jan-73	United Artists 50960
488	Fly Like An Eagle	Steve Miller	19-Feb-77	Capitol 4372
489	Stoned Love	The Supremes	16-Jan-71	Motown 1172
490	Devil Woman	Cliff Richard	2-Oct-76	Rocket/MCA 40574
491	When You're In Love With A Beautiful Woman	Dr. Hook	11-Aug-79	Capitol 4705
492	Dream On	Aerosmith	1-Dec-73 / 27-Mar-76	Columbia 45894
493	The Way I Want To Touch You	Captain & Tennille	15-Nov-75	A&M 1725
494	House Of The Rising Sun	Frijid Pink	4-Apr-70	Parrot 341
495	The Main Event/Fight	Barbra Streisand	25-Aug-79	Columbia 11008
496	Do You Know What I Mean	Lee Michaels	23-Oct-71	A&M 1262
497	Betcha By Golly, Wow	The Stylistics	6-May-72	Avco 4591
498	I Hear You Knocking	Dave Edmunds	13-Feb-71	MAM 3601
499	I Love The Nightlife (Disco 'round)	Alicia Bridges	9-Dec-78	Polydor 14483
500	Hot Line	The Sylvers	22-Jan-77	Capitol 4336
501	Angel In Your Arms	Hot	2-Jul-77	Big Tree 16085
502	Jet Airliner	Steve Miller Band	9-Jul-77	Capitol 4424
503	Something's Burning	Kenny Rogers And The First Edition	9-May-70	Reprise 0888
504	Shannon	Henry Gross	22-May-76	Lifesong 45002
505	Go All The Way	Raspberries	14-Oct-72	Capitol 3348
506	Rock And Roll Heaven	The Righteous Brothers	27-Jul-74	Haven 7002
507	Only Sixteen	Dr. Hook	24-Apr-76	Capitol 4171
508	I Go Crazy	Paul Davis	25-Mar-78	Bang 733
509	You'll Never Find Another Love Like Mine	Lou Rawls	4-Sep-76	Phila. Int'l 3592
510	I'll Never Love This Way Again	Dionne Warwick	29-Sep-79	Arista 0419
511	Dust In The Wind	Kansas	15-Apr-78	Kirshner 4274
512	Last Dance	Donna Summer	5-Aug-78	Casablanca 926
513	She's Gone	Daryl Hall & John Oates	23-Mar-74 / 23-Oct-76	Atlantic 2993
514	Hold The Line	Toto	20-Jan-79	Columbia 10830
515	Midnight At The Oasis	Maria Muldaur	1-Jun-74	Reprise 1183
516	I'll Meet You Halfway	The Partridge Family	19-Jun-71	Bell 996
517	Clean Up Woman	Betty Wright	29-Jan-72	Alston 4601
518	Dazz	Brick	22-Jan-77	Bang 727
519	Fox On The Run	Sweet	10-Jan-76	Capitol 4157
520	Whenever I Call You "Friend"	Kenny Loggins	21-Oct-78	Columbia 10794
521	Jack And Jill	Raydio	15-Apr-78	Arista 0283
522	Rock And Roll Part 2	Gary Glitter	23-Sep-72	Bell 45,237
523	Sugar Daddy	The Jackson 5	29-Jan-72	Motown 1194

'70s Rank	TITLE	ACT	Peak Date	Label & No.
524	Shake Your Body (Down To The Ground)	The Jacksons	19-May-79	Epic 50656
525	Makin' It	David Naughton	28-Jul-79	RSO 916
526	Love You Inside Out	Bee Gees	9-Jun-79	RSO 925
527	Heaven On The 7Th Floor	Paul Nicholas	3-Dec-77	RSO 878
528	Does Anybody Really Know What Time It Is?	Chicago	2-Jan-71	Columbia 45264
529	I Am...I Said	Neil Diamond	24-Apr-71	Uni 55278
530	Let Her In	John Travolta	24-Jul-76	Midland Int'l 10623
531	Take It To The Limit	Eagles	28-Feb-76	Asylum 45293
532	O-o-h Child	The Five Stairsteps	1-Aug-70	Buddah 165
533	On And On	Stephen Bishop	24-Sep-77	ABC 12260
534	The Letter	Joe Cocker	13-Jun-70	A&M 1174
535	25 Or 6 To 4	Chicago	12-Sep-70	Columbia 45194
536	Somebody's Been Sleeping	100 Proof Aged In Soul	14-Nov-70	Hot Wax 7004
537	Don't Cry Daddy	Elvis Presley	24-Jan-70	RCA Victor 47-9768
538	Green-Eyed Lady	Sugarloaf	31-Oct-70	Liberty 56183
539	Let Me Be There	Olivia Newton-John	16-Feb-74	MCA 40101
540	(I Know) I'm Losing You	Rare Earth	10-Oct-70	Rare Earth 5017
541	Psychedelic Shack	The Temptations	7-Mar-70	Gordy 7096
542	That Lady (Part 1)	The Isley Brothers	13-Oct-73	T-Neck 2251
543	Natural High	Bloodstone	21-Jul-73	London 1046
544	Feelings	Morris Albert	4-Oct-75	RCA Victor 10279
545	Looks Like We Made It	Barry Manilow	16-Jul-77	Arista 0244
546	An Old Fashioned Love Song	Three Dog Night	18-Dec-71	Dunhill 4294
547	Lead Me On	Maxine Nightingale	8-Sep-79	Windsong 11530
548	Stay Awhile	The Bells	8-May-71	Polydor 15023
549	Tired Of Being Alone	Al Green	23-Oct-71	Hi 2194
550	Easy	Commodores	27-Aug-77	Motown 1418
551	The Cover Of "Rolling Stone"	Dr. Hook And The Medicine Show	24-Mar-73	Columbia 45732
552	Sara Smile	Daryl Hall & John Oates	12-Jun-76	RCA Victor 10530
553	Junior's Farm	Paul McCartney & Wings	4-Jan-75	Apple 1875
554	Ain't No Way To Treat A Lady	Helen Reddy	25-Oct-75	Capitol 4128
555	Peace Train	Cat Stevens	20-Nov-71	A&M 1291
556	Telephone Line	Electric Light Orchestra	24-Sep-77	United Artists 1000
557	Heaven Knows	Donna Summer	10-Mar-79	Casablanca 959
558	Your Mama Don't Dance	Loggins & Messina	20-Jan-73	Columbia 45719
559	More Than A Feeling	Boston	27-Nov-76	Epic 50266
560	After The Love Has Gone	Earth, Wind & Fire	8-Sep-79	ARC 11033
561	Feels So Good	Chuck Mangione	3-Jun-78	A&M 2001
562	Love Will Find A Way	Pablo Cruise	12-Aug-78	A&M 2048
563	Come And Get It	Badfinger	18-Apr-70	Apple 1815
564	Danny's Song	Anne Murray	14-Apr-73	Capitol 3481

'70s Rank	TITLE	ACT	Peak Date	Label & No.
565	Year Of The Cat	Al Stewart	12-Mar-77	Janus 266
566	The Logical Song	Supertramp	16-Jun-79	A&M 2128
567	Tighter, Tighter	Alive And Kicking	15-Aug-70	Roulette 7078
568	Chick-A-Boom (Don't Ya Jes' Love It)	Daddy Dewdrop	29-May-71	Sunflower 105
569	Just When I Needed You Most	Randy Vanwarmer	9-Jun-79	Bearsville 0334
570	Magic	Pilot	12-Jul-75	EMI 3992
571	Summer Nights	John Travolta, Olivia Newton-John & Cast	30-Sep-78	RSO 906
572	A Cowboy's Work Is Never Done	Sonny & Cher	6-May-72	Kapp 2163
573	I Love Music (Part 1)	The O'Jays	24-Jan-76	Phila. Int'l 3577
574	Send One Your Love	Stevie Wonder	22-Dec-79	Tamla 54303
575	Who Loves You	Four Seasons	1-Nov-75	Warner/Curb 8122
576	Signs	Five Man Electrical Band	4-Sep-71	Lionel 3213
577	Wasted Days And Wasted Nights	Freddy Fender	20-Sep-75	ABC/Dot 17558
578	Swayin' To The Music (Slow Dancin')	Johnny Rivers	15-Oct-77	Big Tree 16094
579	Don't Bring Me Down	Electric Light Orchestra	22-Sep-79	Jet 5060
580	That's Rock 'N' Roll	Shaun Cassidy	22-Oct-77	Warner/Curb 8423
581	Enjoy Yourself	The Jacksons	12-Feb-77	Epic 50289
582	(Last Night) I Didn't Get To Sleep At All	The 5th Dimension	17-Jun-72	Bell 45,195
583	Saturday In The Park	Chicago	30-Sep-72	Columbia 45657
584	Proud Mary	Ike & Tina Turner	27-Mar-71	Liberty 56216
585	After The Lovin'	Engelbert Humperdinck	8-Jan-77	Epic 50270
586	The Devil Went Down To Georgia	Charlie Daniels Band	1-Sep-79	Epic 50700
587	We're All Alone	Rita Coolidge	17-Dec-77	A&M 1965
588	Beach Baby	First Class	19-Oct-74	UK 49022
589	Freddie's Dead (Theme From "Superfly")	Curtis Mayfield	11-Nov-72	Curtom 1975
590	Without Love (There Is Nothing)	Tom Jones	7-Feb-70	Parrot 40045
591	Hocus Pocus	Focus	16-Jun-73	Sire 704
592	Reflections Of My Life	Marmalade	23-May-70	London 20058
593	Shake Your Groove Thing	Peaches & Herb	17-Mar-79	Polydor/MVP 14514
594	I Feel Love	Donna Summer	12-Nov-77	Casablanca 884
595	Superstar	Murray Head	5-Jun-71	Decca 32603
596	Dance With Me	Orleans	18-Oct-75	Asylum 45261
597	School's Out	Alice Cooper	5-Aug-72	Warner Bros. 7596
598	I'm Not Lisa	Jessi Colter	28-Jun-75	Capitol 4009
599	Low Rider	War	8-Nov-75	United Artists 706
600	Shop Around	Captain & Tennille	19-Jun-76	A&M 1817
601	Use Ta Be My Girl	The O'Jays	15-Jul-78	Phila. Int'l 3642
602	Daddy's Home	Jermaine Jackson	17-Mar-73	Motown 1216
603	You Are So Beautiful	Joe Cocker	29-Mar-75	A&M 1641
604	Another Day	Paul McCartney	1-May-71	Apple 1829
605	I've Found Someone Of My Own	The Free Movement	30-Oct-71	Decca 32818
606	Sky High	Jigsaw	20-Dec-75	Chelsea 3022

'70s Rank	TITLE	ACT	Peak Date	Label & No.
607	Chevy Van	Sammy Johns	26-Apr-75	GRC 2046
608	Gold	John Stewart	4-Aug-79	RSO 931
609	Slippin' Into Darkness	War	27-May-72	United Artists 50867
610	Carry On Wayward Son	Kansas	19-Mar-77	Kirshner 4267
611	Baby Hold On	Eddie Money	3-Jun-78	Columbia 10663
612	Boogie Wonderland	Earth, Wind & Fire With The Emotions	7-Jul-79	ARC 10956
613	Travelin' Band	Creedence Clearwater Revival	14-Mar-70	Fantasy 637
614	Sweet And Innocent	Donny Osmond	5-Jun-71	MGM 14227
615	Love Hurts	Nazareth	13-Mar-76	A&M 1671
616	Fly Away	John Denver	10-Jan-76	RCA Victor 10517
617	Hold Your Head Up	Argent	2-Sep-72	Epic 10852
618	Drift Away	Dobie Gray	12-May-73	Decca 33057
619	Only You	Ringo Starr	4-Jan-75	Apple 1876
620	Don't Expect Me To Be Your Friend	Lobo	17-Feb-73	Big Tree 158
621	Never Been To Spain	Three Dog Night	12-Feb-72	Dunhill 4299
622	Goodnight Tonight	Wings	19-May-79	Columbia 10939
623	Here You Come Again	Dolly Parton	21-Jan-78	RCA 11123
624	Vehicle	The Ides Of March	9-May-70	Warner Bros. 7378
625	If You Love Me (Let Me Know)	Olivia Newton-John	29-Jun-74	MCA 40209
626	So In To You	Atlanta Rhythm Section	23-Apr-77	Polydor 14373
627	How Do You Do?	Mouth & MacNeal	12-Aug-72	Philips 40715
628	I'm Gonna Love You Just A Little More Baby	Barry White	23-Jun-73	20th Century 2018
629	Take A Chance On Me	Abba	1-Jul-78	Atlantic 3457
630	Ma Belle Amie	The Tee Set	14-Mar-70	Colossus 107
631	Your Song	Elton John	23-Jan-71	Uni 55265
632	For All We Know	Carpenters	20-Mar-71	A&M 1243
633	I'll Never Fall In Love Again	Dionne Warwick	7-Feb-70	Scepter 12273
634	Rocky Mountain High	John Denver	10-Mar-73	RCA Victor 74-0829
635	Jingle Jangle	The Archies	24-Jan-70	Kirshner 5002
636	Snowbird	Anne Murray	3-Oct-70	Capitol 2738
637	The Morning After	Maureen McGovern	11-Aug-73	20th Century 2010
638	The Twelfth Of Never	Donny Osmond	12-May-73	MGM 14503
639	Poetry Man	Phoebe Snow	12-Apr-75	Shelter 40353
640	Bad Time	Grand Funk	14-Jun-75	Capitol 4046
641	If You Could Read My Mind	Gordon Lightfoot	6-Mar-71	Reprise 0974
642	Everything I Own	Bread	11-Mar-72	Elektra 45765
643	The Bitch Is Back	Elton John	26-Oct-74	MCA 40297
644	Jungle Fever	Chakachas	1-Apr-72	Polydor 15030
645	Jet	Paul McCartney & Wings	23-Mar-74	Apple 1871
646	Sultans Of Swing	Dire Straits	7-Apr-79	Warner Bros. 8736
647	Night Moves	Bob Seger	5-Mar-77	Capitol 4369

'70s Rank	TITLE	ACT	Peak Date	Label & No.
648	Nadia's Theme (The Young And The Restless)	Barry Devorzon And Perry Botkin, Jr.	4-Dec-76	A&M 1856
649	Still The Same	Bob Seger	15-Jul-78	Capitol 4581
650	I Don't Like To Sleep Alone	Paul Anka	24-May-75	United Artists 615
651	Living For The City	Stevie Wonder	12-Jan-74	Tamla 54242
652	Still The One	Orleans	9-Oct-76	Asylum 45336
653	Swearin' To God	Frankie Valli	26-Jul-75	Private Stk 45,021
654	All I Ever Need Is You	Sonny & Cher	1-Jan-72	Kapp 2151
655	An Everlasting Love	Andy Gibb	9-Sep-78	RSO 904
656	Dance, Dance, Dance (Yowsah, Yowsah, Yowsah)	Chic	18-Feb-78	Atlantic 3435
657	My Heart Belongs To Me	Barbra Streisand	30-Jul-77	Columbia 10555
658	Evil Woman	Electric Light Orchestra	14-Feb-76	United Artists 729
659	Superfly	Curtis Mayfield	13-Jan-73	Curtom 1978
660	He Ain't Heavy, He's My Brother	Hollies	14-Mar-70	Epic 10532
661	Do It ('Til You're Satisfied)	B.T. Express	7-Dec-74	Roadshow 12395
662	Sideshow	Blue Magic	10-Aug-74	Atco 6961
663	(Our Love) Don't Throw It All Away	Andy Gibb	23-Dec-78	RSO 911
664	Jane	Jefferson Starship	29-Dec-79	Grunt 11750
665	Longfellow Serenade	Neil Diamond	23-Nov-74	Columbia 10043
666	If	Bread	8-May-71	Elektra 45720
667	The Lord's Prayer	Sister Janet Mead	13-Apr-74	A&M 1491
668	Lady	Styx	15-Mar-75	Wooden Nickel 10102
669	Love Or Let Me Be Lonely	The Friends Of Distinction	2-May-70	RCA Victor 74-0319
670	Could It Be Magic	Barry Manilow	20-Sep-75	Arista 0126
671	You Don't Mess Around With Jim	Jim Croce	9-Sep-72	ABC 11328
672	Lonesome Loser	Little River Band	29-Sep-79	Capitol 4748
673	Get Closer	Seals & Crofts	14-Aug-76	Warner Bros. 8190
674	Until You Come Back To Me (That's What I'm Gonna Do)	Aretha Franklin	9-Feb-74	Atlantic 2995
675	Easy Come, Easy Go	Bobby Sherman	18-Apr-70	Metromedia 177
676	Midnight Blue	Melissa Manchester	9-Aug-75	Arista 0116
677	Hollywood Swinging	Kool & The Gang	6-Jul-74	De-Lite 561
678	Fight The Power Part 1	The Isley Brothers	13-Sep-75	T-Neck 2256
679	Sweet Love	Commodores	24-Apr-76	Motown 1381
680	Evil Ways	Santana	14-Mar-70	Columbia 45069
681	Walk Away From Love	David Ruffin	24-Jan-76	Motown 1376
682	Little Bitty Pretty One	The Jackson 5	3-Jun-72	Motown 1199
683	You Are Everything	The Stylistics	29-Jan-72	Avco 4581
684	What's Your Name	Lynyrd Skynyrd	4-Mar-78	MCA 40819
685	Day Dreaming	Aretha Franklin	6-May-72	Atlantic 2866
686	Help Me	Joni Mitchell	1-Jun-74	Asylum 11034

'70s Rank	TITLE	ACT	Peak Date	Label & No.
687	Baby, What A Big Surprise	Chicago	10-Dec-77	Columbia 10620
688	Feels Like The First Time	Foreigner	25-Jun-77	Atlantic 3394
689	Sweet Hitch-Hiker	Creedence Clearwater Revival	28-Aug-71	Fantasy 665
690	Sweet Mary	Wadsworth Mansion	20-Feb-71	Sussex 209
691	Share The Land	The Guess Who	5-Dec-70	RCA Victor 74-0388
692	Thunder Island	Jay Ferguson	1-Apr-78	Asylum 45444
693	Stand Tall	Burton Cummings	25-Dec-76	Portrait 70001
694	Sing A Song	Earth, Wind & Fire	7-Feb-76	Columbia 10251
695	Stoney End	Barbra Streisand	30-Jan-71	Columbia 45236
696	Slip Slidin' Away	Paul Simon	14-Jan-78	Columbia 10630
697	Emma	Hot Chocolate	26-Apr-75	Big Tree 16031
698	I Believe In You (You Believe In Me)	Johnnie Taylor	1-Sep-73	Stax 0161
699	Two Out Of Three Ain't Bad	Meat Loaf	24-Jun-78	Cleveland Int'l/Epic 50513
700	Come Sail Away	Styx	14-Jan-78	A&M 1977
701	Earache My Eye (Featuring Alice Bowie)	Cheech & Chong	5-Oct-74	Ode 66102
702	The Happiest Girl In The Whole U.S.A.	Donna Fargo	2-Sep-72	Dot 17409
703	Hang On In There Baby	Johnny Bristol	21-Sep-74	MGM 14715
704	Sha-La-La (Make Me Happy)	Al Green	14-Dec-74	Hi 2274
705	Long Tall Glasses (I Can Dance)	Leo Sayer	3-May-75	Warner Bros. 8043
706	The Air That I Breathe	The Hollies	20-Jul-74	Epic 11100
707	Ballroom Blitz	Sweet	18-Oct-75	Capitol 4055
708	Paper Roses	Marie Osmond	17-Nov-73	MGM 14609
709	A Little Bit More	Dr. Hook	25-Sep-76	Capitol 4280
710	Back Home Again	John Denver	16-Nov-74	RCA Victor 10065
711	Magic Man	Heart	23-Oct-76	Mushroom 7011
712	Love Her Madly	The Doors	22-May-71	Elektra 45726
713	What Is Life	George Harrison	10-Apr-71	Apple 1828
714	Happy Days	Pratt & McClain	29-May-76	Reprise 1351
715	Golden Years	David Bowie	20-Mar-76	RCA Victor 10441
716	You Are The Woman	Firefall	27-Nov-76	Atlantic 3335
717	Don't Knock My Love - Pt. I	Wilson Pickett	3-Jul-71	Atlantic 2797
718	Sentimental Lady	Bob Welch	31-Dec-77	Capitol 4479
719	Early In The Morning	Vanity Fare	7-Feb-70	Page One 21,027
720	Drowning In The Sea Of Love	Joe Simon	29-Jan-72	Spring 120
721	Summer Breeze	Seals & Crofts	2-Dec-72	Warner Bros. 7606
722	Funny Face	Donna Fargo	30-Dec-72	Dot 17429
723	You Made Me Believe In Magic	Bay City Rollers	20-Aug-77	Arista 0256
724	Stick-Up	Honey Cone	2-Oct-71	Hot Wax 7106
725	You Decorated My Life	Kenny Rogers	3-Nov-79	United Artists 1315
726	Walkin' In The Rain With The One I Love	Love Unlimited	10-Jun-72	Uni 55319
727	(Every Time I Turn Around) Back In Love Again	L.T.D.	7-Jan-78	A&M 1974

'70s Rank	TITLE	ACT	Peak Date	Label & No.
728	September	Earth, Wind & Fire	20-Jan-79	ARC 10854
729	Lay A Little Lovin' On Me	Robin McNamara	22-Aug-70	Steed 724
730	Immigrant Song	Led Zeppelin	9-Jan-71	Atlantic 2777
731	Space Race	Billy Preston	1-Dec-73	A&M 1463
732	Amos Moses	Jerry Reed	6-Mar-71	RCA Victor 47-9904
733	Money Honey	Bay City Rollers	27-Mar-76	Arista 0170
734	Beth	Kiss	13-Nov-76	Casablanca 863
735	Dance With Me	Peter Brown	1-Jul-78	Drive 6269
736	See Me, Feel Me	The Who	28-Nov-70	Decca 32729
737	Please Come To Boston	Dave Loggins	17-Aug-74	Epic 11115
738	Double Vision	Foreigner	11-Nov-78	Atlantic 3514
739	Where Is The Love	Roberta Flack & Donny Hathaway	5-Aug-72	Atlantic 2879
740	Heat Wave	Linda Ronstadt	15-Nov-75	Asylum 45282
741	One Man Woman/One Woman Man	Paul Anka With Odia Coates	25-Jan-75	United Artists 569
742	Right Time Of The Night	Jennifer Warnes	7-May-77	Arista 0223
743	Arizona	Mark Lindsay	14-Feb-70	Columbia 45037
744	Some Kind Of Wonderful	Grand Funk	15-Feb-75	Capitol 4002
745	You Won't See Me	Anne Murray	20-Jul-74	Capitol 3867
746	Breaking Up Is Hard To Do	Neil Sedaka	14-Feb-76	Rocket/MCA 40500
747	Love Is Like Oxygen	Sweet	17-Jun-78	Capitol 4549
748	She Believes In Me	Kenny Rogers	7-Jul-79	United Artists 1273
749	Watching Scotty Grow	Bobby Goldsboro	20-Feb-71	United Artists 50727
750	Tubular Bells	Mike Oldfield	4-May-74	Virgin 55100
751	Won't Get Fooled Again	The Who	18-Sep-71	Decca 32846
752	Margaritaville	Jimmy Buffett	9-Jul-77	ABC 12254
753	Lido Shuffle	Boz Scaggs	7-May-77	Columbia 10491
754	My Little Town	Simon & Garfunkel	29-Nov-75	Columbia 10230
755	5-10-15-20 (25-30 Years Of Love)	The Presidents	5-Dec-70	Sussex 207
756	Sweet Home Alabama	Lynyrd Skynyrd	19-Oct-74	MCA 40258
757	Weekend In New England	Barry Manilow	12-Feb-77	Arista 0212
758	Stumblin' In	Suzi Quatro And Chris Norman	21-Apr-79	RSO 917
759	She's Not Just Another Woman	The 8th Day	10-Jul-71	Invictus 9087
760	I'm Leaving It (All) Up To You	Donny And Marie Osmond	7-Sep-74	MGM 14735
761	For The Love Of Him	Bobbi Martin	23-May-70	United Artists 50602
762	Gimme Dat Ding	The Pipkins	11-Jul-70	Capitol 2819
763	I Woke Up In Love This Morning	The Partridge Family	2-Oct-71	Bell 45,130
764	When You're Hot, You're Hot	Jerry Reed	3-Jul-71	RCA Victor 47-9976
765	My Maria	B.W. Stevenson	13-Oct-73	RCA Victor 0030
766	The Way We Were/Try To Remember	Gladys Knight & The Pips	12-Jul-75	Buddah 463
767	Sorry Seems To Be The Hardest Word	Elton John	1-Jan-77	MCA/Rocket 40645
768	Rock Steady	Aretha Franklin	11-Dec-71	Atlantic 2838

'70s Rank	TITLE	ACT	Peak Date	Label & No.
769	Mr. Bojangles	Nitty Gritty Dirt Band	27-Feb-71	Liberty 56197
770	Montego Bay	Bobby Bloom	5-Dec-70	L&R/MGM 157
771	All I Know	Garfunkel	10-Nov-73	Columbia 45926
772	Reeling In The Years	Steely Dan	19-May-73	ABC 11352
773	Mama Can't Buy You Love	Elton John	18-Aug-79	MCA 41042
774	Just Don't Want To Be Lonely	The Main Ingredient	11-May-74	RCA Victor 0205
775	Walk This Way	Aerosmith	29-Jan-77	Columbia 10449
776	Sweet City Woman	Stampeders	16-Oct-71	Bell 45,120
777	Takin' Care Of Business	Bachman-Turner Overdrive	17-Aug-74	Mercury 73487
778	Lola	The Kinks	24-Oct-70	Reprise 0930
779	(I've Been) Searchin' So Long	Chicago	1-Jun-74	Columbia 46020
780	Wildflower	Skylark	26-May-73	Capitol 3511
781	You And Me	Alice Cooper	20-Aug-77	Warner Bros. 8349
782	One Of A Kind (Love Affair)	The Spinners	30-Jun-73	Atlantic 2962
783	Bring The Boys Home	Freda Payne	31-Jul-71	Invictus 9092
784	Use Me	Bill Withers	21-Oct-72	Sussex 241
785	You're Only Lonely	J.D. Souther	15-Dec-79	Columbia 11079
786	No Matter What	Badfinger	19-Dec-70	Apple 1822
787	I Just Want To Celebrate	Rare Earth	18-Sep-71	Rare Earth 5031
788	Magnet And Steel	Walter Egan	19-Aug-78	Columbia 10719
789	Don't Look Back	Boston	30-Sep-78	Epic 50590
790	Shame	Evelyn "Champagne" King	2-Sep-78	RCA 11122
791	Couldn't Get It Right	Climax Blues Band	28-May-77	Sire 736
792	It's Only Make Believe	Glen Campbell	7-Nov-70	Capitol 2905
793	The Way Of Love	Cher	25-Mar-72	Kapp 2158
794	Temptation Eyes	The Grass Roots	27-Mar-71	Dunhill 4263
795	Liar	Three Dog Night	4-Sep-71	Dunhill 4282
796	Ooh Baby Baby	Linda Ronstadt	20-Jan-79	Asylum 45546
797	One Toke Over The Line	Brewer And Shipley	24-Apr-71	Kama Sutra 516
798	Oh My My	Ringo Starr	27-Apr-74	Apple 1872
799	Lookin' For A Love	Bobby Womack	27-Apr-74	United Artists 375
800	Cold As Ice	Foreigner	15-Oct-77	Atlantic 3410
801	Day By Day	Godspell	5-Aug-72	Bell 45,210
802	Every 1's A Winner	Hot Chocolate	3-Feb-79	Infinity 50002
803	This Will Be	Natalie Cole	22-Nov-75	Capitol 4109
804	Long Train Runnin'	The Doobie Brothers	7-Jul-73	Warner Bros. 7698
805	Life's Been Good	Joe Walsh	12-Aug-78	Asylum 45493
806	Running On Empty	Jackson Browne	29-Apr-78	Asylum 45460
807	Do It Again	Steely Dan	17-Feb-73	ABC 11338
808	You Can't Change That	Raydio	11-Aug-79	Arista 0399
809	I've Got To Use My Imagination	Gladys Knight & The Pips	19-Jan-74	Buddah 393
810	Love On A Two-Way Street	Moments	13-Jun-70	Stang 5012

'70s Rank	TITLE	ACT	Peak Date	Label & No.
811	Rockin' Chair	Gwen McCrae	19-Jul-75	Cat 1996
812	Gypsy Man	War	22-Sep-73	United Artists 281
813	Lotta Love	Nicolette Larson	10-Feb-79	Warner Bros. 8664
814	Walking In Rhythm	The Blackbyrds	17-May-75	Fantasy 736
815	La La La (If I Had You)	Bobby Sherman	17-Jan-70	Metromedia 150
816	Diamond Girl	Seals & Crofts	4-Aug-73	Warner Bros. 7708
817	Wildwood Weed	Jim Stafford	24-Aug-74	MGM 14737
818	Helen Wheels	Paul McCartney & Wings	12-Jan-74	Apple 1869
819	If I Could Reach You	The 5th Dimension	25-Nov-72	Bell 45,261
820	How Sweet It Is (To Be Loved By You)	James Taylor	16-Aug-75	Warner Bros. 8109
821	Feelin' Stronger Every Day	Chicago	18-Aug-73	Columbia 45880
822	I Wanna Be Where You Are	Michael Jackson	22-Jul-72	Motown 1202
823	I'll Be Good To You	The Brothers Johnson	24-Jul-76	A&M 1806
824	The Wonder Of You	Elvis Presley	4-Jul-70	RCA Victor 47-9835
825	Do You Wanna Make Love	Peter McCann	23-Jul-77	20th Century 2335
826	Jeans On	David Dundas	15-Jan-77	Chrysalis 2094
827	(If You Let Me Make Love To You Then) Why Can't I Touch You?	Ronnie Dyson	15-Aug-70	Columbia 45110
828	Heaven Must Have Sent You	Bonnie Pointer	6-Oct-79	Motown 1459
829	Squeeze Box	The Who	21-Feb-76	MCA 40475
830	Goodbye Girl	David Gates	22-Apr-78	Elektra 45450
831	Joy	Apollo 100	4-Mar-72	Mega 0050
832	Two Divided By Love	The Grass Roots	20-Nov-71	Dunhill 4289
833	Morning Side Of The Mountain	Donny And Marie Osmond	25-Jan-75	MGM 14765
834	Heaven Must Be Missing An Angel (Part 1)	Tavares	11-Sep-76	Capitol 4270
835	Heaven Help Us All	Stevie Wonder	5-Dec-70	Tamla 54200
836	Funky Nassau - Part 1	The Beginning Of The End	24-Jul-71	Alston 4595
837	The Love I Lost (Part 1)	Harold Melvin And The Blue Notes	1-Dec-73	Phila. Int'l 3533
838	Midnight Cowboy	Ferrante & Teicher	10-Jan-70	United Artists 50554
839	I Feel A Song (In My Heart)	Gladys Knight & The Pips	4-Jan-75	Buddah 433
840	Here Comes That Rainy Day Feeling Again	The Fortunes	31-Jul-71	Capitol 3086
841	It Only Takes A Minute	Tavares	1-Nov-75	Capitol 4111
842	Goodbye To Love	Carpenters	2-Sep-72	A&M 1367
843	Anticipation	Carly Simon	12-Feb-72	Elektra 45759
844	Boogie Woogie Bugle Boy	Bette Midler	28-Jul-73	Atlantic 2964
845	Rhiannon (Will You Ever Win)	Fleetwood Mac	29-May-76	Reprise 1345
846	Popcorn	Hot Butter	14-Oct-72	Musicor 1458
847	Make Me Smile	Chicago	13-Jun-70	Columbia 45127
848	We Can Work It Out	Stevie Wonder	8-May-71	Tamla 54202
849	Saturday Night's Alright For Fighting	Elton John	8-Sep-73	MCA 40105
850	Brick House	Commodores	5-Nov-77	Motown 1425
851	Take It Easy	Eagles	22-Jul-72	Asylum 11005

'70s Rank	TITLE	ACT	Peak Date	Label & No.
852	If You Really Love Me	Stevie Wonder	16-Oct-71	Tamla 54208
853	Inner City Blues (Make Me Wanna Holler)	Marvin Gaye	13-Nov-71	Tamla 54209
854	I Don't Want To Do Wrong	Gladys Knight & The Pips	24-Jul-71	Soul 35083
855	Sooner Or Later	The Grass Roots	7-Aug-71	Dunhill 4279
856	Stop And Smell The Roses	Mac Davis	2-Nov-74	Columbia 10018
857	Dancing In The Moonlight	King Harvest	17-Feb-73	Perception 515
858	Fanny (Be Tender With My Love)	Bee Gees	6-Mar-76	RSO 519
859	Stir It Up	Johnny Nash	28-Apr-73	Epic 10949
860	Right Down The Line	Gerry Rafferty	21-Oct-78	United Artists 1233
861	Tryin' To Get The Feeling Again	Barry Manilow	22-May-76	Arista 0172
862	Hot Rod Lincoln	Commander Cody And His Lost Planet Airmen	27-May-72	Paramount 0146
863	Eres Tu (Touch The Wind)	Mocedades	23-Mar-74	Tara 100
864	Daughter Of Darkness	Tom Jones	6-Jun-70	Parrot 40048
865	You Belong To Me	Carly Simon	8-Jul-78	Elektra 45477
866	You're My Best Friend	Queen	24-Jul-76	Elektra 45318
867	Only Women	Alice Cooper	28-Jun-75	Atlantic 3254
868	Give Me Just A Little More Time	Chairmen Of The Board	14-Mar-70	Invictus 9074
869	Free Ride	The Edgar Winter Group	13-Oct-73	Epic 11024
870	Monster Mash	Bobby (Boris) Pickett And The Crypt-Kickers	1-Aug-70 18-Aug-73	Parrot 348
871	Groovy Situation	Gene Chandler	3-Oct-70	Mercury 73083
872	Another Saturday Night	Cat Stevens	5-Oct-74	A&M 1602
873	Just A Song Before I Go	Crosby, Stills & Nash	27-Aug-77	Atlantic 3401
874	For The Good Times	Ray Price	23-Jan-71	Columbia 45178
875	Tin Man	America	16-Nov-74	Warner Bros. 7839
876	Don't Cry Out Loud	Melissa Manchester	10-Mar-79	Arista 0373
877	Sweet Seasons	Carole King	4-Mar-72	Ode 66022
878	Me And You And A Dog Named Boo	Lobo	29-May-71	Big Tree 112
879	Never Can Say Goodbye	Gloria Gaynor	25-Jan-75	MGM 14748
880	China Grove	The Doobie Brothers	13-Oct-73	Warner Bros. 7728
881	It's So Easy	Linda Ronstadt	17-Dec-77	Asylum 45438
882	That's The Way I've Always Heard It Should Be	Carly Simon	17-Jul-71	Elektra 45724
883	What The World Needs Now Is Love/ Abraham, Martin And John	Tom Clay	21-Aug-71	Mowest 5002
884	Just Remember I Love You	Firefall	26-Nov-77	Atlantic 3420
885	Peg	Steely Dan	4-Mar-78	ABC 12320
886	Right Place Wrong Time	Dr. John	30-Jun-73	Atco 6914
887	Hey Girl	Donny Osmond	1-Jan-72	MGM 14322
888	Imaginary Lover	Atlanta Rhythm Section	20-May-78	Polydor 14459
889	Life Is A Rock (But The Radio Rolled Me)	Reunion	16-Nov-74	RCA Victor 10056
890	He's The Greatest Dancer	Sister Sledge	5-May-79	Cotillion 44245

'70s Rank	TITLE	ACT	Peak Date	Label & No.
891	(Don't Fear) The Reaper	Blue Öyster Cult	6-Nov-76	Columbia 10384
892	Love's Lines, Angles And Rhymes	The 5th Dimension	10-Apr-71	Bell 965
893	Only Yesterday	Carpenters	31-May-75	A&M 1677
894	I'm Just A Singer (In A Rock And Roll Band)	The Moody Blues	17-Mar-73	Threshold 67012
895	Don't Let The Green Grass Fool You	Wilson Pickett	6-Mar-71	Atlantic 2781
896	Every Time I Think Of You	The Babys	31-Mar-79	Chrysalis 2279
897	Never Ending Song Of Love	Delaney & Bonnie & Friends	21-Aug-71	Atco 6804
898	Ventura Highway	America	16-Dec-72	Warner Bros. 7641
899	Disco Inferno	The Trammps	20-May-78	Atlantic 3389
900	Here I Am (Come And Take Me)	Al Green	8-Sep-73	Hi 2247
901	Get On The Good Foot - Part 1	James Brown	7-Oct-72	Polydor 14139
902	You Make Loving Fun	Fleetwood Mac	17-Dec-77	Warner Bros. 8483
903	My Baby Loves Lovin'	White Plains	27-Jun-70	Deram 85058
904	It Don't Matter To Me	Bread	7-Nov-70	Elektra 45701
905	Lucille	Kenny Rogers	11-Jun-77	United Artists 929
906	Jambalaya (On The Bayou)	The Blue Ridge Rangers	3-Mar-73	Fantasy 689
907	Help Me Make It Through The Night	Sammi Smith	10-Apr-71	Mega 0015
908	You And Me Against The World	Helen Reddy	14-Sep-74	Capitol 3897
909	Who Are You	The Who	21-Oct-78	MCA 40948
910	Masterpiece	The Temptations	28-Apr-73	Gordy 7126
911	I Need You	America	8-Jul-72	Warner Bros. 7580
912	(Where Do I Begin) Love Story	Andy Williams	17-Apr-71	Columbia 45317
913	Walkin' In The Rain	Jay And The Americans	14-Feb-70	United Artists 50605
914	I Never Cry	Alice Cooper	4-Dec-76	Warner Bros. 8228
915	Me And Baby Brother	War	2-Feb-74	United Artists 350
916	Love Me	Yvonne Elliman	8-Jan-77	RSO 858
917	Love Land	Charles Wright And The Watts 103rd Street Rhythm Band	11-Jul-70	Warner Bros. 7365
918	Ready To Take A Chance Again	Barry Manilow	18-Nov-78	Arista 0357
919	Livin' Thing	Electric Light Orchestra	25-Dec-76	United Artists 888
920	The World Is A Ghetto	War	3-Feb-73	United Artists 50975
921	I Was Made For Lovin' You	Kiss	11-Aug-79	Casablanca 983
922	United We Stand	The Brotherhood Of Man	27-Jun-70	Deram 85059
923	Beast Of Burden	The Rolling Stones	28-Oct-78	Rolling Stones 19309
924	Old Days	Chicago	14-Jun-75	Columbia 10131
925	Never, Never Gonna Give Ya Up	Barry White	12-Jan-74	20th Century 2058
926	Doctor's Orders	Carol Douglas	8-Feb-75	Midland Int'l 10113
927	Lady	Little River Band	31-Mar-79	Harvest 4667
928	Thin Line Between Love And Hate	The Persuaders	23-Oct-71	Atco 6822
929	Keeper Of The Castle	Four Tops	20-Jan-73	Dunhill 4330
930	Starting All Over Again	Mel And Tim	14-Oct-72	Stax 0127
931	Precious, Precious	Jackie Moore	20-Feb-71	Atlantic 2681

'70s Rank	TITLE	ACT	Peak Date	Label & No.
932	Rock And Roll Music	The Beach Boys	24-Jul-76	Brother/Reprise 1354
933	Respect Yourself	The Staple Singers	25-Dec-71	Stax 0104
934	On And On	Gladys Knight & The Pips	27-Jul-74	Buddah 423
935	I'm Easy	Keith Carradine	14-Aug-76	ABC 12117
936	Jungle Boogie	Kool & The Gang	9-Feb-74	De-Lite 559
937	Look What They've Done To My Song Ma	The New Seekers	24-Oct-70	Elektra 45699
938	Power Of Love	Joe Simon	30-Sep-72	Spring 128
939	Remember Me	Diana Ross	13-Feb-71	Motown 1176
940	Strawberry Letter 23	The Brothers Johnson	24-Sep-77	A&M 1949
941	I Only Want To Be With You	Bay City Rollers	16-Oct-76	Arista 0205
942	Heard It In A Love Song	The Marshall Tucker Band	18-Jun-77	Capricorn 0270
943	Tryin' To Love Two	William Bell	7-May-77	Mercury 73839
944	Up The Ladder To The Roof	The Supremes	25-Apr-70	Motown 1162
945	It's Impossible	Perry Como	30-Jan-71	RCA Victor 74-0387
946	Cut The Cake	AWB	14-Jun-75	Atlantic 3261
947	Turn The Beat Around	Vicki Sue Robinson	21-Aug-76	RCA Victor 10562
948	I'm Doin' Fine Now	New York City	16-Jun-73	Chelsea 0113
949	Sweet Life	Paul Davis	2-Dec-78	Bang 738
950	Isn't It Time	The Babys	10-Dec-77	Chrysalis 2173
951	Take The Money And Run	Steve Miller	17-Jul-76	Capitol 4260
952	Winter World Of Love	Engelbert Humperdinck	31-Jan-70	Parrot 40044
953	Fernando	Abba	6-Nov-76	Atlantic 3346
954	Oh Very Young	Cat Stevens	8-Jun-74	A&M 1503
955	Shine A Little Love	Electric Light Orchestra	21-Jul-79	Jet 5057
956	Tusk	Fleetwood Mac	3-Nov-79	Warner Bros. 49077
957	You Take My Breath Away	Rex Smith	23-Jun-79	Columbia 10908
958	Desiree	Neil Diamond	28-Jan-78	Columbia 10657
959	Me And Julio Down By The Schoolyard	Paul Simon	20-May-72	Columbia 45585
960	Stay With Me	Faces	19-Feb-72	Warner Bros. 7545
961	Getaway	Earth, Wind & Fire	2-Oct-76	Columbia 10373
962	Rock 'N' Roll Fantasy	Bad Company	16-Jun-79	Swan Song 70119
963	Bluer Than Blue	Michael Johnson	22-Jul-78	EMI America 8001
964	Shame, Shame, Shame	Shirley (And Company)	22-Mar-75	Vibration 532
965	Walk A Mile In My Shoes	Joe South	21-Feb-70	Capitol 2704
966	Express	B.T. Express	5-Apr-75	Roadshow 7001
967	You Never Done It Like That	Captain & Tennille	28-Oct-78	A&M 2063
968	Beginnings	Chicago	21-Aug-71	Columbia 45417
969	It's All In The Game	Four Tops	20-Jun-70	Motown 1164
970	Feel Like Makin' Love	Bad Company	20-Sep-75	Swan Song 70106
971	Honey Come Back	Glen Campbell	21-Feb-70	Capitol 2718
972	I Wanna Be With You	Raspberries	20-Jan-73	Capitol 3473
973	Lady Blue	Leon Russell	1-Nov-75	Shelter 40378

'70s Rank	TITLE	ACT	Peak Date	Label & No.
974	Good Time Charlie's Got The Blues	Danny O'Keefe	4-Nov-72	Signpost 70006
975	I'll Have To Say I Love You In A Song	Jim Croce	27-Apr-74	ABC 11424
976	Once You Get Started	Rufus Featuring Chaka Khan	12-Apr-75	ABC 12066
977	Out In The Country	Three Dog Night	17-Oct-70	Dunhill 4250
978	Something's Wrong With Me	Austin Roberts	23-Dec-72	Chelsea 0101
979	Easy Loving	Freddie Hart	20-Nov-71	Capitol 3115
980	Shake It	Ian Matthews	17-Feb-79	Mushroom 7039
981	My Angel Baby	Toby Beau	26-Aug-78	RCA 11250
982	Everlasting Love	Carl Carlton	23-Nov-74	Back Beat 27001
983	For The Love Of Money	The O'Jays	22-Jun-74	Phila. Int'l 3544
984	Bang A Gong (Get It On)	T. Rex	18-Mar-72	Reprise 1032
985	Lost Without Your Love	Bread	5-Feb-77	Elektra 45365
986	Call Me (Come Back Home)	Al Green	14-Apr-73	Hi 2235
987	Dynomite - Part I	Bazuka	2-Aug-75	A&M 1666
988	It's Ecstasy When You Lay Down Next To Me	Barry White	19-Nov-77	20th Century 2350
989	I Believe In Music	Gallery	11-Nov-72	Sussex 239
990	Never My Love	The 5th Dimension	6-Nov-71	Bell 45,134
991	I'm Stone In Love With You	The Stylistics	23-Dec-72	Avco 4603
992	I Just Can't Help Believing	B.J. Thomas	15-Aug-70	Scepter 12283
993	Listen To The Music	The Doobie Brothers	4-Nov-72	Warner Bros. 7619
994	Cried Like A Baby	Bobby Sherman	27-Mar-71	Metromedia 206
995	Get Dancin'	Disco Tex & The Sex-O-Lettes	15-Feb-75	Chelsea 3004
996	I Won't Last A Day Without You	Carpenters	1-Jun-74	A&M 1521
997	Say You Love Me	Fleetwood Mac	11-Sep-76	Reprise 1356
998	Rocket Man	Elton John	15-Jul-72	Uni 55328
999	Do It Baby	The Miracles	9-Nov-74	Tamla 54248
1000	Disco Nights (Rock-Freak)	G.Q.	2-Jun-79	Arista 0388
1001	Lonely People	America	1-Mar-75	Warner Bros. 8048
1002	Ain't No Stoppin' Us Now	McFadden & Whitehead	21-Jul-79	Phila. Int'l 3681
1003	Falling	Le Blanc & Carr	18-Mar-78	Big Tree 16100
1004	The Groove Line	Heatwave	8-Jul-78	Epic 50524
1005	The Rockford Files	Mike Post	16-Aug-75	MGM 14772
1006	Money	Pink Floyd	28-Jul-73	Harvest 3609
1007	Get Down, Get Down (Get On The Floor)	Joe Simon	14-Jun-75	Spring 156
1008	This Masquerade	George Benson	28-Aug-76	Warner Bros. 8209
1009	Too Young	Donny Osmond	22-Jul-72	MGM 14407
1010	Call Me	Aretha Franklin	11-Apr-70	Atlantic 2706
1011	Bad Luck (Part 1)	Harold Melvin And The Blue Notes	7-Jun-75	Phila. Int'l 3562
1012	Sealed With A Kiss	Bobby Vinton	19-Aug-72	Epic 10861
1013	Witchy Woman	Eagles	25-Nov-72	Asylum 11008

'70s Rank	TITLE	ACT	Peak Date	Label & No.
1014	Bad Case Of Loving You (Doctor, Doctor)	Robert Palmer	22-Sep-79	Island 49016
1015	Didn't I (Blow Your Mind This Time)	The Delfonics	14-Mar-70	Philly Groove 161
1016	Never Gonna Fall In Love Again	Eric Carmen	26-Jun-76	Arista 0184
1017	Rocky Mountain Way	Joe Walsh	20-Oct-73	Dunhill 4361
1018	What Am I Gonna Do With You	Barry White	26-Apr-75	20th Century 2177
1019	Love Jones	Brighter Side Of Darkness	27-Jan-73	20th Century 2002
1020	If You're Ready (Come Go With Me)	The Staple Singers	29-Dec-73	Stax 0179
1021	Daisy A Day	Jud Strunk	19-May-73	MGM 14463
1022	Nathan Jones	The Supremes	26-Jun-71	Motown 1182
1023	Love Song	Anne Murray	9-Mar-74	Capitol 3776
1024	Trouble Man	Marvin Gaye	3-Feb-73	Tamla 54228
1025	Promises	Eric Clapton	13-Jan-79	RSO 910
1026	Rock And Roll Lullaby	B.J. Thomas	1-Apr-72	Scepter 12344
1027	Clap For The Wolfman	The Guess Who	12-Oct-74	RCA Victor 0324
1028	Don't Play That Song	Aretha Franklin	19-Sep-70	Atlantic 2751
1029	Run To Me	Bee Gees	30-Sep-72	Atco 6896
1030	Vincent	Don McLean	13-May-72	United Artists 50887
1031	Knockin' On Heaven's Door	Bob Dylan	3-Nov-73	Columbia 45913
1032	Barracuda	Heart	20-Aug-77	Portrait 70004
1033	Calling Dr. Love	Kiss	4-Jun-77	Casablanca 880
1034	Pay To The Piper	Chairmen Of The Board	16-Jan-71	Invictus 9081
1035	Somebody To Love	Queen	15-Jan-77	Elektra 45362
1036	Haven't Got Time For The Pain	Carly Simon	29-Jun-74	Elektra 45887
1037	Smoke From A Distant Fire	The Sanford/Townsend Band	24-Sep-77	Warner Bros. 8370
1038	Coconut	Nilsson	26-Aug-72	RCA Victor 74-0718
1039	Uneasy Rider	Charlie Daniels	1-Sep-73	Kama Sutra 576
1040	Keep On Singing	Helen Reddy	27-Apr-74	Capitol 3845
1041	You Got The Love	Rufus Featuring Chaka Khan	21-Dec-74	ABC 12032
1042	Just To Be Close To You	Commodores	20-Nov-76	Motown 1402
1043	The Boys Are Back In Town	Thin Lizzy	17-Jul-76	Mercury 73786
1044	Don't Say You Don't Remember	Beverly Bremers	4-Mar-72	Scepter 12315
1045	Time Passages	Al Stewart	2-Dec-78	Arista 0362
1046	Beautiful Sunday	Daniel Boone	30-Sep-72	Mercury 73281
1047	Yellow River	Christie	5-Dec-70	Epic 10626
1048	Bungle In The Jungle	Jethro Tull	18-Jan-75	Chrysalis 2101
1049	One Hell Of A Woman	Mac Davis	20-Jul-74	Columbia 46004
1050	Strange Way	Firefall	9-Dec-78	Atlantic 3518
1051	Back Off Boogaloo	Ringo Starr	20-May-72	Apple 1849
1052	Yes We Can Can	The Pointer Sisters	27-Oct-73	Blue Thumb 229
1053	Hi, Hi, Hi	Wings	3-Feb-73	Apple 1857
1054	Waterloo	Abba	27-Jul-74	Atlantic 3035
1055	Double Lovin'	The Osmonds	19-Jun-71	MGM 14259

'70s Rank	TITLE	ACT	Peak Date	Label & No.
1056	Tumbling Dice	The Rolling Stones	3-Jun-72	Rolling Stones 19103
1057	Doctor My Eyes	Jackson Browne	20-May-72	Asylum 11004
1058	It Was Almost Like A Song	Ronnie Milsap	29-Oct-77	RCA 10976
1059	Layla	Derek And The Dominos	15-May-71 5-Aug-72	Atco 6809
1060	Love The One You're With	The Isley Brothers	14-Aug-71	T-Neck 930
1061	If You Want Me To Stay	Sly & The Family Stone	1-Sep-73	Epic 11017
1062	Rocky	Austin Roberts	18-Oct-75	Private Stk 45,020
1063	A Very Special Love Song	Charlie Rich	13-Apr-74	Epic 11091
1064	It's A Shame	The Spinners	10-Oct-70	V.I.P. 25057
1065	Go Your Own Way	Fleetwood Mac	5-Mar-77	Warner Bros. 8304
1066	Thinking Of You	Loggins & Messina	2-Jun-73	Columbia 45815
1067	It's A Miracle	Barry Manilow	17-May-75	Arista 0108
1068	Everybody's Everything	Santana	27-Nov-71	Columbia 45472
1069	Radar Love	Golden Earring	10-Aug-74	Track/MCA 40202
1070	Cruel To Be Kind	Nick Lowe	20-Oct-79	Columbia 11018
1071	Trapped By A Thing Called Love	Denise LaSalle	30-Oct-71	Westbound 182
1072	Nights Are Forever Without You	England Dan & John Ford Coley	11-Dec-76	Big Tree 16079
1073	Roundabout	Yes	22-Apr-72	Atlantic 2854
1074	El Condor Pasa	Simon & Garfunkel	24-Oct-70	Columbia 45237
1075	Break Up To Make Up	The Stylistics	14-Apr-73	Avco 4611
1076	Do You Want To Dance?	Bette Midler	3-Mar-73	Atlantic 2928
1077	Dead Skunk	Loudon Wainwright III	14-Apr-73	Columbia 45726
1078	I Love You For All Seasons	The Fuzz	15-May-71	Calla 174
1079	Killer Queen	Queen	24-May-75	Elektra 45226
1080	Do It Any Way You Wanna	People's Choice	25-Oct-75	TSOP 4769
1081	Wishing You Were Here	Chicago	7-Dec-74	Columbia 10049
1082	The Guitar Man	Bread	16-Sep-72	Elektra 45803
1083	Every Kinda People	Robert Palmer	24-Jun-78	Island 100
1084	On Broadway	George Benson	10-Jun-78	Warner Bros. 8542
1085	Love Is In The Air	John Paul Young	14-Oct-78	Scotti Brothers 402
1086	Count On Me	Jefferson Starship	13-May-78	Grunt 11196
1087	I Just Fall In Love Again	Anne Murray	14-Apr-79	Capitol 4675
1088	(I Believe) There's Nothing Stronger Than Our Love	Paul Anka	13-Sep-75	United Artists 685
1089	Celebrate	Three Dog Night	28-Mar-70	Dunhill 4229
1090	The Story In Your Eyes	The Moody Blues	25-Sep-71	Threshold 67006
1091	Morning Has Broken	Cat Stevens	3-Jun-72	A&M 1335
1092	Amazing Grace	Judy Collins	27-Feb-71	Elektra 45709
1093	Don't Call Us, We'll Call You	Sugarloaf/Jerry Corbetta	29-Mar-75	Claridge 402
1094	Don't Worry Baby	B.J. Thomas	8-Oct-77	MCA 40735
1095	Evil Woman Don't Play Your Games With Me	Crow	10-Jan-70	Amaret 112

'70s Rank	TITLE	ACT	Peak Date	Label & No.
1096	I Want Your Love	Chic	21-Apr-79	Atlantic 3557
1097	Supernatural Thing - Part I	Ben E. King	26-Apr-75	Atlantic 3241
1098	Whatcha See Is Whatcha Get	The Dramatics	11-Sep-71	Volt 4058
1099	Let's Pretend	Raspberries	23-Jun-73	Capitol 3546
1100	Copacabana (At The Copa)	Barry Manilow	12-Aug-78	Arista 0339
1101	Rain Dance	The Guess Who	9-Oct-71	RCA Victor 74-0522
1102	There's A Kind Of Hush (All Over The World)	Carpenters	10-Apr-76	A&M 1800
1103	Ohio	Crosby, Stills, Nash & Young	1-Aug-70	Atlantic 2740
1104	Roll On Down The Highway	Bachman-Turner Overdrive	8-Mar-75	Mercury 73656
1105	I Wanna Get Next To You	Rose Royce	7-May-77	MCA 40662
1106	Baby, I Love Your Way	Peter Frampton	28-Aug-76	A&M 1832
1107	Black Betty	Ram Jam	20-Aug-77	Epic 50357
1108	Thunder And Lightning	Chi Coltrane	11-Nov-72	Columbia 45640
1109	Our Day Will Come	Frankie Valli	13-Dec-75	Private Stk 45,043
1110	Can't Get It Out Of My Head	Electric Light Orchestra	22-Mar-75	United Artists 573
1111	You Don't Have To Say You Love Me	Elvis Presley	28-Nov-70	RCA Victor 47-9916
1112	The Gambler	Kenny Rogers	24-Feb-79	United Artists 1250
1113	Woodstock	Crosby, Stills, Nash & Young	16-May-70	Atlantic 2723
1114	One Man Band	Three Dog Night	9-Jan-71	Dunhill 4262
1115	I (Who Have Nothing)	Tom Jones	19-Sep-70	Parrot 40051
1116	Oye Como Va	Santana	3-Apr-71	Columbia 45330
1117	Hand Me Down World	The Guess Who	12-Sep-70	RCA Victor 74-0367
1118	Strange Magic	Electric Light Orchestra	8-May-76	United Artists 770
1119	Fool (If You Think It's Over)	Chris Rea	9-Sep-78	United Artists 1198
1120	How Much Love	Leo Sayer	10-Sep-77	Warner Bros. 8319
1121	Still Water (Love)	Four Tops	31-Oct-70	Motown 1170
1122	High School Dance	The Sylvers	9-Jul-77	Capitol 4405
1123	SOS	Abba	22-Nov-75	Atlantic 3265
1124	Riders On The Storm	The Doors	4-Sep-71	Elektra 45738
1125	Come Saturday Morning	The Sandpipers	20-Jun-70	A&M 1134
1126	(Theme From) Love Story	Henry Mancini, His Orchestra & Chorus	27-Feb-71	RCA Victor 47-9927
1127	Black Dog	Led Zeppelin	19-Feb-72	Atlantic 2849
1128	Wham Bam Shang-A-Lang	Silver	25-Sep-76	Arista 0189
1129	One Monkey Don't Stop No Show Part 1	Honey Cone	22-Jan-72	Hot Wax 7110
1130	I'd Like To Teach The World To Sing (In Perfect Harmony)	The New Seekers	22-Jan-72	Elektra 45762
1131	I Saw The Light	Todd Rundgren	17-Jun-72	Bearsville 0003
1132	Super Bad (Part 1 & Part 2)	James Brown	7-Nov-70	King 6329
1133	Hi-De-Ho	Blood, Sweat & Tears	5-Sep-70	Columbia 45204
1134	Peaceful	Helen Reddy	5-May-73	Capitol 3527
1135	That'll Be The Day	Linda Ronstadt	23-Oct-76	Asylum 45340

'70s Rank	TITLE	ACT	Peak Date	Label & No.
1136	With Your Love	Jefferson Starship	18-Sep-76	Grunt 10746
1137	D'yer Mak'Er	Led Zeppelin	29-Dec-73	Atlantic 2986
1138	Good Girls Don't	The Knack	3-Nov-79	Capitol 4771
1139	Take Me Home	Cher	12-May-79	Casablanca 965
1140	Baby Take Me In Your Arms	Jefferson	14-Feb-70	Janus 106
1141	A Song Of Joy (Himno A La Alegria)	Miguel Rios	11-Jul-70	A&M 1193
1142	L-O-V-E (Love)	Al Green	26-Apr-75	Hi 2282
1143	Engine Number 9	Wilson Pickett	5-Dec-70	Atlantic 2765
1144	Are You Man Enough	Four Tops	1-Sep-73	Dunhill 4354
1145	Little Green Bag	George Baker Selection	16-May-70	Colossus 112
1146	Summer	War	18-Sep-76	United Artists 834
1147	You're My World	Helen Reddy	6-Aug-77	Capitol 4418
1148	Fool To Cry	The Rolling Stones	12-Jun-76	Rolling Stones 19304
1149	I Only Have Eyes For You	Art Garfunkel	29-Nov-75	Columbia 10190
1150	Give A Little Bit	Supertramp	3-Sep-77	A&M 1938
1151	Lovin', Touchin', Squeezin'	Journey	20-Oct-79	Columbia 11036
1152	One Tin Soldier, The Legend Of Billy Jack [version 1]	Coven	27-Nov-71 9-Feb-74	Warner Bros. 7509
1153	Take Me In Your Arms (Rock Me)	The Doobie Brothers	21-Jun-75	Warner Bros. 8092
1154	Don't You Worry 'Bout A Thing	Stevie Wonder	1-Jun-74	Tamla 54245
1155	Domino	Van Morrison	9-Jan-71	Warner Bros. 7434
1156	Ariel	Dean Friedman	6-Aug-77	Lifesong 45022
1157	Misty	Ray Stevens	12-Jul-75	Barnaby 614
1158	Action	Sweet	10-Apr-76	Capitol 4220
1159	Always And Forever	Heatwave	8-Apr-78	Epic 50490
1160	Steamroller Blues	Elvis Presley	2-Jun-73	RCA Victor 74-0910
1161	Wake Up Everybody (Part 1)	Harold Melvin And The Blue Notes	14-Feb-76	Phila. Int'l 3579
1162	Teach Your Children	Crosby, Stills, Nash & Young	25-Jul-70	Atlantic 2735
1163	Maybe I'm Amazed	Wings	2-Apr-77	Capitol 4385
1164	Eighteen With A Bullet	Pete Wingfield	6-Dec-75	Island 026
1165	Call On Me	Chicago	17-Aug-74	Columbia 46062
1166	Funky Worm	Ohio Players	2-Jun-73	Westbound 214
1167	Because The Night	Patti Smith Group	17-Jun-78	Arista 0318
1168	Never My Love	Blue Swede	19-Oct-74	EMI 3938
1169	Are You Ready?	Pacific Gas & Electric	1-Aug-70	Columbia 45158
1170	Kentucky Rain	Elvis Presley	14-Mar-70	RCA Victor 47-9791
1171	Soul Man	Blues Brothers	10-Feb-79	Atlantic 3545
1172	Suavecito	Malo	13-May-72	Warner Bros. 7559
1173	Got To Be Real	Cheryl Lynn	3-Feb-79	Columbia 10808
1174	We've Got Tonite	Bob Seger	20-Jan-79	Capitol 4653
1175	Slow Ride	Foghat	20-Mar-76	Bearsville 0306

'70s Rank	TITLE	ACT	Peak Date	Label & No.
1176	Send In The Clowns	Judy Collins	16-Aug-75 19-Nov-77	Elektra 45253
1177	It's Sad To Belong	England Dan & John Ford Coley	23-Jul-77	Big Tree 16088
1178	Superstar (Remember How You Got Where You Are)	The Temptations	11-Dec-71	Gordy 7111
1179	Be My Baby	Andy Kim	26-Dec-70	Steed 729
1180	Crazy Love	Poco	7-Apr-79	ABC 12439
1181	Power To The People	John Lennon/Plastic Ono Band	8-May-71	Apple 1830
1182	Love Me For A Reason	The Osmonds	26-Oct-74	MGM 14746
1183	Movin'	Brass Construction	12-Jun-76	United Artists 775
1184	Big City Miss Ruth Ann	Gallery	17-Mar-73	Sussex 248
1185	Last Time I Saw Him	Diana Ross	9-Mar-74	Motown 1278
1186	Baby Let Me Take You (In My Arms)	Detroit Emeralds	26-Aug-72	Westbound 203
1187	Stones	Neil Diamond	18-Dec-71	Uni 55310
1188	So Far Away	Carole King	2-Oct-71	Ode 66019
1189	Separate Ways	Elvis Presley	27-Jan-73	RCA Victor 74-0815
1190	The Right Thing To Do	Carly Simon	26-May-73	Elektra 45843
1191	Baby Blue	Badfinger	6-May-72	Apple 1844
1192	Livin' For You	Al Green	19-Jan-74	Hi 2257
1193	The Family Of Man	Three Dog Night	6-May-72	Dunhill 4306
1194	Native New Yorker	Odyssey	18-Feb-78	RCA 11129
1195	Aubrey	Bread	31-Mar-73	Elektra 45832
1196	Behind Closed Doors	Charlie Rich	28-Jul-73	Epic 10950
1197	Mind Games	John Lennon	29-Dec-73	Apple 1868
1198	One Fine Morning	Lighthouse	6-Nov-71	Evolution 1048
1199	Everybody's Got The Right To Love	The Supremes	5-Sep-70	Motown 1167
1200	Turn To Stone	Electric Light Orchestra	21-Jan-78	Jet 1099
1201	After Midnight	Eric Clapton	26-Dec-70	Atco 6784
1202	Takin' It To The Streets	The Doobie Brothers	3-Jul-76	Warner Bros. 8196
1203	Back In The U.S.A.	Linda Ronstadt	21-Oct-78	Asylum 45519
1204	Ebony Eyes	Bob Welch	15-Apr-78	Capitol 4543
1205	Tight Rope	Leon Russell	28-Oct-72	Shelter 7325
1206	Skin Tight	Ohio Players	19-Oct-74	Mercury 73609
1207	Hot Pants Pt. 1 (She Got To Use What She Got To Get What She Wants)	James Brown	7-Aug-71	People 2501
1208	Don't Let Me Be Misunderstood	Santa Esmeralda	4-Feb-78	Casablanca 902
1209	Get Off	Foxy	11-Nov-78	Dash 5046
1210	Knowing Me, Knowing You	Abba	23-Jul-77	Atlantic 3387
1211	Taurus	Dennis Coffey And The Detroit Guitar Band	22-Apr-72	Sussex 233
1212	#9 Dream	John Lennon	22-Feb-75	Apple 1878
1213	Kiss An Angel Good Mornin'	Charley Pride	5-Feb-72	RCA Victor 74-0550

'70s Rank	TITLE	ACT	Peak Date	Label & No.
1214	That's The Way Of The World	Earth, Wind & Fire	13-Sep-75	Columbia 10172
1215	We Just Disagree	Dave Mason	26-Nov-77	Columbia 10575
1216	What You Won't Do For Love	Bobby Caldwell	24-Mar-79	Clouds 11
1217	New York Groove	Ace Frehley	3-Feb-79	Casablanca 941
1218	It's One Of Those Nights (Yes Love)	The Partridge Family	22-Jan-72	Bell 45,160
1219	I Don't Know How To Love Him	Helen Reddy	12-Jun-71	Capitol 3027
1220	Runnin' Away	Sly & The Family Stone	11-Mar-72	Epic 10829
1221	Your Smiling Face	James Taylor	10-Dec-77	Columbia 10602
1222	Who Do You Think You Are	Bo Donaldson And The Heywoods	5-Oct-74	ABC 12006
1223	Wild Thing	Fancy	31-Aug-74	Big Tree 15004
1224	Woodstock	Matthews' Southern Comfort	29-May-71	Decca 32774
1225	Times Of Your Life	Paul Anka	31-Jan-76	United Artists 737
1226	Let's Go	The Cars	1-Sep-79	Elektra 46063
1227	Let It Ride	Bachman-Turner Overdrive	27-Apr-74	Mercury 73457
1228	No Love At All	B.J. Thomas	24-Apr-71	Scepter 12307
1229	My Girl Bill	Jim Stafford	15-Jun-74	MGM 14718
1230	You Can't Turn Me Off (In The Middle Of Turning Me On)	High Inergy	14-Jan-78	Gordy 7155
1231	Questions 67 And 68	Chicago	27-Nov-71	Columbia 45467
1232	Grow Some Funk Of Your Own	Elton John	28-Feb-76	MCA 40505
1233	Give It To Me	The J. Geils Band	30-Jun-73	Atlantic 2953
1234	Brazil	The Ritchie Family	18-Oct-75	20th Century 2218
1235	Tennessee Bird Walk	Jack Blanchard & Misty Morgan	9-May-70	Wayside 010
1236	Desiderata	Les Crane	11-Dec-71	Warner Bros. 7520
1237	I Really Don't Want To Know	Elvis Presley	6-Feb-71	RCA Victor 47-9960
1238	Love Takes Time	Orleans	19-May-79	Infinity 50,006
1239	Help Is On Its Way	Little River Band	19-Nov-77	Harvest 4428
1240	Born To Wander	Rare Earth	6-Feb-71	Rare Earth 5021
1241	Thank You For Being A Friend	Andrew Gold	22-Apr-78	Asylum 45456
1242	Timothy	The Buoys	8-May-71	Scepter 12275
1243	Express Yourself	Charles Wright And The Watts 103rd Street Rhythm Band	24-Oct-70	Warner Bros. 7417
1244	Amazing Grace	The Pipes And Drums And The Military Band Of The Royal Scots Dragoon Guards	1-Jul-72	RCA Victor 74-0709
1245	Stagger Lee	Tommy Roe	23-Oct-71	ABC 11307
1246	Westbound #9	Flaming Ember	8-Aug-70	Hot Wax 7003
1247	I Was Made For Dancin'	Leif Garrett	10-Feb-79	Scotti Brothers 403
1248	God, Love And Rock & Roll	Teegarden & Van Winkle	7-Nov-70	Westbound 170
1249	Walk On Water	Neil Diamond	30-Dec-72	Uni 55352
1250	Deep Purple	Donny And Marie Osmond	10-Apr-76	MGM/Kolob 14840
1251	Rings	Cymarron	21-Aug-71	Entrance 7500

'70s Rank	TITLE	ACT	Peak Date	Label & No.
1252	That's Where I Went Wrong	The Poppy Family	17-Oct-70	London 139
1253	Right On The Tip Of My Tongue	Brenda & The Tabulations	29-May-71	Top & Bottom 407
1254	Reach Out And Touch (Somebody's Hand)	Diana Ross	30-May-70	Motown 1165
1255	Take The Long Way Home	Supertramp	15-Dec-79	A&M 2193
1256	The Bells	The Originals	18-Apr-70	Soul 35069
1257	The Thrill Is Gone	B.B. King	28-Feb-70	BluesWay 61032
1258	Jim Dandy	Black Oak Arkansas	9-Feb-74	Atco 6948
1259	Serpentine Fire	Earth, Wind & Fire	4-Feb-78	Columbia 10625
1260	The Last Farewell	Roger Whittaker	14-Jun-75	RCA Victor 50030
1261	Ships	Barry Manilow	24-Nov-79	Arista 0464
1262	The Best Disco In Town	The Ritchie Family	20-Nov-76	Marlin 3306
1263	Puppet Man	Tom Jones	26-Jun-71	Parrot 40062/40064
1264	Shoeshine Boy	Eddie Kendricks	17-May-75	Tamla 54257
1265	Every Day Of My Life	Bobby Vinton	22-Apr-72	Epic 10822
1266	Why Me	Kris Kristofferson	24-Nov-73	Monument 8571
1267	My Music	Loggins & Messina	22-Dec-73	Columbia 45952
1268	I've Got The Music In Me	The Kiki Dee Band	30-Nov-74	Rocket/MCA 40293
1269	Let's Put It All Together	The Stylistics	14-Sep-74	Avco 4640
1270	Tell It All Brother	Kenny Rogers And The First Edition	29-Aug-70	Reprise 0923
1271	Sweet Surrender	John Denver	15-Feb-75	RCA Victor 10148
1272	Talking In Your Sleep	Crystal Gayle	4-Nov-78	United Artists 1214
1273	Love Is The Answer	England Dan & John Ford Coley	26-May-79	Big Tree 16131
1274	Baby Face	The Wing And A Prayer Fife And Drum Corps.	24-Jan-76	Wing & A Prayer 103
1275	Long Time	Boston	19-Mar-77	Epic 50329
1276	Basketball Jones Featuring Tyrone Shoelaces	Cheech & Chong	3-Nov-73	Ode 66038
1277	Keep On Smilin'	Wet Willie	24-Aug-74	Capricorn 0043
1278	Overture From Tommy (A Rock Opera)	The Assembled Multitude	22-Aug-70	Atlantic 2737
1279	Birds Of A Feather	Raiders	6-Nov-71	Columbia 45453
1280	Mighty Love - Pt. I	The Spinners	30-Mar-74	Atlantic 3006
1281	Oh Me Oh My (I'm A Fool For You Baby)	Lulu	14-Mar-70	Atco 6722
1282	What Is Truth	Johnny Cash	9-May-70	Columbia 45134
1283	Wonderful World, Beautiful People	Jimmy Cliff	31-Jan-70	A&M 1146
1284	Gotta Hold On To This Feeling	Jr. Walker & The All Stars	4-Apr-70	Soul 35070
1285	Rubber Duckie	Ernie (Jim Henson)	26-Sep-70	Columbia 45207
1286	Floy Joy	The Supremes	11-Mar-72	Motown 1195
1287	Young Hearts Run Free	Candi Staton	14-Aug-76	Warner Bros. 8181
1288	Born To Be Alive	Patrick Hernandez	6-Oct-79	Columbia 10986
1289	Long Lonesome Highway	Michael Parks	25-Apr-70	MGM 14104
1290	How You Gonna See Me Now	Alice Cooper	30-Dec-78	Warner Bros. 8695
1291	And I Love You So	Perry Como	14-Jul-73	RCA Victor 74-0906

'70s Rank	TITLE	ACT	Peak Date	Label & No.
1292	(Do The) Push And Pull - Part 1	Rufus Thomas	20-Feb-71	Stax 0079
1293	Love The One You're With	Stephen Stills	6-Feb-71	Atlantic 2778
1294	Could It Be Forever	David Cassidy	1-Apr-72	Bell 45,187
1295	Got To Get You Into My Life	Earth, Wind & Fire	9-Sep-78	Columbia 10796
1296	Corner Of The Sky	The Jackson 5	23-Dec-72	Motown 1214
1297	Steppin' Out (Gonna Boogie Tonight)	Tony Orlando And Dawn	26-Oct-74	Bell 45,601
1298	I'd Like To Teach The World To Sing (In Perfect Harmony)	The Hillside Singers	22-Jan-72	Metromedia 231
1299	Flash Light	Parliament	22-Apr-78	Casablanca 909
1300	Sweet Surrender	Bread	23-Dec-72	Elektra 45818
1301	Theme From Cleopatra Jones	Joe Simon	6-Oct-73	Spring 138
1302	Whodunit	Tavares	18-Jun-77	Capitol 4398
1303	Taxi	Harry Chapin	20-May-72	Elektra 45770
1304	Livin' It Up (Friday Night)	Bell & James	14-Apr-79	A&M 2069
1305	We've Got To Get It On Again	The Addrisi Brothers	25-Mar-72	Columbia 45521
1306	River Deep - Mountain High	The Supremes & Four Tops	2-Jan-71	Motown 1173
1307	You And I	Rick James	30-Sep-78	Gordy 7156
1308	Maybe Tomorrow	The Jackson 5	14-Aug-71	Motown 1186
1309	Living In The Past	Jethro Tull	6-Jan-73	Chrysalis 2006
1310	Carefree Highway	Gordon Lightfoot	16-Nov-74	Reprise 1309
1311	Blow Away	George Harrison	5-May-79	Dark Horse 8763
1312	Wild World	Cat Stevens	17-Apr-71	A&M 1231
1313	Free	Deniece Williams	19-Mar-77	Columbia 10429
1314	Summertime Blues	The Who	22-Aug-70	Decca 32708
1315	Armed And Extremely Dangerous	First Choice	26-May-73	Philly Groove 175
1316	Who'll Stop The Rain	Creedence Clearwater Revival	7-Mar-70	Fantasy 637
1317	Goodbye Stranger	Supertramp	8-Sep-79	A&M 2162
1318	Who's In The Strawberry Patch With Sally	Tony Orlando And Dawn	29-Dec-73	Bell 45,424
1319	Misdemeanor	Foster Sylvers	28-Jul-73	MGM 14580
1320	Driver's Seat	Sniff 'N' The Tears	6-Oct-79	Atlantic 3604
1321	Winners And Losers	Hamilton, Joe Frank And Reynolds	24-Jan-76	Playboy 6054
1322	This Night Won't Last Forever	Michael Johnson	24-Nov-79	EMI America 8019
1323	Cry Me A River	Joe Cocker	21-Nov-70	A&M 1200
1324	I Don't Blame You At All	Smokey Robinson & The Miracles	8-May-71	Tamla 54205
1325	Tear The Roof Off The Sucker (Give Up The Funk)	Parliament	24-Jul-76	Casablanca 856
1326	Rock And Roll All Nite (Live)	Kiss	24-Jan-76	Casablanca 850
1327	We Gotta Get You A Woman	Runt	13-Feb-71	Ampex 31001
1328	Swingtown	Steve Miller Band	10-Dec-77	Capitol 4496
1329	Trying To Hold On To My Woman	Lamont Dozier	23-Mar-74	ABC 11407
1330	My World	Bee Gees	4-Mar-72	Atco 6871

'70s Rank	TITLE	ACT	Peak Date	Label & No.
1331	How Can I Tell Her	Lobo	1-Sep-73	Big Tree 16,004
1332	Speak To The Sky	Rick Springfield	7-Oct-72	Capitol 3340
1333	How Long (Betcha' Got A Chick On The Side)	Pointer Sisters	4-Oct-75	ABC/Blue Thumb 265
1334	Renegade	Styx	26-May-79	A&M 2110
1335	The Name Of The Game	Abba	18-Mar-78	Atlantic 3449
1336	Summer (The First Time)	Bobby Goldsboro	10-Nov-73	United Artists 251
1337	Alive Again	Chicago	9-Dec-78	Columbia 10845
1338	I Do, I Do, I Do, I Do, I Do	Abba	1-May-76	Atlantic 3310
1339	Junk Food Junkie	Larry Groce	27-Mar-76	Warner/Curb 8165
1340	Living Next Door To Alice	Smokie	26-Feb-77	RSO 860
1341	Diary	Bread	24-Jun-72	Elektra 45784
1342	Lookin' Through The Windows	The Jackson 5	26-Aug-72	Motown 1205
1343	Ain't Gonna Bump No More (With No Big Fat Woman)	Joe Tex	4-Jun-77	Epic 50313
1344	Boogie Child	Bee Gees	5-Mar-77	RSO 867
1345	Runaway	Jefferson Starship	29-Jul-78	Grunt 11274
1346	This Time I'm In It For Love	Player	27-May-78	RSO 890
1347	Silver Bird	Mark Lindsay	1-Aug-70	Columbia 45180
1348	You're The One - Part II	Little Sister	18-Apr-70	Stone Flower 9000
1349	Space Oddity	David Bowie	14-Apr-73	RCA Victor 74-0876
1350	Do You Feel Like We Do	Peter Frampton	20-Nov-76	A&M 1867
1351	Does Your Mother Know	Abba	14-Jul-79	Atlantic 3574
1352	Chirpy Chirpy Cheep Cheep	Mac And Katie Kissoon	9-Oct-71	ABC 11306
1353	Already Gone	Eagles	29-Jun-74	Asylum 11036
1354	Movin' Out (Anthony's Song)	Billy Joel	3-Jun-78	Columbia 10708
1355	Our Love	Natalie Cole	8-Apr-78	Capitol 4509
1356	The City Of New Orleans	Arlo Guthrie	4-Nov-72	Reprise 1103
1357	Question	The Moody Blues	27-Jun-70	Threshold 67004
1358	You Wear It Well	Rod Stewart	21-Oct-72	Mercury 73330
1359	He Ain't Heavy...He's My Brother	Neil Diamond	26-Dec-70	Uni 55264
1360	Daddy Could Swear, I Declare	Gladys Knight & The Pips	7-Jul-73	Soul 35105
1361	Motorcycle Mama	Sailcat	2-Sep-72	Elektra 45782
1362	Joanne	Michael Nesmith & The First National Band	3-Oct-70	RCA Victor 74-0368
1363	Life In The Fast Lane	Eagles	2-Jul-77	Asylum 45403
1364	Signed, Sealed, Delivered (I'm Yours)	Peter Frampton	22-Oct-77	A&M 1972
1365	Where Were You When I Was Falling In Love	Lobo	20-Oct-79	MCA/Curb 41065
1366	Operator (That's Not The Way It Feels)	Jim Croce	9-Dec-72	ABC 11335
1367	Is She Really Going Out With Him?	Joe Jackson	18-Aug-79	A&M 2132
1368	I Want You	Marvin Gaye	3-Jul-76	Tamla 54264
1369	Sugar Sugar	Wilson Pickett	27-Jun-70	Atlantic 2722
1370	The Need To Be	Jim Weatherly	16-Nov-74	Buddah 420

'70s Rank	TITLE	ACT	Peak Date	Label & No.
1371	Star	Stealers Wheel	16-Mar-74	A&M 1483
1372	The Witch Queen Of New Orleans	Redbone	19-Feb-72	Epic 10749
1373	Straight On	Heart	9-Dec-78	Portrait 70020
1374	Finally Got Myself Together (I'm A Changed Man)	The Impressions	3-Aug-74	Curtom 1997
1375	Must Of Got Lost	The J. Geils Band	4-Jan-75	Atlantic 3214
1376	If Not For You	Olivia Newton-John	4-Sep-71	Uni 55281
1377	Suspicions	Eddie Rabbitt	1-Sep-79	Elektra 46053
1378	Why	Donny Osmond	14-Oct-72	MGM 14424
1379	Hummingbird	Seals & Crofts	24-Mar-73	Warner Bros. 7671
1380	I Don't Know If It's Right	Evelyn "Champagne" King	24-Mar-79	RCA 11386
1381	This Heart	Gene Redding	27-Jul-74	Haven 7000
1382	She Did It	Eric Carmen	22-Oct-77	Arista 0266
1383	Machine Gun	Commodores	10-Aug-74	Motown 1307
1384	You Turn Me On, I'm A Radio	Joni Mitchell	27-Jan-73	Asylum 11010
1385	Country Boy (You Got Your Feet In L.A.)	Glen Campbell	10-Jan-76	Capitol 4155
1386	Hollywood Nights	Bob Seger	7-Oct-78	Capitol 4618
1387	Play Me	Neil Diamond	7-Oct-72	Uni 55346
1388	Point Of Know Return	Kansas	14-Jan-78	Kirshner 4273
1389	Hurts So Good	Millie Jackson	27-Oct-73	Spring 139
1390	A Natural Man	Lou Rawls	11-Dec-71	MGM 14262
1391	Smoke Gets In Your Eyes	Blue Haze	20-Jan-73	A&M 1357
1392	Hello Stranger	Yvonne Elliman	21-May-77	RSO 871
1393	Toast And Marmalade For Tea	Tin Tin	29-May-71	Atco 6794
1394	Fancy	Bobbie Gentry	7-Feb-70	Capitol 2675
1395	Put Your Hands Together	The O'Jays	16-Feb-74	Phila. Int'l 3535
1396	Blowing Away	The 5th Dimension	31-Jan-70	Soul City 780
1397	Theme From "Close Encounters Of The Third Kind"	John Williams	11-Mar-78	Arista 0300
1398	Dancin' Shoes	Nigel Olsson	10-Mar-79	Bang 740
1399	Give Your Baby A Standing Ovation	The Dells	7-Jul-73	Cadet 5696
1400	Let Me Serenade You	Three Dog Night	15-Dec-73	Dunhill 4370
1401	Part-Time Love	Elton John	23-Dec-78	MCA 40973
1402	Tush	ZZ Top	6-Sep-75	London 220
1403	Ooh Baby	Gilbert O'Sullivan	1-Dec-73	MAM 3633
1404	Check Out Your Mind	Impressions	25-Jul-70	Curtom 1951
1405	Fire And Water	Wilson Pickett	19-Feb-72	Atlantic 2852
1406	Jesse	Roberta Flack	27-Oct-73	Atlantic 2982
1407	Wedding Song (There Is Love)	Paul Stookey	2-Oct-71	Warner Bros. 7511
1408	Ain't Understanding Mellow	Jerry Butler And Brenda Lee Eager	18-Mar-72	Mercury 73255
1409	Angel	Aretha Franklin	8-Sep-73	Atlantic 2969
1410	We'll Never Have To Say Goodbye Again	England Dan & John Ford Coley	22-Apr-78	Big Tree 16110

'70s Rank	TITLE	ACT	Peak Date	Label & No.
1411	Me And My Arrow	Nilsson	19-Jun-71	RCA Victor 74-0443
1412	I'm In Love	Aretha Franklin	1-Jun-74	Atlantic 2999
1413	I Want'a Do Something Freaky To You	Leon Haywood	29-Nov-75	20th Century 2228
1414	So Very Hard To Go	Tower Of Power	28-Jul-73	Warner Bros. 7687
1415	Piano Man	Billy Joel	20-Apr-74	Columbia 45963
1416	The Day I Found Myself	Honey Cone	22-Apr-72	Hot Wax 7113
1417	Somewhere In The Night	Barry Manilow	10-Feb-79	Arista 0382
1418	I've Been Lonely For So Long	Frederick Knight	1-Jul-72	Stax 0117
1419	How Can I Be Sure	David Cassidy	1-Jul-72	Bell 45,220
1420	Here Comes The Sun	Richie Havens	29-May-71	Stormy Forest 656
1421	Rockin' Roll Baby	The Stylistics	29-Dec-73	Avco 4625
1422	Save The Last Dance For Me	The DeFranco Family Featuring Tony DeFranco	22-Jun-74	20th Century 2088
1423	Spirit Of The Boogie	Kool & The Gang	5-Jul-75	De-Lite 1567
1424	Get Used To It	Roger Voudouris	16-Jun-79	Warner Bros. 8762
1425	People Make The World Go Round	The Stylistics	22-Jul-72	Avco 4595
1426	Minute By Minute	The Doobie Brothers	23-Jun-79	Warner Bros. 8828
1427	If You Know What I Mean	Neil Diamond	31-Jul-76	Columbia 10366
1428	You're All I Need To Get By	Aretha Franklin	27-Mar-71	Atlantic 2787
1429	Are You Lonesome Tonight	Donny Osmond	26-Jan-74	MGM 14677
1430	Stand By Your Man	Candi Staton	21-Nov-70	Fame 1472
1431	Love Ballad	George Benson	5-May-79	Warner Bros. 8759
1432	Somewhere In The Night	Helen Reddy	14-Feb-76	Capitol 4192
1433	I Am Love	The Jackson 5	15-Mar-75	Motown 1310
1434	No Tell Lover	Chicago	10-Mar-79	Columbia 10879
1435	You're A Special Part Of Me	Diana Ross & Marvin Gaye	17-Nov-73	Motown 1280
1436	I Can't Stand The Rain	Eruption	8-Jul-78	Ariola/Hansa 7686
1437	Half The Way	Crystal Gayle	15-Dec-79	Columbia 11087
1438	Up In A Puff Of Smoke	Polly Brown	15-Mar-75	GTO 1002
1439	Precious Love	Bob Welch	28-Apr-79	Capitol 4685
1440	Doo Doo Doo Doo Doo (Heartbreaker)	The Rolling Stones	23-Feb-74	Rolling Stones 19109
1441	Rock N' Roll (I Gave You The Best Years Of My Life)	Mac Davis	1-Feb-75	Columbia 10070
1442	Over My Head	Fleetwood Mac	3-Jan-76	Warner Bros. 1339
1443	Hold Her Tight	The Osmonds	5-Aug-72	MGM 14405
1444	Something Better To Do	Olivia Newton-John	1-Nov-75	MCA 40459
1445	Leaving Me	The Independents	9-Jun-73	Wand 11252
1446	Happy	The Rolling Stones	26-Aug-72	Rolling Stones 19104
1447	I Love	Tom T. Hall	2-Mar-74	Mercury 73436
1448	Somebody's Watching You	Little Sister	13-Feb-71	Stone Flower 9001
1449	She's Always A Woman	Billy Joel	21-Oct-78	Columbia 10788
1450	Say You'll Stay Until Tomorrow	Tom Jones	26-Mar-77	Epic 50308
1451	We May Never Pass This Way (Again)	Seals & Crofts	10-Nov-73	Warner Bros. 7740

'70s Rank	TITLE	ACT	Peak Date	Label & No.
1452	Black Superman - "Muhammad Ali"	Johnny Wakelin And The Kinshasa Band	13-Sep-75	Pye 71012
1453	Here Come Those Tears Again	Jackson Browne	2-Apr-77	Asylum 45379
1454	Walk Like A Man	Grand Funk	19-Jan-74	Capitol 3760
1455	Change Of Heart	Eric Carmen	16-Dec-78	Arista 0354
1456	Sweet Talkin' Woman	Electric Light Orchestra	22-Apr-78	Jet 1145
1457	I'm Not Gonna Let It Bother Me Tonight	Atlanta Rhythm Section	12-Aug-78	Polydor 14484
1458	King Tut	Steve Martin	5-Aug-78	Warner Bros. 8577
1459	What A Diff'rence A Day Makes	Esther Phillips	25-Oct-75	Kudu 925
1460	Disco Lucy (I Love Lucy Theme)	Wilton Place Street Band	2-Apr-77	Island 078
1461	Cool Aid	Paul Humphrey & His Cool Aid Chemists	12-Jun-71	Lizard 21006
1462	Games	Redeye	30-Jan-71	Pentagram 204
1463	Baby Let Me Kiss You	King Floyd	8-May-71	Chimneyville 437
1464	The White Knight	Cledus Maggard	6-Mar-76	Mercury 73751
1465	Before My Heart Finds Out	Gene Cotton	15-Apr-78	Ariola America 7675
1466	If You Remember Me	Chris Thompson	24-Nov-79	Planet 45909
1467	Up On Cripple Creek	The Band	17-Jan-70	Capitol 2635
1468	Holdin' On To Yesterday	Ambrosia	23-Aug-75	20th Century 2207
1469	Ain't Too Proud To Beg	The Rolling Stones	21-Dec-74	Rolling Stones 19302
1470	Slow Dancin' Don't Turn Me On	The Addrisi Brothers	18-Jun-77	Buddah 566
1471	Conquistador	Procol Harum	29-Jul-72	A&M 1347
1472	To The Door Of The Sun (Alle Porte Del Sole)	Al Martino	22-Mar-75	Capitol 3987
1473	You Little Trustmaker	The Tymes	12-Oct-74	RCA Victor 10022
1474	Way Down	Elvis Presley	1-Oct-77	RCA 10998
1475	Deeper And Deeper	Freda Payne	7-Nov-70	Invictus 9080
1476	Mississippi Queen	Mountain	18-Jul-70	Windfall 532
1477	The Way I Feel Tonight	Bay City Rollers	14-Jan-78	Arista 0272
1478	Love Really Hurts Without You	Billy Ocean	22-May-76	Ariola America 7621
1479	Hey You	Bachman-Turner Overdrive	5-Jul-75	Mercury 73683
1480	Blue Eyes Crying In The Rain	Willie Nelson	6-Dec-75	Columbia 10176
1481	Go Back	Crabby Appleton	18-Jul-70	Elektra 45687
1482	It's Going To Take Some Time	Carpenters	3-Jun-72	A&M 1351
1483	Third Rate Romance	The Amazing Rhythm Aces	13-Sep-75	ABC 12078
1484	Love Ballad	L.T.D.	11-Dec-76	A&M 1847
1485	Don't Let Me Be Lonely Tonight	James Taylor	20-Jan-73	Warner Bros. 7655
1486	Nightingale	Carole King	1-Mar-75	Ode 66106
1487	Ask Me What You Want	Millie Jackson	17-Jun-72	Spring 123
1488	Heartless	Heart	17-Jun-78	Mushroom 7031
1489	Promised Land	Elvis Presley	4-Jan-75	RCA Victor 10074
1490	After The Goldrush	Prelude	30-Nov-74	Island 002
1491	A Brand New Me	Dusty Springfield	10-Jan-70	Atlantic 2685

'70s Rank	TITLE	ACT	Peak Date	Label & No.
1492	Born To Run	Bruce Springsteen	8-Nov-75	Columbia 10209
1493	So You Are A Star	Hudson Brothers	23-Nov-74	Casablanca 0108
1494	The Boss	Diana Ross	6-Oct-79	Motown 1462
1495	Hey Deanie	Shaun Cassidy	14-Jan-78	Warner/Curb 8488
1496	Whispering/Cherchez La Femme/Se Si Bon	Dr. Buzzard's Original "Savannah" Band	15-Jan-77	RCA 10827
1497	Pop That Thang	The Isley Brothers	23-Sep-72	T-Neck 935
1498	Midnight Rider	Gregg Allman	16-Feb-74	Capricorn 0035
1499	Baretta's Theme ("Keep Your Eye On The Sparrow")	Rhythm Heritage	19-Jun-76	ABC 12177
1500	Do Ya	Electric Light Orchestra	2-Apr-77	United Artists 939
1501	Come To Me	France Joli	10-Nov-79	Prelude 8001
1502	My Mistake (Was To Love You)	Diana Ross & Marvin Gaye	20-Apr-74	Motown 1269
1503	Get Up I Feel Like Being Like A Sex Machine (Part 1)	James Brown	15-Aug-70	King 6318
1504	My Boy	Elvis Presley	15-Mar-75	RCA Victor 10191
1505	Hey Big Brother	Rare Earth	15-Jan-72	Rare Earth 5038
1506	Honky Cat	Elton John	23-Sep-72	Uni 55343
1507	I'm Not My Brother's Keeper	Flaming Ember	19-Dec-70	Hot Wax 7006
1508	Spooky	Atlanta Rhythm Section	13-Oct-79	Polydor/BGO 2001
1509	Don't Hold Back	Chanson	3-Feb-79	Ariola America 7717
1510	Even Now	Barry Manilow	1-Jul-78	Arista 0330
1511	Let's Work Together	Canned Heat	5-Dec-70	Liberty 56151
1512	Ride 'Em Cowboy	Paul Davis	4-Jan-75	Bang 712
1513	Your Love	Marilyn McCoo & Billy Davis Jr.	7-May-77	ABC 12262
1514	Big Shot	Billy Joel	31-Mar-79	Columbia 10913
1515	Lucretia Mac Evil	Blood, Sweat & Tears	7-Nov-70	Columbia 45235
1516	Love Is The Drug	Roxy Music	13-Mar-76	Atco 7042
1517	You're Still A Young Man	Tower Of Power	9-Sep-72	Warner Bros. 7612
1518	One Man Band (Plays All Alone)	Ronnie Dyson	28-Apr-73	Columbia 45776
1519	Hard Luck Woman	Kiss	12-Feb-77	Casablanca 873
1520	Look In My Eyes Pretty Woman	Tony Orlando And Dawn	15-Feb-75	Bell 45,620
1521	Runaround Sue	Leif Garrett	14-Jan-78	Atlantic 3440
1522	Deacon Blues	Steely Dan	10-Jun-78	ABC 12355
1523	Do It Or Die	Atlanta Rhythm Section	28-Jul-79	Polydor 14568
1524	No One To Depend On	Santana	25-Mar-72	Columbia 45552
1525	Mornin' Beautiful	Tony Orlando And Dawn	9-Aug-75	Elektra 45260
1526	Dreidel	Don McLean	24-Feb-73	United Artists 51100
1527	Your Time To Cry	Joe Simon	20-Feb-71	Spring 108
1528	Back When My Hair Was Short	Gunhill Road	23-Jun-73	Kama Sutra 569
1529	Dirty White Boy	Foreigner	3-Nov-79	Atlantic 3618
1530	The Payback - Part I	James Brown	11-May-74	Polydor 14223
1531	My Sweet Lady	Cliff Deyoung	9-Mar-74	MCA 40156

'70s Rank	TITLE	ACT	Peak Date	Label & No.
1532	Our House	Crosby, Stills, Nash & Young	31-Oct-70	Atlantic 2760
1533	Eighteen	Alice Cooper	24-Apr-71	Warner Bros. 7449
1534	Behind Blue Eyes	The Who	25-Dec-71	Decca 32888
1535	Chicago	Graham Nash	31-Jul-71	Atlantic 2804
1536	Rock And Roll, Hoochie Koo	Rick Derringer	23-Mar-74	Blue Sky 2751
1537	La Grange	ZZ Top	13-Jul-74	London 203
1538	Star Wars (Main Title)	John Williams/London Symphony Orchestra	17-Sep-77	20th Century 2345
1539	Peaceful Easy Feeling	Eagles	10-Mar-73	Asylum 11013
1540	Jungle Love	Steve Miller Band	1-Oct-77	Capitol 4466
1541	Love In The Shadows	Neil Sedaka	29-May-76	Rocket/MCA 40543
1542	(Don't Worry) If There's A Hell Below We're All Going To Go	Curtis Mayfield	30-Jan-71	Curtom 1955
1543	I'll Play For You	Seals & Crofts	28-Jun-75	Warner Bros. 8075
1544	Making Our Dreams Come True	Cyndi Grecco	10-Jul-76	Private Stk 45,086
1545	Solitary Man	Neil Diamond	19-Sep-70	Bang 578
1546	Pieces Of April	Three Dog Night	6-Jan-73	Dunhill 4331
1547	You	Rita Coolidge	26-Aug-78	A&M 2058
1548	Paloma Blanca	George Baker Selection	7-Feb-76	Warner Bros. 8115
1549	Forever In Blue Jeans	Neil Diamond	31-Mar-79	Columbia 10897
1550	Summer Sand	Dawn	24-Jul-71	Bell 45,107
1551	Make It Funky (Part 1)	James Brown	9-Oct-71	Polydor 14088
1552	The Bertha Butt Boogie - Part 1	The Jimmy Castor Bunch	19-Apr-75	Atlantic 3232
1553	Give Me Your Love	Barbara Mason	17-Mar-73	Buddah 331
1554	Shinin' On	Grand Funk	31-Aug-74	Capitol 3917
1555	Werewolves Of London	Warren Zevon	13-May-78	Asylum 45472
1556	The King Is Gone	Ronnie McDowell	8-Oct-77	Scorpion 135
1557	Ffun	Con Funk Shun	25-Feb-78	Mercury 73959
1558	I'd Love To Change The World	Ten Years After	20-Nov-71	Columbia 45457
1559	Pinball Wizard/See Me, Feel Me	The New Seekers	5-May-73	MGM/Verve 10709
1560	Booty Butt	The Ray Charles Orchestra	22-May-71	Tangerine 1015
1561	Tracks Of My Tears	Linda Ronstadt	21-Feb-76	Asylum 45295
1562	Save It For A Rainy Day	Stephen Bishop	19-Feb-77	ABC 12232
1563	Young Blood	Bad Company	15-May-76	Swan Song 70108
1564	Saturday Nite	Earth, Wind & Fire	22-Jan-77	Columbia 10439
1565	Love's Grown Deep	Kenny Nolan	2-Jul-77	20th Century 2331
1566	Neanderthal Man	Hotlegs	3-Oct-70	Capitol 2886
1567	Levon	Elton John	5-Feb-72	Uni 55314
1568	I'm Every Woman	Chaka Khan	23-Dec-78	Warner Bros. 8683
1569	Last Child	Aerosmith	31-Jul-76	Columbia 10359
1570	Bicycle Race//Fat Bottomed Girls	Queen	30-Dec-78	Elektra 45541
1571	Cupid	Tony Orlando And Dawn	27-Mar-76	Elektra 45302
1572	Two Tickets To Paradise	Eddie Money	2-Sep-78	Columbia 10765

'70s Rank	TITLE	ACT	Peak Date	Label & No.
1573	Star Baby	The Guess Who	8-Jun-74	RCA Victor 0217
1574	Different Worlds	Maureen McGovern	6-Oct-79	Warner/Curb 8835
1575	Only You Know And I Know	Delaney & Bonnie	30-Oct-71	Atco 6838
1576	Convention '72	The Delegates	25-Nov-72	Mainstream 5525
1577	Solitaire	Carpenters	20-Sep-75	A&M 1721
1578	Cheaper To Keep Her	Johnnie Taylor	24-Nov-73	Stax 0176
1579	Friends	Elton John	1-May-71	Uni 55277
1580	The First Cut Is The Deepest	Rod Stewart	2-Apr-77	Warner Bros. 8321
1581	Monster	Steppenwolf	31-Jan-70	Dunhill 4221
1582	Sad Sweet Dreamer	Sweet Sensation	29-Mar-75	Pye 71002
1583	Gone Too Far	England Dan & John Ford Coley	3-Dec-77	Big Tree 16102
1584	Can't Stop Dancin'	Captain & Tennille	30-Apr-77	A&M 1912
1585	Walk On The Wild Side	Lou Reed	28-Apr-73	RCA Victor 74-0887
1586	In The Midnight Hour	Cross Country	6-Oct-73	Atco 6934
1587	Blue Morning, Blue Day	Foreigner	24-Feb-79	Atlantic 3543
1588	Union Man	Cate Brothers	22-May-76	Asylum 45294
1589	I Can't Stand It No More	Peter Frampton	14-Jul-79	A&M 2148
1590	Play Something Sweet (Brickyard Blues)	Three Dog Night	9-Nov-74	Dunhill/ABC 15013
1591	No More Mr. Nice Guy	Alice Cooper	9-Jun-73	Warner Bros. 7691
1592	Nutbush City Limits	Ike & Tina Turner	24-Nov-73	United Artists 298
1593	It's Only Rock 'N Roll (But I Like It)	The Rolling Stones	21-Sep-74	Rolling Stones 19301
1594	Jennifer Tomkins	Street People	14-Feb-70	Musicor 1365
1595	Only Love Can Break Your Heart	Neil Young	19-Dec-70	Reprise 0958
1596	Moon Shadow	Cat Stevens	14-Aug-71	A&M 1265
1597	I Shall Sing	Garfunkel	2-Feb-74	Columbia 45983
1598	Don't Ever Be Lonely (A Poor Little Fool Like Me)	Cornelius Brothers & Sister Rose	4-Nov-72	United Artists 50954
1599	Don't Want To Live Without It	Pablo Cruise	2-Dec-78	A&M 2076
1600	Dialogue (Parts I & II)	Chicago	9-Dec-72	Columbia 45717
1601	Luckenbach, Texas (Back To The Basics Of Love)	Waylon Jennings	9-Jul-77	RCA 10924
1602	Theme From "Summer Of '42"	Peter Nero	8-Jan-72	Columbia 45399
1603	I Know A Heartache When I See One	Jennifer Warnes	27-Oct-79	Arista 0430
1604	You're The Love	Seals & Crofts	8-Jul-78	Warner Bros. 8551
1605	Blue Money	Van Morrison	10-Apr-71	Warner Bros. 7462
1606	Shakey Ground	The Temptations	14-Jun-75	Gordy 7142
1607	She	Tommy James And The Shondells	17-Jan-70	Roulette 7066
1608	Do Your Thing	Isaac Hayes	15-Apr-72	Enterprise 9042
1609	Instant Replay	Dan Hartman	30-Dec-78	Blue Sky 2772
1610	You'll Never Get To Heaven (If You Break My Heart)	The Stylistics	7-Jul-73	Avco 4618

'70s Rank	TITLE	ACT	Peak Date	Label & No.
1611	Make Me The Woman That You Go Home To	Gladys Knight & The Pips	29-Jan-72	Soul 35091
1612	As The Years Go By	Mashmakhan	21-Nov-70	Epic 10634
1613	That's The Way I Feel About Cha	Bobby Womack	12-Feb-72	United Artists 50847
1614	Fairytale	Pointer Sisters	21-Dec-74	ABC/Blue Thumb 254
1615	Looking For Space	John Denver	10-Apr-76	RCA Victor 10586
1616	Together Let's Find Love	The 5th Dimension	19-Feb-72	Bell 45,170
1617	There's No Me Without You	The Manhattans	28-Jul-73	Columbia 45838
1618	Gone At Last	Paul Simon/Phoebe Snow	27-Sep-75	Columbia 10197
1619	Isn't Life Strange	The Moody Blues	17-Jun-72	Threshold 67009
1620	Close The Door	Teddy Pendergrass	9-Sep-78	Phila. Int'l 3648
1621	(What A) Wonderful World	Art Garfunkel With James Taylor & Paul Simon	18-Mar-78	Columbia 10676
1622	You've Never Been This Far Before	Conway Twitty	20-Oct-73	MCA 40094
1623	Daisy Jane	America	27-Sep-75	Warner Bros. 8118
1624	Don't Change On Me	Ray Charles	15-May-71	ABC/TRC 11291
1625	Closer To Home	Grand Funk Railroad	24-Oct-70	Capitol 2877
1626	Saturday Morning Confusion	Bobby Russell	2-Oct-71	United Artists 50788
1627	Been To Canaan	Carole King	13-Jan-73	Ode 66031
1628	Glory Bound	The Grass Roots	8-Apr-72	Dunhill 4302
1629	Wild Horses	The Rolling Stones	24-Jul-71	Rolling Stones 19101
1630	Heed The Call	Kenny Rogers And The First Edition	28-Nov-70	Reprise 0953
1631	Livin' For The Weekend	The O'Jays	1-May-76	Phila. Int'l 3587
1632	Crazy Horses	The Osmonds	9-Dec-72	MGM 14450
1633	White Lies, Blue Eyes	Bullet	22-Jan-72	Big Tree 123
1634	Sitting	Cat Stevens	30-Dec-72	A&M 1396
1635	Free Bird	Lynyrd Skynyrd	18-Jan-75	MCA 40328
1636	Train Of Thought	Cher	6-Jul-74	MCA 40245
1637	Ain't Love A Bitch	Rod Stewart	2-Jun-79	Warner Bros. 8810
1638	Be	Neil Diamond	1-Dec-73	Columbia 45942
1639	Calling Occupants Of Interplanetary Craft	Carpenters	10-Dec-77	A&M 1978
1640	Come Get To This	Marvin Gaye	15-Dec-73	Tamla 54241
1641	Tell Me A Lie	Sami Jo	13-Apr-74	MGM South 7029
1642	Satin Sheets	Jeanne Pruett	21-Jul-73	MCA 40015
1643	Out Of The Question	Gilbert O'Sullivan	19-May-73	MAM 3628
1644	Don't Do It	The Band	18-Nov-72	Capitol 3433
1645	Inseparable	Natalie Cole	13-Mar-76	Capitol 4193
1646	Living In A House Divided	Cher	1-Jul-72	Kapp 2171
1647	I've Lost You	Elvis Presley	5-Sep-70	RCA Victor 47-9873
1648	I'm A Woman	Maria Muldaur	1-Mar-75	Reprise 1319
1649	Reelin' & Rockin'	Chuck Berry	10-Feb-73	Chess 2136
1650	Absolutely Right	Five Man Electrical Band	13-Nov-71	Lionel 3220

'70s Rank	TITLE	ACT	Peak Date	Label & No.
1651	(I Don't Want To Love You But) You Got Me Anyway	Sutherland Brothers And Quiver	20-Oct-73	Island 1217
1652	She's Not There	Santana	10-Dec-77	Columbia 10616
1653	Maybe	The Three Degrees	15-Aug-70	Roulette 7079
1654	Something He Can Feel	Aretha Franklin	31-Jul-76	Atlantic 3326
1655	Free Man In Paris	Joni Mitchell	14-Sep-74	Asylum 11041
1656	I Was Only Joking	Rod Stewart	1-Jul-78	Warner Bros. 8568
1657	You	George Harrison	8-Nov-75	Apple 1884
1658	Friends With You	John Denver	1-Jan-72	RCA Victor 74-0567
1659	Lady Love	Lou Rawls	8-Apr-78	Phila. Int'l 3634
1660	Women's Love Rights	Laura Lee	23-Oct-71	Hot Wax 7105
1661	Cry Baby	Janis Joplin	19-Jun-71	Columbia 45379
1662	I Do Love You	GQ	15-Sep-79	Arista 0426
1663	Get It On	Chase	17-Jul-71	Epic 10738
1664	Get It Together	The Jackson 5	20-Oct-73	Motown 1277
1665	I Want You Tonight	Pablo Cruise	22-Dec-79	A&M 2195
1666	Elected	Alice Cooper	18-Nov-72	Warner Bros. 7631
1667	Crackerbox Palace	George Harrison	19-Mar-77	Dark Horse 8313
1668	Reach Out I'll Be There	Diana Ross	5-Jun-71	Motown 1184
1669	WOLD	Harry Chapin	23-Mar-74	Elektra 45874
1670	Venus And Mars Rock Show	Wings	6-Dec-75	Capitol 4175
1671	The Way You Do The Things You Do	Rita Coolidge	18-Mar-78	A&M 2004
1672	Living Together, Growing Together	The 5th Dimension	3-Mar-73	Bell 45,310
1673	For The Love Of You (Part 1 & 2)	The Isley Brothers	13-Dec-75	T-Neck 2259
1674	Shilo	Neil Diamond	25-Apr-70	Bang 575
1675	Every Time You Touch Me (I Get High)	Charlie Rich	2-Aug-75	Epic 50103
1676	Rub It In	Billy "Crash" Craddock	31-Aug-74	ABC 12013
1677	I'm On Fire	Dwight Twilley Band	2-Aug-75	Shelter 40380
1678	Carolina In The Pines	Michael Murphey	11-Oct-75	Epic 50131
1679	Rock 'N Roll Soul	Grand Funk Railroad	25-Nov-72	Capitol 3363
1680	Steal Away	Johnnie Taylor	1-Aug-70	Stax 0068
1681	What Are You Doing Sunday	Dawn Featuring Tony Orlando	6-Nov-71	Bell 45,141
1682	Slide	Slave	20-Aug-77	Cotillion 44218
1683	Dance The Night Away	Van Halen	30-Jun-79	Warner Bros. 8823
1684	Mamma Mia	Abba	10-Jul-76	Atlantic 3315
1685	Nobody Wants You When You're Down And Out	Bobby Womack	1-Sep-73	United Artists 255
1686	Let's All Chant	Michael Zager Band	13-May-78	Private Stk 45,184
1687	Such A Woman	Tycoon	19-May-79	Arista 0398
1688	Teddy Bear Song	Barbara Fairchild	9-Jun-73	Columbia 45743
1689	Long Ago And Far Away	James Taylor	30-Oct-71	Warner Bros. 7521
1690	Ring The Living Bell	Melanie	11-Mar-72	Neighborhood 4202
1691	Close Your Eyes	Edward Bear	23-Jun-73	Capitol 3581

'70s Rank	TITLE	ACT	Peak Date	Label & No.
1692	Sure As I'm Sittin' Here	Three Dog Night	24-Aug-74	Dunhill/ABC 15001
1693	Follow You Follow Me	Genesis	15-Jul-78	Atlantic 3474
1694	Fooling Yourself (The Angry Young Man)	Styx	22-Apr-78	A&M 2007
1695	Always Something There To Remind Me	R.B. Greaves	28-Feb-70	Atco 6726
1696	If You Talk In Your Sleep	Elvis Presley	27-Jul-74	RCA Victor 0280
1697	Straight Shootin' Woman	Steppenwolf	26-Oct-74	Mums 6031
1698	This Song	George Harrison	8-Jan-77	Dark Horse 8294
1699	Cat Scratch Fever	Ted Nugent	1-Oct-77	Epic 50425
1700	Free	Chicago	3-Apr-71	Columbia 45331
1701	High Time We Went	Joe Cocker	3-Jul-71	A&M 1258
1702	Let Me In	The Osmonds	27-Oct-73	MGM 14617
1703	Part Time Love	Ann Peebles	28-Nov-70	Hi 2178
1704	Save The Country	The 5th Dimension	25-Jul-70	Bell 895
1705	I Belong To You	Love Unlimited	15-Feb-75	20th Century 2141
1706	Harry Truman	Chicago	5-Apr-75	Columbia 10092
1707	"Cherry Cherry" from Hot August Night	Neil Diamond	12-May-73	MCA 40017
1708	Heart Of The Night	Poco	14-Jul-79	MCA 41023
1709	There Won't Be Anymore	Charlie Rich	23-Mar-74	RCA Victor 0195
1710	Let Your Love Go	Bread	13-Feb-71	Elektra 45711
1711	Mainstreet	Bob Seger	4-Jun-77	Capitol 4422
1712	Dreaming	Blondie	1-Dec-79	Chrysalis 2379
1713	Come Monday	Jimmy Buffett	13-Jul-74	Dunhill 4385
1714	One Way Or Another	Blondie	4-Aug-79	Chrysalis 2336
1715	Telephone Man	Meri Wilson	16-Jul-77	GRT 127
1716	Lovely Day	Bill Withers	11-Feb-78	Columbia 10627
1717	Make It Easy On Yourself	Dionne Warwick	21-Nov-70	Scepter 12294
1718	(I Know) I'm Losing You	Rod Stewart With Faces	1-Jan-72	Mercury 73244
1719	Cupid	Johnny Nash	10-Jan-70	JAD 220
1720	Hot Summer Nights	Night	1-Sep-79	Planet 45903
1721	I Can't Help Myself (Sugar Pie, Honey Bunch)	Donnie Elbert	18-Mar-72	Avco 4587
1722	Hey, Mister Sun	Bobby Sherman	27-Jun-70	Metromedia 188
1723	Baby Hold On	The Grass Roots	20-Jun-70	Dunhill 4237
1724	Soolaimon (African Trilogy II)	Neil Diamond	6-Jun-70	Uni 55224
1725	Who'd She Coo?	Ohio Players	18-Sep-76	Mercury 73814
1726	Hallelujah	Sweathog	15-Jan-72	Columbia 45492
1727	Jump Into The Fire	Nilsson	29-Apr-72	RCA Victor 74-0673
1728	One Nation Under A Groove - Part I	Funkadelic	18-Nov-78	Warner Bros. 8618
1729	So Close	Jake Holmes	28-Nov-70	Polydor 14041
1730	Light Sings	The 5th Dimension	26-Jun-71	Bell 999
1731	Workin' At The Car Wash Blues	Jim Croce	20-Jul-74	ABC 11447
1732	I Got My Mind Made Up (You Can Get It Girl)	Instant Funk	5-May-79	Salsoul 2078

'70s Rank	TITLE	ACT	Peak Date	Label & No.
1733	Shout It Out Loud	Kiss	15-May-76	Casablanca 854
1734	Harry Hippie	Bobby Womack	17-Feb-73	United Artists 50946
1735	Woman To Woman	Shirley Brown	14-Dec-74	Truth 3206
1736	Ain't Nothing Like The Real Thing	Donny & Marie	29-Jan-77	Polydor/Kolob 14363
1737	Can This Be Real	Natural Four	23-Feb-74	Curtom 1990
1738	Doing It To Death	Fred Wesley & The J.B.'s	28-Jul-73	People 621
1739	It's A Laugh	Daryl Hall & John Oates	4-Nov-78	RCA 11371
1740	Blue Collar Man (Long Nights)	Styx	18-Nov-78	A&M 2087
1741	Today's The Day	America	10-Jul-76	Warner Bros. 8212
1742	Gone	Joey Heatherton	12-Aug-72	MGM 14387
1743	I Can't Stand The Rain	Ann Peebles	12-Jan-74	Hi 2248
1744	Let's Get Married	Al Green	4-May-74	Hi 2262
1745	Sweet Charlie Babe	Jackie Moore	22-Sep-73	Atlantic 2956
1746	Operator	The Manhattan Transfer	29-Nov-75	Atlantic 3292
1747	Never Had A Dream Come True	Stevie Wonder	14-Mar-70	Tamla 54191
1748	I Like To Live The Love	B.B. King	16-Mar-74	ABC 11406
1749	Son Of Sagittarius	Eddie Kendricks	22-Jun-74	Tamla 54247
1750	Heavy Makes You Happy (Sha-Na-Boom Boom)	The Staple Singers	3-Apr-71	Stax 0083
1751	Bitter Bad	Melanie	14-Apr-73	Neighborhood 4210
1752	Where Peaceful Waters Flow	Gladys Knight & The Pips	11-Aug-73	Buddah 363
1753	Did You Boogie (With Your Baby)	Flash Cadillac & The Continental Kids	16-Oct-76	Private Stk 45,079
1754	Stuff Like That	Quincy Jones	26-Aug-78	A&M 2043
1755	Join Together	The Who	2-Sep-72	Decca 32983
1756	Changes	David Bowie	13-May-72 / 8-Feb-75	RCA Victor 74-0605
1757	Christine Sixteen	Kiss	27-Aug-77	Casablanca 889
1758	Just What I Needed	The Cars	9-Sep-78	Elektra 45491
1759	Macho Man	Village People	26-Aug-78	Casablanca 922
1760	Breaking Up Is Hard To Do	The Partridge Family	26-Aug-72	Bell 45,235
1761	Fantasy	Earth, Wind & Fire	13-May-78	Columbia 10688
1762	Never Let You Go	Bloodstone	17-Nov-73	London 1051
1763	Sexy Mama	The Moments	9-Mar-74	Stang 5052
1764	Where Did Our Love Go	Donnie Elbert	11-Dec-71	All Platinum 2330
1765	Mother	John Lennon/Plastic Ono Band	6-Feb-71	Apple 1827
1766	Secret Love	Freddy Fender	13-Dec-75	ABC/Dot 17585
1767	Jimmy Loves Mary-Anne	Looking Glass	13-Oct-73	Epic 11001
1768	(If Loving You Is Wrong) I Don't Want To Be Right	Barbara Mandrell	9-Jun-79	ABC/MCA 12451
1769	She Belongs To Me	Rick Nelson And The Stone Canyon Band	31-Jan-70	Decca 32550
1770	Dark Horse	George Harrison	4-Jan-75	Apple 1877

'70s Rank	TITLE	ACT	Peak Date	Label & No.
1771	Drinking Wine Spo-Dee O'Dee	Jerry Lee Lewis	2-Jun-73	Mercury 73374
1772	Can't Stop Loving You	Tom Jones	26-Dec-70	Parrot 40056
1773	Smarty Pants	First Choice	22-Dec-73	Philly Groove 179
1774	Spaceman	Nilsson	11-Nov-72	RCA Victor 74-0788
1775	All The King's Horses	Aretha Franklin	15-Jul-72	Atlantic 2883
1776	Josie	Steely Dan	21-Oct-78	ABC 12404
1777	Street Corner Serenade	Wet Willie	18-Feb-78	Epic 50478
1778	Rockin' All Over The World	John Fogerty	1-Nov-75	Asylum 45274
1779	My Fair Share	Seals & Crofts	19-Nov-77	Warner Bros. 8405
1780	Most Of All	B.J. Thomas	23-Jan-71	Scepter 12299
1781	I Don't Know How To Love Him	Yvonne Elliman	12-Jun-71	Decca 32785
1782	Good Morning Heartache	Diana Ross	10-Mar-73	Motown 1211
1783	Soul Makossa	Manu Dibango	11-Aug-73	Atlantic 2971
1784	I'll Be Your Shelter (In Time Of Storm)	Luther Ingram	27-Jan-73	KoKo 2113
1785	Burning Bridges	The Mike Curb Congregation	13-Mar-71	MGM 14151
1786	Happy Anniversary	Little River Band	11-Mar-78	Harvest 4524
1787	Don't Cross The River	America	17-Mar-73	Warner Bros. 7670
1788	Loving Her Was Easier (Than Anything I'll Ever Do Again)	Kris Kristofferson	23-Oct-71	Monument 8525
1789	So Good, So Right	Brenda Russell	10-Nov-79	Horizon 123
1790	Daybreak	Barry Manilow	12-Nov-77	Arista 0273
1791	Come Together	Aerosmith	7-Oct-78	Columbia 10802
1792	If I Never Knew Your Name	Vic Dana	14-Mar-70	Liberty 56150
1793	Satin Soul	Love Unlimited Orchestra	5-Apr-75	20th Century 2162
1794	I'd Rather Be A Cowboy	John Denver	28-Jul-73	RCA Victor 74-0955
1795	Double Barrel	Dave And Ansil Collins	31-Jul-71	Big Tree 115
1796	This One's For You	Barry Manilow	30-Oct-76	Arista 0206
1797	You've Got A Friend	Roberta Flack & Donny Hathaway	14-Aug-71	Atlantic 2808
1798	Daybreak	Nilsson	1-Jun-74	RCA Victor 0246
1799	Border Song (Holy Moses)	Aretha Franklin	19-Dec-70	Atlantic 2772
1800	Emotion	Helen Reddy	22-Mar-75	Capitol 4021
1801	K-Jee	The Nite-Liters	11-Sep-71	RCA Victor 74-0461
1802	Broken Hearted Me	Anne Murray	24-Nov-79	Capitol 4773
1803	Once You Understand	Think	22-Jan-72 13-Apr-74	Laurie 3583
1804	When Julie Comes Around	The Cuff Links	31-Jan-70	Decca 732592
1805	Go Down Gamblin'	Blood, Sweat & Tears	11-Sep-71	Columbia 45427
1806	Disco Queen	Hot Chocolate	26-Jul-75	Big Tree 16038
1807	Looking Through The Eyes Of Love	The Partridge Family	27-Jan-73	Bell 45,301
1808	Nothing To Hide	Tommy James	1-Jan-72	Roulette 7114
1809	Let's Straighten It Out	Latimore	23-Nov-74	Glades 1722
1810	You Could Have Been A Lady	April Wine	20-May-72	Big Tree 133

'70s Rank	TITLE	ACT	Peak Date	Label & No.
1811	Hearsay	The Soul Children	13-May-72	Stax 0119
1812	Maybe I'm A Fool	Eddie Money	31-Mar-79	Columbia 10900
1813	Autobahn	Kraftwerk	10-May-75	Vertigo 203
1814	Painted Ladies	Ian Thomas	22-Dec-73	Janus 224
1815	Part Of The Plan	Dan Fogelberg	22-Mar-75	Epic 50055
1816	Theme From The Men	Isaac Hayes	2-Dec-72	Enterprise 9058
1817	Wonderful Tonight	Eric Clapton	8-Jul-78	RSO 895
1818	Superwoman (Where Were You When I Needed You)	Stevie Wonder	22-Jul-72	Tamla 54216
1819	The Drum	Bobby Sherman	29-May-71	Metromedia 217
1820	Kissing My Love	Bill Withers	24-Mar-73	Sussex 250
1821	Hijack	Herbie Mann	31-May-75	Atlantic 3246
1822	Stop The War Now	Edwin Starr	9-Jan-71	Gordy 7104
1823	Peace Will Come (According To Plan)	Melanie	26-Sep-70	Buddah 186
1824	I'm Coming Home	The Spinners	6-Jul-74	Atlantic 3027
1825	Part Time Love	Gladys Knight & The Pips	27-Dec-75	Buddah 513
1826	Gotta Get Back To You	Tommy James And The Shondells	4-Apr-70	Roulette 7071
1827	Cold Turkey	Plastic Ono Band	3-Jan-70	Apple 1813
1828	Morning Dance	Spyro Gyra	18-Aug-79	Infinity 50,011
1829	Theme Song From "Which Way Is Up"	Stargard	25-Mar-78	MCA 40825
1830	Sister Mary Elephant (Shudd-Up!)	Cheech & Chong	26-Jan-74	Ode 66041
1831	If You Wanna Get To Heaven	Ozark Mountain Daredevils	6-Jul-74	A&M 1515
1832	Sophisticated Lady (She's A Different Lady)	Natalie Cole	21-Aug-76	Capitol 4259
1833	Stop, Look, Listen (To Your Heart)	The Stylistics	24-Jul-71	Avco Embassy 4572
1834	Dream Baby (How Long Must I Dream)	Glen Campbell	17-Apr-71	Capitol 3062
1835	Stay//The Load-Out	Jackson Browne	12-Aug-78	Asylum 45485
1836	Woman's Gotta Have It	Bobby Womack	24-Jun-72	United Artists 50902
1837	Overnight Sensation (Hit Record)	Raspberries	16-Nov-74	Capitol 3946
1838	Movin' On	Bad Company	8-Mar-75	Swan Song 70101
1839	Take A Look Around	The Temptations	8-Apr-72	Gordy 7115
1840	Puppet Man	The 5th Dimension	30-May-70	Bell 880
1841	The Hurt	Cat Stevens	1-Sep-73	A&M 1418
1842	Loving You Just Crossed My Mind	Sam Neely	11-Nov-72	Capitol 3381
1843	I Need To Be In Love	Carpenters	17-Jul-76	A&M 1828
1844	Just A Little Bit Of You	Michael Jackson	2-Aug-75	Motown 1349
1845	Dancin' Man	Q	7-May-77	Epic 50335
1846	The Nickel Song	Melanie	4-Mar-72	Buddah 268
1847	Never Let Her Go	David Gates	8-Mar-75	Elektra 45223
1848	Love Don't Love Nobody - Pt. I	The Spinners	23-Nov-74	Atlantic 3206
1849	Breaking Up Is Hard To Do	Lenny Welch	21-Feb-70	Commonwealth United 3004
1850	Bangla-Desh	George Harrison	11-Sep-71	Apple 1836

'70s Rank	TITLE	ACT	Peak Date	Label & No.
1851	Get It Right Next Time	Gerry Rafferty	13-Oct-79	United Artists 1316
1852	Slippery When Wet	Commodores	2-Aug-75	Motown 1338
1853	Wigwam	Bob Dylan	29-Aug-70	Columbia 45199
1854	We're Free	Beverly Bremers	22-Jul-72	Scepter 12348
1855	Someday Never Comes	Creedence Clearwater Revival	10-Jun-72	Fantasy 676
1856	7-6-5-4-3-2-1 (Blow Your Whistle)	Gary Toms Empire	27-Sep-75	Pickwick Int'l 6504
1857	My Man, A Sweet Man	Millie Jackson	16-Sep-72	Spring 127
1858	Soul Power Pt. 1	James Brown	3-Apr-71	King 6368
1859	All Day Music	War	25-Sep-71	United Artists 50815
1860	Dance (Disco Heat)	Sylvester	25-Nov-78	Fantasy 827
1861	All I Have To Do Is Dream	Bobbie Gentry & Glen Campbell	28-Mar-70	Capitol 2745
1862	Home And Dry	Gerry Rafferty	3-Feb-79	United Artists 1266
1863	You Are My Starship	Norman Connors	13-Nov-76	Buddah 542
1864	Amie	Pure Prairie League	10-May-75	RCA Victor 10184
1865	Dancin' Fool	The Guess Who	11-Jan-75	RCA Victor 10075
1866	Rainy Jane	Davy Jones	24-Jul-71	Bell 45,111
1867	Struttin'	Billy Preston	1-Feb-75	A&M 1644
1868	Give It Up (Turn It Loose)	Tyrone Davis	27-Nov-76	Columbia 10388
1869	Long Dark Road	The Hollies	23-Dec-72	Epic 10920
1870	Albert Flasher	The Guess Who	26-Jun-71	RCA Victor 74-0458
1871	I Want To Take You Higher	Ike & Tina Turner & The Ikettes	5-Sep-70	Liberty 56177
1872	Ready	Cat Stevens	18-Jan-75	A&M 1645
1873	I Will Be In Love With You	Livingston Taylor	30-Dec-78	Epic 50604
1874	I Play And Sing	Dawn	1-May-71	Bell 970
1875	Long Long Time	Linda Ronstadt	17-Oct-70	Capitol 2846
1876	Deeper Than The Night	Olivia Newton-John	2-Jun-79	MCA 41009
1877	Only Love Is Real	Carole King	27-Mar-76	Ode 66119
1878	Small Beginnings	Flash	26-Aug-72	Capitol 3345
1879	Rock And Roll Love Letter	Bay City Rollers	12-Jun-76	Arista 0185
1880	At Midnight (My Love Will Lift You Up)	Rufus Featuring Chaka Khan	2-Apr-77	ABC 12239
1881	Take Me To The River	Talking Heads	27-Jan-79	Sire 1032
1882	Pretty As You Feel	Jefferson Airplane	25-Dec-71	Grunt 0500
1883	Gettin' Ready For Love	Diana Ross	14-Jan-78	Motown 1427
1884	Let's Work Together (Part 1)	Wilbert Harrison	21-Feb-70	Sue 11
1885	Hurricane (Part I)	Bob Dylan	3-Jan-76	Columbia 10245
1886	Jody's Got Your Girl And Gone	Johnnie Taylor	27-Feb-71	Stax 0085
1887	To Each His Own	Faith, Hope & Charity	4-Oct-75	RCA Victor 10343
1888	Forever Autumn	Justin Hayward	23-Dec-78	Columbia 10799
1889	The South's Gonna Do It	Charlie Daniels Band	22-Mar-75	Kama Sutra 598
1890	Marianne	Stephen Stills	9-Oct-71	Atlantic 2820
1891	Remember What I Told You To Forget	Tavares	7-Jun-75	Capitol 4010

'70s Rank	TITLE	ACT	Peak Date	Label & No.
1892	Another Park, Another Sunday	The Doobie Brothers	22-Jun-74	Warner Bros. 7795
1893	Teenage Lament '74	Alice Cooper	9-Feb-74	Warner Bros. 7762
1894	Mississippi	John Phillips	18-Jul-70	Dunhill 4236
1895	Wild Night	Van Morrison	11-Dec-71	Warner Bros. 7518
1896	I'm Coming Home	Stories	5-Aug-72	Kama Sutra 545
1897	Outside Woman	Bloodstone	27-Apr-74	London 1052
1898	George Jackson	Bob Dylan	8-Jan-72	Columbia 45516
1899	I Feel Like A Bullet (In The Gun Of Robert Ford)	Elton John	6-Mar-76	MCA 40505
1900	Kung Fu	Curtis Mayfield	31-Aug-74	Curtom 1999
1901	Getting Closer	Wings	28-Jul-79	Columbia 11020
1902	Show Me How	The Emotions	5-Feb-72	Volt 4066
1903	Come On Over	Olivia Newton-John	15-May-76	MCA 40525
1904	Mongoose	Elephant's Memory	7-Nov-70	Metromedia 182
1905	Cherry Baby	Starz	7-May-77	Capitol 4399
1906	The Power Of Gold	Dan Fogelberg / Tim Weisberg	25-Nov-78	Full Moon 50606
1907	Only The Good Die Young	Billy Joel	8-Jul-78	Columbia 10750
1908	Big Yellow Taxi	The Neighborhood	22-Aug-70	Big Tree 102
1909	Mighty Clouds Of Joy	B.J. Thomas	21-Aug-71	Scepter 12320
1910	Everybody's Out Of Town	B.J. Thomas	2-May-70	Scepter 12277
1911	Your Move	Yes	11-Dec-71	Atlantic 2819
1912	Over The Hills And Far Away	Led Zeppelin	4-Aug-73	Atlantic 2970
1913	I Know I'm In Love	Chee-Chee And Peppy	10-Jul-71	Buddah 225
1914	If We Make It Through December	Merle Haggard	19-Jan-74	Capitol 3746
1915	Young Americans	David Bowie	10-May-75	RCA Victor 10152
1916	I Ain't Got Time Anymore	The Glass Bottle	25-Sep-71	Avco Embassy 4575
1917	Hallelujah Day	The Jackson 5	28-Apr-73	Motown 1224
1918	Mammy Blue	Stories	8-Dec-73	Kama Sutra 584
1919	Just Seven Numbers (Can Straighten Out My Life)	Four Tops	27-Feb-71	Motown 1175
1920	Two Doors Down	Dolly Parton	13-May-78	RCA 11240
1921	Woman Don't Go Astray	King Floyd	28-Oct-72	Chimneyville 443
1922	Just Too Many People	Melissa Manchester	15-Nov-75	Arista 0146
1923	It's A Long Way There	Little River Band	4-Dec-76	Harvest 4318
1924	The Next Step Is Love	Elvis Presley	19-Sep-70	RCA Victor 47-9873
1925	In The Ghetto	Candi Staton	12-Aug-72	Fame 91000
1926	Hey Lawdy Mama	Steppenwolf	16-May-70	Dunhill 4234
1927	Hot Number	Foxy	2-Jun-79	Dash 5050
1928	When I'm Dead And Gone	McGuinness Flint	20-Feb-71	Capitol 3014
1929	The Runway	The Grass Roots	29-Jul-72	Dunhill 4316
1930	Heavy Fallin' Out	The Stylistics	21-Dec-74	Avco 4647

'70s Rank	TITLE	ACT	Peak Date	Label & No.
1931	American City Suite	Cashman & West	11-Nov-72	Dunhill 4324
1932	Abra-Ca-Dabra	The DeFranco Family Featuring Tony DeFranco	16-Feb-74	20th Century 2070
1933	Stand By Me	John Lennon	26-Apr-75	Apple 1881
1934	Damned If I Do	Alan Parsons Project	22-Dec-79	Arista 0454
1935	Spirit In The Dark	Aretha Franklin	27-Jun-70	Atlantic 2731
1936	Big Yellow Taxi	Joni Mitchell	15-Feb-75	Asylum 45221
1937	I Will Still Love You	Stonebolt	28-Oct-78	Parachute 512
1938	Step By Step	Joe Simon	28-Apr-73	Spring 133
1939	Touch A Hand, Make A Friend	The Staple Singers	20-Apr-74	Stax 0196
1940	I'm Comin' Home	Tommy James	30-Oct-71	Roulette 7110
1941	Honey Please, Can't Ya See	Barry White	6-Apr-74	20th Century 2077
1942	She Came In Through The Bathroom Window	Joe Cocker	31-Jan-70	A&M 1147
1943	That Same Old Feeling	Pickettywitch	25-Jul-70	Janus 118
1944	The Greatest Love Of All	George Benson	8-Oct-77	Arista 0251
1945	Long, Long Way From Home	Foreigner	11-Feb-78	Atlantic 3439
1946	And The Grass Won't Pay No Mind	Mark Lindsay	14-Nov-70	Columbia 45229
1947	Take A Look Around	Smith	21-Mar-70	Dunhill 4228
1948	Mighty Joe	The Shocking Blue	18-Apr-70	Colossus 111
1949	I Wouldn't Want To Be Like You	Alan Parsons	15-Oct-77	Arista 0260
1950	My Thang	James Brown	20-Jul-74	Polydor 14244
1951	I Can Understand It	The New Birth	19-May-73	RCA Victor 74-0912
1952	Gonna Fly Now (Theme From "Rocky")	Maynard Ferguson	11-Jun-77	Columbia 10468
1953	Main Title (Theme From "Jaws")	John Williams	4-Oct-75	MCA 40439
1954	Happiness Is Just Around The Bend	The Main Ingredient	24-Aug-74	RCA Victor 0305
1955	Blue Suede Shoes	Johnny Rivers	5-May-73	United Artists 198
1956	Back Together Again	Daryl Hall & John Oates	18-Jun-77	RCA 10970
1957	Give The People What They Want	The O'Jays	14-Jun-75	Phila. Int'l 3565
1958	If You Leave Me Tonight I'll Cry	Jerry Wallace	7-Oct-72	Decca 32989
1959	Tell Her Love Has Felt The Need	Eddie Kendricks	21-Sep-74	Tamla 54249
1960	Roll Over Beethoven	Electric Light Orchestra	21-Jul-73	United Artists 173
1961	Rainy Day People	Gordon Lightfoot	31-May-75	Reprise 1328
1962	FM (No Static At All)	Steely Dan	29-Jul-78	MCA 40894
1963	Love Theme From "The Godfather" (Speak Softly Love)	Andy Williams	3-Jun-72	Columbia 45579
1964	(You've Got Me) Dangling On A String	Chairmen Of The Board	20-Jun-70	Invictus 9078
1965	Cinderella	Firefall	28-May-77	Atlantic 3392
1966	Shakedown Cruise	Jay Ferguson	30-Jun-79	Asylum 46041
1967	I've Got A Thing About You Baby	Elvis Presley	16-Mar-74	RCA Victor 0196
1968	I Need A Lover	John Cougar	22-Dec-79	Riva 202
1969	I'm On Fire	5000 Volts	6-Dec-75	Philips 40801
1970	Baby Come Close	Smokey Robinson	2-Mar-74	Tamla 54239

'70s Rank	TITLE	ACT	Peak Date	Label & No.
1971	Swamp Witch	Jim Stafford	14-Jul-73	MGM 14496
1972	D.O.A.	Bloodrock	6-Mar-71	Capitol 3009
1973	Now Run And Tell That	Denise LaSalle	18-Mar-72	Westbound 201
1974	It's A New Day (Part 1) & (Part 2)	James Brown	14-Mar-70	King 6292
1975	Loving Arms	Dobie Gray	22-Sep-73	MCA 40100
1976	Looking For A Love	J. Geils Band	29-Jan-72	Atlantic 2844
1977	Believe In Humanity	Carole King	1-Sep-73	Ode 66035
1978	She's All I Got	Freddie North	13-Nov-71	Mankind 12004
1979	You Need Love Like I Do (Don't You)	Gladys Knight & The Pips	2-May-70	Soul 35071
1980	You Want It, You Got It	Detroit Emeralds	11-Mar-72	Westbound 192
1981	Time To Get Down	The O'Jays	14-Jul-73	Phila. Int'l 3531
1982	1900 Yesterday	Liz Damon's Orient Express	20-Feb-71	White Whale 368
1983	People Gotta Move	Gino Vannelli	23-Nov-74	A&M 1614
1984	Days Gone Down (Still Got The Light In Your Eyes)	Gerry Rafferty	14-Jul-79	United Artists 1298
1985	Airport Love Theme (Gwen And Vern)	Vincent Bell	16-May-70	Decca 32659
1986	Let The Music Play	Barry White	7-Feb-76	20th Century 2265
1987	One Love In My Lifetime	Diana Ross	2-Oct-76	Motown 1398
1988	Country Road	James Taylor	20-Mar-71	Warner Bros. 7460
1989	Easy Livin'	Uriah Heep	16-Sep-72	Mercury 73307
1990	Hard Rock Cafe	Carole King	17-Sep-77	Capitol 4455
1991	Baby That's Backatcha	Smokey Robinson	28-Jun-75	Tamla 54258
1992	Love Or Leave	The Spinners	14-Feb-76	Atlantic 3309
1993	Whatever You Got, I Want	The Jackson 5	14-Dec-74	Motown 1308
1994	Fresh As A Daisy	Emitt Rhodes	20-Feb-71	Dunhill 4267
1995	My Marie	Engelbert Humperdinck	1-Aug-70	Parrot 40049
1996	Dreamboat Annie	Heart	29-Jan-77	Mushroom 7023
1997	I Hear Those Church Bells Ringing	Dusk	28-Aug-71	Bell 990
1998	It Sure Took A Long, Long Time	Lobo	2-Jun-73	Big Tree 16,001
1999	Run Run Run	Jo Jo Gunne	20-May-72	Asylum 11003
2000	Hello Old Friend	Eric Clapton	18-Dec-76	RSO 861
2001	The Immigrant	Neil Sedaka	17-May-75	Rocket/MCA 40370
2002	Never Can Say Goodbye	Isaac Hayes	19-Jun-71	Enterprise 9031
2003	Crazy On You	Heart	12-Jun-76 / 28-Jan-78	Mushroom 7021
2004	Viva Tirado - Part 1	El Chicano	30-May-70	Kapp 2085
2005	Dusic	Brick	19-Nov-77	Bang 734
2006	My Elusive Dreams	Bobby Vinton	14-Mar-70	Epic 10576
2007	American Tune	Paul Simon	12-Jan-74	Columbia 45900
2008	The Love We Had (Stays On My Mind)	The Dells	16-Oct-71	Cadet 5683
2009	Superman	Donna Fargo	14-Apr-73	Dot 17444
2010	Mind Bender	Stillwater	4-Feb-78	Capricorn 0280

'70s Rank	TITLE	ACT	Peak Date	Label & No.
2011	Daisy Mae	Hamilton, Joe Frank & Reynolds	29-Jan-72	Dunhill 4296
2012	Walking Through The Country	The Grass Roots	21-Mar-70	Dunhill 4227
2013	Hey Girl (I Like Your Style)	The Temptations	6-Oct-73	Gordy 7131
2014	I'll Always Love My Mama (Part I)	The Intruders	28-Jul-73	Gamble 2506
2015	Silver Moon	Michael Nesmith & The First National Band	9-Jan-71	RCA Victor 74-0399
2016	Boogie Shoes	KC & The Sunshine Band	1-Apr-78	T.K. 1025
2017	I'll Be Right Here	Tyrone Davis	1-Aug-70	Dakar 618
2018	One Less Set Of Footsteps	Jim Croce	24-Mar-73	ABC 11346
2019	Hold On	The Rascals	31-Jan-70	Atlantic 2695
2020	Free Bird (Live)	Lynyrd Skynyrd	8-Jan-77	MCA 40665
2021	Mighty Mighty	Earth, Wind & Fire	1-Jun-74	Columbia 46007
2022	Softly Whispering I Love You	The English Congregation	11-Mar-72	Atco 6865
2023	Hello Hurray	Alice Cooper	24-Mar-73	Warner Bros. 7673
2024	Lorelei	Styx	10-Apr-76	A&M 1786
2025	Do You See My Love (For You Growing)	Jr. Walker & The All Stars	22-Aug-70	Soul 35073
2026	Love Don't Live Here Anymore	Rose Royce	10-Feb-79	Whitfield 8712
2027	A Dose Of Rock 'N' Roll	Ringo Starr	6-Nov-76	Atlantic 3361
2028	The Breakdown Part 1	Rufus Thomas	2-Oct-71	Stax 0098
2029	Smilin'	Sly & The Family Stone	3-Jun-72	Epic 10850
2030	Breakdown	Tom Petty And The Heartbreakers	4-Feb-78	Shelter 62008
2031	Hot Legs	Rod Stewart	1-Apr-78	Warner Bros. 8535
2032	Rockin' Soul	The Hues Corporation	30-Nov-74	RCA Victor 10066
2033	That's When The Music Takes Me	Neil Sedaka	30-Aug-75	Rocket/MCA 40426
2034	Shadows In The Moonlight	Anne Murray	14-Jul-79	Capitol 4716
2035	Drivin' Wheel	Foghat	8-Jan-77	Bearsville 0313
2036	Old Man	Neil Young	10-Jun-72	Reprise 1084
2037	Break Away	Art Garfunkel	14-Feb-76	Columbia 10273
2038	Hold On	Ian Gomm	27-Oct-79	Stiff/Epic 50747
2039	The Homecoming	Hagood Hardy	14-Feb-76	Capitol 4156
2040	Corazon	Carole King	8-Dec-73	Ode 66039
2041	Moody Blue	Elvis Presley	26-Feb-77	RCA 10857
2042	The Sly, Slick, And The Wicked	The Lost Generation	29-Aug-70	Brunswick 55436
2043	Butter Boy	Fanny	5-Apr-75	Casablanca 814
2044	Charity Ball	Fanny	13-Nov-71	Reprise 1033
2045	Dream Merchant	The New Birth	6-Sep-75	Buddah 470
2046	There Goes Another Love Song	Outlaws	25-Oct-75	Arista 0150
2047	Theme From Close Encounters	Meco	25-Feb-78	Millennium 608
2048	Pearl	Tommy Roe	1-Aug-70	ABC 11266
2049	Sweetheart	Engelbert Humperdinck	24-Oct-70	Parrot 40054
2050	Watching The River Flow	Bob Dylan	31-Jul-71	Columbia 45409

'70s Rank	TITLE	ACT	Peak Date	Label & No.
2051	Calypso	John Denver	22-Nov-75	RCA Victor 10353
2052	Hearts Of Stone	The Blue Ridge Rangers	26-May-73	Fantasy 700
2053	Stir It Up And Serve It	Tommy Roe	4-Apr-70	ABC 11258
2054	School Boy Crush	AWB	3-Jan-76	Atlantic 3304
2055	Hurt	Elvis Presley	15-May-76	RCA Victor 10601
2056	You've Got To Crawl (Before You Walk)	The 8th Day	13-Nov-71	Invictus 9098
2057	I Love You	Donna Summer	11-Feb-78	Casablanca 907
2058	Ecstasy	Ohio Players	20-Oct-73	Westbound 216
2059	All The Young Dudes	Mott The Hoople	11-Nov-72	Columbia 45673
2060	Full Of Fire	Al Green	27-Dec-75	Hi 2300
2061	How Can I Forget	Marvin Gaye	7-Feb-70	Tamla 54190
2062	Love Is What You Make It	The Grass Roots	24-Mar-73	Dunhill 4335
2063	Rock Me Baby	David Cassidy	21-Oct-72	Bell 45,260
2064	Edge Of The Universe	Bee Gees	10-Sep-77	RSO 880
2065	I Wanna Dance Wit' Choo (Doo Dat Dance)	Disco Tex & The Sex-O-Lettes	14-Jun-75	Chelsea 3015
2066	Lowdown	Chicago	12-Jun-71	Columbia 45370
2067	I'm A Train	Albert Hammond	4-May-74	Mums 6026
2068	Mr. Blue Sky	Electric Light Orchestra	19-Aug-78	Jet 5050
2069	Bridget The Midget (The Queen Of The Blues)	Ray Stevens	13-Feb-71	Barnaby 2024
2070	Oh What A Day	The Dells	21-Feb-70	Cadet 5663
2071	Sam	Olivia Newton-John	26-Mar-77	MCA 40670
2072	Another Rainy Day In New York City	Chicago	31-Jul-76	Columbia 10360
2073	Attitude Dancing	Carly Simon	28-Jun-75	Elektra 45246
2074	I Believe You	Dorothy Moore	15-Oct-77	Malaco 1042
2075	Thanks For Saving My Life	Billy Paul	4-May-74	Phila. Int'l 3538
2076	When You Say Love	Sonny & Cher	19-Aug-72	Kapp 2176
2077	Alive	Bee Gees	23-Dec-72	Atco 6909
2078	A Million To One	Donny Osmond	22-Sep-73	MGM 14583
2079	Goin' Home	The Osmonds	21-Jul-73	MGM 14562
2080	Hard Work	John Handy	11-Sep-76	ABC Impulse 31005
2081	You Can't Always Get What You Want	The Rolling Stones	16-Jun-73	London 910
2082	Crazy Mama	J.J. Cale	8-Apr-72	Shelter 7314
2083	Weekend	Wet Willie	4-Aug-79	Epic 50714
2084	Highway Song	Blackfoot	25-Aug-79	Atco 7104
2085	Let It Shine	Olivia Newton-John	17-Jan-76	MCA 40495
2086	Pretty Lady	Lighthouse	15-Dec-73	Polydor 14198
2087	I Love My Friend	Charlie Rich	14-Sep-74	Epic 20006
2088	Heartbroken Bopper	The Guess Who	15-Apr-72	RCA Victor 74-0659
2089	Flight '76	The Walter Murphy Band	1-Jan-77	Private Stk 45,123
2090	Until It's Time For You To Go	Elvis Presley	4-Mar-72	RCA Victor 74-0619
2091	Jesus Is Just Alright	The Doobie Brothers	17-Feb-73	Warner Bros. 7661

'70s Rank	TITLE	ACT	Peak Date	Label & No.
2092	Surfin' USA	Leif Garrett	22-Oct-77	Atlantic 3423
2093	King Heroin	James Brown	8-Apr-72	Polydor 14116
2094	In Heaven There Is No Beer	Clean Living	23-Dec-72	Vanguard 35162
2095	From The Beginning	Emerson, Lake & Palmer	21-Oct-72	Cotillion 44158
2096	Virginia (Touch Me Like You Do)	Bill Amesbury	20-Apr-74	Casablanca 0001
2097	One Tin Soldier	The Original Caste	14-Feb-70	T-A 186
2098	I'm So Proud	The Main Ingredient	27-Feb-71	RCA Victor 74-0401
2099	What Cha Gonna Do With My Lovin'	Stephanie Mills	6-Oct-79	20th Cent. Fox 2403
2100	Country Wine	The Raiders	19-Feb-72	Columbia 45535
2101	Do What You Wanna Do	Five Flights Up	24-Oct-70	T-A 202
2102	Love Means (You Never Have To Say You're Sorry)	Sounds Of Sunshine	31-Jul-71	Ranwood 896
2103	Man Sized Job	Denise LaSalle	25-Nov-72	Westbound 206
2104	My Way	Elvis Presley	10-Dec-77	RCA 11165
2105	Soul Song	Joe Stampley	10-Mar-73	Dot 17442
2106	Everybody Is A Star	Sly & The Family Stone	7-Feb-70	Epic 10555
2107	Street Life	The Crusaders	10-Nov-79	MCA 41054
2108	Til The World Ends	Three Dog Night	23-Aug-75	ABC 12114
2109	Raised On Rock	Elvis Presley	3-Nov-73	RCA Victor 0088
2110	Let Your Hair Down	The Temptations	2-Feb-74	Gordy 7133
2111	Where Evil Grows	The Poppy Family	2-Oct-71	London 148
2112	Fallin' In Love	The Souther, Hillman, Furay Band	12-Oct-74	Asylum 45201
2113	You Can Have Her	Sam Neely	9-Nov-74	A&M 1612
2114	That's Where The Happy People Go	The Trammps	26-Jun-76	Atlantic 3306
2115	If You Were Mine	Ray Charles	21-Nov-70	ABC/TRC 11271
2116	Street Singin'	Lady Flash	11-Sep-76	RSO 852
2117	Run For Home	Lindisfarne	16-Dec-78	Atco 7093
2118	Sunshine	The Archies	8-Aug-70	Kirshner 1009
2119	Chameleon	Herbie Hancock	1-Jun-74	Columbia 46002
2120	Fins	Jimmy Buffett	10-Nov-79	MCA 41109
2121	Do I Love You	Paul Anka	13-Nov-71	Buddah 252
2122	Glasshouse	The Temptations	16-Aug-75	Gordy 7144
2123	The End Of Our Road	Marvin Gaye	18-Jul-70	Tamla 54195
2124	So Much Love	Faith, Hope & Charity	4-Jul-70	Maxwell 805
2125	Life And Breath	Climax	10-Jun-72	Rocky Road 30061
2126	I Am Somebody Part II	Johnnie Taylor	28-Nov-70	Stax 0078
2127	Dream On	The Righteous Brothers	21-Dec-74	Haven 7006
2128	People Of The South Wind	Kansas	4-Aug-79	Kirshner 4284
2129	The Proud One	The Osmonds	13-Sep-75	MGM 14791
2130	Trampled Under Foot	Led Zeppelin	31-May-75	Swan Song 70102
2131	I'm Never Gonna Be Alone Anymore	Cornelius Brothers & Sister Rose	10-Feb-73	United Artists 50996

'70s Rank	TITLE	ACT	Peak Date	Label & No.
2132	Every Which Way But Loose	Eddie Rabbitt	31-Mar-79	Elektra 45554
2133	I'm A Greedy Man - Part 1	James Brown	18-Dec-71	Polydor 14100
2134	First Cut Is The Deepest	Keith Hampshire	30-Jun-73	A&M 1432
2135	Oh La De Da	The Staple Singers	28-Apr-73	Stax 0156
2136	Sweet Sticky Thing	Ohio Players	1-Nov-75	Mercury 73713
2137	I Didn't Know I Loved You (Till I Saw You Rock And Roll)	Gary Glitter	9-Dec-72	Bell 45,276
2138	Everybody Needs Love	Stephen Bishop	18-Nov-78	ABC 12406
2139	Do Me Right	Detroit Emeralds	24-Apr-71	Westbound 172
2140	Get The Funk Out Ma Face	The Brothers Johnson	9-Oct-76	A&M 1851
2141	If I Were A Carpenter	Johnny Cash & June Carter	21-Feb-70	Columbia 45064
2142	Freedom For The Stallion	The Hues Corporation	6-Oct-73	RCA Victor 74-0900
2143	Mac Arthur Park (Part II)	Four Tops	23-Oct-71	Motown 1189
2144	You're So Unique	Billy Preston	16-Feb-74	A&M 1492
2145	Grandma's Hands	Bill Withers	4-Dec-71	Sussex 227
2146	To Know You Is To Love You	B.B. King	13-Oct-73	ABC 11373
2147	Who's Your Baby?	The Archies	4-Apr-70	Kirshner 5003
2148	You Said A Bad Word	Joe Tex	1-Jul-72	Dial 1012
2149	Papa Don't Take No Mess - Part I	James Brown	5-Oct-74	Polydor 14255
2150	Cook With Honey	Judy Collins	14-Apr-73	Elektra 45831
2151	The Circle Is Small (I Can See It In Your Eyes)	Gordon Lightfoot	15-Apr-78	Warner Bros. 8518
2152	Ease On Down The Road	Diana Ross & Michael Jackson	11-Nov-78	MCA 40947
2153	Lay-Away	The Isley Brothers	13-May-72	T-Neck 934
2154	Crazy Love	Helen Reddy	25-Sep-71	Capitol 3138
2155	Son Of My Father	Giorgio	8-Apr-72	Dunhill 4304
2156	Ghetto Child	The Spinners	29-Sep-73	Atlantic 2973
2157	Give It To The People	The Righteous Brothers	26-Oct-74	Haven 7004
2158	Honesty	Billy Joel	2-Jun-79	Columbia 10959
2159	Don't Take Away The Music	Tavares	25-Dec-76	Capitol 4348
2160	I Can't Leave Your Love Alone	Clarence Carter	16-May-70	Atlantic 2726
2161	Oh! Darling	Robin Gibb	30-Sep-78	RSO 907
2162	Peace Of Mind	Boston	2-Jul-77	Epic 50381
2163	Can I Get A Witness	Lee Michaels	25-Dec-71	A&M 1303
2164	All Strung Out On You	John Travolta	26-Mar-77	Midland Int'l 10907
2165	Roxanne	The Police	28-Apr-79	A&M 2096
2166	I Was Checkin' Out She Was Checkin' In	Don Covay	1-Sep-73	Mercury 73385
2167	He Called Me Baby	Candi Staton	23-Jan-71	Fame 1476
2168	Letter To Lucille	Tom Jones	30-Jun-73	Parrot 40074
2169	Cheeseburger In Paradise	Jimmy Buffett	3-Jun-78	ABC 12358
2170	New World Coming	Mama Cass Elliot	28-Feb-70	Dunhill 4225
2171	The Last Game Of The Season (A Blind Man In The Bleachers)	David Geddes	13-Dec-75	Big Tree 16052

'70s Rank	TITLE	ACT	Peak Date	Label & No.
2172	The Entertainer	Billy Joel	18-Jan-75	Columbia 10064
2173	Ego	Elton John	20-May-78	MCA 40892
2174	Clouds	David Gates	25-Aug-73	Elektra 45857
2175	Fish Ain't Bitin'	Lamont Dozier	10-Aug-74	ABC 11438
2176	House At Pooh Corner	Nitty Gritty Dirt Band	26-Jun-71	United Artists 50769
2177	I Saw A Man And He Danced With His Wife	Cher	21-Sep-74	MCA 40273
2178	Train, Train	Blackfoot	29-Dec-79	Atco 7207
2179	Let Me Go To Him	Dionne Warwick	16-May-70	Scepter 12276
2180	Judy Mae	Boomer Castleman	14-Jun-75	Mums 6038
2181	Last Kiss	Wednesday	9-Mar-74	Sussex 507
2182	Moon Walk Part I	Joe Simon	14-Feb-70	Sound Stage 7 2651
2183	More Than A Woman	Tavares	29-Apr-78	Capitol 4500
2184	Venus	Frankie Avalon	27-Mar-76	De-Lite 1578
2185	Don't Tell Me Goodnight	Lobo	17-May-75	Big Tree 16033
2186	You Gonna Make Me Love Somebody Else	The Jones Girls	18-Aug-79	Phila. Int'l 3680
2187	Let's Live Together	The Road Apples	17-Jan-76	Polydor 14285
2188	Melting Pot	Booker T. & The M.G.'s	22-May-71	Stax 0082
2189	Walk Away	The James Gang	17-Jul-71	ABC 11301
2190	Livin' Ain't Livin'	Firefall	17-Jul-76	Atlantic 3333
2191	Please Don't Leave	Lauren Wood	17-Nov-79	Warner Bros. 49043
2192	Resurrection Shuffle	Ashton, Gardner & Dyke	24-Jul-71	Capitol 3060
2193	Distant Lover	Marvin Gaye	2-Nov-74	Tamla 54253
2194	C'mon Marianne	Donny Osmond	31-Jul-76	Polydor/Kolob 14320
2195	Tangerine	The Salsoul Orchestra	3-Apr-76	Salsoul 2004
2196	Sugar Pie Guy Pt. 1	The Joneses	28-Dec-74	Mercury 73614
2197	Standing At The End Of The Line	Lobo	25-May-74	Big Tree 15001
2198	Am I Losing You	The Partridge Family	6-May-72	Bell 45,200
2199	Some Guys Have All The Luck	The Persuaders	29-Dec-73	Atco 6943
2200	I Miss You (Part I)	Harold Melvin And The Blue Notes	19-Aug-72	Phila. Int'l 3516
2201	A Song I'd Like To Sing	Kris Kristofferson & Rita Coolidge	5-Jan-74	A&M 1475
2202	I Think Of You	Perry Como	1-May-71	RCA Victor 74-0444
2203	Sweet Emotion	Aerosmith	2-Aug-75	Columbia 10155
2204	Bustin' Loose (Part 1)	Chuck Brown & The Soul Searchers	31-Mar-79	Source 40967
2205	Remember (Christmas)	Nilsson	27-Jan-73	RCA Victor 74-0855
2206	Oh Happy Day	Glen Campbell	16-May-70	Capitol 2787
2207	I Don't Wanna Cry	Ronnie Dyson	21-Nov-70	Columbia 45240
2208	Rolene	Moon Martin	13-Oct-79	Capitol 4765
2209	Kings Of The Party	Brownsville Station	5-Oct-74	Big Tree 16001
2210	Stormy	Santana	24-Feb-79	Columbia 10873
2211	Do The Funky Chicken	Rufus Thomas	14-Mar-70	Stax 0059

'70s Rank	TITLE	ACT	Peak Date	Label & No.
2212	Sweet Feeling	Candi Staton	27-Jun-70	Fame 1466
2213	You'll Lose A Good Thing	Freddy Fender	3-Apr-76	ABC/Dot 17607
2214	Master Of Eyes (The Deepness Of Your Eyes)	Aretha Franklin	31-Mar-73	Atlantic 2941
2215	Control Of Me	Les Emmerson	24-Feb-73	Lion 141
2216	Dependin' On You	The Doobie Brothers	6-Oct-79	Warner Bros. 49029
2217	Tell Her She's Lovely	El Chicano	12-Jan-74	MCA 40104
2218	The Plastic Man	The Temptations	21-Jul-73	Gordy 7129
2219	I'm Gonna Take Care Of Everything	Rubicon	22-Apr-78	20th Century 2362
2220	Put Out The Light	Joe Cocker	10-Aug-74	A&M 1539
2221	I Stand Accused	Isaac Hayes	3-Oct-70	Enterprise 9017
2222	Dream Police	Cheap Trick	24-Nov-79	Epic 50774
2223	Point It Out	Smokey Robinson & The Miracles	24-Jan-70	Tamla 54189
2224	What Am I Crying For?	Dennis Yost & The Classics IV	16-Dec-72	MGM South 7002
2225	Teddy Bear	Red Sovine	4-Sep-76	Starday 142
2226	Songbird	Barbra Streisand	5-Aug-78	Columbia 10756
2227	Almost Summer	Celebration Featuring Mike Love	8-Jul-78	MCA 40891
2228	Prisoner Of Your Love	Player	4-Nov-78	RSO 908
2229	Superman	Herbie Mann	21-Apr-79	Atlantic 3547
2230	I'm Leavin'	Elvis Presley	21-Aug-71	RCA Victor 47-9998
2231	Toast To The Fool	The Dramatics	7-Oct-72	Volt 4082
2232	Springtime Mama	Henry Gross	11-Sep-76	Lifesong 45008
2233	Sugar Baby Love	The Rubettes	14-Sep-74	Polydor 15089
2234	Shower The People	James Taylor	11-Sep-76	Warner Bros. 8222
2235	Good Lovin' Gone Bad	Bad Company	7-Jun-75	Swan Song 70103
2236	The Seeker	The Who	16-May-70	Decca 32670
2237	Found A Cure	Ashford & Simpson	20-Oct-79	Warner Bros. 8870
2238	(How Bout A Little Hand For) The Boys In The Band	The Boys In The Band	25-Jul-70	Spring 103
2239	Higher Plane	Kool & The Gang	19-Oct-74	De-Lite 1562
2240	Midnight Rider	Joe Cocker	21-Oct-72	A&M 1370
2241	I Want To Be Free	Ohio Players	24-May-75	Mercury 73675
2242	Shaving Cream	Benny Bell	3-May-75	Vanguard 35183
2243	Take Me Girl, I'm Ready	Jr. Walker & The All Stars	11-Sep-71	Soul 35084
2244	Jessica	The Allman Brothers Band	23-Feb-74	Capricorn 0036
2245	Took The Last Train	David Gates	21-Oct-78	Elektra 45500
2246	The Relay	The Who	13-Jan-73	Track 33041
2247	Paper Mache	Dionne Warwick	8-Aug-70	Scepter 12285
2248	Keep Your Head To The Sky	Earth, Wind & Fire	19-Jan-74	Columbia 45953
2249	Sing A Song For Freedom	Frijid Pink	5-Sep-70	Parrot 349
2250	Don't Take Your Love	The Manhattans	15-Feb-75	Columbia 10045

'70s Rank	TITLE	ACT	Peak Date	Label & No.
2251	Sunflower	Glen Campbell	27-Aug-77	Capitol 4445
2252	Firecracker	Mass Production	29-Sep-79	Cotillion 44254
2253	A Man I'll Never Be	Boston	20-Jan-79	Epic 50638
2254	Sour Suite	The Guess Who	1-Jan-72	RCA Victor 74-0578
2255	Poor Poor Pitiful Me	Linda Ronstadt	18-Mar-78	Asylum 45462
2256	Tarkio Road	Brewer And Shipley	26-Jun-71	Kama Sutra 524
2257	Dog & Butterfly	Heart	31-Mar-79	Portrait 70025
2258	This World	The Staple Singers	2-Sep-72	Stax 0137
2259	Keep On Dancin'	Gary's Gang	21-Apr-79	Columbia 10884
2260	Little Darling (I Need You)	The Doobie Brothers	24-Sep-77	Warner Bros. 8408
2261	I've Had Enough	Wings	5-Aug-78	Capitol 4594
2262	Little Bit Of Soap	Nigel Olsson	2-Jun-79	Bang 4800
2263	Ballero	War	20-Jul-74	United Artists 432
2264	A Piece Of Paper	Gladstone	7-Oct-72	ABC 11327
2265	It's A Cryin' Shame	Gayle McCormick	20-Nov-71	Dunhill 4288
2266	Dancing In The City	Marshall Hain	17-Feb-79	Harvest 4648
2267	Into The Mystic	Johnny Rivers	13-Jun-70	Imperial 66448
2268	Curious Mind (Um, Um, Um, Um, Um, Um)	Johnny Rivers	4-Feb-78	Big Tree 16106
2269	Song On The Radio	Al Stewart	17-Mar-79	Arista 0389
2270	Themes From The Wizard Of Oz	Meco	28-Oct-78	Millennium 620
2271	Stoned To The Bone - Part 1	James Brown	19-Jan-74	Polydor 14210
2272	Hummingbird	B.B. King	29-Aug-70	ABC 11268
2273	I Got To Know	Starbuck	23-Oct-76	Private Stk 45,104
2274	My Boy	Richard Harris	22-Jan-72	Dunhill 4293
2275	On A Night Like This	Bob Dylan	30-Mar-74	Asylum 11033
2276	Girls' School//Mull Of Kintyre	Wings	31-Dec-77	Capitol 4504
2277	Can We Still Be Friends	Todd Rundgren	5-Aug-78	Bearsville 0324
2278	Do It	Neil Diamond	19-Dec-70	Bang 580
2279	Put It Where You Want It	The Crusaders	26-Aug-72	Blue Thumb 208
2280	Savannah Nights	Tom Johnston	29-Dec-79	Warner Bros. 49096
2281	Automatically Sunshine	The Supremes	17-Jun-72	Motown 1200
2282	He Did With Me	Vicki Lawrence	7-Jul-73	Bell 45,362
2283	Ride With Me	Steppenwolf	21-Aug-71	Dunhill 4283
2284	Up On The Roof	James Taylor	28-Jul-79	Columbia 11005
2285	Hope That We Can Be Together Soon	Sharon Paige	16-Aug-75	Phila. Int'l 3569
2286	Let It Be	Joan Baez	18-Dec-71	Vanguard 35145
2287	Must Be Love	The James Gang	23-Mar-74	Atco 6953
2288	Immigration Man	Graham Nash & David Crosby	17-Jun-72	Atlantic 2873
2289	Time For Livin'	Sly & The Family Stone	24-Aug-74	Epic 11140
2290	Change Partners	Stephen Stills	24-Jul-71	Atlantic 2806
2291	Everyone's Agreed That Everything Will Turn Out Fine	Stealers Wheel	25-Aug-73	A&M 1450

'70s Rank	TITLE	ACT	Peak Date	Label & No.
2292	Love Fire	Jigsaw	3-Apr-76	Chelsea 3037
2293	Ooh Poo Pah Doo	Ike & Tina Turner	19-Jun-71	United Artists 50782
2294	Sweet, Sweet Smile	Carpenters	8-Apr-78	A&M 2008
2295	From His Woman To You	Barbara Mason	18-Jan-75	Buddah 441
2296	An American Trilogy	Mickey Newbury	25-Dec-71	Elektra 45750
2297	If I Ever Lose This Heaven	AWB	11-Oct-75	Atlantic 3285
2298	Twisting The Night Away	Rod Stewart	22-Sep-73	Mercury 73412
2299	Almost Like Being In Love	Michael Johnson	21-Oct-78	EMI America 8004
2300	I've Got So Much To Give	Barry White	22-Sep-73	20th Century 2042
2301	Canned Ham	Norman Greenbaum	18-Jul-70	Reprise 0919
2302	Tongue In Cheek	Sugarloaf	24-Apr-71	Liberty 56218
2303	Help Me Rhonda	Johnny Rivers	23-Aug-75	Epic 50121
2304	Eyes Of Silver	The Doobie Brothers	7-Sep-74	Warner Bros. 7832
2305	In The Mood	Henhouse Five Plus Too	12-Feb-77	Warner Bros. 8301
2306	Get Up, Get Into It, Get Involved (Pt. 1)	James Brown	30-Jan-71	King 6347
2307	Anything You Want	John Valenti	30-Oct-76	Ariola America 7625
2308	Footstompin' Music	Grand Funk Railroad	4-Mar-72	Capitol 3255
2309	I'm The Leader Of The Gang	Brownsville Station	6-Jul-74	Big Tree 15005
2310	Joy, Part 1	Isaac Hayes	9-Feb-74	Enterprise 9085
2311	Tiny Dancer	Elton John	8-Apr-72	Uni 55318
2312	Feeling Alright	Joe Cocker	19-Feb-72	A&M 1063
2313	Miss America	Mark Lindsay	2-May-70	Columbia 45125
2314	Theme From Love Story	Francis Lai And His Orchestra	20-Mar-71	Paramount 0064
2315	Where Did They Go, Lord	Elvis Presley	10-Apr-71	RCA Victor 47-9980
2316	When You Get Right Down To It	The Delfonics	24-Oct-70	Philly Groove 163
2317	This Time I'm Gone For Good	Bobby Blue Bland	12-Jan-74	Dunhill 4369
2318	Early Morning Love	Sammy Johns	30-Nov-74	GRC 2021
2319	And You And I (Part I)	Yes	16-Dec-72	Atlantic 2920
2320	You're A Part Of Me	Gene Cotton	19-Aug-78	Ariola America 7704
2321	Ain't That Loving You (For More Reasons Than One)	Luther Ingram	27-Jun-70	KoKo 2105
2322	Show Biz Kids	Steely Dan	15-Sep-73	ABC 11382
2323	Another Time, Another Place	Engelbert Humperdinck	2-Oct-71	Parrot 40065
2324	Check It Out	Tavares	10-Nov-73	Capitol 3674
2325	Temma Harbour	Mary Hopkin	11-Apr-70	Apple 1816
2326	Love	The Lettermen	4-Dec-71	Capitol 3192
2327	Fire, Baby I'm On Fire	Andy Kim	7-Dec-74	Capitol 3962
2328	You Are The One	Sugar Bears	13-May-72	Big Tree 122
2329	Caribbean Festival	Kool & The Gang	20-Dec-75	De-Lite 1573
2330	My Best Friend's Girl	The Cars	30-Dec-78	Elektra 45537
2331	I Just Want To Make Love To You	Foghat	29-Oct-77	Bearsville 0319
2332	Heaven's Just A Sin Away	The Kendalls	14-Jan-78	Ovation 1103

'70s Rank	TITLE	ACT	Peak Date	Label & No.
2333	Chains And Things	B.B. King	28-Nov-70	ABC 11280
2334	The Message	Cymande	3-Mar-73	Janus 203
2335	Lizzie And The Rainman	Tanya Tucker	14-Jun-75	MCA 40402
2336	Ask Me No Questions	B.B. King	10-Apr-71	ABC 11290
2337	Daytime Friends	Kenny Rogers	1-Oct-77	United Artists 1027
2338	Midnight Wind	John Stewart	20-Oct-79	RSO 1000
2339	Everything's Tuesday	Chairman Of The Board	19-Sep-70	Invictus 9079
2340	Think (About It)	Lyn Collins	7-Oct-72	People 608
2341	Soul Makossa	Afrique	11-Aug-73	Mainstream 5542
2342	Only You Know And I Know	Dave Mason	12-Sep-70	Blue Thumb 114
2343	Zing Went The Strings Of My Heart	The Trammps	9-Sep-72	Buddah 306
2344	Trying To Make A Fool Of Me	The Delfonics	11-Jul-70	Philly Groove 162
2345	Brother Rapp (Part 1) & (Part 2)	James Brown	30-May-70	King 6310
2346	Traces/Memories	The Lettermen	31-Jan-70	Capitol 2697
2347	Fencewalk	Mandrill	9-Jun-73	Polydor 14163
2348	Sunny Days	Lighthouse	9-Dec-72	Evolution 1069
2349	Time Waits For No One	The Friends Of Distinction	14-Nov-70	RCA Victor 74-0385
2350	My Little Lady	Bloodstone	3-May-75	London 1061
2351	Sweet Caroline (Good Times Never Seemed So Good)	Bobby Womack	14-Oct-72	United Artists 50946
2352	Sunrise	Eric Carmen	25-Sep-76	Arista 0200
2353	Showdown	Electric Light Orchestra	9-Feb-74 11-Sep-76	United Artists 337
2354	Mother Freedom	Bread	28-Aug-71	Elektra 45740
2355	We've Come Too Far To End It Now	Smokey Robinson & The Miracles	29-Jul-72	Tamla 54220
2356	Come To Me	Tommy James And The Shondells	27-Jun-70	Roulette 7076
2357	(For God's Sake) Give More Power To The People	The Chi-Lites	15-May-71	Brunswick 55450
2358	Your Love	Graham Central Station	27-Sep-75	Warner Bros. 8105
2359	Shattered	The Rolling Stones	27-Jan-79	Rolling Stones 19310
2360	Rendezvous	Hudson Brothers	30-Aug-75	Rocket/MCA 40417
2361	Powder Blue Mercedes Queen	Raiders	1-Jul-72	Columbia 45601
2362	Hold On	Triumph	1-Sep-79	RCA 11569
2363	Riki Tiki Tavi	Donovan	19-Sep-70	Epic 10649
2364	Baby I'm Burnin'	Dolly Parton	3-Feb-79	RCA 11420
2365	Call My Name, I'll Be There	Wilson Pickett	2-Oct-71	Atlantic 2824
2366	Baby I've Been Missing You	The Independents	1-Sep-73	Wand 11258
2367	Look At Me (I'm In Love)	The Moments	26-Jul-75	Stang 5060
2368	Love Bones	Johnny Taylor	7-Feb-70	Stax 0055
2369	Love Gonna Pack Up (And Walk Out)	The Persuaders	12-Feb-72	Win Or Lose 220
2370	Don't You Write Her Off	McGuinn, Clark & Hillman	12-May-79	Capitol 4693
2371	Hey You! Get Off My Mountain	The Dramatics	16-Jun-73	Volt 4090

'70s Rank	TITLE	ACT	Peak Date	Label & No.
2372	The River Of Love	B.W. Stevenson	5-Jan-74	RCA Victor 0171
2373	Tonight	Raspberries	29-Sep-73	Capitol 3610
2374	The Dream Never Dies	Cooper Brothers	13-Jan-79	Capricorn 0308
2375	I Got A Bag Of My Own	James Brown	23-Dec-72	Polydor 14153
2376	Happiness	Pointer Sisters	5-May-79	Planet 45902
2377	One Chain Don't Make No Prison	Four Tops	15-Jun-74	Dunhill 4386
2378	Money	Gladys Knight & The Pips	27-Sep-75	Buddah 487
2379	You Brought The Joy	Freda Payne	6-Nov-71	Invictus 9100
2380	Your Bulldog Drinks Champagne	Jim Stafford	8-Feb-75	MGM 14775
2381	A Letter To Myself	The Chi-Lites	24-Mar-73	Brunswick 55491
2382	You Can't Be A Beacon (If Your Light Don't Shine)	Donna Fargo	7-Sep-74	Dot 17506
2383	Sunday Morning Coming Down	Johnny Cash	10-Oct-70	Columbia 45211
2384	Black Friday	Steely Dan	28-Jun-75	ABC 12101
2385	Cat's Eye In The Window	Tommy James	1-Jul-72	Roulette 7126
2386	I Still Have Dreams	Richie Furay	29-Dec-79	Asylum 46534
2387	Apeman	The Kinks	13-Feb-71	Reprise 0979
2388	Handbags And Gladrags	Rod Stewart	11-Mar-72	Mercury 73031
2389	I Just Can't Get You Out Of My Mind	Four Tops	9-Mar-74	Dunhill 4377
2390	Hot 'N' Nasty	Humble Pie	24-Jun-72	A&M 1349
2391	Sweet Inspiration/Where You Lead	Barbra Streisand	5-Aug-72	Columbia 45626
2392	Oh What A Night For Dancing	Barry White	10-Jun-78	20th Century 2365
2393	Cherish What Is Dear To You (While It's Near To You)	Freda Payne	27-Mar-71	Invictus 9085
2394	One Last Kiss	The J. Geils Band	27-Jan-79	EMI America 8007
2395	It's All In Your Mind	Clarence Carter	12-Dec-70	Atlantic 2774
2396	Ungena Za Ulimwengu (Unite The World)	The Temptations	24-Oct-70	Gordy 7102
2397	Country Sunshine	Dottie West	17-Nov-73	RCA Victor 0072
2398	(Remember The Days Of The) Old Schoolyard	Cat Stevens	13-Aug-77	A&M 1948
2399	Pushbike Song	The Mixtures	1-May-71	Sire 350
2400	Down To The Line	Bachman-Turner Overdrive	3-Jan-76	Mercury 73724
2401	Chairman Of The Board	Chairmen Of The Board	27-Mar-71	Invictus 9086
2402	I'll Do For You Anything You Want Me To	Barry White	5-Jul-75	20th Century 2208
2403	Chase	Giorgio Moroder	24-Mar-79	Casablanca 956
2404	Peace Pipe	B.T. Express	15-Nov-75	Roadshow 7003
2405	Honey, Honey	Abba	2-Nov-74	Atlantic 3209
2406	Living A Little, Laughing A Little	The Spinners	19-Apr-75	Atlantic 3252
2407	Love Theme From "Eyes Of Laura Mars" (Prisoner)	Barbra Streisand	23-Sep-78	Columbia 10777
2408	What About Me	Anne Murray	7-Jul-73	Capitol 3600
2409	Don't Stop Believin'	Olivia Newton-John	11-Sep-76	MCA 40600
2410	Happy	Eddie Kendricks	29-Nov-75	Tamla 54263

'70s Rank	TITLE	ACT	Peak Date	Label & No.
2411	Geronimo's Cadillac	Michael Murphey	30-Sep-72	A&M 1368
2412	Black Fox	Freddy Robinson	19-Sep-70	World Pacific Jazz 88155
2413	Love Finds Its Own Way	Gladys Knight & The Pips	29-Mar-75	Buddah 453
2414	Touch Me	Fancy	30-Nov-74	Big Tree 16026
2415	The Harder I Try (The Bluer I Get)	The Free Movement	29-Jan-72	Columbia 45512
2416	I Just Don't Know What To Do With Myself	Gary Puckett	28-Nov-70	Columbia 45249
2417	Let Us Love	Bill Withers	6-Jan-73	Sussex 247
2418	We Can Make Music	Tommy Roe	17-Oct-70	ABC 11273
2419	Maggie	Redbone	4-Sep-71	Epic 10670
2420	Baby Sitter	Betty Wright	18-Nov-72	Alston 4614
2421	In The Mood	Bette Midler	2-Mar-74	Atlantic 3004
2422	Dreaming A Dream	Crown Heights Affair	25-Oct-75	De-Lite 1570
2423	Paradise By The Dashboard Light	Meat Loaf	23-Sep-78	Cleveland Int'l/Epic 50588
2424	Run Sally Run	The Cuff Links	11-Apr-70	Decca 32639
2425	Willie And The Hand Jive	Eric Clapton	7-Dec-74	RSO 503
2426	Hold Me, Touch Me	Paul Stanley	30-Dec-78	Casablanca 940
2427	Old Time Rock & Roll	Bob Seger	26-May-79	Capitol 4702
2428	Growin'	Loggins & Messina	17-May-75	Columbia 10118
2429	Escape-Ism (Part 1)	James Brown	10-Jul-71	People 2500
2430	Glory Glory	The Rascals	15-Aug-70	Atlantic 2743
2431	They Can't Take Away Our Music	Eric Burdon And War	23-Jan-71	MGM 14196
2432	Spill The Wine	The Isley Brothers	30-Oct-71	T-Neck 932
2433	Muskrat Love	America	29-Sep-73	Warner Bros. 7725
2434	Be My Lover	Alice Cooper	29-Apr-72	Warner Bros. 7568
2435	Don't Pull Your Love/Then You Can Tell Me Goodbye	Glen Campbell	8-May-76	Capitol 4245
2436	The Green Grass Starts To Grow	Dionne Warwick	16-Jan-71	Scepter 12300
2437	God Bless Whoever Sent You	The Originals	13-Feb-71	Soul 35079
2438	Till	Tom Jones	20-Nov-71	Parrot 40067
2439	Happy People	The Temptations	8-Feb-75	Gordy 7138
2440	Sister James	Nino Tempo And 5th Ave. Sax	27-Oct-73	A&M 1461
2441	Love Or Something Like It	Kenny Rogers	29-Jul-78	United Artists 1210
2442	You Make Me Real	Doors	9-May-70	Elektra 45685
2443	It's Only Love	ZZ Top	27-Nov-76	London 241
2444	Sweet Understanding Love	Four Tops	17-Nov-73	Dunhill 4366
2445	Come Running	Van Morrison	2-May-70	Warner Bros. 7383
2446	Hollywood	Rufus Featuring Chaka Khan	11-Jun-77	ABC 12269
2447	Give Ireland Back To The Irish	Wings	15-Apr-72	Apple 1847
2448	It's All Down To Goodnight Vienna	Ringo Starr	19-Jul-75	Apple 1882
2449	Ruby Tuesday	Melanie	2-Jan-71	Buddah 202
2450	Good Friend	Mary MacGregor	13-Oct-79	RSO 938

'70s Rank	TITLE	ACT	Peak Date	Label & No.
2451	Like A Sunday In Salem (The Amos & Andy Song)	Gene Cotton	18-Nov-78	Ariola America 7723
2452	Second Avenue	Garfunkel	2-Nov-74	Columbia 10020
2453	Lonely Teardrops	Brian Hyland	20-Mar-71	Uni 55272
2454	Honky Tonk - Part 1	The James Brown Soul Train	22-Jul-72	Polydor 14129
2455	Sit Yourself Down	Stephen Stills	3-Apr-71	Atlantic 2790
2456	There It Is - Part 1	James Brown	10-Jun-72	Polydor 14125
2457	Rainbow	Marmalade	12-Sep-70	London 20059
2458	The Agony And The Ecstasy	Smokey Robinson	8-Nov-75	Tamla 54261
2459	All I See Is Your Face	Dan Hill	7-Oct-78	20th Cent. Fox 2378
2460	That's How Love Goes	Jermaine Jackson	28-Oct-72	Motown 1201
2461	Hang On To Your Life	The Guess Who	6-Mar-71	RCA Victor 74-0414
2462	Your Cash Ain't Nothin' But Trash	Steve Miller Band	13-Apr-74	Capitol 3837
2463	Volare	Al Martino	20-Dec-75	Capitol 4134
2464	On The Beach (In The Summertime)	The 5th Dimension	12-Sep-70	Bell 913
2465	I've Gotta Make You Love Me	Steam	28-Feb-70	Mercury 73020
2466	Spinning Around (I Must Be Falling In Love)	The Main Ingredient	26-Jun-71	RCA Victor 74-0456
2467	If You're Not Back In Love By Monday	Millie Jackson	31-Dec-77	Spring 175
2468	We're On Our Way	Chris Hodge	8-Jul-72	Apple 1850
2469	Do Ya Wanna Get Funky With Me	Peter Brown	5-Nov-77	Drive 6258
2470	Mozart Symphony No. 40 In G Minor K.550, 1st Movement	Waldo De Los Ríos	24-Jul-71	United Artists 50772
2471	I Knew Jesus (Before He Was A Star)	Glen Campbell	19-May-73	Capitol 3548
2472	Life	Elvis Presley	12-Jun-71	RCA Victor 47-9985
2473	My Woman, My Woman, My Wife	Marty Robbins	25-Apr-70	Columbia 45091
2474	Daytime Night-Time	Keith Hampshire	10-Feb-73	A&M 1403
2475	Dance Across The Floor	Jimmy "Bo" Horne	10-Jun-78	Sunshine Sound 1003
2476	Afro-Strut	The Nite-Liters	8-Apr-72	RCA Victor 74-0591
2477	Energy Crisis '74	Dickie Goodman	16-Mar-74	Rainy Wednesday 206
2478	Rubber Bullets	10 C. C.	3-Nov-73	UK 49015
2479	All You Get From Love Is A Love Song	Carpenters	16-Jul-77	A&M 1940
2480	I Don't Know Why	The Rolling Stones	19-Jul-75	Abkco 4701
2481	Never, Never, Never (Grande, Grande, Grande)	Shirley Bassey	21-Jul-73	United Artists 211
2482	Angel	Rod Stewart	23-Dec-72	Mercury 73344
2483	Guilty	Al Green	28-Oct-72	Bell 45,258
2484	Long Haired Lover From Liverpool	Little Jimmy Osmond	10-Jun-72	MGM 14376
2485	Annabella	Hamilton, Joe Frank & Reynolds	2-Oct-71	Dunhill 4287
2486	Funky Stuff	Kool & The Gang	3-Nov-73	De-Lite 557
2487	It's O.K.	The Beach Boys	9-Oct-76	Brother/Reprise 1368
2488	Love Song	Tommy James	9-Sep-72	Roulette 7130

'70s Rank	TITLE	ACT	Peak Date	Label & No.
2489	That's The Way A Woman Is	The Messengers	23-Oct-71	Rare Earth 5032
2490	Too Hot Ta Trot	Commodores	11-Feb-78	Motown 1432
2491	It's You That I Need	Enchantment	25-Mar-78	Roadshow 1124
2492	The Same Love That Made Me Laugh	Bill Withers	1-Jun-74	Sussex 513
2493	I Love Makin' Love To You	Evie Sands	27-Sep-75	Haven 7013
2494	Ain't That Peculiar	Diamond Reo	15-Feb-75	Big Tree 16030
2495	Video Killed The Radio Star	The Buggles	22-Dec-79	Island 49114
2496	The Last Thing On My Mind	Neil Diamond	22-Sep-73	MCA 40092
2497	You Took The Words Right Out Of My Mouth	Meat Loaf	27-Jan-79	Cleveland Int'l/Epic 50634
2498	(We're Gonna) Rock Around The Clock	Bill Haley And His Comets	1-Jun-74	MCA 60025
2499	Mean Mistreater	Grand Funk Railroad	23-Jan-71	Capitol 2996
2500	Will You Still Love Me Tomorrow	Dave Mason	29-Jul-78	Columbia 10749
2501	Three Ring Circus	Blue Magic	23-Nov-74	Atco 7004
2502	Ain't That A Shame	Cheap Trick	22-Sep-79	Epic 50743
2503	You Need A Woman Tonight	Captain & Tennille	3-Feb-79	A&M 2106
2504	Walk In The Night	Jr. Walker & The All Stars	20-May-72	Soul 35095
2505	Talking Loud And Saying Nothing - Pt. I	James Brown	19-Feb-72	Polydor 14109
2506	Saturdaynight	Herman Brood	15-Sep-79	Ariola America 7754
2507	Don't Wanna Live Inside Myself	Bee Gees	20-Nov-71	Atco 6847
2508	Where You Lead	Barbra Streisand	28-Aug-71	Columbia 45414
2509	Rings	Lobo	24-Aug-74	Big Tree 15008
2510	Super Fly Meets Shaft	John & Ernest	26-May-73	Rainy Wednesday 201
2511	Today I Started Loving You Again	Bettye Swann	10-Mar-73	Atlantic 2921
2512	Love Has No Pride	Linda Ronstadt	19-Jan-74	Asylum 11026
2513	Rainbow Connection	Kermit (Jim Henson)	1-Dec-79	Atlantic 3610
2514	Gloria	Enchantment	9-Apr-77	United Artists 912
2515	Linda On My Mind	Conway Twitty	12-Apr-75	MCA 40339
2516	Good Hearted Woman	Waylon & Willie	20-Mar-76	RCA Victor 10529
2517	Cinnamon Girl	The Gentrys	13-Jun-70	Sun 1114
2518	Pretty Girls	Melissa Manchester	15-Dec-79	Arista 0456
2519	Help Me Make It Through The Night	Gladys Knight & The Pips	29-Apr-72	Soul 35094
2520	Me And Mrs. Jones	Ron Banks And The Dramatics	21-Jun-75	ABC 12090
2521	I Wanna Learn A Love Song	Harry Chapin	29-Mar-75	Elektra 45236
2522	Everybody Loves A Love Song	Mac Davis	23-Dec-72	Columbia 45727
2523	I Just Wanna Keep It Together	Paul Davis	31-Oct-70	Bang 579
2524	I Got Ants In My Pants - Part 1 And I Want To Dance	James Brown	24-Feb-73	Polydor 14162
2525	Screaming Night Hog	Steppenwolf	19-Sep-70	Dunhill 4248
2526	No	Bulldog	2-Dec-72	Decca 32996
2527	Hold Back The Night	The Trammps	6-Mar-76	Buddah 507
2528	America, Communicate With Me	Ray Stevens	29-Aug-70	Barnaby 2016

'70s Rank	TITLE	ACT	Peak Date	Label & No.
2529	Warm Ride	Rare Earth	24-Jun-78	Prodigal 0640
2530	Draw The Line	Aerosmith	26-Nov-77	Columbia 10637
2531	One Piece At A Time	Johnny Cash	22-May-76	Columbia 10321
2532	Someone Who Cares	Kenny Rogers And The First Edition	1-May-71	Reprise 0999
2533	992 Arguments	The O'Jays	16-Dec-72	Phila. Int'l 3522
2534	Happiness Is Me And You	Gilbert O'Sullivan	27-Apr-74	MAM 3636
2535	Mister Can't You See	Buffy Sainte-Marie	6-May-72	Vanguard 35151
2536	A Real Mother For Ya	Johnny "Guitar" Watson	3-Sep-77	DJM 1024
2537	You Thrill Me	Exile	3-Feb-79	Warner/Curb 8711
2538	Don't Try To Lay No Boogie Woogie On The "King Of Rock & Roll"	Crow	5-Dec-70	Amaret 125
2539	13 Questions	Seatrain	12-Jun-71	Capitol 3067
2540	(Baby) Turn On To Me	The Impressions	17-Oct-70	Curtom 1954
2541	Another Star	Stevie Wonder	1-Oct-77	Tamla 54286
2542	How Can I Leave You Again	John Denver	21-Jan-78	RCA 11036
2543	Get Down	Curtis Mayfield	18-Dec-71	Curtom 1966
2544	It's The Same Old Song	KC & The Sunshine Band	24-Jun-78	T.K. 1028
2545	Woman Tonight	America	3-Jan-76	Warner Bros. 8157
2546	Let's Give Adam And Eve Another Chance	Gary Puckett And The Union Gap	4-Apr-70	Columbia 45097
2547	Good Timin'	The Beach Boys	9-Jun-79	Caribou 9029
2548	You've Been My Inspiration	The Main Ingredient	29-Aug-70	RCA Victor 74-0340
2549	Oh Well	Rockets	1-Sep-79	RSO 935
2550	I Don't Love You Anymore	Teddy Pendergrass	30-Jul-77	Phila. Int'l 3622
2551	Keep On Singing	Austin Roberts	10-Mar-73	Chelsea 0110
2552	Victim Of Love	Elton John	10-Nov-79	MCA 41126
2553	When There's No You	Engelbert Humperdinck	3-Apr-71	Parrot 40059
2554	She Didn't Do Magic	Lobo	7-Aug-71	Big Tree 116
2555	Don't Ever Wanna Lose Ya	New England	23-Jun-79	Infinity 50,013
2556	Fopp	Ohio Players	10-Apr-76	Mercury 73775
2557	It Could Have Been Me	Sami Jo	21-Sep-74	MGM South 7034
2558	You've Got To Take It (If You Want It)	The Main Ingredient	27-Jan-73	RCA Victor 74-0856
2559	If You Let Me	Eddie Kendricks	25-Nov-72	Tamla 54222
2560	Runaway	Charlie Kulis	3-May-75	Playboy 6023
2561	Touch And Go	Al Wilson	20-Apr-74	Rocky Road 30076
2562	Tonight I'll Say A Prayer	Eydie Gorme	24-Jan-70	RCA Victor 74-0250
2563	River	Joe Simon	15-Dec-73	Spring 141
2564	Rocket Ride	Kiss	15-Apr-78	Casablanca 915
2565	With A Child's Heart	Michael Jackson	9-Jun-73	Motown 1218
2566	Beer Barrel Polka	Bobby Vinton	26-Apr-75	ABC 12056
2567	Reach	Orleans	12-Mar-77	Asylum 45375
2568	Rock And Roll	Led Zeppelin	22-Apr-72	Atlantic 2865

'70s Rank	TITLE	ACT	Peak Date	Label & No.
2569	Katmandu	Bob Seger	11-Oct-75	Capitol 4116
2570	Gotta Serve Somebody	Bob Dylan	3-Nov-79	Columbia 11072
2571	Superstar	Paul Davis	18-Sep-76	Bang 726
2572	T-R-O-U-B-L-E	Elvis Presley	21-Jun-75	RCA Victor 10278
2573	Volunteers	Jefferson Airplane	3-Jan-70	RCA Victor 74-0245
2574	(I'm A) Yoyo Man	Rick Cunha	25-May-74	GRC 2016
2575	Hum A Song (From Your Heart)	Lulu	23-May-70	Atco 6749
2576	Come On And Say It	The Grass Roots	17-Oct-70	Dunhill 4249
2577	Feelin' Alright	Grand Funk Railroad	5-Jun-71	Capitol 3095
2578	5.7.0.5.	City Boy	14-Oct-78	Mercury 73999
2579	I've Got A Feeling (We'll Be Seeing Each Other Again)	Al Wilson	15-May-76	Playboy 6062
2580	Who Needs Ya	Steppenwolf	5-Dec-70	Dunhill 4261
2581	Thunder In My Heart	Leo Sayer	12-Nov-77	Warner Bros. 8465
2582	Heavenly	The Temptations	27-Apr-74	Gordy 7135
2583	Mexico	James Taylor	15-Nov-75	Warner Bros. 8137
2584	Bluebird	Helen Reddy	2-Aug-75	Capitol 4108
2585	Ain't Nobody Home	B.B. King	25-Dec-71	ABC 11316
2586	Thank God It's Friday	Love And Kisses	15-Jul-78	Casablanca 925
2587	Two Fine People	Cat Stevens	30-Aug-75	A&M 1700
2588	The Killing Of Georgie (Part I And II)	Rod Stewart	23-Jul-77	Warner Bros. 8396
2589	Without Your Love (Mr. Jordan)	Charlie Ross	10-Apr-76	Big Tree 16056
2590	Goodbye, I Love You	Firefall	10-Mar-79	Atlantic 3544
2591	So Sad The Song	Gladys Knight & The Pips	27-Nov-76	Buddah 544
2592	Work To Do	The Isley Brothers	9-Dec-72	T-Neck 936
2593	Sing For The Day	Styx	17-Feb-79	A&M 2110
2594	Bongo Rock	The Incredible Bongo Band	18-Aug-73	MGM 14588
2595	Tangled Up In Blue	Bob Dylan	19-Apr-75	Columbia 10106
2596	Second Avenue	Tim Moore	12-Oct-74 / 14-Jan-78	Asylum 45208
2597	Living In The U.S.A.	Steve Miller Band	29-Jun-74	Capitol 3884
2598	Chicken Strut	The Meters	16-May-70	Josie 1018
2599	Let Me Get To Know You	Paul Anka	16-Feb-74	Fame 345
2600	Saturday Night Special	Lynyrd Skynyrd	2-Aug-75	MCA 40416
2601	If Ever I See You Again	Roberta Flack	15-Jul-78	Atlantic 3483
2602	Can't You Hear The Song?	Wayne Newton	4-Nov-72	Chelsea 0105
2603	Save Your Kisses For Me	The Brotherhood Of Man	3-Jul-76	Pye 71066
2604	Tequila Sunrise	Eagles	28-Jul-73	Asylum 11017
2605	Good Guys Only Win In The Movies	Mel And Tim	14-Mar-70	Bamboo 109
2606	That Same Old Feeling	The Fortunes	27-Jun-70	World Pacific 77937
2607	Happy Music	The Blackbyrds	1-May-76	Fantasy 762
2608	It's Summer	The Temptations	21-Aug-71	Gordy 7109
2609	Old Fashioned Boy (You're The One)	Stallion	30-Apr-77	Casablanca 877

'70s Rank	TITLE	ACT	Peak Date	Label & No.
2610	You Sure Love To Ball	Marvin Gaye	2-Mar-74	Tamla 54244
2611	Don't Knock My Love	Diana Ross & Marvin Gaye	24-Aug-74	Motown 1296
2612	If I Didn't Care	The Moments	26-Sep-70	Stang 5016
2613	Can't Find The Time	Rose Colored Glass	3-Jul-71	Bang 584
2614	It Keeps You Runnin'	The Doobie Brothers	5-Feb-77	Warner Bros. 8282
2615	Children	Joe South	18-Apr-70	Capitol 2755
2616	Since I Met You Baby	Freddy Fender	29-Nov-75	GRT 031
2617	Hit The Road Jack	Stampeders	3-Apr-76	Quality 501
2618	It's Over	Boz Scaggs	22-May-76	Columbia 10319
2619	Slaughter	Billy Preston	14-Oct-72	A&M 1380
2620	Shake Your Rump To The Funk	Bar-Kays	22-Jan-77	Mercury 73833
2621	Can't Hide Love	Earth, Wind & Fire	1-May-76	Columbia 10309
2622	The Black-Eyed Boys	Paper Lace	16-Nov-74	Mercury 73620
2623	I Want To Take You Higher	Sly & The Family Stone	27-Jun-70	Epic 10450
2624	Resurrection Shuffle	Tom Jones	24-Jul-71	Parrot 40064
2625	A Rock 'N' Roll Fantasy	The Kinks	9-Sep-78	Arista 0342
2626	Georgy Porgy	Toto	16-Jun-79	Columbia 10944
2627	(Not Just) Knee Deep - Part 1	Funkadelic	3-Nov-79	Warner Bros. 49040
2628	Get Down	Gene Chandler	24-Feb-79	Chi-Sound 2386
2629	Stoned Out Of My Mind	The Chi-Lites	8-Sep-73	Brunswick 55500
2630	Wildflower	The New Birth	22-Jun-74	RCA Victor 0265
2631	Sexy	MFSB	26-Jul-75	Phila. Int'l 3567
2632	(Wish I Could Fly Like) Superman	The Kinks	23-Jun-79	Arista 0409
2633	Don't It Make You Want To Go Home	Brook Benton	27-Jun-70	Cotillion 44078
2634	Here Comes The Night	Nick Gilder	23-Dec-78	Chrysalis 2264
2635	Hangin' Around	The Edgar Winter Group	19-Jan-74	Epic 11069
2636	Everything Good Is Bad	100 Proof Aged In Soul	20-May-72	Hot Wax 7202
2637	Can You Fool	Glen Campbell	9-Dec-78	Capitol 4584
2638	Saturday Night, Sunday Morning	Thelma Houston	2-Jun-79	Tamla 54297
2639	Keep On Tryin'	Poco	8-Nov-75	ABC 12126
2640	When A Child Is Born	Michael Holm	25-Jan-75	Mercury 73642
2641	So You Win Again	Hot Chocolate	3-Sep-77	Big Tree 16096
2642	Why Can't We Be Lovers	Holland-Dozier	25-Nov-72	Invictus 9125
2643	It's Impossible	The New Birth	27-Nov-71	RCA Victor 74-0520
2644	I Think We're Alone Now	The Rubinoos	14-May-77	Beserkley 5741
2645	Cottage Cheese	Crow	15-Aug-70	Amaret 119
2646	Lady (Put The Light On Me)	Brownsville Station	30-Jul-77	Private Stk 45,149
2647	You've Got Me Runnin'	Gene Cotton	5-Feb-77	ABC 12227
2648	There It Is	Tyrone Davis	15-Sep-73	Dakar 4523
2649	Battle Hymn Of Lt. Calley	C Company Featuring Terry Nelson	15-May-71	Plantation 73
2650	I'll Be The Other Woman	The Soul Children	30-Mar-74	Stax 0182
2651	Runaway/Happy Together	Dawn Featuring Tony Orlando	19-Feb-72	Bell 45,175

'70s Rank	TITLE	ACT	Peak Date	Label & No.
2652	New Orleans Ladies	Le Roux	2-Sep-78	Capitol 4586
2653	Tupelo Honey	Van Morrison	5-Feb-72	Warner Bros. 7543
2654	Que Sera, Sera (Whatever Will Be, Will Be)	Mary Hopkin	25-Jul-70	Apple 1823
2655	Outlaw Man	Eagles	13-Oct-73	Asylum 11025
2656	Arrow Through Me	Wings	6-Oct-79	Columbia 11070
2657	'Til It's Time To Say Goodbye	Jonathan Cain	28-Feb-76	October 1001
2658	Triangle Of Love (Hey Diddle Diddle)	The Presidents	13-Mar-71	Sussex 212
2659	You're The Man (Part 1)	Marvin Gaye	17-Jun-72	Tamla 54221
2660	The Free Electric Band	Albert Hammond	30-Jun-73	Mums 6018
2661	Live It Up Part 1	The Isley Brothers	19-Oct-74	T-Neck 2254
2662	Please Come Home For Christmas	Eagles	30-Dec-78	Asylum 45555
2663	It Must Be Love	Alton McClain & Destiny	2-Jun-79	Polydor 14532
2664	On The Border	Al Stewart	28-May-77	Janus 267
2665	Diamonds And Rust	Joan Baez	15-Nov-75	A&M 1737
2666	Framed	Cheech & Chong	17-Jul-76	Ode 66124
2667	I Cried	James Brown	29-May-71	King 6363
2668	Summer Of '42	Biddu Orchestra	1-Nov-75	Epic 50139
2669	Your Love (Means Everything To Me)	Charles Wright And The Watts 103rd Street Band	29-May-71	Warner Bros. 7475
2670	Lucky Man	Starbuck	22-Jan-77	Private Stk 45,125
2671	Future Shock	Curtis Mayfield	8-Sep-73	Curtom 1987
2672	Raised On Robbery	Joni Mitchell	9-Feb-74	Asylum 11029
2673	I've Been This Way Before	Neil Diamond	15-Mar-75	Columbia 10084
2674	(You're My) Soul And Inspiration	Donny & Marie	21-Jan-78	Polydor/Kolob 14439
2675	I'm Tired	Savoy Brown	3-Jan-70	Parrot 40042
2676	Open Up My Heart	The Dells	30-May-70	Cadet 5667
2677	Blockbuster	Sweet	4-Aug-73	Bell 45,361
2678	Walk Right Up To The Sun	The Delfonics	11-Dec-71	Philly Groove 169
2679	Keep It In The Family	Leon Haywood	11-May-74	20th Century 2065
2680	Capture The Moment	Jay And The Americans	18-Apr-70	United Artists 50654
2681	Son Of Shaft	Bar-Kays	12-Feb-72	Volt 4073
2682	It Keeps You Runnin'	Carly Simon	31-Jul-76	Elektra 45323
2683	Cryin' In The Streets (Part I)	George Perkins & The Silver Stars	2-May-70	Silver Fox 18
2684	Who's Sorry Now	Marie Osmond	12-Apr-75	MGM 14786
2685	Yesterday's Hero	John Paul Young	7-Feb-76	Ariola America 7607
2686	Werewolf	Five Man Electrical Band	11-May-74	Polydor 14221
2687	Without You In My Life	Tyrone Davis	2-Jun-73	Dakar 4519
2688	Girl Of My Dreams	Bram Tchaikovsky	18-Aug-79	Polydor 14575
2689	If Walls Could Talk	Little Milton	14-Feb-70	Checker 1226
2690	Who Is He And What Is He To You	Creative Source	11-May-74	Sussex 509
2691	Good Vibrations	Todd Rundgren	17-Jul-76	Bearsville 0309
2692	You Really Got Me	Van Halen	18-Mar-78	Warner Bros. 8515

'70s Rank	TITLE	ACT	Peak Date	Label & No.
2693	Ease On Down The Road	Consumer Rapport	24-May-75	Wing & A Prayer 101
2694	You're The Reason Why	The Ebonys	17-Jul-71	Phila. Int'l 3503
2695	Ko-Ko Joe	Jerry Reed	18-Sep-71	RCA Victor 48-1011
2696	Bloat On Featuring The Bloaters	Cheech & Chong	17-Dec-77	Ode 50471
2697	Rock Me On The Water	Jackson Browne	9-Sep-72	Asylum 11006
2698	I Don't Wanna Lose Your Love	The Emotions	29-Jan-77	Columbia 10347
2699	Don't Stop Now	Eddie Holman	9-May-70	ABC 11261
2700	Carolina In My Mind	Crystal Mansion	12-Dec-70	Colossus 128
2701	Who Was It?	Hurricane Smith	28-Apr-73	Capitol 3455
2702	Take A Hand	Rick Springfield	25-Sep-76	Chelsea 3051
2703	Highfly	John Miles	13-Mar-76	London 20084
2704	Snow Blind Friend	Steppenwolf	3-Apr-71	Dunhill 4269
2705	Cindy Incidentally	Faces	28-Apr-73	Warner Bros. 7681
2706	Woman To Woman	Joe Cocker	13-Jan-73	A&M 1370
2707	Think It Over	Cheryl Ladd	16-Sep-78	Capitol 4599
2708	Brian's Song	Michel Legrand	25-Mar-72	Bell 45,171
2709	I Dreamed Last Night	Justin Hayward And John Lodge	21-Jun-75	Threshold 67019
2710	Sneakin' Up Behind You	The Brecker Brothers	26-Jul-75	Arista 0122
2711	The Americans (A Canadian's Opinion)	Gordon Sinclair	16-Feb-74	Avco 4628
2712	Love Power	Willie Hutch	29-Nov-75	Motown 1360
2713	Sure Know Something	Kiss	27-Oct-79	Casablanca 2205
2714	It's All I Can Do	The Cars	24-Nov-79	Elektra 46546
2715	Waiting At The Bus Stop	Bobby Sherman	11-Sep-71	Metromedia 222
2716	Let Me Back In	Tyrone Davis	31-Oct-70	Dakar 621
2717	Oh Me, Oh My (Dreams In My Arms)	Al Green	2-Aug-75	Hi 2288
2718	Easy To Love	Leo Sayer	4-Feb-78	Warner Bros. 8502
2719	I'm Gonna Let My Heart Do The Walking	The Supremes	14-Aug-76	Motown 1391
2720	Jennifer	Bobby Sherman	6-Nov-71	Metromedia 227
2721	I Won't Mention It Again	Ray Price	17-Apr-71	Columbia 45329
2722	What Am I Gonna Do	Smith	27-Jun-70	Dunhill 4238
2723	Please Pardon Me (You Remind Me Of A Friend)	Rufus Featuring Chaka Khan	28-Jun-75	ABC 12099
2724	She Cried	The Lettermen	18-Jul-70	Capitol 2820
2725	I Believe In Love	Kenny Loggins	24-Sep-77	Columbia 10569
2726	Until It's Time For You To Go	Neil Diamond	14-Mar-70	Uni 55204
2727	Where Are You Going To My Love	The Brotherhood Of Man	3-Oct-70	Deram 85065
2728	I Love You Lady Dawn	The Bells	24-Jul-71	Polydor 15027
2729	The Touch Of You	Brenda & The Tabulations	28-Feb-70	Top & Bottom 401
2730	America	Yes	9-Sep-72	Atlantic 2899
2731	Shoes	Brook Benton	6-Feb-71	Cotillion 44093
2732	Boo, Boo, Don't 'Cha Be Blue	Tommy James	17-Mar-73	Roulette 7140
2733	Don't Hide Your Love	Cher	7-Oct-72	Kapp 2184

'70s Rank	TITLE	ACT	Peak Date	Label & No.
2734	Such A Night	Dr. John	20-Oct-73	Atco 6937
2735	You Stepped Into My Life	Melba Moore	3-Mar-79	Epic 50600
2736	Most Likely You Go Your Way (And I'll Go Mine)	Bob Dylan / The Band	7-Sep-74	Asylum 11043
2737	Rock And Roll Never Forgets	Bob Seger	20-Aug-77	Capitol 4449
2738	Without Love	Aretha Franklin	21-Dec-74	Atlantic 3224
2739	Billion Dollar Babies	Alice Cooper	8-Sep-73	Warner Bros. 7724
2740	Can You Handle It?	Graham Central Station	8-Jun-74	Warner Bros. 7782
2741	Ding Dong; Ding Dong	George Harrison	8-Feb-75	Apple 1879
2742	I Do Take You	The Three Degrees	17-Oct-70	Roulette 7088
2743	Freedom	The Isley Brothers	20-Feb-71	T-Neck 927
2744	Rip Off	Laura Lee	8-Jul-72	Hot Wax 7204
2745	Magical Mystery Tour	Ambrosia	9-Apr-77	20th Century 2327
2746	A Simple Man	Lobo	19-Aug-72	Big Tree 141
2747	Why Should I Cry	The Gentrys	21-Feb-70	Sun 1108
2748	She Lets Her Hair Down (Early In The Morning)	The Tokens	31-Jan-70	Buddah 151
2749	(I Will Be Your) Shadow In The Street	Allan Clarke	20-May-78	Atlantic 3459
2750	Renegade	Michael Murphey	28-Feb-76	Epic 50184
2751	Where Did Our Love Go	The J. Geils Band	22-May-76	Atlantic 3320
2752	Since I Fell For You	Laura Lee	25-Mar-72	Hot Wax 7201
2753	Let's Stay Together	Isaac Hayes	15-Apr-72	Enterprise 9045
2754	Sadie	The Spinners	7-Jun-75	Atlantic 3268
2755	Carry Me	David Crosby / Graham Nash	13-Dec-75	ABC 12140
2756	Surrender	Diana Ross	25-Sep-71	Motown 1188
2757	Do You Believe In Magic	Shaun Cassidy	6-May-78	Warner/Curb 8533
2758	Black Lassie (Featuring Johnny Stash)	Cheech & Chong	30-Nov-74	Ode 66104
2759	Skybird	Tony Orlando And Dawn	29-Nov-75	Arista 0156
2760	Ain't Nothing Like The Real Thing	Aretha Franklin	5-Oct-74	Atlantic 3200
2761	Love Me, Love Me Love	Frank Mills	11-Mar-72	Sunflower 118
2762	There'll Never Be	Switch	16-Dec-78	Gordy 7159
2763	I Fought The Law	Sam Neely	1-Mar-75	A&M 1651
2764	Heartbreak Hotel	Frijid Pink	16-Jan-71	Parrot 352
2765	Forever Came Today	The Jackson 5	30-Aug-75	Motown 1356
2766	Rag Doll	Sammy Johns	19-Jul-75	GRC 2062
2767	I'm Movin' On	John Kay	3-Jun-72	Dunhill 4309
2768	Make You Feel Love Again	Wet Willie	29-Apr-78	Epic 50528
2769	Rhumba Girl	Nicolette Larson	12-May-79	Warner Bros. 8795
2770	Anthem	Wayne Newton	20-Jan-73	Chelsea 0109
2771	Evil	Earth, Wind & Fire	29-Sep-73	Columbia 45888
2772	The Court Room	Clarence Carter	5-Jun-71	Atlantic 2801
2773	As Long As He Takes Care Of Home	Candi Staton	8-Feb-75	Warner Bros. 8038
2774	Sooner Or Later	The Impressions	26-Jul-75	Curtom 0103

'70s Rank	TITLE	ACT	Peak Date	Label & No.
2775	The Girls' Song	The 5th Dimension	2-May-70	Soul City 781
2776	Look-Ka Py Py	The Meters	31-Jan-70	Josie 1015
2777	Tumbling Dice	Linda Ronstadt	10-Jun-78	Asylum 45479
2778	A Dream Goes On Forever	Todd Rundgren	27-Apr-74	Bearsville 0020
2779	Roller	April Wine	21-Apr-79	Capitol 4660
2780	Change With The Times	Van McCoy	8-Nov-75	Avco 4660
2781	Lucky Man	Emerson, Lake & Palmer	8-May-71 3-Feb-73	Cotillion 44106
2782	Everything A Man Could Ever Need	Glen Campbell	8-Aug-70	Capitol 2843
2783	I Can't Hear You No More	Helen Reddy	4-Sep-76	Capitol 4312
2784	Remember (Walking In The Sand)	Louise Goffin	6-Oct-79	Asylum 46521
2785	Ball And Chain	Tommy James	5-Sep-70	Roulette 7084
2786	Secretary	Betty Wright	17-Aug-74	Alston 4622
2787	Play On Love	Jefferson Starship	17-Jan-76	Grunt 10456
2788	Sixty Minute Man	Clarence Carter	25-Aug-73	Fame 250
2789	Soul Shake	Delaney & Bonnie & Friends	26-Sep-70	Atco 6756
2790	Haven't Stopped Dancing Yet	Gonzalez	10-Mar-79	Capitol 4674
2791	I Want You To Be Mine	Kayak	17-Jun-78	Janus 274
2792	Flesh And Blood	Johnny Cash	16-Jan-71	Columbia 45269
2793	Over And Over	The Delfonics	24-Jul-71	Philly Groove 166
2794	I'm A Believer	Neil Diamond	7-Aug-71	Bang 586
2795	Sail Around The World	David Gates	1-Dec-73	Elektra 45868
2796	(Just Like) Romeo And Juliet	Sha Na Na	7-Jun-75	Kama Sutra 602
2797	I Don't Wanna Lose You	Daryl Hall & John Oates	3-Feb-79	RCA 11424
2798	I Likes To Do It	People's Choice	11-Sep-71	Phil-L.A. Of Soul 349
2799	Until Now	Bobby Arvon	25-Feb-78	First Artists 41000
2800	I Need Your Help Barry Manilow	Ray Stevens	28-Apr-79	Warner Bros. 8785
2801	Just You And I	Melissa Manchester	20-Mar-76	Arista 0168
2802	Yesterday's Hero	Bay City Rollers	1-Jan-77	Arista 0216
2803	No Sad Song	Helen Reddy	22-Jan-72	Capitol 3231
2804	Changes In Latitudes, Changes In Attitudes	Jimmy Buffett	29-Oct-77	ABC 12305
2805	Stealing In The Name Of The Lord	Paul Kelly	22-Aug-70	Happy Tiger 541
2806	Dance Wit Me	Rufus Featuring Chaka Khan	29-May-76	ABC 12179
2807	Silver Dreams	The Babys	18-Mar-78	Chrysalis 2201
2808	Every Day I Have To Cry Some	Arthur Alexander	18-Oct-75	Buddah 492
2809	Substitute	Clout	4-Nov-78	Epic 50591
2810	Last Of The Singing Cowboys	The Marshall Tucker Band	11-Aug-79	Warner Bros. 8841
2811	How Can I Tell You	Travis Wammack	10-Mar-73	Fame 91008
2812	But For Love	Jerry Naylor	25-Apr-70	Columbia 45106
2813	Rhapsody In Blue	Deodato	6-Oct-73	CTI 16
2814	We're Getting Careless With Our Love	Johnnie Taylor	16-Mar-74	Stax 0193
2815	Day Tripper	Anne Murray	1-Feb-75	Capitol 4000

'70s Rank	TITLE	ACT	Peak Date	Label & No.
2816	Mr. Melody	Natalie Cole	20-Nov-76	Capitol 4328
2817	Gotta See Jane	R. Dean Taylor	15-May-71	Rare Earth 5026
2818	I'll Make You Music	Beverly Bremers	28-Oct-72	Scepter 12363
2819	Come Together	Ike & Tina Turner	21-Mar-70	Minit 32087
2820	Friends	Bette Midler	3-Nov-73	Atlantic 2980
2821	Steppin' Out	Neil Sedaka	31-Jul-76	Rocket/MCA 40582
2822	The Funniest Thing	Dennis Yost & The Classics IV	25-Apr-70	Imperial 66439
2823	Get It Up	Ronnie Milsap	1-Dec-79	RCA 11695
2824	Sexy, Sexy, Sexy	James Brown	29-Sep-73	Polydor 14194
2825	Come Live With Me	Ray Charles	8-Dec-73	Crossover 973
2826	Special Someone	The Heywoods	25-Nov-72	Family 0911
2827	Dance With The Devil	Cozy Powell	4-May-74	Chrysalis 2029
2828	Now That We Found Love	Third World	24-Mar-79	Island 8663
2829	Giving It All Away	Roger Daltrey	7-Jul-73	Track 40053
2830	Fire On The Mountain	The Marshall Tucker Band	3-Jan-76	Capricorn 0244
2831	It Doesn't Matter	Stephen Stills	17-Jun-72	Atlantic 2876
2832	Give It What You Got	B.T. Express	13-Sep-75	Roadshow 7003
2833	Lord, Mr. Ford	Jerry Reed	18-Aug-73	RCA Victor 74-0960
2834	Swing Your Daddy	Jim Gilstrap	26-Apr-75	Roxbury 2006
2835	Stealer	Free	2-Jan-71	A&M 1230
2836	The Martian Boogie	Brownsville Station	1-Oct-77	Private Stk 45,167
2837	Raining In My Heart	Leo Sayer	11-Nov-78	Warner Bros. 8682
2838	Children Of The Sun	Billy Thorpe	15-Sep-79	Capricorn 0321/ Polydor 2018
2839	Wheel In The Sky	Journey	20-May-78	Columbia 10700
2840	Young Love	Donny Osmond	18-Aug-73	MGM 14583
2841	Good Times, Rock & Roll	Flash Cadillac & The Continental Kids	8-Mar-75	Private Stk 45,006
2842	(It's The Way) Nature Planned It	Four Tops	21-Oct-72	Motown 1210
2843	Don't Let Him Take Your Love From Me	Four Tops	10-Jan-70	Motown 1159
2844	Fallen Angel	Frankie Valli	8-May-76	Private Stk 45,074
2845	Time And Love	Barbra Streisand	24-Apr-71	Columbia 45341
2846	Show You The Way To Go	The Jacksons	21-May-77	Epic 50350
2847	A Little Bit Of Soap	Paul Davis	18-Jul-70	Bang 576
2848	Sweet Maxine	The Doobie Brothers	6-Sep-75	Warner Bros. 8126
2849	Funky Drummer (Part 1)	James Brown	18-Apr-70	King 6290
2850	Skybird	Neil Diamond	30-Mar-74	Columbia 45998
2851	Rub It In	Layng Martine	6-Nov-71	Barnaby 2041
2852	No Charge	Melba Montgomery	1-Jun-74	Elektra 45883
2853	Men Of Learning	Vigrass & Osborne	15-Jul-72	Uni 55330
2854	Magic Woman Touch	The Hollies	24-Mar-73	Epic 10951
2855	Fair Game	Crosby, Stills & Nash	26-Nov-77	Atlantic 3432
2856	You Brought The Woman Out Of Me	Evie Sands	10-May-75	Haven 7010

'70s Rank	TITLE	ACT	Peak Date	Label & No.
2857	Dreadlock Holiday	10 C. C.	11-Nov-78	Polydor 14511
2858	Winter Melody	Donna Summer	12-Mar-77	Casablanca 874
2859	Daddy What If	Bobby Bare	2-Mar-74	RCA Victor 0197
2860	Could I Forget You	Tyrone Davis	1-May-71	Dakar 623
2861	Waking Up Alone	Paul Williams	15-Apr-72	A&M 1325
2862	Hot Stuff	The Rolling Stones	21-Aug-76	Rolling Stones 19304
2863	Bite Your Lip (Get Up And Dance!)	Elton John	12-Mar-77	MCA/Rocket 40677
2864	Midnight Man	The James Gang	23-Oct-71	ABC 11312
2865	Simply Call It Love	Gene Chandler	12-Dec-70	Mercury 73121
2866	Everybody Loves A Rain Song	B.J. Thomas	11-Mar-78	MCA 40854
2867	There Won't Be No Country Music (There Won't Be No Rock 'N' Roll)	C.W. McCall	24-Apr-76	Polydor 14310
2868	Satisfaction	Smokey Robinson & The Miracles	11-Dec-71	Tamla 54211
2869	Diamonds	Chris Rea	5-May-79	United Artists 1285
2870	Doraville	Atlanta Rhythm Section	16-Nov-74	Polydor 14248
2871	Pool Of Bad Luck	Joe Simon	29-Apr-72	Spring 124
2872	Take Me To The River	Syl Johnson	19-Jul-75	Hi 2285
2873	Ob-La-Di, Ob-La-Da	The Beatles	18-Dec-76	Capitol 4347
2874	Rags To Riches	Elvis Presley	27-Mar-71	RCA Victor 47-9980
2875	Stay	Rufus/Chaka Khan	3-Jun-78	ABC 12349
2876	I Heard It Through The Grapevine	Creedence Clearwater Revival	6-Mar-76	Fantasy 759
2877	Married Men	Bette Midler	14-Jul-79	Atlantic 3582
2878	Funk #49	James Gang	24-Oct-70	ABC 11272
2879	London Town	Wings	21-Oct-78	Capitol 4625
2880	Sometimes	Facts Of Life	16-Apr-77	Kayvette 5128
2881	Happy	Bobby Darin	3-Mar-73	Motown 1217
2882	Do You Wanna Go Party	KC & The Sunshine Band	28-Jul-79	T.K. 1033
2883	Would You Lay With Me (In A Field Of Stone)	Tanya Tucker	20-Apr-74	Columbia 45991
2884	Pardon Me Sir	Joe Cocker	24-Mar-73	A&M 1407
2885	My Honey And Me	Luther Ingram	7-Feb-70	KoKo 2104
2886	Fancy Dancer	Commodores	19-Feb-77	Motown 1408
2887	To The Other Woman (I'm The Other Woman)	Doris Duke	11-Apr-70	Canyon 28
2888	Young Blood	Rickie Lee Jones	1-Sep-79	Warner Bros. 49018
2889	You're Welcome, Stop On By	Bobby Womack	10-Aug-74	United Artists 439
2890	Make The World Go Away	Donny And Marie Osmond	12-Jul-75	MGM 14807
2891	Keep On Doin'	The Isley Brothers	14-Mar-70	T-Neck 914
2892	Here Comes Summer	Wildfire	23-Jul-77	Casablanca 885
2893	Chantilly Lace	Jerry Lee Lewis	22-Apr-72	Mercury 73273
2894	Sleepin'	Diana Ross	8-Jun-74	Motown 1295
2895	Good Enough To Be Your Wife	Jeannie C. Riley	21-Aug-71	Plantation 75

'70s Rank	TITLE	ACT	Peak Date	Label & No.
2896	He's So Fine	Jody Miller	14-Aug-71	Epic 10734
2897	Sailing	Rod Stewart	22-Nov-75	Warner Bros. 8146
2898	Reach For It	George Duke	4-Feb-78	Epic 50463
2899	Still Crazy After All These Years	Paul Simon	29-May-76	Columbia 10332
2900	Patch Of Blue	Frankie Valli & The 4 Seasons	23-May-70	Philips 40662
2901	Love Corporation	The Hues Corporation	22-Mar-75	RCA Victor 10200
2902	The Next Hundred Years	Al Martino	4-Feb-78	Capitol 4508
2903	If You Go Away	Terry Jacks	6-Jul-74	Bell 45,467
2904	Please, Daddy	John Denver	12-Jan-74	RCA Victor 0182
2905	King Of Nothing	Seals & Crofts	22-Jun-74	Warner Bros. 7810
2906	A Place In The Sun	Pablo Cruise	5-Nov-77	A&M 1976
2907	Sail On Sailor	The Beach Boys	3-Mar-73 21-Jun-75	Brother/Reprise 1138
2908	Watching The River Run	Loggins & Messina	30-Mar-74	Columbia 46010
2909	I Could Write A Book	Jerry Butler	18-Apr-70	Mercury 73045
2910	You're All I Need To Get By	Tony Orlando And Dawn	27-Sep-75	Elektra 45275
2911	Kiss In The Dark	Pink Lady	28-Jul-79	Elektra/Curb 46040
2912	Mary Had A Little Lamb	Wings	15-Jul-72	Apple 1851
2913	La La Peace Song	Al Wilson	30-Nov-74	Rocky Road 30200
2914	So In Love	Curtis Mayfield	8-Nov-75	Curtom 0105
2915	You Got Me Hummin	Cold Blood	28-Feb-70	San Francisco 60
2916	Do What You Want, Be What You Are	Daryl Hall & John Oates	1-Jan-77	RCA 10808
2917	What Can I Do For You?	Labelle	14-Jun-75	Epic 50097
2918	What My Baby Needs Now Is A Little More Lovin'	James Brown - Lyn Collins	3-Feb-73	Polydor 14157
2919	Rubber Biscuit	Blues Brothers	7-Apr-79	Atlantic 3564
2920	Funk Factory	Wilson Pickett	24-Jun-72	Atlantic 2878
2921	Bless You	Martha Reeves & The Vandellas	6-Nov-71	Gordy 7110
2922	Rivers Of Babylon	Boney M	5-Aug-78	Sire 1027
2923	Get The Cream Off The Top	Eddie Kendricks	16-Aug-75	Tamla 54260
2924	Fell For You	The Dramatics	1-Dec-73	Volt 4099
2925	My Way	Brook Benton	9-May-70	Cotillion 44072
2926	It Doesn't Have To Be That Way	Jim Croce	2-Feb-74	ABC 11413
2927	I Am What I Am	Lois Fletcher	4-May-74	Playboy 50049
2928	Long Ago Tomorrow	B.J. Thomas	4-Dec-71	Scepter 12335
2929	Hot Love	T. Rex	12-Jun-71	Reprise 1006
2930	Just Let It Come	Alive And Kicking	17-Oct-70	Roulette 7087
2931	Wish That I Could Talk To You	The Sylvers	17-Mar-73	Pride 1019
2932	When We Get Married	The Intruders	25-Jul-70	Gamble 4004
2933	My Old School	Steely Dan	22-Dec-73	ABC 11396
2934	The End Is Not In Sight (The Cowboy Tune)	The Amazing Rhythm Aces	20-Nov-76	ABC 12202
2935	Rhyme Tyme People	Kool & The Gang	22-Feb-75	De-Lite 1563

'70s Rank	TITLE	ACT	Peak Date	Label & No.
2936	Welcome To My Nightmare	Alice Cooper	29-Nov-75	Atlantic 3298
2937	Burnin' Thing	Mac Davis	19-Jul-75	Columbia 10148
2938	Silver Lady	David Soul	19-Nov-77	Private Stk 45,163
2939	Rebel Rebel	David Bowie	20-Jul-74	RCA Victor 0287
2940	Who's Gonna Take The Blame	Smokey Robinson & The Miracles	27-Jun-70	Tamla 54194
2941	Kalimba Story	Earth, Wind & Fire	10-Aug-74	Columbia 46070
2942	Love Pains	Yvonne Elliman	15-Dec-79	RSO 1007
2943	I Can't Live A Dream	The Osmonds	20-Nov-76	Polydor/Kolob 14348
2944	Crazy Love	The Allman Brothers Band	28-Apr-79	Capricorn 0320
2945	Searching For A Thrill	Starbuck	11-Nov-78	United Artists 1245
2946	We Can't Hide It Anymore	Larry Santos	3-Apr-76	Casablanca 844
2947	We Were Always Sweethearts	Boz Scaggs	22-May-71	Columbia 45353
2948	Across 110th Street	Bobby Womack	28-Apr-73	United Artists 196
2949	Darlin'	Paul Davis	24-Jun-78	Bang 736
2950	Hot Love, Cold World	Bob Welch	15-Jul-78	Capitol 4588
2951	Angel Baby	Dusk	20-Mar-71	Bell 961
2952	Keep Your Eye On The Sparrow	Merry Clayton	20-Sep-75	Ode 66110
2953	Together Alone	Melanie	18-Nov-72	Neighborhood 4207
2954	You Were Made For Me	Luther Ingram	29-Apr-72	KoKo 2110
2955	Confusion	Electric Light Orchestra	24-Nov-79	Jet 5064
2956	Cinnamon Girl	Neil Young	1-Aug-70	Reprise 0911
2957	I Get Lifted	George McCrae	8-Mar-75	T.K. 1007
2958	(The System Of) Doctor Tarr And Professor Fether	Alan Parsons Project	18-Sep-76	20th Century 2297
2959	Love Of My Life	Gino Vannelli	30-Oct-76	A&M 1861
2960	Be My Girl	The Dramatics	26-Feb-77	ABC 12235
2961	From Graceland To The Promised Land	Merle Haggard	19-Nov-77	MCA 40804
2962	Going In With My Eyes Open	David Soul	18-Jun-77	Private Stk 45,150
2963	Jubilation	Paul Anka	13-May-72	Buddah 294
2964	Let Your Yeah Be Yeah	Brownsville Station	28-Apr-73	Big Tree 161
2965	Fool For The City	Foghat	26-Jun-76	Bearsville 0307
2966	You Know Like I Know	The Ozark Mountain Daredevils	2-Apr-77	A&M 1888
2967	Fun Time	Joe Cocker	2-Dec-78	Asylum 45540
2968	Dance Away	Roxy Music	9-Jun-79	Atco 7100
2969	She Didn't Know (She Kept On Talking)	Dee Dee Warwick	20-Jun-70	Atco 6754
2970	Will You Love Me Tomorrow?	Melanie	5-Jan-74	Neighborhood 4213
2971	Blood Is Thicker Than Water	William Devaughn	26-Oct-74	Roxbury 2001
2972	Look What They've Done To My Song, Ma	Ray Charles	29-Jul-72	ABC/TRC 11329
2973	Morning	Jim Ed Brown	16-Jan-71	RCA Victor 47-9909
2974	Gimme Some More	The J.B.'s	11-Mar-72	People 602
2975	Add Some Music To Your Day	The Beach Boys	4-Apr-70	Brother/Reprise 0894

'70s Rank	TITLE	ACT	Peak Date	Label & No.
2976	I Believe I'm Gonna Love You	Frank Sinatra	6-Sep-75	Reprise 1335
2977	Keep Playin' That Rock 'N' Roll	Edgar Winter's White Trash	12-Feb-72	Epic 10788
2978	You Gotta Make Your Own Sunshine	Neil Sedaka	20-Nov-76	Rocket/MCA 40614
2979	Brighton Hill	Jackie Deshannon	4-Apr-70	Imperial 66438
2980	You Make Me Feel (Mighty Real)	Sylvester	17-Feb-79	Fantasy 846
2981	Your Sweetness Is My Weakness	Barry White	30-Dec-78	20th Cent. Fox 2380
2982	After Midnight	J.J. Cale	8-Jul-72	Shelter 7321
2983	Tried To Love	Peter Frampton	7-Jan-78	A&M 1988
2984	You're Moving Out Today	Carole Bayer Sager	19-Nov-77	Elektra 45422
2985	Everybody Be Dancin'	Starbuck	28-May-77	Private Stk 45,144
2986	Everybody Dance	Chic	17-Jun-78	Atlantic 3469
2987	Turn Off The Lights	Teddy Pendergrass	11-Aug-79	Phila. Int'l 3696
2988	No Arms Can Ever Hold You	Bobby Vinton	1-Aug-70	Epic 10629
2989	Ain't Got No Home	The Band	5-Jan-74	Capitol 3758
2990	My Elusive Dreams	Charlie Rich	8-Mar-75	Epic 50064
2991	Holding On (When Love Is Gone)	L.T.D.	21-Oct-78	A&M 2057
2992	I.O.U.	Jimmy Dean	5-Jun-76	Casino 052
2993	Stop To Start	Blue Magic	16-Mar-74	Atco 6949
2994	Love Is The Message	MFSB Featuring The Three Degrees	20-Jul-74	Phila. Int'l 3547
2995	A Fool Such As I	Bob Dylan	26-Jan-74	Columbia 45982
2996	Don't Leave Me Starvin' For Your Love (Part 1)	Holland-Dozier	17-Feb-73	Invictus 9133
2997	Long Haired Country Boy	Charlie Daniels Band	14-Jun-75	Kama Sutra 601
2998	I Just Can't Say No To You	Parker McGee	19-Mar-77	Big Tree 16082
2999	I' Been Watchin' You	The South Side Movement	2-Jun-73	Wand 11251
3000	I Don't See Me In Your Eyes Anymore	Charlie Rich	22-Jun-74	RCA Victor 0260
3001	The More You Do It (The More I Like It Done To Me)	Ronnie Dyson	18-Sep-76	Columbia 10356
3002	I'm Dreaming	Jennifer Warnes	10-Sep-77	Arista 0252
3003	Rainbow In Your Eyes	Leon & Mary Russell	28-Aug-76	Paradise 8208
3004	I Get High On You	Sly Stone	11-Oct-75	Epic 50135
3005	Portrait (He Knew)	Kansas	1-Jul-78	Kirshner 4276
3006	I'll Be Your Everything	Percy Sledge	21-Dec-74	Capricorn 0209
3007	I Started Loving You Again	Al Martino	17-Jan-70	Capitol 2674
3008	Stand By Me	David & Jimmy Ruffin	21-Nov-70	Soul 35076
3009	Baby Don't You Know	Wild Cherry	12-Feb-77	Sweet City/Epic 50306
3010	I Like You	Donovan	2-Jun-73	Epic 10983
3011	And My Heart Sang (Tra La La)	Brenda & The Tabulations	20-Jun-70	Top & Bottom 403
3012	Back To The Island	Leon Russell	31-Jan-76	Shelter 40483
3013	There Ain't No Way	Lobo	24-Nov-73	Big Tree 16,012
3014	Hot Pants	Salvage	17-Apr-71	Odax 420
3015	Keep The Customer Satisfied	Gary Puckett	27-Feb-71	Columbia 45303

'70s Rank	TITLE	ACT	Peak Date	Label & No.
3016	Rock Me	Nick Gilder	14-Jul-79	Chrysalis 2332
3017	Dance The Kung Fu	Carl Douglas	15-Mar-75	20th Century 2168
3018	Brand New Love Affair Parts I & II	Chicago	4-Oct-75	Columbia 10200
3019	Sweet Lui-Louise	Ironhorse	28-Apr-79	Scotti Brothers 406
3020	Mozambique	Bob Dylan	10-Apr-76	Columbia 10298
3021	Anytime (I'll Be There)	Paul Anka	8-May-76	United Artists 789
3022	Pepper Box	The Peppers	13-Apr-74	Event 213
3023	Hey Baby	Ringo Starr	12-Feb-77	Atlantic 3371
3024	Stone Cold Sober	Crawler	17-Dec-77	Epic 50442
3025	You've Got My Soul On Fire	The Temptations	20-Jul-74	Gordy 7136
3026	Let There Be Music	Orleans	31-May-75	Asylum 45243
3027	Goin' Places	The Jacksons	26-Nov-77	Epic 50454
3028	Don't Change Horses (In The Middle Of A Stream)	Tower Of Power	21-Sep-74	Warner Bros. 7828
3029	Reason To Be	Kansas	13-Oct-79	Kirshner 4285
3030	Bloody Well Right	Supertramp	24-May-75	A&M 1660
3031	On The Shelf	Donny & Marie	25-Nov-78	Polydor/Kolob 14510
3032	Brown Eyed Girl	El Chicano	22-Jul-72	Kapp 2173
3033	Falling Apart At The Seams	Marmalade	1-May-76	Ariola America 7619
3034	Crazy About The La La La	Smokey Robinson & The Miracles	17-Jul-71	Tamla 54206
3035	Radioactive	Gene Simmons	13-Jan-79	Casablanca 951
3036	Dancin' Fool	Frank Zappa	26-May-79	Zappa 10
3037	Everything's The Same (Ain't Nothing Changed)	Billy Swan	6-Dec-75	Monument 8661
3038	City In The Sky	The Staple Singers	31-Aug-74	Stax 0215
3039	Let It Rain	Eric Clapton	21-Oct-72	Polydor 15049
3040	Victoria	The Kinks	21-Mar-70	Reprise 0863
3041	Can't Help Falling In Love	Al Martino	21-Mar-70	Capitol 2746
3042	Ace Of Spade	O.V. Wright	26-Dec-70	Back Beat 615
3043	Harvest For The World	The Isley Brothers	9-Oct-76	T-Neck 2261
3044	I'll Supply The Love	Toto	24-Mar-79	Columbia 10898
3045	That's Your Secret	Sea Level	29-Apr-78	Capricorn 0287
3046	Gypsy Queen (Part 1)	Gypsy	16-Jan-71	Metromedia 202
3047	Ain't Got Time	The Impressions	3-Apr-71	Curtom 1957
3048	Let It Go, Let It Flow	Dave Mason	4-Mar-78	Columbia 10662
3049	So Long Dixie	Blood, Sweat & Tears	25-Nov-72	Columbia 45661
3050	Big Time Operator	Keith Hampshire	5-Jan-74	A&M 1486
3051	Tweedlee Dee	Little Jimmy Osmond	3-Feb-73	MGM 14468
3052	One Tear	Eddie Kendricks	11-Jan-75	Tamla 54255
3053	One Beautiful Day	Ecstasy, Passion & Pain	10-May-75	Roulette 7163
3054	Don't Cry Joni	Conway Twitty	17-Jan-76	MCA 40407
3055	Ooh Boy	Rose Royce	28-Jan-78	Whitfield 8491

'70s Rank	TITLE	ACT	Peak Date	Label & No.
3056	Take It Slow (Out In The Country)	Lighthouse	22-Jan-72	Evolution 1052
3057	I'm So Glad I Fell For You	David Ruffin	10-Jan-70	Motown 1158
3058	Hold On	Sons Of Champlin	31-Jul-76	Ariola America 7627
3059	Brother's Gonna Work It Out	Willie Hutch	2-Jun-73	Motown 1222
3060	Me And Bobby McGee	Jerry Lee Lewis	15-Jan-72	Mercury 73248
3061	Do You Know What Time It Is?	P-Nut Gallery	10-Jul-71	Buddah 239
3062	The Pill	Loretta Lynn	12-Apr-75	MCA 40358
3063	Door To Your Heart	The Dramatics	28-Sep-74	Cadet 5704
3064	In The Bottle	Brother To Brother	9-Nov-74	Turbo 039
3065	Can't Give You Anything (But My Love)	The Stylistics	30-Aug-75	Avco 4656
3066	Sing It, Shout It	Starz	30-Jul-77	Capitol 4434
3067	Silly Wasn't I	Valerie Simpson	3-Feb-73	Tamla 54224
3068	We've Got Love	Peaches & Herb	11-Aug-79	Polydor/MVP 14577
3069	Cocomotion	El Coco	18-Feb-78	AVI 147
3070	I Hate Hate	Razzy	29-Jun-74	MGM 14728
3071	Woman From Tokyo	Deep Purple	27-Oct-73	Warner Bros. 7672/ Warner Bros. 7737
3072	Superman	The Ides Of March	25-Jul-70	Warner Bros. 7403
3073	Kong	Dickie Goodman	12-Mar-77	Shock 6
3074	Love, Reign O'Er Me	The Who	22-Dec-73	Track 40152
3075	Just One Look	Linda Ronstadt	31-Mar-79	Asylum 46011
3076	You're The One For Me	Joe Simon	7-Aug-71	Spring 115
3077	Killer Joe	Quincy Jones	23-May-70	A&M 1163
3078	Since I Don't Have You	Art Garfunkel	14-Jul-79	Columbia 10999
3079	What Can I Say	Boz Scaggs	8-Jan-77	Columbia 10440
3080	Devoted To You	Carly Simon & James Taylor	30-Sep-78	Elektra 45506
3081	Greased Lightnin'	John Travolta	4-Nov-78	RSO 909
3082	Mammas Don't Let Your Babies Grow Up To Be Cowboys	Waylon & Willie	25-Mar-78	RCA 11198
3083	River's Risin'	Edgar Winter	31-Aug-74	Epic 11143
3084	Together Again	Bobby Sherman	4-Mar-72	Metromedia 240
3085	Devil's Gun	C.J. & Co.	29-Oct-77	Westbound 55400
3086	Songman	Cashman & West	27-Jan-73	Dunhill 4333
3087	Ruby, Baby	Billy "Crash" Craddock	11-Jan-75	ABC 12036
3088	Only In Your Heart	America	19-May-73	Warner Bros. 7694
3089	What Am I Living For	Ray Charles	5-Feb-72	ABC/TRC 11317
3090	Surfin' U.S.A.	The Beach Boys	21-Sep-74	Capitol 3924
3091	Do It In The Name Of Love	Candi Staton	17-Mar-73	Fame 91009
3092	Got To Have Loving	Don Ray	4-Nov-78	Polydor 14489
3093	Going Down Slowly	Pointer Sisters	20-Dec-75	ABC/Blue Thumb 268
3094	Deeper (In Love With You)	O'Jays	9-May-70	Neptune 22
3095	Welfare Cadillac	Guy Drake	28-Mar-70	Royal American 1

'70s Rank	TITLE	ACT	Peak Date	Label & No.
3096	Diamonds Are Forever	Shirley Bassey	4-Mar-72	United Artists 50845
3097	Walk On	Neil Young	31-Aug-74	Reprise 1209
3098	That's Not How It Goes	Bloodstone	7-Sep-74	London 1055
3099	Together	The Illusion	10-Jan-70	Steed 722
3100	(Shu-Doo-Pa-Poo-Poop) Love Being Your Fool	Travis Wammack	16-Aug-75	Capricorn 0239
3101	You + Me = Love	The Undisputed Truth	9-Apr-77	Whitfield 8306
3102	You're A Lady	Peter Skellern	6-Jan-73	London 20075
3103	It's So Hard For Me To Say Good-Bye	Eddie Kendricks	5-Jun-71	Tamla 54203
3104	The Last Time I Saw Her	Glen Campbell	31-Jul-71	Capitol 3123
3105	It Only Hurts When I Try To Smile	Tony Orlando And Dawn	4-May-74	Bell 45,450
3106	Mr. Penguin - Pt. 1	Lunar Funk	18-Mar-72	Bell 45,172
3107	Gimme Some Lovin' Part One	Traffic, Etc.	20-Nov-71	United Artists 50841
3108	No Sugar Tonight	The Guess Who	18-Apr-70	RCA Victor 74-0325
3109	Chain Gang Medley	Jim Croce	7-Feb-76	Lifesong 45001
3110	Banapple Gas	Cat Stevens	6-Mar-76	A&M 1785
3111	Sally G	Paul McCartney & Wings	15-Feb-75	Apple 1875
3112	Easy To Be Free	Rick Nelson	4-Apr-70	Decca 732635
3113	James Dean	Eagles	12-Oct-74	Asylum 45202
3114	You've Lost That Lovin' Feelin'	Roberta Flack & Donny Hathaway	20-Nov-71	Atlantic 2837
3115	Oh, Singer	Jeannie C. Riley	1-May-71	Plantation 72
3116	Galaxy	War	18-Feb-78	MCA 40820
3117	Baby, Hang Up The Phone	Carl Graves	18-Jan-75	A&M 1620
3118	Flying High	Commodores	11-Nov-78	Motown 1452
3119	Beautiful People	The New Seekers	13-Feb-71	Elektra 45710
3120	Stealin'	Uriah Heep	24-Nov-73	Warner Bros. 7738
3121	Only You Can	Fox	27-Sep-75	Ariola America 7601
3122	Pain (Part 1)	Ohio Players	29-Jan-72	Westbound 188
3123	Take It Like A Man	Bachman-Turner Overdrive	6-Mar-76	Mercury 73766
3124	This Old Man	Purple Reign	3-Jan-76	Private Stk 45,052
3125	Ashes To Ashes	The 5th Dimension	20-Oct-73	Bell 45,380
3126	Stone Blue	Foghat	1-Jul-78	Bearsville 0325
3127	You're My Man	Lynn Anderson	22-May-71	Columbia 45356
3128	Message In Our Music	The O'Jays	16-Oct-76	Phila. Int'l 3601
3129	Do The Funky Penguin, Part 1	Rufus Thomas	19-Feb-72	Stax 0112
3130	In The Quiet Morning (For Janis Joplin)	Joan Baez	26-Aug-72	A&M 1362
3131	Man In Black	Johnny Cash	17-Apr-71	Columbia 45339
3132	Get A Move On	Eddie Money	6-Oct-79	Columbia 11064
3133	This Is The Way That I Feel	Marie Osmond	28-May-77	Polydor/Kolob 14385
3134	Spanish Hustle	The Fatback Band	1-May-76	Event 229
3135	Life Is A Song Worth Singing	Johnny Mathis	16-Mar-74	Columbia 45975
3136	Isn't It A Pity	George Harrison	12-Dec-70	Apple 2995

'70s Rank	TITLE	ACT	Peak Date	Label & No.
3137	Little Queen	Heart	15-Oct-77	Portrait 70008
3138	Silly Milly	Blue Swede	6-Jul-74	EMI 3893
3139	Truckin'	Grateful Dead	8-Jan-72	Warner Bros. 7464
3140	If You Do Believe In Love	The Tee Set	6-Jun-70	Colossus 114
3141	Oh Honey	Delegation	14-Apr-79	Shady Brook 1048
3142	Watch Out For Lucy	Eric Clapton	31-Mar-79	RSO 910
3143	You	The McCrarys	16-Sep-78	Portrait 70014
3144	Jive Turkey (Part 1)	Ohio Players	20-Jul-74	Mercury 73480
3145	Let This Be A Lesson To You	The Independents	7-Dec-74	Wand 11279
3146	I Need To Know	And The Heart-breakers	5-Aug-78	Shelter 62010
3147	I Had It All The Time	Tyrone Davis	22-Apr-72	Dakar 4501
3148	If Loving You Is Wrong I Don't Want To Be Right	Millie Jackson	1-Mar-75	Spring 155
3149	The Year That Clayton Delaney Died	Tom T. Hall	30-Oct-71	Mercury 73221
3150	How Can I Unlove You	Lynn Anderson	25-Sep-71	Columbia 45429
3151	Houston (I'm Comin' To See You)	Glen Campbell	9-Mar-74	Capitol 3808
3152	Cuz It's You, Girl	James Walsh Gypsy Band	9-Dec-78	RCA 11403
3153	If You Gotta Break Another Heart	Albert Hammond	24-Mar-73	Mums 6015
3154	Do What You Set Out To Do	Bobby Bland	1-Apr-72	Duke 472
3155	Stay The Night	The Faragher Brothers	7-Apr-79	Polydor 14533
3156	Guess Who	B.B. King	7-Oct-72	ABC 11330
3157	Like An Open Door	The Fuzz	24-Jul-71	Calla 177
3158	As Time Goes By	Nilsson	29-Sep-73	RCA Victor 0039
3159	Part Two (Let A Man Come In And Do The Popcorn)	James Brown	31-Jan-70	King 6275
3160	Love, Love, Love	Donny Hathaway	1-Sep-73	Atco 6928
3161	Peter Piper	Frank Mills	15-Dec-79	Polydor 2002
3162	Take Me To The Kaptin	Prism	4-Feb-78	Ariola America 7678
3163	C.B. Savage	Rod Hart	22-Jan-77	Plantation 144
3164	Iko Iko	Dr. John	6-May-72	Atco 6882
3165	I Am I Am	Smokey Robinson	25-Jan-75	Tamla 54251
3166	Letting Go	Wings	25-Oct-75	Capitol 4145
3167	Same Thing It Took	The Impressions	22-Nov-75	Curtom 0106
3168	Prove It All Night	Bruce Springsteen	29-Jul-78	Columbia 10763
3169	Whoever Finds This, I Love You	Mac Davis	13-Jun-70	Columbia 45117
3170	Heartbreaker	Dolly Parton	30-Sep-78	RCA 11296
3171	Our World	Blue Mink	31-Oct-70	Philips 40686
3172	Gudbuy T' Jane	Slade	14-Apr-73	Polydor 15060
3173	The Coldest Days Of My Life (Part 1)	The Chi-Lites	12-Aug-72	Brunswick 55478
3174	Go West	Village People	30-Jun-79	Casablanca 984
3175	Then You Can Tell Me Goodbye	Toby Beau	29-Sep-79	RCA 11670
3176	Sweet Harmony	Smokey Robinson	8-Sep-73	Tamla 54233
3177	Devil You	Stampeders	1-Jan-72	Bell 45,154

'70s Rank	TITLE	ACT	Peak Date	Label & No.
3178	So Excited	B.B. King	2-May-70	BluesWay 61035
3179	We're Almost There	Michael Jackson	29-Mar-75	Motown 1341
3180	It's All Right	Jim Capaldi	1-Mar-75	Island 003
3181	The Young New Mexican Puppeteer	Tom Jones	3-Jun-72	Parrot 40070
3182	Lady Bump	Penny McLean	14-Feb-76	Atco 7038
3183	Big Leg Woman (With A Short Short Mini Skirt)	Israel "Popper Stopper" Tolbert	19-Dec-70	Warren 106
3184	Roll With The Changes	REO Speedwagon	24-Jun-78	Epic 50545
3185	New Orleans	The Staple Singers	27-Mar-76	Curtom 0113
3186	Legend In Your Own Time	Carly Simon	6-May-72	Elektra 45774
3187	Help Me Make It (To My Rockin' Chair)	B.J. Thomas	25-Oct-75	ABC 12121
3188	C'mon	Poco	1-May-71	Epic 10714
3189	Help Me Find A Way (To Say I Love You)	Little Anthony And The Imperials	26-Dec-70	United Artists 50720
3190	You're A Lady	Dawn Featuring Tony Orlando	6-Jan-73	Bell 45,285
3191	Little Girl Gone	Donna Fargo	24-Nov-73	Dot 17476
3192	Everything's Been Changed	The 5th Dimension	5-May-73	Bell 45,338
3193	It's The Real Thing - Pt I	The Electric Express	21-Aug-71	Linco 1001
3194	Don't Let Go	Commander Cody And His Lost Planet Airmen	29-Mar-75	Warner Bros. 8073
3195	I Like To Do It	KC & The Sunshine Band	5-Feb-77	T.K. 1020
3196	Funky Music Sho Nuff Turns Me On	Edwin Starr	15-May-71	Gordy 7107
3197	I Can't Leave You Alone	George McCrae	16-Nov-74	T.K. 1007
3198	Everybody Knows About My Good Thing Pt. 1	Little Johnny Taylor	22-Jan-72	Ronn 55
3199	Sylvia	Focus	25-Aug-73	Sire 708
3200	Let Me Party With You (Part 1) (Party, Party, Party)	Bunny Sigler	15-Apr-78	Gold Mind 4008
3201	Can't Sleep	Rockets	2-Jun-79	RSO 926
3202	My Sweet Lady	John Denver	7-May-77	RCA 10911
3203	The Heartbreak Kid	Bo Donaldson And The Heywoods	21-Dec-74	ABC 12039
3204	Cheer	Potliquor	25-Mar-72	Janus 179
3205	Runaway	Bonnie Raitt	16-Jul-77	Warner Bros. 8382
3206	You And I	Johnny Bristol	7-Dec-74	MGM 14762
3207	Ghetto Woman	B.B. King	2-Oct-71	ABC 11310
3208	Amarillo	Neil Sedaka	16-Jul-77	Elektra 45406
3209	Ajax Liquor Store	Hudson And Landry	19-Jun-71	Dore 855
3210	It's A Crazy World	Mac McAnally	20-Aug-77	Ariola America 7665
3211	Keep Holding On	The Temptations	13-Mar-76	Gordy 7146
3212	He's A Friend	Eddie Kendricks	24-Apr-76	Tamla 54266
3213	Chattanooga Choo Choo	Tuxedo Junction	15-Jul-78	Butterfly 1205
3214	Since You Been Gone	Rainbow	22-Dec-79	Polydor 2014
3215	Silly, Silly, Fool	Dusty Springfield	21-Mar-70	Atlantic 2705

'70s Rank	TITLE	ACT	Peak Date	Label & No.
3216	Sexy Ida (Part 2)	Ike & Tina Turner	11-Jan-75	United Artists 528
3217	We're All Playing In The Same Band	Bert Sommer	12-Sep-70	Eleuthera 470
3218	Farther On Down The Road	Joe Simon	23-May-70	Sound Stage 7 2656
3219	Moonlight Special	Ray Stevens	31-Aug-74	Barnaby 604
3220	If I Said You Had A Beautiful Body Would You Hold It Against Me	Bellamy Brothers	14-Jul-79	Warner/Curb 8790
3221	Down By The River	Albert Hammond	9-Sep-72	Mums 6009
3222	Easy As Pie	Billy "Crash" Craddock	17-Jan-76	ABC/Dot 17584
3223	Where Did All The Good Times Go	Dennis Yost & The Classics IV	12-Dec-70	Liberty 56200
3224	I Won't Last A Day Without You/Let Me Be The One	Al Wilson	1-Mar-75	Rocky Road 30202
3225	Whatever Turns You On	Travis Wammack	30-Sep-72	Fame 91001
3226	If I Could Only Win Your Love	Emmylou Harris	4-Oct-75	Reprise 1332
3227	Louisiana	Mike Kennedy	1-Apr-72	ABC 11309
3228	Nobody	The Doobie Brothers	30-Nov-74	Warner Bros. 8041
3229	War Song	Neil Young And Graham Nash	22-Jul-72	Reprise 1099
3230	I'd Rather Be Sorry	Ray Price	11-Sep-71	Columbia 45425
3231	Dear Prudence	Katfish	25-Oct-75	Big Tree 16045
3232	Someone To Lay Down Beside Me	Linda Ronstadt	8-Jan-77	Asylum 45361
3233	The Cat Walk	The Village Soul Choir	11-Apr-70	Abbott 2010
3234	Yes, Yes, Yes	Bill Cosby	26-Jun-76	Capitol 4258
3235	You Can Do Magic	Limmie & Family Cookin'	13-Jan-73	Avco 4602
3236	I Can't Stand To See You Cry	Smokey Robinson & The Miracles	27-Jan-73	Tamla 54225
3237	Isn't It About Time	Stephen Stills -- Manassas	2-Jun-73	Atlantic 2959
3238	One Man Parade	James Taylor	24-Mar-73	Warner Bros. 7682
3239	Daybreaker	Electric Light Orchestra	1-Jun-74	United Artists 405
3240	Love Gun	Kiss	22-Oct-77	Casablanca 895
3241	Rosalie	Sam Neely	10-Mar-73	Capitol 3510
3242	Ca Plane Pour Moi	Plastic Bertrand	24-Jun-78	Sire 1020
3243	Roland The Roadie And Gertrude The Groupie	Dr. Hook And The Medicine Show	28-Jul-73	Columbia 45878
3244	Steppin' In A Slide Zone	The Moody Blues	2-Sep-78	London 270
3245	Ain't Gonna Eat Out My Heart Anymore	Angel	29-Apr-78	Casablanca 914
3246	Some Of Shelly's Blues	Nitty Gritty Dirt Band	23-Oct-71	United Artists 50817
3247	Department Of Youth	Alice Cooper	13-Sep-75	Atlantic 3280
3248	Do It To My Mind	Johnny Bristol	8-Jan-77	Atlantic 3360
3249	Look What You've Done To My Heart	Marilyn McCoo & Billy Davis Jr.	1-Oct-77	ABC 12298
3250	Whole Lotta Love	C.C.S.	20-Feb-71	Rak 4501
3251	Fly At Night	Chilliwack	4-Jun-77	Mushroom 7024
3252	Always	Luther Ingram	12-May-73	KoKo 2115
3253	Sweet Music Man	Kenny Rogers	4-Feb-78	United Artists 1095
3254	Baby I Want You	Funky Communication Committee	1-Sep-79	Free Flight 11595

'70s Rank	TITLE	ACT	Peak Date	Label & No.
3255	Touch Me Baby (Reaching Out For Your Love)	Tamiko Jones	10-May-75	Arista 0110
3256	Ride A White Swan	Tyrannosaurus Rex	13-Feb-71	Blue Thumb 7121
3257	Farewell Andromeda (Welcome To My Morning)	John Denver	6-Oct-73	RCA Victor 0067
3258	Captain Howdy	Simon Stokes	24-Aug-74	Casablanca 0007
3259	Oh No, Not My Baby	Merry Clayton	10-Feb-73	Ode 66030
3260	Hard Times	Boz Scaggs	26-Nov-77	Columbia 10606
3261	You Angel You	Manfred Mann's Earth Band	21-Jul-79	Warner Bros. 8850
3262	Changes	Loggins & Messina	15-Feb-75	Columbia 10077
3263	Hill Where The Lord Hides	Chuck Mangione	7-Aug-71	Mercury 73208
3264	Indian Summer	Poco	1-Oct-77	ABC 12295
3265	Slipped, Tripped And Fell In Love	Clarence Carter	14-Aug-71	Atlantic 2818
3266	Seaside Woman	Suzy And The Red Stripes	16-Jul-77	Epic 50403
3267	Yesterday I Had The Blues	Harold Melvin And The Blue Notes	7-Apr-73	Phila. Int'l 3525
3268	Whenever I'm Away From You	John Travolta	4-Dec-76	Midland Int'l 10780
3269	It's Only Love	Elvis Presley	6-Nov-71	RCA Victor 48-1017
3270	Old Home Filler-Up An' Keep On-A-Truckin' Cafe	C.W. McCall	3-Aug-74	MGM 14738
3271	Black Byrd	Donald Byrd	4-Aug-73	Blue Note 212
3272	I'm Gonna Love You	The Intrigues	17-Jan-70	Yew 1002
3273	Vaya Con Dios	Dawn Featuring Tony Orlando	22-Jul-72	Bell 45,225
3274	The Whistler	Jethro Tull	7-May-77	Chrysalis 2135
3275	Something About You	Le Blanc & Carr	30-Jul-77	Big Tree 16092
3276	Virgin Man	Smokey Robinson	19-Oct-74	Tamla 54250
3277	Loving You	Johnny Nash	20-Apr-74	Epic 11070
3278	Oh! No Not My Baby	Rod Stewart	3-Nov-73	Mercury 73426
3279	Ride, Sally, Ride	Dennis Coffey	24-Jun-72	Sussex 237
3280	California Girl	Eddie Floyd	2-May-70	Stax 0060
3281	You're The One	The Three Degrees	13-Feb-71	Roulette 7091
3282	The Fonz Song	The Heyettes	15-May-76	London 232
3283	I Don't Want Nobody Else (To Dance With You)	Narada Michael Walden	19-May-79	Atlantic 3541
3284	Bigfoot	Bro Smith	5-Jun-76	Big Tree 16061
3285	Long Lonely Nights	The Dells	15-Aug-70	Cadet 5672
3286	Hound Dog Man (Play It Again)	Lenny Le Blanc	1-Oct-77	Big Tree 16062
3287	Good Things Don't Last Forever	Ecstasy, Passion & Pain	24-Aug-74	Roulette 7156
3288	Hard Times For Lovers	Judy Collins	28-Apr-79	Elektra 46020
3289	Ask Me	Ecstasy, Passion & Pain	23-Nov-74	Roulette 7159
3290	Lonely School Year	Hudson Brothers	20-Dec-75	Rocket/MCA 40464
3291	No Chance	Moon Martin	15-Dec-79	Capitol 4794
3292	I Can't Tell The Bottom From The Top	The Hollies	27-Jun-70	Epic 10613
3293	Let Me Make Love To You	The O'Jays	9-Aug-75	Phila. Int'l 3573

'70s Rank	TITLE	ACT	Peak Date	Label & No.
3294	Mama Weer All Crazee Now	Slade	13-Jan-73	Polydor 15053
3295	(I Remember) Summer Morning	Vanity Fare	12-Sep-70	Page One 21,033
3296	Here Comes The Night	The Beach Boys	7-Apr-79	Caribou 9026
3297	Survivor	Cindy Bullens	17-Mar-79	United Artists 1261
3298	Shades Of Green	The Flaming Ember	14-Feb-70	Hot Wax 6907
3299	Whole Lotta Love	King Curtis & The Kingpins	20-Feb-71	Atco 6779
3300	Sweets For My Sweet	Tony Orlando	11-Aug-79	Casablanca 991
3301	Indian Love Call	Ray Stevens	1-Nov-75	Barnaby 616
3302	I've Had It	Fanny	20-Jul-74	Casablanca 0009
3303	In The Bush	Musique	2-Dec-78	Prelude 71110
3304	(If You Add) All The Love In The World	Mac Davis	19-Apr-75	Columbia 10111
3305	You'll Love Again	Hotel	6-May-78	Mercury 73979
3306	This Is Love	Oak	25-Aug-79	Mercury 74076
3307	One Night Affair	Jerry Butler	16-Dec-72	Mercury 73335
3308	Lay Lady Lay	The Isley Brothers	25-Dec-71	T-Neck 933
3309	If Not You	Dr. Hook	29-Jan-77	Capitol 4364
3310	Baby Don't Change Your Mind	Gladys Knight & The Pips	30-Jul-77	Buddah 569
3311	Easy Driver	Kenny Loggins	20-Jan-79	Columbia 10866
3312	Buffalo Soldier	The Flamingos	18-Apr-70	Polydor 14019
3313	California	Debby Boone	18-Mar-78	Warner/Curb 8511
3314	A Passion Play (Edit #8)	Jethro Tull	23-Jun-73	Chrysalis 2012
3315	It Hurts So Bad	Kim Carnes	31-Mar-79	EMI America 8011
3316	I Have A Dream	Donny Osmond	22-Mar-75	MGM 14781
3317	She's Gone	Tavares	14-Dec-74	Capitol 3957
3318	If You Can't Give Me Love	Suzi Quatro	30-Jun-79	RSO 929
3319	I Don't Wanna Go	Joey Travolta	15-Jul-78	Millennium 615
3320	Ready For The Times To Get Better	Crystal Gayle	29-Apr-78	United Artists 1136
3321	Por Amor Viviremos	The Captain & Tennille	6-Sep-75	A&M 1715
3322	Touch	The Supremes	23-Oct-71	Motown 1190
3323	Thanks For The Smiles	Charlie Ross	15-Feb-75	Big Tree 16025
3324	She Said Yes	Wilson Pickett	12-Sep-70	Atlantic 2753
3325	All Shook Up	Suzi Quatro	7-Sep-74	Bell 45,477
3326	Starman	David Bowie	5-Aug-72	RCA Victor 74-0719
3327	I Wanna Do It To You	Jerry Butler	7-May-77	Motown 1414
3328	Gimme Shelter	Grand Funk Railroad	25-Sep-71	Capitol 3160
3329	Wombling Summer Party	The Wombles	14-Sep-74	Columbia 10013
3330	Money, Money, Money	Abba	26-Nov-77	Atlantic 3434
3331	Nothing Succeeds Like Success	Bill Deal & The Rhondels	25-Apr-70	Heritage 821
3332	Rag Mama Rag	The Band	7-Mar-70	Capitol 2705
3333	Free Ride	Tavares	10-Jan-76	Capitol 4184
3334	Mademoiselle	Styx	18-Dec-76	A&M 1877
3335	5:15	The Who	3-Nov-79	Polydor 2022

'70s Rank	TITLE	ACT	Peak Date	Label & No.
3336	Livin' In The Life	The Isley Brothers	30-Jul-77	T-Neck 2264
3337	Highway To Hell	AC/DC	24-Nov-79	Atlantic 3617
3338	Mary Hartman, Mary Hartman	The Deadly Nightshade	21-Aug-76	Phantom 10709
3339	Talking In Your Sleep	Gordon Lightfoot	31-Jul-71	Reprise 1020
3340	Love Uprising	Otis Leavill	31-Oct-70	Dakar 620
3341	Vengeance	Carly Simon	7-Jul-79	Elektra 46051
3342	Make Love To Your Mind	Bill Withers	14-Feb-76	Columbia 10255
3343	Fresh Air	Quicksilver Messenger Service	31-Oct-70	Capitol 2920
3344	Give A Woman Love	Bobbi Martin	18-Jul-70	United Artists 50687
3345	Phantom Writer	Gary Wright	2-Apr-77	Warner Bros. 8331
3346	All In Love Is Fair	Barbra Streisand	4-May-74	Columbia 46024
3347	Happy Xmas (War Is Over)	John & Yoko And The Plastic Ono Band	1-Jan-72	Apple 1842
3348	Goin' Down (On The Road To L.A.)	Terry Black And Laurel Ward	18-Mar-72	Kama Sutra 540
3349	I Miss You	The Dells	23-Feb-74	Cadet 5700
3350	Feelin' Satisfied	Boston	28-Apr-79	Epic 50677
3351	Showdown	Odia Coates	5-Apr-75	United Artists 601
3352	This Night Won't Last Forever	Bill LaBounty	15-Jul-78	Warner/Curb 8529
3353	Since You Been Gone	Head East	20-May-78	A&M 2026
3354	Someday	Dave Loggins	21-Dec-74	Epic 50035
3355	Don't Cha Love It	The Miracles	8-Feb-75	Tamla 54256
3356	Animal House	Stephen Bishop	27-Jan-79	ABC 12435
3357	Spirit In The Night	Manfred Mann's Earth Band	4-Jun-77	Warner Bros. 8355
3358	Manhattan Spiritual	Mike Post	8-Nov-75	MGM 14829
3359	(All I Have To Do Is) Dream	Nitty Gritty Dirt Band	27-Sep-75	United Artists 655
3360	Pretzel Logic	Steely Dan	9-Nov-74	ABC 12033
3361	Just The Same Way	Journey	12-May-79	Columbia 10928
3362	Flyin'	Prism	9-Sep-78	Ariola America 7714
3363	Duncan	Paul Simon	5-Aug-72	Columbia 45638
3364	Got To Get You Into My Life	Blood, Sweat & Tears	19-Jul-75	Columbia 10151
3365	Take Me	Grand Funk Railroad	14-Feb-76	Capitol 4199
3366	Oh Well - Part I	Fleetwood Mac	21-Mar-70	Reprise 0883
3367	Problem Child	Mark Lindsay	23-Jan-71	Columbia 45286
3368	I've Never Been In Love	Suzi Quatro	13-Oct-79	RSO 1001
3369	Redneck Friend	Jackson Browne	10-Nov-73	Asylum 11023
3370	You Gotta Have Love In Your Heart	The Supremes & Four Tops	26-Jun-71	Motown 1181
3371	L.A. Sunshine	War	3-Sep-77	Blue Note 1009
3372	The Biggest Parakeets In Town	Jud Strunk	16-Aug-75	Melodyland 6015
3373	I'm A Stranger Here	Five Man Electrical Band	19-May-73	Lion 149
3374	Travelin' Shoes	Elvin Bishop	9-Nov-74	Capricorn 0202
3375	Get That Gasoline Blues	NRBQ	2-Mar-74	Kama Sutra 586
3376	Hijackin' Love	Johnnie Taylor	2-Oct-71	Stax 0096

'70s Rank	TITLE	ACT	Peak Date	Label & No.
3377	Rock And Roll All Nite (Studio)	Kiss	14-Jun-75	Casablanca 829
3378	Red Hot	Robert Gordon	19-Nov-77	Private Stk 45,156
3379	Evil Boll-Weevil	Grand Canyon	30-Nov-74	Bang 713
3380	Didn't We	Barbra Streisand	20-Jan-73	Columbia 45739
3381	Hoppy, Gene And Me	Roy Rogers	1-Feb-75	20th Century 2154
3382	He's Gonna Step On You Again	John Kongos	14-Aug-71	Elektra 45729
3383	I Never Said Goodbye	Engelbert Humperdinck	3-Feb-73	Parrot 40072
3384	(I Can Feel Those Vibrations) This Love Is Real	Jackie Wilson	6-Feb-71	Brunswick 55443
3385	You're Movin' Out Today	Bette Midler	18-Jun-77	Atlantic 3379
3386	It's For You	Springwell	16-Oct-71	Parrot 359
3387	In France They Kiss On Main Street	Joni Mitchell	6-Mar-76	Asylum 45296
3388	I Need Help (I Can't Do It Alone) (Part 1)	Bobby Byrd	21-Nov-70	King 6323
3389	"Roots" Medley	Quincy Jones	2-Apr-77	A&M 1909
3390	Misty Blue	Joe Simon	18-Nov-72	Sound Stage 7 1508
3391	Boogie Bands And One Night Stands	Kathy Dalton	12-Oct-74	DiscReet 1210
3392	Reach Out, I'll Be There	Gloria Gaynor	12-Apr-75	MGM 14790
3393	I Got Some Help I Don't Need	B.B. King	27-May-72	ABC 11321
3394	It's Been A Long Time	The New Birth	6-Apr-74	RCA Victor 0185
3395	Popsicle Toes	Michael Franks	11-Sep-76	Reprise 1360
3396	Mr. D.J. (5 For The D.J.)	Aretha Franklin	18-Oct-75	Atlantic 3289
3397	What It Comes Down To	The Isley Brothers	2-Feb-74	T-Neck 2252
3398	Hot Summer Nights	Walter Egan	18-Nov-78	Columbia 10824
3399	Uptown Festival (Part 1)	Shalamar	18-Jun-77	Soul Train 10885
3400	West Coast Woman	Painter	10-Nov-73	Elektra 45862
3401	Mammy Blue	Pop-Tops	13-Nov-71	ABC 11311
3402	You Make Your Own Heaven And Hell Right Here On Earth	The Undisputed Truth	1-Jan-72	Gordy 7112
3403	I'm Comin' Home	Dave Edmunds	22-May-71	MAM 3608
3404	Where Are All My Friends	Harold Melvin And The Blue Notes	18-Jan-75	Phila. Int'l 3552
3405	How Do You Feel The Morning After	Millie Jackson	27-Jul-74	Spring 147
3406	Sally From Syracuse	Stu Nunnery	1-Dec-73	Evolution 1084
3407	Get It While You Can	Janis Joplin	25-Sep-71	Columbia 45433
3408	Devil In The Bottle	T.G. Sheppard	22-Mar-75	Melodyland 6002
3409	Star On A TV Show	The Stylistics	1-Mar-75	Avco 4649
3410	Can The Can	Suzi Quatro	28-Feb-76	Big Tree 16053
3411	Mama Was A Rock And Roll Singer, Papa Used To Write All Her Songs	Sonny & Cher	7-Apr-73	MCA 40026
3412	Travelin' Prayer	Billy Joel	28-Sep-74	Columbia 10015
3413	9,999,999 Tears	Dickey Lee	11-Dec-76	RCA 10764
3414	If It Feels Good, Do It	Ian Lloyd & Stories	27-Apr-74	Kama Sutra 588
3415	Sun Goddess	Ramsey Lewis And Earth, Wind & Fire	26-Apr-75	Columbia 10103

'70s Rank	TITLE	ACT	Peak Date	Label & No.
3416	Elena	Marc Tanner Band	14-Apr-79	Elektra 46003
3417	Unborn Child	Seals & Crofts	30-Mar-74	Warner Bros. 7771
3418	Working Class Hero	Tommy Roe	26-May-73	MGM South 7013
3419	I Call My Baby Candy	The Jaggerz	30-May-70	Kama Sutra 509
3420	Baby Boy	Mary Kay Place as Loretta Haggers	20-Nov-76	Columbia 10422
3421	Take A Closer Look At The Woman You're With	Wilson Pickett	20-Oct-73	RCA Victor 0049
3422	I Got Stoned And I Missed It	Jim Stafford	11-Oct-75	MGM 14819
3423	You Are On My Mind	Chicago	7-May-77	Columbia 10523
3424	You Don't Love Me Anymore	Eddie Rabbitt	29-Jul-78	Elektra 45488
3425	Sailing Ships	Mesa	16-Apr-77	Ariola America 7654
3426	Lamplight	David Essex	29-Jun-74	Columbia 46041
3427	Mary Jane	Rick James	16-Dec-78	Gordy 7162
3428	Seems Like I Gotta Do Wrong	The Whispers	7-Nov-70	Soul Clock 1004
3429	Wavelength	Van Morrison	4-Nov-78	Warner Bros. 8661
3430	If You Want It	Niteflyte	1-Dec-79	Ariola America 7747
3431	Badlands	Bruce Springsteen	23-Sep-78	Columbia 10801
3432	Room Full Of Roses	Mickey Gilley	27-Jul-74	Playboy 50056
3433	Tightrope Ride	The Doors	1-Jan-72	Elektra 45757
3434	You Can Do It	Dobie Gray	17-Feb-79	Infinity 50,003
3435	You're My Everything	Lee Garrett	26-Jun-76	Chrysalis 2112
3436	Been Too Long On The Road	Mark Lindsay	26-Jun-71	Columbia 45385
3437	Blue Collar	Bachman-Turner Overdrive	12-Jan-74	Mercury 73417
3438	Don't Eat The Yellow Snow	Frank Zappa	16-Nov-74	DiscReet 1312
3439	The Morning Of Our Lives	Arkade	13-Mar-71	Dunhill 4268
3440	Message In A Bottle	The Police	29-Dec-79	A&M 2190
3441	Good Times Roll	The Cars	28-Apr-79	Elektra 46014
3442	You've Got Another Thing Coming	Hotel	18-Aug-79	MCA 41050
3443	You Keep Me Dancing	Samantha Sang	17-Jun-78	Private Stk 45,188
3444	I Go To Rio	Pablo Cruise	17-Feb-79	A&M 2112
3445	Beyond The Blue Horizon	Lou Christie	6-Apr-74	Three Brothers 402
3446	Lu	Peggy Lipton	31-Jan-70	Ode 124
3447	I'll Erase Away Your Pain	Whatnauts	5-Jun-71	Stang 5023
3448	Lovin' You Baby	White Plains	10-Oct-70	Deram 85066
3449	My Pretending Days Are Over	The Dells	27-Oct-73	Cadet 5698
3450	If You Only Believe (Jesus For Tonite)	Michael Polnareff	20-Mar-76	Atlantic 3314
3451	Tell 'Em Willie Boy 's A'Comin'	Tommy James	4-Mar-72	Roulette 7119
3452	Church Street Soul Revival	Tommy James	23-Jan-71	Roulette 7093
3453	Gone, Gone, Gone	Bad Company	8-Sep-79	Swan Song 71000
3454	Help Me Make It Through The Night	Joe Simon	5-Jun-71	Spring 113
3455	Cry To Me	Loleatta Holloway	19-Apr-75	Aware 047
3456	Heartaches	BTO	31-Mar-79	Mercury 74046

'70s Rank	TITLE	ACT	Peak Date	Label & No.
3457	I Need You, You Need Me	Joe Simon	21-Feb-76	Spring 163
3458	Tenth Avenue Freeze-Out	Bruce Springsteen	14-Feb-76	Columbia 10274
3459	Come And Get Your Love	Roger Daltrey	29-Nov-75	MCA 40453
3460	Power Of Love	Martha Reeves	27-Apr-74	MCA 40194
3461	Dancer	Gino Soccio	12-May-79	Warner/RFC 8757
3462	Love Music	Raiders	17-Feb-73	Columbia 45759
3463	Don't Let The Flame Burn Out	Jackie DeShannon	24-Dec-77	Amherst 725
3464	Keep Me Cryin'	Al Green	1-Jan-77	Hi 2319
3465	Georgia Porcupine	George Fischoff	13-Jul-74	United Artists 410
3466	Sad Girl	Carl Graves	7-May-77	Ariola America 7660
3467	I've Been Born Again	Johnnie Taylor	27-Jul-74	Stax 0208
3468	That's Why You Remember	Kenny Karen	22-Sep-73	Big Tree 16,007
3469	I Will Never Pass This Way Again	Glen Campbell	7-Oct-72	Capitol 3411
3470	Stop! In The Name Of Love	Margie Joseph	17-Apr-71	Volt 4056
3471	Down By The River	Buddy Miles	29-Aug-70	Mercury 73086
3472	She Loves To Be In Love	Charlie	2-Sep-78	Janus 276
3473	Roll On	The New Colony Six	2-Oct-71	Sunlight 1001
3474	Run Through The Jungle	Creedence Clearwater Revival	2-May-70	Fantasy 641
3475	Sunshine Roses	Gene Cotton	14-Dec-74	Myrrh 137
3476	Boogie Woogie Dancin' Shoes	Claudja Barry	28-Apr-79	Chrysalis 2313
3477	Tell The World How I Feel About 'Cha Baby	Harold Melvin And The Blue Notes	1-May-76	Phila. Int'l 3588
3478	Where Will Your Heart Take You	Buckeye	29-Sep-79	Polydor 14578
3479	Hush/I'm Alive	Blue Swede	22-Mar-75	EMI 4029
3480	As	Stevie Wonder	17-Dec-77	Tamla 54291
3481	Neon Nites	Atlanta Rhythm Section	16-Jul-77	Polydor 14397
3482	You're A Big Girl Now	The Stylistics	6-Feb-71	Avco Embassy 4555
3483	Can You Get To That	Funkadelic	2-Oct-71	Westbound 185
3484	You Light Up My Life	Carole King	4-Aug-73	Ode 66035
3485	Watching The Detectives//Alison	Elvis Costello	8-Apr-78	Columbia 10705
3486	It's Her Turn To Live	Smokey Robinson	6-Jul-74	Tamla 54246
3487	Bed Of Rose's	The Statler Brothers	20-Feb-71	Mercury 73141
3488	I Wish I Were	Andy Kim	17-Apr-71	Steed 731
3489	Watergrate	Dickie Goodman	21-Jul-73	Rainy Wednesday 202
3490	You're All I Need To Get By	Johnny Mathis/Deniece Williams	19-Aug-78	Columbia 10772
3491	Victim Of A Foolish Heart	Bettye Swann	15-Jul-72	Atlantic 2869
3492	Lies	J.J. Cale	9-Dec-72	Shelter 7326
3493	You Ain't Never Been Loved (Like I'm Gonna Love You)	Jessi Colter	27-Sep-75	Capitol 4087
3494	Don't Make Me Pay For His Mistakes	Z.Z. Hill	20-Mar-71	Hill 222
3495	Hang On Sloopy	Rick Derringer	3-May-75	Blue Sky 2755
3496	Never My Love	The Addrisi Brothers	14-Jan-78	Buddah 587

'70s Rank	TITLE	ACT	Peak Date	Label & No.
3497	California Soul	Marvin Gaye & Tammi Terrell	2-May-70	Tamla 54192
3498	Ain't That Loving You (For More Reasons Than One)	Isaac Hayes & David Porter	20-May-72	Enterprise 9049
3499	All The Time In The World	Dr. Hook	10-Mar-79	Capitol 4677
3500	Merry Christmas Darling	Carpenters	26-Dec-70	A&M 1236
3501	Ain't Nothing Gonna Keep Me From You	Teri Desario	26-Aug-78	Casablanca 929
3502	Brand New Love Affair	Jigsaw	23-Oct-76	Chelsea 3043
3503	Future Shock	Hello People	22-Feb-75	ABC/Dunhill 15023
3504	Shake And Dance With Me	Con Funk Shun	16-Sep-78	Mercury 74008
3505	California Dreamin'	America	28-Apr-79	American Int'l 700
3506	Storybook Children (Daybreak)	Bette Midler	4-Mar-78	Atlantic 3431
3507	Moonshine (Friend Of Mine)	John Kay	30-Jun-73	Dunhill 4351
3508	A Little Lovin' (Keeps The Doctor Away)	The Raes	3-Feb-79	A&M 2091
3509	Inspiration	Paul Williams	19-Jan-74	A&M 1479
3510	Dancin' Shoes	Faith Band	3-Feb-79	Mercury 74037
3511	Sugar Lump	Leon Haywood	14-Sep-74	20th Century 2103
3512	Blame It On The Boogie	The Jacksons	9-Dec-78	Epic 50595
3513	Chocolate Chip	Isaac Hayes	30-Aug-75	HBS/ABC 12118
3514	Contact	Edwin Starr	10-Mar-79	20th Cent. Fox 2396
3515	Thank You Baby	The Stylistics	10-May-75	Avco 4652
3516	Got To Give In To Love	Bonnie Boyer	1-Sep-79	Columbia 11028
3517	I Like What You Give	Nolan	13-Nov-71	Lizard 21008
3518	Solution For Pollution	Charles Wright And The Watts 103rd Street Rhythm Band	16-Jan-71	Warner Bros. 7451
3519	Ain't It A Sad Thing	R. Dean Taylor	6-Mar-71	Rare Earth 5023
3520	Rock And Roll Dancin'	Beckmeier Brothers	25-Aug-79	Casablanca 1000
3521	Just Don't Want To Be Lonely	Ronnie Dyson	22-Sep-73	Columbia 45867
3522	Queen Of My Soul	Average White Band	9-Oct-76	Atlantic 3354
3523	For A Dancer	Prelude	17-Jan-76	Pye 71045
3524	Primrose Lane	O.C. Smith	11-Jul-70	Columbia 45160
3525	Do You Think I'm Disco?	Steve Dahl And Teenage Radiation	27-Oct-79	Ovation 1132
3526	When Love Is New	Arthur Prysock	29-Jan-77	Old Town 1000
3527	One-Way Ticket	Tyrone Davis	7-Aug-71	Dakar 624
3528	Doing My Own Thing (Part I)	Johnnie Taylor	13-May-72	Stax 0122
3529	I Don't Know What It Is, But It Sure Is Funky	Ripple	1-Dec-73	GRC 1004
3530	That Song Is Driving Me Crazy	Tom T. Hall	27-Jul-74	Mercury 73488
3531	Tie Your Mother Down	Queen	9-Apr-77	Elektra 45385
3532	One Day At A Time	Marilyn Sellars	12-Oct-74	Mega 1205
3533	I Love You	Otis Leaville	17-Jan-70	Dakar 614
3534	This Time It's Real	Tower Of Power	13-Oct-73	Warner Bros. 7733
3535	Don't Let It Show	Alan Parsons Project	7-Jan-78	Arista 0288

'70s Rank	TITLE	ACT	Peak Date	Label & No.
3536	I'm Going Down	Rose Royce	25-Jun-77	MCA 40721
3537	(They Long To Be) Close To You	Jerry Butler	2-Sep-72	Mercury 73301
3538	Dog Days	Atlanta Rhythm Section	1-Oct-77	Polydor 14411
3539	You're My Weakness	Faith Band	14-Jul-79	Mercury 74068
3540	Like A Sad Song	John Denver	2-Oct-76	RCA 10774
3541	Hurt	The Manhattans	21-Jun-75	Columbia 10140
3542	Make Love To Me	Helen Reddy	23-Jun-79	Capitol 4712
3543	Wang Dang Doodle	Pointer Sisters	9-Feb-74	Blue Thumb 243
3544	Get Up Offa That Thing	James Brown	11-Sep-76	Polydor 14326
3545	Lost Horizon	Shawn Phillips	17-Mar-73	A&M 1405
3546	Leona	Wet Willie	29-Mar-75	Capricorn 0224
3547	Border Song	Elton John	3-Oct-70	Uni 55246
3548	Give Me A Reason To Be Gone	Maureen McGovern	23-Nov-74	20th Century 2109
3549	Let Me Try Again (Laisse Moi Le Temps)	Frank Sinatra	22-Dec-73	Reprise 1181
3550	I Kinda Miss You	The Manhattans	1-Jan-77	Columbia 10430
3551	Rain, Oh Rain	Fools Gold	10-Jul-76	Morning Sky 700
3552	Cole, Cooke And Redding	Wilson Pickett	18-Apr-70	Atlantic 2722
3553	Lover's Cross	Melanie	14-Sep-74	Neighborhood 4215
3554	Don't Stop It Now	Hot Chocolate	15-May-76	Big Tree 16060
3555	Lady Writer	Dire Straits	1-Sep-79	Warner Bros. 49006
3556	Yours Love	Joe Simon	22-Aug-70	Sound Stage 7 2664
3557	A Friend In The City	Andy Kim	14-Feb-70	Steed 723
3558	There's Got To Be Rain In Your Life (To Appreciate The Sunshine)	Dorothy Norwood	9-Mar-74	GRC 1011
3559	Let Me Know (I Have A Right)	Gloria Gaynor	20-Oct-79	Polydor 2021
3560	Don't Cost You Nothing	Ashford & Simpson	8-Apr-78	Warner Bros. 8514
3561	Beaucoups Of Blues	Ringo Starr	5-Dec-70	Apple 2969
3562	Art For Art's Sake	10CC	3-Jan-76	Mercury 73725
3563	You Send Me	Ponderosa Twins + One	16-Oct-71	Horoscope 102
3564	Evil Ways	Carlos Santana & Buddy Miles	30-Sep-72	Columbia 45666
3565	Stop Doggin' Me	Johnnie Taylor	14-Oct-72	Stax 0142
3566	Take Me Back To Chicago	Chicago	17-Jun-78	Columbia 10737
3567	Lights	Journey	7-Oct-78	Columbia 10800
3568	No Time To Lose	The Tarney/Spencer Band	23-Jun-79	A&M 2124
3569	Tell Me This Is A Dream	The Delfonics	15-Jul-72	Philly Groove 172
3570	Beautiful	Gordon Lightfoot	1-Jul-72	Reprise 1088
3571	Sorrow	David Bowie	22-Dec-73	RCA Victor 0160
3572	Fire And Rain	Johnny Rivers	19-Sep-70	Imperial 66453
3573	Got To See If I Can't Get Mommy (To Come Back Home)	Jerry Butler	7-Feb-70	Mercury 73015
3574	Lovin' You, Lovin' Me	Candi Staton	16-Dec-72	Fame 91005
3575	In And Out Of My Life	Martha Reeves & The Vandellas	18-Mar-72	Gordy 7113

'70s Rank	TITLE	ACT	Peak Date	Label & No.
3576	Blanket On The Ground	Billie Jo Spears	14-Jun-75	United Artists 584
3577	American Girls	Rick Springfield	10-Aug-74	Columbia 46057
3578	Sixteen Tons	The Don Harrison Band	5-Jun-76	Atlantic 3323
3579	In The Middle	Tim Moore	20-Aug-77	Asylum 45394
3580	If You've Got A Heart	Bobby Bland	28-Feb-70	Duke 458
3581	School Of Life	Tommy Tate	22-Jul-72	KoKo 2112
3582	Foxy Lady	Crown Heights Affair	31-Jul-76	De-Lite 1581
3583	Baby, I Need Your Lovin'	Eric Carmen	24-Feb-79	Arista 0384
3584	Somewhere In The Night	Batdorf & Rodney	10-Jan-76	Arista 0159
3585	Empty Pages	Traffic	3-Oct-70	United Artists 50692
3586	The Golden Age Of Rock 'N' Roll	Mott The Hoople	22-Jun-74	Columbia 46035
3587	Simple Song Of Freedom	Buckwheat	6-May-72	London 176
3588	We Can Make It Together	Steve & Eydie	4-Nov-72	MGM 14383
3589	Who Gets The Guy	Dionne Warwick	3-Apr-71	Scepter 12309
3590	L.A. Goodbye	The Ides Of March	8-May-71	Warner Bros. 7466
3591	Never Let Her Slip Away	Andrew Gold	29-Jul-78	Asylum 45489
3592	Sub-Rosa Subway	Klaatu	30-Apr-77	Capitol 4412
3593	Light The Sky On Fire	Jefferson Starship	30-Dec-78	Grunt 11426
3594	You've Really Got A Hold On Me	Eddie Money	30-Dec-78	Columbia 10842
3595	A Woman's Story	Cher	4-Jan-75	Warner-Spector 0400
3596	Mama Let Him Play	Doucette	29-Apr-78	Mushroom 7030
3597	Everything Is Good About You	The Lettermen	6-Mar-71	Capitol 3020
3598	Dream Me Home	Mac Davis	3-Mar-73	Columbia 45773
3599	Try Some, Buy Some	Ronnie Spector	29-May-71	Apple 1832
3600	Mr. And Mrs. Untrue	Candi Staton	5-Jun-71	Fame 1478
3601	You Got It	Diana Ross	17-Jun-78	Motown 1442
3602	Sweet Sixteen	B.B. King	25-Mar-72	ABC 11319
3603	Shoe Shoe Shine	Dynamic Superiors	14-Dec-74	Motown 1324
3604	I Love You More Than You'll Ever Know	Donny Hathaway	25-Nov-72	Atco 6903
3605	Josie	Kris Kristofferson	8-Apr-72	Monument 8536
3606	Girls Talk	Dave Edmunds	29-Sep-79	Swan Song 71001
3607	I Only Have Eyes For You	Jerry Butler	3-Jun-72	Mercury 73290
3608	Never Been Any Reason	Head East	20-Dec-75	A&M 1718
3609	Wooden Heart	Bobby Vinton	12-Jul-75	ABC 12100
3610	Costafine Town	Splinter	18-Jan-75	Dark Horse 10002
3611	Freedom Blues	Little Richard	27-Jun-70	Reprise 0907
3612	(How I Spent My Summer Vacation) Or A Day At The Beach With Pedro And Man - Part I	Cheech & Chong	8-Nov-75	Ode 66115
3613	I Miss You Baby	Millie Jackson	13-Jan-73	Spring 131
3614	Little One	Chicago	18-Mar-78	Columbia 10683
3615	Won't Find Better (Than Me)	The New Hope	7-Feb-70	Jamie 1381

'70s Rank	TITLE	ACT	Peak Date	Label & No.
3616	The Long Way Home	Neil Diamond	1-Sep-73	Bang 703
3617	It's Up To You Petula	Edison Lighthouse	13-Feb-71	Bell 960
3618	What Can I Do With This Broken Heart	England Dan & John Ford Coley	24-Nov-79	Big Tree 17000
3619	Summer Breeze (Part I)	The Isley Brothers	4-May-74	T-Neck 2253
3620	Do Your Dance - Part I	Rose Royce	12-Nov-77	Whitfield 8440
3621	Is It Love That We're Missin'	Quincy Jones	15-Nov-75	A&M 1743
3622	Pops, We Love You (A Tribute To Father)	Diana Ross, Marvin Gaye, Smokey Robinson & Stevie Wonder	17-Feb-79	Tamla 54306
3623	Somethin' 'Bout 'Cha	Latimore	19-Mar-77	Glades 1739
3624	Julianna	Five Man Electrical Band	25-Mar-72	Lionel 3224
3625	Bootzilla	Bootsy's Rubber Band	8-Apr-78	Warner Bros. 8512
3626	Bombs Away	Bob Weir	22-Apr-78	Arista 0315
3627	For Ladies Only	Steppenwolf	4-Dec-71	Dunhill 4292
3628	Heavy Love	David Ruffin	1-May-76	Motown 1388
3629	Back In The Saddle	Aerosmith	21-May-77	Columbia 10516
3630	Feel So Bad	Ray Charles	4-Sep-71	ABC/TRC 11308
3631	Morning Much Better	Ten Wheel Drive With Genya Ravan	5-Sep-70	Polydor 14037
3632	Honey Honey	Sweet Dreams	5-Oct-74	ABC 12008
3633	Say Maybe	Neil Diamond	16-Jun-79	Columbia 10945
3634	A Mama And A Papa	Ray Stevens	15-May-71	Barnaby 2029
3635	(One More Year Of) Daddy's Little Girl	Ray Sawyer	11-Dec-76	Capitol 4344
3636	Sitting In Limbo	Don Brown	15-Apr-78	1st American 102
3637	Trying To Live My Life Without You	Otis Clay	20-Jan-73	Hi 2226
3638	Ode To Billie Joe	Bobbie Gentry	28-Aug-76	Capitol 4294
3639	Colour My World	Chicago	17-Jul-71	Columbia 45417
3640	Too Late	Tavares	20-Jul-74	Capitol 3882
3641	Turn To Stone	Joe Walsh	15-Mar-75	ABC/Dunhill 15026
3642	Lost In Your Love	John Paul Young	20-Jan-79	Scotti Brothers 405
3643	He's So Fine	Jane Olivor	17-Jun-78	Columbia 10724
3644	Country Side Of Life	Wet Willie	23-Nov-74	Capricorn 0212
3645	Last Kiss	J. Frank Wilson And The Cavaliers	12-Jan-74	Virgo 506
3646	Feelin' That Glow	Roberta Flack	28-Jun-75	Atlantic 3271
3647	Dreams Are Ten A Penny	First Class	14-Dec-74	UK 49028
3648	Finder's Keepers	Chairman Of The Board	7-Jul-73	Invictus 1251
3649	Last Tango In Paris	Herb Alpert & The TJB	14-Apr-73	A&M 1420
3650	Your Wonderful, Sweet Sweet Love	The Supremes	9-Sep-72	Motown 1206
3651	Hello It's Me	Nazz	14-Feb-70	SGC 001
3652	Devotion	Earth, Wind & Fire	26-Oct-74	Columbia 10026
3653	The Pretender	Jackson Browne	18-Jun-77	Asylum 45399
3654	Can You Do It	Grand Funk Railroad	25-Sep-76	MCA 40590

'70s Rank	TITLE	ACT	Peak Date	Label & No.
3655	Telegram Sam	T. Rex	13-May-72	Reprise 1078
3656	I'm Girl Scoutin'	The Intruders	24-Apr-71	Gamble 4009
3657	Remember Me	Willie Nelson	14-Feb-76	Columbia 10275
3658	Try (Try To Fall In Love)	Cooker	9-Mar-74	Scepter 12388
3659	Reach Out Your Hand	The Brotherhood Of Man	15-May-71	Deram 85073
3660	Sea Cruise	Johnny Rivers	5-Jun-71	United Artists 50778
3661	Military Madness	Graham Nash	25-Sep-71	Atlantic 2827
3662	Love Minus Zero - No Limit	Turley Richards	25-Apr-70	Warner Bros. 7376
3663	Open Sesame - Part I	Kool & The Gang	22-Jan-77	De-Lite 1586
3664	Long As I Can See The Light	Creedence Clearwater Revival	22-Aug-70	Fantasy 645
3665	Wholy Holy	Aretha Franklin	26-Aug-72	Atlantic 2901
3666	Let's Get Crazy Tonight	Rupert Holmes	23-Sep-78	Private Stk 45,199
3667	Poor Boy	Casey Kelly	4-Nov-72	Elektra 45804
3668	Reaching For The Sky	Peabo Bryson	8-Apr-78	Capitol 4522
3669	Sad Eyes	Brooklyn Dreams	17-Dec-77	Millennium 606
3670	The Wanderer	Leif Garrett	27-May-78	Atlantic 3476
3671	Losers Weepers - Part I	Etta James	7-Nov-70	Cadet 5676
3672	Romeo	Mr. Big	30-Apr-77	Arista 0229
3673	Summer Sun	Jamestown Massacre	2-Sep-72	Warner Bros. 7603
3674	Postcard	The Who	14-Dec-74	Track/MCA 40330
3675	Is That The Way	Tin Tin	2-Oct-71	Atco 6821
3676	Be What You Are	The Staple Singers	7-Jul-73	Stax 0164
3677	Peggy Sue	The Beach Boys	30-Sep-78	Brother/Reprise 1394
3678	Coldblooded	James Brown	28-Dec-74	Polydor 14258
3679	Driftwood	The Moody Blues	9-Dec-78	London 273
3680	Avenging Annie	Andy Pratt	30-Jun-73	Columbia 45804
3681	For Yasgur's Farm	Mountain	10-Oct-70	Windfall 533
3682	Time For Me To Fly	REO Speedwagon	12-Aug-78	Epic 50582
3683	Follow Your Daughter Home	The Guess Who	3-Mar-73	RCA Victor 74-0880
3684	Was Dog A Doughnut	Cat Stevens	24-Dec-77	A&M 1971
3685	I Hope We Get To Love In Time	Marilyn McCoo & Billy Davis Jr.	17-Jul-76	ABC 12170
3686	Music Everywhere	Tufano & Giammarese	26-May-73	Ode 66033
3687	Boom Boom (Out Go The Lights)	Pat Travers	6-Oct-79	Polydor 2003
3688	I'm Not Gonna Cry Anymore	Nancy Brooks	24-Mar-79	Arista 0385
3689	Don't Take My Kindness For Weakness	The Soul Children	26-Aug-72	Stax 0132
3690	Come Back Home	Bobby Goldsboro	28-Aug-71	United Artists 50807
3691	My Girl	Eddie Floyd	8-Aug-70	Stax 0072
3692	It Makes Me Giggle	John Denver	5-Jun-76	RCA Victor 10687
3693	I'm A Man	Chicago	30-Oct-71	Columbia 45467
3694	Grover Henson Feels Forgotten	Bill Cosby	16-May-70	Uni 55223
3695	Hollywood	Boz Scaggs	18-Mar-78	Columbia 10679

'70s Rank	TITLE	ACT	Peak Date	Label & No.
3696	Wholesale Love	Buddy Miles	19-Jun-71	Mercury 73205
3697	Done Too Soon	Neil Diamond	12-Jun-71	Uni 55278
3698	Music In My Bones	Joe Simon	20-Sep-75	Spring 159
3699	Out Of Time	The Rolling Stones	13-Sep-75	Abkco 4702
3700	I'm Still Waiting	Diana Ross	27-Nov-71	Motown 1192
3701	Man Smart, Woman Smarter	Robert Palmer	15-Jan-77	Island 075
3702	Having A Party Medley	The Ovations	24-Nov-73	MGM 14623
3703	I Don't Wanna Lose You	Johnnie Taylor	12-Jun-71	Stax 0089
3704	Love Gone By	Dan Fogelberg	20-Aug-77	Full Moon/Epic 50412
3705	Silver Star	The Four Seasons	26-Jun-76	Warner/Curb 8203
3706	Follow Me	Mary Travers	31-Jul-71	Warner Bros. 7481
3707	Billy--Don't Be A Hero	Paper Lace	25-May-74	Mercury 73479
3708	Down And Out In New York City	James Brown	7-Apr-73	Polydor 14168
3709	She's Ready	The Spiral Starecase	24-Jan-70	Columbia 45048
3710	I Believe You	Carpenters	23-Dec-78	A&M 2097
3711	Got To Believe In Love	Robin McNamara	24-Oct-70	Steed 728
3712	Fire And Rain	R.B. Greaves	2-May-70	Atco 6745
3713	Isn't It Lonely Together	Stark & McBrien	1-Mar-75	RCA Victor 10109
3714	In The Stone	Earth, Wind & Fire	10-Nov-79	ARC 11093
3715	Bed And Board	Barbara Mason	15-Jul-72	Buddah 296
3716	I'll Be Holding On	Al Downing	22-Mar-75	Chess 2158
3717	1984	Spirit	14-Mar-70	Ode 128
3718	Raise A Little Hell	Trooper	26-Aug-78	MCA 40924
3719	Killer Cut	Charlie	29-Sep-79	Arista 0449
3720	When Love Has Gone Away	Richard Cocciante	1-May-76	20th Century 2275
3721	My Love	Margie Joseph	17-Aug-74	Atlantic 3032
3722	Platinum Heroes	Bruce Foster	30-Jul-77	Millennium 602
3723	Slowdown	John Miles	18-Jun-77	London 20092
3724	Guns, Guns, Guns	The Guess Who	10-Jun-72	RCA Victor 74-0708
3725	Rhapsody In White	Love Unlimited Orchestra	1-Jun-74	20th Century 2090
3726	Love Is Better In The A.M. (Part 1)	Johnnie Taylor	16-Apr-77	Columbia 10478
3727	Rock & Roll Runaway	Ace	23-Aug-75	Anchor 21002
3728	Hell On Wheels	Cher	13-Oct-79	Casablanca 2208
3729	Feel The Need	Leif Garrett	2-Jun-79	Scotti Brothers 407
3730	After All This Time	Merry Clayton	15-Jan-72	Ode 66018
3731	Can You Read My Mind	Maureen McGovern	14-Apr-79	Warner/Curb 8750
3732	Help The Poor	B.B. King	26-Jun-71	ABC 11302
3733	There Goes My Everything	Elvis Presley	2-Jan-71	RCA Victor 47-9960
3734	I Can't Hold On	Karla Bonoff	18-Mar-78	Columbia 10618
3735	One Tin Soldier (The Legend Of Billy Jack) [version 2]	Coven	18-Aug-73	MGM 14308
3736	I Thought It Took A Little Time (But Today I Fell In Love)	Diana Ross	10-Apr-76	Motown 1387

'70s Rank	TITLE	ACT	Peak Date	Label & No.
3737	Deep Enough For Me	Ocean	10-Jul-71	Kama Sutra 525
3738	Our Love Is Insane	Desmond Child And Rouge	31-Mar-79	Capitol 4669
3739	Hot Fun In The Summertime	David T. Walker	1-Jul-72	Ode 66025
3740	He Made A Woman Out Of Me	Bobbie Gentry	2-May-70	Capitol 2788
3741	Four Strong Winds	Neil Young	3-Mar-79	Reprise 1396
3742	Trouble In My Home	Joe Simon	23-Dec-72	Spring 130
3743	Sing	Tony Orlando And Dawn	16-Apr-77	Elektra 45387
3744	Good Morning Judge	10CC	24-Sep-77	Mercury 73943
3745	My Wife, The Dancer	Eddie & Dutch	9-May-70	Ivanhoe 502
3746	Lisa, Listen To Me	Blood, Sweat & Tears	13-Nov-71	Columbia 45477
3747	Down To The Nightclub	Tower Of Power	11-Nov-72	Warner Bros. 7635
3748	Stay Away From Me (I Love You Too Much)	Major Lance	12-Sep-70	Curtom 1953
3749	Free Spirit	Atlanta Rhythm Section	6-Nov-76	Polydor 14339
3750	Hold On	Wild Cherry	1-Oct-77	Sweet City/Epic 50401
3751	Way Back Home	The Jazz Crusaders	30-Jan-71	Chisa 8010
3752	Guess Who	Ruby Winters	24-Jan-70	Diamond 269
3753	Take Me To The Next Phase	The Isley Brothers	3-Jun-78	T-Neck 2272
3754	Star Love	Cheryl Lynn	26-May-79	Columbia 10907
3755	Walk Right In	Dr. Hook	23-Jul-77	Capitol 4423
3756	Put A Little Love Away	The Emotions	27-Apr-74	Volt 4106
3757	Red Eye Blues	Redeye	22-May-71	Pentagram 206
3758	My Part/Make It Funky (Part 3)	James Brown	27-Nov-71	Polydor 14098
3759	Arms Of Mary	Sutherland Brothers And Quiver	1-May-76	Columbia 10284
3760	One Chain (Don't Make No Prison)	Santana	12-May-79	Columbia 10938
3761	Who Loves You Better - Part 1	The Isley Brothers	19-Jun-76	T-Neck 2260
3762	Worse Comes To Worst	Billy Joel	27-Jul-74	Columbia 46055
3763	Ghost Dancer	The Addrisi Brothers	8-Sep-79	Scotti Brothers 500
3764	I Can't Get Next To You	Al Green	19-Dec-70	Hi 2182
3765	Baby, I Need Your Loving	O.C. Smith	10-Oct-70	Columbia 45206
3766	The Other Woman	Vicki Lawrence	25-Oct-75	Private Stk 45,036
3767	Slow Dancing	Funky Kings	1-Jan-77	Arista 0209
3768	Midnight Flower	Four Tops	28-Sep-74	Dunhill/ABC 15005
3769	Do Your Thing	James & Bobby Purify	11-Jan-75	Casablanca 812
3770	Do It In The Name Of Love	Ben E. King	28-Jun-75	Atlantic 3274
3771	It's Late	Queen	3-Jun-78	Elektra 45478
3772	(Everybody Wanna Get Rich) Rite Away	Dr. John	8-Jun-74	Atco 6957
3773	Dance Master Pt. 1	Willie Henderson	3-Aug-74	Playboy 50057
3774	Howzat	Sherbet	25-Sep-76	MCA 40610
3775	If I Only Knew	The Ozark Mountain Daredevils	14-Feb-76	A&M 1772
3776	Fox Hunt	Herb Alpert And The T.J.B.	29-Jun-74	A&M 1526
3777	We Did It	Syl Johnson	17-Mar-73	Hi 2229

'70s Rank	TITLE	ACT	Peak Date	Label & No.
3778	Lonely Feelin'	War	8-May-71	United Artists 50746
3779	Dancin'	Crown Heights Affair	7-May-77	De-Lite 1588
3780	Didn't It Look So Easy	The Stairsteps	6-Mar-71	Buddah 213
3781	Move 'Em Out	Delaney & Bonnie	19-Feb-72	Atco 6866
3782	Who Listens To The Radio	The Sports	10-Nov-79	Arista 0468
3783	Love Me	The Rascals	24-Jul-71	Columbia 45400
3784	Circus	Mike Quatro Jam Band	5-Aug-72	Evolution 1062
3785	Honey I	George McCrae	7-Feb-76	T.K. 1016
3786	An American Trilogy	Elvis Presley	27-May-72	RCA Victor 74-0672
3787	Warpath	The Isley Brothers	3-Apr-71	T-Neck 929
3788	My Love Is Music	Space	26-May-79	Casablanca 974
3789	Heartbreaker	Grand Funk Railroad	7-Mar-70	Capitol 2732
3790	Shackin' Up	Barbara Mason	24-May-75	Buddah 459
3791	Reason To Believe	Rod Stewart	4-Sep-71	Mercury 73224
3792	Yank Me, Crank Me	Ted Nugent	29-Apr-78	Epic 50533
3793	The Lone Ranger	Oscar Brown, Jr.	8-Jun-74	Atlantic 3001
3794	Gotta Find A Way	The Moments	27-Oct-73	Stang 5050
3795	Willpower Weak, Temptation Strong	Bullet	18-Mar-72	Big Tree 131
3796	Outlaw Man	David Blue	26-May-73	Asylum 11015
3797	But I Do	Bobby Vinton	10-Feb-73	Epic 10936
3798	The Player - Part 1	First Choice	19-Oct-74	Philly Groove 200
3799	This Is Love	Paul Anka	4-Nov-78	RCA 11395
3800	Bridge Over Troubled Water	Linda Clifford	14-Apr-79	RSO/Curtom 921
3801	When The Party Is Over	Robert John	19-Dec-70	A&M 1210
3802	Drop By My Place	Little Carl Carlton	1-Aug-70	Back Beat 613
3803	Don't Worry Baby	The Tokens	21-Mar-70	Buddah 159
3804	Jolene	Dolly Parton	12-Jan-74	RCA Victor 0145
3805	Midnight Sky (Part 1)	The Isley Brothers	1-Feb-75	T-Neck 2255
3806	That Magic Touch	Angel	28-May-77	Casablanca 878
3807	It's All Over	The Independents	15-Dec-73	Wand 11263
3808	Could It Be Magic	Donna Summer	29-May-76	Oasis 405
3809	You're The Only One	Dolly Parton	28-Jul-79	RCA 11577
3810	I Cheat The Hangman	The Doobie Brothers	24-Jan-76	Warner Bros. 8161
3811	What A Wonderful Thing We Have	The Fabulous Rhinestones	29-Jul-72	Just Sunshine 500
3812	Check It Out	Bobby Womack	24-May-75	United Artists 621
3813	Are You Old Enough	Mark Lindsay	23-Oct-71	Columbia 45462
3814	Girls Will Be Girls, Boys Will Be Boys	The Isley Brothers	15-Aug-70	T-Neck 921
3815	All The Way Down	Etta James	10-Nov-73	Chess 2144
3816	Thinking Of You	Paul Davis	29-May-76	Bang 724
3817	I'm Coming Home	Johnny Mathis	20-Oct-73	Columbia 45908
3818	You Better Think Twice	Poco	5-Dec-70	Epic 10636
3819	Love Like A Man	Ten Years After	30-May-70	Deram 7529

'70s Rank	TITLE	ACT	Peak Date	Label & No.
3820	Are You Sure Hank Done It This Way	Waylon Jennings	1-Nov-75	RCA Victor 10379
3821	Candy's Going Bad	Golden Earring	2-Nov-74	Track/MCA 40309
3822	If We Try	Don McLean	28-Apr-73	United Artists 206
3823	My Main Man	The Staple Singers	18-Jan-75	Stax 0227
3824	Help Wanted	Hudson Brothers	4-Dec-76	Arista 0208
3825	Teenage Love Affair	Rick Derringer	1-Jun-74	Blue Sky 2752
3826	Get Up And Get Down	The Dramatics	12-Feb-72	Volt 4071
3827	Scotch On The Rocks	The Band Of The Black Watch	13-Mar-76	Private Stk 45,055
3828	Holly Holy	Jr. Walker & The All Stars	16-Jan-71	Soul 35081
3829	The Declaration	The 5th Dimension	28-Feb-70	Bell 860
3830	My Merry-Go-Round	Johnny Nash	28-Jul-73	Epic 11003
3831	This Girl (Has Turned Into A Woman)	Mary MacGregor	11-Jun-77	Ariola America 7662
3832	To Get To You	Jerry Wallace	3-Jun-72	Decca 32914
3833	I Won't Last A Day Without You	Maureen McGovern	17-Nov-73	20th Century 2051
3834	Put Your Head On My Shoulder	Leif Garrett	18-Mar-78	Atlantic 3466
3835	Comin' Back To Me (Ooh Baby)	Smith	29-Aug-70	Dunhill 4246
3836	Iron Man	Black Sabbath	4-Mar-72	Warner Bros. 7530
3837	Scratch	The Crusaders	15-Jun-74	Blue Thumb 249
3838	Treat Me Like A Good Piece Of Candy	Dusk	18-Dec-71	Bell 45,148
3839	Sunset Strip	Ray Stevens	14-Nov-70	Barnaby 2021
3840	Back For A Taste Of Your Love	Syl Johnson	24-Nov-73	Hi 2250
3841	I Need You	The Friends Of Distinction	13-Feb-71	RCA Victor 74-0416
3842	Suspicious Minds	Dee Dee Warwick	24-Jul-71	Atco 6810
3843	Destiny	Jose Feliciano	11-Jul-70	RCA Victor 74-0358
3844	Friends	Feather	13-Jun-70	White Whale 353
3845	Under The Boardwalk	Billy Joe Royal	17-Jun-78	Private Stk 45,192
3846	Lonely Wind	Kansas	10-Feb-79	Kirshner 4280
3847	You Were Always There	Donna Fargo	28-Jul-73	Dot 17460
3848	Missing You	Luther Ingram	19-Feb-72	KoKo 2110
3849	Quiet Storm	Smokey Robinson	28-Feb-76	Tamla 54265
3850	Closer To The Heart	Rush	17-Dec-77	Mercury 73958
3851	You, Me And Mexico	Edward Bear	13-Jun-70	Capitol 2801
3852	Don't Think...Feel	Neil Diamond	23-Oct-76	Columbia 10405
3853	We Need Order	The Chi-Lites	6-Jan-73	Brunswick 55489
3854	You Don't Know What Love Is	Susan Jacks	19-May-73	London 182
3855	Blame It On The Boogie	Mick Jackson	9-Sep-78	Atco 7091
3856	Mornin' Mornin'	Bobby Goldsboro	7-Feb-70	United Artists 50614
3857	Soul Train "75"	Soul Train Gang	3-Jan-76	Soul Train 10400
3858	There Will Come A Day (I'm Gonna Happen To You)	Smokey Robinson	16-Apr-77	Tamla 54279
3859	Indian Summer	Audience	21-Aug-71	Elektra 45732
3860	Blue Sky	Joan Baez	9-Aug-75	A&M 1703

'70s Rank	TITLE	ACT	Peak Date	Label & No.
3861	Echoes Of Love	The Doobie Brothers	19-Nov-77	Warner Bros. 8471
3862	Love Me Tonight	Blackjack	11-Aug-79	Polydor 14572
3863	Best Thing That Ever Happened To Me	The Persuaders	9-Mar-74	Atco 6956
3864	So Long	Firefall	18-Feb-78	Atlantic 3452
3865	Let's Be Young Tonight	Jermaine Jackson	18-Dec-76	Motown 1401
3866	Baby--Get It On	Ike & Tina Turner	28-Jun-75	United Artists 598
3867	I'm Just A Prisoner (Of Your Good Lovin')	Candi Staton	14-Feb-70	Fame 1460
3868	You're The Best Thing That Ever Happened To Me	Ray Price	6-Oct-73	Columbia 45889
3869	Mother-In-Law	Clarence Carter	23-Jun-73	Fame 250
3870	One More Minute	Saint Tropez	26-May-79	Butterfly 41080
3871	Hey, You Love	Mouth & MacNeal	28-Oct-72	Philips 40717
3872	Paranoid	Black Sabbath	26-Dec-70	Warner Bros. 7437
3873	Miles Away	Fotomaker	16-Dec-78	Atlantic 3531
3874	Dear Prudence	The Five Stairsteps	18-Apr-70	Buddah 165
3875	Alvin Stone (The Birth & Death Of A Gangster)	Fantastic Four	30-Aug-75	Westbound 5009
3876	Runaway Love	Linda Clifford	22-Jul-78	Curtom 0138
3877	Here Is Where Your Love Belongs	Sons Of Champlin	26-Feb-77	Ariola America 7653
3878	Just Seventeen	Raiders	7-Mar-70	Columbia 45082
3879	Bold Soul Sister	Ike & Tina Turner	7-Feb-70	Blue Thumb 104
3880	Under My Wheels	Alice Cooper	29-Jan-72	Warner Bros. 7529
3881	Nevada Fighter	Michael Nesmith & The First National Band	8-May-71	RCA Victor 74-0453
3882	The Animal Trainer And The Toad	Mountain	1-May-71	Windfall 534
3883	Oh Woman Oh Why	Paul McCartney	13-Mar-71	Apple 1829
3884	Love Is Funny That Way	Jackie Wilson	18-Dec-71	Brunswick 55461
3885	Money Back Guarantee	Five Man Electrical Band	7-Oct-72	Lion 127
3886	For Emily, Whenever I May Find Her	Simon & Garfunkel	30-Sep-72	Columbia 45663
3887	Hot Dawgit	Ramsey Lewis And Earth, Wind & Fire	8-Feb-75	Columbia 10056
3888	Can't You See	The Marshall Tucker Band	24-Sep-77	Capricorn 0278
3889	Wasn't It Good	Cher	30-Jun-79	Casablanca 987
3890	Delta Queen	Don Fardon	28-Apr-73	Chelsea 0115
3891	Theme From Superman (Main Title)	John Williams/London Symphony Orchestra	3-Feb-79	Warner Bros. 8729
3892	Too Beautiful To Last	Engelbert Humperdinck	15-Apr-72	Parrot 40069
3893	You Got That Right	Lynyrd Skynyrd	29-Apr-78	MCA 40888
3894	I Can Make It Thru The Days (But Oh Those Lonely Nights)	Ray Charles	7-Jul-73	ABC/TRC 11351
3895	I Wish It Was Me	Tyrone Davis	30-Mar-74	Dakar 4529
3896	Leftovers	Millie Jackson	25-Oct-75	Spring 161
3897	Jukin	Atlanta Rhythm Section	26-Jun-76	Polydor 14323
3898	El Bimbo	Bimbo Jet	26-Jul-75	Scepter 12406

'70s Rank	TITLE	ACT	Peak Date	Label & No.
3899	Carolina In My Mind	James Taylor	12-Dec-70	Apple 1805
3900	You Got To Keep On Bumpin'	The Kay-Gees	21-Sep-74	Gang 1321
3901	I've Never Found A Man (To Love Me Like You Do)	Esther Phillips	27-Jan-73	Kudu 910
3902	Give Me An Inch	Ian Matthews	21-Apr-79	Mushroom 7040
3903	Mama Don't Allow No Parkin'	Brownsville Station	11-Jan-75	Big Tree 16029
3904	Oh Me Oh My (I'm A Fool For You Baby)	Aretha Franklin	29-Jan-72	Atlantic 2838
3905	Another Puff	Jerry Reed	5-Feb-72	RCA Victor 74-0613
3906	Sparkle And Shine	The Clique	7-Mar-70	White Whale 338
3907	People In Love	10cc	25-Jun-77	Mercury 73917
3908	White Lies	Grin	11-Mar-72	Spindizzy 4005
3909	The Doodle Song	Frankie Miller	16-Jul-77	Chrysalis 2145
3910	Cheryl Moana Marie	John Rowles	30-Jan-71	Kapp 2102
3911	Sixteen Reasons	Laverne & Shirley	18-Dec-76	Atlantic 3367
3912	Hello Darlin'	Conway Twitty	25-Jul-70	Decca 32661
3913	Only The Lucky	Walter Egan	9-Jul-77	Columbia 10531
3914	Carolyn	Merle Haggard	1-Jan-72	Capitol 3222
3915	Shambala	B.W. Stevenson	23-Jun-73	RCA Victor 74-0952
3916	Can't Keep A Good Man Down	Eddie Money	2-Jun-79	Columbia 10981
3917	Ready For The '80s	Village People	8-Dec-79	Casablanca 2220
3918	It's Your Life	Andy Kim	22-Aug-70	Steed 727
3919	Apartment 21	Bobbie Gentry	18-Jul-70	Capitol 2849
3920	Love Is Life	Earth, Wind & Fire	31-Jul-71	Warner Bros. 7492
3921	You Won't Find Another Fool Like Me	The New Seekers	23-Feb-74	MGM 14691
3922	Long Live Rock	The Who	28-Jul-79	MCA 41053
3923	Smoke! Smoke! Smoke! (That Cigarette)	Commander Cody And His Lost Planet Airmen	21-Jul-73	Paramount 0216
3924	Where Is The Love	Betty Wright	3-May-75	Alston 3713
3925	Santa Claus Is Comin' To Town	The Jackson 5	26-Dec-70	Motown 1174
3926	July 12, 1939	Charlie Rich	11-Apr-70	Epic 10585
3927	(Sittin' On) The Dock Of The Bay	Sammy Hagar	28-Apr-79	Capitol 4699
3928	Kick It Out	Heart	3-Dec-77	Portrait 70010
3929	Take Good Care Of Her	Elvis Presley	16-Feb-74	RCA Victor 0196
3930	Freedom	Jimi Hendrix	17-Apr-71	Reprise 1000
3931	We'll Have It Made	The Spinners	6-Feb-71	V.I.P. 25060
3932	Indian Lady	Lou Christie	31-Oct-70	Buddah 192
3933	Somebody's Gettin' It	Johnnie Taylor	10-Jul-76	Columbia 10334
3934	The Fez	Steely Dan	13-Nov-76	ABC 12222
3935	I Don't Need No Doctor	Humble Pie	30-Oct-71	A&M 1282
3936	Free As The Wind	Brooklyn Bridge	21-Mar-70	Buddah 162
3937	If I Only Could	The Rowans	20-Nov-76	Elektra 45237
3938	You Keep Tightening Up On Me	The Box Tops	4-Apr-70	Bell 865
3939	If Only I Had My Mind On Something Else	Bee Gees	4-Apr-70	Atco 6741

'70s Rank	TITLE	ACT	Peak Date	Label & No.
3940	Will You Still Love Me Tomorrow	Roberta Flack	5-Feb-72	Atlantic 2851
3941	Watch Closely Now	Kris Kristofferson	18-Jun-77	Columbia 10525
3942	That's Why I Love You	Andrew Gold	31-Jan-76	Asylum 45286
3943	If It Don't Fit, Don't Force It	Kellee Patterson	4-Feb-78	Shady Brook 1041
3944	So Young, So Bad	Starz	11-Nov-78	Capitol 4637
3945	Queen Of Clubs	K.C. & The Sunshine Band	3-Apr-76	T.K. 1005
3946	Got To Have Your Lovin'	King Floyd	7-Aug-71	Chimneyville 439
3947	In A Broken Dream	Python Lee Jackson	22-Jul-72	GNP Crescendo 449
3948	The Look Of Love	Isaac Hayes	6-Mar-71	Enterprise 9028
3949	That's What Love Will Make You Do	Little Milton	11-Mar-72	Stax 0111
3950	Keep On Running	Stevie Wonder	30-Sep-72	Tamla 54223
3951	Those Were The Days	Carroll O'Connor And Jean Stapleton	8-Jan-72	Atlantic 2847
3952	Ajax Airlines	Hudson And Landry	29-Jan-72	Dore 868
3953	My Baby's Baby	Liquid Gold	2-Jun-79	Parachute 524
3954	Ophelia	The Band	10-Apr-76	Capitol 4230
3955	Think His Name	Johnny Rivers	2-Oct-71	United Artists 50822
3956	Let Me Down Easy	Cornelius Brothers & Sister Rose	19-May-73	United Artists 208
3957	Live Your Life Before You Die	Pointer Sisters	29-Mar-75	ABC/Blue Thumb 262
3958	Shady Lady	Shepstone & Dibbens	20-Oct-73	Buddah 379
3959	Standing In For Jody	Johnnie Taylor	19-Feb-72	Stax 0114
3960	Flyin' High	The Blackbyrds	30-Aug-75	Fantasy 747
3961	Meadows	Joe Walsh	2-Feb-74	Dunhill 4373
3962	A Lonely Man	The Chi-Lites	21-Oct-72	Brunswick 55483
3963	Hooked On You	Bread	21-May-77	Elektra 45389
3964	Five Hundred Miles	Heaven Bound	25-Dec-71	MGM 14314
3965	Can't Change My Heart	Cate Brothers	21-Aug-76	Asylum 45326
3966	Step Into Christmas	Elton John	29-Dec-73	MCA 65018
3967	It's A Small Small World	The Mike Curb Congregation	6-Oct-73	MGM 14494
3968	Flim Flam Man	Barbra Streisand	29-May-71	Columbia 45384
3969	Holy Man	Diane Kolby	10-Oct-70	Columbia 45169
3970	Slipping Into Darkness	Ramsey Lewis	26-Aug-72	Columbia 45634
3971	Gimme Shelter	Merry Clayton	11-Jul-70	Ode '70 66003
3972	Crazy Feelin'	Jefferson Starship	21-Oct-78	Grunt 11374
3973	Where Are You Going	Jerry Butler	29-Aug-70	Mercury 73101
3974	You Make Me Crazy	Sammy Hagar	21-Jan-78	Capitol 4502
3975	I'll Play The Blues For You	Albert King	12-Aug-72	Stax 0135
3976	I'm Sorry	Joey Heatherton	30-Dec-72	MGM 14434
3977	Hot Pants - I'm Coming, Coming, I'm Coming	Bobby Byrd	16-Oct-71	BrownStone 4203
3978	Take Life A Little Easier	Rodney Allen Rippy	3-Nov-73	Bell 45,403

'70s Rank	TITLE	ACT	Peak Date	Label & No.
3979	Brandy	The O'Jays	26-Aug-78	Phila. Int'l 3652
3980	Champagne Jam	Atlanta Rhythm Section	21-Oct-78	Polydor 14504
3981	Men Are Getting Scarce	Chairmen Of The Board	11-Dec-71	Invictus 9103
3982	On And Off (Part 1)	Anacostia	20-Jan-73	Columbia 45685
3983	Inside My Love	Minnie Riperton	23-Aug-75	Epic 50128
3984	Superman	Celi Bee & The Buzzy Bunch	23-Jul-77	APA 17001
3985	Dancing To Your Music	Archie Bell & The Drells	21-Apr-73	Glades 1707
3986	Turning Point	Tyrone Davis	7-Feb-76	Dakar 4550
3987	Don't Touch Me There	The Tubes	24-Jul-76	A&M 1826
3988	I Just Can't Control Myself	Nature's Divine	8-Dec-79	Infinity 50,027
3989	Mammy Blue	James Darren	13-Nov-71	Kirshner 5015
3990	Stillsane	Carolyne Mas	6-Oct-79	Mercury 76004
3991	So High (Rock Me Baby And Roll Me Away)	Dave Mason	18-Jun-77	Columbia 10509
3992	Detroit Rock City	Kiss	28-Aug-76	Casablanca 863
3993	Bustin' Out	Rick James	16-Jun-79	Gordy 7167
3994	Woodstock	The Assembled Multitude	17-Oct-70	Atlantic 2764
3995	Black Seeds Keep On Growing	The Main Ingredient	2-Oct-71	RCA Victor 74-0517
3996	Black Hands White Cotton	The Caboose	15-Aug-70	Enterprise 9015
3997	Reaching For The World	Harold Melvin And The Blue Notes	2-Apr-77	ABC 12240
3998	I'm Her Fool	Billy Swan	5-Apr-75	Monument 8641
3999	Lucifer	The Bob Seger System	16-May-70	Capitol 2748
4000	Let Me Start Tonite	Lamont Dozier	1-Feb-75	ABC 12044
4001	Number Wonderful	Rock Flowers	12-Feb-72	Wheel 0032
4002	Ridin' My Thumb To Mexico	Johnny Rodriguez	10-Nov-73	Mercury 73416
4003	Desdemona	The Searchers	11-Sep-71	RCA Victor 74-0484
4004	We're Together	The Hillside Singers	4-Mar-72	Metromedia 241
4005	Ten To Eight	David Castle	12-Nov-77	Parachute 501
4006	Make Me Happy	Bobby Bloom	13-Feb-71	MGM 14212
4007	Reality	James Brown	22-Mar-75	Polydor 14268
4008	On The Strip	Paul Nicholas	19-Aug-78	RSO 887
4009	Dedication	Bay City Rollers	12-Mar-77	Arista 0233
4010	Lay Lady Lay	Ferrante & Teicher	14-Mar-70	United Artists 50646
4011	Roll In My Sweet Baby's Arms	Hank Wilson	27-Oct-73	Shelter 7336
4012	Wild World	The Gentrys	13-Mar-71	Sun 1122
4013	Saw A New Morning	Bee Gees	7-Apr-73	RSO 401
4014	Dancin' Kid	Disco Tex & The Sex-O-Lettes	7-Aug-76	Chelsea 3045
4015	The Football Card	Glenn Sutton	27-Jan-79	Mercury 55052
4016	This Old Heart Of Mine	Rod Stewart	31-Jan-76	Warner Bros. 8170
4017	We Got To Live Together - Part I	Buddy Miles	16-Jan-71	Mercury 73159
4018	The Jam	Graham Central Station	6-Mar-76	Warner Bros. 8175
4019	Help Yourself	The Undisputed Truth	1-Jun-74	Gordy 7134

'70s Rank	TITLE	ACT	Peak Date	Label & No.
4020	Your Own Back Yard	Dion	18-Jul-70	Warner Bros. 7401
4021	That Once In A Lifetime	Demis Roussos	15-Jul-78	Mercury 73992
4022	Jealousy	Major Harris	8-May-76	Atlantic 3321
4023	Once You Hit The Road	Dionne Warwick	7-Feb-76	Warner Bros. 8154
4024	Brand New Me	Aretha Franklin	26-Jun-71	Atlantic 2796
4025	Number One	Billy Swan	19-Jun-76	Monument 8697
4026	Rockin' And Rollin' On The Streets Of Hollywood	Buddy Miles	27-Sep-75	Casablanca 839
4027	Locomotive Breath	Jethro Tull	27-Mar-76	Chrysalis 2110
4028	Listen To The Buddha	Ozo	28-Aug-76	DJM 1012
4029	Minnesota	Northern Light	7-Jun-75	Columbia 10136
4030	Lay It On The Line	Triumph	15-Dec-79	RCA 11690
4031	Your Love Is So Good For Me	Diana Ross	15-Apr-78	Motown 1436
4032	Everything's Coming Up Love	David Ruffin	31-Jul-76	Motown 1393
4033	Make Me Feel Like A Woman	Jackie Moore	13-Sep-75	Kayvette 5122
4034	Baby Won't You Let Me Rock 'N Roll You	Ten Years After	12-Feb-72	Columbia 45530
4035	Bringing It Back	Elvis Presley	29-Nov-75	RCA Victor 10401
4036	One Man's Leftovers (Is Another Man's Feast)	100 Proof Aged In Soul	13-Mar-71	Hot Wax 7009
4037	My Best Friend's Wife	Paul Anka	7-May-77	United Artists 972
4038	Love And Happiness	Earnest Jackson	16-Jun-73	Stone 200
4039	Roadhouse Blues	The Doors	16-May-70	Elektra 45685
4040	Touch The Hand	Conway Twitty	12-Jul-75	MCA 40407
4041	Come Live With Me	Roy Clark	16-Jun-73	Dot 17449
4042	Angeleyes	Abba	13-Oct-79	Atlantic 3609
4043	This Is My Love Song	The Intruders	31-Oct-70	Gamble 4007
4044	I Feel Sanctified	Commodores	14-Dec-74	Motown 1319
4045	Runnin' Back To Saskatoon	The Guess Who	28-Oct-72	RCA Victor 74-0803
4046	Just A Smile	Pilot	8-Nov-75	EMI 4135
4047	He'd Rather Have The Rain	Heaven Bound	2-Oct-71	MGM 14284
4048	I'll Always Call Your Name	Little River Band	19-Mar-77	Harvest 4380
4049	Make Me Twice The Man	New York City	22-Sep-73	Chelsea 0025
4050	Action Speaks Louder Than Words	Chocolate Milk	9-Aug-75	RCA Victor 10290
4051	Because I Love You//America/Standing	The Five Stairsteps	24-Oct-70	Buddah 188
4052	Talk It Over In The Morning	Anne Murray	9-Oct-71	Capitol 3159
4053	Colorado Call	Shad O'Shea & The 18 Wheelers	27-Mar-76	Private Stk 45,071
4054	Quick, Fast, In A Hurry	New York City	9-Mar-74	Chelsea 0150
4055	Hey There Little Firefly Part I	Firefly	20-Dec-75	A&M 1736
4056	Fire Sign	Cory	12-Mar-77	Phantom 10856
4057	Sixty Minute Man	Rufus Thomas	18-Jul-70	Stax 0071
4058	On The Wrong Track	Kevin Lamb	8-Jul-78	Arista 0316
4059	Rock And Roll Star	Champagne	2-Apr-77	Ariola America 7658

'70s Rank	TITLE	ACT	Peak Date	Label & No.
4060	Good Friends?	The Poppy Family	4-Mar-72	London 172
4061	Frisky	Sly & The Family Stone	15-Dec-73	Epic 11060
4062	Brooklyn	Cody Jameson	16-Apr-77	Atco 7073
4063	Every Face Tells A Story	Olivia Newton-John	11-Dec-76	MCA 40642
4064	If You Wanna Do A Dance	The Spinners	26-Aug-78	Atlantic 3493
4065	Nice, Nice, Very Nice	Ambrosia	6-Dec-75	20th Century 2244
4066	Life Is A Carnival	The Band	13-Nov-71	Capitol 3199
4067	Silver Lining	Player	27-Jan-79	RSO 914
4068	Don't Ask My Neighbors	The Emotions	24-Dec-77	Columbia 10622
4069	All I Have	The Moments	19-Dec-70	Stang 5017
4070	Who Do You Love	George Thorogood And The Destroyers	21-Apr-79	Rounder 4519
4071	I Say A Little Prayer/By The Time I Get To Phoenix	Glen Campbell/Anne Murray	13-Nov-71	Capitol 3200
4072	Save Me	Merrilee Rush	2-Jul-77	United Artists 993
4073	Teen Angel	Wednesday	8-Jun-74	Sussex 515
4074	Between Her Goodbye And My Hello	Gladys Knight & The Pips	10-Aug-74	Soul 35111
4075	There You Go	Edwin Starr	4-Aug-73	Soul 35103
4076	Listen To Her Heart	Tom Petty And The Heartbreakers	14-Oct-78	Shelter 62011
4077	Philadelphia	B.B. King	18-Jan-75	ABC 12029
4078	Baby I Love You	Little Milton	23-May-70	Checker 1227
4079	Half A Million Miles From Home	Albert Hammond	22-Dec-73	Mums 6024
4080	Mister Magic	Grover Washington, Jr.	31-May-75	Kudu 924
4081	How Glad I Am	Kiki Dee	21-Jun-75	Rocket/MCA 40401
4082	Angel (What In The World's Come Over Us)	Atlanta Rhythm Section	22-Mar-75	Polydor 14262
4083	Starry Eyes	The Records	20-Oct-79	Virgin 67000
4084	Comin' Home	Delaney & Bonnie And Friends Featuring Eric Clapton	7-Mar-70	Atco 6725
4085	I'm Yours (Use Me Anyway You Wanna)	Ike & Tina Turner	4-Dec-71	United Artists 50837
4086	Going Through The Motions	Hot Chocolate	11-Aug-79	Infinity 50,016
4087	Gone Long Gone	Chicago	5-May-79	Columbia 10935
4088	It's In His Kiss (The Shoop Shoop Song)	Kate Taylor	1-Oct-77	Columbia 10596
4089	Homely Girl	The Chi-Lites	23-Mar-74	Brunswick 55505
4090	Jesahel	The English Congregation	29-Jul-72	Signpost 70004
4091	Something	Shirley Bassey	14-Nov-70	United Artists 50698
4092	Traveling Boy	Garfunkel	20-Apr-74	Columbia 46030
4093	Good Morning	Michael Redway	17-Feb-73	Philips 40720
4094	In For The Night	Dirt Band	23-Sep-78	United Artists 1228
4095	Darlin' Darlin' Baby (Sweet, Tender, Love)	The O'Jays	29-Jan-77	Phila. Int'l 3610
4096	Wolf Creek Pass	C.W. McCall	8-Mar-75	MGM 14764
4097	Alabama Wild Man	Jerry Reed	26-Aug-72	RCA Victor 74-0738
4098	Feel That You're Feelin'	Maze	7-Jul-79	Capitol 4686

'70s Rank	TITLE	ACT	Peak Date	Label & No.
4099	One Last Time	Glen Campbell	3-Feb-73	Capitol 3483
4100	I'm Your Man Rock 'N' Roll	The Tarney/Spencer Band	21-Aug-76	Private Stk 45,108
4101	Sinner Man	Sarah Dash	3-Mar-79	Kirshner 4278
4102	Love Me Again	Rita Coolidge	25-Nov-78	A&M 2090
4103	Somethin' 'Bout You Baby I Like	Trini Lopez	19-Jul-75	Private Stk 45,024
4104	If I Could See The Light	The 8th Day	22-Jan-72	Invictus 9107
4105	Pass The Peas	The J.B.'s	10-Jun-72	People 607
4106	In My Father's Footsteps	Terry Jacks	24-Jul-76	Private Stk 45,094
4107	Sing High--Sing Low	Anne Murray	2-Jan-71	Capitol 2988
4108	When The Morning Comes	Hoyt Axton	20-Jul-74	A&M 1497
4109	I'm A Ramblin' Man	Waylon Jennings	12-Oct-74	RCA Victor 10020
4110	You Says It All	Randy Brown	28-Apr-79	Parachute 523
4111	Lonesome Mary	Chilliwack	19-Feb-72	A&M 1310
4112	Mama Liked The Roses	Elvis Presley	16-May-70	RCA Victor 47-9835
4113	The Loneliest Man On The Moon	David Castle	28-Jan-78	Parachute 505
4114	Broken	The Guess Who	24-Apr-71	RCA Victor 74-0458
4115	Turn Back The Pages	Stephen Stills	23-Aug-75	Columbia 10179
4116	Funny How Time Slips Away	Dorothy Moore	11-Sep-76	Malaco 1033
4117	Livingston Saturday Night	Jimmy Buffett	9-Sep-78	ABC 12391
4118	Open The Door (Song For Judith)	Judy Collins	29-Jan-72	Elektra 45755
4119	If We Only Have Love	Dionne Warwicke	18-Mar-72	Warner Bros. 7560
4120	The Girl Who Loved Me When	The Glass Bottle	11-Dec-71	Avco 4584
4121	A Lover's Question	Jacky Ward	22-Apr-78	Mercury 55018
4122	King Kong - Pt. 1	The Jimmy Castor Bunch	8-Nov-75	Atlantic 3295
4123	Colorado	Danny Holien	21-Oct-72	Tumbleweed 1004
4124	After The Feeling Is Gone	Five Flights Up	9-Jan-71	T-A 207
4125	The Game Is Over (What's The Matter With You)	Brown Sugar	13-Mar-76	Capitol 4198
4126	Please, Mr. President	Paula Webb	22-Feb-75	20th Century/ Westbound 5001
4127	Jackie Wilson Said (I'm In Heaven When You Smile)	Van Morrison	9-Sep-72	Warner Bros. 7616
4128	Home Is Where The Hatred Is	Esther Phillips	13-May-72	Kudu 904
4129	Time To Get It Together	Country Coalition	28-Mar-70	BluesWay 61034
4130	Some Day I'll Be A Farmer	Melanie	3-Jun-72	Neighborhood 4204
4131	What You See Is What You Get	Stoney And Meatloaf	5-Jun-71	Rare Earth 5027
4132	Six White Horses	Tommy Cash	17-Jan-70	Epic 10540
4133	Glory, Glory	The Byrds	25-Sep-71	Columbia 45440
4134	Almost Saturday Night	John Fogerty	10-Jan-76	Asylum 45291
4135	Save The Country	Thelma Houston	14-Feb-70	Dunhill 4222
4136	I Can't Believe That You've Stopped Loving Me	Charley Pride	5-Dec-70	RCA Victor 47-9902
4137	Palace Guard	Rick Nelson And The Stone Canyon Band	24-Feb-73	MCA 40001

'70s Rank	TITLE	ACT	Peak Date	Label & No.
4138	Think It Over	The Delfonics	10-Feb-73	Philly Groove 174
4139	Good Thing Man	Frank Lucas	18-Jun-77	ICA 001
4140	99 Miles From L.A.	Albert Hammond	31-May-75	Mums 6037
4141	Upsetter	Grand Funk Railroad	13-May-72	Capitol 3316
4142	Totally Hot	Olivia Newton-John	18-Aug-79	MCA 41074
4143	Just As Long As You Need Me, Part I	Independents	3-Jun-72	Wand 11245
4144	Belle	Al Green	21-Jan-78	Hi 77505
4145	Long And Lonesome Road	The Shocking Blue	27-Jun-70	Colossus 116
4146	Weekend Lover	Odyssey	10-Jun-78	RCA 11245
4147	I'll Come Running	Livingston Taylor	21-Apr-79	Epic 50667
4148	Groovin' (Out On Life)	The Newbeats	17-Jan-70	Hickory 1552
4149	Didn't I	Sylvia	11-Aug-73	Vibration 524
4150	Slip Away	Ian Lloyd	17-Nov-79	Scotti Brothers 505
4151	Best Beat In Town	Switch	1-Sep-79	Gordy 7168
4152	Are You Getting Any Sunshine?	Lou Christie	10-Jan-70	Buddah 149
4153	Arrested For Driving While Blind	ZZ Top	2-Apr-77	London 251
4154	Buzzy Brown	Tim Davis	30-Sep-72	Metromedia 253
4155	Baby, I'm Yours	Jody Miller	9-Oct-71	Epic 10785
4156	Stay Awhile	Continental Miniatures	27-May-78	London 266
4157	Too Late	Shoes	24-Nov-79	Elektra 46557
4158	For You And I	10cc	10-Feb-79	Polydor 14528
4159	While I'm Alone	Maze	2-Jul-77	Capitol 4392
4160	Free Man	South Shore Commission	9-Aug-75	Wand 11287
4161	Cotton Candy	The Sylvers	7-Aug-76	Capitol 4255
4162	Blue Guitar	Justin Hayward And John Lodge	3-Jan-76	Threshold 67021
4163	Jerusalem	Herb Alpert & The Tijuana Brass	31-Oct-70	A&M 1225
4164	I'm The Only One	Lobo	26-Jun-71	Big Tree 116
4165	Goin' Down Slow	Bobby Blue Bland	20-Apr-74	Dunhill 4379
4166	All My Trials	Ray Stevens	11-Sep-71	Barnaby 2039
4167	Hello, Hello, Hello	New England	29-Sep-79	Infinity 50,021
4168	I Love My Music	Wild Cherry	8-Apr-78	Sweet City/Epic 50500
4169	Love Is A Rose	Linda Ronstadt	20-Sep-75	Asylum 45282
4170	Down The Hall	The Four Seasons	20-Aug-77	Warner/Curb 8407
4171	Handbags And Gladrags	Chase	25-Sep-71	Epic 10775
4172	Let's Groove	Archie Bell & The Drells	10-Apr-76	TSOP 4775
4173	Wedding Song (There Is Love)	Petula Clark	4-Nov-72	MGM 14431
4174	Carry Me, Carrie	Dr. Hook And The Medicine Show	7-Oct-72	Columbia 45667
4175	Long Promised Road	The Beach Boys	27-Nov-71	Brother/Reprise 1047
4176	I Who Have Nothing	Liquid Smoke	9-May-70	Avco Embassy 4522

'70s Rank	TITLE	ACT	Peak Date	Label & No.
4177	I Want To (Do Everything For You)	The Raeletts	6-Jun-70	Tangerine 1006
4178	You Keep Me Holding On	Tyrone Davis	18-Dec-71	Dakar 626
4179	What Would The Children Think	Rick Springfield	16-Dec-72	Capitol 3466
4180	Make It Last	Brooklyn Dreams	24-Mar-79	Casablanca 962
4181	Air Disaster	Albert Hammond	27-Jul-74	Mums 6030
4182	I Want To Dance With You (Dance With Me)	The Ritchie Family	17-Jan-76	20th Century 2252
4183	Sure Feels Good	Elvin Bishop	2-Aug-75	Capricorn 0237
4184	Up Your Nose	Gabriel Kaplan	29-Jan-77	Elektra 45369
4185	What'd I Say	Rare Earth	29-Apr-72	Rare Earth 5043
4186	You Got To Be The One	The Chi-Lites	28-Sep-74	Brunswick 55514
4187	Let's Make A Baby	Billy Paul	10-Apr-76	Phila. Int'l 3584
4188	Celebration	Tommy James	11-Nov-72	Roulette 7135
4189	You Just Can't Win (By Making The Same Mistake)	Gene & Jerry	16-Jan-71	Mercury 73163
4190	What's Happened To Blue Eyes	Jessi Colter	8-Nov-75	Capitol 4087
4191	She's Got To Be A Saint	Ray Price	10-Feb-73	Columbia 45724
4192	Could You Put Your Light On, Please	Harry Chapin	19-Aug-72	Elektra 45792
4193	Night Dancin'	Taka Boom	19-May-79	Ariola America 7748
4194	You Think You're Hot Stuff	Jean Knight	30-Oct-71	Stax 0105
4195	Better Place To Be (Parts 1 & 2)	Harry Chapin	26-Jun-76	Elektra 45327
4196	Wrap Your Arms Around Me	KC & The Sunshine Band	24-Dec-77	T.K. 1022
4197	Over The Rainbow	Gary Tanner	17-Jun-78	20th Century 2373
4198	Music, Harmony And Rhythm	Brooklyn Dreams	22-Apr-78	Millennium 610
4199	Georgia Rhythm	Atlanta Rhythm Section	19-Nov-77	Polydor 14432
4200	Dedicated To The One I Love	The Temprees	16-Sep-72	We Produce 1808
4201	Hymn 43	Jethro Tull	7-Aug-71	Reprise 1024
4202	Light My Fire/137 Disco Heaven	Amii Stewart	14-Jul-79	Ariola/Hansa 7753
4203	Love Makes The World Go Round	Odds & Ends	3-Apr-71	Today 1003
4204	Francene	ZZ Top	17-Jun-72	London 179
4205	I Found Sunshine	The Chi-Lites	22-Dec-73	Brunswick 55503
4206	Christmas For Cowboys	John Denver	27-Dec-75	RCA Victor 10464
4207	Love's Street And Fool's Road	Solomon Burke	6-May-72	MGM 14353
4208	Down To The Station	B.W. Stevenson	7-May-77	Warner Bros. 8343
4209	Since I Fell For You	Charlie Rich	14-Feb-76	Epic 50182
4210	Walking On Back	Edward Bear	8-Sep-73	Capitol 3683
4211	You Can't Dance	England Dan & John Ford Coley	24-Jun-78	Big Tree 16117
4212	For You Blue	The Beatles	23-May-70	Apple 2832
4213	Theme from Charlie's Angels	Henry Mancini And His Orchestra	23-Apr-77	RCA 10888
4214	Head First	The Babys	16-Jun-79	Chrysalis 2323
4215	Amazing Grace (Used To Be Her Favorite Song)	The Amazing Rhythm Aces	31-Jan-76	ABC 12142

'70s Rank	TITLE	ACT	Peak Date	Label & No.
4216	Good Morning Freedom	Daybreak	11-Jul-70	Uni 55234
4217	Church	Bob Welch	16-Jun-79	Capitol 4719
4218	It's Hard To Stop (Doing Something When It's Good To You)	Betty Wright	14-Apr-73	Alston 4617
4219	Ticket To Ride	Carpenters	7-Mar-70	A&M 1142
4220	Nursery Rhymes (Part I)	People's Choice	6-Mar-76	TSOP 4773
4221	Safe At Home	The Souther, Hillman, Furay Band	11-Jan-75	Asylum 45217
4222	Loving Power	The Impressions	14-Feb-76	Curtom 0110
4223	Top Of The World	Lynn Anderson	21-Jul-73	Columbia 45857
4224	Dig The Way I Feel	Mary Wells	7-Feb-70	Jubilee 5684
4225	Skating Away On The Thin Ice Of The New Day	Jethro Tull	22-Mar-75	Chrysalis 2103
4226	One Life To Live	The Manhattans	11-Nov-72	DeLuxe 139
4227	The Peacemaker	Albert Hammond	8-Sep-73	Mums 6021
4228	Kissin' Time	Kiss	22-Jun-74	Casablanca 0011
4229	Hey, St. Peter	Flash & The Pan	11-Aug-79	Epic 50715
4230	Sally	Grand Funk Railroad	10-Apr-76	Capitol 4235
4231	When I Fall In Love	Donny Osmond	15-Dec-73	MGM 14677
4232	Hushabye	Robert John	24-Jun-72	Atlantic 2884
4233	Satisfaction Guaranteed (Or Take Your Love Back)	Harold Melvin And The Blue Notes	27-Apr-74	Phila. Int'l 3543
4234	When You Get Right Down To It	Ronnie Dyson	24-Jul-71	Columbia 45387
4235	Suzie Girl	Redbone	21-Sep-74	Epic 50015
4236	I'll Know Her When I See Her	Cooper Brothers Band	7-Jul-79	Capricorn 0325
4237	Mississippi Mama	Owen B.	14-Mar-70	Janus 107
4238	Make Up Your Mind	The J. Geils Band	25-Aug-73	Atlantic 2974
4239	BLT	Lee Oskar	24-Jul-76	United Artists 807
4240	Everybody's Had The Blues	Merle Haggard	6-Oct-73	Capitol 3641
4241	Lookin' Out For #1	Bachman-Turner Overdrive	22-May-76	Mercury 73784
4242	Up In Heah	Ike & Tina Turner	11-Mar-72	United Artists 50881
4243	I've Got To Have You	Sammi Smith	7-Oct-72	Mega 0079
4244	Be My Lady	The Meters	22-Oct-77	Warner Bros. 8434
4245	Valentine Love	Norman Connors	20-Dec-75	Buddah 499
4246	Hurry Sundown	Outlaws	20-Aug-77	Arista 0258
4247	Out Of The Darkness	David Crosby / Graham Nash	21-Aug-76	ABC 12199
4248	You Are A Song	Batdorf & Rodney	13-Sep-75	Arista 0132
4249	Dis-Gorilla (Part 1)	Rick Dees & His Cast Of Idiots	19-Feb-77	RSO 866
4250	Rolling Down A Mountainside	The Main Ingredient	21-Jun-75	RCA Victor 10224
4251	Seven Lonely Nights	Four Tops	28-Jun-75	ABC 12096
4252	(I've Been Lookin' For) A New Way To Say I Love You	Driver	17-Sep-77	A&M 1966
4253	Hold Back The Night	Graham Parker And The Rumour	28-May-77	Mercury 74000

'70s Rank	TITLE	ACT	Peak Date	Label & No.
4254	Caledonia	Robin Trower	8-Jan-77	Chrysalis 2122
4255	Percolator	Hot Butter	19-May-73	Musicor 1473
4256	Freedom Comes, Freedom Goes	The Fortunes	16-Oct-71	Capitol 3179
4257	Never Get Enough Of Your Love	L.T.D.	15-Apr-78	A&M 2005
4258	Stop, Wait And Listen	Circus	17-Feb-73	Metromedia 265
4259	Can't Stop Groovin' Now, Wanna Do It Some More	B.T. Express	26-Jun-76	Columbia 10346
4260	Down In The Alley	Ronnie Hawkins	21-Feb-70	Cotillion 44060
4261	Down On Me	Janis Joplin	29-Jul-72	Columbia 45630
4262	Boogie Woogie Man	Paul Davis	3-Feb-73	Bang 599
4263	Beautiful Girls	Van Halen	15-Sep-79	Warner Bros. 49035
4264	Battle Of New Orleans	Nitty Gritty Dirt Band	2-Nov-74	United Artists 544
4265	Give It To Me	The Mob	10-Apr-71	Colossus 134
4266	Us And Them	Pink Floyd	9-Mar-74	Harvest 3832
4267	Just Another Night	Ian Hunter	8-Sep-79	Chrysalis 2352
4268	Honey Don't Leave L.A.	James Taylor	18-Mar-78	Columbia 10689
4269	Kings And Queens	Aerosmith	15-Apr-78	Columbia 10699
4270	Do It, Fluid	The Blackbyrds	12-Oct-74	Fantasy 729
4271	I Wanna Know Your Name	The Intruders	15-Dec-73	Gamble 2508
4272	Sunday Morning Sunshine	Harry Chapin	25-Nov-72	Elektra 45811
4273	Gee Baby	Peter Shelley	4-Jan-75	Bell 45,614
4274	You Can Call Me Rover	The Main Ingredient	9-Jun-73	RCA Victor 74-0939
4275	Breakaway	Millie Jackson	5-May-73	Spring 134
4276	Dancin' (On A Saturday Night)	Flash Cadillac & The Continental Kids	29-Jun-74	Epic 11102
4277	Together We Can Make Such Sweet Music	The Spinners	19-May-73	Motown 1235
4278	I Think I Love You Again	Brenda Lee	13-Jun-70	Decca 32675
4279	What's Your Name	Andy & David Williams	20-Jul-74	Barnaby 601
4280	The Happy Girls	Helen Reddy	5-Nov-77	Capitol 4487
4281	Ain't Wastin' Time No More	The Allman Brothers Band	13-May-72	Capricorn 0003
4282	Many Rivers To Cross	Nilsson	17-Aug-74	RCA Victor 10001
4283	Catfish	Four Tops	27-Nov-76	ABC 12214
4284	Doctor Love	First Choice	15-Oct-77	Gold Mind 4004
4285	One Fine Day	Rita Coolidge	29-Sep-79	A&M 2169
4286	Back To The River	Damnation Of Adam Blessing	2-Jan-71	United Artists 50726
4287	The Blind Man In The Bleachers	Kenny Starr	3-Jan-76	MCA 40474
4288	I Love The Way You Love	Betty Wright	4-Sep-71	Alston 4594
4289	It's All Up To You	The Dells	11-Mar-72	Cadet 5689
4290	Run Home Girl	Sad Cafe	10-Mar-79	A&M 2111
4291	The Music Never Stopped	Grateful Dead	15-Nov-75	Grateful Dead 718
4292	Sweet Baby	Donnie Elbert	12-Feb-72	All Platinum 2333
4293	After Midnight	Maggie Bell	18-May-74	Atlantic 3018
4294	Wake Up Susan	The Spinners	14-Aug-76	Atlantic 3341

'70s Rank	TITLE	ACT	Peak Date	Label & No.
4295	Wear This Ring (With Love)	Detroit Emeralds	11-Sep-71	Westbound 181
4296	I'm A Rocker	Raspberries	8-Dec-73	Capitol 3765
4297	Gypsy	Abraham's Children	17-Mar-73	Buddah 340
4298	I Found My Dad	Joe Simon	11-Nov-72	Spring 130
4299	Humphrey The Camel	Jack Blanchard & Misty Morgan	11-Jul-70	Wayside 013
4300	Valley To Pray	Arlo Guthrie	21-Nov-70	Reprise 0951
4301	Tell Laura I Love Her	Johnny T. Angel	29-Jun-74	Bell 45,472
4302	Waterfall	Carly Simon	9-Aug-75	Elektra 45263
4303	I Received A Letter	Delbert & Glen	9-Dec-72	Clean 60003
4304	Train Of Glory	Jonathan Edwards	25-Mar-72	Atco 6881
4305	My Country	Jud Strunk	12-Oct-74	Capitol 3960
4306	Tranquillo	Carly Simon	20-Jan-79	Elektra 45544
4307	Standing In The Rain	The James Gang	8-Jun-74	Atco 6966
4308	Midnight Show	Bobby Vinton	11-Oct-75	ABC 12131
4309	Look At You	George McCrae	14-Jun-75	T.K. 1011
4310	I'll Still Love You	Jim Weatherly	15-Feb-75	Buddah 444
4311	Eh! Cumpari	Gaylord & Holiday	3-Apr-76	Prodigal 0622
4312	Good Night & Good Morning	Jim Capaldi	6-Nov-76	Island 067
4313	How High The Moon	Gloria Gaynor	20-Dec-75	MGM 14838
4314	Take Me Bak 'Ome	Slade	14-Oct-72	Polydor 15046
4315	Jump	Aretha Franklin	6-Nov-76	Atlantic 3358
4316	I Wouldn't Treat A Dog (The Way You Treated Me)	Bobby Bland	18-Jan-75	Dunhill/ABC 15015
4317	Golden Rainbow	Looking Glass	2-Dec-72	Epic 10900
4318	Love Theme From "The Godfather"	Nino Rota	27-May-72	Paramount 0152
4319	Hand Clapping Song	The Meters	27-Jun-70	Josie 1021
4320	Ain't Gonna' Hurt Nobody	Brick	11-Feb-78	Bang 735
4321	Sleepwalker	The Kinks	16-Apr-77	Arista 0240
4322	Fancy Lady	Billy Preston	1-Nov-75	A&M 1735
4323	As Soon As I Hang Up The Phone	Loretta Lynn/Conway Twitty	14-Sep-74	MCA 40251
4324	Everyday Without You	Hamilton, Joe Frank & Reynolds	8-May-76	Playboy 6068
4325	(Ain't Nothin' But A) House Party	The J. Geils Band	28-Aug-76	Atlantic 3350
4326	Nice 'N' Naasty	The Salsoul Orchestra	13-Nov-76	Salsoul 2011
4327	90 Day Freeze (On Her Love)	100 Proof Aged In Soul	13-Nov-71	Hot Wax 7108
4328	I'll Play The Fool	Dr. Buzzard's Original "Savannah" Band	16-Oct-76	RCA 10762
4329	Day And Night	The Wackers	16-Dec-72	Elektra 45816
4330	January	Pilot	6-Mar-76	EMI 4202
4331	This Is Your Life	Commodores	22-Nov-75	Motown 1361
4332	I Wish It Was Me You Loved	The Dells	29-Jun-74	Cadet 5702
4333	Your Side Of The Bed	Mac Davis	26-May-73	Columbia 45839
4334	Slow Motion (Part 1)	Johnny Williams	3-Feb-73	Phila. Int'l 3518

'70s Rank	TITLE	ACT	Peak Date	Label & No.
4335	Roots, Rock, Reggae	Bob Marley & The Wailers	31-Jul-76	Island 060
4336	Lady Eleanor	Lindisfarne	7-Oct-72	Elektra 45799
4337	Annabelle	Daniel Boone	9-Dec-72	Mercury 73339
4338	Rumour Has It	Donna Summer	25-Mar-78	Casablanca 916
4339	This Is Your Song	Don Goodwin	26-Jan-74	Silver Blue 806
4340	She's A Disco Queen	Oliver Sain	27-Mar-76	Abet 9463
4341	No, No, Joe	Silver Convention	11-Sep-76	Midland Int'l 10723
4342	Cosmic Sea	The Mystic Moods	19-May-73	Warner Bros. 7686
4343	Put On Your Shoes And Walk	Clarence Carter	10-Mar-73	Fame 179
4344	Could You Ever Love Me Again	Gary & Dave	5-Jan-74	London 200
4345	Son Of My Father	Chicory	18-Mar-72	Epic 10837
4346	I Knew You When	Donny Osmond	4-Dec-71	MGM 14322
4347	Nobody Wins	Brenda Lee	21-Apr-73	MCA 40003
4348	Energy Crisis '79	Dickie Goodman	14-Jul-79	Hotline 1017
4349	Groovy People	Lou Rawls	20-Nov-76	Phila. Int'l 3604
4350	Baby, You Look Good To Me Tonight	John Denver	22-Jan-77	RCA 10854
4351	Machines	John LiVigni	22-Nov-75	Raintree 2204
4352	Feet Start Walking	Doris Duke	13-Jun-70	Canyon 35
4353	Does She Do It Like She Dances	The Addrisi Brothers	17-Sep-77	Buddah 579
4354	Don't Stop Me Now	Queen	24-Feb-79	Elektra 46008
4355	Johnny Cool	Steve Gibbons Band	3-Jul-76	MCA 40551
4356	Sweet Loving Man	Morris Albert	10-Jan-76	RCA Victor 10437
4357	Sunshine	Mickey Newbury	11-Aug-73	Elektra 45853
4358	Glamour Boy	The Guess Who	4-Aug-73	RCA Victor 74-0977
4359	The Long Way Around	Linda Ronstadt	23-Jan-71	Capitol 3021
4360	Keep On Loving Me (You'll See The Change)	Bobby Bland	19-Dec-70	Duke 464
4361	Don't Make Me Over	Brenda & The Tabulations	5-Sep-70	Top & Bottom 404
4362	I Wanna Know If It's Good To You?	Funkadelic	19-Sep-70	Westbound 167
4363	I Wanna Be With You (Part I)	The Isley Brothers	19-May-79	T-Neck 2279
4364	We Are Neighbors	The Chi-Lites	4-Sep-71	Brunswick 55455
4365	Can't Take My Eyes Off You	Nancy Wilson	3-Jan-70	Capitol 2644
4366	You To Me Are Everything	The Real Thing	28-Aug-76	United Artists 833
4367	White Bird	David Laflamme	8-Jan-77	Amherst 717
4368	Sorry Doesn't Always Make It Right	Diana Ross	5-Apr-75	Motown 1335
4369	Money Runner	Quincy Jones	15-Apr-72	Reprise 1072
4370	Birmingham Blues	Charlie Daniels Band	6-Dec-75	Kama Sutra 606
4371	Music Is My Life	Helen Reddy	28-Aug-76	Capitol 4312
4372	L.A. Freeway	Jerry Jeff Walker	11-Aug-73	MCA 40054
4373	Mighty High	Mighty Clouds Of Joy	17-Apr-76	ABC 12164
4374	Solsbury Hill	Peter Gabriel	21-May-77	Atco 7079
4375	It Feels So Good To Be Loved So Bad	The Manhattans	18-Jun-77	Columbia 10495

'70s Rank	TITLE	ACT	Peak Date	Label & No.
4376	You Brought The Woman Out Of Me	Hot	25-Feb-78	Big Tree 16108
4377	Teddy Bear's Last Ride	Diana Williams	16-Oct-76	Capitol 4317
4378	Vaya Con Dios	Freddy Fender	12-Jun-76	ABC/Dot 17627
4379	I Pity The Fool	Ann Peebles	3-Apr-71	Hi 2186
4380	Shotgun Shuffle	The Sunshine Band	4-Oct-75	T.K. 1010
4381	Mama Told Me Not To Come	Wilson Pickett	25-Nov-72	Atlantic 2909
4382	Let's Rock	Ellison Chase	2-Oct-76	Big Tree 16072
4383	I Do Believe In You	Pages	15-Dec-79	Epic 50769
4384	Somebody's Gotta Win, Somebody's Gotta Lose	The Controllers	21-Jan-78	Juana 3414
4385	Life Ain't Easy	Dr. Hook And The Medicine Show	20-Oct-73	Columbia 45925
4386	The Taker	Waylon Jennings	14-Nov-70	RCA Victor 47-9885
4387	Ma! (He's Making Eyes At Me)	Lena Zavaroni	24-Aug-74	Stax 0206
4388	I Wanna Stay With You	Gallagher And Lyle	12-Jun-76	A&M 1778
4389	Real Man	Todd Rundgren	10-May-75	Bearsville 0304
4390	Hey Baby	Ted Nugent	1-May-76	Epic 50197
4391	Sittin' On A Time Bomb (Waitin' For The Hurt To Come)	Honey Cone	5-Aug-72	Hot Wax 7205
4392	Tulsa	Billy Joe Royal	20-Mar-71	Columbia 45289
4393	You're Gettin' A Little Too Smart	Detroit Emeralds	21-Jul-73	Westbound 213
4394	A Simple Game	Four Tops	19-Feb-72	Motown 1196
4395	I Want To Live	John Denver	6-May-78	RCA 11267
4396	Demonstration	Otis Redding	11-Apr-70	Atco 6742
4397	Madelaine	Stu Nunnery	27-Apr-74	Evolution 1088
4398	Cry	Lynn Anderson	19-Feb-72	Columbia 45529
4399	Part Time Love	Kerry Chater	19-Mar-77	Warner Bros. 8310
4400	Yu-Ma/Go Away Little Boy	Marlena Shaw	25-Jun-77	Columbia 10542
4401	Wrapped Up In Your Warm And Tender Love	Tyrone Davis	10-Nov-73	Dakar 4526
4402	Bump Me Baby Pt. 1	Dooley Silverspoon	29-Mar-75	Cotton 636
4403	The Topical Song	The Barron Knights	8-Sep-79	Epic 50755
4404	Little Bit O' Soul	Bullet	1-Jul-72	Big Tree 140
4405	Love My Life Away	The Hagers	9-Nov-74	Elektra 45209
4406	Nutbush City Limits	Bob Seger	10-Jul-76	Capitol 4269
4407	Don't Leave Me In The Morning	Odia Coates	10-May-75	United Artists 601
4408	You Need Love	Styx	31-May-75	Wooden Nickel 10272
4409	I Gotta Let You Go	Martha Reeves & The Vandellas	12-Dec-70	Gordy 7103
4410	Give Up Your Guns	The Buoys	3-Jul-71	Scepter 12318
4411	Get Out Of Denver	Bob Seger	24-Aug-74	Palladium 1205
4412	Christina	Terry Jacks	28-Jun-75	Private Stk 45,023
4413	Look Into Your Heart	Aretha Franklin	19-Mar-77	Atlantic 3373

'70s Rank	TITLE	ACT	Peak Date	Label & No.
4414	Bad Water	The Raeletts	29-May-71	Tangerine 1014
4415	That's What Friends Are For	B.J. Thomas	29-Jul-72	Scepter 12354
4416	Wake Up And Love Me	April	6-Jul-74	A&M 1528
4417	Mistrusted Love	Mistress	22-Dec-79	RSO 1009
4418	Nobody (Tellin' Me 'Bout My Baby)	Charles Wright And The Watts 103rd Street Rhythm Band	31-Jul-71	Warner Bros. 7504
4419	Speak Softly Love	Al Martino	20-May-72	Capitol 3313
4420	In Time	Engelbert Humperdinck	2-Sep-72	Parrot 40071
4421	Two Lane Highway	Pure Prairie League	28-Jun-75	RCA Victor 10302
4422	California Kid And Reemo	Lobo	25-Sep-71	Big Tree 119
4423	Slick	Willie Hutch	15-Sep-73	Motown 1252
4424	Love Hangover	The 5th Dimension	24-Apr-76	ABC 12181
4425	No Good To Cry	The Poppy Family	25-Dec-71	London 164
4426	Spinning Wheel Pt. 1	James Brown	20-Feb-71	King 6366
4427	Charmer	Tim Moore	22-Feb-75	Asylum 45214
4428	The Good Book	Melanie	1-May-71	Buddah 224
4429	Take That To The Bank	Shalamar	10-Feb-79	Solar 11379
4430	Keep On Running Away	Lazy Racer	28-Jul-79	A&M 2152
4431	America, The Beautiful	Charlie Rich	29-May-76	Epic 50222
4432	Kool's Back Again	Kool & The Gang	24-Jan-70	De-Lite 523
4433	Theme From King Kong (Pt. 1)	Love Unlimited Orchestra	12-Mar-77	20th Century 2325
4434	Don't Send Nobody Else	Ace Spectrum	26-Oct-74	Atlantic 3012
4435	Voodoo Woman	Simon Stokes & The Nighthawks	10-Jan-70	Elektra 45670
4436	We're All Alone	Frankie Valli	21-Aug-76	Private Stk 45,098
4437	How Can I Tell My Mom And Dad	The Lovelites	14-Feb-70	Uni 55181
4438	Names, Tags, Numbers & Labels	The Association	10-Mar-73	Mums 6016
4439	Baby Love	Mother's Finest	29-Oct-77	Epic 50407
4440	If You Can Beat Me Rockin' (You Can Have My Chair)	Laura Lee	28-Oct-72	Hot Wax 7207
4441	My Sweet Lord	Billy Preston	6-Mar-71	Apple 1826
4442	Hey Shirley (This Is Squirrely)	Shirley & Squirrely	17-Jul-76	GRT 054
4443	I'm So Glad	The Fuzz	9-Oct-71	Calla 179
4444	Mixed Up Guy	Joey Scarbury	6-Feb-71	Lionel 3208
4445	All I Need Is Time	Gladys Knight & The Pips	1-Sep-73	Soul 35107
4446	Rescue Me	Cher	19-Apr-75	MCA 40375
4447	Break It To Them Gently	Burton Cummings	29-Jul-78	Portrait 70016
4448	Avenging Annie	Roger Daltrey	5-Nov-77	MCA 40800
4449	Shake It Well	The Dramatics	12-Nov-77	ABC 12299
4450	Take It Back	The J. Geils Band	31-Mar-79	EMI America 8012
4451	If It's The Last Thing I Do	Thelma Houston	2-Jul-77	Tamla 54283
4452	A Friend Of Mine Is Going Blind	John Dawson Read	18-Oct-75	Chrysalis 2105
4453	Mamacita	The Grass Roots	11-Oct-75	Haven 7015

'70s Rank	TITLE	ACT	Peak Date	Label & No.
4454	Be Nice To Me	Runt--Todd Rundgren	22-May-71	Bearsville 31002
4455	I'll Have To Go Away	Skylark	29-Sep-73	Capitol 3661
4456	Satin Sheets	Bellamy Brothers	11-Sep-76	Warner/Curb 8248
4457	Fly Little White Dove Fly	The Bells	23-Jan-71	Polydor 15016
4458	Tragedy	Argent	2-Dec-72	Epic 10919
4459	The Jean Genie	David Bowie	30-Dec-72	RCA Victor 74-0838
4460	Martha (Your Lovers Come And Go)	Gabriel	4-Nov-78	Epic 50594
4461	Spider Jiving	Andy Fairweather Low	26-Apr-75	A&M 1649
4462	Can't Help Falling In Love	Andy Williams	7-Mar-70	Columbia 45094
4463	Le Spank	Le Pamplemousse	11-Mar-78	AVI 153
4464	Save Me	Donna McDaniel	2-Jul-77	Midsong Int'l 11005
4465	You And Your Folks, Me And My Folks	Funkadelic	24-Apr-71	Westbound 175
4466	You Are Beautiful	The Stylistics	27-Mar-76	Avco 4664
4467	With Pen In Hand	Bobby Goldsboro	14-Oct-72	United Artists 50938
4468	(What A) Wonderful World	Johnny Nash	22-May-76	Epic 50219
4469	It Amazes Me	John Denver	25-Mar-78	RCA 11214
4470	Flaming Youth	Kiss	10-Jul-76	Casablanca 858
4471	Must Have Been Crazy	Chicago	8-Sep-79	Columbia 11061
4472	Baby, Baby I Love You	Terry Cashman	4-Dec-76	Lifesong 45015
4473	Uhh	Dyke And The Blazers	2-May-70	Original Sound 89
4474	Mr. Skin	Spirit	18-Aug-73	Epic 10701
4475	Come On Say It	Henry Gross	27-Jul-74	A&M 1534
4476	I'm Better Off Without You	The Main Ingredient	31-Oct-70	RCA Victor 74-0382
4477	New York City	Zwol	4-Nov-78	EMI America 8005
4478	Time Bomb	Lake	10-Dec-77	Columbia 10614
4479	Honey Trippin'	The Mystic Moods	26-Jul-75	Sound Bird 5002
4480	Something There Is About You	Bob Dylan	11-May-74	Asylum 11035
4481	I Can't Move No Mountains	Blood, Sweat & Tears	13-Jan-73	Columbia 45755
4482	God Only Knows	Marilyn Scott	28-Jan-78	Big Tree 16105
4483	Feel The Need In Me	Detroit Emeralds	16-Dec-72	Westbound 209
4484	Wheels Of Life	Gino Vannelli	17-Mar-79	A&M 2114
4485	All Down The Line	The Rolling Stones	29-Jul-72	Rolling Stones 19104
4486	Be My Baby	Cissy Houston	15-May-71	Janus 145
4487	San Bernadino	Christie	20-Feb-71	Epic 10695
4488	Love Is Gonna Come At Last	Badfinger	21-Apr-79	Elektra 46025
4489	Hold On To The Night	Hotel	6-Oct-79	MCA 41113
4490	Race Among The Ruins	Gordon Lightfoot	19-Mar-77	Reprise 1380
4491	A Part Of You	Brenda & The Tabulations	25-Sep-71	Top & Bottom 408
4492	Spring Affair	Donna Summer	22-Jan-77	Casablanca 872
4493	Feelings	Barry Mann	20-Jun-70	Scepter 12281
4494	Once A Fool	Kiki Dee	17-Apr-76	Rocket/MCA 40506
4495	Deeply	Anson Williams	16-Apr-77	Chelsea 3061

'70s Rank	TITLE	ACT	Peak Date	Label & No.
4496	Breaking Up Somebody's Home	Ann Peebles	26-Feb-72	Hi 2205
4497	Nothing But A Breeze	Jesse Winchester	20-Aug-77	Bearsville 0318
4498	Prisoner (Captured By Your Eyes)	L.A. Jets	1-Jan-77	RCA 10826
4499	Whatever Happened To Benny Santini?	Chris Rea	25-Nov-78	United Artists 1252
4500	You're Throwing A Good Love Away	The Spinners	30-Apr-77	Atlantic 3382
4501	Going To The Country	The Steve Miller Band	29-Aug-70	Capitol 2878
4502	The Language Of Love	The Intrigues	10-Jul-71	Yew 1012
4503	Do What You Wanna Do	T-Connection	11-Jun-77	Dash 5032
4504	Dream Lover	The Marshall Tucker Band	15-Jul-78	Capricorn 0300
4505	A Whiter Shade Of Pale	R.B. Greaves	12-Dec-70	Atco 6789
4506	Dog Eat Dog	Ted Nugent	4-Dec-76	Epic 50301
4507	The People Tree	Sammy Davis, Jr.	18-Nov-72	MGM 14426
4508	Lady Love	The Klowns	19-Dec-70	RCA Victor 74-0393
4509	Sympathy	Rare Bird	2-May-70	Probe 477
4510	Melting Pot	Blue Mink	28-Feb-70	Philips 40658
4511	The Hungry Years	Wayne Newton	3-Jul-76	Chelsea 3041
4512	He's So Fine	Kristy And Jimmy McNichol	12-Aug-78	RCA 11271
4513	Knock Knock Who's There	Mary Hopkin	16-Dec-72	Apple 1855
4514	I'm On My Way	Captain & Tennille	27-May-78	A&M 2027
4515	Day By Day (Every Minute Of The Hour)	The Continental 4	10-Jul-71	Jay Walking 011
4516	(Oh Lord Won't You Buy Me A) Mercedes Benz	Goose Creek Symphony	18-Mar-72	Capitol 3246
4517	Heaven On The Seventh Floor	The Mighty Pope	27-Aug-77	Private Stk 45,157
4518	Should Anybody Ask	Garry Bonner	25-Jan-75	Atlantic 3234
4519	Come An' Get Yourself Some	Leon Haywood	2-Aug-75	20th Century 2191
4520	Man Of Constant Sorrow	Ginger Baker's Air Force	6-Jun-70	Atco 6750
4521	Amanda	Waylon	7-Jul-79	RCA 11596
4522	Don't Try To Lay No Boogie-Woogie On The King Of Rock And Roll	John Baldry	18-Sep-71	Warner Bros. 7506
4523	My Pearl	Automatic Man	22-Jan-77	Island 063
4524	Feel Alright	Cargoe	23-Sep-72	Ardent 2901
4525	Eddie's Love	Eddie Kendricks	8-Jul-72	Tamla 54218
4526	People Are Changin'	Timmy Thomas	5-May-73	Glades 1709
4527	Let The Music Take Your Mind	Kool & The Gang	11-Jul-70	De-Lite 529
4528	My Guy	Petula Clark	19-Aug-72	MGM 14392
4529	Gimme Your Money Please	Bachman-Turner Overdrive	16-Oct-76	Mercury 73843
4530	Mother	Barbra Streisand	30-Oct-71	Columbia 45471
4531	Beat Me Daddy Eight To The Bar	Commander Cody And His Lost Planet Airmen	9-Sep-72	Paramount 0169
4532	I Dig Everything About You	The Mob	16-Jan-71	Colossus 130
4533	Steam Heat	Pointer Sisters	13-Apr-74	ABC/Blue Thumb 248
4534	After The Fire Is Gone	Conway Twitty Loretta Lynn	20-Mar-71	Decca 32776
4535	I Got Over Love	Major Harris	31-Jan-76	Atlantic 3303

'70s Rank	TITLE	ACT	Peak Date	Label & No.
4536	Everybody Needs A Rainbow	Ray Stevens	14-Dec-74	Barnaby 610
4537	I've Been Lovin' You	Easy Street	31-Jul-76	Capricorn 0255
4538	Gotta Be The One	Maxine Nightingale	7-Aug-76	United Artists 820
4539	So Hard Livin' Without You	Airwaves	24-Jun-78	A&M 2032
4540	Trouble	Frederick Knight	23-Sep-72	Stax 0139
4541	Am I Blue	Cher	5-May-73	MCA 40039
4542	Dear Ann	George Baker Selection	27-Jun-70	Colossus 117
4543	The Ghetto - Part 1	Donny Hathaway	14-Mar-70	Atco 6719
4544	Why Do Lovers (Break Each Other's Heart?)	Daryl Hall & John Oates	19-Nov-77	RCA 11132
4545	Jasper	Jim Stafford	8-May-76	Polydor 14309
4546	Enjoy And Get It On	ZZ Top	11-Jun-77	London 252
4547	Kate	Johnny Cash	10-Jun-72	Columbia 45590
4548	Love For You	Sonoma	22-Dec-73	Dunhill 4365
4549	Got Pleasure	Ohio Players	1-Jul-72	Westbound 204
4550	Too Many Lovers	Shack	13-Mar-71	Volt 4051
4551	If	Telly Savalas	14-Dec-74	MCA 40301
4552	Mr. Magic Man	Wilson Pickett	31-Mar-73	RCA Victor 74-0898
4553	It Doesn't Matter Anymore	Linda Ronstadt	16-Aug-75	Capitol 4050
4554	My Honey And Me	The Emotions	18-Mar-72	Volt 4077
4555	Endlessly	Mavis Staples	21-Oct-72	Volt 4086
4556	Who Do Ya Love	KC & The Sunshine Band	20-Jan-79	T.K. 1031
4557	Them Changes	Buddy Miles	2-Oct-71	Mercury 73228
4558	A New Rock And Roll	Mahogany Rush	24-Aug-74	20th Century 2111
4559	California Nights	Sweet	2-Sep-78	Capitol 4610
4560	Keep On Doin' What You're Doin'	Bobby Byrd	18-Mar-72	BrownStone 4205
4561	Oh Lori	Alessi	17-Sep-77	A&M 1955
4562	Easy To Be Hard	Hair (Original Soundtrack)/ Cheryl Barnes	2-Jun-79	RCA 11548
4563	Give Me An Inch Girl	Robert Palmer	13-Mar-76	Island 049
4564	Here, There And Everywhere	Emmylou Harris	27-Mar-76	Reprise 1346
4565	Surrender	Cheap Trick	19-Aug-78	Epic 50570
4566	Walkin' The Fence	Couchois	21-Apr-79	Warner Bros. 8749
4567	Vahevala	Kenny Loggins With Jim Messina	13-May-72	Columbia 45550
4568	Isn't It Always Love	Karla Bonoff	6-May-78	Columbia 10710
4569	Lonely Teardrops	Narvel Felts	19-Jun-76	ABC/Dot 17620
4570	It's Uncanny	Daryl Hall & John Oates	20-Aug-77	Atlantic 3397
4571	Why Don't They Understand	Bobby Vinton	3-Oct-70	Epic 10651
4572	My Wheels Won't Turn	Bachman-Turner Overdrive	4-Jun-77	Mercury 73903
4573	Music Eyes	Heartsfield	6-Apr-74	Mercury 73449
4574	Love Me Right	Denise LaSalle	4-Mar-78	ABC 12312
4575	Everyday	John Denver	25-Mar-72	RCA Victor 74-0647
4576	Why Leave Us Alone	Five Special	18-Aug-79	Elektra 46032

'70s Rank	TITLE	ACT	Peak Date	Label & No.
4577	Fool	Elvis Presley	19-May-73	RCA Victor 74-0910
4578	Gonna Be Alright Now	Gayle McCormick	7-Aug-71	Dunhill 4281
4579	Then She's A Lover	Roy Clark	7-Feb-70	Dot 17335
4580	Silver Threads And Golden Needles	Linda Ronstadt	18-May-74	Asylum 11032
4581	Caught In A Dream	Alice Cooper	3-Jul-71	Warner Bros. 7490
4582	Mr. President	Dickie Goodman	29-Jun-74	Rainy Wednesday 207
4583	You Stepped Into My Life	Wayne Newton	6-Oct-79	Aries II 101
4584	Stone Of Years	Emerson, Lake & Palmer	18-Sep-71	Cotillion 44131
4585	Jesus Was A Capricorn	Kris Kristofferson	20-Jan-73	Monument 8558
4586	We All Gotta Stick Together	Four Tops	29-Nov-75	ABC 12123
4587	Where Have You Been All My Life	Fotomaker	13-May-78	Atlantic 3471
4588	Crazy Legs	Donald Austin	3-Mar-73	Eastbound 603
4589	Brown Paper Bag	Syndicate Of Sound	18-Apr-70	Buddah 156
4590	Funky Weekend	The Stylistics	31-Jan-76	Avco 4661
4591	Do You Feel All Right	KC & The Sunshine Band	11-Nov-78	T.K. 1030
4592	Love In 'C' Minor - Pt. 1	Cerrone	2-Apr-77	Cotillion 44215
4593	Pinball	Brian Protheroe	26-Apr-75	Chrysalis 2104
4594	Let Me Be Your Lovemaker	Betty Wright	20-Oct-73	Alston 4619
4595	California Blues	Redwing	1-May-71	Fantasy 657
4596	Girls (Part I)	Moments And Whatnauts	1-Feb-75	Stang 5057
4597	What's On My Mind	Kansas	16-Jul-77	Kirshner 4270
4598	Joyful Resurrection	Tom Fogerty	6-Oct-73	Fantasy 702
4599	Workin' Together	Ike & Tina Turner	12-Dec-70	Liberty 56207
4600	Bad Sneakers	Steely Dan	20-Sep-75	ABC 12128
4601	Lady Lay	Wayne Newton	30-Nov-74	Chelsea 3003
4602	All My Hard Times	Joe Simon	9-Oct-71	Spring 118
4603	Uncle John's Band	Grateful Dead	5-Sep-70	Warner Bros. 7410
4604	This Moment In Time	Engelbert Humperdinck	20-Jan-79	Epic 50632
4605	Guava Jelly	Barbra Streisand	18-Jan-75	Columbia 10075
4606	We Got To Have Peace	Curtis Mayfield	11-Mar-72	Curtom 1968
4607	Mother Nature	The Temptations	8-Jul-72	Gordy 7119
4608	Living For The City	Ray Charles	27-Sep-75	Crossover 981
4609	I Can't Get Over You	The Dramatics	25-Jun-77	ABC 12258
4610	Only One Love In My Life	Ronnie Milsap	15-Jul-78	RCA 11270
4611	Just One Minute More	Mike Finnigan	15-Jul-78	Columbia 10741
4612	You'd Better Believe It	The Manhattans	13-Oct-73	Columbia 45927
4613	This I Swear	Tyrone Davis	23-Jul-77	Columbia 10528
4614	Sing A Song	David Clayton-Thomas	15-Apr-72	Columbia 45569
4615	Fox Huntin' (On The Weekend)	Daddy Dewdrop	24-Jul-71	Sunflower 111
4616	Just For Me And You	Poco	20-Nov-71	Epic 10804
4617	Double Trouble	Lynyrd Skynyrd	24-Apr-76	MCA 40532

'70s Rank	TITLE	ACT	Peak Date	Label & No.
4618	Goin' Home (Sing A Song Of Christmas Cheer)	Bobby Sherman	26-Dec-70	Metromedia 204
4619	A Change Is Gonna Come & People Gotta Be Free	The 5th Dimension	14-Mar-70	Bell 860
4620	The Real Me	The Who	9-Feb-74	Track/MCA 40182
4621	One More Chance	Ocean	14-Oct-72	Kama Sutra 556
4622	Pray For Me	The Intruders	17-Jul-71	Gamble 4014
4623	Everybody Ought To Be In Love	Paul Anka	23-Jul-77	United Artists 1018
4624	If It's All Right With You	Dottie West	3-Feb-73	RCA Victor 74-0828
4625	A Little Bit Like Magic	King Harvest	9-Jun-73	Perception 527
4626	There It Goes Again	Barbara And The Uniques	23-Jan-71	Arden 3001
4627	Queen Of The Roller Derby	Leon Russell	29-Sep-73	Shelter 7337
4628	Brownsville	Joy Of Cooking	8-May-71	Capitol 3075
4629	Co-Co	Sweet	9-Oct-71	Bell 45,126
4630	Time To Kill	The Band	31-Oct-70	Capitol 2870
4631	Don't Turn The Light Out	Cliff Richard	2-Jul-77	Rocket/MCA 40724
4632	Can't Let A Woman	Ambrosia	25-Dec-76	20th Century 2310
4633	Feliz Navidad	Jose Feliciano	26-Dec-70	RCA Victor 74-0404
4634	Trans-Europe Express	Kraftwerk	24-Jun-78	Capitol 4460
4635	Love's Made A Fool Of You	Cochise	8-May-71	United Artists 50756
4636	To Be Young, Gifted And Black	Nina Simone	24-Jan-70	RCA Victor 74-0269
4637	Harpo's Blues	Phoebe Snow	7-Jun-75	Shelter 40400
4638	Too Late To Worry, Too Blue To Cry	Ronnie Milsap	10-May-75	RCA Victor 10228
4639	Save Me	Silver Convention	17-May-75	Midland Int'l 10212
4640	Angelica	Oliver	18-Apr-70	Crewe 341
4641	Tell It Like It Is	Andy Williams	7-Feb-76	Columbia 10263
4642	Song Seller	Raiders	21-Oct-72	Columbia 45688
4643	If It's Real What I Feel	Jerry Butler	27-Mar-71	Mercury 73169
4644	Daddy Cool	Boney M	22-Jan-77	Atco 7063
4645	The Lord Knows I'm Drinking	Cal Smith	21-Apr-73	Decca 33040
4646	Jingle Bells	The Singing Dogs	1-Jan-72	RCA Victor 48-1020
4647	Better Days	Melissa Manchester	29-May-76	Arista 0183
4648	Rocky Mountain Music	Eddie Rabbitt	11-Sep-76	Elektra 45315
4649	Might Just Take Your Life	Deep Purple	13-Apr-74	Warner Bros. 7784
4650	Vado Via	Drupi	3-Nov-73	A&M 1460
4651	I Just Can't Stop Loving You	Cornelius Brothers & Sister Rose	1-Dec-73	United Artists 313
4652	I Do The Rock	Tim Curry	8-Dec-79	A&M 2166
4653	It May Be Winter Outside (But In My Heart It's Spring)	Love Unlimited	12-Jan-74	20th Century 2062
4654	I Like Your Lovin' (Do You Like Mine)	Chi-Lites	29-Aug-70	Brunswick 55438
4655	The Wall Street Shuffle	10 C. C.	3-Aug-74	UK 49023
4656	Good Lovin'	Grateful Dead	13-Jan-79	Arista 0383

'70s Rank	TITLE	ACT	Peak Date	Label & No.
4657	Mr. Natural	Bee Gees	23-Mar-74	RSO 408
4658	Ain't No Love In The Heart Of The City	Bobby Bland	14-Sep-74	Dunhill/ABC 15003
4659	Norma Jean Wants To Be A Movie Star	Sundown Company	12-Jun-76	Polydor 14312
4660	Crank It Up (Funk Town) Pt. 1	Peter Brown	22-Sep-79	Drive 6278
4661	The Man That Turned My Mama On	Tanya Tucker	31-Aug-74	Columbia 46047
4662	A Hurricane Is Coming Tonite	Carol Douglas	19-Apr-75	Midland Int'l 10229
4663	Burnin' Sky	Bad Company	4-Jun-77	Swan Song 70112
4664	Dance And Shake Your Tambourine	Universal Robot Band	7-May-77	Red Greg 207
4665	Way Back Home	Jr. Walker & The All Stars	25-Dec-71	Soul 35090
4666	Good Time Sally	Rare Earth	2-Dec-72	Rare Earth 5048
4667	Can't Get Over Losing You	Donnie Elbert	5-Dec-70	Rare Bullet 101
4668	Big Noise From Winnetka	Spaghetti Head	31-May-75	Private Stk 45,014
4669	I Need Someone (To Love Me)	Z.Z. Hill	3-Jul-71	Kent 4547
4670	Roberta	Bones	4-Nov-72	Signpost 70008
4671	Never Had A Love	Pablo Cruise	18-Feb-78	A&M 1999
4672	Beg, Steal Or Borrow	The New Seekers	6-May-72	Elektra 45780
4673	I Can't Be You (You Can't Be Me)	The Glass House	8-Aug-70	Invictus 9076
4674	Apple Of My Eye	Badfinger	2-Feb-74	Apple 1864
4675	Long Hot Summer Nights	Wendy Waldman	2-Sep-78	Warner Bros. 8617
4676	Julie Ann	Ginger	16-Oct-76	Shock 3
4677	She Called Me Baby	Charlie Rich	2-Nov-74	RCA Victor 10062
4678	We May Never Love Like This Again	Maureen McGovern	15-Feb-75	20th Century 2158
4679	Can't It All Be Love	Randy Edelman	12-Nov-77	Arista 0268
4680	Honey Child	Bad Company	7-Aug-76	Swan Song 70109
4681	Day Is Done	Brooklyn Bridge	10-Oct-70	Buddah 193
4682	Street Talk (Var. III)	B. C. G. (B.C. Generation)	3-Apr-76	20th Century 2271
4683	The Princess And The Punk	Barry Mann	11-Sep-76	Arista 0194
4684	Hickory	Frankie Valli And The 4 Seasons	15-Jun-74	Motown 1288
4685	Moondance	Van Morrison	3-Dec-77	Warner Bros. 8450
4686	Nobody	Doucette	11-Aug-79	Mushroom 7042
4687	Givin' It All Up	The J. Geils Band	1-Mar-75	Atlantic 3251
4688	How Could I Let You Get Away	The Spinners	26-Aug-72	Atlantic 2904
4689	It's So Nice	Jackie DeShannon	22-Aug-70	Liberty 56187
4690	Step By Step	The Kiki Dee Band	15-Mar-75	Rocket/MCA 40355
4691	For Love	Pousette-Dart Band	22-Sep-79	Capitol 4764
4692	One Night Stand	The Magic Lanterns	20-Feb-71	Big Tree 109 / Atlantic 2715
4693	Some Enchanted Evening	Jane Olivor	24-Sep-77	Columbia 10527
4694	You And Me Together Forever	Freddie North	11-Mar-72	Mankind 12009
4695	I'm Mandy Fly Me	10cc	1-May-76	Mercury 73779
4696	Goofus	Carpenters	9-Oct-76	A&M 1859
4697	I Don't Want To Make You Wait	The Delfonics	19-May-73	Philly Groove 176

'70s Rank	TITLE	ACT	Peak Date	Label & No.
4698	I Bet He Don't Love You (Like I Love You)	The Intruders	13-Nov-71	Gamble 4016
4699	Darling Come Back Home	Eddie Kendricks	21-Jul-73	Tamla 54236
4700	Party	Van McCoy	4-Sep-76	H&L 4670
4701	Home Tonight	Aerosmith	30-Oct-76	Columbia 10407
4702	Hail! Hail! Rock And Roll!	Starland Vocal Band	22-Jan-77	Windsong 10855
4703	This Is What You Mean To Me	Engelbert Humperdinck	6-Dec-75	Parrot 40085
4704	Laughin And Clownin	Ray Charles	25-Apr-70	ABC/TRC 11259
4705	Gotta Be Funky	Monk Higgins & The Specialties	17-Jun-72	United Artists 50897
4706	The Last Time	The Buchanan Brothers	10-Jan-70	Event 3307
4707	See You When I Git There	Lou Rawls	20-Aug-77	Phila. Int'l 3623
4708	Loving You Is Just An Old Habit	Jim Weatherly	13-Jan-73	RCA Victor 74-0822
4709	Reconsider Me	Narvel Felts	28-Jun-75	ABC/Dot 17549
4710	Like They Say In L.A.	East L.A. Car Pool	23-Aug-75	GRC 2064
4711	Gypsy	Van Morrison	20-Jan-73	Warner Bros. 7665
4712	Funky Man	Kool & The Gang	10-Oct-70	De-Lite 534
4713	Daylight	Bobby Womack	17-Apr-76	United Artists 763
4714	Move Me, O Wondrous Music	The Ray Charles Singers	13-Jun-70	Command 4135
4715	Easy Street	The Edgar Winter Group	12-Oct-74	Epic 50034
4716	Come On Over To My House	Layng Martine	15-Jan-72	Barnaby 2053
4717	A Whiter Shade Of Pale	Procol Harum	2-Dec-72	A&M 1389
4718	I'm Leavin' You	Engelbert Humperdinck	19-May-73	Parrot 40073
4719	You've Got To Earn It	The Staple Singers	24-Jul-71	Stax 0093
4720	Where There's Smoke There's Fire	The Grass Roots	21-Jul-73	Dunhill 4345
4721	Barbara, I Love You	The New Colony Six	17-Jan-70	Mercury 73004
4722	It's Really You	The Tarney/Spencer Band	5-Aug-78	A&M 2049
4723	I (Who Have Nothing)	Sylvester	12-May-79	Fantasy 855
4724	Daylight And Darkness	Smokey Robinson	22-Jul-78	Tamla 54293
4725	Somewhere Between Love And Tomorrow	Roy Clark	12-Jan-74	Dot 17480
4726	Like A Sunday Morning	Lana Cantrell	22-Mar-75	Polydor 14261
4727	Fanny (Be Tender With My Love)	Gino Cunico	3-Jan-76	Arista 0162
4728	All The Way Lover	Millie Jackson	29-Apr-78	Spring 179
4729	Song For Anna (Chanson D'Anna)	Herb Ohta	20-Jul-74	A&M 1505
4730	Am I Losing You	The Manhattans	1-Apr-78	Columbia 10674
4731	Plain And Simple Girl	Garland Green	24-Apr-71	Cotillion 44098
4732	N.Y., You Got Me Dancing	Andrea True Connection	26-Mar-77	Buddah 564
4733	C'est La Vie	Greg Lake	24-Sep-77	Atlantic 3405
4734	Louie, Louie	John Belushi	28-Oct-78	MCA 40950
4735	High On Love	Elliott Randall	21-May-77	Kirshner 4269
4736	Darkness, Darkness	The Youngbloods	16-May-70	RCA Victor 74-0342
4737	Don't Let It Get You Down	The Crusaders	9-Jun-73	Blue Thumb 225
4738	Stoned Cowboy	Fantasy	26-Sep-70	Liberty 56190
4739	If I Have To Go Away	Jigsaw	17-Sep-77	20th Century 2347

'70s Rank	TITLE	ACT	Peak Date	Label & No.
4740	Don't Want To Say Goodbye	Raspberries	13-May-72	Capitol 3280
4741	The Red Back Spider	Brownsville Station	16-Dec-72	Big Tree 156
4742	Seems Like I Can't Live With You, But I Can't Live Without You	The Guess Who	24-May-75	RCA Victor 10075
4743	I Just Want To Be	Cameo	13-Oct-79	Chocolate City 019
4744	Since You've Been Gone	Cherie & Marie Currie	3-Nov-79	Capitol 4754
4745	Why Not Start All Over Again	The Counts	25-Mar-72	Westbound 191
4746	Take It Off The Top	The Dixie Dregs	24-Jun-78	Capricorn 0291
4747	Boomerang	Frankie Valli	30-Oct-76	Private Stk 45,109
4748	Boats Against The Current	Eric Carmen	11-Feb-78	Arista 0295
4749	Greatest Love	Judy Clay	25-Apr-70	Atlantic 2697
4750	Close To You	B.T. Express	7-Feb-76	Roadshow 7005
4751	Ready Or Not	Helen Reddy	5-Aug-78	Capitol 4582
4752	Three Steps From True Love	The Reflections	2-Aug-75	Capitol 4078
4753	The Day That Curly Billy Shot Down Crazy Sam McGee	The Hollies	17-Nov-73	Epic 11051
4754	Look Away	The Ozark Mountain Daredevils	16-Nov-74	A&M 1623
4755	Ce Soir	Golden Earring	29-Mar-75	Track/MCA 40369
4756	The Glory Of Love	The Dells	13-Feb-71	Cadet 5679
4757	(Call Me) The Traveling Man	The Masqueraders	3-Apr-76	HBS/ABC 12157
4758	Go On Fool	Marion Black	13-Mar-71	Avco Embassy 4559
4759	La La Peace Song	O.C. Smith	9-Nov-74	Columbia 10031
4760	Your Own Special Way	Genesis	2-Apr-77	Atco 7076
4761	Sunshine	Enchantment	23-Jul-77	Roadshow 991
4762	I Got Love	Melba Moore	20-Jun-70	Mercury 73072
4763	Baby, I'll Give It To You	Seals & Crofts	27-Nov-76	Warner Bros. 8277
4764	Silver Heels	Blaze	18-Dec-76	Epic 50292
4765	Chocolate City	Parliament	12-Jul-75	Casablanca 831
4766	Not Fade Away	Tanya Tucker	3-Feb-79	MCA 40976
4767	Flashback	The 5th Dimension	12-Jan-74	Bell 45,425
4768	(Love Me) Love The Life I Lead	The Fantastics	11-Mar-72	Bell 45,157
4769	Happier Than The Morning Sun	B.J. Thomas	23-Sep-72	Scepter 12364
4770	Back In My Arms Again	Genya Ravan	26-Aug-78	20th Cen. Fox 2374
4771	My First Day Without Her	Dennis Yost & The Classics IV	12-Apr-75	MGM 14785
4772	One Fine Day	Julie	14-Feb-76	Tom Cat 10454
4773	If It's Good To You (It's Good For You)	Flaming Ember	20-Nov-71	Hot Wax 7109
4774	She Lets Her Hair Down (Early In The Morning)	Gene Pitney	31-Jan-70	Musicor 1384
4775	Nobody But You	Kenny Loggins With Jim Messina	1-Jul-72	Columbia 45617
4776	I Can't Turn You Loose	Edgar Winter's White Trash	27-May-72	Epic 10855
4777	Be Good To Me Baby	Luther Ingram	29-May-71	KoKo 2107
4778	Let's Have Some Fun	Bar-Kays	4-Mar-78	Mercury 73971
4779	The Ballad Of Evel Knievel	John Culliton Mahoney	21-Sep-74	Amherst 701

'70s Rank	TITLE	ACT	Peak Date	Label & No.
4780	Voulez-Vous	Abba	1-Sep-79	Atlantic 3609
4781	Turning To You	Charlie	20-Aug-77	Janus 270
4782	I'm The Midnight Special	Clarence Carter	22-Dec-73	Fame 330
4783	Oh Atlanta	Little Feat	27-May-78	Warner Bros. 8566
4784	Love Me Tonight	Head East	13-Mar-76	A&M 1784
4785	Sandy	The Hollies	26-Apr-75	Epic 50086
4786	Shoes	Reparata	2-Aug-75	Polydor 14271
4787	My Crew	Rita Coolidge	13-Jan-73	A&M 1398
4788	Hum Along And Dance	The Temptations	7-Nov-70	Gordy 7102
4789	Preacher Man	The Impressions	31-Mar-73	Curtom 1982
4790	Mother Nature's Wine	Sugarloaf	17-Jul-71	United Artists 50784
4791	Goodbye Again	John Denver	12-Aug-72	RCA Victor 74-0737
4792	Young Love	Ray Stevens	7-Feb-76	Barnaby 618
4793	Bend Me, Shape Me	Storm	25-Sep-71	Sunflower 113
4794	Time Will Tell	Tower Of Power	8-Jun-74	Warner Bros. 7796
4795	Careful Man	John Edwards	30-Nov-74	Aware 043
4796	Theme From Ice Castles (Through The Eyes Of Love)	Melissa Manchester	19-May-79	Arista 0405
4797	Hot Shot	Karen Young	14-Oct-78	West End 1211
4798	Giving Up	Donny Hathaway	27-May-72	Atco 6884
4799	A Mother For My Children	The Whispers	23-Feb-74	Janus 231
4800	Jambalaya (On The Bayou)	Nitty Gritty Dirt Band	22-Apr-72	United Artists 50890
4801	Can't Say Nothin'	Curtis Mayfield	26-Jan-74	Curtom 1993
4802	Texas	Charlie Daniels Band	28-Feb-76	Kama Sutra 607
4803	Loose Booty	Sly & The Family Stone	23-Nov-74	Epic 50033
4804	Any Way You Want Me	The Sylvers	3-Dec-77	Capitol 4493
4805	Slip 'N Slide	Rufus	12-May-73	ABC 11356
4806	Dancin' Thru The Night	L.A. Jets	3-Jul-76	RCA Victor 10668
4807	25th Of Last December	Roberta Flack	14-Jan-78	Atlantic 3441
4808	That's The Sound That Lonely Makes	Tavares	2-Mar-74	Capitol 3794
4809	Summer In The City	Quincy Jones	8-Sep-73	A&M 1455
4810	Heart On My Sleeve	Gallagher And Lyle	18-Dec-76	A&M 1850
4811	Shout It Out	B.T. Express	4-Mar-78	Columbia 10649
4812	Get Into Something	The Isley Brothers	7-Nov-70	T-Neck 924
4813	So Many People	Chase	8-Jan-72	Epic 10806
4814	Give A Little	Robert John	13-May-78	Ariola America 7693
4815	Capture Your Heart	Blue	28-May-77	Rocket/MCA 40706
4816	This Magic Moment	Richie Furay	1-Jul-78	Asylum 45487
4817	Some Things A Man's Gotta Do	Shango	1-Aug-70	Dunhill 4242
4818	I Got A Thing, You Got A Thing, Everybody's Got A Thing	Funkadelic	18-Apr-70	Westbound 158
4819	Nutrocker	Emerson, Lake & Palmer	15-Apr-72	Cotillion 44151
4820	Everybody But Me	G.W. Kenny	8-Sep-73	Kama Sutra 581

'70s Rank	TITLE	ACT	Peak Date	Label & No.
4821	Everything That 'Cha Do (Will Come Back To You)	Wet Willie	5-Jun-76	Capricorn 0254
4822	Make It With You	The Whispers	27-Aug-77	Soul Train 10996
4823	The Crude Oil Blues	Jerry Reed	2-Mar-74	RCA Victor 0224
4824	Keep Our Love Alive	Paul Davis	26-Jul-75	Bang 718
4825	Adrienne	Tommy James	27-Mar-71	Roulette 7100
4826	The Man On Page 602	Zoot Fenster	6-Dec-75	Antique 106
4827	Christmas Dream	Perry Como	11-Jan-75	RCA Victor 10122
4828	I Could Never Be Happy	The Emotions	26-Aug-72	Volt 4083
4829	Love Is For The Best In Us	James Walsh Gypsy Band	26-May-79	RCA 11480
4830	Come Softly To Me	The New Seekers	10-Feb-73	MGM/Verve 10698
4831	More Power To You	Tommy Tate	23-Dec-72	KoKo 2114
4832	More Than I Can Stand	Bobby Womack	16-May-70	Minit 32093
4833	Soft And Wet	Prince	11-Nov-78	Warner Bros. 8619
4834	Deteriorata	National Lampoon	4-Nov-72	Banana 218
4835	Only The Strong Survive	REO Speedwagon	15-Dec-79	Epic 50790
4836	I Can Feel You	The Addrisi Brothers	17-Jun-72	Columbia 45610
4837	48 Crash	Suzi Quatro	11-May-74	Bell 45,401
4838	Hey, Little Girl	Foster Sylvers	10-Nov-73	MGM 14630
4839	Bad Side Of The Moon	April Wine	12-Aug-72	Big Tree 142
4840	I'll Be Standing By	Foghat	2-Apr-77	Bearsville 0315
4841	Easy Way Out	Roy Orbison	7-Jul-79	Asylum 46048
4842	Country Woman	The Magic Lantern	22-Jul-72	Charisma 100
4843	Dancing In The Moonlight (It's Caught Me In Its Spotlight)	Thin Lizzy	29-Oct-77	Mercury 73945
4844	Sound And Vision	David Bowie	7-May-77	RCA 10905
4845	And I Love You So	Bobby Goldsboro	22-May-71	United Artists 50776
4846	Full Circle	The Byrds	12-May-73	Asylum 11016
4847	Is Anybody Goin' To San Antone	Charley Pride	28-Mar-70	RCA Victor 47-9806
4848	Take It Off Him And Put It On Me	Clarence Carter	28-Feb-70	Atlantic 2702
4849	Sgt. Pepper's Lonely Hearts Club Band/With A Little Help From My Friends	The Beatles	23-Sep-78	Capitol 4612
4850	Roll Away The Stone	Leon Russell	27-Jun-70	Shelter 301
4851	Rock 'N Roll (I Gave You The Best Years Of My Life)	Terry Jacks	14-Dec-74	Bell 45,606
4852	Sometimes It's Got To Rain	Jackie Moore	15-May-71	Atlantic 2798
4853	Under The Influence Of Love	Love Unlimited	4-May-74	20th Century 2082
4854	Sneaky Snake	Tom T. Hall	8-Mar-75	Mercury 73641
4855	I'm Gonna Be A Country Girl Again	Buffy Sainte-Marie	11-Dec-71	Vanguard 35143
4856	Saved By The Grace Of Your Love	Sons Of Champlin	9-Jul-77	Ariola America 7664
4857	Slow Down	Crow	4-Apr-70	Amaret 119
4858	Sho Nuff Boogie (Part 1)	Sylvia & The Moments	29-Jun-74	All Platinum 2350
4859	Memphis At Sunrise	Bar-Kays	4-Nov-72	Volt 4081

'70s Rank	TITLE	ACT	Peak Date	Label & No.
4860	Wake Up	Law	25-Oct-75	GRC 2072
4861	Love Is The Answer	Van Mc Coy	14-Sep-74	Avco 4639
4862	Something Better	Chilliwack	3-Sep-77	Mushroom 7025
4863	Fifteen Years Ago	Conway Twitty	28-Nov-70	Decca 32742
4864	Funky President (People It's Bad)	James Brown	16-Nov-74	Polydor 14258
4865	Put It Where You Want It	Nino & April	7-Jul-73	A&M 1443
4866	Willie Pass The Water	Ripple	9-Mar-74	GRC 1013
4867	One Woman Band	Carol Chase	17-Jan-76	Janus 256
4868	Ocean Of Thoughts And Dreams	The Dramatics	29-Apr-78	ABC 12331
4869	He Ain't Heavy...He's My Brother	Olivia Newton-John	29-Nov-75	MCA 40495
4870	I Was Wondering	The Poppy Family	10-Apr-71	London 148
4871	Chestnut Mare	Byrds	28-Nov-70	Columbia 45259
4872	Rosanna	Dennis Yost & The Classics IV	17-Mar-73	MGM South 7012
4873	Everything Is Going To Be Alright	Teegarden & Van Winkle	9-Jan-71	Westbound 171
4874	Granddaddy (Part 1)	The New Birth	17-May-75	Buddah 464
4875	(Bringing Out) The Girl In Me	Maxine Nightingale	1-Dec-79	Windsong 11729
4876	What Made America Famous	Harry Chapin	13-Jul-74	Elektra 45893
4877	Party Music	Pat Lundi	18-Oct-75	Vigor 1723
4878	Keep Yourself Alive	Queen	30-Aug-75	Elektra 45268
4879	Drive My Car	Gary Toms Empire	20-Dec-75	Pickwick Int'l 6509
4880	Makin' The Best Of A Bad Situation	Dick Feller	29-Jun-74	Asylum 11037
4881	Funk It Up (David's Song)	Sweet	24-Sep-77	Capitol 4454
4882	For A While	Mary MacGregor	27-Aug-77	Ariola America 7667
4883	Heart To Heart	Errol Sober	31-Mar-79	Number 1 Record 215
4884	Candy Apple Red	R. Dean Taylor	14-Aug-71	Rare Earth 5030
4885	Holly Go Softly	Cornerstone	11-Apr-70	Liberty 56148
4886	I Been Moved	Andy Kim	17-Jul-71	Steed 734
4887	Friend And A Lover	The Partridge Family	14-Apr-73	Bell 45,336
4888	You Can't Go Halfway	Johnny Nash	5-Oct-74	Epic 50021
4889	A Song For You	Andy Williams	4-Sep-71	Columbia 45434
4890	You	Aretha Franklin	31-Jan-76	Atlantic 3311
4891	More And More	Carly Simon	25-Oct-75	Elektra 45278
4892	The House On Telegraph Hill	Bo Donaldson And The Heywoods	19-Apr-75	ABC 12072
4893	I Love My Wife	Frank Sinatra	22-Jan-77	Reprise 1383
4894	It's Forever	The Ebonys	4-Aug-73	Phila. Int'l 3529
4895	Rumor At The Honky Tonk	Spellbound	12-Aug-78	EMI America 8002
4896	You'll Never Walk Alone	Blue Haze	23-Jun-73	A&M 1426
4897	You're In Good Hands	Jermaine Jackson	13-Oct-73	Motown 1244
4898	I Never Said I Love You	Orsa Lia	14-Apr-79	Infinity 50,004
4899	What's Come Over Me	Blue Magic	13-Dec-75	Atco/WMOT 7030
4900	There But For The Grace Of God Go I	Machine	12-May-79	RCA/Hologram 11456

'70s Rank	TITLE	ACT	Peak Date	Label & No.
4901	The Call	Anne Murray	6-Mar-76	Capitol 4207
4902	Harlem	The 5th Dimension	7-Dec-74	Bell 45,612
4903	Let Me Be Good To You	Lou Rawls	28-Jul-79	Phila. Int'l 3684
4904	Still The Lovin' Is Fun	B.J. Thomas	10-Dec-77	MCA 40812
4905	What's A Matter Baby	Ellen Foley	24-Nov-79	Cleveland Int'l/Epic 50770
4906	Peace In The Valley Of Love	The Persuaders	2-Dec-72	Win Or Lose 225
4907	Fever	Rita Coolidge	27-Jan-73	A&M 1398
4908	Hot Wire	Al Green	3-Feb-73	Bell 45,305
4909	Jam Band	Disco Tex & The Sex-O-Lettes	20-Sep-75	Chelsea 3026
4910	Gas Lamps And Clay	Blues Image	10-Oct-70	Atco 6777
4911	Country Preacher	Cannonball Adderley Quintet	7-Feb-70	Capitol 2698
4912	Back To Dreamin' Again	Pat Shannon	31-Jan-70	Uni 55191
4913	Arms Of Mary	Chilliwack	26-Aug-78	Mushroom 7033
4914	Darling Be Home Soon	The Association	3-Jun-72	Columbia 45602
4915	She	Southcote	23-Mar-74	Buddah 399
4916	I'm Scared	Burton Cummings	12-Mar-77	Portrait 70002
4917	Carey	Joni Mitchell	28-Aug-71	Reprise 1029
4918	Hang Loose	Mandrill	18-Aug-73	Polydor 14187
4919	Party Line	Andrea True Connection	25-Sep-76	Buddah 538
4920	Crazy Talk	Chilliwack	11-Jan-75	Sire 716
4921	Je T'Aime...Moi Non Plus	Jane Birkin & Serge Gainsbourg	14-Feb-70	Fontana 1665
4922	Started Out Dancing, Ended Up Making Love	Alan O'Day	29-Oct-77	Pacific 002
4923	Taos New Mexico	R. Dean Taylor	22-Apr-72	Rare Earth 5041
4924	(She's A) Very Lovely Woman	Linda Ronstadt	13-Feb-71	Capitol 3021
4925	Don't Throw Our Love Away	Orleans	18-Aug-79	Infinity 50,017
4926	Cum On Feel The Noize	Slade	9-Jun-73	Polydor 15069
4927	Warmin' Up The Band	Don Everly	20-Jul-74	Ode 66046
4928	In The Rain	Arthur Prysock	20-Oct-73	Old Town 100
4929	Take Me Home	Balcones Fault	20-Aug-77	Cream 7714
4930	Carrie's Gone	J.C. Stone	19-Oct-74	Private Stk 45,002
4931	Rings	Reuben Howell	3-Aug-74	Motown 1305
4932	I Can't Help It	The Moments	17-Apr-71	Stang 5020
4933	Keep Me In Mind	Lynn Anderson	3-Mar-73	Columbia 45768
4934	The Seeker	Dolly Parton	16-Aug-75	RCA Victor 10310
4935	Words (Are Impossible)	Donny Gerrard	1-May-76	Greedy 101
4936	Soledad	Eric Burdon & Jimmy Witherspoon	6-Nov-71	MGM 14296
4937	Who Gets Your Love	Dusty Springfield	31-Mar-73	Dunhill 4341
4938	A Sunday Kind Of Love	Lenny Welch	26-Aug-72	Atco 6894
4939	Sweet Lorraine	Uriah Heep	27-Jan-73	Mercury 73349
4940	Sheena Is A Punk Rocker	The Ramones	13-Aug-77	Sire 746

'70s Rank	TITLE	ACT	Peak Date	Label & No.
4941	Needles And Pins	Smokie	15-Oct-77	RSO 881
4942	It Hurts A Little Even Now	John Reid	24-May-75	Arista 0114
4943	I Have Learned To Do Without You	Mavis Staples	26-Sep-70	Volt 4044
4944	What's The Name Of This Funk (Spider Man)	Ramsey Lewis	7-Feb-76	Columbia 10235
4945	If Love Ruled The World	Bobby Bland	30-May-70	Duke 460
4946	Kentucky	Sammi Smith	12-Feb-72	Mega 0056
4947	You Are My Love	Liverpool Express	9-Oct-76	Atco 7058
4948	Down The Road	B.T.O.	15-Apr-78	Mercury 73987
4949	L.A. International Airport	Susan Raye	15-May-71	Capitol 3035
4950	Only One Song	Sha Na Na	22-May-71	Kama Sutra 522
4951	Something	Booker T. & The M.G.'s	1-Aug-70	Stax 0073
4952	Love And Desire (Part I)	Arpeggio	7-Apr-79	Polydor 14535
4953	Souvenirs	Voyage	10-Mar-79	Marlin 3330
4954	Goodbye Media Man (Part 1)	Tom Fogerty	14-Aug-71	Fantasy 661
4955	Georgia On My Mind	Willie Nelson	8-Jul-78	Columbia 10704
4956	You Know The Feelin'	Steve Wightman	29-May-76	Farr 003
4957	Midnight Love Affair	Tony Orlando And Dawn	29-May-76	Elektra 45319
4958	Daydream	David Cassidy	25-Aug-73	Bell 45,386
4959	Music	John Miles	12-Jun-76	London 20086
4960	What A Shame	Foghat	26-May-73	Bearsville 0014
4961	Easy Evil	John Kay	22-Sep-73	Dunhill 4360
4962	Funny How Love Can Be	First Class	28-Jun-75	UK 49033
4963	Only One Woman	Nigel Olsson	15-Mar-75	Rocket/MCA 40337
4964	Maria (You Were The Only One)	Jimmy Ruffin	27-Feb-71	Soul 35077
4965	God Bless	Arthur Conley	16-May-70	Atco 6747
4966	Bye Bye Baby	U.S. 1	6-Dec-75	Private Stk 45,045
4967	Wonder Girl	Sparks	11-Nov-72	Bearsville 0006
4968	Everybody Wants To Find A Bluebird	Randy Edelman	29-Mar-75	20th Century 2155
4969	I'm Falling In Love With You	Little Anthony And The Imperials	6-Jul-74	Avco 4635
4970	I Like It Like That	Loggins & Messina	13-Sep-75	Columbia 10188
4971	Free	Fresh Start	24-Aug-74	Dunhill/ABC 15002
4972	Rock 'N Roll (I Gave You The Best Years Of My Life)	Kevin Johnson	24-Nov-73	Mainstream 5548
4973	Come On Down	Savage Grace	25-Jul-70	Reprise 0924
4974	What A Difference You've Made In My Life	Ronnie Milsap	4-Feb-78	RCA 11146
4975	Nickel Song	The New Seekers	27-Mar-71	Elektra 45719
4976	In Thee	Blue Öyster Cult	15-Sep-79	Columbia 11055
4977	Touch Of Magic	James Leroy	25-Aug-73	Janus 219
4978	Passport To The Future	Jean Jacques Perrey	20-Jun-70	Vanguard 35105
4979	Melanie Makes Me Smile	Tony Burrows	27-Jun-70	Bell 884
4980	Fool Me	Joe South	11-Dec-71	Capitol 3204

'70s Rank	TITLE	ACT	Peak Date	Label & No.
4981	Baby Fat	Robert Byrne	23-Jun-79	Mercury 74070
4982	Baby, Baby My Love's All For You	Deniece Williams	18-Feb-78	Columbia 10648
4983	One More Tomorrow	Henry Gross	3-May-75	A&M 1682
4984	Bad Weather	The Supremes	30-Jun-73	Motown 1225
4985	Sunday Sunrise	Anne Murray	6-Dec-75	Capitol 4142
4986	Never Marry A Railroad Man	The Shocking Blue	6-Feb-71	Colossus 123
4987	Salsoul Hustle	The Salsoul Orchestra	11-Oct-75	Salsoul 2002
4988	Roller Coaster	Blood, Sweat & Tears	3-Nov-73	Columbia 45937
4989	You Know How It Is With A Woman	Jefferson	9-May-70	Janus 117
4990	Hikky Burr - Part One	Bill Cosby With The Bunions Bradford Band	10-Jan-70	Uni 55184
4991	Let This Be A Letter (To My Baby)	Jackie Wilson	30-May-70	Brunswick 55435
4992	This Bitter Earth	The Satisfactions	11-Jul-70	Lionel 3201
4993	Bra	Cymande	9-Jun-73	Janus 215
4994	Living It Down	Freddy Fender	27-Nov-76	ABC/Dot 17652
4995	Wonderful Baby	Don McLean	28-Jun-75	United Artists 614
4996	Celia Of The Seals	Donovan	6-Mar-71	Epic 10694
4997	Georgia Took Her Back	R.B. Greaves	3-Oct-70	Atco 6778
4998	Santo Domingo	The Sandpipers	12-Sep-70	A&M 1208
4999	Love Struck	Stonebolt	10-Mar-79	Parachute 522
5000	Battle Of New Orleans	Bert Sommer	19-Dec-70	Eleuthera 472
5001	Yankee Lady	Brewer And Shipley	29-Jul-72	Kama Sutra 547
5002	Hard Times	Peter Skellern	7-Feb-76	Private Stk 45,054
5003	Answer Me, My Love	The Happenings	31-Jan-70	Jubilee 5686
5004	You Are You	Gilbert O'Sullivan	22-Feb-75	MAM 3642
5005	Can I	Eddie Kendricks	27-Nov-71	Tamla 54210
5006	You Should Do It	Peter Brown	7-Oct-78	Drive 6272
5007	Everything's Alright	Yvonne Elliman	16-Oct-71	Decca 32870
5008	Africanism/Gimme Some Lovin'	Kongas	13-May-78	Polydor 14461
5009	I'm So Anxious	Southside Johnny & The Asbury Jukes	13-Oct-79	Mercury 76007
5010	Touch Me When We're Dancing	Bama	20-Oct-79	Free Flight 11629
5011	I Can Stand A Little Rain	Joe Cocker	2-Nov-74	A&M 1626
5012	Newsy Neighbors	First Choice	23-Mar-74	Philly Groove 183
5013	The Star Wars Stars	The Force	30-Jul-77	Lifesong 45031
5014	Room To Move	John Mayall	10-Jan-70	Polydor 14010
5015	Oh My My	The Monkees	9-May-70	Colgems 5011
5016	I Believe In Father Christmas	Greg Lake	3-Jan-76	Atlantic 3305
5017	Do You Wanna Dance	Ramones	29-Apr-78	Sire 1017
5018	Don't Mess Up A Good Thing	Gregg Allman	27-Apr-74	Capricorn 0042
5019	His Song Shall Be Sung	Lou Rawls	26-Feb-72	MGM 14349
5020	Song From M*A*S*H	Al DeLory	8-Aug-70	Capitol 2811
5021	Take It Any Way You Want It	Outlaws	13-Jan-79	Arista 0378

'70s Rank	TITLE	ACT	Peak Date	Label & No.
5022	Endlessly	Sonny James	24-Oct-70	Capitol 2914
5023	Strange	Jellyroll	12-Sep-70	Kapp 2107
5024	Dick And Jane	Bobby Vinton	1-Mar-75	ABC 12056
5025	Butterfly	Danyel Gérard	8-Jul-72	MGM/Verve 10670
5026	We All Need Love	Troiano	7-Jul-79	Capitol 4709
5027	All Over Me	Charlie Rich	27-Sep-75	Epic 50142
5028	When You Feel Love	Bob McGilpin	14-Oct-78	Butterfly 1211
5029	Bell Bottom Blues	Eric Clapton	3-Mar-73	Polydor 15056
5030	Take Me To Your Heart	Monkey Meeks	22-Dec-73	Roxbury 0133
5031	Flame	Steve Sperry	16-Jul-77	Mercury 73905
5032	Nice To Be Around	Maureen McGovern	23-Feb-74	20th Century 2072
5033	Love Hurts	Jim Capaldi	10-Jan-76	Island 045
5034	Black Night	Deep Purple	2-Jan-71	Warner Bros. 7405
5035	Satin Red And Black Velvet Woman	Dave Mason	19-Dec-70	Blue Thumb 7117
5036	Rust Never Sleeps (My My, Hey Hey [Into The Black])	Neil Young	10-Nov-79	Reprise 49031
5037	My Sweet Summer Suite	Love Unlimited Orchestra	6-Nov-76	20th Century 2301
5038	Who Are You	B.B. King	29-Jun-74	ABC 11433
5039	Come Go With Me	Pockets	21-Jan-78	Columbia 10632
5040	Just About The Same	The Association	14-Mar-70	Warner Bros. 7372
5041	You're Right, Ray Charles	Joe Tex	7-Mar-70	Dial 4096
5042	One Way Sunday	Mark-Almond	11-Mar-72	Blue Thumb 206
5043	Thank God For You Baby	PG&E	1-Apr-72	Columbia 45519
5044	Anytime (I'll Be There)	Frank Sinatra	3-May-75	Reprise 1327
5045	Good, Good Feelin'	War	12-May-79	MCA 40995
5046	Goodnight And Goodmorning	Cecilio & Kapono	24-Jan-76	Columbia 10223
5047	Tryin' To Beat The Morning Home	T.G. Sheppard	14-Jun-75	Melodyland 6006
5048	Midnight Light	Le Blanc & Carr	24-Jun-78	Big Tree 16114
5049	Ain't That Peculiar	Fanny	13-May-72	Reprise 1080
5050	If I Were A Carpenter	Bob Seger	22-Jul-72	Palladium 1079
5051	Anybody Wanna Party?	Gloria Gaynor	14-Jul-79	Polydor 14558
5052	The Witch	The Rattles	8-Aug-70	Probe 480
5053	Amerikan Music	Steve Alaimo	22-Apr-72	Entrance 7507
5054	'Til I Make It On My Own	Tammy Wynette	8-May-76	Epic 50196
5055	Hell Cat	Bellamy Brothers	17-Jul-76	Warner/Curb 8220
5056	So Long, Marianne	Brian Hyland	10-Jul-71	Uni 55287
5057	Ride The Tiger	Jefferson Starship	14-Dec-74	Grunt 10080
5058	Breaking Up Somebody's Home	Albert King	3-Feb-73	Stax 0147
5059	Chokin' Kind	Z.Z. Hill	16-Oct-71	Mankind 12017
5060	Just One Look	Anne Murray	12-Oct-74	Capitol 3955
5061	I Need You	Euclid Beach Band	14-Apr-79	Epic/Cleveland Int'l 50676

'70s Rank	TITLE	ACT	Peak Date	Label & No.
5062	Funky Party	Clarence Reid	3-Aug-74	Alston 4621
5063	Walk Easy My Son	Jerry Butler	6-Nov-71	Mercury 73241
5064	Baby Make It Soon	The Flying Machine	28-Feb-70	Congress 6012
5065	Walk Right Back	Anne Murray	1-Apr-78	Capitol 4527
5066	It's Just A Matter Of Time	Sonny James	14-Feb-70	Capitol 2700
5067	Call Out My Name	Zwol	10-Feb-79	EMI America 8009
5068	Sharing The Night Together	Arthur Alexander	12-Jun-76	Buddah 522
5069	Love Me Now	Ruby Winters	30-Nov-74	Polydor 14249
5070	Love Is All	Engelbert Humperdinck	6-Oct-73	Parrot 40076
5071	You And I	Black Ivory	6-May-72	Today 1508
5072	Love Makes The World Go Round	Kiki Dee	10-Apr-71	Rare Earth 5025
5073	Red Red Wine	Vic Dana	23-May-70	Liberty 56163
5074	After The Feeling Is Gone	Lulu	11-Jul-70	Atco 6761
5075	Hollywood Hot	The Eleventh Hour	27-Sep-75	20th Century 2215
5076	Chase Me	Con Funk Shun	4-Aug-79	Mercury 74059
5077	Calico	Tommy James	27-Oct-73	Roulette 7147
5078	Let There Be Drums	The Incredible Bongo Band	17-Nov-73	MGM 14635
5079	All Things Are Possible	Dan Peek	20-Oct-79	MCA/Songbird 41123
5080	River Road	Uncle Dog	24-Mar-73	MCA 40005
5081	You Can't Do It Right (With The One You Love)	Deep Purple	4-Jan-75	Warner Bros. 8049
5082	Circles	The New Seekers	12-Aug-72	Elektra 45787
5083	Looky Looky (Look At Me Girl)	The O'Jays	29-Aug-70	Neptune 31
5084	Special Memory	Jerry Butler	7-Nov-70	Mercury 73131
5085	I Believe In Music	Marian Love	13-Mar-71	A&R 7100/505
5086	Who's Gonna Take The Weight (Part One)	Kool & The Gang	16-Jan-71	De-Lite 538
5087	Holy Cow	Stefan	4-Nov-72	Stax 0145
5088	Love Potion Number Nine	The Coasters	1-Jan-72	King 6385
5089	Day By Day (Godspell Medley)	Holly Sherwood	2-Oct-71	Carousel 30,057
5090	Don't Pull Your Love	Sam & Dave	20-Nov-71	Atlantic 2839
5091	Lady Blue	George Benson	29-Jul-78	Warner Bros. 8604
5092	Bell Bottom Blues	Derek And The Dominos	13-Feb-71	Atco 6803
5093	O-H-I-O	Ohio Players	27-Aug-77	Mercury 73932
5094	Love Me One Time (Just For Old Times' Sake)	Karen Nelson And Billy T	3-Sep-77	Amherst 724
5095	Compared To What	Les McCann & Eddie Harris	17-Jan-70	Atlantic 2694
5096	Theme From "The Prophet" (Pleasure Is A Freedom Song/On Love)	Richard Harris	15-Mar-75	Atlantic 3238
5097	Blood Red And Goin' Down	Tanya Tucker	22-Sep-73	Columbia 45892
5098	Clap Your Hands	The Manhattan Transfer	16-Aug-75	Atlantic 3277
5099	It's A Heartache	Juice Newton	15-Apr-78	Capitol 4552
5100	Hustle!!! (Dead On It)	James Brown	2-Aug-75	Polydor 14281
5101	Rock 'N Roll	Detroit	29-Jan-72	Paramount 0133

'70s Rank	TITLE	ACT	Peak Date	Label & No.
5102	Soulsville	Isaac Hayes	6-May-72	Enterprise 9045
5103	Gone Movin' On	Raiders	2-May-70	Columbia 45150
5104	If You've Got The Time	The Babys	12-Mar-77	Chrysalis 2132
5105	One Day Of Your Life	Andy Williams	18-Jul-70	Columbia 45175
5106	I Go To Pieces	Cotton, Lloyd And Christian	25-Oct-75	20th Century 2217
5107	Rainbow Man	Looking Glass	3-Mar-73	Epic 10953
5108	Rollin' With The Flow	Charlie Rich	24-Sep-77	Epic 50392
5109	It's Alright	Graham Central Station	13-Dec-75	Warner Bros. 8148
5110	Honey I Still Love You	The Mark IV	14-Oct-72	Mercury 73319
5111	A Lover's Question	Loggins & Messina	8-Nov-75	Columbia 10222
5112	Unloved	Walter Egan	17-Mar-79	Columbia 10916
5113	Some Beautiful	Jack Wild	13-Jun-70	Capitol 2742
5114	Tell Mama	Savoy Brown	13-Nov-71	Parrot 40066
5115	Nanu Nanu (I Wanna Get Funky Wich You)	Daddy Dewdrop	24-Feb-79	Inphasion 7201
5116	That's The Way I Want Our Love	Joe Simon	24-Oct-70	Sound Stage 7 2667
5117	Lazy Eyes	T.M.G.	17-Mar-79	Atco 7096
5118	Stealing Moments From Another Woman's Life	The Glass House	12-Dec-70	Invictus 9082
5119	Midnight Love Affair	Carol Douglas	15-Jan-77	Midland Int'l 10753
5120	You Take My Heart Away	James Darren	23-Apr-77	Private Stk 45,136
5121	I've Just Begun To Care	Michael Nesmith & The First National Band	13-Nov-71	RCA Victor 74-0540
5122	Trying To Slip (Away)	Lloyd Price	8-Sep-73	GSF 6904
5123	What You Got	Duke & The Drivers	13-Sep-75	ABC 12110
5124	I Wrote A Simple Song	Billy Preston	12-Feb-72	A&M 1320
5125	I'll Go To My Grave Loving You	The Statler Brothers	25-Oct-75	Mercury 73687
5126	The Funky Gibbon	The Goodies	24-May-75	20th Century 2189
5127	We Been Singin' Songs	Baron Stewart	11-Oct-75	United Artists 686
5128	If I Were A Carpenter	Leon Russell	18-May-74	Shelter 40210
5129	Wolfman Jack	Todd Rundgren	25-Jan-75	Bearsville 0301
5130	Woman To Woman	Barbara Mandrell	18-Mar-78	ABC/Dot 17736
5131	Bicycle Morning	Billy Sans	2-Feb-74	Atco 6945
5132	Darling Baby	Jackie Moore	15-Apr-72	Atlantic 2861
5133	Please Don't Tell Me How The Story Ends	Ronnie Milsap	21-Sep-74	RCA Victor 0313
5134	Your Precious Love	Linda Jones	11-Mar-72	Turbo 021
5135	Living Without You	Manfred Mann's Earth Band	18-Mar-72	Polydor 14113
5136	Simone	Henry Gross	13-Apr-74	A&M 1494
5137	Roxy Roller	Sweeney Todd	4-Sep-76	London 240
5138	When You Dance I Can Really Love	Neil Young	17-Apr-71	Reprise 0992
5139	Take Me With You	The Honey Cone	9-May-70	Hot Wax 7001
5140	Get Down People	Fabulous Counts	16-May-70	Moira 108
5141	Awaiting On You All	Silver Hawk	29-May-71	Westbound 178
5142	Theme From "Baa Baa Black Sheep"	Mike Post	9-Apr-77	Epic 50325

'70s Rank	TITLE	ACT	Peak Date	Label & No.
5143	Send A Little Love My Way	Anne Murray	11-Aug-73	Capitol 3648
5144	You're A Lady	Gene Chandler	3-Jul-71	Mercury 73206
5145	Will You Love Me Tomorrow	Dana Valery	3-Jul-76	Phantom 10566
5146	Standing Here Wondering Which Way To Go	Marion Williams	27-Feb-71	Atlantic 2788
5147	Where Are We Going	Bobby Bloom	30-Jan-71	Roulette 7095
5148	Instigating (Trouble Making Fool)	Whatnauts	19-May-73	GSF 6897
5149	Funky L.A.	Paul Humphrey & His Cool Aid Chemists	24-Jul-71	Lizard 21009
5150	I Really Love You	Davy Jones	30-Oct-71	Bell 45,136
5151	What's Your Mama's Name	Tanya Tucker	23-Jun-73	Columbia 45799
5152	Midnight Show	Ron Dante	8-Mar-75	Arista 0111
5153	Dolly Dagger	Jimi Hendrix	30-Oct-71	Reprise 1044
5154	You're A Part Of Me	Susan Jacks	22-Mar-75	Mercury 73649
5155	Too Hot To Handle	UFO	3-Sep-77	Chrysalis 2157
5156	God Bless Our Love	Charles Brimmer	26-Jul-75	Chelsea 3017
5157	Spanish Wine	Lou Christie	18-Jun-77	Midsong Int'l 10959
5158	Stormy Monday	Latimore	22-Dec-73	Glades 1716
5159	Tulsa Time	Don Williams	9-Dec-78	ABC 12425
5160	Woman Is The Nigger Of The World	John Lennon/Plastic Ono Band	3-Jun-72	Apple 1848
5161	Papa Was A Rollin' Stone	The Undisputed Truth	17-Jun-72	Gordy 7117
5162	Spring Rain	Silvetti	19-Mar-77	Salsoul 2014
5163	Mendelssohn's 4th (Second Movement)	Apollo 100	22-Apr-72	Mega 0069
5164	The Lonely One	Special Delivery featuring Terry Huff	19-Jun-76	Mainstream 5581
5165	Only Love Can Break A Heart	Jackie Deshannon	2-Sep-72	Atlantic 2871
5166	Suite: Man And Woman	Tony Cole	18-Nov-72	20th Century 2001
5167	You Are My Sunshine	Dyke And The Blazers	31-Jan-70	Original Sound 90
5168	I Can Remember	Oliver	18-Jul-70	Crewe 346
5169	Oh How Happy	The Skyliners	29-Apr-78	Tortoise Int'l 11243
5170	(Any Way That You Want It) I'll Be There	Starz	18-Mar-78	Capitol 4546
5171	Stay Away From Me	The Sylvers	25-Aug-73	MGM 14579
5172	Top Forty (Of The Lord)	Sha Na Na	21-Aug-71	Kama Sutra 528
5173	Sunshine Ship	Arthur, Hurley & Gottlieb	4-Aug-73	Columbia 45881
5174	The Sound Of Silence	Peaches & Herb	3-Jul-71	Columbia 45386
5175	I Just Can't Say Goodbye	Philly Devotions	22-Feb-75	Columbia 10076
5176	Secrets	Sutherland Brothers & Quiver	29-Jan-77	Columbia 10460
5177	How Did We Lose It Baby	Jerry Butler	17-Jul-71	Mercury 73210
5178	Sweet Sweetheart	Bobby Vee	7-Nov-70	Liberty 56208
5179	Daylight	Vicki Sue Robinson	23-Oct-76	RCA 10775
5180	Banks Of The Ohio	Olivia Newton-John	23-Oct-71	Uni 55304
5181	Sneakin' Sally Through The Alley	Robert Palmer	2-Aug-75	Island 006
5182	You Don't Owe Me	The Blue Ridge Rangers	13-Oct-73	Fantasy 710

'70s Rank	TITLE	ACT	Peak Date	Label & No.
5183	Olena	Don Nix	6-Nov-71	Elektra 45746
5184	What Do You Know About Love	Apple & Appleberry	20-Apr-74	ABC 11415
5185	Theme From Rocky (Gonna Fly Now)	Rhythm Heritage	2-Apr-77	ABC 12243
5186	Calling Occupants	Klaatu	2-Apr-77	Capitol 4412
5187	In The Winter	Janis Ian	13-Dec-75	Columbia 10228
5188	Six Packs A Day	Billy Lemmons	2-Apr-77	Ariola America 7661
5189	It's The Same Old Love	The Courtship	3-Jun-72	Tamla 54217
5190	Vanilla Olay	Jackie DeShannon	15-Jul-72	Atlantic 2871
5191	Questions	Bang	13-May-72	Capitol 3304
5192	Grandmother's Song	Steve Martin	10-Dec-77	Warner Bros. 8503
5193	Freight Train	Duane Eddy	17-Jan-70	Congress 6010
5194	Do I Love You (Yes In Every Way)	Donna Fargo	25-Mar-78	Warner Bros. 8509
5195	Slipping Into Christmas	Leon Russell	9-Dec-72	Shelter 7328
5196	Fool Like You	Tim Moore	21-Apr-73	Dunhill 4337
5197	The Mosquito	The Doors	21-Oct-72	Elektra 45807
5198	She's Got A Whole Number	Keith Herman	1-Dec-79	Radio 418
5199	Don't Get Close	Little Anthony & The Imperials	28-Feb-70	United Artists 50625
5200	Shaker Song	Spyro Gyra	15-Jul-78	Amherst 730
5201	Birds Of All Nations	George McCannon III	16-May-70	Amos 135
5202	Save Your Sugar For Me	Tony Joe White	18-Jul-70	Monument 1206
5203	After The First One	Yonah	15-Sep-79	Free Flight 11696
5204	(She's Just A) Fallen Angel	Starz	11-Dec-76	Capitol 4343
5205	Every Little Teardrop	Gallagher And Lyle	2-Apr-77	A&M 1904
5206	Mandrill	Mandrill	12-Jun-71	Polydor 14070
5207	The Electronic Magnetism (That's Heavy, Baby)	Solomon Burke	13-Mar-71	MGM 14221
5208	Easy Rider (Let The Wind Pay The Way)	Iron Butterfly	14-Nov-70	Atco 6782
5209	If I Were Only A Child Again	Curtis Mayfield	10-Nov-73	Curtom 1991
5210	No Charge	Shirley Caesar	31-May-75	Hob/Scepter 12402
5211	The Sound Of Silence	Paul Simon	18-May-74	Columbia 46038
5212	I Got To Tell Somebody	Betty Everett	23-Jan-71	Fantasy 652
5213	Keep On Keeping On	N.F. Porter	18-Dec-71	Lizard 1010
5214	I Want To Pay You Back (For Loving Me)	The Chi-Lites	25-Sep-71	Brunswick 55458
5215	Valerie	Cymarron	9-Oct-71	Entrance 7502
5216	Loving Arms	Kris Kristofferson & Rita Coolidge	6-Apr-74	A&M 1498
5217	Let's Live Together	Cazz	11-Mar-78	Number 1 Record 210
5218	Tryin' To Stay 'live	The Asylum Choir	5-Feb-72	Shelter 7313
5219	All I Wanna Do	Doucette	28-Oct-78	Mushroom 7036
5220	Happier	Paul Anka	15-Jan-77	United Artists 911
5221	My Mind Keeps Telling Me (That I Really Love You, Girl)	Eddie Holman	30-Sep-72	GSF 6873

'70s Rank	TITLE	ACT	Peak Date	Label & No.
5222	All His Children	Charley Pride/Henry Mancini	4-Mar-72	RCA Victor 74-0624
5223	I Wanna Be Your Baby	The Three Degrees	22-Jul-72	Roulette 7125
5224	Melanie Makes Me Smile	Terry Williams	16-Dec-72	Verve 10686
5225	Little Woman Love	Wings	22-Jul-72	Apple 1851
5226	The Pride (Part 1)	The Isley Brothers	28-May-77	T-Neck 2262
5227	If That's The Way You Want It	Diamond Head	26-May-73	Dunhill 4342
5228	What It Takes To Get A Good Woman (That's What It's Gonna Take To Keep Her)	Denise LaSalle	19-May-73	Westbound 215
5229	House Of Strangers	Jim Gilstrap	30-Aug-75	Roxbury 2013
5230	Can You Feel It	Bobby Goldsboro	2-May-70	United Artists 50650
5231	Top Of The World (Make My Reservation)	Canyon	28-Jun-75	Magna-Glide 323
5232	Greenwood Mississippi	Little Richard	26-Sep-70	Reprise 0942
5233	Baby, Is There Something On Your Mind	McKinley Travis	1-Aug-70	Pride 2
5234	I Could Have Loved You	The Moments	22-Apr-78	Stang 5075
5235	Can't Stop Lovin' You	The Flirtations	11-Jul-70	Deram 85062
5236	Drivin' Home	Jerry Smith	27-Jun-70	Decca 32679
5237	Music Is Love	David Crosby	24-Apr-71	Atlantic 2792
5238	What Time Of Day	Billy Thunderkloud & The Chieftones	19-Jul-75	20th Century 2181
5239	Our Last Song Together	Bo Donaldson And The Heywoods	26-Jul-75	ABC 12108
5240	It's Better To Have (And Don't Need)	Don Covay	20-Jul-74	Mercury 73469
5241	1984	David Bowie	7-Sep-74	RCA Victor 10026
5242	Funky	The Chambers Brothers	27-Feb-71	Columbia 45277
5243	See The Light	The Flame	21-Nov-70	Brother 3500
5244	What's Going On	Quincy Jones	18-Dec-71	A&M 1316
5245	Lookin' Back	Bob Seger	27-Nov-71	Capitol 3187
5246	Every Beat Of My Heart	Crown Heights Affair	10-Jan-76	De-Lite 1575
5247	Another Love	Ian Lloyd & Stories	31-Aug-74	Kama Sutra 594
5248	Made To Love You	Gary Wright	9-Oct-76	Warner Bros. 8250
5249	Summertime	Billy Hemmans & Clays Composite	21-Nov-70	Blue Fox 102
5250	That's The Way God Planned It	Billy Preston	19-Aug-72	Apple 1808
5251	What It Is	The Undisputed Truth	18-Mar-72	Gordy 7114
5252	If You Love Me Like You Say You Love Me	Betty Wright	22-Apr-72	Alston 4609
5253	Let's Spend The Night Together	David Bowie	11-Aug-73	RCA Victor 0028
5254	A Pirate Looks At Forty	Jimmy Buffett	19-Apr-75	ABC/Dunhill 15029
5255	Castles In The Sand	Seals & Crofts	20-Sep-75	Warner Bros. 8130
5256	Playing Your Game, Baby	Barry White	18-Feb-78	20th Century 2361
5257	What A Man, My Man Is	Lynn Anderson	11-Jan-75	Columbia 10041
5258	1927 Kansas City	Mike Reilly	17-Apr-71	Paramount 0053
5259	Ridin' The Storm Out	REO Speedwagon	11-Jun-77	Epic 50367
5260	Animal Zoo	Spirit	26-Sep-70	Epic 10648

'70s Rank	TITLE	ACT	Peak Date	Label & No.
5261	Michigan Harry Slaughter	Wadsworth Mansion	24-Apr-71	Sussex 215
5262	To The Other Man	Luther Ingram	17-Oct-70	KoKo 2106
5263	Odyssey Rock Park	Al Capps Band	10-Oct-70	Columbia 45219
5264	Bright Lights, Big City	Sonny James	14-Aug-71	Capitol 3114
5265	It's About Time	The Dillards	7-Aug-71	Anthem 101
5266	Growin' Up	Dan Hill	7-Feb-76	20th Century 2254
5267	Will You Love Me Tomorrow?	Linda Ronstadt	4-Apr-70	Capitol 2767
5268	My Woman, My Woman, My Wife	Dean Martin	15-Aug-70	Reprise 0934
5269	We Got A Dream	Ocean	21-Aug-71	Kama Sutra 529
5270	Something In You	Manitoba	28-Nov-70	RCA Victor 47-9908
5271	Scratch My Back (And Mumble In My Ear)	Clarence Carter	18-Dec-71	Atlantic 2842
5272	Lucky Me	The Moments	4-Sep-71	Stang 5031
5273	If It's Alright With You	Rose Colored Glass	30-Oct-71	Bang 588
5274	Girl You Need A Change Of Mind (Part 1)	Eddie Kendricks	10-Mar-73	Tamla 54230
5275	Do Ya	The Move	4-Nov-72	United Artists 50928
5276	Stories??	Chakachas	5-Aug-72	Avco 4596
5277	The King Of Rock 'N' Roll	Cashman & West	25-Aug-73	Dunhill 4349
5278	The Millionaire	Dr. Hook	27-Sep-75	Capitol 4104
5279	Damn It All	Gene Cotton	17-May-75	ABC 12087
5280	We Can't Dance To Your Music	The Grass Roots	15-Dec-73	Dunhill 4371
5281	I'm On Fire	Jim Gilstrap	29-Nov-75	Roxbury 2016
5282	There's So Much Love All Around Me	The Three Degrees	22-May-71	Roulette 7102
5283	Train Called Freedom	South Shore Commission	27-Mar-76	Wand 11294
5284	Come Into My Life	Jimmy Cliff	28-Mar-70	A&M 1167
5285	Detroit City	Dean Martin	24-Oct-70	Reprise 0955
5286	Faithful And True	Z.Z. Hill	17-Jul-71	Mankind 12003
5287	Groovin' With Mr. Bloe	Cool Heat	5-Sep-70	Forward/MGM 152
5288	(Until Then) I'll Suffer	Barbara Lynn	21-Aug-71	Atlantic 2812
5289	Stop The World And Let Me Off	Flaming Ember	27-Feb-71	Hot Wax 7010
5290	Give The Baby Anything The Baby Wants	Joe Tex	2-Oct-71	Dial 1008
5291	Forever And Ever	Slik	8-May-76	Arista 0179
5292	Thank God And Greyhound	Roy Clark	28-Nov-70	Dot 17355
5293	You Took The Words Right Out Of My Mouth (Hot Summer Night)	Meat Loaf	10-Dec-77	Cleveland Int'l/Epic 50467
5294	Where Are You	Cat Stevens	29-Jan-72	Deram 85079
5295	Brandy	Scott English	18-Mar-72	Janus 171
5296	We Both Need Each Other	Norman Connors	28-Aug-76	Buddah 534
5297	Keep That Same Old Feeling	Side Effect	11-Jun-77	Fantasy 792
5298	I Got A Thing About You Baby	Billy Lee Riley	14-Oct-72	Entrance 7508
5299	Only Love	Bill Quateman	21-Apr-73	Columbia 45792
5300	Nothin' Heavy	David Bellamy	11-Oct-75	Warner/Curb 8123
5301	Bad Luck	The Atlanta Disco Band	7-Feb-76	Ariola America 7611

'70s Rank	TITLE	ACT	Peak Date	Label & No.
5302	Sharing The Night Together	Lenny Le Blanc	12-Jun-76	Big Tree 16062
5303	Mr. Limousine Driver	Grand Funk Railroad	17-Jan-70	Capitol 2691
5304	School's Back	Philadelphia	22-Oct-77	Warner Bros. 8470
5305	What's Your Name, What's Your Number	Andrea True Connection	11-Feb-78	Buddah 582
5306	The Fightin' Side Of Me	Merle Haggard	7-Mar-70	Capitol 2719
5307	Amber Cascades	America	18-Sep-76	Warner Bros. 8238
5308	Down To Love Town	The Originals	18-Dec-76	Soul 35119
5309	Never Have To Say Goodbye Again	Deardorff & Joseph	23-Apr-77	Arista 0230
5310	You're Gonna Make It	The Festivals	26-Sep-70	Colossus 122
5311	Some Broken Hearts Never Mend	Don Williams	28-May-77	ABC/Dot 17683
5312	Them Changes	Buddy Miles & The Freedom Express	13-Jun-70	Mercury 73008
5313	It Ain't Easy Comin' Down	Charlene	2-Apr-77	Prodigal 0632
5314	Leave My Man (Woman) Alone	The Raeletts	4-Sep-71	Tangerine 1017
5315	S.T.O.P. (Stop)	The Lorelei	18-Nov-72	Columbia 45629
5316	Don't Let It End ('til You Let It Begin)	The Miracles	11-Aug-73	Tamla 54237
5317	Am I Black Enough For You	Billy Paul	14-Apr-73	Phila. Int'l 3526
5318	Friends Or Lovers	Act I	31-Mar-73	Spring 132
5319	Love Music	Sergio Mendes & Brasil '77	19-May-73	Bell 45,335
5320	Should I Tie A Yellow Ribbon Round The Ole Oak Tree? The Answer	Connie Francis	14-Jul-73	GSF 6901
5321	No Love In The Room	The 5th Dimension	22-Feb-75	Arista 0101
5322	Reach Out I'll Be There	The New Seekers	19-Jan-74	MGM 14683
5323	Easy Evil	Travis Wammack	25-Oct-75	Capricorn 0242
5324	You've Got Me Dangling On A String	Donny Osmond	1-Oct-77	Polydor 14417
5325	Since I Fell For You/I'm Falling In Love	Hodges, James And Smith	20-Aug-77	London 256
5326	Free Me From My Freedom/Tie Me To A Tree (Handcuff Me)	Bonnie Pointer	18-Nov-78	Motown 1451
5327	Big Yellow Taxi	Joni Mitchell	11-Jul-70	Reprise 0906
5328	If My Heart Could Speak	Manhattans	27-Jun-70	DeLuxe 122
5329	Your Love Is So Doggone Good	The Whispers	12-Jun-71	Janus 150
5330	Bring It On Home	Lou Rawls	15-Aug-70	Capitol 2856
5331	Stealing Love	The Emotions	11-Apr-70	Volt 4031
5332	Black-Eyed Blues	Joe Cocker	17-Jul-71	A&M 1258
5333	Pin The Tail On The Donkey	The Newcomers	9-Oct-71	Stax 0099
5334	Louisiana Lady	New Riders Of The Purple Sage	30-Oct-71	Columbia 45469
5335	I Refuse To Smile	Mandrill	1-Jul-72	Polydor 14127
5336	Why Do Fools Fall In Love	Summer Wine	24-Feb-73	Sire 701
5337	I Guess I'll Miss The Man	The Supremes	4-Nov-72	Motown 1213
5338	It's Too Late	Bill Deal & The Rhondels	19-Aug-72	Buddah 318
5339	Sha La Boom Boom	Bobby Bloom	3-Feb-73	MGM 14437
5340	Make My Life A Little Bit Brighter	Chester	1-Sep-73	Bell 45,379
5341	Bad, Bold And Beautiful Girl	The Persuaders	2-Jun-73	Atco 6919

'70s Rank	TITLE	ACT	Peak Date	Label & No.
5342	I Just Can't Turn My Habit Into Love	Buckwheat	19-May-73	London 189
5343	He Did Me Wrong, But He Did It Right	Patti Dahlstrom	12-Oct-74	20th Century 2113
5344	Ms. Grace	The Tymes	4-Jan-75	RCA Victor 10128
5345	Dancing In The Street	The Dovells	10-Aug-74	Event 216
5346	It Should Have Been Me	Yvonne Fair	22-May-76	Motown 1384
5347	Spaceship Superstar	Prism	5-Nov-77	Ariola America 7672
5348	Shake A Leg	Sea Level	18-Jun-77	Capricorn 0272
5349	Let's Clean Up The Ghetto	Philadelphia International All Stars	8-Oct-77	Phila. Int'l 3627
5350	Peter Gunn	Deodato	13-Nov-76	MCA 40631

Section 2

Ranking the Acts

In this section you will find the decade ranking for all 1698 acts that peaked with one or more song titles on the *Cash Box* Top 100 charts for the years 1970 to 1979.

An act is defined in this compilation in accordance with the labeling on its 7" or 45-rpm releases. As a rule, an act is signaled by upper case letters on the record label. Supporting acts such as backup bands that were signaled in lesser ways on the label (lower case, smaller print) were not credited.

An act is distinct from an artist. It was common for artists to be members of more than one act in the '70s and their points were distributed in Section 2 based on their act affiliations. For example, artist David Crosby was affiliated with five acts: Crosby, Stills, Nash & Young, the Byrds, Crosby, Stills & Nash (Groups), David Crosby / Graham Nash (Duos) and as himself (Soloists). He has no ranking as an artist; rather, in being claimed by five acts, David Crosby finds himself ranked at No. 308, No. 548, No. 804, No. 1107 and No. 1662.

The numbers 1-20 represent a 5-point percentile spread showing the act's relative popularity in each year. The Bee Gees' 15 in 1970 means they were in the lower 25 percent of all scoring acts that year. Their 1 in 1971 puts them in the top five percent. That number 15 in 1970 is italicized, indicating that they also had hits in the previous decade, and their italicized 1 in 1979 means they appeared in the following decade. Acts appearing only once in the '70s whose number is italicized also have a dash indicating the adjacent decade.

Since acts, not artists, are the focus, many interesting observations emerged for this ranking. For example, Alice Cooper is ranked twice, once as a group and once as a soloist; Steve Miller shows up twice--as soloist and with his group--reflecting an inconsistency on the labels of his singles; Elton John, the No. 1 *artist* of the decade is ranked the No. 3 *act* of the decade because he graciously shared top billing with his band on "Philadelphia Freedom" (Groups), and another #1 record, "Don't Go Breaking My Heart," was a duet with Kiki Dee, who is, herself, represented in this ranking in three places! No doubt you will find other surprises as you read through the list.

Perhaps the cleanest method of ranking acts is to simply sum the points of the underlying records for each act and rank them accordingly. For this work, however, we have chosen to add a second consideration related to the number of records that each act placed on the charts. The details of this ranking are found in the appendix, "The Scoring System Explained."

Rank	Act	'70	'71	'72	'73	'74	'75	'76	'77	'78	'79
1	Bee Gees	15	1	4	17	19	1	1	1	1	1
2	The Jackson 5 / Jacksons	1	1	1	7	3	6		4	15	3
3	Elton John	13	4	4	1	1	1	5	5	6	4
4	Carpenters	1	1	1	1	6	1	5	7	10	
5	Paul McCartney & Wings / Wings			9	1	1	1	1	5	2	3
6	Stevie Wonder	1	3	9	1	1	2		1		3
7	Chicago	3	2	4	2	3	4	2	4	6	6
8	Three Dog Night	1	1	1	2	3	10				
9	John Denver		2	8	4	1	1	4	11	10	
10	Neil Diamond	1	3	1	5	5	11	7		5	7
11	Tony Orlando And Dawn	3	1	10	1	7	1	8	14		
12	Elvis Presley	1	4	2	4	7	4	9	5		
13	Rod Stewart		1	4	10		12	1	7	2	1
14	Al Green	14	4	1	4	3	4		13	17	
15	Olivia Newton-John		7			1	1	6	8	3	2
16	Helen Reddy		6	2	1	1	3	6	6	19	15
17	Barry Manilow						1	1	2	1	4
18	Gladys Knight & The Pips	9	2	7	1	1	2	10	12		
19	Eagles			4	6	7	1	4	1	12	2
20	Donna Summer							4	4	1	1
21	Aretha Franklin	3	1	4	6	4	14	8	16		
22	The Temptations	1	1	3	4	7	5	12			
23	Diana Ross	2	4		2	6	17	1		8	7
24	KC & The Sunshine Band						1	3	1	7	2
25	Linda Ronstadt	9	17			11	1	5	1	5	4
26	The Rolling Stones		2	5	2	5	10	6		1	10
27	Spinners	6	16	3	2	5	2	3	17	16	
28	Commodores					7	8	4	2	1	1
29	Marvin Gaye	7	1	12	1	9		7	3		
30	The Doobie Brothers			6	3	7	2	6	8		1
31	The 5th Dimension	1	3	2	7	18	20	17			
32	Ringo Starr	13	3	7	2	1	1	9	11		
33	James Brown	3	3	4	9	5	15	13			
34	The Guess Who	1	5	7	14	5	8				
35	Cher		2	4	2	2	13				5
36	The O'Jays	12		3	2	5	8	4	15	4	
37	Bread	2	2	2	7				6		
38	Earth, Wind & Fire		16		12	7	2	3	8	3	2
39	Captain & Tennille						1	1	8	5	11
40	Carly Simon		6	5	1	7	9	11	2	5	13
41	Donny Osmond		1	1	4	8	13	9	20		
42	B.J. Thomas	1	4	6			3		6	12	
43	Barbra Streisand		4	11	14	2	17		1	8	3
44	The Osmonds		1	2	7	7	10	11			
45	Michael Jackson			1	12		8				2
46	Grand Funk Railroad	8	8	7	2	1	3	10			
47	Roberta Flack		1	1	4	15				2	
48	Andy Gibb								1	1	
49	War		9	5	1	5	2	7	12	13	20
50	Glen Campbell	3	8	14	11	14	1	6	2	11	

Rank	Act	'70	'71	'72	'73	'74	'75	'76	'77	'78	'79
51	The Stylistics		9	1	4	1	9	16			
52	James Taylor	3	2		7		4	9	2	17	10
53	Paul Simon			3	1	10		1		4	
54	The Partridge Family	1	1	5	10						
55	Electric Light Orchestra				10	10	6	2	3	4	2
56	Dr. Hook			3	4		20	2	10	3	3
57	America			1	7	6	2	7			
58	George Harrison	1	4		2		5		6		6
59	Creedence Clearwater Revival	1	2	9				11			
60	Abba					6	6	4	2	3	6
61	Jim Croce			4	1	1		12			
62	Carole King		1	6	5	3	7	8	9		
63	Anne Murray	5	15		4	4	12	19		3	3
64	Barry White				4	2	2	9	6	9	
65	Sly & The Family Stone	2	2	5	6	11					
66	Billy Preston		17	3	1	3	8				
67	Isley Brothers	10	5	6	4	9	3	10	12	16	18
68	Fleetwood Mac	13						3	1		5
69	Chic									1	1
70	The Staple Singers		5	2	5	9	3	12			
71	Melanie	3	1	6	10	11					
72	Tom Jones	2	1	13	11				7		
73	Gilbert O'Sullivan			1	1	12	19				
74	Four Tops	4	7	12	1	8	15	16			
75	Eddie Kendricks		13	11	2	1	4	12			
76	The Ohio Players				13	5	6	2	2	19	
77	Lobo		5	3	3	8	10				6
78	The Beatles	1						4		19	
79	Neil Sedaka						1	4	11		
80	Billy Joel					7	10			1	2
81	Frankie Valli						1	10		2	
82	Johnnie Taylor	6	8	11	4	11		2	14		
83	Steely Dan				3	3	10	15		3	
84	Cat Stevens		3	5	10	4	7	12	9		
85	Ray Stevens	3	9			2	6	19			12
86	Bill Withers		3	1	8	12		13		9	
87	Joe Simon	8	7	3	5		5	13			
88	Eric Clapton	7		13	19	2		9		2	5
89	The Who	3	4	9	9	15		5		5	12
90	Gordon Lightfoot		5	15		2	9	3	16	10	
91	Simon & Garfunkel	1		15			5				
92	Styx						4	8		3	1
93	Queen						6	3	6	2	17
94	Leo Sayer						4	2	1	9	
95	Daryl Hall & John Oates					12		2	2	9	12
96	Paul Anka		11	13		2	3	6	13	16	
97	Bachman-Turner Overdrive					1	4	8	17	19	14
98	Sweet		18		3		4	3	18	5	
99	Rufus Featuring Chaka Khan				18	3	5	3	7	12	
100	Kool & The Gang	14	19		12	3	5		13		2

Rank	Act	'70	'71	'72	'73	'74	'75	'76	'77	'78	'79
101	Bay City Rollers						2	3	4	8	
102	Seals & Crofts			5	3	11	7	5	8	8	
103	Charlie Rich	15			2	4	7	14	19		
104	The Chi-Lites	17	3	2	8	15					
105	Nilsson		8	1	9	9					
106	Kiss					17	14	3	3	11	4
107	Rare Earth	2	4	8						11	
108	Bobby Sherman	1	4	13							
109	David Bowie			11	7	13	2	5	18		
110	Jefferson Starship	11	10			20	3	6		4	4
111	Joe Cocker	3	9	8	10	11	4			13	
112	Isaac Hayes	10	1	5		11	14				
113	Led Zeppelin	2	5	6	5		10				
114	Foreigner								3	2	5
115	Hamilton, Joe Frank & Reynolds		2	10			3	7			
116	Don McLean			1	8		19				
117	Mac Davis	13		2	14	4	6				
118	Peter Frampton							2	2	13	8
119	Hollies	4		2	12	5	18				
120	John Lennon/Plastic Ono Band	9	2	14		3					
121	Santana	5	2	8					8		8
122	The Supremes	4	3	6	19			11			
123	The Grass Roots	6	2	7	10		17				
124	Steve Miller Band	17				2			2		
125	Bob Seger		20	19		18	11	17	3	3	5
126	Tommy James	11	2	6	12						
127	Atlanta Rhythm Section					13	16	12	4	4	5
128	Wilson Pickett	4	3	7	14						
129	Cornelius Brothers & Sister Rose		3	2	10						
130	The Main Ingredient	10	8	3	11	5	16				
131	Smokey Robinson & The Miracles	1	6	11	14						
132	Tyrone Davis	3	11	13	9	17		8	17		
133	Harold Melvin And The Blue Notes			3	5	17	5	6	14		
134	Hot Chocolate						3	2	10		4
135	The Sylvers				13			2	3		
136	Robert John	15		3						19	1
137	Bad Company					4	4	8	17		5
138	10cc				12	19	3	13	3	12	17
139	Bobby Vinton	8		4	16	4	9				
140	Honey Cone	19	1	5							
141	Silver Convention						2	3			
142	The Dramatics		6	3	9	13	11		10	19	
143	Engelbert Humperdinck	4	9	14	13		18		4		18
144	Little River Band							8	7	3	3
145	Pointer Sisters				6	8	6				2
146	Gerry Rafferty									1	4
147	Rita Coolidge					18			1	5	17
148	The Manhattans	20		17	8		9	1	12	18	
149	Raiders	14	1	8	15						
150	England Dan & John Ford Coley							3	5	7	6

Rank	Act	'70	'71	'72	'73	'74	'75	'76	'77	'78	'79
151	Tavares				11	12	4	5	7	10	
152	Aerosmith				11		10	4	4	9	
153	The Moody Blues	7	6	3	6					12	
154	Badfinger	3		3		19					18
155	Johnny Rivers	9	14		3		10		4	10	
156	Heart							5	5	5	10
157	Clarence Carter	2	11		11						
158	Curtis Mayfield		7	4	4	10	12				
159	B.B. King	5	7	10	11	9	16				
160	Eric Carmen							1	7	8	15
161	Dionne Warwick	3	11	16				15			3
162	Alice Cooper (Group)		8	4	6	10					
163	Todd Rundgren		7	7	3	13	17	11		11	
164	Neil Young	7	19	1		14					15
165	Debby Boone								1	14	
166	Freddy Fender						1	9			
167	Paul Davis	9			17		7	9		2	
168	Luther Ingram	8	18	2	8						
169	Village People									9	1
170	Kenny Rogers								5	9	1
171	Kansas								4	2	7
172	Peaches & Herb		20								1
173	Pablo Cruise								3	3	7
174	Jim Stafford				10	1	9	18			
175	Boz Scaggs		13					2	4	15	
176	Bobby Womack	18		5	6	5	15	19			
177	Johnny Nash	8		3	5	14		17			
178	Freda Payne	2	4								
179	Loggins & Messina			17	2	13	9				
180	Yvonne Elliman		9						4	2	12
181	The Shocking Blue	1	19								
182	Bob Dylan	9	11	9	6	9	11	8			11
183	John Lennon	2			7		5				
184	Harry Chapin			7		2	11	16			
185	Natalie Cole						5	5	3	7	
186	Average White Band / AWB						1	8			
187	Lynn Anderson		2	17	17		20				
188	The Knack										1-
189	Gary Wright							1	12		
190	Raspberries			4	4	9					
191	Steve Miller							1	4		
192	Edwin Starr	2	8		17						15
193	The Emotions	20		9			16		2		
194	Andy Kim	6	14			2					
195	Gloria Gaynor						5				2
196	Firefall							4	5	6	11
197	Crystal Gayle								2	6	7
198	Player									1	16
199	Donny And Marie Osmond						6	5	7	8	10
200	Boston							4	6	5	8

Rank	Act	'70	'71	'72	'73	'74	'75	'76	'77	'78	'79
201	Shaun Cassidy								1	7	
202	Alice Cooper						4	6	5	7	
203	Albert Hammond			3	9	10	16				
204	Mary MacGregor								1		10
205	Maxine Nightingale							3			3
206	David Cassidy			1	19						
207	Orleans						3	5	10		6
208	Exile									1	11
209	Gallery			1	7						
210	Norman Greenbaum	1									
211	Lynyrd Skynyrd					6	7	18	9	4	
212	Starland Vocal Band							1	18		
213	Al Wilson					1	13	10			
214	Nick Gilder									1	13
215	Jackson Browne			6	14				7	4	
216	Rose Royce								2	13	9
217	Bo Donaldson And The Heywoods			12		1	18				
218	Looking Glass			2	9						
219	Billy Paul			1	20	10		16			
220	Brownsville Station			18	13	3	15		9		
221	Wayne Newton			2	12	19		18			18
222	The Four Seasons						4	3	15		
223	The Edgar Winter Group				1	12					
224	John Travolta And Olivia Newton-John									1	
225	Tommy Roe	2	7		15						
226	Candi Staton	6	10	9	13		12	7			
227	Heatwave								2	4	
228	Stories			9	2	15					
229	C.W. McCall					14	16	1			
230	Joe Tex	19	20	2					7		
231	Supertramp						13		6		2
232	Donna Fargo			3	8	11				20	
233	Joni Mitchell	20	19		8	4	9	13			
234	The Miracles				20	6	14	2			
235	The New Seekers	6	13	7	8	17					
236	Blondie										1-
237	Art Garfunkel				5	7	6	9			13
238	Melissa Manchester						3	11			4
239	Lou Rawls	20	8	19				4	18	8	19
240	Ike & Tina Turner	14	4	17	9		12				
241	The Ozark Mountain Daredevils					9	2	14	11		
242	Marilyn McCoo & Billy Davis Jr.							14	1		
243	Sister Sledge										1-
244	Cheech & Chong				7	4	15	11	10		
245	The Undisputed Truth		3	14		17			11		
246	Meco								2	7	
247	Love Unlimited Orchestra					3	8	20	16		
248	Chairmen Of The Board	4	5		15						
249	Terry Jacks					2	17	16			
250	Millie Jackson				6	7	15	11		9	18

Rank	Act	'70	'71	'72	'73	'74	'75	'76	'77	'78	'79
251	Jerry Reed		3	14	13	19					
252	The Hues Corporation				10	2	12				
253	Blue Swede					2	14				
254	The DeFranco Family Feat. Tony DeFranco				2	6					
255	Ocean		2	18							
256	R. Dean Taylor	2	11	19							
257	The Beach Boys	12	17		20	14	12	5		15	9
258	B.T. Express					5	4	15		19	
259	Samantha Sang									1	
260	King Floyd		2	9							
261	Joan Baez		3	13			10				
262	Mark Lindsay	3	11								
263	Van Morrison	11	4	11	18				18	14	
264	Walter Murphy & The Big Apple Band							1	9		
265	Wild Cherry							2	10	17	
266	The J. Geils Band			10	7		7	10			10
267	Bette Midler				3	12			12	15	12
268	Vicki Lawrence				2		15				
269	Chuck Berry			2	9						
270	Sonny & Cher			2	15						
271	Ambrosia						7	18	10	3	
272	Betty Wright		17	4	16	13	15				
273	The Three Degrees	7	14	20		4					
274	Alan O'Day								1		
275	Rupert Holmes									15	1
276	Brook Benton	2	13								
277	The Moments	5	18		15	9	10			20	
278	Steppenwolf	5	8			9					
279	Jean Knight		2-								
280	Van McCoy					19	2	18			
281	Starbuck							3	9	13	
282	Dickie Goodman				15	11	3		11		17
283	Vanity Fare	2									
284	Jimmy Buffett					9	20		5	10	9
285	Kenny Rogers And The First Edition	2	12								
286	The Dells	7	10	17	7	13					
287	Michael Murphey			11			3	11			
288	Edward Bear	15			2						
289	Anita Ward										1
290	Eddie Holman	2		20							
291	MFSB					2	11				
292	Eddie Money									3	7
293	Bellamy Brothers							2			13
294	Eric Burdon And War	2	12								
295	A Taste Of Honey									1-	
296	Rick Dees & His Cast Of Idiots							1	15		
297	Bloodstone				3	9	10				
298	Dolly Parton						16	19		3	9
299	Andrew Gold							15	3	6	
300	Blood, Sweat & Tears	5	9	13	17		14				

Rank	Act	'70	'71	'72	'73	'74	'75	'76	'77	'78	'79
301	George McCrae					3	11	14			
302	Bob Welch								5	6	7
303	The Poppy Family (Group)	2									
304	Rhythm Heritage							2	20		
305	Five Man Electrical Band		4	13	14	12					
306	The Doors	10	3	14							
307	Al Stewart								4	6	10
308	Crosby, Stills, Nash & Young	2-									
309	Labelle						2				
310	George Benson							6	9	6	7
311	Dorothy Moore							3	9		
312	Barbra & Neil									2	
313	The Elton John Band						2				
314	The Allman Brothers Band				17	3	11				12
315	Minnie Riperton						2				
316	Redbone		12	8		4					
317	Maureen McGovern				5	15	18				7
318	The Impressions	6	13		18	8	9	16			
319	The Delfonics	4	10	14	16						
320	Billy Swan					3	11	15			
321	Janis Joplin		3	17							
322	Paper Lace					2					
323	Climax			2							
324	Stealers Wheel				3	8					
325	David Soul								2		
326	Smokey Robinson				14	8	6	14	14	18	
327	Bobby Goldsboro	15	5	17	8						
328	Carl Douglas					2	13				
329	Andrea True Connection							3	18	20	
330	Sammy Davis, Jr.			-2							
331	Ronnie Dyson	5	17		8			11			
332	John Sebastian							-1			
333	The Jimmy Castor Bunch			3			7				
334	Gino Vannelli					10		11		3	18
335	Stephen Bishop								3	10	14
336	Judy Collins		6	16	11		12		7		14
337	Leon Russell	18		7	18	20	6	12			
338	Jethro Tull		17		7		6	15	12		
339	Elton John and Kiki Dee							2			
340	David Gates				9		9			4	
341	Brian Hyland	3	12								
342	Amii Stewart										2
343	The Kinks	5	12						16	11	11
344	The Babys								6	12	5
345	Manfred Mann's Earth Band			20					3		13
346	Randy Newman									2-	
347	Cheap Trick									18	2
348	Nitty Gritty Dirt Band			4	18		17	14		16	
349	Wet Willie					7	14	19		7	9
350	Dennis Coffey And The Detroit Guitar Band			3							

Rank	Act	'70	'71	'72	'73	'74	'75	'76	'77	'78	'79
351	Henry Gross					18	19	4			
352	Thelma Houston	16							3		11
353	Charlie Daniels Band						7	19			*3*
354	Poco	15	13				11		12		*4*
355	Johnny Mathis/Deniece Williams									2	
356	Raydio									4	4
357	Deep Purple		*19*		4	19	*19*				
358	Ray Charles	*10*	8	10	12		18				
359	Ace						2				
360	Janis Ian						-2-				
361	John Travolta							4	9	13	
362	Kenny Nolan								2-		
363	Rick Nelson And The Stone Canyon Band	9		4	17						
364	Foghat				19			6	7	*13*	
365	Frank Mills			12							3
366	C. Wright/Watts 103rd Street Rhythm Band	*4*	11								
367	Dan Hill							20		2	
368	Major Harris						3	14			
369	Sylvia				3						
370	Hurricane Smith				3						
371	Herb Alpert										-2-
372	The Righteous Brothers					-3-					
373	Marvin Hamlisch					3					
374	Leif Garrett								9	7	6
375	Stephen Stills		5	12			*16*				
376	Barbra Streisand/Donna Summer										2
377	Joe Walsh				6	17	15			*5*	
378	Free	3	13								
379	The Brothers Johnson							5	6		
380	David Essex					3					
381	Frijid Pink	4	13								
382	Timmy Thomas				3						
383	Paul & Linda McCartney		3								
384	Edison Lighthouse	3	15								
385	The Jaggerz	3									
386	Robert Palmer						20	18	13	6	*6*
387	David Geddes						3				
388	"Deliverance" Soundtrack				3						
389	100 Proof Aged In Soul	4	15	12							
390	Mungo Jerry	3									
391	L.T.D.								7	4	
392	Jr. Walker & The All Stars	*6*	10	12							
393	The Persuaders		6	11	11	17					
394	Clint Holmes				3						
395	Perry Como			5	7		18				
396	The Band	7	16	9		13		15			
397	Deodato				3			20			
398	Brick								3	17	
399	Toto										3-
400	The Cars									7	5

Rank	Act	'70	'71	'72	'73	'74	'75	'76	'77	'78	'79
401	The Five Stairsteps	4	15								
402	Jigsaw							4	8	18	
403	Elvin Bishop					14	16	4			
404	Detroit Emeralds		10	5	18						
405	Johnny Cash	6	11	18				10			
406	Kenny Loggins								10	3	14
407	The Archies	-4									
408	The Trammps			11				7		5	
409	ZZ Top			17		8	7	10	14		
410	Jermaine Jackson			11	4			15			
411	Dave Edmunds		4								15
412	Austin Roberts			6	12		6				
413	Maria Muldaur					5	8				
414	Rickie Lee Jones										3-
415	Tower Of Power			8	7	13					
416	Bonnie Tyler									2-	
417	Dave Mason	10							6	9	
418	Meat Loaf								20	4	11
419	Sugarloaf	4	11								
420	The Addrisi Brothers			7					7	14	16
421	M										2
422	Carly Simon & James Taylor					4				13	
423	Sammy Johns					11	3				
424	Jerry Butler	10	17	10					12		
425	Marmalade	4						12			
426	Andy Williams	16	6	10				18			
427	Jonathan Edwards			4							
428	Lee Michaels		3								
429	Dobie Gray				4						14
430	Denise LaSalle		6	7	20					18	
431	Love Unlimited			5		18	8				
432	Gene Cotton					15	20		10	5	
433	The Bells		4								
434	Blues Image	4									
435	Yes		10	5							
436	Michael Johnson									5	6
437	Jennifer Warnes								5		8
438	Rufus Thomas	9	6	13							
439	Byron Mac Gregor					4					
440	Gary Glitter			4							
441	William DeVaughn					4					
442	Jackie Moore		6	20	9		16				
443	Ray Price		5		14						
444	Dionne Warwicke & Spinners					4					
445	Al Martino	10		17			6			12	
446	David Ruffin	12						5			
447	Roberta Flack & Donny Hathaway		8	5							
448	Blue Magic					5					
449	The Marshall Tucker Band							11	5	18	12
450	Flaming Ember	5	18								

Rank	Act	'70	'71	'72	'73	'74	'75	'76	'77	'78	'79
451	B.W. Stevenson				5	11			15		
452	Pilot							4	17		
453	The New Birth		12		10	10	9				
454	The Friends Of Distinction	4	15								
455	The Ides of March	4	15								
456	Cliff Richard								4	17	
457	Lighthouse		7	9	10						
458	Peter Brown								9	5	19
459	Jessi Colter						4				
460	Hot								4	17	
461	The Brotherhood Of Man	5	15					10			
462	First Class						5	19			
463	Bill Conti								3-		
464	Daddy Dewdrop			4							20
465	Marie Osmond					5		11	11		
466	Gene Chandler	5	19								11
467	Dr. John				13	5	16				
468	The Blackbyrds						17	5	10		
469	Kris Kristofferson			9	15	7			14		
470	Paul Nicholas								4	16	
471	Alive And Kicking	4									
472	The 8th Day			5	16						
473	Evelyn "Champagne" King									5	7
474	Chuck Mangione			14						4	
475	John Stewart										-3
476	The Free Movement			5	11						
477	Johnny Bristol						5		12		
478	Ronnie Milsap						20	18	6	17	12
479	Morris Albert							3	17		
480	Stampeders			5	13			10			
481	The Floaters								3		
482	Focus					4					
483	Walter Egan								14	4	20
484	First Choice					5	16		16		
485	Jay Ferguson									4	9
486	The Ritchie Family						6	7			
487	Disco Tex & The Sex-O-Lettes						5	15			
488	T. Rex		11	6							
489	Conway Twitty	14			9		10	12			
490	Crow	5									
491	Beverly Bremers			5							
492	Alicia Bridges									3	
493	Quincy Jones	12	20	17	18		15		12	9	
494	Brewer And Shipley		5	19							
495	Commander Cody & His Lost Planet Airmen			6	16		13				
496	Brenda & The Tabulations	9	7								
497	The Tee Set	4									
498	The Independents			16	6	14					
499	Paul McCartney		5-								
500	Bobby Bloom	5	16		20						

Rank	Act	'70	'71	'72	'73	'74	'75	'76	'77	'78	'79
501	David Naughton										3
502	Burton Cummings							5	19	17	
503	Diana Ross & Marvin Gaye				8	7					
504	George Baker Selection	6						8			
505	The Blue Ridge Rangers				5						
506	Mouth & MacNeal			4							
507	Bobby Bland	13		13		10	17				
508	Parliament						18	7		7	
509	Argent				5						
510	Dire Straits										4-
511	The Fortunes	11	6								
512	Journey									11	5
513	The Intruders	11	14		10						
514	Funkadelic	16	14							9	11
515	The James Gang	12	9			10					
516	Phoebe Snow						4-				
517	Delaney & Bonnie And Friends	11	6								
518	Randy Vanwarmer										3-
519	Chakachas				5						
520	The Presidents	5	12								
521	Eddie Rabbitt							18		14	5
522	G.Q.										4
523	Michael Nesmith & The First National Band	7	9								
524	Sam Neely				9	14	10	12			
525	Murray Head			5-							
526	Dave Loggins						5				
527	Hudson Brothers						8	9	14		
528	Joe South	5	19								
529	Robin McNamara	5									
530	Wadsworth Mansion			5							
531	Rick Springfield				7		16		11		
532	Tommy James And The Shondells	-6									
533	Bobbi Martin	-5									
534	Earth, Wind & Fire With The Emotions										4
535	Nazareth							5-			
536	Nicolette Larson										4-
537	John Paul Young							11		6	15
538	Barbara Mason			15	8		9				
539	Ann Peebles	8	17	18		9					
540	Leon Haywood					11	7				
541	Donnie Elbert	17	9	9							
542	New York City				6	17					
543	People's Choice			13			6	16			
544	Bruce Springsteen						7	13		11	
545	The Crusaders			15	11	18	16				9
546	Barry DeVorzon and Perry Botkin, Jr.							5			
547	Sammi Smith			6	16						
548	Crosby, Stills & Nash								-5-		
549	Little Sister	7	8								
550	Jud Strunk					6	18	14			

Rank	Act	'70	'71	'72	'73	'74	'75	'76	'77	'78	'79
551	Le Blanc & Carr								12	6	
552	Laura Lee		9	9							
553	Jay And The Americans	-5									
554	Mike Post						5		19		
555	Mel and Tim	11		6							
556	Chris Rea									6	12
557	Skylark				5						
558	Sister Janet Mead					5					
559	Carol Douglas						5		19		
560	The Fuzz		6								
561	Lamont Dozier					6	15				
562	Bobbie Gentry	7						14			
563	Tom T. Hall		14			7	19				
564	Faces			6	12						
565	The Lettermen	8	10								
566	The Originals	7	12					20			
567	Fanny		11	19		14	9				
568	Ferrante & Teicher	-6									
569	Foxy									7	8
570	Waylon Jennings	16				17	15		8		18
571	White Plains	6									
572	Golden Earring					6	18				
573	Pratt & McClain							5			
574	Hot Butter			6	17						
575	Bonnie Pointer									20	5
576	Apollo 100			5							
577	Lulu	-6-									
578	Nigel Olsson							19			6
579	King Harvest					5					
580	Toby Beau									6	13
581	Merle Haggard	20		15	17	10			11		
582	Dennis Yost And The Classics IV	10		10	19		18				
583	Paul Anka with Odia Coates						5				
584	Bobby (Boris) Pickett And The Crypt-Kickers	15			6						
585	Coven		7		15	16					
586	Derek And The Dominos		12	7							
587	Blue Öyster Cult							6			20
588	Teddy Pendergrass								10	8	13
589	Mike Oldfield					6					
590	Suzi Quatro And Chris Norman										4
591	The Pipkins	5									
592	Carl Carlton	15				6					
593	Ian Matthews										5
594	Starz							20	8	16	
595	Tanya Tucker				19	13	10				19
596	Fancy					6					
597	Rick James									6	16
598	J.D. Souther										4
599	Vicki Sue Robinson							6			
600	Charley Pride	15		7							

Rank	Act	'70	'71	'72	'73	'74	'75	'76	'77	'78	'79
601	Climax Blues Band								5-		
602	John Williams						9			7	
603	Blues Brothers										5-
604	Pink Floyd				6	17					
605	El Chicano	10		13		11					
606	Godspell			5							
607	Gwen McCrae						5				
608	Emerson, Lake & Palmer		14	10	15						
609	The Amazing Rhythm Aces						7	10			
610	Peter McCann								5		
611	David Dundas								5		
612	Daniel Boone				6						
613	Ben E. King						-6-				
614	The Beginning Of The End		6								
615	Christie	6	17								
616	Thin Lizzy								6	18	
617	Jerry Lee Lewis			*10*	10						
618	Billy "Crash" Craddock						9	13	12		
619	Mocedades						6				
620	Tom Clay		6								
621	Henry Mancini And His Orchestra		7						15		
622	Reunion						6				
623	Keith Hampshire				8	13					
624	Cheryl Lynn										6-
625	Mountain	7	16								
626	Rick Derringer						8	14			
627	Dusty Springfield	*7*			19						
628	Van Halen									12	*8*
629	The Soul Children				*8*	12					
630	Suzi Quatro					14		13			*11*
631	Ted Nugent							15	8	16	
632	Esther Phillips			*16*	16		7				
633	The Sandpipers	-6									
634	Jim Weatherly					18	8	17			
635	Odyssey									6	
636	R.B. Greaves	*-8*									
637	Jefferson	*-6*									
638	Keith Carradine							6			
639	William Bell							-6			
640	The Rascals	*8*	15								
641	Pacific Gas & Electric	6		19							
642	Rex Smith										5
643	Willie Nelson						7	14		*20*	
644	Shirley (And Company)						5				
645	The J.B.'s			12	9						
646	Danny O'Keefe			6							
647	Ten Years After	15	8	16							
648	The Supremes & Four Tops		7								
649	Freddie Hart			6							
650	Flash Cadillac & The Continental Kids					17	12	8			

Rank	Act	'70	'71	'72	'73	'74	'75	'76	'77	'78	'79
651	Graham Central Station					12	10	15			
652	Jack Blanchard & Misty Morgan	6									
653	Bazuka						6				
654	Smith	-8									
655	Con Funk Shun									7	20
656	Alan Parsons Project								11	15	8
657	The Buoys		7								
658	McFadden & Whitehead										5
659	The Assembled Multitude	7									
660	April Wine				9						12
661	Brighter Side Of Darkness				6						
662	Teegarden & Van Winkle	7	18								
663	The Meters	8							15		
664	The Hillside Singers			7							
665	The Sanford/Townsend Band								6		
666	Charlie Daniels				6						
667	Cymarron		7								
668	The Kiki Dee Band					7	18				
669	J.J. Cale			8							
670	Bullet			8							
671	Roxy Music							8			13
672	Dusk		8								
673	Sami Jo					7					
674	Nick Lowe										6
675	Travis Wammack			14	12		13				
676	Faith, Hope & Charity	10					9				
677	Tin Tin		7								
678	Sylvester									9	12
679	Herbie Mann						9				10
680	Loudon Wainwright III				6						
681	Jimmy Cliff	7									
682	Sugarloaf/Jerry Corbetta						6				
683	Bar-Kays			12					10	19	
684	Ram Jam								6		
685	Chi Coltrane			7							
686	Arlo Guthrie	16		8							
687	Sutherland Brothers And Quiver				9			14	19		
688	Deniece Williams								7	20	
689	Foster Sylvers				8						
690	Silver							6			
691	The Cuff Links	-7									
692	Tom Petty And The Heartbreakers									8-	
693	Smokie								7		
694	Prelude					8		13			
695	Miguel Rios	6									
696	The Nite-Liters		10	12							
697	Merry Clayton	15		15	14		12				
698	Redeye		7								
699	Chase			9	18						
700	Dean Friedman								6		

Rank	Act	'70	'71	'72	'73	'74	'75	'76	'77	'78	'79
701	Tim Moore				20	12	17		13	18	
702	Crown Heights Affair						11	13	14		
703	The Poppy Family (Duo)		10	16							
704	Cashman & West			10	13						
705	Pete Wingfield						6				
706	Patti Smith Group									6	
707	Malo			7							
708	Mary Hopkin	*8*		18							
709	Blackfoot										7-
710	Blue Haze				8						
711	Brass Construction							7			
712	Uriah Heep			10	13						
713	Frederick Knight			8							
714	Latimore				20	9			13		
715	Enchantment								9	11	
716	Graham Nash		8-								
717	Santa Esmeralda									7	
718	The Gentrys	*9*	16								
719	Bobby Caldwell										6-
720	Ace Frehley										6
721	John Williams/London Symphony Orchestra								8		16
722	Matthews' Southern Comfort		7								
723	High Inergy								7		
724	Buddy Miles	13	13				15				
725	Dr. Buzzard's Original "Savannah" Band							17	8		
726	Procol Harum			-8							
727	Les Crane		7								
728	Paul Humphrey & His Cool Aid Chemists		8								
729	Steve Martin								20	8	
730	Delaney & Bonnie		9	15							
731	The Royal Scots Dragoon Guards				7						
732	The Tymes					*8*	20				
733	Black Oak Arkansas					7					
734	Roger Whittaker							7			
735	Ike & Tina Turner & The Ikettes	-8									
736	Giorgio Moroder			10							10
737	Gregg Allman						8				
738	Cate Brothers							7			
739	Jackie DeShannon	*12*		19					13		
740	Shirley Bassey	*16*		13	12						
741	The Wing And A Prayer Fife And Drum Corps.							7			
742	Donovan	*10*	19		13						
743	Norman Connors							16	8		
744	Ernie (Jim Henson)	7									
745	Patrick Hernandez										6
746	Michael Parks	7									
747	Bell & James										6
748	Sniff 'n' The Tears										6
749	Larry Groce							7			
750	Mac And Katie Kissoon		7								

Rank	Act	'70	'71	'72	'73	'74	'75	'76	'77	'78	'79
751	Ecstasy, Passion & Pain					12	13				
752	Sailcat			8							
753	Joe Jackson										7-
754	Outlaws						9		15		20
755	Joey Heatherton			8							
756	Gene Redding					8					
757	Willie Hutch					12		12			
758	Slade				17	11					
759	Dan Fogelberg						8		13		
760	The Mike Curb Congregation		9			16					
761	Paul Stookey		8								
762	Jerry Butler and Brenda Lee Eager			8							
763	Genesis								18	9	
764	Richie Havens			8							
765	Roger Voudouris										7
766	John Fogerty						8	16			
767	Eruption									8	
768	Polly Brown						7				
769	Mandrill		20	20	11						
770	Johnny Wakelin And The Kinshasa Band						7				
771	The Salsoul Orchestra						19	9			
772	Wilton Place Street Band								7		
773	Cledus Maggard							7			
774	Chris Thompson										7
775	Frank Sinatra					15		12		19	
776	Billy Ocean								7-		
777	The Manhattan Transfer							8-			
778	Crabby Appleton	8									
779	Chilliwack				16			19	11	19	
780	Donny Hathaway	17		14	13						
781	Livingston Taylor									9	17
782	Kraftwerk						8			18	
783	Jerry Wallace				-9						
784	France Joli										7
785	Mott The Hoople				10	16					
786	Barbara Mandrell									20	8
787	Chanson										7
788	Canned Heat	-8									
789	The Glass Bottle		9								
790	Vic Dana	-9									
791	Pure Prairie League						8-				
792	Moon Martin										8
793	Evie Sands						-8				
794	Gunhill Road				8						
795	The Police										8-
796	Cliff DeYoung					8					
797	Gary Puckett	11	13								
798	Think				11	14					
799	Lenny Welch	9			19						
800	Spyro Gyra									20	8

Rank	Act	'70	'71	'72	'73	'74	'75	'76	'77	'78	'79
801	Gary Toms Empire						8				
802	Cyndi Grecco							8			
803	Little Milton		*11*	16							
804	David Crosby / Graham Nash			11			12	16			
805	Roger Daltrey				12		14		*16*		
806	Syl Johnson				*13*		12				
807	Warren Zevon									8-	
808	Ronnie McDowell								8		
809	The Ray Charles Orchestra		9								
810	Little Jimmy Osmond			12	13						
811	The English Congregation			9							
812	Davy Jones		-10								
813	Hotlegs	8									
814	Chaka Khan									8-	
815	The Delegates				8						
816	REO Speedwagon								20	11	*19*
817	Sweet Sensation						8				
818	Waylon & Willie								10	13	
819	Ashford & Simpson									15	*10*
820	Lou Reed				8						
821	Cross Country				9						
822	John Kay			12	14						
823	Street People	8									
824	Stonebolt									10	20
825	Martha Reeves & The Vandellas		*17*	13	15						
826	Peter Nero			8							
827	Freddie North		10	18							
828	Dan Hartman									8-	
829	Grateful Dead		*17*		13		17				*18*
830	Mashmakhan	8									
831	Five Flights Up	10	16								
832	John Miles								10	14	
833	Holland-Dozier			12	13						
834	Paul Simon/Phoebe Snow						8				
835	Lou Christie	*13*				15			19		
836	Art Garfunkel w/ James Taylor & Paul Simon									8	
837	Bobby Russell		-9								
838	The Souther, Hillman, Furay Band					10	16				
839	Rockets									9-	
840	Jeanne Pruett				9						
841	Wednesday					10					
842	Lindisfarne			17						10	
843	Dwight Twilley Band						8				
844	Slave								8-		
845	Michael Zager Band									8	
846	Tycoon										8
847	Barbara Fairchild				9						
848	Charlie Ross							14	10		
849	Bettye Swann			*14*	12						
850	Prism								20	*11*	

Rank	Act	'70	'71	'72	'73	'74	'75	'76	'77	'78	'79
851	Meri Wilson								8		
852	Hotel									14	*13*
853	Night										8
854	Sweathog			9							
855	Jake Holmes	8									
856	Instant Funk										8
857	Shirley Brown					9					
858	Natural Four					9					
859	Humble Pie			16	11						
860	Triumph										9-
861	Jeannie C. Riley		*-11*								
862	Booker T. & The M.G.'s	18	11								
863	Mickey Newbury			11	17						
864	Don Covay				*11*	20					
865	Gayle McCormick			11							
866	Manu Dibango				10						
867	Brenda Russell										8-
868	Sons Of Champlin							12	13		
869	Dave And Ansil Collins			10							
870	Kris Kristofferson & Rita Coolidge						11				
871	Cooper Brothers										9
872	Ian Thomas				10						
873	Stargard									9	
874	Head East						14	19		14	
875	Q								8		
876	Richard Harris			*10*			19				
877	Bobbie Gentry & Glen Campbell	-9									
878	Flash			9							
879	Talking Heads										8-
880	Wilbert Harrison	-9									
881	Cymande				11						
882	Justin Hayward									9	
883	Dottie West				*11-*						
884	John Phillips	9									
885	Elephant's Memory	9									
886	Dan Fogelberg / Tim Weisberg									9	
887	The Neighborhood	9									
888	Richie Furay									19	10
889	Paul Williams				13	15					
890	Chee-Chee and Peppy		10								
891	Sha Na Na		18				12				
892	New England										10
893	Herb Alpert & The Tijuana Brass	16				15	16				
894	McGuinness Flint			10							
895	Pickettywitch	9									
896	Alan Parsons								9		
897	Maynard Ferguson								9		
898	Bobby Byrd	13	16	18							
899	The Tokens	-10									
900	Charlie								18	14	*15*

Rank	Act	'70	'71	'72	'73	'74	'75	'76	'77	'78	'79
901	John Cougar										9-
902	5000 Volts						9				
903	Bloodrock		10								
904	Frank Zappa					15					13
905	Liz Damon's Orient Express		10								
906	Vincent Bell	9									
907	Emitt Rhodes		10								
908	Jackie Wilson	19	13								
909	Jo Jo Gunne				10						
910	Jim Gilstrap							12			
911	Stillwater									10	
912	O.C. Smith	12				19					
913	Carl Graves							13	13		
914	Jim Capaldi							13	16		
915	Buffy Sainte-Marie			18	12						
916	Justin Hayward And John Lodge							11	16		
917	Ian Gomm										9
918	Hagood Hardy							9			
919	The Lost Generation	10									
920	The Whispers	13	20			19			18		
921	Switch									12	17
922	Traffic	14	14								
923	John Handy							9			
924	Clean Living				10						
925	Bill Amesbury						10				
926	The Original Caste	10									
927	Stephanie Mills										9-
928	Sounds Of Sunshine		11								
929	Joe Stampley				10						
930	Brooklyn Dreams								13	17	17
931	Dee Dee Warwick	12	16								
932	Lady Flash							9			
933	Herbie Hancock						10-				
934	The Incredible Bongo Band					12					
935	Z.Z. Hill		-14								
936	Johnny Cash & June Carter	10									
937	Diana Ross & Michael Jackson									10	
938	Robin Gibb									10-	
939	Mama Cass Elliot	-10									
940	Rose Colored Glass		12								
941	Jody Miller		-12								
942	Boomer Castleman						10				
943	The Tarney/Spencer Band							16		18	15
944	Frankie Avalon						-9				
945	The Ebonys			12	19						
946	The Jones Girls										9
947	The Road Apples								9		
948	Lauren Wood										9
949	Ashton, Gardner & Dyke		11								
950	The Joneses					11					

Rank	Act	'70	'71	'72	'73	'74	'75	'76	'77	'78	'79
951	Savoy Brown	11	19								
952	Chuck Brown & The Soul Searchers										9
953	Melba Moore	18									11
954	Otis Leavill	11									
955	Johnny Mathis					16	14				
956	Les Emmerson					11					
957	Rubicon									10	
958	Doris Duke	11									
959	Red Sovine							-9			
960	Celebration featuring Mike Love									10	
961	The Rubettes						11				
962	Bill Cosby	14							12		
963	The Boys In The Band	10									
964	Benny Bell							10			
965	Little Anthony And The Imperials	13				20					
966	Mass Production										10
967	Gary's Gang										10
968	Gladstone			10							
969	Marshall Hain										10
970	Eddie Floyd	-11									
971	Tom Johnston										10
972	Sharon Paige						10				
973	Angel								14	14	
974	Layng Martine		13	18							
975	Henhouse Five Plus Too								9		
976	John Valenti								9		
977	Francis Lai and His Orchestra			12							
978	Faith Band										11
979	Hudson and Landry		14	16							
980	Arthur Alexander							12	20		
981	Frankie Valli & The 4 Seasons	12				19					
982	Sugar Bears				11						
983	Boney M								17	13	
984	The Kendalls									11	
985	Lyn Collins				11						
986	Afrique					11					
987	McGuinn, Clark & Hillman										10
988	The Mixtures			12							
989	Margie Joseph			15			16				
990	Edgar Winter's White Trash				12						
991	Freddy Robinson	11									
992	Paul Stanley									11	
993	Ramsey Lewis and Earth, Wind & Fire							12			
994	Nino Tempo And 5th Ave. Sax					11					
995	The James Brown Soul Train				11						
996	Steam	-11									
997	Roy Clark	17				17	19				
998	Chris Hodge			12							
999	Waldo De Los Ríos			12							
1000	Marty Robbins	-11									

Rank	Act	'70	'71	'72	'73	'74	'75	'76	'77	'78	'79
1001	Jimmy "Bo" Horne									11	
1002	The Messengers		12								
1003	Diamond REO						11				
1004	The Buggles										11
1005	Bill Haley And His Comets					-12					
1006	Herman Brood										*11*
1007	John & Ernest				12						
1008	Blue Mink	12									
1009	Kermit (Jim Henson)										11
1010	Bulldog				12						
1011	Johnny "Guitar" Watson								10		
1012	Seatrain			12							
1013	Gary Puckett And The Union Gap	-11									
1014	Peter Skellern					13		19			
1015	Charlie Kulis						11				
1016	Eydie Gorme	-11									
1017	Sea Level								20	13	
1018	Doucette									15	19
1019	Emmylou Harris						13	*18*			
1020	James Walsh Gypsy Band									13	19
1021	Rick Cunha					12					
1022	City Boy									11	
1023	Love And Kisses									11	
1024	The Intrigues	*13*	17								
1025	Etta James	*14*				16					
1026	Odia Coates						13				
1027	Spirit	*14*				18					
1028	Stallion								10		
1029	Michael Holm						11				
1030	The Rubinoos								10		
1031	C Company Featuring Terry Nelson		12								
1032	Stu Nunnery					14	18				
1033	Le Roux									12	
1034	Jonathan Cain							10			
1035	Shalamar								13		*18*
1036	Alton McClain & Destiny										11
1037	Biddu Orchestra						11				
1038	Bert Sommer	12									
1039	George Perkins & The Silver Stars	11									
1040	Bram Tchaikovsky										11
1041	Creative Source					12					
1042	Consumer Rapport						11				
1043	Crystal Mansion	-11									
1044	Cheryl Ladd									12	
1045	Michel LeGrand			12							
1046	Linda Clifford									16	*16*
1047	The Brecker Brothers						11				
1048	Gordon Sinclair					12					
1049	Black Sabbath	15		15							
1050	Bob Dylan / The Band					12					

Rank	Act	'70	'71	'72	'73	'74	'75	'76	'77	'78	'79
1051	Batdorf & Rodney						16	14			
1052	Allan Clarke									12-	
1053	Louise Goffin										12
1054	Gonzalez										12
1055	Kayak									12	
1056	Bobby Arvon									12	
1057	Paul Kelly	12									
1058	Lenny Le Blanc							20	12		
1059	Clout									12	
1060	Jerry Naylor	12									
1061	Cozy Powell					13					
1062	Third World										12
1063	Billy Thorpe										12
1064	The New Colony Six	18	15								
1065	Sammy Hagar									16	16
1066	Melba Montgomery					13					
1067	Vigrass & Osborne			12							
1068	Bobby Bare					-13					
1069	Bill Deal & The Rhondels	13		20							
1070	Kiki Dee		19				16	18			
1071	T.G. Sheppard						14-				
1072	Facts Of Life								10		
1073	Bobby Darin				-13						
1074	Wildfire								11		
1075	George Duke									12-	
1076	Pink Lady										12
1077	Cold Blood	12									
1078	James Brown - Lyn Collins					13					
1079	Lois Fletcher					13					
1080	Heaven Bound		14								
1081	Larry Santos								11		
1082	Whatnauts		15			20					
1083	Ripple					15	19				
1084	Jim Ed Brown		13								
1085	Arthur Prysock					19			13		
1086	Carole Bayer Sager								11-		
1087	The Raeletts	16	17								
1088	The Statler Brothers		15					20			
1089	Jimmy Dean							-11			
1090	Parker McGee								11		
1091	The South Side Movement					13					
1092	Leon & Mary Russell								11		
1093	Sly Stone							13			
1094	Percy Sledge					-13					
1095	David & Jimmy Ruffin	12									
1096	Salvage		13								
1097	Tommy Tate				14						
1098	Ironhorse										13-
1099	David Castle								15	17	
1100	The Peppers					13					

Rank	Act	'70	'71	'72	'73	'74	'75	'76	'77	'78	'79
1101	Crawler								11		
1102	Jane Olivor								18	15	
1103	Gene Simmons										13
1104	Archie Bell & The Drells				16			16			
1105	O.V. Wright	-12									
1106	Gypsy		13								
1107	The Byrds	18	16		19						
1108	P-Nut Gallery		13								
1109	Loretta Lynn						13				
1110	Brother To Brother					14					
1111	Billy Joe Royal		17							16	
1112	Valerie Simpson				13						
1113	El Coco									13	
1114	Razzy					14					
1115	Karla Bonoff									15-	
1116	Edgar Winter					14					
1117	C.J. & Co.								11		
1118	Don Ray									13	
1119	Guy Drake	12									
1120	The Illusion	-12									
1121	Lunar Funk			13							
1122	Rick Nelson	-12									
1123	Maze								15		17
1124	Fox						13				
1125	Klaatu								13		
1126	Purple Reign							12			
1127	The Fatback Band							12			
1128	Delegation										13
1129	The McCrarys									13	
1130	The Faragher Brothers										13
1131	Little Richard	-13-									
1132	Rod Hart								11		
1133	Buckwheat			15	20						
1134	Penny McLean							12			
1135	Israel "Popper Stopper" Tolbert	13									
1136	Fotomaker									15	
1137	The Electric Express		14								
1138	Jose Feliciano	-14									
1139	Little Johnny Taylor			-14							
1140	Bunny Sigler									-14	
1141	Potliquor			14							
1142	Bonnie Raitt								11-		
1143	Mac McAnally								12-		
1144	Tuxedo Junction									14	
1145	Rainbow										13-
1146	Mike Kennedy			14							
1147	Neil Young and Graham Nash			14							
1148	Katfish						13				
1149	The Village Soul Choir	13									
1150	Limmie & Family Cookin'					14					

Rank	Act	'70	'71	'72	'73	'74	'75	'76	'77	'78	'79
1151	Stephen Stills – Manassas				14						
1152	Plastic Bertrand									14	
1153	C.C.S.		14								
1154	Funky Communication Committee										13
1155	Tamiko Jones						13				
1156	Simon Stokes					14					
1157	Suzy And The Red Stripes								12		
1158	Donald Byrd					14					
1159	Ruby Winters	14					20				
1160	Dennis Coffey				14						
1161	The Heyettes							12			
1162	Narada Michael Walden										14-
1163	Brooklyn Bridge	-14									
1164	Bro Smith							13			
1165	Cindy Bullens										14-
1166	King Curtis & The Kingpins		-14								
1167	Tony Orlando										-14
1168	Musique									14	
1169	Oak										14-
1170	The Flamingos	-13									
1171	Kim Carnes										14-
1172	Joey Travolta									14	
1173	The Wombles					14					
1174	AC/DC										14-
1175	The Deadly Nightshade							13			
1176	Quicksilver Messenger Service	-13									
1177	Terry Black And Laurel Ward				14						
1178	Bill LaBounty									14	
1179	NRBQ						15				
1180	Robert Gordon								12-		
1181	Grand Canyon						15				
1182	Brenda Lee	16			17						
1183	Roy Rogers							14			
1184	John Kongos		14								
1185	Springwell		14								
1186	Kathy Dalton						15				
1187	Michael Franks							13			
1188	Gallagher and Lyle							16	20		
1189	Painter					14					
1190	Pop-Tops		-14								
1191	Susan Jacks					16	20				
1192	Petula Clark			-15-							
1193	Dickey Lee							-13			
1194	Marc Tanner Band										14
1195	Mary Kay Place							13			
1196	Mesa								13		
1197	Ramsey Lewis			16				19			
1198	Niteflyte										14
1199	The Association	19		19	18						
1200	Mickey Gilley					15-					

Rank	Act	'70	'71	'72	'73	'74	'75	'76	'77	'78	'79
1201	Lee Garrett							13			
1202	Arkade		14								
1203	Peggy Lipton	13									
1204	Michael Polnareff							13			
1205	Loleatta Holloway						14				
1206	Martha Reeves					15					
1207	Gino Soccio										14
1208	Jimi Hendrix		-15								
1209	George Fischoff						15				
1210	Kenny Karen				15						
1211	Albert King			16	19						
1212	Claudja Barry										14
1213	Buckeye										14
1214	The Mob		16								
1215	Elvis Costello									14-	
1216	Marvin Gaye & Tammi Terrell	-13									
1217	Isaac Hayes & David Porter			14							
1218	Teri DeSario									15-	
1219	The Mystic Moods				17		17				
1220	Hello People						14				
1221	America (Duo)										15-
1222	The Raes										15
1223	James Darren			16					19		
1224	Bonnie Boyer										15
1225	Nolan			15							
1226	Beckmeier Brothers										15
1227	Steve Dahl and Teenage Radiation										15
1228	Marilyn Sellars					15					
1229	Shawn Phillips				15						
1230	Fools Gold							13			
1231	Loretta Lynn/Conway Twitty		18			18					
1232	Dorothy Norwood					15					
1233	Ponderosa Twins + One		15								
1234	Carlos Santana & Buddy Miles			14							
1235	Billie Jo Spears						-14				
1236	The Don Harrison Band							14			
1237	Steve & Eydie			-15							
1238	Ronnie Spector		15								
1239	Dynamic Superiors						16				
1240	Splinter						14				
1241	The New Hope	14									
1242	Ross/Gaye/Robinson/Wonder										15
1243	Bootsy's Rubber Band									15	
1244	Bob Weir									15	
1245	Ten Wheel Drive With Genya Ravan	14									
1246	Sweet Dreams					16					
1247	Ray Sawyer								14		
1248	Don Brown									15	
1249	Otis Clay				-15						
1250	J. Frank Wilson & The Cavaliers					-16					

Rank	Act	'70	'71	'72	'73	'74	'75	'76	'77	'78	'79
1251	Nazz	-14									
1252	Cooker						16				
1253	Turley Richards	14-									
1254	Casey Kelly				15						
1255	Peabo Bryson									15-	
1256	Mr. Big								13		
1257	Jamestown Massacre			15							
1258	Andy Pratt					15					
1259	Tufano & Giammarese					15					
1260	Pat Travers										15
1261	Nancy Brooks										15
1262	The Ovations					-15					
1263	Mary Travers			15							
1264	The Spiral Starecase	-14									
1265	Stark & McBrien							15			
1266	Al Downing							15			
1267	Trooper									16	
1268	Richard Cocciante							14			
1269	Bruce Foster								14		
1270	South Shore Commission							16	20		
1271	Desmond Child and Rouge										16
1272	David T. Walker				15						
1273	Solomon Burke		20	17							
1274	Eddie & Dutch	14									
1275	Major Lance	-14									
1276	Barry Mann	17							18		
1277	Funky Kings								14		
1278	James & Bobby Purify						-15				
1279	Willie Henderson						16				
1280	Sherbet								14		
1281	The Sports										16
1282	Mike Quatro Jam Band			15							
1283	Space										16
1284	Oscar Brown, Jr.						16				
1285	David Blue				16						
1286	The Fabulous Rhinestones			15							
1287	The Band Of The Black Watch							14			
1288	Feather	15									
1289	Rush								14-		
1290	Narvel Felts							18	18		
1291	Mick Jackson									16	
1292	Soul Train Gang							15			
1293	L.A. Jets							19	17		
1294	Audience		16								
1295	Blackjack									16	
1296	Saint Tropez									16	
1297	Fantastic Four						-15				
1298	Don Fardon				-16						
1299	Bimbo Jet						15				
1300	The Kay-Gees					17					

Rank	Act	'70	'71	'72	'73	'74	'75	'76	'77	'78	'79
1301	The Clique	-15									
1302	Grin			15							
1303	Frankie Miller								14-		
1304	John Rowles		16								
1305	LaVerne & Shirley							15			
1306	The Rowans							15			
1307	The Box Tops	-15									
1308	Kellee Patterson									16	
1309	Python Lee Jackson			16							
1310	Carroll O'Connor And Jean Stapleton			16							
1311	Liquid Gold										16-
1312	Shepstone & Dibbens				16						
1313	Diane Kolby	15									
1314	Rodney Allen Rippy				16						
1315	Anacostia				16						
1316	Celi Bee & The Buzzy Bunch								14		
1317	The Tubes						15-				
1318	Nature's Divine										16
1319	Zwol									18	20
1320	Carolyne Mas										16
1321	The Caboose	15									
1322	The Bob Seger System	-15									
1323	Mavis Staples	18		18							
1324	Rock Flowers			16							
1325	Johnny Rodriguez				16						
1326	The Searchers		-16								
1327	Hank Wilson				16						
1328	Glenn Sutton										16
1329	Dion	-15-									
1330	Demis Roussos									16	
1331	Ozo							15			
1332	Northern Light						16				
1333	Dyke And The Blazers	-16									
1334	Earnest Jackson				17						
1335	Tom Fogerty		19		18						
1336	Chocolate Milk							16			
1337	Shad O'Shea & The 18 Wheelers								15		
1338	Firefly							16			
1339	Cory								15		
1340	Kevin Lamb									16	
1341	Champagne								15		
1342	Cody Jameson								15		
1343	George Thorogood And The Destroyers										16-
1344	Glen Campbell/Anne Murray			16							
1345	Merrilee Rush								-15		
1346	Grover Washington, Jr.						16-				
1347	The Records										16
1348	The Magic Lanterns		18	19							
1349	Kate Taylor									15	
1350	Michael Redway				17						

Rank	Act	'70	'71	'72	'73	'74	'75	'76	'77	'78	'79
1351	Sarah Dash										17
1352	Trini Lopez						-16				
1353	Hoyt Axton					17					
1354	Randy Brown										17
1355	Jacky Ward									17	
1356	Danny Holien				16						
1357	Brown Sugar							16			
1358	Paula Webb							16			
1359	Country Coalition	16									
1360	Stoney And Meatloaf			16							
1361	Tommy Cash	16									
1362	Frank Lucas								15		
1363	Randy Edelman							19	18		
1364	The Newbeats	-16									
1365	Ian Lloyd										17
1366	Tim Davis				16						
1367	Continental Miniatures									17	
1368	Shoes										17
1369	Liquid Smoke	16									
1370	Gabriel Kaplan								15		
1371	Gene & Jerry		17								
1372	Taka Boom										17
1373	Gary Tanner									17	
1374	The Temprees				16						
1375	Odds & Ends		17								
1376	Daybreak	16									
1377	Mary Wells	-16									
1378	Sonny James	18	20								
1379	Greg Lake							20	18		
1380	Flash & The Pan										17
1381	Oliver	-17									
1382	Owen B.	16									
1383	Lee Oskar							16			
1384	The Glass House	-17									
1385	Driver								16		
1386	Graham Parker And The Rumour								16		
1387	Robin Trower								16		
1388	Circus					17					
1389	Ronnie Hawkins	-16									
1390	Ian Hunter										17
1391	Peter Shelley							17			
1392	Andy & David Williams						17				
1393	Damnation Of Adam Blessing			17							
1394	Kenny Starr								17		
1395	Sad Cafe										17
1396	Maggie Bell					17					
1397	Abraham's Children					17					
1398	Johnny T. Angel					18					
1399	Delbert & Glen				17						
1400	Gaylord & Holiday								17		

Rank	Act	'70	'71	'72	'73	'74	'75	'76	'77	'78	'79
1401	Nino Rota			17							
1402	Fabulous Counts	19		18							
1403	The Wackers			17							
1404	Johnny Williams					17					
1405	Bob Marley & The Wailers							17			
1406	Don Goodwin						18				
1407	Oliver Sain							17			
1408	Gary & Dave						18				
1409	Chicory				17						
1410	John LiVigni						17				
1411	Steve Gibbons Band							17			
1412	Nancy Wilson	-16									
1413	The Real Thing							17			
1414	David Laflamme								16		
1415	Jerry Jeff Walker					-18					
1416	Mighty Clouds Of Joy							17			
1417	Peter Gabriel								16-		
1418	Diana Williams							17			
1419	The Sunshine Band						17				
1420	Ellison Chase							17			
1421	Pages										18
1422	The Controllers									17	
1423	Lena Zavaroni					18					
1424	Otis Redding	-16									
1425	Kerry Chater								16		
1426	Marlena Shaw								-16		
1427	Dooley Silverspoon						17				
1428	The Barron Knights										18
1429	The Hagers					18					
1430	Ramones								19	20	
1431	April					18					
1432	Mistress										18
1433	Lazy Racer										18
1434	Ace Spectrum					18					
1435	Simon Stokes & The Nighthawks	17									
1436	The Lovelites	17									
1437	Mother's Finest								16		
1438	Shirley & Squirrely							17			
1439	Joey Scarbury		17-								
1440	John Dawson Read						17				
1441	Gabriel									17	
1442	Andy Fairweather Low						17				
1443	Le Pamplemousse									17	
1444	Donna McDaniel								16		
1445	Terry Cashman							17			
1446	Lake								16		
1447	Marilyn Scott									18	
1448	Cissy Houston		17								
1449	Anson Williams								17		
1450	Jesse Winchester								17-		

Rank	Act	'70	'71	'72	'73	'74	'75	'76	'77	'78	'79
1451	T-Connection								17		
1452	The Klowns	17									
1453	Rare Bird	17									
1454	Kristy And Jimmy McNichol									18	
1455	The Continental 4		17								
1456	Goose Creek Symphony				18						
1457	The Mighty Pope								17		
1458	Garry Bonner						17				
1459	Ginger Baker's Air Force	17									
1460	John Baldry		-18								
1461	Automatic Man								17		
1462	Cargoe				18						
1463	Easy Street							18			
1464	Airwaves									18	
1465	Sonoma					18					
1466	Shack			18							
1467	Telly Savalas						18				
1468	Mahogany Rush						18				
1469	Alessi								17-		
1470	Hair (Original Soundtrack)/Cheryl Barnes										18
1471	Couchois										18
1472	Heartsfield						19				
1473	Five Special										18
1474	Donald Austin					18					
1475	Syndicate Of Sound	-17									
1476	Cerrone								17		
1477	Brian Protheroe						17				
1478	Redwing			18							
1479	Moments and Whatnauts							17			
1480	Mike Finnigan									18	
1481	David Clayton-Thomas				18						
1482	Barbara And The Uniques			18							
1483	Joy Of Cooking			18							
1484	Cochise			18							
1485	Nina Simone	-17									
1486	Cal Smith					18					
1487	The Singing Dogs				-18						
1488	Drupi					18					
1489	Tim Curry										18
1490	Sundown Company							18			
1491	Universal Robot Band								17		
1492	Spaghetti Head						18				
1493	Bones				18						
1494	Wendy Waldman									18	
1495	Ginger							18			
1496	B.C. Generation							-18			
1497	Pousette-Dart Band										19
1498	Monk Higgins & The Specialties				18						
1499	The Buchanan Brothers	-17									
1500	East L.A. Car Pool						18				

Rank	Act	'70	'71	'72	'73	'74	'75	'76	'77	'78	'79
1501	The Ray Charles Singers	-17									
1502	Lana Cantrell						18				
1503	Gino Cunico							19			
1504	Herb Ohta					19					
1505	Garland Green		-18								
1506	John Belushi									18	
1507	Elliott Randall								18		
1508	The Youngbloods	-18									
1509	Fantasy	18									
1510	Cameo										19-
1511	Cherie & Marie Currie										19
1512	The Dixie Dregs									19	
1513	Judy Clay	-18									
1514	The Reflections							18			
1515	The Masqueraders							-19			
1516	Marion Black		18								
1517	Blaze							19			
1518	The Fantastics			18							
1519	Genya Ravan									19	
1520	Julie							19			
1521	Gene Pitney	-18									
1522	John Culliton Mahoney					19					
1523	Little Feat									19	
1524	Reparata							18			
1525	Storm		18								
1526	John Edwards					19					
1527	Karen Young									19	
1528	Blue								18		
1529	Shango	-18									
1530	G.W. Kenny					19					
1531	Zoot Fenster							18			
1532	Prince									19-	
1533	National Lampoon			19							
1534	Roy Orbison										-19-
1535	Sylvia & The Moments					19					
1536	Law						19				
1537	Nino & April				-19						
1538	Carol Chase							19			
1539	Pat Lundi						19				
1540	Dick Feller					20					
1541	Errol Sober										19
1542	Cornerstone	18									
1543	Spellbound									19	
1544	Orsa Lia										19
1545	Margie Joseph & Blue Magic						19				
1546	Machine										19
1547	Ellen Foley										19
1548	Cannonball Adderley Quintet	-18									
1549	Pat Shannon	18									
1550	Southcote					20					

Rank	Act	'70	'71	'72	'73	'74	'75	'76	'77	'78	'79
1551	Jane Birkin & Serge Gainsbourg	18									
1552	Don Everly					20					
1553	Balcones Fault								19		
1554	J.C. Stone					20					
1555	Reuben Howell					20					
1556	Donny Gerrard							19			
1557	Eric Burdon & Jimmy Witherspoon		19								
1558	John Reid						19				
1559	Don Williams								20	20-	
1560	Liverpool Express							19			
1561	Susan Raye			19							
1562	Arpeggio										19
1563	Voyage										19
1564	Steve Wightman							19			
1565	Jimmy Ruffin			-19							
1566	Arthur Conley	-18									
1567	U.S. 1						19				
1568	Sparks				19-						
1569	Fresh Start					20					
1570	Kevin Johnson				19						
1571	Savage Grace	18									
1572	James Leroy				19						
1573	Tony Burrows		19								
1574	Jean Jacques Perrey		19								
1575	Robert Byrne										20
1576	Bill Cosby With The Bunions Bradford Band		19								
1577	The Satisfactions		19								
1578	The Happenings		-19								
1579	Kongas									20	
1580	Southside Johnny & The Asbury Jukes										20-
1581	Bama										20
1582	The Force								19		
1583	John Mayall		-19								
1584	The Monkees		-19-								
1585	Al DeLory		19								
1586	Jellyroll		19								
1587	Danyel Gérard				19						
1588	Troiano										20
1589	Bob McGilpin									20	
1590	Monkey Meeks					19					
1591	Steve Sperry								19		
1592	Pockets									20	
1593	Mark-Almond				19						
1594	Cecilio & Kapono							20			
1595	Dean Martin		-19								
1596	The Rattles		19								
1597	Steve Alaimo				-19						
1598	Tammy Wynette							-20			
1599	Euclid Beach Band										20
1600	Clarence Reid					-20					

Rank	Act	'70	'71	'72	'73	'74	'75	'76	'77	'78	'79
1601	The Flying Machine	-19									
1602	Black Ivory			19							
1603	The Eleventh Hour						19				
1604	Dan Peek										20
1605	Uncle Dog				19						
1606	Marian Love		19								
1607	Stefan			19							
1608	The Coasters			-19							
1609	Holly Sherwood			19							
1610	Sam & Dave			-19							
1611	Karen Nelson And Billy T								19		
1612	Les McCann & Eddie Harris	19									
1613	Juice Newton									20-	
1614	Detroit				20						
1615	Cotton, Lloyd and Christian						19				
1616	The Mark IV				20						
1617	Jack Wild		19								
1618	T.M.G.										20
1619	Lloyd Price				-20						
1620	Duke & The Drivers						20				
1621	The Goodies						20				
1622	Baron Stewart						20				
1623	Billy Sans					20					
1624	Linda Jones			-20							
1625	Sweeney Todd							20			
1626	Silver Hawk		19								
1627	Dana Valery							20			
1628	Marion Williams			20							
1629	Ron Dante						20				
1630	UFO								19		
1631	Charles Brimmer						20				
1632	Silvetti								19		
1633	Special Delivery featuring Terry Huff							20			
1634	Tony Cole			20							
1635	The Skyliners									-20	
1636	Arthur, Hurley & Gottlieb					20					
1637	Philly Devotions							20			
1638	Bobby Vee	-20									
1639	Don Nix		20								
1640	Apple & Appleberry						20				
1641	Billy Lemmons								20		
1642	The Courtship				20						
1643	Bang				20						
1644	Duane Eddy	-20-									
1645	Keith Herman										20
1646	George McCannon III	20									
1647	Tony Joe White	-20-									
1648	Yonah										20
1649	Iron Butterfly	-20									
1650	Shirley Caesar						20				

Rank	Act	'70	'71	'72	'73	'74	'75	'76	'77	'78	'79
1651	Betty Everett		-20								
1652	N.F. Porter		20								
1653	Cazz									20	
1654	The Asylum Choir			20							
1655	Charley Pride/Henry Mancini			20							
1656	Terry Williams			20							
1657	Diamond Head				20						
1658	Canyon							20			
1659	McKinley Travis	20									
1660	The Flirtations	-20									
1661	Jerry Smith	-20									
1662	David Crosby		20								
1663	Billy Thunderkloud & The Chieftones							20			
1664	The Chambers Brothers		-20								
1665	The Flame	20									
1666	Billy Hemmans & Clays Composite	20									
1667	Mike Reilly			20							
1668	Al Capps Band	20									
1669	The Dillards			20							
1670	Manitoba	20									
1671	The Move				20						
1672	Cool Heat	20									
1673	Barbara Lynn		-20								
1674	Slik							20			
1675	Scott English				-20						
1676	Side Effect								20		
1677	Billy Lee Riley			20							
1678	Bill Quateman				20						
1679	David Bellamy						20				
1680	The Atlanta Disco Band							20			
1681	Philadelphia								20		
1682	Deardorff & Joseph								20		
1683	The Festivals	20									
1684	Buddy Miles & The Freedom Express	20									
1685	Charlene								20-		
1686	The Lorelei			20							
1687	Act I				20						
1688	Sergio Mendes & Brasil '77				-20						
1689	Connie Francis				-20						
1690	Hodges, James and Smith								20		
1691	The Newcomers			20							
1692	New Riders Of The Purple Sage			20							
1693	Summer Wine					20					
1694	Chester					20					
1695	Patti Dahlstrom					20					
1696	The Dovells					-20					
1697	Yvonne Fair								20		
1698	Philadelphia International All Stars								20		
	Total Number of Acts Per Year	383	363	369	341	330	372	330	314	306	324

Section 3

Act Index

Here you will find every Top 100 act of the 1970s alphabetized and categorized as Soloists, Duos and Groups along with their '70s chart hits weighted and numbered according to chart strength.

To the right of each act's name is its decade rank. The decade rank is also given in Section 2, so the number here is a convenient way to direct you to that section in order that you may see other acts ranked above and below, thereby providing a clearer impression of the relative popularity of an act.

The designation (s) after an act name indicates that the act was a studio or recording project and at least not initially an ongoing band. An example would be the Blue Ridge Rangers (s), a studio project of John Fogerty of the disbanded Creedence Clearwater Revival. Members of such assemblages were often unheralded studio musicians and session players, not unlike the now-famous Wrecking Crew or Funk Brothers. Fogerty's project was unusual in that it was a totally solo effort.

An act with members who were affiliated with another charting act is noted directly under the act's name. The bold lettering signifies that the individual or group has its own main entry. Artists whose names are in parentheses were members of more than one charting act during the '70s. Artists who were members of a group and left before that group charted or who had joined a group after its final chart record were not noted.

Each act's 1970s chart output is listed below its name in order of chart strength. The year, peak rank and points are shown for each song title. Weeks at peak rank are designated by the superscript. The points were used to determine this compilation's song rankings for Section 1. Because the titles are arranged with chart performance in mind, it is an easy matter to compare the popularity of an act's singles. In this way, music chart fans can learn, for example, that, based on the Ranking the '70s scoring system, the second most popular hit by James Taylor, "Fire and Rain," was actually his third highest peaking title in the Top 100 (#4) behind "Handy Man" (#2) and that Linda Ronstadt's "Blue Bayou" was her most popular hit even though it peaked at #2 behind her two #1s, "When Will I be Loved" and "You're No Good."

Italicized lettering under a song title indicates that the act was known by an alternative name on the record label.

For help in finding an act's configuration more quickly, you may want to first skim the listings beginning on the next page. The first number after the act indicates the act rank; the second is its number of charted records for the decade.

Soloists

Alaimo, Steve	1597-1	Bristol, Johnny	477-3	Charles, Ray	358-9
Albert, Morris	479-2	Brood, Herman	1006-1	Chase, Carol	1538-1
Alexander, Arthur	980-2	Brooks, Nancy	1261-1	Chase, Ellison	1420-1
Allman, Gregg	737-2	Brown, Don	1248-1	Chater, Kerry	1425-1
Alpert, Herb	371-1	Brown, James	33-32	Cher	35-14
Amesbury, Bill	925-1	Brown, Jim Ed	1084-1	Christie, Lou	835-4
Anderson, Lynn	187-7	Brown Jr., Oscar	1284-1	Clapton, Eric	88-10
Anka, Paul	96-12	Brown, Peter	458-4	Clark, Petula	1192-2
April	1431-1	Brown, Polly	768-1	Clark, Roy	997-4
Arvon, Bobby	1056-1	Brown, Randy	1354-1	Clarke, Allan	1052-1
Austin, Donald	1474-1	Brown, Shirley	857-1	Clay, Judy	1513-1
Avalon, Frankie	944-1	Brown Sugar	1357-1	Clay, Otis	1249-1
Axton, Hoyt	1353-1	Browne, Jackson	215-8	Clay, Tom	620-1
Baez, Joan	261-5	Bryson, Peabo	1255-1	Clayton, Merry	697-4
Baldry, John	1460-1	Buffett, Jimmy	284-7	Clayton-Thomas, David	1481-1
Bare, Bobby	1068-1	Bullens, Cindy	1165-1	Cliff, Jimmy	681-2
Barry, Claudja	1212-1	Burke, Solomon	1273-2	Clifford, Linda	1046-2
Bassey, Shirley	740-3	Burrows, Tony	1574-1	Coates, Odia	1026-2
Bell, Benny	964-1	Butler, Jerry	424-11	Cocciante, Richard	1268-1
Bell, Maggie	1396-1	Byrd, Bobby	898-3	Cocker, Joe	111-13
Bell, Vincent	906-1	Byrd, Donald	1158-1	Coffey, Dennis	1160-1
Bell, William	639-1	Byrne, Robert	1575-1	Cole, Natalie	185-6
Bellamy, David	1679-1	Caesar, Shirley	1650-1	Cole, Tony	1634-1
Belushi, John	1506-1	Cain, Jonathan	1034-1	Collins, Judy	336-6
Benson, George	310-5	Caldwell, Bobby	719-1	Collins, Lyn	985-1
Benton, Brook	276-4	Cale, J.J.	669-3	Colter, Jessi	459-3
Berry, Chuck	269-2	Campbell, Glen	50-16	Coltrane, Chi	685-1
Bertrand, Plastic	1152-1	Cantrell, Lana	1502-1	Como, Perry	395-4
Bishop, Elvin	403-3	Capaldi, Jim	914-3	Conley, Arthur	1566-1
Bishop, Stephen	335-4	Carlton, Carl	592-2	Connors, Norman	743-3
Black, Marion	1516-1	Carmen, Eric	160-7	Conti, Bill	463-1
Bland, Bobby	507-8	Carnes, Kim	1171-1	Cooker	1252-1
Bloom, Bobby	500-4	Carradine, Keith	638-1	Coolidge, Rita	147-8
Blue Ridge Rangers (s)	505-3	Carter, Clarence	157-11	Cooper, Alice	202-6
Blue, David	1285-1	Cash, Johnny	405-6	Cory	1339-1
Bonner, Garry	1458-1	Cash, Tommy	1361-1	Cosby, Bill	962-2
Bonoff, Karla	1115-2	Cashman, Terry	1445-1	Costello, Elvis	1215-1
Boom, Taka	1372-1	Cassidy, David	206-5	Cotton, Gene	432-6
Boone, Daniel	612-2	Cassidy, Shaun	201-4	Cougar, John	901-1
Boone, Debby	165-2	Castle, David	1099-2	Covay, Don	864-2
Bowie, David	109-13	Castleman, Boomer	942-1	Craddock, Billy "Crash"	618-3
Boyer, Bonnie	1224-1	Cazz	1653-1	Crane, Les	727-1
Bremers, Beverly	491-3	Cerrone	1476-1	Croce, Jim	61-10
Bridges, Alicia	492-1	Chandler, Gene	466-4	Crosby, David	1662-1
Brimmer, Charles	1631-1	Chapin, Harry	184-8	Cuff Links	691-2
		Charlene	1685-1	Cummings, Burton	502-3

Cunha, Rick	1021-1	Edmunds, Dave	411-3	Gates, David	340-5
Cunico, Gino	1503-1	Edwards, John	1526-1	Gaye, Marvin	29-13
Curry, Tim	1489-1	Edwards, Jonathan	427-2	Gayle, Crystal	197-4
Daddy Dewdrop	464-3	Egan, Walter	483-4	Gaynor, Gloria	195-6
Dahlstrom, Patti	1695-1	Elbert, Donnie	541-4	Geddes, David	387-2
Dalton, Kathy	1186-1	Elliman, Yvonne	180-6	Gentry, Bobbie	562-4
Daltrey, Roger	805-3	Elliot, Mama Cass	939-1	Gérard, Danyel	1587-1
Dana, Vic	790-2	Emmerson, Les	956-1	Gerrard, Donny	1556-1
Daniels, Charlie	666-1	English, Scott	1675-1	Gibb, Andy	48-5
Dante, Ron	1629-1	Ernie (Jim Henson)	744-1	Gibb, Robin	938-1
Darin, Bobby	1073-1	Essex, David	380-2	Gilder, Nick	214-3
Darren, James	1223-2	Everett, Betty	1651-1	Gilley, Mickey	1200-1
Dash, Sarah	1351-1	Everly, Don	1552-1	Gilstrap, Jim	910-3
Davis, Mac	117-10	Fair, Yvonne	1697-1	Glitter, Gary	440-2
Davis, Paul	167-10	Fairchild, Barbara	847-1	Goffin, Louise	1053-1
Davis Jr., Sammy	330-2	Fardon, Don	1298-1	Gold, Andrew	299-4
Davis, Tim	1366-1	Fargo, Donna	232-7	Goldsboro, Bobby	327-7
Davis, Tyrone	132-14	Feliciano, Jose	1138-2	Gomm, Ian	917-1
Dean, Jimmy	1089-1	Feller, Dick	1540-1	Goodman, Dickie	282-6
Dee, Kiki	1070-3	Felts, Narvel	1290-2	Goodwin, Don	1406-1
DeLory, Al	1585-1	Fender, Freddy	166-7	Gordon, Robert	1180-1
Denver, John	9-25	Fenster, Zoot	1531-1	Gorme, Eydie	1016-1
Deodato	397-3	Ferguson, Jay	485-2	Graves, Carl	913-2
Derringer, Rick	626-3	Ferguson, Maynard	897-1	Gray, Dobie	429-3
DeSario, Teri	1218-1	Finnigan, Mike	1480-1	Greaves, R.B.	636-4
DeShannon, Jackie	739-5	Fischoff, George	1209-1	Grecco, Cyndi	802-1
DeVaughn, William	441-2	Flack, Roberta	47-9	Green, Al	14-18
DeYoung, Cliff	796-1	Fletcher, Lois	1079-1	Green, Garland	1505-1
Diamond, Neil	10-27	Floyd, Eddie	970-2	Greenbaum, Norman	210-2
Dibango, Manu	866-1	Floyd, King	260-4	Groce, Larry	749-1
Dion	1329-1	Fogelberg, Dan	759-2	Gross, Henry	351-5
Doctor John	467-4	Fogerty, John	766-2	Guthrie, Arlo	686-2
Donovan	742-3	Fogerty, Tom	1335-2	Hagar, Sammy	1065-2
Douglas, Carl	328-2	Foley, Ellen	1547-1	Haggard, Merle	581-5
Douglas, Carol	559-3	Foster, Bruce	1269-1	Hall, Tom T.	563-4
Downing, Al	1266-1	Frampton, Peter	118-7	Hamlisch, Marvin	373-1
Dozier, Lamont	561-3	Francis, Connie	1689-1	Hammond, Albert	203-9
Drake, Guy	1119-1	Franklin, Aretha	21-24	Hampshire, Keith	623-3
Drupi	1488-1	Franks, Michael	1187-1	Hancock, Herbie	933-1
Duke, Doris	958-2	Frehley, Ace	720-1	Handy, John	923-1
Duke, George	1075-1	Friedman, Dean	700-1	Hardy, Hagood	918-1
Dundas, David	611-1	Furay, Richie	888-2	Harris, Emmylou	1019-2
Dylan, Bob	182-11	Gabriel, Peter	1417-1	Harris, Major	368-3
Dyson, Ronnie	331-6	Garfunkel, Art	237-7	Harris, Richard	876-2
Eddy, Duane	1644-1	Garrett, Lee	1201-1	Harrison, George	58-11
Edelman, Randy	1363-2	Garrett, Leif	374-6	Harrison, Wilbert	880-1

Hart, Freddie	649-1	James, Etta	1025-2	Kristofferson, Kris	469-5
Hart, Rod	1132-1	James, Rick	597-3	Kulis, Charlie	1015-1
Hartman, Dan	828-1	James, Sonny	1378-3	LaBounty, Bill	1178-1
Hathaway, Donny	780-4	James, Tommy	126-12	Ladd, Cheryl	1044-1
Havens, Richie	764-1	Jameson, Cody	1342-1	Laflamme, David	1414-1
Hawkins, Ronnie	1389-1	Jefferson	637-2	Lake, Greg	1379-2
Hayes, Isaac	112-10	Jennings, Waylon	570-5	Lamb, Kevin	1340-1
Hayward, Justin	882-1	Joel, Billy	80-11	Lance, Major	1275-1
Haywood, Leon	540-4	John, Elton	3-26	Larson, Nicolette	536-2
Head, Murray	525-1	John, Robert	136-5	LaSalle, Denise	430-5
Heatherton, Joey	755-2	Johnny T. Angel	1398-1	Latimore	714-3
Henderson, Willie	1279-1	Johns, Sammy	423-3	Lawrence, Vicki	268-3
Hendrix, Jimi	1208-2	Johnson, Kevin	1570-1	Leavill, Otis	954-2
Henhouse Five Plus Too	975-1	Johnson, Michael	436-3	LeBlanc, Lenny	1058-2
Herman, Keith	1645-1	Johnson, Syl	806-3	Lee, Brenda	1182-2
Hernandez, Patrick	745-1	Johnston, Tom	971-1	Lee, Dickey	1193-1
Hill, Dan	367-3	Joli, France	784-1	Lee, Laura	552-4
Hill, Z.Z.	935-4	Jones, Davy	812-2	LeGrand, Michel	1045-1
Hodge, Chris	998-1	Jones, Linda	1624-1	Lemmons, Billy	1641-1
Holien, Danny	1356-1	Jones, Quincy	493-7	Lennon, John	183-4
Holloway, Loleatta	1205-1	Jones, Rickie Lee	414-2	Leroy, James	1572-1
Holm, Michael	1029-1	Jones, Tamiko	1155-1	Lewis, Jerry Lee	617-3
Holman, Eddie	290-3	Jones, Tom	72-11	Lewis, Ramsey	1197-2
Holmes, Clint	394-1	Joplin, Janis	321-4	Lia, Orsa	1544-1
Holmes, Jake	855-1	Joseph, Margie	989-2	Lightfoot, Gordon	90-9
Holmes, Rupert	275-2	Julie	1520-1	Lindsay, Mark	262-7
Hopkin, Mary	708-3	Kaplan, Gabriel	1370-1	Lipton, Peggy	1203-1
Horne, Jimmy "Bo"	1001-1	Karen, Kenny	1210-1	Little Milton	803-3
Hot Butter (s)	574-2	Kay, John	822-3	Little Richard	1131-2
Houston, Cissy	1448-1	Kelly, Casey	1254-1	LiVigni, John	1410-1
Houston, Thelma	352-4	Kelly, Paul	1057-1	Lloyd, Ian	1365-1
Howell, Reuben	1555-1	Kendricks, Eddie	75-15	Lobo	77-14
Humperdinck, Engelbert	143-13	Kennedy, Mike	1146-1	Loggins, Dave	526-2
Hunter, Ian	1390-1	Kenny, G.W.	1530-1	Loggins, Kenny	406-3
Hutch, Willie	757-3	Kermit (Jim Henson)	1009-1	Lopez, Trini	1352-1
Hyland, Brian	341-3	Khan, Chaka	814-1	Love, Marian	1606-1
Ian, Janis	360-2	Kim, Andy	194-7	Low, Andy Fairweather	1442-1
Ingram, Luther	168-9	King, Albert	1211-2	Lowe, Nick	674-1
Jacks, Susan	1191-2	King, B.B.	159-15	Lucas, Frank	1362-1
Jacks, Terry	249-5	King, Ben E.	613-2	Lulu	577-3
Jackson, Earnest	1334-1	King, Carole	62-11	Lundi, Pat	1539-1
Jackson, Jermaine	410-4	King, Evelyn "Champagne"	473-2	Lynn, Barbara	1673-1
Jackson, Joe	753-1	Knight, Frederick	713-2	Lynn, Cheryl	624-2
Jackson, Michael	45-8	Knight, Jean	279-2	Lynn, Loretta	1109-1
Jackson, Mick	1291-1	Kolby, Diane	1313-1	M	421-1
Jackson, Millie	250-10	Kongos, John	1184-1	Mac Gregor, Byron	439-1

Name	Ref	Name	Ref	Name	Ref
MacGregor, Mary	204-4	Mighty Pope	1457-1	Ohta, Herb	1504-1
Maggard, Cledus	773-1	Miles, Buddy	724-5	O'Keefe, Danny	646-1
Mahoney, John Culliton	1522-1	Miles, John	832-3	Oldfield, Mike	589-1
Manchester, Melissa	238-7	Miller, Frankie	1303-1	Oliver	1381-2
Mandrell, Barbara	786-2	Miller, Jody	941-2	Olivor, Jane	1102-2
Mangione, Chuck	474-2	Miller, Steve	191-3	Olsson, Nigel	578-3
Manilow, Barry	17-15	Mills, Frank	365-3	Orbison, Roy	1534-1
Mann, Barry	1276-2	Mills, Stephanie	927-1	Orlando, Tony	1167-1
Mann, Herbie	679-2	Milsap, Ronnie	478-6	Oskar, Lee	1383-1
Martin, Bobbi	533-2	Mitchell, Joni	233-8	Osmond, Donny	41-15
Martin, Dean	1595-2	Money, Eddie	292-6	Osmond, Little Jimmy	810-2
Martin, Moon	792-2	Montgomery, Melba	1066-1	Osmond, Marie	465-3
Martin, Steve	729-2	Moore, Dorothy	311-3	O'Sullivan, Gilbert	73-7
Martine, Layng	974-2	Moore, Jackie	442-5	Paige, Sharon	972-1
Martino, Al	445-6	Moore, Melba	953-2	Palmer, Robert	386-5
Mas, Carolyne	1320-1	Moore, Tim	701-5	Parks, Michael	746-1
Mason, Barbara	538-4	Moroder, Giorgio	736-2	Parsons, Alan	896-1
Mason, Dave	417-6	Morrison, Van	263-9	Parton, Dolly	298-7
Mathis, Johnny	955-2	Muldaur, Maria	413-2	Patterson, Kellee	1308-1
Matthews, Ian	593-2	Murphey, Michael	287-4	Paul, Billy	219-4
Mayall, John	1583-1	Murray, Anne	63-17	Payne, Freda	178-5
Mayfield, Curtis	158-10	Nash, Graham	#REF!	Peebles, Ann	539-4
McAnally, Mac	1143-1	Nash, Johnny	177-7	Peek, Dan	1604-1
McCall, C.W.	229-4	Naughton, David	501-1	Pendergrass, Teddy	588-3
McCann, Peter	610-1	Naylor, Jerry	1060-1	Perrey, Jean Jacques	1573-1
McCannon III, George	1646-1	Neely, Sam	524-4	Phillips, Esther	632-3
McCartney, Paul	499-2	Nelson, Rick	1122-1	Phillips, John	884-1
McCormick, Gayle	865-2	Nelson, Willie	643-3	Phillips, Shawn	1229-1
McCoy, Van	280-4	Nero, Peter	826-1	Pickett, Bobby (Boris) And The Crypt-Kickers	584-2
McCrae, George	301-5	Newbury, Mickey	863-2	Pickett, Wilson	128-12
McCrae, Gwen	607-1	Newman, Randy	346-1	Pitney, Gene	1521-1
McDaniel, Donna	1444-1	Newton, Juice	1613-1	Place, Mary Kay	1195-1
McDowell, Ronnie	808-1	Newton, Wayne	221-6	Pointer, Bonnie	575-2
McGee, Parker	1090-1	Newton-John, Olivia	15-19	Polnareff, Michael	1204-1
McGilpin, Bob	1589-1	Nicholas, Paul	470-2	Porter, N.F.	1652-1
McGovern, Maureen	317-7	Nightingale, Maxine	205-4	Post, Mike	554-3
McLean, Don	116-5	Nilsson	105-9	Powell, Cozy	1061-1
McLean, Penny	1134-1	Nix, Don	1639-1	Pratt, Andy	1258-1
McNamara, Robin	529-2	Nolan	1225-1	Presley, Elvis	12-32
Mead, Sister Janet	558-1	Nolan, Kenny	362-2	Preston, Billy	66-11
Meat Loaf	418-4	North, Freddie	827-2	Price, Lloyd	1619-1
Meco	246-3	Norwood, Dorothy	1232-1	Price, Ray	443-5
Meeks, Monkey	1590-1	Nugent, Ted	631-4	Pride, Charley	600-3
Melanie	71-12	Nunnery, Stu	1032-2	Prince	1532-1
Michaels, Lee	428-2	Ocean, Billy	776-1	Protheroe, Brian	1477-1
Midler, Bette	267-7	O'Day, Alan	274-2	Pruett, Jeanne	840-1

Prysock, Arthur	1085-2	Ronstadt, Linda	25-21	Simone, Nina	1485-1
Puckett, Gary	797-2	Ross, Charlie	848-2	Simpson, Valerie	1112-1
Quateman, Bill	1678-1	Ross, Diana	23-19	Sinatra, Frank	775-4
Quatro, Suzi	630-5	Rota, Nino	1401-1	Sinclair, Gordon	1048-1
Rabbitt, Eddie	521-4	Roussos, Demis	1330-1	Skellern, Peter	1014-2
Rafferty, Gerry	146-5	Rowles, John	1304-1	Sledge, Percy	1094-1
Raitt, Bonnie	1142-1	Royal, Billy Joe	1111-2	Smith, Bro	1164-1
Randall, Elliott	1507-1	Ruffin, David	446-4	Smith, Cal	1486-1
Ravan, Genya	1519-1	Ruffin, Jimmy	1565-1	Smith, Hurricane	370-2
Rawls, Lou	239-8	Rundgren, Todd	163-9	Smith, Jerry	1661-1
Ray, Don	1118-1	Rush, Merrilee	1345-1	Smith, O.C.	912-3
Raye, Susan	1561-1	Russell, Bobby	837-1	Smith, Rex	642-1
Razzy	1114-1	Russell, Brenda	867-1	Smith, Sammi	547-3
Rea, Chris	556-3	Russell, Leon	337-7	Snow, Phoebe	516-2
Read, John Dawson	1440-1	Sager, Carole Bayer	1086-1	Sober, Errol	1541-1
Redding, Gene	756-1	Sain, Oliver	1407-1	Soccio, Gino	1207-1
Redding, Otis	1424-1	Sainte-Marie, Buffy	915-2	Sommer, Bert	1038-2
Reddy, Helen	16-20	Sami Jo	673-2	Soul, David	325-3
Redway, Michael	1350-1	Sands, Evie	793-2	South, Joe	528-3
Reed, Jerry	251-7	Sang, Samantha	259-2	Souther, J.D.	598-1
Reed, Lou	820-1	Sans, Billy	1623-1	Sovine, Red	959-1
Reeves, Martha	1206-1	Santos, Larry	1081-1	Spears, Billie Jo	1235-1
Reid, Clarence	1600-1	Savalas, Telly	1467-1	Spector, Ronnie	1238-1
Reid, John	1558-1	Sawyer, Ray	1247-1	Sperry, Steve	1591-1
Reilly, Mike	1667-1	Sayer, Leo	94-7	Springfield, Dusty	627-3
Reparata	1524-1	Scaggs, Boz	175-7	Springfield, Rick	531-4
Rhodes, Emitt	907-1	Scarbury, Joey	1439-1	Springsteen, Bruce	544-4
Rich, Charlie	103-14	Scott, Marilyn	1447-1	Stafford, Jim	174-7
Richard, Cliff	456-2	Sebastian, John	332-1	Stampley, Joe	929-1
Richards, Turley	1253-1	Sedaka, Neil	79-9	Stanley, Paul	992-1
Riley, Billy Lee	1677-1	Seger, Bob	125-12	Staples, Mavis	1323-2
Riley, Jeannie C.	861-2	Sellars, Marilyn	1228-1	Starr, Edwin	192-5
Rios, Miguel	695-1	Shannon, Pat	1549-1	Starr, Kenny	1394-1
Ríos, Waldo De Los	999-1	Shaw, Marlena	1426-1	Starr, Ringo	32-11
Riperton, Minnie	315-2	Shelley, Peter	1391-1	Staton, Candi	226-10
Rippy, Rodney Allen	1314-1	Sheppard, T.G.	1071-2	Stefan	1607-1
Rivers, Johnny	155-9	Sherman, Bobby	108-10	Stevens, Cat	84-14
Robbins, Marty	1000-1	Sherwood, Holly	1609-1	Stevens, Ray	85-13
Roberts, Austin	412-3	Shirley & Squirrely (s)	1438-1	Stevenson, B.W.	451-4
Robinson, Freddy	991-1	Sigler, Bunny	1140-1	Stewart, Al	307-4
Robinson, Smokey	326-10	Silverspoon, Dooley	1427-1	Stewart, Amii	342-2
Robinson, Vicki Sue	599-2	Silvetti	1632-1	Stewart, Baron	1622-1
Rodriguez, Johnny	1325-1	Simmons, Gene	1103-1	Stewart, John	475-2
Roe, Tommy	225-6	Simon, Carly	40-14	Stewart, Rod	13-18
Rogers, Kenny	170-7	Simon, Joe	87-20	Stills, Stephen	375-6
Rogers, Roy	1183-1	Simon, Paul	53-10	Stokes, Simon	1156-1

Artist	Ref
Stone, J.C.	1554-1
Stone, Sly	1093-1
Stookey, Paul	761-1
Streisand, Barbra	43-15
Strunk, Jud	550-3
Summer, Donna	20-13
Sutton, Glenn	1328-1
Swan, Billy	320-4
Swann, Bettye	849-2
Sylvers, Foster	689-2
Sylvester	678-3
Sylvia	369-2
Tanner, Gary	1373-1
Tate, Tommy	1097-2
Taylor, James	52-14
Taylor, Johnnie	82-16
Taylor, Kate	1349-1
Taylor, Little Johnny	1139-1
Taylor, Livingston	781-2
Taylor, R. Dean	256-5
Tex, Joe	230-5
Thomas, B.J.	42-15
Thomas, Ian	872-1
Thomas, Rufus	438-5
Thomas, Timmy	382-2
Thompson, Chris	774-1
Thorpe, Billy	1063-1
Tolbert, Israel "Popper Stopper"	1135-1
Travers, Mary	1263-1
Travers, Pat	1260-1
Travis, McKinley	1659-1
Travolta, Joey	1172-1
Travolta, John	361-4
Troiano	1588-1
Trower, Robin	1387-1
Tucker, Tanya	595-6
Twitty, Conway	489-6
Tyler, Bonnie	416-1
Valenti, John	976-1
Valery, Dana	1627-1
Valli, Frankie	81-7
Vannelli, Gino	334-4
Vanwarmer, Randy	518-1
Vee, Bobby	1638-1
Vinton, Bobby	139-11
Voudouris, Roger	765-1
Wainwright III, Loudon	680-1
Wakelin, Johnny And The Kinshasa Band	770-1
Walden, Narada Michael	1162-1
Waldman, Wendy	1494-1
Walker, David T.	1272-1
Walker, Jerry Jeff	1415-1
Wallace, Jerry	783-2
Walsh, Joe	377-4
Wammack, Travis	675-4
Ward, Anita	289-1
Ward, Jacky	1355-1
Warnes, Jennifer	437-3
Warwick, Dee Dee	931-2
Warwick, Dionne	161-9
Washington Jr., Grover	1346-1
Watson, Johnny "Guitar"	1011-1
Weatherly, Jim	634-3
Webb, Paula	1358-1
Weir, Bob	1244-1
Welch, Bob	302-5
Welch, Lenny	799-2
Wells, Mary	1377-1
West, Dottie	883-2
White, Barry	64-13
White, Tony Joe	1647-1
Whittaker, Roger	734-1
Wightman, Steve	1564-1
Wild, Jack	1617-1
Williams, Andy	426-6
Williams, Anson	1449-1
Williams, Deniece	688-2
Williams, Diana	1418-1
Williams, Don	1559-2
Williams, John	602-2
Williams, Johnny	1404-1
Williams, Marion	1628-1
Williams, Paul	889-2
Williams, Terry	1656-1
Wilson, Al	213-5
Wilson, Hank	1327-1
Wilson, Jackie	908-3
Wilson, Meri	851-1
Wilson, Nancy	1412-1
Winchester, Jesse	1450-1
Wingfield, Pete	705-1
Winter, Edgar	1116-1
Winters, Ruby	1159-2
Withers, Bill	86-9
Womack, Bobby	176-11
Wonder, Stevie	6-19
Wood, Lauren	948-1
Wright, Betty	272-8
Wright, Gary	189-4
Wright, O.V.	1105-1
Wynette, Tammy	1598-1
Yonah	1648-1
Young, John Paul	537-3
Young, Karen	1527-1
Young, Neil	164-8
Zappa, Frank	904-2
Zavaroni, Lena	1423-1
Zevon, Warren	807-1
Zwol	1319-2

Duos

Artist	Ref
Addrisi Brothers	420-6
Alessi	1469-1
America	1221-1
Anka, Paul, with Odia Coates	583-1
Apple & Appleberry	1640-1
Ashford & Simpson	819-2
Asylum Choir	1654-1
Barbra & Neil	312-1
Batdorf & Rodney	1051-2
Beckmeier Brothers	1226-1
Bell & James	747-1
Bellamy Brothers	293-4
Birkin, Jane, & Serge Gainsbourg	1551-1
Black, Terry, And Laurel Ward	1177-1
Blanchard, Jack, & Misty Morgan	652-2
Blues Brothers	603-2
Brecker Brothers	1047-1
Brewer And Shipley	494-3
Brothers Johnson	379-3
Brown, James - Lyn Collins	1078-1
Buggles	1004-1
Burdon, Eric, & Jimmy Witherspoon	1557-1
Butler, Jerry, and Brenda Lee Eager	762-1
Campbell, Glen / Anne Murray	1344-1

Captain & Tennille	39-10	Kristofferson, Kris, & Rita Coolidge	870-2	Seals & Crofts	102-12
Carpenters	4-24	LaVerne & Shirley	1305-1	Shepstone & Dibbens	1312-1
Cash, Johnny, & June Carter	936-1	Le Blanc & Carr	551-3	Simon & Garfunkel	91-5
Cashman & West	704-3	Loggins & Messina	179-10	Simon, Carly, & James Taylor	422-2
Cate Brothers	738-2	Lynn, Loretta/Conway Twitty	1231-2	Simon, Paul/Phoebe Snow	834-1
Cecilio & Kapono	1594-1	Mark-Almond	1593-1	Sonny & Cher	270-4
Chanson	787-1	Marshall Hain	969-1	Splinter	1240-1
Cheech & Chong	244-7	Mathis, Johnny / Deniece Williams	355-2	Stark & McBrien	1265-1
Chee-Chee and Peppy	890-1	McCann, Les, & Eddie Harris	1612-1	Steve & Eydie	1237-1
Collins, Dave, And Ansil	869-1	McCartney, Paul, & Linda	383-1	Stoney And Meatloaf	1360-1
Crosby, David / Graham Nash	804-3	McCoo, Marilyn, & Billy Davis Jr.	242-4	Streisand, Barbra/ Donna Summer	376-1
Currie, Cherie & Marie	1511-1	McFadden & Whitehead	658-1	Sweet Dreams	1246-1
Deardorff & Joseph	1682-1	Mcichol, Kristy, And Jimmy	1454-1	Tarney/Spencer Band	943-3
Delaney & Bonnie	730-2	Mel and Tim	555-2	Teegarden & Van Winkle	662-2
Delbert & Glen	1399-1	Monkees	1584-1	Tin Tin	677-2
"Deliverance" Soundtrack	388-1	Mouth & MacNeal	506-2	Travolta, John, And Olivia Newton-John	224-2
DeVorzon, Barry, and Perry Botkin, Jr.	546-1	Nash, Graham, & David Crosby	804-3	Tufano & Giammarese	1259-1
Eddie & Dutch	1274-1	Nelson, Karen, And Billy T	1611-1	Turner, Ike, & Tina	240-9
England Dan & John Ford Coley	150-8	Nino & April	1537-1	Twitty, Conway Loretta Lynn	1231-2
Euclid Beach Band	1599-1	O'Connor, Carroll, And Jean Stapleton	1310-1	Vigrass & Osborne	1067-1
Ferrante & Teicher	568-2	Osmond, Donny, And Marie	199-7	Waylon & Willie	818-2
Flack, Roberta, & Donny Hathaway	447-3	Peaches & Herb	172-4	Williams, Andy, & David	1392-1
Flash & The Pan	1380-1	Peppers (s)	1100-1	Young, Neil, and Graham Nash	1147-1
Fogelberg, Dan / Tim Weisberg	886-1	Pink Lady	1076-1		
Force	1582-1	Pipkins (s)	591-1	**Groups**	
Gallagher & Lyle	1188-3	Poppy Family	703-4	Abba	60-15
Gary & Dave	1408-1	Pratt & McClain	573-1	Abraham's Children	1397-1
Gaye, Marvin, & Tammi Terrell	1216-1	Pride, Charley/Henry Mancini	1655-1	AC/DC	1174-1
Gaylord & Holiday	1400-1	Purify, James, & Bobby	1278-1	Ace	359-2
Gene & Jerry	1371-1	Quatro, Suzi, And Chris Norman	590-1	Ace Spectrum	1434-1
Gentry, Bobbie, & Glen Campbell	877-1	Raes	1222-1	Act I	1687-1
Grand Canyon	1181-1	Righteous Brothers	372-3	Adderley, Cannonball, Quintet	1548-1
Hagers	1429-1	Ross, Diana, & Marvin Gaye	503-3	Aerosmith	152-10
Hall, Daryl, & John Oates	95-10	Ross, Diana, & Michael Jackson	937-1	Afrique (s)	986-1
Hayes, Isaac, & David Porter	1217-1	Ruffin, David, & Jimmy	1095-1	Airwaves	1464-1
Hayward, Justin, And John Lodge	916-2	Russell, Leon, & Mary	1092-1	Alice Cooper	162-10
Holland-Dozier	833-2	Sailcat	752-1	Alive And Kicking	471-2
Hudson and Landry	979-2	Sam & Dave	1610-1	Allman Brothers Band	314-4
John & Ernest	1007-1	Sanford/Townsend Band	665-1	Alpert, Herb, & The Tijuana Brass	893-3
John, Elton, and Kiki Dee	339-1	Santana, Carlos, & Buddy Miles	1234-1	Amazing Rhythm Aces	609-3
Kendalls	984-1			Ambrosia	271-5
Kissoon, Mac, And Katie	750-1			America	57-13
				Anacostia	1315-1

Artist	Ref	Artist	Ref	Artist	Ref
Angel	973-2	Blackfoot	709-2	Caboose	1321-1
Apollo 100 (s)	576-2	Blackjack	1295-1	Cameo	1510-1
April Wine	660-3	Blaze	1517-1	Canned Heat	788-1
Archies (s)	407-3	Blondie	236-3	Canyon	1658-1
Argent	509-2	Blood, Sweat & Tears	300-8	Capps, Al, Band	1668-1
Arkade	1202-1	Bloodrock	903-1	Cargoe	1462-1
Arpeggio (s)	1562-1	Bloodstone	297-5	Cars	400-5
Arthur, Hurley & Gottlieb	1636-1	Blue	1528-1	Castor, Jimmy, Bunch	333-3
Ashton, Gardner & Dyke	949-1	Blue Haze (s)	710-2	Celebration featuring Mike Love	960-1
Assembled Multitude (s)	659-2	Blue Magic	448-3		
Association	1199-3	Blue Mink	1008-2	Celi Bee & The Buzzy Bunch	1316-1
Atlanta Disco Band (s)	1680-1	Blue Öyster Cult	587-2	Chairmen Of The Board	248-7
Atlanta Rhythm Section	127-13	Blue Swede	253-4	Chakachas (s)	519-2
Audience	1294-1	Blues Image	434-2	Chambers Brothers	1664-1
Automatic Man	1461-1	Bones	1493-1	Champagne	1341-1
Average White Band / AWB	186-5	Boney M	983-2	Charles, Ray, Orchestra	809-1
B.C. Generation (s)	1496-1	Booker T. & The M.G.'s	862-2	Charles, Ray, Singers	1501-1
B.T. Express	258-7	Bootsy's Rubber Band	1243-1	Charlie	900-3
Babys	344-5	Boston	200-6	Chase	699-3
Bachman-Turner Overdrive	97-13	Box Tops	1307-1	Cheap Trick	347-4
Bad Company	137-9	Boys In The Band (s)	963-1	Chester	1694-1
Badfinger	154-6	Bram Tchaikovsky	1040-1	Chic	69-5
Baker, George, Selection	504-3	Brass Construction	711-1	Chicago	7-29
Baker's, Ginger, Air Force	1459-1	Bread	37-13	Chicory	1409-1
Balcones Fault	1553-1	Brenda & The Tabulations	496-5	Child, Desmond and Rouge	1271-1
Bama (s)	1581-1	Brick	398-3	Chi-Lites	104-14
Band	396-7	Brighter Side Of Darkness	661-1	Chilliwack	779-5
Band Of The Black Watch	1287-1	Brooklyn Bridge	1163-2	Chocolate Milk	1336-1
Bang	1643-1	Brooklyn Dreams	930-3	Christie	615-2
Barbara And The Uniques	1482-1	Brother To Brother	1110-1	Circus	1388-1
Bar-Kays	683-4	Brotherhood Of Man (s)	461-4	City Boy	1022-1
Barron Knights	1428-1	Brown, Chuck, & The Soul Searchers	952-1	Clean Living	924-1
Bay City Rollers	101-8			Climax	323-2
Bazuka (s)	653-1	Brown, James Soul Train	995-1	Climax Blues Band	601-1
Beach Boys	257-10	Brownsville Station	220-8	Clique	1301-1
Beatles	78-6	Buchanan Brothers	1499-1	Clout	1059-1
Bee Gees	1-22	Buckeye	1213-1	Coasters	1608-1
Beginning Of The End	614-1	Buckwheat	1133-2	Cochise	1484-1
Bell, Archie, & The Drells	1104-2	Bulldog	1010-1	Coffey, Dennis And The Detroit Guitar Band	350-2
Bells	433-3	Bullet (s)	670-3		
Biddu Orchestra (s)	1037-1	Buoys	657-2	Cold Blood	1077-1
Bimbo Jet (s)	1299-1	Burdon, Eric And War	294-2	Commander Cody And His Lost Planet Airmen	495-4
Black Ivory	1602-1	Byrds	1107-3		
Black Oak Arkansas	733-1	C Company Featuring Terry Nelson (s)	1031-1	Commodores	28-14
Black Sabbath	1049-2			Con Funk Shun	655-3
Blackbyrds	468-4	C.C.S.	1153-1	Consumer Rapport	1042-1
		C.J. & Co.	1117-1	Continental 4	1455-1
				Continental Miniatures	1367-1

Artist	Code	Artist	Code	Artist	Code
Controllers	1422-1	Detroit	1614-1	Fabulous Rhinestones	1286-1
Cool Heat (s)	1672-1	Detroit Emeralds	404-6	Faces	564-2
Cooper Brothers	871-2	Diamond Head	1657-1	Facts Of Life	1072-1
Cornelius Brothers & Sister Rose	129-6	Diamond REO	1003-1	Faith Band	978-2
Cornerstone	1542-1	Dillards	1669-1	Faith, Hope & Charity	676-2
Cosby, Bill With The Bunions Bradford Band	1576-1	Dire Straits	510-2	Fancy	596-2
Cotton, Lloyd and Christian	1615-1	Disco-Tex & The Sex-O-Lettes	487-4	Fanny	567-4
Couchois	1471-1	Dixie Dregs	1512-1	Fantastic Four	1297-1
Country Coalition	1359-1	Dr. Buzzard's Original "Savannah" Band	725-2	Fantastics	1518-1
Courtship	1642-1	Dr. Hook	56-13	Fantasy	1509-1
Coven	585-3	Donaldson, Bo And The Heywoods	217-6	Faragher Brothers	1130-1
Crabby Appleton	778-1	Doobie Brothers	30-18	Fatback Band	1127-1
Crawler	1101-1	Doors	306-6	Feather	1288-1
Creative Source	1041-1	Doucette	1018-3	Festivals	1683-1
Creedence Clearwater Revival	59-10	Dovells	1696-1	5th Dimension	31-21
Crosby, Stills & Nash	548-2	Dramatics	142-12	Firefall	196-7
Crosby, Stills, Nash & Young	308-4	Driver	1385-1	Firefly (s)	1338-1
Cross Country	821-1	Duke And The Drivers	1620-1	First Choice	484-5
Crow	490-4	Dusk (s)	672-3	First Class (s)	462-3
Crown Heights Affair	702-4	Dyke And The Blazers	1333-2	Five Flights Up	831-2
Crusaders	545-5	Dylan, Bob / The Band	1050-1	Five Man Electrical Band	305-6
Crystal Mansion	1043-1	Dynamic Superiors	1239-1	Five Special	1473-1
Curb, Mike, Congregation	760-2	Eagles	19-16	Five Stairsteps	401-4
Cymande	881-2	Earth, Wind & Fire	38-18	5000 Volts	902-1
Cymarron	667-2	Earth, Wind & Fire With The Emotions	534-1	Flame	1665-1
Dahl, Steve and Teenage Radiation	1227-1	East L.A. Car Pool	1500-1	Flaming Ember	450-5
Damnation Of Adam Blessing	1393-1	Easy Street	1463-1	Flamingos	1170-1
Damon's, Liz, Orient Express	905-1	Ebonys	945-2	Flash	878-1
Daniels, Charlie, Band	353-5	Ecstasy, Passion & Pain	751-3	Flash Cadillac & The Continental Kids	650-3
Daybreak	1376-1	Edison Lighthouse (s)	384-2	Fleetwood Mac	68-9
Deadly Nightshade	1175-1	Edward Bear	288-4	Flirtations	1660-1
Deal, Bill, & The Rhondels	1069-2	8th Day	472-3	Floaters	481-1
Dee, Kiki, Band, The	668-2	El Chicano	605-3	Flying Machine (s)	1601-1
Deep Purple	357-5	El Coco (s)	1113-1	Focus	482-2
Dees, Rick And His Cast Of Idiots	296-2	Electric Express	1137-1	Foghat	364-7
DeFranco Family, The, featuring Tony DeFranco	254-3	Electric Light Orchestra	55-16	Fools Gold	1230-1
Delaney & Bonnie And Friends	517-3	Elephant's Memory	885-1	Foreigner	114-7
Delegates	815-1	Eleventh Hour (s)	1603-1	Fortunes	511-3
Delegation	1128-1	Emerson, Lake & Palmer	608-5	Fotomaker	1136-2
Delfonics	319-8	Emotions	193-8	Four Seasons	222-4
Dells	286-10	Enchantment	715-3	Four Tops	74-17
Derek And The Dominos	586-3	English Congregation	811-2	Fox	1124-1
		Eruption	767-1	Foxy	569-2
		Exile	208-2	Free	378-2
		Fabulous Counts	1402-2	Free Movement	476-2
				Fresh Start	1569-1

Artist	Code	Artist	Code	Artist	Code
Friends Of Distinction	454-3	Heyettes	1161-1	Kansas	171-8
Frijid Pink	381-3	Higgins, Monk & The Specialties	1498-1	Katfish	1148-1
Funkadelic	514-6	High Inergy	723-1	Kayak	1055-1
Funky Communication Committee	1154-1	Hillside Singers	664-2	Kay-Gees	1300-1
Funky Kings	1277-1	Hodges, James and Smith	1690-1	King Curtis & The Kingpins	1166-1
Fuzz	560-3	Hollies	119-8	King Harvest	579-2
G.Q.	522-2	Honey Cone	140-6	Kinks	343-6
Gabriel	1441-1	Hot	460-2	Kiss	106-15
Gallery	209-3	Hot Chocolate	134-7	Klaatu	1125-2
Garfunkel, Art with James Taylor & Paul Simon	836-1	Hotel	852-3	Klowns	1452-1
Gary's Gang	967-1	Hotlegs	813-1	Knack	188-2
Geils, J., Band	266-9	Hudson Brothers	527-4	Knight, Gladys, & The Pips	18-21
Genesis	763-2	Hues Corporation	252-4	Kongas (s)	1579-1
Gentrys	718-3	Humble Pie	859-2	Kool & The Gang	100-13
Gibbons, Steve, Band	1411-1	Humphrey, Paul & His Cool Aid Chemists	728-2	Kraftwerk	782-2
Ginger (s)	1495-1	Ides Of March	455-3	L.A. Jets	1293-2
Gladstone	968-1	Illusion	1120-1	L.T.D.	391-4
Glass Bottle	789-2	Impressions	318-8	Labelle	309-2
Glass House	1384-2	Incredible Bongo Band	934-2	Lady Flash	932-1
Godspell	606-1	Independents	498-5	Lai, Francis and His Orchestra	977-1
Golden Earring	572-3	Instant Funk	856-1	Lake	1446-1
Gonzalez	1054-1	Intrigues	1024-2	Law	1536-1
Goodies	1621-1	Intruders	513-7	Lazy Racer	1433-1
Goose Creek Symphony	1456-1	Iron Butterfly	1649-1	Le Pamplemousse (s)	1443-1
Graham Central Station	651-4	Ironhorse	1098-1	Le Roux	1033-1
Grand Funk Railroad	46-18	Isley Brothers	67-24	Led Zeppelin	113-7
Grass Roots	123-12	Jackson 5	2-23	Lennon, John/Plastic Ono Band	120-7
Grateful Dead	829-4	Jaggerz	385-2	Lettermen	565-4
Grin	1302-1	James Gang	515-5	Lewis, Ramsey, and Earth, Wind and Fire	993-2
Guess Who	34-19	James, Tommy, And The Shondells	532-3	Lighthouse	457-4
Gunhill Road	794-1	Jamestown Massacre	1257-1	Limmie & Family Cookin'	1150-1
Gypsy	1106-1	Jay And The Americans	553-2	Lindisfarne	842-2
Hair (Original Soundtrack)/Cheryl Barnes	1470-1	The J.B.'s, The	645-3	Liquid Gold	1311-1
Haley, Bill And His Comets	1005-1	Jefferson Starship	110-11	Liquid Smoke	1369-1
Hamilton, Joe Frank & Reynolds	115-6	Jellyroll	1586-1	Little Anthony And The Imperials	965-3
Happenings	1578-1	Jethro Tull	338-7	Little Feat	1523-1
Harrison, Don, Band, The	1236-1	Jigsaw	402-4	Little River Band	144-7
Head East	874-3	Jo Jo Gunne	909-1	Little Sister	549-2
Heart	156-10	John, Elton, Band	313-1	Liverpool Express	1560-1
Heartsfield	1472-1	Jones Girls	946-1	Looking Glass	218-4
Heatwave	227-3	Joneses	950-1	Lorelei (s)	1686-1
Heaven Bound	1080-2	Joseph, Margie & Blue Magic	1545-1	Lost Generation	919-1
Hello People	1220-1	Journey	512-4	Love And Kisses (s)	1023-1
Hemmans, Billy & Clays Composite	1666-1	Joy Of Cooking	1483-1	Love Unlimited	431-4
		K.C. & The Sunshine Band	24-14		

Artist	Ref
Love Unlimited Orchestra (s)	247-5
Lovelites	1436-1
Lunar Funk	1121-1
Lynyrd Skynyrd	211-7
MFSB (s)	291-3
Machine	1546-1
Magic Lanterns	1348-2
Mahogany Rush	1468-1
Main Ingredient	130-11
Malo	707-1
Mancini, Henry And His Orchestra	621-2
Mandrill	769-4
Manfred Mann's Earth Band	345-4
Manhattan Transfer	777-2
Manhattans	148-10
Manitoba	1670-1
Mark IV	1616-1
Marley, Bob & The Wailers	1405-1
Marmalade	425-3
Marshall Tucker Band	449-5
Mashmakhan	830-1
Masqueraders	1515-1
Mass Production	966-1
Matthews' Southern Comfort	722-1
Maze	1123-2
McCartney, Paul & Wings	5-25
McClain, Alton & Destiny	1036-1
McCrarys	1129-1
McGuinn, Clark & Hillman	987-1
McGuinness Flint	894-1
Melvin, Harold And The Blue Notes	133-10
Mendes, Sergio, & Brasil '77	1688-1
Mesa	1196-1
Messengers	1002-1
Meters	663-4
Mighty Clouds Of Joy	1416-1
Miles, Buddy & The Freedom Express	1684-1
Miller, Steve, Band	124-7
Miracles	234-4
Mr. Big	1256-1
Mistress	1432-1
Mixtures	988-1
Mob	1214-2
Mocedades	619-1
Moments	277-9
Moments and Whatnauts	1479-1
Moody Blues	153-7
Mother's Finest	1437-1
Mott The Hoople	785-2
Mountain	625-3
Move	1671-1
Mungo Jerry	390-1
Murphy, Walter & The Big Apple Band	264-2
Musique (s)	1168-1
Mystic Moods (s)	1219-2
NRBQ	1179-1
National Lampoon	1533-1
Natural Four	858-1
Nature's Divine	1318-1
Nazareth	535-1
Nazz	1251-1
Neighborhood, The	887-1
Nelson, Rick, And The Stone Canyon Band	363-3
Nesmith, Michael & The First National Band	523-4
New Birth	453-6
New Colony Six	1064-2
New England	892-2
New Hope	1241-1
New Riders Of The Purple Sage	1692-1
New Seekers	235-10
New York City	542-3
Newbeats	1364-1
Newcomers	1691-1
Night	853-1
Niteflyte	1198-1
Nite-Liters	696-2
Nitty Gritty Dirt Band	348-7
Northern Light	1332-1
Oak	1169-1
Ocean	255-4
Odds & Ends	1375-1
Odyssey	635-2
Ohio Players	76-13
O'Jays, The	36-16
100 Proof Aged in Soul	389-4
Original Caste	926-1
Originals	566-3
Tony Orlando and Dawn	11-21
Orleans	207-6
O'Shea, Shad & The 18 Wheelers	1337-1
Osmonds	44-11
Outlaws	754-3
Ovations	1262-1
Owen B.	1382-1
Ozark Mountain Daredevils	241-5
Ozo	1331-1
P-Nut Gallery (s)	1108-1
Pablo Cruise	173-7
Pacific Gas & Electric	641-2
Pages	1421-1
Painter	1189-1
Paper Lace	322-3
Parker, Graham And The Rumour	1386-1
Parliament	508-3
Parsons, Alan, Project	656-3
Partridge Family	54-9
People's Choice	543-3
Perkins, George & The Silver Stars	1039-1
Persuaders	393-6
Petty, Tom And The Heartbreakers	692-3
Philadelphia	1681-1
Philadelphia International All Stars	1698-1
Philly Devotions	1637-1
Pickettywitch	895-1
Pilot	452-3
Pink Floyd	604-2
Pipes And Drums And The Military Band Of The Royal Scots Dragoon Guards, The	731-1
Player	198-4
Pockets	1592-1
Poco	354-7
Pointer Sisters	145-9
Police	795-2
Ponderosa Twins + One	1233-1
Poppy Family	303-2
Pop-Tops	1190-1
Potliquor	1141-1
Pousette-Dart Band	1497-1
Prelude	694-2
Presidents	520-2
Prism	850-3
Procol Harum	726-2

Artist	Code
Puckett, Gary, And The Union Gap	1013-1
Pure Prairie League	791-2
Purple Reign (s)	1126-1
Python Lee Jackson	1309-1
Q	875-1
Quatro, Mike, Jam Band	1282-1
Queen	93-10
Quicksilver Messenger Service	1176-1
Raeletts	1087-3
Raiders	149-8
Rainbow	1145-1
Ram Jam	684-1
Ramones	1430-2
Rare Bird	1453-1
Rare Earth	107-8
Rascals	640-3
Raspberries	190-7
Rattles	1596-1
Raydio	356-2
Real Thing	1413-1
Records	1347-1
Redbone	316-4
Redeye	698-2
Redwing	1478-1
Reeves, Martha & The Vandellas	825-3
Reflections	1514-1
REO Speedwagon	816-4
Reunion (s)	622-1
Rhythm Heritage (s)	304-3
Ripple	1083-2
Ritchie Family	486-3
Road Apples	947-1
Robinson, Smokey & The Miracles	131-8
Rock Flowers	1324-1
Rockets	839-2
Rogers, Kenny And The First Edition	285-4
Rolling Stones	26-17
Rose Colored Glass	940-2
Rose Royce	216-6
Ross, Diana, Marvin Gaye, Smokey Robinson & Stevie Wonder	1242-1
Rowans	1306-1
Roxy Music	671-2
Rubettes	961-1
Rubicon	957-1
Rubinoos	1030-1
Rufus Featuring Chaka Khan	99-10
Rush	1289-1
Sad Cafe	1395-1
Saint Tropez	1296-1
Salsoul Orchestra	771-3
Salvage (s)	1096-1
Sandpipers	633-2
Santa Esmeralda (s)	717-1
Santana	121-8
Satisfactions	1577-1
Savage Grace	1571-1
Savoy Brown	951-2
Sea Level	1017-2
Searchers	1326-1
Seatrain	1012-1
Seger, Bob, System	1322-1
Sha Na Na	891-3
Shack	1466-1
Shalamar	1035-2
Shango	1529-1
Sherbet	1280-1
Shirley (And Company)	644-1
Shocking Blue	181-4
Shoes	1368-1
Side Effect	1676-1
Silver	690-1
Silver Convention	141-4
Silver Hawk	1626-1
Singing Dogs	1487-1
Sister Sledge	243-2
Skylark	557-2
Skyliners	1635-1
Slade	758-4
Slave	844-1
Slik	1674-1
Sly & The Family Stone	65-10
Smith	654-3
Smith, Patti, Group	706-1
Smokie	693-2
Sniff 'n' The Tears	748-1
Sonoma	1465-1
Sons Of Champlin	868-3
Soul Children	629-3
Soul Train Gang (s)	1292-1
Sounds Of Sunshine	928-1
South Shore Commission	1270-2
South Side Movement	1091-1
Southcote	1550-1
Souther, Hillman, Furay Band, The	838-2
Southside Johnny & The Asbury Jukes	1580-1
Space (s)	1283-1
Spaghetti Head	1492-1
Sparks	1568-1
Special Delivery featuring Terry Huff	1633-1
Spellbound	1543-1
Spinners	27-19
Spiral Starecase	1264-1
Spirit	1027-3
Sports	1281-1
Springwell	1185-1
Spyro Gyra	800-2
Stallion	1028-1
Stampeders	480-3
Staple Singers	70-13
Starbuck	281-5
Stargard	873-1
Starland Vocal Band	212-2
Starz	594-5
Statler Brothers	1088-2
Stealers Wheel	324-3
Steam (s)	996-1
Steely Dan	83-13
Steppenwolf	278-8
Stephen Stills -- Manassas	1151-1
Stillwater	911-1
Stokes, Simon & The Nighthawks	1435-1
Stonebolt	824-2
Stories	228-5
Storm	1525-1
Street People (s)	823-1
Stylistics	51-17
Styx	92-10
Sugar Bears (s)	982-1
Sugarloaf	419-3
Sugarloaf/Jerry Corbetta	682-1
Summer Wine	1693-1
Sundown Company (s)	1490-1
Sunshine Band	1419-1

Artist	Ref	Artist	Ref	Artist	Ref
Supertramp	231-5	Three Degrees	273-6	Wadsworth Mansion	530-2
Supremes	122-11	Three Dog Night	8-17	Walker, Jr., & The All Stars	392-6
Supremes, The & Four Tops	648-2	Thunderkloud, Billy, & The Chieftones	1663-1	Walsh, James, Gypsy Band	1020-2
Sutherland Brothers And Quiver	687-3	Toby Beau	580-2	War	49-14
Suzy And The Red Stripes	1157-1	Tokens	899-2	Warwicke, Dionne & Spinners	444-1
Sweathog	854-1	Toms, Gary, Empire	801-2	Wednesday	841-2
Sweeney Todd	1625-1	Toto	399-3	Wet Willie	349-7
Sweet	98-9	Tower Of Power	415-6	Whatnauts	1082-2
Sweet Sensation	817-1	Traffic	922-2	Whispers	920-4
Switch	921-2	Trammps	408-4	White Plains (s)	571-2
Sylvers	135-7	Triumph	860-2	Who	89-14
Sylvia & The Moments	1535-1	Trooper	1267-1	Wild Cherry	265-4
Syndicate Of Sound	1475-1	True, Andrea, Connection	329-4	Wildfire	1074-1
T-Connection	1451-1	Tubes	1317-1	Williams, John/London Symphony Orchestra	721-2
T.M.G.	1618-1	Turner, Ike & Tina & The Ikettes	735-2	Wilson, J. Frank & The Cavaliers	1250-1
T. Rex	488-4	Tuxedo Junction	1144-1	Wilton Place Street Band (s)	772-1
Talking Heads	879-1	Twilley, Dwight, Band	843-1	The Wing And A Prayer Fife And Drum Corps. (s)	741-1
Tanner, Marc, Band	1194-1	Tycoon	846-1	Winter, Edgar, Group	223-4
Taste Of Honey, A	295-1	Tymes	732-2	Winter's, Edgar, White Trash	990-2
Tavares	151-11	UFO	1630-1	Wombles, The (s)	1173-1
Tee Set	497-2	U.S. 1 (s)	1567-1	Wright, Charles And The Watts 103rd Street Rhythm Band	366-5
Tempo, Nino And 5th Ave. Sax	994-1	Uncle Dog	1605-1		
Temprees	1374-1	Undisputed Truth	245-6	Yes	435-4
Temptations	22-20	Universal Robot Band	1491-1	Yost, Dennis, And The Classics IV	582-5
10cc	138-10	Uriah Heep	712-3	Youngbloods	1508-1
Ten Wheel Drive With Genya Ravan	1245-1	Valli, Frankie & The 4 Seasons	981-2	Zager, Michael, Band	845-1
Ten Years After	647-3	Van Halen	628-3	ZZ Top	409-6
Thin Lizzy	616-2	Vanity Fare	283-3		
Think	798-2	Village People	169-5		
Third World	1062-1	Village Soul Choir	1149-1		
Thorogood, George And The Destroyers	1343-1	Voyage	1563-1		
		Wackers	1403-1		

SOLOISTS

Artist / Song	Year	Peak	Points
Steve ALAIMO ▶1597			
1. Amerikan Music	72	94	14
Morris ALBERT ▶479			
1. Feelings	75	10	2951
2. Sweet Loving Man	76	85²	60
Arthur ALEXANDER ▶980			
1. Every Day I Have To Cry Some	75	51²	318
2. Sharing The Night Together	76	94	13
Gregg ALLMAN ▶737			
Groups: The Allman Brothers Band / Gregg Allman Band			
1. Midnight Rider	74	16	967
2. Don't Mess Up A Good Thing	74	91	16
Herb ALPERT ▶371			
Group: Herb Alpert & The Tijuana Brass/T.J.B./TJB			
1. Rise	79	1²	5202
Bill AMESBURY ▶925			
1. Virginia (Touch Me Like You Do)	74	38	564
Lynn ANDERSON ▶187			
1. Rose Garden	71	1	7032
2. You're My Man	71	56	248
3. How Can I Unlove You	71	60	243
4. Top Of The World	73	81	74
5. Cry	72	81	57
6. Keep Me In Mind	73	91	20
7. What A Man, My Man Is	75	99²	5
Paul ANKA ▶96			
Duo: Paul Anka with Odia Coates			
1. (You're) Having My Baby	74	1	5348
2. I Don't Like To Sleep Alone	75	5	2456
#1 & 2: with Odia Coates, uncredited			
3. (I Believe) There's Nothing Stronger Than Our Love — PAUL ANKA with Odia Coates	75	14²	1477
4. Times Of Your Life	76	17²	1296
5. Do I Love You	71	38²	556
6. Let Me Get To Know You	74	54²	380
7. Jubilation	72	58	285
8. Anytime (I'll Be There)	76	50	272
9. This Is Love	78	70	122
10. My Best Friend's Wife	77	74²	92
11. Everybody Ought To Be In Love	77	83	38
12. Happier	77	97	7
APRIL ▶1431			
Duo: Nino & April			
1. Wake Up And Love Me	74	81	55
Bobby ARVON ▶1056			
1. Until Now	78	59	321
Donald AUSTIN ▶1474			
1. Crazy Legs	73	87	40
Frankie AVALON ▶944			
1. Venus	76	32	529
Hoyt AXTON ▶1353			
1. When The Morning Comes	74	72	85
Joan BAEZ ▶261			
1. The Night They Drove Old Dixie Down	71	3	4488
2. Let It Be	71	47²	489
3. Diamonds And Rust	75	48	360
4. In The Quiet Morning (For Janis Joplin)	72	64²	247
5. Blue Sky	75	68	114
John BALDRY ▶1460			
1. Don't Try To Lay No Boogie-Woogie On The King Of Rock And Roll	71	89	45
Bobby BARE ▶1068			
1. Daddy What If	74	50	307
Cheryl BARNES - see **HAIR (O.S.)**			
Claudja BARRY ▶1212			
1. Boogie Woogie Dancin' Shoes	79	65	176
Shirley BASSEY ▶740			
1. Never, Never, Never (Grande, Grande, Grande)	73	58²	421
2. Diamonds Are Forever	72	54	255
3. Something	70	81	87
Benny BELL ▶964			
1. Shaving Cream	75	34	506
Maggie BELL ▶1396			
1. After Midnight	74	76	67
Vincent BELL ▶906			
1. Airport Love Theme (Gwen And Vern)	70	27	615
William BELL ▶639			
1. Tryin' To Love Two	77	8	1705
David BELLAMY ▶1679			
1. Nothin' Heavy	75	98	3
John BELUSHI ▶1506			
Duo: Blues Brothers			
1. Louie, Louie	78	91	30
George BENSON ▶310			
1. This Masquerade	76	12	1596
2. On Broadway	78	11	1480
3. Love Ballad	79	14	1034
4. The Greatest Love Of All	77	29	635
5. Lady Blue	78	94	12
Brook BENTON ▶276			
1. Rainy Night In Georgia	70	2	4792
2. Don't It Make You Want To Go Home	70	48	369

	Year	Peak	Points
Brook BENTON – cont'd			
3. Shoes	71	52	342
#2 & 3: BROOK BENTON With The Dixie Flyers			
4. My Way	70	48^2	294
Chuck BERRY ▶269			
1. My Ding-A-Ling	72	1^2	6157
2. Reelin' & Rockin'	73	30	821
Plastic BERTRAND ▶1152			
1. Ca Plane Pour Moi	78	57	221
Elvin BISHOP ▶403			
1. Fooled Around And Fell In Love	76	3	3414
[uncredited vocal: Mickey Thomas, later of **Jefferson Starship**]			
2. Travelin' Shoes	74	70	198
3. Sure Feels Good	75	76	77
Stephen BISHOP ▶335			
1. On And On	77	5^2	3023
2. Save It For A Rainy Day	77	21^2	903
3. Everybody Needs Love	78	29	549
4. Animal House	79	57	200
Marion BLACK ▶1516			
1. Go On Fool	71	93	28
Bobby BLAND ▶507			
1. This Time I'm Gone For Good	74	44^2	479
2. Do What You Set Out To Do	72	58	242
3. If You've Got A Heart	70	74	157
4. Goin' Down Slow	74	81^2	79
#1 & 4: Bobby Blue Bland			
5. I Wouldn't Treat A Dog (The Way You Treated Me)	75	82	64
6. Keep On Loving Me (You'll See The Change)	70	73	60
7. Ain't No Love In The Heart Of The City	74	90	35
8. If Love Ruled The World	70	93	19
Bobby BLOOM ▶500			
1. Montego Bay	70	6	2055
2. Make Me Happy	71	78	96
3. Where Are We Going	71	97^2	10
4. Sha La Boom Boom	73	100	1
The BLUE RIDGE RANGERS (s) ▶505			
[John Fogerty]			
Solo: **John Fogerty**			
Group: **Creedence Clearwater Revival**			
1. Jambalaya (On The Bayou)	73	10^2	1770
2. Hearts Of Stone	73	33	586
3. You Don't Owe Me	73	93	9
David BLUE ▶1285			
1. Outlaw Man	73	73	122

	Year	Peak	Points
Garry BONNER ▶1458			
1. Should Anybody Ask	75	85	45
Karla BONOFF ▶1115			
1. I Can't Hold On	78	69	130
2. Isn't It Always Love	78	85	41
Taka BOOM ▶1372			
1. Night Dancin'	79	74	76
Daniel BOONE ▶612			
1. Beautiful Sunday	72	16	1532
2. Annabelle	72	81	62
Debby BOONE ▶165			
1. You Light Up My Life	77	1^8	11239
2. California	78	57	207
David BOWIE ▶109			
1. Fame	75	1	5246
2. Golden Years	76	12^2	2239
3. Space Oddity	73	17	1119
4. Young Americans	75	20	649
5. Changes	75	38	539
[reissue--see #8]			
6. Rebel Rebel	74	53	289
7. Starman	72	64	205
8. Changes	72	59	197
9. Sorrow	73	69	159
10. The Jean Genie	72	87	51
11. Sound And Vision	77	88	23
12. Let's Spend The Night Together	73	97	6
13. 1984	74	96	6
Bonnie BOYER ▶1224			
1. Got To Give In To Love	79	56	168
Beverly BREMERS ▶491			
1. Don't Say You Don't Remember	72	16	1533
2. We're Free	72	45	683
3. I'll Make You Music	72	54	315
Alicia BRIDGES ▶492			
1. I Love The Nightlife (Disco 'round)	78	6^3	3229
Charles BRIMMER ▶1631			
1. God Bless Our Love	75	95	10
Johnny BRISTOL ▶477			
1. Hang On In There Baby	74	8^2	2269
2. You And I	74	51	230
3. Do It To My Mind	77	68^2	220
Herman BROOD ▶1006			
1. Saturdaynight	79	44	415
Nancy BROOKS ▶1261			
1. I'm Not Gonna Cry Anymore	79	62	136
Don BROWN ▶1248			
1. Sitting In Limbo	78	64	147

James BROWN ▶33
Duo: James Brown & Lyn Collins

#	Title	Year	Peak	Points
1.	Get On The Good Foot - Part 1	72	10^2	1785
2.	Super Bad (Part 1 & Part 2) [Alt. title: Call Me Super Bad]	70	15^3	1423
3.	Hot Pants Pt. 1 (She Got To Use What She Got To Get What She Wants)	71	10	1327
4.	Get Up I Feel Like Being Like A Sex Machine (Part 1)	70	17^2	964
5.	The Payback - Part I	74	23^2	941
6.	Make It Funky (Part 1) [different version from #29]	71	20^2	914
7.	Soul Power Pt. 1	71	32^2	680
8.	My Thang	74	30^2	633
9.	It's A New Day (Part 1) & (Part 2)	70	26	621
10.	King Heroin	72	32	565
11.	I'm A Greedy Man - Part 1	71	29	551
12.	Papa Don't Take No Mess - Part I	74	27	542
13.	Stoned To The Bone - Part 1 [Alt. title: Stone To The Bone--Part I]	74	46	495
14.	Get Up, Get Into It, Get Involved Pt. 1	71	35	481
15.	Brother Rapp (Part 1) & (Part 2)	70	30^2	470
16.	I Got A Bag Of My Own	72	32	457
17.	Escape-Ism (Part 1)	71	40	436
18.	There It Is - Part 1	72	38	429
20.	Talking Loud And Saying Nothing - Pt. I	72	30^2	416
21.	I Got Ants In My Pants - Part 1 and I want to dance	73	33	410
22.	I Cried	71	43	360
23.	Sexy, Sexy, Sexy	73	46	314
24.	Funky Drummer (Part 1)	70	37	309
25.	Part Two (Let A Man Come In And Do The Popcorn)	70	57	241
26.	Get Up Offa That Thing	76	72	163
27.	Coldblooded	74	78	139
28.	Down And Out In New York City	73	61	133
29.	My Part/Make It Funky-Part 3 [different version from #6]	71	75	126
30.	Reality	75	73	96
31.	Spinning Wheel Pt. 1	71	78	54
32.	Funky President (People It's Bad)	74	87	22
33.	Hustle!!! (Dead On It)	75	95	12

Jim Ed BROWN ▶1084

#	Title	Year	Peak	Points
1.	Morning	71	59	282

Oscar BROWN, Jr. ▶1284

#	Title	Year	Peak	Points
1.	The Lone Ranger	74	71	122

Peter BROWN ▶458

#	Title	Year	Peak	Points
1.	Dance With Me PETER BROWN - Special Background Vocals: Betty Wright	78	8^2	2165
2.	Do Ya Wanna Get Funky With Me	77	41	424
3.	Crank It Up (Funk Town) Pt. 1	79	90^2	34
4.	You Should Do It PETER BROWN - Special Background Vocals: Betty Wright	78	91	16

Polly BROWN ▶768
Groups: Pickettywitch, Sweet Dreams

#	Title	Year	Peak	Points
1.	Up In A Puff Of Smoke	75	16	1023

Randy BROWN ▶1354

#	Title	Year	Peak	Points
1.	You Says It All	79	69	84

Shirley BROWN ▶857

#	Title	Year	Peak	Points
1.	Woman To Woman	74	26	758

BROWN SUGAR ▶1357
[Clydie King, formerly of the Raeletts]

#	Title	Year	Peak	Points
1.	The Game Is Over (What's The Matter With You)	76	76^2	83

Jackson BROWNE ▶215

#	Title	Year	Peak	Points
1.	Running On Empty	78	6	1962
2.	Doctor My Eyes	72	12	1516
3.	Here Come Those Tears Again	77	18	1008
4.	Stay//The Load-Out [TSW]	78	22	621
5.	Rock Me On The Water	72	45	353
6.	Redneck Friend	73	72	198
7.	The Pretender	77	58	145
8.	Stay	78	58	75

Peabo BRYSON ▶1255

#	Title	Year	Peak	Points
1.	Reaching For The Sky	78	60	141

Jimmy BUFFETT ▶284

#	Title	Year	Peak	Points
1.	Margaritaville	77	7^2	2117
2.	Come Monday	74	26	775
3.	Fins	79	25	556
4.	Cheeseburger In Paradise	78	29^3	536
5.	Changes In Latitudes, Changes In Attitudes	77	34	319
6.	Livingston Saturday Night	78	73	84
7.	A Pirate Looks At Forty	75	97	6

Cindy BULLENS ▶1165
Group: Disco Tex & The Sex-O-Lettes

#	Title	Year	Peak	Points
1.	Survivor	79	57	209

Solomon BURKE ▶1273

#	Title	Year	Peak	Points
1.	Love's Street And Fool's Road	72	82	75
2.	The Electronic Magnetism (That's Heavy, Baby)	71	95	8

Tony BURROWS ▶1574
Groups (s): The Brotherhood Of Man, Edison Lighthouse, First Class, White Plains
Duo: The Pipkins (s)

#	Title	Year	Peak	Points
1.	Melanie Makes Me Smile	70	95	18

Jerry BUTLER ▶424
Duo: Jerry Butler and Brenda Lee Eager

#	Title	Year	Peak	Points
1.	I Could Write A Book	70	50	297
2.	One Night Affair	72	57	208
3.	I Wanna Do It To You	77	64	205

	Year	Peak	Points
Jerry BUTLER – cont'd			
4. (They Long To Be) Close To You	72	66	164
5. Got To See If I Can't Get Mommy (To Come Back Home) #4 and 5: *JERRY BUTLER Featuring Brenda Lee Eager*	70	57	159
6. I Only Have Eyes For You	72	67	153
7. Where Are You Going	70	74	101
8. If It's Real What I Feel [#5 and 8: Alt. label, *JERRY BUTLER Featuring Brenda Lee*]	71	89	36
9. Walk Easy My Son	71	93	13
10. Special Memory	70	96	13
11. How Did We Lose It Baby	71	97	9
Bobby BYRD ▶898			
1. I Need Help (I Can't Do It Alone) (Part 1)	70	61	194
2. Hot Pants - I'm Coming, Coming, I'm Coming	71	72	100
3. Keep On Doin' What You're Doin'	72	81	42
Donald BYRD ▶1158 Group: The **Blackbyrds**			
1. Black Byrd	73	71^2	215
Robert BYRNE ▶1575			
1. Baby Fat	79	93	18
Shirley CAESAR ▶1650			
1. No Charge	75	97	8
Jonathan CAIN ▶1034 Group: The **Babys**			
1. 'Til It's Time To Say Goodbye	76	48^2	363
Bobby CALDWELL ▶719			
1. What You Won't Do For Love	79	10	1315
J.J. CALE ▶669			
1. Crazy Mama	72	35	568
2. After Midnight	72	49	280
3. Lies	72	62	172
Glen CAMPBELL ▶50 Duos: **Bobbie Gentry & Glen Campbell** **Glen Campbell/Anne Murray**			
1. Rhinestone Cowboy	75	1	6800
2. Southern Nights	77	1	5048
3. It's Only Make Believe	70	9	2008
4. Honey Come Back	70	11^2	1658
5. Country Boy (You Got Your Feet In L.A.)	76	17^2	1086
6. Dream Baby (How Long Must I Dream)	71	24	696
7. Oh Happy Day	70	34	521
8. Sunflower	77	39^2	503
9. Don't Pull Your Love/Then You Can Tell Me Goodbye	76	41	435
10. I Knew Jesus (Before He Was A Star)	73	46	423
11. Can You Fool	78	39	367

	Year	Peak	Points
12. Everything A Man Could Ever Need	70	45	327
13. The Last Time I Saw Her	71	57	253
14. Houston (I'm Comin' To See You)	74	54	243
15. I Will Never Pass This Way Again	72	65	178
16. One Last Time	73	78	86
Lana CANTRELL ▶1502			
1. Like A Sunday Morning	75	90	31
Jim CAPALDI ▶914 Group: **Traffic**			
1. It's All Right	75	53	235
2. Good Night & Good Morning	76	81	64
3. Love Hurts	76	95	15
Carl CARLTON ▶592			
1. Everlasting Love	74	9	1645
2. Drop By My Place *Little Carl Carlton*	70	77	122
Eric CARMEN ▶160 Group: **Raspberries**			
1. All By Myself	76	1	5343
2. Never Gonna Fall In Love Again	76	9	1578
3. She Did It	77	15^2	1088
4. Change Of Heart	78	19	1005
5. Sunrise	76	38^2	467
6. Baby, I Need Your Lovin'	79	60	157
7. Boats Against The Current	78	92	29
Kim CARNES ▶1171 [see also **Gene Cotton**]			
1. It Hurts So Bad	79	54	206
Keith CARRADINE ▶638			
1. I'm Easy	76	10	1723
Clarence CARTER ▶157			
1. Patches	70	1	5262
2. I Can't Leave Your Love Alone	70	49	539
3. It's All In Your Mind	70	39	448
4. The Court Room	71	49^2	329
5. Sixty Minute Man	73	51	326
6. Slipped, Tripped And Fell In Love	71	50	216
7. Mother-In-Law	73	66	112
8. Put On Your Shoes And Walk	73	83	61
9. I'm The Midnight Special	73	87	27
10. Take It Off Him And Put It On Me	70	95	23
11. Scratch My Back (And Mumble In My Ear)	71	97	5
Johnny CASH ▶405 Duo: **Johnny Cash & June Carter**			
1. What Is Truth	70	11^2	1195
2. Sunday Morning Coming Down	70	41	453
3. One Piece At A Time	76	41	407
4. Flesh And Blood	71	49	323
5. Man In Black	71	56	247

	Year	Peak	Points
Johnny CASH – cont'd			
6. Kate	72	85	43
#3 & 6: JOHNNY CASH And The Tennessee Three			
Tommy CASH ▶1361			
1. Six White Horses	70	81	82
Terry CASHMAN ▶1445			
Duo: Cashman & West			
1. Baby, Baby I Love You	76	81	50
David CASSIDY ▶206			
Group: The Partridge Family			
1. Cherish	72	3^2	4777
2. Could It Be Forever	72	15	1178
3. How Can I Be Sure	72	15^2	1046
4. Rock Me Baby	72	26	579
5. Daydream	73	91	19
Shaun CASSIDY ▶201			
1. Da Doo Ron Ron	77	1^2	4296
2. That's Rock 'N' Roll	77	4	2775
3. Hey Deanie	78	21	971
4. Do You Believe In Magic	78	37	333
David CASTLE ▶1099			
1. Ten To Eight	77	79	96
2. The Loneliest Man On The Moon	78	74	84
Boomer CASTLEMAN ▶942			
1. Judy Mae	75	29	532
CAZZ ▶1653			
1. Let's Live Together	78	96	7
CERRONE ▶1476			
1. Love In 'C' Minor - Pt. 1	77	80	40
Gene CHANDLER ▶466			
Duo: Gene & Jerry			
1. Groovy Situation	70	11	1834
2. Get Down	79	50	370
3. Simply Call It Love	70	62	305
4. You're A Lady	71	93	10
Harry CHAPIN ▶184			
1. Cat's In The Cradle	74	1	4704
2. Taxi	72	20	1165
3. WOLD	74	26^2	803
4. I Wanna Learn A Love Song	75	40^2	410
5. Could You Put Your Light On, Please	72	81	76
6. Better Place To Be (Parts 1 & 2)	76	76^2	76
7. Sunday Morning Sunshine	72	77	68
8. What Made America Famous	74	87	22
CHARLENE ▶1685			
1. It Ain't Easy Comin' Down	77	99	3
Ray CHARLES ▶358			
Group: The Ray Charles Orchestra			
1. Don't Change On Me	71	28	841

	Year	Peak	Points
2. If You Were Mine	70	50	557
3. Come Live With Me	73	52^2	314
4. Look What They've Done To My Song, Ma	72	49	283
5. What Am I Living For	72	61	256
6. Feel So Bad	71	67^2	148
7. I Can Make It Thru The Days (But Oh Those Lonely Nights)	73	79	110
8. Living For The City	75	87	39
9. Laughin And Clownin	70	90^2	32
Carol CHASE ▶1538			
1. One Woman Band	76	92	22
Ellison CHASE ▶1420			
1. Let's Rock	76	82	58
Kerry CHATER ▶1425			
Group: Gary Puckett And The Union Gap			
1. Part Time Love	77	80	57
CHER ▶35			
Duo: Sonny & Cher			
1. Gypsys, Tramps & Thieves	71	1^2	7146
2. Half-Breed	73	1	6403
3. Dark Lady	74	2	4543
4. The Way Of Love	72	9	2007
5. Take Me Home	79	10^2	1412
6. Train Of Thought	74	18	835
7. Living In A House Divided	72	21	824
8. I Saw A Man And He Danced With His Wife	74	33^2	534
9. Don't Hide Your Love	72	50^2	340
10. A Woman's Story	75	66^2	155
11. Hell On Wheels	79	64	131
12. Wasn't It Good	79	69	111
13. Rescue Me	75	84	52
14. Am I Blue	73	79	43
Lou CHRISTIE ▶835			
1. Beyond The Blue Horizon	74	72	182
2. Indian Lady	70	75^2	106
3. Are You Getting Any Sunshine?	70	84	80
4. Spanish Wine	77	95	10
Eric CLAPTON ▶88			
Groups: Delaney & Bonnie And Friends / Derek And The Dominos / Plastic Ono Band			
1. I Shot The Sheriff	74	1	4937
2. Lay Down Sally	78	3^2	4142
3. Promises	79	11	1559
4. After Midnight	70	13	1341
5. Wonderful Tonight	78	24^2	704
6. Hello Old Friend	76	28	605
7. Willie And The Hand Jive	74	40	439
8. Let It Rain	72	57	268

	Year	Peak	Points
Eric CLAPTON – cont'd			
9. Watch Out For Lucy	79	45	244
#3 & 9: ERIC CLAPTON And His Band			
10. Bell Bottom Blues	73	95	15
Petula CLARK ▶1192			
1. Wedding Song (There Is Love)	72	77	78
2. My Guy	72	89	44
Roy CLARK ▶997			
1. Come Live With Me	73	79	92
2. Then She's A Lover	70	83	41
3. Somewhere Between Love And Tomorrow	74	94^2	31
4. Thank God And Greyhound	70	99	4
Allan CLARKE ▶1052			
Group: The **Hollies**			
1. (I Will Be Your) Shadow In The Street	78	47	335
Judy CLAY ▶1513			
1. Greatest Love	70	86	29
Otis CLAY ▶1249			
1. Trying To Live My Life Without You	73	70	147
Tom CLAY ▶620			
1. What The World Needs Now Is Love/Abraham, Martin And John	71	7^2	1815
Merry CLAYTON ▶697			
1. Keep Your Eye On The Sparrow	75	58	287
2. Oh No, Not My Baby	73	61	218
3. After All This Time	72	71	130
4. Gimme Shelter	70	82	101
David CLAYTON-THOMAS ▶1481			
Group: **Blood, Sweat & Tears**			
1. Sing A Song	72	85	38
Jimmy CLIFF ▶681			
1. Wonderful World, Beautiful People	70	18	1194
2. Come Into My Life	70	99	4
Linda CLIFFORD ▶1046			
1. Bridge Over Troubled Water	79	59	122
2. Runaway Love	78	69	112
Odia COATES ▶1026			
Duo: **Paul Anka & Odia Coates**			
Group: The **Edwin Hawkins Singers**			
1. Showdown	75	62	201
2. Don't Leave Me In The Morning	75	80	56
Richard COCCIANTE ▶1268			
1. When Love Has Gone Away	76	62	131
Joe COCKER ▶111			
Group: **Delaney & Bonnie And Friends**			
1. The Letter	70	5^2	3023
JOE COCKER with Leon Russell and the Shelter People			
2. You Are So Beautiful	75	4^2	2650
3. Cry Me A River	70	16	1142
4. High Time We Went	71	29^2	780
5. She Came In Through The Bathroom Window	70	36	635
6. Put Out The Light	74	38	513
7. Midnight Rider	72	31^2	507
8. Feeling Alright	72	36	479
9. Woman To Woman	73	52	349
#7 & 9: JOE COCKER and The Chris Stainton Band			
10. Pardon Me Sir	73	49	301
11. Fun Time	78	45	283
12. I Can Stand A Little Rain	74	91	16
13. Black-Eyed Blues	71	100	1
Dennis COFFEY ▶1160			
Group: **Dennis Coffey And The Detroit Guitar Band**			
1. Ride, Sally, Ride	72	55	212
Natalie COLE ▶185			
1. I've Got Love On My Mind	77	3	3384
2. This Will Be	75	9^2	1966
3. Our Love	78	16	1115
4. Inseparable	76	33	825
5. Sophisticated Lady (She's A Different Lady)	76	40^2	696
6. Mr. Melody	76	54	317
Tony COLE ▶1634			
1. Suite: Man And Woman	72	95	9
Judy COLLINS ▶336			
1. Amazing Grace	71	13	1472
2. Send In The Clowns	77	17^2	1029
[reissue--see #4]			
3. Cook With Honey	73	29	542
4. Send In The Clowns	75	53	342
5. Hard Times For Lovers	79	63	210
6. Open The Door (Song For Judith)	72	82	84
Lyn COLLINS ▶985			
Duo: **James Brown & Lyn Collins**			
1. Think (About It)	72	55	471
Jessi COLTER ▶459			
1. I'm Not Lisa	75	5	2691
2. You Ain't Never Been Loved (Like I'm Gonna Love You)	75	56^2	172
3. What's Happened To Blue Eyes	75	78	77
Chi COLTRANE ▶685			
1. Thunder And Lightning	72	15^2	1455
Perry COMO ▶395			
1. It's Impossible	71	10	1704
2. And I Love You So	73	18	1182
[Alt. title: And I Love Her So]			
3. I Think Of You	71	45	523
4. Christmas Dream	75	88	24

Artist / Song	Year	Peak	Points
Arthur CONLEY ▶1566			
1. God Bless	70	91	18
Norman CONNORS ▶743			
1. You Are My Starship	76	26	677
2. Valentine Love	75	81	71
#1 & 2: NORMAN CONNORS (Featuring Michael Henderson and Jean Cain)			
3. We Both Need Each Other	76	98	3
Bill CONTI ▶463			
1. Gonna Fly Now (Theme From "Rocky")	77	1	3683
COOKER ▶1252			
1. Try (Try To Fall In Love)	74	67	143
Rita COOLIDGE ▶147			
Duo: Kris Kristofferson & Rita Coolidge			
1. (Your Love Has Lifted Me) Higher And Higher	77	1	5387
2. We're All Alone	77	5	2756
3. You	78	17^2	917
4. The Way You Do The Things You Do	78	18	800
5. Love Me Again	78	71	85
6. One Fine Day	79	84	67
7. My Crew	73	87	26
8. Fever	73	90	21
Alice COOPER ▶202			
Group: Alice Cooper			
1. You And Me	77	8	2035
2. Only Women	75	10	1837
3. I Never Cry	76	9^2	1756
4. How You Gonna See Me Now	78	16^3	1183
5. Welcome To My Nightmare	75	40	290
6. Department Of Youth	75	58	220
CORY ▶1339			
1. Fire Sign	77	77	91
Bill COSBY ▶962			
1. Yes, Yes, Yes	76	63^2	223
2. Grover Henson Feels Forgotten	70	70	135
Elvis COSTELLO ▶1215			
1. Watching The Detectives //Alison [TSW]	78	61^2	174
Gene COTTON ▶432			
1. Before My Heart Finds Out	78	16^2	1000
2. You're A Part Of Me	78	35	478
GENE COTTON with Kim Carnes			
3. Like A Sunday In Salem (The Amos & Andy Song)	78	37	430
4. You've Got Me Runnin'	77	49^2	366
5. Sunshine Roses	74	63^2	176
6. Damn It All	75	97	4
John COUGAR ▶901			
1. I Need A Lover	79	32	623
Don COVAY ▶864			
1. I Was Checkin' Out She Was Checkin' In	73	28	537
2. It's Better To Have (And Don't Need)	74	95	6
Billy "Crash" CRADDOCK ▶618			
1. Rub It In	74	22^2	798
2. Ruby, Baby	75	50	257
3. Easy As Pie	76	52	225
Les CRANE ▶727			
1. Desiderata [see also: Deteriorata]	71	11	1279
Jim CROCE ▶61			
1. Bad, Bad Leroy Brown	73	1	5263
2. Time In A Bottle	74	1	4831
3. I Got A Name	73	3^2	3524
4. You Don't Mess Around With Jim	72	7	2388
5. I'll Have To Say I Love You In A Song	74	7	1655
6. Operator (That's Not The Way It Feels)	72	14	1103
7. Workin' At The Car Wash Blues	74	20^2	762
8. One Less Set Of Footsteps	73	30	598
9. It Doesn't Have To Be That Way	74	47	293
10. Chain Gang Medley	76	56	252
David CROSBY ▶1662			
Groups: Crosby, Stills, Nash & Young / Crosby, Stills & Nash			
Duos: Graham Nash & David Crosby / David Crosby / Graham Nash			
1. Music Is Love	71	96	6
The CUFF LINKS (s) ▶691			
[Ron Dante]			
Group: The Archies (s)			
Solo: Ron Dante			
1. When Julie Comes Around	70	31	712
2. Run Sally Run	70	40	440
Burton CUMMINGS ▶502			
Group: The Guess Who			
1. Stand Tall	76	5	2300
2. Break It To Them Gently	78	82	52
3. I'm Scared	77	90	20
Rick CUNHA ▶1021			
1. (I'm A) Yoyo Man	74	47^3	389
Gino CUNICO ▶1503			
1. Fanny (Be Tender With My Love)	76	91	31
Tim CURRY ▶1489			
1. I Do The Rock	79	85	35
DADDY DEWDROP ▶464			
1. Chick-A-Boom (Don't Ya Jes' Love It)	71	5	2836
2. Fox Huntin' (On The Weekend)	71	87	38
3. Nanu Nanu (I Wanna Get Funky Wich You)	79	95	11

Artist / Song	Year	Peak	Points
Patti DAHLSTROM ▶1695			
1. He Did Me Wrong, But He Did It Right	74	100	1
Kathy DALTON ▶1186			
1. Boogie Bands And One Night Stands	74	61	193
Roger DALTREY ▶805			
Group: The **Who**			
1. Giving It All Away	73	60	313
2. Come And Get Your Love	75	63	179
3. Avenging Annie	77	87	52
Vic DANA ▶790			
1. If I Never Knew Your Name	70	39^2	718
2. Red Red Wine	70	94	13
Charlie DANIELS ▶666			
Group: The **Charlie Daniels Band**			
1. Uneasy Rider	73	10	1537
Ron DANTE ▶1629			
Group: The **Archies** (s)			
Solo: The **Cuff Links** (s)			
1. Midnight Show	75	94	10
Bobby DARIN ▶1073			
1. Happy	73	59	301
James DARREN ▶1223			
1. Mammy Blue	71	77	98
2. You Take My Heart Away	77	95	11
Sarah DASH ▶1351			
Group: **Labelle**			
1. Sinner Man	79	72	85
Mac DAVIS ▶117			
1. Baby Don't Get Hooked On Me	72	1	5087
2. Stop And Smell The Roses	74	7^2	1852
3. One Hell Of A Woman	74	14	1528
4. Rock N' Roll (I Gave You The Best Years Of My Life)	75	16	1022
5. Everybody Loves A Love Song	72	41^2	410
6. Burnin' Thing	75	52	290
7. Whoever Finds This, I Love You	70	69	238
8. (If You Add) All The Love In The World	75	62^2	208
9. Dream Me Home	73	66	154
10. Your Side Of The Bed	73	83	62
Paul DAVIS ▶167			
1. I Go Crazy	78	7^2	3174
2. Sweet Life	78	15^3	1696
3. Ride 'Em Cowboy	75	27^2	955
4. I Just Wanna Keep It Together	70	42	410
5. Superstar	76	41	389
6. A Little Bit Of Soap	70	56	310
7. Darlin'	78	45	288
PAUL DAVIS Featuring Susan Collins			
8. Thinking Of You	76	75	120
9. Boogie Woogie Man	73	79	69
10. Keep Our Love Alive	75	90	24
Sammy DAVIS, Jr. ▶330			
1. The Candy Man	72	1	5587
2. The People Tree	72	87	46
#1 & 2: SAMMY DAVIS, JR. with The Mike Curb Congregation			
Tim DAVIS ▶1366			
1. Buzzy Brown	72	80	80
Tyrone DAVIS ▶132			
1. Turn Back The Hands Of Time	70	4^3	3916
2. Give It Up (Turn It Loose)	76	36^2	671
3. I'll Be Right Here	70	33^2	598
4. There It Is	73	39	366
5. Without You In My Life	73	51	355
6. Let Me Back In	70	53	346
7. Could I Forget You	71	58	307
8. I Had It All The Time	72	54	244
9. One-Way Ticket	71	68	166
10. I Wish It Was Me	74	78	110
11. Turning Point	76	78^2	99
12. You Keep Me Holding On	71	80	78
13. Wrapped Up In Your Warm And Tender Love	73	84	57
14. This I Swear	77	88	38
Jimmy DEAN ▶1089			
1. I.O.U.	76	33	278
Kiki DEE ▶1070			
Duo: **Elton John and Kiki Dee**			
Group: **The Kiki Dee Band**			
1. How Glad I Am	75	75	88
2. Once A Fool	76	85	48
3. Love Makes The World Go Round	71	95	13
Al DeLORY ▶1585			
1. Song From M*A*S*H	70	93	15
John DENVER ▶9			
1. Take Me Home, Country Roads	71	1	6219
2. Annie's Song	74	1	5117
3. Thank God I'm A Country Boy	75	1	5069
4. Sunshine On My Shoulders	74	1	4891
5. I'm Sorry	75	1	4688
6. Fly Away	76	6^4	2597
7. Rocky Mountain High	73	7	2514
8. Back Home Again	74	5^2	2249
9. Sweet Surrender	75	14^3	1210
10. Looking For Space	76	18^2	851
11. Friends With You	72	27	813
12. I'd Rather Be A Cowboy	73	27	717
13. Calypso	75	26	586
14. How Can I Leave You Again	78	38	400
15. Please, Daddy	74	51	298

	Year	Peak	Points
John DENVER – cont'd			
16. My Sweet Lady	77	44	231
17. Farewell Andromeda (Welcome To My Morning)	73	59	218
18. Like A Sad Song	76	60^2	163
19. It Makes Me Giggle	76	66	135
20. Christmas For Cowboys	75	59	75
21. Baby, You Look Good To Me Tonight	77	85^2	60
22. I Want To Live	78	76	57
23. It Amazes Me	78	81	50
24. Everyday	72	83	41
25. Goodbye Again	72	87	26
DEODATO ▶397			
1. Also Sprach Zarathustra (2001)	73	4^3	3470
2. Rhapsody In Blue	73	55	317
3. Peter Gunn	76	100	1
Rick DERRINGER ▶626			
Groups: Edgar Winter's White Trash / The Edgar Winter Group			
1. Rock And Roll, Hoochie Koo	74	15	934
2. Hang On Sloopy	75	67	172
3. Teenage Love Affair	74	70	118
Teri DeSARIO ▶1218			
1. Ain't Nothing Gonna Keep Me From You	78	59	171
Jackie DeSHANNON ▶739			
1. Brighton Hill	70	52	280
2. Don't Let The Flame Burn Out	77	70	179
3. It's So Nice	70	92^2	33
4. Only Love Can Break A Heart	72	96	9
5. Vanilla Olay	72	95	8
William DeVAUGHN ▶441			
1. Be Thankful For What You Got	74	3^2	3343
2. Blood Is Thicker Than Water	74	55	283
Cliff DeYOUNG ▶796			
1. My Sweet Lady	74	23	940
Neil DIAMOND ▶10			
Duo: Barbra & Neil			
1. Cracklin' Rosie	70	1	5610
2. Song Sung Blue	72	1	4975
3. Holly Holy	70	4	3954
4. I Am...I Said	71	4^2	3038
5. Longfellow Serenade	74	4^2	2416
6. Desiree	78	9^2	1685
7. Stones	71	13^2	1358
8. Walk On Water	72	16^2	1249
9. He Ain't Heavy...He's My Brother	70	17	1113
10. Play Me	72	16	1081
11. If You Know What I Mean	76	16	1038

	Year	Peak	Points
12. Solitary Man [reissue--first charted in 1966]	70	20	920
13. Forever In Blue Jeans	79	20^2	916
14. Be	73	19^2	835
15. Shilo	70	23	799
16. "Cherry Cherry" From Hot August Night	73	24	778
17. Soolaimon (African Trilogy II)	70	24	767
18. Do It	70	36	492
19. The Last Thing On My Mind	73	42	418
20. I've Been This Way Before	75	43	359
21. Until It's Time For You To Go	70	44^2	343
22. I'm A Believer	71	52	323
23. Skybird	74	48	309
24. The Long Way Home	73	67	150
25. Say Maybe	79	63	148
26. Done Too Soon	71	69	135
27. Don't Think...Feel	76	77	114
Manu DIBANGO ▶866			
1. Soul Makossa	73	22	722
DION ▶1329			
1. Your Own Back Yard	70	69	94
DR. JOHN ▶467			
1. Right Place Wrong Time	73	11^2	1803
2. Such A Night	73	45	340
3. Iko Iko	72	52	240
4. (Everybody Wanna Get Rich) Rite Away	74	72	124
DONOVAN ▶742			
1. Riki Tiki Tavi	70	40	461
2. I Like You	73	57^2	274
3. Celia Of The Seals	71	93	16
Carl DOUGLAS ▶328			
1. Kung Fu Fighting	74	1	5379
2. Dance The Kung Fu	75	46	273
Carol DOUGLAS ▶559			
1. Doctor's Orders	75	10	1738
2. A Hurricane Is Coming Tonite	75	85	34
3. Midnight Love Affair	77	96	11
Al DOWNING ▶1266			
1. I'll Be Holding On	75	71	132
Lamont DOZIER ▶561			
Duo: Holland-Dozier			
1. Trying To Hold On To My Woman	74	14	1135
2. Fish Ain't Bitin'	74	26	534
3. Let Me Start Tonite	75	72	97
Guy DRAKE ▶1119			
1. Welfare Cadillac	70	63	255
DRUPI ▶1488			
1. Vado Via	73	89	35

	Year	Peak	Points
Doris DUKE ▶958			
1. To The Other Woman (I'm The Other Woman)	70	57	300
2. Feet Start Walking	70	86	60
George DUKE ▶1075			
1. Reach For It	78	61^2	299
David DUNDAS ▶611			
1. Jeans On	77	14^2	1918
Bob DYLAN ▶182			
Group: **Bob Dylan / The Band**			
1. Knockin' On Heaven's Door	73	10^2	1548
2. Wigwam	70	28^2	684
3. Hurricane (Part I)	76	27^2	663
4. George Jackson	72	30	655
5. Watching The River Flow	71	31	586
6. On A Night Like This	74	30	494
7. Gotta Serve Somebody	79	37	389
8. Tangled Up In Blue	75	43	380
9. A Fool Such As I	74	47	277
10. Mozambique	76	49	272
11. Something There Is About You	74	76	49
Ronnie DYSON ▶331			
1. (If You Let Me Make Love To You Then) Why Can't I Touch You?	70	10^3	1915
2. One Man Band (Plays All Alone)	73	20	950
3. I Don't Wanna Cry	70	35	520
4. The More You Do It (The More I Like It Done To Me)	76	59	276
5. Just Don't Want To Be Lonely	73	70	167
6. When You Get Right Down To It	71	81	72
Duane EDDY ▶1644			
1. Freight Train	70	95	8
Randy EDELMAN ▶1363			
1. Can't It All Be Love	77	91	33
2. Everybody Wants To Find A Bluebird	75	91	18
Dave EDMUNDS ▶411			
1. I Hear You Knocking	71	4^2	3231
2. I'm Comin' Home	71	53	190
3. Girls Talk	79	65	153
John EDWARDS ▶1526			
1. Careful Man	74	86	26
Jonathan EDWARDS ▶427			
1. Sunshine	72	5^3	3719
2. Train Of Glory	72	69	65
Walter EGAN ▶483			
1. Magnet And Steel	78	9^2	2021
2. Hot Summer Nights	78	57	192
3. Only The Lucky	77	74	108
4. Unloved	79	93	11

	Year	Peak	Points
Donnie ELBERT ▶541			
1. I Can't Help Myself (Sugar Pie, Honey Bunch)	72	19	769
2. Where Did Our Love Go	71	30	731
3. Sweet Baby	72	79	67
4. Can't Get Over Losing You	70	91	34
Yvonne ELLIMAN ▶180			
1. If I Can't Have You	78	1	4814
2. Love Me	77	10	1752
3. Hello Stranger	77	14	1078
4. I Don't Know How To Love Him	71	30	723
5. Love Pains	79	53	289
6. Everything's Alright	71	95	16
Mama Cass ELLIOT ▶939			
1. New World Coming	70	30^2	536
Les EMMERSON ▶956			
Group: **Five Man Electrical Band**			
1. Control Of Me	73	37	515
Scott ENGLISH ▶1675			
1. Brandy	72	98	4
ERNIE (Jim Henson) ▶744			
Solo: **Kermit (Jim Henson)**			
1. Rubber Duckie	70	13^2	1193
David ESSEX ▶380			
1. Rock On	74	1	4412
2. Lamplight	74	65^2	186
Betty EVERETT ▶1651			
1. I Got To Tell Somebody	71	97	7
Don EVERLY ▶1552			
1. Warmin' Up The Band	74	92	20
Yvonne FAIR ▶1697			
1. It Should Have Been Me	76	100	1
Barbara FAIRCHILD ▶847			
1. Teddy Bear Song	73	32^2	788
Don FARDON ▶1298			
1. Delta Queen	73	75	111
Donna FARGO ▶232			
1. The Happiest Girl In The Whole U.S.A.	72	8	2271
2. Funny Face	72	9^2	2200
3. Superman	73	31	602
4. You Can't Be A Beacon (If Your Light Don't Shine)	74	48^2	454
5. Little Girl Gone	73	61	233
6. You Were Always There	73	76^2	115
7. Do I Love You (Yes In Every Way)	78	94	8
Jose FELICIANO ▶1138			
1. Destiny	70	75	116
2. Feliz Navidad	70	71	37

	Year	Peak	Points
Dick FELLER ►1540			
1. Makin' The Best Of A Bad Situation	74	89	22
Narvel FELTS ►1290			
1. Lonely Teardrops	76	85	41
2. Reconsider Me	75	86	32
Freddy FENDER ►166			
1. Before The Next Teardrop Falls	75	1	4751
2. Wasted Days And Wasted Nights	75	6^2	2785
3. Secret Love	75	25	730
4. You'll Lose A Good Thing	76	36	516
5. Since I Met You Baby	75	44^2	374
6. Vaya Con Dios	76	80^2	58
7. Living It Down	76	93	16
Zoot FENSTER ►1531			
[Country singer Jack Barlow]			
1. The Man On Page 602	75	91^2	24
Jay FERGUSON ►485			
Groups: Spirit, Jo Jo Gunne			
1. Thunder Island	78	6^2	2300
2. Shakedown Cruise	79	27	624
Maynard FERGUSON ►897			
1. Gonna Fly Now (Theme From "Rocky")	77	31^2	632
Mike FINNIGAN ►1480			
1. Just One Minute More	78	84	39
George FISCHOFF ►1209			
1. Georgia Porcupine	74	65	178
Roberta FLACK ►47			
Duo: Roberta Flack & Donny Hathaway			
1. The First Time Ever I Saw Your Face	72	1^4	8527
2. Killing Me Softly With His Song	73	1^3	6447
3. The Closer I Get To You	78	2	4453
ROBERTA FLACK with Donny Hathaway			
4. Feel Like Makin' Love	74	1	3548
5. Jesse	73	12^2	1059
6. If Ever I See You Again	78	38	379
7. Feelin' That Glow	75	65	146
8. Will You Still Love Me Tomorrow	72	66	104
9. 25th Of Last December	78	92	25
Lois FLETCHER ►1079			
1. I Am What I Am	74	53^2	293
Eddie FLOYD ►970			
1. California Girl	70	54	212
2. My Girl	70	69	136
King FLOYD ►260			
1. Groove Me	71	4^4	4416
2. Baby Let Me Kiss You	71	19	1003
3. Woman Don't Go Astray	72	35^2	647
4. Got To Have Your Lovin'	71	72	104

	Year	Peak	Points
Dan FOGELBERG ►759			
Duo: Dan Fogelberg /Tim Weisberg			
1. Part Of The Plan	75	24	706
2. Love Gone By	77	75	134
John FOGERTY ►766			
Group: Creedence Clearwater Revival			
Solo: The Blue Ridge Rangers (s)			
1. Rockin' All Over The World	75	25	725
2. Almost Saturday Night	76	78	82
Tom FOGERTY ►1335			
Group: Creedence Clearwater Revival			
1. Joyful Resurrection	73	84	39
2. Goodbye Media Man (Part 1)	71	93	19
Ellen FOLEY ►1547			
1. What's A Matter Baby	79	93	21
Bruce FOSTER ►1269			
1. Platinum Heroes	77	66	131
Peter FRAMPTON ►118			
Group: Humble Pie			
1. I'm In You	77	1	3686
2. Show Me The Way	76	4	3352
3. Baby, I Love Your Way	76	16^2	1459
4. Do You Feel Like We Do	76	13	1117
5. Signed, Sealed, Delivered (I'm Yours)	77	13	1107
6. I Can't Stand It No More	79	18^2	875
7. Tried To Love	78	57	280
Connie FRANCIS ►1689			
1. Should I Tie A Yellow Ribbon Round The Ole Oak Tree? The Answer	73	99	2
Aretha FRANKLIN ►21			
1. Bridge Over Troubled Water	71	2	4771
2. Spanish Harlem	71	1	4230
3. Until You Come Back To Me (That's What I'm Gonna Do)	74	7^3	2362
4. Day Dreaming	72	5	2332
5. Rock Steady	71	7^2	2059
6. Call Me	70	13	1588
7. Don't Play That Song	70	10^2	1549
8. Angel	73	16	1056
9. I'm In Love	74	16^2	1054
10. You're All I Need To Get By	71	15^2	1038
11. Something He Can Feel	76	30	816
12. All The King's Horses	72	20	727
13. Border Song (Holy Moses)	70	23	716
14. Spirit In The Dark	70	25	639
#7 & 14: ARETHA FRANKLIN With The Dixie Flyers			
15. Master Of Eyes (The Deepness Of Your Eyes)	73	36	515
16. Without Love	74	52^2	338
17. Ain't Nothing Like The Real Thing	74	44	332

	Year	Peak	Points
Aretha FRANKLIN – cont'd			
18. Mr. D.J. (5 For The D.J.)	75	50	192
19. Wholy Holy	72	54	141
20. Oh Me Oh My (I'm A Fool For You Baby)	72	70	109
21. Brand New Me	71	72	94
22. Jump	76	77	64
23. Look Into Your Heart	77	75	55
24. You	76	90	21
Michael FRANKS ►1187			
1. Popsicle Toes	76	65^2	192
Ace FREHLEY ►720			
Group: **KISS**			
1. New York Groove	79	16	1311
Dean FRIEDMAN ►700			
1. Ariel	77	17	1393
Richie FURAY ►888			
Groups: The **Souther, Hillman, Furay Band** **Poco**			
1. I Still Have Dreams	79	40^2	453
2. This Magic Moment	78	92	25
Peter GABRIEL ►1417			
Group: **Genesis**			
1. Solsbury Hill	77	81	59
Art GARFUNKEL ►237			
Group: **Art Garfunkel with James Taylor & Paul Simon**			
Duo: **Simon & Garfunkel**			
1. All I Know	73	6	2050
2. I Only Have Eyes For You	75	19	1396
3. I Shall Sing	74	18	871
4. Break Away	76	38	593
5. Second Avenue	74	44	429
6. Since I Don't Have You	79	52	260
7. Traveling Boy	74	70	87
#1, 3, 5 & 7: GARFUNKEL			
Lee GARRETT ►1201			
1. You're My Everything	76	67^2	184
Leif GARRETT ►374			
1. I Was Made For Dancin'	79	15^2	1252
2. Runaround Sue	78	18	949
3. Surfin' Usa	77	29	565
4. The Wanderer	78	62	140
5. Feel The Need	79	63	131
6. Put Your Head On My Shoulder	78	66	116
David GATES ►340			
Group: **Bread**			
1. Goodbye Girl	78	9^2	1903
2. Never Let Her Go	75	26^2	689
3. Clouds	73	36	534
4. Took The Last Train	78	30	504
5. Sail Around The World	73	49	323

	Year	Peak	Points
Marvin GAYE ►29			
Duos: **Marvin Gaye & Tammi Terrell** **Diana Ross & Marvin Gaye**			
Group: **Diana Ross, Marvin Gaye, Smokey Robinson & Stevie Wonder**			
1. Let's Get It On	73	1	6802
2. What's Going On	71	1	4567
3. Got To Give It Up Pt. I	77	1	4230
4. Mercy Mercy Me (The Ecology)	71	4	3547
5. Inner City Blues (Make Me Wanna Holler)	71	6	1855
6. Trouble Man	73	8^2	1560
7. I Want You	76	20^2	1101
8. Come Get To This	73	18^2	831
9. How Can I Forget	70	27	582
10. The End Of Our Road	70	28	555
11. Distant Lover	74	33^2	526
12. You Sure Love To Ball	74	40	375
13. You're The Man (Part 1)	72	41	363
Crystal GAYLE ►197			
1. Don't It Make My Brown Eyes Blue	77	1^2	6216
2. Talking In Your Sleep	78	16	1210
3. Half The Way	79	18	1024
4. Ready For The Times To Get Better	78	66	206
Gloria GAYNOR ►195			
1. I Will Survive	79	1	5552
2. Never Can Say Goodbye	75	8^2	1820
3. Reach Out, I'll Be There	75	60	193
4. Let Me Know (I Have A Right)	79	62	161
5. How High The Moon	75	83	64
6. Anybody Wanna Party?	79	94	14
David GEDDES ►387			
1. Run Joey Run	75	1	3888
2. The Last Game Of The Season (A Blind Man In The Bleachers)	75	22	536
Bobbie GENTRY ►562			
1. Fancy	70	31	1072
2. Ode To Billie Joe [reissue--first charted in 1967]	76	67	147
3. He Made A Woman Out Of Me	70	74^2	128
4. Apartment 21	70	70	107
Danyel GÉRARD ►1587			
1. Butterfly	72	96^2	15
Donny GERRARD ►1556			
Group: **Skylark**			
1. Words (Are Impossible)	76	95^2	20
Andy GIBB ►48			
1. Shadow Dancing	78	1^6	10066
2. I Just Want To Be Your Everything	77	1^3	7100
3. (Love Is) Thicker Than Water	78	1	5256
4. An Everlasting Love	78	5^2	2436

	Year	Peak	Points
Andy GIBB – cont'd			
5. (Our Love) Don't Throw It All Away	78	7	2417
Robin GIBB ▶938			
Group: **Bee Gees**			
1. Oh! Darling	78	24	538
Nick GILDER ▶214			
Group: **Sweeny Todd**			
1. Hot Child In The City	78	1^3	7682
2. Here Comes The Night	78	39	368
3. Rock Me	79	53	273
Mickey GILLEY ▶1200			
1. Room Full Of Roses	74	61	185
Jim GILSTRAP ▶910			
1. Swing Your Daddy	75	57	312
2. House Of Strangers	75	97	7
3. I'm On Fire	75	99	4
GIORGIO - see Giorgio **MORODOR**			
Gary GLITTER ▶440			
1. Rock And Roll Part 2	72	3	3078
2. I Didn't Know I Loved You (Till I Saw You Rock And Roll)	72	30^2	550
Louise GOFFIN ▶1053			
1. Remember (Walking In The Sand)	79	44	326
Andrew GOLD ▶299			
1. Lonely Boy	77	3^2	3890
2. Thank You For Being A Friend	78	11^2	1265
3. Never Let Her Slip Away	78	70	155
4. That's Why I Love You	76	69	104
Bobby GOLDSBORO ▶327			
1. Watching Scotty Grow	71	8^2	2122
2. Summer (The First Time)	73	17^2	1129
3. Come Back Home	71	74	136
4. Mornin' Mornin'	70	78	114
5. With Pen In Hand	72	87	50
6. And I Love You So	71	91	23
7. Can You Feel It	70	98	7
Ian GOMM ▶917			
1. Hold On	79	25	592
Dickie GOODMAN ▶282			
1. Mr. Jaws	75	1	3887
2. Energy Crisis '74	74	37	422
3. Kong	77	50	261
4. Watergrate	73	66	173
5. Energy Crisis '79	79	75	61
6. Mr. President	74	85	41
Don GOODWIN ▶1406			
1. This Is Your Song	74	82	61

	Year	Peak	Points
Robert GORDON ▶1180			
1. Red Hot	77	69	198
ROBERT GORDON With Link Wray			
Eydie GORME ▶1016			
Duo: **Steve & Eydie**			
1. Tonight I'll Say A Prayer	70	54	393
Carl GRAVES ▶913			
Group: **Skylark**			
1. Baby, Hang Up The Phone	75	62	250
2. Sad Girl	77	68^2	178
Dobie GRAY ▶429			
1. Drift Away	73	8^2	2576
2. Loving Arms	73	36	621
3. You Can Do It	79	54	184
R.B. GREAVES ▶636			
1. Always Something There To Remind Me	70	22^2	783
2. Fire And Rain	70	65	133
3. A Whiter Shade Of Pale	70	80	46
4. Georgia Took Her Back	70	92	16
Cyndi GRECCO ▶802			
1. Making Our Dreams Come True	76	21	921
Al GREEN ▶14			
1. Let's Stay Together	72	1^2	8515
2. I'm Still In Love With You	72	1	5185
3. You Ought To Be With Me	72	2	4857
4. Look What You Done For Me	72	3^3	4494
5. Tired Of Being Alone	71	6	2926
6. Sha-La-La (Make Me Happy)	74	7	2262
7. Here I Am (Come And Take Me)	73	10	1786
8. Call Me (Come Back Home)	73	9	1633
9. L-O-V-E (Love)	75	10	1408
10. Livin' For You	74	14^3	1354
11. Let's Get Married	74	21	746
12. Full Of Fire	75	30	582
13. Guilty	72	46	421
14. Oh Me, Oh My (Dreams In My Arms)	75	40	346
15. Keep Me Cryin'	77	63	178
16. I Can't Get Next To You	70	70	125
17. Belle	78	81	82
18. Hot Wire	73	91	20
Garland GREEN ▶1505			
1. Plain And Simple Girl	71	90	30
Norman GREENBAUM ▶210			
1. Spirit In The Sky	70	1^2	8420
2. Canned Ham	70	32	483
Larry GROCE ▶749			
1. Junk Food Junkie	76	20	1128

	Year	Peak	Points
Henry GROSS ▶351			
1. Shannon	76	5²	3210
2. Springtime Mama	76	39	510
3. Come On Say It	74	79	50
4. One More Tomorrow	75	92	18
5. Simone	74	94	10
Arlo GUTHRIE ▶686			
1. The City Of New Orleans	72	21	1115
2. Valley To Pray	70	84	65
Sammy HAGAR ▶1065			
Group: **Van Halen**			
1. (Sittin' On) The Dock Of The Bay	79	66	106
2. You Make Me Crazy	78	83²	101
Merle HAGGARD ▶581			
1. If We Make It Through December	74	29	649
2. From Graceland To The Promised Land	77	58	285
3. Carolyn	72	77²	108
4. Everybody's Had The Blues	73	77	71
5. The Fightin' Side Of Me	70	99	3
#3-5: MERLE HAGGARD And The Strangers			
Tom T. HALL ▶563			
1. I Love	74	17	1013
2. The Year That Clayton Delaney Died	71	58	243
3. That Song Is Driving Me Crazy	74	60	165
4. Sneaky Snake	75	93	23
Marvin HAMLISCH ▶373			
1. The Entertainer	74	1	5169
Albert HAMMOND ▶203			
Group: The **Magic Lanterns**			
1. It Never Rains In Southern California	72	2	4198
2. I'm A Train	74	31²	576
3. The Free Electric Band	73	41	362
4. If You Gotta Break Another Heart	73	57²	242
5. Down By The River	72	64	225
6. Half A Million Miles From Home	73	72	88
7. 99 Miles From L.A.	75	78	82
8. Air Disaster	74	73	77
9. The Peacemaker	73	85	72
Keith HAMPSHIRE ▶623			
1. First Cut Is The Deepest	73	40	551
2. Daytime Night-Time	73	43	423
3. Big Time Operator	74	58²	265
Herbie HANCOCK ▶933			
1. Chameleon	74	41	556
John HANDY ▶923			
1. Hard Work	76	48³	570
Hagood HARDY ▶918			
1. The Homecoming	76	46	591

	Year	Peak	Points
Emmylou HARRIS ▶1019			
1. If I Could Only Win Your Love	75	67	224
2. Here, There And Everywhere	76	82	42
Major HARRIS ▶368			
Group: The **Delfonics**			
1. Love Won't Let Me Wait	75	3²	4226
2. Jealousy	76	77	94
3. I Got Over Love	76	86	44
Richard HARRIS ▶876			
1. My Boy	72	46	494
A musical interpretation featuring RICHARD HARRIS			
2. Theme From "The Prophet" (Pleasure Is A Freedom Song/On Love)	75	94	12
George HARRISON ▶58			
Groups: The **Beatles**			
Plastic Ono Band			
Delaney & Bonnie And Friends [as L'Angelo Misterioso]			
1. My Sweet Lord	70	1⁴	8857
2. Give Me Love (Give Me Peace On Earth)	73	1²	4919
3. What Is Life	71	7	2240
4. Blow Away	79	12²	1155
5. You	75	19	814
6. Crackerbox Palace	77	17	803
7. This Song	77	28	782
8. Dark Horse	75	19	728
9. Bangla-Desh	71	20	685
10. Ding Dong; Ding Dong	75	36	337
11. Isn't It A Pity	70	46²	245
Wilbert HARRISON ▶880			
1. Let's Work Together (Part 1)	70	30	663
Wilbert Harrison One Man Band			
Freddie HART ▶649			
1. Easy Loving	71	12	1651
Rod HART ▶1132			
1. C.B. Savage	77	59²	240
Dan HARTMAN ▶828			
Group: The **Edgar Winter Group**			
1. Instant Replay	78	22²	857
Donny HATHAWAY ▶780			
Duo: Roberta Flack & Donny Hathaway			
1. Love, Love, Love	73	56	241
2. I Love You More Than You'll Ever Know	72	64	153
3. The Ghetto - Part 1	70	89	43
4. Giving Up	72	87	26
Richie HAVENS ▶764			
1. Here Comes The Sun	71	15	1046
Ronnie HAWKINS ▶1389			
1. Down In The Alley	70	78	69

	Year	Peak	Points
Isaac HAYES ▶112			
Duo: **Isaac Hayes & David Porter**			
1. Theme From Shaft	71	1^2	7911
2. Do Your Thing	72	23	858
3. Theme From The Men	72	36^2	705
4. Never Can Say Goodbye	71	33	605
5. I Stand Accused	70	38^2	513
6. Joy, Part 1	74	31	480
7. Let's Stay Together	72	45	334
8. Chocolate Chip	75	65^2	168
9. The Look Of Love	71	68	104
10. Soulsville	72	94	12
Justin HAYWARD ▶882			
Group: The **Moody Blues**			
Duo: **Justin Hayward And John Lodge**			
1. Forever Autumn	78	34	660
Leon HAYWOOD ▶540			
1. I Want'a Do Something Freaky To You	75	20^2	1052
2. Keep It In The Family	74	56	358
3. Sugar Lump	74	68	169
4. Come An' Get Yourself Some	75	82	45
Murray HEAD ▶525			
1. Superstar	71	8^2	2710
MURRAY HEAD with The Trinidad Singers			
Joey HEATHERTON ▶755			
1. Gone	72	26	750
2. I'm Sorry	72	76	100
Willie HENDERSON ▶1279			
1. Dance Master Pt. 1	74	69	124
Jimi HENDRIX ▶1208			
1. Freedom	71	76	106
2. Dolly Dagger	71	94	10
HENHOUSE FIVE PLUS TOO (s) ▶975			
Solo: **Ray Stevens** [Ray Stevens]			
1. In The Mood	77	37^2	482
Keith HERMAN ▶1645			
1. She's Got A Whole Number	79	96	8
Patrick HERNANDEZ ▶745			
1. Born To Be Alive	79	17	1188
Dan HILL ▶367			
1. Sometimes When We Touch	78	4	3937
2. All I See Is Your Face	78	35	427
3. Growin' Up	76	98	5
Z.Z. HILL ▶935			
1. Don't Make Me Pay For His Mistakes	71	65	172
2. I Need Someone (To Love Me)	71	88	34
3. Chokin' Kind	71	94	14
4. Faithful And True	71	99	4

	Year	Peak	Points
Chris HODGE ▶998			
1. We're On Our Way	72	36	424
Danny HOLIEN ▶1356			
1. Colorado	72	80	83
Loleatta HOLLOWAY ▶1205			
1. Cry To Me	75	66^2	180
Michael HOLM ▶1029			
1. When A Child Is Born	75	38	367
Eddie HOLMAN ▶290			
1. Hey There Lonely Girl	70	2^3	5699
2. Don't Stop Now	70	43	353
3. My Mind Keeps Telling Me (That I Really Love You, Girl)	72	98	7
Clint HOLMES ▶394			
1. Playground In My Mind	73	2	4728
Jake HOLMES ▶855			
1. So Close	70	29	762
Rupert HOLMES ▶275			
Group: **Street People**			
1. Escape (The Pina Colada Song)	79	1^3	6661
2. Let's Get Crazy Tonight	78	64	141
Mary HOPKIN ▶708			
1. Temma Harbour	70	43	476
2. Que Sera, Sera (Whatever Will Be, Will Be)	70	49	364
3. Knock Knock Who's There	72	86	46
Jimmy "Bo" HORNE ▶1001			
1. Dance Across The Floor	78	51	422
HOT BUTTER (s) ▶574			
1. Popcorn	72	11	1865
2. Percolator	73	82	70
Cissy HOUSTON ▶1448			
1. Be My Baby	71	86	48
Thelma HOUSTON ▶352			
1. Don't Leave Me This Way	77	3^2	3695
2. Saturday Night, Sunday Morning	79	44	367
3. Save The Country	70	83	82
4. If It's The Last Thing I Do	77	85^2	52
Reuben HOWELL ▶1555			
1. Rings	74	88	20
Engelbert HUMPERDINCK ▶143			
1. After The Lovin'	77	5^2	2759
2. Winter World Of Love	70	13^2	1692
3. My Marie	70	27	608
4. Sweetheart	70	38^2	587
5. Another Time, Another Place	71	40	477
6. When There's No You	71	37	397
7. I Never Said Goodbye	73	70	196
8. Too Beautiful To Last	72	75^2	111

	Year	Peak	Points
Engelbert HUMPERDINCK – cont'd			
9. In Time	72	86	54
10. This Moment In Time	79	88	39
11. This Is What You Mean To Me	75	87	32
12. I'm Leavin' You	73	90^2	31
13. Love Is All	73	95	13
Ian HUNTER ▶ 1390			
Group: **Mott The Hoople**			
1. Just Another Night	79	75	69
Willie HUTCH ▶ 757			
1. Love Power	75	48	347
2. Brother's Gonna Work It Out	73	60^2	263
3. Slick	73	83	54
Brian HYLAND ▶ 341			
1. Gypsy Woman	70	3	4359
2. Lonely Teardrops	71	48^2	429
3. So Long, Marianne	71	93	14
Janis IAN ▶ 360			
1. At Seventeen	75	1	4935
2. In The Winter	75	97	8
Luther INGRAM ▶ 168			
1. (If Loving You Is Wrong) I Don't Want To Be Right	72	3^2	5597
2. I'll Be Your Shelter (In Time Of Storm)	73	32	722
3. Ain't That Loving You (For More Reasons Than One)	70	45	477
4. My Honey And Me	70	47	301
5. You Were Made For Me	72	57	286
6. Always	73	64	219
7. Missing You	72	72	115
8. Be Good To Me Baby	71	88	27
9. To The Other Man	70	97	5
Susan JACKS ▶ 1191			
Group and Duo: The **Poppy Family**			
1. You Don't Know What Love Is *SUSAN JACKS and The Poppy Family*	73	70	114
2. You're A Part Of Me	75	95	10
Terry JACKS ▶ 249			
Group and Duo: The **Poppy Family**			
1. Seasons In The Sun	74	1^2	5523
2. If You Go Away	74	45	298
3. In My Father's Footsteps	76	74	85
4. Christina	75	83	56
5. Rock 'N Roll (I Gave You The Best Years Of My Life)	74	92	23
Earnest JACKSON ▶ 1334			
1. Love And Happiness	73	80	92
Jermaine JACKSON ▶ 410			
Group: The **Jackson 5**			
1. Daddy's Home	73	7	2651

	Year	Peak	Points
2. That's How Love Goes	72	43	427
3. Let's Be Young Tonight	76	66	113
4. You're In Good Hands	73	89	21
Joe JACKSON ▶ 753			
1. Is She Really Going Out With Him?	79	21	1102
Michael JACKSON ▶ 45			
Groups: The **Jackson 5**			
Duo: **Diana Ross Michael Jackson**			
1. Rockin' Robin	72	1	7353
2. Got To Be There	72	1	6050
3. Don't Stop 'til You Get Enough	79	1	5047
4. Ben	72	2	4073
5. I Wanna Be Where You Are	72	7	1926
6. Just A Little Bit Of You	75	30	690
7. With A Child's Heart	73	37	392
8. We're Almost There	75	57	236
Mick JACKSON ▶ 1291			
1. Blame It On The Boogie	78	64	114
Millie JACKSON ▶ 250			
1. Hurts So Good	73	18^2	1080
2. Ask Me What You Want	72	19	976
3. My Man, A Sweet Man	72	34^2	681
4. If You're Not Back In Love By Monday	77	35	425
5. If Loving You Is Wrong I Don't Want To Be Right	75	48	243
6. How Do You Feel The Morning After	74	56	190
7. I Miss You Baby	73	69	151
8. Leftovers	75	74	110
9. Breakaway	73	80	68
10. All The Way Lover	78	88	30
Etta JAMES ▶ 1025			
1. Losers Weepers - Part I	70	76	140
2. All The Way Down	73	70	120
Rick JAMES ▶ 597			
1. You And I	78	15	1162
2. Mary Jane	78	53	186
3. Bustin' Out	79	74	98
Sonny JAMES ▶ 1378			
1. Endlessly	70	91	15
2. It's Just A Matter Of Time *SONNY JAMES The Southern Gentleman*	70	93	13
3. Bright Lights, Big City	71	97	5
Tommy JAMES ▶ 126			
Group: **Tommy James And The Shondells**			
1. Draggin' The Line	71	2^2	6159
2. Nothing To Hide	72	25	709
3. I'm Comin' Home	71	23	637
4. Cat's Eye In The Window	72	48^2	453
5. Love Song	72	50	420
6. Boo, Boo, Don't 'Cha Be Blue	73	40	341

	Year	Peak	Points
Tommy JAMES – cont'd			
7. Ball And Chain	70	45	326
8. Tell 'Em Willie Boy 's A'Comin'	72	58	180
9. Church Street Soul Revival	71	63	180
10. Celebration	72	75	77
11. Adrienne	71	90	24
12. Calico	73	94	13
Cody JAMESON ▶1342			
1. Brooklyn	77	71	90
JEFFERSON ▶637			
1. Baby Take Me In Your Arms	70	19^2	1412
2. You Know How It Is With A Woman	70	96	17
Waylon JENNINGS ▶570			
Duo: **Waylon & Willie**			
1. Luckenbach, Texas (Back To The Basics Of Love)	77	23^2	863
2. Are You Sure Hank Done It This Way	75	74	119
3. I'm A Ramblin' Man	74	77	85
4. The Taker	70	84	58
5. Amanda	79	87	45
WAYLON			
Billy JOEL ▶80			
1. Just The Way You Are	78	2	4785
2. My Life	79	3^2	3918
3. Movin' Out (Anthony's Song)	78	14	1115
4. Piano Man	74	16^2	1051
5. She's Always A Woman	78	18	1011
6. Big Shot	79	13	954
7. Only The Good Die Young	78	25^2	652
8. Honesty	79	23	539
9. The Entertainer	75	37^2	536
10. Travelin' Prayer	74	59	188
11. Worse Comes To Worst	74	70	125
Elton JOHN ▶3			
Duo: **Elton John and Kiki Dee**			
Group: The **Elton John Band**			
1. Crocodile Rock	73	1^2	7708
2. Island Girl	75	1^2	5962
3. Bennie And The Jets	74	1	5168
4. Goodbye Yellow Brick Road	73	1	4721
5. Lucy In The Sky With Diamonds	75	1	4565
6. Don't Let The Sun Go Down On Me	74	1	4427
7. Someone Saved My Life Tonight	75	1	4351
8. Daniel	73	2^2	4159
9. Your Song	71	8	2539
10. The Bitch Is Back	74	5^2	2481
11. Sorry Seems To Be The Hardest Word	77	7	2071
12. Mama Can't Buy You Love	79	10^2	2050
13. Saturday Night's Alright For Fighting	73	9^3	1858
14. Rocket Man	72	11	1610
15. Grow Some Funk Of Your Own	76	9	1285
16. Part-Time Love	78	13^3	1067
17. Honky Cat	72	18^2	961
18. Levon	72	17	898
19. Friends	71	17	883
20. I Feel Like A Bullet (In The Gun Of Robert Ford)	76	18	654
21. Ego	78	22	535
22. Tiny Dancer	72	29	480
23. Victim Of Love	79	38^2	398
24. Bite Your Lip (Get Up And Dance!)	77	42	306
25. Border Song	70	69	162
26. Step Into Christmas	73	56	102
Robert JOHN ▶136			
1. Sad Eyes	79	1^2	6337
2. The Lion Sleeps Tonight	72	2	4929
3. When The Party Is Over	70	69	122
4. Hushabye	72	77	72
5. Give A Little	78	89	25
[Alt. title: Give A Little More]			
JOHNNY T. ANGEL ▶1398			
1. Tell Laura I Love Her	74	80	65
Sammy JOHNS ▶423			
1. Chevy Van	75	5^2	2634
2. Early Morning Love	74	49	478
3. Rag Doll	75	49	330
Kevin JOHNSON ▶1570			
1. Rock 'N Roll (I Gave You The Best Years Of My Life)	73	90	18
Michael JOHNSON ▶436			
1. Bluer Than Blue	78	10^2	1678
2. This Night Won't Last Forever	79	18	1142
3. Almost Like Being In Love	78	37	484
Syl JOHNSON ▶806			
1. Take Me To The River	75	59	303
2. We Did It	73	72	124
3. Back For A Taste Of Your Love	73	74	116
Tom JOHNSTON ▶971			
Group: The **Doobie Brothers**			
1. Savannah Nights	79	34^2	492
France JOLI ▶784			
1. Come To Me	79	15^2	966
Davy JONES ▶812			
Duo: The **Monkees**			
1. Rainy Jane	71	32^2	674
2. I Really Love You	71	96	10
Linda JONES ▶1624			
1. Your Precious Love	72	92	11

	Year	Peak	Points
Quincy JONES ▶493			
1. Stuff Like That	78	21	736
2. Killer Joe	70	55	260
3. "Roots" Medley	77	62	194
4. Is It Love That We're Missin'	75	66	150
5. Money Runner	72	84	59
6. Summer In The City	73	87	25
7. What's Going On	71	96	6
Rickie Lee JONES ▶414			
1. Chuck E.'s In Love	79	4^3	3658
2. Young Blood	79	44	300
Tamiko JONES ▶1155			
1. Touch Me Baby (Reaching Out For Your Love)	75	70^2	219
Tom JONES ▶72			
1. She's A Lady	71	1	6766
2. Without Love (There Is Nothing)	70	5	2737
3. Daughter Of Darkness	70	10^2	1842
4. I (Who Have Nothing)	70	11^2	1444
5. Puppet Man	71	14^2	1220
6. Say You'll Stay Until Tomorrow	77	15	1010
7. Can't Stop Loving You	70	23^2	728
8. Letter To Lucille	73	34	536
9. Till	71	40	434
10. Resurrection Shuffle	71	40	372
11. The Young New Mexican Puppeteer	72	60	235
Janis JOPLIN ▶321			
1. Me And Bobby McGee	71	3^2	3897
2. Cry Baby	71	20	809
3. Get It While You Can	71	58	190
4. Down On Me	72	79	69
Margie JOSEPH ▶989			
1. Stop! In The Name Of Love	71	66	177
2. My Love	74	75	131
JULIE ▶1520			
1. One Fine Day	76	91	27
Gabriel KAPLAN ▶1370			
1. Up Your Nose	77	82^2	77
Kenny KAREN ▶1210			
1. That's Why You Remember	73	60	178
John KAY ▶822			
Group: Steppenwolf			
1. I'm Movin' On	72	45	330
2. Moonshine (Friend Of Mine)	73	67	170
3. Easy Evil	73	92	19
Casey KELLY ▶1254			
1. Poor Boy	72	65	141
Paul KELLY ▶1057			
1. Stealing In The Name Of The Lord	70	54	319

	Year	Peak	Points
Eddie KENDRICKS ▶75			
Group: The Temptations			
1. Keep On Truckin' (Part 1)	73	1	5073
2. Boogie Down	74	1	5010
3. Shoeshine Boy	75	22^2	1220
4. Son Of Sagittarius	74	20	743
5. Tell Her Love Has Felt The Need	74	38	627
6. Happy	75	59^2	444
7. If You Let Me	72	50	394
8. Get The Cream Off The Top	75	58	294
9. One Tear	75	55	264
10. It's So Hard For Me To Say Good-Bye	71	61	253
11. He's A Friend	76	65	228
12. Eddie's Love	72	83	45
13. Darling Come Back Home	73	91	32
14. Can I	71	92	16
15. Girl You Need A Change Of Mind (Part 1)	73	98	5
Mike KENNEDY ▶1146			
1. Louisiana	72	65^2	224
G.W. KENNY ▶1530			
1. Everybody But Me	73	89	24
KERMIT (Jim Henson) ▶1009			
Solo: Ernie (Jim Henson)			
1. Rainbow Connection	79	43	413
Chaka KHAN ▶814			
Group: Rufus Featuring Chaka Khan			
1. I'm Every Woman	78	19	896
Andy KIM ▶194			
Group: The Archies (s)			
1. Rock Me Gently	74	1	4963
2. Be My Baby	70	12	1368
3. Fire, Baby I'm On Fire	74	32	476
4. I Wish I Were	71	68	173
5. A Friend In The City	70	63	161
6. It's Your Life	70	78	107
7. I Been Moved	71	94	21
Albert KING ▶1211			
1. I'll Play The Blues For You	72	73	100
2. Breaking Up Somebody's Home	73	96^2	14
B.B. KING ▶159			
1. The Thrill Is Gone	70	15	1242
2. I Like To Live The Love	74	25^2	743
3. To Know You Is To Love You	73	38	544
4. Hummingbird	70	42	495
5. Chains And Things	70	45	473
6. Ask Me No Questions	71	43	471
7. Ain't Nobody Home	71	56	384
8. Guess Who	72	62	241

	Year	Peak	Points
B.B. KING – cont'd			
9. So Excited	70	50	236
10. Ghetto Woman	71	56	230
11. I Got Some Help I Don't Need	72	68^2	193
12. Sweet Sixteen	72	63	154
13. Help The Poor	71	65	130
14. Philadelphia	75	79	89
15. Who Are You	74	95	14
Ben E. KING ▶613			
1. Supernatural Thing - Part I	75	9	1468
2. Do It In The Name Of Love	75	64^2	125
Carole KING ▶62			
1. It's Too Late	71	1^4	8024
2. Jazzman	74	1	4439
3. Sweet Seasons	72	8	1824
4. So Far Away	71	10	1357
5. Nightingale	75	16	978
6. Been To Canaan	73	20	839
7. Only Love Is Real	76	27^2	666
8. Believe In Humanity	73	24	620
9. Hard Rock Cafe	77	25	611
10. Corazon	73	27	591
11. You Light Up My Life	73	62	174
Evelyn "Champagne" KING ▶473			
1. Shame	78	8^2	2012
2. I Don't Know If It's Right	79	17^2	1090
Frederick KNIGHT ▶713			
1. I've Been Lonely For So Long	72	20	1047
2. Trouble	72	80	43
Jean KNIGHT ▶279			
1. Mr. Big Stuff	71	2	6621
2. You Think You're Hot Stuff	71	75	76
Diane KOLBY ▶1313			
1. Holy Man	70	76	101
John KONGOS ▶1184			
1. He's Gonna Step On You Again	71	64	196
Kris KRISTOFFERSON ▶469			
Duo: Kris Kristofferson & Rita Coolidge			
1. Why Me	73	32	1219
2. Loving Her Was Easier (Than Anything I'll Ever Do Again)	71	33^2	719
3. Josie	72	69	153
4. Watch Closely Now	77	68^2	104
5. Jesus Was A Capricorn	73	86	40
Charlie KULIS ▶1015			
1. Runaway	75	42	394
Bill LaBOUNTY ▶1178			
1. This Night Won't Last Forever	78	68	201

	Year	Peak	Points
Cheryl LADD ▶1044			
1. Think It Over	78	44	348
David LAFLAMME ▶1414			
1. White Bird	77	85^2	59
Greg LAKE ▶1379			
Group: Emerson, Lake & Palmer			
1. C'est La Vie	77	87	30
2. I Believe In Father Christmas	76	92	16
Kevin LAMB ▶1340			
1. On The Wrong Track	78	71	90
Major LANCE ▶1275			
1. Stay Away From Me (I Love You Too Much)	70	79	127
Nicolette LARSON ▶536			
1. Lotta Love	79	8^2	1943
2. Rhumba Girl	79	41	330
Denise LaSALLE ▶430			
1. Trapped By A Thing Called Love	71	13	1494
2. Now Run And Tell That	72	33	621
3. Man Sized Job	72	40	561
4. Love Me Right	78	88	41
5. What It Takes To Get A Good Woman (That's What It's Gonna Take To Keep Her)	73	97	7
LATIMORE ▶714			
1. Let's Straighten It Out	74	32	709
2. Somethin' 'Bout 'Cha	77	66	149
3. Stormy Monday	73	92	10
Vicki LAWRENCE ▶268			
1. The Night The Lights Went Out In Georgia	73	1	5911
2. He Did With Me	73	49	491
3. The Other Woman	75	70	125
Otis LEAVILL ▶954			
1. Love Uprising	70	69	203
2. I Love You Otis Leaville	70	71	165
Lenny LE BLANC ▶1058			
Duo: Le Blanc & Carr			
1. Hound Dog Man (Play It Again)	77	56	211
2. Sharing The Night Together	76	99	3
Brenda LEE ▶1182			
1. I Think I Love You Again	70	84	68
2. Nobody Wins	73	80	61
Dickey LEE ▶1193			
1. 9,999,999 Tears	76	67	188
Laura LEE ▶552			
1. Women's Love Rights	71	20^2	810
2. Rip Off	72	51	336

	Year	Peak	Points
Laura LEE – cont'd			
3. Since I Fell For You	72	43	334
4. If You Can Beat Me Rockin' (You Can Have My Chair)	72	84	53
Michel LeGRAND ▶1045			
1. Brian's Song	72	51	348
Billy LEMMONS ▶1641			
1. Six Packs A Day	77	93	8
John LENNON ▶183			
Groups: **John Lennon/Plastic Ono Band, The Beatles**			
1. Instant Karma (We All Shine On) JOHN ONO LENNON or JOHN ONO LENNON with the Plastic Ono Band	70	3^4	6164
2. Mind Games	73	10	1348
3. #9 Dream	75	10	1321
4. Stand By Me	75	20	639
James LEROY ▶1572			
1. Touch Of Magic	73	94	18
Jerry Lee LEWIS ▶617			
1. Drinking Wine Spo-Dee O'Dee	73	25	728
2. Chantilly Lace	72	56	299
3. Me And Bobby McGee	72	63	263
Ramsey LEWIS ▶1197			
Group: **Ramsey Lewis and Earth, Wind & Fire**			
1. Slipping Into Darkness	72	79	101
2. What's The Name Of This Funk (Spider Man)	76	88	19
Orsa LIA ▶1544			
1. I Never Said I Love You	79	92	21
Gordon LIGHTFOOT ▶90			
1. Sundown	74	1	4939
2. The Wreck Of The Edmund Fitzgerald	76	1	4315
3. If You Could Read My Mind	71	5	2486
4. Carefree Highway	74	13	1157
5. Rainy Day People	75	32	626
6. The Circle Is Small (I Can See It In Your Eyes)	78	31	542
7. Talking In Your Sleep	71	69	203
8. Beautiful	72	67	159
9. Race Among The Ruins	77	78	48
Mark LINDSAY ▶262			
Group: **Raiders**			
1. Arizona	70	9^2	2138
2. Silver Bird	70	20^2	1121
3. And The Grass Won't Pay No Mind	70	37	634
4. Miss America	70	31	479
5. Problem Child	71	59	198
6. Been Too Long On The Road	71	63	184
7. Are You Old Enough	71	69	120

	Year	Peak	Points
Peggy LIPTON ▶1203			
1. Lu	70	70	182
Little MILTON ▶803			
1. If Walls Could Talk	70	52^2	355
2. That's What Love Will Make You Do	72	71	104
3. Baby I Love You	70	82	88
Little RICHARD ▶1131			
Group: **Delaney & Bonnie And Friends**			
1. Freedom Blues	70	62	151
2. Greenwood Mississippi	70	96	6
John LIVIGNI ▶1410			
[John LaVigni--see also John Valenti]			
1. Machines	75	84	60
Ian LLOYD ▶1365			
Group: **Stories / Ian Lloyd & Stories**			
1. Slip Away	79	73	81
LOBO ▶77			
1. I'd Love You To Want Me	72	1	4745
2. Don't Expect Me To Be Your Friend	73	4	2571
3. Me And You And A Dog Named Boo	71	8	1820
4. How Can I Tell Her	73	20	1133
5. Where Were You When I Was Falling In Love	79	16	1103
6. It Sure Took A Long, Long Time	73	27	606
7. Don't Tell Me Goodnight	75	30	529
8. Standing At The End Of The Line	74	30	524
9. Rings	74	37^2	414
10. She Didn't Do Magic	71	44	397
11. A Simple Man	72	52	335
12. There Ain't No Way	73	50	273
13. I'm The Only One	71	76	79
14. California Kid And Reemo	71	82	54
Dave LOGGINS ▶526			
1. Please Come To Boston	74	7^2	2151
2. Someday	74	67	201
Kenny LOGGINS ▶406			
Duo: **Loggins & Messina**			
1. Whenever I Call You "Friend"	78	5^3	3083
2. I Believe In Love	77	53	343
3. Easy Driver	79	54	207
Trini LOPEZ ▶1352			
1. Somethin' 'Bout You Baby I Like	75	76	85
Marian LOVE ▶1606			
1. I Believe In Music	71	97^2	13
Andy Fairweather LOW ▶1442			
1. Spider Jiving	75	83	51
Nick LOWE ▶674			
1. Cruel To Be Kind	79	12	1498
Frank LUCAS ▶1362			
1. Good Thing Man	77	72	82

	Year	Peak	Points
LULU ▶577			
1. Oh Me Oh My (I'm A Fool For You Baby)	70	18	1198
2. Hum A Song (From Your Heart)	70	41	388
3. After The Feeling Is Gone	70	95	13
#2 & 3: LULU with The Dixie Flyers			
Pat LUNDI ▶1539			
1. Party Music	75	91	22
Barbara LYNN ▶1673			
1. (Until Then) I'll Suffer	71	98	4
Cheryl LYNN ▶624			
1. Got To Be Real	79	10^2	1373
2. Star Love	79	65	126
Loretta LYNN ▶1109			
Duos: Loretta Lynn/Conway Twitty			
Conway Twitty Loretta Lynn			
1. The Pill	75	49^2	262
M ▶421			
1. Pop Muzik	79	4^3	4309
Byron Mac GREGOR ▶439			
1. Americans	74	1	4085
Mary MacGREGOR ▶204			
1. Torn Between Two Lovers	77	1^3	7701
2. Good Friend	79	44^2	430
3. This Girl (Has Turned Into A Woman)	77	69	117
4. For A While	77	93	22
Cledus MAGGARD ▶773			
1. The White Knight	76	20	1003
Cledus MAGGARD And The Citizen's Band			
John Culliton MAHONEY ▶1522			
1. The Ballad Of Evel Knievel	74	85	27
Melissa MANCHESTER ▶238			
1. Midnight Blue	75	7	2358
2. Don't Cry Out Loud	79	10^2	1824
3. Just Too Many People	75	32	646
4. Pretty Girls	79	44	411
5. Just You And I	76	46	320
6. Better Days	76	88	36
7. Theme From Ice Castles (Through The Eyes Of Love)	79	87	26
Barbara MANDRELL ▶786			
1. (If Loving You Is Wrong) I Don't Want To Be Right	79	27	729
2. Woman To Woman	78	93	11
Chuck MANGIONE ▶474			
1. Feels So Good	78	6^2	2886
2. Hill Where The Lord Hides	71	61	216
Barry MANILOW ▶17			
1. I Write The Songs	76	1	8120
2. Can't Smile Without You	78	2^4	5595

	Year	Peak	Points
3. Mandy	75	1	5395
4. Looks Like We Made It	77	3^2	2950
5. Could It Be Magic	75	7	2394
6. Weekend In New England	77	9^2	2101
7. Tryin' To Get The Feeling Again	76	10	1845
8. Ready To Take A Chance Again	78	7^2	1747
9. It's A Miracle	75	10	1503
10. Copacabana (At The Copa)	78	10^2	1466
11. Ships	79	11^2	1227
12. Somewhere In The Night	79	13^2	1050
13. Even Now	78	17^2	956
14. Daybreak	77	21^2	718
15. This One's For You	76	21	716
Barry MANN ▶1276			
1. Feelings	70	83	48
2. The Princess And The Punk	76	84	33
Herbie MANN ▶679			
1. Hijack	75	22	701
2. Superman	79	35	510
Bobbi MARTIN ▶533			
1. For The Love Of Him	70	9	2091
2. Give A Woman Love	70	63	202
Dean MARTIN ▶1595			
1. My Woman, My Woman, My Wife	70	97	5
2. Detroit City	70	99	4
Moon MARTIN ▶792			
1. Rolene	79	28	519
2. No Chance	79	55	210
Steve MARTIN ▶729			
1. King Tut	78	18^2	1004
STEVE MARTIN and the Toot Uncommons			
2. Grandmother's Song	77	94	8
Layng MARTINE ▶974			
1. Rub It In	71	63	309
2. Come On Over To My House	72	93	31
Al MARTINO ▶445			
1. To The Door Of The Sun (Alle Porte Del Sole)	75	21	994
2. Volare	75	41^2	426
3. The Next Hundred Years	78	55^2	298
4. I Started Loving You Again	70	74	275
5. Can't Help Falling In Love	70	57	267
6. Speak Softly Love	72	81	54
Carolyne MAS ▶1320			
1. Stillsane	79	72	98
Barbara MASON ▶538			
1. Give Me Your Love	73	18	914
2. From His Woman To You	75	34^2	485
3. Bed And Board	72	66	133

	Year	Peak	Points
Barbara MASON – cont'd			
4. Shackin' Up	75	76	122
Dave MASON ▶417			
Groups: **Delaney & Bonnie And Friends, Traffic**			
1. We Just Disagree	77	15	1315
2. Only You Know And I Know	70	37	470
3. Will You Still Love Me Tomorrow	78	40	417
4. Let It Go, Let It Flow	78	49	266
5. So High (Rock Me Baby And Roll Me Away)	77	69	98
6. Satin Red And Black Velvet Woman	70	95	15
Johnny MATHIS ▶955			
Duo: **Johnny Mathis/Deniece Williams**			
1. Life Is A Song Worth Singing	74	64	245
2. I'm Coming Home	73	72	120
Ian MATTHEWS ▶593			
Group: **Matthew's Southern Comfort**			
1. Shake It	79	10^2	1648
2. Give Me An Inch	79	65	109
John MAYALL ▶1583			
1. Room To Move	70	95	16
Curtis MAYFIELD ▶158			
1. Freddie's Dead (Theme From "Superfly")	72	6^2	2741
2. Superfly	73	6^3	2430
3. (Don't Worry) If There's A Hell Below We're All Going To Go	71	24	922
4. Kung Fu	74	32	654
5. Get Down	71	52^2	399
6. Future Shock	73	39	359
7. So In Love	75	58^2	296
8. We Got To Have Peace	72	81	39
9. Can't Say Nothin'	74	89	26
10. If I Were Only A Child Again	73	94	8
Mac McANALLY ▶1143			
1. It's A Crazy World	77	58	229
C.W. McCALL ▶229			
1. Convoy	76	1^3	6837
2. There Won't Be No Country Music (There Won't Be No Rock 'N' Roll)	76	52^2	305
3. Old Home Filler-Up An' Keep On-A-Truckin' Café	74	52	215
4. Wolf Creek Pass	75	73	86
Peter McCANN ▶610			
1. Do You Wanna Make Love	77	9^2	1919
George McCANNON III ▶1646			
1. Birds Of All Nations	70	97	8
Paul McCARTNEY ▶499			
Duo: **Paul & Linda McCartney**			
Groups: **Paul McCartney/Wings, The Beatles**			
1. Another Day	71	6	2647
2. Oh Woman Oh Why	71	55	112
Gayle McCORMICK ▶865			
Group: **Smith**			
1. It's A Cryin' Shame	71	43	498
2. Gonna Be Alright Now	71	91	41
Van McCOY ▶280			
1. The Hustle	75	1	5355
2. Change With The Times	75	52^2	327
3. Party	76	85	32
4. Love Is The Answer	74	89	23
#1 & 4: *VAN Mc COY & The Soul City Symphony*			
George McCRAE ▶301			
1. Rock Your Baby	74	1	4245
2. I Get Lifted	75	54	286
3. I Can't Leave You Alone	74	58	231
4. Honey I	76	69	123
5. Look At You	75	79	64
Gwen McCRAE ▶607			
1. Rockin' Chair	75	10^2	1947
Donna McDANIEL ▶1444			
1. Save Me	77	84^2	51
Ronnie McDOWELL ▶808			
1. The King Is Gone	77	14	910
Parker McGEE ▶1090			
1. I Just Can't Say No To You	77	55	277
Bob McGILPIN ▶1589			
1. When You Feel Love	78	94^2	15
Maureen McGOVERN ▶317			
1. The Morning After	73	3	2509
2. Different Worlds	79	26^2	888
3. Give Me A Reason To Be Gone	74	68	162
4. Can You Read My Mind	79	69	130
5. I Won't Last A Day Without You	73	72	117
6. We May Never Love Like This Again	75	91^2	33
7. Nice To Be Around	74	96^2	15
Don McLEAN ▶116			
1. American Pie	72	1^4	10352
2. Vincent	72	11^2	1548
3. Dreidel	73	19	944
4. If We Try	73	68	119
5. Wonderful Baby	75	94^2	16
Penny McLEAN ▶1134			
Group: **Silver Convention**			
1. Lady Bump	76	61	235

Artist / Song	Year	Peak	Points
Robin McNAMARA ▶529			
1. Lay A Little Lovin' On Me	70	7	2180
2. Got To Believe In Love	70	75	133
Sister Janet MEAD ▶558			
1. The Lord's Prayer	74	5^2	2397
MEAT LOAF ▶418			
Duo: **Stoney & Meatloaf**			
1. Two Out Of Three Ain't Bad	78	9^2	2274
2. Paradise By The Dashboard Light	78	37	440
3. You Took The Words Right Out Of My Mouth	79	42	418
4. You Took The Words Right Out Of My Mouth (Hot Summer Night)	77	97	4
MECO ▶246			
1. Star Wars Theme/Cantina Band	77	1^2	5942
2. Theme From Close Encounters	78	29	587
3. Themes From The Wizard Of Oz	78	34	495
Monkey MEEKS ▶1590			
1. Take Me To Your Heart	73	93	15
MELANIE ▶71			
1. Brand New Key	71	1^2	8365
2. Lay Down (Candles In The Rain)	70	3	4215
MELANIE with The Edwin Hawkins Singers			
3. Ring The Living Bell	72	21	786
4. Bitter Bad	73	30	740
5. Peace Will Come (According To Plan)	70	20	701
6. The Nickel Song	72	25	689
7. Ruby Tuesday	71	34	430
8. Together Alone	72	57	287
9. Will You Love Me Tomorrow?	74	54^2	283
10. Lover's Cross	74	70	162
11. Some Day I'll Be A Farmer	72	79	83
12. The Good Book	71	78	54
Lee MICHAELS ▶428			
1. Do You Know What I Mean	71	4	3246
2. Can I Get A Witness	71	39^2	538
Bette MIDLER ▶267			
1. Boogie Woogie Bugle Boy	73	6	1871
2. Do You Want To Dance?	73	13	1489
3. In The Mood	74	31	441
4. Friends	73	40	315
5. Married Men	79	46	302
6. You're Movin' Out Today	77	62	195
7. Storybook Children (Daybreak)	78	66	170
The MIGHTY POPE ▶1457			
1. Heaven On The Seventh Floor	77	83^2	45

Artist / Song	Year	Peak	Points
Buddy MILES ▶724			
Group: **Buddy Miles & The Freedom Express**			
Duo: **Carlos Santana & Buddy Miles**			
1. Down By The River	70	68	177
2. Wholesale Love	71	62	135
3. We Got To Live Together - Part I	71	81	95
4. Rockin' And Rollin' On The Streets Of Hollywood	75	80	94
5. Them Changes	71	82	42
John MILES ▶832			
1. Highfly	76	58	351
2. Slowdown	77	64	131
3. Music	76	91	19
Frankie MILLER ▶1303			
1. The Doodle Song	77	69^2	108
Jody MILLER ▶941			
1. He's So Fine	71	57	299
2. Baby, I'm Yours	71	83	80
Steve MILLER ▶191			
Group: **Steve Miller Band**			
1. Rock'n Me	76	1	4622
2. Fly Like An Eagle	77	3^3	3311
3. Take The Money And Run	76	9	1693
Frank MILLS ▶365			
1. Music Box Dancer	79	2^2	3861
2. Love Me, Love Me Love	72	45	331
3. Peter Piper	79	57	240
Stephanie MILLS ▶927			
1. What Cha Gonna Do With My Lovin'	79	28	562
Ronnie MILSAP ▶478			
1. It Was Almost Like A Song	77	11	1514
2. Get It Up	79	50	315
3. Only One Love In My Life	78	80	39
4. Too Late To Worry, Too Blue To Cry	75	87	36
5. What A Difference You've Made In My Life	78	89	18
6. Please Don't Tell Me How The Story Ends	74	96^2	11
Joni MITCHELL ▶233			
1. Help Me	74	8^3	2325
2. You Turn Me On, I'm A Radio	73	20^2	1086
3. Free Man In Paris	74	23	815
4. Big Yellow Taxi [studio version of #8]	75	25	639
5. Raised On Robbery	74	50	359
6. In France They Kiss On Main Street	76	55	194
7. Carey	71	92	20
8. Big Yellow Taxi	70	100	1

	Year	Peak	Points
Eddie MONEY ▶292			
1. Baby Hold On	78	5^2	2618
2. Two Tickets To Paradise	78	20^2	890
3. Maybe I'm A Fool	79	25^2	708
4. Get A Move On	79	55	247
5. You've Really Got A Hold On Me	78	67^2	155
6. Can't Keep A Good Man Down	79	65	107
Melba MONTGOMERY ▶1066			
1. No Charge	74	54	309
Dorothy MOORE ▶311			
1. Misty Blue	76	3^2	4938
2. I Believe You	77	28^2	572
3. Funny How Time Slips Away	76	73	84
Jackie MOORE ▶442			
1. Precious, Precious	71	11	1728
2. Sweet Charlie Babe	73	32^2	746
3. Make Me Feel Like A Woman	75	81	93
4. Sometimes It's Got To Rain	71	91	23
#1 & 4: *JACKIE MOORE With The Dixie Flyers*			
5. Darling Baby	72	97	11
Melba MOORE ▶953			
1. You Stepped Into My Life	79	47	340
2. I Got Love	70	87	28
Tim MOORE ▶701			
1. Second Avenue	74	59	346
2. In The Middle	77	68	157
3. Charmer	75	79	54
4. Second Avenue [reissue--see #1]	78	93^2	34
5. Fool Like You	73	94	8
Giorgio MORODER ▶736			
1. Son Of My Father	72	34^2	540
Giorgio			
2. Chase	79	38	445
Van MORRISON ▶263			
1. Domino	71	9	1394
2. Blue Money	71	23	859
3. Wild Night	71	25	657
4. Come Running	70	30^2	431
5. Tupelo Honey	72	43	364
6. Wavelength	78	61	185
7. Jackie Wilson Said (I'm In Heaven When You Smile)	72	73	83
8. Moondance	77	91	33
9. Gypsy	73	89	32
Maria MULDAUR ▶413			
1. Midnight At The Oasis	74	4	3140
2. I'm A Woman	75	24	821

	Year	Peak	Points
Michael MURPHEY ▶287			
1. Wildfire	75	2	4059
2. Carolina In The Pines	75	23	796
3. Geronimo's Cadillac	72	49	443
4. Renegade	76	42	335
Anne MURRAY ▶63			
Duo: *Glen Campbell/Anne Murray*			
1. You Needed Me	78	4^4	4060
2. Danny's Song	73	6	2857
3. Snowbird	70	6^2	2509
4. You Won't See Me	74	8^2	2130
5. Love Song	74	10	1568
6. I Just Fall In Love Again	79	11^2	1477
7. Broken Hearted Me	79	22^2	715
8. Shadows In The Moonlight	79	27^2	594
9. What About Me	73	37^2	444
10. Day Tripper	75	44	317
11. Talk It Over In The Morning	71	79	91
12. Sing High--Sing Low	71	83	85
13. The Call	76	91	21
14. Sunday Sunrise	75	94	17
15. Just One Look	74	93	14
16. Walk Right Back	78	92	13
17. Send A Little Love My Way	73	96	10
Graham NASH ▶716			
Groups: **Crosby, Stills, Nash & Young** / **Crosby, Stills & Nash**			
Duos: **Neil Young and Graham Nash** / **Graham Nash & David Crosby** / **David Crosby / Graham Nash**			
1. Chicago	71	29	935
2. Military Madness	71	66	142
Johnny NASH ▶177			
1. I Can See Clearly Now	72	1	5242
2. Stir It Up	73	11	1849
3. Cupid	70	36^2	772
4. Loving You	74	67	213
5. My Merry-Go-Round	73	74	117
6. (What A) Wonderful World	76	82	50
7. You Can't Go Halfway	74	90	21
David NAUGHTON ▶501			
1. Makin' It	79	5^2	3059
Jerry NAYLOR ▶1060			
1. But For Love	70	42	317
Sam NEELY ▶524			
1. Loving You Just Crossed My Mind	72	31	691
2. You Can Have Her	74	35	558
3. I Fought The Law	75	41^2	331
4. Rosalie	73	58	222

	Year	Peak	Points
Rick NELSON ▶1122			
Group: Rick Nelson & The Stone Canyon Band			
1. Easy To Be Free	70	50	251
Willie NELSON ▶643			
Duo: Waylon & Willie			
1. Blue Eyes Crying In The Rain	75	25	981
2. Remember Me	76	72	143
3. Georgia On My Mind	78	93	19
Peter NERO ▶826			
1. Theme From "Summer Of '42"	72	21	862
Mickey NEWBURY ▶863			
1. An American Trilogy	71	46	484
2. Sunshine	73	82	60
Randy NEWMAN ▶346			
1. Short People	78	1	5653
Juice NEWTON ▶1613			
1. It's A Heartache	78	93	12
Wayne NEWTON ▶221			
1. Daddy Don't You Walk So Fast	72	1	5850
2. Can't You Hear The Song?	72	38	379
3. Anthem	73	45	330
4. The Hungry Years	76	81	46
5. You Stepped Into My Life	79	91^2	41
6. Lady Lay	74	83	39
Olivia NEWTON-JOHN ▶15			
Duo: John Travolta And Olivia Newton-John			
1. Have You Never Been Mellow	75	1	6119
2. I Honestly Love You	74	1^2	5982
3. Please Mr. Please	75	1	4812
4. Hopelessly Devoted To You	78	3	3942
5. A Little More Love	79	4^3	3742
6. Let Me Be There	74	4	2978
7. If You Love Me (Let Me Know)	74	6^2	2558
8. If Not For You	71	23	1094
9. Something Better To Do	75	15	1017
10. Deeper Than The Night	79	19	667
11. Come On Over	76	30	653
12. Sam	77	34	574
13. Let It Shine	76	28	566
14. Don't Stop Believin'	76	47	444
15. I Honestly Love You	77	60	192
16. Every Face Tells A Story	76	71	90
17. Totally Hot	79	72	82
18. He Ain't Heavy...He's My Brother	75	80	22
19. Banks Of The Ohio	71	94	9
Paul NICHOLAS ▶470			
1. Heaven On The 7Th Floor	77	5	3044
2. On The Strip	78	73	96

	Year	Peak	Points
Maxine NIGHTINGALE ▶205			
1. Right Back Where We Started From	76	1	5260
2. Lead Me On	79	5^2	2940
3. Gotta Be The One	76	84	43
4. (Bringing Out) The Girl In Me	79	91	22
NILSSON ▶105			
1. Without You	72	1^2	7109
2. Coconut	72	12^2	1538
3. Me And My Arrow	71	27	1054
4. Jump Into The Fire	72	22^2	763
5. Spaceman	72	23	728
6. Daybreak	74	23^2	716
7. Remember (Christmas)	73	40	521
8. As Time Goes By	73	64	241
9. Many Rivers To Cross	74	78	67
Don NIX ▶1639			
1. Olena	71	96	9
NOLAN ▶1225			
[Nolan Porter; see also N.F. Porter]			
1. I Like What You Give	71	70	168
Kenny NOLAN ▶362			
1. I Like Dreamin'	77	3	4020
2. Love's Grown Deep	77	25	898
Freddie NORTH ▶827			
1. She's All I Got	71	30	620
2. You And Me Together Forever	72	90	32
Dorothy NORWOOD ▶1232			
1. There's Got To Be Rain In Your Life (To Appreciate The Sunshine)	74	74	161
Ted NUGENT ▶631			
1. Cat Scratch Fever	77	21^2	780
2. Yank Me, Crank Me	78	64	122
3. Hey Baby	76	84^2	58
4. Dog Eat Dog	76	82	46
Stu NUNNERY ▶1032			
1. Sally From Syracuse	73	67^2	190
2. Madelaine	74	86	57
Billy OCEAN ▶776			
1. Love Really Hurts Without You	76	16	987
Alan O'DAY ▶274			
1. Undercover Angel	77	1	6790
2. Started Out Dancing, Ended Up Making Love	77	93	20
Herb OHTA ▶1504			
1. Song For Anna (Chanson D'Anna)	74	88	30
Danny O'KEEFE ▶646			
1. Good Time Charlie's Got The Blues	72	10	1656
Mike OLDFIELD ▶589			
1. Tubular Bells	74	6^2	2122

	Year	Peak	Points
OLIVER ▶1381			
1. Angelica	70	84	36
2. I Can Remember	70	94	9
Jane OLIVOR ▶1102			
1. He's So Fine	78	67^2	146
2. Some Enchanted Evening	77	89	32
Nigel OLSSON ▶578			
1. Dancin' Shoes	79	17	1068
2. Little Bit Of Soap	79	33	499
3. Only One Woman	75	92	19
Roy ORBISON ▶1534			
1. Easy Way Out	79	92	23
Tony ORLANDO ▶1167			
Group: **Tony Orlando And Dawn**			
1. Sweets For My Sweet	79	55^2	209
Lee OSKAR ▶1383			
Groups: **War, Eric Burdon & War**			
1. BLT	76	77	71
Donny OSMOND ▶41			
Group: **Osmonds**			
Duo: **Donny And Marie Osmond**			
1. Go Away Little Girl	71	1	6764
2. Puppy Love	72	3^3	3823
3. Sweet And Innocent	71	7^3	2607
4. The Twelfth Of Never	73	5	2508
5. Hey Girl	72	9^2	1802
6. Too Young	72	8	1596
7. Why	72	16	1093
8. Are You Lonesome Tonight	74	16	1036
9. A Million To One	73	28	570
10. C'mon Marianne	76	44^2	525
11. Young Love	73	41	310
12. I Have A Dream	75	54	206
13. When I Fall In Love	73	73	72
14. I Knew You When	71	83	61
15. You've Got Me Dangling On A String	77	99	2
Little Jimmy OSMOND ▶810			
1. Long Haired Lover From Liverpool LITTLE JIMMY OSMOND with The Mike Curb Congregation	72	41	421
2. Tweedlee Dee	73	49	264
Marie OSMOND ▶465			
Duo: **Donny And Marie Osmond**			
1. Paper Roses	73	6^2	2252
2. Who's Sorry Now	75	39	357
3. This Is The Way That I Feel	77	52	247
Gilbert O'SULLIVAN ▶73			
1. Alone Again (Naturally)	72	1^3	9269
2. Clair	73	3	4323
3. Get Down	73	4	3363

	Year	Peak	Points
4. Ooh Baby	73	11	1062
5. Out Of The Question	73	22	829
6. Happiness Is Me And You	74	34	406
7. You Are You	75	95	16
Sharon PAIGE ▶972			
1. Hope That We Can Be Together Soon SHARON PAIGE and Harold Melvin And The Blue Notes	75	31	489
Robert PALMER ▶386			
1. Bad Case Of Loving You (Doctor, Doctor)	79	10^2	1582
2. Every Kinda People	78	13^2	1482
3. Man Smart, Woman Smarter	77	70	134
4. Give Me An Inch Girl	76	88	42
5. Sneakin' Sally Through The Alley	75	96	9
Michael PARKS ▶746			
1. Long Lonesome Highway	70	13	1185
Alan PARSONS ▶896			
Group: **Alan Parsons Project**			
1. I Wouldn't Want To Be Like You	77	27	633
Dolly PARTON ▶298			
1. Here You Come Again	78	7^2	2563
2. Two Doors Down	78	24	648
3. Baby I'm Burnin'	79	34^2	461
4. Heartbreaker	78	56	238
5. Jolene	74	80	122
6. You're The Only One	79	68	121
7. The Seeker	75	91	20
Kellee PATTERSON ▶1308			
1. If It Don't Fit, Don't Force It	78	77	104
Billy PAUL ▶219			
Group: **Philadelphia International All Stars**			
1. Me And Mrs. Jones	72	1^2	7075
2. Thanks For Saving My Life	74	43	571
3. Let's Make A Baby	76	79^2	77
4. Am I Black Enough For You	73	99	2
Freda PAYNE ▶178			
1. Band Of Gold	70	2	5438
2. Bring The Boys Home	71	7	2025
3. Deeper And Deeper	70	21^2	989
4. You Brought The Joy	71	45	456
5. Cherish What Is Dear To You (While It's Near To You)	71	36	449
Ann PEEBLES ▶539			
1. Part Time Love	70	27	780
2. I Can't Stand The Rain	74	45	748
3. I Pity The Fool	71	84	58
4. Breaking Up Somebody's Home	72	83	48
Dan PEEK ▶1606			
Group: **America**			
1. All Things Are Possible	79	95	13

	Year	Peak	Points
Teddy PENDERGRASS ▶588			
Groups: **Harold Melvin & The Blue Notes** / **Philadelphia International All Stars**			
1. Close The Door	78	19	844
2. I Don't Love You Anymore	77	43	398
3. Turn Off The Lights	79	50	279
Jean Jacques PERREY ▶1573			
1. Passport To The Future	70	94^2	18
Esther PHILLIPS ▶632			
1. What A Diff'rence A Day Makes	75	21^2	1004
2. I've Never Found A Man (To Love Me Like You Do)	73	72	109
3. Home Is Where The Hatred Is	72	86	83
John PHILLIPS ▶884			
1. Mississippi	70	37	657
Shawn PHILLIPS ▶1229			
1. Lost Horizon	73	71	163
Bobby (Boris) PICKETT And The CRYPT-KICKERS ▶584			
1. Monster Mash	73	10^2	1730
2. Monster Mash	70	72	105
[#1 and 2: reisssues--first charted in 1962]			
Wilson PICKETT ▶128			
1. Don't Knock My Love - Pt. I	71	7	2220
2. Don't Let The Green Grass Fool You	71	10^3	1797
3. Engine Number 9	70	14	1407
4. Sugar Sugar	70	16	1100
5. Fire And Water	72	17	1062
6. Call My Name, I'll Be There	71	41	461
7. Funk Factory	72	53	295
8. She Said Yes	70	52	205
9. Take A Closer Look At The Woman You're With	73	58	186
10. Cole, Cooke And Redding	70	61	162
11. Mama Told Me Not To Come	72	81	58
12. Mr. Magic Man	73	83	43
Gene PITNEY ▶1521			
1. She Lets Her Hair Down (Early In The Morning)	70	90	27
Mary Kay PLACE ▶1195			
1. Baby Boy	76	66^3	186
MARY KAY PLACE as Loretta Haggers			
Bonnie POINTER ▶575			
Group: **Pointer Sisters**			
1. Heaven Must Have Sent You	79	10^2	1912
2. Free Me From My Freedom/Tie Me To A Tree (Handcuff Me)	78	99	2
Michael POLNAREFF ▶1204			
1. If You Only Believe (Jesus For Tonite)	76	66^2	180
N.F. PORTER ▶1652			
[Nolan Porter; see also **Nolan**]			
1. Keep On Keeping On	71	95	7
Mike POST ▶554			
1. The Rockford Files	75	10	1601
2. Manhattan Spiritual	75	64	200
3. Theme From "Baa Baa Black Sheep"	77	96	10
Cozy POWELL ▶1061			
Group: **Rainbow**			
1. Dance With The Devil	74	50	314
Andy PRATT ▶1258			
1. Avenging Annie	73	69	138
Elvis PRESLEY ▶12			
1. Burning Love	72	1	5423
2. Don't Cry Daddy	70	6^2	3010
3. The Wonder Of You	70	10	1921
4. You Don't Have To Say You Love Me	70	10^2	1449
5. Steamroller Blues	73	10^2	1390
6. Kentucky Rain	70	10	1377
7. Separate Ways	73	15	1356
8. I Really Don't Want To Know	71	13^2	1278
9. Way Down	77	25	993
10. Promised Land	75	22	976
11. My Boy	75	17	962
12. I've Lost You	70	18	822
13. If You Talk In Your Sleep	74	23^2	782
14. The Next Step Is Love	70	30	645
15. I've Got A Thing About You Baby	74	30^2	624
16. Moody Blue	77	39	590
17. Hurt	76	31^2	585
18. Until It's Time For You To Go	72	31	565
19. My Way	77	31^2	561
20. Raised On Rock	73	27	560
21. I'm Leavin'	71	36	510
22. Where Did They Go, Lord	71	34	479
23. Life	71	40	423
24. T-R-O-U-B-L-E	75	40	389
25. Rags To Riches	71	45^2	303
26. It's Only Love	71	51	215
27. There Goes My Everything	71	57	130
28. An American Trilogy	72	73^2	123
29. Take Good Care Of Her	74	63	106
30. Bringing It Back	75	75	93
31. Mama Liked The Roses	70	65	84
32. Fool	73	79	41
Billy PRESTON ▶66			
Group: **Plastic Ono Band**			
1. Will It Go Round In Circles	73	1	5132
2. Nothing From Nothing	74	1	4620
3. Outa-Space	72	1	4539

	Year	Peak	Points
Billy PRESTON – cont'd			
4. Space Race	73	6	2172
5. Struttin'	75	22	673
6. You're So Unique	74	30	546
7. Slaughter	72	46²	374
8. Fancy Lady	75	81	64
9. My Sweet Lord	71	82	53
10. I Wrote A Simple Song	72	96	11
11. That's The Way God Planned It	72	96	6
[reissue--first charted in 1969]			
Lloyd PRICE ►1619			
1. Trying To Slip (Away)	73	95	11
Ray PRICE ►443			
1. For The Good Times	71	13	1830
2. I Won't Mention It Again	71	51	344
3. I'd Rather Be Sorry	71	63	224
4. You're The Best Thing That Ever Happened To Me	73	75	113
5. She's Got To Be A Saint	73	78	76
Charley PRIDE ►600			
Duo: Charley Pride/Henry Mancini			
1. Kiss An Angel Good Mornin'	72	19	1319
2. I Can't Believe That You've Stopped Loving Me	70	81	82
3. Is Anybody Goin' To San Antone	70	93	23
PRINCE ►1532			
1. Soft And Wet	78	94²	24
Brian PROTHEROE ►1477			
1. Pinball	75	84	40
Jeanne PRUETT ►840			
1. Satin Sheets	73	24	829
Arthur PRYSOCK ►1085			
1. When Love Is New	77	74²	166
2. In The Rain	73	95	20
Gary PUCKETT ►797			
Group: Gary Puckett And The Union Gap			
1. I Just Don't Know What To Do With Myself	70	44	442
2. Keep The Customer Satisfied	71	50	273
Bill QUATEMAN ►1678			
1. Only Love	73	99	3
Suzi QUATRO ►630			
Duo: Suzi Quatro And Chris Norman			
1. If You Can't Give Me Love	79	53	206
2. All Shook Up	74	63	205
3. I've Never Been In Love	79	56	198
4. Can The Can	76	62	189
5. 48 Crash	74	90	24
Eddie RABBITT ►521			
1. Suspicions	79	19	1093

	Year	Peak	Points
2. Every Which Way But Loose	79	34	552
3. You Don't Love Me Anymore	78	64	186
4. Rocky Mountain Music	76	88	36
Gerry RAFFERTY ►146			
Group: Stealers Wheel			
1. Baker Street	78	1²	7330
2. Right Down The Line	78	8²	1848
3. Get It Right Next Time	79	23	685
4. Home And Dry	79	23	678
5. Days Gone Down (Still Got The Light In Your Eyes)	79	22²	616
Bonnie RAITT ►1142			
1. Runaway	77	52	230
Elliott RANDALL ►1507			
1. High On Love	77	91	30
Genya RAVAN ►1519			
Group: Ten Wheel Drive With Genya Ravan			
1. Back In My Arms Again	78	90	27
Lou RAWLS ►239			
Group: Philadelphia International All Stars			
1. You'll Never Find Another Love Like Mine	76	4	3170
2. A Natural Man	71	27	1079
3. Lady Love	78	20	812
4. Groovy People	76	76	60
5. See You When I Git There	77	87	32
6. Let Me Be Good To You	79	92	21
7. His Song Shall Be Sung	72	93	16
8. Bring It On Home	70	100	1
Don RAY ►1118			
1. Got To Have Loving	78	49	256
Susan RAYE ►1561			
1. L.A. International Airport	71	92	19
RAZZY ►1114			
1. I Hate Hate	74	49	261
[Alt label: Razzy And The Neighborhood Kids]			
Chris REA ►556			
1. Fool (If You Think It's Over)	78	10²	1443
2. Diamonds	79	44²	305
3. Whatever Happened To Benny Santini?	78	77	47
John Dawson READ ►1440			
1. A Friend Of Mine Is Going Blind	75	80	52
Gene REDDING ►756			
1. This Heart	74	22	1088
Otis REDDING ►1424			
1. Demonstration	70	75	57
Helen REDDY ►16			
1. Delta Dawn	73	1²	5959
2. I Am Woman	72	1	5833

	Year	Peak	Points
Helen REDDY – cont'd			
3. Leave Me Alone (Ruby Red Dress)	74	1	4846
4. Angie Baby	74	1	4336
5. Ain't No Way To Treat A Lady	75	5	2897
6. You And Me Against The World	74	10	1760
7. Keep On Singing	74	10	1537
8. Peaceful	73	14	1420
9. You're My World	77	16	1399
10. I Don't Know How To Love Him	71	19^2	1308
11. Somewhere In The Night	76	20^2	1033
12. Emotion	75	23	715
13. Crazy Love	71	38	540
14. Bluebird	75	34	385
15. I Can't Hear You No More	76	41^2	326
16. No Sad Song	72	56	320
17. Make Love To Me	79	59	163
18. The Happy Girls	77	75	67
19. Music Is My Life	76	75	59
20. Ready Or Not	78	87	29
Michael REDWAY ▶1350			
1. Good Morning	73	77	86
Jerry REED ▶251			
1. Amos Moses	71	8^2	2171
2. When You're Hot, You're Hot	71	9^2	2084
3. Ko-Ko Joe	71	53^3	353
4. Lord, Mr. Ford	73	52	312
5. Another Puff	72	72	109
6. Alabama Wild Man	72	82	86
7. The Crude Oil Blues	74	93	24
Lou REED ▶820			
1. Walk On The Wild Side	73	17^2	880
Martha REEVES ▶1206			
Group: Martha Reeves & The Vandellas			
1. Power Of Love	74	71	179
Clarence REID ▶1600			
1. Funky Party	74	91	13
John REID ▶1558			
1. It Hurts A Little Even Now	75	91	19
Mike REILLY ▶1667			
Group: Pure Prairie League			
1. 1927 Kansas City	71	98	5
REPARATA ▶1524			
1. Shoes	75	92	26
Emitt RHODES ▶907			
1. Fresh As A Daisy	71	38	609
Charlie RICH ▶103			
1. The Most Beautiful Girl	73	1^2	5101
2. A Very Special Love Song	74	8	1507
3. Behind Closed Doors	73	17	1350

	Year	Peak	Points
4. Every Time You Touch Me (I Get High)	75	22^2	798
5. There Won't Be Anymore	74	22^2	778
6. I Love My Friend	74	29	566
7. My Elusive Dreams	75	49^2	278
8. I Don't See Me In Your Eyes Anymore	74	59	276
9. July 12, 1939	70	72	107
10. Since I Fell For You	76	82^2	75
11. America, The Beautiful	76	78	53
12. She Called Me Baby	74	90	33
13. All Over Me	75	90	15
14. Rollin' With The Flow	77	94	11
Cliff RICHARD ▶456			
1. Devil Woman	76	5^3	3299
2. Don't Turn The Light Out	77	87	37
Turley RICHARDS ▶1253			
1. Love Minus Zero - No Limit	70	76	142
Billy Lee RILEY ▶1677			
1. I Got A Thing About You Baby	72	99	3
Jeannie C. RILEY ▶861			
1. Good Enough To Be Your Wife	71	51	299
2. Oh, Singer	71	61	251
Miguel RIOS ▶695			
1. A Song Of Joy (Himno A La Alegria)	70	9	1410
Waldo de los RÍOS ▶999			
1. Mozart Symphony No. 40 In G Minor K.550, 1st Movement	71	57	424
Minnie RIPERTON ▶315			
[Group: Rotary Connection, peaked Dec. '69]			
1. Lovin' You	75	1	5910
2. Inside My Love	75	72	99
Rodney Allen RIPPY ▶1314			
1. Take Life A Little Easier	73	75	100
Johnny RIVERS ▶155			
1. Rockin' Pneumonia - Boogie Woogie Flu	73	5^2	3311
2. Swayin' To The Music (Slow Dancin') [Alt. title: Slow Dancin']	77	6	2782
3. Blue Suede Shoes	73	27	628
4. Into The Mystic	70	38	497
5. Curious Mind (Um, Um, Um, Um, Um, Um)	78	34^3	496
6. Help Me Rhonda	75	30	482
7. Fire And Rain JOHNNY RIVERS & Friends	70	71	159
8. Sea Cruise	71	74	142
9. Think His Name	71	71	103
Marty ROBBINS ▶1000			
1. My Woman, My Woman, My Wife	70	38	423

Austin ROBERTS ▶412	Year	Peak	Points
1. Something's Wrong With Me	72	10^2	1651
2. Rocky	75	11	1509
3. Keep On Singing	73	39	398

Freddy ROBINSON ▶991	Year	Peak	Points
1. Black Fox	70	45	443

Smokey ROBINSON ▶326
Groups: Smokey Robinson & The Miracles
Diana Ross, Marvin Gaye, Smokey Robinson & Stevie Wonder

	Year	Peak	Points
1. Baby Come Close	74	36	623
2. Baby That's Backatcha	75	38^2	609
3. The Agony And The Ecstasy	75	50	428
4. I Am I Am	75	60	240
5. Sweet Harmony	73	60	237
6. Virgin Man	74	70	213
7. It's Her Turn To Live	74	69	174
8. Quiet Storm	76	77	115
9. There Will Come A Day (I'm Gonna Happen To You)	77	66	114
10. Daylight And Darkness	78	90	31

Vicki Sue ROBINSON ▶599	Year	Peak	Points
1. Turn The Beat Around	76	15	1701
2. Daylight	76	97	9

Johnny RODRIGUEZ ▶1325	Year	Peak	Points
1. Ridin' My Thumb To Mexico	73	75	96

Tommy ROE ▶225	Year	Peak	Points
1. Jam Up Jelly Tight	70	5^2	3523
2. Stagger Lee	71	19^2	1253
3. Pearl	70	30	587
4. Stir It Up And Serve It	70	32	586
5. We Can Make Music	70	35	441
6. Working Class Hero	73	67	187

Kenny ROGERS ▶170
Group: Kenny Rogers And The First Edition

	Year	Peak	Points
1. You Decorated My Life	79	7^3	2189
2. She Believes In Me	79	7^2	2124
3. Lucille	77	6	1771
4. The Gambler	79	13^3	1448
5. Daytime Friends	77	28	471
6. Love Or Something Like It	78	38	434
7. Sweet Music Man	78	60	219

Roy ROGERS ▶1183	Year	Peak	Points
1. Hoppy, Gene And Me	75	61	196

Linda RONSTADT ▶25	Year	Peak	Points
1. Blue Bayou	77	2^2	4628
2. When Will I Be Loved	75	1	4394
3. You're No Good	75	1	4326
4. Heat Wave	75	4	2146
5. Ooh Baby Baby	79	7^2	1998
6. It's So Easy	77	9	1819
7. That'll Be The Day	76	11	1419
8. Back In The U.S.A.	78	11^2	1338
9. Tracks Of My Tears	76	25^2	905
10. Long Long Time	70	26	668
11. Poor Poor Pitiful Me	78	26	502
12. Love Has No Pride	74	45	413
13. Tumbling Dice	78	40	328
14. Just One Look	79	46	261
15. Someone To Lay Down Beside Me	77	65^3	223
16. Love Is A Rose	75	70	78
17. The Long Way Around	71	74	60
18. It Doesn't Matter Anymore	75	80	43
19. Silver Threads And Golden Needles	74	89	41
20. (She's A) Very Lovely Woman	71	94^2	20
21. Will You Love Me Tomorrow?	70	98	5

Charlie ROSS ▶848	Year	Peak	Points
1. Without Your Love (Mr. Jordan)	76	44	383
2. Thanks For The Smiles	75	61	206

Diana ROSS ▶23
Duos: Diana Ross & Marvin Gaye
Diana Ross Michael Jackson
Group: Diana Ross, Marvin Gaye, Smokey Robinson & Stevie Wonder

	Year	Peak	Points
1. Ain't No Mountain High Enough	70	1	6173
2. Touch Me In The Morning	73	1	4800
3. Love Hangover	76	1	4639
4. Theme From Mahogany (Do You Know Where You're Going To)	76	1	4370
5. Remember Me	71	8	1713
6. Last Time I Saw Him	74	9	1361
7. Reach Out And Touch (Somebody's Hand)	70	10	1243
8. The Boss	79	21^2	972
9. Reach Out I'll Be There	71	19	803
10. Good Morning Heartache	73	30	723
11. Gettin' Ready For Love	78	32	663
12. One Love In My Lifetime	76	34	614
13. Surrender	71	47	333
14. Sleepin'	74	53	299
15. You Got It	78	69	154
16. I'm Still Waiting	71	71	134
17. I Thought It Took A Little Time (But Today I Fell In Love)	76	60	129
18. Your Love Is So Good For Me	78	75	93
19. Sorry Doesn't Always Make It Right	75	84	59

Nino ROTA ▶1401	Year	Peak	Points
1. Love Theme From "The Godfather" The Music of NINO ROTA Conducted by Carlo Savina	72	84	64

Demis ROUSSOS ▶1330	Year	Peak	Points
1. That Once In A Lifetime	78	79	94

	Year	Peak	Points
John ROWLES ▶1304			
1. Cheryl Moana Marie	71	78²	108
Billy Joe ROYAL ▶1111			
1. Under The Boardwalk	78	60	115
2. Tulsa	71	88	57
David RUFFIN ▶446			
Duo: David & Jimmy Ruffin			
1. Walk Away From Love	76	8²	2334
2. I'm So Glad I Fell For You	70	59	263
3. Heavy Love	76	69	148
4. Everything's Coming Up Love	76	70	93
Jimmy RUFFIN ▶1565			
Duo: David & Jimmy Ruffin			
1. Maria (You Were The Only One)	71	90	19
Todd RUNDGREN ▶163			
Groups: Nazz, Runt, Utopia			
1. Hello It's Me	73	2	4196
2. I Saw The Light	72	11	1424
3. We Gotta Get You A Woman Runt	71	21	1136
4. Can We Still Be Friends	78	38	493
5. Good Vibrations	76	47	355
6. A Dream Goes On Forever	74	46	328
7. Real Man	75	84	58
8. Be Nice To Me RUNT--Todd Rundgren	71	87	52
9. Wolfman Jack	75	94	11
Merrilee RUSH ▶1345			
1. Save Me	77	78²	89
Bobby RUSSELL ▶837			
1. Saturday Morning Confusion	71	34	840
Brenda RUSSELL ▶867			
1. So Good, So Right	79	26	719
Leon RUSSELL ▶337			
Duo: Leon & Mary Russell			
Group: Delaney & Bonnie And Friends			
[see also Hank Wilson]			
1. Lady Blue	75	8	1657
2. Tight Rope	72	10	1332
3. Back To The Island	76	56	274
4. Queen Of The Roller Derby	73	87	37
5. Roll Away The Stone	70	91	23
6. If I Were A Carpenter	74	96	11
7. Slipping Into Christmas	72	94	8
Carole Bayer SAGER ▶1086			
1. You're Moving Out Today	77	57²	280
Oliver SAIN ▶1407			
1. She's A Disco Queen	76	78	61
Buffy SAINTE-MARIE ▶915			
1. Mister Can't You See	72	40²	405
2. I'm Gonna Be A Country Girl Again	71	89	23

	Year	Peak	Points
SAMI JO ▶673			
1. Tell Me A Lie	74	21²	831
2. It Could Have Been Me	74	49	396
Evie SANDS ▶793			
1. I Love Makin' Love To You	75	44²	419
2. You Brought The Woman Out Of Me	75	63²	308
Samantha SANG ▶259			
1. Emotion	78	1	7018
2. You Keep Me Dancing	78	66	182
Billy SANS ▶1623			
1. Bicycle Morning	74	97	11
Larry SANTOS ▶1081			
1. We Can't Hide It Anymore	76	57	289
Telly SAVALAS ▶1467			
1. If	74	89	43
Ray SAWYER ▶1247			
Group: Dr. Hook			
1. (One More Year Of) Daddy's Little Girl	76	68	147
Leo SAYER ▶94			
1. You Make Me Feel Like Dancing	76	1	5348
2. When I Need You	77	1³	4770
3. Long Tall Glasses (I Can Dance) [Alt. title: Long Tall Glasses]	75	6²	2259
4. How Much Love	77	9	1443
5. Thunder In My Heart	77	35	387
6. Easy To Love	78	51²	346
7. Raining In My Heart	78	43	311
Boz SCAGGS ▶175			
1. Lowdown	76	1	4956
2. Lido Shuffle	77	6²	2117
3. It's Over	76	43	374
4. We Were Always Sweethearts	71	44	289
5. What Can I Say	77	59	260
6. Hard Times	77	58	217
7. Hollywood	78	65	135
Joey SCARBURY ▶1439			
1. Mixed Up Guy	71	87	52
Marilyn SCOTT ▶1447			
1. God Only Knows	78	88	49
John SEBASTIAN ▶332			
1. Welcome Back	76	1²	6067
Neil SEDAKA ▶79			
1. Bad Blood	75	1²	5822
2. Laughter In The Rain	75	1	5106
3. Breaking Up Is Hard To Do	76	7	2128
4. Love In The Shadows	76	17	925
5. The Immigrant	75	28	605
6. That's When The Music Takes Me	75	30	594

	Year	Peak	Points
Neil SEDAKA – cont'd			
7. Steppin' Out	76	53	315
8. You Gotta Make Your Own Sunshine	76	55	281
9. Amarillo	77	50	230
Bob SEGER ▶125			
Group: The **Bob Seger System**			
1. Night Moves	77	6^2	2468
2. Still The Same	78	4^2	2465
3. We've Got Tonite	79	11	1372
4. Hollywood Nights	78	13	1085
5. Mainstreet	77	19	777
6. Old Time Rock & Roll	79	34	438
#2-4, 6: BOB SEGER & The Silver Bullet Band			
7. Katmandu	75	45	390
8. Rock And Roll Never Forgets	77	50	339
9. Nutbush City Limits	76	77	56
10. Get Out Of Denver	74	82	56
11. If I Were A Carpenter	72	91	14
12. Lookin' Back	71	97	6
Marilyn SELLARS ▶1228			
1. One Day At A Time	74	67	165
Pat SHANNON ▶1549			
1. Back To Dreamin' Again	70	92	20
Marlena SHAW ▶1426			
1. Yu-Ma/Go Away Little Boy	77	76	57
Peter SHELLEY ▶1391			
1. Gee Baby	75	82	68
T.G. SHEPPARD ▶1071			
1. Devil In The Bottle	75	64	189
2. Tryin' To Beat The Morning Home	75	94	14
Bobby SHERMAN ▶108			
1. Julie, Do Ya Love Me	70	3	3647
2. Easy Come, Easy Go	70	7	2362
3. La La La (If I Had You)	70	11	1941
4. Cried Like A Baby	71	10	1615
5. Hey, Mister Sun	70	23	767
6. The Drum	71	22^2	702
7. Waiting At The Bus Stop	71	45	346
8. Jennifer	71	38	345
9. Together Again	72	53^2	257
10. Goin' Home (Sing A Song Of Christmas Cheer)	70	70	38
Holly SHERWOOD ▶1609			
1. Day By Day (Godspell Medley)	71	91	12
SHIRLEY & SQUIRRELY (s) ▶1438			
1. Hey Shirley (This Is Squirrely)	76	85^2	52
Bunny SIGLER ▶1140			
1. Let Me Party With You (Part 1) (Party, Party, Party)	78	55	231

	Year	Peak	Points
Dooley SILVERSPOON ▶1427			
1. Bump Me Baby Pt. 1	75	82	57
SILVETTI ▶1632			
1. Spring Rain	77	97^2	9
Gene SIMMONS ▶1103			
Group: KISS			
1. Radioactive	79	51	268
Carly SIMON ▶40			
Duo: Carly Simon & James Taylor			
1. You're So Vain	73	1^2	7028
2. Nobody Does It Better	77	2^4	6578
3. Anticipation	72	10	1873
4. You Belong To Me	78	9^2	1841
5. That's The Way I've Always Heard It Should Be	71	9	1818
6. Haven't Got Time For The Pain	74	7	1540
7. The Right Thing To Do	73	10	1354
8. Attitude Dancing	75	25	572
9. It Keeps You Runnin'	76	49	357
10. Legend In Your Own Time	72	61	234
11. Vengeance	79	52	203
12. Waterfall	75	76	65
13. Tranquillo	79	86	65
14. More And More	75	90	21
Joe SIMON ▶87			
1. Drowning In The Sea Of Love	72	8	2209
2. Power Of Love	72	10	1716
3. Get Down, Get Down (Get On The Floor)	75	9	1598
4. Theme From Cleopatra Jones [Alt. label: JOE SIMON Featuring The Mainstreeters]	73	14	1166
5. Your Time To Cry	71	30^2	944
6. Step By Step	73	29	638
7. Moon Walk Part I	70	40	532
8. River	73	42^2	393
9. Pool Of Bad Luck	72	49	304
10. You're The One For Me	71	63	260
11. Farther On Down The Road	70	58	226
12. Misty Blue	72	62	194
13. Help Me Make It Through The Night	71	65	180
14. I Need You, You Need Me	76	63	179
15. Yours Love	70	74	161
16. Music In My Bones	75	60	135
17. Trouble In My Home	72	69	128
18. I Found My Dad	72	74	66
19. All My Hard Times	71	87	39
20. That's The Way I Want Our Love	70	92	11

Artist / Song	Year	Peak	Points
Paul SIMON ▶53			
Duos: Simon & Garfunkel			
Paul Simon/Phoebe Snow			
Group: Art Garfunkel with James Taylor & Paul Simon			
1. 50 Ways To Leave Your Lover	76	1^3	6430
2. Loves Me Like A Rock	73	1	4820
PAUL SIMON with The Dixie Hummingbirds			
3. Kodachrome	73	2	3600
4. Mother And Child Reunion	72	4^2	3422
5. Slip Slidin' Away	78	6^2	2292
6. Me And Julio Down By The Schoolyard	72	7	1683
7. American Tune	74	27	603
8. Still Crazy After All These Years	76	45	299
9. Duncan	72	58	199
10. The Sound Of Silence	74	97	8
Nina SIMONE ▶1485			
1. To Be Young, Gifted And Black	70	90	36
Valerie SIMPSON ▶1112			
Duo: Ashford & Simpson			
[see also Marvin Gaye & Tammi Terrell]			
1. Silly Wasn't I	73	58	262
Frank SINATRA ▶775			
1. I Believe I'm Gonna Love You	75	52	281
2. Let Me Try Again (Laisse Moi Le Temps)	73	61	162
3. I Love My Wife	77	92^2	21
4. Anytime (I'll Be There)	75	93	14
Gordon SINCLAIR ▶1048			
1. The Americans (A Canadian's Opinion)	74	36	347
Peter SKELLERN ▶1014			
1. You're A Lady	73	59	253
2. Hard Times	76	90	16
Percy SLEDGE ▶1094			
1. I'll Be Your Everything	74	59	275
Bro SMITH ▶1164			
1. Bigfoot	76	58	211
Cal SMITH ▶1486			
1. The Lord Knows I'm Drinking	73	87	36
Hurricane SMITH ▶370			
1. Oh, Babe, What Would You Say?	73	1	4395
2. Who Was It?	73	44	352
Jerry SMITH ▶1661			
1. Drivin' Home	70	98	6
O.C. SMITH ▶912			
1. Primrose Lane	70	72	166
2. Baby, I Need Your Loving	70	72	125
3. La La Peace Song	74	90	28
Rex SMITH ▶642			
1. You Take My Breath Away	79	7^2	1685
Sammi SMITH ▶547			
1. Help Me Make It Through The Night	71	9	1763
2. I've Got To Have You	72	77	71
3. Kentucky	72	92	19
Phoebe SNOW ▶516			
Duo: Paul Simon/Phoebe Snow			
1. Poetry Man	75	5	2496
2. Harpo's Blues	75	81	36
Errol SOBER ▶1541			
1. Heart To Heart	79	90	22
Gino SOCCIO ▶1207			
1. Dancer	79	59^2	179
Bert SOMMER ▶1038			
1. We're All Playing In The Same Band	70	59	226
2. Battle Of New Orleans	70	93	16
David SOUL ▶325			
1. Don't Give Up On Us	77	1	4702
2. Silver Lady	77	53	290
3. Going In With My Eyes Open	77	55^2	285
Joe SOUTH ▶528			
1. Walk A Mile In My Shoes	70	12^2	1676
JOE SOUTH and The Believers			
2. Children	70	48	374
3. Fool Me	71	93	18
J.D. SOUTHER ▶598			
Group: The Souther, Hillman, Furay Band			
1. You're Only Lonely	79	7	2023
Red SOVINE ▶959			
1. Teddy Bear	76	40	512
Billie Jo SPEARS ▶1235			
1. Blanket On The Ground	75	69	158
Ronnie SPECTOR ▶1238			
1. Try Some, Buy Some	71	65	154
Steve SPERRY ▶1591			
1. Flame	77	91	15
Dusty SPRINGFIELD ▶627			
1. A Brand New Me	70	22	974
2. Silly, Silly, Fool	70	60	227
3. Who Gets Your Love	73	93	20
Rick SPRINGFIELD ▶531			
1. Speak To The Sky	72	15	1132
2. Take A Hand	76	47	351
3. American Girls	74	64	158
4. What Would The Children Think	72	76	77
Bruce SPRINGSTEEN ▶544			
1. Born To Run	75	17	974
2. Prove It All Night	78	53	238

	Year	Peak	Points
Bruce SPRINGSTEEN – cont'd			
3. Badlands	78	52	185
4. Tenth Avenue Freeze-Out	76	63	179
Jim STAFFORD ▶174			
1. Spiders And Snakes	74	3^2	3816
2. Wildwood Weed	74	5^2	1936
3. My Girl Bill	74	10	1289
4. Swamp Witch	73	31	623
5. Your Bulldog Drinks Champagne	75	35	455
6. I Got Stoned And I Missed It	75	62	186
7. Jasper	76	86	43
Joe STAMPLEY ▶929			
1. Soul Song	73	33	561
Paul STANLEY ▶992			
Group: KISS			
1. Hold Me, Touch Me	78	41^2	439
Mavis STAPLES ▶1323			
Group: The Staple Singers			
1. Endlessly	72	85	42
2. I Have Learned To Do Without You	70	92	19
Edwin STARR ▶192			
1. War	70	1^2	7205
2. Stop The War Now	71	24^2	701
3. Funky Music Sho Nuff Turns Me On	71	54	232
4. Contact	79	64	168
5. There You Go	73	74	89
Kenny STARR ▶1394			
1. The Blind Man In The Bleachers	76	84^2	67
Ringo STARR ▶32			
Groups: The Beatles			
Plastic Ono Band			
1. Photograph	73	1	5487
2. It Don't Come Easy	71	1	5104
3. You're Sixteen	74	1	4715
4. No No Song	75	1	4062
5. Only You	75	6^2	2574
6. Oh My My	74	6	1983
7. Back Off Boogaloo	72	10^2	1526
8. A Dose Of Rock 'N' Roll	76	26	597
9. It's All Down To Goodnight Vienna	75	29	430
10. Hey Baby	77	62	272
11. Beaucoups Of Blues	70	69	161
Candi STATON ▶226			
1. Young Hearts Run Free	76	25	1189
2. Stand By Your Man	70	21	1035
3. In The Ghetto	72	36	642
4. He Called Me Baby	71	48^2	536
5. Sweet Feeling	70	44	517
6. As Long As He Takes Care Of Home	75	42	328
7. Do It In The Name Of Love	73	63^2	256

	Year	Peak	Points
8. Lovin' You, Lovin' Me	72	70	159
9. Mr. And Mrs. Untrue	71	63	154
10. I'm Just A Prisoner (Of Your Good Lovin')	70	73	113
STEFAN ▶1607			
1. Holy Cow	72	96	12
Cat STEVENS ▶84			
1. Peace Train	71	4	2895
2. Another Saturday Night	74	9^2	1831
3. Oh Very Young	74	10	1690
4. Morning Has Broken	72	11^2	1474
5. Wild World	71	18	1155
6. Moon Shadow	71	26	871
7. Sitting	72	21^2	837
8. The Hurt	73	25	691
9. Ready	75	29	669
10. (Remember The Days Of The) Old Schoolyard	77	38	447
11. Two Fine People	75	45	383
12. Banapple Gas	76	50	252
13. Was Dog A Doughnut	77	68	137
14. Where Are You	72	98	4
Ray STEVENS ▶85			
Solo: Henhouse Five Plus Too (s)			
1. The Streak	74	1	5747
2. Everything Is Beautiful	70	1	4385
3. Misty	75	16^2	1393
4. Bridget The Midget (The Queen Of The Blues)	71	43	575
5. America, Communicate With Me	70	38	409
6. I Need Your Help Barry Manilow	79	34	321
7. Moonlight Special	74	55	226
8. Indian Love Call	75	63	209
9. A Mama And A Papa	71	66^2	147
10. Sunset Strip	70	79^2	116
11. All My Trials	71	74	79
12. Everybody Needs A Rainbow	74	83	43
13. Young Love	76	87	26
B.W. STEVENSON ▶451			
1. My Maria	73	7	2074
2. The River Of Love	74	36^2	458
3. Shambala	73	77	108
4. Down To The Station	77	76	75
Al STEWART ▶307			
1. Year Of The Cat	77	4	2855
2. Time Passages	78	9^2	1532
3. Song On The Radio	79	27	496
4. On The Border	77	39	360

Artist / Song	Year	Peak	Points
Amii STEWART ▶342			
1. Knock On Wood	79	1	5153
2. Light My Fire/137 Disco Heaven	79	72	75
Baron STEWART ▶1622			
1. We Been Singin' Songs	75	97	11
John STEWART ▶475			
1. Gold	79	6^2	2624
2. Midnight Wind	79	33	471
Rod STEWART ▶13			
Group: **Faces** [see also Python Lee Jackson]			
1. Maggie May	71	1^3	9547
2. Da Ya Think I'm Sexy?	79	1^5	8597
[see also: Do You Think I'm Disco?]			
3. Tonight's The Night (Gonna Be Alright)	76	1^5	7317
4. You're In My Heart (The Final Acclaim)	78	3	4104
5. You Wear It Well	72	14	1113
6. The First Cut Is The Deepest	77	17	883
7. Ain't Love A Bitch	79	14^2	835
8. I Was Only Joking	78	19	814
9. (I Know) I'm Losing You	72	22	772
ROD STEWART With Faces			
10. Hot Legs	78	25	595
11. Twisting The Night Away	73	35	484
12. Handbags And Gladrags	72	38	451
13. Angel	72	39	421
14. The Killing Of Georgie (Part I And II)	77	38	383
15. Sailing	75	49	299
16. Oh! No Not My Baby	73	56	212
17. Reason To Believe	71	80	122
18. This Old Heart Of Mine	76	72	95
Stephen STILLS ▶375			
Groups: **Stephen Stills & Manassas** **Crosby, Stills, Nash & Young** **Crosby, Stills & Nash**			
1. Love The One You're With	71	16	1178
2. Marianne	71	31	660
3. Change Partners	71	38	488
4. Sit Yourself Down	71	31	429
5. It Doesn't Matter	72	49	312
6. Turn Back The Pages	75	76	84
Simon STOKES ▶1156			
Group: **Simon Stokes & The Nighthawks**			
1. Captain Howdy	74	64	218
J.C. STONE ▶1554			
1. Carrie's Gone	74	92	20
Sly STONE ▶1093			
Group: **Sly & The Family Stone**			
1. I Get High On You	75	58	275
Paul STOOKEY ▶761			
1. Wedding Song (There Is Love)	71	21^2	1057
Barbra STREISAND ▶43			
Duos: **Barbra Streisand/Donna Summer** **Barbra & Neil**			
1. Love Theme From "A Star Is Born" (Evergreen)	77	1^3	5759
2. The Way We Were	74	1	5516
3. The Main Event/Fight	79	3^2	3246
4. My Heart Belongs To Me	77	5^2	2431
5. Stoney End	71	7	2298
6. Songbird	78	33	511
7. Sweet Inspiration/Where You Lead	72	41	451
8. Love Theme From "Eyes Of Laura Mars" (Prisoner)	78	35	444
9. Where You Lead	71	40	414
10. Time And Love	71	48	310
11. All In Love Is Fair	74	60	201
12. Didn't We	73	65	197
13. Flim Flam Man	71	69	101
14. Mother	71	88^2	44
15. Guava Jelly	75	83	39
Jud STRUNK ▶550			
1. Daisy A Day	73	10	1569
2. The Biggest Parakeets In Town	75	55	198
3. My Country	74	74	65
Donna SUMMER ▶20			
Duo: **Barbra Streisand / Donna Summer**			
1. Bad Girls	79	1^3	7437
2. Hot Stuff	79	1^4	6275
3. Mac Arthur Park	78	1^2	5874
4. Dim All The Lights	79	3^2	3912
5. Love To Love You Baby	76	3^2	3760
6. Last Dance	78	4^2	3151
7. Heaven Knows	79	4^2	2892
DONNA SUMMER with Brooklyn Dreams			
8. I Feel Love	77	4	2711
9. I Love You	78	26	583
10. Winter Melody	77	47^2	308
11. Could It Be Magic	76	63	121
12. Rumour Has It	78	72	62
13. Spring Affair	77	84^2	48
Glenn SUTTON ▶1328			
1. The Football Card	79	60	95
Billy SWAN ▶320			
1. I Can Help	74	1	4522
2. Everything's The Same (Ain't Nothing Changed)	75	67	268
3. I'm Her Fool	75	63	97
4. Number One	76	74	94
Bettye SWANN ▶849			
1. Today I Started Loving You Again	73	44	413
2. Victim Of A Foolish Heart	72	65	172

	Year	Peak	Points
Foster SYLVERS ▶689			
Group: **The Sylvers**			
1. Misdemeanor	73	14²	1143
2. Hey, Little Girl	73	93	24
SYLVESTER ▶678			
1. Dance (Disco Heat)	78	30	678
2. You Make Me Feel (Mighty Real)	79	53²	280
3. I (Who Have Nothing)	79	88	31
SYLVIA ▶369			
Group: **Sylvia & The Moments**			
1. Pillow Talk	73	2	4671
2. Didn't I	73	74	81
Gary TANNER ▶1373			
1. Over The Rainbow	78	74	76
Tommy TATE ▶1097			
1. School Of Life	72	68	157
2. More Power To You	72	93	24
James TAYLOR ▶52			
Duo: **Carly Simon & James Taylor**			
Group: **Art Garfunkel with James Taylor & Paul Simon**			
1. You've Got A Friend	71	1	6064
2. Fire And Rain	70	4³	4236
3. Handy Man	77	2	3546
4. How Sweet It Is (To Be Loved By You)	75	7	1934
5. Your Smiling Face	77	12²	1307
6. Don't Let Me Be Lonely Tonight	73	15	978
7. Long Ago And Far Away	71	16	787
8. Country Road	71	25	612
9. Shower The People	76	49²	509
10. Up On The Roof	79	32	490
11. Mexico	75	38	385
12. One Man Parade	73	53	222
13. Carolina In My Mind	70	72	110
14. Honey Don't Leave L.A.	78	70	69
Johnnie TAYLOR ▶82			
1. Disco Lady	76	1²	5739
2. I Believe In You (You Believe In Me)	73	5	2276
3. Cheaper To Keep Her	73	18	884
4. Steal Away	70	23	796
5. Jody's Got Your Girl And Gone	71	27²	663
6. I Am Somebody Part II	70	30	553
7. Love Bones	70	32	460
JOHNNY TAYLOR (The Soul Philosopher)			
8. We're Getting Careless With Our Love	74	49²	317
9. Hijackin' Love	71	57	198
10. I've Been Born Again	74	62	178
11. Doing My Own Thing (Part I)	72	63	165
12. Stop Doggin' Me	72	70	160
13. I Don't Wanna Lose You	71	67	134

	Year	Peak	Points
14. Love Is Better In The A.M. (Part 1)	77	65	131
15. Somebody's Gettin' It	76	73	106
16. Standing In For Jody	72	70	102
Kate TAYLOR ▶1349			
1. It's In His Kiss (The Shoop Shoop Song)	77	74	87
Little Johnny TAYLOR ▶1139			
1. Everybody Knows About My Good Thing Pt. 1	72	66	231
Livingston TAYLOR ▶781			
1. I Will Be In Love With You	78	28³	668
2. I'll Come Running	79	72	81
R. Dean TAYLOR ▶256			
1. Indiana Wants Me	70	1	5328
2. Gotta See Jane	71	48	316
3. Ain't It A Sad Thing	71	63	167
4. Candy Apple Red	71	92	21
5. Taos New Mexico	72	90	20
Joe TEX ▶230			
1. I Gotcha	72	3²	5228
2. Ain't Gonna Bump No More (With No Big Fat Woman)	77	15²	1124
3. You Said A Bad Word	72	35²	543
4. You're Right, Ray Charles	70	95	14
5. Give The Baby Anything The Baby Wants	71	98	4
B.J. THOMAS ▶42			
1. Raindrops Keep Fallin' On My Head	70	1²	9782
2. (Hey Won't You Play) Another Somebody Done Somebody Wrong Song	75	1	4283
3. I Just Can't Help Believing	70	11²	1623
4. Rock And Roll Lullaby	72	12²	1554
5. Don't Worry Baby	77	13²	1471
6. No Love At All	71	14	1291
7. Most Of All	71	30	724
8. Mighty Clouds Of Joy	71	39²	651
9. Everybody's Out Of Town	70	21	650
10. Everybody Loves A Rain Song	78	44	305
11. Long Ago Tomorrow	71	57	292
12. Help Me Make It (To My Rockin' Chair)	75	62	233
13. That's What Friends Are For	72	85	55
14. Happier Than The Morning Sun	72	86	27
15. Still The Lovin' Is Fun	77	92	21
Ian THOMAS ▶872			
1. Painted Ladies	73	27²	706
Rufus THOMAS ▶438			
1. (Do The) Push And Pull - Part 1	71	20²	1182
2. The Breakdown Part 1	71	31	596

	Year	Peak	Points
Rufus THOMAS – cont'd			
3. Do The Funky Chicken	70	50	517
4. Do The Funky Penguin, Part 1	72	61	247
5. Sixty Minute Man	70	72	90
Timmy THOMAS ▶382			
1. Why Can't We Live Together	73	2	4480
2. People Are Changin'	73	86	45
CHRIS THOMPSON ▶774			
Groups: **Manfred Mann's Earth Band** **Night**			
1. If You Remember Me [later credited to Chris Thompson & Night]	79	19	999
Billy THORPE ▶1063			
1. Children Of The Sun	79	50	311
Israel "Popper Stopper" TOLBERT ▶1135			
1. Big Leg Woman (With A Short Short Mini Skirt)	70	58	235
Mary TRAVERS ▶1263			
1. Follow Me	71	70	133
Pat TRAVERS ▶1260			
1. Boom Boom (Out Go The Lights)	79	65	137
McKinley TRAVIS ▶1659			
1. Baby, Is There Something On Your Mind	70	97	6
Joey TRAVOLTA ▶1172			
1. I Don't Wanna Go	78	59	206
John TRAVOLTA ▶361			
Duo: **John Travolta And Olivia Newton-John**			
1. Let Her In	76	5^2	3028
2. All Strung Out On You	77	28^2	538
3. Greased Lightnin'	78	45	259
4. Whenever I'm Away From You	76	62	215
TROIANO ▶1588			
Groups: The **Guess Who**, The **James Gang** [Domenic Troiano]			
1. We All Need Love	79	93	15
Robin TROWER ▶1387			
1. Caledonia	77	81^2	70
Tanya TUCKER ▶595			
1. Lizzie And The Rainman	75	35^2	471
2. Would You Lay With Me (In A Field Of Stone)	74	54	301
3. The Man That Turned My Mama On	74	91	34
4. Not Fade Away	79	90	28
5. Blood Red And Goin' Down	73	94	12
6. What's Your Mama's Name	73	94	10
Conway TWITTY ▶489			
Duos: **Conway Twitty Loretta Lynn** **Loretta Lynn/Conway Twitty**			
1. You've Never Been This Far Before	73	18	843
2. Linda On My Mind	75	48^2	413

	Year	Peak	Points
3. Don't Cry Joni	76	51	263
4. Hello Darlin'	70	82	108
5. Touch The Hand	75	75	92
6. Fifteen Years Ago	70	90	22
Bonnie TYLER ▶416			
1. It's A Heartache	78	3^3	4382
John VALENTI ▶976			
[John LaVigni--see also John LiVigni]			
1. Anything You Want	76	43^2	481
Dana VALERY ▶1627			
1. Will You Love Me Tomorrow	76	95	10
Frankie VALLI ▶81			
Groups: **Frankie Valli & The Four Seasons** **The Four Seasons** [later '70s lineup]			
1. Grease	78	1	6820
2. My Eyes Adored You	75	1	5675
3. Swearin' To God	75	7^2	2444
4. Our Day Will Come	75	14^2	1455
5. Fallen Angel	76	49	310
6. We're All Alone	76	74	53
7. Boomerang	76	90^2	29
Gino VANNELLI ▶334			
1. I Just Wanna Stop	78	2^2	3739
2. People Gotta Move	74	27	616
3. Love Of My Life	76	57	285
4. Wheels Of Life	79	79	49
Randy VANWARMER ▶518			
1. Just When I Needed You Most	79	5^2	2835
Bobby VEE ▶1638			
1. Sweet Sweetheart	70	94	9
Bobby VINTON ▶139			
1. My Melody Of Love	74	2^2	3864
2. Sealed With A Kiss	72	14	1585
3. Every Day Of My Life [Alt. title: Ev'ry Day Of My Life]	72	18	1219
4. My Elusive Dreams	70	34^2	603
5. Beer Barrel Polka	75	45	391
6. No Arms Can Ever Hold You	70	58	279
7. Wooden Heart	75	70	152
8. But I Do	73	71	122
9. Midnight Show	75	78	65
10. Why Don't They Understand	70	90^2	41
11. Dick And Jane	75	87	15
Roger VOUDOURIS ▶765			
1. Get Used To It	79	22^2	1043
Loudon WAINWRIGHT III ▶680			
1. Dead Skunk	73	12	1486
Johnny WAKELIN And The **KINSHASA BAND** (s) ▶770			
1. Black Superman - "Muhammad Ali"	75	22	1010

	Year	Peak	Points
Narada Michael WALDEN ▶1162			
1. I Don't Want Nobody Else (To Dance With You)	79	52	211
Wendy WALDMAN ▶1494			
1. Long Hot Summer Nights	78	89	33
David T. WALKER ▶1272			
1. Hot Fun In The Summertime	72	66	129
Jerry Jeff WALKER ▶1415			
1. L.A. Freeway	73	78	59
Jerry WALLACE ▶783			
1. If You Leave Me Tonight I'll Cry	72	39	627
2. To Get To You	72	74	117
Joe WALSH ▶377			
Groups: The **James Gang**, **Eagles**			
1. Life's Been Good	78	6^2	1963
2. Rocky Mountain Way	73	13^2	1577
3. Turn To Stone	75	64	147
4. Meadows	74	77	102
Travis WAMMACK ▶675			
1. How Can I Tell You	73	59	317
2. (Shu-Doo-Pa-Poo-Poop) Love Being Your Fool	75	50	254
3. Whatever Turns You On	72	65	225
4. Easy Evil	75	99	2
Anita WARD ▶289			
1. Ring My Bell	79	1^3	7028
Jacky WARD ▶1355			
1. A Lover's Question	78	77	83
Jennifer WARNES ▶437			
1. Right Time Of The Night	77	5	2141
2. I Know A Heartache When I See One	79	21^2	861
3. I'm Dreaming	77	62^2	276
Dee Dee WARWICK ▶931			
1. She Didn't Know (She Kept On Talking)	70	53	283
2. Suspicious Minds	71	78	116
Dionne WARWICK ▶161			
Group: **Dionne Warwicke & Spinners**			
1. I'll Never Love This Way Again	79	5^2	3165
2. I'll Never Fall In Love Again	70	6	2517
3. Make It Easy On Yourself	70	25	773
4. Let Me Go To Him	70	26	532
5. Paper Mache	70	31	504
6. The Green Grass Starts To Grow	71	45	435
7. Who Gets The Guy	71	62	156
8. Once You Hit The Road	76	75	94
9. If We Only Have Love *Dionne Warwicke*	72	71	83
Grover WASHINGTON, Jr. ▶1346			
1. Mister Magic	75	77	88

	Year	Peak	Points
Johnny "Guitar" WATSON ▶1011			
1. A Real Mother For Ya	77	42	404
Jim WEATHERLY ▶634			
1. The Need To Be	74	16^2	1099
2. I'll Still Love You	75	77	64
3. Loving You Is Just An Old Habit	73	90	32
Paula WEBB ▶1358			
1. Please, Mr. President	75	76	83
Bob WEIR ▶1244			
Group: **Grateful Dead**			
1. Bombs Away	78	63	149
Bob WELCH ▶302			
1. Sentimental Lady	77	4	2220
2. Ebony Eyes	78	12^2	1334
3. Precious Love	79	17	1023
4. Hot Love, Cold World	78	49	287
5. Church	79	76	74
Lenny WELCH ▶799			
1. Breaking Up Is Hard To Do	70	32^2	687
2. A Sunday Kind Of Love	72	95^2	20
Mary WELLS ▶1377			
1. Dig The Way I Feel	70	80	73
Dottie WEST ▶883			
1. Country Sunshine	73	45	447
2. If It's All Right With You	73	90^2	37
Barry WHITE ▶64			
1. You're The First, The Last, My Everything	75	1	4703
2. Can't Get Enough Of Your Love, Babe	74	1	3937
3. I'm Gonna Love You Just A Little More Baby	73	4	2544
4. Never, Never Gonna Give Ya Up	74	9	1741
5. It's Ecstasy When You Lay Down Next To Me	77	7	1627
6. What Am I Gonna Do With You	75	8	1573
7. Honey Please, Can't Ya See	74	23	636
8. Let The Music Play	76	31^2	614
9. I've Got So Much To Give	73	38^2	483
10. Oh What A Night For Dancing	78	32^2	451
11. I'll Do For You Anything You Want Me To	75	32	446
12. Your Sweetness Is My Weakness	78	56^2	280
13. Playing Your Game, Baby	78	95	5
Tony Joe WHITE ▶1647			
1. Save Your Sugar For Me	70	99^3	8
Roger WHITTAKER ▶734			
1. The Last Farewell	75	17	1241
Steve WIGHTMAN ▶1564			
1. You Know The Feelin'	76	90	19

	Year	Peak	Points
Jack WILD ▶1617			
1. Some Beautiful	70	94	11
Andy WILLIAMS ▶426			
1. (Where Do I Begin) Love Story	71	10^2	1757
2. Love Theme From "The Godfather" (Speak Softly Love)	72	24	625
3. Can't Help Falling In Love	70	85	51
4. Tell It Like It Is	76	85	36
5. A Song For You	71	95^2	21
6. One Day Of Your Life	70	92	12
Anson WILLIAMS ▶1449			
1. Deeply	77	84	48
Deniece WILLIAMS ▶688			
Duo: Johnny Mathis/Deniece Williams			
1. Free	77	21^2	1155
2. Baby, Baby My Love's All For You	78	91	18
Diana WILLIAMS ▶1418			
1. Teddy Bear's Last Ride	76	84^2	58
Don WILLIAMS ▶1559			
1. Tulsa Time	78	96	10
2. Some Broken Hearts Never Mend	77	99	3
John WILLIAMS ▶602			
Group: John Williams / London Symphony Orchestra			
1. Theme From "Close Encounters Of The Third Kind"	78	13	1068
2. Main Title (Theme From "Jaws")	75	25	631
Johnny WILLIAMS ▶1404			
1. Slow Motion (Part 1)	73	80	62
Marion WILLIAMS ▶1628			
1. Standing Here Wondering Which Way To Go	71	93	10
Paul WILLIAMS ▶889			
1. Waking Up Alone	72	51	307
2. Inspiration	74	69	170
Terry WILLIAMS ▶1656			
1. Melanie Makes Me Smile	72	98^2	7
Al WILSON ▶213			
1. Show And Tell	74	1	6013
2. Touch And Go	74	48	394
3. I've Got A Feeling (We'll Be Seeing Each Other Again)	76	41	387
4. La La Peace Song	74	46	296
5. I Won't Last A Day Without You/Let Me Be The One	75	61	225
Hank WILSON ▶1327			
[see also Leon Russell]			
1. Roll In My Sweet Baby's Arms	73	66	95
Jackie WILSON ▶908			
1. (I Can Feel Those Vibrations) This Love Is Real	71	64	195

	Year	Peak	Points
2. Love Is Funny That Way	71	75	112
3. Let This Be A Letter (To My Baby)	70	95	17
Meri WILSON ▶851			
1. Telephone Man	77	25^2	774
Nancy WILSON ▶1412			
1. Can't Take My Eyes Off You	70	82	59
Jesse WINCHESTER ▶1450			
1. Nothing But A Breeze	77	82	47
Pete WINGFIELD ▶705			
1. Eighteen With A Bullet	75	14	1386
WINGS - see Paul **McCARTNEY & WINGS / WINGS**			
Edgar WINTER ▶1116			
Groups: Edgar Winter's White Trash / The Edgar Winter Group			
1. River's Risin'	74	53	257
Ruby WINTERS ▶1159			
1. Guess Who	70	69	126
2. Love Me Now	74	95	13
Bill WITHERS ▶86			
1. Lean On Me	72	1^2	5779
2. Ain't No Sunshine	71	4^2	4309
3. Use Me	72	5	2024
4. Lovely Day	78	23	774
5. Kissing My Love	73	26^2	702
6. Grandma's Hands	71	31	544
7. Let Us Love	73	42	441
8. The Same Love That Made Me Laugh	74	43^2	419
9. Make Love To Your Mind	76	67	203
Bobby WOMACK ▶176			
1. Lookin' For A Love	74	8	1974
2. That's The Way I Feel About Cha	72	22	855
3. Nobody Wants You When You're Down And Out	73	30^2	791
4. Harry Hippie	73	25	760
5. Woman's Gotta Have It	72	32	695
#2 & 5: (The Preacher) BOBBY WOMACK & Peace			
6. Sweet Caroline (Good Times Never Seemed So Good)	72	42	468
#4 & 6: BOBBY WOMACK & Peace			
7. You're Welcome, Stop On By	74	53^2	300
8. Across 110th Street	73	49	288
(Performed by Bobby Womack & Peace)			
9. Check It Out	75	74	120
10. Daylight	76	88	31
11. More Than I Can Stand	70	90	24
Stevie WONDER ▶6			
Group: Diana Ross, Marvin Gaye, Smokey Robinson & Stevie Wonder			
1. Superstition	73	1^2	6156
2. Signed, Sealed, Delivered I'm Yours	70	1	5676

	Year	Peak	Points
Stevie WONDER – cont'd			
3. Boogie On Reggae Woman	75	1	5012
4. I Wish	77	1	4697
5. You Haven't Done Nothin'	74	1	4684
6. Higher Ground	73	1	4208
7. You Are The Sunshine Of My Life	73	1	3682
8. Sir Duke	77	1	3468
9. Send One Your Love	79	5^3	2818
10. Living For The City	74	6^2	2455
11. Heaven Help Us All	70	9^2	1891
12. We Can Work It Out	71	9	1859
13. If You Really Love Me	71	9^2	1855
14. Don't You Worry 'Bout A Thing	74	10	1394
15. Never Had A Dream Come True	70	22	744
16. Superwoman (Where Were You When I Needed You)	72	32	703
17. Another Star	77	36	400
18. As	77	69^2	175
19. Keep On Running	72	76	103
Lauren WOOD ▶948			
1. Please Don't Leave	79	31^2	526
Betty WRIGHT ▶272			
1. Clean Up Woman	72	4^2	3123
2. Baby Sitter	72	41	441
3. Secretary	74	48	326
4. Where Is The Love	75	73	107
5. It's Hard To Stop (Doing Something When It's Good To You)	73	83	74
6. I Love The Way You Love	71	84	67
7. Let Me Be Your Lovemaker	73	84	40
8. If You Love Me Like You Say You Love Me	72	98	6
Gary WRIGHT ▶189			
1. Dream Weaver	76	1	5579
2. Love Is Alive	76	3	3443
3. Phantom Writer	77	53^2	202
4. Made To Love You	76	97	6
O.V. WRIGHT ▶1105			
1. Ace Of Spade	70	61^2	267
Tammy WYNETTE ▶1598			
1. 'Til I Make It On My Own	76	91	14
YONAH ▶1648			
1. After The First One	79	97	8
John Paul YOUNG ▶537			
1. Love Is In The Air	78	13^2	1479
2. Yesterday's Hero	76	44	357
3. Lost In Your Love	79	68	146
Karen YOUNG ▶1527			
1. Hot Shot	78	90	26

	Year	Peak	Points
Neil YOUNG ▶164			
Group: **Crosby, Stills, Nash & Young**			
Duo: **Neil Young and Graham Nash**			
1. Heart Of Gold	72	1	6473
2. Only Love Can Break Your Heart	70	20	872
3. Old Man	72	26	594
4. Cinnamon Girl	70	56^2	286
5. Walk On	74	54	255
6. Four Strong Winds	79	69^2	128
7. Rust Never Sleeps (My My, Hey Hey [Into The Black])	79	94	15
#4 & 7: NEIL YOUNG With Crazy Horse			
8. When You Dance I Can Really Love	71	93	10
Frank ZAPPA ▶904			
1. Dancin' Fool	79	45	268
2. Don't Eat The Yellow Snow	74	62	183
Lena ZAVARONI ▶1423			
1. Ma! (He's Making Eyes At Me)	74	81	58
Warren ZEVON ▶807			
1. Werewolves Of London	78	15^2	913
ZWOL ▶1319			
1. New York City	78	81	49
2. Call Out My Name	79	95	13

DUOS

	Year	Peak	Points
The ADDRISI BROTHERS ▶420			
1. We've Got To Get It On Again	72	15	1163
2. Slow Dancin' Don't Turn Me On	77	18	997
3. Never My Love	78	69	171
4. Ghost Dancer	79	65	125
5. Does She Do It Like She Dances	77	85^2	60
6. I Can Feel You	72	90	24
ALESSI ▶1469			
1. Oh Lori	77	84^2	42
AMERICA ▶1221			
Group: **America (Gerry Beckley, Dewey Bunnell, Dan Peek)**			
Solo: **Dan Peek**			
1. California Dreamin'	79	62	170
PAUL ANKA With ODIA COATES ▶583			
Solos: **Paul Anka, Odia Coates**			
1. One Man Woman/One Woman Man	75	7	2143
APPLE & APPLEBERRY ▶1640			
1. What Do You Know About Love	74	97	9
ASHFORD & SIMPSON ▶819			
Solo: **Valerie Ashford**			
1. Found A Cure	79	35	508
2. Don't Cost You Nothing	78	66^2	161
Ashford And Simpson			

Artist / Song	Year	Peak	Points
The ASYLUM CHOIR ▶1654			
1. Tryin' To Stay 'live	72	98^2	7
BARBRA & NEIL ▶312			
Solos: Barbra Streisand, Neil Diamond			
Duo: Barbra Streisand/Donna Summer			
1. You Don't Bring Me Flowers	78	1^3	6531
BATDORF & RODNEY ▶1051			
Group: Silver (John Batdorf)			
1. Somewhere In The Night	76	74	157
2. You Are A Song	75	80	70
BECKMEIER BROTHERS ▶1226			
1. Rock And Roll Dancin'	79	57	167
BELL & JAMES ▶747			
1. Livin' It Up (Friday Night)	79	16^2	1165
BELLAMY BROTHERS ▶293			
Solo: David Bellamy			
1. Let Your Love Flow	76	1	5282
2. If I Said You Had A Beautiful Body Would You Hold It Against Me	79	58	225
3. Satin Sheets	76	77	51
4. Hell Cat	76	93	14
Jane BIRKIN & Serge GAINSBOURG ▶1551			
1. Je T'Aime...Moi Non Plus	70	92	20
Terry BLACK And Laurel WARD ▶1177			
1. Goin' Down (On The Road To L.A.)	72	59	201
Jack BLANCHARD & Misty MORGAN ▶652			
1. Tennessee Bird Walk	70	14	1281
2. Humphrey The Camel	70	81	66
BLUES BROTHERS ▶603			
Solo: John Belushi			
1. Soul Man	79	9^2	1377
2. Rubber Biscuit	79	42^2	295
The BRECKER BROTHERS ▶1047			
Group: Spyro Gyra (Michael and Randy Brecker)			
1. Sneakin' Up Behind You	75	47	347
BREWER And SHIPLEY ▶494			
1. One Toke Over The Line Brewer & Shipley	71	8	1989
2. Tarkio Road	71	39	501
3. Yankee Lady	72	90	16
The BROTHERS JOHNSON ▶379			
1. I'll Be Good To You	76	7	1922
2. Strawberry Letter 23	77	8	1713
3. Get The Funk Out Ma Face	76	34	548
James BROWN - Lyn COLLINS ▶1078			
Solos: James Brown, Lyn Collins			
1. What My Baby Needs Now Is A Little More Lovin'	73	51	295

Artist / Song	Year	Peak	Points
The BUGGLES ▶1004			
1. Video Killed The Radio Star	79	40	418
Eric BURDON & Jimmy WITHERSPOON ▶1557			
Group: Eric Burdon & War			
1. Soledad	71	91	20
Jerry BUTLER And Brenda Lee EAGER ▶762			
Duo: Gene & Jerry			
Solo: Jerry Butler			
1. Ain't Understanding Mellow	72	24	1057
Glen CAMPBELL/Anne MURRAY ▶1344			
Solos: Glen Campbell, Anne Murray			
Duo: Bobbie Gentry & Glen Campbell			
1. I Say A Little Prayer/By The Time I Get To Phoenix	71	72	89
CAPTAIN & TENNILLE ▶39			
1. Lonely Night (Angel Face) Captain And Tennille	76	1	6099
2. Love Will Keep Us Together	75	1^2	5787
3. Muskrat Love	76	2^5	5490
4. The Way I Want To Touch You	75	3	3279
5. Shop Around	76	6^2	2673
6. You Never Done It Like That	78	10^3	1670
7. Can't Stop Dancin'	77	17^2	881
8. You Need A Woman Tonight	79	36	416
9. Por Amor Viviremos	75	57	206
#2 & 9: The CAPTAIN & TENNILLE			
10. I'm On My Way	78	86	46
CARPENTERS ▶4			
1. (They Long To Be) Close To You	70	1^2	6997
2. We've Only Just Begun	70	1	6257
3. Superstar	71	2^2	5746
4. Top Of The World	73	1	5421
5. Please Mr. Postman	75	1	5055
6. Hurting Each Other	72	2^2	4861
7. Yesterday Once More	73	1	4436
8. Rainy Days And Mondays	71	2	4430
9. Sing	73	5^3	3463
10. For All We Know	71	6^2	2535
11. Goodbye To Love	72	7	1875
12. Only Yesterday	75	8	1798
13. I Won't Last A Day Without You	74	9	1612
14. There's A Kind Of Hush (All Over The World)	76	12^2	1464
15. It's Going To Take Some Time	72	17	981
16. Solitaire	75	15	885
17. Calling Occupants Of Interplanetary Craft	77	24	831
18. I Need To Be In Love	76	31	691
19. Sweet, Sweet Smile	78	42^2	485

	Year	Peak	Points
CARPENTERS – cont'd			
20. All You Get From Love Is A Love Song	77	43	422
21. Merry Christmas Darling	70	41	171
22. I Believe You	78	70	133
23. Ticket To Ride	70	78	74
24. Goofus	76	87	32
Johnny CASH & June CARTER ▶936			
Solo: Johnny Cash			
1. If I Were A Carpenter	70	26	547
CASHMAN & WEST ▶704			
Duo: The Buchanan Brothers			
Solo: Terry Cashman			
1. American City Suite	72	28	640
2. Songman	73	54	257
3. The King Of Rock 'N' Roll	73	98	4
CATE BROTHERS ▶738			
1. Union Man	76	32^2	876
2. Can't Change My Heart	76	73	102
CECILIO & KAPONO ▶1594			
1. Goodnight And Goodmorning	76	95	14
CHANSON ▶787			
1. Don't Hold Back	79	20	958
CHEECH & CHONG ▶244			
1. Earache My Eye (Featuring Alice Bowie)	74	4^2	2271
2. Basketball Jones Featuring Tyrone Shoelaces	73	13	1207
Cheech Y Chong			
3. Sister Mary Elephant (Shudd-Up!)	74	36^2	697
4. Framed	76	46	360
5. Bloat On Featuring The Bloaters	77	47	353
[see also: Float On]			
6. Black Lassie (Featuring Johnny Stash)	74	47	332
7. (How I Spent My Summer Vacation) Or A Day At The Beach With Pedro And Man - Part I	75	53	151
CHEE-CHEE And PEPPY ▶890			
1. I Know I'm In Love	71	35	649
Dave And Ansil COLLINS ▶869			
1. Double Barrel	71	27	717
David CROSBY / Graham NASH ▶804			
Solos: David Crosby, Graham Nash			
Groups: Crosby, Stills, Nash & Young			
Crosby, Stills & Nash			
Duos: Graham Nash & David Crosby			
Neil Young & Graham Nash			
1. Carry Me	75	44^2	333
2. Out Of The Darkness	76	77	70
Cherie & Marie CURRIE ▶1511			
1. Since You've Been Gone	79	91	30

	Year	Peak	Points
DEARDORFF & JOSEPH ▶1682			
1. Never Have To Say Goodbye Again	77	99	3
DELANEY & BONNIE ▶730			
Group: Delaney & Bonnie & Friends			
1. Only You Know And I Know	71	18^2	888
2. Move 'Em Out	72	68	123
DELBERT & GLEN ▶1399			
1. I Received A Letter	72	80	65
"DELIVERANCE" Soundtrack ▶388			
[Eric Weissberg, Steve Mandell]			
1. Dueling Banjos	73	1	4862
Barry DeVORZON and Perry BOTKIN, Jr. ▶546			
1. Nadia's Theme (The Young And The Restless)	76	5	2466
EDDIE & DUTCH ▶1274			
1. My Wife, The Dancer	70	68	127
ENGLAND DAN & John Ford COLEY ▶150			
1. I'd Really Love To See You Tonight	76	4^2	3478
2. Nights Are Forever Without You	76	10^2	1491
3. It's Sad To Belong	77	13^2	1369
4. Love Is The Answer	79	13	1209
5. We'll Never Have To Say Goodbye Again	78	14^2	1055
6. Gone Too Far	77	17^2	882
7. What Can I Do With This Broken Heart	79	64	150
8. You Can't Dance	78	74	74
EUCLID BEACH BAND ▶1599			
1. I Need You	79	93	14
FERRANTE & TEICHER ▶568			
1. Midnight Cowboy	70	10	1879
2. Lay Lady Lay	70	71	96
Roberta FLACK & Donny HATHAWAY ▶447			
Solos: Roberta Flack, Donny Hathaway			
1. Where Is The Love	72	7^2	2149
2. You've Got A Friend	71	28	716
3. You've Lost That Lovin' Feelin'	71	57	251
FLASH & The PAN ▶1380			
1. Hey, St. Peter	79	76	72
Dan FOGELBERG / Tim WEISBERG ▶886			
Solo: Dan Fogelberg			
1. The Power Of Gold	78	23^2	652
The FORCE ▶1582			
1. The Star Wars Stars	77	94^2	16

	Year	Peak	Points
GALLAGHER and LYLE ▶1188			
Group: **McGuinness Flint** (Benny Gallagher, Graham Lyle)			
1. I Wanna Stay With You	76	79	58
2. Heart On My Sleeve	76	89	25
3. Every Little Teardrop	77	92	8
Gallagher & Lyle			
GARY & DAVE ▶1408			
1. Could You Ever Love Me Again	74	91³	61
Marvin GAYE & Tammi TERRELL ▶1216			
[Marvin Gaye & Valerie Simpson]			
Solos: **Marvin Gaye, Valerie Simpson**			
Duo: **Diana Ross Marvin Gaye**			
Group: **Diana Ross, Marvin Gaye, Smokey Robinson & Stevie Wonder**			
1. California Soul	70	63	171
GAYLORD & HOLIDAY ▶1400			
1. Eh! Cumpari	76	79	64
GENE & JERRY ▶1371			
Solos: **Gene Chandler, Jerry Butler**			
Duo: **Jerry Butler & Brenda Lee Eager**			
1. You Just Can't Win (By Making The Same Mistake)	71	76	77
Bobbie GENTRY & Glen CAMPBELL ▶877			
Solos: **Bobbie Gentry, Glen Campbell**			
Duo: **Glen Campbell/Anne Murray**			
1. All I Have To Do Is Dream	70	31	678
GRAND CANYON ▶1181			
1. Evil Boll-Weevil	74	61	198
The HAGERS ▶1429			
1. Love My Life Away	74	84	57
Daryl HALL & John OATES ▶95			
1. Rich Girl	77	1²	5243
2. Sara Smile	76	6	2903
3. She's Gone	76	6³	2789
[reissue--see #6]			
4. It's A Laugh	78	21	756
5. Back Together Again	77	25	628
6. She's Gone	74	52	353
7. I Don't Wanna Lose You	79	44²	322
8. Do What You Want, Be What You Are	77	55²	295
9. Why Do Lovers (Break Each Other's Heart?)	77	87	43
10. It's Uncanny	77	84	41
Isaac HAYES & David PORTER ▶1217			
Solo: **Isaac Hayes**			
1. Ain't That Loving You (For More Reasons Than One)	72	67	171

	Year	Peak	Points
Justin HAYWARD And John LODGE ▶916			
Solo: **Justin Hayward**			
Group: **The Moody Blues**			
1. I Dreamed Last Night	75	45	348
2. Blue Guitar	76	82	79
Justin Hayward & John Lodge			
HOLLAND-DOZIER ▶833			
Solo: **Lamont Dozier**			
1. Why Can't We Be Lovers	72	48	367
Holland-Dozier featuring Lamont Dozier			
2. Don't Leave Me Starvin' For Your Love (Part 1)	73	49	277
Holland-Dozier featuring Brian Holland			
HUDSON And LANDRY ▶979			
1. Ajax Liquor Store	71	61²	229
2. Ajax Airlines	72	81	103
Hudson & Landry			
JOHN & ERNEST ▶1007			
1. Super Fly Meets Shaft	73	43	414
Elton JOHN and Kiki DEE ▶339			
Solos: **Elton John, Kiki Dee**			
Groups: **The Elton John Band**			
The Kiki Dee Band			
1. Don't Go Breaking My Heart	76	1³	5752
The KENDALLS ▶984			
1. Heaven's Just A Sin Away	78	47	473
Mac And Katie KISSOON ▶750			
1. Chirpy Chirpy Cheep Cheep	71	18	1116
Kris KRISTOFFERSON & Rita COOLIDGE ▶870			
Solos: **Kris Kristofferson, Rita Coolidge**			
1. A Song I'd Like To Sing	74	33	523
2. Loving Arms	74	97	7
LaVERNE & SHIRLEY ▶1305			
1. Sixteen Reasons	76	69	108
LE BLANC & CARR ▶551			
Solo: **Lenny Le Blanc**			
1. Falling	78	11	1603
2. Something About You	77	55	213
3. Midnight Light	78	94	14
LOGGINS & MESSINA ▶179			
Solo: **Kenny Loggins**			
1. Your Mama Don't Dance	73	5²	2892
Kenny Loggins And Jim Messina			
[Alt. label: Ken Loggins With Jim Messina]			
2. Thinking Of You	73	11	1503
3. My Music	73	13	1218
4. Growin'	75	45	437
5. Watching The River Run	74	41	297
6. Changes	75	62²	217
7. Vahevala (Pronounced Va-Hēē-Va-La)	72	83	42
[Alt. label: Vahevella Ken Loggins With Jim Messina]			

Artist / Song	Year	Peak	Points
LOGGINS & MESSINA – cont'd			
8. Nobody But You	72	88	27
#7 & 8: *Kenny Loggins With Jim Messina*			
9. I Like It Like That	75	92	18
10. A Lover's Question	75	94	11
Loretta LYNN/Conway TWITTY ▶1231			
Solos: **Loretta Lynn, Conway Twitty**			
Duo: **Conway Twitty Loretta Lynn**			
1. As Soon As I Hang Up The Phone	74	81	63
MARK-ALMOND ▶1593			
1. One Way Sunday	72	94	14
MARSHALL HAIN ▶969			
1. Dancing In The City	79	39	498
Johnny Mathis/Deniece Williams ▶355			
Solos: **Johnny Mathis, Deniece Williams**			
1. Too Much, Too Little, Too Late	78	2^3	4866
2. You're All I Need To Get By	78	67^2	173
Les McCANN & Eddie HARRIS ▶1612			
1. Compared To What	70	96	12
Paul & Linda McCARTNEY ▶383			
Groups: **Paul McCartney/Wings**			
The Beatles			
Solo: **Paul McCartney**			
1. Uncle Albert/Admiral Halsey	71	1	4963
Marilyn McCOO & Billy DAVIS Jr. ▶242			
Group: **The 5th Dimension**			
1. You Don't Have To Be A Star (To Be In My Show)	77	1^2	5541
2. Your Love	77	16	955
3. Look What You've Done To My Heart	77	61	220
4. I Hope We Get To Love In Time	76	71	137
McFADDEN & WHITEHEAD ▶658			
1. Ain't No Stoppin' Us Now	79	12^2	1604
Kristy And Jimmy McNICHOL ▶1454			
1. He's So Fine	78	83	46
MEL and TIM ▶555			
1. Starting All Over Again	72	18	1729
2. Good Guys Only Win In The Movies	70	42	378
The MONKEES ▶1584			
[Mickey Dolenz and Davy Jones]			
Solo: **Davy Jones**			
1. Oh My My	70	94	16
MOUTH & MacNEAL ▶506			
1. How Do You Do?	72	5	2554
2. Hey, You Love	72	68	112

Artist / Song	Year	Peak	Points
Graham NASH & David CROSBY ▶804			
Solos: **Graham Nash, David Crosby**			
Duos: **Neil Young & Graham Nash**			
David Crosby / Graham Nash			
Groups: **Crosby, Stills, Nash & Young**			
Crosby, Stills & Nash			
1. Immigration Man	72	31	488
Karen NELSON And BILLY T ▶1611			
1. Love Me One Time (Just For Old Times' Sake)	77	96	12
NINO & APRIL ▶1537			
Group: **Nino Tempo And 5th Ave. Sax**			
Solo: **April**			
1. Put It Where You Want It	73	91	22
Carroll O'CONNOR And Jean STAPLETON ▶1310			
1. Those Were The Days	72	79	103
CARROLL O'CONNOR AND JEAN STAPLETON (As The Bunkers)			
Donny And Marie OSMOND ▶199			
Solos: **Donny Osmond, Marie Osmond**			
Group: **Osmond Brothers**			
1. I'm Leaving It (All) Up To You	74	7^2	2093
2. Morning Side Of The Mountain	75	6	1896
[Alt. label: *Donny & Marie Osmond*]			
3. Deep Purple	76	20	1248
4. Ain't Nothing Like The Real Thing	77	30	757
5. (You're My) Soul And Inspiration	78	46	359
6. Make The World Go Away	75	45	300
7. On The Shelf	78	53	269
#4, 5 & 7: *Donny & Marie*			
PEACHES & HERB ▶172			
1. Reunited	79	1^4	7111
2. Shake Your Groove Thing	79	5^3	2720
3. We've Got Love	79	47	262
4. The Sound Of Silence	71	94	9
The PEPPERS (s) ▶1100			
1. Pepper Box	74	61	272
PINK LADY ▶1076			
1. Kiss In The Dark	79	49	296
The PIPKINS (s) ▶591			
Groups (s): **The Brotherhood Of Man, Edison Lighthouse, First Class, White Plains** (Tony Burrows, all groups)			
Solo: **Tony Burrows**			
1. Gimme Dat Ding	70	7^2	2087
The POPPY FAMILY ▶703			
Solos: **Susan Jacks, Terry Jacks**			
Group: **The Poppy Family** (Susan and Terry Jacks, Craig McCaw, Satwant Singh)			
1. Where Evil Grows	71	50^2	559
THE POPPY FAMILY Vocal: Susan and Terry Jacks			
2. Good Friends?	72	74	90
3. No Good To Cry	71	80	54

	Year	Peak	Points
POPPY FAMILY – cont'd			
4. I Was Wondering	71	90	22
#2 & 4: THE POPPY FAMILY Vocal: Susan Jacks			
PRATT & McCLAIN ▶573			
1. Happy Days	76	6^2	2240
Charley PRIDE/Henry MANCINI ▶1655			
Solo: Charley Pride			
Group: Henry Mancini And His Orchestra			
1. All His Children	72	95	7
CHARLEY PRIDE arranged and conducted by HENRY MANCINI			
James & Bobby PURIFY ▶1278			
1. Do Your Thing	75	71	125
Suzi QUATRO And Chris NORMAN ▶590			
Solo: Suzi Quatro			
Group: Smokie (Chris Norman)			
1. Stumblin' In	79	6^2	2098
The RAES ▶1222			
1. A Little Lovin' (Keeps The Doctor Away)	79	66	170
The RIGHTEOUS BROTHERS ▶372			
1. Rock And Roll Heaven	74	4^2	3199
2. Dream On	74	32^3	553
3. Give It To The People	74	27	539
Diana ROSS & Marvin GAYE ▶503			
Solos: Diana Ross, Marvin Gaye			
Duos: Diana Ross & Michael Jackson			
Marvin Gaye & Tammi Terrell			
Group: Diana Ross, Marvin Gaye, Smokey Robinson & Stevie Wonder			
1. You're A Special Part Of Me	73	14^2	1031
2. My Mistake (Was To Love You)	74	20^2	965
3. Don't Knock My Love	74	38	375
Diana ROSS & Michael JACKSON ▶937			
Solos: Diana Ross, Michael Jackson			
Duo: Diana Ross & Marvin Gaye			
Groups: The Jackson 5			
Diana Ross, Marvin Gaye, Smokey Robinson & Stevie Wonder			
1. Ease On Down The Road	78	36	541
David & Jimmy RUFFIN ▶1095			
Solos: David Ruffin, Jimmy Ruffin			
1. Stand By Me	70	57	274
Leon & Mary RUSSELL ▶1092			
Solos: Leon Russell, Hank Snow			
1. Rainbow In Your Eyes	76	62	275
SAILCAT ▶752			
1. Motorcycle Mama	72	19	1111
SAM & DAVE ▶1610			
1. Don't Pull Your Love	71	96	12
The SANFORD/TOWNSEND BAND ▶665			
1. Smoke From A Distant Fire	77	9	1539
Carlos SANTANA & Buddy MILES ▶1234			
Groups: Buddy Miles & The Freedom Express			
Santana (Carlos Santana)			
Solo: Buddy Miles			
1. Evil Ways	72	67	160
SEALS & CROFTS ▶102			
1. Get Closer	76	7	2381
SEALS & CROFTS (Featuring Carolyn Willis)			
2. Summer Breeze	72	6	2203
3. Diamond Girl	73	8	1940
4. Hummingbird	73	15	1092
5. We May Never Pass This Way (Again)	73	18^2	1010
6. I'll Play For You	75	35^2	922
7. You're The Love	78	20	860
8. My Fair Share	77	25^2	724
9. King Of Nothing	74	50	297
10. Unborn Child	74	65	187
11. Baby, I'll Give It To You	76	88	28
12. Castles In The Sand	75	97	5
SHEPSTONE & DIBBENS ▶1312			
1. Shady Lady	73	68	103
SIMON & GARFUNKEL ▶91			
Solos: Paul Simon, Art Garfunkel			
Duo: Paul Simon/Phoebe Snow			
Group: Art Garfunkel with James Taylor & Paul Simon			
1. Bridge Over Troubled Water	70	1^4	8291
2. Cecilia	70	1	4323
3. My Little Town	75	7^3	2112
4. El Condor Pasa	70	11	1490
5. For Emily, Whenever I May Find Her	72	72	111
Carly SIMON & James TAYLOR ▶422			
Solos: Carly Simon, James Taylor			
Group: Art Garfunkel with James Taylor & Paul Simon			
1. Mockingbird	74	3^2	3584
2. Devoted To You	78	48	260
Carly Simon and James Taylor			
Paul SIMON/Phoebe SNOW ▶834			
Solos: Paul Simon, Phoebe Snow			
Duo: Simon & Garfunkel			
Group: Art Garfunkel with James Taylor & Paul Simon			
1. Gone At Last	75	20	848
PAUL SIMON/PHOEBE SNOW and The Jessy Dixon Singers			
SONNY & CHER ▶270			
Solo: Cher			
1. A Cowboy's Work Is Never Done	72	6	2828
2. All I Ever Need Is You	72	6	2440
3. When You Say Love	72	30	571

	Year	Peak	Points
SONNY & CHER – cont'd			
4. Mama Was A Rock And Roll Singer, Papa Used To Write All Her Songs	73	60²	188
SPLINTER ▶1240			
1. Costafine Town	75	69	151
STARK & McBRIEN ▶1265			
1. Isn't It Lonely Together	75	69	133
STEVE & EYDIE ▶1237			
Solo: **Eydie Gorme**			
1. We Can Make It Together STEVE & EYDIE featuring The Osmonds	72	64	156
STONEY AND MEATLOAF ▶1360			
Solo: **Meatloaf**			
1. What You See Is What You Get	71	79	82
Barbra STREISAND/Donna SUMMER ▶376			
Solos: **Barbra Streisand, Donna Summer** Duo: **Barbra & Neil**			
1. No More Tears (Enough Is Enough)	79	1	5100
SWEET DREAMS ▶1246			
Group: **Pickettywitch (Polly Brown)**			
1. Honey Honey	74	69²	148
The TARNEY/SPENCER BAND ▶943			
1. No Time To Lose	79	66	160
2. I'm Your Man Rock 'N' Roll	76	71	85
3. It's Really You	78	89	31
TEEGARDEN & VAN WINKLE ▶662			
1. God, Love And Rock & Roll	70	14²	1251
2. Everything Is Going To Be Alright	71	91	22
TIN TIN ▶677			
1. Toast And Marmalade For Tea	71	16	1074
2. Is That The Way	71	67	140
John TRAVOLTA And Olivia NEWTON-JOHN ▶224			
Solos: **John Travolta, Olivia Newton-John**			
1. You're The One That I Want	78	3⁴	5793
2. Summer Nights John Travolta, Olivia Newton-John & Cast	78	3²	2832
TUFANO & GIAMMARESE ▶1259			
1. Music Everywhere	73	70²	137
Ike & Tina TURNER ▶240			
Group: **Ike & Tina Turner & the Ikettes**			
1. Proud Mary	71	5²	2760
2. Nutbush City Limits	73	26	874
3. Ooh Poo Pah Doo	71	37	486
4. Sexy Ida (Part 2)	75	67	227
5. Baby--Get It On	75	70	113
6. Bold Soul Sister	70	74	112
7. I'm Yours (Use Me Anyway You Wanna)	71	80	88

	Year	Peak	Points
8. Up In Heah	72	70	71
9. Workin' Together	70	91²	39
Conway TWITTY Loretta LYNN ▶1231			
Solos: **Conway Twitty, Loretta Lynn** Duo: **Loretta Lynn/Conway Twitty**			
1. After The Fire Is Gone	71	90	44
VIGRASS & OSBORNE ▶1067			
1. Men Of Learning	72	45	308
WAYLON & WILLIE ▶818			
Solos: **Waylon Jennings, Willie Nelson**			
1. Good Hearted Woman	76	37²	412
2. Mammas Don't Let Your Babies Grow Up To Be Cowboys	78	44	258
Andy & David WILLIAMS ▶1392			
1. What's Your Name	74	73	68
Neil YOUNG and Graham NASH ▶1147			
Solos: **Neil Young, Graham Nash** Duo: **David Crosby & Graham Nash** Groups: **Crosby, Stills, Nash & Young** **Crosby, Stills & Nash**			
1. War Song NEIL YOUNG and GRAHAM NASH with the Stray Gators	72	52	224

GROUPS

	Year	Peak	Points
ABBA ▶60			
1. Dancing Queen	77	1	4541
2. Take A Chance On Me	78	5²	2544
3. Fernando	76	10²	1692
4. Waterloo ABBA (Bjorn, Benny, Anna & Frida)	74	10²	1518
5. SOS	75	12	1438
6. Knowing Me, Knowing You	77	11²	1322
7. The Name Of The Game	78	16²	1129
8. I Do, I Do, I Do, I Do, I Do	76	19	1128
9. Does Your Mother Know	79	16²	1116
10. Mamma Mia	76	36³	791
11. Honey, Honey	74	37	445
12. Money, Money, Money	77	63	204
13. Angeleyes [Alt. title: Angel Eyes]	79	76	78
14. Voulez-Vous//Angeleyes [TSW]	79	85²	28
15. Voulez-Vous	79	86	13
ABRAHAM'S CHILDREN ▶1397			
1. Gypsy	73	78	66
AC/DC ▶1175			
1. Highway To Hell	79	57	203

	Year	Peak	Points
ACE ▶359			
1. How Long	75	1	4818
2. Rock & Roll Runaway	75	63	131
ACE SPECTRUM ▶1434			
1. Don't Send Nobody Else	74	84	53
ACT I ▶1687			
1. Friends Or Lovers	73	99	2
Cannonball ADDERLEY QUINTET ▶1548			
1. Country Preacher	70	93	20
AEROSMITH ▶152			
1. Dream On [reissue--longer version of #6]	76	6^2	2839
2. Walk This Way	77	7	2047
3. Last Child	76	21	894
4. Come Together	78	20	718
5. Sweet Emotion	75	36	522
6. Dream On	73	43	454
7. Draw The Line	77	37	409
8. Back In The Saddle	77	67	148
9. Kings And Queens	78	80	68
10. Home Tonight	76	89	32
AFRIQUE (s) ▶986			
Group: **Paul Humphrey & His Cool Aid Chemists** (Paul Humphrey)			
1. Soul Makossa	73	41	470
AIRWAVES ▶1464			
1. So Hard Livin' Without You	78	82	43
ALICE COOPER ▶162			
Solo: **Alice Cooper**			
1. School's Out	72	6^3	2692
2. Eighteen	71	21^2	935
3. No More Mr. Nice Guy	73	26	874
4. Elected	72	18	804
5. Teenage Lament '74	74	24^2	657
6. Hello Hurray	73	25	597
7. Be My Lover	72	36	435
8. Billion Dollar Babies	73	36	338
9. Under My Wheels	72	74	112
10. Caught In A Dream	71	86	41
ALIVE AND KICKING ▶471			
Group: **Brooklyn Dreams** (Bruce Sudano)			
1. Tighter, Tighter	70	5	2844
2. Just Let It Come *Alive 'N Kickin'*	70	49	292

	Year	Peak	Points
The **ALLMAN BROTHERS BAND** ▶314			
Groups: **Delaney & Bonnie And Friends Featuring Eric Clapton** (Duane Allman) **Sea Level** (Jai Johnny Johanson, Chuck Leavell, Lamar Williams) **Gregg Allman Band** (Gregg Allman) Solo: **Gregg Allman**			
1. Ramblin' Man	73	1	4277
2. Jessica	74	33	505
3. Crazy Love	79	41	289
4. Ain't Wastin' Time No More	72	72	67
Herb ALPERT & The TIJUANA BRASS ▶893			
Solo: **Herb Alpert**			
1. Last Tango In Paris Herb Alpert & The TJB	73	70	146
2. Fox Hunt Herb Alpert and the T.J.B.	74	70	124
3. Jerusalem	70	74	79
The **AMAZING RHYTHM ACES** ▶609			
1. Third Rate Romance	75	17	979
2. The End Is Not In Sight (The Cowboy Tune)	76	56	290
3. Amazing Grace (Used To Be Her Favorite Song)	76	77	74
AMBROSIA ▶271			
1. How Much I Feel	78	2^3	4014
2. Holdin' On To Yesterday	75	18	998
3. Magical Mystery Tour	77	41	335
4. Nice, Nice, Very Nice	75	78	90
5. Can't Let A Woman	76	88^2	37
AMERICA ▶57			
Duo: **America** (Gerry Beckley, Dewey Bunnell) Solo: **Dan Peek**			
1. A Horse With No Name	72	1^3	6631
2. Sister Golden Hair	75	2	3718
3. Tin Man	74	6	1829
4. Ventura Highway	72	8^2	1790
5. I Need You	72	8	1757
6. Lonely People	75	10^2	1605
7. Daisy Jane	75	27	842
8. Today's The Day	76	24	751
9. Don't Cross The River	73	20	720
10. Muskrat Love	73	33	436
11. Woman Tonight	76	42	399
12. Only In Your Heart	73	58^2	257
13. Amber Cascades	76	99	3
ANACOSTIA ▶1315			
Group: **The Presidents** (Tony Boyd, Archie Powell, Billy Shorter)			
1. On And Off (Part 1)	73	76	99

	Year	Peak	Points
ANGEL ▶973			
1. Ain't Gonna Eat Out My Heart Anymore	78	56	221
2. That Magic Touch	77	74	121
APOLLO 100 (s) ▶576			
1. Joy	72	6	1901
2. Mendelssohn's 4th (Second Movement)	72	93	9
APRIL WINE ▶660			
Group: **Mashmakhan** (Jerry Mercer)			
1. You Could Have Been A Lady	72	27^2	709
2. Roller	79	47^2	327
3. Bad Side Of The Moon	72	90	24
The **ARCHIES** (s) ▶407			
Solos: **Andy Kim, Ron Dante**			
The **Cuff Links** (s): (Ron Dante)			
1. Jingle Jangle	70	8^2	2509
2. Sunshine	70	30	556
3. Who's Your Baby?	70	29	543
ARGENT ▶509			
Group: **Charlie** (Bob Henrit)			
1. Hold Your Head Up	72	5	2585
2. Tragedy	72	81	51
ARKADE ▶1202			
Solo: **Austin Roberts**			
1. The Morning Of Our Lives	71	67	183
ARPEGGIO (s) ▶1562			
1. Love And Desire (Part I)	79	91	19
ARTHUR, HURLEY & GOTTLIEB ▶1636			
1. Sunshine Ship	73	96	9
ASHTON, GARDNER & DYKE ▶949			
1. Resurrection Shuffle	71	37	526
The **ASSEMBLED MULTITUDE** (s) ▶659			
1. Overture From Tommy (A Rock Opera)	70	16^2	1205
2. Woodstock	70	78	98
The **ASSOCIATION** ▶1199			
1. Names, Tags, Numbers & Labels	73	85	53
2. Darling Be Home Soon	72	90	20
3. Just About The Same	70	91	14
The **ATLANTA DISCO BAND** (s) ▶1680			
Group: (members of) **MFSB**			
1. Bad Luck	76	99	3
ATLANTA RHYTHM SECTION ▶127			
1. So In To You	77	5^2	2557
2. Imaginary Lover	78	9^2	1802
3. I'm Not Gonna Let It Bother Me Tonight	78	16^2	1005

	Year	Peak	Points
4. Spooky	79	15	960
5. Do It Or Die	79	21^2	948
6. Doraville	74	57	305
7. Neon Nites	77	65	174
8. Dog Days	77	63	164
9. Free Spirit	76	76	126
10. Jukin	76	75^2	110
11. Champagne Jam	78	66	99
12. Angel (What In The World's Come Over Us)	75	74	88
13. Georgia Rhythm	77	77	76
AUDIENCE ▶1294			
1. Indian Summer	71	76	114
AUTOMATIC MAN ▶1461			
Group: **Santana** (Michael Shrieve)			
1. My Pearl	77	88	45
AVERAGE WHITE BAND / AWB ▶186			
1. Pick Up The Pieces	75	1	5857
2. Cut The Cake	75	12^2	1703
3. School Boy Crush	76	31	586
4. If I Ever Lose This Heaven	75	44	484
#1-4: *AWB*			
5. Queen Of My Soul	76	67	167
Average White Band			
B.C. GENERATION (s) ▶1496			
[Bob Crewe]			
1. Street Talk (Var. III)	76	86	33
B.C.G. (B. C. Generation)			
B.T. EXPRESS ▶258			
1. Do It ('Til You're Satisfied)	74	6^2	2423
2. Express	75	9	1674
3. Peace Pipe	75	40	445
4. Give It What You Got	75	46	312
5. Can't Stop Groovin' Now, Wanna Do It Some More	76	74	69
6. Close To You	76	86	29
7. Shout It Out	78	89	25
The **BABYS** ▶344			
Solo: **Jonathan Cain**			
1. Every Time I Think Of You	79	8^2	1795
2. Isn't It Time	77	8	1696
3. Silver Dreams	78	48	319
4. Head First	79	71	74
5. If You've Got The Time	77	95	12
BACHMAN-TURNER OVERDRIVE ▶97			
Groups: The **Guess Who** & **Ironhorse** (Randy Bachman)			
1. You Ain't Seen Nothing Yet	74	1	4765
2. Takin' Care Of Business	74	6	2042
3. Roll On Down The Highway	75	8	1462

	Year	Peak	Points
BACHMAN-TURNER OVERDIRVE – cont'd			
4. Let It Ride	74	14^2	1293
5. Hey You	75	16	983
6. Down To The Line	76	38^2	446
7. Take It Like A Man	76	63^2	249
8. Blue Collar	74	68	184
9. Heartaches *BTO*	79	57^2	180
10. Lookin' Out For #1	76	79	71
11. Gimme Your Money Please	76	86	44
12. My Wheels Won't Turn	77	84	41
13. Down The Road *B.T.O.*	78	92	19
BAD COMPANY ▶137 Groups: **Free** (Paul Rodgers, Simon Kirke) **Mott The Hoople** (Mick Ralphs)			
1. Can't Get Enough	74	1	4096
2. Rock 'N' Roll Fantasy	79	11^2	1680
3. Feel Like Makin' Love	75	10	1658
4. Young Blood	76	22	900
5. Movin' On	75	23^2	694
6. Good Lovin' Gone Bad	75	32	509
7. Gone, Gone, Gone	79	63	180
8. Burnin' Sky	77	83	34
9. Honey Child	76	86	33
BADFINGER ▶154 Group: **Yes** (Tony Kaye)			
1. Day After Day	72	3^3	3981
2. Come And Get It	70	6	2880
3. No Matter What	70	6	2022
4. Baby Blue	72	9^2	1354
5. Love Is Gonna Come At Last	79	79	48
6. Apple Of My Eye	74	88^2	34
George BAKER SELECTION ▶504			
1. Little Green Bag	70	16^2	1407
2. Paloma Blanca	76	22	917
3. Dear Ann	70	85	43
Ginger BAKER'S AIR FORCE ▶1459 Groups: **Traffic** (Steve Winwood, Rick (or Ric) Grech), **Wings** (Denny Laine)			
1. Man Of Constant Sorrow	70	79	45
BALCONES FAULT ▶1553			
1. Take Me Home	77	93	20
BAMA (s) ▶1581			
1. Touch Me When We're Dancing	79	93	16
The BAND ▶396 Group: **Bob Dylan / The Band**			
1. Up On Cripple Creek	70	26	998
2. Don't Do It	72	23	826

	Year	Peak	Points
3. Ain't Got No Home	74	53	279
4. Rag Mama Rag	70	50	204
5. Ophelia	76	66	103
6. Life Is A Carnival	71	80	90
7. Time To Kill	70	88	37
The BAND OF THE BLACK WATCH ▶1287			
1. Scotch On The Rocks	76	77^2	118
BANG ▶1643			
1. Questions	72	94	8
BARBARA And The UNIQUES ▶1482			
1. There It Goes Again	71	88	37
BAR-KAYS ▶683			
1. Shake Your Rump To The Funk	77	53	373
2. Son Of Shaft	72	55	357
3. Let's Have Some Fun	78	91^2	27
4. Memphis At Sunrise	72	90	23
The BARRON KNIGHTS ▶1428			
1. The Topical Song	79	76	57
[see also: The Logical Song]			
BAY CITY ROLLERS ▶101			
1. Saturday Night	75	1	5200
2. You Made Me Believe In Magic	77	7^2	2199
3. Money Honey	76	7^2	2170
4. I Only Want To Be With You	76	8^2	1708
5. The Way I Feel Tonight	78	19	988
6. Rock And Roll Love Letter	76	30^2	666
7. Yesterday's Hero	77	49	320
8. Dedication	77	70	96
BAZUKA (s) ▶653			
1. Dynomite - Part I *Tony Camillo's BAZUKA*	75	12^2	1632
The BEACH BOYS ▶257 Group: **Celebration featuring Mike Love**			
1. Rock And Roll Music	76	11^2	1727
2. It's O.K.	76	39	420
3. Good Timin'	79	33	399
4. Sail On Sailor	75	62	286
5. Add Some Music To Your Day	70	49	281
6. Surfin' U.S.A.	74	51^2	256
7. Here Comes The Night	79	52	209
8. Peggy Sue	78	66	139
9. Long Promised Road	71	79	78
10. Sail On Sailor	73	96	12

Artist / Song	Year	Peak	Points
The BEATLES ▶78			
Solos: George Harrison, John Lennon, Paul McCartney, Ringo Starr			
Duo: Paul & Linda McCartney			
Groups: John Lennon/Plastic Ono Band			
Paul McCartney & Wings / Wings			
Delaney & Bonnie And Friends			
(George Harrison as L'Angelo Misterioso)			
1. Let It Be	70	1^4	8236
2. The Long And Winding Road	70	1^2	5870
3. Got To Get You Into My Life	76	3	3336
4. Ob-La-Di, Ob-La-Da	76	47	303
5. For You Blue	70	71	74
6. Sgt. Pepper's Lonely Hearts Club Band/With A Little Help From My Friends	78	92^2	23
BEE GEES ▶1			
Solo: Robin Gibb			
1. Night Fever	78	1^8	9333
2. Stayin' Alive	78	1^4	8639
3. How Deep Is Your Love	77	1^4	8540
4. How Can You Mend A Broken Heart	71	1^3	7467
5. Jive Talkin'	75	1	6907
6. Too Much Heaven	78	2^5	6471
7. Tragedy	79	1^3	5532
8. You Should Be Dancing	76	1	4707
9. Lonely Days	71	1	4525
10. Love So Right	76	3^2	4040
11. Nights On Broadway	75	4	3323
12. Love You Inside Out	79	2^2	3048
13. Fanny (Be Tender With My Love)	76	9	1849
14. Run To Me	72	11	1549
15. My World	72	15^2	1135
16. Boogie Child	77	14^2	1123
17. Edge Of The Universe	77	26	578
18. Alive	72	26	570
19. Don't Wanna Live Inside Myself	71	39	414
20. If Only I Had My Mind On Something Else	70	76	105
21. Saw A New Morning	73	78	95
22. Mr. Natural	74	87	35
The BEGINNING OF THE END ▶614			
1. Funky Nassau - Part 1	71	10	1887
Archie BELL & The DRELLS ▶1104			
Group: Philadelphia International All Stars (Archie Bell)			
1. Dancing To Your Music	73	78^2	99
2. Let's Groove	76	77	78
The BELLS ▶433			
1. Stay Awhile	71	4^2	2934
2. I Love You Lady Dawn	71	52	343
3. Fly Little White Dove Fly	71	86	51
BIDDU ORCHESTRA (s) ▶1037			
1. Summer Of '42	75	54^2	360
BIMBO JET (s) ▶1299			
1. El Bimbo	75	74	110
BLACK IVORY ▶1602			
1. You And I	72	95	13
BLACK OAK ARKANSAS ▶733			
1. Jim Dandy	74	12^2	1241
BLACK SABBATH ▶1049			
1. Iron Man	72	67	116
2. Paranoid	70	79^2	112
The BLACKBYRDS ▶468			
Solo: Donald Byrd			
1. Walking In Rhythm	75	7	1943
2. Happy Music	76	42	376
3. Flyin' High	75	72	102
4. Do It, Fluid	74	82	68
BLACKFOOT ▶709			
1. Highway Song	79	32^2	567
2. Train, Train	79	36^2	533
BLACKJACK ▶1295			
1. Love Me Tonight	79	69	113
BLAZE ▶1517			
1. Silver Heels	76	88	28
BLONDIE ▶236			
1. Heart Of Glass	79	1	6041
2. Dreaming	79	20^2	776
3. One Way Or Another	79	22	774
BLOOD, SWEAT & TEARS ▶300			
1. Hi-De-Ho	70	9^2	1422
2. Lucretia Mac Evil	70	17	953
3. Go Down Gamblin'	71	21	711
4. So Long Dixie	72	62	266
5. Got To Get You Into My Life	75	62	199
6. Lisa, Listen To Me	71	66	127
7. I Can't Move No Mountains	73	78	49
8. Roller Coaster	73	90	17
BLOODROCK ▶903			
1. D.O.A.	71	36	622
BLOODSTONE ▶297			
1. Natural High	73	5^2	2958
2. Never Let You Go	73	35	732
3. Outside Woman	74	31	656
4. My Little Lady	75	41	468
5. That's Not How It Goes	74	50	254
BLUE ▶1528			
1. Capture Your Heart	77	93^2	25

	Year	Peak	Points
BLUE HAZE (s) ▶710			
1. Smoke Gets In Your Eyes	73	21^2	1078
2. You'll Never Walk Alone	73	93	21
BLUE MAGIC ▶448			
1. Sideshow	74	5^2	2420
2. Three Ring Circus	74	44^2	417
3. Stop To Start	74	56	277
BLUE MINK ▶1008			
1. Our World	70	66	238
2. Melting Pot	70	82	46
BLUE MINK Featuring Madeline Bell			
BLUE ÖYSTER CULT ▶587			
1. (Don't Fear) The Reaper	76	7	1799
2. In Thee	79	92	18
BLUE SWEDE ▶253			
1. Hooked On A Feeling	74	1	4540
2. Never My Love	74	10	1379
3. Silly Milly	74	56	245
4. Hush/I'm Alive	75	58	175
BLUES IMAGE ▶434			
Group: **Iron Butterfly** (Mike Pinera)			
1. Ride Captain Ride	70	5^2	3696
2. Gas Lamps And Clay	70	95^2	20
BONES ▶1493			
1. Roberta	72	85	34
BONEY M ▶983			
1. Rivers Of Babylon	78	54	294
2. Daddy Cool	77	90	36
Booker T. & The M.G.'S ▶862			
1. Melting Pot	71	47	528
2. Something	70	93	19
BOOTSY'S RUBBER BAND ▶1243			
Groups: **Parliament/Funkadelic** (William "Bootsy" Collins, Phelps "Catfish" Collins, Frankie "Kash" Waddy, Gary "Mudbone" Cooper, Joel Johnson, Robert Johnson and The Horny Horns: Fred Wesley, Maceo Parker, Rick Gardner, Richard "Kush" Griffith) The **J.B.'s** (William "Bootsy" Collins)			
1. Bootzilla	78	59	149
BOSTON ▶200			
1. More Than A Feeling	76	4^2	2890
2. Don't Look Back	78	7^3	2013
3. Long Time	77	12	1208
4. Peace Of Mind	77	33	538
5. A Man I'll Never Be	79	36	502
6. Feelin' Satisfied	79	51	201
The **BOX TOPS** ▶1307			
1. You Keep Tightening Up On Me	70	74	105
The **BOYS IN THE BAND** (s) ▶963			
1. (How Bout A Little Hand For) The Boys In The Band	70	41	508

	Year	Peak	Points
BRAM TCHAIKOVSKY ▶1040			
1. Girl Of My Dreams	79	40^2	355
BRASS CONSTRUCTION ▶711			
1. Movin'	76	14^2	1363
BREAD ▶37			
Solo: **David Gates**			
1. Make It With You	70	1	6465
2. Baby I'm-A Want You	71	3^2	3701
3. Everything I Own	72	6	2484
4. If	71	6^2	2400
5. It Don't Matter To Me	70	7^2	1771
6. Lost Without Your Love	77	12^2	1638
7. The Guitar Man	72	10^2	1483
8. Aubrey	73	11	1351
9. Sweet Surrender	72	11	1168
10. Diary	72	15	1126
11. Let Your Love Go	71	20	778
12. Mother Freedom	71	45	467
13. Hooked On You	77	72^2	102
BRENDA & The TABULATIONS ▶496			
1. Right On The Tip Of My Tongue	71	14	1246
2. The Touch Of You	70	54^2	343
3. And My Heart Sang (Tra La La)	70	58	274
4. Don't Make Me Over	70	76	60
5. A Part Of You	71	84	48
BRICK ▶398			
1. Dazz	77	5^2	3120
2. Dusic	77	30	603
3. Ain't Gonna' Hurt Nobody	78	76	64
BRIGHTER SIDE OF DARKNESS ▶661			
1. Love Jones	73	10^2	1572
[see also: Basketball Jones]			
BROOKLYN BRIDGE ▶1163			
1. Free As The Wind	70	67	105
2. Day Is Done	70	89	33
BROOKLYN DREAMS ▶930			
Group: **Alive And Kicking** (Bruce Sudano)			
1. Sad Eyes	77	66	140
2. Make It Last	79	73	77
3. Music, Harmony And Rhythm	78	80^2	76
BROTHER TO BROTHER ▶1110			
1. In The Bottle	74	64	262
The **BROTHERHOOD OF MAN** (s) ▶461			
Groups (s): **Edison Lighthouse, First Class, White Plains** (Tony Burrows, all) Duo: The **Pipkins** (s) (Tony Burrows) Solo: **Tony Burrows**			
1. United We Stand	70	13^3	1744

	Year	Peak	Points
BROTHERHOOD OF MAN – cont'd			
2. Save Your Kisses For Me	76	48	379
3. Where Are You Going To My Love	70	54	343
4. Reach Out Your Hand	71	73	143
Chuck BROWN & The SOUL SEARCHERS ▶952			
1. Bustin' Loose (Part 1)	79	29	522
The James BROWN SOUL TRAIN ▶995			
Group: The **J.B.'s** (Fred Wesley, Maceo Parker, St. Claire Pinckney)			
1. Honky Tonk - Part 1	72	38	429
BROWNSVILLE STATION ▶220			
1. Smokin' In The Boy's Room	74	2	3718
2. Kings Of The Party	74	31	519
3. I'm The Leader Of The Gang	74	26	481
4. Lady (Put The Light On Me)	77	44	366
5. The Martian Boogie	77	45	311
6. Let Your Yeah Be Yeah	73	60	285
7. Mama Don't Allow No Parkin'	75	74	109
8. The Red Back Spider	72	85	30
The BUCHANAN BROTHERS (s) ▶1499			
Duo: **Cashman & West**			
Solo: **Terry Cashman**			
1. The Last Time	70	90	32
BUCKEYE ▶1213			
1. Where Will Your Heart Take You	79	66	176
BUCKWHEAT ▶1133			
1. Simple Song Of Freedom	72	69	156
2. I Just Can't Turn My Habit Into Love	73	100	1
BULLDOG ▶1010			
Groups: The **Rascals**, **Fotomaker** (Gene Cornish & Dino Danelli, both groups)			
1. No	72	51	410
BULLET (s) ▶670			
1. White Lies, Blue Eyes	72	25	838
2. Willpower Weak, Temptation Strong	72	68	122
3. Little Bit O' Soul	72	80	57
The BUOYS ▶657			
1. Timothy	71	13^2	1261
2. Give Up Your Guns	71	81	56
Eric BURDON And WAR ▶294			
Solo: **Lee Oskar**			
Group: **War**			
1. Spill The Wine	70	1	6039
2. They Can't Take Away Our Music	71	37	436
ERIC BURDON And WAR featuring Sharon Scott and the Beautiful New Born Children of Southern California			

	Year	Peak	Points
The BYRDS ▶1107			
Groups: **Firefall** (Mike Clarke)			
McGuinn, Clark & Hillman (Chris Hillman)			
The Souther, Hillman, Furay Band (Chris Hillman)			
1. Glory, Glory	71	65	82
2. Full Circle	73	87	23
3. Chestnut Mare	70	95^3	22
BYRDS			
C COMPANY FEATURING Terry NELSON (s) ▶1031			
1. Battle Hymn Of Lt. Calley	71	26	365
C.C.S. ▶1153			
1. Whole Lotta Love	71	58	220
C.J. & CO. ▶1117			
1. Devil's Gun	77	65	257
The CABOOSE ▶1321			
1. Black Hands White Cotton	70	79	97
CAMEO ▶1510			
1. I Just Want To Be	79	90	30
CANNED HEAT ▶788			
1. Let's Work Together	70	17	955
CANYON ▶1658			
1. Top Of The World (Make My Reservation)	75	98	7
Al CAPPS BAND ▶1668			
1. Odyssey Rock Park	70	97	5
CARGOE ▶1462			
1. Feel Alright	72	91	45
The CARS ▶400			
1. Let's Go	79	14^2	1295
2. Just What I Needed	78	24^2	735
3. My Best Friend's Girl	78	44^2	475
4. It's All I Can Do	79	40	347
5. Good Times Roll	79	60	183
The Jimmy CASTOR BUNCH ▶333			
Group: The **Fatback Band** (Gerry Thomas)			
1. Troglodyte (Cave Man)	72	2	4149
2. The Bertha Butt Boogie - Part 1	75	21^2	914
3. King Kong - Pt. 1	75	81^2	83
CELEBRATION FEATURING MIKE LOVE ▶960			
Groups: The **Beach Boys** (Mike Love)			
King Harvest (Ron Altback, Dave "Doc" Robinson)			
1. Almost Summer	78	35	510
CELI BEE & The BUZZY BUNCH ▶1316			
1. Superman	77	77	99
CHAIRMEN OF THE BOARD ▶248			
1. Give Me Just A Little More Time	70	9	1836
2. Pay To The Piper	71	10^2	1542

	Year	Peak	Points
CHAIRMEN OF THE BOARD – cont'd			
3. (You've Got Me) Dangling On A String	70	30	625
4. Everything's Tuesday	70	39	471
5. Chairman Of The Board	71	37	446
6. Finder's Keepers Chairman Of The Board	73	69^2	146
7. Men Are Getting Scarce	71	68	99
CHAKACHAS (s) ▶519			
1. Jungle Fever	72	6	2479
2. Stories??	72	99^2	5
The **CHAMBERS BROTHERS** ▶1664			
1. Funky	71	96	6
CHAMPAGNE ▶1341			
1. Rock And Roll Star	77	68	90
The **Ray CHARLES ORCHESTRA** ▶809			
1. Booty Butt	71	24	905
The **Ray CHARLES SINGERS** ▶1501			
1. Move Me, O Wondrous Music	70	91	31
CHARLIE ▶900 Group: **Argent** (Bob Henrit)			
1. She Loves To Be In Love	78	61	177
2. Killer Cut	79	70	132
3. Turning To You	77	88	27
CHASE ▶699			
1. Get It On	71	22^2	806
2. Handbags And Gladrags	71	74	78
3. So Many People	72	93	25
CHEAP TRICK ▶347			
1. I Want You To Want Me	79	3^2	3322
2. Dream Police	79	27^2	513
3. Ain't That A Shame	79	35	417
4. Surrender	78	83	42
CHESTER ▶1694			
1. Make My Life A Little Bit Brighter	73	100	1
CHIC ▶69			
1. Le Freak	78	1^7	10002
2. Good Times	79	1	6502
3. Dance, Dance, Dance (Yowsah, Yowsah, Yowsah)	78	6^2	2432
4. I Want Your Love	79	10^2	1469
5. Everybody Dance	78	49	279
CHICAGO ▶7			
1. If You Leave Me Now	76	1	4998
2. Just You 'N' Me	73	1	4101
3. Does Anybody Really Know What Time It Is?	71	5^2	3039

	Year	Peak	Points
4. 25 Or 6 To 4	70	6^2	3012
5. Saturday In The Park	72	3	2765
6. Baby, What A Big Surprise	77	4	2324
7. (I've Been) Searchin' So Long	74	7	2040
8. Feelin' Stronger Every Day	73	8^2	1934
9. Make Me Smile	70	11	1860
10. Old Days	75	6	1742
11. Beginnings	71	11^2	1660
12. Wishing You Were Here	74	9	1483
13. Call On Me	74	10	1383
14. Questions 67 And 68 [longer version charted in 1969]	71	13	1286
15. Alive Again	78	13	1128
16. No Tell Lover	79	14	1031
17. Dialogue (Parts I & II)	72	17	866
18. Free	71	19	780
19. Harry Truman	75	19	779
20. Lowdown	71	25	577
21. Another Rainy Day In New York City	76	33	574
22. Brand New Love Affair Parts I & II	75	43	272
23. You Are On My Mind	77	56	186
24. Take Me Back To Chicago	78	62	160
25. Little One	78	59	150
26. Colour My World	71	75	147
27. I'm A Man	71	67	135
28. Gone Long Gone	79	75	87
29. Must Have Been Crazy	79	84	50
CHICORY ▶1409			
1. Son Of My Father	72	82	61
Desmond CHILD and ROUGE ▶1271			
1. Our Love Is Insane	79	60	129
The **CHI-LITES** ▶104			
1. Oh Girl	72	1	5637
2. Have You Seen Her	71	5	3312
3. (For God's Sake) Give More Power To The People	71	29^2	466
4. A Letter To Myself	73	41	455
5. Stoned Out Of My Mind	73	53^2	370
6. The Coldest Days Of My Life (Part 1)	72	52	237
7. We Need Order	73	74	114
8. A Lonely Man	72	69	102
9. Homely Girl	74	77	87
10. You Got To Be The One	74	75	77
11. I Found Sunshine	73	80	75
12. We Are Neighbors	71	87	59
13. I Like Your Lovin' (Do You Like Mine) Chi-Lites	70	88	35
14. I Want To Pay You Back (For Loving Me)	71	97	7

	Year	Peak	Points
CHILLIWACK ►779			
Group: **Prism** (Ab Bryant)			
1. Fly At Night	77	57	220
2. Lonesome Mary	72	77	84
3. Something Better	77	92	23
4. Arms Of Mary	78	92	20
5. Crazy Talk	75	90	20
CHOCOLATE MILK ►1336			
1. Action Speaks Louder Than Words	75	74	91
CHRISTIE ►615			
1. Yellow River	70	16	1531
2. San Bernadino	71	86	48
CIRCUS ►1388			
1. Stop, Wait And Listen	73	81	69
CITY BOY ►1022			
1. 5.7.0.5.	78	52^2	388
CLEAN LIVING ►924			
Group: **NRBQ** (Al Anderson)			
1. In Heaven There Is No Beer	72	34	565
CLIMAX ►323			
1. Precious And Few	72	1	5228
2. Life And Breath	72	42	553
CLIMAX featuring Sonny Geraci			
CLIMAX BLUES BAND ►601			
1. Couldn't Get It Right	77	7	2010
The **CLIQUE** ►1301			
1. Sparkle And Shine	70	70	109
CLOUT ►1059			
1. Substitute	78	52	318
The **COASTERS** ►1608			
1. Love Potion Number Nine	72	96	12
COCHISE ►1484			
Groups: **Sutherland Brothers And Quiver** (Willie Wilson)			
Foreigner (Rick Wills)			
1. Love's Made A Fool Of You	71	90	37
Dennis **COFFEY** And The **DETROIT GUITAR BAND** ►350			
Solo: **Dennis Coffey**			
1. Scorpio	72	4	3774
2. Taurus	72	13	1321
COLD BLOOD ►1077			
1. You Got Me Hummin	70	64	295
COMMANDER CODY And His **LOST PLANET AIRMEN** ►495			
1. Hot Rod Lincoln	72	7	1843
2. Don't Let Go	75	53^2	232
3. Smoke! Smoke! Smoke! (That Cigarette)	73	71	107
4. Beat Me Daddy Eight To The Bar	72	90	44

	Year	Peak	Points
COMMODORES ►28			
1. Three Times A Lady	78	1^4	7257
2. Sail On	79	1	4997
3. Still	79	1	4402
4. Easy	77	4^2	2926
5. Sweet Love	76	9	2346
6. Brick House	77	6	1857
7. Just To Be Close To You	76	11^2	1536
8. Machine Gun	74	13^2	1086
9. Slippery When Wet	75	29	685
10. Too Hot Ta Trot	78	37^2	419
11. Fancy Dancer	77	63^2	301
12. Flying High	78	52	250
13. I Feel Sanctified	74	78	92
14. This Is Your Life	75	77	62
CON FUNK SHUN ►655			
1. Ffun	78	18	909
2. Shake And Dance With Me	78	59	170
3. Chase Me	79	94	13
CONSUMER RAPPORT ►1042			
1. Ease On Down The Road	75	42	354
The **CONTINENTAL 4** ►1455			
1. Day By Day (Every Minute Of The Hour)	71	83	45
CONTINENTAL MINIATURES ►1367			
1. Stay Awhile	78	74	79
The **CONTROLLERS** ►1422			
1. Somebody's Gotta Win, Somebody's Gotta Lose	78	84	58
COOL HEAT (s) ►1672			
1. Groovin' With Mr. Bloe	70	98	4
COOPER BROTHERS ►871			
1. The Dream Never Dies	79	44	458
2. I'll Know Her When I See Her	79	75	71
Cooper Brothers Band			
CORNELIUS BROTHERS & SISTER ROSE ►129			
1. Too Late To Turn Back Now	72	1	5269
2. Treat Her Like A Lady	71	2	4897
3. Don't Ever Be Lonely (A Poor Little Fool Like Me)	72	23	870
4. I'm Never Gonna Be Alone Anymore	73	31	552
5. Let Me Down Easy	73	72	103
6. I Just Can't Stop Loving You	73	88	35
CORNERSTONE ►1542			
1. Holly Go Softly	70	92	21

	Year	Peak	Points
Bill COSBY With The BUNIONS BRADFORD BAND ▶1576			
1. Hikky Burr - Part One	70	92	17
COTTON, LLOYD And CHRISTIAN ▶1615			
1. I Go To Pieces	75	95	12
COUCHOIS ▶1471			
1. Walkin' The Fence	79	83	42
COUNTRY COALITION ▶1359			
1. Time To Get It Together	70	80	83
COUNTS - see **FABULOUS COUNTS**			
The COURTSHIP ▶1642			
1. It's The Same Old Love	72	96	8
COVEN ▶585			
1. One Tin Soldier The Legend Of Billy Jack [Version 1]	71	18	1259
2. One Tin Soldier The Legend Of Billy Jack [reissue of #1]	74	73	136
3. One Tin Soldier (The Legend Of Billy Jack) [Version 2]	73	68	130
CRABBY APPLETON ▶778			
1. Go Back	70	30	981
CRAWLER ▶1101 [shortened from Back Street Crawler after the death of founder Paul Kossoff (**Free**)]			
1. Stone Cold Sober	77	62^2	272
CREATIVE SOURCE ▶1041			
1. Who Is He And What Is He To You	74	60	355
CREEDENCE CLEARWATER REVIVAL ▶59 Solos: **Tom Fogerty**, **John Fogerty** The **Blue Ridge Rangers** (s) (John Fogerty) Group: The **Don Harrison Band** (Doug Clifford, Stu Cook)			
1. Lookin' Out My Back Door	70	1	5503
2. Up Around The Bend	70	2	4594
3. Have You Ever Seen The Rain	71	3^2	3551
4. Travelin' Band	70	5	2612
5. Sweet Hitch-Hiker	71	5	2309
6. Who'll Stop The Rain	70	13	1149
7. Someday Never Comes	72	25	683
8. I Heard It Through The Grapevine	76	47	302
9. Run Through The Jungle	70	48	176
10. Long As I Can See The Light	70	57	141
CROSBY, STILLS & NASH ▶548 Solos: **David Crosby**, **Stephen Stills**, **Graham Nash** Duos: **Graham Nash & David Crosby** **David Crosby / Graham Nash** **Neil Young and Graham Nash** Groups: **Crosby, Stills, Nash & Young** **Stephen Stills – Manassas**			

	Year	Peak	Points
1. Just A Song Before I Go	77	8^2	1830
2. Fair Game	77	47	308
CROSBY, STILLS, NASH & YOUNG ▶308 Groups: **Crosby, Stills & Nash** **Stephen Stills – Manassas** Duos: **Graham Nash & David Crosby** **Neil Young and Graham Nash** **David Crosby / Graham Nash** Solos: **David Crosby**, **Stephen Stills**, **Graham Nash**, **Neil Young**			
1. Ohio	70	14	1463
2. Woodstock	70	13	1446
3. Teach Your Children	70	16^2	1387
4. Our House	70	20	938
CROSS COUNTRY ▶821 Group: The **Tokens** (Jay Siegel, Mitch and Phil Margo)			
1. In The Midnight Hour	73	18	880
CROW ▶490			
1. Evil Woman Don't Play Your Games With Me	70	16	1469
2. Don't Try To Lay No Boogie Woogie On The "King Of Rock & Roll"	70	40	401
3. Cottage Cheese	70	66^2	366
4. Slow Down	70	94^2	23
CROWN HEIGHTS AFFAIR ▶702			
1. Dreaming A Dream	75	46	440
2. Foxy Lady	76	64	157
3. Dancin'	77	65	123
4. Every Beat Of My Heart	76	97	6
The CRUSADERS ▶545			
1. Street Life	79	29	560
2. Put It Where You Want It	72	40^2	492
3. Way Back Home The Jazz Crusaders	71	73	126
4. Scratch	74	72	116
5. Don't Let It Get You Down	73	90	30
CRYSTAL MANSION ▶1043			
1. Carolina In My Mind CRYSTAL MANSION Featuring Johnny Caswell	70	61	352
The Mike CURB CONGREGATION ▶760			
1. Burning Bridges	71	29^2	721
2. It's A Small Small World	73	79	102
CYMANDE ▶881			
1. The Message	73	39	472
2. Bra	73	93	17
CYMARRON ▶667			
1. Rings	71	17	1247
2. Valerie	71	98^2	7

	Year	Peak	Points
Steve DAHL And TEENAGE RADIATION ▶1227			
1. Do You Think I'm Disco?	79	61	166
[see also: Do Ya Think I'm Sexy?]			
DAMNATION OF ADAM BLESSING ▶1393			
1. Back To The River	71	85^2	67
Liz DAMON'S ORIENT EXPRESS ▶905			
1. 1900 Yesterday	71	29	618
Charlie DANIELS BAND ▶353			
Solo: **Charlie Daniels**			
1. The Devil Went Down To Georgia	79	4^2	2759
2. The South's Gonna Do It	75	26^2	660
3. Long Haired Country Boy	75	50	277
4. Birmingham Blues	75	79	59
5. Texas	76	92^2	26
DAWN - see **Tony ORLANDO And DAWN**			
DAYBREAK ▶1376			
1. Good Morning Freedom	70	83	74
The DEADLY NIGHTSHADE ▶1175			
1. Mary Hartman, Mary Hartman	76	65^2	203
Bill DEAL & The RHONDELS ▶1069			
1. Nothing Succeeds Like Success	70	62	204
2. It's Too Late	72	100	1
The Kiki DEE BAND ▶668			
Duo: **Elton John and Kiki Dee**			
Solo: **Kiki Dee**			
1. I've Got The Music In Me	74	18^2	1217
2. Step By Step	75	85	33
DEEP PURPLE ▶357			
Group: **Rainbow** (Ritchie Blackmore, Roger Glover)			
1. Smoke On The Water	73	3^2	3403
2. Woman From Tokyo	73	59^2	261
3. Might Just Take Your Life	74	87	36
4. Black Night	71	96^2	15
5. You Can't Do It Right (With The One You Love)	75	93	13
Rick DEES & His CAST OF IDIOTS (s) ▶296			
1. Disco Duck (Part 1)	76	1^2	6330
2. Dis-Gorilla (Part 1)	77	81	70
The DeFRANCO FAMILY FEATURING Tony DeFRANCO ▶254			
1. Heartbeat - It's A Lovebeat	73	1	5136
2. Save The Last Dance For Me	74	16^2	1044
3. Abra-Ca-Dabra	74	23	639

	Year	Peak	Points
DELANEY & BONNIE And FRIENDS ▶517			
Duo: **Delaney & Bonnie**			
1. Never Ending Song Of Love	71	9	1795
2. Soul Shake	70	43	325
#1 & 2: *Delaney & Bonnie & Friends*			
3. Comin' Home	70	74	88
Delaney & Bonnie And Friends Featuring Eric Clapton			
The DELEGATES ▶815			
1. Convention '72	72	9	886
DELEGATION ▶1128			
1. Oh Honey	79	60	245
The DELFONICS ▶319			
Solo: **Major Harris**			
1. Didn't I (Blow Your Mind This Time)	70	13^2	1579
2. When You Get Right Down To It	70	41	479
3. Trying To Make A Fool Of Me	70	41	470
4. Walk Right Up To The Sun	71	62	358
5. Over And Over	71	61	323
6. Tell Me This Is A Dream	72	73	160
7. Think It Over	73	75	82
8. I Don't Want To Make You Wait	73	86	32
The DELLS ▶286			
1. Give Your Baby A Standing Ovation	73	20^2	1068
2. The Love We Had (Stays On My Mind)	71	33	602
3. Oh What A Day	70	36^2	574
4. Open Up My Heart	70	51	358
5. Long Lonely Nights	70	64	211
6. I Miss You	74	56	201
7. My Pretending Days Are Over	73	60^2	181
8. It's All Up To You	72	76	67
9. I Wish It Was Me You Loved	74	78	62
10. The Glory Of Love	71	91	29
DEREK And The DOMINOS ▶586			
1. Layla	72	14	1180
[reissue--longer version of #2]			
2. Layla	71	52	330
3. Bell Bottom Blues	71	96^2	12
DETROIT ▶1614			
1. Rock 'N Roll	72	95	12
DETROIT featuring Mitch Ryder			
DETROIT EMERALDS ▶404			
1. Baby Let Me Take You (In My Arms)	72	19	1361
2. You Want It, You Got It	72	35^2	618
3. Do Me Right	71	42	548
4. Wear This Ring (With Love)	71	78	66
5. You're Gettin' A Little Too Smart	73	82	57
6. Feel The Need In Me	72	88	49

	Year	Peak	Points
DIAMOND HEAD ▶1657			
1. If That's The Way You Want It	73	95	7
DIAMOND REO ▶1003			
1. Ain't That Peculiar	75	36	418
The **DILLARDS** ▶1669			
1. It's About Time	71	99^2	5
DIRE STRAITS ▶510			
1. Sultans Of Swing	79	5^2	2470
2. Lady Writer	79	63	161
DISCO TEX & The SEX-O-LETTES (s) ▶487			
Solo: Cindy Bullens			
Group: Sugarloaf (Jerry Corbetta)			
1. Get Dancin'	75	10	1613
2. I Wanna Dance Wit' Choo (Doo Dat Dance)	75	34	577
3. Dancin' Kid	76	69	95
#1 & 3: DISCO TEX & THE SEX-O-LETTES featuring Sir Monti Rock III			
4. Jam Band	75	89	20
The **DIXIE DREGS** ▶1512			
1. Take It Off The Top	78	92	29
DR. BUZZARD'S ORIGINAL "SAVANNAH" BAND ▶725			
1. Whispering/Cherchez La Femme/ Se Si Bon	77	23^2	968
2. I'll Play The Fool	76	83	63
DR. HOOK ▶56			
Solo: Ray Sawyer			
1. Sylvia's Mother	72	1	4171
2. Sharing The Night Together	78	4^3	4070
3. When You're In Love With A Beautiful Woman	79	5^2	3295
4. Only Sixteen	76	5	3181
5. The Cover Of "Rolling Stone"	73	5^2	2926
6. A Little Bit More	76	9^2	2251
7. Roland The Roadie And Gertrude The Groupie	73	59	221
8. If Not You	77	63	207
9. All The Time In The World	79	62	171
10. Walk Right In	77	72^2	126
11. Carry Me, Carrie	72	74	78
12. Life Ain't Easy	73	80	58
#1, 5, 7, 11 & 12: Dr. Hook And The Medicine Show			
13. The Millionaire	75	97	4
Bo DONALDSON And The HEYWOODS ▶217			
1. Billy, Don't Be A Hero	74	1	4883
2. Who Do You Think You Are	74	13	1307
3. Special Someone	72	51	314
The Heywoods			
4. The Heartbreak Kid	74	51	230

	Year	Peak	Points
5. The House On Telegraph Hill	75	89	21
6. Our Last Song Together	75	98	6
The **DOOBIE BROTHERS** ▶30			
Group: Steely Dan (Jeff "Skunk" Baxter, Michael McDonald)			
Solo: Tom Johnston			
1. What A Fool Believes	79	1^2	6476
2. Black Water	75	3	4321
3. Long Train Runnin'	73	9	1964
4. China Grove	73	8^2	1819
5. Listen To The Music	72	9^2	1620
6. Take Me In Your Arms (Rock Me)	75	10	1394
7. Takin' It To The Streets	76	15^2	1340
8. Minute By Minute	79	13	1039
9. Another Park, Another Sunday	74	38	658
10. Jesus Is Just Alright	73	33	565
11. Dependin' On You	79	30	515
12. Little Darling (I Need You)	77	39	500
13. Eyes Of Silver	74	43	482
14. It Keeps You Runnin'	77	50	374
15. Sweet Maxine	75	44^2	310
16. Nobody	74	51	224
17. I Cheat The Hangman	76	76	121
18. Echoes Of Love	77	78^2	113
The **DOORS** ▶306			
1. Love Her Madly	71	7^2	2240
2. Riders On The Storm	71	12	1437
3. You Make Me Real	70	40	433
doors			
4. Tightrope Ride	72	64	184
5. Roadhouse Blues	70	76	92
6. The Mosquito	72	94	8
DOUCETTE ▶1018			
1. Mama Let Him Play	78	69	155
2. Nobody	79	91	33
3. All I Wanna Do	78	97	7
The **DOVELLS** ▶1696			
1. Dancing In The Street	74	100	1
The **DRAMATICS** ▶142			
1. In The Rain	72	3	3699
2. Whatcha See Is Whatcha Get	71	14^2	1467
3. Toast To The Fool	72	52	510
4. Hey You! Get Off My Mountain	73	51	460
5. Me And Mrs. Jones	75	46	410
Ron Banks And The Dramatics			
7. Be My Girl	77	62^2	285
6. Fell For You	73	50	294
8. Door To Your Heart	74	55^2	262
9. Get Up And Get Down	72	69	118
10. Shake It Well	77	86	52
11. I Can't Get Over You	77	84	39

	Year	Peak	Points
DRAMATICS – cont'd			
12. Ocean Of Thoughts And Dreams	78	89	22
DRIVER ▶1385			
1. (I've Been Lookin' For) A New Way To Say I Love You	77	83^2	70
DUKE & The DRIVERS ▶1620			
1. What You Got	75	96	11
DUSK (s) ▶672			
1. I Hear Those Church Bells Ringing	71	41	606
2. Angel Baby	71	62	287
3. Treat Me Like A Good Piece Of Candy	71	71	116
DYKE And The BLAZERS ▶1333			
1. Uhh	70	85	50
2. You Are My Sunshine	70	96	9
Bob DYLAN / The BAND ▶1050			
Group: **The Band**			
Solo: **Bob Dylan**			
1. Most Likely You Go Your Way (And I'll Go Mine)	74	47	339
DYNAMIC SUPERIORS ▶1239			
1. Shoe Shoe Shine	74	72	153
EAGLES ▶19			
Groups: **Poco** (Timothy B. Schmit)			
The **James Gang** (Joe Walsh)			
The **Stone Canyon Band** (Randy Meisner)			
Solo: **Joe Walsh**			
1. One Of These Nights	75	1	5337
2. Heartache Tonight	79	1	4321
3. Hotel California	77	1	4197
4. New Kid In Town	77	2^2	3807
5. Best Of My Love	75	4^3	3748
6. Lyin' Eyes	75	3	3707
7. Take It To The Limit	76	5^2	3025
8. Take It Easy	72	9	1855
9. Witchy Woman	72	11	1583
10. Already Gone	74	17^2	1115
11. Life In The Fast Lane	77	11	1108
12. Peaceful Easy Feeling	73	20	927
13. Tequila Sunrise	73	40	378
14. Outlaw Man	73	49	363
15. Please Come Home For Christmas	78	29^3	361
16. James Dean	74	49	251
EARTH, WIND & FIRE ▶38			
Groups: **Earth, Wind & Fire With The Emotions**			
Ramsey Lewis and Earth, Wind & Fire			
1. Shining Star	75	1	5358
2. After The Love Has Gone	79	3^2	2888
3. Sing A Song	76	7	2299
4. September	79	6^2	2182
5. Getaway	76	10^2	1681
6. That's The Way Of The World	75	13^2	1316
7. Serpentine Fire	78	15^2	1241
8. Got To Get You Into My Life	78	11^2	1175
9. Saturday Nite	77	21	899
10. Fantasy	78	33	732
11. Mighty Mighty	74	35	597
12. Keep Your Head To The Sky	74	34	504
13. Can't Hide Love	76	45^2	373
14. Evil	73	54	329
15. Kalimba Story	74	55	289
16. Devotion	74	57	145
17. In The Stone	79	66	133
18. Love Is Life	71	77	107
EARTH, WIND & FIRE With The EMOTIONS ▶534			
Groups: **Earth, Wind & Fire**			
The **Emotions**			
Ramsey Lewis and Earth, Wind & Fire			
1. Boogie Wonderland	79	5^2	2613
EAST L.A. CAR POOL ▶1500			
1. Like They Say In L.A.	75	84	32
EASY STREET ▶1463			
1. I've Been Lovin' You	76	79	43
The **EBONYS** ▶945			
1. You're The Reason Why	71	46	353
2. It's Forever	73	90	21
ECSTASY, PASSION & PAIN ▶751			
1. One Beautiful Day	75	52	263
2. Good Things Don't Last Forever	74	68	210
3. Ask Me	74	57	210
EDISON LIGHTHOUSE (s) ▶384			
Groups (s): The **Brotherhood of Man, First Class, White Plains** (Tony Burrows, all)			
Duo: The **Pipkins** (s) (Tony Burrows)			
Solo: **Tony Burrows**			
1. Love Grows (Where My Rosemary Goes)	70	4^2	4332
2. It's Up To You Petula	71	69	150
EDWARD BEAR ▶288			
1. Last Song	73	3^3	4652
2. Close Your Eyes	73	24	786
3. You, Me And Mexico	70	78	114
4. Walking On Back	73	77	74
The **8TH DAY** ▶472			
1. She's Not Just Another Woman	71	8^2	2097
2. You've Got To Crawl (Before You Walk)	71	34	585
3. If I Could See The Light	72	78	85
EL CHICANO ▶605			
1. Viva Tirado - Part 1	70	27	604
2. Tell Her She's Lovely	74	28	514
3. Brown Eyed Girl	72	49	269

Artist / Song	Year	Peak	Points
EL COCO (s) ▶1113			
1. Cocomotion	78	52	261
The **ELECTRIC EXPRESS** ▶1137			
1. It's The Real Thing - Pt I	71	65	232
ELECTRIC LIGHT ORCHESTRA ▶55			
Group: **The Move** (Bev Bevan, Jeff Lynne, Roy Wood)			
1. Telephone Line	77	4	2894
2. Don't Bring Me Down	79	4^2	2779
3. Evil Woman	76	9^2	2431
4. Livin' Thing	76	10	1747
5. Shine A Little Love	79	7	1688
6. Can't Get It Out Of My Head	75	14	1455
7. Strange Magic	76	14	1443
8. Turn To Stone	78	11	1342
9. Sweet Talkin' Woman	78	18^2	1005
10. Do Ya	77	16	967
11. Roll Over Beethoven	73	48^2	627
12. Mr. Blue Sky	78	27	575
13. Showdown	74	51	396
14. Confusion	79	47	286
15. Daybreaker	74	61	222
16. Showdown	76	75	72
ELEPHANT'S MEMORY ▶885			
[see also **John Lennon/Plastic Ono Band**]			
1. Mongoose	70	49	652
The **ELEVENTH HOUR** (s) ▶1603			
1. Hollywood Hot	75	94	13
EMERSON, LAKE & PALMER ▶608			
Solo: **Greg Lake**			
1. From The Beginning	72	40	564
2. Lucky Man	71	65	183
3. Lucky Man [reissue of #2]	73	63	144
4. Stone Of Years	71	84	40
5. Nutrocker	72	92	24
The **EMOTIONS** ▶193			
Group: **Earth, Wind & Fire With The Emotions**			
1. Best Of My Love	77	1^3	5500
2. Show Me How	72	33	654
3. I Don't Wanna Lose Your Love	77	55	353
4. Put A Little Love Away	74	72	126
5. Don't Ask My Neighbors	77	73	90
6. My Honey And Me	72	85	42
7. I Could Never Be Happy	72	92	24
8. Stealing Love	70	100	1
ENCHANTMENT ▶715			
1. It's You That I Need	78	36	419
2. Gloria	77	46	413
3. Sunshine	77	93	28
The **ENGLISH CONGREGATION** ▶811			
1. Softly Whispering I Love You	72	28	597
2. Jesahel	72	74	87
ERUPTION ▶767			
1. I Can't Stand The Rain	78	19^2	1030
EXILE ▶208			
1. Kiss You All Over	78	1^2	8678
2. You Thrill Me	79	43	402
FABULOUS COUNTS ▶1402			
1. Why Not Start All Over Again — The Counts	72	89	29
2. Get Down People	70	96	10
The **FABULOUS RHINESTONES** ▶1286			
1. What A Wonderful Thing We Have	72	67	121
FACES ▶564			
Group: **The Who** (Kenney Jones)			
Solo: **Rod Stewart**			
[1960s: The **Small Faces**]			
1. Stay With Me	72	10^2	1681
2. Cindy Incidentally	73	43	349
FACTS OF LIFE ▶1072			
1. Sometimes	77	60^2	302
FAITH BAND ▶978			
1. Dancin' Shoes	79	63	169
2. You're My Weakness	79	67	164
FAITH, HOPE & CHARITY ▶676			
1. To Each His Own	75	42^2	661
2. So Much Love	70	36^2	554
FANCY ▶596			
1. Wild Thing	74	12	1301
2. Touch Me	74	37	443
FANNY ▶567			
1. Butter Boy	75	27	590
2. Charity Ball	71	32	589
3. I've Had It	74	63	209
4. Ain't That Peculiar	72	91	14
FANTASTIC FOUR ▶1297			
1. Alvin Stone (The Birth & Death Of A Gangster)	75	76^2	112
The **FANTASTICS** ▶1518			
1. (Love Me) Love The Life I Lead	72	88	27
FANTASY ▶1509			
1. Stoned Cowboy	70	93^2	30
The **FARAGHER BROTHERS** ▶1130			
1. Stay The Night	79	48	242

	Year	Peak	Points
The **FATBACK BAND** ▶1127			
Group: The **Jimmy Castor Bunch** (Gerry Thomas)			
1. Spanish Hustle	76	60	246
FEATHER ▶1288			
1. Friends	70	76	116
The **FESTIVALS** ▶1683			
1. You're Gonna Make It	70	99	3
The **5TH DIMENSION** ▶31			
Duo: **Marilyn McCoo & Billy Davis, Jr.**			
1. One Less Bell To Answer	70	2	6960
2. (Last Night) I Didn't Get To Sleep At All	72	6³	2768
3. If I Could Reach You	72	10	1935
4. Love's Lines, Angles And Rhymes	71	11²	1799
5. Never My Love	71	14²	1627
6. Blowing Away	70	14²	1071
7. Together Let's Find Love	72	24	850
8. Living Together, Growing Together	73	20	800
9. Save The Country	70	20	780
10. Light Sings	71	22	762
11. Puppet Man	70	22	693
12. On The Beach (In The Summertime)	70	41	426
13. The Girls' Song	70	46	328
14. Ashes To Ashes	73	71	248
15. Everything's Been Changed	73	55	232
16. The Declaration	70	66	117
17. Love Hangover	76	82²	54
18. A Change Is Gonna Come & People Gotta Be Free	70	84	38
19. Flashback	74	92	28
20. Harlem	74	92	21
21. No Love In The Room	75	99	2
FIREFALL ▶196			
Groups: **Spirit** & **Jo Jo Gunne** (Mark Andes) The **Byrds** (Mike Clarke)			
1. You Are The Woman	76	8²	2221
2. Just Remember I Love You	77	9²	1808
3. Strange Way	78	11²	1528
4. Cinderella	77	30	625
5. Livin' Ain't Livin'	76	41	527
6. Goodbye, I Love You	79	40	382
7. So Long	78	67	113
FIREFLY (s) ▶1338			
1. Hey There Little Firefly Part I	75	75	91
FIRST CHOICE ▶484			
1. Armed And Extremely Dangerous	73	19	1149
2. Smarty Pants	73	38³	728
3. The Player - Part 1	74	73	122
4. Doctor Love	77	79	67

	Year	Peak	Points
5. Newsy Neighbors	74	93	16
FIRST CLASS (s) ▶462			
Groups (s): The **Brotherhood Of Man**, **Edison Lighthouse**, **White Plains** (Tony Burrows, all)			
Duo: The **Pipkins** (Tony Burrows)			
Solo: **Tony Burrows**			
1. Beach Baby	74	3	2750
2. Dreams Are Ten A Penny	74	71²	146
3. Funny How Love Can Be	75	90	19
FIVE FLIGHTS UP ▶831			
1. Do What You Wanna Do	70	29	561
2. After The Feeling Is Gone	71	84	83
FIVE MAN ELECTRICAL BAND ▶305			
Solo: **Les Emmerson**			
1. Signs	71	7	2790
2. Absolutely Right	71	20	820
3. Werewolf	74	44	356
4. I'm A Stranger Here	73	65	198
5. Julianna	72	61	149
6. Money Back Guarantee	72	71	111
FIVE SPECIAL ▶1473			
1. Why Leave Us Alone	79	86	41
The **FIVE STAIRSTEPS** ▶401			
1. O-o-h Child [Alt. title: O-O-H Child]	70	4	3025
2. Didn't It Look So Easy *The Stairsteps*	71	65	123
3. Dear Prudence	70	69	112
4. Because I Love You// America/Standing [TSW]	70	71	91
5000 VOLTS ▶902			
1. I'm On Fire	75	24	623
The **FLAME** ▶1665			
1. See The Light	70	96	6
FLAMING EMBER ▶450			
1. Westbound #9	70	23	1253
2. I'm Not My Brother's Keeper	70	22²	960
3. Shades Of Green *The Flaming Ember*	70	56	209
4. If It's Good To You (It's Good For You)	71	91	27
5. Stop The World And Let Me Off	71	98	4
The **FLAMINGOS** ▶1170			
1. Buffalo Soldier	70	56	207
FLASH ▶878			
Group: **Yes** (Peter Banks)			
1. Small Beginnings	72	30	666
FLASH CADILLAC & The CONTINENTAL KIDS ▶650			
Group: **Gary Puckett And The Union Gap** (Dwight Bement, Paul Wheatbread)			
1. Did You Boogie (With Your Baby)	76	25	737

	Year	Peak	Points
FLASH CADILLAC – cont'd			
2. Good Times, Rock & Roll	75	45	310
3. Dancin' (On A Saturday Night)	74	79	68
FLEETWOOD MAC ▶68			
1. Don't Stop	77	1	4505
2. Dreams	77	1	4400
3. Rhiannon (Will You Ever Win)	76	9	1867
4. You Make Loving Fun	77	7^2	1783
5. Tusk	79	8^2	1686
6. Say You Love Me	76	12^2	1612
7. Go Your Own Way	77	10	1507
8. Over My Head	76	18^2	1019
9. Oh Well - Part I	70	62	198
The **FLIRTATIONS** ▶1660			
1. Can't Stop Lovin' You	70	96	6
The **FLOATERS** ▶481			
1. Float On	77	3^2	3360
[see also: Bloat On Featuring The Bloaters]			
The **FLYING MACHINE** (s) ▶1601			
1. Baby Make It Soon	70	97^2	13
FOCUS ▶482			
1. Hocus Pocus	73	4	2728
2. Sylvia	73	58	231
FOGHAT ▶364			
Group: **Savoy Brown** (Roger Earl, "Lonesome" Dave Peverett, Tony "Tone" Stevens)			
1. Slow Ride	76	20	1371
2. Drivin' Wheel	77	37	594
3. I Just Want To Make Love To You	77	31	474
4. Fool For The City	76	57^2	285
5. Stone Blue	78	47	248
6. I'll Be Standing By	77	90^2	23
7. What A Shame	73	92	19
FOOLS GOLD ▶1230			
[backup band for **Dan Fogelberg**]			
1. Rain, Oh Rain	76	67	162
FOREIGNER ▶114			
Group: **Cochise** (Rick Wills)			
1. Hot Blooded	78	4^3	3602
2. Feels Like The First Time	77	5	2320
3. Double Vision	78	5^2	2151
4. Cold As Ice	77	10	1974
5. Dirty White Boy	79	16	942
6. Blue Morning, Blue Day	79	19^2	879
7. Long, Long Way From Home	78	27	635
The **FORTUNES** ▶511			
1. Here Comes That Rainy Day Feeling Again	71	8	1876
2. That Same Old Feeling	70	59	378
3. Freedom Comes, Freedom Goes	71	80	69

	Year	Peak	Points
FOTOMAKER ▶1136			
Groups: **Raspberries** (Wally Bryson) The **Rascals**, **Bulldog** (Gene Cornish & Dino Danelli, both groups)			
1. Miles Away	78	70	112
2. Where Have You Been All My Life	78	88	40
The **FOUR SEASONS** ▶222			
Group: **Frankie Valli & The 4 Seasons** (Frankie Valli)			
Solo: **Frankie Valli**			
1. December, 1963 (Oh, What A Night)	76	1	4662
2. Who Loves You	75	7^3	2795
Four Seasons			
3. Silver Star	76	68	133
4. Down The Hall	77	77	78
FOUR TOPS ▶74			
Group: The **Supremes & Four Tops**			
1. Ain't No Woman (Like The One I've Got)	73	1	4303
2. Keeper Of The Castle	73	9	1729
3. It's All In The Game	70	14^2	1659
4. Still Water (Love)	70	12	1442
5. Are You Man Enough	73	14^2	1407
6. Just Seven Numbers (Can Straighten Out My Life)	71	26	648
7. Mac Arthur Park (Part II)	71	36	547
8. One Chain Don't Make No Prison	74	36	457
9. I Just Can't Get You Out Of My Mind	74	41^2	451
10. Sweet Understanding Love	73	30	431
11. (It's The Way) Nature Planned It	72	53	310
12. Don't Let Him Take Your Love From Me	70	52	310
13. Midnight Flower	74	76	125
14. Seven Lonely Nights	75	79	70
15. Catfish	76	75	67
16. A Simple Game	72	80	57
17. We All Gotta Stick Together	75	87	40
FOX ▶1124			
1. Only You Can	75	58^2	249
FOXY ▶569			
1. Get Off	78	17	1324
2. Hot Number	79	29	642
FREE ▶378			
Group: **Bad Company** (Paul Rodgers, Simon Kirke) [see also **Crawler**]			
1. All Right Now	70	3	4315
2. Stealer	71	46	311
The **FREE MOVEMENT** ▶476			
1. I've Found Someone Of My Own	71	6^2	2644
2. The Harder I Try (The Bluer I Get)	72	43	442
FRESH START ▶1569			
1. Free	74	91	18

	Year	Peak	Points
The **FRIENDS OF DISTINCTION** ▶454			
1. Love Or Let Me Be Lonely	70	8²	2397
2. Time Waits For No One	70	44	468
3. I Need You	71	79	116
FRIJID PINK ▶381			
1. House Of The Rising Sun	70	6²	3259
2. Sing A Song For Freedom	70	39	504
3. Heartbreak Hotel	71	53	331
FUNKADELIC ▶514			
Groups: **Parliament** (with the same personnel, led by George Clinton)			
Bootsy's Rubber Band (led by William "Bootsy" Collins)			
The **J.B.'s** (Fred Wesley)			
1. One Nation Under A Groove - Part I	78	22²	762
2. (Not Just) Knee Deep - Part 1	79	45	372
3. Can You Get To That	71	61	174
4. I Wanna Know If It's Good To You?	70	85	60
5. You And Your Folks, Me And My Folks	71	85	51
6. I Got A Thing, You Got A Thing, Everybody's Got A Thing	70	91	25
FUNKY COMMUNICATION COMMITTEE ▶1154			
1. Baby I Want You	79	59	219
FUNKY KINGS ▶1277			
1. Slow Dancing	77	66	125
The **FUZZ** ▶560			
1. I Love You For All Seasons	71	20²	1486
2. Like An Open Door	71	70	241
3. I'm So Glad	71	90²	52
G.Q. ▶522			
1. Disco Nights (Rock-Freak)	79	10	1606
2. I Do Love You	79	27²	806
GQ			
GABRIEL ▶1441			
1. Martha (Your Lovers Come And Go)	78	82	51
GALLERY ▶209			
1. Nice To Be With You	72	1	5457
2. I Believe In Music	72	13	1627
3. Big City Miss Ruth Ann	73	12	1363
Art **GARFUNKEL With James TAYLOR & Paul SIMON** ▶836			
Solos: **Art Garfunkel, James Taylor, Paul Simon**			
Duos: **Simon & Garfunkel**			
Paul Simon/Phoebe Snow			
Carly Simon & James Taylor			
1. (What A) Wonderful World	78	15	844
GARY'S GANG ▶967			
1. Keep On Dancin'	79	33	500
The **J. GEILS BAND** ▶266			
1. Give It To Me	73	15	1285

	Year	Peak	Points
2. Must Of Got Lost	75	17²	1094
3. Looking For A Love	72	37	620
J. Geils Band			
4. One Last Kiss	79	37	448
5. Where Did Our Love Go	76	62²	334
6. Make Up Your Mind	73	76	71
7. (Ain't Nothin' But A) House Party	76	77	63
8. Take It Back	79	80²	52
9. Givin' It All Up	75	86	33
GENESIS ▶763			
1. Follow You Follow Me	78	22	784
2. Your Own Special Way	77	87	28
The **GENTRYS** ▶718			
1. Cinnamon Girl	70	45	412
2. Why Should I Cry	70	50	335
3. Wild World	71	78	95
Steve **GIBBONS BAND** ▶1411			
1. Johnny Cool	76	77	60
GINGER (s) ▶1495			
1. Julie Ann	76	89	33
GLADSTONE ▶968			
1. A Piece Of Paper	72	38	498
The **GLASS BOTTLE** ▶789			
1. I Ain't Got Time Anymore	71	26	648
THE GLASS BOTTLE Featuring Gary Criss			
2. The Girl Who Loved Me When	71	78	83
The **GLASS HOUSE** ▶1384			
Group: The **Originals** (Ty Hunter)			
1. I Can't Be You (You Can't Be Me)	70	90	34
2. Stealing Moments From Another Woman's Life	70	92	11
GODSPELL ▶606			
1. Day By Day	72	9	1971
GOLDEN EARRING ▶572			
1. Radar Love	74	10	1501
2. Candy's Going Bad	74	78	119
3. Ce Soir	75	90²	29
GONZALEZ ▶1054			
1. Haven't Stopped Dancing Yet	79	46	325
The **GOODIES** ▶1621			
1. The Funky Gibbon	75	94	11
GOOSE CREEK SYMPHONY ▶1456			
1. (Oh Lord Won't You Buy Me A) Mercedes Benz	72	83	45
GRAHAM CENTRAL STATION ▶651			
Group: **Sly & The Family Stone** (Larry Graham)			
1. Your Love	75	42	465
2. Can You Handle It?	74	49	338

	Year	Peak	Points
GRAHAM CENTRAL STATION – cont'd			
3. The Jam	76	79^2	95
4. It's Alright	75	95	11
GRAND FUNK RAILROAD ▶46			
1. The Loco-Motion	74	1	5152
2. We're An American Band	73	1	4961
3. Bad Time	75	5	2490
4. Some Kind Of Wonderful	75	7	2134
5. Walk Like A Man	74	17	1008
6. Shinin' On	74	18	913
#1-6: GRAND FUNK			
7. Closer To Home	70	27	841
8. Rock 'N Roll Soul	72	24^2	796
9. Footstompin' Music	72	40	481
10. Mean Mistreater	71	44^2	417
11. Feelin' Alright	71	45	388
12. Gimme Shelter	71	57	205
13. Take Me	76	50	199
14. Can You Do It	76	70	144
15. Heartbreaker	70	72	122
16. Upsetter	72	82^2	82
17. Sally	76	69	72
18. Mr. Limousine Driver	70	99	3
The **GRASS ROOTS** ▶123			
1. Temptation Eyes	71	16^2	2004
2. Two Divided By Love	71	8^2	1900
3. Sooner Or Later	71	12	1853
4. Glory Bound	72	22	839
5. Baby Hold On	70	25	767
6. The Runway	72	29^2	641
7. Walking Through The Country	70	30	601
8. Love Is What You Make It	73	32	580
9. Come On And Say It	70	39	388
10. Mamacita	75	84	52
11. Where There's Smoke There's Fire	73	88	31
12. We Can't Dance To Your Music	73	97	4
GRATEFUL DEAD ▶829			
Solo: **Bob Weir**			
1. Truckin'	72	64	245
2. The Music Never Stopped	75	78	67
3. Uncle John's Band	70	84	39
4. Good Lovin'	79	87	35
GRIN ▶1302			
1. White Lies	72	69	108
The **GUESS WHO** ▶34			
Groups: **Bachman-Turner Overdrive & Ironhorse** (Randy Bachman) The **James Gang** (Domenic Troiano) Solos: **Burton Cummings, Troiano**			
1. American Woman	70	1^2	7259

	Year	Peak	Points
2. No Time	70	4^2	3612
3. Share The Land	70	5	2306
4. Clap For The Wolfman	74	10	1552
5. Rain Dance	71	15^2	1465
6. Hand Me Down World	70	13^2	1443
7. Star Baby	74	30	889
8. Dancin' Fool	75	24	674
9. Albert Flasher	71	35	670
10. Heartbroken Bopper	72	26	566
11. Sour Suite	72	41^2	502
12. Hang On To Your Life	71	35	427
13. No Sugar Tonight	70	39	253
14. Follow Your Daughter Home	73	71^2	137
15. Guns, Guns, Guns	72	66	131
16. Runnin' Back To Saskatoon	72	74	92
17. Broken	71	77	84
18. Glamour Boy	73	83	60
19. Seems Like I Can't Live With You, But I Can't Live Without You	75	88	30
GUNHILL ROAD ▶794			
1. Back When My Hair Was Short	73	25^2	942
GYPSY ▶1106			
Group: **James Walsh Gypsy Band** (James Walsh)			
1. Gypsy Queen (Part 1)	71	66	267
HAIR (ORIGINAL SOUNDTRACK)/ CHERYL BARNES ▶1470			
1. Easy To Be Hard	79	89^2	42
Bill **HALEY** And His **COMETS** ▶1005			
1. (We're Gonna) Rock Around The Clock	74	36	418
HAMILTON, JOE FRANK & REYNOLDS ▶115			
1. Don't Pull Your Love	71	1	6041
2. Fallin' In Love	75	1	4409
3. Winners And Losers	76	18	1142
Hamilton, Joe Frank And Reynolds			
4. Daisy Mae	72	39	601
5. Annabella	71	42	421
6. Everyday Without You	76	82	63
The **HAPPENINGS** ▶1578			
1. Answer Me, My Love	70	95	16
The Don **HARRISON BAND** ▶1236			
Group: **Creedence Clearwater Revival** (Doug Clifford, Stu Cook)			
1. Sixteen Tons	76	65	158
HEAD EAST ▶874			
1. Since You Been Gone	78	65	201
2. Never Been Any Reason	75	71	152
3. Love Me Tonight	76	92^2	27

	Year	Peak	Points
HEART ▶156			
1. Magic Man	76	7²	2246
2. Barracuda	77	10²	1548
3. Straight On	78	18	1097
4. Heartless	78	18²	976
5. Dreamboat Annie	77	32	607
6. Dog & Butterfly	79	31²	501
7. Crazy On You	76	40²	486
8. Little Queen	77	48	245
9. Crazy On You [reissue--see #7]	78	69³	118
10. Kick It Out	77	69	106
HEARTSFIELD ▶1472			
1. Music Eyes	74	85	41
HEATWAVE ▶227			
1. Boogie Nights	77	2	5046
2. The Groove Line	78	10²	1602
3. Always And Forever	78	12	1391
HEAVEN BOUND ▶1080			
1. Five Hundred Miles	71	79	102
2. He'd Rather Have The Rain	71	80	91
#1 & 2: HEAVEN BOUND with Tony Scotti			
HELLO PEOPLE ▶1220			
1. Future Shock	75	70	170
Billy HEMMANS & CLAYS COMPOSITE ▶1666			
1. Summertime	70	97	6
The HEYETTES ▶1161			
1. The Fonz Song	76	66²	212
Monk HIGGINS & The SPECIALTIES ▶1498			
1. Gotta Be Funky	72	86	32
HIGH INERGY ▶723			
1. You Can't Turn Me Off (In The Middle Of Turning Me On)	78	12	1287
The HILLSIDE SINGERS ▶664			
1. I'd Like To Teach The World To Sing (In Perfect Harmony)	72	16²	1172
2. We're Together	72	73	96
HODGES, JAMES And SMITH ▶1690			
1. Since I Fell For You/I'm Falling In Love	77	100²	2
The HOLLIES ▶119			
Solo: Allan Clarke			
1. Long Cool Woman (In A Black Dress)	72	1	5552
2. He Ain't Heavy, He's My Brother *Hollies*	70	8³	2427
3. The Air That I Breathe	74	7²	2258
4. Long Dark Road	72	24	671
5. Magic Woman Touch	73	43	308

	Year	Peak	Points
6. I Can't Tell The Bottom From The Top	70	64	210
7. The Day That Curly Billy Shot Down Crazy Sam McGee	73	86	29
8. Sandy	75	86	26
HONEY CONE ▶140			
[for Carolyn Willis – see also **Seals & Crofts**]			
1. Want Ads	71	1²	6164
2. Stick-Up	71	7	2195
3. One Monkey Don't Stop No Show Part 1	72	14	1426
4. The Day I Found Myself	72	15	1051
5. Sittin' On A Time Bomb (Waitin' For The Hurt To Come)	72	75	58
6. Take Me With You	70	93	10
#1 & 6: *The Honey Cone*			
HOT ▶460			
1. Angel In Your Arms	77	6	3226
2. You Brought The Woman Out Of Me	78	83	58
HOT CHOCOLATE ▶134			
1. You Sexy Thing	76	2	5240
2. Emma	75	6	2287
3. Every 1's A Winner	79	7²	1971
4. Disco Queen	75	21	711
5. So You Win Again	77	48²	367
6. Don't Stop It Now	76	68	162
7. Going Through The Motions	79	71	88
HOTEL ▶852			
1. You'll Love Again	78	67²	208
2. You've Got Another Thing Coming	79	63	182
3. Hold On To The Night	79	77	48
HOTLEGS ▶813			
Group: **10cc** (Graham Gouldman, Kevin Godley, Lol Creme, Eric Stewart)			
1. Neanderthal Man	70	20²	898
HUDSON BROTHERS ▶527			
1. So You Are A Star	74	20	973
2. Rendezvous	75	32	465
3. Lonely School Year	75	68²	210
4. Help Wanted	76	70	118
The HUES CORPORATION ▶252			
1. Rock The Boat	74	1	4904
2. Rockin' Soul	74	28	594
3. Freedom For The Stallion	73	38	547
4. Love Corporation	75	49	298
HUMBLE PIE ▶859			
Solo: **Peter Frampton**			
1. Hot 'N' Nasty	72	44	451
2. I Don't Need No Doctor	71	70	105

	Year	Peak	Points
PAUL HUMPHREY & HIS COOL AID CHEMISTS ▶728			
Group: **Afrique** (Paul Humphrey, David T. Walker)			
1. Cool Aid	71	22^2	1003
2. Funky L.A.	71	97^2	10
The **IDES OF MARCH** ▶455			
1. Vehicle	70	6^2	2561
2. Superman	70	50	261
3. L.A. Goodbye	71	72	156
The **ILLUSION** ▶1120			
1. Together	70	55	254
The **IMPRESSIONS** ▶318			
Solo: **Curtis Mayfield**			
1. Finally Got Myself Together (I'm A Changed Man)	74	17	1095
2. Check Out Your Mind	70	21	1062
Impressions			
3. (Baby) Turn On To Me	70	47	400
4. Sooner Or Later	75	63^2	328
5. Ain't Got Time	71	50	266
6. Same Thing It Took	75	62	238
7. Loving Power	76	79	74
8. Preacher Man	73	90	26
The **INCREDIBLE BONGO BAND(s)** ▶934			
1. Bongo Rock	73	57^2	381
2. Let There Be Drums	73	93	13
The **INDEPENDENTS** ▶498			
1. Leaving Me	73	18	1016
2. Baby I've Been Missing You	73	36	461
3. Let This Be A Lesson To You	74	63	244
4. It's All Over	73	69	121
5. Just As Long As You Need Me, Part I	72	77	82
Independents			
INSTANT FUNK ▶856			
1. I Got My Mind Made Up (You Can Get It Girl)	79	22	761
The **INTRIGUES** ▶1024			
1. I'm Gonna Love You	70	68	214
2. The Language Of Love	71	82	47
The **INTRUDERS** ▶513			
1. I'll Always Love My Mama (Part I)	73	25	600
2. When We Get Married	70	48	291
3. I'm Girl Scoutin'	71	74	144
4. This Is My Love Song	70	80	92
5. I Wanna Know Your Name	73	80	68
6. Pray For Me	71	88	38
7. I Bet He Don't Love You (Like I Love You)	71	86	32

	Year	Peak	Points
IRON BUTTERFLY ▶1649			
Group: **Blues Image** (Mike Pinera)			
1. Easy Rider (Let The Wind Pay The Way)	70	98	8
IRONHORSE ▶1098			
Groups: The **Guess Who**, **Bachman-Turner Overdrive** (Randy Bachman)			
1. Sweet Lui-Louise	79	42	272
The **ISLEY BROTHERS** ▶67			
1. That Lady (Part 1)	73	6^2	2963
2. Fight The Power Part 1	75	6	2348
3. Love The One You're With	71	10^2	1509
4. Pop That Thang	72	23	967
5. For The Love Of You (Part 1 & 2)	75	26^2	800
6. Lay-Away	72	36	541
7. Spill The Wine	71	39	436
8. Work To Do	72	43	381
9. Live It Up Part 1	74	62	362
10. Freedom	71	53^2	336
11. Keep On Doin'	70	55	300
12. Harvest For The World	76	63	267
13. Lay Lady Lay	71	57	208
14. Livin' In The Life	77	60	203
15. What It Comes Down To	74	63	192
16. Summer Breeze (Part I)	74	71	150
17. Take Me To The Next Phase	78	69	126
18. Who Loves You Better - Part 1	76	62	126
19. Warpath	71	76^2	123
20. Midnight Sky (Part 1)	75	65	121
21. Girls Will Be Girls, Boys Will Be Boys	70	69	120
22. I Wanna Be With You (Part I)	79	76	60
23. Get Into Something	70	93	25
24. The Pride (Part 1)	77	96	7
The **JACKSON 5** ▶2			
Duo: **Diana Ross Michael Jackson**			
Solos: **Michael Jackson, Jermaine Jackson**			
1. I'll Be There	70	1^2	9964
2. ABC	70	1	9272
3. I Want You Back	70	1	7696
4. Never Can Say Goodbye	71	1	7580
5. The Love You Save	70	1^2	5814
6. Mama's Pearl	71	1	5370
7. Dancing Machine	74	1	4254
8. Sugar Daddy	72	6^2	3075
9. Shake Your Body (Down To The Ground)	79	5^2	3069
10. Enjoy Yourself	77	4^2	2772
11. Little Bitty Pretty One	72	5^2	2333
12. Corner Of The Sky	72	12	1174
13. Maybe Tomorrow	71	16	1162
14. Lookin' Through The Windows	72	15^2	1125

	Year	Peak	Points
JACKSON 5 –cont'd			
15. I Am Love	75	18	1031
16. Get It Together	73	24^2	805
17. Hallelujah Day	73	21	648
18. Whatever You Got, I Want	74	27	609
19. Forever Came Today	75	55	330
20. Show You The Way To Go	77	45	310
21. Goin' Places	77	55	270
22. Blame It On The Boogie	78	63	169
#9, 10, 20, 21, 22: *The Jacksons*			
23. Santa Claus Is Comin' To Town	70	51	107
The JAGGERZ ▶385			
1. The Rapper	70	2	4267
2. I Call My Baby Candy	70	56	187
The JAMES GANG ▶515			
Solos: **Joe Walsh, Troiano**			
Groups: The **Guess Who** (Domenic Troiano) **Eagles** (Joe Walsh)			
1. Walk Away	71	29	528
2. Must Be Love	74	45	489
3. Midnight Man	71	51	305
4. Funk #49	70	60	302
James Gang			
5. Standing In The Rain	74	82	65
Tommy JAMES And The SHONDELLS ▶532			
Solo: **Tommy James**			
1. She	70	19	858
2. Gotta Get Back To You	70	28	699
3. Come To Me	70	36	466
JAMESTOWN MASSACRE ▶1257			
1. Summer Sun	72	78	140
JAY And The AMERICANS ▶553			
1. Walkin' In The Rain	70	14	1756
2. Capture The Moment	70	45^2	357
The J.B.'s ▶645			
Groups: **Parliament/Funkadelic** (Fred Wesley) **The James Brown Soul Train** (Fred Wesley, Maceo Parker, St. Claire Pinckney)			
1. Doing It To Death	73	21	756
Fred Wesley & The J.B.'s			
2. Gimme Some More	72	55	281
3. Pass The Peas	72	76	85
#2 & 3: *The J.B.'s*			
JEFFERSON STARSHIP ▶110			
Groups: **New Riders Of The Purple Sage** (Spencer Dryden) **Journey** (Aynsley Dunbar)			
1. Miracles	75	4^2	3335
2. Jane	79	6^3	2416
3. Count On Me	78	9	1478
4. With Your Love	76	13^2	1419
5. Runaway	78	13	1123

	Year	Peak	Points
6. Pretty As You Feel	71	35^2	664
7. Volunteers	70	60	389
#6 & 7: *Jefferson Airplane*			
8. Play On Love	76	47	326
9. Light The Sky On Fire	78	65^2	155
10. Crazy Feelin'	78	73	101
11. Ride The Tiger	74	94	14
JELLYROLL ▶1586			
1. Strange	70	97^3	15
JETHRO TULL ▶338			
1. Bungle In The Jungle	75	12	1528
2. Living In The Past	73	15^2	1160
3. The Whistler	77	52^2	214
4. A Passion Play (Edit #8)	73	60^2	206
5. Locomotive Breath	76	74	94
6. Hymn 43	71	77	75
7. Skating Away On The Thin Ice Of The New Day	75	75	73
JIGSAW ▶402			
1. Sky High	75	5	2644
2. Love Fire	76	34	487
3. Brand New Love Affair	76	72	170
4. If I Have To Go Away	77	89	30
JO JO GUNNE ▶909			
Groups: **Spirit** (Jay Ferguson, Mark Andes) **Firefall** (Mark Andes)			
Solo: **Jay Ferguson**			
1. Run Run Run	72	31	606
The Elton JOHN BAND ▶313			
Solo: **Elton John**			
Duo: **Elton John and Kiki Dee**			
1. Philadelphia Freedom	75	1^2	6531
The JONES GIRLS ▶946			
1. You Gonna Make Me Love Somebody Else	79	32	529
The JONESES ▶950			
1. Sugar Pie Guy Pt. 1	74	54^3	524
Margie JOSEPH & BLUE MAGIC ▶1545			
Group: **Blue Magic**			
1. What's Come Over Me	75	89	21
JOURNEY ▶512			
Groups: **Santana** (Neil Schon, Gregg Rolie) **Jefferson Starship** (Aynsley Dunbar)			
1. Lovin', Touchin', Squeezin'	79	15	1395
2. Wheel In The Sky	78	52^2	311
3. Just The Same Way	79	63	199
4. Lights	78	67	160
JOY OF COOKING ▶1483			
1. Brownsville	71	87	37

Artist / Song	Year	Peak	Points
KC & The SUNSHINE BAND ▶24			
1. That's The Way (I Like It)	75	1^3	6341
2. (Shake, Shake, Shake) Shake Your Booty	76	1	4942
3. Please Don't Go	79	3^3	4789
4. I'm Your Boogie Man	77	1	4754
5. Get Down Tonight	75	1^2	4588
6. Keep It Comin' Love	77	2^2	4167
7. Boogie Shoes	78	33	598
8. It's The Same Old Song	78	41^2	399
9. Do You Wanna Go Party	79	43	301
10. I Like To Do It	77	63	232
11. Queen Of Clubs	76	63	104
#1, 5 & 11: *K.C. & The Sunshine Band*			
12. Wrap Your Arms Around Me	77	80	76
13. Who Do Ya Love	79	87	42
14. Do You Feel All Right	78	83	40
KANSAS ▶171			
1. Dust In The Wind	78	3^2	3156
2. Carry On Wayward Son	77	7^2	2619
3. Point Of Know Return	78	17	1080
4. People Of The South Wind	79	28	553
5. Portrait (He Knew)	78	53^3	275
6. Reason To Be	79	51^2	269
7. Lonely Wind	79	64	115
8. What's On My Mind	77	85	39
KATFISH ▶1148			
1. Dear Prudence	75	57	224
KAYAK ▶1055			
1. I Want You To Be Mine	78	50	325
The KAY-GEES ▶1300			
1. You Got To Keep On Bumpin'	74	81	109
KING CURTIS & The KINGPINS ▶1166			
Group: **Delaney & Bonnie And Friends** (King Curtis)			
1. Whole Lotta Love	71	60	209
KING HARVEST ▶579			
Group: **Celebration** (Ron Altback, Dave "Doc" Robinson)			
1. Dancing In The Moonlight	73	10	1850
2. A Little Bit Like Magic	73	87	37
The KINKS ▶343			
1. Lola	70	8^2	2041
2. Apeman	71	39	452
3. A Rock 'N' Roll Fantasy	78	36	372
4. (Wish I Could Fly Like) Superman	79	42	369
5. Victoria	70	54	267
6. Sleepwalker	77	69	64
KISS ▶106			
Solos: **Ace Frehley, Gene Simmons, Paul Stanley**			
1. Beth	76	7^2	2077
2. I Was Made For Lovin' You	79	8	1746
3. Calling Dr. Love	77	10	1547
4. Rock And Roll All Nite (Live)	76	17	1138
5. Hard Luck Woman	77	19	950
6. Shout It Out Loud	76	24	761
7. Christine Sixteen	77	20	735
8. Rocket Ride	78	46^2	392
9. Sure Know Something	79	44	347
10. Love Gun	77	55	222
11. Rock And Roll All Nite (Studio)	75	57	198
12. Detroit Rock City//Beth [TSW]	76	25	184
13. Kissin' Time	74	79	72
14. Flaming Youth	76	80	50
15. Detroit Rock City	76	94	6
KLAATU ▶1125			
1. Sub-Rosa Subway	77	57^2	155
2. Calling Occupants	77	91	8
The KLOWNS ▶1452			
1. Lady Love	70	81	46
The KNACK ▶188			
1. My Sharona	79	1^6	8758
2. Good Girls Don't	79	11^2	1413
Gladys KNIGHT & The PIPS ▶18			
1. Midnight Train To Georgia	73	1	5470
2. Neither One Of Us (Wants To Be The First To Say Goodbye)	73	1	4555
3. Best Thing That Ever Happened To Me	74	3^2	3596
4. If I Were Your Woman	71	5^2	3344
5. The Way We Were/Try To Remember	75	10	2072
6. I've Got To Use My Imagination	74	7	1957
7. I Feel A Song (In My Heart)	75	11	1878
8. I Don't Want To Do Wrong	71	9^2	1853
9. On And On	74	9	1725
10. Daddy Could Swear, I Declare	73	15	1112
11. Make Me The Woman That You Go Home To	72	22^2	857
12. Where Peaceful Waters Flow	73	23	739
13. Part Time Love	75	27	700
14. You Need Love Like I Do (Don't You)	70	28	618
15. Money	75	40^2	457
16. Love Finds Its Own Way	75	33	443
17. Help Me Make It Through The Night	72	37	411
18. So Sad The Song	76	56	382
19. Baby Don't Change Your Mind	77	51	207

	Year	Peak	Points
Gladys KNIGHT & The PIPS – cont'd			
20. Between Her Goodbye And My Hello	74	76	89
21. All I Need Is Time	73	81	52
KONGAS (s) ▶1579			
1. Africanism/Gimme Some Lovin'	78	92	16
KOOL & The GANG ▶100			
1. Ladies Night	79	4^4	4376
2. Hollywood Swinging	74	7^2	2358
3. Jungle Boogie	74	8	1719
4. Spirit Of The Boogie	75	27^2	1044
5. Higher Plane	74	39	507
6. Caribbean Festival	75	45	475
7. Funky Stuff	73	44	420
8. Rhyme Tyme People	75	52	290
9. Open Sesame - Part I	77	73	142
10. Kool's Back Again	70	80	53
11. Let The Music Take Your Mind	70	88	45
12. Funky Man	70	91	31
13. Who's Gonna Take The Weight (Part One)	71	94	12
KRAFTWERK ▶782			
1. Autobahn	75	19	708
2. Trans-Europe Express	78	91^2	37
L.A. JETS ▶1293			
1. Prisoner (Captured By Your Eyes)	77	80	47
2. Dancin' Thru The Night	76	91^2	25
L.T.D. ▶391			
1. (Every Time I Turn Around) Back In Love Again	78	6	2186
2. Love Ballad	76	22	979
3. Holding On (When Love Is Gone)	78	54	278
4. Never Get Enough Of Your Love	78	81^2	69
LABELLE ▶309			
1. Lady Marmalade	75	1	5815
2. What Can I Do For You?	75	52	295
LADY FLASH ▶932			
1. Street Singin'	76	34	557
Francis LAI and His ORCHESTRA ▶977			
1. Theme From Love Story	71	36	479
LAKE ▶1446			
1. Time Bomb	77	88	49
LAW ▶1536			
1. Wake Up	75	92	23
LAZY RACER ▶1433			
1. Keep On Running Away	79	81	53
LE PAMPLEMOUSSE (s) ▶1443			
1. Le Spank	78	80	51

	Year	Peak	Points
LE ROUX ▶1033			
1. New Orleans Ladies *Louisiana's Le Roux*	78	55	365
LED ZEPPELIN ▶113			
1. Whole Lotta Love	70	2^2	5899
2. Immigrant Song	71	8^2	2174
3. Black Dog	72	9	1430
4. D'yer Mak'er	73	16^2	1417
5. Over The Hills And Far Away	73	28^2	649
6. Trampled Under Foot	75	28	552
7. Rock And Roll	72	42	390
John LENNON/PLASTIC ONO BAND ▶120 Solos: **John Lennon, Eric Clapton, George Harrison, Billy Preston, Ringo Starr** Groups: The **Beatles** (John Lennon, Ringo Starr) **Delaney & Bonnie And Friends** (Eric Clapton)			
1. Imagine	71	2	4529
2. Whatever Gets You Thru The Night *John Lennon With The Plastic Ono Nuclear Band [guest vocal: Elton John]*	74	1	4209
3. Power To The People *#1 & 3: John Lennon/Plastic Ono Band*	71	10	1366
4. Mother *[Alt label: includes Yoko Ono / Plastic Ono Band]*	71	19	730
5. Cold Turkey *Plastic Ono Band*	70	32	698
6. Happy Xmas (War Is Over) *John & Yoko and the Plastic Ono Band with The Harlem Community Choir*	72	36	201
7. Woman Is The Nigger Of The World *JOHN LENNON/PLASTIC ONO Band With Elephants Memory and The Invisible Strings*	72	93	9
The LETTERMEN ▶565			
1. Love	71	44	476
2. Traces/Memories	70	51	469
3. She Cried	70	54	344
4. Everything Is Good About You	71	78	155
Ramsey LEWIS And EARTH, WIND & FIRE ▶993 Solo: **Ramsey Lewis** Groups: **Earth, Wind & Fire** **Earth, Wind & Fire With The Emotions**			
1. Sun Goddess	75	67	188
2. Hot Dawgit	75	72	111
LIGHTHOUSE ▶457			
1. One Fine Morning	71	16^2	1348
2. Pretty Lady	73	31^2	566
3. Sunny Days	72	37	468
4. Take It Slow (Out In The Country)	72	63	263
LIMMIE & FAMILY COOKIN' ▶1150			
1. You Can Do Magic	73	64	222

	Year	Peak	Points
LINDISFARNE ▶842			
1. Run For Home	78	35	557
2. Lady Eleanor	72	79	62
LIQUID GOLD ▶1311			
1. My Baby's Baby	79	66	103
LIQUID SMOKE ▶1369			
1. I Who Have Nothing	70	78	78
LITTLE ANTHONY And The IMPERIALS ▶965			
Group: The **O'Jays** (Sammy Strain)			
1. Help Me Find A Way (To Say I Love You)	70	65	233
2. I'm Falling In Love With You	74	90	18
3. Don't Get Close	70	98^2	8
Little Anthony & The Imperials			
LITTLE FEAT ▶1523			
1. Oh Atlanta	78	92^2	27
LITTLE RIVER BAND ▶144			
1. Reminiscing	78	3^2	3587
2. Lonesome Loser	79	7^2	2382
3. Lady	79	10^2	1735
4. Help Is On Its Way	77	14	1275
5. Happy Anniversary	78	22^2	721
6. It's A Long Way There	76	31	645
7. I'll Always Call Your Name	77	71	91
LITTLE SISTER ▶549			
[backing singers for **Sly & The Family Stone**]			
1. You're The One - Part II	70	20^3	1121
2. Somebody's Watching You	71	22	1011
LIVERPOOL EXPRESS ▶1560			
1. You Are My Love	76	96^3	19
Ian **LLOYD & STORIES** - see **STORIES**			
LOOKING GLASS ▶218			
Group: **Starz** (Pieter Sweval)			
1. Brandy (You're A Fine Girl)	72	1	6949
2. Jimmy Loves Mary-Anne	73	31	730
3. Golden Rainbow	72	75	64
4. Rainbow Man	73	94	12
The **LORELEI** (s) ▶1686			
1. S.T.O.P. (Stop)	72	99	2
The **LOST GENERATION** ▶919			
1. The Sly, Slick, And The Wicked	70	39	590
LOVE AND KISSES (s) ▶1023			
1. Thank God It's Friday	78	44	384
LOVE UNLIMITED ▶431			
1. Walkin' In The Rain With The One I Love	72	7^2	2188
2. I Belong To You	75	29	779

	Year	Peak	Points
3. It May Be Winter Outside (But In My Heart It's Spring)	74	87	35
4. Under The Influence Of Love	74	87	23
LOVE UNLIMITED ORCHESTRA (s) ▶247			
[conducted by **Barry White**]			
1. Love's Theme	74	1	5080
2. Satin Soul	75	28^2	717
3. Rhapsody In White	74	66	131
4. Theme From King Kong (Pt. 1)	77	78	53
5. My Sweet Summer Suite	76	95	15
The **LOVELITES** ▶1436			
1. How Can I Tell My Mom And Dad	70	86	53
LUNAR FUNK ▶1121			
1. Mr. Penguin - Pt. 1	72	56	253
LYNYRD SKYNYRD ▶211			
1. What's Your Name	78	7^2	2332
2. Sweet Home Alabama	74	7	2102
3. Free Bird	75	25	837
4. Free Bird (Live)	77	32^2	598
5. Saturday Night Special	75	41	380
6. You Got That Right	78	68	110
7. Double Trouble	76	86	38
MFSB (s) ▶291			
Groups: The **Atlanta Disco Band** (s), The **Salsoul Orchestra**			
1. TSOP (The Sound Of Philadelphia)	74	1^2	5412
2. Sexy	75	43	369
3. Love Is The Message	74	48	277
#1 & 3: MFSB featuring The Three Degrees			
MACHINE ▶1546			
1. There But For The Grace Of God Go I	79	93	21
The **MAGIC LANTERNS** ▶1348			
Solo: **Albert Hammond**			
1. One Night Stand	71	91	32
2. Country Woman	72	90	23
The Magic Lantern			
MAHOGANY RUSH ▶1468			
1. A New Rock And Roll	74	88	42
The **MAIN INGREDIENT** ▶130			
1. Everybody Plays The Fool	72	1	5073
2. Just Don't Want To Be Lonely	74	8	2050
3. Happiness Is Just Around The Bend	74	26	629
4. I'm So Proud	71	41	562
5. Spinning Around (I Must Be Falling In Love)	71	47	426
6. You've Been My Inspiration	70	53	398
7. You've Got To Take It (If You Want It)	73	48	395
8. Black Seeds Keep On Growing	71	74	98
9. Rolling Down A Mountainside	75	80	70

	Year	Peak	Points
MAIN INGREDIENT – cont'd			
10. You Can Call Me Rover	73	78	68
11. I'm Better Off Without You	70	83	50
MALO ▶707			
1. Suavecito	72	12	1374
Henry MANCINI And His ORCHESTRA ▶621			
Duo: **Charley Pride**/Henry Mancini			
1. (Theme From) Love Story	71	11^2	1432
HENRY MANCINI, HIS ORCHESTRA & CHORUS Henry Mancini, Piano Soloist			
2. Theme from Charlie's Angels	77	73	74
MANDRILL ▶769			
1. Fencewalk	73	47	468
2. Hang Loose	73	92^2	20
3. Mandrill	71	98^2	8
4. I Refuse To Smile	72	100	1
Manfred MANN'S EARTH BAND ▶345			
Groups: **McGuiness Flint** (Tom McGuiness) **Night** (Chris Thompson)			
Solo: **Chris Thompson**			
1. Blinded By The Light	77	1	3872
2. You Angel You	79	53	217
3. Spirit In The Night	77	59^2	200
4. Living Without You	72	93	11
The MANHATTAN TRANSFER ▶777			
1. Operator	75	24	745
2. Clap Your Hands	75	95	12
The MANHATTANS ▶148			
1. Kiss And Say Goodbye	76	1^2	6645
2. There's No Me Without You	73	29^2	850
3. Don't Take Your Love	75	37	504
4. Hurt	75	70	163
5. I Kinda Miss You	77	71	162
6. One Life To Live	72	72	73
7. It Feels So Good To Be Loved So Bad	77	74	59
8. You'd Better Believe It	73	84	39
9. Am I Losing You	78	89	30
10. If My Heart Could Speak	70	100	1
Manhattans			
MANITOBA ▶1670			
1. Something In You	70	98	5
The MARK IV ▶1616			
1. Honey I Still Love You	72	96	11
Bob MARLEY & The WAILERS ▶1405			
1. Roots, Rock, Reggae	76	75	62
MARMALADE ▶425			
1. Reflections Of My Life	70	7	2724

	Year	Peak	Points
2. Rainbow	70	48	428
3. Falling Apart At The Seams	76	55^2	268
The MARSHALL TUCKER BAND ▶449			
1. Heard It In A Love Song	77	10^2	1706
2. Last Of The Singing Cowboys	79	43	317
3. Fire On The Mountain	76	55^2	313
4. Can't You See	77	70	111
5. Dream Lover	78	81	46
MASHMAKHAN ▶830			
Group: **April Wine** (Jerry Mercer)			
1. As The Years Go By	70	30	856
The MASQUERADERS ▶1515			
1. (Call Me) The Traveling Man	76	94	29
MASS PRODUCTION ▶966			
1. Firecracker	79	33^2	502
MATTHEWS' SOUTHERN COMFORT ▶722			
Solo: **Ian Matthews**			
1. Woodstock	71	17	1298
MAZE ▶1123			
1. Feel That You're Feelin'	79	73	86
2. While I'm Alone	77	71	79
#1 & 2: MAZE Featuring Frankie Beverly			
Paul McCARTNEY & WINGS / WINGS ▶5			
Groups: **The Beatles** (Paul McCartney) **Ginger Baker's Air Force** (Denny Laine)			
Duo: **Paul & Linda McCartney**			
Solo: **Paul McCartney**			
1. My Love	73	1^4	7880
2. Silly Love Songs	76	1^2	7833
3. Live And Let Die	73	1	4880
4. With A Little Luck	78	1^2	4802
5. Band On The Run	74	1^2	4779
6. Listen To What The Man Said	75	1	4634
7. Let 'Em In	76	1	4202
8. Junior's Farm	75	4	2903
9. Goodnight Tonight	79	4	2567
10. Jet	74	5	2476
11. Helen Wheels	74	5	1935
12. Hi, Hi, Hi	73	6	1521
13. Maybe I'm Amazed	77	10	1386
14. Venus And Mars Rock Show	75	16^2	801
15. Getting Closer	79	20	654
16. I've Had Enough	78	28	499
17. Give Ireland Back To The Irish	72	38	430
18. Arrow Through Me	79	36	363
19. Girls' School//Mull Of Kintyre [TSW]	77	31	336
20. London Town	78	42	302
21. Mary Had A Little Lamb	72	48	296

	Year	Peak	Points
Paul McCARTNEY & WINGS – cont'd			
22. Sally G	75	49²	251
#1, 5, 8, 10, 11, 22: *Paul McCartney & Wings*			
23. Letting Go	75	41	240
24. Girls' School	77	38	157
25. Little Woman Love	72	95	7
#2-4, 6, 7, 9, 12-21, 23-25: *Wings*			
Alton McCLAIN & DESTINY ▶1036			
1. It Must Be Love	79	45	361
The McCRARYS ▶1129			
1. You	78	51	244
McGUINN, CLARK & HILLMAN ▶987			
Groups: **The Byrds** (Roger McGuinn, Gene Clark, (Chris Hillman)			
The Souther, Hillman, Furay Band (Chris Hillman)			
1. Don't You Write Her Off	79	33	460
McGUINNESS FLINT ▶894			
Duo: **Gallagher and Lyle** (Benny Gallagher, Graham Lyle)			
Group: **Manfred Mann's Earth Band** (Tom McGuiness)			
1. When I'm Dead And Gone	71	35	642
Harold MELVIN And The BLUE NOTES ▶133			
Solo: **Teddy Pendergrass**			
1. If You Don't Know Me By Now	72	2	3625
2. The Love I Lost (Part 1)	73	9	1884
3. Bad Luck (Part 1)	75	13²	1586
4. Wake Up Everybody (Part 1)	76	15²	1387
5. I Miss You (Part I)	72	40	523
6. Yesterday I Had The Blues	73	52	215
7. Where Are All My Friends	75	67	190
8. Tell The World How I Feel About 'Cha Baby	76	67	176
9. Reaching For The World	77	73	97
10. Satisfaction Guaranteed (Or Take Your Love Back)	74	79	72
Sergio MENDES & BRASIL '77 ▶1688			
1. Love Music	73	99	2
MESA ▶1196			
1. Sailing Ships	77	64	186
The MESSENGERS ▶1002			
1. That's The Way A Woman Is	71	42	420
The METERS ▶663			
1. Chicken Strut	70	53	380
2. Look-Ka Py Py	70	55	328
3. Be My Lady	77	83²	71
4. Hand Clapping Song	70	84	64
MIGHTY CLOUDS OF JOY ▶1416			
1. Mighty High	76	77	59

	Year	Peak	Points
Buddy MILES & The FREEDOM EXPRESS ▶1684			
Solo: **Buddy Miles**			
Duo: **Carlos Santana & Buddy Miles**			
1. Them Changes	70	99	3
Steve MILLER BAND ▶124			
Solo: **Steve Miller**			
1. The Joker	74	1	5462
2. Jet Airliner	77	3	3224
3. Swingtown	77	13²	1136
4. Jungle Love	77	17	926
5. Your Cash Ain't Nothin' But Trash	74	40	427
6. Living In The U.S.A.	74	38	380
7. Going To The Country	70	81	47
The Steve Miller Band			
The MIRACLES ▶234			
Group: **Smokey Robinson & The Miracles** (Warren Moore, Bobby Rogers, Ronnie White)			
1. Love Machine (Part 1)	76	1	5368
2. Do It Baby	74	10	1609
3. Don't Cha Love It	75	63	200
4. Don't Let It End ('til You Let It Begin)	73	99	2
MR. BIG ▶1256			
1. Romeo	77	64	140
MISTRESS ▶1432			
1. Mistrusted Love	79	81	55
The MIXTURES ▶988			
1. Pushbike Song	71	44	446
The MOB ▶1214			
1. Give It To Me	71	87	69
2. I Dig Everything About You	71	90	44
MOCEDADES ▶619			
1. Eres Tu (Touch The Wind)	74	9²	1842
The MOMENTS ▶277			
Groups: **Sylvia & The Moments**			
Moments And Whatnauts			
1. Love On A Two-Way Street	70	8	1954
Moments			
2. Sexy Mama	74	20	731
3. Look At Me (I'm In Love)	75	39²	460
4. If I Didn't Care	70	37	374
5. Gotta Find A Way	73	71	122
6. All I Have	70	74	90
7. I Can't Help It	71	90	20
8. I Could Have Loved You	78	97	6
9. Lucky Me	71	97	5
MOMENTS And WHATNAUTS ▶1479			
Groups: The **Moments**, **Whatnauts**			
1. Girls (Part I)	75	85	39

Artist / Song	Year	Peak	Points
The MOODY BLUES ▶153 Duo: **Justin Hayward And John Lodge** Solo: **Justin Hayward**			
1. Nights In White Satin	72	1	4348
2. I'm Just A Singer (In A Rock And Roll Band)	73	8^2	1798
3. The Story In Your Eyes	71	14^2	1476
4. Question	70	19^2	1114
5. Isn't Life Strange	72	20	847
6. Steppin' In A Slide Zone	78	46	221
7. Driftwood	78	68	138
MOTHER'S FINEST ▶1437			
1. Baby Love	77	86	53
MOTT THE HOOPLE ▶785 Group: **Bad Company** (Mick Ralphs) Solo: **Ian Hunter**			
1. All The Young Dudes	72	34^2	583
2. The Golden Age Of Rock 'N' Roll	74	72	157
MOUNTAIN ▶625			
1. Mississippi Queen	70	24	988
2. For Yasgur's Farm	70	73	138
3. The Animal Trainer And The Toad	71	71	112
The MOVE ▶1671 Group: **Electric Light Orchestra** (Bev Bevan, Jeff Lynne, Roy Wood)			
1. Do Ya	72	97	5
MUNGO JERRY ▶390			
1. In The Summertime	70	2	4797
Walter MURPHY & The BIG APPLE BAND ▶264			
1. A Fifth Of Beethoven	76	1	6506
2. Flight '76 *The Walter Murphy Band*	77	36^2	566
MUSIQUE (s) ▶1168			
1. In The Bush	78	58	209
The MYSTIC MOODS (s) ▶1219			
1. Cosmic Sea	73	78	61
2. Honey Trippin'	75	84^2	49
NRBQ ▶1179 Group: **Clean Living** (Al Anderson)			
1. Get That Gasoline Blues	74	55	198
NATIONAL LAMPOON ▶1533			
1. Deteriorata [see also: Desiderata]	72	88	24
NATURAL FOUR ▶858			
1. Can This Be Real	74	25	756
NATURE'S DIVINE ▶1318			
1. I Just Can't Control Myself	79	70	99
NAZARETH ▶535			
1. Love Hurts	76	9^2	2604
NAZZ ▶1251 Groups: **Runt, Utopia** (Todd Rundgren) Solo: **Todd Rundgren** [Todd Rundgren had left Nazz by 1970]			
1. Hello It's Me [reissue--first charted in 1969]	70	69	145
The NEIGHBORHOOD ▶887			
1. Big Yellow Taxi	70	24	651
Rick NELSON And The STONE CANYON BAND ▶363 Solo: **Rick Nelson**			
1. Garden Party	72	3	3652
2. She Belongs To Me	70	30	729
3. Palace Guard	73	79	82
Michael NESMITH & The FIRST NATIONAL BAND ▶523			
1. Joanne	70	17^2	1111
2. Silver Moon	71	28	599
3. Nevada Fighter	71	73	112
4. I've Just Begun To Care	71	95	11
The NEW BIRTH ▶453 Group: **The Nite-Liters**			
1. I Can Understand It	73	28	632
2. Dream Merchant	75	31	589
3. Wildflower	74	49	369
4. It's Impossible	71	46	366
5. It's Been A Long Time	74	59	192
6. Granddaddy (Part 1)	75	87	22
The NEW COLONY SIX ▶1064			
1. Roll On	71	63^2	177
2. Barbara, I Love You	70	93^2	31
NEW ENGLAND ▶892			
1. Don't Ever Wanna Lose Ya	79	40^2	397
2. Hello, Hello, Hello	79	75	78
The NEW HOPE ▶1241			
1. Won't Find Better (Than Me)	70	75	150
NEW RIDERS OF THE PURPLE SAGE ▶1692 Group: **Jefferson Airplane** (Spencer Dryden)			
1. Louisiana Lady	71	100	1
The NEW SEEKERS ▶235			
1. Look What They've Done To My Song Ma	70	10^2	1716
2. I'd Like To Teach The World To Sing (In Perfect Harmony)	72	11^2	1425
3. Pinball Wizard/See Me, Feel Me	73	21	906
4. Beautiful People	71	53	249
5. You Won't Find Another Fool Like Me *THE NEW SEEKERS Featuring Lyn Paul*	74	75	107
6. Beg, Steal Or Borrow	72	86	34
7. Come Softly To Me *The NEW SEEKERS Featuring Marty Kristian*	73	92	24

	Year	Peak	Points
NEW SEEKERS – cont'd			
8. Nickel Song	71	96^2	18
#1, 4 & 8: THE NEW SEEKERS Featuring Eve Graham			
9. Circles	72	94	13
10. Reach Out I'll Be There	74	99	2
NEW YORK CITY ▶542			
1. I'm Doin' Fine Now	73	12	1701
2. Make Me Twice The Man	73	78	91
3. Quick, Fast, In A Hurry	74	78	91
The **NEWBEATS** ▶1364			
1. Groovin' (Out On Life)	70	85	81
The **NEWCOMERS** ▶1691			
1. Pin The Tail On The Donkey	71	100	1
NIGHT ▶853			
Group: **Manfred Mann's Earth Band** (Chris Thompson)			
Solo: **Chris Thompson**			
1. Hot Summer Nights	79	26^3	770
NITEFLYTE ▶1198			
1. If You Want It	79	59	185
The **NITE-LITERS** ▶696			
Group: The **New Birth**			
1. K-Jee	71	39	715
2. Afro-Strut	72	39	422
NITTY GRITTY DIRT BAND ▶348			
1. Mr. Bojangles	71	9	2058
[alt. label adds (Prologue: Uncle Charlie And His Dog Teddy)]			
2. House At Pooh Corner	71	38	534
3. Some Of Shelly's Blues	71	64	220
4. (All I Have To Do Is) Dream	75	57	199
5. In For The Night	78	76	86
The Dirt Band			
6. Battle Of New Orleans	74	77	69
7. Jambalaya (On The Bayou)	72	91	26
NORTHERN LIGHT ▶1332			
1. Minnesota	75	77	93
OAK ▶1169			
1. This Is Love	79	55	208
OCEAN ▶255			
1. Put Your Hand In The Hand	71	2^3	6150
2. Deep Enough For Me	71	70	129
3. One More Chance	72	88	38
4. We Got A Dream	71	99	5
ODDS & ENDS ▶1375			
1. Love Makes The World Go Round	71	83	75
ODYSSEY ▶635			
1. Native New Yorker	78	15^2	1353
2. Weekend Lover	78	80	81

	Year	Peak	Points
OHIO PLAYERS ▶76			
1. Love Rollercoaster	76	3^2	4712
2. Fire	75	1	4427
3. Funky Worm	73	13	1383
4. Skin Tight	74	11	1328
5. Who'd She Coo?	76	35^2	765
6. Ecstasy	73	31	583
7. Sweet Sticky Thing	75	31	550
8. I Want To Be Free	75	32	507
9. Fopp	76	41	396
10. Pain (Part 1)	72	71	249
11. Jive Turkey (Part 1)	74	51	244
12. Got Pleasure	72	90^2	43
13. O-H-I-O	77	95	12
The **O'JAYS** ▶36			
Groups: **Philadelphia International All Stars**			
Little Anthony & The Imperials (Sammy Strain)			
1. Love Train	73	1	6626
2. Back Stabbers	72	1	4991
3. I Love Music (Part 1)	76	7	2818
4. Use Ta Be My Girl	78	5^2	2671
5. For The Love Of Money	74	7	1644
6. Put Your Hands Together	74	14	1071
7. Livin' For The Weekend	76	24	838
8. Give The People What They Want	75	33	628
9. Time To Get Down	73	30^2	618
10. 992 Arguments	72	43^2	406
11. Deeper (In Love With You)	70	58	255
O'Jays			
12. Message In Our Music	76	66	248
13. Let Me Make Love To You	75	56^2	210
14. Brandy	78	76^2	100
15. Darlin' Darlin' Baby (Sweet, Tender, Love)	77	79	86
16. Looky Looky (Look At Me Girl)	70	97	13
100 PROOF AGED IN SOUL ▶389			
1. Somebody's Been Sleeping	70	6^3	3010
2. Everything Good Is Bad	72	49	368
3. One Man's Leftovers (Is Another Man's Feast)	71	79^2	92
4. 90 Day Freeze (On Her Love)	71	83^2	63
The **ORIGINAL CASTE** ▶926			
1. One Tin Soldier	70	50	563
The **ORIGINALS** ▶566			
Group: The **Glass House** (Ty Hunter)			
1. The Bells	70	18	1242
2. God Bless Whoever Sent You	71	52	435
3. Down To Love Town	76	99	3

	Year	Peak	Points
Tony ORLANDO And DAWN ▶11			
Solo: Tony Orlando			
1. Knock Three Times	71	1^2	9172
2. Tie A Yellow Ribbon Round The Ole Oak Tree	73	1^3	8603
3. Candida	70	1	4962
4. He Don't Love You (Like I Love You)	75	1	4388
5. Say, Has Anybody Seen My Sweet Gypsy Rose	73	4^2	3655
6. Steppin' Out (Gonna Boogie Tonight)	74	14	1174
7. Who's In The Strawberry Patch With Sally	73	13	1144
8. Look In My Eyes Pretty Woman	75	20^2	950
9. Mornin' Beautiful	75	15	945
10. Summer Sand	71	19	916
11. Cupid	76	21	891
12. What Are You Doing Sunday	71	26^2	796
13. I Play And Sing	71	22	668
#1, 3, 10 & 13: DAWN			
14. Runaway/Happy Together	72	41	365
15. Skybird	75	52	332
16. You're All I Need To Get By	75	38	296
17. It Only Hurts When I Try To Smile	74	56	253
18. You're A Lady	73	68	233
19. Vaya Con Dios	72	60	214
#2, 5, 12, 14, 18 & 19: DAWN Featuring TONY ORLANDO			
20. Sing	77	62	127
21. Midnight Love Affair	76	93	19
ORLEANS ▶207			
1. Dance With Me	75	5	2701
2. Still The One	76	6^2	2452
3. Love Takes Time	79	12^2	1278
4. Reach	77	45^2	391
5. Let There Be Music	75	53	270
6. Don't Throw Our Love Away	79	92	20
Shad O'SHEA & The 18 WHEELERS ▶1337			
1. Colorado Call	76	79	91
The OSMONDS ▶44			
Solos: Donny Osmond, Marie Osmond			
Duo: Donny And Marie Osmond			
[see also Steve & Eydie]			
1. One Bad Apple	71	1^4	7752
2. Yo-Yo	71	2	5130
3. Down By The Lazy River	72	3^3	4503
4. Double Lovin'	71	9	1517
5. Love Me For A Reason	74	8^2	1363
6. Hold Her Tight	72	15^2	1017
7. Crazy Horses	72	19	838
8. Let Me In	73	19	780
9. Goin' Home	73	21	570

	Year	Peak	Points
10. The Proud One	75	33^2	553
11. I Can't Live A Dream	76	53	289
OUTLAWS ▶754			
1. There Goes Another Love Song	75	26	588
2. Hurry Sundown	77	78	70
3. Take It Any Way You Want It	79	94	15
The OVATIONS ▶1262			
1. Having A Party Medley	73	73	134
[Alt. label: The Ovations Featuring Louis Williams]			
OWEN B. ▶1382			
1. Mississippi Mama	70	81	71
The OZARK MOUNTAIN DAREDEVILS ▶241			
1. Jackie Blue	75	1^2	5297
2. If You Wanna Get To Heaven	74	21	696
Ozark Mountain Daredevils			
3. You Know Like I Know	77	55	284
4. If I Only Knew	76	71	124
5. Look Away	74	88	29
OZO ▶1331			
1. Listen To The Buddha	76	72	94
P-NUT GALLERY (s) ▶1108			
1. Do You Know What Time It Is?	71	54	263
PABLO CRUISE ▶173			
1. Whatcha Gonna Do?	77	3^2	3367
2. Love Will Find A Way	78	5^3	2884
3. Don't Want To Live Without It	78	18	869
4. I Want You Tonight	79	21	804
5. A Place In The Sun	77	42	297
6. I Go To Rio	79	56	182
7. Never Had A Love	78	89^2	34
PACIFIC GAS & ELECTRIC ▶641			
1. Are You Ready?	70	12	1378
PACIFIC GAS & ELECTRIC With The Blackberries			
2. Thank God For You Baby	72	95	14
PG&E			
PAGES ▶1421			
1. I Do Believe In You	79	80	58
PAINTER ▶1189			
1. West Coast Woman	73	64	191
PAPER LACE ▶322			
1. The Night Chicago Died	74	1	4872
2. The Black-Eyed Boys	74	41	373
3. Billy--Don't Be A Hero	74	68	133
Graham PARKER And The RUMOUR ▶1386			
1. Hold Back The Night	77	77	70

PARLIAMENT ▶508	Year	Peak	Points
Groups: **Funkadelic** (with the same personnel, led by George Clinton) **Bootsy's Rubber Band** (led by William "Bootsy" Collins) **The J.B.'s** (Fred Wesley)			
1. Flash Light	78	15^2	1171
2. Tear The Roof Off The Sucker (Give Up The Funk)	76	20^2	1141
3. Chocolate City	75	86	28

Alan PARSONS PROJECT ▶656	Year	Peak	Points
1. Damned If I Do	79	30	639
2. (The System Of) Doctor Tarr And Professor Fether	76	54	286
3. Don't Let It Show	78	65	164

The PARTRIDGE FAMILY ▶54	Year	Peak	Points
Solo: **David Cassidy**			
1. I Think I Love You	70	1^3	9173
2. Doesn't Somebody Want To Be Wanted	71	1	6056
3. I'll Meet You Halfway	71	2	3132
4. I Woke Up In Love This Morning	71	9	2084
5. It's One Of Those Nights (Yes Love)	72	13^2	1308
6. Breaking Up Is Hard To Do	72	25	734
7. Looking Through The Eyes Of Love	73	25^2	709
8. Am I Losing You	72	31	523
9. Friend And A Lover	73	92	21
#1-9: THE PARTRIDGE FAMILY Starring Shirley Jones & Featuring David Cassidy			

PEOPLE'S CHOICE ▶543	Year	Peak	Points
1. Do It Any Way You Wanna	75	14	1484
2. I Likes To Do It	71	50	322
3. Nursery Rhymes (Part I)	76	78	74

George PERKINS & The SILVER STARS ▶1039	Year	Peak	Points
1. Cryin' In The Streets (Part I)	70	52	357

The PERSUADERS ▶393	Year	Peak	Points
1. Thin Line Between Love And Hate	71	10	1730
2. Some Guys Have All The Luck	73	39	523
3. Love Gonna Pack Up (And Walk Out)	72	54	460
4. Best Thing That Ever Happened To Me	74	64	113
5. Peace In The Valley Of Love	72	92	21
6. Bad, Bold And Beautiful Girl	73	100	1

Tom PETTY And The HEARTBREAKERS ▶692	Year	Peak	Points
1. Breakdown	78	33^3	595
2. I Need To Know	78	53	244
3. Listen To Her Heart	78	73	89

PHILADELPHIA ▶1681	Year	Peak	Points
1. School's Back	77	99	3

PHILADELPHIA INTERNATIONAL ALL STARS ▶1698	Year	Peak	Points
Solos: Billy Paul, Teddy Pendergrass, Lou Rawls			
Groups: **Archie Bell & The Drells** (Archie Bell) **The O'Jays** (Eddie Levert, Walter Williams, Sammy Strain)			
1. Let's Clean Up The Ghetto	77	100	1

PHILLY DEVOTIONS ▶1637	Year	Peak	Points
1. I Just Can't Say Goodbye	75	96	9

PICKETTYWITCH ▶895	Year	Peak	Points
Group: **Sweet Dreams** (Polly Brown)			
1. That Same Old Feeling	70	40	635

PILOT ▶452	Year	Peak	Points
1. Magic	75	5^2	2834
2. Just A Smile	75	75	92
3. January	76	87^2	62

PINK FLOYD ▶604	Year	Peak	Points
1. Money	73	10^2	1599
2. Us And Them	74	72	69

The PIPES AND DRUMS And The MILITARY BAND Of The ROYAL SCOTS DRAGOON GUARDS ▶731	Year	Peak	Points
1. Amazing Grace	72	10^2	1256

PLASTIC ONO BAND - see **John LENNON/PLASTIC ONO BAND**

PLAYER ▶198	Year	Peak	Points
1. Baby Come Back	78	1^2	6788
2. This Time I'm In It For Love	78	13	1121
3. Prisoner Of Your Love	78	30	510
4. Silver Lining	79	74	90

POCKETS ▶1592	Year	Peak	Points
1. Come Go With Me	78	94	14

POCO ▶354	Year	Peak	Points
Groups: **Eagles** (Timothy B. Schmit) **The Souther, Hillman, Furay Band** (Richie Furay)			
Solo: **Richie Furay**			
1. Crazy Love	79	14	1367
2. Heart Of The Night	79	19^2	778
3. Keep On Tryin'	75	45^2	367
4. C'mon	71	63	233
5. Indian Summer	77	62	216
6. You Better Think Twice	70	74	119
7. Just For Me And You	71	88	38

POINTER SISTERS ▶145	Year	Peak	Points
Solo: **Bonnie Pointer**			
1. Fire	79	2^2	4841
2. Yes We Can Can *The Pointer Sisters*	73	10	1523
3. How Long (Betcha' Got A Chick On The Side)	75	17^2	1130
4. Fairytale	74	19	855
5. Happiness	79	28	457

	Year	Peak	Points
POINTER SISTERS – cont'd			
6. Going Down Slowly	75	51	256
7. Wang Dang Doodle	74	69	163
8. Live Your Life Before You Die	75	72	103
9. Steam Heat	74	84	44
The **POLICE** ▶795			
1. Roxanne	79	31	537
2. Message In A Bottle	79	62^2	183
PONDEROSA TWINS + ONE ▶1233			
1. You Send Me	71	63	160
The **POPPY FAMILY** ▶303			
Duo: The **Poppy Family**			
Solos: **Susan Jacks, Terry Jacks**			
1. Which Way You Goin' Billy?	70	2^2	4993
2. That's Where I Went Wrong	70	20^2	1246
#1 & 2: THE POPPY FAMILY (Featuring Susan Jacks)			
POP-TOPS ▶1190			
1. Mammy Blue	71	68^2	191
POTLIQUOR ▶1141			
1. Cheer	72	64	230
POUSETTE-DART BAND ▶1497			
1. For Love	79	91^2	33
PRELUDE ▶694			
1. After The Goldrush	74	17	975
2. For A Dancer	76	66^2	167
The **PRESIDENTS** ▶520			
Group: **Anacostia** (Tony Boyd, Archie Powell, Billy Shorter)			
1. 5-10-15-20 (25-30 Years Of Love)	70	7^2	2102
2. Triangle Of Love (Hey Diddle Diddle)	71	52	363
PRISM ▶850			
Group: **Chilliwack** (Ab Bryant)			
1. Take Me To The Kaptin	78	56^2	240
2. Flyin'	78	63	199
3. Spaceship Superstar	77	100	1
PROCOL HARUM ▶726			
1. Conquistador	72	18	995
2. A Whiter Shade Of Pale	72	86	31
Gary PUCKETT And The UNION GAP ▶1013			
Solos: **Gary Puckett, Kerry Chater**			
Group: **Flash Cadillac & The Continental Kids** (Dwight Bement, Paul Wheatbread)			
1. Let's Give Adam And Eve Another Chance	70	38	399
PURE PRAIRIE LEAGUE ▶791			
Solo: **Mike Reilly**			
1. Amie	75	27	675
2. Two Lane Highway	75	87^2	54
PURPLE REIGN (s) ▶1126			
1. This Old Man	76	48	248

	Year	Peak	Points
PYTHON LEE JACKSON ▶1309			
1. In A Broken Dream	72	75	104
[**Rod Stewart**, guest vocalist; recorded in 1969]			
Q ▶875			
1. Dancin' Man	77	20^2	690
Mike QUATRO JAM BAND (s) ▶1282			
1. Circus	72	74	123
QUEEN ▶93			
1. We Are The Champions	78	3^2	4159
2. Bohemian Rhapsody	76	6^2	3311
3. You're My Best Friend	76	9^2	1839
4. Somebody To Love	77	9^2	1541
5. Killer Queen	75	12	1485
6. Bicycle Race//Fat Bottomed Girls [TSW]	78	18^3	892
7. Tie Your Mother Down	77	54	165
8. It's Late	78	66	124
9. Don't Stop Me Now	79	77	60
10. Keep Yourself Alive	75	89	22
QUICKSILVER MESSENGER SERVICE ▶1176			
1. Fresh Air	70	71	202
The **RAELETTS** ▶1087			
1. I Want To (Do Everything For You)	70	83	78
2. Bad Water	71	80	55
3. Leave My Man (Woman) Alone	71	99	2
The RAELETTS Featuring Vernita Moss			
RAIDERS ▶149			
Solo: **Mark Lindsay**			
1. Indian Reservation (The Lament Of The Cherokee)	71	1	7243
2. Birds Of A Feather	71	13	1202
3. Country Wine	72	28^2	562
The Raiders			
4. Powder Blue Mercedes Queen	72	43	464
5. Love Music	73	61	179
6. Just Seventeen	70	73	112
7. Song Seller	72	89	36
8. Gone Movin' On	70	92	12
RAINBOW ▶1145			
Group: **Deep Purple** (Ritchie Blackmore, Roger Glover)			
Solo: **Cozy Powell**			
1. Since You Been Gone	79	56	227
RAM JAM ▶684			
1. Black Betty	77	14^2	1458
RAMONES ▶1430			
1. Sheena Is A Punk Rocker	77	96^3	19
The Ramones			
2. Do You Wanna Dance	78	91	16

Artist / Song	Year	Peak	Points
RARE BIRD ▶1453			
1. Sympathy	70	82	46
RARE EARTH ▶107			
1. Get Ready	70	2	5097
2. (I Know) I'm Losing You	70	5	2965
3. I Just Want To Celebrate	71	7^2	2021
4. Born To Wander	71	18^2	1268
5. Hey Big Brother	72	24^2	962
6. Warm Ride	78	42^2	409
7. What'd I Say	72	76	77
8. Good Time Sally	72	83	34
The RASCALS ▶640			
Groups: **Bulldog, Fotomaker** (Gene Cornish, Dino Danelli, both groups)			
1. Hold On	70	29	598
2. Glory Glory	70	42^2	436
3. Love Me	71	74	123
RASPBERRIES ▶190			
Solo: **Eric Carmen**			
Group: **Fotomaker** (Wally Bryson)			
1. Go All The Way	72	4	3208
2. I Wanna Be With You	73	10	1658
3. Let's Pretend	73	18^2	1466
4. Overnight Sensation (Hit Record)	74	24	694
5. Tonight	73	37^2	458
6. I'm A Rocker	73	75	66
7. Don't Want To Say Goodbye	72	90	30
The RATTLES ▶1596			
1. The Witch	70	95	14
RAYDIO ▶356			
1. Jack And Jill	78	6^2	3080
2. You Can't Change That	79	10	1958
The REAL THING ▶1413			
1. You To Me Are Everything	76	78	59
The RECORDS ▶1347			
1. Starry Eyes	79	76	88
REDBONE ▶316			
1. Come And Get Your Love	74	5	3505
2. The Witch Queen Of New Orleans	72	19	1098
3. Maggie	71	60	441
4. Suzie Girl	74	76	71
REDEYE ▶698			
1. Games	71	22	1003
2. Red Eye Blues	71	77	126
REDWING ▶1478			
1. California Blues	71	83	40
Martha REEVES & The VANDELLAS ▶825			
Solo: **Martha Reeves**			
1. Bless You	71	44	294
2. In And Out Of My Life	72	70^2	158
3. I Gotta Let You Go	70	83	56
The REFLECTIONS ▶1514			
1. Three Steps From True Love	75	90	29
REO SPEEDWAGON ▶816			
1. Roll With The Changes	78	48	235
2. Time For Me To Fly	78	70	137
3. Only The Strong Survive	79	91	24
4. Ridin' The Storm Out	77	97	5
REUNION (s) ▶622			
1. Life Is A Rock (But The Radio Rolled Me)	74	7	1802
RHYTHM HERITAGE (s) ▶304			
1. Theme From S.W.A.T.	76	1	4790
2. Baretta's Theme ("Keep Your Eye On The Sparrow")	76	16	967
3. Theme From Rocky (Gonna Fly Now)	77	95	9
RIPPLE ▶1083			
1. I Don't Know What It Is, But It Sure Is Funky	73	59	165
2. Willie Pass The Water	74	94	22
The RITCHIE FAMILY ▶486			
1. Brazil	75	10	1284
2. The Best Disco In Town	76	18	1225
3. I Want To Dance With You (Dance With Me)	76	81	77
The ROAD APPLES ▶947			
1. Let's Live Together	76	48	528
Smokey ROBINSON & The MIRACLES ▶131			
Solo: **Smokey Robinson**			
Groups: The **Miracles** (Warren Moore, Bobby Rogers, Ronnie White)			
Diana Ross, Marvin Gaye, Smokey Robinson & Stevie Wonder			
1. The Tears Of A Clown	70	1	7684
2. I Don't Blame You At All	71	18^2	1141
3. Point It Out	70	41	513
4. We've Come Too Far To End It Now	72	46	466
5. Satisfaction	71	55	305
6. Who's Gonna Take The Blame	70	52	289
7. Crazy About The La La La	71	49^2	268
8. I Can't Stand To See You Cry	73	64	222
ROCK FLOWERS ▶1324			
1. Number Wonderful	72	78	96
ROCKETS ▶839			
1. Oh Well	79	39	398
2. Can't Sleep	79	56^2	231
Kenny ROGERS And The FIRST EDITION ▶285			
Solo: **Kenny Rogers**			
1. Something's Burning	70	5	3218

	Year	Peak	Points
Kenny ROGERS/FIRST EDITION – cont'd			
2. Tell It All Brother	70	17	1210
3. Heed The Call	70	21	838
4. Someone Who Cares	71	48	407
The ROLLING STONES ▶26			
Group: **Faces** (Ron Wood)			
1. Miss You	78	1^2	6525
2. Brown Sugar	71	2^2	5007
3. Angie	73	1	4909
4. Beast Of Burden	78	7^3	1743
5. Tumbling Dice	72	10^2	1517
6. Fool To Cry	76	9	1398
7. Doo Doo Doo Doo Doo (Heartbreaker)	74	10	1022
8. Happy	72	14	1016
9. Ain't Too Proud To Beg	74	15^2	998
10. It's Only Rock 'N Roll (But I Like It)	74	18	872
11. Wild Horses	71	18	838
12. You Can't Always Get What You Want	73	34	569
13. Shattered	79	27^2	465
14. I Don't Know Why	75	37	421
15. Hot Stuff	76	60	307
16. Out Of Time	75	65	135
17. All Down The Line	72	77	49
ROSE COLORED GLASS ▶940			
Group: **Blood, Sweat & Tears** (Bill Tillman)			
1. Can't Find The Time	71	53	374
2. If It's Alright With You	71	97	5
ROSE ROYCE ▶216			
1. Car Wash	77	1^2	4139
2. I Wanna Get Next To You	77	10^2	1461
3. Love Don't Live Here Anymore	79	28	597
4. Ooh Boy	78	48	263
5. I'm Going Down	77	64	164
6. Do Your Dance - Part I	77	67	150
Diana ROSS, Marvin GAYE, Smokey ROBINSON & Stevie WONDER ▶1242			
[see solo entries for configurations]			
1. Pops, We Love You (A Tribute To Father)	79	65	150
The ROWANS ▶1306			
Group: **Seatrain** (Peter Rowan)			
1. If I Only Could	76	69	105
The ROYAL SCOTS DRAGOON GUARDS - see **The PIPES AND DRUMS OF**			
ROXY MUSIC ▶671			
Solo: **Bryan Ferry**			
1. Love Is The Drug	76	24^2	953
2. Dance Away	79	51	283
The RUBETTES ▶961			
1. Sugar Baby Love	74	30	509
RUBICON ▶957			
Group: **Sly & The Family Stone** (Jerry Martini)			
1. I'm Gonna Take Care Of Everything	78	31	513
The RUBINOOS ▶1030			
1. I Think We're Alone Now	77	46	366
RUFUS Featuring CHAKA KHAN ▶99			
1. Tell Me Something Good	74	1	3700
2. Sweet Thing	76	5^2	3594
3. Once You Get Started	75	6	1652
4. You Got The Love	74	10	1536
5. At Midnight (My Love Will Lift You Up)	77	30^2	665
6. Hollywood	77	39	430
7. Please Pardon Me (You Remind Me Of A Friend)	75	44	344
8. Dance Wit Me	76	37	319
9. Stay	78	45^2	302
Rufus / Chaka Khan			
10. Slip 'N Slide	73	90	25
#1 & 10: *Rufus*			
RUSH ▶1289			
1. Closer To The Heart	77	79	115
SAD CAFE ▶1395			
1. Run Home Girl	79	81	67
SAINT TROPEZ ▶1296			
1. One More Minute	79	70	112
The SALSOUL ORCHESTRA ▶771			
Group: **MFSB** (s)			
1. Tangerine	76	40	524
2. Nice 'N' Naasty	76	77	63
[Alt. title: Hot 'N' Nasty]			
3. Salsoul Hustle	75	90	17
SALVAGE (s) **▶1096**			
1. Hot Pants	71	64	273
The SANDPIPERS ▶633			
1. Come Saturday Morning	70	13	1434
2. Santo Domingo	70	94	16
SANTA ESMERALDA (s) **▶717**			
1. Don't Let Me Be Misunderstood	78	14^2	1327
SANTA ESMERALDA Starring Leroy Gómez			
SANTANA ▶121			
Duo: **Carlos Santana & Buddy Miles**			
Groups: **Journey** (Gregg Rolie, Neil Schon), **Automatic Man** (Michael Schrieve)			
1. Black Magic Woman	71	4^2	3680
2. Evil Ways	70	7^2	2345
3. Everybody's Everything	71	10	1501
4. Oye Como Va	71	10	1444
5. No One To Depend On	72	17	947
6. She's Not There	77	20	818

Artist / Song	Year	Peak	Points
SANTANA – cont'd			
7. Stormy	79	33	518
8. One Chain (Don't Make No Prison)	79	68	126
The SATISFACTIONS ▶1577			
1. This Bitter Earth	70	93	17
SAVAGE GRACE ▶1571			
1. Come On Down	70	92	18
SAVOY BROWN ▶951			
Group: **Foghat** (Roger Earl, "Lonesome" Dave Peverett, Tony "Tone" Stevens)			
1. I'm Tired	70	42	359
2. Tell Mama	71	92	11
SEA LEVEL ▶1017			
Group: The **Allman Brothers Band** (Jai Johnny Johanson, Chuck Leavell, Lamar Williams)			
1. That's Your Secret	78	53	267
2. Shake A Leg	77	100	1
The SEARCHERS ▶1326			
1. Desdemona	71	79	96
SEATRAIN ▶1012			
Group: The **Rowans** (Peter Rowan)			
1. 13 Questions	71	53	400
The Bob SEGER SYSTEM ▶1322			
Solo: **Bob Seger**			
1. Lucifer	70	72	97
SHA NA NA ▶891			
1. (Just Like) Romeo And Juliet	75	46	323
2. Only One Song	71	94	19
3. Top Forty (Of The Lord)	71	97	9
SHACK ▶1466			
1. Too Many Lovers	71	81	43
SHALAMAR ▶1035			
1. Uptown Festival (Part 1)	77	61	191
2. Take That To The Bank	79	82	54
SHANGO ▶1529			
1. Some Things A Man's Gotta Do	70	90	25
SHERBET ▶1280			
1. Howzat	76	73	124
SHIRLEY (AND COMPANY) ▶644			
1. Shame, Shame, Shame	75	8^2	1676
The SHOCKING BLUE ▶181			
1. Venus	70	1^3	8842
Shocking Blue			
2. Mighty Joe	70	30	633
3. Long And Lonesome Road	70	75	81
4. Never Marry A Railroad Man	71	93	17
SHOES ▶1368			
1. Too Late	79	74	79
SIDE EFFECT ▶1676			
1. Keep That Same Old Feeling	77	98	3
SILVER ▶690			
Duo: **Batdorf & Rodney** (John Batdorf)			
1. Wham Bam Shang-A-Lang	76	16^2	1429
SILVER CONVENTION (s) ▶141			
[first charted as studio session singers--see #4] Solo: **Penny McLean**			
1. Fly, Robin, Fly	75	1	6322
2. Get Up And Boogie (That's Right)	76	1	5227
3. No, No, Joe	76	78	61
4. Save Me	75	88	36
SILVER HAWK ▶1626			
1. Awaiting On You All	71	94	10
The SINGING DOGS ▶1487			
1. Jingle Bells	72	72	36
Don Charles Presents THE SINGING DOGS directed by Carl Weissman with Instrumental Accomp.			
SISTER SLEDGE ▶243			
1. We Are Family	79	2^2	5893
2. He's The Greatest Dancer	79	8^2	1801
SKYLARK ▶557			
Solo: **Carl Graves**			
1. Wildflower	73	9^2	2039
2. I'll Have To Go Away	73	85	52
The SKYLINERS ▶1635			
1. Oh How Happy	78	96^2	9
SLADE ▶758			
1. Gudbuy T' Jane	73	62	237
2. Mama Weer All Crazee Now	73	60	209
3. Take Me Bak 'Ome	72	80	64
4. Cum On Feel The Noize	73	91	20
SLAVE ▶844			
1. Slide	77	27	793
SLIK ▶1674			
1. Forever And Ever	76	98	4
SLY & The FAMILY STONE ▶65			
Solo: **Sly Stone** Group: **Rubicon** (Jerry Martini)			
1. Family Affair	71	1^4	8067
2. Thank You (Falettinme Be Mice Elf Agin)	70	1	6543
3. If You Want Me To Stay	73	15^2	1509
4. Runnin' Away	72	11^2	1308
5. Smilin'	72	25	595
6. Everybody Is A Star	70	40	561
7. Time For Livin'	74	39^2	488
8. I Want To Take You Higher	70	40	373
9. Frisky	73	65	90
10. Loose Booty	74	90	26
SMITH ▶654			
Solo: **Gayle McCormick**			
1. Take A Look Around	70	26	633

	Year	Peak	Points
SMITH – cont'd			
2. What Am I Gonna Do	70	50	344
3. Comin' Back To Me (Ooh Baby)	70	72	116
Patti SMITH GROUP ▶706			
1. Because The Night	78	10^2	1382
SMOKIE ▶693			
Duo: **Suzi Quatro And Chris Norman** (Chris Norman)			
1. Living Next Door To Alice	77	18^2	1127
2. Needles And Pins	77	93	19
SNIFF 'n' The TEARS ▶748			
1. Driver's Seat	79	15	1143
SONOMA ▶1465			
1. Love For You	73	83	43
SONS OF CHAMPLIN ▶868			
1. Hold On	76	59	263
2. Here Is Where Your Love Belongs	77	71	112
3. Saved By The Grace Of Your Love	77	89	23
The **SOUL CHILDREN** ▶629			
1. Hearsay	72	22	708
2. I'll Be The Other Woman	74	52^2	365
3. Don't Take My Kindness For Weakness	72	73	136
SOUL TRAIN GANG (s) ▶1292			
1. Soul Train "75"	76	74	114
SOUNDS OF SUNSHINE ▶928			
1. Love Means (You Never Have To Say You're Sorry)	71	40	561
SOUTH SHORE COMMISSION ▶1270			
1. Free Man	75	79	79
2. Train Called Freedom	76	98	4
The **SOUTH SIDE MOVEMENT** ▶1091			
1. I' Been Watchin' You	73	54	277
SOUTHCOTE ▶1550			
1. She	74	91	20
The **SOUTHER, HILLMAN, FURAY BAND** ▶838			
Solos: **J.D. Souther, Richie Furay**			
Groups: The **Byrds** (Chris Hillman)			
Poco (Richie Furay)			
McGuinn, Clark & Hillman (Chris Hillman)			
1. Fallin' In Love	74	24	559
2. Safe At Home	75	80	74
SOUTHSIDE JOHNNY & The ASBURY JUKES ▶1580			
1. I'm So Anxious	79	92	16
SPACE (s) ▶1283			
1. My Love Is Music	79	67	123

	Year	Peak	Points
SPAGHETTI HEAD ▶1492			
1. Big Noise From Winnetka	75	90	34
SPARKS ▶1568			
1. Wonder Girl	72	92	18
SPECIAL DELIVERY FEATURING TERRY HUFF ▶1633			
1. The Lonely One	76	96	9
SPELLBOUND ▶1543			
1. Rumor At The Honky Tonk	78	89	21
The **SPINNERS** ▶27			
Group: **Dionne Warwicke And Spinners**			
1. They Just Can't Stop It the (Games People Play) [Alt. title: Games People Play]	75	2	5275
2. I'll Be Around	72	1	4920
3. Could It Be I'm Falling In Love	73	1	4515
4. The Rubberband Man	76	3	3467
5. One Of A Kind (Love Affair)	73	8^2	2033
6. It's A Shame	70	15	1507
7. Mighty Love - Pt. I	74	15	1199
8. I'm Coming Home	74	20	700
9. Love Don't Love Nobody - Pt. I	74	24	688
10. Love Or Leave	76	35	609
11. Ghetto Child	73	24	539
12. Living A Little, Laughing A Little	75	33	445
13. Sadie	75	45	333
14. We'll Have It Made	71	75	106
15. If You Wanna Do A Dance	78	73	90
16. Together We Can Make Such Sweet Music	73	76	68
17. Wake Up Susan	76	76	66
18. You're Throwing A Good Love Away	77	83	47
19. How Could I Let You Get Away	72	89	33
The **SPIRAL STARECASE** ▶1264			
1. She's Ready [Alt label: SPIRAL STARECASE Featuring: Pat Upton]	70	75	133
SPIRIT ▶1027			
Groups: **Firefall** (Mark Andes)			
Jo Jo Gunne (Mark Andes, Jay Ferguson)			
Solo: Jay Ferguson			
1. 1984	70	69	132
2. Mr. Skin	73	85	50
3. Animal Zoo	70	98	5
The **SPORTS** ▶1281			
1. Who Listens To The Radio	79	70	123
SPRINGWELL ▶1185			
1. It's For You	71	60	194
SPYRO GYRA ▶800			
Duo: The **Brecker Brothers** (Michael and Randy Brecker)			
1. Morning Dance	79	27^2	698
2. Shaker Song	78	95	8

Artist / Song	Year	Peak	Points
STALLION ▶1028			
1. Old Fashioned Boy (You're The One)	77	42^3	376
STAMPEDERS ▶480			
1. Sweet City Woman	71	7^2	2043
2. Hit The Road Jack	76	41	374
3. Devil You	72	60^2	236
The STAPLE SINGERS ▶70			
Solo: **Mavis Staples**			
1. I'll Take You There	72	1^2	5249
2. Let's Do It Again	75	1	4677
3. Respect Yourself	71	10	1726
4. If You're Ready (Come Go With Me)	73	9	1569
5. Heavy Makes You Happy (Sha-Na-Boom Boom)	71	24^2	740
6. Touch A Hand, Make A Friend	74	23	637
7. Oh La De Da	73	35	550
8. This World	72	36	500
9. City In The Sky	74	58	268
10. New Orleans	76	57	235
11. Be What You Are	73	71	139
12. My Main Man	75	70	118
13. You've Got To Earn It	71	85	31
STARBUCK ▶281			
1. Moonlight Feels Right	76	3	3872
2. I Got To Know	76	40	494
3. Lucky Man	77	48	359
4. Searching For A Thrill	78	45	289
5. Everybody Be Dancin'	77	48	280
STARGARD ▶873			
1. Theme Song From "Which Way Is Up"	78	24^2	698
STARLAND VOCAL BAND ▶212			
1. Afternoon Delight	76	1^4	8818
2. Hail! Hail! Rock And Roll!	77	89	32
STARZ ▶594			
Group: **Looking Glass** (Pieter Sweval)			
1. Cherry Baby	77	27	652
2. Sing It, Shout It	77	53	262
3. So Young, So Bad	78	73^2	104
4. (Any Way That You Want It) I'll Be There	78	96^2	9
5. (She's Just A) Fallen Angel	76	98^2	8
The STATLER BROTHERS ▶1088			
1. Bed Of Rose's	71	73	173
2. I'll Go To My Grave Loving You	75	96	11
STEALERS WHEEL ▶324			
Solo: **Gerry Rafferty**			
1. Stuck In The Middle With You	73	3	3748
2. Star	74	20^3	1098
3. Everyone's Agreed That Everything Will Turn Out Fine	73	33^2	488
STEAM (s) ▶996			
1. I've Gotta Make You Love Me	70	38	426
STEELY DAN ▶83			
Group: **Doobie Brothers** (Jeff "Skunk" Baxter, Michael McDonald)			
1. Rikki Don't Lose That Number	74	3^2	4052
2. Reeling In The Years	73	7^2	2050
3. Do It Again	73	7	1960
4. Peg	78	8^2	1806
5. Deacon Blues	78	17	949
6. Josie	78	21	726
7. FM (No Static At All)	78	24	625
8. Show Biz Kids	73	30	477
9. Black Friday	75	31	453
10. My Old School	73	56	291
11. Pretzel Logic	74	59	199
12. The Fez	76	71	105
13. Bad Sneakers	75	90	39
STEPPENWOLF ▶278			
Solo: **John Kay**			
1. Monster	70	23	883
2. Straight Shootin' Woman	74	20^2	782
3. Hey Lawdy Mama	70	21	642
4. Ride With Me	71	31	490
5. Screaming Night Hog	70	42^2	410
6. Who Needs Ya	70	45	387
7. Snow Blind Friend	71	51	350
8. For Ladies Only	71	61	149
Stephen STILLS – MANASSAS ▶1151			
Solo: **Stephen Stills**			
Groups: **Crosby, Stills & Nash**			
Crosby, Stills, Nash & Young			
1. Isn't It About Time	73	62^2	222
STILLWATER ▶911			
1. Mind Bender	78	43^2	602
Simon STOKES & The NIGHTHAWKS ▶1435			
Solo: **Simon Stokes**			
1. Voodoo Woman	70	87^2	53
STONEBOLT ▶824			
1. I Will Still Love You	78	30	638
2. Love Struck	79	91	16
STORIES ▶228			
Solo: **Ian Lloyd**			
1. Brother Louie	73	1	5471
2. I'm Coming Home	72	26	656
3. Mammy Blue	73	21	648
4. If It Feels Good, Do It	74	69	188
5. Another Love	74	98	6
#4 & 5: *Ian Lloyd & Stories*			

	Year	Peak	Points
STORM ▶1525			
1. Bend Me, Shape Me	71	89	26
STREET PEOPLE (s) ▶823			
Solo: Rupert Holmes			
1. Jennifer Tomkins	70	36	872
The **STYLISTICS** ▶51			
1. You Make Me Feel Brand New	74	1	5098
2. Betcha By Golly, Wow	72	4	3239
#1 & 2: THE STYLISTICS Featurng Airrion Love & Russell Thompkins, Jr.			
3. You Are Everything	72	9	2332
4. I'm Stone In Love With You	72	9	1624
5. Break Up To Make Up	73	10	1489
6. Let's Put It All Together	74	14^2	1212
7. Rockin' Roll Baby	73	20	1044
8. People Make The World Go Round	72	18	1040
9. You'll Never Get To Heaven (If You Break My Heart)	73	16	857
10. Stop, Look, Listen (To Your Heart)	71	34	696
11. Heavy Fallin' Out	74	31	641
12. Can't Give You Anything (But My Love)	75	54	262
13. Star On A TV Show	75	58	189
14. You're A Big Girl Now	71	66^2	174
15. Thank You Baby	75	67^2	168
16. You Are Beautiful	76	81	50
17. Funky Weekend	76	85	40
STYX ▶92			
1. Babe	79	1^3	5107
2. Lady	75	6	2397
3. Come Sail Away	78	9^2	2272
4. Renegade	79	18^2	1130
5. Fooling Yourself (The Angry Young Man)	78	23	784
6. Blue Collar Man (Long Nights)	78	20	753
7. Lorelei	76	30^2	597
8. Sing For The Day	79	41^2	381
9. Mademoiselle	76	57^2	204
10. You Need Love	75	81	56
SUGAR BEARS (s) ▶982			
1. You Are The One	72	38^2	475
SUGARLOAF ▶419			
Groups: Sugarloaf/Jerry Corbetta			
Disco Tex & The Sex-O-Lettes (Jerry Corbetta)			
1. Green-Eyed Lady	70	5	2979
2. Tongue In Cheek	71	40	482
3. Mother Nature's Wine	71	89	26

	Year	Peak	Points
SUGARLOAF/JERRY CORBETTA ▶682			
Groups: Sugarloaf			
Disco Tex & The Sex-O-Lettes (Jerry Corbetta)			
1. Don't Call Us, We'll Call You	75	12	1471
SUMMER WINE ▶1693			
1. Why Do Fools Fall In Love	73	100	1
SUNDOWN COMPANY (s) ▶1490			
1. Norma Jean Wants To Be A Movie Star	76	86	35
The **SUNSHINE BAND** ▶1419			
Group: KC & The Sunshine Band			
1. Shotgun Shuffle	75	84	58
SUPERTRAMP ▶231			
1. The Logical Song	79	4^2	2854
[see also: The Topical Song]			
2. Give A Little Bit	77	12	1396
3. Take The Long Way Home	79	15	1243
4. Goodbye Stranger	79	16^2	1146
5. Bloody Well Right	75	53	269
The **SUPREMES** ▶122			
Group: The Supremes & Four Tops			
1. Stoned Love	71	5	3309
2. Up The Ladder To The Roof	70	9	1705
3. Nathan Jones	71	10	1569
4. Everybody's Got The Right To Love	70	14^2	1348
5. Floy Joy	72	16	1190
6. Automatically Sunshine	72	37	492
7. I'm Gonna Let My Heart Do The Walking	76	54	345
8. Touch	71	53	206
9. Your Wonderful, Sweet Sweet Love	72	70	145
10. Bad Weather	73	92	18
11. I Guess I'll Miss The Man	72	100	1
The **SUPREMES & FOUR TOPS** ▶648			
Groups: Four Tops, The Supremes			
1. River Deep - Mountain High	71	15	1162
2. You Gotta Have Love In Your Heart	71	51	198
SUTHERLAND BROTHERS And QUIVER ▶687			
Group: Cochise (Willie Wilson)			
1. (I Don't Want To Love You But) You Got Me Anyway	73	20	820
2. Arms Of Mary	76	71^2	126
3. Secrets	77	97	9
Sutherland Brothers & Quiver			
SUZY And The RED STRIPES ▶1157			
Duo: Paul & Linda McCartney			
Group: Paul McCartney & Wings / Wings			
1. Seaside Woman	77	58^2	216
[Linda McCartney & Wings]			

	Year	Peak	Points
SWEATHOG ▶854			
1. Hallelujah	72	28	765
SWEENEY TODD ▶1625			
Solo: Nick Gilder			
1. Roxy Roller	76	93	10
SWEET ▶98			
1. Little Willy	73	3^2	3727
2. Fox On The Run	76	5^3	3103
3. Ballroom Blitz	75	9	2254
4. Love Is Like Oxygen	78	8^2	2128
5. Action	76	10	1392
6. Blockbuster	73	43	358
7. California Nights	78	88	42
8. Co-Co	71	85	37
9. Funk It Up (David's Song)	77	90	22
SWEET SENSATION ▶817			
1. Sad Sweet Dreamer	75	17	883
SWITCH ▶921			
1. There'll Never Be	78	46	331
2. Best Beat In Town	79	81	80
The SYLVERS ▶135			
Solo: Foster Sylvers			
1. Boogie Fever	76	1	5661
2. Hot Line	77	4^3	3228
3. High School Dance	77	13	1439
4. Wish That I Could Talk To You	73	57	291
5. Cotton Candy	76	74	79
6. Any Way You Want Me	77	92	26
7. Stay Away From Me	73	93	9
SYLVIA & The MOMENTS ▶1535			
Solo: Sylvia			
Group: The Moments			
1. Sho Nuff Boogie (Part 1)	74	91	23
SYNDICATE OF SOUND ▶1475			
1. Brown Paper Bag	70	82	40
T-CONNECTION ▶1451			
1. Do What You Wanna Do	77	80	47
T.M.G. ▶1618			
1. Lazy Eyes	79	94	11
T. REX ▶488			
1. Bang A Gong (Get It On)	72	12	1641
2. Hot Love	71	54	292
3. Ride A White Swan	71	60	219
Tyrannosaurus Rex			
4. Telegram Sam	72	64	144
TALKING HEADS ▶879			
1. Take Me To The River	79	31^2	665
MARC TANNER BAND ▶1194			
1. Elena	79	52	188

	Year	Peak	Points
A TASTE Of HONEY ▶295			
1. Boogie Oogie Oogie	78	1^3	6935
TAVARES ▶151			
1. Heaven Must Be Missing An Angel (Part 1)	76	10	1896
2. It Only Takes A Minute	75	10	1875
3. Whodunit	77	16	1166
4. Remember What I Told You To Forget	75	23	659
5. Don't Take Away The Music	76	40^2	539
6. More Than A Woman	78	39	531
7. Check It Out	73	34	477
8. She's Gone	74	66	206
9. Free Ride	76	56	204
10. Too Late	74	66	147
11. That's The Sound That Lonely Makes	74	94	25
The TEE SET ▶497			
1. Ma Belle Amie	70	6^2	2542
2. If You Do Believe In Love	70	58	245
Nino TEMPO And 5th AVE. SAX ▶994			
Duo: Nino & April			
1. Sister James	73	40	434
The TEMPREES ▶1374			
1. Dedicated To The One I Love	72	75	75
The TEMPTATIONS ▶22			
Solo: Eddie Kendricks			
1. Just My Imagination (Running Away With Me)	71	1	6557
2. Ball Of Confusion (That's What The World Is Today)	70	1	6033
3. Papa Was A Rollin' Stone	72	1	4337
4. Psychedelic Shack	70	4	2965
5. Masterpiece	73	9	1757
6. Superstar (Remember How You Got Where You Are)	71	13	1368
7. Shakey Ground	75	28	859
8. Take A Look Around	72	28	694
9. Hey Girl (I Like Your Style)	73	27	600
10. Let Your Hair Down	74	27	559
11. Glasshouse	75	41	555
12. The Plastic Man	73	33	514
13. Ungena Za Ulimwengu (Unite The World)	70	30	447
14. Happy People	75	44	434
15. Heavenly	74	45	387
16. It's Summer	71	40	376
17. You've Got My Soul On Fire	74	56	272
18. Keep Holding On	76	53	229
19. Mother Nature	72	82	39
20. Hum Along And Dance	70	88	26

	Year	Peak	Points
10cc ▶138			
Group: **Hotlegs** (Kevin Godley, Lol Creme, Eric Stewart)			
1. I'm Not In Love	75	3^2	4240
2. The Things We Do For Love	77	4^2	3471
10 CC			
3. Rubber Bullets	73	43	422
4. Dreadlock Holiday	78	46^2	308
5. Art For Art's Sake	76	63	160
6. Good Morning Judge	77	75	127
#5 & 6: 10CC			
7. People In Love	77	72^2	109
8. For You And I	79	73	79
9. The Wall Street Shuffle	74	84	35
#3, 4, & 9: 10 C.C.			
10. I'm Mandy Fly Me	76	88	32
TEN WHEEL DRIVE With GENYA RAVAN ▶1245			
Solo: **Genya Ravan**			
Group: **Michael Zager Band** (Michael Zager)			
1. Morning Much Better	70	74	148
TEN YEARS AFTER ▶647			
1. I'd Love To Change The World	71	28^2	907
2. Love Like A Man	70	73	119
3. Baby Won't You Let Me Rock 'N Roll You	72	73	93
THIN LIZZY ▶616			
1. The Boys Are Back In Town	76	10^2	1535
2. Dancing In The Moonlight (It's Caught Me In Its Spotlight)	77	92	23
THINK (s) ▶798			
1. Once You Understand	72	29	464
2. Once You Understand	74	53	250
THINK (Featuring Lou Stallman) [reissue of #1]			
THIRD WORLD ▶1062			
1. Now That We Found Love	79	41	314
GEORGE THOROGOOD And The DESTROYERS ▶1343			
1. Who Do You Love	79	71	89
The THREE DEGREES ▶273			
[see also **MFSB**]			
1. When Will I See You Again	74	1	3667
2. Maybe	70	24	816
3. I Do Take You	70	43	336
4. You're The One	71	57	212
5. I Wanna Be Your Baby	72	96	7
6. There's So Much Love All Around Me	71	99	4
THREE DOG NIGHT ▶8			
1. Joy To The World	71	1^6	10356
2. Mama Told Me (Not To Come)	70	1^2	6389
3. Shambala	73	1	4892
4. Black And White	72	1	4833
5. The Show Must Go On	74	1	3455
6. An Old Fashioned Love Song	71	4^2	2943
7. Never Been To Spain	72	5^2	2568
8. Liar	71	8	2001
9. Out In The Country	70	9^2	1651
10. Celebrate	70	12^2	1477
11. One Man Band	71	13^2	1444
12. The Family Of Man	72	10	1354
13. Let Me Serenade You	73	12	1068
14. Pieces Of April	73	18	918
15. Play Something Sweet (Brickyard Blues)	74	26	875
16. Sure As I'm Sittin' Here	74	18	785
17. Til The World Ends	75	29^2	560
BILLY THUNDERKLOUD & The CHIEFTONES ▶1663			
1. What Time Of Day	75	97	6
TOBY BEAU ▶580			
1. My Angel Baby	78	10	1647
2. Then You Can Tell Me Goodbye	79	62	237
The TOKENS ▶899			
Group: **Cross Country** (Mitch and Phil Margo, Jay Seigel)			
1. She Lets Her Hair Down (Early In The Morning)	70	59	335
2. Don't Worry Baby	70	71	122
GARY TOMS EMPIRE ▶801			
1. 7-6-5-4-3-2-1 (Blow Your Whistle)	75	35	682
2. Drive My Car	75	93	22
TOTO ▶399			
1. Hold The Line	79	5^2	3141
2. Georgy Porgy	79	44^2	372
3. I'll Supply The Love	79	46	267
TOWER Of POWER ▶415			
1. So Very Hard To Go	73	19	1051
2. You're Still A Young Man	72	22^2	952
3. Don't Change Horses (In The Middle Of A Stream)	74	59	269
4. This Time It's Real	73	62	165
5. Down To The Nightclub	72	67	127
6. Time Will Tell	74	93	26
TRAFFIC ▶922			
Solos: **Jim Capaldi**, **Dave Mason**			
Group: **Ginger Baker's Air Force** (Steve Winwood, Rick (or Ric) Grech)			
1. Gimme Some Lovin' Part One	71	56	253
Traffic, Etc.			
2. Empty Pages	70	73	157
The TRAMMPS ▶408			
1. Disco Inferno	78	8^2	1790
2. That's Where The Happy People Go	76	44	558

	Year	Peak	Points
TRAMMPS – cont'd			
3. Zing Went The Strings Of My Heart	72	55	470
4. Hold Back The Night	76	44	409
TRIUMPH ▶860			
1. Hold On	79	42	463
2. Lay It On The Line	79	77	93
TROOPER ▶1267			
1. Raise A Little Hell	78	71	132
ANDREA TRUE CONNECTION ▶329			
1. More, More, More (Pt. 1)	76	3^3	4695
2. N.Y., You Got Me Dancing	77	86	30
3. Party Line	76	87	20
4. What's Your Name, What's Your Number	78	99	3
The **TUBES** ▶1317			
1. Don't Touch Me There	76	68	99
IKE & TINA TURNER & The IKETTES ▶735			
Duo: Ike & Tina Turner			
1. I Want To Take You Higher	70	42	670
2. Come Together	70	52	315
[Alt. label: IKE & TINA TURNER & The Ikettes]			
TUXEDO JUNCTION ▶1144			
1. Chattanooga Choo Choo	78	62	227
DWIGHT TWILLEY BAND ▶843			
1. I'm On Fire	75	23	796
TYCOON ▶846			
1. Such A Woman	79	21^2	790
The **TYMES** ▶732			
1. You Little Trustmaker	74	16	993
2. Ms. Grace	75	100	1
UFO ▶1630			
1. Too Hot To Handle	77	94	10
U.S. 1 (s) ▶1567			
1. Bye Bye Baby	75	90	18
UNCLE DOG ▶1605			
1. River Road	73	95	13
The **UNDISPUTED TRUTH** ▶245			
1. Smiling Faces Sometimes	71	1	5197
Undisputed Truth			
2. You + Me = Love	77	56	253
3. You Make Your Own Heaven And Hell Right Here On Earth	72	71	190
4. Help Yourself	74	74	94
5. Papa Was A Rollin' Stone	72	93	9
6. What It Is	72	96	6
UNIVERSAL ROBOT BAND ▶1491			
1. Dance And Shake Your Tambourine	77	87	34

	Year	Peak	Points
URIAH HEEP ▶712			
1. Easy Livin'	72	32^2	612
2. Stealin'	73	62	249
3. Sweet Lorraine	73	91	19
Frankie VALLI & The 4 SEASONS ▶981			
Solo: Frankie Valli			
Group: The 4 Seasons [mid '70s lineup, only (Frankie Valli)]			
1. Patch Of Blue	70	53	298
2. Hickory	74	90^2	33
Frankie Valli And The Four Seasons			
VAN HALEN ▶628			
Solo: Sammy Hagar			
1. Dance The Night Away	79	22	793
2. You Really Got Me	78	44	354
3. Beautiful Girls	79	80^2	69
VANITY FARE ▶283			
1. Hitchin' A Ride	70	4	3710
2. Early In The Morning	70	10	2217
3. (I Remember) Summer Morning	70	61	209
VILLAGE PEOPLE ▶169			
1. Y.M.C.A.	79	3^2	5623
2. In The Navy	79	3	3327
3. Macho Man	78	28	734
4. Go West	79	48	237
5. Ready For The '80s	79	72	107
The **VILLAGE SOUL CHOIR** ▶1149			
1. The Cat Walk	70	63	223
VOYAGE ▶1563			
1. Souvenirs	79	92	19
The **WACKERS** ▶1403			
1. Day And Night	72	79	63
WADSWORTH MANSION ▶530			
1. Sweet Mary	71	5^2	2306
2. Michigan Harry Slaughter	71	99^2	5
Jr. WALKER & The ALL STARS ▶392			
1. Gotta Hold On To This Feeling	70	14^2	1194
2. Do You See My Love (For You Growing)	70	25	597
3. Take Me Girl, I'm Ready	71	44	506
4. Walk In The Night	72	50	416
5. Holly Holy	71	67	118
6. Way Back Home	71	91	34
JAMES WALSH GYPSY BAND ▶1020			
Group: Gypsy (James Walsh)			
1. Cuz It's You, Girl	78	58	242
2. Love Is For The Best In Us	79	91^2	24

WAR ▶49
Group: **Eric Burdon & War**
Solo: **Lee Oskar**

	Year	Peak	Points
1. The Cisco Kid	73	2	4283
2. Why Can't We Be Friends?	75	5²	3515
3. Low Rider	75	5²	2689
4. Slippin' Into Darkness	72	12	2622
5. Gypsy Man	73	7	1947
6. Me And Baby Brother	74	12	1754
7. The World Is A Ghetto	73	9²	1746
8. Summer	76	15	1401
9. All Day Music	71	28²	679
10. Ballero	74	35	498
11. Galaxy	78	46²	250
12. L.A. Sunshine	77	62	198
13. Lonely Feelin'	71	71	124
14. Good, Good Feelin'	79	94	14

DIONNE WARWICKE & SPINNERS ▶444
Solo: **Dionne Warwick**
Group: **Spinners**

	Year	Peak	Points
1. Then Came You	74	1	4011

WEDNESDAY ▶841

	Year	Peak	Points
1. Last Kiss	74	45	532
2. Teen Angel	74	73	89

WET WILLIE ▶349

	Year	Peak	Points
1. Keep On Smilin'	74	16	1207
2. Street Corner Serenade	78	26	725
3. Weekend	79	29	568
4. Make You Feel Love Again	78	45²	330
5. Leona	75	65	163
6. Country Side Of Life	74	62	146
7. Everything That 'Cha Do (Will Come Back To You)	76	84	24

WHATNAUTS ▶1082
Group: **Moments And Whatnauts**

	Year	Peak	Points
1. I'll Erase Away Your Pain	71	64	181
2. Instigating (Trouble Making Fool)	73	96	10

The WHISPERS ▶920

	Year	Peak	Points
1. Seems Like I Gotta Do Wrong	70	62	185
2. A Mother For My Children	74	92	26
3. Make It With You	77	90	24
4. Your Love Is So Doggone Good	71	100	1

WHITE PLAINS (s) ▶571
Groups (s): The **Brotherhood Of Man**, **Edison Lighthouse**, **First Class** (Tony Burrows, all)
Duo: The **Pipkins** (Tony Burrows)
Solo: **Tony Burrows**

	Year	Peak	Points
1. My Baby Loves Lovin'	70	10	1777
2. Lovin' You Baby	70	63	181

The WHO ▶89
Group: **Faces** (Kenney Jones)

	Year	Peak	Points
1. See Me, Feel Me	70	8²	2160
2. Won't Get Fooled Again	71	9	2119
3. Squeeze Box	76	11²	1912
4. Who Are You	78	9³	1757
5. Summertime Blues	70	14	1151
6. Behind Blue Eyes	71	24²	935
7. Join Together	72	28²	736
8. The Seeker	70	30	508
9. The Relay	73	33	504
10. Love, Reign O'er Me	73	54	261
11. 5:15	79	53	203
12. Postcard	74	64	140
13. Long Live Rock	79	66	107
14. The Real Me	74	82	38

WILD CHERRY ▶265

	Year	Peak	Points
1. Play That Funky Music	76	1²	5621
2. Baby Don't You Know	77	57	274
3. Hold On	77	69	126
4. I Love My Music	78	74	78

WILDFIRE ▶1074

	Year	Peak	Points
1. Here Comes Summer	77	43	299

John WILLIAMS/LONDON SYMPHONY ORCHESTRA ▶721
Solo: **John Williams**

	Year	Peak	Points
1. Star Wars (Main Title)	77	18	932
2. Theme From Superman (Main Title)	79	69²	111

J. Frank WILSON & The CAVALIERS ▶1250

	Year	Peak	Points
1. Last Kiss	74	74	146

J. Frank Wilson And The Cavaliers [reissue--first charted in 1964]

WILTON PLACE STREET BAND (s) ▶772

	Year	Peak	Points
1. Disco Lucy (I Love Lucy Theme)	77	19²	1004

The WING AND A PRAYER FIFE AND DRUM CORPS. (s) ▶741

	Year	Peak	Points
1. Baby Face	76	26²	1209

The EDGAR WINTER GROUP ▶223
Group: **Edgar Winter's White Trash** (Edgar Winter, Rick Derringer)
Solos: **Edgar Winter**, **Dan Hartman**, **Rick Derringer**

	Year	Peak	Points
1. Frankenstein	73	1	5425
2. Free Ride	73	10²	1836
3. Hangin' Around	74	39	368
4. Easy Street	74	88	31

EDGAR WINTER'S WHITE TRASH ▶990
Solos: **Edgar Winter**, **Rick Derringer**
Group: The **Edgar Winter Group** (Edgar Winter, Rick Derringer)

	Year	Peak	Points
1. Keep Playin' That Rock 'N' Roll	72	58²	281
2. I Can't Turn You Loose	72	89	27

	Year	Peak	Points
The WOMBLES (s) ▶1173			
1. Wombling Summer Party	74	59	204
Charles WRIGHT And The WATTS 103RD STREET RHYTHM BAND ▶366			
1. Love Land	70	16	1749
2. Express Yourself	70	17	1261
3. Your Love (Means Everything To Me) Charles Wright And The Watts 103rd Street Band	71	56	359
4. Solution For Pollution	71	61	167
5. Nobody (Tellin' Me 'Bout My Baby)	71	81	54
YES ▶435 Group: **Flash** (Peter Banks)			
1. Roundabout	72	10	1491
2. Your Move	71	29	649
3. And You And I (Part I)	72	32	478
4. America	72	44	343
Dennis YOST And The CLASSICS IV ▶582			
1. What Am I Crying For?	72	31	512

	Year	Peak	Points
2. The Funniest Thing	70	50	315
3. Where Did All The Good Times Go	70	67	225
#1 & 3: Dennis Yost & The Classics IV			
4. My First Day Without Her	75	88	27
5. Rosanna	73	90	22
The YOUNGBLOODS ▶1508			
1. Darkness, Darkness	70	87	30
MICHAEL ZAGER BAND ▶845 Group: **Ten Wheel Drive With Genya Ravan** (Michael Zager)			
1. Let's All Chant	78	25^2	790
ZZ TOP ▶409			
1. Tush	75	12	1065
2. La Grange	74	24	933
3. It's Only Love	76	46	433
4. Arrested For Driving While Blind	77	74	80
5. Francene	72	81^2	75
6. Enjoy And Get It On	77	82	43

Section 4

Song Title Index

This is an alphabetical listing of the song titles, with their decade rankings cross-referenced to Section 1.

You will find special features in this index for titles with multiple versions.

- A song title without a number to the left indicates a "head title." Its multiple versions are ranked and identified by act just beneath it. See "After Midnight."
- A title with double hyphenation (--) refers to a version whose title is in variation with that of the version just above it. See, for example, "Americans" by Byron Mac Gregor and "The Americans (A Canadian's Opinion)" by Gordon Sinclair.
- It is not uncommon to find a version whose title is longer than the head title. For these, a title extension appears after the name of the act that recorded it. See, for example, "Bad Luck" and the extension "(Part 1)" after Harold Melvin And The Blue Notes.
- A [P] following the act's name denotes a version of a title that differs in punctuation from the head title. See "All I Have To Do Is Dream" by Nitty Gritty Dirt Band.

There is one other class of linked songs. Though not versions of the same song, two songs that share an [R:] still have something in common. The [R:] may be read as "responds to." It classifies the preceding title as a response or an answer to the title inside the brackets. See "Basketball Jones Featuring Tyrone Shoelaces [R: Love Jones]."

A

- 10 **ABC** *Jackson 5*
- 1932 **ABRA-CA-DABRA** *DeFranco Family Feat. Tony DeFranco*
- **ABRAHAM, MARTIN AND JOHN**...see **WHAT THE WORLD NEEDS NOW IS LOVE**
- 1650 **ABSOLUTELY RIGHT** *Five Man Electrical Band*
- 3042 **ACE OF SPADE** *O.V. Wright*
- 2948 **ACROSS 110TH STREET** *Bobby Womack*
- 1158 **ACTION** *Sweet*
- 4050 **ACTION SPEAKS LOUDER THAN WORDS** *Chocolate Milk*
- 2975 **ADD SOME MUSIC TO YOUR DAY** *Beach Boys*
- 4825 **ADRIENNE** *Tommy James*
- **AFRICANISM**...see **GIMME SOME LOVIN'**
- 2476 **AFRO-STRUT** *Nite-Liters*
- 3730 **AFTER ALL THIS TIME** *Merry Clayton*
- **AFTER MIDNIGHT**
- 1201 *Eric Clapton*
- 2982 *J.J. Cale*
- 4293 *Maggie Bell*
- **AFTER THE FEELING IS GONE**
- 4124 *Five Flights Up*
- 5074 *Lulu*
- 4534 **AFTER THE FIRE IS GONE** *Conway Twitty & Loretta Lynn*
- 5203 **AFTER THE FIRST ONE** *Yonah*
- 1490 **AFTER THE GOLDRUSH** *Prelude*
- 560 **AFTER THE LOVE HAS GONE** *Earth, Wind & Fire*
- 585 **AFTER THE LOVIN'** *Engelbert Humperdinck*
- 16 **AFTERNOON DELIGHT** *Starland Vocal Band*
- 2458 **THE AGONY AND THE ECSTASY** *Smokey Robinson*
- 1343 **AIN'T GONNA BUMP NO MORE (With No Big Fat Woman)** *Joe Tex*
- 3245 **AIN'T GONNA EAT OUT MY HEART ANYMORE** *Angel*
- 4320 **AIN'T GONNA' HURT NOBODY** *Brick*
- 2989 **AIN'T GOT NO HOME** *Band*
- 3047 **AIN'T GOT TIME** *Impressions*
- 3519 **AIN'T IT A SAD THING** *R. Dean Taylor*
- 1637 **AIN'T LOVE A BITCH** *Rod Stewart*
- 4658 **AIN'T NO LOVE IN THE HEART OF THE CITY** *Bobby Bland*
- 103 **AIN'T NO MOUNTAIN HIGH ENOUGH** *Diana Ross*
- 1002 **AIN'T NO STOPPIN' US NOW** *McFadden & Whitehead*
- 358 **AIN'T NO SUNSHINE** *Bill Withers*
- 554 **AIN'T NO WAY TO TREAT A LADY** *Helen Reddy*
- 360 **AIN'T NO WOMAN (Like The One I've Got)** *Four Tops*
- 2585 **AIN'T NOBODY HOME** *B.B. King*
- 4325 **(Ain't Nothin' But A) HOUSE PARTY** *J. Geils Band*
- 3501 **AIN'T NOTHING GONNA KEEP ME FROM YOU** *Teri DeSario*
- **AIN'T NOTHING LIKE THE REAL THING**
- 1736 *Donny & Marie*
- 2760 *Aretha Franklin*
- 2502 **AIN'T THAT A SHAME** *Cheap Trick*
- **AIN'T THAT LOVING YOU (For More Reasons Than One)**
- 2321 *Luther Ingram*
- 3498 *Isaac Hayes & David Porter*
- **AIN'T THAT PECULIAR**
- 2494 *Diamond REO*
- 5049 *Fanny*
- 1469 **AIN'T TOO PROUD TO BEG** *Rolling Stones*
- 1408 **AIN'T UNDERSTANDING MELLOW** *Jerry Butler & Brenda Lee Eager*
- 4281 **AIN'T WASTIN' TIME NO MORE** *Allman Brothers Band*
- 4181 **AIR DISASTER** *Albert Hammond*
- 706 **THE AIR THAT I BREATHE** *Hollies*
- 1985 **AIRPORT LOVE THEME (Gwen And Vern)** *Vincent Bell*
- 3952 **AJAX AIRLINES** *Hudson & Landry*
- 3209 **AJAX LIQUOR STORE** *Hudson & Landry*
- 4097 **ALABAMA WILD MAN** *Jerry Reed*
- 1870 **ALBERT FLASHER** *Guess Who*
- **ALISON** *Elvis Costello* see: **WATCHING THE DETECTIVES**
- 2077 **ALIVE** *Bee Gees*
- 1337 **ALIVE AGAIN** *Chicago*
- 185 **ALL BY MYSELF** *Eric Carmen*
- 1859 **ALL DAY MUSIC** *War*
- 4485 **ALL DOWN THE LINE** *Rolling Stones*
- 5222 **ALL HIS CHILDREN** *Charley Pride*
- 654 **ALL I EVER NEED IS YOU** *Sonny & Cher*
- 4069 **ALL I HAVE** *Moments*
- **ALL I HAVE TO DO IS DREAM**
- 1861 *Bobbie Gentry & Glen Campbell*
- 3359 *Nitty Gritty Dirt Band* [P]
- 771 **ALL I KNOW** *Garfunkel*
- 4445 **ALL I NEED IS TIME** *Gladys Knight & The Pips*
- 2459 **ALL I SEE IS YOUR FACE** *Dan Hill*
- 5219 **ALL I WANNA DO** *Doucette*
- 3346 **ALL IN LOVE IS FAIR** *Barbra Streisand*
- 4602 **ALL MY HARD TIMES** *Joe Simon*
- 4166 **ALL MY TRIALS** *Ray Stevens*
- 5027 **ALL OVER ME** *Charlie Rich*
- 356 **ALL RIGHT NOW** *Free*
- 3325 **ALL SHOOK UP** *Suzi Quatro*
- 2164 **ALL STRUNG OUT ON YOU** *John Travolta*
- 1775 **ALL THE KING'S HORSES** *Aretha Franklin*
- 3499 **ALL THE TIME IN THE WORLD** *Dr. Hook*
- 3815 **ALL THE WAY DOWN** *Etta James*
- 4728 **ALL THE WAY LOVER** *Millie Jackson*
- 2059 **ALL THE YOUNG DUDES** *Mott The Hoople*
- 5079 **ALL THINGS ARE POSSIBLE** *Dan Peek*
- 2479 **ALL YOU GET FROM LOVE IS A LOVE SONG** *Carpenters*
- 2299 **ALMOST LIKE BEING IN LOVE** *Michael Johnson*
- 4134 **ALMOST SATURDAY NIGHT** *John Fogerty*
- 2227 **ALMOST SUMMER** *Celebration Feat. Mike Love*
- 11 **ALONE AGAIN (Naturally)** *Gilbert O'Sullivan*
- 1353 **ALREADY GONE** *Eagles*
- 464 **ALSO SPRACH ZARATHUSTRA (2001)** *Deodato*
- 3875 **ALVIN STONE (The Birth & Death Of A Gangster)** *Fantastic Four*
- 3252 **ALWAYS** *Luther Ingram*
- 1159 **ALWAYS AND FOREVER** *Heatwave*
- 1695 **ALWAYS SOMETHING THERE TO REMIND ME** *R.B. Greaves*
- 5317 **AM I BLACK ENOUGH FOR YOU** *Billy Paul*
- 4541 **AM I BLUE** *Cher*
- 2198 **AM I LOSING YOU** *Partridge Family*
- 4730 **AM I LOSING YOU** *Manhattans*
- 4521 **AMANDA** *Waylon*
- 3208 **AMARILLO** *Neil Sedaka*
- **AMAZING GRACE**
- 1092 *Judy Collins*
- 1244 *Royal Scots Dragoon Guards*
- 4215 **AMAZING GRACE (Used To Be Her Favorite Song)** *Amazing Rhythm Aces*
- 5307 **AMBER CASCADES** *America*
- 2730 **AMERICA** *Yes*
- 2528 **AMERICA, COMMUNICATE WITH ME** *Ray Stevens*
- 4431 **AMERICA, THE BEAUTIFUL** *Charlie Rich*
- **AMERICA/STANDING** *Five Stairsteps* see: **BECAUSE I LOVE YOU**
- 1931 **AMERICAN CITY SUITE** *Cashman & West*
- 3577 **AMERICAN GIRLS** *Rick Springfield*
- 3 **AMERICAN PIE** *Don McLean*
- **AN AMERICAN TRILOGY**
- 2296 *Mickey Newbury*
- 3786 *Elvis Presley*
- 2007 **AMERICAN TUNE** *Paul Simon*
- 47 **AMERICAN WOMAN** *Guess Who*
- 390 **AMERICANS** *Byron Mac Gregor*
- 2711 **--THE AMERICANS (A Canadian's Opinion)** *Gordon Sinclair*
- 5053 **AMERIKAN MUSIC** *Steve Alaimo*
- 1864 **AMIE** *Pure Prairie League*
- 732 **AMOS MOSES** *Jerry Reed*
- **AND I LOVE YOU SO**
- 1291 *Perry Como*
- 4845 *Bobby Goldsboro*
- 3011 **AND MY HEART SANG (Tra La La)** *Brenda & The Tabulations*
- 1946 **AND THE GRASS WON'T PAY NO MIND** *Mark Lindsay*
- 2319 **AND YOU AND I (Part 1)** *Yes*
- 1409 **ANGEL** *Aretha Franklin*
- 2482 **ANGEL** *Rod Stewart*
- 2951 **ANGEL BABY** *Dusk*
- 4042 **ANGELEYES** *ABB*
- 501 **ANGEL IN YOUR ARMS** *Hot*
- 4082 **ANGEL (What In The World's Come Over Us)** *Atlanta Rhythm Section*

4640	ANGELICA Oliver	
253	ANGIE Rolling Stones	
349	ANGIE BABY Helen Reddy	
3356	ANIMAL HOUSE Stephen Bishop	
3882	THE ANIMAL TRAINER AND THE TOAD Mountain	
5260	ANIMAL ZOO Spirit	
2485	ANNABELLA Hamilton, Joe Frank & Reynolds	
4337	ANNABELLE Daniel Boone	
215	ANNIE'S SONG John Denver	
604	ANOTHER DAY Paul McCartney	
5247	ANOTHER LOVE Ian Lloyd & Stories	
1892	ANOTHER PARK, ANOTHER SUNDAY Doobie Brothers	
3905	ANOTHER PUFF Jerry Reed	
2072	ANOTHER RAINY DAY IN NEW YORK CITY Chicago	
872	ANOTHER SATURDAY NIGHT Cat Stevens	
	ANOTHER SOMEBODY DONE SOMEBODY WRONG SONG...see (Hey Won't You Play)	
2541	ANOTHER STAR Stevie Wonder	
2323	ANOTHER TIME, ANOTHER PLACE Engelbert Humperdinck	
5003	ANSWER ME, MY LOVE Happenings	
2770	ANTHEM Wayne Newton	
843	ANTICIPATION Carly Simon	
5170	(Any Way That You Want It) I'LL BE THERE Starz	
4804	ANY WAY YOU WANT ME Sylvers	
5051	ANYBODY WANNA PARTY? Gloria Gaynor	
2307	ANYTHING YOU WANT John Valenti	
	ANYTIME (I'll Be There)	
3021	Paul Anka	
5044	Frank Sinatra	
3919	APARTMENT 21 Bobbie Gentry	
2387	APEMAN Kinks	
4674	APPLE OF MY EYE Badfinger	
4152	ARE YOU GETTING ANY SUNSHINE? Lou Christie	
1429	ARE YOU LONESOME TONIGHT Donny Osmond	
1144	ARE YOU MAN ENOUGH Four Tops	
3813	ARE YOU OLD ENOUGH Mark Lindsay	
1169	ARE YOU READY? Pacific Gas & Electric	
3820	ARE YOU SURE HANK DONE IT THIS WAY Waylon Jennings	
1156	ARIEL Dean Friedman	
743	ARIZONA Mark Lindsay	
1315	ARMED AND EXTREMELY DANGEROUS First Choice	
	ARMS OF MARY	
3759	Sutherland Brothers & Quiver	
4913	Chilliwack	
4153	ARRESTED FOR DRIVING WHILE BLIND ZZ Top	
2656	ARROW THROUGH ME Wings	
3562	ART FOR ART'S SAKE 10cc	
3480	AS Stevie Wonder	
2773	AS LONG AS HE TAKES CARE OF HOME Candi Staton	
4323	AS SOON AS I HANG UP THE PHONE Loretta Lynn/Conway Twitty	
1612	AS THE YEARS GO BY Mashmakhan	
3158	AS TIME GOES BY Nilsson	
3125	ASHES TO ASHES 5th Dimension	
3289	ASK ME Ecstasy, Passion & Pain	
2336	ASK ME NO QUESTIONS B.B. King	
1487	ASK ME WHAT YOU WANT Millie Jackson	
1880	AT MIDNIGHT (My Love Will Lift You Up) Rufus, Feat. Chaka Khan	
249	AT SEVENTEEN Janis Ian	
2073	ATTITUDE DANCING Carly Simon	
1195	AUBREY Bread	
1813	AUTOBAHN Kraftwerk	
2281	AUTOMATICALLY SUNSHINE Supremes	
	AVENGING ANNIE	
3680	Andy Pratt	
4448	Roger Daltrey	
5141	AWAITING ON YOU ALL Silver Hawk	

B

216	BABE Styx	
4472	BABY, BABY I LOVE YOU Terry Cashman	
4982	BABY, BABY MY LOVE'S ALL FOR YOU Deniece Williams	
1191	BABY BLUE Badfinger	
3420	BABY BOY Mary Kay Place as Loretta Haggers	
70	BABY COME BACK Player	
1970	BABY COME CLOSE Smokey Robinson	
3310	BABY DON'T CHANGE YOUR MIND Gladys Knight & The Pips	
223	BABY DON'T GET HOOKED ON ME Mac Davis	
3009	BABY DON'T YOU KNOW Wild Cherry	
1274	BABY FACE Wing And A Prayer Fife & Drum Corps.	
4981	BABY FAT Robert Byrne	
3117	BABY, HANG UP THE PHONE Carl Graves	
611	BABY HOLD ON Eddie Money	
1723	BABY HOLD ON Grass Roots	
4078	BABY I LOVE YOU Little Milton	
1106	BABY, I LOVE YOUR WAY Peter Frampton	
	BABY, I NEED YOUR LOVING	
3583	Eric Carmen [P]	
3765	O.C. Smith	
3254	BABY I WANT YOU Funky Communication Committee	
4763	BABY, I'LL GIVE IT TO YOU Seals & Crofts	
432	BABY I'M-A WANT YOU Bread	
2364	BABY I'M BURNIN' Dolly Parton	
4155	BABY, I'M YOURS Jody Miller	
2366	BABY I'VE BEEN MISSING YOU Independents	
5233	BABY, IS THERE SOMETHING ON YOUR MIND McKinley Travis	
1463	BABY LET ME KISS YOU King Floyd	
1186	BABY LET ME TAKE YOU (In My Arms) Detroit Emeralds	
4439	BABY LOVE Mother's Finest	
5064	BABY MAKE IT SOON Flying Machine	
2420	BABY SITTER Betty Wright	
1140	BABY TAKE ME IN YOUR ARMS Jefferson	
1991	BABY THAT'S BACKATCHA Smokey Robinson	
2540	(Baby) TURN ON TO ME Impressions	
687	BABY, WHAT A BIG SURPRISE Chicago	
4034	BABY WON'T YOU LET ME ROCK 'N ROLL YOU Ten Years After	
4350	BABY, YOU LOOK GOOD TO ME TONIGHT John Denver	
3866	BABY--GET IT ON Ike & Tina Turner	
3840	BACK FOR A TASTE OF YOUR LOVE Syl Johnson	
710	BACK HOME AGAIN John Denver	
	BACK IN LOVE AGAIN...see (Every Time I Turn Around)	
4770	BACK IN MY ARMS AGAIN Genya Raven	
3629	BACK IN THE SADDLE Aerosmith	
1203	BACK IN THE U.S.A. Linda Ronstadt	
1051	BACK OFF BOOGALOO Ringo Starr	
238	BACK STABBERS O'Jays	
4912	BACK TO DREAMIN' AGAIN Pat Shannon	
3012	BACK TO THE ISLAND Leon Russell	
4286	BACK TO THE RIVER Damnation Of Adam Blessing	
1956	BACK TOGETHER AGAIN Daryl Hall & John Oates	
1528	BACK WHEN MY HAIR WAS SHORT Gunhill Road	
192	BAD, BAD LEROY BROWN Jim Croce	
133	BAD BLOOD Neil Sedaka	
5341	BAD, BOLD AND BEAUTIFUL, GIRL Persuaders	
1014	BAD CASE OF LOVING YOU (Doctor, Doctor) Robert Palmer	
43	BAD GIRLS Donna Summer	
	BAD LUCK	
1011	Harold Melvin And The Blue Notes (Part 1)	
5301	Atlanta Disco Band	
4839	BAD SIDE OF THE MOON April Wine	
4600	BAD SNEAKERS Steely Dan	
640	BAD TIME Grand Funk	
4414	BAD WATER Raeletts	
4984	BAD WEATHER Supremes	
3431	BADLANDS Bruce Springsteen	
45	BAKER STREET Gerry Rafferty	
2785	BALL AND CHAIN Tommy James	
119	BALL OF CONFUSION (That's What The World Is Today) Temptations	
4779	THE BALLAD OF EVEL KNIEVEL John Culliton Mahoney	
2263	BALLERO War	
707	BALLROOM BLITZ Sweet	
3110	BANAPPLE GAS Cat Stevens	
171	BAND OF GOLD Freda Payne	
280	BAND ON THE RUN Paul McCartney & Wings	
984	BANG A GONG (Get It On) T. Rex	
1850	BANGLA-DESH George Harrison	
5180	BANKS OF THE OHIO Olivia Newton-John	
4721	BARBARA, I LOVE YOU New Colony Six	

#	Title	Artist
1499	BARETTA'S THEME ("Keep Your Eye On The Sparrow")	Rhythm Heritage
2952	--KEEP YOUR EYE ON THE SPARROW	Merry Clayton
1032	BARRACUDA	Heart
1276	BASKETBALL JONES FEATURING TYRONE SHOELACES	Cheech & Chong [R: LOVE JONES]
2649	BATTLE HYMN OF LT. CALLEY	C Company Feat. Terry Nelson
	BATTLE OF NEW ORLEANS	
4264		Nitty Gritty Dirt Band
5000		Bert Sommer
1638	BE	Neil Diamond
4777	BE GOOD TO ME BABY	Luther Ingram
	BE MY BABY	
1179		Andy Kim
4486		Cissy Houston
2960	BE MY GIRL	Dramatics
4244	BE MY LADY	Meters
2434	BE MY LOVER	Alice Cooper
4454	BE NICE TO ME	Runt--Todd Rundgren
479	BE THANKFUL FOR WHAT YOU GOT	William DeVaughn
3676	BE WHAT YOU ARE	Staple Singers
588	BEACH BABY	First Class
923	BEAST OF BURDEN	Rolling Stones
4531	BEAT ME DADDY EIGHT TO THE BAR	Commander Cody And His Lost Planet Airmen
3561	BEAUCOUPS OF BLUES	Ringo Starr
3570	BEAUTIFUL	Gordon Lightfoot
4263	BEAUTIFUL GIRLS	Van Halen
3119	BEAUTIFUL PEOPLE	New Seekers
1046	BEAUTIFUL SUNDAY	Daniel Boone
4051	BECAUSE I LOVE YOU / AMERICA/STANDING*	Five Stairsteps
1167	BECAUSE THE NIGHT	Patti Smith Group
3715	BED AND BOARD	Barbara Mason
3487	BED OF ROSE'S	Statler Brothers
1627	BEEN TO CANAAN	Carole King
3436	BEEN TOO LONG ON THE ROAD	Mark Lindsay
2566	BEER BARREL POLKA	Bobby Vinton
1465	BEFORE MY HEART FINDS OUT	Gene Cotton
286	BEFORE THE NEXT TEARDROP FALLS	Freddy Fender
4672	BEG, STEAL OR BORROW	New Seekers
968	BEGINNINGS	Chicago
1534	BEHIND BLUE EYES	Who
1196	BEHIND CLOSED DOORS	Charlie Rich
1977	BELIEVE IN HUMANITY	Carole King
	BELL BOTTOM BLUES	
5029		Eric Clapton
5092		Derek & The Dominos
4144	BELLE	Al Green
1256	THE BELLS	Originals
391	BEN	Michael Jackson
4793	BEND ME, SHAPE ME	Storm
209	BENNIE AND THE JETS	Elton John
1552	THE BERTHA BUTT BOOGIE (Part 1)	Jimmy Castor Bunch
4151	BEST BEAT IN TOWN	Switch
1262	THE BEST DISCO IN TOWN	Ritchie Family
164	BEST OF MY LOVE	Emotions
422	BEST OF MY LOVE	Eagles
	BEST THING THAT EVER HAPPENED TO ME	
450		Gladys Knight & The Pips
3863		Persuaders
3868	--YOU'RE THE BEST THING THAT EVER HAPPENED TO ME	Ray Price
497	BETCHA BY GOLLY, WOW	Stylistics Feat. Russell Thompkins, Jr.
734	BETH	Kiss
4647	BETTER DAYS	Melissa Manchester
4195	BETTER PLACE TO BE (Parts 1 & 2)	Harry Chapin
4074	BETWEEN HER GOODBYE AND MY HELLO	Gladys Knight & The Pips
3445	BEYOND THE BLUE HORIZON	Lou Christie
5131	BICYCLE MORNING	Billy Sans
1570	BICYCLE RACE / FAT BOTTOMED GIRLS*	Queen
1184	BIG CITY MISS RUTH ANN	Gallery
3183	BIG LEG WOMAN (With A Short Short Mini Skirt)	Israel "Popper Stopper" Tolbert
4668	BIG NOISE FROM WINNETKA	Spaghetti Head
1514	BIG SHOT	Billy Joel
3050	BIG TIME OPERATOR	Keith Hampshire
	BIG YELLOW TAXI	
1908		Neighborhood
1936		Joni Mitchell [Studio]
5327		Joni Mitchell
3284	BIGFOOT	Bro Smith
3372	THE BIGGEST PARAKEETS IN TOWN	Jud Strunk
2739	BILLION DOLLAR BABIES	Alice Cooper
	BILLY, DON'T BE A HERO	
258		Bo Donaldson & The Heywoods
3707		Paper Lace [P]
1279	BIRDS OF A FEATHER	Raiders
5201	BIRDS OF ALL NATIONS	George McCannon III
4370	BIRMINGHAM BLUES	Charlie Daniels Band
643	THE BITCH IS BACK	Elton John
2863	BITE YOUR LIP (Get Up And Dance!)	Elton John
1751	BITTER BAD	Melanie
267	BLACK & WHITE	Three Dog Night
1107	BLACK BETTY	Ram Jam
3271	BLACK BYRD	Donald Byrd
1127	BLACK DOG	Led Zeppelin
5332	BLACK-EYED BLUES	Joe Cocker
2622	THE BLACK-EYED BOYS	Paper Lace
2412	BLACK FOX	Freddy Robinson
2384	BLACK FRIDAY	Steely Dan
3996	BLACK HANDS WHITE COTTON	Caboose
2758	BLACK LASSIE	Cheech & Chong
440	BLACK MAGIC WOMAN	Santana
5034	BLACK NIGHT	Deep Purple
3995	BLACK SEEDS KEEP ON GROWING	Main Ingredient
1452	BLACK SUPERMAN--"MUHAMMAD ALI"	Johnny Wakelin & The Kinshasa Band
355	BLACK WATER	Doobie Brothers
	BLAME IT ON THE BOOGIE	
3512		Jacksons
3855		Mick Jackson
3576	BLANKET ON THE GROUND	Billie Jo Spears
2921	BLESS YOU	Martha Reeves & The Vandellas
	THE BLIND MAN IN THE BLEACHERS ...see THE LAST GAME OF THE SEASON	
414	BLINDED BY THE LIGHT	Manfred Mann's Earth Band
2696	BLOAT ON (Featuring The Bloaters)	Cheech & Chong's [R: FLOAT ON]
2677	BLOCKBUSTER	Sweet
2971	BLOOD IS THICKER THAN WATER	William DeVaughn
5097	BLOOD RED AND GOIN' DOWN	Tanya Tucker
3030	BLOODY WELL RIGHT	Supertramp
1311	BLOW AWAY	George Harrison
1396	BLOWING AWAY	5th Dimension
4239	BLT	Lee Oskar
306	BLUE BAYOU	Linda Ronstadt
3437	BLUE COLLAR	Bachman-Turner Overdrive
1740	BLUE COLLAR MAN (Long Nights)	Styx
1480	BLUE EYES CRYING IN THE RAIN	Willie Nelson
4162	BLUE GUITAR	Justin Hayward & John Lodge
1605	BLUE MONEY	Van Morrison
1587	BLUE MORNING, BLUE DAY	Foreigner
3860	BLUE SKY	Joan Baez
1955	BLUE SUEDE SHOES	Johnny Rivers
2584	BLUEBIRD	Helen Reddy
963	BLUER THAN BLUE	Michael Johnson
4748	BOATS AGAINST THE CURRENT	Eric Carmen
486	BOHEMIAN RHAPSODY	Queen
3879	BOLD SOUL SISTER	Ike & Tina Turner
3626	BOMBS AWAY	Bob Weir
2594	BONGO ROCK	Incredible Bongo Band
2732	BOO, BOO, DON'T 'CHA BE BLUE	Tommy James
3391	BOOGIE BANDS AND ONE NIGHT STANDS	Kathy Dalton
1344	BOOGIE CHILD	Bee Gees
233	BOOGIE DOWN	Eddie Kendricks
147	BOOGIE FEVER	Sylvers
231	BOOGIE NIGHTS	Heatwave
232	BOOGIE ON REGGAE WOMAN	Stevie Wonder
63	BOOGIE OOGIE OOGIE	A Taste Of Honey
2016	BOOGIE SHOES	K C & The Sunshine Band
612	BOOGIE WONDERLAND	Earth, Wind & Fire with The Emotions
844	BOOGIE WOOGIE BUGLE BOY	Bette Midler
3476	BOOGIE WOOGIE DANCIN' SHOES	Claudja Barry

#	Title	Artist
4262	BOOGIE WOOGIE MAN	Paul Davis
3687	BOOM BOOM (Out Go The Lights)	Pat Travers
4747	BOOMERANG	Frankie Valli
1560	BOOTY BUTT	Ray Charles Orchestra
3625	BOOTZILLA	Bootsy's Rubber Band
	BORDER SONG	
1799		Aretha Franklin (Holy Moses)
3547		Elton John
1288	BORN TO BE ALIVE	Patrick Hernandez
1492	BORN TO RUN	Bruce Springsteen
1240	BORN TO WANDER	Rare Earth
1494	THE BOSS	Diana Ross
1043	THE BOYS ARE BACK IN TOWN	Thin Lizzy
	THE BOYS IN THE BAND...see (How Bout A Little Hand For)	
4993	BRA	Cymande
26	BRAND NEW KEY	Melanie
3502	BRAND NEW LOVE AFFAIR	Jigsaw
3018	BRAND NEW LOVE AFFAIR (Part 1 & 2)	Chicago
1491	A BRAND NEW ME	Dusty Springfield
4024	--BRAND NEW ME	Aretha Franklin
3979	BRANDY	O'Jays
62	BRANDY (You're A Fine Girl)	Looking Glass
	see also MANDY	
1234	BRAZIL	Ritchie Family
2037	BREAK AWAY	Art Garfunkel
4447	BREAK IT TO THEM GENTLY	Burton Cummings
1075	BREAK UP TO MAKE UP	Stylistics
4275	BREAKAWAY	Millie Jackson
2030	BREAKDOWN	Tom Petty And The Heartbreakers
2028	THE BREAKDOWN (Part 1)	Rufus Thomas
	BREAKING UP IS HARD TO DO	
746		Neil Sedaka
1760		Partridge Family
1849		Lenny Welch
	BREAKING UP SOMEBODY'S HOME	
4496		Ann Peebles
5058		Albert King
2708	BRIAN'S SONG	Michel LeGrand
850	BRICK HOUSE	Commodores
	BRIDGE OVER TROUBLED WATER	
27		Simon & Garfunkel
282		Aretha Franklin
3800		Linda Clifford
2069	BRIDGET THE MIDGET (The Queen Of The Blues)	Ray Stevens
5264	BRIGHT LIGHTS, BIG CITY	Sonny James
2979	BRIGHTON HILL	Jackie DeShannon
5330	BRING IT ON HOME	Lou Rawls
783	BRING THE BOYS HOME	Freda Payne
4035	BRINGING IT BACK	Elvis Presley
4875	(Bringing Out) THE GIRL IN ME	Maxine Nightingale
4114	BROKEN	Guess Who
1802	BROKEN HEARTED ME	Anne Murray
4062	BROOKLYN	Cody Jameson
167	BROTHER LOUIE	Stories
2345	BROTHER RAPP (Part 1) & (Part 2)	James Brown
3059	BROTHER'S GONNA WORK IT OUT	Willie Hutch
3032	BROWN EYED GIRL	El Chicano
4589	BROWN PAPER BAG	Syndicate Of Sound
234	BROWN SUGAR	Rolling Stones
4628	BROWNSVILLE	Joy Of Cooking
3312	BUFFALO SOLDIER	Flamingos
4402	BUMP ME BABY (Part 1)	Dooley Silverspoon
1048	BUNGLE IN THE JUNGLE	Jethro Tull
4663	BURNIN' SKY	Bad Company
2937	BURNIN' THING	Mac Davis
1785	BURNING BRIDGES	Mike Curb Congregation
173	BURNING LOVE	Elvis Presley
2204	BUSTIN' LOOSE Part 1	Chuck Brown & The Soul Searchers
3993	BUSTIN' OUT	Rick James
2812	BUT FOR LOVE	Jerry Naylor
3797	BUT I DO	Bobby Vinton
2043	BUTTER BOY	Fanny
5025	BUTTERFLY	Danyel Gerard
4154	BUZZY BROWN	Tim Davis
	BY THE TIME I GET TO PHOENIX...see I SAY A LITTLE PRAYER	
4966	BYE BYE BABY	U.S. 1

C

#	Title	Artist
3163	C.B. SAVAGE	Rod Hart
3242	CA PLANE POUR MOI	Plastic Bertrand
4254	CALEDONIA	Robin Trower
5077	CALICO	Tommy James
3313	CALIFORNIA	Debby Boone
4595	CALIFORNIA BLUES	Redwing
3505	CALIFORNIA DREAMIN'	America
3280	CALIFORNIA GIRL	Eddie Floyd
4422	CALIFORNIA KID AND REEMO	Lobo
4559	CALIFORNIA NIGHTS	Sweet
3497	CALIFORNIA SOUL	Marvin Gaye & Tammi Terrell
4901	THE CALL	Anne Murray
1010	CALL ME	Aretha Franklin
986	CALL ME (Come Back Home)	Al Green
4757	(Call Me) THE TRAVELING MAN	Masqueraders
2365	CALL MY NAME, I'LL BE THERE	Wilson Pickett
1165	CALL ON ME	Chicago
5067	CALL OUT MY NAME	Zwol
1033	CALLING DR. LOVE	Kiss
1639	CALLING OCCUPANTS OF INTER-PLANETARY CRAFT	Carpenters
5186	--CALLING OCCUPANTS	Klaatu
2051	CALYPSO	John Denver
5005	CAN I	Eddie Kendricks
2163	CAN I GET A WITNESS	Lee Michaels
3410	CAN THE CAN	Suzi Quatro
1737	CAN THIS BE REAL	Natural Four
2277	CAN WE STILL BE FRIENDS	Todd Rundgren
3654	CAN YOU DO IT	Grand Funk Railroad
5230	CAN YOU FEEL IT	Bobby Goldsboro
2637	CAN YOU FOOL	Glen Campbell
3483	CAN YOU GET TO THAT	Funkadelic
2740	CAN YOU HANDLE IT?	Graham Central Station
3731	CAN YOU READ MY MIND	Maureen McGovern
3965	CAN'T CHANGE MY HEART	Cate Bros.
2613	CAN'T FIND THE TIME	Rose Colored Glass
389	CAN'T GET ENOUGH	Bad Company
404	CAN'T GET ENOUGH OF YOUR LOVE, BABE	Barry White
1110	CAN'T GET IT OUT OF MY HEAD	Electric Light Orchestra
4667	CAN'T GET OVER LOSING YOU	Donnie Elbert
3065	CAN'T GIVE YOU ANYTHING (But My Love)	Stylistics
	CAN'T HELP FALLING IN LOVE	
3041		Al Martino
4462		Andy Williams
2621	CAN'T HIDE LOVE	Earth, Wind & Fire
4679	CAN'T IT ALL BE LOVE	Randy Edelman
3916	CAN'T KEEP A GOOD MAN DOWN	Eddie Money
4632	CAN'T LET A WOMAN	Ambrosia
4801	CAN'T SAY NOTHIN'	Curtis Mayfield
3201	CAN'T SLEEP	Rockets
154	CAN'T SMILE WITHOUT YOU	Barry Manilow
1584	CAN'T STOP DANCIN'	Captain & Tennille
4259	CAN'T STOP GROOVIN' NOW, WANNA DO IT SOME MORE	B.T. Express
	CAN'T STOP LOVING YOU	
1772		Tom Jones
5235		Flirtations [P]
4365	CAN'T TAKE MY EYES OFF YOU	Nancy Wilson
2602	CAN'T YOU HEAR THE SONG?	Wayne Newton
3888	CAN'T YOU SEE	Marshall Tucker Band
242	CANDIDA	Dawn
4884	CANDY APPLE RED	R. Dean Taylor
155	THE CANDY MAN	Sammy Davis, Jr.
3821	CANDY'S GOING BAD	Golden Earring
2301	CANNED HAM	Norman Greenbaum
	CANTINA BAND...see STAR WARS THEME	
3258	CAPTAIN HOWDY	Simon Stokes
2680	CAPTURE THE MOMENT	Jay & The Americans
4815	CAPTURE YOUR HEART	Blue
386	CAR WASH	Rose Royce
1310	CAREFREE HIGHWAY	Gordon Lightfoot
4795	CAREFUL MAN	John Edwards
4917	CAREY	Joni Mitchell
2329	CARIBBEAN FESTIVAL	Kool & The Gang
	CAROLINA IN MY MIND	
2700		Crystal Mansion
3899		James Taylor
1678	CAROLINA IN THE PINES	Michael Murphey
3914	CAROLYN	Merle Haggard
4930	CARRIE'S GONE	J.C. Stone
2755	CARRY ME	David Crosby/Graham Nash
4174	CARRY ME, CARRIE	Dr. Hook And The Medicine Show
610	CARRY ON WAYWARD SON	Kansas
5255	CASTLES IN THE SAND	Seals & Crofts
1699	CAT SCRATCH FEVER	Ted Nugent
3233	THE CAT WALK	Village Soul Choir

#	Title	Artist
2385	CAT'S EYE IN THE WINDOW	Tommy James
293	CAT'S IN THE CRADLE	Harry Chapin
4283	CATFISH	Four Tops
4581	CAUGHT IN A DREAM	Alice Cooper
4755	CE SOIR	Golden Earring
352	CECILIA	Simon & Garfunkel
1089	CELEBRATE	Three Dog Night
4188	CELEBRATION	Tommy James
4996	CELIA OF THE SEALS	Donovan
4733	C'EST LA VIE	Greg Lake
3109	CHAIN GANG MEDLEY	Jim Croce
2333	CHAINS AND THINGS	B.B. King
2401	CHAIRMAN OF THE BOARD	Chairmen Of The Board
2119	CHAMELEON	Herbie Hancock
3980	CHAMPAGNE JAM	Atlanta Rhythm Section
4619	A CHANGE IS GONNA COME & PEOPLE GOTTA BE FREE	5th Dimension
1455	CHANGE OF HEART	Eric Carmen
2290	CHANGE PARTNERS	Stephen Stills
2780	CHANGE WITH THE TIMES	Van McCoy
1756	CHANGES	David Bowie
3262	CHANGES	Loggins & Messina
2804	CHANGES IN LATITUDES, CHANGES IN ATTITUDES	Jimmy Buffett
2893	CHANTILLY LACE	Jerry Lee Lewis
2044	CHARITY BALL	Fanny
4427	CHARMER	Tim Moore
2403	CHASE	Giorgio Moroder
5076	CHASE ME	Con Funk Shun
3213	CHATTANOOGA CHOO CHOO	Tuxedo Junction
1578	CHEAPER TO KEEP HER	Johnnie Taylor
2324	CHECK IT OUT	Tavares
3812	CHECK IT OUT	Bobby Womack
1404	CHECK OUT YOUR MIND	Impressions
3204	CHEER	Potliquor
2169	CHEESEBURGER IN PARADISE	Jimmy Buffett
	CHERCHEZ LA FEMME...see WHISPERING	
281	CHERISH	David Cassidy
2393	CHERISH WHAT IS DEAR TO YOU (While It's Near To You)	Freda Payne
1905	CHERRY BABY	Starz
1707	CHERRY CHERRY	Neil Diamond
3910	CHERYL MOANA MARIE	John Rowles
4871	CHESTNUT MARE	Byrds
607	CHEVY VAN	Sammy Johns
1535	CHICAGO	Graham Nash
568	CHICK-A-BOOM (Don't Ya Jes' Love It)	Daddy Dewdrop
2598	CHICKEN STRUT	Meters
2615	CHILDREN	Joe South
2838	CHILDREN OF THE SUN	Billy Thorpe
3124	THE CHILDREN'S MARCHING SONG ...see THIS OLD MAN	
880	CHINA GROVE	Doobie Brothers
1352	CHIRPY CHIRPY CHEEP CHEEP	Mac & Katie Kissoon
3513	CHOCOLATE CHIP	Isaac Hayes
4765	CHOCOLATE CITY	Parliament
5059	CHOKIN' KIND	Z.Z. Hill
4412	CHRISTINA	Terry Jacks
1757	CHRISTINE SIXTEEN	Kiss
4827	CHRISTMAS DREAM	Perry Como
4206	CHRISTMAS FOR COWBOYS	John Denver
442	CHUCK E.'S IN LOVE	Rickie Lee Jones
4217	CHURCH	Bob Welch
3452	CHURCH STREET SOUL REVIVAL	Tommy James
1965	CINDERELLA	Firefall
2705	CINDY INCIDENTALLY	Faces
	CINNAMON GIRL	
2517		Gentrys
2956		Neil Young
2151	THE CIRCLE IS SMALL (I Can See It In Your Eyes)	Gordon Lightfoot
5082	CIRCLES	New Seekers
3784	CIRCUS	Mike Quatro Jam Band
363	THE CISCO KID	War
3038	CITY IN THE SKY	Staple Singers
1356	THE CITY OF NEW ORLEANS	Arlo Guthrie
353	CLAIR	Gilbert O'Sullivan
1027	CLAP FOR THE WOLFMAN	Guess Who
5098	CLAP YOUR HANDS	Manhattan Transfer
517	CLEAN UP WOMAN	Betty Wright
1620	CLOSE THE DOOR	Teddy Pendergrass
4750	CLOSE TO YOU	B.T. Express
	see also (They Long To Be)	
1691	CLOSE YOUR EYES	Edward Bear
327	THE CLOSER I GET TO YOU	Roberta Flack & Donny Hathaway
1625	CLOSER TO HOME	Grand Funk Railroad
3850	CLOSER TO THE HEART	Rush
2174	CLOUDS	David Gates
	C'MON...see also COME ON	
3188	C'MON	Poco
2194	C'MON MARIANNE	Donny Osmond
4629	CO-CO	Sweet
3069	COCOMOTION	El Coco
1038	COCONUT	Nilsson
800	COLD AS ICE	Foreigner
1827	COLD TURKEY	Plastic Ono Band
3678	COLDBLOODED	James Brown
3173	THE COLDEST DAYS OF MY LIFE (Part 1)	Chi-Lites
3552	COLE, COOKE AND REDDING	Wilson Pickett
4123	COLORADO	Danny Holien
4053	COLORADO CALL	Shad O'Shea & The 18 Wheelers
3639	COLOUR MY WORLD	Chicago
4519	COME AN' GET YOURSELF SOME	Leon Haywood
563	COME AND GET IT	Badfinger
3459	COME AND GET YOUR LOVE	Roger Daltrey
461	COME AND GET YOUR LOVE	Redbone
3690	COME BACK HOME	Bobby Goldsboro
1640	COME GET TO THIS	Marvin Gaye
5039	COME GO WITH ME	Pockets
5284	COME INTO MY LIFE	Jimmy Cliff
	COME LIVE WITH ME	
2825		Ray Charles
4041		Roy Clark
1713	COME MONDAY	Jimmy Buffett
	COME ON...see also C'MON	
2576	COME ON AND SAY IT	Grass Roots
4973	COME ON DOWN	Savage Grace
1903	COME ON OVER	Olivia Newton-John
4716	COME ON OVER TO MY HOUSE	Layng Martine
4475	COME ON SAY IT	Henry Gross
2445	COME RUNNING	Van Morrison
700	COME SAIL AWAY	Styx
1125	COME SATURDAY MORNING	Sandpipers
4830	COME SOFTLY TO ME	New Seekers Feat. Marty Kristian
1501	COME TO ME	France Joli
2356	COME TO ME	Tommy James & The Shondells
	COME TOGETHER	
1791		Aerosmith
2819		Ike & Tina Turner
3835	COMIN' BACK TO ME (Ooh Baby)	Smith
4084	COMIN' HOME	Delaney & Bonnie & Friends Feat. Eric Clapton
5095	COMPARED TO WHAT	Les McCann & Eddie Harris
2955	CONFUSION	Electric Light Orchestra
1471	CONQUISTADOR	Procol Harum
3514	CONTACT	Edwin Starr
2215	CONTROL OF ME	Les Emmerson
1576	CONVENTION '72	Delegates
65	CONVOY	C.W. McCall
2150	COOK WITH HONEY	Judy Collins
1461	COOL AID	Paul Humphrey & His Cool Aid Chemists
1100	COPACABANA (At The Copa)	Barry Manilow
2040	CORAZON	Carole King
1296	CORNER OF THE SKY	Jackson 5
4342	COSMIC SEA	Mystic Moods
3610	COSTAFINE TOWN	Splinter
2645	COTTAGE CHEESE	Crow
4161	COTTON CANDY	Sylvers
2860	COULD I FORGET YOU	Tyrone Davis
1294	COULD IT BE FOREVER	David Cassidy
321	COULD IT BE I'M FALLING IN LOVE	Spinners
	COULD IT BE MAGIC	
670		Barry Manilow
3808		Donna Summer
4344	COULD YOU EVER LOVE ME AGAIN	Gary & Dave
4192	COULD YOU PUT YOUR LIGHT ON PLEASE	Harry Chapin
791	COULDN'T GET IT RIGHT	Climax Blues Band
1086	COUNT ON ME	Jefferson Starship
1385	COUNTRY BOY (You Got Your Feet In L.A.)	Glen Campbell
4911	COUNTRY PREACHER	Cannonball Adderley Quintet
1988	COUNTRY ROAD	James Taylor
3644	COUNTRY SIDE OF LIFE	Wet Willie
2397	COUNTRY SUNSHINE	Dottie West
2100	COUNTRY WINE	Raiders
4842	COUNTRY WOMAN	Magic Lantern
2772	THE COURT ROOM	Clarence Carter
551	THE COVER OF "ROLLING STONE"	Dr. Hook & The Medicine Show

572	**A COWBOYS WORK IS NEVER DONE**	
	Sonny & Cher	
1667	**CRACKERBOX PALACE**	
	George Harrison	
152	**CRACKLIN' ROSIE** *Neil Diamond*	
4660	**CRANK IT UP (Funk Town) (Part 1)**	
	Peter Brown	
3034	**CRAZY ABOUT THE LA LA LA**	
	Smokey Robinson & The Miracles	
3972	**CRAZY FEELIN'** *Jefferson Starship*	
1632	**CRAZY HORSES** *Osmonds*	
4588	**CRAZY LEGS** *Donald Austin*	
1180	**CRAZY LOVE** *Poco*	
2154	**CRAZY LOVE** *Helen Reddy*	
2944	**CRAZY LOVE** *Allman Brothers Band*	
2082	**CRAZY MAMA** *J.J. Cale*	
2003	**CRAZY ON YOU** *Heart*	
4920	**CRAZY TALK** *Chilliwack*	
994	**CRIED LIKE A BABY** *Bobby Sherman*	
36	**CROCODILE ROCK** *Elton John*	
4823	**THE CRUDE OIL BLUES** *Jerry Reed*	
1070	**CRUEL TO BE KIND** *Nick Lowe*	
4398	**CRY** *Lynn Anderson*	
1661	**CRY BABY** *Janis Joplin*	
1323	**CRY ME A RIVER** *Joe Cocker*	
3455	**CRY TO ME** *Loleatta Holloway*	
2683	**CRYIN' IN THE STREETS (Part 1)**	
	George Perkins & The Silver Stars	
4926	**CUM ON FEEL THE NOIZE** *Slade*	
	CUPID	
1571	*Tony Orlando & Dawn*	
1719	*Johnny Nash*	
2268	**CURIOUS MIND (Um, Um, Um, Um, Um, Um)** *Johnny Rivers*	
946	**CUT THE CAKE** *AWB*	
3152	**CUZ IT'S YOU, GIRL**	
	James Walsh Gypsy Band	

D

1972	**D.O.A.** *Bloodrock*	
361	**DA DOO RON RON** *Shaun Cassidy*	
21	**DA YA THINK I'M SEXY?** *Rod Stewart*	
4644	**DADDY COOL** *Boney M*	
1360	**DADDY COULD SWEAR, I DECLARE**	
	Gladys Knight & The Pips	
131	**DADDY DON'T YOU WALK SO FAST**	
	Wayne Newton	
2859	**DADDY WHAT IF** *Bobby Bare*	
602	**DADDY'S HOME** *Jermaine Jackson*	
	DADDY'S LITTLE GIRL...see **(One More Year Of)**	
1021	**DAISY A DAY** *Jud Strunk*	
1623	**DAISY JANE** *America*	
2011	**DAISY MAE**	
	Hamilton, Joe Frank & Reynolds	
5279	**DAMN IT ALL** *Gene Cotton*	
1934	**DAMNED IF I DO** *Alan Parsons Project*	
2475	**DANCE ACROSS THE FLOOR**	
	Jimmy "Bo" Horne	
4664	**DANCE AND SHAKE YOUR TAM-BOURINE** *Universal Robot Band*	
2968	**DANCE AWAY** *Roxy Music*	
656	**DANCE, DANCE, DANCE (Yowsah, Yowsah, Yowsah)** *Chic*	
1860	**DANCE (Disco Heat)** *Sylvester*	
3773	**DANCE MASTER** *Willie Henderson*	
3017	**DANCE THE KUNG FU** *Carl Douglas*	
1683	**DANCE THE NIGHT AWAY** *Van Halen*	
2806	**DANCE WIT ME**	
	Rufus Feat. Chaka Khan	
596	**DANCE WITH ME** *Orleans*	
735	**DANCE WITH ME** *Peter Brown*	
2827	**DANCE WITH THE DEVIL** *Cozy Powell*	
3461	**DANCER** *Gino Soccio*	
3779	**DANCIN'** *Crown Heights Affair*	
1865	**DANCIN' FOOL** *Guess Who*	
3036	**DANCIN' FOOL** *Frank Zappa*	
4014	**DANCIN' KID**	
	Disco Tex & The Sex-O-Lettes	
1845	**DANCIN' MAN** *Q*	
4276	**DANCIN' (On A Saturday Night)**	
	Flash Cadillac & The Continental Kids	
	DANCIN' SHOES	
1398	*Nigel Olsson*	
3510	*Faith Band*	
4806	**DANCIN' THRU THE NIGHT** *L.A. Jets*	
2266	**DANCING IN THE CITY** *Marshall Hain*	
857	**DANCING IN THE MOONLIGHT**	
	King Harvest	
4843	**DANCING IN THE MOONLIGHT (It's Caught Me In Its Spotlight)** *Thin Lizzy*	
5345	**DANCING IN THE STREET** *Dovells*	
366	**DANCING MACHINE** *Jackson 5*	
315	**DANCING QUEEN** *ABBA*	
3985	**DANCING TO YOUR MUSIC**	
	Archie Bell & The Drells	
	DANGLING ON A STRING...see **(You've Got Me)**	
382	**DANIEL** *Elton John*	
564	**DANNY'S SONG** *Anne Murray*	
1770	**DARK HORSE** *George Harrison*	
314	**DARK LADY** *Cher*	
4736	**DARKNESS, DARKNESS** *Youngbloods*	
2949	**DARLIN'** *Paul Davis*	
4095	**DARLIN' DARLIN' BABY (Sweet, Tender, Love)** *O'Jays*	
5132	**DARLING BABY** *Jackie Moore*	
4914	**DARLING BE HOME SOON**	
	Association	
4699	**DARLING COME BACK HOME**	
	Eddie Kendricks	
864	**DAUGHTER OF DARKNESS** *Tom Jones*	
401	**DAY AFTER DAY** *Badfinger*	
4329	**DAY AND NIGHT** *Wackers*	
	DAY BY DAY	
801	*Godspell*	
5089	*Holly Sherwood* **(Godspell Medley)**	
4515	**DAY BY DAY (Every Minute Of The Hour)** *Continental 4*	
685	**DAY DREAMING** *Aretha Franklin*	
1416	**THE DAY I FOUND MYSELF**	
	Honey Cone	
4681	**DAY IS DONE** *Brooklyn Bridge*	
	A DAY AT THE BEACH WITH PEDRO & MAN...see **(How I Spent My Summer Vacation)**	
4753	**THE DAY THAT CURLY BILLY SHOT DOWN CRAZY SAM McGEE** *Hollies*	
2815	**DAY TRIPPER** *Anne Murray*	
1790	**DAYBREAK** *Barry Manilow*	
1798	**DAYBREAK** *Nilsson*	
3239	**DAYBREAKER**	
	Electric Light Orchestra	
4958	**DAYDREAM** *David Cassidy*	
	DAYLIGHT	
4713	*Bobby Womack*	
5179	*Vickie Sue Robinson*	
4724	**DAYLIGHT AND DARKNESS**	
	Smokey Robinson	
1984	**DAYS GONE DOWN (Still Got The Light In Your Eyes)** *Gerry Rafferty*	
2337	**DAYTIME FRIENDS** *Kenny Rogers*	
2474	**DAYTIME NIGHT-TIME**	
	Keith Hampshire	
518	**DAZZ** *Brick*	
1522	**DEACON BLUES** *Steely Dan*	
1077	**DEAD SKUNK** *Loudon Wainwright III*	
4542	**DEAR ANN** *George Baker Selection*	
	DEAR PRUDENCE	
3231	*Katfish*	
3874	*Five Stairsteps*	
302	**DECEMBER, 1963 (Oh, What A Night)**	
	Four Seasons	
3829	**THE DECLARATION** *5th Dimension*	
4200	**DEDICATED TO THE ONE I LOVE**	
	Temprees	
4009	**DEDICATION** *Bay City Rollers*	
3737	**DEEP ENOUGH FOR ME** *Ocean*	
1250	**DEEP PURPLE**	
	Donny & Marie Osmond	
1475	**DEEPER & DEEPER** *Freda Payne*	
3094	**DEEPER (In Love With You)** *O'Jays*	
1876	**DEEPER THAN THE NIGHT**	
	Olivia Newton-John	
4495	**DEEPLY** *Anson Williams*	
122	**DELTA DAWN** *Helen Reddy*	
3890	**DELTA QUEEN** *Don Fardon*	
4396	**DEMONSTRATION** *Otis Redding*	
3247	**DEPARTMENT OF YOUTH**	
	Alice Cooper	
2216	**DEPENDIN' ON YOU** *Doobie Brothers*	
4003	**DESDEMONA** *Searchers*	
1236	**DESIDERATA** *Les Crane*	
	see also **DETERIORATA**	
958	**DESIREE** *Neil Diamond*	
3843	**DESTINY** *Jose Feliciano*	
4834	**DETERIORATA**	
	National Lampoon [R: **DESIDERATA**]	
5285	**DETROIT CITY** *Dean Martin*	
3992	**DETROIT ROCK CITY** *KISS*	
3408	**DEVIL IN THE BOTTLE** *T.G. Sheppard*	
586	**THE DEVIL WENT DOWN TO GEORGIA**	
	Charlie Daniels Band	
490	**DEVIL WOMAN** *Cliff Richard*	
3177	**DEVIL YOU** *Stampeders*	
3085	**DEVIL'S GUN** *C.J. & Co.*	
3080	**DEVOTED TO YOU**	
	Carly Simon & James Taylor	
3652	**DEVOTION** *Earth, Wind & Fire*	
1600	**DIALOGUE (Part 1 & 2)** *Chicago*	
816	**DIAMOND GIRL** *Seals & Crofts*	
2869	**DIAMONDS** *Chris Rea*	
2665	**DIAMONDS AND RUST** *Joan Baez*	
3096	**DIAMONDS ARE FOREVER**	
	Shirley Bassey	
1341	**DIARY** *Bread*	
5024	**DICK AND JANE** *Bobby Vinton*	
1753	**DID YOU BOOGIE (With Your Baby)**	
	Flash Cadillac & The Continental Kids	
4149	**DIDN'T I** *Sylvia*	
1015	**DIDN'T I (Blow Your Mind This Time)**	
	Delfonics	
3780	**DIDN'T IT LOOK SO EASY** *Stairsteps*	

3380	**DIDN'T WE** Barbra Streisand	
1574	**DIFFERENT WORLDS**	
	Maureen McGovern	
4224	**DIG THE WAY I FEEL** Mary Wells	
408	**DIM ALL THE LIGHTS** Donna Summer	
2741	**DING DONG; DING DONG**	
	George Harrison	
1529	**DIRTY WHITE BOY** Foreigner	
4249	**DIS-GORILLA (Part 1)** Rick Dees	
96	**DISCO DUCK (Part 1)**	
	Rick Dees & His Cast of Idiots	
899	**DISCO INFERNO** Trammps	
143	**DISCO LADY** Johnnie Taylor	
1460	**DISCO LUCY (I Love Lucy Theme)**	
	Wilton Place Street Band	
1000	**DISCO NIGHTS (Rock-Freak)** G.Q.	
1806	**DISCO QUEEN** Hot Chocolate	
2193	**DISTANT LOVER** Marvin Gaye	
	DO I LOVE YOU	
2121	Paul Anka	
5194	Donna Fargo **(Yes In Every Way)**	
2278	**DO IT** Neil Diamond	
807	**DO IT AGAIN** Steely Dan	
1080	**DO IT ANY WAY YOU WANNA**	
	People's Choice	
999	**DO IT BABY** Miracles	
4270	**DO IT, FLUID** Blackbyrds	
3770	**DO IT IN THE NAME OF LOVE**	
	Ben E. King	
3091	**DO IT IN THE NAME OF LOVE**	
	Candi Staton	
1523	**DO IT OR DIE** Atlanta Rhythm Section	
661	**DO IT ('Til You're Satisfied)**	
	B.T. Express	
3248	**DO IT TO MY MIND** Johnny Bristol	
2139	**DO ME RIGHT** Detroit Emeralds	
2211	**DO THE FUNKY CHICKEN**	
	Rufus Thomas	
3129	**DO THE FUNKY PENGUIN (Part 1)**	
	Rufus Thomas	
1292	**(Do The) PUSH AND PULL (Part 1)**	
	Rufus Thomas	
3154	**DO WHAT YOU SET OUT TO DO**	
	Bobby Bland	
2101	**DO WHAT YOU WANNA DO**	
	Five Flights Up	
4503	**DO WHAT YOU WANNA DO**	
	T-Connection	
2916	**DO WHAT YOU WANT, BE WHAT YOU ARE** Daryl Hall & John Oates	
	DO YA	
1500	Electric Light Orchestra	
5275	Move	
2469	**DO YA WANNA GET FUNKY WITH ME**	
	Peter Brown	
2757	**DO YOU BELIEVE IN MAGIC**	
	Shaun Cassidy	
4591	**DO YOU FEEL ALL RIGHT**	
	K C & The Sunshine Band	
1350	**DO YOU FEEL LIKE WE DO**	
	Peter Frampton	
496	**DO YOU KNOW WHAT I MEAN**	
	Lee Michaels	
3061	**DO YOU KNOW WHAT TIME IT IS?**	
	P-Nut Gallery	
2025	**DO YOU SEE MY LOVE (For You Growing)** Jr. Walker & The All Stars	
3525	**DO YOU THINK I'M DISCO?**	
	Steve Dahl & Teenage Radiation	
2882	**DO YOU WANNA GO PARTY**	
	K C & The Sunshine Band	
825	**DO YOU WANNA MAKE LOVE**	
	Peter McCann	
1076	**DO YOU WANT TO DANCE?**	
	Bette Midler	
5017	**--DO YOU WANNA DANCE** Ramones	
3620	**DO YOUR DANCE (Part 1)** Rose Royce	
	DO YOUR THING	
1608	Isaac Hayes	
3769	James & Bobby Purify	
	DOCK OF THE BAY...see **(Sittin' On)**	
4284	**DOCTOR LOVE** First Choice	
1057	**DOCTOR MY EYES** Jackson Browne	
	DOCTOR TARR AND PROFESSOR FETHER...see **(The System Of)**	
926	**DOCTOR'S ORDERS** Carol Douglas	
528	**DOES ANYBODY REALLY KNOW WHAT TIME IT IS?** Chicago	
4353	**DOES SHE DO IT LIKE SHE DANCES**	
	Addrisi Brothers	
1351	**DOES YOUR MOTHER KNOW** ABBA	
114	**DOESN'T SOMEBODY WANT TO BE WANTED** Partridge Family	
2257	**DOG & BUTTERFLY** Heart	
3538	**DOG DAYS** Atlanta Rhythm Section	
4506	**DOG EAT DOG** Ted Nugent	
1738	**DOING IT TO DEATH**	
	Fred Wesley & The J.B.'s	
3528	**DOING MY OWN THING (Part 1)**	
	Johnnie Taylor	
5153	**DOLLY DAGGER** Jimi Hendrix	
1155	**DOMINO** Van Morrison	
4068	**DON'T ASK MY NEIGHBORS** Emotions	
579	**DON'T BRING ME DOWN**	
	Electric Light Orchestra	
1093	**DON'T CALL US, WE'LL CALL YOU**	
	Sugarloaf/Jerry Corbetta	
3355	**DON'T CHA LOVE IT** Miracles	
3028	**DON'T CHANGE HORSES (In The Middle Of A Stream)** Tower Of Power	
1624	**DON'T CHANGE ON ME** Ray Charles	
3560	**DON'T COST YOU NOTHING**	
	Ashford & Simpson	
1787	**DON'T CROSS THE RIVER** America	
537	**DON'T CRY DADDY** Elvis Presley	
3054	**DON'T CRY JONI** Conway Twitty	
876	**DON'T CRY OUT LOUD**	
	Melissa Manchester	
1644	**DON'T DO IT** Band	
3438	**DON'T EAT THE YELLOW SNOW**	
	Frank Zappa	
1598	**DON'T EVER BE LONELY (A Poor Little Fool Like Me)**	
	Cornelius Brothers & Sister Rose	
2555	**DON'T EVER WANNA LOSE YA**	
	New England	
620	**DON'T EXPECT ME TO BE YOUR FRIEND** Lobo	
891	**(Don't Fear) THE REAPER**	
	Blue Öyster Cult	
5199	**DON'T GET CLOSE**	
	Little Anthony & The Imperials	
295	**DON'T GIVE UP ON US** David Soul	
140	**DON'T GO BREAKING MY HEART**	
	Elton John & Kiki Dee	
2733	**DON'T HIDE YOUR LOVE** Cher	
1509	**DON'T HOLD BACK** Chanson	
101	**DON'T IT MAKE MY BROWN EYES BLUE** Crystal Gayle	
2633	**DON'T IT MAKE YOU WANT TO GO HOME** Brook Benton	
	DON'T KNOCK MY LOVE	
717	Wilson Pickett **(Part 1)**	
2611	Diana Ross & Marvin Gaye	
4407	**DON'T LEAVE ME IN THE MORNING**	
	Odia Coates	
2996	**DON'T LEAVE ME STARVIN' FOR YOUR LOVE (Part 1)**	
	Holland-Dozier Feat. Brian Holland	
436	**DON'T LEAVE ME THIS WAY**	
	Thelma Houston	
3194	**DON'T LET GO** Commander Cody & His Lost Planet Airmen	
2843	**DON'T LET HIM TAKE YOUR LOVE FROM ME** Four Tops	
5316	**DON'T LET IT END ('Til You Let It Begin)**	
	Miracles	
4737	**DON'T LET IT GET YOU DOWN**	
	Crusaders	
3535	**DON'T LET IT SHOW**	
	Alan Parsons Project	
1485	**DON'T LET ME BE LONELY TONIGHT**	
	James Taylor	
1208	**DON'T LET ME BE MISUNDERSTOOD**	
	Santa Esmeralda	
3463	**DON'T LET THE FLAME BURN OUT**	
	Jackie DeShannon	
895	**DON'T LET THE GREEN GRASS FOOL YOU** Wilson Pickett	
331	**DON'T LET THE SUN GO DOWN ON ME**	
	Elton John	
789	**DON'T LOOK BACK** Boston	
4361	**DON'T MAKE ME OVER**	
	Brenda & The Tabulations	
3494	**DON'T MAKE ME PAY FOR HIS MISTAKES** Z.Z. Hill	
5018	**DON'T MESS UP A GOOD THING**	
	Gregg Allman	
1028	**DON'T PLAY THAT SONG**	
	Aretha Franklin	
	DON'T PULL YOUR LOVE	
116	Hamilton, Joe Frank & Reynolds	
5090	Sam & Dave	
2435	**--/THEN YOU CAN TELL ME GOODBYE**	
	Glen Campbell	
1044	**DON'T SAY YOU DON'T REMEMBER**	
	Beverly Bremers	
4434	**DON'T SEND NOBODY ELSE**	
	Ace Spectrum	
322	**DON'T STOP** Fleetwood Mac	
230	**DON'T STOP 'TIL YOU GET ENOUGH**	
	Michael Jackson	
2409	**DON'T STOP BELIEVIN'**	
	Olivia Newton-John	
3554	**DON'T STOP IT NOW** Hot Chocolate	
4354	**DON'T STOP ME NOW** Queen	
2699	**DON'T STOP NOW** Eddie Holman	
2159	**DON'T TAKE AWAY THE MUSIC**	
	Tavares	
3689	**DON'T TAKE MY KINDNESS FOR WEAKNESS** Soul Children	
2250	**DON'T TAKE YOUR LOVE** Manhattans	
2185	**DON'T TELL ME GOODNIGHT** Lobo	
3852	**DON'T THINK...FEEL** Neil Diamond	
	DON'T THROW IT ALL AWAY...see **(Our Love)**	

4925	DON'T THROW OUR LOVE AWAY *Orleans*	
3987	DON'T TOUCH ME THERE *Tubes*	
	DON'T TRY TO LAY NO BOOGIE WOOGIE ON THE "KING OF ROCK & ROLL"	
2538	*Crow*	
4522	*John Baldry*	
4631	DON'T TURN THE LIGHT OUT *Cliff Richard*	
2507	DON'T WANNA LIVE INSIDE MYSELF *Bee Gees*	
1599	DON'T WANT TO LIVE WITHOUT IT *Pablo Cruise*	
4740	DON'T WANT TO SAY GOODBYE *Raspberries*	
	DON'T WORRY BABY	
1094	*B.J. Thomas*	
3803	*Tokens*	
1542	(Don't Worry) IF THERE'S A HELL BELOW WE'RE ALL GOING TO GO *Curtis Mayfield*	
	DON'T YOU...see also DON'T CHA	
1154	DON'T YOU WORRY 'BOUT A THING *Stevie Wonder*	
2370	DON'T YOU WRITE HER OFF *McGuinn, Clark & Hillman*	
3697	DONE TOO SOON *Neil Diamond*	
1440	DOO DOO DOO DOO DOO (Heartbreaker) *Rolling Stones*	
3909	THE DOODLE SONG *Frankie Miller*	
3063	DOOR TO YOUR HEART *Dramatics*	
2870	DORAVILLE *Atlanta Rhythm Section*	
2027	A DOSE OF ROCK 'N' ROLL *Ringo Starr*	
1795	DOUBLE BARREL *Dave & Ansil Collins*	
1055	DOUBLE LOVIN' *Osmonds*	
4617	DOUBLE TROUBLE *Lynyrd Skynyrd*	
738	DOUBLE VISION *Foreigner*	
3708	DOWN AND OUT IN NEW YORK CITY *James Brown*	
323	DOWN BY THE LAZY RIVER *Osmonds*	
3221	DOWN BY THE RIVER *Albert Hammond*	
3471	DOWN BY THE RIVER *Buddy Miles*	
4260	DOWN IN THE ALLEY *Ronnie Hawkins*	
4261	DOWN ON ME *Janis Joplin*	
4170	DOWN THE HALL *Four Seasons*	
4948	DOWN THE ROAD *B.T.O.*	
5308	DOWN TO LOVE TOWN *Originals*	
2400	DOWN TO THE LINE *Bachman-Turner Overdrive*	
3747	DOWN TO THE NIGHTCLUB *Tower Of Power*	
4208	DOWN TO THE STATION *B.W. Stevenson*	
106	DRAGGIN' THE LINE *Tommy James*	
2530	DRAW THE LINE *Aerosmith*	
2857	DREADLOCK HOLIDAY *10 CC*	
1834	DREAM BABY (How Long Must I Dream) *Glen Campbell*	
2778	A DREAM GOES ON FOREVER *Todd Rundgren*	
4504	DREAM LOVER *Marshall Tucker Band*	
3598	DREAM ME HOME *Mac Davis*	
2045	DREAM MERCHANT *New Birth*	
2374	THE DREAM NEVER DIES *Cooper Brothers*	
492	DREAM ON *Aerosmith*	
2127	DREAM ON *Righteous Brothers*	
2222	DREAM POLICE *Cheap Trick*	
156	DREAM WEAVER *Gary Wright*	
1996	DREAMBOAT ANNIE *Heart*	
1712	DREAMING *Blondie*	
2422	DREAMING A DREAM *Crown Heights Affair*	
337	DREAMS *Fleetwood Mac*	
3647	DREAMS ARE TEN A PENNY *First Class*	
1526	DREIDEL *Don McLean*	
618	DRIFT AWAY *Dobie Gray*	
3679	DRIFTWOOD *Moody Blues*	
1771	DRINKING WINE SPO-DEE O'DEE *Jerry Lee Lewis*	
4879	DRIVE MY CAR *Gary Toms Empire*	
1320	DRIVER'S SEAT *Sniff 'n' The Tears*	
5236	DRIVIN' HOME *Jerry Smith*	
2035	DRIVIN' WHEEL *Foghat*	
3802	DROP BY MY PLACE *Little Carl Carlton*	
720	DROWNING IN THE SEA OF LOVE *Joe Simon*	
1819	THE DRUM *Bobby Sherman*	
262	DUELING BANJOS *Deliverance Soundtrack (Eric Weissberg & Steve Mandell)*	
3363	DUNCAN *Paul Simon*	
2005	DUSIC *Brick*	
511	DUST IN THE WIND *Kansas*	
1137	D'YER MAK'ER *Led Zeppelin*	
987	DYNOMITE (Part 1) *Bazuka*	

E

701	EARACHE MY EYE Featuring Alice Bowie *Cheech & Chong*	
719	EARLY IN THE MORNING *Vanity Fare*	
2318	EARLY MORNING LOVE *Sammy Johns*	
	EASE ON DOWN THE ROAD	
2152	*Diana Ross & Michael Jackson*	
2693	*Consumer Rapport*	
550	EASY *Commodores*	
3222	EASY AS PIE *Billy "Crash" Craddock*	
675	EASY COME, EASY GO *Bobby Sherman*	
3311	EASY DRIVER *Kenny Loggins*	
	EASY EVIL	
4961	*John Kay*	
5323	*Travis Wammack*	
1989	EASY LIVIN *Uriah Heep*	
979	EASY LOVING *Freddie Hart*	
5208	EASY RIDER (Let The Wind Pay The Way) *Iron Butterfly*	
4715	EASY STREET *Edgar Winter Group*	
3112	EASY TO BE FREE *Rick Nelson*	
4562	EASY TO BE HARD *Hair (Original Soundtrack)/Cheryl Barnes*	
2718	EASY TO LOVE *Leo Sayer*	
4841	EASY WAY OUT *Roy Orbison*	
1204	EBONY EYES *Bob Welch*	
3861	ECHOES OF LOVE *Doobie Brothers*	
2058	ECSTASY *Ohio Players*	
4525	EDDIE'S LOVE *Eddie Kendricks*	
2064	EDGE OF THE UNIVERSE *Bee Gees*	
2173	EGO *Elton John*	
4311	EH! CUMPARI *Gaylord & Holiday*	
1533	EIGHTEEN *Alice Cooper*	
1164	EIGHTEEN WITH A BULLET *Pete Wingfield*	
3898	EL BIMBO *Bimbo Jet*	
1074	EL CONDOR PASA *Simon & Garfunkel*	
1666	ELECTED *Alice Cooper*	
5207	THE ELECTRONIC MAGNETISM (That's Heavy, Baby) *Solomon Burke*	
3416	ELENA *Marc Tanner Band*	
697	EMMA *Hot Chocolate*	
59	EMOTION *Samantha Sang*	
1800	EMOTION *Helen Reddy*	
3585	EMPTY PAGES *Traffic*	
2934	THE END IS NOT IN SIGHT (The Cowboy Tune) *Amazing Rhythm Aces*	
2123	THE END OF OUR ROAD *Marvin Gaye*	
	ENDLESSLY	
4555	*Mavis Staples*	
5022	*Sonny James*	
2477	ENERGY CRISIS '74 *Dickie Goodman*	
4348	ENERGY CRISIS '79 *Dickie Goodman*	
1143	ENGINE NUMBER 9 *Wilson Pickett*	
4546	ENJOY AND GET IT ON *ZZ Top*	
581	ENJOY YOURSELF *Jacksons*	
208	THE ENTERTAINER *Marvin Hamlisch*	
2172	THE ENTERTAINER *Billy Joel*	
863	ERES TU (Touch The Wind) *Mocedades*	
73	ESCAPE (The Pina Colada Song) *Rupert Holmes*	
2429	ESCAPE-ISM (Part 1) *James Brown*	
1510	EVEN NOW *Barry Manilow*	
982	EVERLASTING LOVE *Carl Carlton*	
655	AN EVERLASTING LOVE *Andy Gibb*	
5246	EVERY BEAT OF MY HEART *Crown Heights Affair*	
	EVERY DAY...see also EVERYDAY	
2808	EVERY DAY I HAVE TO CRY SOME *Arthur Alexander*	
1265	EVERY DAY OF MY LIFE *Bobby Vinton*	
4063	EVERY FACE TELLS A STORY *Olivia Newton-John*	
1083	EVERY KINDA PEOPLE *Robert Palmer*	
5205	EVERY LITTLE TEARDROP *Gallagher & Lyle*	
896	EVERY TIME I THINK OF YOU *Babys*	
727	(Every Time I Turn Around) BACK IN LOVE AGAIN *L.T.D.*	
1675	EVERY TIME YOU TOUCH ME (I Get High) *Charlie Rich*	
2132	EVERY WHICH WAY BUT LOOSE *Eddie Rabbitt*	
2985	EVERYBODY BE DANCIN' *Starbuck*	
4820	EVERYBODY BUT ME *G.W. Kenny*	
2986	EVERYBODY DANCE *Chic*	
2106	EVERYBODY IS A STAR *Sly & The Family Stone*	
3198	EVERYBODY KNOWS ABOUT MY GOOD THING (Part 1) *Little Johnny Taylor*	
2522	EVERYBODY LOVES A LOVE SONG *Mac Davis*	
2866	EVERYBODY LOVES A RAIN SONG *B.J. Thomas*	
4536	EVERYBODY NEEDS A RAINBOW *Ray Stevens*	
2138	EVERYBODY NEEDS LOVE *Stephen Bishop*	
4623	EVERYBODY OUGHT TO BE IN LOVE *Paul Anka*	
225	EVERYBODY PLAYS THE FOOL *Main Ingredient*	

#	Title	Artist
3772	(Everybody Wanna Get Rich) RITE AWAY	Dr. John
4968	EVERYBODY WANTS TO FIND A BLUEBIRD	Randy Edelman
1068	EVERYBODY'S EVERYTHING	Santana
1199	EVERYBODY'S GOT THE RIGHT TO LOVE	Supremes
4240	EVERYBODY'S HAD THE BLUES	Merle Haggard
1910	EVERYBODY'S OUT OF TOWN	B.J. Thomas
	EVERYDAY...see also EVERY DAY	
4575	EVERYDAY	John Denver
4324	EVERYDAY WITHOUT YOU	Hamilton, Joe Frank & Reynolds
802	EVERY 1'S A WINNER	Hot Chocolate
2291	EVERYONE'S AGREED THAT EVERYTHING WILL TURN OUT FINE	Stealers Wheel
2782	EVERYTHING A MAN COULD EVER NEED	Glen Campbell
2636	EVERYTHING GOOD IS BAD	100 Proof Aged In Soul
642	EVERYTHING I OWN	Bread
341	EVERYTHING IS BEAUTIFUL	Ray Stevens
4873	EVERYTHING IS GOING TO BE ALRIGHT	Teegarden & Van Winkle
3597	EVERYTHING IS GOOD ABOUT YOU	Lettermen
4821	EVERYTHING THAT 'CHA DO (Will Come Back To You)	Wet Willie
5007	EVERYTHING'S ALRIGHT	Yvonne Elliman
3192	EVERYTHING'S BEEN CHANGED	5th Dimension
4032	EVERYTHING'S COMING UP LOVE	David Ruffin
3037	EVERYTHING'S THE SAME (Ain't Nothing Changed)	Billy Swan
2339	EVERYTHING'S TUESDAY	Chairmen Of The Board
2771	EVIL	Earth, Wind & Fire
3379	EVIL BOLL-WEEVIL	Grand Canyon
	EVIL WAYS	
680		Santana
3564		Carlos Santana & Buddy Miles
658	EVIL WOMAN	Electric Light Orchestra
1095	EVIL WOMAN DON'T PLAY YOUR GAMES WITH ME	Crow
966	EXPRESS	B.T. Express
1243	EXPRESS YOURSELF	Charles Wright & The Watts 103rd Street Rhythm Band
2304	EYES OF SILVER	Doobie Brothers

F

#	Title	Artist
1962	FM (No Static At All)	Steely Dan
2855	FAIR GAME	Crosby, Stills & Nash
1614	FAIRYTALE	Pointer Sisters
5286	FAITHFUL AND TRUE	Z.Z. Hill
2844	FALLEN ANGEL	Frankie Valli
	see also (She's Just A)	
335	FALLIN' IN LOVE	Hamilton, Joe Frank & Reynolds
2112	FALLIN' IN LOVE	Souther, Hillman, Furay Band
1003	FALLING	LeBlanc & Carr
3033	FALLING APART AT THE SEAMS	Marmalade
197	FAME	David Bowie
30	FAMILY AFFAIR	Sly & The Family Stone
1193	THE FAMILY OF MAN	Three Dog Night
1394	FANCY	Bobbie Gentry
2886	FANCY DANCER	Commodores
4322	FANCY LADY	Billy Preston
	FANNY (Be Tender With My Love)	
858		Bee Gees
4727		Gino Cunico
1761	FANTASY	Earth, Wind & Fire
3257	FAREWELL ANDROMEDA (Welcome To My Morning)	John Denver
3218	FARTHER ON DOWN THE ROAD	Joe Simon
	FAT BOTTOMED GIRLS Queen see: BICYCLE RACE	
4524	FEEL ALRIGHT	Cargoe
455	FEEL LIKE MAKIN' LOVE	Roberta Flack
970	FEEL LIKE MAKIN' LOVE	Bad Company
3630	FEEL SO BAD	Ray Charles
4098	FEEL THAT YOU'RE FEELIN'	Maze
3729	FEEL THE NEED	Leif Garrett
4483	--FEEL THE NEED IN ME	Detroit Emeralds
3350	FEELIN' SATISFIED	Boston
821	FEELIN' STRONGER EVERY DAY	Chicago
3646	FEELIN' THAT GLOW	Roberta Flack
	FEELING ALRIGHT	
2312		Joe Cocker
2577		Grand Funk Railroad [P]
544	FEELINGS	Morris Albert
4493	FEELINGS	Barry Mann
688	FEELS LIKE THE FIRST TIME	Foreigner
561	FEELS SO GOOD	Chuck Mangione
4352	FEET START WALKING	Doris Duke
4633	FELIZ NAVIDAD	Jose Feliciano
2924	FELL FOR YOU	Dramatics
2347	FENCEWALK	Mandrill
953	FERNANDO	ABBA
4907	FEVER	Rita Coolidge
3934	THE FEZ	Steely Dan
1557	FFUN	Con Funk Shun
4863	FIFTEEN YEARS AGO	Conway Twitty
84	A FIFTH OF BEETHOVEN	Walter Murphy & The Big Apple Band
91	50 WAYS TO LEAVE YOUR LOVER	Paul Simon
678	FIGHT THE POWER (Part 1)	Isley Brothers
5306	THE FIGHTIN' SIDE OF ME	Merle Haggard
1374	FINALLY GOT MYSELF TOGETHER (I'm A Changed Man)	Impressions
3648	FINDER'S KEEPERS	Chairmen Of The Board
2120	FINS	Jimmy Buffett
332	FIRE	Ohio Players
266	FIRE	Pointer Sisters
	FIRE AND RAIN	
369		James Taylor
3572		Johnny Rivers
3712		R.B. Greaves
1405	FIRE AND WATER	Wilson Pickett
2327	FIRE, BABY I'M ON FIRE	Andy Kim
2830	FIRE ON THE MOUNTAIN	Marshall Tucker Band
4056	FIRE SIGN	Cory
2252	FIRECRACKER	Mass Production
1580	THE FIRST CUT IS THE DEEPEST	Rod Stewart
2134	--FIRST CUT IS THE DEEPEST	Keith Hampshire
23	THE FIRST TIME EVER I SAW YOUR FACE	Roberta Flack
2175	FISH AIN'T BITIN'	Lamont Dozier
3335	5:15	Who
3964	FIVE HUNDRED MILES	Heaven Bound
2578	5.7.0.5.	City Boy
755	5-10-15-20 (25-30 Years Of Love)	Presidents
5031	FLAME	Steve Sperry
4470	FLAMING YOUTH	Kiss
1299	FLASH LIGHT	Parliament
4767	FLASHBACK	5th Dimension
2792	FLESH AND BLOOD	Johnny Cash
2089	FLIGHT '76	Walter Murphy Band
3968	FLIM FLAM MAN	Barbra Streisand
476	FLOAT ON	Floaters
	see also BLOAT ON	
1286	FLOY JOY	Supremes
3251	FLY AT NIGHT	Chilliwack
616	FLY AWAY	John Denver
488	FLY LIKE AN EAGLE	Steve Miller
4457	FLY LITTLE WHITE DOVE FLY	Bells
97	FLY, ROBIN, FLY	Silver Convention
3362	FLYIN'	Prism
3118	FLYING HIGH	Commodores
3960	FLYING HIGH	Blackbyrds
3706	FOLLOW ME	Mary Travers
1693	FOLLOW YOU FOLLOW ME	Genesis
3683	FOLLOW YOUR DAUGHTER HOME	Guess Who
3282	THE FONZ SONG	Heyettes
4577	FOOL	Elvis Presley
2965	FOOL FOR THE CITY	Foghat
1119	FOOL (If You Think It's Over)	Chris Rea
5196	FOOL LIKE YOU	Tim Moore
4980	FOOL ME	Joe South
2995	A FOOL SUCH AS I	Bob Dylan
1148	FOOL TO CRY	Rolling Stones
471	FOOLED AROUND AND FELL IN LOVE	Elvin Bishop
1694	FOOLING YOURSELF (The Angry Young Man)	Styx
4015	THE FOOTBALL CARD	Glenn Sutton
2308	FOOTSTOMPIN' MUSIC	Grand Funk Railroad
2556	FOPP	Ohio Players
3523	FOR A DANCER	Prelude
4882	FOR A WHILE	Mary MacGregor
632	FOR ALL WE KNOW	Carpenters
3886	FOR EMILY, WHENEVER I MAY FIND HER	Simon & Garfunkel
2357	(For God's Sake) GIVE MORE POWER TO THE PEOPLE	Chi-Lites
3627	FOR LADIES ONLY	Steppenwolf
4691	FOR LOVE	Pousette-Dart Band
874	FOR THE GOOD TIMES	Ray Price
761	FOR THE LOVE OF HIM	Bobbi Martin
983	FOR THE LOVE OF MONEY	O'Jays
1673	FOR THE LOVE OF YOU (Part 1 & 2)	Isley Brothers

#	Title	Artist
3681	FOR YASGUR'S FARM	Mountain
4158	FOR YOU AND I	10cc
4212	FOR YOU BLUE	Beatles
	FOR YOUR PRECIOUS LOVE...see YOUR PRECIOUS LOVE	
5291	FOREVER AND EVER	Slik
1888	FOREVER AUTUMN	Justin Hayward
2765	FOREVER CAME TODAY	Jackson 5
1549	FOREVER IN BLUE JEANS	Neil Diamond
4837	48 CRASH	Suzi Quatro
2237	FOUND A CURE	Ashford & Simpson
3741	FOUR STRONG WINDS	Neil Young
3776	FOX HUNT	Herb Alpert & The TJB
4615	FOX HUNTIN' (On The Weekend)	Daddy Dewdrop
519	FOX ON THE RUN	Sweet
3582	FOXY LADY	Crown Heights Affair
2666	FRAMED	Cheech & Chong
4204	FRANCENE	ZZ Top
172	FRANKENSTEIN	Edgar Winter Group
589	FREDDIE'S DEAD (Theme From "Superfly")	Curtis Mayfield
1313	FREE	Deniece Williams
1700	FREE	Chicago
4971	FREE	Fresh Start
3936	FREE AS THE WIND	Brooklyn Bridge
	FREE BIRD	
1635		Lynyrd Skynyrd [Live]
2020		Lynyrd Skynyrd
2660	THE FREE ELECTRIC BAND	Albert Hammond
4160	FREE MAN	South Shore Commission
1655	FREE MAN IN PARIS	Joni Mitchell
5326	FREE ME FROM MY FREEDOM/TIE ME TO A TREE (Handcuff Me)	Bonnie Pointer
	FREE RIDE	
869		Edgar Winter Group
3333		Tavares
3749	FREE SPIRIT	Atlanta Rhythm Section
2743	FREEDOM	Isley Brothers
3930	FREEDOM	Jimi Hendrix
3611	FREEDOM BLUES	Little Richard
4256	FREEDOM COMES, FREEDOM GOES	Fortunes
2142	FREEDOM FOR THE STALLION	Hues Corporation
5193	FREIGHT TRAIN	Duane Eddy
3343	FRESH AIR	Quicksilver Messenger Service
1994	FRESH AS A DAISY	Emitt Rhodes
4887	FRIEND AND A LOVER	Partridge Family
3557	A FRIEND IN THE CITY	Andy Kim
4452	A FRIEND OF MINE IS GOING BLIND	John Dawson Read
1579	FRIENDS	Elton John
2820	FRIENDS	Bette Midler
3844	FRIENDS	Feather
5318	FRIENDS OR LOVERS	Act I
1658	FRIENDS WITH YOU	John Denver
4061	FRISKY	Sly & The Family Stone
2961	FROM GRACELAND TO THE PROMISED LAND	Merle Haggard
2295	FROM HIS WOMAN TO YOU	Barbara Mason
2095	FROM THE BEGINNING	Emerson, Lake & Palmer
4846	FULL CIRCLE	Byrds
2060	FULL OF FIRE	Al Green
2967	FUN TIME	Joe Cocker
2920	FUNK FACTORY	Wilson Pickett
4881	FUNK IT UP (David's Song)	Sweet
2878	FUNK #49	James Gang
5242	FUNKY	Chambers Brothers
2849	FUNKY DRUMMER (Part 1)	James Brown
5126	THE FUNKY GIBBON	Goodies
5149	FUNKY L.A.	Paul Humphrey & His Cool Aid Chemists
4712	FUNKY MAN	Kool & The Gang
3196	FUNKY MUSIC SHO NUFF TURNS ME ON	Edwin Starr
836	FUNKY NASSAU (Part 1)	Beginning Of The End
5062	FUNKY PARTY	Clarence Reid
4864	FUNKY PRESIDENT (People It's Bad)	James Brown
2486	FUNKY STUFF	Kool & The Gang
4590	FUNKY WEEKEND	Stylistics
1166	FUNKY WORM	Ohio Players
2822	THE FUNNIEST THING	Dennis Yost & The Classics IV
722	FUNNY FACE	Donna Fargo
4962	FUNNY HOW LOVE CAN BE	First Class
4116	FUNNY HOW TIME SLIPS AWAY	Dorothy Moore
2671	FUTURE SHOCK	Curtis Mayfield
3503	FUTURE SHOCK	Hello People

G

#	Title	Artist
3116	GALAXY	War
1112	THE GAMBLER	Kenny Rogers
4125	THE GAME IS OVER (What's The Matter With You)	Brown Sugar
1462	GAMES	Redeye
444	GARDEN PARTY	Rick Nelson & The Stone Canyon Band
4910	GAS LAMPS AND CLAY	Blues Image
4273	GEE BABY	Peter Shelley
1898	GEORGE JACKSON	Bob Dylan
4955	GEORGIA ON MY MIND	Willie Nelson
3465	GEORGIA PORCUPINE	George Fischoff
4199	GEORGIA RHYTHM	Atlanta Rhythm Section
4997	GEORGIA TOOK HER BACK	R.B. Greaves
2626	GEORGY PORGY	Toto
2411	GERONIMO'S CADILLAC	Michael Murphey
3132	GET A MOVE ON	Eddie Money
673	GET CLOSER	Seals & Crofts
995	GET DANCIN'	Disco Tex & The Sex-O-Lettes
2543	GET DOWN	Curtis Mayfield
2628	GET DOWN	Gene Chandler
475	GET DOWN	Gilbert O'Sullivan
1007	GET DOWN, GET DOWN (Get On The Floor)	Joe Simon
5140	GET DOWN PEOPLE	Fabulous Counts
310	GET DOWN TONIGHT	K.C. & The Sunshine Band
4812	GET INTO SOMETHING	Isley Brothers
1663	GET IT ON	Chase
1851	GET IT RIGHT NEXT TIME	Gerry Rafferty
1664	GET IT TOGETHER	Jackson 5
2823	GET IT UP	Ronnie Milsap
3407	GET IT WHILE YOU CAN	Janis Joplin
1209	GET OFF	Foxy
901	GET ON THE GOOD FOOT (Part 1)	James Brown
4411	GET OUT OF DENVER	Bob Seger
222	GET READY	Rare Earth
3375	GET THAT GASOLINE BLUES	NRBQ
2923	GET THE CREAM OFF THE TOP	Eddie Kendricks
2140	GET THE FUNK OUT MA FACE	Brothers Johnson
203	GET UP AND BOOGIE (That's Right)	Silver Convention
3826	GET UP AND GET DOWN	Dramatics
2306	GET UP, GET INTO IT, GET INVOLVED (Part 1)	James Brown
1503	GET UP (I Feel Like Being Like A) SEX MACHINE (Part 1)	James Brown
3544	GET UP OFFA THAT THING	James Brown
1424	GET USED TO IT	Roger Voudouris
961	GETAWAY	Earth, Wind & Fire
1883	GETTIN' READY FOR LOVE	Diana Ross
1901	GETTING CLOSER	Wings
4543	THE GHETTO (Part 1)	Donny Hathaway
2156	GHETTO CHILD	Spinners
3207	GHETTO WOMAN	B.B. King
3763	GHOST DANCER	Addrisi Brothers
	GIMME...see also GIVE ME	
762	GIMME DAT DING	Pipkins
	GIMME SHELTER	
3328		Grand Funk Railroad
3971		Merry Clayton
	GIMME SOME LOVIN'	
3107		Traffic, Etc. (Part 1)
5008		Kongas - /AFRICANISM
2974	GIMME SOME MORE	JB's
4529	GIMME YOUR MONEY PLEASE	Bachman-Turner Overdrive
	THE GIRL IN ME...see (Bringing Out)	
2688	GIRL OF MY DREAMS	Bram Tchaikovsky
4120	THE GIRL WHO LOVED ME WHEN	Glass Bottle
5274	GIRL YOU NEED A CHANGE OF MIND (Part 1)	Eddie Kendricks
4596	GIRLS (Part 1)	Moments & Whatnauts
2276	GIRLS' SCHOOL / MULL OF KINTYRE*	Wings
2775	THE GIRLS' SONG	5th Dimension
3606	GIRLS TALK	Dave Edmunds
3814	GIRLS WILL BE GIRLS, BOYS WILL BE BOYS	Isley Brothers
1150	GIVE A LITTLE BIT	Supertramp
4814	GIVE A LITTLE MORE	Robert John
3344	GIVE A WOMAN LOVE	Bobbi Martin
2447	GIVE IRELAND BACK TO THE IRISH	Wings
1233	GIVE IT TO ME	J. Geils Band
4265	GIVE IT TO ME	The Mob
2157	GIVE IT TO THE PEOPLE	Righteous Brothers
1868	GIVE IT UP (Turn It Loose)	Tyrone Davis

#	Title	Artist
2832	GIVE IT WHAT YOU GOT	B.T. Express
	GIVE ME...see also GIMME	
3548	GIVE ME A REASON TO BE GONE	Maureen McGovern
3902	GIVE ME AN INCH	Ian Matthews
4563	GIVE ME AN INCH GIRL	Robert Palmer
868	GIVE ME JUST A LITTLE MORE TIME	Chairmen Of The Board
252	GIVE ME LOVE - (Give Me Peace On Earth)	George Harrison
1553	GIVE ME YOUR LOVE	Barbara Mason
	GIVE MORE POWER TO THE PEOPLE...see (For God's Sake)	
5290	GIVE THE BABY ANYTHING THE BABY WANTS	Joe Tex
1957	GIVE THE PEOPLE WHAT THEY WANT	O'Jays
4410	GIVE UP YOUR GUNS	Buoys
1399	GIVE YOUR BABY A STANDING OVATION	Dells
4687	GIVIN' IT ALL UP	J. Geils Band
2829	GIVING IT ALL AWAY	Roger Daltrey
4798	GIVING UP	Donny Hathaway
4358	GLAMOUR BOY	Guess Who
2122	GLASSHOUSE	Temptations
2514	GLORIA	Enchantment
1628	GLORY BOUND	Grass Roots
4133	GLORY, GLORY	Byrds
2430	GLORY GLORY	Rascals
4756	THE GLORY OF LOVE	Dells
505	GO ALL THE WAY	Raspberries
	GO AWAY LITTLE BOY...see YU-MA	
72	GO AWAY LITTLE GIRL	Donny Osmond
1481	GO BACK	Crabby Appleton
1805	GO DOWN GAMBLIN'	Blood, Sweat & Tears
4758	GO ON FOOL	Marion Black
3174	GO WEST	Village People
1065	GO YOUR OWN WAY	Fleetwood Mac
4965	GOD BLESS	Arthur Conley
5156	GOD BLESS OUR LOVE	Charles Brimmer
2437	GOD BLESS WHOEVER SENT YOU	Originals
1248	GOD, LOVE AND ROCK & ROLL	Teegarden & Van Winkle
4482	GOD ONLY KNOWS	Marilyn Scott
3348	GOIN' DOWN (On The Road To L.A.)	Terry Black & Laurel Ward
4165	GOIN' DOWN SLOW	Bobby Blue Bland
2079	GOIN' HOME	Osmonds
4618	GOIN' HOME (Sing A Song Of Christmas Cheer)	Bobby Sherman
3027	GOIN' PLACES	Jacksons
3093	GOING DOWN SLOWLY	Pointer Sisters
2962	GOING IN WITH MY EYES OPEN	David Soul
4086	GOING THROUGH THE MOTIONS	Hot Chocolate
4501	GOING TO THE COUNTRY	Steve Miller Band
608	GOLD	John Stewart
3586	THE GOLDEN AGE OF ROCK 'N' ROLL	Mott The Hoople
4317	GOLDEN RAINBOW	Looking Glass
715	GOLDEN YEARS	David Bowie
1742	GONE	Joey Heatherton
1618	GONE AT LAST	Paul Simon/Phoebe Snow
3453	GONE, GONE, GONE	Bad Company
4087	GONE LONG GONE	Chicago
5103	GONE MOVIN' ON	Raiders
1583	GONE TOO FAR	England Dan & John Ford Coley
4578	GONNA BE ALRIGHT NOW	Gayle McCormick
	GONNA FLY NOW (Theme From "Rocky")	
438	Bill Conti	
1952	Maynard Ferguson	
5185	--THEME FROM ROCKY (Gonna Fly Now)	Rhythm Heritage
4428	THE GOOD BOOK	Melanie
2895	GOOD ENOUGH TO BE YOUR WIFE	Jeannie C. Riley
2450	GOOD FRIEND	Mary MacGregor
4060	GOOD FRIENDS?	Poppy Family
1138	GOOD GIRLS DON'T	Knack
5045	GOOD, GOOD FEELIN'	War
2605	GOOD GUYS ONLY WIN IN THE MOVIES	Mel & Tim
2516	GOOD HEARTED WOMAN	Waylon & Willie
4656	GOOD LOVIN'	Grateful Dead
2235	GOOD LOVIN' GONE BAD	Bad Company
4093	GOOD MORNING	Michael Redway
4216	GOOD MORNING FREEDOM	Daybreak
1782	GOOD MORNING HEARTACHE	Diana Ross
3744	GOOD MORNING JUDGE	10cc
4312	GOOD NIGHT & GOOD MORNING	Jim Capaldi
5046	--GOODNIGHT AND GOOD MORNING	Cecilio & Kapono
4139	GOOD THING MAN	Frank Lucas
3287	GOOD THINGS DON'T LAST FOREVER	Ecstasy, Passion & Pain
974	GOOD TIME CHARLIE'S GOT THE BLUES	Danny O'Keefe
4666	GOOD TIME SALLY	Rare Earth
85	GOOD TIMES	Chic
2841	GOOD TIMES, ROCK & ROLL	Flash Cadillac & The Continental Kids
3441	GOOD TIMES ROLL	Cars
2547	GOOD TIMIN'	Beach Boys
2691	GOOD VIBRATIONS	Todd Rundgren
4791	GOODBYE AGAIN	John Denver
830	GOODBYE GIRL	David Gates
2590	GOODBYE, I LOVE YOU	Firefall
4954	GOODBYE MEDIA MAN (Part 1)	Tom Fogerty
1317	GOODBYE STRANGER	Supertramp
842	GOODBYE TO LOVE	Carpenters
289	GOODBYE YELLOW BRICK ROAD	Elton John
622	GOODNIGHT TONIGHT	Wings
4696	GOOFUS	Carpenters
4549	GOT PLEASURE	Ohio Players
1173	GOT TO BE REAL	Cheryl Lynn
115	GOT TO BE THERE	Michael Jackson
3711	GOT TO BELIEVE IN LOVE	Robin McNamara
	GOT TO GET YOU INTO MY LIFE	
480	Beatles	
1295	Earth, Wind & Fire	
3364	Blood, Sweat & Tears	
3516	GOT TO GIVE IN TO LOVE	Bonnie Boyer
370	GOT TO GIVE IT UP (Part 1)	Marvin Gaye
3092	GOT TO HAVE LOVING	Don Ray
3946	GOT TO HAVE YOUR LOVIN'	King Floyd
3573	GOT TO SEE IF I CAN'T GET MOMMY (To Come Back Home)	Jerry Butler
4705	GOTTA BE FUNKY	Monk Higgins & The Specialties
4538	GOTTA BE THE ONE	Maxine Nightingale
3794	GOTTA FIND A WAY	Moments
1826	GOTTA GET BACK TO YOU	Tommy James & The Shondells
1284	GOTTA HOLD ON TO THIS FEELING	Jr. Walker & The All Stars
2817	GOTTA SEE JANE	R. Dean Taylor
2570	GOTTA SERVE SOMEBODY	Bob Dylan
4874	GRANDDADDY (Part 1)	New Birth
2145	GRANDMA'S HANDS	Bill Withers
5192	GRANDMOTHER'S SONG	Steve Martin
66	GREASE	Frankie Valli
3081	GREASED LIGHTNIN'	John Travolta
4749	GREATEST LOVE	Judy Clay
1944	THE GREATEST LOVE OF ALL	George Benson
538	GREEN-EYED LADY	Sugarloaf
2436	THE GREEN GRASS STARTS TO GROW	Dionne Warwick
5232	GREENWOOD MISSISSIPPI	Little Richard
1004	THE GROOVE LINE	Heatwave
333	GROOVE ME	King Floyd
4148	GROOVIN' (Out On Life)	Newbeats
5287	GROOVIN' WITH MR. BLOE	Cool Heat
4349	GROOVY PEOPLE	Lou Rawls
871	GROOVY SITUATION	Gene Chandler
3694	GROVER HENSON FEELS FORGOTTEN	Bill Cosby
1232	GROW SOME FUNK OF YOUR OWN	Elton John
2428	GROWIN'	Loggins & Messina
5266	GROWIN' UP	Dan Hill
4605	GUAVA JELLY	Barbra Streisand
3172	GUDBUY T' JANE	Slade
	GUESS WHO	
3156	B.B. King	
3752	Ruby Winters	
2483	GUILTY	Al Green
1082	THE GUITAR MAN	Bread
3724	GUNS, GUNS, GUNS	Guess Who
4297	GYPSY	Abraham's Children
4711	GYPSY	Van Morrison
812	GYPSY MAN	War
3046	GYPSY QUEEN (Part 1)	Gypsy
345	GYPSY WOMAN	Brian Hyland
51	GYPSYS, TRAMPS AND THIEVES	Cher

H

| 4702 | HAIL! HAIL! ROCK AND ROLL! | Starland Vocal Band |

#	Title	Artist
4079	**HALF A MILLION MILES FROM HOME**	Albert Hammond
92	**HALF-BREED**	Cher
1437	**HALF THE WAY**	Crystal Gayle
1726	**HALLELUJAH**	Sweathog
1917	**HALLELUJAH DAY**	Jackson 5
4319	**HAND CLAPPING SONG**	Meters
1117	**HAND ME DOWN WORLD**	Guess Who
	HANDBAGS AND GLADRAGS	
2388		Rod Stewart
4171		Chase
457	**HANDY MAN**	James Taylor
4918	**HANG LOOSE**	Mandrill
703	**HANG ON IN THERE BABY**	Johnny Bristol
3495	**HANG ON SLOOPY**	Rick Derringer
2461	**HANG ON TO YOUR LIFE**	Guess Who
2635	**HANGIN' AROUND**	Edgar Winter Group
5220	**HAPPIER**	Paul Anka
4769	**HAPPIER THAN THE MORNING SUN**	B.J. Thomas
702	**THE HAPPIEST GIRL IN THE WHOLE U.S.A.**	Donna Fargo
2376	**HAPPINESS**	Pointer Sisters
1954	**HAPPINESS IS JUST AROUND THE BEND**	Main Ingredient
2534	**HAPPINESS IS ME AND YOU**	Gilbert O'Sullivan
1446	**HAPPY**	Rolling Stones
2410	**HAPPY**	Eddie Kendricks
1786	**HAPPY ANNIVERSARY**	Little River Band
714	**HAPPY DAYS**	Pratt & McClain
4280	**THE HAPPY GIRLS**	Helen Reddy
2881	**HAPPY (Love Theme From "Lady Sings The Blues")**	Bobby Darin
2607	**HAPPY MUSIC**	Blackbyrds
2439	**HAPPY PEOPLE**	Temptations
	HAPPY TOGETHER...see RUNAWAY	
3347	**HAPPY XMAS (War Is Over)**	John & Yoko and the Plastic Ono Band with the Harlem Community Choir
1519	**HARD LUCK WOMAN**	Kiss
1990	**HARD ROCK CAFE**	Carole King
3260	**HARD TIMES**	Boz Scaggs
5002	**HARD TIMES**	Peter Skellern
3288	**HARD TIMES FOR LOVERS**	Judy Collins
2080	**HARD WORK**	John Handy
2415	**THE HARDER I TRY (The Bluer I Get)**	Free Movement
4902	**HARLEM**	5th Dimension
4637	**HARPO'S BLUES**	Phoebe Snow
1734	**HARRY HIPPIE**	Bobby Womack
1706	**HARRY TRUMAN**	Chicago
3043	**HARVEST FOR THE WORLD**	Isley Brothers
454	**HAVE YOU EVER SEEN THE RAIN**	Creedence Clearwater Revival
110	**HAVE YOU NEVER BEEN MELLOW**	Olivia Newton-John
485	**HAVE YOU SEEN HER**	Chi-Lites
1036	**HAVEN'T GOT TIME FOR THE PAIN**	Carly Simon
2790	**HAVEN'T STOPPED DANCING YET**	Gonzalez
3702	**HAVING A PARTY Medley**	Ovations
	HAVING MY BABY...see (You're)	
	HE AIN'T HEAVY, HE'S MY BROTHER	
660		Hollies
1359		Neil Diamond [P]
4869		Olivia Newton-John [P]
2167	**HE CALLED ME BABY**	Candi Staton
4677	**--SHE CALLED ME BABY**	Charlie Rich
5343	**HE DID ME WRONG, BUT HE DID IT RIGHT**	Patti Dahlstrom
2282	**HE DID WITH ME**	Vicki Lawrence
340	**HE DON'T LOVE YOU (Like I Love You)**	Tony Orlando & Dawn
3740	**HE MADE A WOMAN OUT OF ME**	Bobbie Gentry
4047	**HE'D RATHER HAVE THE RAIN**	Heaven Bound With Tony Scotti
3212	**HE'S A FRIEND**	Eddie Kendricks
3382	**HE'S GONNA STEP ON YOU AGAIN**	John Kongos
	HE'S SO FINE	
2896		Jody Miller
3643		Jane Olivor
4512		Kristy & Jimmy McNichol
890	**HE'S THE GREATEST DANCER**	Sister Sledge
4214	**HEAD FIRST**	Babys
942	**HEARD IT IN A LOVE SONG**	Marshall Tucker Band
1811	**HEARSAY**	Soul Children
117	**HEART OF GLASS**	Blondie
87	**HEART OF GOLD**	Neil Young
1708	**HEART OF THE NIGHT**	Poco
4810	**HEART ON MY SLEEVE**	Gallagher & Lyle
4883	**HEART TO HEART**	Errol Sober
354	**HEARTACHE TONIGHT**	Eagles
3456	**HEARTACHES**	BTO
212	**HEARTBEAT - IT'S A LOVEBEAT**	DeFranco Family
2764	**HEARTBREAK HOTEL**	Frijid Pink
3203	**THE HEARTBREAK KID**	Bo Donaldson & The Heywoods
3170	**HEARTBREAKER**	Dolly Parton
3789	**HEARTBREAKER**	Grand Funk Railroad
2088	**HEARTBROKEN BOPPER**	Guess Who
1488	**HEARTLESS**	Heart
2052	**HEARTS OF STONE**	Blue Ridge Rangers
740	**HEAT WAVE**	Linda Ronstadt
835	**HEAVEN HELP US ALL**	Stevie Wonder
557	**HEAVEN KNOWS**	Donna Summer
834	**HEAVEN MUST BE MISSING AN ANGEL (Part 1)**	Tavares
828	**HEAVEN MUST HAVE SENT YOU**	Bonnie Pointer
527	**HEAVEN ON THE 7TH FLOOR**	Paul Nicholas
4517	**--HEAVEN ON THE SEVENTH FLOOR**	Mighty Pope
2332	**HEAVEN'S JUST A SIN AWAY**	Kendalls
2582	**HEAVENLY**	Temptations
1930	**HEAVY FALLIN' OUT**	Stylistics
3628	**HEAVY LOVE**	David Ruffin
1750	**HEAVY MAKES YOU HAPPY (Sha-Na-Boom Boom)**	Staple Singers
1630	**HEED THE CALL**	Kenny Rogers & The First Edition
818	**HELEN WHEELS**	Paul McCartney & Wings
5055	**HELL CAT**	Bellamy Brothers
3728	**HELL ON WHEELS**	Cher
3912	**HELLO DARLIN'**	Conway Twitty
4167	**HELLO, HELLO, HELLO**	New England
2023	**HELLO HURRAY**	Alice Cooper
	HELLO IT'S ME	
379		Todd Rundgren
3651		Nazz
2000	**HELLO OLD FRIEND**	Eric Clapton
1392	**HELLO STRANGER**	Yvonne Elliman
1239	**HELP IS ON ITS WAY**	Little River Band
686	**HELP ME**	Joni Mitchell
3189	**HELP ME FIND A WAY (To Say I Love You)**	Little Anthony & The Imperials
	HELP ME MAKE IT THROUGH THE NIGHT	
907		Sammi Smith
2519		Gladys Knight & The Pips
3454		Joe Simon
3187	**HELP ME MAKE IT (To My Rockin' Chair)**	B.J. Thomas
2303	**HELP ME RHONDA**	Johnny Rivers
3732	**HELP THE POOR**	B.B. King
3824	**HELP WANTED**	Hudson Brothers
4019	**HELP YOURSELF**	Undisputed Truth
1453	**HERE COME THOSE TEARS AGAIN**	Jackson Browne
2892	**HERE COMES SUMMER**	Wildfire
840	**HERE COMES THAT RAINY DAY FEELING AGAIN**	Fortunes
2634	**HERE COMES THE NIGHT**	Nick Gilder
3296	**HERE COMES THE NIGHT**	Beach Boys
1420	**HERE COMES THE SUN**	Richie Havens
900	**HERE I AM (Come And Take Me)**	Al Green
3877	**HERE IS WHERE YOUR LOVE BELONGS**	Sons Of Champlin
4564	**HERE, THERE AND EVERYWHERE**	Emmylou Harris
623	**HERE YOU COME AGAIN**	Dolly Parton
3023	**HEY BABY**	Ringo Starr
4390	**HEY BABY**	Ted Nugent
1505	**HEY BIG BROTHER**	Rare Earth
1495	**HEY DEANIE**	Shaun Cassidy
887	**HEY GIRL**	Donny Osmond
2013	**HEY GIRL (I Like Your Style)**	Temptations
1926	**HEY LAWDY MAMA**	Steppenwolf
4838	**HEY, LITTLE GIRL**	Foster Sylvers
1722	**HEY, MISTER SUN**	Bobby Sherman
4442	**HEY SHIRLEY (This Is Squirrely)**	Shirley & Squirrely
4229	**HEY, ST. PETER**	Flash & The Pan
4055	**HEY THERE LITTLE FIREFLY (Part 1)**	Firefly
144	**HEY THERE LONELY GIRL**	Eddie Holman
362	**(Hey Won't You Play) ANOTHER SOMEBODY DONE SOMEBODY WRONG SONG**	B.J. Thomas
1479	**HEY YOU**	Bachman-Turner Overdrive
2371	**HEY YOU! GET OFF MY MOUNTAIN**	Dramatics
3871	**HEY, YOU LOVE**	Mouth & MacNeal
1133	**HI-DE-HO**	Blood, Sweat & Tears
1053	**HI, HI, HI**	Wings
4684	**HICKORY**	Frankie Valli & The Four Seasons
4735	**HIGH ON LOVE**	Elliott Randall
1122	**HIGH SCHOOL DANCE**	Sylvers

#	Title	Artist
1701	HIGH TIME WE WENT	Joe Cocker
	HIGHER AND HIGHER...see (Your Love Has Lifted Me)	
375	HIGHER GROUND	Stevie Wonder
2239	HIGHER PLANE	Kool & The Gang
2703	HIGHFLY	John Miles
2084	HIGHWAY SONG	Blackfoot
3337	HIGHWAY TO HELL	AC/DC
1821	HIJACK	Herbie Mann
3376	HIJACKIN' LOVE	Johnnie Taylor
4990	HIKKY BURR (Part 1)	Bill Cosby With The Bunions Bradford Band
3263	HILL WHERE THE LORD HIDES	Chuck Mangione
5019	HIS SONG SHALL BE SUNG	Lou Rawls
2617	HIT THE ROAD JACK	Stampeders
430	HITCHIN' A RIDE	Vanity Fare
591	HOCUS POCUS	Focus
	HOLD BACK THE NIGHT	
2527		Trammps
4253		Graham Parker & The Rumour
1443	HOLD HER TIGHT	Osmonds
2426	HOLD ME, TOUCH ME	Paul Stanley
2019	HOLD ON	Rascals
2038	HOLD ON	Ian Gomm
2362	HOLD ON	Triumph
3058	HOLD ON	Sons Of Champlin
3750	HOLD ON	Wild Cherry
4489	HOLD ON TO THE NIGHT	Hotel
514	HOLD THE LINE	Toto
617	HOLD YOUR HEAD UP	Argent
1468	HOLDIN' ON TO YESTERDAY	Ambrosia
2991	HOLDING ON (When Love Is Gone)	L.T.D.
4885	HOLLY GO SOFTLY	Cornerstone
	HOLLY HOLY	
402		Neil Diamond
3828		Jr. Walker & The All Stars
2446	HOLLYWOOD	Rufus, Feat. Chaka Khan
3695	HOLLYWOOD	Boz Scaggs
5075	HOLLYWOOD HOT	Eleventh Hour
1386	HOLLYWOOD NIGHTS	Bob Seger
677	HOLLYWOOD SWINGING	Kool & The Gang
5087	HOLY COW	Stefan
3969	HOLY MAN	Diane Kolby
1862	HOME AND DRY	Gerry Rafferty
4128	HOME IS WHERE THE HATRED IS	Esther Phillips
4701	HOME TONIGHT	Aerosmith
2039	THE HOMECOMING	Hagood Hardy
4089	HOMELY GIRL	Chi-Lites
2158	HONESTY	Billy Joel
4680	HONEY CHILD	Bad Company
971	HONEY COME BACK	Glen Campbell
4268	HONEY DON'T LEAVE L.A.	James Taylor
	HONEY HONEY	
2405		ABBA [P]
3632		Sweet Dreams
3785	HONEY I	George McCrae
5110	HONEY I STILL LOVE YOU	Mark IV
1941	HONEY PLEASE, CAN'T YA SEE	Barry White
4479	HONEY TRIPPIN'	Mystic Moods
1506	HONKY CAT	Elton John
2454	HONKY TONK (Part 1)	James Brown Soul Train
316	HOOKED ON A FEELING	Blue Swede
3963	HOOKED ON YOU	Bread
2285	HOPE THAT WE CAN BE TOGETHER SOON	Sharon Paige
403	HOPELESSLY DEVOTED TO YOU	Olivia Newton-John
3381	HOPPY, GENE AND ME	Roy Rogers
75	A HORSE WITH NO NAME	America
448	HOT BLOODED	Foreigner
40	HOT CHILD IN THE CITY	Nick Gilder
3887	HOT DAWGIT	Ramsey Lewis and Earth, Wind & Fire
3739	HOT FUN IN THE SUMMERTIME	David T. Walker
2031	HOT LEGS	Rod Stewart
500	HOT LINE	Sylvers
2929	HOT LOVE	T. Rex
2950	HOT LOVE, COLD WORLD	Bob Welch
2390	HOT 'N' NASTY	Humble Pie
1927	HOT NUMBER	Foxy
3014	HOT PANTS	Salvage
1207	HOT PANTS (Part 1) (She Got To Use What She Got To Get What She Wants)	James Brown
3977	HOT PANTS--I'M COMING, I'M COMING, I'M COMING	Bobby Byrd
862	HOT ROD LINCOLN	Commander Cody & His Lost Planet Airmen
4797	HOT SHOT	Karen Young
98	HOT STUFF	Donna Summer
2862	HOT STUFF	Rolling Stones
	HOT SUMMER NIGHTS	
1720		Night
3398		Walter Egan
4908	HOT WIRE	Al Green
378	HOTEL CALIFORNIA	Eagles
3286	HOUND DOG MAN (Play It Again)	Lenny LeBlanc
2176	HOUSE AT POOH CORNER	Nitty Gritty Dirt Band
5229	HOUSE OF STRANGERS	Jim Gilstrap
494	HOUSE OF THE RISING SUN	Frijid Pink
4892	THE HOUSE ON TELEGRAPH HILL	Bo Donaldson & The Heywoods
	HOUSE PARTY...see (Ain't Nothin' But A)	
3151	HOUSTON (I'm Comin' To See You)	Glen Campbell
2238	(How Bout A Little Hand For) THE BOYS IN THE BAND	Boys In The Band
1419	HOW CAN I BE SURE	David Cassidy
2061	HOW CAN I FORGET	Marvin Gaye
2542	HOW CAN I LEAVE YOU AGAIN	John Denver
1331	HOW CAN I TELL HER	Lobo
4437	HOW CAN I TELL MY MOM AND DAD	Lovelites
2811	HOW CAN I TELL YOU	Travis Wammack
3150	HOW CAN I UNLOVE YOU	Lynn Anderson
42	HOW CAN YOU MEND A BROKEN HEART	Bee Gees
4688	HOW COULD I LET YOU GET AWAY	Spinners
22	HOW DEEP IS YOUR LOVE	Bee Gees
5177	HOW DID WE LOSE IT BABY	Jerry Butler
627	HOW DO YOU DO?	Mouth & MacNeal
3405	HOW DO YOU FEEL THE MORNING AFTER	Millie Jackson
4081	HOW GLAD I AM	Kiki Dee
4313	HOW HIGH THE MOON	Gloria Gaynor
3612	(How I Spent My Summer Vacation) OR A DAY AT THE BEACH WITH PEDRO AND MAN (Part 1)	Cheech & Chong
270	HOW LONG	Ace
1333	HOW LONG (Betcha' Got A Chick On The Side)	Pointer Sisters
399	HOW MUCH I FEEL	Ambrosia
1120	HOW MUCH LOVE	Leo Sayer
820	HOW SWEET IT IS (To Be Loved By You)	James Taylor
1290	HOW YOU GONNA SEE ME NOW	Alice Cooper
3774	HOWZAT	Sherbet
2575	HUM A SONG (From Your Heart)	Lulu
4788	HUM ALONG AND DANCE	Temptations
1379	HUMMINGBIRD	Seals & Crofts
2272	HUMMINGBIRD	B.B. King
4299	HUMPHREY THE CAMEL	Jack Blanchard & Misty Morgan
4511	THE HUNGRY YEARS	Wayne Newton
1885	HURRICANE (Part 1)	Bob Dylan
4662	A HURRICANE IS COMING TONITE	Carol Douglas
4246	HURRY SUNDOWN	Outlaws
1841	THE HURT	Cat Stevens
	HURT	
2055		Elvis Presley
3541		Manhattans
263	HURTING EACH OTHER	Carpenters
1389	HURTS SO GOOD	Millie Jackson
3479	HUSH/I'M ALIVE	Blue Swede
4232	HUSHABYE	Robert John
182	THE HUSTLE	Van Mc Coy
5100	HUSTLE!!! (Dead On It)	James Brown
4201	HYMN 43	Jethro Tull

I

#	Title	Artist
1916	I AIN'T GOT TIME ANYMORE	Glass Bottle
3165	I AM I AM	Smokey Robinson
529	I AM...I SAID	Neil Diamond
1433	I AM LOVE (Parts 1 & 2)	Jackson 5
2126	I AM SOMEBODY (Part 2)	Johnnie Taylor
2927	I AM WHAT I AM	Lois Fletcher
132	I AM WOMAN	Helen Reddy
4886	I BEEN MOVED	Andy Kim
2999	I' BEEN WATCHIN' YOU	South Side Movement
2976	I BELIEVE I'M GONNA LOVE YOU	Frank Sinatra
5016	I BELIEVE IN FATHER CHRISTMAS	Greg Lake
2725	I BELIEVE IN LOVE	Kenny Loggins
	I BELIEVE IN MUSIC	
989		Gallery
5085		Marian Love
698	I BELIEVE IN YOU (You Believe In Me)	Johnnie Taylor

#	Title	Artist
1088	(I Believe) THERE'S NOTHING STRONGER THAN OUR LOVE	Paul Anka
	I BELIEVE YOU	
2074		Dorothy Moore
3710		Carpenters
1705	I BELONG TO YOU	Love Unlimited
4698	I BET HE DON'T LOVE YOU (Like I Love You)	Intruders
3419	I CALL MY BABY CANDY	Jaggerz
3384	(I Can Feel Those Vibrations) THIS LOVE IS REAL	Jackie Wilson
4836	I CAN FEEL YOU	Addrisi Brothers
320	I CAN HELP	Billy Swan
3894	I CAN MAKE IT THRU THE DAYS (But Oh Those Lonely Nights)	Ray Charles
5168	I CAN REMEMBER	Oliver
199	I CAN SEE CLEARLY NOW	Johnny Nash
5011	I CAN STAND A LITTLE RAIN	Joe Cocker
1951	I CAN UNDERSTAND IT	New Birth
4673	I CAN'T BE YOU (You Can't Be Me)	Glass House
4136	I CAN'T BELIEVE THAT YOU'VE STOPPED LOVING ME	Charley Pride
3764	I CAN'T GET NEXT TO YOU	Al Green
4609	I CAN'T GET OVER YOU	Dramatics
2783	I CAN'T HEAR YOU NO MORE	Helen Reddy
4932	I CAN'T HELP IT	Moments
1721	I CAN'T HELP MYSELF (Sugar Pie, Honey Bunch)	Donnie Elbert
3734	I CAN'T HOLD ON	Karla Bonoff
3197	I CAN'T LEAVE YOU ALONE	George McCrae
2160	I CAN'T LEAVE YOUR LOVE ALONE	Clarence Carter
2943	I CAN'T LIVE A DREAM	Osmonds
4481	I CAN'T MOVE NO MOUNTAINS	Blood, Sweat & Tears
1589	I CAN'T STAND IT NO MORE	Peter Frampton
	I CAN'T STAND THE RAIN	
1436		Eruption
1743		Ann Peebles
3236	I CAN'T STAND TO SEE YOU CRY	Smokey Robinson & The Miracles
3292	I CAN'T TELL THE BOTTOM FROM THE TOP	Hollies
4776	I CAN'T TURN YOU LOOSE	Edgar Winter's White Trash
3810	I CHEAT THE HANGMAN	Doobie Brothers
5234	I COULD HAVE LOVED YOU	Moments
4828	I COULD NEVER BE HAPPY	Emotions
2909	I COULD WRITE A BOOK	Jerry Butler
2667	I CRIED	James Brown
	I DIDN'T GET TO SLEEP AT ALL...see (Last Night)	
2137	I DIDN'T KNOW I LOVED YOU (Till I Saw You Rock And Roll)	Gary Glitter
4532	I DIG EVERYTHING ABOUT YOU	The Mob
4383	I DO BELIEVE IN YOU	Pages
1338	I DO, I DO, I DO, I DO, I DO	ABBA
1662	I DO LOVE YOU	GQ
2742	I DO TAKE YOU	Three Degrees
4652	I DO THE ROCK	Tim Curry
1324	I DON'T BLAME YOU AT ALL	Smokey Robinson & The Miracles
	I DON'T KNOW HOW TO LOVE HIM	
1219		Helen Reddy
1781		Yvonne Elliman
1380	I DON'T KNOW IF IT'S RIGHT	Evelyn "Champagne" King
3529	I DON'T KNOW WHAT IT IS, BUT IT SURE IS FUNKY	Ripple
2480	I DON'T KNOW WHY	Rolling Stones
650	I DON'T LIKE TO SLEEP ALONE	Paul Anka
2550	I DON'T LOVE YOU ANYMORE	Teddy Pendergrass
3935	I DON'T NEED NO DOCTOR	Humble Pie
3000	I DON'T SEE ME IN YOUR EYES ANYMORE	Charlie Rich
2207	I DON'T WANNA CRY	Ronnie Dyson
3319	I DON'T WANNA GO	Joey Travolta
2797	I DON'T WANNA LOSE YOU	Daryl Hall & John Oates
3703	I DON'T WANNA LOSE YOU	Johnnie Taylor
2698	I DON'T WANNA LOSE YOUR LOVE	Emotions
3283	I DON'T WANT NOBODY ELSE (To Dance With You)	Narada Michael Walden
854	I DON'T WANT TO DO WRONG	Gladys Knight & The Pips
1651	(I Don't Want To Love You But) YOU GOT ME ANYWAY	Sutherland Brothers & Quiver
4697	I DON'T WANT TO MAKE YOU WAIT	Delfonics
2709	I DREAMED LAST NIGHT	Justin Hayward & John Lodge
839	I FEEL A SONG (In My Heart)	Gladys Knight & The Pips
1899	I FEEL LIKE A BULLET (In The Gun Of Robert Ford)	Elton John
594	I FEEL LOVE	Donna Summer
4044	I FEEL SANCTIFIED	Commodores
2763	I FOUGHT THE LAW	Sam Neely
4298	I FOUND MY DAD	Joe Simon
4205	I FOUND SUNSHINE	Chi-Lites
3004	I GET HIGH ON YOU	Sly Stone
2957	I GET LIFTED	George McCrae
508	I GO CRAZY	Paul Davis
5106	I GO TO PIECES	Cotton, Lloyd & Christian
3444	I GO TO RIO	Pablo Cruise
2375	I GOT A BAG OF MY OWN	James Brown
458	I GOT A NAME	Jim Croce
	I GOT A THING ABOUT YOU BABY...see I'VE GOT A THING ABOUT YOU BABY	
4818	I GOT A THING, YOU GOT A THING, EVERYBODY'S GOT A THING	Funkadelic
2524	I GOT ANTS IN MY PANTS (And I Want To Dance) (Part 1)	James Brown
4762	I GOT LOVE	Melba Moore
1732	I GOT MY MIND MADE UP (You Can Get It Girl)	Instant Funk
4535	I GOT OVER LOVE	Major Harris
3393	I GOT SOME HELP I DON'T NEED	B.B. King
3422	I GOT STONED AND I MISSED IT	Jim Stafford
2273	I GOT TO KNOW	Starbuck
5212	I GOT TO TELL SOMEBODY	Betty Everett
202	I GOTCHA	Joe Tex
4409	I GOTTA LET YOU GO	Martha Reeves & The Vandellas
5337	I GUESS I'LL MISS THE MAN	Supremes
3147	I HAD IT ALL THE TIME	Tyrone Davis
3070	I HATE HATE	Razzy
3316	I HAVE A DREAM	Donny Osmond
4943	I HAVE LEARNED TO DO WITHOUT YOU	Mavis Staples
1997	I HEAR THOSE CHURCH BELLS RINGING	Dusk
498	I HEAR YOU KNOCKING	Dave Edmunds
2876	I HEARD IT THROUGH THE GRAPEVINE	Creedence Clearwater Revival
102	I HONESTLY LOVE YOU	Olivia Newton-John
3685	I HOPE WE GET TO LOVE IN TIME	Marilyn McCoo & Billy Davis Jr.
3988	I JUST CAN'T CONTROL MYSELF	Nature's Divine
2389	I JUST CAN'T GET YOU OUT OF MY MIND	Four Tops
992	I JUST CAN'T HELP BELIEVING	B.J. Thomas
5175	I JUST CAN'T SAY GOODBYE	Philly Devotions
2998	I JUST CAN'T SAY NO TO YOU	Parker McGee
4651	I JUST CAN'T STOP LOVING YOU	Cornelius Brothers & Sister Rose
5342	I JUST CAN'T TURN MY HABIT INTO LOVE	Buckwheat
2416	I JUST DON'T KNOW WHAT TO DO WITH MYSELF	Gary Puckett
1087	I JUST FALL IN LOVE AGAIN	Anne Murray
2523	I JUST WANNA KEEP IT TOGETHER	Paul Davis
425	I JUST WANNA STOP	Gino Vannelli
4743	I JUST WANT TO BE	Cameo
54	I JUST WANT TO BE YOUR EVERYTHING	Andy Gibb
787	I JUST WANT TO CELEBRATE	Rare Earth
2331	I JUST WANT TO MAKE LOVE TO YOU	Foghat
3550	I KINDA MISS YOU	Manhattans
2471	I KNEW JESUS (Before He Was A Star)	Glen Campbell
4346	I KNEW YOU WHEN	Donny Osmond
1603	I KNOW A HEARTACHE WHEN I SEE ONE	Jennifer Warnes
1913	I KNOW I'M IN LOVE	Chee-Chee & Peppy
	(I Know) I'M LOSING YOU	
540		Rare Earth
1718		Rod Stewart
398	I LIKE DREAMIN'	Kenny Nolan
4970	I LIKE IT LIKE THAT	Loggins & Messina
3195	I LIKE TO DO IT	K C & The Sunshine Band
1748	I LIKE TO LIVE THE LOVE	B.B. King

#	Title	Artist
3517	I LIKE WHAT YOU GIVE	Nolan
3010	I LIKE YOU	Donovan
4654	I LIKE YOUR LOVIN' (Do You Like Mine)	Chi-Lites
2798	I LIKES TO DO IT	People's Choice
1447	I LOVE	Tom T. Hall
2493	I LOVE MAKIN' LOVE TO YOU	Evie Sands
573	I LOVE MUSIC (Part 1)	O'Jays
2087	I LOVE MY FRIEND	Charlie Rich
4168	I LOVE MY MUSIC	Wild Cherry
4893	I LOVE MY WIFE	Frank Sinatra
499	I LOVE THE NIGHTLIFE (Disco 'Round)	Alicia Bridges
4288	I LOVE THE WAY YOU LOVE	Betty Wright
2057	I LOVE YOU	Donna Summer
3533	I LOVE YOU	Otis Leavill
1078	I LOVE YOU FOR ALL SEASONS	Fuzz
2728	I LOVE YOU LADY DAWN	Bells
3604	I LOVE YOU MORE THAN YOU'LL EVER KNOW	Donny Hathaway
3349	I MISS YOU	Dells
2200	I MISS YOU (Part 1)	Harold Melvin & The Blue Notes
3613	I MISS YOU BABY	Millie Jackson
1968	I NEED A LOVER	John Cougar
3388	I NEED HELP (I Can't Do It Alone) (Part 1)	Bobby Byrd
4669	I NEED SOMEONE (To Love Me)	Z.Z. Hill
1843	I NEED TO BE IN LOVE	Carpenters
3146	I NEED TO KNOW	Tom Petty & The Heartbreakers
911	I NEED YOU	America
3841	I NEED YOU	Friends Of Distinction
5061	I NEED YOU	Euclid Beach Band
3457	I NEED YOU, YOU NEED ME	Joe Simon
2800	I NEED YOUR HELP BARRY MANILOW	Ray Stevens
914	I NEVER CRY	Alice Cooper
3383	I NEVER SAID GOODBYE	Engelbert Humperdinck
4898	I NEVER SAID I LOVE YOU	Orsa Lia
2992	I.O.U.	Jimmy Dean
	I ONLY HAVE EYES FOR YOU	
1149		Art Garfunkel
3607		Jerry Butler
941	I ONLY WANT TO BE WITH YOU	Bay City Rollers
4379	I PITY THE FOOL	Ann Peebles
1874	I PLAY AND SING	Dawn
1237	I REALLY DON'T WANT TO KNOW	Elvis Presley
5150	I REALLY LOVE YOU	Davy Jones
4303	I RECEIVED A LETTER	Delbert & Glen
5335	I REFUSE TO SMILE	Mandrill
3295	(I Remember) SUMMER MORNING	Vanity Fare
2177	I SAW A MAN AND HE DANCED WITH HIS WIFE	Cher
1131	I SAW THE LIGHT	Todd Rundgren
4071	I SAY A LITTLE PRAYER/BY THE TIME I GET TO PHOENIX	Glen Campbell / Anne Murray
1597	I SHALL SING	Garfunkel
248	I SHOT THE SHERIFF	Eric Clapton
2221	I STAND ACCUSED	Isaac Hayes
3007	I STARTED LOVING YOU AGAIN	Al Martino
2386	I STILL HAVE DREAMS	Richie Furay
12	I THINK I LOVE YOU	Partridge Family
4278	I THINK I LOVE YOU AGAIN	Brenda Lee
2202	I THINK OF YOU	Perry Como
2644	I THINK WE'RE ALONE NOW	Rubinoos
3736	I THOUGHT IT TOOK A LITTLE TIME (But Today I Fell In Love)	Diana Ross
	I WANNA...see also I WANT TO	
822	I WANNA BE WHERE YOU ARE	Michael Jackson
972	I WANNA BE WITH YOU	Raspberries
4363	I WANNA BE WITH YOU (Part 1)	Isley Brothers
5223	I WANNA BE YOUR BABY	Three Degrees
2065	I WANNA DANCE WIT' CHOO (Doo Dat Dance)	Disco Tex & The Sex-O-Lettes
3327	I WANNA DO IT TO YOU	Jerry Butler
1105	I WANNA GET NEXT TO YOU	Rose Royce
4362	I WANNA KNOW IF IT'S GOOD TO YOU?	Funkadelic
4271	I WANNA KNOW YOUR NAME	Intruders
2521	I WANNA LEARN A LOVE SONG	Harry Chapin
4388	I WANNA STAY WITH YOU	Gallagher & Lyle
	I WANT TO...see also I WANNA	
2241	I WANT TO BE FREE	Ohio Players
4182	I WANT TO DANCE WITH YOU (Dance With Me)	Ritchie Family
4177	I WANT TO (Do Everything For You)	Raeletts
4395	I WANT TO LIVE	John Denver
5214	I WANT TO PAY YOU BACK (For Loving Me)	Chi-Lites
	I WANT TO TAKE YOU HIGHER	
1871		Ike & Tina Turner & The Ikettes
2623		Sly & The Family Stone
1368	I WANT YOU	Marvin Gaye
38	I WANT YOU BACK	Jackson 5
2791	I WANT YOU TO BE MINE	Kayak
484	I WANT YOU TO WANT ME	Cheap Trick
1665	I WANT YOU TONIGHT	Pablo Cruise
1096	I WANT YOUR LOVE	Chic
1413	I WANT'A DO SOMETHING FREAKY TO YOU	Leon Haywood
2166	I WAS CHECKIN' OUT SHE WAS CHECKIN' IN	Don Covay
1247	I WAS MADE FOR DANCIN'	Leif Garrett
921	I WAS MADE FOR LOVIN' YOU	Kiss
1656	I WAS ONLY JOKING	Rod Stewart
4870	I WAS WONDERING	Poppy Family
	I (Who Have Nothing)	
1115		Tom Jones
4176		Liquid Smoke [P]
4723		Sylvester
1873	I WILL BE IN LOVE WITH YOU	Livingston Taylor
2749	(I Will Be Your) SHADOW IN THE STREET	Allan Clarke
3469	I WILL NEVER PASS THIS WAY AGAIN	Glen Campbell
1937	I WILL STILL LOVE YOU	Stonebolt
157	I WILL SURVIVE	Gloria Gaynor
296	I WISH	Stevie Wonder
3488	I WISH I WERE	Andy Kim
3895	I WISH IT WAS ME	Tyrone Davis
4332	I WISH IT WAS ME YOU LOVED	Dells
763	I WOKE UP IN LOVE THIS MORNING	Partridge Family
	I WON'T LAST A DAY WITHOUT YOU	
996		Carpenters
3224	Al Wilson - MEDLEY:__ / LET ME BE THE ONE	
3833		Maureen McGovern
2721	I WON'T MENTION IT AGAIN	Ray Price
4316	I WOULDN'T TREAT A DOG (The Way You Treated Me)	Bobby Bland
1949	I WOULDN'T WANT TO BE LIKE YOU	Alan Parsons
29	I WRITE THE SONGS	Barry Manilow
5124	I WROTE A SIMPLE SONG	Billy Preston
	I'D LIKE TO TEACH THE WORLD TO SING (In Perfect Harmony)	
1130		New Seekers
1298		Hillside Singers
1558	I'D LOVE TO CHANGE THE WORLD	Ten Years After
287	I'D LOVE YOU TO WANT ME	Lobo
1794	I'D RATHER BE A COWBOY	John Denver
3230	I'D RATHER BE SORRY	Ray Price
462	I'D REALLY LOVE TO SEE YOU TONIGHT	England Dan & John Ford Coley
4048	I'LL ALWAYS CALL YOUR NAME	Little River Band
2014	I'LL ALWAYS LOVE MY MAMA (Part 1)	Intruders
251	I'LL BE AROUND	Spinners
823	I'LL BE GOOD TO YOU	Brothers Johnson
3716	I'LL BE HOLDING ON	Big Al Downing
2017	I'LL BE RIGHT HERE	Tyrone Davis
4840	I'LL BE STANDING BY	Foghat
2650	I'LL BE THE OTHER WOMAN	Soul Children
6	I'LL BE THERE	Jackson 5
	also see (Any Way That You Want It)	
3006	I'LL BE YOUR EVERYTHING	Percy Sledge
1784	I'LL BE YOUR SHELTER (In Time Of Storm)	Luther Ingram
4147	I'LL COME RUNNING	Livingston Taylor
2402	I'LL DO FOR YOU ANYTHING YOU WANT ME TO	Barry White
3447	I'LL ERASE AWAY YOUR PAIN	Whatnauts
5125	I'LL GO TO MY GRAVE LOVING YOU	Statler Brothers
4455	I'LL HAVE TO GO AWAY	Skylark
975	I'LL HAVE TO SAY I LOVE YOU IN A SONG	Jim Croce
4236	I'LL KNOW HER WHEN I SEE HER	Cooper Brothers Band
2818	I'LL MAKE YOU MUSIC	Beverly Bremers

516	I'LL MEET YOU HALFWAY *Partridge Family*	
633	I'LL NEVER FALL IN LOVE AGAIN *Dionne Warwick*	
510	I'LL NEVER LOVE THIS WAY AGAIN *Dionne Warwick*	
1543	I'LL PLAY FOR YOU *Seals & Crofts*	
3975	I'LL PLAY THE BLUES FOR YOU *Albert King*	
4328	I'LL PLAY THE FOOL *Dr. Buzzard's Original "Savannah" Band*	
4310	I'LL STILL LOVE YOU *Jim Weatherly*	
	I'LL SUFFER...see (Until Then)	
3044	I'LL SUPPLY THE LOVE *Toto*	
196	I'LL TAKE YOU THERE *Staple Singers*	
2794	I'M A BELIEVER *Neil Diamond*	
2133	I'M A GREEDY MAN (Part 1) *James Brown*	
3693	I'M A MAN *Chicago*	
4109	I'M A RAMBLIN' MAN *Waylon Jennings*	
4296	I'M A ROCKER *Raspberries*	
3373	I'M A STRANGER HERE *Five Man Electrical Band*	
2067	I'M A TRAIN *Albert Hammond*	
1648	I'M A WOMAN *Maria Muldaur*	
2574	(I'm A) YOYO MAN *Rick Cunha*	
	I'M ALIVE *Blue Swede* see HUSH	
4476	I'M BETTER OFF WITHOUT YOU *Main Ingredient*	
1940	I'M COMIN' HOME *Tommy James*	
3403	I'M COMIN' HOME *Dave Edmunds*	
	I'M COMING HOME	
1824	*Spinners*	
3817	*Johnny Mathis*	
1896	I'M COMING HOME *Stories*	
948	I'M DOIN' FINE NOW *New York City*	
3002	I'M DREAMING *Jennifer Warnes*	
935	I'M EASY *Keith Carradine*	
1568	I'M EVERY WOMAN *Chaka Khan*	
	I'M FALLING IN LOVE...see SINCE I FELL FOR YOU	
4969	I'M FALLING IN LOVE WITH YOU *Little Anthony & The Imperials*	
3656	I'M GIRL SCOUTIN' *Intruders*	
3536	I'M GOING DOWN *Rose Royce*	
4855	I'M GONNA BE A COUNTRY GIRL AGAIN *Buffy Sainte-Marie*	
2719	I'M GONNA LET MY HEART DO THE WALKING *Supremes*	
3272	I'M GONNA LOVE YOU *Intrigues*	
628	I'M GONNA LOVE YOU JUST A LITTLE MORE BABY *Barry White*	
2219	I'M GONNA TAKE CARE OF EVERYTHING *Rubicon*	
3998	I'M HER FOOL *Billy Swan*	
1412	I'M IN LOVE *Aretha Franklin*	
437	I'M IN YOU *Peter Frampton*	
3867	I'M JUST A PRISONER (Of Your Good Lovin') *Candi Staton*	
894	I'M JUST A SINGER (In A Rock And Roll Band) *Moody Blues*	
2230	I'M LEAVIN' *Elvis Presley*	
4718	I'M LEAVIN' YOU *Engelbert Humperdinck*	
760	I'M LEAVING IT (ALL) UP TO YOU *Donny & Marie Osmond*	
	I'M LOSING YOU...see (I KNOW)	
4695	I'M MANDY FLY ME *10cc*	
2767	I'M MOVIN' ON *John Kay*	
2131	I'M NEVER GONNA BE ALONE ANYMORE *Cornelius Brothers & Sister Rose*	
3688	I'M NOT GONNA CRY ANYMORE *Nancy Brooks*	
1457	I'M NOT GONNA LET IT BOTHER ME TONIGHT *Atlanta Rhythm Section*	
368	I'M NOT IN LOVE *10cc*	
598	I'M NOT LISA *Jessi Colter*	
1507	I'M NOT MY BROTHER'S KEEPER *Flaming Ember*	
1677	I'M ON FIRE *Dwight Twilley Band*	
	I'M ON FIRE	
1969	*5000 Volts*	
5281	*Jim Gilstrap*	
4514	I'M ON MY WAY *Captain & Tennille*	
4916	I'M SCARED *Burton Cummings*	
5009	I'M SO ANXIOUS *Southside Johnny & The Asbury Jukes*	
4443	I'M SO GLAD *Fuzz*	
3057	I'M SO GLAD I FELL FOR YOU *David Ruffin*	
2098	I'M SO PROUD *Main Ingredient*	
298	I'M SORRY *John Denver*	
3976	I'M SORRY *Joey Heatherton*	
207	I'M STILL IN LOVE WITH YOU *Al Green*	
3700	I'M STILL WAITING *Diana Ross*	
991	I'M STONE IN LOVE WITH YOU *Stylistics*	
2309	I'M THE LEADER OF THE GANG *Brownsville Station*	
4782	I'M THE MIDNIGHT SPECIAL *Clarence Carter*	
4164	I'M THE ONLY ONE *Lobo*	
2675	I'M TIRED *Savoy Brown*	
285	I'M YOUR BOOGIE MAN *K C & The Sunshine Band*	
4100	I'M YOUR MAN ROCK 'N' ROLL *Tarney/Spencer Band*	
4085	I'M YOURS (Use Me Anyway You Wanna) *Ike & Tina Turner*	
3467	I'VE BEEN BORN AGAIN *Johnnie Taylor*	
1418	I'VE BEEN LONELY FOR SO LONG *Frederick Knight*	
4252	(I've Been Lookin' For) A NEW WAY TO SAY I LOVE YOU *Driver*	
4537	I'VE BEEN LOVIN' YOU *Easy Street*	
779	(I've Been) SEARCHIN' SO LONG *Chicago*	
2673	I'VE BEEN THIS WAY BEFORE *Neil Diamond*	
605	I'VE FOUND SOMEONE OF MY OWN *Free Movement*	
2579	I'VE GOT A FEELING (We'll Be Seeing Each Other Again) *Al Wilson*	
1967	I'VE GOT A THING ABOUT YOU BABY *Elvis Presley*	
5298	--I GOT A THING ABOUT YOU BABY *Billy Lee Riley*	
473	I'VE GOT LOVE ON MY MIND *Natalie Cole*	
2300	I'VE GOT SO MUCH TO GIVE *Barry White*	
1268	I'VE GOT THE MUSIC IN ME *Kiki Dee Band*	
4243	I'VE GOT TO HAVE YOU *Sammi Smith*	
809	I'VE GOT TO USE MY IMAGINATION *Gladys Knight & The Pips*	
2465	I'VE GOTTA MAKE YOU LOVE ME *Steam*	
2261	I'VE HAD ENOUGH *Wings*	
3302	I'VE HAD IT *Fanny*	
5121	I'VE JUST BEGUN TO CARE *Michael Nesmith & The First National Band*	
1647	I'VE LOST YOU *Elvis Presley*	
3368	I'VE NEVER BEEN IN LOVE *Suzi Quatro*	
3901	I'VE NEVER FOUND A MAN (To Love Me Like You Do) *Esther Phillips*	
	IF	
666	*Bread*	
4551	*Telly Savalas*	
2601	IF EVER I SEE YOU AGAIN *Roberta Flack*	
271	IF I CAN'T HAVE YOU *Yvonne Elliman*	
3226	IF I COULD ONLY WIN YOUR LOVE *Emmylou Harris*	
819	IF I COULD REACH YOU *5th Dimension*	
4104	IF I COULD SEE THE LIGHT *8th Day*	
2612	IF I DIDN'T CARE *Moments*	
2297	IF I EVER LOSE THIS HEAVEN *AWB*	
4739	IF I HAVE TO GO AWAY *Jigsaw*	
1792	IF I NEVER KNEW YOUR NAME *Vic Dana*	
3937	IF I ONLY COULD *Rowans*	
3775	IF I ONLY KNEW *Ozark Mountain Daredevils*	
3220	IF I SAID YOU HAD A BEAUTIFUL BODY WOULD YOU HOLD IT AGAINST ME *Bellamy Brothers*	
	IF I WERE A CARPENTER	
2141	*Johnny Cash & June Carter*	
5050	*Bob Seger*	
5128	*Leon Russell*	
5209	IF I WERE ONLY A CHILD AGAIN *Curtis Mayfield*	
478	IF I WERE YOUR WOMAN *Gladys Knight & The Pips*	
3943	IF IT DON'T FIT, DON'T FORCE IT *Kellee Patterson*	
3414	IF IT FEELS GOOD, DO IT *Ian Lloyd & Stories*	
4624	IF IT'S ALL RIGHT WITH YOU *Dottie West*	
5273	--IF IT'S ALRIGHT WITH YOU *Rose Colored Glass*	
4773	IF IT'S GOOD TO YOU (It's Good For You) *Flaming Ember*	
4643	IF IT'S REAL WHAT I FEEL *Jerry Butler*	
4451	IF IT'S THE LAST THING I DO *Thelma Houston*	
4945	IF LOVE RULED THE WORLD *Bobby Bland*	
	(If Loving You Is Wrong) I DON'T WANT TO BE RIGHT	
153	*Luther Ingram*	
1768	*Barbara Mandrell*	
3148	*Millie Jackson* [P]	
5328	IF MY HEART COULD SPEAK *Manhattans*	
1376	IF NOT FOR YOU *Olivia Newton-John*	
3309	IF NOT YOU *Dr. Hook*	

#	Title	Artist
3939	IF ONLY I HAD MY MIND ON SOMETHING ELSE	Bee Gees
5227	IF THAT'S THE WAY YOU WANT IT	Diamond Head
	IF THERE'S A HELL BELOW...see (Don't Worry)	
2689	IF WALLS COULD TALK	Little Milton
1914	IF WE MAKE IT THROUGH DECEMBER	Merle Haggard
4119	IF WE ONLY HAVE LOVE	Dionne Warwicke
3822	IF WE TRY	Don McLean
3304	(If You Add) ALL THE LOVE IN THE WORLD	Mac Davis
4440	IF YOU CAN BEAT ME ROCKIN' (You Can Have My Chair)	Laura Lee
3318	IF YOU CAN'T GIVE ME LOVE	Suzi Quatro
641	IF YOU COULD READ MY MIND	Gordon Lightfoot
3140	IF YOU DO BELIEVE IN LOVE	Tee Set
446	IF YOU DON'T KNOW ME BY NOW	Harold Melvin & The Bluenotes
2903	IF YOU GO AWAY	Terry Jacks
3153	IF YOU GOTTA BREAK ANOTHER HEART	Albert Hammond
1427	IF YOU KNOW WHAT I MEAN	Neil Diamond
235	IF YOU LEAVE ME NOW	Chicago
1958	IF YOU LEAVE ME TONIGHT I'LL CRY	Jerry Wallace
2559	IF YOU LET ME	Eddie Kendricks
827	(If You Let Me Make Love To You Then) WHY CAN'T I TOUCH YOU?	Ronnie Dyson
625	IF YOU LOVE ME (Let Me Know)	Olivia Newton-John
5252	IF YOU LOVE ME LIKE YOU SAY YOU LOVE ME	Betty Wright
3450	IF YOU ONLY BELIEVE (Jesus For Tonite)	Michael Polnareff
852	IF YOU REALLY LOVE ME	Stevie Wonder
1466	IF YOU REMEMBER ME	Chris Thompson & Night
1696	IF YOU TALK IN YOUR SLEEP	Elvis Presley
4064	IF YOU WANNA DO A DANCE	Spinners
1831	IF YOU WANNA GET TO HEAVEN	Ozark Mountain Daredevils
3430	IF YOU WANT IT	Niteflyte
1061	IF YOU WANT ME TO STAY	Sly & The Family Stone
2115	IF YOU WERE MINE	Ray Charles
2467	IF YOU'RE NOT BACK IN LOVE BY MONDAY	Millie Jackson
1020	IF YOU'RE READY (Come Go With Me)	Staple Singers
3580	IF YOU'VE GOT A HEART	Bobby Bland
5104	IF YOU'VE GOT THE TIME	Babys
3164	IKO IKO	Dr. John
888	IMAGINARY LOVER	Atlanta Rhythm Section
318	IMAGINE	John Lennon
2001	THE IMMIGRANT	Neil Sedaka
730	IMMIGRANT SONG	Led Zeppelin
2288	IMMIGRATION MAN	David Crosby & Graham Nash
3947	IN A BROKEN DREAM	Python Lee Jackson
3575	IN AND OUT OF MY LIFE	Martha Reeves & The Vandellas
4094	IN FOR THE NIGHT	Dirt Band
3387	IN FRANCE THEY KISS ON MAIN STREET	Joni Mitchell
2094	IN HEAVEN THERE IS NO BEER	Clean Living
4106	IN MY FATHER'S FOOTSTEPS	Terry Jacks
3064	IN THE BOTTLE	Brother To Brother
3303	IN THE BUSH	Musique
1925	IN THE GHETTO	Candi Staton
3579	IN THE MIDDLE	Tim Moore
1586	IN THE MIDNIGHT HOUR	Cross Country
	IN THE MOOD	
2305		Henhouse Five Plus Too
2421		Bette Midler
482	IN THE NAVY	Village People
3130	IN THE QUIET MORNING (For Janis Joplin)	Joan Baez
	IN THE RAIN	
434		Dramatics
4928		Arthur Prysock
3714	IN THE STONE	Earth, Wind & Fire
275	IN THE SUMMERTIME	Mungo Jerry
5187	IN THE WINTER	Janis Ian
4976	IN THEE	Blue Öyster Cult
4420	IN TIME	Engelbert Humperdinck
3932	INDIAN LADY	Lou Christie
3301	INDIAN LOVE CALL	Ray Stevens
49	INDIAN RESERVATION (The Lament Of The Cherokee)	Raiders
3264	INDIAN SUMMER	Poco
3859	INDIAN SUMMER	Audience
187	INDIANA WANTS ME	R. Dean Taylor
853	INNER CITY BLUES (Make Me Wanna Holler)	Marvin Gaye
1645	INSEPARABLE	Natalie Cole
3983	INSIDE MY LOVE	Minnie Riperton
3509	INSPIRATION	Paul Williams
104	INSTANT KARMA (We All Shine On)	John Ono Lennon
1609	INSTANT REPLAY	Dan Hartman
5148	INSTIGATING (Trouble Making Fool)	Whatnauts
2267	INTO THE MYSTIC	Johnny Rivers
3836	IRON MAN	Black Sabbath
4847	IS ANYBODY GOIN' TO SAN ANTONE	Charley Pride
3621	IS IT LOVE THAT WE'RE MISSIN'	Quincy Jones
1367	IS SHE REALLY GOING OUT WITH HIM?	Joe Jackson
3675	IS THAT THE WAY	Tin Tin
121	ISLAND GIRL	Elton John
3136	ISN'T IT A PITY	George Harrison
3237	ISN'T IT ABOUT TIME	Stephen Stills -- Manassas
4568	ISN'T IT ALWAYS LOVE	Karla Bonoff
3713	ISN'T IT LONELY TOGETHER	Stark & McBrien
950	ISN'T IT TIME	Babys
1619	ISN'T LIFE STRANGE	Moody Blues
5313	IT AIN'T EASY COMIN' DOWN	Charlene
4469	IT AMAZES ME	John Denver
2557	IT COULD HAVE BEEN ME	Sami Jo
2926	IT DOESN'T HAVE TO BE THAT WAY	Jim Croce
2831	IT DOESN'T MATTER	Stephen Stills
4553	IT DOESN'T MATTER ANYMORE	Linda Ronstadt
218	IT DON'T COME EASY	Ringo Starr
904	IT DON'T MATTER TO ME	Bread
4375	IT FEELS SO GOOD TO BE LOVED SO BAD	Manhattans
4942	IT HURTS A LITTLE EVEN NOW	John Reid
3315	IT HURTS SO BAD	Kim Carnes
	IT KEEPS YOU RUNNIN'	
2614		Doobie Brothers
2682		Carly Simon
3692	IT MAKES ME GIGGLE	John Denver
4653	IT MAY BE WINTER OUTSIDE (But In My Heart It's Spring)	Love Unlimited
2663	IT MUST BE LOVE	Alton McClain & Destiny
377	IT NEVER RAINS IN SOUTHERN CALIFORNIA	Albert Hammond
3105	IT ONLY HURTS WHEN I TRY TO SMILE	Dawn
841	IT ONLY TAKES A MINUTE	Tavares
5346	IT SHOULD HAVE BEEN ME	Yvonne Fair
1998	IT SURE TOOK A LONG, LONG TIME	Lobo
1058	IT WAS ALMOST LIKE A SONG	Ronnie Milsap
3210	IT'S A CRAZY WORLD	Mac McAnally
2265	IT'S A CRYIN' SHAME	Gayle McCormick
	IT'S A HEARTACHE	
342		Bonnie Tyler
5099		Juice Newton
1739	IT'S A LAUGH	Daryl Hall & John Oates
1923	IT'S A LONG WAY THERE	Little River Band
1067	IT'S A MIRACLE	Barry Manilow
1974	IT'S A NEW DAY (Parts 1 & 2)	James Brown
1064	IT'S A SHAME	Spinners
3967	IT'S A SMALL SMALL WORLD	Mike Curb Congregation
5265	IT'S ABOUT TIME	Dillards
2448	IT'S ALL DOWN TO GOODNIGHT VIENNA	Ringo Starr
2714	IT'S ALL I CAN DO	Cars
969	IT'S ALL IN THE GAME	Four Tops
2395	IT'S ALL IN YOUR MIND	Clarence Carter
3807	IT'S ALL OVER	Independents
3180	IT'S ALL RIGHT	Jim Capaldi
4289	IT'S ALL UP TO YOU	Dells
5109	IT'S ALRIGHT	Graham Central Station
3394	IT'S BEEN A LONG TIME	New Birth
5240	IT'S BETTER TO HAVE (And Don't Need)	Don Covay
988	IT'S ECSTASY WHEN YOU LAY DOWN NEXT TO ME	Barry White
3386	IT'S FOR YOU	Springwell
4894	IT'S FOREVER	Ebonys
1482	IT'S GOING TO TAKE SOME TIME	Carpenters
4218	IT'S HARD TO STOP (Doing Something When It's Good To You)	Betty Wright

3486	IT'S HER TURN TO LIVE *Smokey Robinson*	
	IT'S IMPOSSIBLE	
945	*Perry Como*	
2643	*New Birth*	
4088	IT'S IN HIS KISS (The Shoop Shoop Song) *Kate Taylor*	
5066	IT'S JUST A MATTER OF TIME *Sonny James*	
3771	IT'S LATE *Queen*	
2487	IT'S O.K. *Beach Boys*	
1218	IT'S ONE OF THOSE NIGHTS (Yes Love) *Partridge Family*	
2443	IT'S ONLY LOVE *Z.Z. Top*	
3269	IT'S ONLY LOVE *Elvis Presley*	
792	IT'S ONLY MAKE BELIEVE *Glen Campbell*	
1593	IT'S ONLY ROCK 'N ROLL (But I Like It) *Rolling Stones*	
2618	IT'S OVER *Boz Scaggs*	
4722	IT'S REALLY YOU *Tarney/Spencer Band*	
1177	IT'S SAD TO BELONG *England Dan & John Ford Coley*	
881	IT'S SO EASY *Linda Ronstadt*	
3103	IT'S SO HARD FOR ME TO SAY GOOD-BYE *Eddie Kendricks*	
4689	IT'S SO NICE *Jackie DeShannon*	
2608	IT'S SUMMER *Temptations*	
3193	IT'S THE REAL THING (Part 1) *Electric Express*	
5189	IT'S THE SAME OLD LOVE *Courtship*	
2544	IT'S THE SAME OLD SONG *K C & The Sunshine Band*	
2842	(It's The Way) NATURE PLANNED IT *Four Tops*	
	IT'S TOO LATE	
31	*Carole King*	
5338	*Bill Deal & The Rhondels*	
4570	IT'S UNCANNY *Daryl Hall & John Oates*	
3617	IT'S UP TO YOU PETULA *Edison Lighthouse*	
2491	IT'S YOU THAT I NEED *Enchantment*	
3918	IT'S YOUR LIFE *Andy Kim*	

J

521	JACK AND JILL *Raydio*	
188	JACKIE BLUE *Ozark Mountain Daredevils*	
4127	JACKIE WILSON SAID (I'm In Heaven When You Smile) *Van Morrison*	
4018	THE JAM *Graham Central Station*	
4909	JAM BAND *Disco Tex & The Sex-O-Lettes*	
459	JAM UP JELLY TIGHT *Tommy Roe*	
	JAMBALAYA (On The Bayou)	
906	*Blue Ridge Rangers*	
4800	*Nitty Gritty Dirt Band*	
3113	JAMES DEAN *Eagles*	
664	JANE *Jefferson Starship*	
4330	JANUARY *Pilot*	
4545	JASPER *Jim Stafford*	
328	JAZZMAN *Carole King*	
4921	JE T'AIME...MOI NON PLUS *Jane Birkin & Serge Gainsbourg*	
4022	JEALOUSY *Major Harris*	

4459	THE JEAN GENIE *David Bowie*	
826	JEANS ON *David Dundas*	
2720	JENNIFER *Bobby Sherman*	
1594	JENNIFER TOMKINS *Street People*	
4163	JERUSALEM *Herb Alpert & The Tijuana Brass*	
4090	JESAHEL *English Congregation*	
1406	JESSE *Roberta Flack*	
2244	JESSICA *Allman Brothers Band*	
2091	JESUS IS JUST ALRIGHT *Doobie Brothers*	
4585	JESUS WAS A CAPRICORN *Kris Kristofferson*	
645	JET *Paul McCartney & Wings*	
502	JET AIRLINER *Steve Miller Band*	
1258	JIM DANDY *Black Oak Arkansas*	
1767	JIMMY LOVES MARY-ANNE *Looking Glass*	
4646	JINGLE BELLS *Singing Dogs*	
635	JINGLE JANGLE *Archies*	
64	JIVE TALKIN' *Bee Gees*	
3144	JIVE TURKEY (Part 1) *Ohio Players*	
1362	JOANNE *Michael Nesmith*	
1886	JODY'S GOT YOUR GIRL AND GONE *Johnnie Taylor*	
4355	JOHNNY COOL *Steve Gibbons Band*	
1755	JOIN TOGETHER *Who*	
169	THE JOKER *Steve Miller Band*	
3804	JOLENE *Dolly Parton*	
1776	JOSIE *Steely Dan*	
3605	JOSIE *Kris Kristofferson*	
831	JOY *Apollo 100*	
2310	JOY (Part 1) *Isaac Hayes*	
2	JOY TO THE WORLD *Three Dog Night*	
4598	JOYFUL RESURRECTION *Tom Fogerty*	
2963	JUBILATION *Paul Anka*	
2180	JUDY MAE *Boomer Castleman*	
3897	JUKIN' *Atlanta Rhythm Section*	
3624	JULIANNA *Five Man Electrical Band*	
4676	JULIE ANN *Ginger*	
445	JULIE, DO YA LOVE ME *Bobby Sherman*	
3926	July 12, 1939 *Charlie Rich*	
4315	JUMP *Aretha Franklin*	
1727	JUMP INTO THE FIRE *Nilsson*	
936	JUNGLE BOOGIE *Kool & The Gang*	
644	JUNGLE FEVER *Chakachas*	
1540	JUNGLE LOVE *Steve Miller Band*	
553	JUNIOR'S FARM *Paul McCartney & Wings*	
1339	JUNK FOOD JUNKIE *Larry Groce*	
1844	JUST A LITTLE BIT OF YOU *Michael Jackson*	
4046	JUST A SMILE *Pilot*	
873	JUST A SONG BEFORE I GO *Crosby, Stills & Nash*	
5040	JUST ABOUT THE SAME *Association*	
4267	JUST ANOTHER NIGHT *Ian Hunter*	
4143	JUST AS LONG AS YOU NEED ME (Part 1) *Independents*	
	JUST DON'T WANT TO BE LONELY	
774	*Main Ingredient*	
3521	*Ronnie Dyson*	
4616	JUST FOR ME AND YOU *Poco*	
2930	JUST LET IT COME *Alive 'n' Kickin'*	
2796	(Just Like) ROMEO AND JULIET *Sha Na Na*	
79	JUST MY IMAGINATION (Running Away With Me) *Temptations*	

	JUST ONE LOOK	
3075	*Linda Ronstadt*	
5060	*Anne Murray*	
4611	JUST ONE MINUTE MORE *Mike Finnigan*	
884	JUST REMEMBER I LOVE YOU *Firefall*	
1919	JUST SEVEN NUMBERS (Can Straighten Out My Life) *Four Tops*	
3878	JUST SEVENTEEN *Raiders*	
3361	JUST THE SAME WAY *Journey*	
279	JUST THE WAY YOU ARE *Billy Joel*	
1042	JUST TO BE CLOSE TO YOU *Commodores*	
1922	JUST TOO MANY PEOPLE *Melissa Manchester*	
1758	JUST WHAT I NEEDED *Cars*	
569	JUST WHEN I NEEDED YOU MOST *Randy Vanwarmer*	
2801	JUST YOU AND I *Melissa Manchester*	
388	JUST YOU 'N' ME *Chicago*	

K

1801	K-JEE *Nite-Liters*	
2941	KALIMBA STORY *Earth, Wind & Fire*	
4547	KATE *Johnny Cash*	
2569	KATMANDU *Bob Seger*	
3211	KEEP HOLDING ON *Temptations*	
381	KEEP IT COMIN' LOVE *K C & The Sunshine Band*	
2679	KEEP IT IN THE FAMILY *Leon Haywood*	
3464	KEEP ME CRYIN' *Al Green*	
4933	KEEP ME IN MIND *Lynn Anderson*	
2259	KEEP ON DANCIN' *Gary's Gang*	
2891	KEEP ON DOIN' *Isley Brothers*	
4560	KEEP ON DOIN' WHAT YOU'RE DOIN' *Bobby Byrd*	
5213	KEEP ON KEEPING ON *N.F. Porter*	
4360	KEEP ON LOVING ME (You'll See The Change) *Bobby Bland*	
3950	KEEP ON RUNNING *Stevie Wonder*	
4430	KEEP ON RUNNING AWAY *Lazy Racer*	
	KEEP ON SINGING	
1040	*Helen Reddy*	
2551	*Austin Roberts*	
1277	KEEP ON SMILIN' *Wet Willie*	
226	KEEP ON TRUCKIN' (Part 1) *Eddie Kendricks*	
2639	KEEP ON TRYIN' *Poco*	
4824	KEEP OUR LOVE ALIVE *Paul Davis*	
2977	KEEP PLAYIN' THAT ROCK 'N' ROLL *Edgar Winter's White Trash*	
5297	KEEP THAT SAME OLD FEELING *Side Effect*	
3015	KEEP THE CUSTOMER SATISFIED *Gary Puckett*	
	KEEP YOUR EYE ON THE SPARROW...see BARETTA'S THEME	
2248	KEEP YOUR HEAD TO THE SKY *Earth, Wind & Fire*	
4878	KEEP YOURSELF ALIVE *Queen*	
929	KEEPER OF THE CASTLE *Four Tops*	
4946	KENTUCKY *Sammi Smith*	
1170	KENTUCKY RAIN *Elvis Presley*	
3928	KICK IT OUT *Heart*	
3719	KILLER CUT *Charlie*	
3077	KILLER JOE *Quincy Jones*	

#	Title	Artist
1079	KILLER QUEEN	Queen
90	KILLING ME SOFTLY WITH HIS SONG	Roberta Flack
2588	THE KILLING OF GEORGIE (Part 1 & 2)	Rod Stewart
2093	KING HEROIN	James Brown
1556	THE KING IS GONE	Ronnie McDowell
4122	KING KONG (Parts 1 & 2)	Jimmy Castor Bunch
2905	KING OF NOTHING	Seals & Crofts
5277	THE KING OF ROCK 'N' ROLL	Cashman & West
1458	KING TUT	Steve Martin
4269	KINGS AND QUEENS	Aerosmith
2209	KINGS OF THE PARTY	Brownsville Station
1213	KISS AN ANGEL GOOD MORNIN'	Charley Pride
74	KISS AND SAY GOODBYE	Manhattans
2911	KISS IN THE DARK	Pink Lady
18	KISS YOU ALL OVER	Exile
4228	KISSIN' TIME	Kiss
1820	KISSING MY LOVE	Bill Withers
	KNEE DEEP...see (Not Just)	
4513	KNOCK KNOCK WHO'S THERE	Mary Hopkin
210	KNOCK ON WOOD	Amii Stewart
13	KNOCK THREE TIMES	Dawn
1031	KNOCKIN' ON HEAVEN'S DOOR	Bob Dylan
1210	KNOWING ME, KNOWING YOU	ABBA
2695	KO-KO JOE	Jerry Reed
449	KODACHROME	Paul Simon
3073	KONG	Dickie Goodman
4432	KOOL'S BACK AGAIN	Kool & The Gang
1900	KUNG FU	Curtis Mayfield
178	KUNG FU FIGHTING	Carl Douglas

L

#	Title	Artist
4372	L.A. FREEWAY	Jerry Jeff Walker
3590	L.A. GOODBYE	Ides Of March
4949	L.A. INTERNATIONAL AIRPORT	Susan Raye
3371	L.A. SUNSHINE	War
1537	LA GRANGE	ZZ Top
815	LA LA LA (If I Had You)	Bobby Sherman
	LA LA PEACE SONG	
2913		Al Wilson
4759		O.C. Smith
343	LADIES NIGHT	Kool & The Gang
668	LADY	Styx
927	LADY	Little River Band
	LADY BLUE	
973		Leon Russell
5091		George Benson
3182	LADY BUMP	Penny McLean
4336	LADY ELEANOR	Lindisfarne
4601	LADY LAY	Wayne Newton
1659	LADY LOVE	Lou Rawls
4508	LADY LOVE	Klowns
134	LADY MARMALADE	LaBelle
2646	LADY (Put The Light On Me)	Brownsville Station
3555	LADY WRITER	Dire Straits
3426	LAMPLIGHT	David Essex
4502	THE LANGUAGE OF LOVE	Intrigues
1569	LAST CHILD	Aerosmith
512	LAST DANCE	Donna Summer
1260	THE LAST FAREWELL	Roger Whittaker
2171	THE LAST GAME OF THE SEASON (A Blind Man In The Bleachers)	David Geddes
4287	--THE BLIND MAN IN THE BLEACHERS	Kenny Starr
	LAST KISS	
2181		Wednesday
3645		J. Frank Wilson & The Cavaliers
582	(Last Night) I DIDN'T GET TO SLEEP AT ALL	5th Dimension
2810	LAST OF THE SINGING COWBOYS	Marshall Tucker Band
303	LAST SONG	Edward Bear
3649	LAST TANGO IN PARIS	Herb Alpert & The TJB
2496	THE LAST THING ON MY MIND	Neil Diamond
4706	THE LAST TIME	Buchanan Brothers
3104	THE LAST TIME I SAW HER	Glen Campbell
1185	LAST TIME I SAW HIM	Diana Ross
4704	LAUGHIN AND CLOWNIN	Ray Charles
217	LAUGHTER IN THE RAIN	Neil Sedaka
729	LAY A LITTLE LOVIN' ON ME	Robin McNamara
2153	LAY-AWAY	Isley Brothers
373	LAY DOWN (Candles In The Rain)	Melanie
385	LAY DOWN SALLY	Eric Clapton
4030	LAY IT ON THE LINE	Triumph
	LAY LADY LAY	
3308		Isley Brothers
4010		Ferrante & Teicher
1059	LAYLA	Derek & The Dominos
5117	LAZY EYES	T.M.G.
5	LE FREAK	Chic
4463	LE SPANK	Le Pamplemousse
547	LEAD ME ON	Maxine Nightingale
138	LEAN ON ME	Bill Withers
265	LEAVE ME ALONE (Ruby Red Dress)	Helen Reddy
5314	LEAVE MY MAN (Woman) ALONE	Raeletts
1445	LEAVING ME	Independents
3896	LEFTOVERS	Millie Jackson
3186	LEGEND IN YOUR OWN TIME	Carly Simon
3546	LEONA	Wet Willie
376	LET 'EM IN	Wings
530	LET HER IN	John Travolta
	LET IT BE	
28		Beatles
2286		Joan Baez
3048	LET IT GO, LET IT FLOW	Dave Mason
3039	LET IT RAIN	Eric Clapton
1227	LET IT RIDE	Bachman-Turner Overdrive
2085	LET IT SHINE	Olivia Newton-John
2716	LET ME BACK IN	Tyrone Davis
4903	LET ME BE GOOD TO YOU	Lou Rawls
	LET ME BE THE ONE...see I WON'T LAST A DAY WITHOUT YOU	
539	LET ME BE THERE	Olivia Newton-John
4594	LET ME BE YOUR LOVEMAKER	Betty Wright
3956	LET ME DOWN EASY	Cornelius Brothers & Sister Rose
2599	LET ME GET TO KNOW YOU	Paul Anka
2179	LET ME GO TO HIM	Dionne Warwick
1702	LET ME IN	Osmonds
3559	LET ME KNOW (I Have A Right)	Gloria Gaynor
3293	LET ME MAKE LOVE TO YOU	O'Jays
3200	LET ME PARTY WITH YOU (Part 1) (Party, Party, Party)	Bunny Sigler
1400	LET ME SERENADE YOU	Three Dog Night
4000	LET ME START TONITE	Lamont Dozier
3549	LET ME TRY AGAIN	Frank Sinatra
1986	LET THE MUSIC PLAY	Barry White
4527	LET THE MUSIC TAKE YOUR MIND	Kool & The Gang
5078	LET THERE BE DRUMS	Incredible Bongo Band
3026	LET THERE BE MUSIC	Orleans
3145	LET THIS BE A LESSON TO YOU	Independents
4991	LET THIS BE A LETTER (To My Baby)	Jackie Wilson
2417	LET US LOVE	Bill Withers
2110	LET YOUR HAIR DOWN	Temptations
189	LET YOUR LOVE FLOW	Bellamy Brothers
1710	LET YOUR LOVE GO	Bread
2964	LET YOUR YEAH BE YEAH	Brownsville Station
1686	LET'S ALL CHANT	Michael Zager Band
3865	LET'S BE YOUNG TONIGHT	Jermaine Jackson
5349	LET'S CLEAN UP THE GHETTO	Philadelphia International All Stars: Lou Rawls, Billy Paul, Archie Bell, Teddy Pendergrass, O'Jays, Dee Dee Sharp Gamble
300	LET'S DO IT AGAIN	Staple Singers
3666	LET'S GET CRAZY TONIGHT	Rupert Holmes
67	LET'S GET IT ON	Marvin Gaye
1744	LET'S GET MARRIED	Al Green
2546	LET'S GIVE ADAM AND EVE ANOTHER CHANCE	Gary Puckett & The Union Gap
1226	LET'S GO	Cars
4172	LET'S GROOVE (Part 1)	Archie Bell & The Drells
4778	LET'S HAVE SOME FUN	Bar-Kays
	LET'S LIVE TOGETHER	
2187		Road Apples
5217		Cazz
4187	LET'S MAKE A BABY	Billy Paul
1099	LET'S PRETEND	Raspberries
1269	LET'S PUT IT ALL TOGETHER	Stylistics
4382	LET'S ROCK	Ellison Chase
5253	LET'S SPEND THE NIGHT TOGETHER	David Bowie
	LET'S STAY TOGETHER	
24		Al Green
2753		Isaac Hayes
1809	LET'S STRAIGHTEN IT OUT	Latimore
	LET'S WORK TOGETHER	
1511		Canned Heat
1884		Wilbert Harrison One Man Band (Part 1)

534 **THE LETTER** *Joe Cocker*	2190 **LIVIN' AIN'T LIVIN'** *Firefall*	4675 **LONG HOT SUMMER NIGHTS** *Wendy Waldman*
2168 **LETTER TO LUCILLE** *Tom Jones*	1631 **LIVIN' FOR THE WEEKEND** *O'Jays*	3922 **LONG LIVE ROCK** *Who*
2381 **A LETTER TO MYSELF** *Chi-Lites*	1192 **LIVIN' FOR YOU** *Al Green*	3285 **LONG LONELY NIGHTS** *Dells*
3166 **LETTING GO** *Wings*	3336 **LIVIN' IN THE LIFE** *Isley Brothers*	1289 **LONG LONESOME HIGHWAY** *Michael Parks*
1567 **LEVON** *Elton John*	1304 **LIVIN' IT UP (Friday Night)** *Bell & James*	1875 **LONG LONG TIME** *Linda Ronstadt*
795 **LIAR** *Three Dog Night*	919 **LIVIN' THING** *Electric Light Orchestra*	1945 **LONG, LONG WAY FROM HOME** *Foreigner*
753 **LIDO SHUFFLE** *Boz Scaggs*	2406 **LIVING A LITTLE, LAUGHING A LITTLE** *Spinners*	4175 **LONG PROMISED ROAD** *Beach Boys*
3492 **LIES** *J.J. Cale*	**LIVING FOR THE CITY**	705 **LONG TALL GLASSES (I Can Dance)** *Leo Sayer*
2472 **LIFE** *Elvis Presley*	651 *Stevie Wonder*	1275 **LONG TIME** *Boston*
4385 **LIFE AIN'T EASY** *Dr. Hook & The Medicine Show*	4608 *Ray Charles*	804 **LONG TRAIN RUNNIN'** *Doobie Brothers*
2125 **LIFE AND BREATH** *Climax*	1646 **LIVING IN A HOUSE DIVIDED** *Cher*	4359 **THE LONG WAY AROUND** *Linda Ronstadt*
1363 **LIFE IN THE FAST LANE** *Eagles*	1309 **LIVING IN THE PAST** *Jethro Tull*	3616 **THE LONG WAY HOME** *Neil Diamond*
4066 **LIFE IS A CARNIVAL** *Band*	2597 **LIVING IN THE U.S.A.** *Steve Miller Band*	665 **LONGFELLOW SERENADE** *Neil Diamond*
889 **LIFE IS A ROCK (But The Radio Rolled Me)** *Reunion*	4994 **LIVING IT DOWN** *Freddy Fender*	2367 **LOOK AT ME (I'm In Love)** *Moments*
3135 **LIFE IS A SONG WORTH SINGING** *Johnny Mathis*	1340 **LIVING NEXT DOOR TO ALICE** *Smokie*	4309 **LOOK AT YOU** *George McCrae*
805 **LIFE'S BEEN GOOD** *Joe Walsh*	1672 **LIVING TOGETHER, GROWING TOGETHER** *5th Dimension*	4754 **LOOK AWAY** *Ozark Mountain Daredevils*
4202 **LIGHT MY FIRE/137 DISCO HEAVEN** *Amii Stewart*	5135 **LIVING WITHOUT YOU** *Manfred Mann's Earth Band*	1520 **LOOK IN MY EYES PRETTY WOMAN** *Tony Orlando & Dawn*
1730 **LIGHT SINGS** *5th Dimension*	4117 **LIVINGSTON SATURDAY NIGHT** *Jimmy Buffett*	4413 **LOOK INTO YOUR HEART** *Aretha Franklin*
3593 **LIGHT THE SKY ON FIRE** *Jefferson Starship*	2335 **LIZZIE AND THE RAINMAN** *Tanya Tucker*	2776 **LOOK-KA PY PY** *Meters*
3567 **LIGHTS** *Journey*	**THE LOAD-OUT** *Jackson Browne* see: **STAY**	3948 **THE LOOK OF LOVE** *Isaac Hayes*
3540 **LIKE A SAD SONG** *John Denver*	211 **THE LOCO-MOTION** *Grand Funk*	**LOOK WHAT THEY'VE DONE TO MY SONG MA**
2451 **LIKE A SUNDAY IN SALEM (The Amos & Andy Song)** *Gene Cotton*	4027 **LOCOMOTIVE BREATH** *Jethro Tull*	937 *New Seekers*
4726 **LIKE A SUNDAY MORNING** *Lana Cantrell*	566 **THE LOGICAL SONG** *Supertramp*	2972 *Ray Charles* [P]
3157 **LIKE AN OPEN DOOR** *Fuzz*	778 **LOLA** *Kinks*	324 **LOOK WHAT YOU DONE FOR ME** *Al Green*
4710 **LIKE THEY SAY IN L.A.** *East L.A. Car Pool*	2879 **LONDON TOWN** *Wings*	3249 **LOOK WHAT YOU'VE DONE TO MY HEART** *Marilyn McCoo & Billy Davis Jr.*
2515 **LINDA ON MY MIND** *Conway Twitty*	3793 **THE LONE RANGER** *Oscar Brown Jr.*	5245 **LOOKIN' BACK** *Bob Seger*
250 **THE LION SLEEPS TONIGHT** *Robert John*	4113 **THE LONELIEST MAN ON THE MOON** *David Castle*	4241 **LOOKIN' OUT FOR #1** *Bachman-Turner Overdrive*
3746 **LISA, LISTEN TO ME** *Blood, Sweat & Tears*	410 **LONELY BOY** *Andrew Gold*	163 **LOOKIN' OUT MY BACK DOOR** *Creedence Clearwater Revival*
4076 **LISTEN TO HER HEART** *Tom Petty & The Heartbreakers*	319 **LONELY DAYS** *Bee Gees*	1342 **LOOKIN' THROUGH THE WINDOWS** *Jackson 5*
4028 **LISTEN TO THE BUDDHA** *Ozo*	3778 **LONELY FEELIN'** *War*	**LOOKING FOR A LOVE**
993 **LISTEN TO THE MUSIC** *Doobie Brothers*	3962 **A LONELY MAN** *Chi-Lites*	799 *Bobby Womack* [P]
305 **LISTEN TO WHAT THE MAN SAID** *Wings*	111 **LONELY NIGHT (Angel Face)** *Captain & Tennille*	1976 *J. Geils Band*
4625 **A LITTLE BIT LIKE MAGIC** *King Harvest*	5164 **THE LONELY ONE** *Special Delivery Feat. Terry Huff*	1615 **LOOKING FOR SPACE** *John Denver*
709 **A LITTLE BIT MORE** *Dr. Hook*	1001 **LONELY PEOPLE** *America*	1807 **LOOKING THROUGH THE EYES OF LOVE** *Partridge Family*
4404 **LITTLE BIT O' SOUL** *Bullet*	3290 **LONELY SCHOOL YEAR** *Hudson Brothers*	545 **LOOKS LIKE WE MADE IT** *Barry Manilow*
2847 **A LITTLE BIT OF SOAP** *Paul Davis*	**LONELY TEARDROPS**	5083 **LOOKY LOOKY (Look At Me Girl)** *O'Jays*
2262 **--LITTLE BIT OF SOAP** *Nigel Olsson*	2453 *Brian Hyland*	4803 **LOOSE BOOTY** *Sly & The Family Stone*
682 **LITTLE BITTY PRETTY ONE** *Jackson 5*	4569 *Narvel Felts*	4645 **THE LORD KNOWS I'M DRINKING** *Cal Smith*
2260 **LITTLE DARLING (I Need You)** *Doobie Brothers*	3846 **LONELY WIND** *Kansas*	2833 **LORD, MR. FORD** *Jerry Reed*
3191 **LITTLE GIRL GONE** *Donna Fargo*	672 **LONESOME LOSER** *Little River Band*	667 **THE LORD'S PRAYER** *Sister Janet Mead*
1145 **LITTLE GREEN BAG** *George Baker Selection*	4111 **LONESOME MARY** *Chilliwack*	2024 **LORELEI** *Styx*
3508 **A LITTLE LOVIN' (Keeps The Doctor Away)** *Raes*	1689 **LONG AGO AND FAR AWAY** *James Taylor*	3671 **LOSERS WEEPERS (Part 1)** *Etta James*
424 **A LITTLE MORE LOVE** *Olivia Newton-John*	2928 **LONG AGO TOMORROW** *B.J. Thomas*	3545 **LOST HORIZON** *Shawn Phillips*
3614 **LITTLE ONE** *Chicago*	4145 **LONG AND LONESOME ROAD** *Shocking Blue*	3642 **LOST IN YOUR LOVE** *John Paul Young*
3137 **LITTLE QUEEN** *Heart*	129 **THE LONG AND WINDING ROAD** *Beatles*	985 **LOST WITHOUT YOUR LOVE** *Bread*
426 **LITTLE WILLY** *Sweet*	3664 **LONG AS I CAN SEE THE LIGHT** *Creedence Clearwater Revival*	813 **LOTTA LOVE** *Nicolette Larson*
5225 **LITTLE WOMAN LOVE** *Wings*	158 **LONG COOL WOMAN (In A Black Dress)** *Hollies*	2024 **LORELEI** *Styx*
259 **LIVE AND LET DIE** *Paul McCartney & Wings*	1869 **LONG DARK ROAD** *Hollies*	
2661 **LIVE IT UP (Part 1)** *Isley Brothers*	2997 **LONG HAIRED COUNTRY BOY** *Charlie Daniels Band*	
3957 **LIVE YOUR LIFE BEFORE YOU DIE** *Pointer Sisters*	2484 **LONG HAIRED LOVER FROM LIVERPOOL** *Little Jimmy Osmond*	4734 **LOUIE, LOUIE** *John Belushi*

#	Title	Artist
3227	LOUISIANA	Mike Kennedy
5334	LOUISIANA LADY	New Riders Of The Purple Sage
2326	LOVE	Lettermen
4952	LOVE AND DESIRE (Part 1)	Arpeggio
4038	LOVE AND HAPPINESS	Earnest Jackson
	LOVE BALLAD	
1431		George Benson
1484		L.T.D.
	LOVE BEING YOUR FOOL...see (Shu-Doo-Pa-Poo-Poop)	
2368	LOVE BONES	Johnnie Taylor
2901	LOVE CORPORATION	Hues Corporation
2026	LOVE DON'T LIVE HERE ANYMORE	Rose Royce
1848	LOVE DON'T LOVE NOBODY (Part 1)	Spinners
2413	LOVE FINDS ITS OWN WAY	Gladys Knight & The Pips
2292	LOVE FIRE	Jigsaw
4548	LOVE FOR YOU	Sonoma
3704	LOVE GONE BY	Dan Fogelberg
2369	LOVE GONNA PACK UP (And Walk Out)	Persuaders
350	LOVE GROWS (Where My Rosemary Goes)	Edison Lighthouse
3240	LOVE GUN	Kiss
	LOVE HANGOVER	
304		Diana Ross
4424		5th Dimension
2512	LOVE HAS NO PRIDE	Linda Ronstadt
712	LOVE HER MADLY	Doors
	LOVE HURTS	
615		Nazareth
5033		Jim Capaldi
837	THE LOVE I LOST (Part 1)	Harold Melvin & The Blue Notes
4592	LOVE IN 'C' MINOR (Part 1)	Cerrone
1541	LOVE IN THE SHADOWS	Neil Sedaka
4169	LOVE IS A ROSE	Linda Ronstadt
469	LOVE IS ALIVE	Gary Wright
5070	LOVE IS ALL	Engelbert Humperdinck
3726	LOVE IS BETTER IN THE A.M. (Part 1)	Johnnie Taylor
4829	LOVE IS FOR THE BEST IN US	James Walsh Gypsy Band
3884	LOVE IS FUNNY THAT WAY	Jackie Wilson
4488	LOVE IS GONNA COME AT LAST	Badfinger
1085	LOVE IS IN THE AIR	John Paul Young
3920	LOVE IS LIFE	Earth, Wind & Fire
747	LOVE IS LIKE OXYGEN	Sweet
1273	LOVE IS THE ANSWER	England Dan & John Ford Coley
4861	LOVE IS THE ANSWER	Van McCoy
1516	LOVE IS THE DRUG	Roxy Music
2994	LOVE IS THE MESSAGE	MFSB
195	(Love Is) THICKER THAN WATER	Andy Gibb
2062	LOVE IS WHAT YOU MAKE IT	Grass Roots
1019	LOVE JONES	Brighter Side Of Darkness
	see also BASKETBALL JONES	
917	LOVE LAND	Charles Wright & The Watts 103rd Street Rhythm Band
3819	LOVE LIKE A MAN	Ten Years After
1142	L-O-V-E (Love)	Al Green
3160	LOVE, LOVE, LOVE	Donny Hathaway
180	LOVE MACHINE (Part 1)	Miracles
	LOVE MAKES THE WORLD GO ROUND	
4203		Odds & Ends
5072		Kiki Dee
916	LOVE ME	Yvonne Elliman
3783	LOVE ME	Rascals
4102	LOVE ME AGAIN	Rita Coolidge
1182	LOVE ME FOR A REASON	Osmonds
2761	LOVE ME, LOVE ME LOVE	Frank Mills
4768	(Love Me) LOVE THE LIFE I LEAD	Fantastics
5069	LOVE ME NOW	Ruby Winters
5094	LOVE ME ONE TIME (Just For Old Times Sake)	Karen Nelson & Billy T
4574	LOVE ME RIGHT	Denise La Salle
3862	LOVE ME TONIGHT	Blackjack
4784	LOVE ME TONIGHT	Head East
2102	LOVE MEANS (You Never Have To Say You're Sorry)	Sounds Of Sunshine
3662	LOVE MINUS ZERO-NO LIMIT	Turley Richards
	LOVE MUSIC	
3462		Raiders
5319		Sergio Mendes & Brasil '77
4405	LOVE MY LIFE AWAY	Hagers
2959	LOVE OF MY LIFE	Gino Vannelli
810	LOVE ON A TWO-WAY STREET	Moments
1992	LOVE OR LEAVE	Spinners
669	LOVE OR LET ME BE LONELY	Friends Of Distinction
2441	LOVE OR SOMETHING LIKE IT	Kenny Rogers
2942	LOVE PAINS	Yvonne Elliman
5088	LOVE POTION NUMBER NINE	Coasters
2712	LOVE POWER	Willie Hutch
1478	LOVE REALLY HURTS WITHOUT YOU	Billy Ocean
3074	LOVE, REIGN O'ER ME	Who
291	LOVE ROLLERCOASTER	Ohio Players
397	LOVE SO RIGHT	Bee Gees
1023	LOVE SONG	Anne Murray
2488	LOVE SONG	Tommy James
	LOVE STORY...see THEME FROM LOVE STORY	
4999	LOVE STRUCK	Stonebolt
1238	LOVE TAKES TIME	Orleans
	LOVE THE LIFE I LEAD...see (Love Me)	
	LOVE THE ONE YOU'RE WITH	
1060		Isley Brothers
1293		Stephen Stills
139	LOVE THEME FROM "A STAR IS BORN" (Evergreen)	Barbra Streisand
2407	LOVE THEME FROM "EYES OF LAURA MARS" (Prisoner)	Barbra Streisand
	LOVE THEME FROM "THE GODFATHER"	
1963		Andy Williams (Speak Softly Love)
4318		Nino Rota
4419	--SPEAK SOFTLY LOVE	Al Martino
421	LOVE TO LOVE YOU BABY	Donna Summer
76	LOVE TRAIN	O'Jays
3340	LOVE UPRISING	Otis Leaville
2008	THE LOVE WE HAD (Stays On My Mind)	Dells
562	LOVE WILL FIND A WAY	Pablo Cruise
137	LOVE WILL KEEP US TOGETHER	Captain & Tennille
3321	--POR AMOR VIVIREMOS (Love Will Keep Us Together)	Captain & Tennille
372	LOVE WON'T LET ME WAIT	Major Harris
526	LOVE YOU INSIDE OUT	Bee Gees
135	THE LOVE YOU SAVE	Jackson 5
1565	LOVE'S GROWN DEEP	Kenny Nolan
892	LOVE'S LINES, ANGLES AND RHYMES	5th Dimension
4635	LOVE'S MADE A FOOL OF YOU	Cochise
4207	LOVE'S STREET AND FOOL'S ROAD	Solomon Burke
224	LOVE'S THEME	Love Unlimited Orchestra
1716	LOVELY DAY	Bill Withers
3553	LOVER'S CROSS	Melanie
	A LOVER'S QUESTION	
4121		Jacky Ward
5111		Loggins & Messina
269	LOVES ME LIKE A ROCK	Paul Simon
1151	LOVIN', TOUCHIN', SQUEEZIN'	Journey
125	LOVIN' YOU	Minnie Riperton
3448	LOVIN' YOU BABY	White Plains
3574	LOVIN' YOU, LOVIN' ME	Candi Staton
	LOVING ARMS	
1975		Dobie Gray
5216		Kris Kristofferson & Rita Coolidge
1788	LOVING HER WAS EASIER (Than Anything I'll Ever Do Again)	Kris Kristofferson
4222	LOVING POWER	Impressions
3277	LOVING YOU	Johnny Nash
4708	LOVING YOU IS JUST AN OLD HABIT	Jim Weatherly
1842	LOVING YOU JUST CROSSED MY MIND	Sam Neely
599	LOW RIDER	War
244	LOWDOWN	Boz Scaggs
2066	LOWDOWN	Chicago
3446	LU	Peggy Lipton
3999	LUCIFER	Bob Seger System
905	LUCILLE	Kenny Rogers
1601	LUCKENBACH, TEXAS (Back to the Basics of Love)	Waylon Jennings
2670	LUCKY MAN	Starbuck
2781	LUCKY MAN	Emerson, Lake & Palmer
5272	LUCKY ME	Moments
1515	LUCRETIA MAC EVIL	Blood, Sweat & Tears
312	LUCY IN THE SKY WITH DIAMONDS	Elton John
431	LYIN' EYES	Eagles

M

#	Title	Artist
630	MA BELLE AMIE	Tee Set
4387	MA! (He's Making Eyes At Me)	Lena Zavaroni
	Mac ARTHUR PARK	
128		Donna Summer
2143		Four Tops (Part 2)

#	Title	Artist
1383	**MACHINE GUN**	*Commodores*
4351	**MACHINES**	*John LiVigni*
1759	**MACHO MAN**	*Village People*
5248	**MADE TO LOVE YOU**	*Gary Wright*
4397	**MADELAINE**	*Stu Nunnery*
3334	**MADEMOISELLE**	*Styx*
2419	**MAGGIE**	*Redbone*
8	**MAGGIE MAY**	*Rod Stewart*
570	**MAGIC**	*Pilot*
711	**MAGIC MAN**	*Heart*
2854	**MAGIC WOMAN TOUCH**	*Hollies*
2745	**MAGICAL MYSTERY TOUR**	*Ambrosia*
788	**MAGNET AND STEEL**	*Walter Egan*
495	**THE MAIN EVENT/FIGHT**	*Barbra Streisand*
1953	**MAIN TITLE (Theme From "JAWS")**	*John Williams*
1711	**MAINSTREET**	*Bob Seger*
1717	**MAKE IT EASY ON YOURSELF**	*Dionne Warwick*
1551	**MAKE IT FUNKY (Part 1)**	*James Brown*
	MAKE IT FUNKY-Part 3...see **MY PART**	
4180	**MAKE IT LAST**	*Brooklyn Dreams*
	MAKE IT WITH YOU	
89		*Bread*
4822		*Whispers*
3542	**MAKE LOVE TO ME**	*Helen Reddy*
3342	**MAKE LOVE TO YOUR MIND**	*Bill Withers*
4033	**MAKE ME FEEL LIKE A WOMAN**	*Jackie Moore*
4006	**MAKE ME HAPPY**	*Bobby Bloom*
847	**MAKE ME SMILE**	*Chicago*
1611	**MAKE ME THE WOMAN THAT YOU GO HOME TO**	*Gladys Knight & The Pips*
4049	**MAKE ME TWICE THE MAN**	*New York City*
5340	**MAKE MY LIFE A LITTLE BIT BRIGHTER**	*Chester*
2890	**MAKE THE WORLD GO AWAY**	*Donny & Marie Osmond*
4238	**MAKE UP YOUR MIND**	*J. Geils Band*
2768	**MAKE YOU FEEL LOVE AGAIN**	*Wet Willie*
525	**MAKIN' IT**	*David Naughton*
4880	**MAKIN' THE BEST OF A BAD SITUATION**	*Dick Feller*
1544	**MAKING OUR DREAMS COME TRUE**	*Cyndi Grecco*
3634	**A MAMA AND A PAPA**	*Ray Stevens*
773	**MAMA CAN'T BUY YOU LOVE**	*Elton John*
3903	**MAMA DON'T ALLOW NO PARKIN'**	*Brownsville Station*
3596	**MAMA LET HIM PLAY**	*Doucette*
4112	**MAMA LIKED THE ROSES**	*Elvis Presley*
	MAMA TOLD ME (Not To Come)	
93		*Three Dog Night*
4381		*Wilson Pickett* [P]
3411	**MAMA WAS A ROCK AND ROLL SINGER PAPA USED TO WRITE ALL HER SONGS (Part 1)**	*Sonny & Cher*
3294	**MAMA WEER ALL CRAZEE NOW**	*Slade*
179	**MAMA'S PEARL**	*Jackson 5*
4453	**MAMACITA**	*Grass Roots*
1684	**MAMMA MIA**	*ABBA*
3082	**MAMMAS DON'T LET YOUR BABIES GROW UP TO BE COWBOYS**	*Waylon & Willie*
	MAMMY BLUE	
1918		*Stories*
3401		*Pop-Tops*
3989		*James Darren*
2253	**A MAN I'LL NEVER BE**	*Boston*
3131	**MAN IN BLACK**	*Johnny Cash*
4520	**MAN OF CONSTANT SORROW**	*Ginger Baker's Air Force*
4826	**THE MAN ON PAGE 602**	*Zoot Fenster*
2103	**A MAN SIZED JOB**	*Denise La Salle*
3701	**MAN SMART, WOMAN SMARTER**	*Robert Palmer*
4661	**THE MAN THAT TURNED MY MAMA ON**	*Tanya Tucker*
5206	**MANDRILL**	*Mandrill*
176	**MANDY**	*Barry Manilow*
5295	**--BRANDY**	*Scott English*
3358	**MANHATTAN SPIRITUAL**	*Mike Post*
4282	**MANY RIVERS TO CROSS**	*Nilsson*
752	**MARGARITAVILLE**	*Jimmy Buffett*
4964	**MARIA (You Were The Only One)**	*Jimmy Ruffin*
1890	**MARIANNE**	*Stephen Stills*
2877	**MARRIED MEN**	*Bette Midler*
4460	**MARTHA (Your Lovers Come And Go)**	*Gabriel*
2836	**THE MARTIAN BOOGIE**	*Brownsville Station*
2912	**MARY HAD A LITTLE LAMB**	*Wings*
3338	**MARY HARTMAN, MARY HARTMAN (Theme)**	*Deadly Nightshade*
3427	**MARY JANE**	*Rick James*
2214	**MASTER OF EYES (The Deepness Of Your Eyes)**	*Aretha Franklin*
910	**MASTERPIECE**	*Temptations*
1653	**MAYBE**	*Three Degrees*
1812	**MAYBE I'M A FOOL**	*Eddie Money*
1163	**MAYBE I'M AMAZED**	*Wings*
1308	**MAYBE TOMORROW**	*Jackson 5*
915	**ME AND BABY BROTHER**	*War*
	ME AND BOBBY McGEE	
409		*Janis Joplin*
3060		*Jerry Lee Lewis*
959	**ME AND JULIO DOWN BY THE SCHOOLYARD**	*Paul Simon*
	ME AND MRS. JONES	
55		*Billy Paul*
2520		*Ron Banks & The Dramatics*
1411	**ME AND MY ARROW**	*Nilsson*
878	**ME AND YOU AND A DOG NAMED BOO**	*Lobo*
3961	**MEADOWS**	*Joe Walsh*
2499	**MEAN MISTREATER**	*Grand Funk Railroad*
	MEDLEY...see **I WON'T LAST A DAY WITHOUT YOU**	
	MELANIE MAKES ME SMILE	
4979		*Tony Burrows*
5224		*Terry Williams*
2188	**MELTING POT**	*Booker T. & The M.G.'s*
4510	**MELTING POT**	*Blue Mink*
	MEMORIES...see **TRACES**	
4859	**MEMPHIS AT SUNRISE**	*Bar-Kays*
3981	**MEN ARE GETTING SCARCE**	*Chairmen Of The Board*
2853	**MEN OF LEARNING**	*Vigrass & Osborne*
5163	**MENDELSSOHN'S 4TH (Second Movement)**	*Apollo 100*
	MERCEDES BENZ...see **(Oh Lord Won't You Buy Me A)**	
456	**MERCY MERCY ME (The Ecology)**	*Marvin Gaye*
3500	**MERRY CHRISTMAS DARLING**	*Carpenters*
2334	**THE MESSAGE**	*Cymande*
3440	**MESSAGE IN A BOTTLE**	*Police*
3128	**MESSAGE IN OUR MUSIC**	*O'Jays*
2583	**MEXICO**	*James Taylor*
5261	**MICHIGAN HARRY SLAUGHTER**	*Wadsworth Mansion*
515	**MIDNIGHT AT THE OASIS**	*Maria Muldaur*
676	**MIDNIGHT BLUE**	*Melissa Manchester*
838	**MIDNIGHT COWBOY**	*Ferrante & Teicher*
3768	**MIDNIGHT FLOWER**	*Four Tops*
5048	**MIDNIGHT LIGHT**	*Le Blanc & Carr*
	MIDNIGHT LOVE AFFAIR	
4957		*Tony Orlando & Dawn*
5119		*Carol Douglas*
2864	**MIDNIGHT MAN**	*James Gang*
	MIDNIGHT RIDER	
1498		*Gregg Allman*
2240		*Joe Cocker*
	MIDNIGHT SHOW	
4308		*Bobby Vinton*
5152		*Ron Dante*
3805	**MIDNIGHT SKY (Part 1)**	*Isley Brothers*
168	**MIDNIGHT TRAIN TO GEORGIA**	*Gladys Knight & The Pips*
2338	**MIDNIGHT WIND**	*John Stewart*
4649	**MIGHT JUST TAKE YOUR LIFE**	*Deep Purple*
1909	**MIGHTY CLOUDS OF JOY**	*B.J. Thomas*
4373	**MIGHTY HIGH**	*Mighty Clouds Of Joy*
1948	**MIGHTY JOE**	*Shocking Blue*
1280	**MIGHTY LOVE (Part 1)**	*Spinners*
2021	**MIGHTY MIGHTY**	*Earth, Wind & Fire*
3873	**MILES AWAY**	*Fotomaker*
3661	**MILITARY MADNESS**	*Graham Nash*
2078	**A MILLION TO ONE**	*Donny Osmond*
5278	**THE MILLIONAIRE**	*Dr. Hook*
2010	**MIND BENDER**	*Stillwater*
1197	**MIND GAMES**	*John Lennon*
4029	**MINNESOTA**	*Northern Light*
1426	**MINUTE BY MINUTE**	*Doobie Brothers*
481	**MIRACLES**	*Jefferson Starship*
1319	**MISDEMEANOR**	*Foster Sylvers*
2313	**MISS AMERICA**	*Mark Lindsay*
83	**MISS YOU**	*Rolling Stones*
3848	**MISSING YOU**	*Luther Ingram*
1894	**MISSISSIPPI**	*John Phillips*
4237	**MISSISSIPPI MAMA**	*Owen B.*
1476	**MISSISSIPPI QUEEN**	*Mountain*
	MISTER...see also **MR.**	
2535	**MISTER CAN'T YOU SEE**	*Buffy Sainte-Marie*
4080	**MISTER MAGIC**	*Grover Washington, Jr.*
4417	**MISTRUSTED LOVE**	*Mistress*
1157	**MISTY**	*Ray Stevens*

	MISTY BLUE	4714	MOVE ME, O WONDROUS MUSIC	657	MY HEART BELONGS TO ME
247	Dorothy Moore		Ray Charles Singers		Barbra Streisand
3390	Joe Simon	1183	MOVIN' Brass Construction		MY HONEY AND ME
4444	MIXED UP GUY Joey Scarbury	1838	MOVIN' ON Bad Company	2885	Luther Ingram
453	MOCKINGBIRD	1354	MOVIN' OUT (Anthony's Song)	4554	Emotions
	Carly Simon & James Taylor		Billy Joel	406	MY LIFE Billy Joel
1006	MONEY Pink Floyd	3020	MOZAMBIQUE Bob Dylan	2350	MY LITTLE LADY Bloodstone
2378	MONEY Gladys Knight & The Pips	2470	MOZART SYMPHONY NO. 40 IN G MINOR K.550, 1ST MOVEMENT	754	MY LITTLE TOWN Simon & Garfunkel
3885	MONEY BACK GUARANTEE				MY LOVE
	Five Man Electrical Band		Waldo De Los Rios	33	Paul McCartney & Wings
733	MONEY HONEY Bay City Rollers		MR….see also MISTER	3721	Margie Joseph
3330	MONEY, MONEY, MONEY ABBA	3600	MR. AND MRS. UNTRUE Candi Staton	3788	MY LOVE IS MUSIC Space
4369	MONEY RUNNER Quincy Jones	77	MR. BIG STUFF Jean Knight	3823	MY MAIN MAN Staple Singers
1904	MONGOOSE Elephant's Memory	2068	MR. BLUE SKY Electric Light Orchestra	1857	MY MAN, A SWEET MAN
1581	MONSTER Steppenwolf	769	MR. BOJANGLES		Millie Jackson
870	MONSTER MASH Bobby (Boris) Pickett & The Crypt-Kickers		Nitty Gritty Dirt Band	765	MY MARIA B.W. Stevenson
		3396	MR. D.J. (5 For The D.J.)	1995	MY MARIE Engelbert Humperdinck
770	MONTEGO BAY Bobby Bloom		Aretha Franklin	415	MY MELODY OF LOVE Bobby Vinton
2041	MOODY BLUE Elvis Presley	412	MR. JAWS Dickie Goodman	3830	MY MERRY-GO-ROUND Johnny Nash
1596	MOON SHADOW Cat Stevens	5303	MR. LIMOUSINE DRIVER	5221	MY MIND KEEPS TELLING ME (That I Really Love You Girl) Eddie Holman
2182	MOON WALK (Part 1) Joe Simon		Grand Funk Railroad		
4685	MOONDANCE Van Morrison	4552	MR. MAGIC MAN Wilson Pickett	1502	MY MISTAKE (Was To Love You)
413	MOONLIGHT FEELS RIGHT Starbuck	2816	MR. MELODY Natalie Cole		Diana Ross & Marvin Gaye
3219	MOONLIGHT SPECIAL Ray Stevens	4657	MR. NATURAL Bee Gees	1267	MY MUSIC Loggins & Messina
3507	MOONSHINE (Friend Of Mine)	3106	MR. PENGUIN (Part 1) Lunar Funk	2933	MY OLD SCHOOL Steely Dan
	John Kay	4582	MR. PRESIDENT Dickie Goodman	3758	MY PART/MAKE IT FUNKY (Part 3)
4891	MORE AND MORE Carly Simon	4474	MR. SKIN Spirit		James Brown
297	MORE, MORE, MORE (Part 1)	5344	MS. GRACE Tymes	4523	MY PEARL Automatic Man
	Andrea True Connection		MULL OF KINTYRE Wings see: GIRLS' SCHOOL	3449	MY PRETENDING DAYS ARE OVER
4831	MORE POWER TO YOU Tommy Tate				Dells
559	MORE THAN A FEELING Boston	4959	MUSIC John Miles	17	MY SHARONA Knack
2183	MORE THAN A WOMAN Tavares	416	MUSIC BOX DANCER Frank Mills		MY SWEET LADY
4832	MORE THAN I CAN STAND	3686	MUSIC EVERYWHERE	1531	Cliff DeYoung
	Bobby Womack		Tufano & Giammarese	3202	John Denver
3001	THE MORE YOU DO IT (The More I Like It Done To Me) Ronnie Dyson	4573	MUSIC EYES Heartsfield		MY SWEET LORD
		4198	MUSIC, HARMONY AND RHYTHM	14	George Harrison
1525	MORNIN' BEAUTIFUL		Brooklyn Dreams	4441	Billy Preston
	Tony Orlando & Dawn	3698	MUSIC IN MY BONES Joe Simon	5037	MY SWEET SUMMER SUITE
3856	MORNIN' MORNIN' Bobby Goldsboro	5237	MUSIC IS LOVE David Crosby		Love Unlimited Orchestra
2973	MORNING Jim Ed Brown	4371	MUSIC IS MY LIFE Helen Reddy	1950	MY THANG James Brown
637	THE MORNING AFTER	4291	THE MUSIC NEVER STOPPED		MY WAY
	Maureen McGovern		Grateful Dead	2104	Elvis Presley
1828	MORNING DANCE Spyro Gyra		MUSKRAT LOVE	2925	Brook Benton
1091	MORNING HAS BROKEN Cat Stevens	165	Captain & Tennille	4572	MY WHEELS WON'T TURN
3631	MORNING MUCH BETTER	2433	America		Bachman-Turner Overdrive
	Ten Wheel Drive With Genya Ravan	2287	MUST BE LOVE James Gang	3745	MY WIFE, THE DANCER
3439	THE MORNING OF OUR LIVES Arkade	4471	MUST HAVE BEEN CRAZY Chicago		Eddie & Dutch
833	MORNING SIDE OF THE MOUNTAIN	1375	MUST OF GOT LOST J. Geils Band		MY WOMAN, MY WOMAN, MY WIFE
	Donny & Marie Osmond	981	MY ANGEL BABY Toby Beau	2473	Marty Robbins
5197	THE MOSQUITO Doors	903	MY BABY LOVES LOVIN' White Plains	5268	Dean Martin
219	THE MOST BEAUTIFUL GIRL	3953	MY BABY'S BABY Liquid Gold	1330	MY WORLD Bee Gees
	Charlie Rich	2330	MY BEST FRIEND'S GIRL Cars		
2736	MOST LIKELY YOU GO YOUR WAY (And I'll Go Mine) Bob Dylan / The Band	4037	MY BEST FRIEND'S WIFE Paul Anka		# N
			MY BOY		
1780	MOST OF ALL B.J. Thomas	1504	Elvis Presley	4732	N.Y., YOU GOT ME DANCING
	MOTHER	2274	Richard Harris		Andrea True Connection
1765	John Lennon / Plastic Ono Band	4305	MY COUNTRY Jud Strunk	648	NADIA'S THEME (The Young And The Restless)
4530	Barbra Streisand	4787	MY CREW Rita Coolidge		
470	MOTHER AND CHILD REUNION	107	MY DING-A-LING Chuck Berry		Barry DeVorzon & Perry Botkin, Jr.
	Paul Simon		MY ELUSIVE DREAMS	1335	THE NAME OF THE GAME ABBA
4799	A MOTHER FOR MY CHILDREN	2006	Bobby Vinton	4438	NAMES, TAGS, NUMBERS & LABELS
	Whispers	2990	Charlie Rich		Association
2354	MOTHER FREEDOM Bread	146	MY EYES ADORED YOU Frankie Valli	5115	NANU, NANU (I Wanna Get Funky Wich You) Daddy Dewdrop
3869	MOTHER-IN-LAW Clarence Carter	1779	MY FAIR SHARE Seals & Crofts		
4607	MOTHER NATURE Temptations	4771	MY FIRST DAY WITHOUT HER	1022	NATHAN JONES Supremes
4790	MOTHER NATURE'S WINE Sugarloaf		Dennis Yost & The Classics IV	1194	NATIVE NEW YORKER Odyssey
1361	MOTORCYCLE MAMA Sailcat	3691	MY GIRL Eddie Floyd	543	NATURAL HIGH Bloodstone
3781	MOVE 'EM OUT Delaney & Bonnie	1229	MY GIRL BILL Jim Stafford	1390	A NATURAL MAN Lou Rawls
		4528	MY GUY Petula Clark		

#	Title	Artist
1566	**NEANDERTHAL MAN**	Hotlegs
1370	**THE NEED TO BE**	Jim Weatherly
4941	**NEEDLES AND PINS**	Smokie
313	**NEITHER ONE OF US (Wants To Be The First To Say Goodbye)**	Gladys Knight & The Pips
3481	**NEON NITES**	Atlanta Rhythm Section
3881	**NEVADA FIGHTER**	Michael Nesmith & The First National Band
3608	**NEVER BEEN ANY REASON**	Head East
621	**NEVER BEEN TO SPAIN**	Three Dog Night
	NEVER CAN SAY GOODBYE	
41		Jackson 5
879		Gloria Gaynor
2002		Isaac Hayes
897	**NEVER ENDING SONG OF LOVE**	Delaney & Bonnie & Friends
4257	**NEVER GET ENOUGH OF YOUR LOVE**	L.T.D.
1016	**NEVER GONNA FALL IN LOVE AGAIN**	Eric Carmen
1747	**NEVER HAD A DREAM COME TRUE**	Stevie Wonder
4671	**NEVER HAD A LOVE**	Pablo Cruise
	NEVER HAVE TO SAY GOODBYE AGAIN...see **WE'LL NEVER HAVE TO SAY GOODBYE AGAIN**	
1847	**NEVER LET HER GO**	David Gates
3591	**NEVER LET HER SLIP AWAY**	Andrew Gold
1762	**NEVER LET YOU GO**	Bloodstone
4986	**NEVER MARRY A RAILROAD MAN**	Shocking Blue
	NEVER MY LOVE	
990		5th Dimension
1168		Blue Swede
3496		Addrisi Brothers
925	**NEVER, NEVER GONNA GIVE YA UP**	Barry White
2481	**NEVER, NEVER, NEVER (Grande, Grande, Grande)**	Shirley Bassey
419	**NEW KID IN TOWN**	Eagles
3185	**NEW ORLEANS**	Staple Singers
2652	**NEW ORLEANS LADIES**	Louisiana's Le Roux
4558	**A NEW ROCK AND ROLL**	Mahogany Rush
2170	**NEW WORLD COMING**	Mama Cass Elliot
4477	**NEW YORK CITY**	Zwol
1217	**NEW YORK GROOVE**	Ace Frehley
5012	**NEWSY NEIGHBORS**	First Choice
2902	**THE NEXT HUNDRED YEARS**	Al Martino
1924	**THE NEXT STEP IS LOVE**	Elvis Presley
4326	**NICE 'N' NAASTY**	Salsoul Orchestra
4065	**NICE, NICE, VERY NICE**	Ambrosia
5032	**NICE TO BE AROUND**	Maureen McGovern
170	**NICE TO BE WITH YOU**	Gallery
1846	**NICKEL SONG**	Melanie
4975	**--THE NICKEL SONG**	New Seekers
260	**THE NIGHT CHICAGO DIED**	Paper Lace
4193	**NIGHT DANCIN'**	Taka Boom
9	**NIGHT FEVER**	Bee Gees
647	**NIGHT MOVES**	Bob Seger
124	**THE NIGHT THE LIGHTS WENT OUT IN GEORGIA**	Vicki Lawrence
325	**THE NIGHT THEY DROVE OLD DIXIE DOWN**	Joan Baez
1486	**NIGHTINGALE**	Carole King
1072	**NIGHTS ARE FOREVER WITHOUT YOU**	England Dan & John Ford Coley
347	**NIGHTS IN WHITE SATIN**	Moody Blues
483	**NIGHTS ON BROADWAY**	Bee Gees
2533	**992 ARGUMENTS**	O'Jays
3413	**9,999,999 TEARS**	Dickey Lee
3717	**1984**	Spirit
5241	**1984**	David Bowie
1982	**1900 YESTERDAY**	Liz Damon's Orient Express
5258	**1927 KANSAS CITY**	Mike Reilly
4327	**90 DAY FREEZE (On Her Love)**	100 Proof Aged In Soul
4140	**99 MILES FROM L.A.**	Albert Hammond
2526	**NO**	Bulldog
2988	**NO ARMS CAN EVER HOLD YOU**	Bobby Vinton
3291	**NO CHANCE**	Moon Martin
	NO CHARGE	
2852		Melba Montgomery
5210		Shirley Caesar
4425	**NO GOOD TO CRY**	Poppy Family
1228	**NO LOVE AT ALL**	B.J. Thomas
5321	**NO LOVE IN THE ROOM**	5th Dimension
786	**NO MATTER WHAT**	Badfinger
1591	**NO MORE MR. NICE GUY**	Alice Cooper
220	**NO MORE TEARS (Enough Is Enough)**	Barbra Streisand / Donna Summer
4341	**NO, NO, JOE**	Silver Convention
393	**NO NO SONG**	Ringo Starr
1524	**NO ONE TO DEPEND ON**	Santana
2803	**NO SAD SONG**	Helen Reddy
3108	**NO SUGAR TONIGHT**	Guess Who
1434	**NO TELL LOVER**	Chicago
447	**NO TIME**	Guess Who
3568	**NO TIME TO LOSE**	Tarney/Spencer Band
3228	**NOBODY**	Doobie Brothers
4686	**NOBODY**	Doucette
4775	**NOBODY BUT YOU**	Kenny Loggins With Jim Messina
78	**NOBODY DOES IT BETTER**	Carly Simon
1685	**NOBODY KNOWS YOU WHEN YOU'RE DOWN AND OUT**	Bobby Womack
4418	**NOBODY (Tellin' Me 'Bout My Baby)**	Charles Wright & The Watts 103rd Street Rhythm Band
4347	**NOBODY WINS**	Brenda Lee
4659	**NORMA JEAN WANTS TO BE A MOVIE STAR**	Sundown Company
4766	**NOT FADE AWAY**	Tanya Tucker
2627	**(not just) KNEE DEEP (Part 1)**	Funkadelic
5300	**NOTHIN' HEAVY**	David Bellamy
4497	**NOTHING BUT A BREEZE**	Jesse Winchester
308	**NOTHING FROM NOTHING**	Billy Preston
3331	**NOTHING SUCCEEDS LIKE SUCCESS**	Bill Deal & The Rhondels
1808	**NOTHING TO HIDE**	Tommy James
1973	**NOW RUN AND TELL THAT**	Denise LaSalle
2828	**NOW THAT WE FOUND LOVE**	Third World
1212	**#9 DREAM**	John Lennon
4025	**NUMBER ONE**	Billy Swan
4001	**NUMBER WONDERFUL**	Rock Flowers
4220	**NURSERY RHYMES (Part 1)**	People's Choice
	NUTBUSH CITY LIMITS	
1592		Ike & Tina Turner
4406		Bob Seger
4819	**NUTROCKER**	Emerson, Lake & Palmer

O

#	Title	Artist
2873	**OB-LA-DI, OB-LA-DA**	Beatles
4868	**OCEAN OF THOUGHTS AND DREAMS**	Dramatics
3638	**ODE TO BILLIE JOE**	Bobbie Gentry
5263	**ODYSSEY PARK ROCK**	Al Capps Band
4783	**OH ATLANTA**	Little Feat
338	**OH, BABE, WHAT WOULD YOU SAY?**	Hurricane Smith
2161	**OH! DARLING**	Robin Gibb
149	**OH GIRL**	Chi-Lites
2206	**OH HAPPY DAY**	Glen Campbell
3141	**OH HONEY**	Delegation
5169	**OH HOW HAPPY**	Skyliners
2135	**OH LA DE DA**	Staple Singers
4516	**(Oh Lord Won't You Buy Me A) MERCEDES BENZ**	Goose Creek Symphony
4561	**OH LORI**	Alessi
2717	**OH ME, OH MY (Dreams In My Arms)**	Al Green
	OH ME OH MY (I'm A Fool For You Baby)	
1281		Lulu
3904		Aretha Franklin
798	**OH MY MY**	Ringo Starr
5015	**OH MY MY**	Monkees
	OH NO, NOT MY BABY	
3259		Merry Clayton
3278		Rod Stewart [P]
3115	**OH, SINGER**	Jeannie C. Riley
954	**OH VERY YOUNG**	Cat Stevens
	OH WELL	
2549		Rockets
3366		Fleetwood Mac **(Part 1)**
2070	**OH WHAT A DAY**	Dells
2392	**OH WHAT A NIGHT FOR DANCING**	Barry White
3883	**OH WOMAN OH WHY**	Paul McCartney
5093	**O-H-I-O**	Ohio Players
1103	**OHIO**	Crosby, Stills, Nash & Young
924	**OLD DAYS**	Chicago
2609	**OLD FASHIONED BOY (You're The One)**	Stallion
546	**AN OLD FASHIONED LOVE SONG**	Three Dog Night
3270	**OLD HOME FILLER-UP AN' KEEP ON-A-TRUCKIN' CAFE**	C.W. McCall
2036	**OLD MAN**	Neil Young

	OLD SCHOOLYARD...see (Remember The Days Of The)
2427	**OLD TIME ROCK & ROLL** *Bob Seger & The Silver Bullet Band*
5183	**OLENA** *Don Nix*
2275	**ON A NIGHT LIKE THIS** *Bob Dylan*
3982	**ON AND OFF (Part 1)** *Anacostia*
533	**ON AND ON** *Stephen Bishop*
934	**ON AND ON** *Gladys Knight & The Pips*
1084	**ON BROADWAY** *George Benson*
2464	**ON THE BEACH (In The Summertime)** *5th Dimension*
2664	**ON THE BORDER** *Al Stewart*
3031	**ON THE SHELF** *Donny & Marie*
4008	**ON THE STRIP** *Paul Nicholas*
4058	**ON THE WRONG TRACK** *Kevin Lamb*
4494	**ONCE A FOOL** *Kiki Dee*
976	**ONCE YOU GET STARTED** *Rufus Feat. Chaka Khan*
4023	**ONCE YOU HIT THE ROAD** *Dionne Warwicke*
1803	**ONCE YOU UNDERSTAND** *Think*
35	**ONE BAD APPLE** *Osmonds*
3053	**ONE BEAUTIFUL DAY** *Ecstasy, Passion & Pain*
	ONE CHAIN (Don't Make No Prison)
2377	*Four Tops* [P]
3760	*Santana*
3532	**ONE DAY AT A TIME** *Marilyn Sellars*
5105	**ONE DAY OF YOUR LIFE** *Andy Williams*
	ONE FINE DAY
4285	*Rita Coolidge*
4772	*Julie*
1198	**ONE FINE MORNING** *Lighthouse*
1049	**ONE HELL OF A WOMAN** *Mac Davis*
2394	**ONE LAST KISS** *J. Geils Band*
4099	**ONE LAST TIME** *Glen Campbell*
61	**ONE LESS BELL TO ANSWER** *5th Dimension*
2018	**ONE LESS SET OF FOOTSTEPS** *Jim Croce*
4226	**ONE LIFE TO LIVE** *Manhattans*
1987	**ONE LOVE IN MY LIFETIME** *Diana Ross*
1114	**ONE MAN BAND** *Three Dog Night*
1518	**ONE MAN BAND (Plays All Alone)** *Ronnie Dyson*
3238	**ONE MAN PARADE** *James Taylor*
741	**ONE MAN WOMAN/ONE WOMAN MAN** *Paul Anka with Odia Coates*
4036	**ONE MAN'S LEFTOVERS (Is Another Man's Feast)** *100 Proof Aged In Soul*
1129	**ONE MONKEY DON'T STOP NO SHOW (Part 1)** *Honey Cone*
4621	**ONE MORE CHANCE** *Ocean*
3870	**ONE MORE MINUTE** *Saint Tropez*
4983	**ONE MORE TOMORROW** *Henry Gross*
3635	**(One More Year Of) DADDY'S LITTLE GIRL** *Ray Sawyer*
1728	**ONE NATION UNDER A GROOVE (Part 1)** *Funkadelic*
3307	**ONE NIGHT AFFAIR** *Jerry Butler*
4692	**ONE NIGHT STAND** *Magic Lanterns*
782	**ONE OF A KIND (Love Affair)** *Spinners*
186	**ONE OF THESE NIGHTS** *Eagles*
2531	**ONE PIECE AT A TIME** *Johnny Cash & The Tennessee Three*
3052	**ONE TEAR** *Eddie Kendricks*
	137 DISCO HEAVEN...see **LIGHT MY FIRE**
	ONE TIN SOLDIER
1152	*Coven* **(The Legend of Billy Jack)** [version 1]
2097	*Original Caste*
3735	*Coven* **(The Legend of Billy Jack)** [version 2]
797	**ONE TOKE OVER THE LINE** *Brewer & Shipley*
1714	**ONE WAY OR ANOTHER** *Blondie*
5042	**ONE WAY SUNDAY** *Mark-Almond*
3527	**ONE-WAY TICKET** *Tyrone Davis*
4867	**ONE WOMAN BAND** *Carol Chase*
3088	**ONLY IN YOUR HEART** *America*
5299	**ONLY LOVE** *Bill Quateman*
	ONLY LOVE CAN BREAK YOUR HEART
1595	*Neil Young*
5165	*Jackie DeShannon*
1877	**ONLY LOVE IS REAL** *Carole King*
4610	**ONLY ONE LOVE IN MY LIFE** *Ronnie Milsap*
4950	**ONLY ONE SONG** *Sha Na Na*
4963	**ONLY ONE WOMAN** *Nigel Olsson*
507	**ONLY SIXTEEN** *Dr. Hook*
1907	**ONLY THE GOOD DIE YOUNG** *Billy Joel*
3913	**ONLY THE LUCKY** *Walter Egan*
4835	**ONLY THE STRONG SURVIVE** *REO Speedwagon*
867	**ONLY WOMEN** *Alice Cooper*
893	**ONLY YESTERDAY** *Carpenters*
619	**ONLY YOU** *Ringo Starr*
3121	**ONLY YOU CAN** *Fox*
	ONLY YOU KNOW AND I KNOW
1575	*Delaney & Bonnie*
2342	*Dave Mason*
1403	**OOH BABY** *Gilbert O'Sullivan*
796	**OOH BABY BABY** *Linda Ronstadt*
3055	**OOH BOY** *Rose Royce*
532	**O-o-h CHILD** *Five Stairsteps*
2293	**OOH POO PAH DOO** *Ike & Tina Turner*
3663	**OPEN SESAME (Part 1)** *Kool & The Gang*
4118	**OPEN THE DOOR (Song For Judith)** *Judy Collins*
2676	**OPEN UP MY HEART** *Dells*
1746	**OPERATOR** *Manhattan Transfer*
1366	**OPERATOR (That's Not The Way It Feels)** *Jim Croce*
3954	**OPHELIA** *Band*
3766	**THE OTHER WOMAN** *Vicki Lawrence*
1109	**OUR DAY WILL COME** *Frankie Valli*
1532	**OUR HOUSE** *Crosby, Stills, Nash & Young*
5239	**OUR LAST SONG TOGETHER** *Bo Donaldson & The Heywoods*
1355	**OUR LOVE** *Natalie Cole*
663	**(Our Love) DON'T THROW IT ALL AWAY** *Andy Gibb*
3738	**OUR LOVE IS INSANE** *Desmond Child & Rouge*
3171	**OUR WORLD** *Blue Mink*
977	**OUT IN THE COUNTRY** *Three Dog Night*
4247	**OUT OF THE DARKNESS** *David Crosby / Graham Nash*
1643	**OUT OF THE QUESTION** *Gilbert O'Sullivan*
3699	**OUT OF TIME** *Rolling Stones*
317	**OUTA-SPACE** *Billy Preston*
	OUTLAW MAN
2655	*Eagles*
3796	*David Blue*
1897	**OUTSIDE WOMAN** *Bloodstone*
2793	**OVER AND OVER** *Delfonics*
1442	**OVER MY HEAD** *Fleetwood Mac*
1912	**OVER THE HILLS AND FAR AWAY** *Led Zeppelin*
4197	**OVER THE RAINBOW** *Gary Tanner*
1837	**OVERNIGHT SENSATION (Hit Record)** *Raspberries*
1278	**OVERTURE FROM TOMMY (A Rock Opera)** *Assembled Multitude*
1116	**OYE COMO VA** *Santana*

P

3122	**PAIN (Part 1)** *Ohio Players*
1814	**PAINTED LADIES** *Ian Thomas*
4137	**PALACE GUARD** *Rick Nelson & The Stone Canyon Band*
1548	**PALOMA BLANCA** *George Baker Selection*
2149	**PAPA DON'T TAKE NO MESS (Part 1)** *James Brown*
	PAPA WAS A ROLLIN' STONE
348	*Temptations*
5161	*Undisputed Truth*
2247	**PAPER MACHE** *Dionne Warwick*
708	**PAPER ROSES** *Marie Osmond*
2423	**PARADISE BY THE DASHBOARD LIGHT** *Meat Loaf*
3872	**PARANOID** *Black Sabbath*
2884	**PARDON ME SIR** *Joe Cocker*
1815	**PART OF THE PLAN** *Dan Fogelberg*
4491	**A PART OF YOU** *Brenda & The Tabulations*
1401	**PART-TIME LOVE** *Elton John*
1703	**PART TIME LOVE** *Ann Peebles*
1825	**PART TIME LOVE** *Gladys Knight & The Pips*
4399	**PART TIME LOVE** *Kerry Chater*
3159	**PART TWO (Let A Man Come In And Do The Popcorn)** *James Brown*
4700	**PARTY** *Van McCoy*
4919	**PARTY LINE** *Andrea True Connection*
4877	**PARTY MUSIC** *Pat Lundi*
4105	**PASS THE PEAS** *JB's*
3314	**A PASSION PLAY (Edit #8)** *Jethro Tull*
4978	**PASSPORT TO THE FUTURE** *Jean Jacques Perrey*
2900	**PATCH OF BLUE** *Frankie Valli & The 4 Seasons*
193	**PATCHES** *Clarence Carter*
1034	**PAY TO THE PIPER** *Chairmen Of The Board*
1530	**THE PAYBACK (Part 1)** *James Brown*
4906	**PEACE IN THE VALLEY OF LOVE** *Persuaders*
2162	**PEACE OF MIND** *Boston*
2404	**PEACE PIPE** *B.T. Express*
555	**PEACE TRAIN** *Cat Stevens*
1823	**PEACE WILL COME (According To Plan)** *Melanie*

#	Title	Artist
1134	PEACEFUL	Helen Reddy
1539	PEACEFUL EASY FEELING	Eagles
4227	THE PEACEMAKER	Albert Hammond
2048	PEARL	Tommy Roe
885	PEG	Steely Dan
3677	PEGGY SUE	Beach Boys
4526	PEOPLE ARE CHANGIN'	Timmy Thomas
	PEOPLE GOTTA BE FREE...see A CHANGE IS GONNA COME	
1983	PEOPLE GOTTA MOVE	Gino Vannelli
3907	PEOPLE IN LOVE	10cc
1425	PEOPLE MAKE THE WORLD GO ROUND	Stylistics
2128	PEOPLE OF THE SOUTH WIND	Kansas
4507	THE PEOPLE TREE	Sammy Davis, Jr.
3022	PEPPER BOX	Peppers
4255	PERCOLATOR	Hot Butter
5350	PETER GUNN	Deodato
3161	PETER PIPER	Frank Mills
3345	PHANTOM WRITER	Gary Wright
4077	PHILADELPHIA	B.B. King
82	PHILADELPHIA FREEDOM	Elton John Band
166	PHOTOGRAPH	Ringo Starr
1415	PIANO MAN	Billy Joel
130	PICK UP THE PIECES	AWB
2264	A PIECE OF PAPER	Gladstone
1546	PIECES OF APRIL	Three Dog Night
3062	THE PILL	Loretta Lynn
301	PILLOW TALK	Sylvia
5333	PIN THE TAIL ON THE DONKEY	Newcomers
4593	PINBALL	Brian Protheroe
1559	PINBALL WIZARD/SEE ME, FEEL ME	New Seekers
5254	A PIRATE LOOKS AT FORTY	Jimmy Buffett
2906	A PLACE IN THE SUN	Pablo Cruise
4731	PLAIN AND SIMPLE GIRL	Garland Green
2218	THE PLASTIC MAN	Temptations
3722	PLATINUM HEROES	Bruce Foster
1387	PLAY ME	Neil Diamond
2787	PLAY ON LOVE	Jefferson Starship
1590	PLAY SOMETHING SWEET (Brickyard Blues)	Three Dog Night
151	PLAY THAT FUNKY MUSIC	Wild Cherry
3798	THE PLAYER (Part 1)	First Choice
288	PLAYGROUND IN MY MIND	Clint Holmes
5256	PLAYING YOUR GAME, BABY	Barry White
2662	PLEASE COME HOME FOR CHRISTMAS	Eagles
737	PLEASE COME TO BOSTON	Dave Loggins
2904	PLEASE, DADDY	John Denver
278	PLEASE DON'T GO	K C & The Sunshine Band
2191	PLEASE DON'T LEAVE	Lauren Wood
5133	PLEASE DON'T TELL ME HOW THE STORY ENDS	Ronnie Milsap
272	PLEASE MR. PLEASE	Olivia Newton-John
228	PLEASE MR. POSTMAN	Carpenters
4126	PLEASE, MR. PRESIDENT	Paula Webb
2723	PLEASE PARDON ME (You Remind Me Of A Friend)	Rufus Feat. Chaka Khan
639	POETRY MAN	Phoebe Snow
2223	POINT IT OUT	Smokey Robinson & The Miracles
1388	POINT OF KNOW RETURN	Kansas
2871	POOL OF BAD LUCK	Joe Simon
3667	POOR BOY	Casey Kelly
2255	POOR POOR PITIFUL ME	Linda Ronstadt
359	POP MUZIK	M
1497	POP THAT THANG	Isley Brothers
846	POPCORN	Hot Butter
3622	POPS, WE LOVE YOU (A Tribute To Father)	Diana Ross, Marvin Gaye, Smokey Robinson & Stevie Wonder
3395	POPSICLE TOES	Michael Franks
	POR AMOR VIVIREMOS...see LOVE WILL KEEP US TOGETHER	
3005	PORTRAIT (He Knew)	Kansas
3674	POSTCARD	Who
2361	POWDER BLUE MERCEDES QUEEN	Raiders
1906	THE POWER OF GOLD	Dan Fogelberg / Tim Weisberg
	POWER OF LOVE	
938		Joe Simon
3460		Martha Reeves
1181	POWER TO THE PEOPLE	John Lennon Plastic Ono Band
4622	PRAY FOR ME	Intruders
4789	PREACHER MAN	Impressions
201	PRECIOUS AND FEW	Climax
1439	PRECIOUS LOVE	Bob Welch
931	PRECIOUS, PRECIOUS	Jackie Moore
3653	THE PRETENDER	Jackson Browne
1882	PRETTY AS YOU FEEL	Jefferson Airplane
2518	PRETTY GIRLS	Melissa Manchester
2086	PRETTY LADY	Lighthouse
3360	PRETZEL LOGIC	Steely Dan
5226	THE PRIDE (Part 1)	Isley Brothers
3524	PRIMROSE LANE	O.C. Smith
4683	THE PRINCESS AND THE PUNK	Barry Mann
4498	PRISONER (Captured By Your Eyes)	L.A. Jets
2228	PRISONER OF YOUR LOVE	Player
3367	PROBLEM CHILD	Mark Lindsay
1489	PROMISED LAND	Elvis Presley
1025	PROMISES	Eric Clapton & His Band
584	PROUD MARY	Ike & Tina Turner
2129	THE PROUD ONE	Osmonds
3168	PROVE IT ALL NIGHT	Bruce Springsteen
541	PSYCHEDELIC SHACK	Temptations
	PUPPET MAN	
1263		Tom Jones
1840		5th Dimension
417	PUPPY LOVE	Donny Osmond
	PUSH AND PULL...see (Do The)	
2399	PUSHBIKE SONG	Mixtures
3756	PUT A LITTLE LOVE AWAY	Emotions
	PUT IT WHERE YOU WANT IT	
2279		Crusaders
4865		Nino & April
4343	PUT ON YOUR SHOES AND WALK	Clarence Carter
2220	PUT OUT THE LIGHT	Joe Cocker
109	PUT YOUR HAND IN THE HAND	Ocean
1395	PUT YOUR HANDS TOGETHER	O'Jays
3834	PUT YOUR HEAD ON MY SHOULDER	Leif Garrett

Q

#	Title	Artist
2654	QUE SERA, SERA (Whatever Will Be, Will Be)	Mary Hopkin
3945	QUEEN OF CLUBS	K.C. & The Sunshine Band
3522	QUEEN OF MY SOUL	Average White Band
4627	QUEEN OF THE ROLLER DERBY	Leon Russell
1357	QUESTION	Moody Blues
5191	QUESTIONS	Bang
1231	QUESTIONS 67 AND 68	Chicago
4054	QUICK, FAST, IN A HURRY	New York City
3849	QUIET STORM	Smokey Robinson

R

#	Title	Artist
4490	RACE AMONG THE RUINS	Gordon Lightfoot
1069	RADAR LOVE	Golden Earring
3035	RADIOACTIVE	Gene Simmons
2766	RAG DOLL	Sammy Johns
3332	RAG MAMA RAG	Band
2874	RAGS TO RICHES	Elvis Presley
1101	RAIN DANCE	Guess Who
3551	RAIN, OH RAIN	Fools Gold
2457	RAINBOW	Marmalade
2513	RAINBOW CONNECTION	Kermit (Jim Henson)
3003	RAINBOW IN YOUR EYES	Leon & Mary Russell
5107	RAINBOW MAN	Looking Glass
7	RAINDROPS KEEP FALLIN' ON YOUR HEAD	B.J. Thomas
2837	RAINING IN MY HEART	Leo Sayer
1961	RAINY DAY PEOPLE	Gordon Lightfoot
330	RAINY DAYS AND MONDAYS	Carpenters
1866	RAINY JANE	Davy Jones
276	RAINY NIGHT IN GEORGIA	Brook Benton
3718	RAISE A LITTLE HELL	Trooper
2672	RAISED ON ROBBERY	Joni Mitchell
2109	RAISED ON ROCK	Elvis Presley
364	RAMBLIN' MAN	Allman Brothers Band
365	THE RAPPER	Jaggerz
2567	REACH	Orleans
2898	REACH FOR IT	George Duke
1254	REACH OUT AND TOUCH (Somebody's Hand)	Diana Ross
	REACH OUT I'LL BE THERE	
1668		Diana Ross
3392		Gloria Gaynor [P]
5322		New Seekers
3659	REACH OUT YOUR HAND	Brotherhood Of Man
3668	REACHING FOR THE SKY	Peabo Bryson

#	Title	Artist
3997	REACHING FOR THE WORLD	Harold Melvin & The Blue Notes
1872	READY	Cat Stevens
3917	READY FOR THE 80's	Village People
3320	READY FOR THE TIMES TO GET BETTER	Crystal Gayle
4751	READY OR NOT	Helen Reddy
918	READY TO TAKE A CHANCE AGAIN	Barry Manilow
4389	REAL MAN	Todd Rundgren
4620	THE REAL ME	Who
2536	A REAL MOTHER FOR YA	Johnny "Guitar" Watson
4007	REALITY	James Brown
	THE REAPER...see (Don't Fear)	
3029	REASON TO BE	Kansas
3791	REASON TO BELIEVE	Rod Stewart
2939	REBEL REBEL	David Bowie
4709	RECONSIDER ME	Narvel Felts
4741	THE RED BACK SPIDER	Brownsville Station
3757	RED EYE BLUES	Redeye
3378	RED HOT	Robert Gordon
5073	RED RED WINE	Vic Dana
3369	REDNECK FRIEND	Jackson Browne
1649	REELIN' & ROCKIN'	Chuck Berry
772	REELING IN THE YEARS	Steely Dan
592	REFLECTIONS OF MY LIFE	Marmalade
2246	THE RELAY	Who
2205	REMEMBER (Christmas)	Nilsson
939	REMEMBER ME	Diana Ross
3657	REMEMBER ME	Willie Nelson
2398	(Remember The Days Of The) OLD SCHOOLYARD	Cat Stevens
2784	REMEMBER (Walking In The Sand)	Louise Goffin
1891	REMEMBER WHAT I TOLD YOU TO FORGET	Tavares
452	REMINISCING	Little River Band
2360	RENDEZVOUS	Hudson Brothers
1334	RENEGADE	Styx
2750	RENEGADE	Michael Murphey
4446	RESCUE ME	Cher
933	RESPECT YOURSELF	Staple Singers
	RESURRECTION SHUFFLE	
2192		Ashton, Gardner & Dyke
2624		Tom Jones
52	REUNITED	Peaches & Herb
2813	RHAPSODY IN BLUE	Deodato
3725	RHAPSODY IN WHITE	Love Unlimited Orchestra
845	RHIANNON (Will You Ever Win)	Fleetwood Mac
68	RHINESTONE COWBOY	Glen Campbell
2769	RHUMBA GIRL	Nicolette Larson
2935	RHYME TYME PEOPLE	Kool & The Gang
198	RICH GIRL	Daryl Hall & John Oates
3256	RIDE A WHITE SWAN	Tyrannosaurus Rex
435	RIDE CAPTAIN RIDE	Blues Image
1512	RIDE 'EM COWBOY	Paul Davis
3279	RIDE, SALLY, RIDE	Dennis Coffey
5057	RIDE THE TIGER	Jefferson Starship
2283	RIDE WITH ME	Steppenwolf
1124	RIDERS ON THE STORM	Doors
4002	RIDIN' MY THUMB TO MEXICO	Johnny Rodriguez
5259	RIDIN' THE STORM OUT	REO Speedwagon
194	RIGHT BACK WHERE WE STARTED FROM	Maxine Nightingale
860	RIGHT DOWN THE LINE	Gerry Rafferty
1253	RIGHT ON THE TIP OF MY TONGUE	Brenda & The Tabulations
886	RIGHT PLACE WRONG TIME	Dr. John
1190	THE RIGHT THING TO DO	Carly Simon
742	RIGHT TIME OF THE NIGHT	Jennifer Warnes
2363	RIKI TIKI TAVI	Donovan
396	RIKKI DON'T LOSE THAT NUMBER	Steely Dan
57	RING MY BELL	Anita Ward
1690	RING THE LIVING BELL	Melanie
	RINGS	
1251		Cymarron
2509		Lobo
4931		Reuben Howell
2744	RIP OFF	Laura Lee
204	RISE	Herb Alpert
	RITE AWAY...see (Everybody Wanna Get Rich)	
2563	RIVER	Joe Simon
1306	RIVER DEEP-MOUNTAIN HIGH	Supremes & Four Tops
2372	THE RIVER OF LOVE	B.W. Stevenson
5080	RIVER ROAD	Uncle Dog
3083	RIVER'S RISIN'	Edgar Winter
2922	RIVERS OF BABYLON	Boney M
4039	ROADHOUSE BLUES	Doors
4670	ROBERTA	Bones
	ROCK AND ROLL...see also ROCK 'N ROLL	
2568	ROCK AND ROLL	Led Zeppelin
522	ROCK AND ROLL (Part 2)	Gary Glitter
	ROCK AND ROLL ALL NITE	
1326		Kiss (Live Version)
3377		Kiss
3520	ROCK AND ROLL DANCIN'	Beckmeier Brothers
506	ROCK AND ROLL HEAVEN	Righteous Brothers
1536	ROCK AND ROLL, HOOCHIE KOO	Rick Derringer
1879	ROCK AND ROLL LOVE LETTER	Bay City Rollers
1026	ROCK AND ROLL LULLABY	B.J. Thomas
932	ROCK AND ROLL MUSIC	Beach Boys
2737	ROCK AND ROLL NEVER FORGETS	Bob Seger
3727	ROCK & ROLL RUNAWAY	Ace
4059	ROCK AND ROLL STAR	Champagne
	ROCK AROUND THE CLOCK...see (We're Gonna)	
3016	ROCK ME	Nick Gilder
2063	ROCK ME BABY	David Cassidy
240	ROCK ME GENTLY	Andy Kim
2697	ROCK ME ON THE WATER	Jackson Browne
	ROCK 'N ROLL...see also ROCK AND ROLL	
5101	ROCK 'N ROLL	Detroit
962	ROCK 'N' ROLL FANTASY	Bad Company
2625	A ROCK 'N' ROLL FANTASY	Kinks
	ROCK N' ROLL (I Gave You The Best Years Of My Life)	
1441		Mac Davis
4851		Terry Jacks
4972		Kevin Johnson [P]
1679	ROCK 'N ROLL SOUL	Grand Funk Railroad
334	ROCK ON	David Essex
768	ROCK STEADY	Aretha Franklin
254	ROCK THE BOAT	Hues Corporation
367	ROCK YOUR BABY	George McCrae
998	ROCKET MAN	Elton John
2564	ROCKET RIDE	Kiss
1005	THE ROCKFORD FILES	Mike Post
1778	ROCKIN' ALL OVER THE WORLD	John Fogerty
4026	ROCKIN' AND ROLLIN' ON THE STREETS OF HOLLYWOOD	Buddy Miles
811	ROCKIN' CHAIR	Gwen McCrae
487	ROCKIN' PNEUMONIA -- BOOGIE WOOGIE FLU	Johnny Rivers
44	ROCKIN' ROBIN	Michael Jackson
1421	ROCKIN' ROLL BABY	Stylistics
2032	ROCKIN' SOUL	Hues Corporation
307	ROCK'N ME	Steve Miller
1062	ROCKY	Austin Roberts
634	ROCKY MOUNTAIN HIGH	John Denver
4648	ROCKY MOUNTAIN MUSIC	Eddie Rabbitt
1017	ROCKY MOUNTAIN WAY	Joe Walsh
3243	ROLAND THE ROADIE AND GERTRUDE THE GROUPIE	Dr. Hook & The Medicine Show
2208	ROLENE	Moon Martin
4850	ROLL AWAY THE STONE	Leon Russell
4011	ROLL IN MY SWEET BABY'S ARMS	Hank Wilson
3473	ROLL ON	New Colony Six
1104	ROLL ON DOWN THE HIGHWAY	Bachman-Turner Overdrive
1960	ROLL OVER BEETHOVEN	Electric Light Orchestra
3184	ROLL WITH THE CHANGES	REO Speedwagon
2779	ROLLER	April Wine
4988	ROLLER COASTER	Blood, Sweat & Tears
5108	ROLLIN' WITH THE FLOW	Charlie Rich
4250	ROLLING DOWN A MOUNTAINSIDE	Main Ingredient
3672	ROMEO	Mr. Big
	ROMEO AND JULIET...see (Just Like)	
3432	ROOM FULL OF ROSES	Mickey Gilley
5014	ROOM TO MOVE	John Mayall
3389	"ROOTS" MEDLEY	Quincy Jones
4335	ROOTS, ROCK, REGGAE	Bob Marley & The Wailers
3241	ROSALIE	Sam Neely
4872	ROSANNA	Dennis Yost & The Classics IV
56	ROSE GARDEN	Lynn Anderson
1073	ROUNDABOUT	Yes
2165	ROXANNE	Police
5137	ROXY ROLLER	Sweeney Todd
	RUB IT IN	
1676		Billy "Crash" Craddock
2851		Layng Martine

#	Title	Artist
2919	**RUBBER BISCUIT**	Blues Brothers
2478	**RUBBER BULLETS**	10 C.C.
1285	**RUBBER DUCKIE**	Ernie
466	**THE RUBBERBAND MAN**	Spinners
3087	**RUBY, BABY**	Billy "Crash" Craddock
2449	**RUBY TUESDAY**	Melanie
4895	**RUMOR AT THE HONKY TONK**	Spellbound
4338	**RUMOUR HAS IT**	Donna Summer
2117	**RUN FOR HOME**	Lindisfarne
4290	**RUN HOME GIRL**	Sad Café
411	**RUN JOEY RUN**	David Geddes
1999	**RUN RUN RUN**	Jo Jo Gunne
2424	**RUN SALLY RUN**	Cuff Links
3474	**RUN THROUGH THE JUNGLE**	Creedence Clearwater Revival
1029	**RUN TO ME**	Bee Gees
1521	**RUNAROUND SUE**	Leif Garrett
1345	**RUNAWAY**	Jefferson Starship
	RUNAWAY	
2560		Charlie Kulis
3205		Bonnie Raitt
2651		Dawn - / HAPPY TOGETHER
3876	**RUNAWAY LOVE**	Linda Clifford
1220	**RUNNIN' AWAY**	Sly & The Family Stone
4045	**RUNNIN' BACK TO SASKATOON**	Guess Who
806	**RUNNING ON EMPTY**	Jackson Browne
1929	**THE RUNWAY**	Grass Roots
5036	**RUST NEVER SLEEPS (My My, Hey Hey [Into The Black])**	Neil Young & Crazy Horse

S

#	Title	Artist
1123	**SOS**	ABBA
95	**SAD EYES**	Robert John
3669	**SAD EYES**	Brooklyn Dreams
3466	**SAD GIRL**	Carl Graves
1582	**SAD SWEET DREAMER**	Sweet Sensation
2754	**SADIE**	Spinners
4221	**SAFE AT HOME**	Souther, Hillman, Furay Band
2795	**SAIL AROUND THE WORLD**	David Gates
236	**SAIL ON**	Commodores
2907	**SAIL ON SAILOR**	Beach Boys
2897	**SAILING**	Rod Stewart
3425	**SAILING SHIPS**	Mesa
4230	**SALLY**	Grand Funk Railroad
3406	**SALLY FROM SYRACUSE**	Stu Nunnery
3111	**SALLY G**	Paul McCartney & Wings
4987	**SALSOUL HUSTLE**	Salsoul Orchestra
2071	**SAM**	Olivia Newton-John
2492	**THE SAME LOVE THAT MADE ME LAUGH**	Bill Withers
3167	**SAME THING IT TOOK**	Impressions
4487	**SAN BERNADINO**	Christie
4785	**SANDY**	Hollies
3925	**SANTA CLAUS IS COMIN' TO TOWN**	Jackson 5
4998	**SANTO DOMINGO**	Sandpipers
552	**SARA SMILE**	Daryl Hall & John Oates
5035	**SATIN RED AND BLACK VELVET WOMAN**	Dave Mason
1642	**SATIN SHEETS**	Jeanne Pruett
4456	**SATIN SHEETS**	Bellamy Brothers
1793	**SATIN SOUL**	Love Unlimited Orchestra
2868	**SATISFACTION**	Smokey Robinson & The Miracles
4233	**SATISFACTION GUARANTEED (Or Take Your Love Back)**	Harold Melvin & The Bluenotes
583	**SATURDAY IN THE PARK**	Chicago
1626	**SATURDAY MORNING CONFUSION**	Bobby Russell
205	**SATURDAY NIGHT**	Bay City Rollers
2600	**SATURDAY NIGHT SPECIAL**	Lynyrd Skynyrd
2638	**SATURDAY NIGHT, SUNDAY MORNING**	Thelma Houston
849	**SATURDAY NIGHT'S ALRIGHT FOR FIGHTING**	Elton John
1564	**SATURDAY NITE**	Earth, Wind & Fire
2506	**SATURDAYNIGHT**	Herman Brood
2280	**SAVANNAH NIGHTS**	Tom Johnston
1562	**SAVE IT FOR A RAINY DAY**	Stephen Bishop
4639	**SAVE ME**	Silver Convention
	SAVE ME	
4072		Merrilee Rush
4464		Donna McDaniel
	SAVE THE COUNTRY	
1704		5th Dimension
4135		Thelma Houston
1422	**SAVE THE LAST DANCE FOR ME**	DeFranco Family
2603	**SAVE YOUR KISSES FOR ME**	Brotherhood Of Man
5202	**SAVE YOUR SUGAR FOR ME**	Tony Joe White
4856	**SAVED BY THE GRACE OF YOUR LOVE**	Sons Of Champlin
4013	**SAW A NEW MORNING**	Bee Gees
443	**SAY, HAS ANYBODY SEEN MY SWEET GYPSY ROSE**	Dawn Feat. Tony Orlando
3633	**SAY MAYBE**	Neil Diamond
997	**SAY YOU LOVE ME**	Fleetwood Mac
1450	**SAY YOU'LL STAY UNTIL TOMORROW**	Tom Jones
2054	**SCHOOL BOY CRUSH**	AWB
3581	**SCHOOL OF LIFE**	Tommy Tate
5304	**SCHOOL'S BACK**	Philadelphia
597	**SCHOOL'S OUT**	Alice Cooper
420	**SCORPIO**	Dennis Coffey & The Detroit Guitar Band
3827	**SCOTCH ON THE ROCKS**	Band Of The Black Watch
3837	**SCRATCH**	Crusaders
5271	**SCRATCH MY BACK (And Mumble In My Ear)**	Clarence Carter
2525	**SCREAMING NIGHT HOG**	Steppenwolf
	SE SI BON...see WHISPERING	
3660	**SEA CRUISE**	Johnny Rivers
1012	**SEALED WITH A KISS**	Bobby Vinton
2945	**SEARCHING FOR A THRILL**	Starbuck
3266	**SEASIDE WOMAN**	Suzy & The Red Stripes
161	**SEASONS IN THE SUN**	Terry Jacks
	SECOND AVENUE	
2452		Garfunkel
2596		Tim Moore
1766	**SECRET LOVE**	Freddy Fender
2786	**SECRETARY**	Betty Wright
5176	**SECRETS**	Sutherland Brothers & Quiver
	SEE ME, FEEL ME	
736		Who
	see also **PINBALL WIZARD**	
5243	**SEE THE LIGHT**	Flame
4707	**SEE YOU WHEN I GIT THERE**	Lou Rawls
2236	**THE SEEKER**	Who
4934	**THE SEEKER**	Dolly Parton
4742	**SEEMS LIKE I CAN'T LIVE WITH YOU, BUT I CAN'T LIVE WITHOUT YOU**	Guess Who
3428	**SEEMS LIKE I GOTTA DO WRONG**	Whispers
5143	**SEND A LITTLE LOVE MY WAY**	Anne Murray
1176	**SEND IN THE CLOWNS**	Judy Collins
574	**SEND ONE YOUR LOVE**	Stevie Wonder
718	**SENTIMENTAL LADY**	Bob Welch
1189	**SEPARATE WAYS**	Elvis Presley
728	**SEPTEMBER**	Earth, Wind & Fire
1259	**SERPENTINE FIRE**	Earth, Wind & Fire
4251	**SEVEN LONELY NIGHTS**	Four Tops
1856	**7-6-5-4-3-2-1 (Blow Your Whistle)**	Gary Toms Empire
2631	**SEXY**	MFSB
3216	**SEXY IDA (Part 1)**	Ike & Tina Turner
1763	**SEXY MAMA**	Moments
2824	**SEXY, SEXY, SEXY**	James Brown
4849	**SGT. PEPPER'S LONELY HEARTS CLUB BAND/WITH A LITTLE HELP FROM MY FRIENDS**	Beatles
5339	**SHA LA BOOM BOOM**	Bobby Bloom
704	**SHA-LA-LA (Make Me Happy)**	Al Green
3790	**SHACKIN' UP**	Barbara Mason
3298	**SHADES OF GREEN**	Flaming Ember
4	**SHADOW DANCING**	Andy Gibb
2034	**SHADOWS IN THE MOONLIGHT**	Anne Murray
3958	**SHADY LADY**	Shepstone & Dibbens
5348	**SHAKE A LEG**	Sea Level
3504	**SHAKE AND DANCE WITH ME**	Con Funk Shun
980	**SHAKE IT**	Ian Matthews
4449	**SHAKE IT WELL**	Dramatics
245	**(Shake, Shake, Shake) SHAKE YOUR BOOTY**	K C & The Sunshine Band
524	**SHAKE YOUR BODY (Down To The Ground)**	Jacksons
593	**SHAKE YOUR GROOVE THING**	Peaches & Herb
2620	**SHAKE YOUR RUMP TO THE FUNK**	Bar-Kays
1966	**SHAKEDOWN CRUISE**	Jay Ferguson
5200	**SHAKER SONG**	Spyro Gyra
1606	**SHAKEY GROUND**	Temptations
	SHAMBALA	
256		Three Dog Night
3915		B.W. Stevenson
790	**SHAME**	Evelyn "Champagne" King
964	**SHAME, SHAME, SHAME**	Shirley (And Company)
504	**SHANNON**	Henry Gross
691	**SHARE THE LAND**	Guess Who

	SHARING THE NIGHT TOGETHER	477	SHOW ME THE WAY	4391	SITTIN' ON A TIME BOMB (Waitin' For
392	Dr. Hook		Peter Frampton		The Hurt To Come) Honey Cone
5068	Arthur Alexander	468	THE SHOW MUST GO ON	3927	(Sittin' On) THE DOCK OF THE BAY
5302	Lenny Le Blanc		Three Dog Night		Sammy Hagar
2359	SHATTERED Rolling Stones	2846	SHOW YOU THE WAY TO GO	1634	SITTING Cat Stevens
2242	SHAVING CREAM Benny Bell		Jacksons	3636	SITTING IN LIMBO Don Brown
1607	SHE Tommy James & The Shondells		SHOWDOWN	5188	SIX PACKS A DAY Billy Lemmons
4915	SHE Southcote	2353	Electric Light Orchestra	4132	SIX WHITE HORSES Tommy Cash
748	SHE BELIEVES IN ME Kenny Rogers	3351	Odia Coates	3911	SIXTEEN REASONS LaVerne & Shirley
1769	SHE BELONGS TO ME Rick Nelson &	2234	SHOWER THE PEOPLE James Taylor	3578	SIXTEEN TONS Don Harrison Band
	The Stone Canyon Band	3100	(Shu-Doo-Pa-Poo-Poop) LOVE BEING		SIXTY MINUTE MAN
	SHE CALLED ME BABY...see HE CALLED		YOUR FOOL Travis Wammack	2788	Clarence Carter
	ME BABY	662	SIDESHOW Blue Magic	4057	Rufus Thomas (Part 2)
1942	SHE CAME IN THROUGH THE		SIGNED, SEALED, DELIVERED I'M	4225	SKATING AWAY ON THE THIN ICE OF
	BATHROOM WINDOW Joe Cocker		YOURS		THE NEW DAY Jethro Tull
2724	SHE CRIED Lettermen	145	Stevie Wonder	1206	SKIN TIGHT Ohio Players
1382	SHE DID IT Eric Carmen	1364	Peter Frampton [P]	606	SKY HIGH Jigsaw
2554	SHE DIDN'T DO MAGIC Lobo	576	SIGNS Five Man Electrical Band	2759	SKYBIRD Tony Orlando & Dawn
2969	SHE DIDN'T KNOW (She Kept On	34	SILLY LOVE SONGS Wings	2850	SKYBIRD Neil Diamond
	Talking) Dee Dee Warwick	3138	SILLY MILLY Blue Swede	2619	SLAUGHTER Billy Preston
	SHE LETS HER HAIR DOWN (Early In	3215	SILLY, SILLY, FOOL Dusty Springfield	2894	SLEEPIN' Diana Ross
	The Morning)	3067	SILLY WASN'T I Valerie Simpson	4321	SLEEPWALKER Kinks
2748	Tokens	1347	SILVER BIRD Mark Lindsay	4423	SLICK Willie Hutch
4774	Gene Pitney	2807	SILVER DREAMS Babys	1682	SLIDE Slave
3472	SHE LOVES TO BE IN LOVE Charlie	4764	SILVER HEELS Blaze	4805	SLIP 'N SLIDE Rufus
3324	SHE SAID YES Wilson Pickett	2938	SILVER LADY David Soul	4150	SLIP AWAY Ian Lloyd
4340	SHE'S A DISCO QUEEN Oliver Sain	4067	SILVER LINING Player	696	SLIP SLIDIN' AWAY Paul Simon
71	SHE'S A LADY Tom Jones	2015	SILVER MOON Michael Nesmith &	3265	SLIPPED, TRIPPED AND FELL IN LOVE
4924	(She's A) VERY LOVELY WOMAN		The First National Band		Clarence Carter
	Linda Ronstadt	3705	SILVER STAR Four Seasons	1852	SLIPPERY WHEN WET Commodores
1978	SHE'S ALL I GOT Freddie North	4580	SILVER THREADS AND GOLDEN		SLIPPING INTO DARKNESS
1449	SHE'S ALWAYS A WOMAN Billy Joel		NEEDLES Linda Ronstadt	609	War [P]
	SHE'S GONE	5136	SIMONE Henry Gross	3970	Ramsey Lewis
513	Daryl Hall & John Oates	4394	A SIMPLE GAME Four Tops	5195	SLIPPING INTO CHRISTMAS
3317	Tavares	2746	A SIMPLE MAN Lobo		Leon Russell
5198	SHE'S GOT A WHOLE NUMBER	3587	SIMPLE SONG OF FREEDOM	1470	SLOW DANCIN' DON'T TURN ME ON
	Keith Herman		Buckwheat		Addrisi Brothers
4191	SHE'S GOT TO BE A SAINT Ray Price	2865	SIMPLY CALL IT LOVE Gene Chandler		SLOW DANCING...see SWAYIN' TO THE
5204	(She's Just A) FALLEN ANGEL Starz	3078	SINCE I DON'T HAVE YOU		MUSIC
759	SHE'S NOT JUST ANOTHER WOMAN		Art Garfunkel	4857	SLOW DOWN Crow
	8th Day		SINCE I FELL FOR YOU	4334	SLOW MOTION (Part 1)
1652	SHE'S NOT THERE Santana	2752	Laura Lee		Johnny Williams
3709	SHE'S READY Spiral Starecase	4209	Charlie Rich	1175	SLOW RIDE Foghat
4940	SHEENA IS A PUNK ROCKER Ramones	5325	Hodges, James & Smith - /I'M FAL-	3723	SLOWDOWN John Miles
1674	SHILO Neil Diamond		LING IN LOVE	2042	THE SLY, SLICK, AND THE WICKED
955	SHINE A LITTLE LOVE	2616	SINCE I MET YOU BABY		Lost Generation
	Electric Light Orchestra		Freddy Fender	1878	SMALL BEGINNINGS Flash
1554	SHININ' ON Grand Funk		SINCE YOU BEEN GONE	1773	SMARTY PANTS First Choice
181	SHINING STAR Earth, Wind & Fire	3214	Rainbow	2029	SMILIN' Sly & The Family Stone
1261	SHIPS Barry Manilow	3353	Head East	206	SMILING FACES SOMETIMES
4858	SHO NUFF BOOGIE (Part 1)	4744	--SINCE YOU'VE BEEN GONE		Undisputed Truth
	Sylvia & The Moments		Cherie & Marie Currie	1037	SMOKE FROM A DISTANT FIRE
3603	SHOE SHOE SHINE Dynamic Superiors	467	SING Carpenters		Sanford/Townsend Band
2731	SHOES Brook Benton	3743	SING Tony Orlando & Dawn	1391	SMOKE GETS IN YOUR EYES
4786	SHOES Reparata	694	SING A SONG Earth, Wind & Fire		Blue Haze
1264	SHOESHINE BOY Eddie Kendricks	4614	SING A SONG David Clayton-Thomas	472	SMOKE ON THE WATER Deep Purple
600	SHOP AROUND Captain & Tennille	2249	SING A SONG FOR FREEDOM	3923	SMOKE! SMOKE! SMOKE! (That
148	SHORT PEOPLE Randy Newman		Frijid Pink		Cigarette) Commander Cody & His
4380	SHOTGUN SHUFFLE Sunshine Band	2593	SING FOR THE DAY Styx		Lost Planet Airmen
4518	SHOULD ANYBODY ASK Garry Bonner	4107	SING HIGH--SING LOW Anne Murray	428	SMOKIN' IN THE BOY'S ROOM
5320	SHOULD I TIE A YELLOW RIBBON	3066	SING IT, SHOUT IT Starz		Brownsville Station
	ROUND THE OLE OAK TREE? (THE	4101	SINNER MAN Sarah Dash	5181	SNEAKIN' SALLY THROUGH THE ALLEY
	ANSWER) Connie Francis [R: TIE A	465	SIR DUKE Stevie Wonder		Robert Palmer
	YELLOW RIBBON...OLE OAK TREE]	429	SISTER GOLDEN HAIR America	2710	SNEAKIN' UP BEHIND YOU
4811	SHOUT IT OUT B.T. Express	2440	SISTER JAMES		Brecker Brothers
1733	SHOUT IT OUT LOUD Kiss		Nino Tempo & 5th Ave. Sax	4854	SNEAKY SNAKE Tom T. Hall
120	SHOW AND TELL Al Wilson	1830	SISTER MARY ELEPHANT (Shudd-Up!)	2704	SNOW BLIND FRIEND Steppenwolf
2322	SHOW BIZ KIDS Steely Dan		Cheech & Chong	636	SNOWBIRD Anne Murray
1902	SHOW ME HOW Emotions	2455	SIT YOURSELF DOWN Stephen Stills	1729	SO CLOSE Jake Holmes

#	Title	Artist
3178	SO EXCITED	B.B. King
1188	SO FAR AWAY	Carole King
1789	SO GOOD, SO RIGHT	Brenda Russell
4539	SO HARD LIVIN' WITHOUT YOU	Airwaves
3991	SO HIGH (Rock Me Baby And Roll Me Away)	Dave Mason
2914	SO IN LOVE	Curtis Mayfield
626	SO IN TO YOU	Atlanta Rhythm Section
3864	SO LONG	Firefall
3049	SO LONG DIXIE	Blood, Sweat & Tears
5056	SO LONG, MARIANNE	Brian Hyland
4813	SO MANY PEOPLE	Chase
2124	SO MUCH LOVE	Faith, Hope & Charity
2591	SO SAD THE SONG	Gladys Knight & The Pips
1414	SO VERY HARD TO GO	Tower Of Power
1493	SO YOU ARE A STAR	Hudson Brothers
2641	SO YOU WIN AGAIN	Hot Chocolate
3944	SO YOUNG, SO BAD	Starz
4833	SOFT AND WET	Prince
2022	SOFTLY WHISPERING I LOVE YOU	English Congregation
4936	SOLEDAD	Eric Burdon & Jimmy Witherspoon
1577	SOLITAIRE	Carpenters
1545	SOLITARY MAN	Neil Diamond
4374	SOLSBURY HILL	Peter Gabriel
3518	SOLUTION FOR POLLUTION	Charles Wright & The Watts 103rd Street Rhythm Band
5113	SOME BEAUTIFUL	Jack Wild
5311	SOME BROKEN HEARTS NEVER MEND	Don Williams
4130	SOME DAY I'LL BE A FARMER	Melanie
4693	SOME ENCHANTED EVENING	Jane Olivor
2199	SOME GUYS HAVE ALL THE LUCK	Persuaders
744	SOME KIND OF WONDERFUL	Grand Funk
3246	SOME OF SHELLY'S BLUES	Nitty Gritty Dirt Band
4817	SOME THINGS A MAN'S GOTTA DO	Shango
1035	SOMEBODY TO LOVE	Queen
536	SOMEBODY'S BEEN SLEEPING	100 Proof Aged In Soul
3933	SOMEBODY'S GETTIN' IT	Johnnie Taylor
4384	SOMEBODY'S GOTTA WIN, SOMEBODY'S GOTTA LOSE	Controllers
1448	SOMEBODY'S WATCHING YOU	Little Sister
3354	SOMEDAY	Dave Loggins
1855	SOMEDAY NEVER COMES	Creedence Clearwater Revival
346	SOMEONE SAVED MY LIFE TONIGHT	Elton John
3232	SOMEONE TO LAY DOWN BESIDE ME	Linda Ronstadt
2532	SOMEONE WHO CARES	Kenny Rogers & The First Edition
3623	SOMETHIN' 'BOUT 'CHA	Latimore
4103	SOMETHIN' 'BOUT YOU BABY I LIKE	Trini Lopez
	SOMETHING	
4091		Shirley Bassey
4951		Booker T. & The M.G.'s
3275	SOMETHING ABOUT YOU	Le Blanc & Carr
4862	SOMETHING BETTER	Chilliwack
1444	SOMETHING BETTER TO DO	Olivia Newton-John
1654	SOMETHING HE CAN FEEL	Aretha Franklin
5270	SOMETHING IN YOU	Manitoba
4480	SOMETHING THERE IS ABOUT YOU	Bob Dylan
503	SOMETHING'S BURNING	Kenny Rogers & The First Edition
978	SOMETHING'S WRONG WITH ME	Austin Roberts
2880	SOMETIMES	Facts Of Life
4852	SOMETIMES IT'S GOT TO RAIN	Jackie Moore
405	SOMETIMES WHEN WE TOUCH	Dan Hill
4725	SOMEWHERE BETWEEN LOVE AND TOMORROW	Roy Clark
	SOMEWHERE IN THE NIGHT	
1417		Barry Manilow
1432		Helen Reddy
3584		Batdorf & Rodney
	SON OF MY FATHER	
2155		Giorgio
4345		Chicory
1749	SON OF SAGITTARIUS	Eddie Kendricks
2681	SON OF SHAFT	Bar-Kays
4729	SONG FOR ANNA (Chanson D'Anna)	Herb Ohta
4889	A SONG FOR YOU	Andy Williams
5020	SONG FROM M*A*S*H	Al DeLory
2201	A SONG I'D LIKE TO SING	Kris Kristofferson & Rita Coolidge
1141	A SONG OF JOY (Himno A La Alegria)	Miguel Rios
2269	SONG ON THE RADIO	Al Stewart
4642	SONG SELLER	Raiders
239	SONG SUNG BLUE	Neil Diamond
2226	SONGBIRD	Barbra Streisand
3086	SONGMAN	Cashman & West
1724	SOOLAIMÓN (African Trilogy II)	Neil Diamond
855	SOONER OR LATER	Grass Roots
2774	SOONER OR LATER	Impressions
1832	SOPHISTICATED LADY (She's A Different Lady)	Natalie Cole
3571	SORROW	David Bowie
4368	SORRY DOESN'T ALWAYS MAKE IT RIGHT	Diana Ross
767	SORRY SEEMS TO BE THE HARDEST WORD	Elton John
	SOUL AND INSPIRATION...see (You're My)	
	SOUL MAKOSSA	
1783		Manu Dibango
2341		Afrique
1171	SOUL MAN	Blues Brothers
1858	SOUL POWER (Part 1)	James Brown
2789	SOUL SHAKE	Delaney & Bonnie & Friends
2105	SOUL SONG	Joe Stampley
3857	SOUL TRAIN "75"	Soul Train Gang
5102	SOULSVILLE	Isaac Hayes
4844	SOUND AND VISION	David Bowie
	THE SOUND OF SILENCE	
5174		Peaches & Herb
5211		Paul Simon
2254	SOUR SUITE	Guess Who
1889	THE SOUTH'S GONNA DO IT	Charlie Daniels Band
229	SOUTHERN NIGHTS	Glen Campbell
4953	SOUVENIRS	Voyage
1349	SPACE ODDITY	David Bowie
731	SPACE RACE	Billy Preston
1774	SPACEMAN	Nilsson
5347	SPACESHIP SUPERSTAR	Prism
371	SPANISH HARLEM	Aretha Franklin
3134	SPANISH HUSTLE	Fatback Band
5157	SPANISH WINE	Lou Christie
3906	SPARKLE AND SHINE	Clique
	SPEAK SOFTLY LOVE...see LOVE THEME FROM "THE GODFATHER"	
1332	SPEAK TO THE SKY	Rick Springfield
5084	SPECIAL MEMORY	Jerry Butler
2826	SPECIAL SOMEONE	Heywoods
4461	SPIDER JIVING	Andy Fairweather Low
418	SPIDERS & SNAKES	Jim Stafford
	SPILL THE WINE	
118		Eric Burdon & War
2432		Isley Brothers
2466	SPINNING AROUND (I Must Be Falling In Love)	Main Ingredient
4426	SPINNING WHEEL (Part 1)	James Brown
1935	SPIRIT IN THE DARK	Aretha Franklin
3357	SPIRIT IN THE NIGHT	Manfred Mann's Earth Band
25	SPIRIT IN THE SKY	Norman Greenbaum
1423	SPIRIT OF THE BOOGIE	Kool & The Gang
1508	SPOOKY	Atlanta Rhythm Section
4492	SPRING AFFAIR	Donna Summer
5162	SPRING RAIN	Silvetti
2232	SPRINGTIME MAMA	Henry Gross
829	SQUEEZE BOX	Who
1245	STAGGER LEE	Tommy Roe
	STAND BY ME	
1933		John Lennon
3008		David & Jimmy Ruffin
1430	STAND BY YOUR MAN	Candi Staton
693	STAND TALL	Burton Cummings
	STANDING...see AMERICA	
2197	STANDING AT THE END OF THE LINE	Lobo
5146	STANDING HERE WONDERING WHICH WAY TO GO	Marion Williams
3959	STANDING IN FOR JODY	Johnnie Taylor
4307	STANDING IN THE RAIN	James Gang
1371	STAR	Stealers Wheel
1573	STAR BABY	Guess Who
3754	STAR LOVE	Cheryl Lynn
3409	STAR ON A TV SHOW	Stylistics
1538	STAR WARS (Main Title)	John Williams/London Symphony Orchestra
123	--STAR WARS THEME/CANTINA BAND	Meco
5013	THE "STAR WARS STARS"	Force
3326	STARMAN	David Bowie

#	Title	Artist
4083	STARRY EYES	Records
4922	STARTED OUT DANCING, ENDED UP MAKING LOVE	Alan O'Day
930	STARTING ALL OVER AGAIN	Mel & Tim
1835	STAY / THE LOAD OUT*	Jackson Browne
2875	STAY	Rufus/Chaka Khan
5171	STAY AWAY FROM ME	Sylvers
3748	STAY AWAY FROM ME (I Love You Too Much)	Major Lance
548	STAY AWHILE	Bells
4156	STAY AWHILE	Continental Miniatures
3155	STAY THE NIGHT	Faragher Brothers
960	STAY WITH ME	Faces
19	STAYIN' ALIVE	Bee Gees
1680	STEAL AWAY	Johnnie Taylor
2835	STEALER	Free
3120	STEALIN'	Uriah Heep
2805	STEALING IN THE NAME OF THE LORD	Paul Kelly
5331	STEALING LOVE	Emotions
5118	STEALING MOMENTS FROM ANOTHER WOMAN'S LIFE	Glass House
4533	STEAM HEAT	Pointer Sisters
1160	STEAMROLLER BLUES	Elvis Presley
4690	STEP BY STEP	Kiki Dee
1938	STEP BY STEP	Joe Simon
3966	STEP INTO CHRISTMAS	Elton John
3244	STEPPIN' IN A SLIDE ZONE	Moody Blues
2821	STEPPIN' OUT	Neil Sedaka
1297	STEPPIN' OUT (Gonna Boogie Tonight)	Tony Orlando & Dawn
724	STICK-UP	Honey Cone
336	STILL	Commodores
2899	STILL CRAZY AFTER ALL THESE YEARS	Paul Simon
4904	STILL THE LOVIN' IS FUN	B.J. Thomas
652	STILL THE ONE	Orleans
649	STILL THE SAME	Bob Seger & The Silver Bullet Band
1121	STILL WATER (Love)	Four Tops
3990	STILLSANE	Carolyne Mas
859	STIR IT UP	Johnny Nash
2053	STIR IT UP AND SERVE IT	Tommy Roe
3126	STONE BLUE	Foghat
3024	STONE COLD SOBER	Crawler
4584	STONE OF YEARS	Emerson, Lake & Palmer
4738	STONED COWBOY	Fantasy
489	STONED LOVE	Supremes
2629	STONED OUT OF MY MIND	Chi-Lites
2271	STONED TO THE BONE (Part 1)	James Brown
1187	STONES	Neil Diamond
695	STONEY END	Barbra Streisand
5315	S.T.O.P. (Stop)	Lorelei
856	STOP AND SMELL THE ROSES	Mac Davis
3565	STOP DOGGIN' ME	Johnnie Taylor
3470	STOP! IN THE NAME OF LOVE	Margie Joseph
1833	STOP, LOOK, LISTEN (To Your Heart)	Stylistics
1822	STOP THE WAR NOW	Edwin Starr
5289	STOP THE WORLD AND LET ME OFF	Flaming Ember
2993	STOP TO START	Blue Magic
4258	STOP, WAIT & LISTEN	Circus
5276	STORIES??	Chakachas
2210	STORMY	Santana
5158	STORMY MONDAY	Latimore
1090	THE STORY IN YOUR EYES	Moody Blues
3506	STORYBOOK CHILDREN (Daybreak)	Bette Midler
1373	STRAIGHT ON	Heart
1697	STRAIGHT SHOOTIN' WOMAN	Steppenwolf
5023	STRANGE	Jellyroll
1118	STRANGE MAGIC	Electric Light Orchestra
1050	STRANGE WAY	Firefall
940	STRAWBERRY LETTER 23	Brothers Johnson
141	THE STREAK	Ray Stevens
1777	STREET CORNER SERENADE	Wet Willie
2107	STREET LIFE	Crusaders
2116	STREET SINGIN'	Lady Flash
4682	STREET TALK (Var. II)	B. C. G. (B. C. Generation)
1867	STRUTTIN'	Billy Preston
423	STUCK IN THE MIDDLE WITH YOU	Stealers Wheel
1754	STUFF LIKE THAT	Quincy Jones
758	STUMBLIN' IN	Suzi Quatro & Chris Norman
1172	SUAVECITO	Malo
3592	SUB-ROSA SUBWAY	Klaatu
2809	SUBSTITUTE	Clout
2734	SUCH A NIGHT	Dr. John
1687	SUCH A WOMAN	Tycoon
2233	SUGAR BABY LOVE	Rubettes
523	SUGAR DADDY	Jackson 5
3511	SUGAR LUMP	Leon Haywood
2196	SUGAR PIE GUY (Part 1)	Joneses
1369	SUGAR SUGAR	Wilson Pickett
5166	SUITE: MAN AND WOMAN	Tony Cole
646	SULTANS OF SWING	Dire Straits
1146	SUMMER	War
	SUMMER BREEZE	
721		Seals & Crofts
3619		Isley Brothers (Part 1)
4809	SUMMER IN THE CITY	Quincy Jones
571	SUMMER NIGHTS	John Travolta, Olivia Newton-John & Cast
	SUMMER OF '42...see THEME FROM "SUMMER OF '42"	
1550	SUMMER SAND	Dawn
3673	SUMMER SUN	Jamestown Massacre
1336	SUMMER (The First Time)	Bobby Goldsboro
5219	SUMMERTIME (Part 1)	Bill Hemmans & Clays Composite
1314	SUMMERTIME BLUES	Who
3415	SUN GODDESS	Ramsey Lewis and Earth, Wind & Fire
4938	A SUNDAY KIND OF LOVE	Lenny Welch
2383	SUNDAY MORNING COMING DOWN	Johnny Cash
4272	SUNDAY MORNING SUNSHINE	Harry Chapin
4985	SUNDAY SUNRISE	Anne Murray
246	SUNDOWN	Gordon Lightfoot
2251	SUNFLOWER	Glen Campbell
2348	SUNNY DAYS	Lighthouse
2352	SUNRISE	Eric Carmen
3839	SUNSET STRIP	Ray Stevens
427	SUNSHINE	Jonathan Edwards
2118	SUNSHINE	Archies
4357	SUNSHINE	Mickey Newbury
4761	SUNSHINE	Enchantment
257	SUNSHINE ON MY SHOULDERS	John Denver
3475	SUNSHINE ROSES	Gene Cotton
5173	SUNSHINE SHIP	Arthur, Hurley & Gottlieb
1132	SUPER BAD (Part 1 & Part 2)	James Brown
2510	SUPER FLY MEETS SHAFT	John & Ernest
659	SUPERFLY	Curtis Mayfield
2009	SUPERMAN	Donna Fargo
3072	SUPERMAN	Ides Of March
	SUPERMAN	
2229		Herbie Mann
3984		Celi Bee & The Buzzy Bunch
	see also (WISH I COULD FLY LIKE)	
1097	SUPERNATURAL THING (Part 1)	Ben E. King
142	SUPERSTAR	Carpenters
595	SUPERSTAR (From "Jesus Christ")	Murray Head
2571	SUPERSTAR	Paul Davis
1178	SUPERSTAR (Remember How You Got Where You Are)	Temptations
108	SUPERSTITION	Stevie Wonder
1818	SUPERWOMAN (Where Were You When I Needed You)	Stevie Wonder
1692	SURE AS I'M SITTIN' HERE	Three Dog Night
4183	SURE FEELS GOOD	Elvin Bishop
	SURE KNOW SOMETHING	Kiss
	SURFIN' U.S.A.	
2092		Leif Garrett [P]
3090		Beach Boys
2756	SURRENDER	Diana Ross
4565	SURRENDER	Cheap Trick
3297	SURVIVOR	Cindy Bullens
1377	SUSPICIONS	Eddie Rabbitt
3842	SUSPICIOUS MINDS	Dee Dee Warwick
4235	SUZIE GIRL	Redbone
1971	SWAMP WITCH	Jim Stafford
578	SWAYIN' TO THE MUSIC (Slow Dancin')	Johnny Rivers
3767	--SLOW DANCING	Funky Kings
653	SWEARIN' TO GOD	Frankie Valli
614	SWEET AND INNOCENT	Donny Osmond
4292	SWEET BABY	Donnie Elbert
2351	SWEET CAROLINE (Good Times Never Seemed So Good)	Bobby Womack
1745	SWEET CHARLIE BABE	Jackie Moore
776	SWEET CITY WOMAN	Stampeders
2203	SWEET EMOTION	Aerosmith
2212	SWEET FEELING	Candi Staton
3176	SWEET HARMONY	Smokey Robinson
689	SWEET HITCH-HIKER	Creedence Clearwater Revival
756	SWEET HOME ALABAMA	Lynyrd Skynyrd
2391	SWEET INSPIRATION/WHERE YOU LEAD	Barbra Streisand

#	Title	Artist
949	SWEET LIFE	Paul Davis
4939	SWEET LORRAINE	Uriah Heep
679	SWEET LOVE	Commodores
4356	SWEET LOVING MAN	Morris Albert
3019	SWEET LUI-LOUISE	Ironhorse
690	SWEET MARY	Wadsworth Mansion
2848	SWEET MAXINE	Doobie Brothers
3253	SWEET MUSIC MAN	Kenny Rogers
877	SWEET SEASONS	Carole King
3602	SWEET SIXTEEN	B.B. King
2136	SWEET STICKY THING	Ohio Players
1271	SWEET SURRENDER	John Denver
1300	SWEET SURRENDER	Bread
2294	SWEET, SWEET SMILE	Carpenters
5178	SWEET SWEETHEART	Bobby Vee
1456	SWEET TALKIN' WOMAN	Electric Light Orchestra
451	SWEET THING	Rufus Feat. Chaka Khan
2444	SWEET UNDERSTANDING LOVE	Four Tops
2049	SWEETHEART	Engelbert Humperdinck
3300	SWEETS FOR MY SWEET	Tony Orlando
2834	SWING YOUR DADDY	Jim Gilstrap
1328	SWINGTOWN	Steve Miller Band
3199	SYLVIA	Focus
380	SYLVIA'S MOTHER	Dr. Hook & The Medicine Show
4509	SYMPATHY	Rare Bird
2958	(The System Of) DOCTOR TARR AND PROFESSOR FETHER	Alan Parsons Project

T

#	Title	Artist
175	T.S.O.P. (The Sound Of Philadelphia)	MFSB
629	TAKE A CHANCE ON ME	ABBA
3421	TAKE A CLOSER LOOK AT THE WOMAN YOU'RE WITH	Wilson Pickett
2702	TAKE A HAND	Rick Springfield
1839	TAKE A LOOK AROUND	Temptations
1947	TAKE A LOOK AROUND	Smith
3929	TAKE GOOD CARE OF HER	Elvis Presley
5021	TAKE IT ANY WAY YOU WANT IT	Outlaws
4450	TAKE IT BACK	J. Geils Band
851	TAKE IT EASY	Eagles
3123	TAKE IT LIKE A MAN	Bachman-Turner Overdrive
4848	TAKE IT OFF HIM AND PUT IT ON ME	Clarence Carter
4746	TAKE IT OFF THE TOP	Dixie Dregs
3056	TAKE IT SLOW (Out In The Country)	Lighthouse
531	TAKE IT TO THE LIMIT	Eagles
3978	TAKE LIFE A LITTLE EASIER	Rodney Allen Rippy
3365	TAKE ME	Grand Funk Railroad
3566	TAKE ME BACK TO CHICAGO	Chicago
4314	TAKE ME BAK 'OME	Slade
2243	TAKE ME GIRL, I'M READY	Jr. Walker & The All Stars
4929	TAKE ME HOME	Balcones Fault
1139	TAKE ME HOME	Cher
100	TAKE ME HOME, COUNTRY ROADS	John Denver
1153	TAKE ME IN YOUR ARMS (Rock Me)	Doobie Brothers
3162	TAKE ME TO THE KAPTIN	Prism
3753	TAKE ME TO THE NEXT PHASE	Isley Brothers
	TAKE ME TO THE RIVER	
1881	Talking Heads (Edit)	
2872	Syl Johnson	
5030	TAKE ME TO YOUR HEART	Monkey Meeks
5139	TAKE ME WITH YOU	Honey Cone
4429	TAKE THAT TO THE BANK	Shalamar
1255	TAKE THE LONG WAY HOME	Supertramp
951	TAKE THE MONEY AND RUN	Steve Miller
4386	THE TAKER	Waylon Jennings
777	TAKIN' CARE OF BUSINESS	Bachman-Turner Overdrive
1202	TAKIN' IT TO THE STREETS	Doobie Brothers
4052	TALK IT OVER IN THE MORNING	Anne Murray
1272	TALKING IN YOUR SLEEP	Crystal Gayle
3339	TALKING IN YOUR SLEEP	Gordon Lightfoot
2505	TALKING LOUD AND SAYING NOTHING (Part 1)	James Brown
2195	TANGERINE	Salsoul Orchestra
2595	TANGLED UP IN BLUE	Bob Dylan
4923	TAOS NEW MEXICO	R. Dean Taylor
2256	TARKIO ROAD	Brewer & Shipley
1211	TAURUS	Dennis Coffey & The Detroit Guitar Band
1303	TAXI	Harry Chapin
1162	TEACH YOUR CHILDREN	Crosby, Stills, Nash & Young
1325	TEAR THE ROOF OFF THE SUCKER (Give Up The Funk)	Parliament
39	THE TEARS OF A CLOWN	Smokey Robinson & The Miracles
2225	TEDDY BEAR	Red Sovine
1688	TEDDY BEAR SONG	Barbara Fairchild
4377	TEDDY BEAR'S LAST RIDE	Diana Williams
4073	TEEN ANGEL	Wednesday
1893	TEENAGE LAMENT '74	Alice Cooper
3825	TEENAGE LOVE AFFAIR	Rick Derringer
3655	TELEGRAM SAM	T. Rex
556	TELEPHONE LINE	Electric Light Orchestra
1715	TELEPHONE MAN	Meri Wilson
3451	TELL 'EM WILLIE BOY 'S A'COMIN'	Tommy James
1959	TELL HER LOVE HAS FELT THE NEED	Eddie Kendricks
2217	TELL HER SHE'S LOVELY	El Chicano
1270	TELL IT ALL BROTHER	Kenny Rogers & The First Edition
4641	TELL IT LIKE IT IS	Andy Williams
4301	TELL LAURA I LOVE HER	Johnny T. Angel
5114	TELL MAMA	Savoy Brown
1641	TELL ME A LIE	Sami Jo
433	TELL ME SOMETHING GOOD	Rufus
3569	TELL ME THIS IS A DREAM	Delfonics
3477	TELL THE WORLD HOW I FEEL ABOUT 'CHA BABY	Harold Melvin & The Blue Notes
2325	TEMMA HARBOUR	Mary Hopkin
794	TEMPTATION EYES	Grass Roots
4005	TEN TO EIGHT	David Castle
1235	TENNESSEE BIRD WALK	Jack Blanchard & Misty Morgan
3458	TENTH AVENUE FREEZE-OUT	Bruce Springsteen
2604	TEQUILA SUNRISE	Eagles
4802	TEXAS	Charlie Daniels Band
5292	THANK GOD AND GREYHOUND	Roy Clark
5043	THANK GOD FOR YOU BABY	PG&E
227	THANK GOD I'M A COUNTRY BOY	John Denver
2586	THANK GOD IT'S FRIDAY	Love & Kisses
3515	THANK YOU BABY	Stylistics
80	THANK YOU (Falettinme Be Mice Elf Agin)	Sly & The Family Stone
1241	THANK YOU FOR BEING A FRIEND	Andrew Gold
2075	THANKS FOR SAVING MY LIFE	Billy Paul
3323	THANKS FOR THE SMILES	Charlie Ross
542	THAT LADY (Part 1)	Isley Brothers
3806	THAT MAGIC TOUCH	Angel
4021	THAT ONCE IN A LIFETIME	Demis Roussos
	THAT SAME OLD FEELING	
1943	Pickettywitch	
2606	Fortunes	
3530	THAT SONG IS DRIVING ME CRAZY	Tom T. Hall
1135	THAT'LL BE THE DAY	Linda Ronstadt
2460	THAT'S HOW LOVE GOES	Jermaine Jackson
3098	THAT'S NOT HOW IT GOES	Bloodstone
580	THAT'S ROCK 'N' ROLL	Shaun Cassidy
4808	THAT'S THE SOUND THAT LONELY MAKES	Tavares
2489	THAT'S THE WAY A WOMAN IS	Messengers
5250	THAT'S THE WAY GOD PLANNED IT	Billy Preston
1613	THAT'S THE WAY I FEEL ABOUT CHA	Bobby Womack
94	THAT'S THE WAY (I Like It)	K.C. & The Sunshine Band
5116	THAT'S THE WAY I WANT OUR LOVE	Joe Simon
882	THAT'S THE WAY I'VE ALWAYS HEARD IT SHOULD BE	Carly Simon
1214	THAT'S THE WAY OF THE WORLD	Earth, Wind & Fire
4415	THAT'S WHAT FRIENDS ARE FOR	B.J. Thomas
3949	THAT'S WHAT LOVE WILL MAKE YOU DO	Little Milton
2033	THAT'S WHEN THE MUSIC TAKES ME	Neil Sedaka
1252	THAT'S WHERE I WENT WRONG	Poppy Family
2114	THAT'S WHERE THE HAPPY PEOPLE GO	Trammps

3942 THAT'S WHY I LOVE YOU *Andrew Gold*	2046 THERE IT IS *Tyrone Davis*	2317 THIS TIME I'M GONE FOR GOOD *Bobby Blue Bland*
3468 THAT'S WHY YOU REMEMBER *Kenny Karen*	2456 THERE IT IS (Part 1) *James Brown*	1346 THIS TIME I'M IN IT FOR LOVE *Player*
3045 THAT'S YOUR SECRET *Sea Level*	3858 THERE WILL COME A DAY (I'm Gonna Happen To You) *Smokey Robinson*	3534 THIS TIME IT'S REAL *Tower Of Power*
THEM CHANGES	1709 THERE WON'T BE ANYMORE *Charlie Rich*	803 THIS WILL BE *Natalie Cole*
4557 *Buddy Miles*	2867 THERE WON'T BE NO COUNTRY MUSIC (There Won't Be No Rock 'N' Roll) *C.W. McCall*	2258 THIS WORLD *Staple Singers*
5312 *Buddy Miles & The Freedom Express*		3951 THOSE WERE THE DAYS *Carroll O'Connor & Jean Stapleton*
5142 THEME FROM "BAA BAA BLACK SHEEP" *Mike Post*	4075 THERE YOU GO *Edwin Starr*	2501 THREE RING CIRCUS *Blue Magic*
4213 Theme from CHARLIE'S ANGELS *Henry Mancini & His Orchestra*	2762 THERE'LL NEVER BE *Switch*	4752 THREE STEPS FROM TRUE LOVE *Reflections*
1301 THEME FROM CLEOPATRA JONES *Joe Simon*	1102 THERE'S A KIND OF HUSH (All Over The World) *Carpenters*	48 THREE TIMES A LADY *Commodores*
1397 THEME FROM "CLOSE ENCOUNTERS OF THE THIRD KIND" *John Williams*	3558 THERE'S GOT TO BE RAIN IN YOUR LIFE (To Appreciate The Sunshine) *Dorothy Norwood*	1257 THE THRILL IS GONE *B.B. King*
		1108 THUNDER AND LIGHTNING *Chi Coltrane*
2047 -- THEME FROM CLOSE ENCOUNTERS *Meco*	1617 THERE'S NO ME WITHOUT YOU *Manhattans*	2581 THUNDER IN MY HEART *Leo Sayer*
4796 THEME FROM ICE CASTLES (Through The Eyes Of Love) *Melissa Manchester*	THERE'S NOTHING STRONGER THAN OUR LOVE...see (I Believe)	692 THUNDER ISLAND *Jay Ferguson*
		4219 TICKET TO RIDE *Carpenters*
THEME FROM "JAWS"...see MAIN TITLE	5282 THERE'S SO MUCH LOVE ALL AROUND ME *Three Degrees*	20 TIE A YELLOW RIBBON ROUND THE OLE OAK TREE *Dawn Feat. Tony Orlando*
4433 THEME FROM KING KONG (Part 1) *Love Unlimited Orchestra*	2431 THEY CAN'T TAKE AWAY OUR MUSIC *Eric Burdon & War*	see also SHOULD I TIE...
THEME FROM LOVE STORY	190 THEY JUST CAN'T STOP IT The (Games People Play) *Spinners*	3531 TIE YOUR MOTHER DOWN *Queen*
1126 *Henry Mancini, His Orchestra & Chorus*		1205 TIGHT ROPE *Leon Russell*
	(They Long To Be) CLOSE TO YOU	567 TIGHTER, TIGHTER *Alive & Kicking*
2314 *Francis Lai & His Orchestra*	60 *Carpenters*	3433 TIGHTROPE RIDE *Doors*
912 --(Where Do I Begin) LOVE STORY *Andy Williams*	3537 *Jerry Butler*	5054 'TIL I CAN MAKE IT ON MY OWN *Tammy Wynette*
	THICKER THAN WATER...see (Love Is)	
344 THEME FROM MAHOGANY (Do You Know Where You're Going To) *Diana Ross*	928 THIN LINE BETWEEN LOVE AND HATE *Persuaders*	2657 'TIL IT'S TIME TO SAY GOODBYE *Jonathan Cain*
		2108 TIL THE WORLD ENDS *Three Dog Night*
THEME FROM ROCKY...see GONNA FLY NOW	463 THE THINGS WE DO FOR LOVE *10CC*	2438 TILL *Tom Jones*
	2340 THINK (About It) *Lyn Collins*	2845 TIME AND LOVE *Barbra Streisand*
277 THEME FROM S.W.A.T. *Rhythm Heritage*	3955 THINK HIS NAME *Johnny Rivers*	4478 TIME BOMB *Lake*
32 THEME FROM SHAFT *Isaac Hayes*	2707 THINK IT OVER *Cheryl Ladd*	2289 TIME FOR LIVIN' *Sly & The Family Stone*
1602 THEME FROM "SUMMER OF '42" *Peter Nero*	4138 THINK IT OVER *Delfonics*	
	1066 THINKING OF YOU *Loggins & Messina*	3682 TIME FOR ME TO FLY *REO Speedwagon*
2668 -- SUMMER OF '42 BIDDU ORCHESTRA	3816 THINKING OF YOU *Paul Davis*	268 TIME IN A BOTTLE *Jim Croce*
	1483 THIRD RATE ROMANCE *Amazing Rhythm Aces*	1045 TIME PASSAGES *Al Stewart*
3891 THEME FROM SUPERMAN (MAIN TITLE) *John Williams/London Symphony Orchestra*		1981 TIME TO GET DOWN *O'Jays*
	2539 13 QUESTIONS *Seatrain*	4129 TIME TO GET IT TOGETHER *Country Coalition*
	4992 THIS BITTER EARTH *Satisfactions*	
1816 THEME FROM THE MEN *Isaac Hayes*	3831 THIS GIRL (Has Turned Into A Woman) *Mary MacGregor*	4630 TIME TO KILL *Band*
5096 THEME FROM "THE PROPHET" (Pleasure Is A Freedom Song/On Love) *Richard Harris*		2349 TIME WAITS FOR NO ONE *Friends Of Distinction*
	1381 THIS HEART *Gene Redding*	
	4613 THIS I SWEAR *Tyrone Davis*	4794 TIME WILL TELL *Tower Of Power*
1829 THEME SONG FROM "WHICH WAY IS UP" *Stargard*	3306 THIS IS LOVE *Oak*	1225 TIMES OF YOUR LIFE *Paul Anka*
	3799 THIS IS LOVE *Paul Anka*	1242 TIMOTHY *Buoys*
2270 THEMES FROM THE WIZARD OF OZ *Meco*	4043 THIS IS MY LOVE SONG *Intruders*	875 TIN MAN *America*
	3133 THIS IS THE WAY THAT I FEEL *Marie Osmond*	2311 TINY DANCER *Elton John*
400 THEN CAME YOU *Dionne Warwicke & Spinners*		549 TIRED OF BEING ALONE *Al Green*
	4703 THIS IS WHAT YOU MEAN TO ME *Engelbert Humperdinck*	4636 TO BE YOUNG, GIFTED AND BLACK *Nina Simone*
4579 THEN SHE'S A LOVER *Roy Clark*		
3175 THEN YOU CAN TELL ME GOODBYE *Toby Beau*	4331 THIS IS YOUR LIFE *Commodores*	1887 TO EACH HIS OWN *Faith, Hope & Charity*
	4339 THIS IS YOUR SONG *Don Goodwin*	
see also DON'T PULL YOUR LOVE	4816 THIS MAGIC MOMENT *Richie Furay*	3832 TO GET TO YOU *Jerry Wallace*
3013 THERE AIN'T NO WAY *Lobo*	1008 THIS MASQUERADE *George Benson*	2146 TO KNOW YOU IS TO LOVE YOU *B.B. King*
4900 THERE BUT FOR THE GRACE OF GOD GO I *Machine*	4604 THIS MOMENT IN TIME *Engelbert Humperdinck*	
		1472 TO THE DOOR OF THE SUN (Alle Porte Del Sole) *Al Martino*
2046 THERE GOES ANOTHER LOVE SONG *Outlaws*	THIS NIGHT WON'T LAST FOREVER	
	1322 *Michael Johnson*	5262 TO THE OTHER MAN *Luther Ingram*
3733 THERE GOES MY EVERYTHING *Elvis Presley*	3352 *Bill LaBounty*	2887 TO THE OTHER WOMAN (I'm The Other Woman) *Doris Duke*
	4016 THIS OLD HEART OF MINE *Rod Stewart*	
4626 THERE IT GOES AGAIN *Barbara & The Uniques*		1393 TOAST AND MARMALADE FOR TEA *Tin Tin*
	3124 THIS OLD MAN *Purple Reign*	
	1796 THIS ONE'S FOR YOU *Barry Manilow*	2231 TOAST TO THE FOOL *Dramatics*
	1698 THIS SONG *George Harrison*	

#	Title	Artist
2511	TODAY I STARTED LOVING YOU AGAIN	Bettye Swann
1741	TODAY'S THE DAY	America
3099	TOGETHER	Illusion
3084	TOGETHER AGAIN	Bobby Sherman
2953	TOGETHER ALONE	Melanie
1616	TOGETHER LET'S FIND LOVE	5th Dimension
4277	TOGETHER WE CAN MAKE SUCH SWEET MUSIC	Spinners
2302	TONGUE IN CHEEK	Sugarloaf
2373	TONIGHT	Raspberries
2562	TONIGHT I'LL SAY A PRAYER	Eydie Gorme
46	TONIGHT'S THE NIGHT (Gonna Be Alright)	Rod Stewart
3892	TOO BEAUTIFUL TO LAST	Engelbert Humperdinck
2490	TOO HOT TA TROT	Commodores
5155	TOO HOT TO HANDLE	UFO
3640	TOO LATE	Tavares
4157	TOO LATE	Shoes
191	TOO LATE TO TURN BACK NOW	Cornelius Brothers & Sister Rose
4638	TOO LATE TO WORRY, TOO BLUE TO CRY	Ronnie Milsap
4550	TOO MANY LOVERS	Shack
88	TOO MUCH HEAVEN	Bee Gees
261	TOO MUCH, TOO LITTLE, TOO LATE	Johnny Mathis/Deniece Williams
1009	TOO YOUNG	Donny Osmond
2245	TOOK THE LAST TRAIN	David Gates
5172	TOP FORTY (Of The Lord)	Sha Na Na
	TOP OF THE WORLD	
174		Carpenters
4223		Lynn Anderson
5231	TOP OF THE WORLD (Make My Reservation)	Canyon
4403	THE TOPICAL SONG	Barron Knights
37	TORN BETWEEN TWO LOVERS	Mary MacGregor
4142	TOTALLY HOT	Olivia Newton-John
3322	TOUCH	Supremes
1939	TOUCH A HAND, MAKE A FRIEND	Staple Singers
2561	TOUCH AND GO	Al Wilson
2414	TOUCH ME	Fancy
3255	TOUCH ME BABY (Reaching Out For Your Love)	Tamiko Jones
274	TOUCH ME IN THE MORNING	Diana Ross
5010	TOUCH ME WHEN WE'RE DANCING	Bama
4977	TOUCH OF MAGIC	James Leroy
2729	THE TOUCH OF YOU	Brenda & The Tabulations
4040	TOUCH THE HAND	Conway Twitty
2346	TRACES/MEMORIES MEDLEY	Lettermen
1561	TRACKS OF MY TEARS	Linda Ronstadt
160	TRAGEDY	Bee Gees
4458	TRAGEDY	Argent
5283	TRAIN CALLED FREEDOM	South Shore Commission
4304	TRAIN OF GLORY	Jonathan Edwards
1636	TRAIN OF THOUGHT	Cher
2178	TRAIN, TRAIN	Blackfoot
2130	TRAMPLED UNDER FOOT	Led Zeppelin
4306	TRANQUILLO	Carly Simon
4634	TRANS-EUROPE EXPRESS	Kraftwerk
1071	TRAPPED BY A THING CALLED LOVE	Denise LaSalle
613	TRAVELIN' BAND	Creedence Clearwater Revival
3412	TRAVELIN' PRAYER	Billy Joel
3374	TRAVELIN' SHOES	Elvin Bishop
4092	TRAVELING BOY	Garfunkel
	THE TRAVELING MAN...see (Call Me)	
255	TREAT HER LIKE A LADY	Cornelius Brothers & Sister Rose
3838	TREAT ME LIKE A GOOD PIECE OF CANDY	Dusk
2658	TRIANGLE OF LOVE (Hey Diddle Diddle)	Presidents
2983	TRIED TO LOVE	Peter Frampton
384	TROGLODYTE (Cave Man)	Jimmy Castor Bunch
2572	T-R-O-U-B-L-E	Elvis Presley
4540	TROUBLE	Frederick Knight
3742	TROUBLE IN MY HOME	Joe Simon
1024	TROUBLE MAN	Marvin Gaye
3139	TRUCKIN'	Grateful Dead
3599	TRY SOME, BUY SOME	Ronnie Spector
	TRY TO REMEMBER...see THE WAY WE WERE	
3658	TRY (Try To Fall In Love)	Cooker
5047	TRYIN' TO BEAT THE MORNING HOME	T.G. Sheppard
861	TRYIN' TO GET THE FEELING AGAIN	Barry Manilow
943	TRYIN' TO LOVE TWO	William Bell
5218	TRYIN' TO STAY 'LIVE	Asylum Choir
1329	TRYING TO HOLD ON TO MY WOMAN	Lamont Dozier
3637	TRYING TO LIVE MY LIFE WITHOUT YOU	Otis Clay
2344	TRYING TO MAKE A FOOL OF ME	Delfonics
5122	TRYING TO SLIP (Away)	Lloyd Price
750	TUBULAR BELLS	Mike Oldfield
4392	TULSA	Billy Joe Royal
5159	TULSA TIME	Don Williams
	TUMBLING DICE	
1056		Rolling Stones
2777		Linda Ronstadt
2653	TUPELO HONEY	Van Morrison
407	TURN BACK THE HANDS OF TIME	Tyrone Davis
4115	TURN BACK THE PAGES	Stephen Stills
2987	TURN OFF THE LIGHTS	Teddy Pendergrass
	TURN ON TO ME...see (Baby)	
947	TURN THE BEAT AROUND	Vicki Sue Robinson
1200	TURN TO STONE	Electric Light Orchestra
3641	TURN TO STONE	Joe Walsh
3986	TURNING POINT	Tyrone Davis
4781	TURNING TO YOU	Charlie
1402	TUSH	ZZ Top
956	TUSK	Fleetwood Mac
3051	TWEEDLEE DEE	Little Jimmy Osmond
638	THE TWELFTH OF NEVER	Donny Osmond
4807	25TH OF LAST DECEMBER	Roberta Flack
535	25 OR 6 TO 4	Chicago
2298	TWISTING THE NIGHT AWAY	Rod Stewart
832	TWO DIVIDED BY LOVE	Grass Roots
1920	TWO DOORS DOWN	Dolly Parton
2587	TWO FINE PEOPLE	Cat Stevens
4421	TWO LANE HIGHWAY	Pure Prairie League
699	TWO OUT OF THREE AIN'T BAD	Meat Loaf
1572	TWO TICKETS TO PARADISE	Eddie Money

U

#	Title	Artist
4473	UHH	Dyke & The Blazers
3417	UNBORN CHILD	Seals & Crofts
241	UNCLE ALBERT/ADMIRAL HALSEY	Paul & Linda McCartney
4603	UNCLE JOHN'S BAND	Grateful Dead
3880	UNDER MY WHEELS	Alice Cooper
3845	UNDER THE BOARDWALK	Billy Joe Royal
4853	UNDER THE INFLUENCE OF LOVE	Love Unlimited
69	UNDERCOVER ANGEL	Alan O'Day
1039	UNEASY RIDER	Charlie Daniels
2396	UNGENA ZA ULIMWENGU (Unite The World)	Temptations
1588	UNION MAN	Cate Bros.
922	UNITED WE STAND	Brotherhood Of Man
5112	UNLOVED	Walter Egan
	UNTIL IT'S TIME FOR YOU TO GO	
2090		Elvis Presley
2726		Neil Diamond
2799	UNTIL NOW	Bobby Arvon
5288	(Until Then) I'LL SUFFER	Barbara Lynn
674	UNTIL YOU COME BACK TO ME (That's What I'm Gonna Do)	Aretha Franklin
309	UP AROUND THE BEND	Creedence Clearwater Revival
1438	UP IN A PUFF OF SMOKE	Polly Brown
4242	UP IN HEAH	Ike & Tina Turner
1467	UP ON CRIPPLE CREEK	Band
2284	UP ON THE ROOF	James Taylor
944	UP THE LADDER TO THE ROOF	Supremes
4184	UP YOUR NOSE	Gabriel Kaplan
4141	UPSETTER	Grand Funk Railroad
3399	UPTOWN FESTIVAL (Part 1)	Shalamar
4266	US AND THEM	Pink Floyd
784	USE ME	Bill Withers
601	USE TA BE MY GIRL	O'Jays

V

VADO VIA...see WORDS (Are Impossible)

#	Title	Artist
4567	VAHEVELLA	Ken Loggins With Jim Messina
4245	VALENTINE LOVE	Norman Connors (Featuring Michael Henderson and Jean Cain)
5215	VALERIE	Cymarron
4300	VALLEY TO PRAY	Arlo Guthrie
5190	VANILLA OLAY	Jackie DeShannon

	VAYA CON DIOS	3543	**WANG DANG DOODLE** *Pointer Sisters*	4678	**WE MAY NEVER LOVE LIKE THIS AGAIN**
3273	*Dawn Feat. Tony Orlando*	105	**WANT ADS** *Honey Cone*		*Maureen McGovern*
4378	*Freddy Fender*	50	**WAR** *Edwin Starr*	1451	**WE MAY NEVER PASS THIS WAY (Again)** *Seals & Crofts*
624	**VEHICLE** *Ides of March*	3229	**WAR SONG**	3853	**WE NEED ORDER** *Chi-Lites*
3341	**VENGEANCE** *Carly Simon*		*Neil Young & Graham Nash*	2947	**WE WERE ALWAYS SWEETHEARTS**
898	**VENTURA HIGHWAY** *America*	2529	**WARM RIDE** *Rare Earth*		*Boz Scaggs*
15	**VENUS** *Shocking Blue*	4927	**WARMIN' UP THE BAND** *Don Everly*	3931	**WE'LL HAVE IT MADE** *Spinners*
2184	**VENUS** *Frankie Avalon*	3787	**WARPATH** *Isley Brothers*	1410	**WE'LL NEVER HAVE TO SAY GOODBYE AGAIN** *England Dan & John Ford Coley*
1670	**VENUS AND MARS ROCK SHOW** *Wings*	3684	**WAS DOG A DOUGHNUT** *Cat Stevens*	5309	**--NEVER HAVE TO SAY GOODBYE AGAIN** *Deardorff & Joseph*
	VERY LOVELY WOMAN...see (She's A)	3889	**WASN'T IT GOOD** *Cher*		**WE'RE ALL ALONE**
1063	**A VERY SPECIAL LOVE SONG** *Charlie Rich*	577	**WASTED DAYS AND WASTED NIGHTS** *Freddy Fender*	587	*Rita Coolidge*
3491	**VICTIM OF A FOOLISH HEART** *Bettye Swann*	3941	**WATCH CLOSELY NOW** *Kris Kristofferson*	4436	*Frankie Valli*
2552	**VICTIM OF LOVE** *Elton John*	3142	**WATCH OUT FOR LUCY** *Eric Clapton*	3217	**WE'RE ALL PLAYING IN THE SAME BAND** *Bert Sommer*
3040	**VICTORIA** *Kinks*	749	**WATCHING SCOTTY GROW** *Bobby Goldsboro*	3179	**WE'RE ALMOST THERE** *Michael Jackson*
2495	**VIDEO KILLED THE RADIO STAR** *Buggles*	3485	**WATCHING THE DETECTIVES / ALISON*** *Elvis Costello*	243	**WE'RE AN AMERICAN BAND** *Grand Funk*
1030	**VINCENT** *Don McLean*	2050	**WATCHING THE RIVER FLOW** *Bob Dylan*	1854	**WE'RE FREE** *Beverly Bremers*
3276	**VIRGIN MAN** *Smokey Robinson*	2908	**WATCHING THE RIVER RUN** *Loggins & Messina*	2814	**WE'RE GETTING CARELESS WITH OUR LOVE** *Johnnie Taylor*
2096	**VIRGINIA (Touch Me Like You Do)** *Bill Amesbury*	4302	**WATERFALL** *Carly Simon*	2498	**(We're Gonna) ROCK AROUND THE CLOCK** *Bill Haley & His Comets*
2004	**VIVA TIRADO (Part 1)** *El Chicano*	3489	**WATERGRATE** *Dickie Goodman*	2468	**WE'RE ON OUR WAY** *Chris Hodge*
2463	**VOLARE** *Al Martino*	1054	**WATERLOO** *ABBA*	4004	**WE'RE TOGETHER** *Hillside Singers*
2573	**VOLUNTEERS** *Jefferson Airplane*	3429	**WAVELENGTH** *Van Morrison*	2355	**WE'VE COME TOO FAR TO END IT NOW** *Smokey Robinson & The Miracles*
4435	**VOODOO WOMAN** *Simon Stokes & The Nighthawks*		**WAY BACK HOME**	3068	**WE'VE GOT LOVE** *Peaches & Herb*
4780	**VOULEZ-VOUS** *ABBA*	3751	*Jazz Crusaders*	1305	**WE'VE GOT TO GET IT ON AGAIN** *Addrisi Brothers*
	W	4665	*Jr. Walker & The All Stars*	1174	**WE'VE GOT TONITE** *Bob Seger & The Silver Bullet Band*
1669	**WOLD** *Harry Chapin*	1474	**WAY DOWN** *Elvis Presley*	99	**WE'VE ONLY JUST BEGUN** *Carpenters*
2715	**WAITING AT THE BUS STOP** *Bobby Sherman*	1477	**THE WAY I FEEL TONIGHT** *Bay City Rollers*	4295	**WEAR THIS RING (With Love)** *Detroit Emeralds*
4860	**WAKE UP** *Law*	493	**THE WAY I WANT TO TOUCH YOU** *Captain & Tennille*		**WEDDING SONG (There Is Love)**
4416	**WAKE UP AND LOVE ME** *April*	793	**THE WAY OF LOVE** *Cher*	1407	*Paul Stookey*
1161	**WAKE UP EVERYBODY (Part 1)** *Harold Melvin & The Blue Notes*		**THE WAY WE WERE**	4173	*Petula Clark*
4294	**WAKE UP SUSAN** *Spinners*	162	*Barbra Streisand*	2083	**WEEKEND** *Wet Willie*
2861	**WAKING UP ALONE** *Paul Williams*	766	*Gladys Knight & The Pips* - **/TRY TO REMEMBER**	757	**WEEKEND IN NEW ENGLAND** *Barry Manilow*
965	**WALK A MILE IN MY SHOES** *Joe South*	1671	**THE WAY YOU DO THE THINGS YOU DO** *Rita Coolidge*	4146	**WEEKEND LOVER** *Odyssey*
2189	**WALK AWAY** *James Gang*	4586	**WE ALL GOTTA STICK TOGETHER** *Four Tops*	112	**WELCOME BACK** *John Sebastian*
681	**WALK AWAY FROM LOVE** *David Ruffin*	5026	**WE ALL NEED LOVE** *Troiano*	2936	**WELCOME TO MY NIGHTMARE** *Alice Cooper*
5063	**WALK EASY MY SON** *Jerry Butler*	127	**WE ARE FAMILY** *Sister Sledge*	3095	**WELFARE CADILLAC** *Guy Drake*
2504	**WALK IN THE NIGHT** *Jr. Walker & The All Stars*	4364	**WE ARE NEIGHBORS** *Chi-Lites*	2686	**WEREWOLF** *Five Man Electrical Band*
1454	**WALK LIKE A MAN** *Grand Funk*	383	**WE ARE THE CHAMPIONS** *Queen*	1555	**WEREWOLVES OF LONDON** *Warren Zevon*
3097	**WALK ON** *Neil Young*	5127	**WE BEEN SINGIN' SONGS** *Baron Stewart*	3400	**WEST COAST WOMAN** *Painter*
1585	**WALK ON THE WILD SIDE** *Lou Reed*	5296	**WE BOTH NEED EACH OTHER** *Norman Connors*	1246	**WESTBOUND #9** *Flaming Ember*
1249	**WALK ON WATER** *Neil Diamond*	3588	**WE CAN MAKE IT TOGETHER** *Steve & Eydie*	1128	**WHAM BAM SHANG-A-LANG** *Silver*
5065	**WALK RIGHT BACK** *Anne Murray*	2418	**WE CAN MAKE MUSIC** *Tommy Roe*	1459	**WHAT A DIFF'RENCE A DAY MAKES** *Esther Phillips*
3755	**WALK RIGHT IN** *Dr. Hook*	848	**WE CAN WORK IT OUT** *Stevie Wonder*	4974	**WHAT A DIFFERENCE YOU'VE MADE IN MY LIFE** *Ronnie Milsap*
2678	**WALK RIGHT UP TO THE SUN** *Delfonics*	5280	**WE CAN'T DANCE TO YOUR MUSIC** *Grass Roots*	86	**WHAT A FOOL BELIEVES** *Doobie Brothers*
775	**WALK THIS WAY** *Aerosmith*	2946	**WE CAN'T HIDE IT ANYMORE** *Larry Santos*	5257	**WHAT A MAN, MY MAN IS** *Lynn Anderson*
913	**WALKIN' IN THE RAIN** *Jay & The Americans*	3777	**WE DID IT** *Syl Johnson*	4960	**WHAT A SHAME** *Foghat*
726	**WALKIN' IN THE RAIN WITH THE ONE I LOVE** *Love Unlimited*	5269	**WE GOT A DREAM** *Ocean*	3811	**WHAT A WONDERFUL THING WE HAVE** *Fabulous Rhinestones*
4566	**WALKIN' THE FENCE** *Couchois*	4606	**WE GOT TO HAVE PEACE** *Curtis Mayfield*		**(What A) WONDERFUL WORLD**
814	**WALKING IN RHYTHM** *Blackbyrds*	4017	**WE GOT TO LIVE TOGETHER (Part 1)** *Buddy Miles*	1621	*Art Garfunkel with James Taylor & Paul Simon*
4210	**WALKING ON BACK** *Edward Bear*	1327	**WE GOTTA GET YOU A WOMAN** *Runt*	4468	*Johnny Nash*
2012	**WALKING THROUGH THE COUNTRY** *Grass Roots*	1215	**WE JUST DISAGREE** *Dave Mason*		
4655	**THE WALL STREET SHUFFLE** *10 C.C.*				
3670	**THE WANDERER** *Leif Garrett*				

#	Title	Artist
2408	WHAT ABOUT ME	Anne Murray
2224	WHAT AM I CRYING FOR?	Dennis Yost & The Classics IV
2722	WHAT AM I GONNA DO	Smith
1018	WHAT AM I GONNA DO WITH YOU	Barry White
3089	WHAT AM I LIVING FOR	Ray Charles
1681	WHAT ARE YOU DOING SUNDAY	Dawn Feat. Tony Orlando
2917	WHAT CAN I DO FOR YOU?	LaBelle
3618	WHAT CAN I DO WITH THIS BROKEN HEART	England Dan & John Ford Coley
3079	WHAT CAN I SAY	Boz Scaggs
2099	WHAT CHA GONNA DO WITH MY LOVIN'	Stephanie Mills
5184	WHAT DO YOU KNOW ABOUT LOVE	Apple & Appleberry
713	WHAT IS LIFE	George Harrison
1282	WHAT IS TRUTH	Johnny Cash
3397	WHAT IT COMES DOWN TO	Isley Brothers
5251	WHAT IT IS	Undisputed Truth
5228	WHAT IT TAKES TO GET A GOOD WOMAN (That's What It's Gonna Take To Keep Her)	Denise La Salle
4876	WHAT MADE AMERICA FAMOUS	Harry Chapin
2918	WHAT MY BABY NEEDS NOW IS A LITTLE MORE LOVIN'	James Brown & Lyn Collins
883	WHAT THE WORLD NEEDS NOW IS LOVE/ABRAHAM, MARTIN AND JOHN	Tom Clay
5238	WHAT TIME OF DAY	Billy Thunderkloud & The Chieftones
4179	WHAT WOULD THE CHILDREN THINK	Rick Springfield
	WHAT YOU...see also WHATCHA	
5123	WHAT YOU GOT	Duke & The Drivers
4131	WHAT YOU SEE IS WHAT YOU GET	Stoney & Meatloaf
1216	WHAT YOU WON'T DO FOR LOVE	Bobby Caldwell
4185	WHAT'D I SAY	Rare Earth
4905	WHAT'S A MATTER BABY	Ellen Foley
4899	WHAT'S COME OVER ME	Margie Joseph & Blue Magic
	WHAT'S GOING ON	
311		Marvin Gaye
5244		Quincy Jones (Part 1)
4190	WHAT'S HAPPENED TO BLUE EYES	Jessi Colter
4597	WHAT'S ON MY MIND	Kansas
4944	WHAT'S THE NAME OF THIS FUNK (Spider Man)	Ramsey Lewis
5151	WHAT'S YOUR MAMA'S NAME	Tanya Tucker
684	WHAT'S YOUR NAME	Lynyrd Skynyrd
4279	WHAT'S YOUR NAME	Andy & David Williams
5305	WHAT'S YOUR NAME, WHAT'S YOUR NUMBER	Andrea True Connection
	WHATCHA...see also WHAT YOU	
474	WHATCHA GONNA DO?	Pablo Cruise
1098	WHATCHA SEE IS WHATCHA GET	Dramatics
374	WHATEVER GETS YOU THRU THE NIGHT	John Lennon
4499	WHATEVER HAPPENED TO BENNY SANTINI?	Chris Rea
3225	WHATEVER TURNS YOU ON	Travis Wammack
1993	WHATEVER YOU GOT, I WANT	Jackson 5
2839	WHEEL IN THE SKY	Journey
4484	WHEELS OF LIFE	Gino Vannelli
2640	WHEN A CHILD IS BORN	Michael Holm
4231	WHEN I FALL IN LOVE	Donny Osmond
283	WHEN I NEED YOU	Leo Sayer
1928	WHEN I'M DEAD AND GONE	McGuinness Flint
1804	WHEN JULIE COMES AROUND	Cuff Links
3720	WHEN LOVE HAS GONE AWAY	Richard Cocciante
3526	WHEN LOVE IS NEW	Arthur Prysock
4108	WHEN THE MORNING COMES	Hoyt Axton
3801	WHEN THE PARTY IS OVER	Robert John
2553	WHEN THERE'S NO YOU	Engelbert Humperdinck
2932	WHEN WE GET MARRIED	Intruders
339	WHEN WILL I BE LOVED	Linda Ronstadt
441	WHEN WILL I SEE YOU AGAIN	Three Degrees
5138	WHEN YOU DANCE I CAN REALLY LOVE	Neil Young
5028	WHEN YOU FEEL LOVE	Bob McGilpin
	WHEN YOU GET RIGHT DOWN TO IT	
2316		Delfonics
4234		Ronnie Dyson
2076	WHEN YOU SAY LOVE	Sonny & Cher
764	WHEN YOU'RE HOT, YOU'RE HOT	Jerry Reed
491	WHEN YOU'RE IN LOVE WITH A BEAUTIFUL WOMAN	Dr. Hook
520	WHENEVER I CALL YOU "FRIEND"	Kenny Loggins
3268	WHENEVER I'M AWAY FROM YOU	John Travolta
3404	WHERE ARE ALL MY FRIENDS	Harold Melvin And The Blue Notes
5147	WHERE ARE WE GOING	Bobby Bloom
5294	WHERE ARE YOU	Cat Stevens
3973	WHERE ARE YOU GOING	Jerry Butler
2727	WHERE ARE YOU GOING TO MY LOVE	Brotherhood Of Man
3223	WHERE DID ALL THE GOOD TIMES GO	Dennis Yost & The Classics IV
	WHERE DID OUR LOVE GO	
1764		Donnie Elbert
2751		J. Geils Band
2315	WHERE DID THEY GO, LORD	Elvis Presley
	WHERE DO I BEGIN...see THEME FROM LOVE STORY	
2111	WHERE EVIL GROWS	Poppy Family
4587	WHERE HAVE YOU BEEN ALL MY LIFE	Fotomaker
739	WHERE IS THE LOVE	Roberta Flack & Donny Hathaway
3924	WHERE IS THE LOVE	Betty Wright
1752	WHERE PEACEFUL WATERS FLOW	Gladys Knight & The Pips
4720	WHERE THERE'S SMOKE THERE'S FIRE	Grass Roots
1365	WHERE WERE YOU WHEN I WAS FALLING IN LOVE	Lobo
3478	WHERE WILL YOUR HEART TAKE YOU	Buckeye
2508	WHERE YOU LEAD	Barbra Streisand
	see also SWEET INSPIRATION	
237	WHICH WAY YOU GOIN' BILLY?	Poppy Family
4159	WHILE I'M ALONE	Maze
1496	WHISPERING/CHERCHEZ LA FEMME/SE SI BON	Dr. Buzzard's Original "Savannah" Band
3274	THE WHISTLER	Jethro Tull
4367	WHITE BIRD	David LaFlamme
1464	THE WHITE KNIGHT	Cledus Maggard
3908	WHITE LIES	Grin
1633	WHITE LIES, BLUE EYES	Bullet
4717	A WHITER SHADE OF PALE	Procol Harum
4505	--WHITER SHADE OF PALE	R.B. Greaves
909	WHO ARE YOU	Who
5038	WHO ARE YOU	B.B. King
4556	WHO DO YA LOVE	K C & The Sunshine Band
4070	WHO DO YOU LOVE	George Thorogood And The Destroyers
1222	WHO DO YOU THINK YOU ARE	Bo Donaldson & The Heywoods
3589	WHO GETS THE GUY	Dionne Warwick
4937	WHO GETS YOUR LOVE	Dusty Springfield
2690	WHO IS HE AND WHAT IS HE TO YOU	Creative Source
3782	WHO LISTENS TO THE RADIO	Sports
575	WHO LOVES YOU	Four Seasons
3761	WHO LOVES YOU BETTER (Part 1)	Isley Brothers
2580	WHO NEEDS YA	Steppenwolf
2701	WHO WAS IT?	Hurricane Smith
1725	WHO'D SHE COO?	Ohio Players
1316	WHO'LL STOP THE RAIN	Creedence Clearwater Revival
2940	WHO'S GONNA TAKE THE BLAME	Smokey Robinson & The Miracles
5086	WHO'S GONNA TAKE THE WEIGHT (Part 1)	Kool & The Gang
1318	WHO'S IN THE STRAWBERRY PATCH WITH SALLY	Tony Orlando & Dawn
2684	WHO'S SORRY NOW	Marie Osmond
2147	WHO'S YOUR BABY?	Archies
1302	WHODUNIT	Tavares
3169	WHOEVER FINDS THIS, I LOVE YOU	Mac Davis
	WHOLE LOTTA LOVE	
126		Led Zeppelin
3250		C.C.S.
3299		King Curtis & The Kingpins
3696	WHOLESALE LOVE	Buddy Miles
3665	WHOLY HOLY	Aretha Franklin
1378	WHY	Donny Osmond
460	WHY CAN'T WE BE FRIENDS?	War
2642	WHY CAN'T WE BE LOVERS	Holland-Dozier
326	WHY CAN'T WE LIVE TOGETHER	Timmy Thomas

5336	WHY DO FOOLS FALL IN LOVE *Summer Wine*	
4544	WHY DO LOVERS (Break Each Other's Heart?) *Daryl Hall & John Oates*	
4571	WHY DON'T THEY UNDERSTAND *Bobby Vinton*	
4576	WHY LEAVE US ALONE *Five Special*	
1266	WHY ME *Kris Kristofferson*	
4745	WHY NOT START ALL OVER AGAIN *Counts*	
2747	WHY SHOULD I CRY *Gentrys*	
1853	WIGWAM *Bob Dylan*	
1629	WILD HORSES *Rolling Stones*	
1895	WILD NIGHT *Van Morrison*	
1223	WILD THING *Fancy*	
	WILD WORLD	
1312	*Cat Stevens*	
4012	*Gentrys*	
395	WILDFIRE *Michael Murphey*	
	WILDFLOWER	
780	*Skylark*	
2630	*New Birth*	
817	WILDWOOD WEED *Jim Stafford*	
213	WILL IT GO ROUND IN CIRCLES *Billy Preston*	
	WILL YOU LOVE ME TOMORROW	
2970	*Melanie* [P]	
5145	*Dana Valery*	
5267	*Linda Ronstadt* [P]	
	--WILL YOU STILL LOVE ME TOMORROW	
2500	*Dave Mason*	
3940	*Roberta Flack*	
2425	WILLIE AND THE HAND JIVE *Eric Clapton*	
4866	WILLIE PASS THE WATER *Ripple*	
3795	WILLPOWER WEAK, TEMPTATION STRONG *Bullet*	
1321	WINNERS AND LOSERS *Hamilton, Joe Frank & Reynolds*	
2858	WINTER MELODY *Donna Summer*	
952	WINTER WORLD OF LOVE *Engelbert Humperdinck*	
2632	(Wish I Could Fly Like) SUPERMAN *Kinks*	
2931	WISH THAT I COULD TALK TO YOU *Sylvers*	
1081	WISHING YOU WERE HERE *Chicago*	
5052	THE WITCH *Rattles*	
1372	THE WITCH QUEEN OF NEW ORLEANS *Redbone*	
1013	WITCHY WOMAN *Eagles*	
2565	WITH A CHILD'S HEART *Michael Jackson*	
	WITH A LITTLE HELP FROM MY FRIENDS...see SGT. PEPPER'S LONELY HEARTS CLUB BAND	
273	WITH A LITTLE LUCK *Wings*	
4467	WITH PEN IN HAND *Bobby Goldsboro*	
1136	WITH YOUR LOVE *Jefferson Starship*	
2738	WITHOUT LOVE *Aretha Franklin*	
590	WITHOUT LOVE (There Is Nothing) *Tom Jones*	
53	WITHOUT YOU *Nilsson*	
2687	WITHOUT YOU IN MY LIFE *Tyrone Davis*	
2589	WITHOUT YOUR LOVE (Mr. Jordan) *Charlie Ross*	
4096	WOLF CREEK PASS *C.W. McCall*	

5129	WOLFMAN JACK *Todd Rundgren*	
1921	WOMAN DON'T GO ASTRAY *King Floyd*	
3071	WOMAN FROM TOKYO *Deep Purple*	
5160	WOMAN IS THE NIGGER OF THE WORLD *John Lennon/Plastic Ono Band with Elephant's Memory and Invisible Strings*	
	WOMAN TO WOMAN	
1735	*Shirley Brown*	
5130	*Barbara Mandrell*	
2706	WOMAN TO WOMAN *Joe Cocker*	
2545	WOMAN TONIGHT *America*	
1836	WOMAN'S GOTTA HAVE IT *Bobby Womack*	
3595	A WOMAN'S STORY *Cher*	
3329	WOMBLING SUMMER PARTY *Wombles*	
1660	WOMEN'S LOVE RIGHTS *Laura Lee*	
3615	WON'T FIND BETTER (Than Me) *New Hope*	
751	WON'T GET FOOLED AGAIN *Who*	
4967	WONDER GIRL *Sparks*	
824	THE WONDER OF YOU *Elvis Presley*	
4995	WONDERFUL BABY *Don McLean*	
1817	WONDERFUL TONIGHT *Eric Clapton*	
	WONDERFUL WORLD...see (What A)	
1283	WONDERFUL WORLD, BEAUTIFUL PEOPLE *Jimmy Cliff*	
3609	WOODEN HEART *Bobby Vinton*	
	WOODSTOCK	
1113	*Crosby, Stills, Nash & Young*	
1224	*Matthews' Southern Comfort*	
3994	*Assembled Multitude*	
4935	WORDS (Are Impossible) *Donny Gerrard*	
4650	--VADO VIA *Drupi*	
2592	WORK TO DO *Isley Brothers*	
1731	WORKIN' AT THE CAR WASH BLUES *Jim Croce*	
4599	WORKIN' TOGETHER *Ike & Tina Turner*	
3418	WORKING CLASS HERO *Tommy Roe*	
920	THE WORLD IS A GHETTO *War*	
3762	WORSE COMES TO WORST *Billy Joel*	
2883	WOULD YOU LAY WITH ME (In A Field Of Stone) *Tanya Tucker*	
4196	WRAP YOUR ARMS AROUND ME *K C & The Sunshine Band*	
4401	WRAPPED UP IN YOUR WARM AND TENDER LOVE *Tyrone Davis*	
357	THE WRECK OF THE EDMUND FITZGERALD *Gordon Lightfoot*	

Y

150	Y.M.C.A. *Village People*	
3792	YANK ME, CRANK ME *Ted Nugent*	
5001	YANKEE LADY *Brewer & Shipley*	
565	YEAR OF THE CAT *Al Stewart*	
3149	THE YEAR THAT CLAYTON DELANEY DIED *Tom T. Hall*	
1047	YELLOW RIVER *Christie*	
1052	YES WE CAN CAN *Pointer Sisters*	
3234	YES, YES, YES *Bill Cosby*	
3267	YESTERDAY I HAD THE BLUES *Harold Melvin & The Blue Notes*	
329	YESTERDAY ONCE MORE *Carpenters*	

	YESTERDAY'S HERO	
2685	*John Paul Young*	
2802	*Bay City Rollers*	
214	YO-YO *Osmonds*	
1547	YOU *Rita Coolidge*	
1657	YOU *George Harrison*	
3143	YOU *McCrarys*	
4890	YOU *Aretha Franklin*	
3493	YOU AIN'T NEVER BEEN LOVED (Like I'm Gonna Love You) *Jessi Colter*	
284	YOU AIN'T SEEN NOTHING YET *Bachman-Turner Overdrive*	
1307	YOU AND I *Rick James*	
3206	YOU AND I *Johnny Bristol*	
5071	YOU AND I *Black Ivory*	
781	YOU AND ME *Alice Cooper*	
908	YOU AND ME AGAINST THE WORLD *Helen Reddy*	
4694	YOU AND ME TOGETHER FOREVER *Freddie North*	
4465	YOU AND YOUR FOLKS, ME AND MY FOLKS *Funkadelic*	
3261	YOU ANGEL YOU *Manfred Mann's Earth Band*	
4248	YOU ARE A SONG *Batdorf & Rodney*	
4466	YOU ARE BEAUTIFUL *Stylistics*	
683	YOU ARE EVERYTHING *Stylistics*	
4947	YOU ARE MY LOVE *Liverpool Express*	
1863	YOU ARE MY STARSHIP *Norman Connors*	
5167	YOU ARE MY SUNSHINE *Dyke & The Blazers*	
3423	YOU ARE ON MY MIND *Chicago*	
603	YOU ARE SO BEAUTIFUL *Joe Cocker*	
2328	YOU ARE THE ONE *Sugar Bears*	
439	YOU ARE THE SUNSHINE OF MY LIFE *Stevie Wonder*	
716	YOU ARE THE WOMAN *Firefall*	
5004	YOU ARE YOU *Gilbert O'Sullivan*	
865	YOU BELONG TO ME *Carly Simon*	
3818	YOU BETTER THINK TWICE *Poco*	
2379	YOU BROUGHT THE JOY *Freda Payne*	
	YOU BROUGHT THE WOMAN OUT OF ME	
2856	*Evie Sands*	
4376	*Hot*	
4274	YOU CAN CALL ME ROVER *Main Ingredient*	
3434	YOU CAN DO IT *Dobie Gray*	
3235	YOU CAN DO MAGIC *Limmie & Family Cookin'*	
2113	YOU CAN HAVE HER *Sam Neely*	
2081	YOU CAN'T ALWAYS GET WHAT YOU WANT *Rolling Stones*	
2382	YOU CAN'T BE A BEACON (If Your Light Don't Shine) *Donna Fargo*	
808	YOU CAN'T CHANGE THAT *Raydio*	
4211	YOU CAN'T DANCE *England Dan & John Ford Coley*	
5081	YOU CAN'T DO IT RIGHT (With The One You Love) *Deep Purple*	
4888	YOU CAN'T GO HALFWAY *Johnny Nash*	
1230	YOU CAN'T TURN ME OFF (In The Middle Of Turning Me On) *High Inergy*	
1810	YOU COULD HAVE BEEN A LADY *April Wine*	

#	Title	Artist
725	YOU DECORATED MY LIFE	Kenny Rogers
81	YOU DON'T BRING ME FLOWERS	Barbra & Neil
159	YOU DON'T HAVE TO BE A STAR (To Be In My Show)	Marilyn McCoo & Billy Davis Jr.
1111	YOU DON'T HAVE TO SAY YOU LOVE ME	Elvis Presley
3854	YOU DON'T KNOW WHAT LOVE IS	Susan Jacks
3424	YOU DON'T LOVE ME ANYMORE	Eddie Rabbitt
671	YOU DON'T MESS AROUND WITH JIM	Jim Croce
5182	YOU DON'T OWE ME	Blue Ridge Rangers
2186	YOU GONNA MAKE ME LOVE SOMEBODY ELSE	Jones Girls
3601	YOU GOT IT	Diana Ross
2915	YOU GOT ME HUMMIN	Cold Blood
3893	YOU GOT THAT RIGHT	Lynyrd Skynyrd
1041	YOU GOT THE LOVE	Rufus
4186	YOU GOT TO BE THE ONE	Chi-Lites
3370	YOU GOTTA HAVE LOVE IN YOUR HEART	Supremes & Four Tops
2978	YOU GOTTA MAKE YOUR OWN SUNSHINE	Neil Sedaka
299	YOU HAVEN'T DONE NOTHIN	Stevie Wonder
4189	YOU JUST CAN'T WIN (By Making The Same Mistake)	Gene & Jerry
3443	YOU KEEP ME DANCING	Samantha Sang
4178	YOU KEEP ME HOLDING ON	Tyrone Davis
3938	YOU KEEP TIGHTENING UP ON ME	Box Tops
4989	YOU KNOW HOW IT IS WITH A WOMAN	Jefferson
2966	YOU KNOW LIKE I KNOW	Ozark Mountain Daredevils
4956	YOU KNOW THE FEELIN'	Steve Wightman
1	YOU LIGHT UP MY LIFE	Debby Boone
3484	YOU LIGHT UP MY LIFE	Carole King
1473	YOU LITTLE TRUSTMAKER	Tymes
723	YOU MADE ME BELIEVE IN MAGIC	Bay City Rollers
902	YOU MAKE LOVING FUN	Fleetwood Mac
3974	YOU MAKE ME CRAZY	Sammy Hagar
221	YOU MAKE ME FEEL BRAND NEW	Stylistics
184	YOU MAKE ME FEEL LIKE DANCING	Leo Sayer
2980	YOU MAKE ME FEEL (Mighty Real)	Sylvester
2442	YOU MAKE ME REAL	Doors
3402	YOU MAKE YOUR OWN HEAVEN AND HELL RIGHT HERE ON EARTH	Undisputed Truth
3851	YOU, ME AND MEXICO	Edward Bear
2503	YOU NEED A WOMAN TONIGHT	Captain & Tennille
4408	YOU NEED LOVE	Styx
1979	YOU NEED LOVE LIKE I DO (Don't You)	Gladys Knight & The Pips
394	YOU NEEDED ME	Anne Murray
967	YOU NEVER DONE IT LIKE THAT	Captain & Tennille
264	YOU OUGHT TO BE WITH ME	Al Green
3101	YOU + ME = LOVE	Undisputed Truth
2692	YOU REALLY GOT ME	Van Halen
2148	YOU SAID A BAD WORD	Joe Tex
4110	YOU SAYS IT ALL	Randy Brown
3563	YOU SEND ME	Ponderosa Twins + One
200	YOU SEXY THING	Hot Chocolate
292	YOU SHOULD BE DANCING	Bee Gees
5006	YOU SHOULD DO IT	Peter Brown
	YOU STEPPED INTO MY LIFE	
2735	Melba Moore	
4583	Wayne Newton	
2610	YOU SURE LOVE TO BALL	Marvin Gaye
957	YOU TAKE MY BREATH AWAY	Rex Smith
5120	YOU TAKE MY HEART AWAY	James Darren
4194	YOU THINK YOU'RE HOT STUFF	Jean Knight
2537	YOU THRILL ME	Exile
4366	YOU TO ME ARE EVERYTHING	Real Thing
	YOU TOOK THE WORDS RIGHT OUT OF MY MOUTH	
2497	Meat Loaf	
5293	Meat Loaf (Hot Summer Night)	
1384	YOU TURN ME ON, I'M A RADIO	Joni Mitchell
1980	YOU WANT IT, YOU GOT IT	Detroit Emeralds
1358	YOU WEAR IT WELL	Rod Stewart
3847	YOU WERE ALWAYS THERE	Donna Fargo
2954	YOU WERE MADE FOR ME	Luther Ingram
3921	YOU WON'T FIND ANOTHER FOOL LIKE ME	New Seekers
745	YOU WON'T SEE ME	Anne Murray
4612	YOU'D BETTER BELIEVE IT	Manhattans
2213	YOU'LL LOSE A GOOD THING	Freddy Fender
3305	YOU'LL LOVE AGAIN	Hotel
509	YOU'LL NEVER FIND ANOTHER LOVE LIKE MINE	Lou Rawls
1610	YOU'LL NEVER GET TO HEAVEN (If You Break My Heart)	Stylistics
4896	YOU'LL NEVER WALK ALONE	Blue Haze
3482	YOU'RE A BIG GIRL NOW	Stylistics
	YOU'RE A LADY	
3102	Peter Skellern	
3190	Dawn	
5144	YOU'RE A LADY	Gene Chandler
	YOU'RE A PART OF ME	
2320	Gene Cotton	
5154	Susan Jacks	
1435	YOU'RE A SPECIAL PART OF ME	Diana Ross & Marvin Gaye
	YOU'RE ALL I NEED TO GET BY	
1428	Aretha Franklin	
2910	Tony Orlando & Dawn	
3490	Johnny Mathis & Deniece Williams	
4393	YOU'RE GETTIN' A LITTLE TOO SMART	Detroit Emeralds
5310	YOU'RE GONNA MAKE IT	Festivals
183	(You're) HAVING MY BABY	Paul Anka
4897	YOU'RE IN GOOD HANDS	Jermaine Jackson
387	YOU'RE IN MY HEART (The Final Acclaim)	Rod Stewart
	YOU'RE MOVING OUT TODAY	
2984	Carole Bayer Sager	
3385	Bette Midler [P]	
866	YOU'RE MY BEST FRIEND	Queen
3435	YOU'RE MY EVERYTHING	Lee Garrett
3127	YOU'RE MY MAN	Lynn Anderson
2674	(You're My) SOUL AND INSPIRATION	Donny & Marie
3539	YOU'RE MY WEAKNESS	Faith Band
1147	YOU'RE MY WORLD	Helen Reddy
351	YOU'RE NO GOOD	Linda Ronstadt
785	YOU'RE ONLY LONELY	J.D. Souther
5041	YOU'RE RIGHT, RAY CHARLES	Joe Tex
290	YOU'RE SIXTEEN	Ringo Starr
2144	YOU'RE SO UNIQUE	Billy Preston
58	YOU'RE SO VAIN	Carly Simon
1517	YOU'RE STILL A YOUNG MAN	Tower Of Power
	YOU'RE THE BEST THING THAT EVER HAPPENED TO ME…see BEST THING THAT EVER HAPPENED TO ME	
294	YOU'RE THE FIRST, THE LAST, MY EVERYTHING	Barry White
1604	YOU'RE THE LOVE	Seals & Crofts
2659	YOU'RE THE MAN (Part 1)	Marvin Gaye
	YOU'RE THE ONE	
1348	Little Sister (Part 2)	
3281	Three Degrees	
3076	YOU'RE THE ONE FOR ME	Joe Simon
136	YOU'RE THE ONE THAT I WANT	John Travolta & Olivia Newton-John
3809	YOU'RE THE ONLY ONE	Dolly Parton
2694	YOU'RE THE REASON WHY	Ebonys
4500	YOU'RE THROWING A GOOD LOVE AWAY	Spinners
2889	YOU'RE WELCOME, STOP ON BY	Bobby Womack
2548	YOU'VE BEEN MY INSPIRATION	Main Ingredient
	YOU'VE GOT A FRIEND	
113	James Taylor	
1797	Robert Flack & Donny Hathaway	
3442	YOU'VE GOT ANOTHER THING COMING	Hotel
	(You've Got Me) DANGLING ON A STRING	
1964	Chairmen Of The Board	
5324	Donny Osmond [P]	
2647	YOU'VE GOT ME RUNNIN'	Gene Cotton
3025	YOU'VE GOT MY SOUL ON FIRE	Temptations
2056	YOU'VE GOT TO CRAWL (Before You Walk)	8th Day
4719	YOU'VE GOT TO EARN IT	Staple Singers
3900	YOU'VE GOT TO KEEP ON BUMPIN' (Part 1)	Kay-Gees
2558	YOU'VE GOT TO TAKE IT (If You Want It)	Main Ingredient

3114 **YOU'VE LOST THAT LOVIN' FEELIN'** *Roberta Flack & Donny Hathaway*	1513 **YOUR LOVE** *Marilyn McCoo & Billy Davis Jr.*	631 **YOUR SONG** *Elton John*
1622 **YOU'VE NEVER BEEN THIS FAR BEFORE** *Conway Twitty*	2358 **YOUR LOVE** *Graham Central Station*	2981 **YOUR SWEETNESS IS MY WEAKNESS** *Barry White*
3594 **YOU'VE REALLY GOT A HOLD ON ME** *Eddie Money*	177 **(Your Love Has Lifted Me) HIGHER AND HIGHER** *Rita Coolidge*	1527 **YOUR TIME TO CRY** *Joe Simon*
1915 **YOUNG AMERICANS** *David Bowie*	5329 **YOUR LOVE IS SO DOGGONE GOOD** *Whispers*	3650 **YOUR WONDERFUL, SWEET SWEET LOVE** *Supremes*
1563 **YOUNG BLOOD** *Bad Company*	4031 **YOUR LOVE IS SO GOOD FOR ME** *Diana Ross*	3556 **YOURS LOVE** *Joe Simon*
2888 **YOUNG BLOOD** *Rickie Lee Jones*	2669 **YOUR LOVE (Means Everything To Me)** *Charles Wright & The Watts 103rd Street Band*	4400 **YU-MA/GO AWAY LITTLE BOY** *Marlena Shaw*
1287 **YOUNG HEARTS RUN FREE** *Candi Staton*		

YOUNG LOVE
2840 Donny Osmond
4792 Ray Stevens

3181 **THE YOUNG NEW MEXICAN PUPPETEER** *Tom Jones*

2380 **YOUR BULLDOG DRINKS CHAMPAGNE** *Jim Stafford*

2462 **YOUR CASH AIN'T NOTHIN' BUT TRASH** *Steve Miller Band*

558 **YOUR MAMA DON'T DANCE** *Kenny Loggins & Jim Messina*

1911 **YOUR MOVE** *Yes*

4020 **YOUR OWN BACK YARD** *Dion*

4760 **YOUR OWN SPECIAL WAY** *Genesis*

5134 **YOUR PRECIOUS LOVE** *Linda Jones*

4333 **YOUR SIDE OF THE BED** *Mac Davis*

1221 **YOUR SMILING FACE** *James Taylor*

Z

2343 **ZING WENT THE STRINGS OF MY HEART** *Trammps*

* Denotes Two-Sided Hit

Section 5

Appendix

The Scoring System Explained

The calculations for *Ranking the '70s* are based on data obtained with permission from *Cash Box* magazine. *Cash Box* was one of the three major national trade magazines dedicated to the broadcasting and music businesses. It operated from July, 1942 to November 16, 1996, and has recently been revitalized as an online vehicle. *Cash Box* historical charts are transcribed and available on the web at:

http://www.cashboxmagazine.com/cashbox-archives.html

There are at least eight published chart methodologies for ranking records.[1] (Carroll, 2014) In all cases there are two important variables: rank; that is, how high up the chart the record went, and duration; that is, how many weeks it spent on the chart in total or at a given rank. The most complete methodologies award points for the rank attained by a record each week, then sum the points earned through its lifecycle. Many will recognize this as an area-under-the-curve approach (AUC).

The simplest chart methodology awards points as follows: #1 = 100 points, #2 = 99 points and so on to #100 = 1 point. This scoring system, which we call *Reverse Rank*, has the effect of emphasizing duration and, in our minds, is incomplete. In Reverse Rank, a record spending three weeks at #67 scores more points than a record spending one week at #1. To more properly reward achievement of high rank we accorded additional points at the upper reaches of the chart. In differing ways, this approach is used by most of the published methodologies. Our system builds upon Reverse Rank between #30 and #1, and a list of points by rank is shown in Table 1. This system is derived from that used in *Ranking the '60s*, but it is slightly smoothed and augmented to place a bit more emphasis on the points of ranks 2-10.

Table 1. Allocation of points by chart rank used in *Ranking the '70s*.

Rank	Points	Rank	Points	Rank	Points
1	1000	11	190	21	100
2	824	12	184	22	97
3	658	13	178	23	94
4	529	14	172	24	91
5	434	15	166	25	88
6	345	16	145	26	85
7	310	17	140	27	82
8	277	18	135	28	79
9	246	19	130	29	76
10	217	20	125	30	73

All other positions score 101 minus Rank.

---

[1] Seven of the methodologies are described in detail in Carroll, 2014. They include Reverse Rank and methodologies put forward in other publications by Joel Whitburn, Jim Quirin and Barry Cohen, Howard Drake, Randy Price, Dann Isbell and Bill Carroll. The eighth is used by Fred Bronson in *Billboard's Hottest Hot 100 Hits*, 4th Edition, Billboard Books, 2007.

The AUC method is demonstrated graphically in Figure 1.

Figure 1. A comparison of "Me And Mrs. Jones" by Billy Paul (left) and "Clair" by Gilbert O'Sullivan (right) using the *Ranking the '70s* scoring system. Numerical raw scores are 6250 and 3819 respectively. The two records shown in Figure 1 debuted the same day, October 21, 1972.

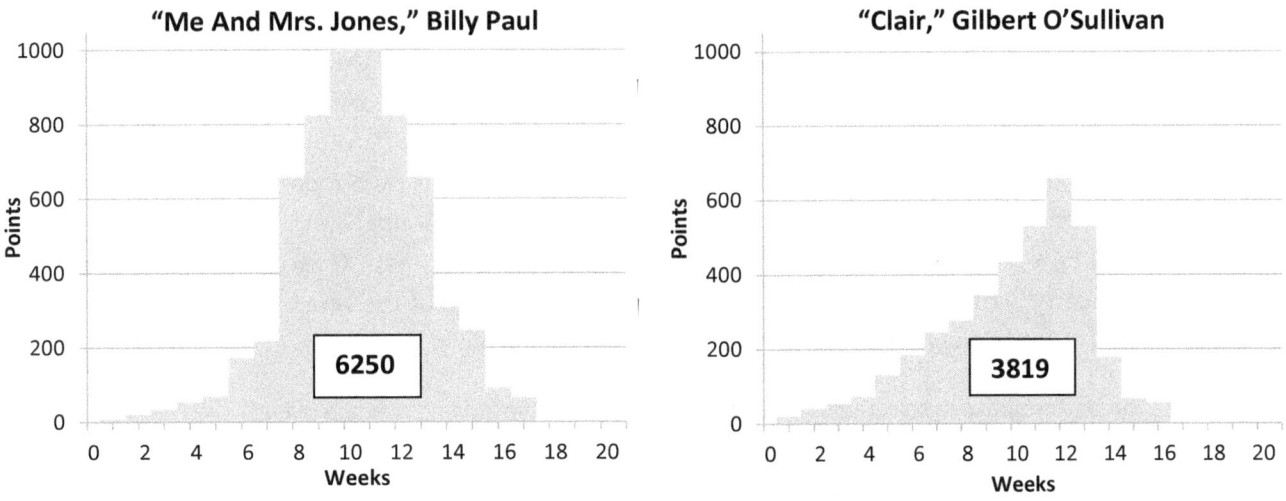

It is not necessary to graph each record's lifecycle to make comparisons. Because each bar of the graph is the same width--one week--one need only total the points, week to week. This is how the raw score for each record is calculated.

But there is more complexity. The music and broadcast businesses--the bases of the data used to construct the charts--were changing throughout the '70s. Additionally, the methodologies used by *Cash Box* in obtaining data and constructing the charts may also have changed a number of times, although such changes are not always documented.

Whether as a direct outcome or not, the number of new records entering the charts on a weekly basis changed during this period. At the beginning of the decade, new entries averaged 12.8 per week (665 per 52 week period). By January of 1978 the average was 8.65 (450 per 52 weeks), a decrease of 33%. As a result, the average time on the chart for records increased, and an "average" record scored very differently over the decade. (Figure 2)

Figure 2. Number of records entering the charts per rolling 52 week period (left) and average record score (right).

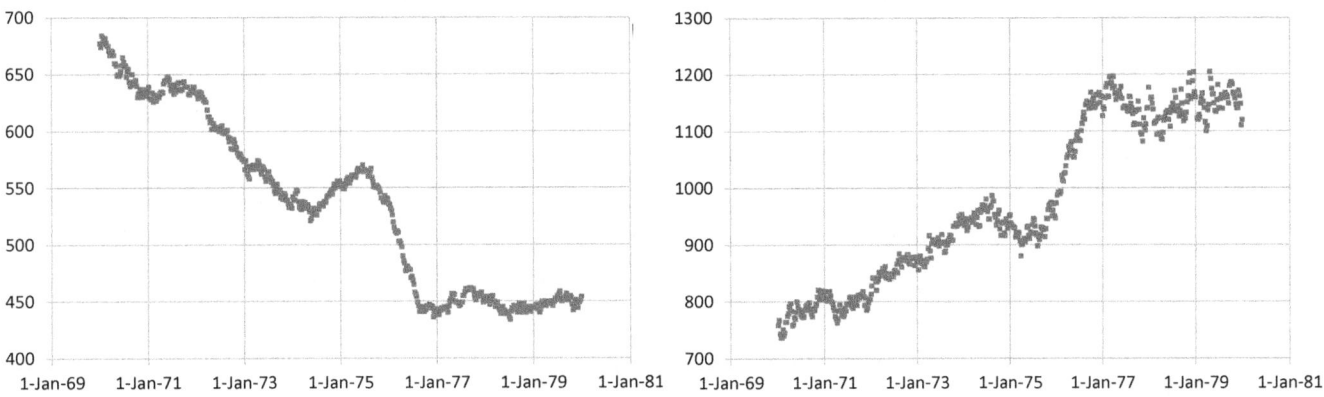

A Baseball Analogy

The problem of comparing performances over time in a changing environment is common to many fields. As an example, if the question is: "Who had the best season ever for hitting home runs?" the answer depends on the metric. If the metric is Most Home Runs in a Year the answer is simple: Barry Bonds, 2001: 73. That is an *absolute metric*, and absolute metrics are most appropriate where all variables can be controlled and all results are comparable.

However, as with most comparisons over a long time, conditions change; not all variables can be controlled and not all results are comparable. In this case, 2001 was in the steroid era, and there are questions about how to compare performance in that era with historical performance. In 1961, when Roger Maris hit 61 home runs, breaking Babe Ruth's 1927 season record of 60, he did so in a 162-game season, while the 1927 season was 154 games. Babe Ruth's 1927 season broke his own record of 59 in 1921. Which was the greatest season: Babe Ruth's 59 or 60, Roger Maris' 61 or Barry Bonds' 73?

For us, the answer is "none of the above." It is 1920, when Ruth hit 54 with George Sisler in second place at 19. Ruth had nearly 3 times Sisler's output and *44 times* the average of the rest of the league. That year, Babe Ruth hit 15% of the home runs in the league, truly an outlier. (Table 2)

Table 2. Home run performance in selected years by league leader, runner-up and average player.

Year	League Batters	League HRs	League Leader	League Runner-up	Average HR, Others	Leader/ Average	Leader/ Runner-up	Leader, Pct. Total
1920	261	369	54	19	1.21	44.6	2.84	14.6
1921	250	477	59	24	1.68	35.1	2.46	12.4
1927	259	439	60	47	1.47	40.8	1.28	13.7
1961	359	1534	61	54	4.11	14.8	1.13	4.0
2001	688	2952	73	64	4.19	17.4	1.14	2.5

Percent of Total, Ratio of Leader to Average Player or Ratio of Leader to Runner-Up are alternate means to distinguish performances in the context of their times. These are *relative metrics*, which are most appropriate where variables cannot be controlled and results may not be comparable over time. Relative metrics take context into account. The goal of such metrics is to find the outliers: the truly transcendent performances versus their peers, in the era they performed.

Now Back to Records

In a similar way, we can devise absolute and relative metrics for records in the 1970s. The simplest metric for the best chart performance could be highest raw score, regardless of year. However, since the average record score rose by nearly 60% over the decade, the absolute metric populates the top of the list nearly exclusively with records from the late 1970s.

Our preferred metric is a relative metric: the ratio of a record's raw score to the average raw score of contemporaneous records, that is, those entering the chart during the 52 weeks centered at the date of entry of the subject recording. Thus, an "average" record always has a score ratio of 1. Records scoring the highest multiple of the average of their contemporaries are the transcendent outliers, and the highest ranking records of the decade are those with the highest ratio. To make the scores comparable in magnitude to the original scoring system, we multiply that ratio by 1000.[2] (Table 3) We call this process *normalization over time*.

---

[2] Those with a statistical background will note the skewness of the distribution. While we have chosen to use average as our operative statistic for simplicity of calculation, the results are similar if median is used. The median of this distribution over the period is 359.

Table 3. Normalization calculation for records entering the chart 27 August 1977.

Title	Act	Natural Points	52 Week Moving Avg.	Ratio, Natural Points to Mvg. Avg.	Normalized Points (Ratio * 1000)
Another Star	Stevie Wonder	452	1131	0.400	400
Brick House	Commodores	2100	1131	1.857	1857
C'est La Vie	Greg Lake	34	1131	0.030	30
Does She Do It Like She Dances	Addrisi Brothers	68	1131	0.060	60
Hold On	Wild Cherry	143	1131	0.126	126
I Go Crazy	Paul Davis	3589	1131	3.174	3174
She Did It	Eric Carmen	1230	1131	1.088	1088
Signed, Sealed, Delivered (I'm Yours)	Peter Frampton	1252	1131	1.107	1107
Surfin' USA	Leif Garrett	639	1131	0.565	565
Too Hot To Handle	UFO	11	1131	0.010	10
You Light Up My Life	Debby Boone	12709	1131	11.239	11239

"She Did It" and "Signed, Sealed, Delivered" scored virtually the 52-week average, yielding a ratio of nearly 1. On the other hand, "You Light Up My Life" was the ultimate outlier, the number one record of the decade, scoring over 11 times the 52-week moving average.

By entering the chart in the same week, each record in Table 3 is subject to the same 52-week moving average. The following example compares three records that entered the chart at different times and are subject to different 52-week moving averages. Consider "ABC" by The Jackson 5, "Kiss And Say Goodbye" by The Manhattans and "My Sharona" by The Knack.

Table 4. Comparing the effect of normalization on three records across the decade.

Title	Act	Entry Date	52-Week Mvg. Avg. Score for that week	Natural Points	Ratio, Natural Points to Mvg. Avg.	Normalized Points
ABC	Jackson 5	14 Mar 1970	774	7185	9.272	9272
Kiss And Say Goodbye	Manhattans	24 Apr 1976	1076	7148	6.645	6645
My Sharona	Knack	23 Jun 1979	1181	10347	8.758	8758

Normalization provides a means of "grading on the curve" to account for times when average records scored higher or lower due to the average duration on the chart. "ABC" scored 7185 points, with 1 week at #1, 5 weeks at #2 and 2 weeks at #3 in its 13-week lifecycle. Nearly 2/3 of its lifecycle was spent in the top 3. "Kiss And Say Goodbye" has the next highest natural score to "ABC," but only spent 2 weeks at #1 and 2 weeks at #2 in a 27-week lifecycle. To us, "ABC" had the more potent lifecycle and should be the higher rated record. It was also over 9 times the average score for its time and "Kiss And Say Goodbye" was about 6.5 times the average for its time.

"My Sharona" had 6 weeks at #1, 1 at #2 and 3 weeks at #3 in 25 total weeks for 10347 points--a higher score, more weeks at #1, but only about 40% of its lifecycle in the top 3. It scored a bit below 9 times the average for its day. Its lifecycle is much more comparable to that of "ABC" despite the fact that it scored 30%

more points before normalization. But "ABC" still appears to have had the more potent run, and the normalized score demonstrates that, as does the Scoring Intensity System described below.

The highest scoring records by raw score disproportionately entered the charts from 1976 to 1979, the period of fewest new entries, longest duration on the chart and least competition. After normalization, it is clear that there are outliers for their time at the beginning of the decade and at the end; there are curiously few in the middle (Figure 3, 4). Examination of the raw natural scores in the next appendix piece, "The Top 300 Records of Each Year," shows that the highest scores of the year in the middle of the decade are relatively low, confirming the observation.

Figure 3. Natural scores by peak date. (n=5368). Note that virtually all high scores occur between 1976 and 1980, and the lowest scores occur between 1974 and 1976.

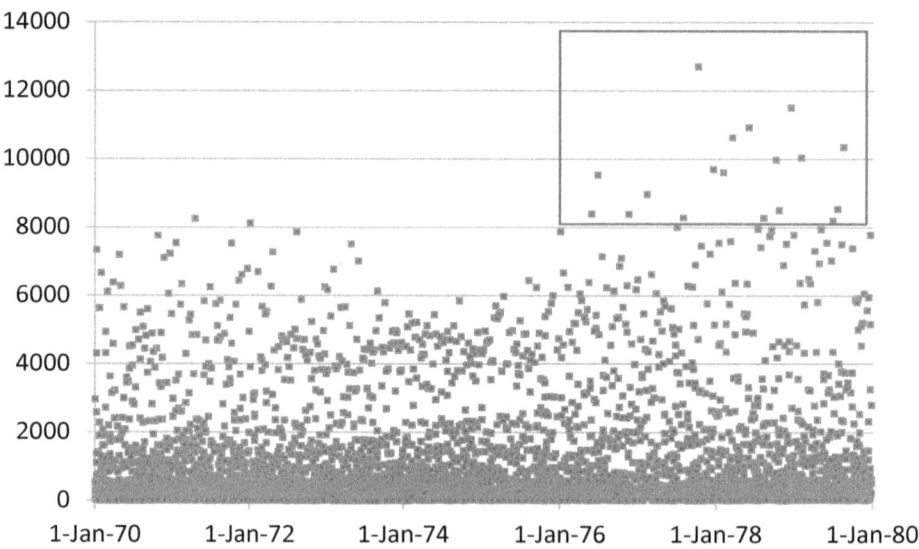

Figure 4. Normalized scores by peak date. (n=5368). Note a more even distribution of high scores, but still low scores in 1974-1976.

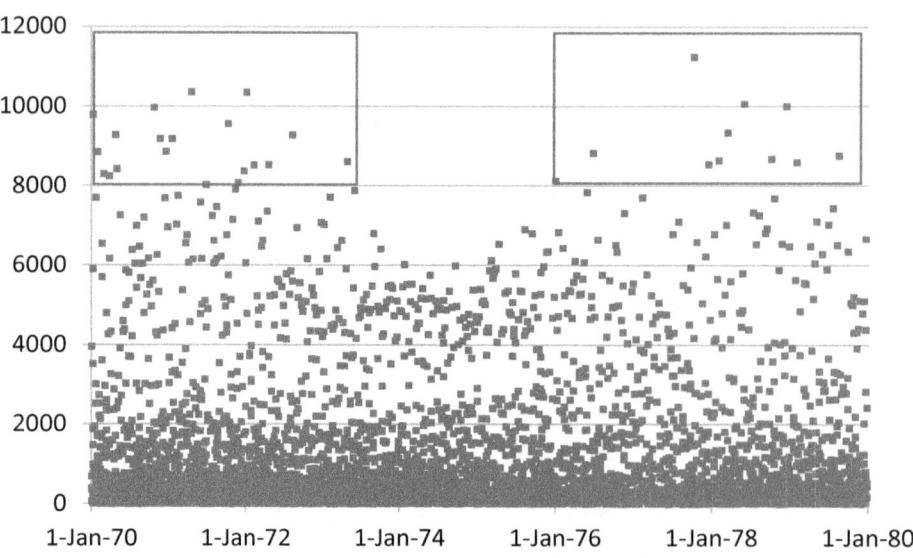

Ranking the Acts

Perhaps the cleanest method of ranking acts is to simply sum the points of the underlying records for each act and rank them accordingly. For this work, however, we have chosen to add a second consideration related to the number of records that each act placed on the charts.

Nearly half the acts (839) have a single entry. They range from acts with one week at #100 to Anita Ward who scored about 7028 normalized points and spent 3 weeks at #1. Her one hit, "Ring My Bell," ranked No. 57 in Section 1[3]. That so many acts are "one-hit wonders"[4] illustrates how difficult it is to chart a second record, even if the first was highly successful. To acknowledge that, we developed a reward for repeat appearances based on a percentage of the act's score. That percentage reward declines with more repeat appearances; as difficult as it is for an act to chart its second record, it is substantially less difficult to chart record number 30 after 29 relative successes.

Specifically, here is the way the "entries" bonus is calculated. First is the factor that decreases with entries:

Table 5. Act Entries Bonus scaling factor.

Act Points	Factor Calculation
0-500	Factor = 60 - (score-0)/20
501-1000	Factor = 35 - (score-500)/50
1001-2000	Factor = 25 - (score-1000)/100
2001-5000	Factor = 15 - (score-2000)/500
5001-10000	Factor = 9 - (score-5000)/1000
10001-20000	Factor = 4 - (score-10000)/10000
20001-40000	Factor = 3 - (score-20000)/20000
Above 40000	Factor = 2

This gives a continuous array of factors from 60 to 2, with the largest factors reserved for the lowest scoring acts. Then, the act point total is multiplied by that factor expressed as percent, and then by number of entries minus 1:

$$\text{Final Score} = \text{Act Total} + [\text{Act Total} * (\text{Factor}/100) * (\text{Entries}-1)]$$

As an example, on points alone, Elvis Presley ranked 23rd with 28764 normalized points; however, he also charted 32 records, most in the decade. Utilizing this formula increased his score to 51947, ranking him 12th.

The Entries Bonus only accrues to acts with more than one charted record. It increases the highest act scores by about 4% and scores of acts that score low but have numerous entries up to 300%. The few ties among the acts were broken by total weeks on the charts.

Scoring for Intensity: The High Intensity 300

The scoring system used in *Ranking the '70s* rewards both longevity and rank over a record's lifecycle. The normalization process attempts to level the playing field over the decade when the number of records charting and consequently the average chart longevity of records varies greatly. But neither system adequately values the hot record that burns out quickly compared to its longer-lived competition.

Scoring for intensity does that by averaging the points earned in a lifecycle over weeks on the chart, then putting that average on a 1-100 rank basis according to Table 1. It transforms the lifecycle from a bar graph with variable heights into a rectangle--the total weeks on the chart expressed as one rank.

---

[3] Anita Ward had a second charted record in Billboard.
[4] The definition of "One-Hit Wonder" varies. Some consider "Hit" to mean Top 40; our definition is entry into the Top 100.

Thus, a record that averages 529 points would have an average rank of 4. One that averages 434 points would have an average rank of 5. For intermediate point levels the rank is scaled between the two values.

"My Sweet Lord" by George Harrison lived on the charts for 14 weeks at an average rank of 4.14. "Night Fever" by the Bee Gees occupied the charts for 21 weeks at an average rank of 4.24. Based on total points, "Night Fever" far outscores "My Sweet Lord." But on an intensity basis they are nearly equivalent. (Figure 5) This is another way of normalizing score between shorter and longer average lifecycle eras, generating an equals-to-equals comparison.

Figure 5. Scoring total and average for "Night Fever" (left) and "My Sweet Lord" (right).

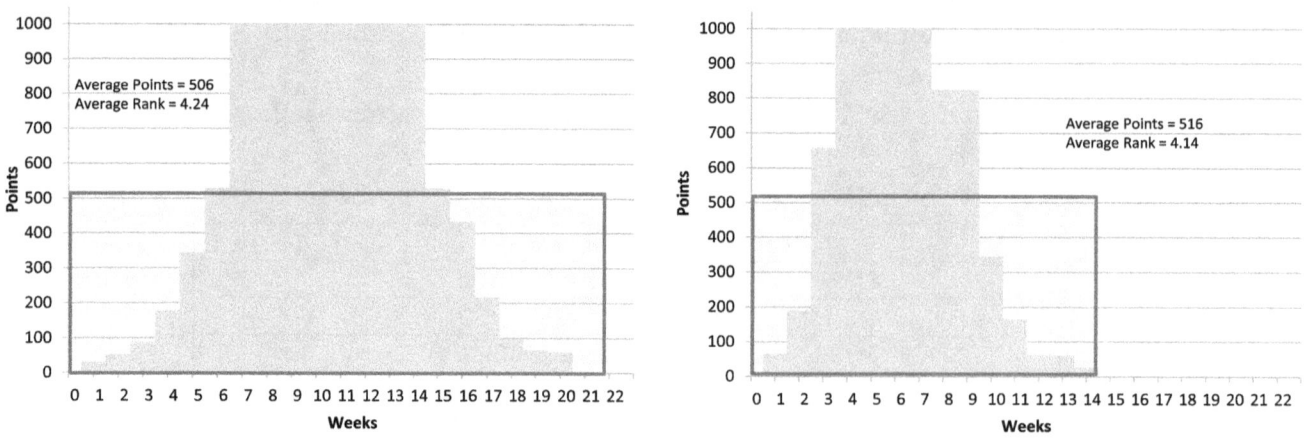

Using this method to compare the records in the previous normalization example, "ABC" by the Jackson 5 is the most intense single of the decade, achieving an average rank of 3.82. "My Sharona" by The Knack is No. 26 with average rank of 5.26 and "Kiss And Say Goodbye" by the Manhattans is No. 260 with average rank of 8.40. This is the same order as when normalized over time by the outliers method, and the difference between "ABC" and "Kiss And Say Goodbye--near ties by natural score--is even more striking.

The application of this simple average of points over lifecycle provides a unique means of showcasing the songs in this decade that have made the most out of their time on the charts, however long. We call this list the "High Intensity Singles," and it can be found in the appendix.

A Note About Breaking Ties

The calculations in this book seldom give whole number results, and so ties are infrequent. In some cases, there are apparent ties that are broken by truncated, and thus unseen, decimal places. Where there are actual ties, if the list allows, they are broken first by a record's peak rank, then by weeks at that peak. If the tie cannot be broken, the records are given the same rank in the list.

REFERENCES

http://www.baseball-reference.com Accessed January 31, 2015.

Carroll, William F. "Not So Lonely At The Top: Billboard #1s and a New Methodology for Comparing Records, 1958-1975." Popular Music and Society, Published online December 22, 2014. DOI: 10.1080/03007766.2014.991188

Top 300 Songs of Each Year

Trajectory = Peak--Wks to Peak/Peak Weeks/Weeks to Exit; Pts. are natural scoring before normalization.

1970

Rank	Title - Act	Trajectory	Pts.
1	I'll Be There - Jackson 5	1--6/2/9	7757
2	Raindrops Keep Fallin' On My Head - B.J. Thomas	1--12/2/9	7330
3	My Sweet Lord - George Harrison	1--4/4/7	7222
4	ABC - Jackson 5	1--7/1/6	7185
5	I Think I Love You - Partridge Family	1--9/3/8	7100
6	Venus - Shocking Blue	1--9/3/5	6656
7	Let It Be - Beatles	1--3/4/7	6382
8	Spirit In The Sky - Norman Greenbaum	1--11/2/5	6278
9	Bridge Over Troubled Water - Simon & Garfunkel	1--5/4/6	6107
10	The Tears Of A Clown - Smokey Robinson & The Miracles	1--10/1/6	6051
11	American Woman - Guess Who	1--9/2/4	5657
12	I Want You Back - Jackson 5	1--11/1/6	5631
13	War - Edwin Starr	1--9/2/5	5603
14	(They Long To Be) Close To You - Carpenters	1--8/2/7	5503
15	One Less Bell To Answer - 5th Dimension	2--11/1/7	5463
16	Make It With You - Bread	1--10/1/6	5085
17	Mama Told Me (Not To Come) - Three Dog Night	1--8/2/5	4993
18	Thank You (Falettinme Be Mice Elf Agin) - Sly & The Family Stone	1--9/1/6	4936
19	We've Only Just Begun - Carpenters	1--9/1/6	4912
20	Ain't No Mountain High Enough - Diana Ross	1--8/1/4	4889
21	Spill The Wine - Eric Burdon & War	1--14/1/5	4830
22	Ball Of Confusion (That's What The World Is Today) - Temptations	1--10/1/4	4715
23	Instant Karma (We All Shine On) - John Ono Lennon	3--6/4/5	4596
24	The Love You Save - Jackson 5	1--6/2/7	4544
25	The Long And Winding Road - Beatles	1--5/2/5	4520
26	Signed, Sealed, Delivered I'm Yours - Stevie Wonder	1--10/1/4	4451
27	Cracklin' Rosie - Neil Diamond	1--10/1/5	4449
28	Lookin' Out My Back Door - Creedence Clearwater Revival	1--9/1/3	4358
29	Hey There Lonely Girl - Eddie Holman	2--10/3/4	4325
30	Whole Lotta Love - Led Zeppelin	2--9/2/6	4316
31	Indiana Wants Me - R. Dean Taylor	1--12/1/3	4195
32	Band Of Gold - Freda Payne	2--14/1/5	4135
33	Patches - Clarence Carter	1--10/1/4	4065
34	Get Ready - Rare Earth	2--16/1/4	3950
35	Candida – Dawn	1--11/1/5	3895
36	Which Way You Goin' Billy? - Poppy Family	2--14/2/4	3869
37	In The Summertime - Mungo Jerry	2--9/1/4	3730
38	Rainy Night In Georgia - Brook Benton	2--11/1/4	3633
39	Up Around The Bend - Creedence Clearwater Revival	2--7/1/5	3599
40	Everything Is Beautiful - Ray Stevens	1--11/1/4	3472
41	Cecilia - Simon & Garfunkel	1--8/1/4	3445
42	Gypsy Woman - Brian Hyland	3--15/1/5	3432
43	All Right Now – Free	3--11/1/5	3426
44	Fire And Rain - James Taylor	4--9/3/4	3325
45	Lay Down (Candles In The Rain) - Melanie	3--13/1/4	3302
46	Love Grows (Where My Rosemary Goes) - Edison Lighthouse	4--8/2/4	3208
47	The Rapper – Jaggerz	2--9/1/5	3146
48	Turn Back The Hands Of Time - Tyrone Davis	4--11/3/2	2993
49	Holly Holy - Neil Diamond	4--11/1/3	2963
50	Hitchin' A Ride - Vanity Fare	4--15/1/6	2891
51	Julie, Do Ya Love Me - Bobby Sherman	3--10/1/5	2823
52	Ride Captain Ride - Blues Image	5--10/2/5	2810
53	No Time - Guess Who	4--11/2/4	2719
54	Jam Up Jelly Tight - Tommy Roe	5--9/2/4	2578
55	Something's Burning - Kenny Rogers & The First Edition	5--14/1/3	2417
56	House Of The Rising Sun - Frijid Pink	6--11/2/4	2403
57	O-O-H Child - Five Stairsteps	4--9/1/4	2394
58	Somebody's Been Sleeping - 100 Proof Aged In Soul	6--12/3/2	2370
59	The Letter - Joe Cocker	5--9/2/3	2368
60	Green-Eyed Lady - Sugarloaf	5--13/1/5	2359
61	(I Know) I'm Losing You - Rare Earth	5--11/1/4	2327
62	25 Or 6 To 4 – Chicago	6--9/2/3	2327
63	Tighter, Tighter - Alive And Kicking	5--12/1/4	2275
64	Don't Cry Daddy - Elvis Presley	6--9/2/3	2273
65	Psychedelic Shack - Temptations	4--8/1/4	2205
66	Come And Get It - Badfinger	6--11/1/4	2163
67	Reflections Of My Life - Marmalade	7--13/1/3	2082
68	Without Love (There Is Nothing) - Tom Jones	5--7/1/3	2065
69	Vehicle - Ides of March	6--8/2/4	1996
70	Snowbird - Anne Murray	6--12/2/4	1938
71	Travelin' Band - Creedence Clearwater Revival	5--8/1/3	1926
72	I'll Never Fall In Love Again - Dionne Warwick	6--7/1/4	1899
73	Jingle Jangle – Archies	8--9/2/3	1895
74	Ma Belle Amie - Tee Set	6--9/2/3	1891
75	He Ain't Heavy, He's My Brother - Hollies	8--13/3/2	1842
76	Love Or Let Me Be Lonely - Friends Of Distinction	8--9/2/3	1832
77	Share The Land - Guess Who	5--8/1/4	1810
78	Easy Come, Easy Go - Bobby Sherman	7--11/1/3	1774
79	Evil Ways – Santana	7--7/2/4	1727
80	Lay A Little Lovin' On Me - Robin McNamara	7--14/1/3	1704
81	See Me, Feel Me - The Who	8--10/2/2	1672
82	5-10-15-20 (25-30 Years Of Love) - Presidents	7--10/2/4	1649
83	Early In The Morning - Vanity Fare	10--14/1/2	1626
84	For The Love Of Him - Bobbi Martin	9--11/1/3	1620
85	Lola – Kinks	8--11/2/4	1619
86	Arizona - Mark Lindsay	9--12/2/3	1615
87	Gimme Dat Ding - Pipkins	7--9/2/3	1607
88	It's Only Make Believe - Glen Campbell	9--10/1/3	1602
89	Montego Bay - Bobby Bloom	6--12/1/3	1600
90	No Matter What - Badfinger	6--10/1/4	1587
91	Love On A Two-Way Street - Moments	8--9/1/4	1531
92	(If You Let Me Make Love To You Then) Why Can't I Touch You? - Ronnie Dyson	10--10/3/3	1506
93	Heaven Help Us All - Stevie Wonder	9--8/2/2	1484
94	The Wonder Of You - Elvis Presley	10--9/1/4	1483
95	Make Me Smile - Chicago	11--12/1/4	1473
96	Groovy Situation - Gene Chandler	11--15/1/3	1427

Rank	Title - Act	Trajectory	Pts.
97	**La La La (If I Had You)** *Bobby Sherman*	11--10/1/3	1420
98	**My Baby Loves Lovin'** - *White Plains*	10--12/1/4	1416
99	**Daughter Of Darkness** - *Tom Jones*	10--7/2/3	1396
100	**Love Land** - *Charles Wright And The Watts 103rd Street Rhythm Band*	16--16/1/4	1385
101	**Midnight Cowboy** - *Ferrante & Teicher*	10--11/1/4	1382
102	**It Don't Matter To Me** - *Bread*	7--7/2/3	1371
103	**United We Stand** - *Brotherhood Of Man*	13--11/3/2	1366
104	**Give Me Just A Little More Time** *Chairmen Of The Board*	9--8/1/4	1354
105	**Look What They've Done To My Song Ma** - *New Seekers*	10--9/2/2	1351
106	**Up The Ladder To The Roof** *Supremes*	9--8/1/3	1303
107	**Out In The Country** - *Three Dog Night*	9--8/2/3	1300
108	**Walkin' In The Rain** *Jay & The Americans*	14--14/1/2	1285
109	**Winter World Of Love** *Engelbert Humperdinck*	13--10/2/2	1278
110	**I Just Can't Help Believing** *B.J. Thomas*	11--9/2/3	1273
111	**Walk A Mile In My Shoes** - *Joe South*	12--10/2/2	1272
112	**It's All In The Game** - *Four Tops*	14--9/2/2	1257
113	**Honey Come Back** - *Glen Campbell*	11--6/2/3	1233
114	**Don't Play That Song** - *Aretha Franklin*	10--7/2/3	1227
115	**Didn't I (Blow Your Mind This Time)** *Delfonics*	13--10/2/3	1212
116	**El Condor Pasa** - *Simon & Garfunkel*	11--8/1/3	1189
117	**Yellow River** - *Christie*	16--23/1/2	1185
118	**Call Me** - *Aretha Franklin*	13--9/1/2	1176
119	**It's A Shame** – *Spinners*	15--13/1/3	1164
120	**You Don't Have To Say You Love Me** *Elvis Presley*	10--6/2/2	1153
121	**Ohio** - *Crosby, Stills, Nash & Young*	14--7/1/3	1147
122	**I (Who Have Nothing)** - *Tom Jones*	11--6/2/3	1145
123	**Still Water (Love)** - *Four Tops*	12--10/1/3	1135
124	**Woodstock** *Crosby, Stills, Nash & Young*	13--9/1/3	1127
125	**Hi-De-Ho** - *Blood, Sweat & Tears*	9--6/2/2	1116
126	**A Song Of Joy (Himno A La Alegria)** *Miguel Rios*	9--6/1/4	1116
127	**Super Bad (Part 1 & Part 2)** *James Brown*	15--6/3/2	1116
128	**Hand Me Down World** - *Guess Who*	13--9/2/2	1115
129	**Celebrate** - *Three Dog Night*	12--6/2/2	1101
130	**Evil Woman Don't Play Your Games With Me** - *Crow*	16--12/1/2	1101
131	**Teach Your Children** *Crosby, Stills, Nash & Young*	16--8/2/2	1098
132	**Little Green Bag** *George Baker Selection*	16--10/2/1	1090
133	**Engine Number 9** - *Wilson Pickett*	14--11/1/2	1089
134	**Be My Baby** - *Andy Kim*	12--9/1/3	1086
135	**Come Saturday Morning** - *Sandpipers*	13--26/1/2	1082
136	**Are You Ready?** - *Pacific Gas & Electric*	12--11/1/2	1077
137	**Baby Take Me In Your Arms** - *Jefferson*	19--11/2/1	1063
138	**After Midnight** - *Eric Clapton*	13--12/1/2	1056
139	**Everybody's Got The Right To Love** *Supremes*	14--9/2/1	1048
140	**Kentucky Rain** - *Elvis Presley*	10--5/1/4	1020
141	**Express Yourself** - *Charles Wright And The Watts 103rd Street Rhythm Band*	17--11/1/3	1000
142	**Tennessee Bird Walk** *Jack Blanchard & Misty Morgan*	14--9/1/2	993
143	**God, Love And Rock & Roll** *Teegarden & Van Winkle*	14--9/2/1	982
144	**That's Where I Went Wrong** *Poppy Family*	20--12/2/1	978
145	**Reach Out And Touch (Somebody's Hand)** - *Diana Ross*	10--7/1/2	974
146	**Westbound #9** - *Flaming Ember*	23--13/1/3	965
147	**What Is Truth** - *Johnny Cash*	11--5/2/3	952
148	**Overture From Tommy (A Rock Opera)** *Assembled Multitude*	16--11/2/3	948
149	**Rubber Duckie** - *Ernie*	13--8/2/1	945
150	**The Thrill Is Gone** - *B.B. King*	15--10/1/2	937
151	**Tell It All Brother** *Kenny Rogers & The First Edition*	17--9/1/3	937
152	**The Bells** - *Originals*	18--12/1/1	915
153	**Long Lonesome Highway** *Michael Parks*	13--9/1/3	906
154	**Wonderful World, Beautiful People** *Jimmy Cliff*	18--10/1/2	902
155	**Oh Me Oh My (I'm A Fool For You Baby)** - *Lulu*	18--14/1/3	902
156	**He Ain't Heavy...He's My Brother** *Neil Diamond*	17--8/1/2	900
157	**Cry Me A River** - *Joe Cocker*	16--8/1/2	896
158	**Summertime Blues** - *The Who*	14--8/1/3	891
159	**Gotta Hold On To This Feeling** *Jr. Walker & The All Stars*	14--7/2/1	890
160	**Silver Bird** - *Mark Lindsay*	20--8/2/2	882
161	**Joanne** - *Michael Nesmith & The First National Band*	17--8/2/1	881
162	**Who'll Stop The Rain** *Creedence Clearwater Revival*	13--7/1/1	847
163	**Question** - *Moody Blues*	19--9/2/1	847
164	**Sugar Sugar** - *Wilson Pickett*	16--9/1/2	836
165	**You're The One** - *Part II* - *Little Sister*	20--10/3/1	830
166	**Stand By Your Man** - *Candi Staton*	21--12/1/1	826
167	**Check Out Your Mind** - *Impressions*	21--11/1/2	818
168	**Blowing Away** - *5th Dimension*	14--5/2/2	812
169	**Fancy** - *Bobbie Gentry*	31--13/1/3	784
170	**Deeper And Deeper** - *Freda Payne*	21--9/2/1	776
171	**I'm Not My Brother's Keeper** *Flaming Ember*	22--9/2/2	764
172	**Mississippi Queen** – *Mountain*	24--11/1/2	763
173	**Up On Cripple Creek** - *The Band*	26--14/1/1	752
174	**Let's Work Together** - *Canned Heat*	17--10/1/2	749
175	**Go Back** - *Crabby Appleton*	30--12/1/2	746
176	**Get Up I Feel Like Being Like A Sex Machine (Part 1)** - *James Brown*	17--5/2/3	745
177	**Lucretia Mac Evil** *Blood, Sweat & Tears*	17--7/1/2	738
178	**Our House** *Crosby, Stills, Nash & Young*	20--7/1/3	730
179	**A Brand New Me** - *Dusty Springfield*	22--9/1/2	713
180	**Neanderthal Man** – *Hotlegs*	20--8/2/1	712
181	**Solitary Man** - *Neil Diamond*	20--10/1/1	711
182	**Only Love Can Break Your Heart** *Neil Young*	20--8/1/2	692
183	**As The Years Go By** - *Mashmakhan*	30--13/1/2	674
184	**Monster** – *Steppenwolf*	23--6/1/3	666
185	**Closer To Home** - *Grand Funk Railroad*	27--12/1/1	666
186	**Heed The Call** *Kenny Rogers & The First Edition*	21--8/1/2	660
187	**Jennifer Tomkins** - *Street People*	36--10/1/4	656
188	**She** - *Tommy James & Shondells*	19--6/1/2	646

Rank	Title - Act	Trajectory	Pts.
189	I've Lost You - Elvis Presley	18--6/1/2	645
190	Maybe - Three Degrees	24--10/1/2	642
191	Steal Away - Johnnie Taylor	23--11/1/1	622
192	Save The Country - 5th Dimension	20--8/1/1	617
193	Part Time Love - Ann Peebles	27--11/1/2	607
194	Make It Easy On Yourself - Dionne Warwick	25--8/1/1	606
195	Can't Stop Loving You - Tom Jones	23--7/2/1	598
196	Shilo - Neil Diamond	23--10/1/1	596
197	Hey, Mister Sun - Bobby Sherman	23--7/1/2	591
198	So Close - Jake Holmes	29--10/1/2	590
199	Border Song (Holy Moses) - Aretha Franklin	23--6/1/3	588
200	Baby Hold On - Grass Roots	25--8/1/2	583
201	Soolaimon (African Trilogy II) - Neil Diamond	24--7/1/2	581
202	Always Something There To Remind Me - R.B. Greaves	22--6/2/1	577
203	Cupid - Johnny Nash	36--10/2/2	566
204	Peace Will Come (According To Plan) - Melanie	20--7/1/1	556
205	Puppet Man - 5th Dimension	22--8/1/1	552
206	She Belongs To Me - Rick Nelson & The Stone Canyon Band	30--16/1/1	549
207	Never Had A Dream Come True - Stevie Wonder	22--7/1/1	548
208	When Julie Comes Around - Cuff Links	31--10/1/1	538
209	If I Never Knew Your Name - Vic Dana	39--9/2/1	534
210	Long Long Time - Linda Ronstadt	26--9/1/1	530
211	I Want To Take You Higher - Ike & Tina Turner & The Ikettes	42--14/1/1	530
212	Wigwam - Bob Dylan	28--7/2/1	528
213	Breaking Up Is Hard To Do - Lenny Welch	32--8/2/2	521
214	Gotta Get Back To You - Tommy James & The Shondells	28--8/1/1	518
215	Everybody's Out Of Town - B.J. Thomas	21--6/1/1	515
216	Mongoose - Elephant's Memory	49--15/1/1	512
217	Cold Turkey - Plastic Ono Band	32--8/1/2	511
218	Mississippi - John Phillips	37--11/1/1	507
219	The Next Step Is Love - Elvis Presley	30--8/1/1	506
220	Hey Lawdy Mama - Steppenwolf	21--7/1/0	505
221	Big Yellow Taxi - Neighborhood	24--8/1/1	504
222	All I Have To Do Is Dream - Bobbie Gentry & Glen Campbell	31--7/1/2	502
223	Spirit In The Dark - Aretha Franklin	25--6/1/2	499
224	Let's Work Together (Part 1) - Wilbert Harrison	30--11/1/0	499
225	And The Grass Won't Pay No Mind - Mark Lindsay	37--8/1/2	491
226	That Same Old Feeling - Pickettywitch	40--11/1/1	489
227	Airport Love Theme (Gwen And Vern) - Vincent Bell	27--8/1/2	487
228	Mighty Joe - Shocking Blue	30--7/1/1	484
229	You Need Love Like I Do (Don't You) - Gladys Knight & The Pips	28--7/1/1	482
230	She Came In Through The Bathroom Window - Joe Cocker	36--8/1/2	478
231	Viva Tirado - Part 1 - El Chicano	27--9/1/2	475
232	(You've Got Me) Dangling On A String - Chairmen Of The Board	30--8/1/1	475
233	My Marie - Engelbert Humperdinck	27--6/1/2	473
234	Take A Look Around - Smith	26--6/1/2	469
235	I'll Be Right Here - Tyrone Davis	33--7/2/2	469
236	Do You See My Love (For You Growing) - Jr. Walker & The All Stars	25--7/1/1	464
237	It's A New Day (Part 1) & (Part 2) - James Brown	26--5/1/2	460
238	Pearl - Tommy Roe	30--7/1/2	460
239	The Sly, Slick, And The Wicked - Lost Generation	39--10/1/1	459
240	Sweetheart - Engelbert Humperdinck	38--5/2/3	454
241	Hold On - Rascals	29--6/1/2	451
242	Walking Through The Country - Grass Roots	30--6/1/2	445
243	My Elusive Dreams - Bobby Vinton	34--7/2/1	444
244	Do What You Wanna Do - Five Flights Up	29--9/1/1	442
245	How Can I Forget - Marvin Gaye	27--6/1/1	441
246	The End Of Our Road - Marvin Gaye	28--7/1/1	439
247	Stir It Up And Serve It - Tommy Roe	32--7/1/1	437
248	I Am Somebody Part II - Johnnie Taylor	30--9/1/1	434
249	If You Were Mine - Ray Charles	50--10/1/9	434
250	Sunshine - Archies	30--7/1/1	433
251	So Much Love - Faith, Hope & Charity	36--7/2/1	433
252	Oh What A Day - Dells	36--6/2/1	427
253	Everybody Is A Star - Sly & The Family Stone	40--7/1/2	423
254	I Can't Leave Your Love Alone - Clarence Carter	49--5/1/5	422
255	Let Me Go To Him - Dionne Warwick	26--5/1/2	417
256	Who's Your Baby? - Archies	29--6/1/1	415
257	Oh Happy Day - Glen Campbell	34--6/1/2	415
258	One Tin Soldier - Original Caste	50--16/1/0	414
259	I Don't Wanna Cry - Ronnie Dyson	35--6/1/1	408
260	If I Were A Carpenter - Johnny Cash & June Carter	26--6/1/1	407
261	The Seeker - The Who	30--6/1/2	405
262	I Stand Accused - Isaac Hayes	38--6/2/1	404
263	Moon Walk Part I - Joe Simon	40--8/1/1	401
264	Do It - Neil Diamond	36--7/1/1	398
265	(How Bout A Little Hand For) The Boys In The Band - Boys In The Band	41--10/1/1	397
266	New World Coming - Mama Cass Elliot	30--6/2/0	395
267	Paper Mache - Dionne Warwick	31--5/1/2	392
268	Sweet Feeling - Candi Staton	44--10/1/1	392
269	Sing A Song For Freedom - Frijid Pink	39--7/1/1	390
270	Point It Out - Smokey Robinson & The Miracles	41--8/1/0	386
271	Canned Ham - Norman Greenbaum	32--7/1/0	382
272	When You Get Right Down To It - Delfonics	41--8/1/1	382
273	Hummingbird - B.B. King	42--7/1/1	382
274	Do The Funky Chicken - Rufus Thomas	50--7/1/4	381
275	Into The Mystic - Johnny Rivers	38--7/1/1	378
276	Miss America - Mark Lindsay	31--5/1/2	377
277	Trying To Make A Fool Of Me - Delfonics	41--7/1/1	376
278	Chains And Things - B.B. King	45--6/1/2	376
279	Everything's Tuesday - Chairmen Of The Board	39--7/1/1	373
280	Ain't That Loving You (For More Reasons Than One) - Luther Ingram	45--6/1/3	373
281	Only You Know And I Know - Dave Mason	37--7/1/1	369

Rank	Title - Act	Trajectory	Pts.
282	Time Waits For No One - Friends Of Distinction	44--7/1/1	367
283	Riki Tiki Tavi - Donovan	40--6/1/2	366
284	It's All In Your Mind - Clarence Carter	39--6/1/1	362
285	Come To Me - Tommy James & The Shondells	36--7/1/1	359
286	Brother Rapp (Part 1) & (Part 2) - James Brown	30--5/2/0	357
287	Sunday Morning Coming Down - Johnny Cash	41--7/1/1	357
288	Temma Harbour - Mary Hopkin	43--8/1/0	355
289	Traces/Memories - Lettermen	51--8/1/1	353
290	We Can Make Music - Tommy Roe	35--7/1/0	352
291	Ungena Za Ulimwengu (Unite The World) - Temptations	30--4/1/2	351
292	Love Bones - Johnnie Taylor	32--6/1/1	349
293	Black Fox - Freddy Robinson	45--8/1/0	348
294	I Just Don't Know What To Do With Myself - Gary Puckett	44--7/1/1	347
295	Come Running - Van Morrison	30--6/2/0	341
296	You Make Me Real - Doors	40--6/1/1	341
297	On The Beach (In The Summertime) - 5th Dimension	41--5/1/2	338
298	Glory Glory - Rascals	42--5/2/1	337
299	Run Sally Run - Cuff Links	40--7/1/0	336
300	Rainbow - Marmalade	48--7/1/2	336

1971

Rank	Title - Act	Trajectory	Pts.
1	Joy To The World - Three Dog Night	1--7/6/6	8259
2	Knock Three Times - Dawn	1--10/2/7	7534
3	Maggie May - Rod Stewart	1--9/3/7	7525
4	Brand New Key - Melanie	1--10/2/6	6782
5	Family Affair - Sly & The Family Stone	1--5/4/7	6599
6	Theme From Shaft - Isaac Hayes	1--5/2/8	6433
7	One Bad Apple - Osmonds	1--8/4/4	6331
8	It's Too Late - Carole King	1--7/4/7	6246
9	How Can You Mend A Broken Heart - Bee Gees	1--9/3/4	5852
10	Never Can Say Goodbye - Jackson 5	1--9/1/3	5836
11	Indian Reservation (The Lament Of The Cherokee) - Raiders	1--13/1/7	5753
12	Gypsys, Tramps & Thieves - Cher	1--7/2/7	5737
13	Rose Garden - Lynn Anderson	1--11/1/7	5734
14	She's A Lady - Tom Jones	1--9/1/7	5447
15	Go Away Little Girl - Donny Osmond	1--9/1/5	5349
16	Just My Imagination (Running Away With Me) - Temptations	1--8/1/8	5279
17	Mr. Big Stuff - Jean Knight	2--10/1/6	5121
18	Take Me Home, Country Roads - John Denver	1--18/1/4	4881
19	Doesn't Somebody Want To Be Wanted - Partridge Family	1--9/1/4	4857
20	Put Your Hand In The Hand - Ocean	2--7/3/6	4857
21	Draggin' The Line - Tommy James	2--11/2/3	4786
22	Don't Pull Your Love - Hamilton, Joe Frank & Reynolds	1--12/1/3	4703
23	Want Ads - Honey Cone	1--9/2/5	4698
24	You've Got A Friend - James Taylor	1--11/1/5	4690
25	Superstar - Carpenters	2--7/2/7	4602
26	Mama's Pearl - Jackson 5	1--7/1/4	4304
27	Smiling Faces Sometimes - Undisputed Truth	1--13/1/5	4130
28	Yo-Yo - Osmonds	2--7/1/7	4072
29	It Don't Come Easy - Ringo Starr	1--9/1/4	4000
30	Brown Sugar - Rolling Stones	2--7/2/4	3924
31	Uncle Albert/Admiral Halsey - Paul & Linda McCartney	1--7/1/5	3912
32	Treat Her Like A Lady - Cornelius Brothers & Sister Rose	2--17/1/6	3867
33	What's Going On - Marvin Gaye	1--8/1/6	3701
34	Lonely Days - Bee Gees	1--10/1/6	3690
35	Imagine - John Lennon/Plastic Ono Band	2--6/1/5	3683
36	Bridge Over Troubled Water - Aretha Franklin	2--7/1/4	3669
37	The Night They Drove Old Dixie Down - Joan Baez	3--9/1/6	3549
38	Groove Me - King Floyd	4--12/4/5	3506
39	Rainy Days And Mondays - Carpenters	2--8/1/4	3477
40	Ain't No Sunshine - Bill Withers	4--14/2/3	3428
41	Spanish Harlem - Aretha Franklin	1--7/1/5	3390
42	Me And Bobby McGee - Janis Joplin	3--8/2/5	3137
43	Baby I'm-A Want You - Bread	3--8/2/5	3010
44	Black Magic Woman - Santana	4--9/2/4	2976
45	Have You Ever Seen The Rain - Creedence Clearwater Revival	3--6/2/3	2859
46	Mercy Mercy Me (The Ecology) - Marvin Gaye	4--10/1/3	2819
47	If I Were Your Woman - Gladys Knight & The Pips	5--11/2/4	2690
48	Have You Seen Her - Chi-Lites	5--5/1/8	2685
49	Stoned Love - Supremes	5--12/1/3	2627
50	I Hear You Knocking - Dave Edmunds	4--9/2/4	2608
51	Do You Know What I Mean - Lee Michaels	4--12/1/4	2567
52	I'll Meet You Halfway - Partridge Family	2--7/1/3	2458
53	Does Anybody Really Know What Time It Is? - Chicago	5--9/2/2	2458
54	I Am...I Said - Neil Diamond	4--6/2/4	2383
55	An Old Fashioned Love Song - Three Dog Night	4--7/2/5	2382
56	Peace Train - Cat Stevens	4--9/1/4	2350
57	Tired Of Being Alone - Al Green	6--13/1/4	2345
58	Stay Awhile - Bells	4--10/2/3	2340
59	Chick-A-Boom (Don't Ya Jes' Love It) - Daddy Dewdrop	5--13/1/3	2262
60	Proud Mary - Ike & Tina Turner	5--9/2/3	2222
61	Signs - Five Man Electrical Band	7--17/1/3	2172
62	Another Day - Paul McCartney	6--9/1/2	2111
63	I've Found Someone Of My Own - Free Movement	6--23/2/4	2045
64	Sweet And Innocent - Donny Osmond	7--12/3/4	2045
65	Your Song - Elton John	8--10/1/6	2042
66	For All We Know - Carpenters	6--7/2/5	2033
67	If You Could Read My Mind - Gordon Lightfoot	5--11/1/4	2030
68	Superstar - Murray Head	8--72/2/3	1998
69	Sweet Mary - Wadsworth Mansion	5--12/2/4	1889
70	If – Bread	6--8/2/4	1883
71	Sweet Hitch-Hiker - Creedence Clearwater Revival	5--7/1/3	1865
72	What Is Life - George Harrison	7--8/1/3	1815
73	Stoney End - Barbra Streisand	7--16/1/4	1804
74	Amos Moses - Jerry Reed	8--15/2/5	1770
75	Stick-Up - Honey Cone	7--10/1/4	1759
76	Immigrant Song - Led Zeppelin	8--8/2/4	1749

Rank	Title - Act	Trajectory	Pts.
77	Don't Knock My Love - *Pt. I* Wilson Pickett	7--11/1/2	1740
78	Love Her Madly - *Doors*	7--8/2/3	1725
79	Watching Scotty Grow Bobby Goldsboro	8--10/2/3	1713
80	Won't Get Fooled Again - *The Who*	9--11/1/3	1687
81	Rock Steady - *Aretha Franklin*	7--7/2/2	1684
82	I Woke Up In Love This Morning Partridge Family	9--9/1/3	1648
83	She's Not Just Another Woman 8th Day	8--10/2/3	1646
84	Sweet City Woman - *Stampeders*	7--12/2/2	1637
85	I Just Want To Celebrate - *Rare Earth*	7--9/2/2	1635
86	Mr. Bojangles - *Nitty Gritty Dirt Band*	9--18/1/5	1634
87	When You're Hot, You're Hot Jerry Reed	9--11/2/2	1633
88	Temptation Eyes - *Grass Roots*	16--15/2/3	1618
89	One Toke Over The Line Brewer & Shipley	8--12/1/3	1595
90	Liar - *Three Dog Night*	8--10/1/3	1592
91	Bring The Boys Home - *Freda Payne*	7--10/1/4	1566
92	Two Divided By Love - *Grass Roots*	8--7/2/3	1544
93	Funky Nassau - *Part 1* Beginning Of The End	10--13/1/2	1499
94	Inner City Blues (Make Me Wanna Holler) - *Marvin Gaye*	6--7/1/4	1497
95	We Can Work It Out - *Stevie Wonder*	9--9/1/3	1468
96	If You Really Love Me - *Stevie Wonder*	9--11/2/2	1467
97	Here Comes That Rainy Day Feeling Again - *Fortunes*	8--12/1/3	1460
98	For The Good Times - *Ray Price*	13--21/1/2	1460
99	Love's Lines, Angles And Rhymes 5th Dimension	11--8/2/3	1458
100	What The World Needs Now Is Love/ Abraham, Martin And John - *Tom Clay*	7--7/2/2	1445
101	Don't Let The Green Grass Fool You Wilson Pickett	10--8/3/2	1443
102	I Don't Want To Do Wrong Gladys Knight & The Pips	9--10/2/3	1439
103	Sooner Or Later - *Grass Roots*	12--11/1/2	1433
104	That's The Way I've Always Heard It Should Be - *Carly Simon*	9--13/1/3	1425
105	Help Me Make It Through The Night Sammi Smith	9--12/1/3	1413
106	(Where Do I Begin) Love Story Andy Williams	10--11/2/2	1409
107	Me And You And A Dog Named Boo Lobo	8--10/1/3	1408
108	Remember Me - *Diana Ross*	8--8/1/3	1399
109	Respect Yourself - *Staple Singers*	10--13/1/4	1393
110	Precious, Precious - *Jackie Moore*	11--14/1/3	1390
111	Never Ending Song Of Love Delaney & Bonnie & Friends	9--13/1/3	1388
112	Thin Line Between Love And Hate Persuaders	10--11/1/4	1364
113	It's Impossible - *Perry Como*	10--14/1/3	1353
114	Easy Loving - *Freddie Hart*	12--13/1/4	1322
115	Beginnings - *Chicago*	11--9/2/3	1319
116	Never My Love - *5th Dimension*	14--8/2/3	1306
117	Cried Like A Baby - *Bobby Sherman*	10--8/1/3	1295
118	Pay To The Piper Chairmen Of The Board	10--11/2/1	1247
119	Light Sings - *Supremes*	10--9/1/1	1246
120	Everybody's Everything - *Santana*	10--8/1/3	1220
121	I Love You For All Seasons - *Fuzz*	20--16/2/2	1196
122	Trapped By A Thing Called Love Denise LaSalle	13--11/1/4	1193
123	Amazing Grace - *Judy Collins*	13--11/1/3	1188
124	One Man Band - *Three Dog Night*	13--9/2/2	1186
125	Love The One You're With Isley Brothers	10--9/2/2	1183
126	Double Lovin' - *Osmonds*	9--6/1/4	1181
127	Oye Como Va - *Santana*	10--7/1/2	1170
128	Whatcha See Is Whatcha Get Dramatics	14--10/2/3	1168
129	The Story In Your Eyes - *Moody Blues*	14--8/2/2	1167
130	Rain Dance - *Guess Who*	15--9/2/1	1155
131	(Theme From) Love Story Henry Mancini & His Orchestra	11--7/2/4	1150
132	Riders On The Storm - *Doors*	12--10/1/2	1143
133	Domino - *Van Morrison*	9--10/1/2	1127
134	Superstar (Remember How You Got Where You Are) - *Temptations*	13--6/1/4	1107
135	Stones - *Neil Diamond*	13--7/2/3	1099
136	So Far Away - *Carole King*	10--6/1/4	1087
137	One Fine Morning - *Lighthouse*	16--9/2/3	1070
138	Hot Pants Pt. 1 (She Got To Use What She Got To Get What She Wants) James Brown	10--6/1/4	1056
139	Power To The People John Lennon/Plastic Ono Band	10--6/1/3	1052
140	No Love At All - *B.J. Thomas*	14--10/1/2	1046
141	I Really Don't Want To Know Elvis Presley	13--7/2/2	1044
142	I Don't Know How To Love Him Helen Reddy	19--15/2/1	1043
143	Desiderata - *Les Crane*	11--9/1/2	1040
144	Questions 67 And 68 - *Chicago*	13--9/1/2	1038
145	Woodstock Matthews' Southern Comfort	17--13/1/2	1035
146	Born To Wander - *Rare Earth*	18--9/2/1	1018
147	One Tin Soldier, The Legend Of Billy Jack [version 1] - *Coven*	18--12/1/3	999
148	Timothy - *Buoys*	13--9/2/2	996
149	Stagger Lee - *Tommy Roe*	19--11/2/2	988
150	Rings - *Cymarron*	17--12/1/2	969
151	Birds Of A Feather - *Raiders*	13--8/1/1	965
152	Love The One You're With Stephen Stills	16--10/1/1	965
153	Right On The Tip Of My Tongue Brenda & The Tabulations	14--9/1/3	959
154	(Do The) Push And Pull - *Part 1* Rufus Thomas	20--11/2/3	949
155	Nathan Jones - *Tom Jones*	14--6/2/2	947
156	Wild World - *Cat Stevens*	18--10/1/2	945
157	River Deep - *Mountain High* Supremes & Four Tops	15--7/1/4	935
158	Maybe Tomorrow - *Jackson 5*	16--6/1/4	925
159	We Gotta Get You A Woman - *Runt*	21--15/1/2	919
160	I Don't Blame You At All Smokey Robinson & The Miracles	18--9/2/2	901
161	Chirpy Chirpy Cheep Cheep Mac & Katie Kissoon	18--11/1/2	894
162	A Natural Man - *Lou Rawls*	27--16/1/1	864
163	If Not For You - *Olivia Newton-John*	23--13/1/2	861
164	Wedding Song (There Is Love) Paul Stookey	21--10/2/2	847
165	You're All I Need To Get By Aretha Franklin	15--6/2/1	841

Rank	Title - Act	Trajectory	Pts.
166	Toast And Marmalade For Tea - Tin Tin	16--9/1/2	827
167	Games - Redeye	22--12/1/2	824
168	Me And My Arrow - Nilsson	27--13/1/1	815
169	Somebody's Watching You - Little Sister	22--10/1/2	812
170	Here Comes The Sun - Richie Havens	15--10/1/2	809
171	Baby Let Me Kiss You - King Floyd	19--10/1/1	800
172	Cool Aid - Paul Humphrey & His Cool Aid Chemists	22--12/2/1	776
173	Behind Blue Eyes - The Who	24--9/2/2	765
174	Eighteen - Alice Cooper	21--10/2/1	758
175	Your Time To Cry - Joe Simon	30--11/2/1	758
176	(Don't Worry) If There's A Hell Below We're All Going To Go - Curtis Mayfield	24--10/1/2	752
177	Make It Funky (Part 1) - James Brown	20--8/2/1	730
178	I'd Love To Change The World - Ten Years After	28--10/2/1	728
179	Chicago - Graham Nash	29--10/1/3	723
180	Only You Know And I Know - Delaney & Bonnie	18--6/2/2	721
181	Summer Sand - Dawn	19--7/1/3	721
182	Booty Butt - Ray Charles Orchestra	24--10/1/2	710
183	Friends - Elton John	17--7/1/1	693
184	Blue Money - Van Morrison	23--10/1/2	689
185	Moon Shadow - Cat Stevens	26--9/1/2	683
186	Don't Change On Me - Ray Charles	28--11/1/1	671
187	Saturday Morning Confusion - Bobby Russell	34--13/1/2	669
188	Absolutely Right - Five Man Electrical Band	20--6/1/3	666
189	Wild Horses - Rolling Stones	18--6/1/2	657
190	Women's Love Rights - Laura Lee	20--8/2/1	655
191	What Are You Doing Sunday - Dawn	26--7/2/3	646
192	Reach Out I'll Be There - Diana Ross	19--6/1/2	638
193	Long Ago And Far Away - James Taylor	16--5/1/2	635
194	Let Your Love Go - Bread	20--8/1/2	635
195	Cry Baby - Janis Joplin	20--7/1/1	635
196	Free - Chicago	19--7/1/1	632
197	Get It On - Chase	22--8/2/2	623
198	High Time We Went - Joe Cocker	29--8/2/2	607
199	Heavy Makes You Happy (Sha-Na-Boom Boom) - Staple Singers	24--7/2/2	600
200	Where Did Our Love Go - Donnie Elbert	30--10/1/4	594
201	Puppet Man - 5th Dimension	22--7/1/1	593
202	Mother - John Lennon/Plastic Ono Band	19--5/1/2	590
203	Most Of All - B.J. Thomas	30--9/1/1	590
204	Burning Bridges - Mike Curb Congregation	29--14/2/1	579
205	Loving Her Was Easier (Than Anything I'll Ever Do Again) - Kris Kristofferson	33--10/2/1	574
206	K-Jee - Nite-Liters	39--7/1/6	573
207	Go Down Gamblin' - Blood, Sweat & Tears	21--7/1/1	570
208	Stop The War Now - Edwin Starr	24--5/2/2	563
209	The Drum - Bobby Sherman	22--5/2/1	558
210	Double Barrel - Dave & Ansil Collins	27--9/1/2	557
211	I Don't Know How To Love Him - Yvonne Elliman	30--9/1/2	556
212	Dream Baby (How Long Must I Dream) - Glen Campbell	24--7/1/1	555
213	You've Got A Friend - Roberta Flack & Donny Hathaway	28--12/1/1	554
214	Soul Power Pt. 1 - James Brown	32--7/2/2	551
215	Bangla-Desh - George Harrison	20--6/1/1	542
216	Stop, Look, Listen (To Your Heart) - Stylistics	34--8/1/9	541
217	All Day Music - War	28--8/2/1	537
218	Wild Night - Van Morrison	25--9/1/1	534
219	Jody's Got Your Girl And Gone - Johnnie Taylor	27--7/2/1	532
220	Rainy Jane - Davy Jones	32--6/2/3	528
221	Pretty As You Feel - Jefferson Airplane	35--7/2/2	527
222	I Play And Sing - Dawn	22--7/1/1	524
223	Your Move - Yes	29--11/1/1	524
224	When I'm Dead And Gone - McGuinness Flint	35--9/1/1	524
225	Just Seven Numbers (Can Straighten Out My Life) - Four Tops	26--7/1/2	520
226	Marianne - Stephen Stills	31--9/1/1	520
227	Mighty Clouds Of Joy - B.J. Thomas	39--9/2/0	517
228	I Ain't Got Time Anymore - Glass Bottle	26--12/1/1	516
229	Albert Flasher - Guess Who	35--11/1/2	515
230	I'm Comin' Home - Tommy James	23--7/1/1	511
231	D.O.A. - Bloodrock	36--11/1/2	508
232	I Know I'm In Love - Chee-Chee & Peppy	35--8/1/10	504
233	She's All I Got - Freddie North	30--7/1/3	500
234	1900 Yesterday - Liz Damon's Orient Express	29--10/1/1	499
235	Fresh As A Daisy - Emitt Rhodes	38--9/1/2	497
236	Country Road - James Taylor	25--7/1/1	491
237	Silver Moon - Michael Nesmith & The First National Band	28--8/1/1	482
238	The Love We Had (Stays On My Mind) - Dells	33--9/1/1	481
239	Charity Ball - Fanny	32--8/1/1	478
240	Never Can Say Goodbye - Isaac Hayes	33--7/1/3	475
241	The Breakdown Part 1 - Rufus Thomas	31--9/1/2	471
242	I Hear Those Church Bells Ringing - Dusk	41--14/1/0	469
243	Watching The River Flow - Bob Dylan	31--6/1/2	466
244	You've Got To Crawl (Before You Walk) - 8th Day	34--10/1/1	464
245	Bridget The Midget (The Queen Of The Blues) - Ray Stevens	43--9/1/2	464
246	I'm So Proud - Main Ingredient	41--11/1/2	454
247	Lowdown - Chicago	25--6/1/1	453
248	Do I Love You - Paul Anka	38--8/2/2	451
249	Where Evil Grows - Poppy Family	50--10/2/1	448
250	I'm A Greedy Man - Part 1 - James Brown	29--7/1/1	446
251	Grandma's Hands - Bill Withers	31--6/1/2	445
252	Do Me Right - Detroit Emeralds	42--14/1/1	439
253	Mac Arthur Park (Part II) - Four Tops	36--9/1/0	438
254	He Called Me Baby - Candi Staton	48--5/2/2	438
255	Crazy Love - Helen Reddy	38--10/1/1	437
256	Can I Get A Witness - Lee Michaels	39--6/2/2	434
257	Love Means (You Never Have To Say You're Sorry) - Sounds Of Sunshine	40--10/1/2	434
258	House At Pooh Corner - Nitty Gritty Dirt Band	38--9/1/1	424
259	Resurrection Shuffle - Ashton, Gardner & Dyke	37--5/1/4	418

Rank	Title - Act	Trajectory	Pts.
260	Melting Pot - *Booker T. & MG's*	47--11/1/0	417
261	I Think Of You - *Perry Como*	45--8/1/1	413
262	Walk Away - *James Gang*	29--9/1/0	410
263	I'm Leavin' - *Elvis Presley*	36--7/1/1	406
264	It's A Cryin' Shame - *Gayle McCormick*	43--9/1/1	404
265	Take Me Girl, I'm Ready *Jr. Walker & The All Stars*	44--6/1/2	400
266	Ride With Me - *Steppenwolf*	31--6/1/1	396
267	Get Up, Get Into It, Get Involved (Pt. 1) *James Brown*	35--6/1/1	393
268	An American Trilogy - *Mickey Newbury*	46--8/1/3	392
269	Tarkio Road - *Brewer & Shipley*	39--7/1/1	390
270	Let It Be - *Joan Baez*	47--6/2/2	388
271	Tongue In Cheek - *Sugarloaf*	40--9/1/0	386
272	Theme From Love Story - *Francis Lai & His Orchestra*	36--9/1/1	384
273	Change Partners - *Stephen Stills*	38--7/1/1	384
274	Love - *Lettermen*	44--10/1/0	384
275	Where Did They Go, Lord *Elvis Presley*	34--6/1/1	382
276	Ask Me No Questions - *B.B. King*	43--8/1/1	382
277	Another Time, Another Place *Engelbert Humperdinck*	40--7/1/1	381
278	Ooh Poo Pah Doo - *Ike & Tina Turner*	37--6/1/1	378
279	Mother Freedom - *Bread*	45--8/1/1	372
280	Apeman - *Kinks*	39--7/1/2	370
281	You Brought The Joy - *Freda Payne*	45--7/1/2	370
282	Call My Name, I'll Be There *Wilson Pickett*	41--7/1/0	368
283	Chairman Of The Board *Chairmen Of The Board*	37--7/1/0	365
284	Cherish What Is Dear To You (While It's Near To You) - *Freda Payne*	36--8/1/0	360
285	Pushbike Song - *Mixtures*	44--9/1/1	356
286	The Green Grass Starts To Grow *Dionne Warwick*	45--7/1/1	356
287	(For God's Sake) Give More Power To The People - *Chi-Lites*	29--6/2/1	355
288	Spill The Wine - *Isley Brothers*	39--6/1/1	354
289	Maggie - *Redbone*	60--39/1/1	354
290	Ruby Tuesday - *Melanie*	34--5/1/1	352
291	They Can't Take Away Our Music *Eric Burdon & War*	37--6/1/1	352
292	Till - *Tom Jones*	40--5/1/2	352
293	God Bless Whoever Sent You *Originals*	52--10/1/2	349
294	Hang On To Your Life - *Guess Who*	35--6/1/1	344
295	Lonely Teardrops - *Brian Hyland*	48--7/2/1	344
296	Sit Yourself Down - *Stephen Stills*	31--5/1/1	342
297	Escape-Ism (Part 1) - *James Brown*	40--6/1/2	339
298	Don't Wanna Live Inside Myself *Bee Gees*	39--6/1/1	337
299	Mean Mistreater - *Grand Funk Railroad*	44--6/2/0	337
300	Annabella *Hamilton, Joe Frank & Reynolds*	42--7/1/1	336

1972

Rank	Title - Act	Trajectory	Pts.
1	American Pie - *Don McLean*	1--7/4/9	8129
2	Alone Again (Naturally) *Gilbert O'Sullivan*	1--9/3/7	7867
3	The First Time Ever I Saw Your Face *Roberta Flack*	1--8/4/5	7266
4	Let's Stay Together - *Al Green*	1--12/2/4	6687
5	Rockin' Robin - *Michael Jackson*	1--7/1/7	6265
6	Me And Mrs. Jones - *Billy Paul*	1--10/2/6	6250
7	Brandy (You're A Fine Girl) *Looking Glass*	1--13/1/3	5885
8	Without You - *Nilsson*	1--13/2/5	5673
9	A Horse With No Name - *America*	1--6/3/5	5541
10	Heart Of Gold - *Neil Young*	1--8/1/7	5452
11	My Ding-A-Ling - *Chuck Berry*	1--13/2/4	5238
12	Daddy Don't You Walk So Fast *Wayne Newton*	1--17/1/5	5014
13	I Am Woman - *Helen Reddy*	1--23/1/5	4980
14	Got To Be There - *Michael Jackson*	1--10/1/4	4949
15	Lean On Me - *Bill Withers*	1--12/2/5	4866
16	Oh Girl - *Chi-Lites*	1--9/1/5	4817
17	(If Loving You Is Wrong) I Don't Want To Be Right - *Luther Ingram*	3--13/2/4	4746
18	The Candy Man - *Sammy Davis, Jr.*	1--13/1/7	4723
19	Burning Love - *Elvis Presley*	1--13/1/3	4722
20	Long Cool Woman (In A Black Dress) *Hollies*	1--14/1/2	4712
21	Nice To Be With You - *Gallery*	1--17/1/4	4650
22	I Can See Clearly Now - *Johnny Nash*	1--13/1/8	4585
23	I'll Take You There - *Staple Singers*	1--8/2/5	4507
24	Too Late To Turn Back Now *Cornelius Brothers & Sister Rose*	1--11/1/4	4468
25	I'm Still In Love With You - *Al Green*	1--11/1/3	4422
26	I Gotcha - *Joe Tex*	3--14/2/4	4403
27	Everybody Plays The Fool *Main Ingredient*	1--15/1/5	4339
28	Baby Don't Get Hooked On Me *Mac Davis*	1--15/1/4	4338
29	You Ought To Be With Me - *Al Green*	2--10/1/4	4291
30	Back Stabbers - *O'Jays*	1--12/1/5	4269
31	I'll Be Around - *Spinners*	1--13/1/3	4236
32	Precious And Few - *Climax*	1--10/1/7	4205
33	Song Sung Blue - *Neil Diamond*	1--10/1/4	4189
34	I'd Love You To Want Me - *Lobo*	1--12/1/3	4167
35	Black And White - *Three Dog Night*	1--10/1/4	4112
36	Hurting Each Other - *Carpenters*	2--8/2/4	4095
37	The Lion Sleeps Tonight - *Robert John*	2--13/1/6	3964
38	Outa-Space - *Billy Preston*	1--12/1/4	3914
39	Cherish - *David Cassidy*	3--11/2/3	3908
40	Papa Was A Rollin' Stone - *Temptations*	1--9/1/5	3827
41	Look What You Done For Me *Al Green*	3--9/3/3	3820
42	Nights In White Satin - *Moody Blues*	1--14/1/4	3795
43	Down By The Lazy River - *Osmonds*	3--7/3/4	3790
44	It Never Rains In Southern California *Albert Hammond*	2--12/1/4	3705
45	Ben - *Michael Jackson*	2--12/1/4	3555
46	Sylvia's Mother *Dr. Hook & The Medicine Show*	1--14/1/3	3526
47	Troglodyte (Cave Man) *Jimmy Castor Bunch*	2--11/1/3	3510
48	Garden Party - *Rick Nelson & The Stone Canyon Band*	3--14/1/4	3229
49	Puppy Love - *Donny Osmond*	3--6/3/4	3195
50	If You Don't Know Me By Now *Harold Melvin & The Blue Notes*	2--10/1/5	3166
51	Day After Day - *Badfinger*	3--9/3/2	3138
52	In The Rain – *Dramatics*	3--10/1/4	3091
53	Scorpio - *Dennis Coffey & The Detroit Guitar Band*	4--13/1/3	3087
54	Sunshine - *Jonathan Edwards*	5--11/3/3	2952

Rank	Title - Act	Trajectory	Pts.
55	Mother And Child Reunion - Paul Simon	4--8/2/5	2858
56	Go All The Way - Raspberries	4--15/1/3	2744
57	Betcha By Golly, Wow - Stylistics	4--12/1/3	2707
58	Rock And Roll Part 2 - Gary Glitter	3--11/1/2	2628
59	Clean Up Woman - Betty Wright	4--11/2/3	2520
60	Sugar Daddy - Jackson 5	6--8/2/3	2454
61	Freddie's Dead (Theme From "Superfly") - Curtis Mayfield	6--13/2/3	2387
62	A Cowboy's Work Is Never Done - Sonny & Cher	6--12/1/3	2363
63	(Last Night) I Didn't Get To Sleep At All - 5th Dimension	6--13/3/2	2353
64	Saturday In The Park - Chicago	3--10/1/2	2352
65	School's Out - Alice Cooper	6--11/3/2	2261
66	Hold Your Head Up - Argent	5--14/1/3	2189
67	How Do You Do? - Mouth & MacNeal	5--16/1/3	2151
68	Slippin' Into Darkness - War	12--23/1/2	2109
69	Everything I Own - Bread	6--8/1/5	2091
70	Never Been To Spain - Three Dog Night	5--8/2/2	2065
71	You Don't Mess Around With Jim - Jim Croce	7--12/1/3	2016
72	Little Bitty Pretty One - Jackson 5	5--7/2/2	2012
73	Jungle Fever - Chakachas	6--15/1/4	1994
74	All I Ever Need Is You - Sonny & Cher	6--12/1/3	1984
75	Day Dreaming - Aretha Franklin	5--9/1/2	1978
76	Summer Breeze - Seals & Crofts	6--11/1/4	1923
77	The Happiest Girl In The Whole U.S.A. - Donna Fargo	8--14/1/2	1923
78	Funny Face - Donna Fargo	9--14/2/4	1921
79	You Are Everything - Stylistics	9--14/1/3	1908
80	Walkin' In The Rain With The One I Love - Love Unlimited	7--13/2/2	1850
81	Where Is The Love - Roberta Flack & Donny Hathaway	7--9/2/3	1820
82	Use Me - Bill Withers	5--10/1/2	1762
83	Drowning In The Sea Of Love - Joe Simon	8--12/1/3	1753
84	The Way Of Love - Cher	9--10/1/4	1689
85	Day By Day - Godspell	9--13/1/3	1675
86	If I Could Reach You - 5th Dimension	10--13/1/3	1666
87	I Wanna Be Where You Are - Michael Jackson	7--10/1/2	1633
88	Goodbye To Love - Carpenters	7--9/1/3	1604
89	Popcorn - Hot Butter	11--16/1/3	1590
90	Ventura Highway - America	8--10/2/2	1580
91	Take It Easy - Eagles	9--10/1/3	1573
92	Hot Rod Lincoln - Commander Cody & His Lost Planet Airmen	7--10/1/3	1567
93	Joy - Apollo 100	6--10/1/4	1547
94	Sweet Seasons - Carole King	8--7/1/4	1535
95	Get On The Good Foot - Part 1 - James Brown	10--11/2/2	1519
96	I Need You - America	8--9/1/2	1493
97	Anticipation - Carly Simon	10--11/1/3	1476
98	Power Of Love - Joe Simon	10--14/1/1	1463
99	Starting All Over Again - Mel & Tim	18--17/1/5	1460
100	Hey Girl - Donny Osmond	9--7/2/3	1454
101	Good Time Charlie's Got The Blues - Danny O'Keefe	10--11/1/3	1448
102	Me And Julio Down By The Schoolyard - Paul Simon	7--8/1/3	1445
103	Something's Wrong With Me - Austin Roberts	10--16/2/2	1445
104	I'm Stone In Love With You - Stylistics	9--11/1/3	1433
105	I Believe In Music - Gallery	13--15/1/2	1420
106	Listen To The Music - Doobie Brothers	9--10/2/2	1395
107	Witchy Woman - Eagles	11--14/1/2	1385
108	Stay With Me - Faces	10--8/2/2	1368
109	Rocket Man - Elton John	11--12/1/2	1356
110	Too Young - Donny Osmond	8--7/1/3	1352
111	Sealed With A Kiss - Bobby Vinton	14--12/1/3	1342
112	Run To Me - Bee Gees	11--11/1/2	1341
113	Bang A Gong (Get It On) - T. Rex	12--14/1/3	1320
114	Vincent - Don McLean	11--9/2/1	1309
115	Tumbling Dice - Rolling Stones	10--7/2/3	1308
116	Coconut - Nilsson	12--13/2/2	1302
117	Rock And Roll Lullaby - B.J. Thomas	12--9/2/2	1298
118	Back Off Boogaloo - Ringo Starr	10--9/2/1	1297
119	Beautiful Sunday - Daniel Boone	16--18/1/2	1297
120	Doctor My Eyes - Jackson Browne	12--11/2/2	1286
121	The Guitar Man - Bread	10--9/2/1	1284
122	Morning Has Broken - Cat Stevens	11--11/2/2	1253
123	Thunder And Lightning - Chi Coltrane	15--11/2/2	1253
124	Roundabout - Yes	10--12/1/2	1245
125	I Saw The Light - Todd Rundgren	11--12/1/2	1223
126	Don't Say You Don't Remember - Beverly Bremers	16--16/1/3	1186
127	Tight Rope - Leon Russell	10--11/1/2	1160
128	Suavecito - Malo	12--12/1/2	1153
129	One Monkey Don't Stop No Show Part 1 - Honey Cone	14--10/1/2	1151
130	The Family Of Man - Three Dog Night	10--7/1/2	1151
131	Black Dog - Led Zeppelin	9--10/1/2	1150
132	Baby Blue - Badfinger	9--8/2/1	1145
133	Baby Let Me Take You (In My Arms) - Detroit Emeralds	19--14/1/2	1143
134	I'd Like To Teach The World To Sing (In Perfect Harmony) - New Seekers	11--9/2/2	1119
135	Runnin' Away - Sly & The Family Stone	11--6/2/3	1092
136	Taurus - Dennis Coffey & The Detroit Guitar Band	13--11/1/2	1084
137	Walk On Water - Neil Diamond	16--9/2/2	1082
138	Amazing Grace - Royal Scots Dragoon Guards	10--8/2/1	1067
139	It's One Of Those Nights (Yes Love) - Partridge Family	13--7/2/1	1044
140	Kiss An Angel Good Mornin' - Charley Pride	19--11/1/3	1036
141	Every Day Of My Life - Bobby Vinton	18--13/1/3	1027
142	Corner Of The Sky - Jackson 5	12--9/1/2	1019
143	Sweet Surrender - Bread	11--8/1/3	1012
144	Taxi - Harry Chapin	20--12/1/4	993
145	Layla - Derek & The Dominos	14--11/1/2	991
146	Floy Joy - Supremes	16--10/1/3	986
147	We've Got To Get It On Again - Addrisi Brothers	15--11/1/3	980
148	The City Of New Orleans - Arlo Guthrie	21--14/1/2	973
149	Operator (That's Not The Way It Feels) - Jim Croce	14--9/1/2	973
150	Diary - Bread	15--10/1/1	971
151	You Wear It Well - Rod Stewart	14--10/1/1	969
152	Could It Be Forever - David Cassidy	15--8/1/3	966
153	Why - Donny Osmond	16--10/1/3	966

Rank	Title - Act	Trajectory	Pts.
154	Speak To The Sky - Rick Springfield	15--11/1/3	963
155	Lookin' Through The Windows Jackson 5	15--8/2/1	962
156	Play Me - Neil Diamond	16--9/1/2	956
157	My World - Bee Gees	15--7/2/2	955
158	Motorcycle Mama - Sailcat	19--11/1/3	938
159	I'd Like To Teach The World To Sing (In Perfect Harmony) - Hillside Singers	16--9/2/1	920
160	I've Been Lonely For So Long Frederick Knight	20--11/1/3	903
161	How Can I Be Sure - David Cassidy	15--8/2/1	889
162	The Day I Found Myself - Honey Cone	15--10/1/1	878
163	People Make The World Go Round Stylistics	18--9/1/2	873
164	Happy - Rolling Stones	14--8/1/2	869
165	The Witch Queen Of New Orleans Redbone	19--13/1/1	862
166	Hold Her Tight - Osmonds	15--7/2/1	859
167	Fire And Water - Wilson Pickett	17--9/1/2	854
168	Ain't Understanding Mellow Jerry Butler & Brenda Lee Eager	24--13/1/3	850
169	Honky Cat - Elton John	18--7/2/2	850
170	Conquistador - Procol Harum	18--10/1/2	836
171	Ask Me What You Want - Millie Jackson	19--13/1/1	830
172	It's Going To Take Some Time Carpenters	17--6/1/3	826
173	Pop That Thang - Isley Brothers	23--13/1/1	825
174	You're Still A Young Man Tower Of Power	22--10/2/2	814
175	No One To Depend On - Santana	17--8/1/2	791
176	Convention '72 - Delegates	9--6/1/1	783
177	Hey Big Brother - Rare Earth	24--9/2/2	776
178	Dialogue (Parts I & II) - Chicago	17--7/1/3	751
179	Don't Ever Be Lonely (A Poor Little Fool Like Me) Cornelius Brothers & Sister Rose	23--10/1/1	749
180	Crazy Horses - Osmonds	19--8/1/2	740
181	Sitting - Cat Stevens	21--8/2/2	734
182	Isn't Life Strange - Moody Blues	20--9/1/1	730
183	Don't Do It - The Band	23--10/1/2	725
184	Levon - Elton John	17--8/1/1	722
185	Do Your Thing - Isaac Hayes	23--9/1/2	717
186	Elected - Alice Cooper	18--7/1/2	701
187	Living In A House Divided - Cher	21--8/1/1	700
188	Rock 'N Roll Soul Grand Funk Railroad	24--11/2/1	699
189	Theme From "Summer Of '42" Peter Nero	21--12/1/1	699
190	That's The Way I Feel About Cha Bobby Womack	22--13/1/2	690
191	Glory Bound - Grass Roots	22--9/1/1	688
192	Make Me The Woman That You Go Home To - Gladys Knight & The Pips	22--8/2/1	684
193	Together Let's Find Love 5th Dimension	24--9/1/2	684
194	White Lies, Blue Eyes - Bullet	25--14/1/1	679
195	Ring The Living Bell - Melanie	21--8/1/1	662
196	Friends With You - John Denver	27--9/1/2	658
197	I Can't Help Myself (Sugar Pie, Honey Bunch) - Donnie Elbert	19--9/1/1	647
198	Jump Into The Fire - Nilsson	22--7/2/1	645
199	Spaceman - Nilsson	23--9/1/1	639
200	Gone - Joey Heatherton	26--13/1/1	636
201	Join Together - The Who	28--8/2/2	628
202	Breaking Up Is Hard To Do Partridge Family	25--9/1/1	626
203	(I Know) I'm Losing You Rod Stewart	22--7/1/2	623
204	All The King's Horses - Aretha Franklin	20--7/1/1	616
205	Theme From The Men - Isaac Hayes	36--9/2/2	615
206	Loving You Just Crossed My Mind Sam Neely	31--14/1/1	611
207	Hallelujah - Sweathog	28--10/1/1	607
208	Hearsay - Soul Children	22--8/1/2	602
209	You Could Have Been A Lady April Wine	27--10/2/0	599
210	Woman's Gotta Have It Bobby Womack	32--10/1/2	599
211	Superwoman (Where Were You When I Needed You) - Stevie Wonder	32--10/1/1	596
212	We're Free - Beverly Bremers	45--14/1/1	589
213	Long Dark Road - Hollies	24--8/1/2	581
214	The Nickel Song - Melanie	25--7/1/2	580
215	Take A Look Around - Temptations	28--8/1/2	580
216	My Man, A Sweet Man - Millie Jackson	34--8/2/2	579
217	Someday Never Comes Creedence Clearwater Revival	25--7/1/2	575
218	Nothing To Hide - Tommy James	25--7/1/2	572
219	Small Beginnings - Flash	30--12/1/1	564
220	American City Suite Cashman & West	28--9/1/2	562
221	Woman Don't Go Astray - King Floyd	35--9/2/1	557
222	I'm Coming Home - Stories	26--9/1/1	556
223	In The Ghetto - Candi Staton	36--10/1/2	544
224	The Runway - Grass Roots	29--8/2/1	543
225	If You Leave Me Tonight I'll Cry Jerry Wallace	39--12/1/1	543
226	Love Theme From "The Godfather" (Speak Softly Love) - Andy Williams	24--9/1/1	534
227	Easy Livin' - Uriah Heep	32--9/2/1	530
228	Now Run And Tell That Denise LaSalle	33--9/1/2	523
229	You Want It, You Got It Detroit Emeralds	35--9/2/1	521
230	Show Me How - Emotions	33--13/1/1	519
231	George Jackson - Bob Dylan	30--6/1/3	516
232	Run Run Run - Jo Jo Gunne	31--10/1/1	512
233	Smilin' - Sly & The Family Stone	25--8/1/1	510
234	All The Young Dudes - Mott The Hoople	34--8/2/1	509
235	Rock Me Baby - David Cassidy	26--7/1/1	507
236	Softly Whispering I Love You English Congregation	28--9/1/1	503
237	Old Man - Neil Young	26--7/1/1	500
238	Alive - Bee Gees	26--8/1/1	494
239	From The Beginning Emerson, Lake & Palmer	40--9/1/2	493
240	In Heaven There Is No Beer Clean Living	34--9/1/1	490
241	Man Sized Job - Denise LaSalle	40--9/1/2	490
242	When You Say Love - Sonny & Cher	30--7/1/2	488
243	Looking For A Love - J. Geils Band	37--10/1/0	487
244	Heartbroken Bopper - Guess Who	26--7/1/1	482
245	I Didn't Know I Loved You (Till I Saw You Rock And Roll) - Gary Glitter	30--7/2/1	477
246	Until It's Time For You To Go Elvis Presley	31--7/1/1	476
247	Crazy Mama - J.J. Cale	35--8/1/2	475
248	King Heroin - James Brown	32--7/1/2	474

Rank	Title - Act	Trajectory	Pts.
249	Country Wine - *Raiders*	28--5/2/1	473
250	Daisy Mae *Hamilton, Joe Frank & Reynolds*	39--10/1/1	472
251	Life And Breath - *Climax*	42--7/1/8	466
252	You Said A Bad Word - *Joe Tex*	35--7/2/1	460
253	Lay-Away - *Isley Brothers*	36--9/1/1	457
254	What Am I Crying For? *Dennis Yost & The Classics IV*	31--10/1/1	452
255	Son Of My Father - *Giorgio*	34--8/2/1	451
256	Midnight Rider - *Joe Cocke*	31--6/2/1	445
257	Am I Losing You - *Partridge Family*	31--7/1/1	445
258	Toast To The Fool - *Dramatics*	52--10/1/3	445
259	I Miss You (Part I) *Harold Melvin & The Blue Notes*	40--9/1/2	442
260	A Piece Of Paper - *Gladstone*	38--9/1/2	440
261	This World - *Staple Singers*	36--7/1/2	433
262	Put It Where You Want It - *Crusaders*	40--16/2/1	418
263	Think (About It) - *Lyn Collins*	55--9/1/2	416
264	And You And I (Part I) - *Yes*	32--7/1/1	414
265	Automatically Sunshine - *Supremes*	37--8/1/1	414
266	Immigration Man *Graham Nash & David Crosby*	31--7/1/1	413
267	Sunny Days - *Lighthouse*	37--9/1/2	413
268	Tiny Dancer - *Elton John*	29--6/1/1	409
269	Sweet Caroline (Good Times Never Seemed So Good) - *Bobby Womack*	42--8/1/1	409
270	Footstompin' Music *Grand Funk Railroad*	40--8/1/1	405
271	You Are The One - *Sugar Bears*	38--10/2/0	403
272	I Got A Bag Of My Own - *James Brown*	32--7/1/1	401
273	Zing Went The Strings Of My Heart *Trammps*	55--13/1/1	399
274	We've Come Too Far To End It Now *Smokey Robinson & The Miracles*	46--9/1/1	395
275	Sour Suite - *Guess Who*	41--6/2/1	394
276	Powder Blue Mercedes Queen *Raiders*	43--8/1/1	394
277	My Boy - *Richard Harris*	46--11/1/1	392
278	Geronimo's Cadillac *Michael Murphey*	49--8/1/2	392
279	Feeling Alright - *Joe Cocker*	36--8/1/1	390
280	Baby Sitter - *Betty Wright*	41--8/1/1	385
281	Cat's Eye In The Window *Tommy James*	48--8/2/0	385
282	Sweet Inspiration/Where You Lead *Barbra Streisand*	41--7/1/2	381
283	Hot 'N' Nasty - *Humble Pie*	44--9/1/1	380
284	Handbags And Gladrags - *Rod Stewart*	38--6/1/2	377
285	That's How Love Goes *Jermaine Jackson*	43--8/1/1	374
286	Once You Understand - *Think*	29--7/1/1	370
287	Guilty - *Al Green*	46--7/1/3	370
288	Angel - *Rod Stewart*	39--6/1/2	369
289	Be My Lover - *Alice Cooper*	36--7/1/1	368
290	Love Gonna Pack Up (And Walk Out) *Persuaders*	54--10/1/0	367
291	Give Ireland Back To The Irish - *Wings*	38--6/1/2	365
292	Honky Tonk - **Part 1** - *James Brown*	38--6/1/2	364
293	Long Haired Lover From Liverpool *Little Jimmy Osmond*	41--8/1/1	363
294	No - *Bulldog*	51--7/1/4	362
295	There It Is - **Part 1** - *James Brown*	38--7/1/1	361
296	Everybody Loves A Love Song *Mac Davis*	41--6/2/1	359
297	Walk In The Night *Jr. Walker & The All Stars*	50--8/1/2	357
298	Love Song - *Tommy James*	50--7/1/2	357
299	We're On Our Way - *Chris Hodge*	36--7/1/1	356
300	992 Arguments - *O'Jays*	43--6/2/1	356

1973

Rank	Title - Act	Trajectory	Pts.
1	Tie A Yellow Ribbon Round The Ole Oak Tree - *Dawn*	1--13/3/8	7509
2	My Love - *Paul McCartney & Wings*	1--8/4/5	7007
3	Crocodile Rock - *Elton John*	1--9/2/7	6758
4	You're So Vain - *Carly Simon*	1--6/2/10	6161
5	Let's Get It On - *Marvin Gaye*	1--9/1/9	6138
6	Half-Breed - *Cher*	1--12/1/7	5792
7	Love Train - *O'Jays*	1--12/1/3	5671
8	Killing Me Softly With His Song *Roberta Flack*	1--8/3/5	5648
9	Superstition - *Stevie Wonder*	1--11/2/5	5396
10	Delta Dawn - *Helen Reddy*	1--12/2/6	5350
11	The Night The Lights Went Out In Georgia - *Vicki Lawrence*	1--11/1/7	5127
12	Photograph - *Ringo Starr*	1--8/1/6	4982
13	Brother Louie - *Stories*	1--12/1/7	4973
14	Midnight Train To Georgia *Gladys Knight & The Pips*	1--11/1/5	4957
15	Top Of The World - *Carpenters*	1--10/1/9	4923
16	Frankenstein - *Edgar Winter Group*	1--11/1/5	4722
17	The Most Beautiful Girl - *Charlie Rich*	1--13/2/8	4633
18	Heartbeat - **It's A Lovebeat** *DeFranco Family*	1--13/1/4	4623
19	Bad, Bad Leroy Brown - *Jim Croce*	1--15/1/7	4615
20	Keep On Truckin' (Part 1) *Eddie Kendricks*	1--12/1/5	4562
21	We're An American Band - *Grand Funk*	1--10/1/6	4488
22	Angie - *Rolling Stones*	1--8/1/6	4470
23	Shambala - *Three Dog Night*	1--10/1/5	4449
24	Give Me Love (Give Me Peace On Earth) - *George Harrison*	1--8/2/4	4448
25	Will It Go Round In Circles *Billy Preston*	1--20/1/4	4422
26	Live And Let Die - *Wings*	1--8/1/6	4415
27	Goodbye Yellow Brick Road *Elton John*	1--7/1/8	4403
28	Loves Me Like A Rock - *Paul Simon*	1--10/1/5	4363
29	Touch Me In The Morning - *Diana Ross*	1--11/1/8	4353
30	Dueling Banjos *"Deliverance" Soundtrack*	1--9/1/6	4224
31	Pillow Talk - *Sylvia*	2--13/1/3	4176
32	Playground In My Mind - *Clint Holmes*	2--16/1/6	4115
33	Last Song - *Edward Bear*	3--13/3/2	4089
34	Yesterday Once More - *Carpenters*	1--10/1/4	4023
35	Neither One Of Us (Wants To Be The First To Say Goodbye) *Gladys Knight & The Pips*	1--12/1/4	3990
36	Could It Be I'm Falling In Love *Spinners*	1--9/1/5	3943
37	Why Can't We Live Together *Timmy Thomas*	2--12/1/4	3935
38	Oh, Babe, What Would You Say? *Hurricane Smith*	1--14/1/3	3849
39	Ramblin' Man - *Allman Brothers Band*	1--10/1/4	3846
40	Clair - *Gilbert O'Sullivan*	3--12/1/4	3819
41	Hello It's Me - *Todd Rundgren*	2--13/1/6	3811

Rank	Title - Act	Trajectory	Pts.
42	Daniel - Elton John	2--10/2/4	3810
43	Higher Ground - Stevie Wonder	1--9/1/4	3784
44	Just You 'N' Me - Chicago	1--13/1/4	3759
45	Ain't No Woman (Like The One I've Got) - Four Tops	1--11/1/4	3756
46	The Cisco Kid - War	2--10/1/3	3737
47	Say, Has Anybody Seen My Sweet Gypsy Rose - Dawn	4--11/2/3	3355
48	Kodachrome - Paul Simon	2--9/1/4	3274
49	Stuck In The Middle With You - Stealers Wheel	3--12/1/4	3270
50	Little Willy - Sweet	3--14/2/5	3265
51	You Are The Sunshine Of My Life - Stevie Wonder	1--10/1/4	3205
52	I Got A Name - Jim Croce	3--9/2/6	3200
53	Smoke On The Water - Deep Purple	3--10/2/3	3066
54	Also Sprach Zarathustra (2001) - Deodato	4--8/3/2	3029
55	Get Down - Gilbert O'Sullivan	4--8/1/7	3019
56	Sing - Carpenters	5--9/3/3	3013
57	Rockin' Pneumonia - **Boogie Woogie Flu** - Johnny Rivers	5--13/2/4	2922
58	Natural High - Bloodstone	5--16/2/3	2710
59	That Lady (Part 1) - Isley Brothers	6--12/2/4	2682
60	The Cover Of "Rolling Stone" - Dr. Hook & The Medicine Show	5--18/2/2	2570
61	Danny's Song - Anne Murray	6--17/1/3	2511
62	Your Mama Don't Dance - Kenny Loggins & Jim Messina	5--12/2/4	2505
63	Hocus Pocus - Focus	4--14/1/3	2374
64	I'm Gonna Love You Just A Little More Baby - Barry White	4--12/1/3	2331
65	Daddy's Home - Jermaine Jackson	7--14/1/3	2290
66	The Morning After - Maureen McGovern	3--9/1/6	2289
67	Don't Expect Me To Be Your Friend - Lobo	4--8/1/4	2245
68	Drift Away - Dobie Gray	8--13/2/6	2241
69	Rocky Mountain High - John Denver	7--15/1/3	2204
70	The Twelfth Of Never - Donny Osmond	5--11/1/2	2161
71	Superfly - Curtis Mayfield	6--10/3/2	2130
72	Paper Roses - Marie Osmond	6--11/2/3	2051
73	I Believe In You (You Believe In Me) - Johnnie Taylor	5--11/1/4	2043
74	Space Race - Billy Preston	6--12/1/3	1992
75	My Maria - B.W. Stevenson	7--12/1/3	1877
76	All I Know - Garfunkel	6--10/1/4	1867
77	Gypsy Man - War	7--11/1/3	1787
78	Reeling In The Years - Steely Dan	7--10/2/2	1784
79	One Of A Kind (Love Affair) - Spinners	8--11/2/2	1783
80	Diamond Girl - Seals & Crofts	8--12/1/4	1764
81	Wildflower - Skylark	9--14/2/2	1762
82	Feelin' Stronger Every Day - Chicago	8--9/2/3	1736
83	The Love I Lost (Part 1) - Harold Melvin & The Blue Notes	9--11/1/4	1727
84	Do It Again - Steely Dan	7--13/1/3	1722
85	Long Train Runnin' - Doobie Brothers	9--12/1/4	1722
86	Boogie Woogie Bugle Boy - Bette Midler	6--13/1/3	1701
87	Saturday Night's Alright For Fighting - Elton John	9--7/3/3	1682
88	China Grove - Doobie Brothers	8--9/2/2	1636
89	Free Ride - Edgar Winter Group	10--11/2/3	1627
90	Here I Am (Come And Take Me) - Al Green	10--11/1/3	1616
91	Stir It Up - Johnny Nash	11--13/1/2	1614
92	Dancing In The Moonlight - King Harvest	10--17/1/3	1605
93	Right Place Wrong Time - Dr. John	11--12/2/3	1603
94	I'm Just A Singer (In A Rock And Roll Band) - Moody Blues	8--9/2/3	1575
95	Monster Mash - Bobby (Boris) Pickett & The Crypt Kickers	10--15/2/2	1564
96	Jambalaya (On The Bayou) - Blue Ridge Rangers	10--13/2/1	1552
97	The World Is A Ghetto - War	9--11/2/3	1534
98	Masterpiece - Temptations	9--11/1/2	1529
99	Keeper Of The Castle - Four Tops	9--12/1/1	1498
100	If You're Ready (Come Go With Me) - Staple Singers	9--9/1/4	1471
101	I'm Doin' Fine Now - New York City	12--17/1/3	1470
102	Money - Pink Floyd	10--11/2/3	1454
103	I Wanna Be With You - Raspberries	10--11/1/3	1453
104	Call Me (Come Back Home) - Al Green	9--9/1/2	1421
105	Knockin' On Heaven's Door - Bob Dylan	10--10/2/3	1403
106	Rocky Mountain Way - Joe Walsh	13--12/2/3	1398
107	Uneasy Rider - Charlie Daniels	10--14/1/2	1394
108	Love Jones - Brighter Side Of Darkness	10--10/2/3	1381
109	Yes We Can Can - Pointer Sisters	10--11/1/3	1370
110	Daisy A Day - Jud Strunk	10--15/1/1	1361
111	If You Want Me To Stay - Sly & The Family Stone	15--11/2/3	1355
112	Trouble Man - Marvin Gaye	8--8/2/2	1348
113	D'yer Mak'er - Led Zeppelin	16--12/2/3	1322
114	Thinking Of You - Loggins & Messina	11--11/1/2	1315
115	Hi, Hi, Hi - Wings	6--8/1/2	1314
116	Do You Want To Dance? - Bette Midler	13--11/1/3	1309
117	Dead Skunk - Loudon Wainwright III	12--13/1/3	1302
118	Break Up To Make Up - Stylistics	10--10/1/2	1292
119	Let's Pretend - Raspberries	18--15/2/1	1276
120	Are You Man Enough - Four Tops	14--11/2/2	1263
121	Mind Games - John Lennon	10--8/1/4	1257
122	Steamroller Blues - Elvis Presley	10--8/2/2	1236
123	Peaceful - Helen Reddy	14--13/1/1	1232
124	Behind Closed Doors - Charlie Rich	17--12/1/5	1221
125	Funky Worm - Ohio Players	13--16/1/2	1203
126	Big City Miss Ruth Ann - Gallery	12--13/1/3	1198
127	Separate Ways - Elvis Presley	15--10/1/4	1191
128	The Right Thing To Do - Carly Simon	10--10/1/1	1185
129	Aubrey - Bread	11--9/1/2	1179
130	Give It To Me - J. Geils Band	15--14/1/2	1149
131	My Music - Loggins & Messina	13--9/1/3	1136
132	Why Me - Kris Kristofferson	32--30/1/3	1108
133	Basketball Jones Featuring Tyrone Shoelaces - Cheech & Chong	13--10/1/2	1094
134	And I Love You So - Perry Como	18--15/1/1	1083
135	Who's In The Strawberry Patch With Sally - Tony Orlando & Dawn	13--8/1/3	1067
136	Theme From Cleopatra Jones - Joe Simon	14--12/1/2	1055
137	How Can I Tell Her - Lobo	20--12/1/3	1034
138	Misdemeanor - Foster Sylvers	14--10/2/2	1030
139	Living In The Past - Jethro Tull	15--9/2/1	1017
140	Summer (The First Time) - Bobby Goldsboro	17--13/2/1	1015
141	Daddy Could Swear, I Declare - Gladys Knight & The Pips	15--11/1/2	1003

Rank	Title - Act	Trajectory	Pts.
142	Let Me Serenade You - *Three Dog Night*	12--7/1/2	1001
143	Armed And Extremely Dangerous *First Choice*	19--14/1/2	993
144	Ooh Baby - *Gilbert O'Sullivan*	11--8/1/2	991
145	Space Oddity - *David Bowie*	17--12/1/1	985
146	Rockin' Roll Baby - *Stylistics*	20--12/1/2	974
147	Hurts So Good - *Millie Jackson*	18--10/2/2	972
148	Jesse - *Roberta Flack*	12--6/2/2	971
149	Hummingbird - *Seals & Crofts*	15--9/1/3	961
150	So Very Hard To Go - *Tower Of Power*	19--11/1/3	956
151	Angel - *Aretha Franklin*	16--11/1/2	955
152	You Turn Me On, I'm A Radio *Joni Mitchell*	20--12/2/2	952
153	Give Your Baby A Standing Ovation *Dells*	20--13/2/1	950
154	You're A Special Part Of Me *Diana Ross & Marvin Gaye*	14--8/2/2	936
155	Smoke Gets In Your Eyes - *Blue Haze*	21--12/2/2	934
156	We May Never Pass This Way (Again) *Seals & Crofts*	18--8/2/2	926
157	Leaving Me - *Independents*	18--12/1/2	889
158	Don't Let Me Be Lonely Tonight *James Taylor*	15--9/1/1	859
159	Back When My Hair Was Short *Gunhill Road*	25--13/2/1	842
160	Dreidel - *Don McLean*	19--10/1/1	830
161	One Man Band (Plays All Alone) *Ronnie Dyson*	20--12/1/1	824
162	Peaceful Easy Feeling - *Eagles*	20--11/1/1	810
163	Pieces Of April - *Three Dog Night*	18--9/1/2	805
164	Cheaper To Keep Her - *Johnnie Taylor*	18--8/1/3	803
165	No More Mr. Nice Guy - *Alice Cooper*	26--10/1/4	801
166	Give Me Your Love - *Barbara Mason*	18--12/1/1	798
167	Pinball Wizard/See Me, Feel Me *New Seekers*	21--12/1/1	788
168	Nutbush City Limits - *Ike & Tina Turner*	26--14/1/2	787
169	In The Midnight Hour - *Cross Country*	18--9/1/3	782
170	Come Get To This - *Marvin Gaye*	18--7/2/2	779
171	Be - *Neil Diamond*	19--7/2/2	778
172	You'll Never Get To Heaven (If You Break My Heart) - *Stylistics*	16--9/1/1	775
173	There's No Me Without You *Manhattans*	29--13/2/2	773
174	Walk On The Wild Side - *Lou Reed*	17--11/2/1	766
175	You've Never Been This Far Before *Conway Twitty*	18--10/1/2	758
176	Satin Sheets - *Jeanne Pruett*	24--11/1/1	750
177	Been To Canaan - *Carole King*	20--8/1/2	737
178	(I Don't Want To Love You But) You Got Me Anyway *Sutherland Brothers & Quiver*	20--11/1/1	728
179	Get It Together - *Jackson 5*	24--9/2/1	725
180	Out Of The Question - *Gilbert O'Sullivan*	22--11/1/1	723
181	Reelin' & Rockin' - *Chuck Berry*	30--12/1/1	721
182	Nobody Wants You When You're Down And Out - *Bobby Womack*	30--13/2/1	719
183	Let Me In - *Osmonds*	19--8/1/2	710
184	Close Your Eyes - *Edward Bear*	24--11/1/1	699
185	Living Together, Growing Together *5th Dimension*	20--9/1/1	695
186	Doing It To Death *Fred Wesley & J.B.'s*	21--10/1/2	681
187	Smarty Pants - *First Choice*	38--11/3/0	679
188	"Cherry Cherry" from Hot August Night - *Neil Diamond*	24--10/1/1	679
189	Teddy Bear Song - *Barbara Fairchild*	32--15/2/1	679
190	Sweet Charlie Babe - *Jackie Moore*	32--13/2/1	675
191	Where Peaceful Waters Flow *Gladys Knight & The Pips*	23--10/1/1	672
192	Jimmy Loves Mary-Anne *Looking Glass*	31--14/1/2	670
193	Harry Hippie - *Bobby Womack*	25--11/1/1	666
194	Never Let You Go - *Bloodstone*	35--12/1/2	663
195	Soul Makossa - *Manu Dibango*	22--9/1/2	659
196	Painted Ladies - *Ian Thomas*	27--10/2/2	658
197	Drinking Wine Spo-Dee O'Dee *Jerry Lee Lewis*	25--10/1/1	651
198	I'd Rather Be A Cowboy - *John Denver*	27--10/1/2	646
199	Bitter Bad - *Melanie*	30--10/1/2	642
200	Don't Cross The River - *America*	20--8/1/1	634
201	I'll Be Your Shelter (In Time Of Storm) *Luther Ingram*	32--10/1/2	634
202	Good Morning Heartache - *Diana Ross*	30--10/1/2	628
203	The Hurt - *Cat Stevens*	25--9/1/2	624
204	Looking Through The Eyes Of Love *Partridge Family*	25--8/2/1	622
205	Kissing My Love - *Bill Withers*	26--8/2/1	613
206	Mammy Blue - *Stories*	21--8/1/1	604
207	Over The Hills And Far Away *Led Zeppelin*	28--9/2/1	590
208	Roll Over Beethoven *Electric Light Orchestra*	48--10/2/1	570
209	Believe In Humanity - *Carole King*	24--8/1/2	569
210	Hallelujah Day - *Jackson 5*	21--7/1/1	564
211	Swamp Witch - *Jim Stafford*	31--10/1/2	563
212	Loving Arms - *Dobie Gray*	36--9/1/2	562
213	Time To Get Down - *O'Jays*	30--8/2/1	557
214	It Sure Took A Long, Long Time - *Lobo*	27--9/1/1	555
215	Corazon - *Carole King*	27--8/1/2	551
216	Step By Step - *Joe Simon*	29--10/1/1	551
217	I Can Understand It - *New Birth*	28--10/1/1	550
218	Blue Suede Shoes - *Johnny Rivers*	27--9/1/1	548
219	I'll Always Love My Mama (Part I) *Intruders*	25--8/1/2	545
220	Hey Girl (I Like Your Style) *Temptations*	27--8/1/1	540
221	Pretty Lady - *Lighthouse*	31--10/2/1	528
222	Superman - *Donna Fargo*	31--9/1/1	524
223	Hearts Of Stone - *Blue Ridge Rangers*	33--9/1/1	524
224	One Less Set Of Footsteps - *Jim Croce*	30--8/1/2	522
225	Hello Hurray - *Alice Cooper*	25--8/1/1	521
226	Goin' Home - *Osmonds*	21--7/1/1	518
227	Ecstasy - *Ohio Players*	31--12/1/1	517
228	A Million To One - *Donny Osmond*	28--9/1/1	516
229	Raised On Rock - *Elvis Presley*	27--7/1/2	513
230	Love Is What You Make It *Grass Roots*	32--8/1/1	506
231	You Can't Always Get What You Want *Rolling Stones*	34--9/1/1	499
232	Jesus Is Just Alright - *Doobie Brothers*	33--9/1/1	497
233	Freedom For The Stallion *Hues Corporation*	38--12/1/0	495
234	First Cut Is The Deepest *Keith Hampshire*	40--12/1/1	490
235	Some Guys Have All The Luck *Persuaders*	39--11/1/1	488
236	Letter To Lucille - *Tom Jones*	34--9/1/1	487
237	Ghetto Child - *Spinners*	24--7/1/1	485

Rank	Title - Act	Trajectory	Pts.
238	I'm Never Gonna Be Alone Anymore - Cornelius Brothers & Sister Rose	31--8/1/1	485
239	Clouds - David Gates	36--9/1/1	483
240	To Know You Is To Love You - B.B. King	38--10/1/2	483
241	I Was Checkin' Out She Was Checkin' In - Don Covay	28--11/1/1	482
242	Soul Song - Joe Stampley	33--9/1/1	480
243	Oh La De Da - Staple Singers	35--8/1/1	480
244	Cook With Honey - Judy Collins	29--10/1/1	470
245	The Plastic Man - Temptations	33--8/1/1	466
246	Remember (Christmas) - Nilsson	40--8/1/1	457
247	Control Of Me - Les Emmerson	37--9/1/1	450
248	Master Of Eyes (The Deepness Of Your Eyes) - Aretha Franklin	36--8/1/1	447
249	He Did With Me - Vicki Lawrence	49--5/1/5	446
250	The Relay - The Who	33--6/1/2	442
251	Everyone's Agreed That Everything Will Turn Out Fine - Stealers Wheel	33--8/2/0	440
252	Check It Out - Tavares	34--7/1/2	433
253	Twisting The Night Away - Rod Stewart	35--8/1/1	429
254	I've Got So Much To Give - Barry White	38--7/2/1	429
255	Soul Makossa - Afrique	41--9/1/1	429
256	Fencewalk - Mandrill	47--10/1/1	429
257	Show Biz Kids - Steely Dan	30--7/1/1	423
258	Baby I've Been Missing You - Independents	36--8/1/1	423
259	Tonight - Raspberries	37--7/2/1	412
260	Dream On - Aerosmith	43--9/1/2	412
261	The Message - Cymande	39--9/1/1	410
262	Country Sunshine - Dottie West	45--10/1/0	410
263	Hey You! Get Off My Mountain - Dramatics	51--9/1/1	403
264	Sweet Understanding Love - Four Tops	30--6/1/1	402
265	What About Me - Anne Murray	37--7/2/0	400
266	A Letter To Myself - Chi-Lites	41--8/1/2	397
267	Sister James - Nino Tempo & 5th Ave. Sax	40--8/1/2	395
268	Muskrat Love - America	33--8/1/1	387
269	Let Us Love - Bill Withers	42--6/1/2	387
270	Funky Stuff - Kool & The Gang	44--7/1/2	385
271	Rubber Bullets - 10 C.C.	43--9/1/1	384
272	Never, Never, Never (Grande, Grande, Grande) - Shirley Bassey	58--12/2/1	383
273	Super Fly Meets Shaft - John & Ernest	43--8/1/1	379
274	The Last Thing On My Mind - Neil Diamond	42--6/1/2	376
275	I Knew Jesus (Before He Was A Star) - Glen Campbell	46--9/1/1	370
276	River - Joe Simon	42--7/2/1	368
277	Daytime Night-Time - Keith Hampshire	43--9/1/1	365
278	Today I Started Loving You Again - Bettye Swann	44--8/1/1	362
279	I Got Ants In My Pants - Part 1 and I want to dance - James Brown	33--6/1/1	359
280	With A Child's Heart - Michael Jackson	37--6/1/1	356
281	Keep On Singing - Austin Roberts	39--7/1/1	350
282	You've Got To Take It (If You Want It) - Main Ingredient	48--6/1/3	347
283	Bongo Rock - Incredible Bongo Band	57--11/2/0	346
284	Tequila Sunrise - Eagles	40--8/1/1	344
285	Stoned Out Of My Mind - Chi-Lites	53--4/2/4	333
286	The Free Electric Band - Albert Hammond	41--9/1/1	329
287	Outlaw Man - Eagles	49--7/1/2	329
288	Blockbuster - Sweet	43--8/1/1	327
289	Future Shock - Curtis Mayfield	39--7/1/1	325
290	There It Is - Tyrone Davis	39--7/1/1	324
291	Without You In My Life - Tyrone Davis	51--8/1/2	316
292	Such A Night - Dr. John	45--7/1/3	310
293	Who Was It? - Hurricane Smith	44--7/1/1	306
294	Woman To Woman - Joe Cocker	52--7/1/1	306
295	Cindy Incidentally - Faces	43--7/1/0	304
296	Sail Around The World - David Gates	49--8/1/1	301
297	Billion Dollar Babies - Alice Cooper	36--5/1/1	300
298	Boo, Boo, Don't 'Cha Be Blue - Tommy James	40--6/1/1	296
299	Evil - Earth, Wind & Fire	54--6/1/2	296
300	Sixty Minute Man - Clarence Carter	51--8/1/1	294

1974

Rank	Title - Act	Trajectory	Pts.
1	I Honestly Love You - Olivia Newton-John	1--6/2/4	5841
2	Show And Tell - Al Wilson	1--17/1/5	5460
3	The Streak - Ray Stevens	1--7/1/8	5448
4	Seasons In The Sun - Terry Jacks	1--8/2/9	5224
5	The Way We Were - Barbra Streisand	1--11/1/8	5200
6	TSOP (The Sound Of Philadelphia) - MFSB	1--8/2/7	5128
7	(You're) Having My Baby - Paul Anka	1--8/1/8	5123
8	The Joker - Steve Miller Band	1--14/1/5	5092
9	Annie's Song - John Denver	1--10/1/6	4961
10	Kung Fu Fighting - Carl Douglas	1--9/1/9	4929
11	Bennie And The Jets - Elton John	1--9/1/8	4883
12	The Entertainer - Marvin Hamlisch	1--12/1/4	4882
13	The Loco-Motion - Grand Funk	1--9/1/8	4838
14	You Make Me Feel Brand New - Stylistics	1--15/1/4	4815
15	Rock Me Gently - Andy Kim	1--16/1/3	4807
16	Love's Theme - Love Unlimited Orchestra	1--13/1/4	4789
17	The Night Chicago Died - Paper Lace	1--9/1/8	4719
18	Boogie Down - Eddie Kendricks	1--12/1/4	4718
19	Rock The Boat - Hues Corporation	1--9/1/9	4715
20	Sundown - Gordon Lightfoot	1--12/1/5	4682
21	I Shot The Sheriff - Eric Clapton	1--9/1/5	4667
22	Billy, Don't Be A Hero - Bo Donaldson & The Heywoods	1--13/1/3	4629
23	You Haven't Done Nothin' - Stevie Wonder	1--13/1/2	4622
24	Sunshine On My Shoulders - John Denver	1--11/1/7	4584
25	Band On The Run - Paul McCartney & Wings	1--9/2/6	4530
26	Time In A Bottle - Jim Croce	1--9/1/5	4522
27	Leave Me Alone (Ruby Red Dress) - Helen Reddy	1--11/1/4	4520
28	You Ain't Seen Nothing Yet - Bachman-Turner Overdrive	1--11/1/5	4453
29	Cat's In The Cradle - Harry Chapin	1--15/1/5	4430
30	You're Sixteen - Ringo Starr	1--9/1/6	4419
31	Nothing From Nothing - Billy Preston	1--14/1/4	4368
32	Don't Let The Sun Go Down On Me - Elton John	1--7/1/6	4339
33	I Can Help - Billy Swan	1--10/1/8	4313
34	Dark Lady - Cher	2--12/1/3	4297
35	Hooked On A Feeling - Blue Swede	1--9/1/7	4286

Rank	Title - Act	Trajectory	Pts.
36	**Jazzman** - Carole King	1--11/1/4	4230
37	**Rock On** - David Essex	1--18/1/4	4193
38	**Rock Your Baby** - George McCrae	1--9/1/8	4116
39	**Whatever Gets You Thru The Night** John Lennon	1--8/1/5	4014
40	**Dancing Machine** - Jackson 5	1--11/1/6	3995
41	**Angie Baby** - Helen Reddy	1--10/1/5	3973
42	**Can't Get Enough** - Bad Company	1--13/1/3	3967
43	**Americans** - Byron MacGregor	1--8/1/2	3847
44	**Can't Get Enough Of Your Love, Babe** Barry White	1--8/1/6	3800
45	**Then Came You** Dionne Warwicke & Spinners	1--12/1/4	3789
46	**Rikki Don't Lose That Number** Steely Dan	3--13/2/4	3781
47	**My Melody Of Love** - Bobby Vinton	2--10/2/5	3639
48	**Tell Me Something Good** - Rufus	1--11/1/5	3627
49	**Spiders And Snakes** - Jim Stafford	3--18/2/3	3578
50	**When Will I See You Again** Three Degrees	1--11/1/7	3497
51	**Smokin' In The Boy's Room** Brownsville Station	2--14/1/4	3468
52	**Feel Like Makin' Love** - Roberta Flack	1--10/1/6	3436
53	**Best Thing That Ever Happened To Me** - Gladys Knight & The Pips	3--10/2/4	3398
54	**Mockingbird** Carly Simon & James Taylor	3--9/2/4	3340
55	**Come And Get Your Love** - Redbone	5--17/1/5	3273
56	**The Show Must Go On** Three Dog Night	1--9/1/5	3263
57	**Be Thankful For What You Got** William DeVaughn	3--12/2/3	3169
58	**Rock And Roll Heaven** Righteous Brothers	4--11/2/4	3076
59	**Midnight At The Oasis** - Maria Muldaur	4--13/1/5	2949
60	**Let Me Be There** - Olivia Newton-John	4--17/1/3	2778
61	**Beach Baby** - First Class	3--13/1/2	2654
62	**If You Love Me (Let Me Know)** Olivia Newton-John	6--13/2/4	2394
63	**Longfellow Serenade** - Neil Diamond	4--8/2/5	2320
64	**The Bitch Is Back** - Elton John	5--7/2/2	2319
65	**Jet** - Paul McCartney & Wings	5--8/1/4	2307
66	**Living For The City** - Stevie Wonder	6--10/2/4	2289
67	**Do It ('Til You're Satisfied)** B.T. Express	6--12/2/6	2282
68	**The Lord's Prayer** - Sister Janet Mead	5--9/2/4	2265
69	**Sideshow** - Blue Magic	5--15/2/3	2258
70	**Earache My Eye (Featuring Alice Bowie)** - Cheech & Chong	4--9/2/2	2241
71	**Hollywood Swinging** - Kool & The Gang	7--13/2/3	2235
72	**Until You Come Back To Me (That's What I'm Gonna Do)** - Aretha Franklin	7--13/3/2	2211
73	**Help Me** - Joni Mitchell	8--14/3/3	2203
74	**Hang On In There Baby** - Johnny Bristol	8--13/2/2	2185
75	**The Air That I Breathe** - Hollies	7--14/2/3	2168
76	**Sha-La-La (Make Me Happy)** - Al Green	7--12/1/5	2157
77	**Back Home Again** - John Denver	5--9/2/4	2118
78	**Please Come To Boston** - Dave Loggins	7--15/2/5	2059
79	**You Won't See Me** - Anne Murray	8--14/2/2	2045
80	**Sweet Home Alabama** - Lynyrd Skynyrd	7--13/1/4	2029
81	**Tubular Bells** - Mike Oldfield	6--11/2/4	2007
82	**I'm Leaving It (All) Up To You** Donny & Marie Osmond	7--10/2/3	2005
83	**Takin' Care Of Business** Bachman-Turner Overdrive	6--13/1/5	1980
84	**(I've Been) Searchin' So Long** - Chicago	7--11/1/3	1950
85	**Just Don't Want To Be Lonely** Main Ingredient	8--14/1/5	1935
86	**Oh My My** - Ringo Starr	6--9/1/4	1879
87	**Lookin' For A Love** - Bobby Womack	8--12/1/3	1864
88	**I've Got To Use My Imagination** Gladys Knight & The Pips	7--9/1/5	1860
89	**Wildwood Weed** - Jim Stafford	5--8/2/4	1855
90	**Helen Wheels** - Paul McCartney & Wings	5--9/1/3	1811
91	**Stop And Smell The Roses** - Mac Davis	7--12/2/2	1808
92	**Tin Man** - America	6--14/1/4	1786
93	**Another Saturday Night** - Cat Stevens	9--10/2/2	1773
94	**Eres Tu (Touch The Wind)** - Mocedades	9--13/2/3	1735
95	**Life Is A Rock (But The Radio Rolled Me)** - Reunion	7--11/1/3	1708
96	**You And Me Against The World** - Helen Reddy	10--15/1/3	1692
97	**On And On** - Gladys Knight & The Pips	9--12/1/2	1651
98	**Jungle Boogie** - Kool & The Gang	8--9/1/7	1639
99	**Me And Baby Brother** - War	12--13/1/2	1635
100	**Never, Never Gonna Give Ya Up** Barry White	9--11/1/5	1632
101	**Oh Very Young** - Cat Stevens	10--13/1/3	1596
102	**For The Love Of Money** - O'Jays	7--10/1/3	1578
103	**I'll Have To Say I Love You In A Song** Jim Croce	7--9/1/4	1568
104	**Do It Baby** - Miracles	10--15/1/2	1558
105	**Everlasting Love** - Carl Carlton	9--10/1/4	1549
106	**I Won't Last A Day Without You** Carpenters	9--9/1/3	1509
107	**Love Song** - Anne Murray	10--13/1/2	1495
108	**Waterloo** - Abba	10--10/2/3	1472
109	**Clap For The Wolfman** - Guess Who	10--14/1/2	1467
110	**One Hell Of A Woman** - Mac Davis	14--17/1/3	1456
111	**Radar Love** - Golden Earring	10--13/1/2	1443
112	**Keep On Singing** - Helen Reddy	10--8/1/4	1443
113	**Haven't Got Time For The Pain** Carly Simon	7--9/1/3	1437
114	**You Got The Love** Rufus Featuring Chaka Khan	10--11/1/4	1425
115	**A Very Special Love Song** Charlie Rich	8--9/1/4	1424
116	**Wishing You Were Here** - Chicago	9--9/1/3	1376
117	**Call On Me** - Chicago	10--9/1/3	1356
118	**Never My Love** - Blue Swede	10--9/1/3	1347
119	**Don't You Worry 'Bout A Thing** Stevie Wonder	10--10/1/2	1328
120	**Love Me For A Reason** - Osmonds	8--9/2/2	1299
121	**Livin' For You** - Al Green	14--9/3/1	1287
122	**Skin Tight** - Ohio Players	11--12/1/4	1286
123	**Last Time I Saw Him** - Diana Ross	9--11/1/2	1282
124	**Who Do You Think You Are** Bo Donaldson & The Heywoods	13--10/1/2	1266
125	**Wild Thing** - Fancy	12--14/1/3	1254
126	**Let It Ride** - Bachman-Turner Overdrive	14--9/2/3	1225
127	**My Girl Bill** - Jim Stafford	10--10/1/2	1222
128	**Keep On Smilin'** - Wet Willie	16--14/1/3	1170
129	**Jim Dandy** - Black Oak Arkansas	12--10/2/2	1163
130	**Steppin' Out (Gonna Boogie Tonight)** Tony Orlando & Dawn	14--11/1/3	1146
131	**Let's Put It All Together** - Stylistics	14--9/2/2	1145

Rank	Title - Act	Trajectory	Pts.
132	I've Got The Music In Me - *Kiki Dee Band*	18--12/2/3	1137
133	Mighty Love - Pt. I – *Spinners*	15--11/1/2	1124
134	Carefree Highway - *Gordon Lightfoot*	13--12/1/2	1102
135	The Need To Be - *Jim Weatherly*	16--13/2/1	1074
136	Trying To Hold On To My Woman - *Lamont Dozier*	14--13/1/2	1069
137	Machine Gun - *Commodores*	13--9/2/2	1052
138	Already Gone - *Eagles*	17--9/2/2	1041
139	Star - *Stealers Wheel*	20--13/3/1	1038
140	This Heart - *Gene Redding*	22--20/1/2	1028
141	Finally Got Myself Together (I'm A Changed Man) - *Impressions*	17--14/1/2	1022
142	Put Your Hands Together - *O'Jays*	14--8/1/4	1009
143	Piano Man - *Billy Joel*	16--11/2/2	992
144	I'm In Love - *Aretha Franklin*	16--9/2/2	986
145	You Little Trustmaker - *Tymes*	16--10/1/3	980
146	Save The Last Dance For Me - *DeFranco Family Featuring Tony DeFranco*	16--9/2/2	973
147	Are You Lonesome Tonight - *Donny Osmond*	16--11/1/2	970
148	Doo Doo Doo Doo Doo (Heartbreaker) - *Rolling Stones*	10--7/1/1	967
149	I Love - *Tom T. Hall*	17--11/1/3	958
150	Walk Like A Man - *Grand Funk*	17--10/1/2	943
151	Ain't Too Proud To Beg - *Rolling Stones*	15--7/2/2	938
152	So You Are A Star - *Hudson Brothers*	20--12/1/2	922
153	Midnight Rider - *Gregg Allman*	16--9/1/2	914
154	My Mistake (Was To Love You) - *Diana Ross & Marvin Gaye*	20--10/2/3	912
155	After The Goldrush - *Prelude*	17--12/1/3	911
156	My Sweet Lady - *Cliff DeYoung*	23--12/1/4	889
157	La Grange - *ZZ Top*	24--14/1/2	884
158	The Payback - Part I - *James Brown*	23--10/2/2	884
159	Shinin' On - *Grand Funk*	18--9/1/3	875
160	Rock And Roll, Hoochie Koo - *Rick Derringer*	15--10/1/2	875
161	It's Only Rock 'N Roll (But I Like It) - *Rolling Stones*	18--7/1/2	860
162	Star Baby - *Guess Who*	30--15/1/2	842
163	Play Something Sweet (Brickyard Blues) - *Three Dog Night*	26--8/1/5	824
164	I Shall Sing - *Garfunkel*	18--7/1/3	823
165	Train Of Thought - *Cher*	18--8/1/2	803
166	Fairytale - *Pointer Sisters*	19--11/1/2	793
167	Tell Me A Lie - *Sami Jo*	21--11/2/1	774
168	Free Man In Paris - *Joni Mitchell*	23--9/1/4	770
169	Rub It In - *Billy "Crash" Craddock*	22--9/2/2	764
170	WOLD - *Harry Chapin*	26--13/2/1	756
171	If You Talk In Your Sleep - *Elvis Presley*	23--9/2/2	754
172	Sure As I'm Sittin' Here - *Three Dog Night*	18--8/1/2	752
173	Straight Shootin' Woman - *Steppenwolf*	20--9/2/1	745
174	Workin' At The Car Wash Blues - *Jim Croce*	20--7/2/2	732
175	There Won't Be Anymore - *Charlie Rich*	22--8/2/2	725
176	Come Monday - *Jimmy Buffett*	26--12/1/2	722
177	Can This Be Real - *Natural Four*	25--10/1/2	715
178	I Like To Live The Love - *B.B. King*	25--14/2/1	708
179	Let's Get Married - *Al Green*	21--8/1/3	705
180	Woman To Woman - *Shirley Brown*	26--10/1/3	703
181	Son Of Sagittarius - *Eddie Kendricks*	20--8/1/2	693
182	I Can't Stand The Rain - *Ann Peebles*	45--18/1/1	686
183	Sexy Mama - *Moments*	20--10/1/2	683
184	Let's Straighten It Out - *Latimore*	32--9/1/5	676
185	I'm Coming Home – *Spinners*	20--9/1/1	670
186	Daybreak - *Nilsson*	23--9/2/1	670
187	Sister Mary Elephant (Shudd-Up!) - *Cheech & Chong*	36--11/2/1	652
188	If You Wanna Get To Heaven - *Ozark Mountain Daredevils*	21--11/1/1	649
189	Overnight Sensation (Hit Record) - *Raspberries*	24--10/1/1	649
190	Love Don't Love Nobody - Pt. I - *Spinners*	24--10/1/1	648
191	Kung Fu - *Curtis Mayfield*	32--10/1/1	630
192	Teenage Lament '74 - *Alice Cooper*	24--8/2/1	621
193	Another Park, Another Sunday - *Doobie Brothers*	38--12/1/2	616
194	Outside Woman - *Bloodstone*	31--13/1/1	611
195	Happiness Is Just Around The Bend - *Main Ingredient*	26--11/1/2	609
196	My Thang - *James Brown*	30--7/2/3	608
197	If We Make It Through December - *Merle Haggard*	29--11/1/2	605
198	Tell Her Love Has Felt The Need - *Eddie Kendricks*	38--9/1/3	605
199	Abra-Ca-Dabra - *DeFranco Family Featuring Tony DeFranco*	23--8/1/2	602
200	Touch A Hand, Make A Friend - *Staple Singers*	23--9/1/2	602
201	Honey Please, Can't Ya See - *Barry White*	23--8/1/2	601
202	Baby Come Close - *Smokey Robinson*	36--15/1/1	592
203	Heavy Fallin' Out - *Stylistics*	31--10/1/2	587
204	People Gotta Move - *Gino Vannelli*	27--12/1/1	584
205	I've Got A Thing About You Baby - *Elvis Presley*	30--7/2/2	581
206	American Tune - *Paul Simon*	27--7/1/3	568
207	Mighty Mighty - *Earth, Wind & Fire*	35--12/1/1	564
208	Whatever You Got, I Want - *Jackson 5*	27--9/1/1	558
209	Rockin' Soul - *Hues Corporation*	28--8/1/2	551
210	I Love My Friend - *Charlie Rich*	29--7/1/3	548
211	Fallin' In Love - *Souther, Hillman, Furay Band*	24--8/1/2	546
212	I'm A Train - *Albert Hammond*	31--10/2/1	546
213	Let Your Hair Down - *Temptations*	27--8/1/1	533
214	You Can Have Her - *Sam Neely*	35--11/1/2	532
215	Virginia (Touch Me Like You Do) - *Bill Amesbury*	38--11/1/1	532
216	Thanks For Saving My Life - *Billy Paul*	43--14/1/1	532
217	Papa Don't Take No Mess - Part I - *James Brown*	27--7/1/2	530
218	Chameleon - *Herbie Hancock*	41--12/1/1	525
219	Dream On - *Righteous Brothers*	32--7/3/1	520
220	I Saw A Man And He Danced With His Wife - *Cher*	33--8/2/1	517
221	Fish Ain't Bitin' - *Lamont Dozier*	26--7/1/1	514
222	You're So Unique - *Billy Preston*	30--8/1/2	514
223	Give It To The People - *Righteous Brothers*	27--8/1/2	511
224	Kings Of The Party - *Brownsville Station*	31--8/1/2	507
225	Standing At The End Of The Line - *Lobo*	30--9/1/1	499
226	Last Kiss - *Wednesday*	45--17/1/1	498
227	Put Out The Light - *Joe Cocker*	38--9/1/2	497
228	Distant Lover - *Marvin Gaye*	33--7/2/1	495

Rank	Title - Act	Trajectory	Pts.
229	A Song I'd Like To Sing - Kris & Rita	33--9/1/1	488
230	Sugar Pie Guy Pt. 1 – Joneses	54--12/3/0	486
231	Higher Plane - Kool & The Gang	39--8/1/2	483
232	Tell Her She's Lovely - El Chicano	28--9/1/1	481
233	Sugar Baby Love - Rubettes	30--9/1/1	481
234	Ballero - War	35--8/1/2	480
235	Keep Your Head To The Sky Earth, Wind & Fire	34--9/1/1	479
236	Jessica - Allman Brothers Band	33--9/1/1	476
237	Time For Livin' - Sly & Family Stone	39--9/2/1	470
238	On A Night Like This - Bob Dylan	30--6/1/2	467
239	I'm The Leader Of The Gang Brownsville Station	26--7/1/1	466
240	Stoned To The Bone - Part 1 James Brown	46--10/1/1	463
241	Must Be Love - James Gang	45--10/1/1	458
242	Eyes Of Silver - Doobie Brothers	43--8/1/2	455
243	Joy, Part 1 - Isaac Hayes	31--8/1/1	454
244	This Time I'm Gone For Good Bobby Blue Bland	44--9/2/1	448
245	Early Morning Love - Sammy Johns	49--12/1/1	447
246	Fire, Baby I'm On Fire - Andy Kim	32--7/1/2	446
247	You Can't Be A Beacon (If Your Light Don't Shine) - Donna Fargo	48--11/2/0	437
248	The River Of Love - B.W. Stevenson	36--8/2/1	429
249	One Chain Don't Make No Prison Four Tops	36--8/1/1	426
250	I Just Can't Get You Out Of My Mind - Four Tops	41--8/2/1	423
251	Honey, Honey - Abba	37--8/1/1	416
252	In The Mood - Bette Midler	31--7/1/1	413
253	Willie And The Hand Jive - Eric Clapton	40--7/1/2	412
254	Touch Me - Fancy	37--8/1/1	411
255	Second Avenue - Garfunkel	44--9/1/1	407
256	Your Cash Ain't Nothin' But Trash Steve Miller Band	40--8/1/1	404
257	(We're Gonna) Rock Around The Clock - Bill Haley & Comets	36--10/1/1	398
258	The Same Love That Made Me Laugh Bill Withers	43--8/2/1	397
259	Rings - Lobo	37--6/2/1	391
260	Energy Crisis '74 - Dickie Goodman	37--8/1/1	390
261	Three Ring Circus - Blue Magic	44--7/2/1	387
262	Love Has No Pride - Linda Ronstadt	45--7/1/2	387
263	Happiness Is Me And You Gilbert O'Sullivan	34--8/1/1	381
264	It Could Have Been Me - Sami Jo	49--12/1/1	379
265	(I'm A) Yoyo Man - Rick Cunha	47--6/3/1	373
266	Touch And Go - Al Wilson	48--8/1/1	373
267	Showdown - Electric Light Orchestra	51--10/1/1	371
268	Living In The U.S.A. - Steve Miller Band	38--7/1/1	365
269	Heavenly - Temptations	45--8/1/1	363
270	Let Me Get To Know You - Paul Anka	54--10/2/0	362
271	The Black-Eyed Boys - Paper Lace	41--7/1/1	358
272	Don't Knock My Love Diana Ross & Marvin Gaye	38--6/1/1	354
273	Live It Up Part 1 - Isley Brothers	62--10/1/3	353
274	You Sure Love To Ball - Marvin Gaye	40--6/1/1	347
275	Hangin' Around - Edgar Winter Group	39--7/1/1	345
276	Wildflower - New Birth	49--9/1/1	344
277	I'll Be The Other Woman - Soul Children	52--9/2/1	340
278	Werewolf - Five Man Electrical Band	44--7/1/1	339

Rank	Title - Act	Trajectory	Pts.
279	Raised On Robbery - Joni Mitchell	50--7/1/1	338
280	Keep It In The Family - Leon Haywood	56--10/1/2	336
281	Who Is He And What Is He To You Creative Source	60--9/1/1	335
282	Second Avenue - Tim Moore	59--12/1/1	334
283	She's Gone - Daryl Hall & John Oates	52--8/1/2	329
284	The Americans (A Canadian's Opinion) Gordon Sinclair	36--6/1/1	328
285	Most Likely You Go Your Way (And I'll Go Mine) - Bob Dylan & The Band	47--7/1/1	327
286	Can You Handle It? Graham Central Station	49--9/1/2	320
287	Ain't Nothing Like The Real Thing Aretha Franklin	44--6/1/1	316
288	Secretary - Betty Wright	48--8/1/1	314
289	A Dream Goes On Forever Todd Rundgren	46--6/1/2	313
290	Black Lassie (Featuring Johnny Stash) Cheech & Chong	47--5/1/2	312
291	Without Love - Aretha Franklin	52--6/2/1	311
292	Dance With The Devil - Cozy Powell	50--7/1/1	300
293	We're Getting Careless With Our Love Johnnie Taylor	49--7/2/0	295
294	You're Welcome, Stop On By Bobby Womack	53--8/2/1	294
295	No Charge - Melba Montgomery	54--10/1/1	294
296	Skybird - Neil Diamond	48--5/1/2	293
297	If You Go Away - Terry Jacks	45--6/1/1	287
298	Daddy What If - Bobby Bare	50--9/1/0	287
299	Doraville - Atlanta Rhythm Section	57--9/1/1	287
300	King Of Nothing - Seals & Crofts	50--6/1/1	286

1975

Rank	Title - Act	Trajectory	Pts.
1	Jive Talkin' - Bee Gees	1--12/1/7	6444
2	Rhinestone Cowboy - Glen Campbell	1--16/1/7	6233
3	That's The Way (I Like It) K.C. & The Sunshine Band	1--7/3/7	6001
4	Philadelphia Freedom Elton John Band	1--6/2/10	5975
5	Fly, Robin, Fly - Silver Convention	1--8/1/10	5779
6	Have You Never Been Mellow Olivia Newton-John	1--7/1/8	5709
7	Island Girl - Elton John	1--5/2/9	5533
8	Lovin' You - Minnie Riperton	1--10/1/6	5514
9	Lady Marmalade – LaBelle	1--11/1/6	5457
10	Bad Blood - Neil Sedaka	1--7/2/6	5401
11	Pick Up The Pieces Average White Band	1--15/1/5	5363
12	My Eyes Adored You - Frankie Valli	1--19/1/5	5335
13	Love Will Keep Us Together Captain & Tennille	1--10/2/10	5273
14	Shining Star - Earth, Wind & Fire	1--16/1/5	4982
15	Mandy - Barry Manilow	1--10/1/7	4963
16	Jackie Blue - Ozark Mountain Daredevils	1--14/2/4	4926
17	Fame - David Bowie	1--14/1/7	4910
18	One Of These Nights - Eagles	1--9/1/7	4892
19	The Hustle - Van Mc Coy	1--13/1/6	4879
20	They Just Can't Stop It the (Games People Play) - Spinners	2--13/1/6	4840
21	Saturday Night - Bay City Rollers	1--13/1/7	4754
22	Boogie On Reggae Woman Stevie Wonder	1--14/1/3	4712
23	Laughter In The Rain - Neil Sedaka	1--16/1/4	4679
24	Please Mr. Postman - Carpenters	1--10/1/5	4628

Rank	Title - Act	Trajectory	Pts.
25	Thank God I'm A Country Boy - John Denver	1--13/1/4	4598
26	At Seventeen - Janis Ian	1--14/1/5	4539
27	How Long - Ace	1--12/1/3	4441
28	Let's Do It Again - Staple Singers	1--10/1/6	4426
29	You're The First, The Last, My Everything - Barry White	1--11/1/4	4415
30	Please Mr. Please - Olivia Newton-John	1--10/1/4	4411
31	Before The Next Teardrop Falls - Freddy Fender	1--17/1/2	4341
32	Lucy In The Sky With Diamonds - Elton John	1--6/1/7	4313
33	Get Down Tonight - K.C. & The Sunshine Band	1--9/2/8	4294
34	Listen To What The Man Said - Wings	1--7/1/7	4247
35	I'm Sorry - John Denver	1--10/1/7	4211
36	Someone Saved My Life Tonight - Elton John	1--7/1/5	4117
37	Fire - Ohio Players	1--11/1/5	4111
38	Fallin' In Love - Hamilton, Joe Frank & Reynolds	1--12/1/5	4055
39	Black Water - Doobie Brothers	3--10/1/7	4054
40	You're No Good - Linda Ronstadt	1--11/1/4	4052
41	He Don't Love You (Like I Love You) - Tony Orlando & Dawn	1--9/1/5	4015
42	(Hey Won't You Play) Another Somebody Done Somebody Wrong Song - B.J. Thomas	1--13/1/5	3988
43	When Will I Be Loved - Linda Ronstadt	1--11/1/5	3958
44	I'm Not In Love - 10cc	3--14/2/3	3862
45	No No Song - Ringo Starr	1--9/1/5	3777
46	Love Won't Let Me Wait - Major Harris	3--13/2/4	3720
47	Wildfire - Michael Murphey	2--15/1/5	3682
48	Run Joey Run - David Geddes	1--10/1/3	3568
49	Best Of My Love - Eagles	4--12/3/4	3541
50	Mr. Jaws - Dickie Goodman	1--9/1/4	3533
51	Lyin' Eyes - Eagles	3--6/1/7	3447
52	Sister Golden Hair - America	2--10/1/5	3349
53	Why Can't We Be Friends? - War	5--16/2/4	3184
54	The Way I Want To Touch You - Captain & Tennille	3--9/1/9	3049
55	Nights On Broadway - Bee Gees	4--10/1/7	3038
56	Miracles - Jefferson Starship	4--10/2/5	3031
57	Junior's Farm - Paul McCartney & Wings	4--9/1/3	2729
58	Feelings - Morris Albert	10--17/1/15	2723
59	Ain't No Way To Treat A Lady - Helen Reddy	5--12/1/4	2602
60	Wasted Days And Wasted Nights - Freddy Fender	6--15/2/3	2569
61	Who Loves You - Four Seasons	7--10/3/4	2565
62	Magic - Pilot	5--15/2/3	2551
63	Dance With Me - Orleans	5--14/1/4	2519
64	Low Rider - War	5--9/2/5	2495
65	You Are So Beautiful - Joe Cocker	4--11/2/3	2477
66	Sky High - Jigsaw	5--16/1/5	2461
67	Chevy Van - Sammy Johns	5--13/2/3	2452
68	I'm Not Lisa - Jessi Colter	5--14/1/5	2369
69	Only You - Ringo Starr	6--8/2/3	2368
70	Poetry Man - Phoebe Snow	5--14/1/2	2342
71	I Don't Like To Sleep Alone - Paul Anka	5--11/1/3	2264
72	Bad Time - Grand Funk	5--11/1/3	2241
73	Lady - Styx	6--14/1/3	2226
74	Swearin' To God - Frankie Valli	7--12/2/3	2226
75	Could It Be Magic - Barry Manilow	7--14/1/4	2202
76	Fight The Power Part I - Isley Brothers	6--14/1/4	2166
77	Midnight Blue - Melissa Manchester	7--14/1/5	2148
78	Emma - Hot Chocolate	6--13/1/3	2129
79	Long Tall Glasses (I Can Dance) - Leo Sayer	6--11/2/3	2081
80	Ballroom Blitz - Sweet	9--18/1/3	2073
81	One Man Woman/One Woman Man - Paul Anka with Odia Coates	7--12/1/3	2015
82	My Little Town - Simon & Garfunkel	7--7/3/4	1999
83	Heat Wave - Linda Ronstadt	4--8/1/4	1989
84	Some Kind Of Wonderful - Grand Funk	7--10/1/3	1982
85	The Way We Were/Try To Remember - Gladys Knight & The Pips	10--12/1/5	1888
86	How Sweet It Is (To Be Loved By You) - James Taylor	7--8/1/5	1810
87	Walking In Rhythm - Blackbyrds	7--15/1/2	1807
88	This Will Be - Natalie Cole	9--13/2/2	1804
89	Rockin' Chair - Gwen McCrae	10--12/2/4	1764
90	I Feel A Song (In My Heart) - Gladys Knight & The Pips	11--13/1/3	1742
91	Morning Side Of The Mountain - Donny & Marie Osmond	6--10/1/4	1736
92	It Only Takes A Minute - Tavares	10--15/1/3	1727
93	Never Can Say Goodbye - Gloria Gaynor	8--13/2/2	1709
94	Only Women - Alice Cooper	10--13/1/3	1653
95	Doctor's Orders - Carol Douglas	10--12/1/4	1591
96	Old Days - Chicago	6--8/1/3	1587
97	Only Yesterday - Carpenters	8--10/1/2	1583
98	Shame, Shame, Shame - Shirley (And Company)	8--10/2/3	1567
99	Express - B.T. Express	9--10/1/4	1559
100	Once You Get Started - Rufus Featuring Chaka Khan	6--10/1/3	1536
101	Cut The Cake - Average White Band	12--11/2/4	1533
102	Lady Blue - Leon Russell	8--15/1/5	1526
103	Feel Like Makin' Love - Bad Company	10--14/1/2	1525
104	Get Dancin' - Disco Tex & The Sex-O-Lettes	10--12/1/2	1524
105	Lonely People - America	10--11/2/2	1506
106	The Rockford Files - Mike Post	10--13/1/3	1494
107	Dynomite - Part I - Bazuka	12--15/2/2	1487
108	What Am I Gonna Do With You - Barry White	8--8/1/3	1439
109	Get Down, Get Down (Get On The Floor) - Joe Simon	9--11/1/4	1438
110	Bungle In The Jungle - Jethro Tull	12--13/1/3	1433
111	Rocky - Austin Roberts	11--14/1/2	1407
112	Don't Call Us, We'll Call You - Sugarloaf/Jerry Corbetta	12--14/1/3	1399
113	Bad Luck (Part 1) - Harold Melvin & The Blue Notes	13--11/2/3	1396
114	It's A Miracle - Barry Manilow	10--12/1/2	1378
115	(I Believe) There's Nothing Stronger Than Our Love - Paul Anka with Odia Coates	14--9/2/3	1377
116	Our Day Will Come - Frankie Valli	14--9/2/3	1377
117	Supernatural Thing - Part I - Ben E. King	9--14/1/2	1370
118	Roll On Down The Highway - Bachman-Turner Overdrive	8--7/1/2	1364
119	Killer Queen - Queen	12--15/1/2	1357

Rank	Title - Act	Trajectory	Pts.
120	Can't Get It Out Of My Head - Electric Light Orchestra	14--15/1/2	1351
121	Do It Any Way You Wanna - People's Choice	14--12/1/6	1333
122	SOS - Abba	12--15/1/3	1315
123	L-O-V-E (Love) - Al Green	10--9/1/3	1291
124	Eighteen With A Bullet - Pete Wingfield	14--15/1/3	1272
125	I Only Have Eyes For You - Art Garfunkel	19--15/1/2	1269
126	Take Me In Your Arms (Rock Me) - Doobie Brothers	10--8/1/4	1263
127	#9 Dream - John Lennon	10--9/1/2	1256
128	Misty - Ray Stevens	16--14/2/2	1255
129	That's The Way Of The World - Earth, Wind & Fire	13--11/2/1	1245
130	Brazil - Ritchie Family	10--10/1/3	1174
131	Sweet Surrender - John Denver	14--8/3/1	1151
132	Shoeshine Boy - Eddie Kendricks	22--15/2/3	1134
133	The Last Farewell - Roger Whittaker	17--12/1/4	1092
134	How Long (Betcha' Got A Chick On The Side) - Pointer Sisters	17--11/2/1	1041
135	Must Of Got Lost - J. Geils Band	17--10/2/2	1027
136	Tush - ZZ Top	12--8/1/2	993
137	I Want'a Do Something Freaky To You - Leon Haywood	20--12/2/2	976
138	Up In A Puff Of Smoke - Polly Brown	16--12/1/2	973
139	I Am Love - Jackson 5	18--9/1/4	964
140	Rock N' Roll (I Gave You The Best Years Of My Life) - Mac Davis	16--9/1/2	957
141	Something Better To Do - Olivia Newton-John	15--7/1/3	946
142	Spirit Of The Boogie - Kool & The Gang	27--13/2/2	940
143	Black Superman - "Muhammad Ali" - Johnny Wakelin & The Kinshasa Band	22--27/1/3	931
144	Nightingale - Carole King	16--10/1/2	930
145	To The Door Of The Sun (Alle Porte Del Sole) - Al Martino	21--15/1/1	923
146	Holdin' On To Yesterday - Ambrosia	18--10/1/3	918
147	What A Diff'rence A Day Makes - Esther Phillips	21--11/2/2	918
148	Ride 'Em Cowboy - Paul Davis	27--14/2/2	917
149	Third Rate Romance - Amazing Rhythm Aces	17--12/1/2	916
150	Hey You - Bachman-Turner Overdrive	16--8/1/3	915
151	Born To Run - Bruce Springsteen	17--9/1/3	904
152	My Boy - Elvis Presley	17--8/1/3	898
153	Promised Land - Elvis Presley	22--12/1/2	894
154	Blue Eyes Crying In The Rain - Willie Nelson	25--16/1/2	892
155	Look In My Eyes Pretty Woman - Tony Orlando & Dawn	20--10/2/1	882
156	Mornin' Beautiful - Tony Orlando & Dawn	15--8/1/2	869
157	The Bertha Butt Boogie - Part 1 - Jimmy Castor Bunch	21--11/2/2	850
158	I'll Play For You - Seals & Crofts	35--15/2/1	836
159	Sad Sweet Dreamer - Sweet Sensation	17--11/1/2	825
160	Solitaire - Carpenters	15--8/1/1	812
161	Daisy Jane - America	27--10/1/2	775
162	For The Love Of You (Part 1 & 2) - Isley Brothers	26--6/2/6	775
163	Venus And Mars Rock Show - Wings	16--6/2/2	770
164	I'm A Woman - Maria Muldaur	24--11/1/2	770
165	Free Bird - Lynyrd Skynyrd	25--9/1/3	766
166	Gone At Last - Paul Simon & Phoebe Snow	20--8/1/3	762
167	You - George Harrison	19--8/1/2	757
168	Shakey Ground - Temptations	28--12/1/1	756
169	I'm On Fire - Dwight Twilley Band	23--12/1/2	741
170	Every Time You Touch Me (I Get High) - Charlie Rich	22--10/2/1	731
171	Carolina In The Pines - Michael Murphey	23--9/1/3	728
172	I Belong To You - Love Unlimited	29--14/1/1	717
173	Harry Truman - Chicago	19--8/1/2	712
174	Operator - Manhattan Transfer	24--11/1/2	693
175	Secret Love - Freddy Fender	25--9/1/2	691
176	Part Time Love - Gladys Knight & The Pips	27--9/1/3	673
177	Part Of The Plan - Dan Fogelberg	24--13/1/1	671
178	Satin Soul - Love Unlimited Orchestra	28--10/2/2	668
179	Dark Horse - George Harrison	19--7/1/2	667
180	Emotion - Helen Reddy	23--8/1/2	666
181	Rockin' All Over The World - John Fogerty	25--10/1/2	665
182	Disco Queen - Hot Chocolate	21--10/1/2	663
183	Never Let Her Go - David Gates	26--11/2/1	655
184	Movin' On - Bad Company	23--8/2/1	649
185	Hijack - Herbie Mann	22--15/1/1	646
186	Autobahn - Kraftwerk	19--8/1/1	642
187	Just A Little Bit Of You - Michael Jackson	30--12/1/1	642
188	7-6-5-4-3-2-1 (Blow Your Whistle) - Gary Toms Empire	35--14/1/1	638
189	Slippery When Wet - Commodores	29--12/1/2	637
190	Ready - Cat Stevens	29--8/1/3	632
191	Struttin' - Billy Preston	22--9/1/1	630
192	Amie - Pure Prairie League	27--11/1/2	619
193	Dancin' Fool - Guess Who	24--8/1/2	617
194	The South's Gonna Do It - Charlie Daniels Band	26--10/2/1	617
195	To Each His Own - Faith, Hope & Charity	42--8/2/5	604
196	Just Too Many People - Melissa Manchester	32--9/1/2	601
197	Big Yellow Taxi - Joni Mitchell	25--9/1/1	599
198	Young Americans - David Bowie	20--9/1/2	598
199	Remember What I Told You To Forget - Tavares	23--9/1/2	594
200	I'm On Fire - 5000 Volts	24--8/1/2	590
201	Stand By Me - John Lennon	20--7/1/1	589
202	Main Title (Theme From "Jaws") - John Williams	25--8/1/2	577
203	Give The People What They Want - O'Jays	33--8/1/3	572
204	Full Of Fire - Al Green	30--8/1/3	564
205	That's When The Music Takes Me - Neil Sedaka	30--9/1/1	562
206	Dream Merchant - New Birth	31--10/1/1	557
207	Baby That's Backatcha - Smokey Robinson	38--10/2/0	555
208	Rainy Day People - Gordon Lightfoot	32--10/1/1	551
209	Butter Boy - Fanny	27--10/1/1	549
210	The Immigrant - Neil Sedaka	28--9/1/1	549
211	There Goes Another Love Song - Outlaws	26--8/1/2	547
212	Calypso - John Denver	26--7/1/2	544

Rank	Title - Act	Trajectory	Pts.
213	Til The World Ends - *Three Dog Night*	29--8/2/1	530
214	Glasshouse – *Temptations*	41--7/1/4	525
215	Attitude Dancing - *Carly Simon*	25--8/1/1	521
216	I Wanna Dance Wit' Choo (Doo Dat Dance) - *Disco Tex & The Sex-O-Lettes*	34--10/1/1	520
217	The Last Game Of The Season (A Blind Man In The Bleachers) *David Geddes*	22--6/1/3	519
218	Sweet Sticky Thing - *Ohio Players*	31--9/1/1	512
219	The Proud One - *Osmonds*	33--8/2/1	509
220	Changes - *David Bowie*	38--11/1/0	509
221	The Entertainer - *Billy Joel*	37--8/2/1	506
222	Trampled Under Foot - *Led Zeppelin*	28--8/1/1	497
223	Judy Mae - *Boomer Castleman*	29--7/1/1	482
224	Don't Tell Me Goodnight - *Lobo*	30--9/1/1	480
225	Don't Take Your Love - *Manhattans*	37--8/1/2	479
226	Sweet Emotion - *Aerosmith*	36--9/1/1	476
227	Shaving Cream - *Benny Bell*	34--10/1/1	464
228	Hope That We Can Be Together Soon *Sharon Paige*	31--7/1/2	463
229	Good Lovin' Gone Bad - *Bad Company*	32--8/1/1	461
230	From His Woman To You *Barbara Mason*	34--8/2/1	458
231	I Want To Be Free - *Ohio Players*	32--8/1/1	456
232	Help Me Rhonda - *Johnny Rivers*	30--7/1/2	455
233	Caribbean Festival - *Kool & The Gang*	45--9/1/2	449
234	Rendezvous - *Hudson Brothers*	32--10/1/1	435
235	If I Ever Lose This Heaven *Average White Band*	44--10/1/0	435
236	My Little Lady - *Bloodstone*	41--9/1/1	428
237	Lizzie And The Rainman *Tanya Tucker*	35--7/2/1	427
238	Your Bulldog Drinks Champagne *Jim Stafford*	35--8/1/1	427
239	Your Love - *Graham Central Station*	42--9/1/1	427
240	Black Friday - *Steely Dan*	31--6/1/2	423
241	Look At Me (I'm In Love) - *Moments*	39--9/2/1	422
242	Happy - *Eddie Kendricks*	59--7/2/4	420
243	I'll Do For You Anything You Want Me To - *Barry White*	32--7/1/1	416
244	Money - *Gladys Knight & The Pips*	40--6/2/2	415
245	Peace Pipe - *B.T. Express*	40--9/1/1	414
246	Volare - *Al Martino*	41--8/2/1	410
247	Living A Little, Laughing A Little *Spinners*	33--8/1/0	408
248	Love Finds Its Own Way *Gladys Knight & The Pips*	33--7/1/1	405
249	Happy People - *Temptations*	44--9/1/1	403
250	Ain't That Peculiar - *Diamond REO*	36--8/1/1	398
251	It's All Down To Goodnight Vienna - *Ringo Starr*	29--6/1/1	397
252	Dreaming A Dream *Crown Heights Affair*	46--12/1/1	395
253	The Agony And The Ecstasy *Smokey Robinson*	50--13/1/1	391
254	Growin' - *Loggins & Messina*	45--8/1/1	385
255	I Don't Know Why - *Rolling Stones*	37--7/1/1	384
256	I Wanna Learn A Love Song *Harry Chapin*	40--6/2/1	378
257	Linda On My Mind - *Conway Twitty*	48--9/2/0	377
258	I Love Makin' Love To You *Evie Sands*	44--8/2/1	376
259	Me And Mrs. Jones *Ron Banks And The Dramatics*	46--9/1/1	374
260	Runaway - *Charlie Kulis*	42--8/1/1	363
261	Two Fine People - *Cat Stevens*	45--8/1/1	362
262	Bluebird - *Helen Reddy*	34--6/1/1	360
263	Beer Barrel Polka - *Bobby Vinton*	45--8/1/1	358
264	Mexico - *James Taylor*	38--6/1/1	357
265	T-R-O-U-B-L-E - *Elvis Presley*	40--7/1/1	354
266	Since I Met You Baby - *Freddy Fender*	44--7/2/1	354
267	Katmandu - *Bob Seger*	45--10/1/0	350
268	Tangled Up In Blue - *Bob Dylan*	43--7/1/1	348
269	Saturday Night Special *Lynyrd Skynyrd*	41--9/1/1	346
270	When A Child Is Born - *Michael Holm*	38--6/1/1	344
271	Keep On Tryin' - *Poco*	45--8/2/0	341
272	Sexy - *MFSB*	43--8/1/1	336
273	I've Been This Way Before *Neil Diamond*	43--7/1/0	334
274	Diamonds And Rust - *Joan Baez*	48--8/1/1	334
275	Summer Of '42 - *Biddu Orchestra*	54--8/2/1	334
276	Who's Sorry Now - *Marie Osmond*	39--7/1/1	327
277	Oh Me, Oh My (Dreams In My Arms) *Al Green*	40--6/1/1	324
278	Carry Me - *Crosby & Nash*	44--6/2/1	323
279	Please Pardon Me (You Remind Me Of A Friend) - *Rufus Featuring Chaka Khan*	44--6/1/1	321
280	Sneakin' Up Behind You *Brecker Brothers*	47--7/1/1	320
281	Send In The Clowns - *Judy Collins*	53--8/1/1	320
282	Ease On Down The Road *Consumer Rapport*	42--7/1/2	319
283	I Dreamed Last Night *Justin Hayward & John Lodge*	45--7/1/1	317
284	Love Power - *Willie Hutch*	48--9/1/1	317
285	Ding Dong; Ding Dong *George Harrison*	36--5/1/1	316
286	Skybird - *Tony Orlando & Dawn*	52--7/1/1	314
287	Forever Came Today - *Jackson 5*	55--8/1/0	312
288	I Fought The Law - *Sam Neely*	41--6/2/0	309
289	As Long As He Takes Care Of Home - *Candi Staton*	42--9/1/0	305
290	Sadie - *Spinners*	45--6/1/1	302
291	Rag Doll - *Sammy Johns*	49--7/1/1	301
292	Sooner Or Later - *Impressions*	63--9/2/1	301
293	Change With The Times - *Van McCoy*	52--6/2/1	299
294	Day Tripper - *Anne Murray*	44--7/1/0	297
295	(Just Like) Romeo And Juliet *Sha Na Na*	46--7/1/1	294
296	Every Day I Have To Cry Some *Arthur Alexander*	51--8/2/1	292
297	Good Times, Rock & Roll - *Flash Cadillac & The Continental Kids*	45--8/1/1	290
298	Give It What You Got - *B.T. Express*	46--5/1/2	285
299	Swing Your Daddy - *Jim Gilstrap*	57--8/1/1	285
300	Sailing - *Rod Stewart*	49--6/1/1	283

1976

Rank	Title - Act	Trajectory	Pts.
1	Afternoon Delight - *Starland Vocal Band*	1--9/4/10	9537
2	Silly Love Songs - *Wings*	1--8/2/12	8405
3	Tonight's The Night (Gonna Be Alright) *Rod Stewart*	1--7/5/11	8395
4	I Write The Songs - *Barry Manilow*	1--9/1/11	7868
5	Kiss And Say Goodbye - *Manhattans*	1--13/2/13	7148
6	Disco Duck (Part 1) *Rick Dees & His Cast Of Idiots*	1--10/2/8	7096

Rank	Title - Act	Trajectory	Pts.
7	**A Fifth Of Beethoven** - Walter Murphy & The Big Apple Band	1--21/1/9	6859
8	**Convoy** - C.W. McCall	1--9/3/5	6663
9	**Welcome Back** - John Sebastian	1--8/2/9	6391
10	**Muskrat Love** - Captain & Tennille	2--8/5/10	6305
11	**50 Ways To Leave Your Lover** - Paul Simon	1--9/3/9	6248
12	**Don't Go Breaking My Heart** - Elton John & Kiki Dee	1--6/3/12	6238
13	**You Make Me Feel Like Dancing** - Leo Sayer	1--11/1/12	6180
14	**Play That Funky Music** - Wild Cherry	1--14/2/10	6143
15	**Lonely Night (Angel Face)** - Captain & Tennille	1--11/1/8	6050
16	**Disco Lady** - Johnnie Taylor	1--9/2/9	5865
17	**If You Leave Me Now** - Chicago	1--12/1/7	5664
18	**Boogie Fever** - Sylvers	1--15/1/9	5603
19	**Dream Weaver** - Gary Wright	1--12/1/9	5506
20	**Get Up And Boogie (That's Right)** - Silver Convention	1--14/1/9	5431
21	**Right Back Where We Started From** - Maxine Nightingale	1--11/1/9	5375
22	**Lowdown** - Boz Scaggs	1--14/1/9	5374
23	**(Shake, Shake, Shake) Shake Your Booty** - KC & The Sunshine Band	1--12/1/9	5353
24	**Let Your Love Flow** - Bellamy Brothers	1--13/1/8	5246
25	**Love Machine (Part 1)** - Miracles	1--18/1/8	5202
26	**All By Myself** - Eric Carmen	1--14/1/8	5192
27	**Rock'n Me** - Steve Miller	1--13/1/11	5181
28	**You Should Be Dancing** - Bee Gees	1--10/1/10	5104
29	**Misty Blue** - Dorothy Moore	3--16/2/8	5063
30	**Love Hangover** - Diana Ross	1--10/1/7	4978
31	**You Sexy Thing** - Hot Chocolate	2--18/1/7	4959
32	**The Wreck Of The Edmund Fitzgerald** - Gordon Lightfoot	1--11/1/7	4948
33	**More, More, More (Pt. 1)** - Andrea True Connection	3--16/3/8	4878
34	**Theme From S.W.A.T.** - Rhythm Heritage	1--16/1/9	4653
35	**Love So Right** - Bee Gees	3--12/2/11	4607
36	**Love Rollercoaster** - Ohio Players	3--10/2/7	4577
37	**Let 'Em In** - Wings	1--10/1/8	4564
38	**December, 1963 (Oh, What A Night)** - Four Seasons	1--13/1/10	4414
39	**Theme From Mahogany (Do You Know Where You're Going To)** - Diana Ross	1--11/1/5	4203
40	**Moonlight Feels Right** - Starbuck	3--16/1/7	4130
41	**The Rubberband Man** - Spinners	3--15/1/10	3987
42	**I'd Really Love To See You Tonight** - England Dan & John Ford Coley	4--14/2/9	3801
43	**Love Is Alive** - Gary Wright	3--15/1/8	3672
44	**Love To Love You Baby** - Donna Summer	3--15/2/5	3643
45	**Got To Get You Into My Life** - Beatles	3--10/1/7	3613
46	**Devil Woman** - Cliff Richard	5--15/3/7	3583
47	**Fooled Around And Fell In Love** - Elvin Bishop	3--12/1/7	3501
48	**Sweet Thing** - Rufus Featuring Chaka Khan	5--14/2/8	3403
49	**You'll Never Find Another Love Like Mine** - Lou Rawls	4--15/1/10	3373
50	**More Than A Feeling** - Boston	4--12/2/10	3324
51	**Shannon** - Henry Gross	5--12/2/8	3291
52	**Let Her In** - John Travolta	5--12/2/9	3229
53	**Show Me The Way** - Peter Frampton	4--44/1/7	3165
54	**Bohemian Rhapsody** - Queen	6--18/2/7	3135
55	**Only Sixteen** - Dr. Hook	5--17/1/6	3096
56	**She's Gone** - Daryl Hall & John Oates	6--15/3/7	3070
57	**Fox On The Run** - Sweet	5--9/3/4	3014
58	**Sara Smile** - Daryl Hall & John Oates	6--18/1/9	2967
59	**Take It To The Limit** - Eagles	5--11/2/10	2876
60	**Shop Around** - Captain & Tennille	6--9/2/10	2875
61	**Nadia's Theme (The Young And The Restless)** - Barry DeVorzon & Perry Botkin, Jr.	5--14/1/10	2828
62	**Dream On** - Aerosmith	6--13/2/8	2763
63	**Still The One** - Orleans	6--12/2/8	2730
64	**Stand Tall** - Burton Cummings	5--13/1/9	2687
65	**I Love Music (Part 1)** - O'Jays	7--14/1/5	2665
66	**Get Closer** - Seals & Crofts	7--19/1/8	2555
67	**Love Hurts** - Nazareth	9--17/2/6	2538
68	**Fly Away** - John Denver	6--6/4/2	2495
69	**You Are The Woman** - Firefall	8--16/2/7	2490
70	**A Little Bit More** - Dr. Hook	9--15/2/9	2473
71	**Magic Man** - Heart	7--16/2/7	2433
72	**Beth** – Kiss	7--7/2/9	2427
73	**Happy Days** - Pratt & McClain	6--9/2/6	2371
74	**Evil Woman** - Electric Light Orchestra	9--14/2/4	2361
75	**Walk Away From Love** - David Ruffin	8--11/2/4	2267
76	**Sing A Song** - Earth, Wind & Fire	7--12/1/5	2240
77	**Sweet Love** - Commodores	9--19/1/5	2230
78	**Golden Years** - David Bowie	12--15/2/7	2176
79	**Money Honey** - Bay City Rollers	7--8/2/7	2155
80	**I'll Be Good To You** - Brothers Johnson	7--13/1/8	2079
81	**Breaking Up Is Hard To Do** - Neil Sedaka	7--10/1/4	2068
82	**Heaven Must Be Missing An Angel (Part 1)** - Tavares	10--15/1/9	2053
83	**(Don't Fear) The Reaper** - Blue Öyster Cult	7--15/1/6	2022
84	**I Never Cry** - Alice Cooper	9--11/2/10	2017
85	**Livin' Thing** - Electric Light Orchestra	10--9/1/11	1994
86	**I Only Want To Be With You** - Bay City Rollers	8--7/2/7	1958
87	**You're My Best Friend** - Queen	9--9/2/8	1957
88	**Fernando** - Abba	10--11/2/7	1950
89	**Rhiannon (Will You Ever Win)** - Fleetwood Mac	9--13/1/7	1914
90	**Tryin' To Get The Feeling Again** - Barry Manilow	10--11/1/6	1894
91	**Rock And Roll Music** - Beach Boys	11--8/2/13	1870
92	**Squeeze Box** - The Who	11--15/2/4	1857
93	**Getaway** - Earth, Wind & Fire	10--12/2/7	1850
94	**I'm Easy** - Keith Carradine	10--15/1/7	1837
95	**Turn The Beat Around** - Vicki Sue Robinson	15--16/1/8	1814
96	**Take The Money And Run** - Steve Miller	9--11/1/7	1805
97	**Just To Be Close To You** - Commodores	11--11/2/7	1766
98	**Fanny (Be Tender With My Love)** - Bee Gees	9--12/1/6	1758
99	**Say You Love Me** - Fleetwood Mac	12--11/2/9	1748
100	**This Masquerade** - George Benson	12--13/1/9	1729
101	**Nights Are Forever Without You** - England Dan & John Ford Coley	10--10/2/7	1711
102	**Never Gonna Fall In Love Again** - Eric Carmen	9--9/1/6	1707

Rank	Title - Act	Trajectory	Pts.
103	That'll Be The Day - Linda Ronstadt	11--10/1/6	1627
104	The Boys Are Back In Town - Thin Lizzy	10--10/2/6	1620
105	Baby, I Love Your Way - Peter Frampton	16--11/2/10	1603
106	With Your Love - Jefferson Starship	13--8/2/8	1594
107	Wham Bam Shang-A-Lang - Silver	16--14/2/7	1552
108	Summer - War	15--11/1/6	1518
109	Fool To Cry - Rolling Stones	9--8/1/6	1504
110	There's A Kind Of Hush (All Over The World) - Carpenters	12--7/2/6	1481
111	Strange Magic - Electric Light Orchestra	14--10/1/7	1480
112	Takin' It To The Streets Doobie Brothers	15--11/2/5	1441
113	Action – Sweet	10--9/1/6	1423
114	Movin' - Brass Construction	14--13/2/4	1416
115	The Best Disco In Town - Ritchie Family	18--12/1/8	1405
116	Wake Up Everybody (Part 1) - Harold Melvin & The Blue Notes	15--13/2/4	1352
117	Slow Ride - Foghat	20--15/1/4	1332
118	Do You Feel Like We Do Peter Frampton	13--8/1/5	1305
119	Grow Some Funk Of Your Own Elton John	9--6/1/3	1275
120	Times Of Your Life - Paul Anka	17--12/2/3	1259
121	Young Hearts Run Free - Candi Staton	25--13/1/7	1253
122	Deep Purple - Donny & Marie Osmond	20--18/1/4	1213
123	Tear The Roof Off The Sucker (Give Up The Funk) - Parliament	20--11/2/7	1204
124	I Want You - Marvin Gaye	20--12/2/4	1174
125	Baby Face Wing And A Prayer Fife & Drum Corps	26--11/2/8	1174
126	I Do, I Do, I Do, I Do, I Do - Abba	19--11/1/5	1144
127	If You Know What I Mean Neil Diamond	16--8/1/7	1135
128	Love Ballad - L.T.D.	22--12/1/11	1124
129	Winners And Losers Hamilton, Joe Frank & Reynolds	18--12/1/2	1107
130	Rock And Roll All Nite (Live) - Kiss	17--12/1/3	1103
131	Junk Food Junkie - Larry Groce	20--13/1/3	1098
132	Country Boy (You Got Your Feet In L.A.) - Glen Campbell	17--10/2/3	1052
133	Love Really Hurts Without You Billy Ocean	16--8/1/5	1045
134	Baretta's Theme ("Keep Your Eye On The Sparrow") - Rhythm Heritage	16--10/1/4	1031
135	Love In The Shadows - Neil Sedaka	17--8/1/5	992
136	Making Our Dreams Come True Cyndi Grecco	21--12/1/4	991
137	Over My Head - Fleetwood Mac	18--9/2/4	987
138	Somewhere In The Night - Helen Reddy	20--12/2/2	982
139	The White Knight - Cledus Maggard	20--10/1/4	976
140	Last Child - Aerosmith	21--9/1/7	968
141	Young Blood - Bad Company	22--10/1/5	924
142	Love Is The Drug - Roxy Music	24--13/2/2	906
143	Union Man - Cate Brothers	32--14/2/3	888
144	Cupid - Tony Orlando & Dawn	21--8/1/4	885
145	Something He Can Feel Aretha Franklin	30--9/1/7	884
146	Paloma Blanca George Baker Selection	22--11/1/3	871
147	Looking For Space - John Denver	18--7/2/3	861
148	Tracks Of My Tears - Linda Ronstadt	25--10/2/3	860
149	Livin' For The Weekend - O'Jays	24--9/1/4	859
150	Mamma Mia – Abba	36--7/3/3	842
151	Who'd She Coo? - Ohio Players	35--11/2/7	829
152	Did You Boogie (With Your Baby) Flash Cadillac & The Continental Kids	25--13/1/6	821
153	This One's For You - Barry Manilow	21--7/1/5	817
154	Today's The Day - America	24--9/1/4	793
155	Inseparable - Natalie Cole	33--13/1/3	784
156	Shout It Out Loud - Kiss	24--10/1/3	781
157	Give It Up (Turn It Loose) Tyrone Davis	36--14/2/2	774
158	You Are My Starship - Norman Connors	26--9/1/5	772
159	I Need To Be In Love - Carpenters	31--7/1/7	748
160	It's A Long Way There Little River Band	31--11/1/4	741
161	Sophisticated Lady (She's A Different Lady) - Natalie Cole	40--13/2/3	741
162	Rock And Roll Love Letter Bay City Rollers	30--8/2/4	716
163	A Dose Of Rock 'N' Roll - Ringo Starr	26--6/1/5	697
164	Hello Old Friend - Eric Clapton	28--8/1/5	691
165	One Love In My Lifetime - Diana Ross	34--10/1/6	690
166	Only Love Is Real - Carole King	27--7/2/3	681
167	Come On Over - Olivia Newton-John	30--10/1/2	670
168	I Feel Like A Bullet (In The Gun Of Robert Ford) - Elton John	18--7/1/2	649
169	Hurricane (Part I) - Bob Dylan	27--7/2/3	646
170	Hard Work - John Handy	48--13/3/3	626
171	Another Rainy Day In New York City Chicago	33--6/1/7	623
172	Hurt - Elvis Presley	31--8/2/2	616
173	Don't Take Away The Music - Tavares	40--9/2/5	615
174	Get The Funk Out Ma Face Brothers Johnson	34--9/1/5	614
175	Street Singin' - Lady Flash	34--9/1/4	613
176	Lorelei - Styx	30--9/2/3	610
177	That's Where The Happy People Go Trammps	44--14/1/4	588
178	Let The Music Play - Barry White	31--8/2/2	584
179	Love Or Leave - Spinners	35--9/1/2	579
180	Shower The People - James Taylor	49--7/2/7	572
181	Livin' Ain't Livin' - Firefall	41--7/1/5	571
182	I Got To Know - Starbuck	40--9/1/4	570
183	School Boy Crush Average White Band	31--8/1/3	569
184	The Homecoming - Hagood Hardy	46--11/1/4	568
185	Break Away - Art Garfunkel	38--8/1/3	561
186	C'mon Marianne - Donny Osmond	44--10/2/1	559
187	Teddy Bear - Red Sovine	40--10/1/3	555
188	Springtime Mama - Henry Gross	39--10/1/2	552
189	Let It Shine - Olivia Newton-John	28--7/1/2	544
190	Anything You Want - John Valenti	43--12/2/3	539
191	Sunrise - Eric Carmen	38--6/2/4	536
192	Venus - Frankie Avalon	32--10/1/1	525
193	Crazy On You – Heart	40--8/2/10	523
194	Tangerine - Salsoul Orchestra	40--10/1/2	519
195	You'll Lose A Good Thing Freddy Fender	36--9/1/1	513
196	Don't Stop Believin' Olivia Newton-John	47--6/1/8	503
197	It's Only Love - ZZ Top	46--13/1/1	496
198	Love Fire – Jigsaw	34--9/1/2	484
199	It's O.K. - Beach Boys	39--7/1/3	484
200	Let's Live Together - Road Apples	48--16/1/1	483
201	Don't Pull Your Love/Then You Can Tell Me Goodbye - Glen Campbell	41--7/1/3	458

Rank	Title - Act	Trajectory	Pts.
202	**Superstar** - Paul Davis	41--7/1/2	441
203	**So Sad The Song** - Gladys Knight & The Pips	56--7/1/7	441
204	**One Piece At A Time** - Johnny Cash	41--7/1/3	437
205	**Down To The Line** - Bachman-Turner Overdrive	38--7/2/1	435
206	**Good Hearted Woman** - Waylon & Willie	37--6/2/2	421
207	**I've Got A Feeling (We'll Be Seeing Each Other Again)** - Al Wilson	41--8/1/2	408
208	**Hold Back The Night** – Trammps	44--9/1/2	404
209	**Save Your Kisses For Me** - Brotherhood Of Man	48--9/1/2	404
210	**Take A Hand** - Rick Springfield	47--6/1/4	403
211	**Fopp** - Ohio Players	41--7/1/2	401
212	**It's Over** - Boz Scaggs	43--7/1/2	401
213	**Can't Hide Love** - Earth, Wind & Fire	45--6/2/2	393
214	**Framed** - Cheech & Chong	46--7/1/2	390
215	**It Keeps You Runnin'** - Carly Simon	49--8/1/2	390
216	**Woman Tonight** - America	42--7/1/2	389
217	**Without Your Love (Mr. Jordan)** - Charlie Ross	44--8/1/1	388
218	**Happy Music** - Blackbyrds	42--9/1/2	386
219	**Good Vibrations** - Todd Rundgren	47--7/1/2	384
220	**Hit The Road Jack** - Stampeders	41--8/1/1	382
221	**I'm Gonna Let My Heart Do The Walking** - Supremes	54--11/1/1	374
222	**I Can't Hear You No More** - Helen Reddy	41--5/2/2	370
223	**Mr. Melody** - Natalie Cole	54--10/1/1	361
224	**'Til It's Time To Say Goodbye** - Jonathan Cain	48--8/2/0	358
225	**Ob-La-Di, Ob-La-Da** - Beatles	47--6/1/2	353
226	**Where Did Our Love Go** - J. Geils Band	62--9/2/3	352
227	**Highfly** - John Miles	58--6/1/26	349
228	**Steppin' Out** - Neil Sedaka	53--7/1/2	346
229	**Dance Wit Me** - Rufus Featuring Chaka Khan	37--6/1/1	343
230	**Yesterday's Hero** - John Paul Young	44--8/1/1	339
231	**Hot Stuff** - Rolling Stones	60--10/1/1	337
232	**The End Is Not In Sight (The Cowboy Tune)** - Amazing Rhythm Aces	56--11/1/1	334
233	**Renegade** - Michael Murphey	42--7/1/1	332
234	**I Can't Live A Dream** - Osmonds	53--9/1/1	332
235	**Fallen Angel** - Frankie Valli	49--6/1/2	328
236	**Just You And I** - Melissa Manchester	46--6/1/2	327
237	**Love Of My Life** - Gino Vannelli	57--9/1/2	327
238	**Still Crazy After All These Years** - Paul Simon	45--5/1/2	323
239	**You Gotta Make Your Own Sunshine** - Neil Sedaka	55--10/1/0	320
240	**(The System Of) Doctor Tarr And Professor Fether** - Alan Parsons Project	54--9/1/3	318
241	**There Won't Be No Country Music (There Won't Be No Rock 'N' Roll)** - C.W. McCall	52--6/2/1	317
242	**Play On Love** - Jefferson Starship	47--7/1/1	313
243	**Harvest For The World** - Isley Brothers	63--7/1/5	308
244	**The More You Do It (The More I Like It Done To Me)** - Ronnie Dyson	59--10/1/0	304
245	**Fire On The Mountain** - Marshall Tucker Band	55--10/2/0	301
246	**I Heard It Through The Grapevine** - Creedence Clearwater Revival	47--7/1/1	300
247	**Fool For The City** - Foghat	57--6/2/2	300
248	**Rainbow In Your Eyes** - Leon & Mary Russell	62--10/1/1	299
249	**I.O.U.** - Jimmy Dean	33--4/1/1	293
250	**We Can't Hide It Anymore** - Larry Santos	57--7/1/2	293
251	**Hold On** - Sons Of Champlin	59--7/1/2	289
252	**Anytime (I'll Be There)** - Paul Anka	50--6/1/2	288
253	**Message In Our Music** - O'Jays	66--6/1/5	285
254	**Falling Apart At The Seams** - Marmalade	55--5/2/2	284
255	**Mozambique** - Bob Dylan	49--6/1/1	279
256	**Back To The Island** - Leon Russell	56--6/1/1	259
257	**Spanish Hustle** - Fatback Band	60--6/1/2	259
258	**Don't Cry Joni** - Conway Twitty	51--6/1/2	256
259	**Banapple Gas** - Cat Stevens	50--5/1/1	250
260	**Chain Gang Medley** - Jim Croce	56--5/1/2	249
261	**Whenever I'm Away From You** - John Travolta	62--9/1/0	247
262	**Take It Like A Man** - Bachman-Turner Overdrive	63--6/2/1	246
263	**New Orleans** - Staple Singers	57--6/1/1	238
264	**This Old Man** - Purple Reign	48--6/1/1	236
265	**Yes, Yes, Yes** - Bill Cosby	63--7/2/1	235
266	**Mademoiselle** - Styx	57--7/2/2	233
267	**He's A Friend** - Eddie Kendricks	65--11/1/0	233
268	**Lady Bump** - Penny McLean	61--6/1/2	232
269	**Keep Holding On** - Temptations	53--6/1/1	227
270	**Bigfoot** - Bro Smith	58--7/1/1	227
271	**The Fonz Song** - Heyettes	66--6/2/1	227
272	**Mary Hartman, Mary Hartman** - Deadly Nightshade	65--8/2/0	220
273	**9,999,999 Tears** - Dickey Lee	67--5/1/7	219
274	**Popsicle Toes** - Michael Franks	65--7/2/2	216
275	**Baby Boy** - Mary Kay Place	66--5/3/0	216
276	**Easy As Pie** - Billy "Crash" Craddock	52--5/1/1	214
277	**Detroit Rock City** - Kiss	25--4/1/0	211
278	**Free Ride** - Tavares	56--5/1/1	198
279	**Take Me** - Grand Funk Railroad	50--4/1/1	197
280	**Make Love To Your Mind** - Bill Withers	67--10/1/1	197
281	**Brand New Love Affair** - Jigsaw	72--8/1/2	195
282	**You're My Everything** - Lee Garrett	67--7/2/0	194
283	**In France They Kiss On Main Street** - Joni Mitchell	55--5/1/1	193
284	**Queen Of My Soul** - Average White Band	67--6/1/4	191
285	**Like A Sad Song** - John Denver	60--4/2/1	188
286	**Can The Can** - Suzi Quatro	62--6/1/0	187
287	**Tell The World How I Feel About 'Cha Baby** - Harold Melvin & The Blue Notes	67--5/1/3	186
288	**If You Only Believe (Jesus For Tonite)** - Michael Polnareff	66--5/2/1	183
289	**Get Up Offa That Thing** - James Brown	72--7/1/2	183
290	**I Need You, You Need Me** - Joe Simon	63--6/1/0	178
291	**Tenth Avenue Freeze-Out** - Bruce Springsteen	63--6/1/0	177
292	**Rain, Oh Rain** - Fools Gold	67--9/1/0	171
293	**Don't Stop It Now** - Hot Chocolate	68--7/1/1	171
294	**Foxy Lady** - Crown Heights Affair	64--9/1/1	170
295	**Sixteen Tons** - Don Harrison Band	65--8/1/1	168
296	**(One More Year Of) Daddy's Little Girl** - Ray Sawyer	68--7/1/0	168
297	**Can You Do It** - Grand Funk Railroad	70--8/1/1	163
298	**Ode To Billie Joe** - Bobbie Gentry	67--7/1/0	162

Rank	Title - Act	Trajectory	Pts.
299	For A Dancer - *Prelude*	66--7/2/0	160
300	Art For Art's Sake - *10cc*	63--5/1/0	154

1977

Rank	Title - Act	Trajectory	Pts.
1	You Light Up My Life - *Debby Boone*	1--7/8/13	12709
2	How Deep Is Your Love - *Bee Gees*	1--13/4/12	9706
3	Torn Between Two Lovers *Mary MacGregor*	1--14/3/9	8971
4	I Just Want To Be Your Everything *Andy Gibb*	1--15/3/12	8292
5	Undercover Angel - *Alan O'Day*	1--14/1/11	8004
6	Nobody Does It Better - *Carly Simon*	2--14/4/8	7464
7	Don't It Make My Brown Eyes Blue *Crystal Gayle*	1--18/2/8	7214
8	Star Wars Theme/Cantina Band - *Meco*	1--9/2/11	6899
9	Love Theme From "A Star Is Born" (Evergreen) - *Barbra Streisand*	1--13/3/10	6625
10	You Don't Have To Be A Star (To Be In My Show) *Marilyn McCoo & Billy Davis, Jr.*	1--14/2/9	6474
11	Best Of My Love - *Emotions*	1--10/3/9	6281
12	(Your Love Has Lifted Me) Higher And Higher - *Rita Coolidge*	1--19/1/5	6253
13	Rich Girl - *Daryl Hall & John Oates*	1--10/2/6	6074
14	Southern Nights - *Glen Campbell*	1--11/1/11	5858
15	Boogie Nights - *Heatwave*	2--20/1/7	5767
16	When I Need You - *Leo Sayer*	1--11/3/8	5703
17	I'm Your Boogie Man *KC & The Sunshine Band*	1--14/1/8	5632
18	Don't Give Up On Us - *David Soul*	1--12/1/7	5537
19	I Wish - *Stevie Wonder*	1--9/1/10	5485
20	Dancing Queen - *Abba*	1--17/1/7	5223
21	Blue Bayou - *Linda Ronstadt*	2--16/2/7	5154
22	Don't Stop - *Fleetwood Mac*	1--11/1/6	5149
23	Dreams - *Fleetwood Mac*	1--9/1/11	5085
24	Da Doo Ron Ron - *Shaun Cassidy*	1--9/2/9	5030
25	Hotel California - *Eagles*	1--8/1/12	4972
26	Got To Give It Up Pt. I - *Marvin Gaye*	1--10/1/9	4889
27	Car Wash - *Rose Royce*	1--11/2/8	4736
28	Keep It Comin' Love *KC & The Sunshine Band*	2--12/2/7	4729
29	I Like Dreamin' - *Kenny Nolan*	3--18/1/9	4683
30	Lonely Boy - *Andrew Gold*	3--15/2/7	4574
31	Blinded By The Light *Manfred Mann's Earth Band*	1--12/1/9	4447
32	New Kid In Town - *Eagles*	2--11/2/7	4379
33	I'm In You - *Peter Frampton*	1--9/1/8	4344
34	Don't Leave Me This Way *Thelma Houston*	3--16/2/7	4290
35	Gonna Fly Now (Theme From "Rocky") *Bill Conti*	1--11/1/8	4256
36	Sir Duke - *Stevie Wonder*	1--9/1/7	4088
37	Handy Man - *James Taylor*	2--14/1/5	4045
38	I've Got Love On My Mind - *Natalie Cole*	3--13/1/10	4005
39	Whatcha Gonna Do? - *Pablo Cruise*	3--19/2/5	3927
40	The Things We Do For Love - *10cc*	4--15/2/7	3913
41	Fly Like An Eagle - *Steve Miller*	3--10/3/6	3848
42	Float On - *Floaters*	3--13/2/5	3844
43	Angel In Your Arms - *Hot*	6--21/1/9	3749
44	Jet Airliner - *Steve Miller Band*	3--11/1/7	3745
45	Hot Line - *Sylvers*	4--13/3/6	3685
46	Dazz - *Brick*	5--14/2/7	3614
47	Heaven On The 7th Floor *Paul Nicholas*	5--17/1/9	3496
48	Easy - *Commodores*	4--14/2/6	3448
49	On And On - *Stephen Bishop*	5--16/2/7	3448
50	Looks Like We Made It - *Barry Manilow*	3--11/2/8	3424
51	Telephone Line *Electric Light Orchestra*	4--15/1/6	3305
52	Year Of The Cat - *Al Stewart*	4--14/1/7	3284
53	Enjoy Yourself - *Jacksons*	4--14/2/7	3229
54	That's Rock 'N' Roll - *Shaun Cassidy*	4--13/1/7	3222
55	After The Lovin' *Engelbert Humperdinck*	5--13/2/7	3189
56	Swayin' To The Music (Slow Dancin') *Johnny Rivers*	6--17/1/9	3183
57	I Feel Love - *Donna Summer*	4--15/1/6	3146
58	We're All Alone - *Rita Coolidge*	5--15/1/5	3070
59	Carry On Wayward Son - *Kansas*	7--15/2/9	3013
60	So In To You - *Atlanta Rhythm Section*	5--14/2/5	2962
61	Night Moves - *Bob Seger*	6--14/2/6	2882
62	My Heart Belongs To Me *Barbra Streisand*	5--11/2/5	2826
63	Feels Like The First Time - *Foreigner*	5--14/1/8	2775
64	Baby, What A Big Surprise - *Chicago*	4--12/1/5	2641
65	Sentimental Lady - *Bob Welch*	4--13/1/6	2559
66	You Made Me Believe In Magic *Bay City Rollers*	7--12/2/5	2546
67	Right Time Of The Night *Jennifer Warnes*	5--14/1/5	2534
68	Margaritaville - *Jimmy Buffett*	7--16/2/7	2532
69	Lido Shuffle - *Boz Scaggs*	6--9/2/6	2510
70	Weekend In New England *Barry Manilow*	9--12/2/13	2444
71	You And Me - *Alice Cooper*	8--18/1/5	2377
72	Sorry Seems To Be The Hardest Word *Elton John*	7--9/1/10	2369
73	Walk This Way - *Aerosmith*	7--11/1/9	2351
74	Couldn't Get It Right *Climax Blues Band*	7--16/1/6	2335
75	Do You Wanna Make Love *Peter McCann*	9--14/2/6	2241
76	Cold As Ice - *Foreigner*	10--13/1/6	2240
77	Jeans On - *David Dundas*	14--18/2/9	2187
78	Just A Song Before I Go *Crosby, Stills & Nash*	8--14/2/5	2157
79	Brick House - *Commodores*	6--11/1/5	2100
80	It's So Easy - *Linda Ronstadt*	9--11/1/7	2097
81	Lucille - *Kenny Rogers*	6--11/1/7	2087
82	Just Remember I Love You - *Firefall*	9--16/2/3	2077
83	Love Me - *Yvonne Elliman*	10--15/1/6	2047
84	You Make Loving Fun - *Fleetwood Mac*	7--10/2/4	2029
85	Heard It In A Love Song *Marshall Tucker Band*	10--15/2/6	2023
86	Tryin' To Love Two - *William Bell*	8--12/1/5	1979
87	Strawberry Letter 23 - *Brothers Johnson*	8--11/1/7	1945
88	Isn't It Time - *Babys*	8--11/1/8	1886
89	Lost Without Your Love - *Bread*	12--12/2/7	1881
90	Calling Dr. Love - *Kiss*	10--13/1/5	1834
91	Barracuda - *Heart*	10--13/2/5	1824
92	It's Ecstasy When You Lay Down Next To Me - *Barry White*	7--12/1/5	1807
93	Somebody To Love - *Queen*	9--9/2/6	1770
94	Smoke From A Distant Fire *Sanford/Townsend Band*	9--14/1/4	1761

Rank	Title - Act	Trajectory	Pts.
95	It Was Almost Like A Song - Ronnie Milsap	11--19/1/4	1732
96	I Wanna Get Next To You - Rose Royce	10--10/2/5	1731
97	Go Your Own Way - Fleetwood Mac	10--9/1/7	1721
98	Black Betty - Ram Jam	14--12/2/7	1688
99	Don't Worry Baby - B.J. Thomas	13--14/2/4	1681
100	High School Dance - Sylvers	13--13/1/7	1663
101	How Much Love - Leo Sayer	9--10/1/4	1649
102	Give A Little Bit - Supertramp	12--17/1/4	1634
103	You're My World - Helen Reddy	16--15/1/7	1625
104	Ariel - Dean Friedman	17--18/1/6	1625
105	Maybe I'm Amazed - Wings	10--8/1/7	1611
106	It's Sad To Belong - England Dan & John Ford Coley	13--12/2/5	1589
107	Knowing Me, Knowing You - Abba	11--11/2/5	1548
108	Help Is On Its Way - Little River Band	14--17/1/4	1480
109	We Just Disagree - Dave Mason	15--13/1/7	1461
110	Your Smiling Face - James Taylor	12--11/2/4	1454
111	Long Time - Boston	12--9/1/6	1400
112	Whodunit - Tavares	16--14/1/4	1371
113	Ain't Gonna Bump No More (With No Big Fat Woman) - Joe Tex	15--11/2/5	1344
114	Free - Deniece Williams	21--18/2/6	1326
115	Living Next Door To Alice - Smokie	18--13/2/5	1316
116	Life In The Fast Lane - Eagles	11--8/1/6	1297
117	Swingtown - Steve Miller Band	13--9/2/5	1292
118	Boogie Child - Bee Gees	14--8/2/5	1279
119	Hello Stranger - Yvonne Elliman	14--10/1/7	1267
120	Signed, Sealed, Delivered (I'm Yours) - Peter Frampton	13--9/1/4	1252
121	She Did It - Eric Carmen	15--9/2/4	1230
122	Slow Dancin' Don't Turn Me On - Addrisi Brothers	18--13/1/5	1192
123	Here Come Those Tears Again - Jackson Browne	18--10/1/6	1187
124	Say You'll Stay Until Tomorrow - Tom Jones	15--14/1/5	1173
125	Send In The Clowns - Judy Collins	17--9/2/7	1169
126	Disco Lucy (I Love Lucy Theme) - Wilton Place Street Band	19--11/2/5	1163
127	Do Ya - Electric Light Orchestra	16--9/1/5	1144
128	Way Down - Elvis Presley	25--16/1/5	1134
129	Your Love - Marilyn McCoo & Billy Davis, Jr.	16--9/1/6	1132
130	Whispering/Cherchez La Femme/Se Si Bon - Dr. Buzzard's Original "Savannah" Band	23--10/2/6	1128
131	Hard Luck Woman - Kiss	19--9/1/7	1104
132	Jungle Love - Steve Miller Band	17--9/1/5	1075
133	Star Wars (Main Title) - John Williams/London Symphony Orchestra	18--10/1/6	1058
134	Save It For A Rainy Day - Stephen Bishop	21--12/2/4	1055
135	Love's Grown Deep - Kenny Nolan	25--13/1/6	1047
136	Saturday Nite - Earth, Wind & Fire	21--9/1/7	1045
137	Can't Stop Dancin' - Captain & Tennille	17--7/2/5	1036
138	The First Cut Is The Deepest - Rod Stewart	17--8/1/5	1026
139	The King Is Gone - Ronnie McDowell	14--5/1/7	1014
140	Luckenbach, Texas (Back To The Basics Of Love) - Waylon Jennings	23--12/2/6	1008
141	Gone Too Far - England Dan & John Ford Coley	17--10/2/2	981
142	Crackerbox Palace - George Harrison	17--8/1/4	946
143	Calling Occupants Of Interplanetary Craft - Carpenters	24--12/1/6	945
144	She's Not There - Santana	20--11/1/5	910
145	Mainstreet - Bob Seger	19--7/1/6	908
146	Slide - Slave	27--11/1/7	905
147	This Song - George Harrison	28--8/1/8	898
148	Telephone Man - Meri Wilson	25--7/2/6	896
149	Cat Scratch Fever - Ted Nugent	21--11/2/4	885
150	Ain't Nothing Like The Real Thing - Donny & Marie	30--11/1/5	869
151	Christine Sixteen - Kiss	20--7/1/4	835
152	Dancin' Man - Q	20--9/2/3	818
153	My Fair Share - Seals & Crofts	25--12/2/3	804
154	Daybreak - Barry Manilow	21--7/2/4	799
155	At Midnight (My Love Will Lift You Up) - Rufus Featuring Chaka Khan	30--9/2/4	787
156	Cherry Baby - Starz	27--8/1/5	767
157	Cinderella - Firefall	30--10/1/5	747
158	The Greatest Love Of All - George Benson	29--11/1/3	737
159	Gonna Fly Now (Theme From "Rocky") - Maynard Ferguson	31--9/2/4	730
160	Back Together Again - Daryl Hall & John Oates	25--7/1/5	729
161	I Wouldn't Want To Be Like You - Alan Parsons	27--10/1/3	727
162	Free Bird (Live) - Lynyrd Skynyrd	32--6/2/6	698
163	Dreamboat Annie - Heart	32--8/1/5	698
164	Hard Rock Cafe - Carole King	25--9/1/3	693
165	Moody Blue - Elvis Presley	39--11/1/5	686
166	Drivin' Wheel - Foghat	37--8/1/6	682
167	Sam - Olivia Newton-John	34--9/1/5	676
168	Dusic - Brick	30--12/1/3	670
169	Edge Of The Universe - Bee Gees	26--8/1/3	656
170	I Believe You - Dorothy Moore	28--13/2/1	649
171	Flight '76 - Walter Murphy Band	36--9/2/4	647
172	Surfin' Usa - Leif Garrett	29--9/1/3	639
173	Peace Of Mind - Boston	33--8/1/4	630
174	All Strung Out On You - John Travolta	28--6/2/4	624
175	My Way - Elvis Presley	31--5/2/6	607
176	Sunflower - Glen Campbell	39--9/2/3	575
177	Little Darling (I Need You) - Doobie Brothers	39--10/1/2	567
178	In The Mood - Henhouse Five Plus Too	37--8/2/3	559
179	Daytime Friends - Kenny Rogers	28--9/1/2	547
180	I Just Want To Make Love To You - Foghat	31--9/1/2	527
181	(Remember The Days Of The) Old Schoolyard - Cat Stevens	38--9/1/2	510
182	Hollywood - Rufus Featuring Chaka Khan	39--7/1/5	500
183	All You Get From Love Is A Love Song - Carpenters	43--9/1/2	490
184	If You're Not Back In Love By Monday - Millie Jackson	35--7/1/3	478
185	Gloria - Enchantment	46--12/1/3	478
186	Do Ya Wanna Get Funky With Me - Peter Brown	41--9/1/2	472
187	I Don't Love You Anymore - Teddy Pendergrass	43--10/1/2	469
188	Draw The Line - Aerosmith	37--7/1/2	465
189	A Real Mother For Ya - Johnny "Guitar" Watson	42--10/1/2	461
190	Reach - Orleans	45--8/2/1	453

Rank	Title - Act	Trajectory	Pts.
191	Another Star - Stevie Wonder	36--6/1/3	452
192	Old Fashioned Boy (You're The One) - Stallion	42--8/3/1	446
193	I Think We're Alone Now - Rubinoos	46--12/1/2	438
194	The Killing Of Georgie (Part I And II) - Rod Stewart	38--7/1/2	437
195	Shake Your Rump To The Funk - Bar-Kays	53--11/1/4	435
196	Lady (Put The Light On Me) - Brownsville Station	44--10/1/2	431
197	Thunder In My Heart - Leo Sayer	35--7/1/2	430
198	It Keeps You Runnin' - Doobie Brothers	50--12/1/3	430
199	You've Got Me Runnin' - Gene Cotton	49--10/2/2	427
200	On The Border - Al Stewart	39--6/1/3	421
201	So You Win Again - Hot Chocolate	48--9/2/0	419
202	Lucky Man - Starbuck	48--9/1/3	418
203	I Don't Wanna Lose Your Love - Emotions	55--12/1/3	411
204	Magical Mystery Tour - Ambrosia	41--7/1/2	401
205	I Believe In Love - Kenny Loggins	53--11/1/2	390
206	Rock And Roll Never Forgets - Bob Seger	50--7/1/3	387
207	Bloat On Featuring The Bloaters - Cheech & Chong	47--6/1/4	382
208	Girls' School//Mull Of Kintyre - Wings	31--7/1/4	377
209	Yesterday's Hero - Bay City Rollers	49--6/1/3	372
210	Winter Melody - Donna Summer	47--6/2/1	364
211	Changes In Latitudes, Changes In Attitudes - Jimmy Buffett	34--7/1/1	362
212	Show You The Way To Go - Jacksons	45--7/1/2	361
213	Bite Your Lip (Get Up And Dance!) - Elton John	42--5/1/2	355
214	The Martian Boogie - Brownsville Station	45--7/1/2	355
215	Fair Game - Crosby, Stills & Nash	47--8/1/1	355
216	Sometimes - Facts Of Life	60--9/2/3	350
217	Fancy Dancer - Commodores	63--9/2/2	349
218	Here Comes Summer - Wildfire	43--6/1/2	342
219	A Place In The Sun - Pablo Cruise	42--7/1/1	338
220	Do What You Want, Be What You Are - Daryl Hall & John Oates	55--9/2/1	338
221	Going In With My Eyes Open - David Soul	55--8/2/1	331
222	Be My Girl - Dramatics	62--10/2/0	331
223	You Know Like I Know - Ozark Mountain Daredevils	55--11/1/1	329
224	Everybody Be Dancin' - Starbuck	48--8/1/2	326
225	Silver Lady - David Soul	53--8/1/1	322
226	You're Moving Out Today - Carole Bayer Sager	57--10/2/1	317
227	From Graceland To The Promised Land - Merle Haggard	58--8/1/2	317
228	Hey Baby - Ringo Starr	62--9/1/3	316
229	I Just Can't Say No To You - Parker McGee	55--10/1/1	315
230	Baby Don't You Know - Wild Cherry	57--6/1/3	313
231	I'm Dreaming - Jennifer Warnes	62--8/2/2	313
232	Goin' Places - Jacksons	55--8/1/1	311
233	Kong - Dickie Goodman	50--7/1/1	307
234	What Can I Say - Boz Scaggs	59--7/1/3	302
235	Stone Cold Sober - Crawler	62--12/2/2	302
236	You + Me = Love - Undisputed Truth	56--10/1/0	300
237	Sing It, Shout It - Starz	53--7/1/2	299
238	Devil's Gun - C.J. & Co.	65--16/1/1	292
239	This Is The Way That I Feel - Marie Osmond	52--7/1/2	285
240	C.B. Savage - Rod Hart	59--7/2/2	276
241	Little Queen - Heart	48--6/1/1	273
242	My Sweet Lady - John Denver	44--6/1/1	272
243	I Like To Do It - KC & The Sunshine Band	63--8/1/2	270
244	Runaway - Bonnie Raitt	52--7/1/1	266
245	Amarillo - Neil Sedaka	50--6/1/1	262
246	It's A Crazy World - Mac McAnally	58--9/1/3	262
247	Someone To Lay Down Beside Me - Linda Ronstadt	65--6/3/2	261
248	Do It To My Mind - Johnny Bristol	68--7/2/4	256
249	Fly At Night - Chilliwack	57--8/1/0	254
250	Love Gun - Kiss	55--5/1/2	252
251	Look What You've Done To My Heart - Marilyn McCoo & Billy Davis, Jr.	61--7/1/1	251
252	The Whistler - Jethro Tull	52--5/2/0	250
253	Hard Times - Boz Scaggs	58--7/1/1	247
254	Seaside Woman - Suzy & The Red Stripes	58--6/2/0	246
255	Indian Summer - Poco	62--11/1/0	245
256	Something About You - Le Blanc & Carr	55--6/1/1	244
257	I Wanna Do It To You - Jerry Butler	64--9/1/2	243
258	If Not You - Dr. Hook	63--10/1/1	241
259	Phantom Writer - Gary Wright	53--5/2/0	239
260	Baby Don't Change Your Mind - Gladys Knight & The Pips	51--6/1/1	237
261	Hound Dog Man (Play It Again) - Lenny Le Blanc	56--5/1/1	234
262	Spirit In The Night - Manfred Mann's Earth Band	59--7/2/0	234
263	Livin' In The Life - Isley Brothers	60--7/1/1	232
264	Money, Money, Money - Abba	63--7/1/1	232
265	L.A. Sunshine - War	62--6/1/1	230
266	You're Movin' Out Today - Bette Midler	62--7/1/2	226
267	"Roots" Medley - Quincy Jones	62--7/1/1	225
268	Red Hot - Robert Gordon	69--10/1/1	224
269	Uptown Festival (Part 1) - Shalamar	61--10/1/1	221
270	Sailing Ships - Mesa	64--10/1/0	216
271	You Are On My Mind - Chicago	56--4/1/2	215
272	I Honestly Love You - Olivia Newton-John	60--6/1/0	208
273	Sad Girl - Carl Graves	68--5/2/2	208
274	Keep Me Cryin' - Al Green	63--7/1/3	205
275	Neon Nites - Atlanta Rhythm Section	65--7/1/1	202
276	Don't Let The Flame Burn Out - Jackie DeShannon	70--9/1/2	196
277	Tie Your Mother Down - Queen	54--4/1/1	194
278	When Love Is New - Arthur Prysock	74--6/2/4	193
279	I'm Going Down - Rose Royce	64--7/1/1	192
280	As - Stevie Wonder	69--6/2/5	189
281	I Kinda Miss You - Manhattans	71--8/1/2	189
282	Dog Days - Atlanta Rhythm Section	63--7/1/0	187
283	Sub-Rosa Subway - Klaatu	57--4/2/0	181
284	In The Middle - Tim Moore	68--7/1/2	180
285	Somethin' 'Bout 'Cha - Latimore	66--8/1/1	176
286	Girls' School - Wings	38--3/1/0	173
287	Back In The Saddle - Aerosmith	67--5/1/1	173
288	Do Your Dance - Part I - Rose Royce	67--6/1/1	173
289	The Pretender - Jackson Browne	58--5/1/0	168

Rank	Title - Act	Trajectory	Pts.
290	**Romeo** - *Mr. Big*	64--9/1/0	166
291	**Open Sesame - Part I** - *Kool & The Gang*	73--7/1/2	163
292	**Man Smart, Woman Smarter** - *Robert Palmer*	70--8/1/0	156
293	**Love Is Better In The A.M. (Part 1)** - *Johnnie Taylor*	65--7/1/0	155
294	**Was Dog A Doughnut** - *Cat Stevens*	68--6/1/2	154
295	**Slowdown** - *John Miles*	64--7/1/0	152
296	**Sad Eyes** - *Brooklyn Dreams*	66--6/1/0	152
297	**Love Gone By** - *Dan Fogelberg*	75--6/1/3	152
298	**Sing** - *Tony Orlando & Dawn*	62--6/1/0	151
299	**Platinum Heroes** - *Bruce Foster*	66--6/1/0	150
300	**Slow Dancing** - *Funky Kings*	66--5/1/1	146

1978

Rank	Title - Act	Trajectory	Pts.
1	**Le Freak** - *Chic*	1--8/7/12	11508
2	**Shadow Dancing** - *Andy Gibb*	1--8/6/11	10931
3	**Night Fever** - *Bee Gees*	1--7/8/7	10627
4	**Kiss You All Over** - *Exile*	1--14/2/13	9970
5	**Stayin' Alive** - *Bee Gees*	1--9/4/15	9612
6	**Hot Child In The City** - *Nick Gilder*	1--19/3/10	8511
7	**Three Times A Lady** - *Commodores*	1--8/4/10	8281
8	**Baker Street** - *Gerry Rafferty*	1--14/2/9	7960
9	**Boogie Oogie Oogie** - *Taste Of Honey*	1--13/3/10	7914
10	**Too Much Heaven** - *Bee Gees*	2--7/5/9	7777
11	**Grease** - *Frankie Valli*	1--16/1/7	7745
12	**Emotion** - *Samantha Sang*	1--18/1/10	7595
13	**Baby Come Back** - *Player*	1--16/2/10	7549
14	**You Don't Bring Me Flowers** - *Barbra & Neil*	1--5/3/11	7514
15	**Miss You** - *Rolling Stones*	1--10/2/12	7411
16	**Mac Arthur Park** - *Donna Summer*	1--10/2/11	6894
17	**Can't Smile Without You** - *Barry Manilow*	2--9/4/8	6371
18	**You're The One That I Want** - *John Travolta & Olivia Newton-John*	3--9/4/13	6354
19	**Short People** - *Randy Newman*	1--12/1/9	6118
20	**(Love Is) Thicker Than Water** - *Andy Gibb*	1--18/1/10	5752
21	**If I Can't Have You** - *Yvonne Elliman*	1--15/1/6	5481
22	**Too Much, Too Little, Too Late** - *Johnny Mathis & Deniece Williams*	2--11/3/8	5470
23	**With A Little Luck** - *Wings*	1--9/2/8	5393
24	**Just The Way You Are** - *Billy Joel*	2--15/1/8	5179
25	**The Closer I Get To You** - *Roberta Flack & Donny Hathaway*	2--15/1/8	4958
26	**It's A Heartache** - *Bonnie Tyler*	3--14/3/10	4922
27	**Lay Down Sally** - *Eric Clapton*	3--14/2/8	4874
28	**Sharing The Night Together** - *Dr. Hook*	4--13/3/7	4677
29	**You Needed Me** - *Anne Murray*	4--16/4/6	4664
30	**We Are The Champions** - *Queen*	3--14/2/9	4623
31	**You're In My Heart (The Final Acclaim)** - *Rod Stewart*	3--13/1/10	4562
32	**How Much I Feel** - *Ambrosia*	2--12/3/7	4559
33	**Hopelessly Devoted To You** - *Olivia Newton-John*	3--12/1/7	4529
34	**I Just Wanna Stop** - *Gino Vannelli*	2--14/2/6	4388
35	**Sometimes When We Touch** - *Dan Hill*	4--13/1/9	4365
36	**Reminiscing** - *Little River Band*	3--13/2/7	4202
37	**Hot Blooded** - *Foreigner*	4--8/3/9	4109
38	**I Love The Nightlife (Disco 'round)** - *Alicia Bridges*	6--24/3/9	3683
39	**Dust In The Wind** - *Kansas*	3--12/2/7	3625
40	**I Go Crazy** - *Paul Davis*	7--31/2/4	3589
41	**Whenever I Call You "Friend"** - *Kenny Loggins*	5--13/3/7	3572
42	**Last Dance** - *Donna Summer*	4--13/2/8	3568
43	**Jack And Jill** - *Raydio*	6--17/2/7	3514
44	**Feels So Good** - *Chuck Mangione*	6--19/2/8	3314
45	**Love Will Find A Way** - *Pablo Cruise*	5--12/3/7	3275
46	**Summer Nights** - *John Travolta & Olivia Newton-John*	3--9/2/5	3240
47	**Baby Hold On** - *Eddie Money*	5--19/2/6	3007
48	**Use Ta Be My Girl** - *O'Jays*	5--11/2/8	3004
49	**Here You Come Again** - *Dolly Parton*	7--16/2/7	2955
50	**Take A Chance On Me** - *Abba*	5--11/2/7	2792
51	**Still The Same** - *Bob Seger*	4--10/2/8	2791
52	**An Everlasting Love** - *Andy Gibb*	5--9/2/6	2766
53	**(Our Love) Don't Throw It All Away** - *Andy Gibb*	7--11/1/7	2712
54	**Dance, Dance, Dance (Yowsah, Yowsah, Yowsah)** - *Chic*	6--18/2/5	2704
55	**Thunder Island** - *Jay Ferguson*	6--16/2/6	2623
56	**Slip Slidin' Away** - *Paul Simon*	6--14/2/5	2608
57	**What's Your Name** - *Lynyrd Skynyrd*	7--15/2/6	2586
58	**Two Out Of Three Ain't Bad** - *Meat Loaf*	9--14/2/10	2554
59	**Come Sail Away** - *Styx*	9--19/2/7	2530
60	**(Every Time I Turn Around) Back In Love Again** - *L.T.D.*	6--17/1/7	2479
61	**Dance With Me** - *Peter Brown*	8--16/2/7	2434
62	**Double Vision** - *Foreigner*	5--8/2/9	2427
63	**Love Is Like Oxygen** - *Sweet*	8--17/2/6	2377
64	**Don't Look Back** - *Boston*	7--7/3/5	2295
65	**Shame** - *Evelyn "Champagne" King*	8--15/2/8	2285
66	**Magnet And Steel** - *Walter Egan*	9--14/2/8	2264
67	**Life's Been Good** - *Joe Walsh*	6--11/2/7	2200
68	**Running On Empty** - *Jackson Browne*	6--12/1/5	2185
69	**Goodbye Girl** - *David Gates*	9--20/2/4	2117
70	**Right Down The Line** - *Gerry Rafferty*	8--11/2/5	2097
71	**Disco Inferno** - *Trammps*	8--59/2/5	2087
72	**Ready To Take A Chance Again** - *Barry Manilow*	7--11/2/7	2050
73	**Beast Of Burden** - *Rolling Stones*	7--8/3/5	2046
74	**Peg** - *Steely Dan*	8--15/2/4	2002
75	**You Belong To Me** - *Carly Simon*	9--13/2/5	1999
76	**Who Are You** - *The Who*	9--9/3/5	1979
77	**Imaginary Lover** - *Atlanta Rhythm Section*	9--12/2/5	1972
78	**You Never Done It Like That** - *Captain & Tennille*	10--14/3/5	1935
79	**Sweet Life** - *Paul Davis*	15--17/3/5	1925
80	**My Angel Baby** - *Toby Beau*	10--14/1/5	1871
81	**Desiree** - *Neil Diamond*	9--10/2/5	1868
82	**Bluer Than Blue** - *Michael Johnson*	10--14/2/4	1842
83	**Falling** – *Le Blanc & Carr*	11--22/1/5	1782
84	**The Groove Line** - *Heatwave*	10--13/2/7	1740
85	**Time Passages** - *Al Stewart*	9--10/2/6	1712
86	**Strange Way** - *Firefall*	11--11/2/7	1707
87	**Love Is In The Air** - *John Paul Young*	13--14/2/4	1679
88	**Every Kinda People** - *Robert Palmer*	13--14/2/6	1665
89	**On Broadway** - *George Benson*	11--13/1/7	1664
90	**Copacabana (At The Copa)** - *Barry Manilow*	10--10/2/6	1660
91	**Count On Me** - *Jefferson Starship*	9--10/1/6	1658
92	**Fool (If You Think It's Over)** - *Chris Rea*	10--11/2/4	1646

Rank	Title - Act	Trajectory	Pts.
93	**Always And Forever** - *Heatwave*	12--16/1/5	1587
94	**Get Off** – *Foxy*	17--16/1/6	1534
95	**Ebony Eyes** - *Bob Welch*	12--12/2/4	1532
96	**Back In The U.S.A.** - *Linda Ronstadt*	11--10/2/5	1526
97	**Turn To Stone** - *Electric Light Orchestra*	11--10/1/5	1508
98	**Because The Night** - *Patti Smith Group*	10--11/2/6	1502
99	**Native New Yorker** - *Odyssey*	15--15/2/4	1464
100	**Don't Let Me Be Misunderstood** *Santa Esmeralda*	14--14/2/4	1452
101	**You Can't Turn Me Off (In The Middle Of Turning Me On)** - *High Inergy*	12--13/1/4	1431
102	**Thank You For Being A Friend** *Andrew Gold*	11--11/2/3	1408
103	**Talking In Your Sleep** - *Crystal Gayle*	16--18/1/5	1390
104	**Got To Get You Into My Life** *Earth, Wind & Fire*	11--8/2/5	1377
105	**Serpentine Fire** - *Earth, Wind & Fire*	15--14/2/3	1358
106	**How You Gonna See Me Now** *Alice Cooper*	16--11/3/3	1340
107	**You And I** - *Rick James*	15--14/1/5	1326
108	**Flash Light** - *Parliament*	15--11/2/4	1304
109	**Our Love** - *Natalie Cole*	16--13/1/5	1291
110	**The Name Of The Game** - *Abba*	16--13/2/4	1288
111	**Alive Again** - *Chicago*	13--8/1/5	1278
112	**Runaway** - *Jefferson Starship*	13--10/1/5	1275
113	**Straight On** - *Heart*	18--13/1/6	1261
114	**This Time I'm In It For Love** - *Player*	13--12/1/4	1258
115	**Movin' Out (Anthony's Song)** *Billy Joel*	14--12/1/3	1254
116	**Part-Time Love** - *Elton John*	13--8/3/4	1240
117	**Hollywood Nights** - *Bob Seger*	13--9/1/4	1231
118	**Theme From "Close Encounters Of The Third Kind"** - *John Williams*	13--12/1/3	1219
119	**Point Of Know Return** - *Kansas*	17--11/1/4	1182
120	**We'll Never Have To Say Goodbye Again** - *England Dan & John Ford Coley*	14--9/2/3	1178
121	**Before My Heart Finds Out** *Gene Cotton*	16--13/2/2	1159
122	**She's Always A Woman** - *Billy Joel*	18--12/1/7	1156
123	**Change Of Heart** - *Eric Carmen*	19--14/1/4	1155
124	**The Way I Feel Tonight** *Bay City Rollers*	19--15/1/3	1139
125	**I'm Not Gonna Let It Bother Me Tonight** - *Atlanta Rhythm Section*	16--10/2/5	1138
126	**I Can't Stand The Rain** - *Eruption*	19--15/2/3	1130
127	**King Tut** *Steve Martin & The Toot Uncommons*	18--12/2/4	1125
128	**Sweet Talkin' Woman** *Electric Light Orchestra*	18--10/2/5	1122
129	**Even Now** - *Barry Manilow*	17--9/2/4	1075
130	**Heartless** - *Heart*	18--11/2/5	1061
131	**Bicycle Race//Fat Bottomed Girls** *Queen*	18--8/3/3	1058
132	**Hey Deanie** - *Shaun Cassidy*	21--10/1/6	1051
133	**You** - *Rita Coolidge*	17--10/2/4	1046
134	**Deacon Blues** - *Steely Dan*	17--11/1/4	1041
135	**Runaround Sue** - *Leif Garrett*	18--11/1/3	1039
136	**Werewolves Of London** - *Warren Zevon*	15--8/2/4	1025
137	**Two Tickets To Paradise** - *Eddie Money*	20--10/2/4	1015
138	**I'm Every Woman** - *Chaka Khan*	19--12/1/5	1014
139	**Ffun** - *Con Funk Shun*	18--12/1/3	1011
140	**Don't Want To Live Without It** *Pablo Cruise*	18--11/1/5	980
141	**(What A) Wonderful World** - *Art Garfunkel with James Taylor & Paul Simon*	15--9/1/3	978
142	**Close The Door** - *Teddy Pendergrass*	19--11/1/5	963
143	**Instant Replay** - *Dan Hartman*	22--12/2/4	962
144	**Lady Love** - *Lou Rawls*	20--12/1/5	942
145	**You're The Love** - *Seals & Crofts*	20--14/1/4	935
146	**The Way You Do The Things You Do** *Rita Coolidge*	18--9/1/3	928
147	**I Was Only Joking** - *Rod Stewart*	19--10/1/4	911
148	**Blue Collar Man (Long Nights)** - *Styx*	20--11/1/3	884
149	**Let's All Chant** - *Michael Zager Band*	25--12/2/3	883
150	**One Nation Under A Groove - Part I** - *Funkadelic*	22--10/2/4	876
151	**Fooling Yourself (The Angry Young Man)** - *Styx*	23--11/1/4	873
152	**Lovely Day** - *Bill Withers*	23--13/1/2	869
153	**Follow You Follow Me** - *Genesis*	22--13/1/4	861
154	**It's A Laugh** - *Daryl Hall & John Oates*	21--11/1/4	851
155	**Macho Man** - *Village People*	28--10/1/7	838
156	**Stuff Like That** - *Quincy Jones*	21--15/1/4	825
157	**Happy Anniversary** - *Little River Band*	22--13/2/3	822
158	**Fantasy** - *Earth, Wind & Fire*	33--12/1/3	818
159	**Josie** - *Steely Dan*	21--9/1/4	817
160	**Come Together** - *Aerosmith*	20--9/1/4	815
161	**Just What I Needed** - *Cars*	24--13/2/4	814
162	**Theme Song From "Which Way Is Up"** *Stargard*	24--11/2/4	808
163	**Street Corner Serenade** - *Wet Willie*	26--12/1/3	799
164	**Wonderful Tonight** - *Eric Clapton*	24--9/2/3	797
165	**Dance (Disco Heat)** - *Sylvester*	30--14/1/4	764
166	**I Will Be In Love With You** *Livingston Taylor*	28--11/3/2	757
167	**Forever Autumn** - *Justin Hayward*	34--14/1/4	745
168	**I Will Still Love You** - *Stonebolt*	30--14/1/2	739
169	**The Power Of Gold** *Dan Fogelberg & Tim Weisberg*	23--8/2/6	738
170	**Only The Good Die Young** - *Billy Joel*	25--8/2/4	730
171	**Two Doors Down** - *Dolly Parton*	24--9/1/3	728
172	**Gettin' Ready For Love** - *Diana Ross*	32--12/1/3	728
173	**Stay//The Load-Out** - *Jackson Browne*	22--7/1/5	708
174	**Long, Long Way From Home** *Foreigner*	27--10/1/3	706
175	**FM (No Static At All)** - *Steely Dan*	24--9/1/4	701
176	**Boogie Shoes** *KC & The Sunshine Band*	33--9/1/7	681
177	**Theme From Close Encounters** - *Meco*	29--10/1/3	670
178	**Hot Legs** - *Rod Stewart*	25--8/1/3	662
179	**Mind Bender** - *Stillwater*	43--14/2/2	659
180	**Mr. Blue Sky** - *Electric Light Orchestra*	27--9/1/3	656
181	**Breakdown** *Tom Petty & The Heartbreakers*	33--10/3/3	655
182	**I Love You** - *Donna Summer*	26--10/1/3	649
183	**Everybody Needs Love** *Stephen Bishop*	29--11/1/3	644
184	**Run For Home** - *Lindisfarne*	35--12/1/4	622
185	**Ease On Down The Road** *Diana Ross & Michael Jackson*	36--11/1/3	614
186	**Oh! Darling** - *Robin Gibb*	24--8/1/3	611
187	**The Circle Is Small (I Can See It In Your Eyes)** - *Gordon Lightfoot*	31--10/1/2	603
188	**Prisoner Of Your Love** - *Player*	30--9/1/4	599
189	**More Than A Woman** - *Tavares*	39--11/1/4	593

Rank	Title - Act	Trajectory	Pts.
190	**Cheeseburger In Paradise** - Jimmy Buffett	29--7/3/3	588
191	**Ego** - Elton John	22--6/1/2	581
192	**Songbird** - Barbra Streisand	33--9/1/4	579
193	**Poor Poor Pitiful Me** - Linda Ronstadt	26--8/1/2	576
194	**I'm Gonna Take Care Of Everything** - Rubicon	31--10/1/2	573
195	**Almost Summer** - Celebration Featuring Mike Love	35--11/1/2	571
196	**Took The Last Train** - David Gates	30--9/1/2	568
197	**Curious Mind (Um, Um, Um, Um, Um, Um)** - Johnny Rivers	34--8/3/3	566
198	**Themes From The Wizard Of Oz** - Meco	34--9/1/3	562
199	**I've Had Enough** - Wings	28--8/1/4	553
200	**Can We Still Be Friends** - Todd Rundgren	38--10/1/3	552
201	**Sweet, Sweet Smile** - Carpenters	42--10/2/2	552
202	**Almost Like Being In Love** - Michael Johnson	37--11/1/2	549
203	**My Best Friend's Girl** - Cars	44--10/2/3	546
204	**You're A Part Of Me** - Gene Cotton	35--11/1/2	541
205	**Heaven's Just A Sin Away** - Kendalls	47--14/1/2	538
206	**Love Theme From "Eyes Of Laura Mars" (Prisoner)** - Barbra Streisand	35--9/1/2	515
207	**Hold Me, Touch Me** - Paul Stanley	41--9/2/2	510
208	**Paradise By The Dashboard Light** - Meat Loaf	37--7/1/3	499
209	**Oh What A Night For Dancing** - Barry White	32--8/2/2	495
210	**Love Or Something Like It** - Kenny Rogers	38--9/1/3	486
211	**All I See Is Your Face** - Dan Hill	35--9/1/1	485
212	**Like A Sunday In Salem (The Amos & Andy Song)** - Gene Cotton	37--8/1/3	480
213	**Too Hot Ta Trot** - Commodores	37--9/2/3	478
214	**It's You That I Need** - Enchantment	36--8/1/3	477
215	**Will You Still Love Me Tomorrow** - Dave Mason	40--10/1/3	474
216	**Dance Across The Floor** - Jimmy "Bo" Horne	51--11/1/4	463
217	**Warm Ride** - Rare Earth	42--8/2/2	460
218	**How Can I Leave You Again** - John Denver	38--10/1/1	449
219	**It's The Same Old Song** - KC & The Sunshine Band	41--8/2/2	449
220	**5.7.0.5.** - City Boy	52--14/2/1	440
221	**Thank God It's Friday** - Love And Kisses	44--9/1/3	430
222	**Please Come Home For Christmas** - Eagles	29--4/3/2	429
223	**Rocket Ride** - Kiss	46--7/2/2	429
224	**Here Comes The Night** - Nick Gilder	39--8/1/3	428
225	**If Ever I See You Again** - Roberta Flack	38--7/1/3	425
226	**A Rock 'N' Roll Fantasy** - Kinks	36--9/1/2	422
227	**Can You Fool** - Glen Campbell	39--8/1/4	416
228	**New Orleans Ladies** - Le Roux	55--10/1/3	416
229	**You Really Got Me** - Van Halen	44--9/1/2	411
230	**Think It Over** - Cheryl Ladd	44--9/1/2	408
231	**(You're My) Soul And Inspiration** - Donny & Marie	46--10/1/1	403
232	**Easy To Love** - Leo Sayer	51--9/2/2	385
233	**(I Will Be Your) Shadow In The Street** - Allan Clarke	47--9/1/1	376
234	**There'll Never Be** - Switch	46--11/1/3	375
235	**Do You Believe In Magic** - Shaun Cassidy	37--7/1/2	374
236	**Silver Dreams** - Babys	48--8/1/1	366
237	**Make You Feel Love Again** - Wet Willie	45--5/2/2	362
238	**Substitute** - Clout	52--10/1/1	361
239	**Tumbling Dice** - Linda Ronstadt	40--8/1/1	360
240	**Until Now** - Bobby Arvon	59--12/1/2	357
241	**London Town** - Wings	42--7/1/2	354
242	**Everybody Loves A Rain Song** - B.J. Thomas	44--8/1/1	354
243	**I Want You To Be Mine** - Kayak	50--11/1/2	353
244	**Raining In My Heart** - Leo Sayer	43--8/1/2	351
245	**Dreadlock Holiday** - 10cc	46--7/2/2	344
246	**Wheel In The Sky** - Journey	52--8/2/1	341
247	**Rivers Of Babylon** - Boney M	54--9/1/2	333
248	**Stay** - Rufus/Chaka Khan	45--7/2/0	332
249	**Your Sweetness Is My Weakness** - Barry White	56--8/2/2	332
250	**Reach For It** - George Duke	61--10/2/1	329
251	**The Next Hundred Years** - Al Martino	55--10/2/1	328
252	**Darlin'** - Paul Davis	45--7/1/2	326
253	**Searching For A Thrill** - Starbuck	45--8/1/2	326
254	**Hot Love, Cold World** - Bob Welch	49--7/1/3	322
255	**Fun Time** - Joe Cocker	45--8/1/1	318
256	**Everybody Dance** - Chic	49--7/1/1	314
257	**Holding On (When Love Is Gone)** - L.T.D.	54--9/1/1	313
258	**Let It Go, Let It Flow** - Dave Mason	49--8/1/1	308
259	**Portrait (He Knew)** - Kansas	53--5/3/1	308
260	**Tried To Love** - Peter Frampton	57--6/1/3	308
261	**On The Shelf** - Donny & Marie	53--8/1/2	304
262	**Cocomotion** - El Coco	52--9/1/2	298
263	**Devoted To You** - Carly Simon & James Taylor	48--7/1/1	296
264	**Galaxy** - War	46--8/2/1	294
265	**Got To Have Loving** - Don Ray	49--8/1/1	294
266	**That's Your Secret** - Sea Level	53--9/1/2	292
267	**Ooh Boy** - Rose Royce	48--9/1/1	290
268	**Greased Lightnin'** - John Travolta	45--6/1/3	289
269	**Mammas Don't Let Your Babies Grow Up To Be Cowboys** - Waylon & Willie	44--7/1/1	287
270	**You** - McCrarys	51--7/1/2	279
271	**Flying High** - Commodores	52--7/1/2	279
272	**Stone Blue** - Foghat	47--7/1/2	278
273	**I Need To Know** - Tom Petty & The Heartbreakers	53--7/1/2	278
274	**Take Me To The Kaptin** - Prism	56--7/2/1	274
275	**Cuz It's You, Girl** - James Walsh Gypsy Band	58--8/1/1	274
276	**Prove It All Night** - Bruce Springsteen	53--6/1/2	272
277	**Heartbreaker** - Dolly Parton	56--7/1/2	271
278	**Roll With The Changes** - REO Speedwagon	48--7/1/0	266
279	**Let Me Party With You (Part 1) (Party, Party, Party)** - Bunny Sigler	55--6/1/2	259
280	**Steppin' In A Slide Zone** - Moody Blues	46--6/1/2	256
281	**Chattanooga Choo Choo** - Tuxedo Junction	62--11/1/1	255
282	**Sweet Music Man** - Kenny Rogers	60--8/1/1	250
283	**Ca Plane Pour Moi** - Plastic Bertrand	57--8/1/0	249
284	**Ain't Gonna Eat Out My Heart Anymore** - Angel	56--4/1/3	240

Rank	Title - Act	Trajectory	Pts.
285	In The Bush - Musique	58--8/1/2	234
286	Flyin' - Prism	63--8/1/2	233
287	I Don't Wanna Go - Joey Travolta	59--7/1/1	231
288	California - Debby Boone	57--6/1/1	230
289	Ready For The Times To Get Better Crystal Gayle	66--11/1/0	230
290	You'll Love Again - Hotel	67--10/2/0	228
291	This Night Won't Last Forever Bill LaBounty	68--9/1/1	225
292	Mary Jane - Rick James	53--6/1/1	220
293	Since You Been Gone - Head East	65--7/1/1	218
294	Hot Summer Nights - Walter Egan	57--6/1/2	215
295	Badlands - Bruce Springsteen	52--4/1/2	210
296	Wavelength - Van Morrison	61--7/1/1	209
297	You Don't Love Me Anymore Eddie Rabbitt	64--7/1/1	206
298	She Loves To Be In Love - Charlie	61--6/1/3	205
299	You Keep Me Dancing Samantha Sang	66--7/1/1	205
300	Shake And Dance With Me Con Funk Shun	59--8/1/2	197

1979

Rank	Title - Act	Trajectory	Pts.
1	My Sharona - Knack	1--9/6/11	10347
2	Da Ya Think I'm Sexy? - Rod Stewart	1--7/5/11	10042
3	Bad Girls - Donna Summer	1--9/3/10	8549
4	Ring My Bell - Anita Ward	1--7/3/11	8189
5	Reunited - Peaches & Herb	1--8/4/10	7937
6	Escape (The Pina Colada Song) Rupert Holmes	1--10/3/9	7779
7	Hot Stuff - Donna Summer	1--7/4/11	7559
8	Good Times - Chic	1--9/1/12	7507
9	Sad Eyes - Robert John	1--20/2/9	7384
10	What A Fool Believes - Doobie Brothers	1--11/2/9	7309
11	We Are Family - Sister Sledge	2--9/2/8	7023
12	Heart Of Glass - Blondie	1--12/1/11	6941
13	I Will Survive - Gloria Gaynor	1--12/1/11	6486
14	Y.M.C.A. - Village People	3--15/2/12	6370
15	Tragedy - Bee Gees	1--6/3/8	6356
16	Babe - Styx	1--8/3/10	6061
17	No More Tears (Enough Is Enough) Barbra Streisand & Donna Summer	1--9/1/8	5956
18	Rise - Herb Alpert	1--14/2/10	5927
19	Don't Stop 'til You Get Enough Michael Jackson	1--10/1/10	5872
20	Knock On Wood - Amii Stewart	1--13/1/9	5816
21	Sail On - Commodores	1--11/1/9	5814
22	Fire - Pointer Sisters	2--15/2/7	5740
23	Please Don't Go KC & The Sunshine Band	3--16/3/11	5571
24	Still - Commodores	1--8/1/11	5216
25	Ladies Night - Kool & The Gang	4--11/4/10	5176
26	Heartache Tonight - Eagles	1--6/1/10	5129
27	Pop Muzik - M	4--12/3/10	5013
28	My Life - Billy Joel	3--11/2/8	4552
29	Dim All The Lights - Donna Summer	3--12/2/8	4551
30	Chuck E.'s In Love - Rickie Lee Jones	4--10/3/7	4360
31	Music Box Dancer - Frank Mills	2--12/2/7	4358
32	A Little More Love - Olivia Newton-John	4--13/3/6	4328
33	I Want You To Want Me - Cheap Trick	3--15/2/7	4002
34	When You're In Love With A Beautiful Woman - Dr. Hook	5--18/2/7	3776
35	The Main Event/Fight - Barbra Streisand	3--11/2/7	3748
36	I'll Never Love This Way Again Dionne Warwick	5--15/2/10	3739
37	In The Navy - Village People	3--10/1/7	3713
38	Love You Inside Out - Bee Gees	2--8/2/5	3671
39	Shake Your Body (Down To The Ground) - Jacksons	5--14/2/9	3555
40	Hold The Line – Toto	5--16/2/7	3554
41	Lead Me On - Maxine Nightingale	5--19/2/9	3453
42	Makin' It - David Naughton	5--20/2/7	3414
43	After The Love Has Gone Earth, Wind & Fire	3--10/2/6	3294
44	Send One Your Love - Stevie Wonder	5--8/3/6	3262
45	The Devil Went Down To Georgia Charlie Daniels Band	4--11/2/8	3259
46	Heaven Knows - Donna Summer	4--9/2/6	3247
47	The Logical Song - Supertramp	4--11/2/7	3244
48	Shake Your Groove Thing Peaches & Herb	5--15/3/5	3231
49	Don't Bring Me Down Electric Light Orchestra	4--9/2/7	3166
50	Just When I Needed You Most Randy Vanwarmer	5--13/2/7	3164
51	Gold - John Stewart	6--12/2/7	3057
52	Boogie Wonderland Earth, Wind & Fire with The Emotions	5--9/2/7	3043
53	Goodnight Tonight - Wings	4--8/1/7	2847
54	Jane - Jefferson Starship	6--9/3/6	2796
55	Sultans Of Swing - Dire Straits	5--10/2/5	2778
56	Lonesome Loser - Little River Band	7--12/2/7	2755
57	September - Earth, Wind & Fire	6--10/2/7	2622
58	She Believes In Me - Kenny Rogers	7--12/2/7	2558
59	You Decorated My Life - Kenny Rogers	7--9/3/8	2538
60	Ooh Baby Baby - Linda Ronstadt	7--11/2/4	2369
61	Stumblin' In Suzi Quatro & Chris Norman	6--13/2/5	2368
62	You Can't Change That - Raydio	10--17/1/8	2358
63	Every 1's A Winner - Hot Chocolate	7--13/2/5	2337
64	Mama Can't Buy You Love Elton John	10--11/2/6	2325
65	You're Only Lonely - J.D. Souther	7--14/1/7	2324
66	Heaven Must Have Sent You Bonnie Pointer	10--16/2/6	2259
67	Lotta Love - Nicolette Larson	8--12/2/5	2248
68	Don't Cry Out Loud Melissa Manchester	10--18/2/4	2163
69	Every Time I Think Of You - Babys	8--14/2/6	2082
70	You Take My Breath Away - Rex Smith	7--10/2/5	2030
71	He's The Greatest Dancer Sister Sledge	8--14/2/5	2026
72	I Was Made For Lovin' You - Kiss	8--12/1/7	2007
73	Tusk - Fleetwood Mac	8--5/2/10	2001
74	Shine A Little Love Electric Light Orchestra	7--10/1/4	1967
75	Lady - Little River Band	10--12/2/7	1948
76	Ain't No Stoppin' Us Now McFadden & Whitehead	12--13/2/6	1912
77	Shake It - Ian Matthews	10--13/2/4	1906
78	Rock 'N' Roll Fantasy - Bad Company	11--14/2/6	1875
79	Bad Case Of Loving You (Doctor, Doctor) - Robert Palmer	10--10/2/7	1841
80	Disco Nights (Rock-Freak) - G.Q.	10--12/1/7	1792
81	Promises - Eric Clapton	11--14/1/6	1749
82	Cruel To Be Kind - Nick Lowe	12--14/1/6	1743

Rank	Title - Act	Trajectory	Pts.
83	The Gambler - *Kenny Rogers*	13--15/3/5	1740
84	I Want Your Love - *Chic*	10--11/2/6	1688
85	I Just Fall In Love Again - *Anne Murray*	11--13/2/4	1655
86	Good Girls Don't - *Knack*	11--9/2/6	1638
87	Soul Man - *Blues Brothers*	9--10/2/6	1635
88	Take Me Home - *Cher*	10--14/2/4	1623
89	Lovin', Touchin', Squeezin' - *Journey*	15--15/1/8	1614
90	Got To Be Real - *Cheryl Lynn*	10--11/2/5	1588
91	What You Won't Do For Love *Bobby Caldwell*	10--15/1/4	1583
92	We've Got Tonite - *Bob Seger*	11--13/1/5	1579
93	Crazy Love - *Poco*	14--13/1/5	1535
94	Let's Go - *Cars*	14--10/2/5	1476
95	New York Groove - *Ace Frehley*	16--17/1/4	1471
96	Take The Long Way Home - *Supertramp*	15--10/1/7	1470
97	I Was Made For Dancin' - *Leif Garrett*	15--15/2/3	1455
98	Ships - *Barry Manilow*	11--7/2/6	1451
99	Love Takes Time - *Orleans*	12--9/2/5	1406
100	Love Is The Answer *England Dan & John Ford Coley*	13--12/1/5	1380
101	Blow Away - *George Harrison*	12--11/2/4	1348
102	Born To Be Alive - *Patrick Hernandez*	17--18/1/5	1348
103	Driver's Seat - *Sniff 'n' The Tears*	15--12/1/5	1330
104	This Night Won't Last Forever *Michael Johnson*	18--17/1/4	1323
105	Livin' It Up (Friday Night) - *Bell & James*	16--12/2/5	1315
106	Goodbye Stranger - *Supertramp*	16--10/2/5	1307
107	Does Your Mother Know - *Abba*	16--9/2/5	1300
108	Is She Really Going Out With Him? *Joe Jackson*	21--15/1/7	1283
109	Dancin' Shoes - *Nigel Olsson*	17--14/1/5	1269
110	Somewhere In The Night *Barry Manilow*	13--9/2/4	1264
111	I Don't Know If It's Right *Evelyn "Champagne" King*	17--13/2/6	1264
112	Renegade - *Styx*	18--11/2/6	1261
113	Where Were You When I Was Falling In Love - *Lobo*	16--13/1/5	1257
114	Suspicions - *Eddie Rabbitt*	19--13/1/5	1240
115	Minute By Minute - *Doobie Brothers*	13--8/1/6	1220
116	Half The Way - *Crystal Gayle*	18--13/1/6	1208
117	Love Ballad - *George Benson*	14--11/1/4	1207
118	No Tell Lover - *Chicago*	14--12/1/3	1204
119	Precious Love - *Bob Welch*	17--12/1/4	1175
120	If You Remember Me *Chris Thompson & Night*	19--15/1/7	1166
121	Get Used To It - *Roger Voudouris*	22--14/2/3	1164
122	Spooky - *Atlanta Rhythm Section*	15--9/1/5	1120
123	Don't Hold Back - *Chanson*	20--14/1/5	1113
124	The Boss - *Diana Ross*	21--14/2/4	1109
125	Come To Me - *France Joli*	15--9/2/5	1109
126	Big Shot - *Billy Joel*	13--8/1/3	1096
127	Dirty White Boy - *Foreigner*	16--9/1/5	1092
128	Do It Or Die - *Atlanta Rhythm Section*	21--10/2/4	1090
129	Forever In Blue Jeans - *Neil Diamond*	20--10/2/4	1034
130	Blue Morning, Blue Day - *Foreigner*	19--10/2/3	1027
131	Different Worlds - *Maureen McGovern*	26--15/2/3	1012
132	I Can't Stand It No More *Peter Frampton*	18--8/2/5	1006
133	Ain't Love A Bitch - *Rod Stewart*	14--6/2/4	995
134	I Know A Heartache When I See One - *Jennifer Warnes*	21--17/2/4	982
135	I Want You Tonight - *Pablo Cruise*	21--11/1/4	951
136	Dance The Night Away - *Van Halen*	22--10/1/6	945
137	Dreaming - *Blondie*	20--10/2/5	919
138	I Do Love You - *GQ*	27--11/2/6	919
139	Hot Summer Nights - *Night*	26--11/3/3	910
140	Heart Of The Night - *Poco*	19--10/2/3	906
141	Such A Woman - *Tycoon*	21--11/2/3	902
142	I Got My Mind Made Up (You Can Get It Girl) - *Instant Funk*	22--11/1/4	888
143	One Way Or Another - *Blondie*	22--10/1/4	879
144	Broken Hearted Me - *Anne Murray*	22--10/2/3	843
145	So Good, So Right - *Brenda Russell*	26--14/1/4	836
146	(If Loving You Is Wrong) I Don't Want To Be Right - *Barbara Mandrell*	27--13/1/3	814
147	Maybe I'm A Fool - *Eddie Money*	25--10/2/3	799
148	Get It Right Next Time - *Gerry Rafferty*	23--10/1/4	797
149	Morning Dance - *Spyro Gyra*	27--12/2/4	793
150	Home And Dry - *Gerry Rafferty*	23--11/1/4	784
151	Take Me To The River - *Talking Heads*	31--13/2/5	772
152	Deeper Than The Night *Olivia Newton-John*	19--8/1/4	765
153	Damned If I Do - *Alan Parsons Project*	30--13/1/4	757
154	Getting Closer - *Wings*	20--7/1/5	755
155	I Need A Lover - *John Cougar*	32--12/1/4	740
156	Shakedown Cruise - *Jay Ferguson*	27--9/1/4	733
157	Love Don't Live Here Anymore *Rose Royce*	28--13/1/3	717
158	Hot Number - *Foxy*	29--11/1/4	706
159	Days Gone Down (Still Got The Light In Your Eyes) - *Gerry Rafferty*	22--7/2/3	699
160	Shadows In The Moonlight *Anne Murray*	27--9/2/3	692
161	Hold On - *Ian Gomm*	25--9/1/4	688
162	Highway Song - *Blackfoot*	32--10/2/3	670
163	Street Life - *Crusaders*	29--13/1/4	654
164	Weekend - *Wet Willie*	29--11/1/3	653
165	What Cha Gonna Do With My Lovin' *Stephanie Mills*	28--10/1/3	651
166	Honesty - *Billy Joel*	23--7/1/4	649
167	Fins - *Jimmy Buffett*	25--11/1/2	646
168	People Of The South Wind - *Kansas*	28--10/1/2	628
169	You Gonna Make Me Love Somebody Else - *Jones Girls*	32--9/1/3	625
170	Train, Train - *Blackfoot*	36--11/2/2	622
171	Please Don't Leave - *Lauren Wood*	31--9/2/3	621
172	Every Which Way But Loose *Eddie Rabbitt*	34--11/1/2	618
173	Roxanne - *Police*	31--12/1/3	617
174	Dream Police - *Cheap Trick*	27--8/2/3	609
175	Rolene - *Moon Martin*	28--9/1/3	606
176	Stormy - *Santana*	33--10/1/4	605
177	Dependin' On You - *Doobie Brothers*	30--9/1/3	599
178	A Man I'll Never Be - *Boston*	36--11/1/2	595
179	Found A Cure - *Ashford & Simpson*	35--10/1/4	593
180	Dancing In The City - *Marshall Hain*	39--11/1/3	591
181	Bustin' Loose (Part 1) *Chuck Brown & The Soul Searchers*	29--9/1/3	587
182	Firecracker - *Mass Production*	33--8/2/5	584
183	Keep On Dancin' - *Gary's Gang*	33--10/1/3	579
184	Superman - *Herbie Mann*	35--13/1/2	576
185	Little Bit Of Soap - *Nigel Olsson*	33--9/1/4	567
186	Savannah Nights - *Tom Johnston*	34--8/2/4	564

Rank	Title - Act	Trajectory	Pts.
187	Dog & Butterfly - *Heart*	31--9/2/2	563
188	Shattered - *Rolling Stones*	27--7/2/3	560
189	Song On The Radio - *Al Stewart*	27--8/1/2	560
190	Up On The Roof - *James Taylor*	32--9/1/3	556
191	Baby I'm Burnin' - *Dolly Parton*	34--8/2/4	555
192	Midnight Wind - *John Stewart*	33--9/1/3	548
193	One Last Kiss - *J. Geils Band*	37--11/1/2	539
194	Hold On - *Triumph*	42--12/1/3	534
195	I Still Have Dreams - *Richie Furay*	40--10/2/2	528
196	Happiness - *Pointer Sisters*	28--9/1/2	522
197	The Dream Never Dies *Cooper Brothers*	44--14/1/2	514
198	Don't You Write Her Off *McGuinn, Clark & Hillman*	33--9/1/3	513
199	You Took The Words Right Out Of My Mouth - *Meat Loaf*	42--11/1/1	502
200	Good Friend - *Mary MacGregor*	44--10/2/2	500
201	Chase - *Giorgio Moroder*	38--10/1/2	499
202	Old Time Rock & Roll - *Bob Seger*	34--8/1/3	498
203	Rainbow Connection *Kermit (Jim Henson)*	43--10/1/3	489
204	Pretty Girls - *Melissa Manchester*	44--10/1/5	486
205	Ain't That A Shame - *Cheap Trick*	35--8/1/3	483
206	You Need A Woman Tonight *Captain & Tennille*	36--10/1/2	483
207	You Thrill Me - *Exile*	43--12/1/1	483
208	Video Killed The Radio Star - *Buggles*	40--7/1/4	480
209	Saturdaynight - *Herman Brood*	44--10/1/3	480
210	Good Timin' - *Beach Boys*	33--7/1/3	475
211	Victim Of Love - *Elton John*	38--7/2/3	471
212	Don't Ever Wanna Lose Ya *New England*	40--8/2/2	466
213	Oh Well - *Rockets*	39--9/1/3	454
214	Gotta Serve Somebody - *Bob Dylan*	37--8/1/3	447
215	Georgy Porgy - *Toto*	44--8/2/1	443
216	Sing For The Day - *Styx*	41--8/2/3	442
217	Get Down - *Gene Chandler*	50--12/1/2	440
218	(Wish I Could Fly Like) Superman *Kinks*	42--8/1/2	433
219	(Not Just) Knee Deep - Part 1 - *Funkadelic*	45--9/1/4	431
220	Goodbye, I Love You - *Firefall*	40--8/1/1	428
221	Arrow Through Me - *Wings*	36--7/1/3	422
222	It's All I Can Do - *Cars*	40--7/1/2	410
223	You Stepped Into My Life *Melba Moore*	47--12/1/1	409
224	Girl Of My Dreams - *Bram Tchaikovsky*	40--7/2/1	405
225	Saturday Night, Sunday Morning *Thelma Houston*	44--11/1/2	404
226	Sure Know Something - *Kiss*	44--9/1/2	403
227	It Must Be Love *Alton McClain & Destiny*	45--11/1/3	397
228	I Don't Wanna Lose You *Daryl Hall & John Oates*	44--8/2/1	388
229	Remember (Walking In The Sand) *Louise Goffin*	44--8/1/2	381
230	Roller - *April Wine*	47--8/2/2	377
231	Last Of The Singing Cowboys *Marshall Tucker Band*	43--8/1/2	375
232	Get It Up - *Ronnie Milsap*	50--11/1/2	371
233	Rhumba Girl - *Nicolette Larson*	41--7/1/2	366
234	Haven't Stopped Dancing Yet *Gonzalez*	46--8/1/2	364
235	Children Of The Sun - *Billy Thorpe*	50--9/1/2	362
236	I Need Your Help Barry Manilow *Ray Stevens*	34--6/1/3	353
237	Now That We Found Love - *Third World*	41--8/1/2	353
238	Do You Wanna Go Party *KC & The Sunshine Band*	43--7/1/2	348
239	Married Men - *Bette Midler*	46--7/1/2	343
240	Young Blood - *Rickie Lee Jones*	44--6/1/2	342
241	Love Pains - *Yvonne Elliman*	53--10/1/3	342
242	Dance Away - *Roxy Music*	51--8/1/3	341
243	Rubber Biscuit - *Blues Brothers*	42--6/2/1	340
244	Diamonds - *Chris Rea*	44--6/2/2	338
245	Confusion - *Electric Light Orchestra*	47--7/1/2	338
246	Kiss In The Dark - *Pink Lady*	49--8/1/2	336
247	You Make Me Feel (Mighty Real) *Sylvester*	53--8/2/2	325
248	Crazy Love - *Allman Brothers Band*	41--6/1/3	318
249	Turn Off The Lights *Teddy Pendergrass*	50--7/1/2	318
250	Rock Me - *Nick Gilder*	53--8/1/1	314
251	Reason To Be - *Kansas*	51--7/2/2	313
252	Radioactive - *Gene Simmons*	51--7/1/2	311
253	Dancin' Fool - *Frank Zappa*	45--7/1/3	307
254	I'll Supply The Love - *Toto*	46--7/1/1	307
255	Sweet Lui-Louise - *Ironhorse*	42--7/1/2	304
256	Just One Look - *Linda Ronstadt*	46--7/1/1	302
257	We've Got Love - *Peaches & Herb*	47--7/1/2	298
258	Since I Don't Have You - *Art Garfunkel*	52--7/1/2	295
259	Get A Move On - *Eddie Money*	55--7/1/2	287
260	Watch Out For Lucy - *Eric Clapton*	45--7/1/1	283
261	Stay The Night - *Faragher Brothers*	48--7/1/1	282
262	Peter Piper - *Frank Mills*	57--8/1/3	280
263	Can't Sleep - *Rockets*	56--7/2/1	278
264	Oh Honey - *Delegation*	60--12/1/1	276
265	Then You Can Tell Me Goodby *Toby Beau*	62--9/1/1	274
266	Go West - *Village People*	48--6/1/2	272
267	Since You Been Gone - *Rainbow*	56--7/1/3	260
268	If I Said You Had A Beautiful Body Would You Hold It Against Me *Bellamy Brothers*	58--8/1/1	259
269	Baby I Want You *Funky Communication Committee*	59--9/1/1	250
270	You Angel You *Manfred Mann's Earth Band*	53--7/1/1	246
271	Easy Driver - *Kenny Loggins*	54--7/1/1	246
272	No Chance - *Moon Martin*	55--7/1/1	243
273	Here Comes The Night - *Beach Boys*	52--6/1/1	241
274	5:15 - *The Who*	53--6/1/1	241
275	This Is Love - *Oak*	55--7/1/1	241
276	Animal House - *Stephen Bishop*	57--7/1/1	241
277	I Don't Want Nobody Else (To Dance With You) - *Narada Michael Walden*	52--7/1/2	240
278	Hard Times For Lovers - *Judy Collins*	63--8/1/1	240
279	It Hurts So Bad - *Kim Carnes*	54--7/1/1	239
280	Sweets For My Sweet - *Tony Orlando*	55--6/2/1	238
281	If You Can't Give Me Love *Suzi Quatro*	53--6/1/2	237
282	Highway To Hell - *AC/DC*	57--6/1/2	237
283	Survivor - *Cindy Bullens*	57--7/1/1	235
284	Vengeance - *Carly Simon*	52--5/1/2	230
285	I've Never Been In Love - *Suzi Quatro*	56--6/1/2	230

Rank	Title - Act	Trajectory	Pts.
286	**Just The Same Way** - *Journey*	63--9/1/2	222
287	**Feelin' Satisfied** - *Boston*	51--6/1/1	221
288	**If You Want It** - *Niteflyte*	59--8/1/2	219
289	**Elena** - *Marc Tanner Band*	52--6/1/1	214
290	**Message In A Bottle** - *Police*	62--7/2/2	209
291	**You've Got Another Thing Coming** *Hotel*	63--7/1/1	208
292	**Heartaches** - *BTO*	57--5/2/1	207
293	**You Can Do It** - *Dobie Gray*	54--5/1/2	206

Rank	Title - Act	Trajectory	Pts.
294	**Dancer** - *Gino Soccio*	59--5/2/1	205
295	**Gone, Gone, Gone** - *Bad Company*	63--7/1/1	205
296	**Where Will Your Heart Take You** *Buckeye*	66--7/1/1	205
297	**I Go To Rio** - *Pablo Cruise*	56--5/1/2	204
298	**Dancin' Shoes** - *Faith Band*	63--8/1/1	204
299	**Good Times Roll** - *Cars*	60--6/1/2	201
300	**Boogie Woogie Dancin' Shoes** *Claudja Barry*	65--4/1/5	200

300 High Intensity Singles

A ranking of the hottest records of the decade during their chart lifetimes. Records of varying duration are given equal treatment in a system that normalizes performance by averaging the points earned in a lifecycle by weeks on the chart, then putting that average on a rank basis.

Rank	Title - Act	Pk Yr	Wks	Avg Pts/Wk	Avg Pos
1	ABC - Jackson 5	1970	13	552.7	3.82
2	My Sweet Lord - George Harrison	1970	14	515.9	4.14
3	Night Fever - Bee Gees	1978	21	506.0	4.24
4	Let It Be - Beatles	1970	13	490.9	4.40
5	Never Can Say Goodbye - Jackson 5	1971	12	486.3	4.45
6	I'll Be There - Jackson 5	1970	16	484.8	4.47
7	You Light Up My Life - Debby Boone	1977	27	470.7	4.61
8	Theme From Shaft - Isaac Hayes	1971	14	459.5	4.73
9	Joy To The World - Three Dog Night	1971	18	458.8	4.74
10	Da Ya Think I'm Sexy? - Rod Stewart	1979	22	456.5	4.76
11	Shadow Dancing - Andy Gibb	1978	24	455.5	4.77
12	The First Time Ever I Saw Your Face - Roberta Flack	1972	16	454.1	4.79
13	Rockin' Robin - Michael Jackson	1972	14	447.5	4.86
14	Le Freak - Chic	1978	26	442.6	4.91
15	Family Affair - Sly & The Family Stone	1971	15	439.9	4.94
16	My Love - Paul McCartney & Wings	1973	16	437.9	4.96
17	Alone Again (Naturally) - Gilbert O'Sullivan	1972	18	437.1	4.97
18	Bridge Over Troubled Water - Simon & Garfunkel	1970	14	436.2	4.98
19	A Horse With No Name - America	1972	13	426.2	5.09
20	Knock Three Times - Dawn	1971	18	418.6	5.17
21	Maggie May - Rod Stewart	1971	18	418.1	5.18
22	You Don't Bring Me Flowers - Barbra & Neil	1978	18	417.4	5.19
23	I Honestly Love You - Olivia Newton-John	1974	14	417.2	5.19
24	Convoy - C.W. McCall	1976	16	416.4	5.20
25	Venus - Shocking Blue	1970	16	416.0	5.20
26	My Sharona - Knack	1979	25	413.9	5.23
27	The Long And Winding Road - Beatles	1970	11	410.9	5.26
28	Ring My Bell - Anita Ward	1979	20	409.5	5.28
29	Ain't No Mountain High Enough - Diana Ross	1970	12	407.4	5.30
30	Bad Girls - Donna Summer	1979	21	407.1	5.30
31	American Pie - Don McLean	1972	20	406.5	5.31
32	American Woman - Guess Who	1970	14	404.1	5.34
33	Silly Love Songs - Wings	1976	21	400.2	5.38
34	Crocodile Rock - Elton John	1973	17	397.5	5.41
35	Afternoon Delight - Starland Vocal Band	1976	24	397.4	5.41
36	Tragedy - Bee Gees	1979	16	397.3	5.41
37	One Bad Apple - Osmonds	1971	16	395.7	5.43
38	Three Times A Lady - Commodores	1978	21	394.3	5.45
39	I Write The Songs - Barry Manilow	1976	20	393.4	5.46
39	Let's Stay Together - Al Green	1972	17	393.4	5.46
41	Mama's Pearl - Jackson 5	1971	11	391.3	5.48
42	We Are Family - Sister Sledge	1979	18	390.2	5.49
43	How Can You Mend A Broken Heart - Bee Gees	1971	15	390.1	5.49
44	Too Much Heaven - Bee Gees	1978	20	388.9	5.51
45	Bad Blood - Neil Sedaka	1975	14	385.8	5.54
46	Americans - Byron Mac Gregor	1974	10	384.7	5.55
47	Gypsys, Tramps & Thieves - Cher	1971	15	382.5	5.58
48	Go Away Little Girl - Donny Osmond	1971	14	382.1	5.58
49	Tonight's The Night (Gonna Be Alright) - Rod Stewart	1976	22	381.6	5.59
50	Have You Never Been Mellow - Olivia Newton-John	1975	15	380.6	5.60
51	The Tears Of A Clown - Smokey Robinson & The Miracles	1970	16	378.2	5.63
52	Love Train - O'Jays	1973	15	378.1	5.63
53	Reunited - Peaches & Herb	1979	21	378.0	5.63
54	Killing Me Softly With His Song - Roberta Flack	1973	15	376.5	5.65
55	That's The Way (I Like It) - K.C. & The Sunshine Band	1975	16	375.1	5.66
56	I Think I Love You - Partridge Family	1970	19	373.7	5.68
57	Doesn't Somebody Want To Be Wanted - Partridge Family	1971	13	373.6	5.68
58	War - Edwin Starr	1970	15	373.5	5.68
59	Escape (The Pina Colada Song) - Rupert Holmes	1979	21	370.4	5.71
60	Spirit In The Sky - Norman Greenbaum	1970	17	369.3	5.73
61	Island Girl - Elton John	1975	15	368.9	5.73
62	Brandy (You're A Fine Girl) - Looking Glass	1972	16	367.8	5.74
63	Me And Mrs. Jones - Billy Paul	1972	17	367.6	5.75
64	It's Too Late - Carole King	1971	17	367.4	5.75
65	Heart Of Gold - Neil Young	1972	15	363.5	5.79
66	The Streak - Ray Stevens	1974	15	363.2	5.80
67	Lookin' Out My Back Door - Creedence Clearwater Revival	1970	12	363.2	5.80
68	You're So Vain - Carly Simon	1973	17	362.4	5.80
69	Hot Stuff - Donna Summer	1979	21	360.0	5.83
70	Torn Between Two Lovers - Mary MacGregor	1977	25	358.8	5.84
71	Good Times - Chic	1979	21	357.5	5.86
72	Brand New Key - Melanie	1971	19	356.9	5.87
73	Mama Told Me (Not To Come) - Three Dog Night	1970	14	356.6	5.87
74	Kiss You All Over - Exile	1978	28	356.1	5.88
75	Stayin' Alive - Bee Gees	1978	27	356.0	5.88
76	Photograph - Ringo Starr	1973	14	355.9	5.88
77	Welcome Back - John Sebastian	1976	18	355.1	5.89

Rank	Title - Act	Pk Yr	Wks	Avg Pts/Wk	Avg Pos
78	Disco Duck (Part 1) - Rick Dees & His Cast Of Idiots	1976	20	354.8	5.89
79	Got To Be There - Michael Jackson	1972	14	353.5	5.90
80	Philadelphia Freedom - Elton John Band	1975	17	351.5	5.93
81	No More Tears (Enough Is Enough) - Barbra Streisand/Donna Summer	1979	17	350.4	5.94
82	What A Fool Believes - Doobie Brothers	1979	21	348.0	5.97
83	How Deep Is Your Love - Bee Gees	1977	28	346.6	5.98
84	Lovin' You - Minnie Riperton	1975	16	344.6	6.01
85	Oh Girl - Chi-Lites	1972	14	344.1	6.03
86	(They Long To Be) Close To You - Carpenters	1970	16	343.9	6.03
87	Someone Saved My Life Tonight - Elton John	1975	12	343.1	6.05
88	Give Me Love (Give Me Peace On Earth) - George Harrison	1973	13	342.2	6.08
89	Let's Get It On - Marvin Gaye	1973	18	341.0	6.11
90	She's A Lady - Tom Jones	1971	16	340.4	6.13
91	Jive Talkin' - Bee Gees	1975	19	339.2	6.17
92	Rich Girl - Daryl Hall & John Oates	1977	18	337.4	6.22
93	Ball Of Confusion (That's What The World Is Today) - Temptations	1970	14	336.8	6.23
94	Grease - Frankie Valli	1978	23	336.7	6.24
95	Imagine - John Lennon/Plastic Ono Band	1971	11	334.8	6.29
96	Don't Let The Sun Go Down On Me - Elton John	1974	13	333.8	6.32
97	Bridge Over Troubled Water - Aretha Franklin	1971	11	333.5	6.33
98	I Shot The Sheriff - Eric Clapton	1974	14	333.4	6.33
99	Raindrops Keep Fallin' On My Head - B.J. Thomas	1970	22	333.2	6.34
100	Lucy In The Sky With Diamonds - Elton John	1975	13	331.8	6.38
101	Baker Street - Gerry Rafferty	1978	24	331.7	6.38
102	I Want You Back - Jackson 5	1970	17	331.2	6.39
103	Just My Imagination (Running Away With Me) - Temptations	1971	16	329.9	6.43
104	Thank You (Falettinme Be Mice Elf Agin) - Sly & The Family Stone	1970	15	329.1	6.46
105	Star Wars Theme/Cantina Band - Meco	1977	21	328.5	6.47
106	Instant Karma (We All Shine On) - John Ono Lennon	1970	14	328.3	6.48
107	We've Only Just Begun - Carpenters	1970	15	327.5	6.50
108	Brown Sugar - Rolling Stones	1971	12	327.0	6.51
109	Tie A Yellow Ribbon Round The Ole Oak Tree - Dawn	1973	23	326.5	6.53
110	Uncle Albert/Admiral Halsey - Paul & Linda McCartney	1971	12	326.0	6.54
111	The Love You Save - Jackson 5	1970	14	324.6	6.58
112	Put Your Hand In The Hand - Ocean	1971	15	323.8	6.61
113	Time In A Bottle - Jim Croce	1974	14	323.0	6.63
114	Miss You - Rolling Stones	1978	23	322.2	6.65
115	I'll Take You There - Staple Singers	1972	14	321.9	6.66
116	Fly, Robin, Fly - Silver Convention	1975	18	321.1	6.68
117	Lady Marmalade - Labelle	1975	17	321.0	6.69
118	Heartache Tonight - Eagles	1979	16	320.6	6.70
119	TSOP (The Sound Of Philadelphia) - MFSB	1974	16	320.5	6.70
120	(You're) Having My Baby - Paul Anka	1974	16	320.2	6.71
121	Undercover Angel - Alan O'Day	1977	25	320.2	6.71
122	Mr. Big Stuff - Jean Knight	1971	16	320.1	6.71
123	Angie - Rolling Stones	1973	14	319.3	6.73
124	Draggin' The Line - Tommy James	1971	15	319.1	6.74
125	Rose Garden - Lynn Anderson	1971	18	318.6	6.76
125	Can't Smile Without You - Barry Manilow	1978	20	318.6	6.76
127	Lonely Night (Angel Face) - Captain And Tennille	1976	19	318.4	6.76
128	Signed, Sealed, Delivered I'm Yours - Stevie Wonder	1970	14	317.9	6.77
129	Make It With You - Bread	1970	16	317.8	6.78
130	Superstition - Stevie Wonder	1973	17	317.4	6.79
131	Boogie Oogie Oogie - A Taste Of Honey	1978	25	316.6	6.81
132	I'm Still In Love With You - Al Green	1972	14	315.9	6.83
133	Live And Let Die - Wings	1973	14	315.4	6.85
134	Please Mr. Please - Olivia Newton-John	1975	14	315.1	6.86
135	Hurting Each Other - Carpenters	1972	13	315.0	6.86
136	Don't Pull Your Love - Hamilton, Joe Frank & Reynolds	1971	15	313.5	6.90
137	Mac Arthur Park - Donna Summer	1978	22	313.4	6.90
138	Want Ads - Honey Cone	1971	15	313.2	6.91
139	50 Ways To Leave Your Lover - Paul Simon	1976	20	312.4	6.93
140	Don't Go Breaking My Heart - Elton John & Kiki Dee	1976	20	311.9	6.95
141	Annie's Song - John Denver	1974	16	310.1	7.00
142	Midnight Train To Georgia - Gladys Knight & The Pips	1973	16	309.8	7.01
143	Whatever Gets You Thru The Night - John Lennon	1974	13	308.8	7.04
144	Disco Lady - Johnnie Taylor	1976	19	308.7	7.04
145	Please Mr. Postman - Carpenters	1975	15	308.5	7.04
146	You Haven't Done Nothin' - Stevie Wonder	1974	15	308.1	7.06
147	It Don't Come Easy - Ringo Starr	1971	13	307.7	7.07
148	Superstar - Carpenters	1971	15	306.8	7.10
149	You Ought To Be With Me - Al Green	1972	14	306.5	7.11
150	One Of These Nights - Eagles	1975	16	305.8	7.13
151	The Entertainer - Marvin Hamlisch	1974	16	305.1	7.15
152	Half-Breed - Cher	1973	19	304.8	7.16
153	One Less Bell To Answer - 5th Dimension	1970	18	303.5	7.20
154	Listen To What The Man Said - Wings	1975	14	303.4	7.20
155	Babe – Styx	1979	20	303.1	7.21
156	Don't Stop - Fleetwood Mac	1977	17	302.9	7.22
157	Heart Of Glass - Blondie	1979	23	301.8	7.25
158	Leave Me Alone (Ruby Red Dress) - Helen Reddy	1974	15	301.3	7.26
159	Up Around The Bend - Creedence Clearwater Revival	1970	12	299.9	7.31
160	With A Little Luck - Wings	1978	18	299.6	7.31

Rank	Title - Act	Pk Yr	Wks	Avg Pts/Wk	Avg Pos
161	Song Sung Blue - Neil Diamond	1972	14	299.2	7.33
162	Best Of My Love - Emotions	1977	21	299.1	7.33
163	Without You - Nilsson	1972	19	298.6	7.35
164	Nobody Does It Better - Carly Simon	1977	25	298.6	7.35
165	If You Leave Me Now - Chicago	1976	19	298.1	7.36
166	Too Late To Turn Back Now - Cornelius Brothers & Sister Rose	1972	15	297.9	7.37
167	Cracklin' Rosie - Neil Diamond	1970	15	296.6	7.41
167	Shambala - Three Dog Night	1973	15	296.6	7.41
169	How Long - Ace	1975	15	296.1	7.42
170	Frankenstein - Edgar Winter Group	1973	16	295.1	7.45
170	Burning Love - Elvis Presley	1972	16	295.1	7.45
172	Boogie Down - Eddie Kendricks	1974	16	294.9	7.46
173	You're Sixteen - Ringo Starr	1974	15	294.6	7.47
174	Long Cool Woman (In A Black Dress) - Hollies	1972	16	294.5	7.47
175	You're The First, The Last, My Everything - Barry White	1975	15	294.3	7.47
176	Black And White - Three Dog Night	1972	14	293.7	7.49
177	Don't Stop 'til You Get Enough - Michael Jackson	1979	20	293.6	7.50
178	Goodbye Yellow Brick Road - Elton John	1973	15	293.5	7.50
179	You've Got A Friend - James Taylor	1971	16	293.1	7.51
180	Love Hangover - Diana Ross	1976	17	292.8	7.52
181	Mandy - Barry Manilow	1975	17	291.9	7.55
182	Down By The Lazy River - Osmonds	1972	13	291.5	7.56
183	Don't Give Up On Us - David Soul	1977	19	291.4	7.56
184	Short People - Randy Newman	1978	21	291.3	7.57
185	Higher Ground - Stevie Wonder	1973	13	291.1	7.57
186	My Ding-A-Ling - Chuck Berry	1972	18	291.0	7.58
187	Loves Me Like A Rock - Paul Simon	1973	15	290.9	7.58
187	Yo-Yo - Osmonds	1971	14	290.9	7.58
189	Sail On - Commodores	1979	20	290.7	7.58
190	Patches - Clarence Carter	1970	14	290.4	7.60
191	Seasons In The Sun - Terry Jacks	1974	18	290.2	7.60
192	Rainy Days And Mondays - Carpenters	1971	12	289.8	7.61
193	Billy, Don't Be A Hero - Bo Donaldson And The Heywoods	1974	16	289.3	7.63
194	I Wish - Stevie Wonder	1977	19	288.7	7.65
195	Indian Reservation (The Lament Of The Cherokee) - Raiders	1971	20	287.7	7.68
196	The Cisco Kid - War	1973	13	287.5	7.68
197	Yesterday Once More - Carpenters	1973	14	287.4	7.69
198	Bennie And The Jets - Elton John	1974	17	287.2	7.69
199	Cecilia - Simon & Garfunkel	1970	12	287.1	7.69
200	In The Summertime - Mungo Jerry	1970	13	286.9	7.70
201	He Don't Love You (Like I Love You) - Tony Orlando & Dawn	1975	14	286.8	7.70
202	Muskrat Love - Captain & Tennille	1976	22	286.6	7.71
203	Dark Lady - Cher	1974	15	286.5	7.71
204	I Just Want To Be Your Everything - Andy Gibb	1977	29	285.9	7.73
205	Have You Ever Seen The Rain - Creedence Clearwater Revival	1971	10	285.9	7.73
206	The Night The Lights Went Out In Georgia - Vicki Lawrence	1973	18	284.8	7.76
207	The Loco-Motion - Grand Funk	1974	17	284.6	7.77
208	Band On The Run - Paul McCartney & Wings	1974	16	283.1	7.81
209	Spanish Harlem - Aretha Franklin	1971	12	282.5	7.83
210	I Will Survive - Gloria Gaynor	1979	23	282.0	7.85
210	Jazzman - Carole King	1974	15	282.0	7.85
212	Love's Theme - Love Unlimited Orchestra	1974	17	281.7	7.86
213	Could It Be I'm Falling In Love - Spinners	1973	14	281.6	7.86
213	Dueling Banjos - "Deliverance" Soundtrack	1973	15	281.6	7.86
213	Delta Dawn - Helen Reddy	1973	19	281.6	7.86
216	We're An American Band - Grand Funk	1973	16	280.5	7.89
217	Indiana Wants Me - R. Dean Taylor	1970	15	279.7	7.92
218	Baby Come Back - Player	1978	27	279.6	7.92
219	You Ain't Seen Nothing Yet - Bachman-Turner Overdrive	1974	16	278.3	7.96
220	I'd Love You To Want Me - Lobo	1972	15	277.8	7.98
221	The Night Chicago Died - Paper Lace	1974	17	277.6	7.98
222	Boogie On Reggae Woman - Stevie Wonder	1975	17	277.2	7.99
223	Let's Do It Again - Staple Singers	1975	16	276.6	8.01
224	Sundown - Gordon Lightfoot	1974	17	275.4	8.05
225	The Wreck Of The Edmund Fitzgerald - Gordon Lightfoot	1976	18	274.9	8.07
226	Ramblin' Man - Allman Brothers Band	1973	14	274.7	8.07
227	Hot Child In The City - Nick Gilder	1978	31	274.5	8.08
228	Still - Commodores	1979	19	274.5	8.08
229	Run Joey Run - David Geddes	1975	13	274.5	8.08
230	Kung Fu Fighting - Carl Douglas	1974	18	273.8	8.10
231	The Way We Were - Barbra Streisand	1974	19	273.7	8.11
232	Papa Was A Rollin' Stone - Temptations	1972	14	273.4	8.12
233	Look What You Done For Me - Al Green	1972	14	272.9	8.13
234	Heartbeat - It's A Lovebeat - DeFranco Family	1973	17	271.9	8.16
235	Mr. Jaws - Dickie Goodman	1975	13	271.8	8.17
236	When I Need You - Leo Sayer	1977	21	271.6	8.18
237	Can't Get Enough Of Your Love, Babe - Barry White	1974	14	271.4	8.18
238	Emotion - Samantha Sang	1978	28	271.3	8.19
239	Rhinestone Cowboy - Glen Campbell	1975	23	271.0	8.19
240	Thank God I'm A Country Boy - John Denver	1975	17	270.5	8.21
241	Lean On Me - Bill Withers	1972	18	270.3	8.22
241	Hey There Lonely Girl - Eddie Holman	1970	16	270.3	8.22
243	You're No Good - Linda Ronstadt	1975	15	270.1	8.22
244	No No Song - Ringo Starr	1975	14	269.8	8.23
245	Whole Lotta Love - Led Zeppelin	1970	16	269.8	8.23
245	You Don't Have To Be A Star (To Be In My Show) - Marilyn McCoo & Billy Davis Jr.	1977	24	269.8	8.23

Rank	Title - Act	Pk Yr	Wks	Avg Pts/Wk	Avg Pos
247	**Right Back Where We Started From** - *Maxine Nightingale*	1976	20	268.8	8.27
248	**You Make Me Feel Like Dancing** - *Leo Sayer*	1976	23	268.7	8.27
249	**Keep On Truckin' (Part 1)** - *Eddie Kendricks*	1973	17	268.4	8.28
250	**Pick Up The Pieces** - *Average White Band*	1975	20	268.2	8.29
251	**The Joker** - *Steve Miller Band*	1974	19	268.0	8.29
252	**Hooked On A Feeling** - *Blue Swede*	1974	16	267.9	8.29
253	**Don't It Make My Brown Eyes Blue** - *Crystal Gayle*	1977	27	267.2	8.32
254	**Southern Nights** - *Glen Campbell*	1977	22	266.3	8.35
255	**Puppy Love** - *Donny Osmond*	1972	12	266.3	8.35
256	**Lyin' Eyes** - *Eagles*	1975	13	265.2	8.38
257	**Love Theme From "A Star Is Born" (Evergreen)** - *Barbra Streisand*	1977	25	265.0	8.39
258	**Angie Baby** - *Helen Reddy*	1974	15	264.9	8.39
259	**I'll Be Around** - *Spinners*	1972	16	264.8	8.40
260	**Kiss And Say Goodbye** - *Manhattans*	1976	27	264.7	8.40
261	**Da Doo Ron Ron** - *Shaun Cassidy*	1977	19	264.7	8.40
262	**Knock On Wood** - *Amii Stewart*	1979	22	264.4	8.41
262	**What's Going On** - *Marvin Gaye*	1971	14	264.4	8.41
264	**(If Loving You Is Wrong) I Don't Want To Be Right** - *Luther Ingram*	1972	18	263.7	8.43
265	**Theme From Mahogany (Do You Know Where You're Going To)** - *Diana Ross*	1976	16	262.7	8.46
266	**Love You Inside Out** - *Bee Gees*	1979	14	262.2	8.48
267	**Dream Weaver** - *Gary Wright*	1976	21	262.2	8.48
268	**Rock The Boat** - *Hues Corporation*	1974	18	261.9	8.49
269	**Brother Louie** - *Stories*	1973	19	261.7	8.49
270	**If I Can't Have You** - *Yvonne Elliman*	1978	21	261.0	8.52
270	**Pillow Talk** - *Sylvia*	1973	16	261.0	8.52
272	**(Your Love Has Lifted Me) Higher And Higher** - *Rita Coolidge*	1977	24	260.5	8.53
273	**Cherish** - *David Cassidy*	1972	15	260.5	8.53
274	**Too Much, Too Little, Too Late** - *Johnny Mathis/Deniece Williams*	1978	21	260.5	8.53
275	**Jackie Blue** - *Ozark Mountain Daredevils*	1975	19	259.3	8.57
276	**Top Of The World** - *Carpenters*	1973	19	259.1	8.58
277	**Got To Give It Up Pt. I** - *Marvin Gaye*	1977	19	257.3	8.63
278	**Fire** - *Ohio Players*	1975	16	256.9	8.65
279	**The Hustle** - *Van Mc Coy*	1975	19	256.8	8.65
280	**I'm Your Boogie Man** - *K.C. & The Sunshine Band*	1977	22	256.0	8.68
281	**I'm In You** - *Peter Frampton*	1977	17	255.5	8.69
282	**Sir Duke** - *Stevie Wonder*	1977	16	255.5	8.69
283	**You Should Be Dancing** - *Bee Gees*	1976	20	255.2	8.70
284	**(Shake, Shake, Shake) Shake Your Booty** - *K.C. & The Sunshine Band*	1976	21	254.9	8.71
285	**They Just Can't Stop It the (Games People Play)** - *Spinners*	1975	19	254.7	8.72
286	**Sunshine On My Shoulders** - *John Denver*	1974	18	254.7	8.72
287	**Love Rollercoaster** - *Ohio Players*	1976	18	254.3	8.73
288	**Dreams** - *Fleetwood Mac*	1977	20	254.3	8.73
289	**Spill The Wine** - *Eric Burdon & War*	1970	19	254.2	8.74
290	**You're The One That I Want** - *John Travolta And Olivia Newton-John*	1978	25	254.2	8.74
291	**Daniel** - *Elton John*	1973	15	254.0	8.74
292	**Let 'Em In** - *Wings*	1976	18	253.6	8.76
293	**You Make Me Feel Brand New** - *Stylistics*	1974	19	253.4	8.76
294	**Rock Me Gently** - *Andy Kim*	1974	19	253.0	8.77
295	**Also Sprach Zarathustra (2001)** - *Deodato*	1973	12	252.4	8.79
296	**Kodachrome** - *Paul Simon*	1973	13	251.8	8.81
297	**Back Stabbers** - *O'Jays*	1972	17	251.1	8.83
298	**Love Will Keep Us Together** - *Captain & Tennille*	1975	21	251.1	8.84
299	**Troglodyte (Cave Man)** - *Jimmy Castor Bunch*	1972	14	250.7	8.85
300	**Ain't No Woman (Like The One I've Got)** - *Four Tops*	1973	15	250.4	8.86

Records Charting Only on the Cash Box Top 100

No.	Title - Act	Peak Date	Peak
	1970		
1	Merry Christmas Darling - Carpenters	26-Dec-70	41
2	Santa Claus Is Comin' To Town Jackson 5	26-Dec-70	51
3	Goin' Home (Sing A Song Of Christmas Cheer - Bobby Sherman	26-Dec-70	70
4	Feliz Navidad - Jose Feliciano	26-Dec-70	71
5	Dig The Way I Feel - Mary Wells	7-Feb-70	80
6	Kools Back Again - Kool & The Gang	24-Jan-70	80
7	Some Things A Man's Gotta Do Shango	1-Aug-70	90
8	Just About The Same - Association	14-Mar-70	91
9	Endlessly - Sonny James	24-Oct-70	91
10	Holly Go Softly - Cornerstone	11-Apr-70	92
11	Gone Movin' On - Raiders	2-May-70	92
12	Come On Down - Savage Grace	25-Jul-70	92
13	Stealing Moments From Another Woman's Life - Glass House	12-Dec-70	92
14	Battle Of New Orleans - Bert Sommer	19-Dec-70	93
15	Santo Domingo - Sandpipers	12-Sep-70	94
16	Freight Train - Duane Eddy	17-Jan-70	95
17	Chestnut Mare - Byrds	28-Nov-70	95
18	Special Memory - Jerry Butler	7-Nov-70	96
19	You Know How It Is With A Woman Jefferson	9-May-70	96
20	Can't Stop Lovin' You - Flirtations	11-Jul-70	96
21	Birds Of All Nations George McCannon III	16-May-70	97
22	My Woman, My Woman, My Wife Dean Martin	15-Aug-70	97
23	To The Other Man - Luther Ingram	17-Oct-70	97
24	Odyssey Rock Park - Al Capps Band	10-Oct-70	97
25	Summertime Billy Hemmans & Clays Composite	21-Nov-70	97
26	Don't Get Close Little Anthony & The Imperials	28-Feb-70	98
27	Will You Love Me Tomorrow? Linda Ronstadt	4-Apr-70	98
28	Something In You – Manitoba	28-Nov-70	98
29	Detroit City - Dean Martin	24-Oct-70	99
30	Stealing Love - The Emotions	11-Apr-70	100
	1971		
1	Glory, Glory - Byrds	25-Sep-71	65
2	Nobody (Tellin' Me 'Bout My Baby) Charles Wright And The Watts 103rd Street Rhythm Band	31-Jul-71	81
3	California Blues - Redwing	1-May-71	83
4	90 Day Freeze (On Her Love) 100 Proof Aged In Soul	13-Nov-71	83
5	Pray For Me - Intruders	17-Jul-71	88
6	I Can't Help It - Moments	17-Apr-71	90
7	Plain And Simple Girl - Garland Green	24-Apr-71	90
8	If It's Good To You (It's Good For You) Flaming Ember	20-Nov-71	91
9	Never Marry A Railroad Man Shocking Blue	6-Feb-71	93
10	Go On Fool - Marion Black	13-Mar-71	93
11	You're A Lady - Gene Chandler	3-Jul-71	93
12	Goodbye Media Man (Part 1) Tom Fogerty	14-Aug-71	93
13	Standing Here Wondering Which Way To Go - Marion Williams	27-Feb-71	93
14	Who's Gonna Take The Weight (Part One) - Kool & The Gang	16-Jan-71	94
15	Awaiting On You All - Silver Hawk	29-May-71	94
16	Funky - Chambers Brothers	27-Feb-71	96
17	I Really Love You - Davy Jones	30-Oct-71	96
18	Funky L.A. - Paul Humphrey & His Cool Aid Chemists	24-Jul-71	97
19	Stop The World And Let Me Off Flaming Ember	27-Feb-71	98
20	(Until Then) I'll Suffer - Barbara Lynn	21-Aug-71	98
21	Michigan Harry Slaughter Wadsworth Mansion	24-Apr-71	99
22	Faithful And True - Z.Z. Hill	17-Jul-71	99
23	Leave My Man (Woman) Alone Raeletts	4-Sep-71	99
24	Louisiana Lady New Riders Of The Purple Sage	30-Oct-71	100
25	In And Out Of My Life Martha Reeves & The Vandellas	18-Mar-72	70
	1972		
1	Jingle Bells - Singing Dogs	1-Jan-72	72
2	Don't Take My Kindness For Weakness Soul Children	26-Aug-72	73
3	I'll Play The Blues For You - Albert King	12-Aug-72	73
4	Good Friends? - Poppy Family	4-Mar-72	74
5	We Got To Have Peace - Curtis Mayfield	11-Mar-72	81
6	Tragedy - Argent	2-Dec-72	81
7	Endlessly - Mavis Staples	21-Oct-72	85
8	Home Is Where The Hatred Is Esther Phillips	13-May-72	86
9	Why Not Start All Over Again - Counts	25-Mar-72	89
10	I Can Feel You - Addrisi Brothers	17-Jun-72	90
11	Got Pleasure - Ohio Players	1-Jul-72	90
12	Yankee Lady - Brewer And Shipley	29-Jul-72	90
13	Memphis At Sunrise - Bar-Kays	4-Nov-72	90
14	His Song Shall Be Sung - Lou Rawls	26-Feb-72	93
15	Soulsville - Isaac Hayes	6-May-72	94
16	Slipping Into Christmas - Leon Russell	9-Dec-72	94
17	You And I - Black Ivory	6-May-72	95
18	Holy Cow - Stefan	4-Nov-72	96
19	Darling Baby - Jackie Moore	15-Apr-72	97
20	Tryin' To Stay 'live - Asylum Choir	5-Feb-72	98
21	Where Are You - Cat Stevens	29-Jan-72	98
22	I Refuse To Smile - Mandrill	1-Jul-72	100
	1973		
1	Sorrow - David Bowie	22-Dec-73	69
2	You Don't Know What Love Is Susan Jacks	19-May-73	70
3	All The Way Down - Etta James	10-Nov-73	70
4	I've Never Found A Man (To Love Me Like You Do) - Esther Phillips	27-Jan-73	72
5	Think It Over - Delfonics	10-Feb-73	75
6	Take Life A Little Easier Rodney Allen Rippy	3-Nov-73	75

No.	Title - Act	Peak Date	Peak
7	Walking On Back - *Edward Bear*	8-Sep-73	77
8	Gypsy - *Abraham's Children*	17-Mar-73	78
9	Breakaway - *Millie Jackson*	5-May-73	80
10	Joyful Resurrection - *Tom Fogerty*	6-Oct-73	84
11	The Day That Curly Billy Shot Down Crazy Sam McGee - *Hollies*	17-Nov-73	86
12	Summer In The City - *Quincy Jones*	8-Sep-73	87
13	I'm The Midnight Special *Clarence Carter*	22-Dec-73	87
14	Everybody But Me - *G.W. Kenny*	8-Sep-73	89
15	Roller Coaster - *Blood, Sweat & Tears*	3-Nov-73	90
16	Keep Me In Mind - *Lynn Anderson*	3-Mar-73	91
17	Daydream - *David Cassidy*	25-Aug-73	91
18	Stormy Monday - *Latimore*	22-Dec-73	92
19	Who Gets Your Love - *Dusty Springfield*	31-Mar-73	93
20	Bra - *Cymande*	9-Jun-73	93
21	Let There Be Drums *Incredible Bongo Band*	17-Nov-73	93
22	You'll Never Walk Alone - *Blue Haze*	23-Jun-73	93
23	You Don't Owe Me - *Blue Ridge Rangers*	13-Oct-73	93
24	Calico - *Tommy James*	27-Oct-73	94
25	If That's The Way You Want It *Diamond Head*	26-May-73	95
26	Trying To Slip (Away) - *Lloyd Price*	8-Sep-73	95
27	Instigating (Trouble Making Fool) *Whatnauts*	19-May-73	96
28	What It Takes To Get A Good Woman (That's What It's Gonna Take To Keep Her) - *Denise Lasalle*	19-May-73	97
29	We Can't Dance To Your Music *Grass Roots*	15-Dec-73	97
30	Friends Or Lovers - *Act I*	31-Mar-73	99
31	Love Music - *Sergio Mendes & Brasil '77*	19-May-73	99
32	Should I Tie A Yellow Ribbon Round The Ole Oak Tree? The Answer *Connie Francis*	14-Jul-73	99
33	Sha La Boom Boom - *Bobby Bloom*	3-Feb-73	100
34	Why Do Fools Fall In Love *Summer Wine*	24-Feb-73	100
35	Bad, Bold And Beautiful Girl *Persuaders*	2-Jun-73	100
36	I Just Can't Turn My Habit Into Love *Buckwheat*	19-May-73	100
37	Make My Life A Little Bit Brighter *Chester*	1-Sep-73	100

1974

No.	Title - Act	Peak Date	Peak
1	Postcard - *Who*	14-Dec-74	64
2	Inspiration - *Paul Williams*	19-Jan-74	69
3	Traveling Boy - *Garfunkel*	20-Apr-74	70
4	Us And Them - *Pink Floyd*	9-Mar-74	72
5	Something There Is About You *Bob Dylan*	11-May-74	76
6	As Soon As I Hang Up The Phone *Loretta Lynn/Conway Twitty*	14-Sep-74	81
7	Lady Lay - *Wayne Newton*	30-Nov-74	83
8	Everybody Needs A Rainbow *Ray Stevens*	14-Dec-74	83
9	Steam Heat - *Pointer Sisters*	13-Apr-74	84
10	The Wall Street Shuffle - *10 C. C.*	3-Aug-74	84
11	Careful Man - *John Edwards*	30-Nov-74	86
12	What Made America Famous *Harry Chapin*	13-Jul-74	87
13	Apple Of My Eye - *Badfinger*	2-Feb-74	88
14	If - *Telly Savalas*	14-Dec-74	89
15	48 Crash - *Suzi Quatro*	11-May-74	90
16	Don't Mess Up A Good Thing *Gregg Allman*	27-Apr-74	91
17	I Can Stand A Little Rain - *Joe Cocker*	2-Nov-74	91
18	Warmin' Up The Band - *Don Everly*	20-Jul-74	92
19	Carrie's Gone - *J.C. Stone*	19-Oct-74	92
20	Harlem - *5th Dimension*	7-Dec-74	92
21	Willie Pass The Water - *Ripple*	9-Mar-74	94
22	Nice To Be Around *Maureen McGovern*	23-Feb-74	96
23	1984 - *David Bowie*	7-Sep-74	96
24	What Do You Know About Love *Apple & Appleberry*	20-Apr-74	97
25	The Sound Of Silence - *Paul Simon*	18-May-74	97
26	Another Love - *Ian Lloyd & Stories*	31-Aug-74	98
27	Reach Out I'll Be There - *New Seekers*	19-Jan-74	99
28	Dancing In The Street - *Dovells*	10-Aug-74	100
29	He Did Me Wrong, But He Did It Right *Patti Dahlstrom*	12-Oct-74	100

1975

No.	Title - Act	Peak Date	Peak
1	Skating Away On The Thin Ice Of The New Day - *Jethro Tull*	22-Mar-75	75
2	Touch The Hand - *Conway Twitty*	12-Jul-75	75
3	Midnight Show - *Bobby Vinton*	11-Oct-75	78
4	Birmingham Blues *Charlie Daniels Band*	6-Dec-75	79
5	Harpo's Blues - *Phoebe Snow*	7-Jun-75	81
6	Christina - *Terry Jacks*	28-Jun-75	83
7	Guava Jelly - *Barbra Streisand*	18-Jan-75	83
8	Sorry Doesn't Always Make It Right *Diana Ross*	5-Apr-75	84
9	Should Anybody Ask - *Garry Bonner*	25-Jan-75	85
10	Step By Step - *Kiki Dee Band*	15-Mar-75	85
11	Givin' It All Up - *J. Geils Band*	1-Mar-75	86
12	Too Late To Worry, Too Blue To Cry *Ronnie Milsap*	10-May-75	87
13	This Is What You Mean To Me *Engelbert Humperdinck*	6-Dec-75	87
14	Seems Like I Can't Live With You, But I Can't Live Without You - *Guess Who*	24-May-75	88
15	The House On Telegraph Hill *Bo Donaldson And The Heywoods*	19-Apr-75	89
16	Keep Yourself Alive - *Queen*	30-Aug-75	89
17	What's Come Over Me *Margie Joseph & Blue Magic*	13-Dec-75	89
18	Bad Sneakers - *Steely Dan*	20-Sep-75	90
19	Ce Soir - *Golden Earring*	29-Mar-75	90
20	Big Noise From Winnetka *Spaghetti Head*	31-May-75	90
21	All Over Me - *Charlie Rich*	27-Sep-75	90
22	The Man On Page 602 - *Zoot Fenster*	6-Dec-75	91
23	You Can't Do It Right (With The One You Love) - *Deep Purple*	4-Jan-75	93
24	Wolfman Jack - *Todd Rundgren*	25-Jan-75	94
25	Midnight Show - *Ron Dante*	8-Mar-75	94
26	You Are You - *Gilbert O'Sullivan*	22-Feb-75	95
27	Clap Your Hands - *Manhattan Transfer*	16-Aug-75	95
28	Sneakin' Sally Through The Alley *Robert Palmer*	2-Aug-75	96
29	A Pirate Looks At Forty - *Jimmy Buffett*	19-Apr-75	97
30	Castles In The Sand - *Seals & Crofts*	20-Sep-75	97
31	In The Winter - *Janis Ian*	13-Dec-75	97
32	No Love In The Room - *5th Dimension*	22-Feb-75	99

No.	Title - Act	Peak Date	Peak
	1976		
1	I'm Your Man Rock 'N' Roll - Tarney/Spencer Band	21-Aug-76	71
2	(Ain't Nothin' But A) House Party - J. Geils Band	28-Aug-76	77
3	She's A Disco Queen - Oliver Sain	27-Mar-76	78
4	America, The Beautiful - Charlie Rich	29-May-76	78
5	Colorado Call - Shad O'Shea & The 18 Wheelers	27-Mar-76	79
6	Good Night & Good Morning - Jim Capaldi	6-Nov-76	81
7	(What A) Wonderful World - Johnny Nash	22-May-76	82
8	I Got Over Love - Major Harris	31-Jan-76	86
9	Give Me An Inch Girl - Robert Palmer	13-Mar-76	88
10	Julie Ann – Ginger	16-Oct-76	89
11	You Know The Feelin' - Steve Wightman	29-May-76	90
12	You - Aretha Franklin	31-Jan-76	90
13	Hard Times - Peter Skellern	7-Feb-76	90
14	Boomerang - Frankie Valli	30-Oct-76	90
15	Fanny (Be Tender With My Love) - Gino Cunico	3-Jan-76	91
16	Dancin' Thru The Night - L.A. Jets	3-Jul-76	91
17	One Woman Band - Carol Chase	17-Jan-76	92
18	Midnight Love Affair - Tony Orlando And Dawn	29-May-76	93
19	Sharing The Night Together - Arthur Alexander	12-Jun-76	94
20	Goodnight And Goodmorning - Cecilio & Kapono	24-Jan-76	95
21	You Are My Love - Liverpool Express	9-Oct-76	96
22	We Both Need Each Other - Norman Connors	28-Aug-76	98
23	Forever And Ever – Slik	8-May-76	98
24	Sharing The Night Together - Lenny Le Blanc	12-Jun-76	99
	1977		
1	Love Gone By - Dan Fogelberg	20-Aug-77	75
2	Yu-Ma/Go Away Little Boy - Marlena Shaw	25-Jun-77	76
3	Enjoy And Get It On - ZZ Top	11-Jun-77	82
4	(I've Been Lookin' For) A New Way To Say I Love You – Driver	17-Sep-77	83
5	Heaven On The Seventh Floor - Mighty Pope	27-Aug-77	83
6	I Can't Get Over You – Dramatics	25-Jun-77	84
7	Saved By The Grace Of Your Love - Sons Of Champlin	9-Jul-77	89
8	High On Love - Elliott Randall	21-May-77	91
9	Every Little Teardrop – Gallagher & Lyle	2-Apr-77	92
10	I Love My Wife - Frank Sinatra	22-Jan-77	92
11	Something Better – Chilliwack	3-Sep-77	92
12	Dancing In The Moonlight (It's Caught Me In Its Spotlight) - Thin Lizzy	29-Oct-77	92
13	Take Me Home - Balcones Fault	20-Aug-77	93
14	Too Hot To Handle – UFO	3-Sep-77	94
15	Rollin' With The Flow - Charlie Rich	24-Sep-77	94
16	Spanish Wine - Lou Christie	18-Jun-77	95
17	Midnight Love Affair - Carol Douglas	15-Jan-77	96
18	Theme From "Baa Baa Black Sheep" - Mike Post	9-Apr-77	96
19	Secrets - Sutherland Brothers & Quiver	29-Jan-77	97
20	Keep That Same Old Feeling - Side Effect	11-Jun-77	98
21	Some Broken Hearts Never Mend - Don Williams	28-May-77	99
22	School's Back – Philadelphia	22-Oct-77	99
23	Shake A Leg - Sea Level	18-Jun-77	100
	1978		
1	Just One Minute More - Mike Finnigan	15-Jul-78	84
2	Isn't It Always Love - Karla Bonoff	6-May-78	85
3	All The Way Lover - Millie Jackson	29-Apr-78	88
4	Ocean Of Thoughts And Dreams - Dramatics	29-Apr-78	89
5	Shout It Out - B.T. Express	4-Mar-78	89
6	Give A Little - Robert John	13-May-78	89
7	Let's Have Some Fun - Bar-Kays	4-Mar-78	91
8	Walk Right Back - Anne Murray	1-Apr-78	92
9	Take It Off The Top - Dixie Dregs	24-Jun-78	92
10	This Magic Moment - Richie Furay	1-Jul-78	92
11	25th Of Last December - Roberta Flack	14-Jan-78	92
12	Down The Road - B.T.O.	15-Apr-78	92
13	Oh Atlanta - Little Feat	27-May-78	92
14	Do I Love You (Yes In Every Way) - Donna Fargo	25-Mar-78	94
15	Lady Blue - George Benson	29-Jul-78	94
16	Tulsa Time - Don Williams	9-Dec-78	96
17	All I Wanna Do – Doucette	28-Oct-78	97
	1979		
1	Tranquillo - Carly Simon	20-Jan-79	86
2	Love Is For The Best In Us - James Walsh Gypsy Band	26-May-79	91
3	Nobody – Doucette	11-Aug-79	91
4	Easy Way Out - Roy Orbison	7-Jul-79	92
5	Don't Throw Our Love Away - Orleans	18-Aug-79	92
6	Baby Fat - Robert Byrne	23-Jun-79	93
7	Unloved - Walter Egan	17-Mar-79	93
8	We All Need Love – Troiano	7-Jul-79	93
9	Anybody Wanna Party? - Gloria Gaynor	14-Jul-79	94
10	Take It Any Way You Want It - Outlaws	13-Jan-79	94
11	After The First One - Yonah	15-Sep-79	97

The No. 1s

Title - Act	'70s Rank	Year
Eight Weeks		
You Light Up My Life - *Debby Boone*	1	1977
Night Fever - *Bee Gees*	9	1978
Seven Weeks		
Le Freak - *Chic*	5	1978
Six Weeks		
Joy To The World - *Three Dog Night*	2	1971
Shadow Dancing - *Andy Gibb*	4	1978
My Sharona - *Knack*	17	1979
Five Weeks		
Tonight's The Night (Gonna Be Alright) *Rod Stewart*	46	1976
Da Ya Think I'm Sexy? - *Rod Stewart*	21	1979
Four Weeks		
My Sweet Lord - *George Harrison*	14	1970
Bridge Over Troubled Water - *Simon & Garfunkel*	27	1970
Let It Be - *Beatles*	28	1970
Family Affair - *Sly & The Family Stone*	30	1971
It's Too Late - *Carole King*	31	1971
One Bad Apple - *Osmonds*	35	1971
American Pie - *Don McLean*	3	1972
The First Time Ever I Saw Your Face *Roberta Flack*	23	1972
My Love - *Paul McCartney & Wings*	33	1973
Afternoon Delight - *Starland Vocal Band*	16	1976
How Deep Is Your Love - *Bee Gees*	22	1977
Stayin' Alive - *Bee Gees*	19	1978
Three Times A Lady - *Commodores*	48	1978
Reunited - *Peaches & Herb*	52	1979
Hot Stuff - *Donna Summer*	98	1979
Three Weeks		
I Think I Love You - *Partridge Family*	12	1970
Venus - *Shocking Blue*	15	1970
Maggie May - *Rod Stewart*	8	1971
How Can You Mend A Broken Heart - *Bee Gees*	42	1971
Alone Again (Naturally) - *Gilbert O'Sullivan*	11	1972
A Horse With No Name - *America*	75	1972
Tie A Yellow Ribbon Round The Ole Oak Tree *Dawn*	20	1973
Killing Me Softly With His Song - *Roberta Flack*	90	1973
That's The Way (I Like It) *K.C. & The Sunshine Band*	94	1975
Convoy - *C.W. McCall*	65	1976
50 Ways To Leave Your Lover - *Paul Simon*	91	1976
Don't Go Breaking My Heart *Elton John & Kiki Dee*	140	1976
Torn Between Two Lovers - *Mary MacGregor*	37	1977
I Just Want To Be Your Everything - *Andy Gibb*	54	1977
Love Theme From "A Star Is Born" (Evergreen) *Barbra Streisand*	139	1977

Title - Act	'70s Rank	Year
Best Of My Love - *Emotions*	164	1977
When I Need You - *Leo Sayer*	283	1977
Hot Child In The City - *Nick Gilder*	40	1978
Boogie Oogie Oogie - *Taste Of Honey*	63	1978
You Don't Bring Me Flowers - *Barbra & Neil*	81	1978
Bad Girls - *Donna Summer*	43	1979
Ring My Bell - *Anita Ward*	57	1979
Escape (The Pina Colada Song) - *Rupert Holmes*	73	1979
Tragedy - *Bee Gees*	160	1979
Babe - *Styx*	216	1979
Two Weeks		
I'll Be There - *Jackson 5*	6	1970
Raindrops Keep Fallin' On My Head - *B.J. Thomas*	7	1970
Spirit In The Sky - *Norman Greenbaum*	25	1970
American Woman - *Guess Who*	47	1970
War - *Edwin Starr*	50	1970
(They Long To Be) Close To You - *Carpenters*	60	1970
Mama Told Me (Not To Come) - *Three Dog Night*	93	1970
The Love You Save - *Jackson 5*	135	1970
The Long And Winding Road - *Beatles*	129	1970
Knock Three Times - *Dawn*	13	1971
Brand New Key - *Melanie*	26	1971
Theme From Shaft - *Isaac Hayes*	32	1971
Gypsys, Tramps & Thieves - *Cher*	51	1971
Want Ads - *Honey Cone*	105	1971
Let's Stay Together - *Al Green*	24	1972
Without You - *Nilsson*	53	1972
Me And Mrs. Jones - *Billy Paul*	55	1972
My Ding-A-Ling - *Chuck Berry*	107	1972
Lean On Me - *Bill Withers*	138	1972
I'll Take You There - *Staple Singers*	196	1972
Crocodile Rock - *Elton John*	36	1973
You're So Vain - *Carly Simon*	58	1973
Superstition - *Stevie Wonder*	108	1973
Delta Dawn - *Helen Reddy*	122	1973
The Most Beautiful Girl - *Charlie Rich*	219	1973
Give Me Love (Give Me Peace On Earth) *George Harrison*	252	1973
I Honestly Love You - *Olivia Newton-John*	102	1974
Seasons In The Sun - *Terry Jacks*	161	1974
TSOP (The Sound Of Philadelphia) - *MFSB*	175	1974
Band On The Run - *Paul McCartney & Wings*	280	1974
Philadelphia Freedom - *Elton John Band*	82	1975
Island Girl - *Elton John*	121	1975
Bad Blood - *Neil Sedaka*	133	1975
Love Will Keep Us Together - *Captain & Tennille*	137	1975
Jackie Blue - *Ozark Mountain Daredevils*	188	1975
Get Down Tonight - *K.C. & Sunshine Band*	310	1975
Silly Love Songs - *Wings*	34	1976

Title - Act	'70s Rank	Year
Kiss And Say Goodbye - *Manhattans*	74	1976
Disco Duck (Part 1) - *Rick Dees & His Cast Of Idiots*	96	1976
Welcome Back - *John Sebastian*	112	1976
Disco Lady - *Johnnie Taylor*	143	1976
Play That Funky Music - *Wild Cherry*	151	1976
Don't It Make My Brown Eyes Blue - *Crystal Gayle*	101	1977
Star Wars Theme/Cantina Band - *Meco*	123	1977
You Don't Have To Be A Star (To Be In My Show) - *Marilyn McCoo & Billy Davis Jr.*	159	1977
Rich Girl - *Daryl Hall & John Oates*	198	1977
Da Doo Ron Ron - *Shaun Cassidy*	361	1977
Car Wash - *Rose Royce*	386	1977
Kiss You All Over - *Exile*	18	1978
Baker Street - *Gerry Rafferty*	45	1978
Baby Come Back - *Player*	70	1978
Miss You - *Rolling Stones*	83	1978
Mac Arthur Park - *Donna Summer*	128	1978
With A Little Luck - *Wings*	273	1978
Sad Eyes - *Robert John*	95	1979
What A Fool Believes - *Doobie Brothers*	86	1979
Rise - *Herb Alpert*	204	1979

One Week

Title - Act	'70s Rank	Year
ABC - *Jackson 5*	10	1970
I Want You Back - *Jackson 5*	38	1970
The Tears Of A Clown - *Smokey Robinson & The Miracles*	39	1970
Thank You (Falettinme Be Mice Elf Agin) - *Sly & The Family Stone*	80	1970
Make It With You - *Bread*	89	1970
We've Only Just Begun - *Carpenters*	99	1970
Ain't No Mountain High Enough - *Diana Ross*	103	1970
Spill The Wine - *Eric Burdon And War*	118	1970
Ball Of Confusion (That's What The World Is Today) - *Temptations*	119	1970
Signed, Sealed, Delivered I'm Yours - *Stevie Wonder*	145	1970
Cracklin' Rosie - *Neil Diamond*	152	1970
Lookin' Out My Back Door - *Creedence Clearwater Revival*	163	1970
Indiana Wants Me - *R. Dean Taylor*	187	1970
Patches - *Clarence Carter*	193	1970
Candida - *Dawn*	242	1970
Everything Is Beautiful - *Ray Stevens*	341	1970
Cecilia - *Simon & Garfunkel*	352	1970
Never Can Say Goodbye - *Jackson 5*	41	1971
Indian Reservation (The Lament Of The Cherokee) - *Raiders*	49	1971
Rose Garden - *Lynn Anderson*	56	1971
She's A Lady - *Tom Jones*	71	1971
Go Away Little Girl - *Donny Osmond*	72	1971
Just My Imagination (Running Away With Me) - *Temptations*	79	1971
Take Me Home, Country Roads - *John Denver*	100	1971
You've Got A Friend - *James Taylor*	113	1971

Title - Act	'70s Rank	Year
Doesn't Somebody Want To Be Wanted - *Partridge Family*	114	1971
Don't Pull Your Love - *Hamilton, Joe Frank & Reynolds*	116	1971
Mama's Pearl - *Jackson 5*	179	1971
Smiling Faces Sometimes - *Undisputed Truth*	206	1971
It Don't Come Easy - *Ringo Starr*	218	1971
Uncle Albert/Admiral Halsey - *Paul & Linda McCartney*	241	1971
What's Going On - *Marvin Gaye*	311	1971
Lonely Days - *Bee Gees*	319	1971
Spanish Harlem - *Aretha Franklin*	371	1971
Rockin' Robin - *Michael Jackson*	44	1972
Brandy (You're A Fine Girl) - *Looking Glass*	62	1972
Heart Of Gold - *Neil Young*	87	1972
Got To Be There - *Michael Jackson*	115	1972
Daddy Don't You Walk So Fast - *Wayne Newton*	131	1972
I Am Woman - *Helen Reddy*	132	1972
Oh Girl - *Chi-Lites*	149	1972
The Candy Man - *Sammy Davis, Jr.*	155	1972
Long Cool Woman (In A Black Dress) - *Hollies*	158	1972
Nice To Be With You - *Gallery*	170	1972
Burning Love - *Elvis Presley*	173	1972
Too Late To Turn Back Now - *Cornelius Brothers & Sister Rose*	191	1972
I Can See Clearly Now - *Johnny Nash*	199	1972
Precious And Few - *Climax*	201	1972
I'm Still In Love With You - *Al Green*	207	1972
Baby Don't Get Hooked On Me - *Mac Davis*	223	1972
Everybody Plays The Fool - *Main Ingredient*	225	1972
Back Stabbers - *O'Jays*	238	1972
Song Sung Blue - *Neil Diamond*	239	1972
I'll Be Around - *Spinners*	251	1972
Black And White - *Three Dog Night*	267	1972
I'd Love You To Want Me - *Lobo*	287	1972
Outa-Space - *Billy Preston*	317	1972
Nights In White Satin - *Moody Blues*	347	1972
Papa Was A Rollin' Stone - *Temptations*	348	1972
Sylvia's Mother - *Dr. Hook & The Medicine Show*	380	1972
Let's Get It On - *Marvin Gaye*	67	1973
Love Train - *O'Jays*	76	1973
Half-Breed - *Cher*	92	1973
The Night The Lights Went Out In Georgia - *Vicki Lawrence*	124	1973
Photograph - *Ringo Starr*	166	1973
Brother Louie - *Stories*	167	1973
Midnight Train To Georgia - *Gladys Knight & The Pips*	168	1973
Frankenstein - *Edgar Winter Group*	172	1973
Top Of The World - *Carpenters*	174	1973
Bad, Bad Leroy Brown - *Jim Croce*	192	1973
Heartbeat - It's A Lovebeat - *DeFranco Family Featuring Tony DeFranco*	212	1973
Will It Go Round In Circles - *Billy Preston*	213	1973

Title - Act	'70s Rank	Year
Keep On Truckin' (Part 1) - Eddie Kendricks	226	1973
We're An American Band - Grand Funk	243	1973
Angie - Rolling Stones	253	1973
Shambala - Three Dog Night	256	1973
Live And Let Die - Wings	259	1973
Dueling Banjos - "Deliverance" Soundtrack	262	1973
Loves Me Like A Rock - Paul Simon	269	1973
Touch Me In The Morning - Diana Ross	274	1973
Goodbye Yellow Brick Road - Elton John	289	1973
Neither One Of Us (Wants To Be The First To Say Goodbye) - Gladys Knight & The Pips	313	1973
Could It Be I'm Falling In Love - Spinners	321	1973
Yesterday Once More - Carpenters	329	1973
Oh, Babe, What Would You Say? - Hurricane Smith	338	1973
Ain't No Woman (Like The One I've Got) - Four Tops	360	1973
Ramblin' Man - Allman Brothers Band	364	1973
Higher Ground - Stevie Wonder	375	1973
Just You 'N' Me - Chicago	388	1973
You Are The Sunshine Of My Life - Stevie Wonder	439	1973
Show And Tell - Al Wilson	120	1974
The Streak - Ray Stevens	141	1974
The Way We Were - Barbra Streisand	162	1974
The Joker - Steve Miller Band	169	1974
Kung Fu Fighting - Carl Douglas	178	1974
(You're) Having My Baby - Paul Anka	183	1974
The Entertainer - Marvin Hamlisch	208	1974
Bennie And The Jets - Elton John	209	1974
The Loco-Motion - Grand Funk	211	1974
Annie's Song - John Denver	215	1974
You Make Me Feel Brand New - Stylistics	221	1974
Love's Theme - Love Unlimited Orchestra	224	1974
Boogie Down - Eddie Kendricks	233	1974
Rock Me Gently - Andy Kim	240	1974
Sundown - Gordon Lightfoot	246	1974
I Shot The Sheriff - Eric Clapton	248	1974
Rock The Boat - Hues Corporation	254	1974
Sunshine On My Shoulders - John Denver	257	1974
Billy, Don't Be A Hero - Bo Donaldson And The Heywoods	258	1974
The Night Chicago Died - Paper Lace	260	1974
Leave Me Alone (Ruby Red Dress) - Helen Reddy	265	1974
Time In A Bottle - Jim Croce	268	1974
You Ain't Seen Nothing Yet - Bachman-Turner Overdrive	284	1974
You're Sixteen - Ringo Starr	290	1974
Cat's In The Cradle - Harry Chapin	293	1974
You Haven't Done Nothin' - Stevie Wonder	299	1974
Nothing From Nothing - Billy Preston	308	1974
Hooked On A Feeling - Blue Swede	316	1974
I Can Help - Billy Swan	320	1974
Jazzman - Carole King	328	1974
Don't Let The Sun Go Down On Me - Elton John	331	1974
Rock On - David Essex	334	1974
Angie Baby - Helen Reddy	349	1974
Dancing Machine - Jackson 5	366	1974
Rock Your Baby - George McCrae	367	1974
Whatever Gets You Thru The Night - John Lennon	374	1974
Can't Get Enough - Bad Company	389	1974
Americans - Byron MacGregor	390	1974
Then Came You - Dionne Warwicke & Spinners	400	1974
Can't Get Enough Of Your Love, Babe - Barry White	404	1974
Tell Me Something Good - Rufus	433	1974
When Will I See You Again - Three Degrees	441	1974
Feel Like Makin' Love - Roberta Flack	455	1974
The Show Must Go On - Three Dog Night	468	1974
Jive Talkin' - Bee Gees	64	1975
Rhinestone Cowboy - Glen Campbell	68	1975
Fly, Robin, Fly - Silver Convention	97	1975
Have You Never Been Mellow - Olivia Newton-John	110	1975
Lovin' You - Minnie Riperton	125	1975
Pick Up The Pieces - Average White Band	130	1975
Lady Marmalade - Labelle	134	1975
My Eyes Adored You - Frankie Valli	146	1975
Mandy - Barry Manilow	176	1975
Shining Star - Earth, Wind & Fire	181	1975
The Hustle - Van McCoy & The Soul City Symphony	182	1975
One Of These Nights - Eagles	186	1975
Fame - David Bowie	197	1975
Saturday Night - Bay City Rollers	205	1975
Laughter In The Rain - Neil Sedaka	217	1975
Thank God I'm A Country Boy - John Denver	227	1975
Please Mr. Postman - Carpenters	228	1975
Boogie On Reggae Woman - Stevie Wonder	232	1975
At Seventeen - Janis Ian	249	1975
How Long - Ace	270	1975
Please Mr. Please - Olivia Newton-John	272	1975
Before The Next Teardrop Falls - Freddy Fender	286	1975
You're The First, The Last, My Everything - Barry White	294	1975
I'm Sorry - John Denver	298	1975
Let's Do It Again - Staple Singers	300	1975
Listen To What The Man Said - Wings	305	1975
Lucy In The Sky With Diamonds - Elton John	312	1975
Fire - Ohio Players	332	1975
Fallin' In Love - Hamilton, Joe Frank & Reynolds	335	1975
When Will I Be Loved - Linda Ronstadt	339	1975
He Don't Love You (Like I Love You) - Tony Orlando & Dawn	340	1975
Someone Saved My Life Tonight - Elton John	346	1975
You're No Good - Linda Ronstadt	351	1975
(Hey Won't You Play) Another Somebody Done Somebody Wrong Song - B.J. Thomas	362	1975

Title - Act	'70s Rank	Year
No No Song - Ringo Starr	393	1975
Run Joey Run - David Geddes	411	1975
Mr. Jaws - Dickie Goodman	412	1975
I Write The Songs - Barry Manilow	29	1976
A Fifth Of Beethoven Walter Murphy & The Big Apple Band	84	1976
Lonely Night (Angel Face) - Captain And Tennille	111	1976
Boogie Fever – Sylvers	147	1976
Dream Weaver - Gary Wright	156	1976
Love Machine (Part 1) – Miracles	180	1976
You Make Me Feel Like Dancing - Leo Sayer	184	1976
All By Myself - Eric Carmen	185	1976
Let Your Love Flow - Bellamy Brothers	189	1976
Right Back Where We Started From Maxine Nightingale	194	1976
Get Up And Boogie (That's Right) Silver Convention	203	1976
If You Leave Me Now – Chicago	235	1976
Lowdown - Boz Scaggs	244	1976
(Shake, Shake, Shake) Shake Your Booty K.C. & The Sunshine Band	245	1976
Theme From S.W.A.T. - Rhythm Heritage	277	1976
You Should Be Dancing - Bee Gees	292	1976
December, 1963 (Oh, What A Night) Four Seasons	302	1976
Love Hangover - Diana Ross	304	1976
Rock'n Me - Steve Miller	307	1976
Theme From Mahogany (Do You Know Where You're Going To) - Diana Ross	344	1976
The Wreck Of The Edmund Fitzgerald Gordon Lightfoot	357	1976
Let 'Em In - Wings	376	1976
Undercover Angel - Alan O'Day	69	1977
(Your Love Has Lifted Me) Higher And Higher Rita Coolidge	177	1977
Southern Nights - Glen Campbell	229	1977
I'm Your Boogie Man - K.C. & The Sunshine Band	285	1977
Don't Give Up On Us - David Soul	295	1977
I Wish - Stevie Wonder	296	1977
Dancing Queen - Abba	315	1977
Don't Stop - Fleetwood Mac	322	1977
Dreams - Fleetwood Mac	337	1977
Got To Give It Up Pt. I - Marvin Gaye	370	1977
Hotel California - Eagles	378	1977
Blinded By The Light - Manfred Mann's Earth Band	414	1977
I'm In You - Peter Frampton	437	1977
Gonna Fly Now (Theme From "Rocky") - Bill Conti	438	1977
Sir Duke - Stevie Wonder	465	1977
Emotion - Samantha Sang	59	1978
Grease - Frankie Valli	66	1978
Short People - Randy Newman	148	1978
(Love Is) Thicker Than Water - Andy Gibb	195	1978
If I Can't Have You - Yvonne Elliman	271	1978
Good Times - Chic	85	1979
Heart Of Glass - Blondie	117	1979
I Will Survive - Gloria Gaynor	157	1979
Knock On Wood - Amii Stewart	210	1979
No More Tears (Enough Is Enough) Barbra Streisand/Donna Summer	220	1979
Don't Stop 'til You Get Enough - Michael Jackson	230	1979
Sail On - Commodores	236	1979
Still - Commodores	336	1979
Heartache Tonight - Eagles	354	1979

Year	No. 1s	Year	No. 1s
1970	31	1975	44
1971	28	1976	33
1972	36	1977	28
1973	39	1978	19
1974	48	1979	21

Fastest and Slowest Records to No. 1

	Title - Act	Rank	Year
	Three Weeks		
1	Let It Be - *Beatles*	28	1970
	Four Weeks		
2	My Sweet Lord - *George Harrison*	14	1970
	Five Weeks		
3	Bridge Over Troubled Water *Simon & Garfunkel*	27	1970
4	Family Affair - *Sly & The Family Stone*	30	1971
5	Theme From Shaft - *Isaac Hayes*	32	1971
6	You Don't Bring Me Flowers - *Barbra & Neil*	81	1978
7	Island Girl - *Elton John*	121	1975
8	The Long And Winding Road - *Beatles*	129	1970
	Six Weeks		
9	I'll Be There - *Jackson 5*	6	1970
10	You're So Vain - *Carly Simon*	58	1973
11	A Horse With No Name - *America*	75	1972
12	Philadelphia Freedom - *Elton John Band*	82	1975
13	I Honestly Love You - *Olivia Newton-John*	102	1974
14	The Love You Save - *Jackson 5*	135	1970
15	Don't Go Breaking My Heart *Elton John & Kiki Dee*	140	1976
16	Tragedy - *Bee Gees*	160	1979
17	Lucy In The Sky With Diamonds - *Elton John*	312	1975
18	Heartache Tonight - *Eagles*	354	1979
	Seven Weeks		
19	You Light Up My Life - *Debby Boone*	1	1977
20	Joy To The World - *Three Dog Night*	2	1971
21	American Pie - *Don McLean*	3	1972
22	Night Fever - *Bee Gees*	9	1978
23	ABC - *Jackson 5*	10	1970
24	Da Ya Think I'm Sexy? - *Rod Stewart*	21	1979
25	It's Too Late - *Carole King*	31	1971
26	Rockin' Robin - *Michael Jackson*	44	1972
27	Tonight's The Night (Gonna Be Alright) *Rod Stewart*	46	1976
28	Gypsys, Tramps & Thieves - *Cher*	51	1971
29	Ring My Bell - *Anita Ward*	57	1979
30	That's The Way (I Like It) *K.C. & The Sunshine Band*	94	1975
31	Hot Stuff - *Donna Summer*	98	1979
32	Have You Never Been Mellow *Olivia Newton-John*	110	1975
33	Bad Blood - *Neil Sedaka*	133	1975
34	The Streak - *Ray Stevens*	141	1974
35	Mama's Pearl - *Jackson 5*	179	1971
36	Uncle Albert/Admiral Halsey *Paul & Linda McCartney*	241	1971
37	Goodbye Yellow Brick Road - *Elton John*	289	1973
38	Listen To What The Man Said - *Wings*	305	1975
39	Don't Let The Sun Go Down On Me *Elton John*	331	1974
40	Someone Saved My Life Tonight - *Elton John*	346	1975
41	Spanish Harlem - *Aretha Franklin*	371	1971

	Title - Act	Rank	Year
	Twenty-One Weeks		
327	A Fifth Of Beethoven *Walter Murphy & The Big Apple Band*	84	1976
	Twenty Weeks		
326	Will It Go Round In Circles - *Billy Preston*	213	1973
325	Sad Eyes - *Robert John*	95	1979
	Nineteen Weeks		
324	(Your Love Has Lifted Me) Higher And Higher - *Rita Coolidge*	177	1977
323	My Eyes Adored You - *Frankie Valli*	146	1975
322	Hot Child In The City - *Nick Gilder*	40	1978
	Eighteen Weeks		
321	Rock On - *David Essex*	334	1974
320	(Love Is) Thicker Than Water - *Andy Gibb*	195	1978
319	Love Machine (Part 1) - *Miracles*	180	1976
318	Don't It Make My Brown Eyes Blue *Crystal Gayle*	101	1977
317	Take Me Home, Country Roads *John Denver*	100	1971
316	Emotion - *Samantha Sang*	59	1978
	Seventeen Weeks		
315	Dancing Queen - *Abba*	315	1977
314	Before The Next Teardrop Falls *Freddy Fender*	286	1975
313	Nice To Be With You - *Gallery*	170	1972
312	I Am Woman - *Helen Reddy*	132	1972
311	Daddy Don't You Walk So Fast *Wayne Newton*	131	1972
310	Show And Tell - *Al Wilson*	120	1974
	Sixteen Weeks		
309	Theme From S.W.A.T. *Rhythm Heritage*	277	1976
308	Rock Me Gently - *Andy Kim*	240	1974
307	Laughter In The Rain - *Neil Sedaka*	217	1975
306	Shining Star - *Earth, Wind & Fire*	181	1975
305	Baby Come Back - *Player*	70	1978
304	Rhinestone Cowboy - *Glen Campbell*	68	1975
303	Grease - *Frankie Valli*	66	1978
	Fifteen Weeks		
302	Cat's In The Cradle - *Harry Chapin*	293	1974
301	If I Can't Have You - *Yvonne Elliman*	271	1978
300	Everybody Plays The Fool - *Main Ingredient*	225	1972
299	Baby Don't Get Hooked On Me - *Mac Davis*	223	1972
298	You Make Me Feel Brand New - *Stylistics*	221	1974
297	Bad, Bad Leroy Brown - *Jim Croce*	192	1973
296	Boogie Fever - *Sylvers*	147	1976
295	Pick Up The Pieces - *Average White Band*	130	1975
294	I Just Want To Be Your Everything *Andy Gibb*	54	1977

Chart Singles of 25 Weeks or More

Records are ordered by their number of weeks in the weekly Top 100. All but 4 charted after 1974.

#	Title - Act	Wks	Rank	Peak Year
1	I Go Crazy - Paul Davis	36	508	1978
2	I Love The Nightlife (Disco 'round) - Alicia Bridges	35	499	1978
3	Feelings - Morris Albert	32	544	1975
4	Hot Child In The City - Nick Gilder	31	40	1978
5	Why Me - Kris Kristofferson	31	1266	1973
6	A Fifth Of Beethoven - Walter Murphy & The Big Apple Band	30	84	1976
7	Sad Eyes - Robert John	30	95	1979
8	Angel In Your Arms - Hot	30	501	1977
9	Superstar - Murray Head	30	595	1971
10	I Just Want To Be Your Everything - Andy Gibb	29	54	1977
11	Please Don't Go - KC & The Sunshine Band	29	278	1979
12	Lead Me On - Maxine Nightingale	29	547	1979
13	Kiss You All Over - Exile	28	18	1978
14	How Deep Is Your Love - Bee Gees	28	22	1977
15	Emotion - Samantha Sang	28	59	1978
16	Y.M.C.A. - Village People	28	150	1979
17	(Love Is) Thicker Than Water - Andy Gibb	28	195	1978
18	Makin' It - David Naughton	28	525	1979
19	Feels So Good - Chuck Mangione	28	561	1978
20	Jeans On - David Dundas	28	826	1977
21	You Light Up My Life - Debby Boone	27	1	1977
22	Stayin' Alive - Bee Gees	27	19	1978
23	Baby Come Back - Player	27	70	1978
24	Kiss And Say Goodbye - Manhattans	27	74	1976
25	Don't It Make My Brown Eyes Blue - Crystal Gayle	27	101	1977
26	Boogie Nights - Heatwave	27	231	1977
27	I Like Dreamin' - Kenny Nolan	27	398	1977
28	Sara Smile - Daryl Hall & John Oates	27	552	1976
29	Get Closer - Seals & Crofts	27	673	1976
30	Come Sail Away - Styx	27	700	1978
31	Disco Inferno - Trammps	27	899	1978
32	Falling - Le Blanc & Carr	27	1003	1978
33	Le Freak - Chic	26	5	1978
34	Love Machine (Part 1) - Miracles	26	180	1976
35	More, More, More (Pt. 1) - Andrea True Connection	26	297	1976
36	It's A Heartache - Bonnie Tyler	26	342	1978
37	Bohemian Rhapsody – Queen	26	486	1976
38	When You're In Love With A Beautiful Woman - Dr. Hook	26	491	1979
39	I'll Never Love This Way Again - Dionne Warwick	26	510	1979
40	Heaven On The 7th Floor - Paul Nicholas	26	527	1977
41	Swayin' To The Music (Slow Dancin') - Johnny Rivers	26	578	1977
42	Baby Hold On - Eddie Money	26	611	1978
43	Weekend In New England - Barry Manilow	26	757	1977
44	My Sharona - The Knack	25	17	1979
45	Torn Between Two Lovers - Mary MacGregor	25	37	1977
46	Boogie Oogie Oogie - A Taste Of Honey	25	63	1978
47	Undercover Angel - Alan O'Day	25	69	1977
48	Nobody Does It Better - Carly Simon	25	78	1977
49	You're The One That I Want - John Travolta And Olivia Newton-John	25	136	1978
50	Love Theme From "A Star Is Born" (Evergreen) - Barbra Streisand	25	139	1977
51	Play That Funky Music - Wild Cherry	25	151	1976
52	You Sexy Thing - Hot Chocolate	25	200	1976
53	Rise - Herb Alpert	25	204	1979
54	Misty Blue - Dorothy Moore	25	247	1976
55	Theme From S.W.A.T. - Rhythm Heritage	25	277	1976
56	You Needed Me - Anne Murray	25	394	1978
57	The Rubberband Man - Spinners	25	466	1976
58	Whatcha Gonna Do? - Pablo Cruise	25	474	1977
59	You'll Never Find Another Love Like Mine - Lou Rawls	25	509	1976
60	Jack And Jill - Raydio	25	521	1978
61	Slippin' Into Darkness - War	25	609	1972
62	Carry On Wayward Son - Kansas	25	610	1977
63	Two Out Of Three Ain't Bad - Meat Loaf	25	699	1978
64	A Little Bit More - Dr. Hook	25	709	1976
65	You Can't Change That - Raydio	25	808	1979
66	Goodbye Girl - David Gates	25	830	1978
67	Yellow River - Christie	25	1047	1970
68	Free - Deniece Williams	25	1313	1977

Records in Top 1000 by Natural Score Charting Fewer Than 14 Weeks

These '70s records required the fewest weeks to earn their coveted rank among the Top 1000 for the decade. The list is heavily weighted to the earlier years when less average time on the Top 100 was a reflection of a higher number of records entering the weekly survey.

#	Title - Act	Wks	Rank	Peak Year
1	ABC - Jackson 5	13	47	1970
2	Let It Be - Beatles	13	69	1970
3	Never Can Say Goodbye - Jackson 5	12	105	1971
4	A Horse With No Name - America	13	128	1972
5	Ain't No Mountain High Enough - Diana Ross	12	204	1970
6	Doesn't Somebody Want To Be Wanted - Partridge Family	13	213	1971
7	The Long And Winding Road - Beatles	11	273	1970
8	Give Me Love (Give Me Peace On Earth) - George Harrison	13	283	1973
9	Lookin' Out My Back Door - Creedence Clearwater Revival	12	303	1970
10	Don't Let The Sun Go Down On Me - Elton John	13	309	1974
11	Lucy In The Sky With Diamonds - Elton John	13	315	1975
12	Mama's Pearl - Jackson 5	11	316	1971
13	Someone Saved My Life Tonight - Elton John	12	340	1975
14	Hurting Each Other - Carpenters	13	346	1972
15	Whatever Gets You Thru The Night - John Lennon	13	357	1974
16	It Don't Come Easy - Ringo Starr	13	360	1971
17	Brown Sugar - Rolling Stones	12	373	1971
18	Uncle Albert/Admiral Halsey - Paul & Linda McCartney	12	376	1971
19	Americans - Byron Mac Gregor	10	384	1974
20	Down By The Lazy River - Osmonds	13	395	1972
21	Higher Ground - Stevie Wonder	13	397	1973
22	The Cisco Kid - War	13	407	1973
23	In The Summertime - Mungo Jerry	13	408	1970
24	Imagine - John Lennon	11	415	1971
25	Bridge Over Troubled Water - Aretha Franklin	11	420	1971
26	Up Around The Bend - Creedence Clearwater Revival	12	428	1970
27	Run Joey Run - David Geddes	13	433	1975
28	Mr. Jaws - Dickie Goodman	13	440	1975
29	Rainy Days And Mondays - Carpenters	12	448	1971
30	Lyin' Eyes - Eagles	13	454	1975
31	Cecilia - Simon & Garfunkel	12	455	1970
32	Spanish Harlem - Aretha Franklin	12	464	1971
33	Kodachrome - Paul Simon	13	478	1973
34	Love Grows (Where My Rosemary Goes) - Edison Lighthouse	13	493	1970
35	Puppy Love - Donny Osmond	12	496	1972
36	Day After Day - Badfinger	13	507	1972
37	Also Sprach Zarathustra (2001) - Deodato	12	522	1973
38	Have You Ever Seen The Rain - Creedence Clearwater Revival	10	543	1971
39	Mercy Mercy Me (The Ecology) - Marvin Gaye	13	549	1971
40	Junior's Farm - Paul McCartney & Wings	12	562	1975
41	Have You Seen Her - Chi-Lites	13	571	1971
42	Rock And Roll Part 2 - Gary Glitter	13	576	1972
43	Fly Away - John Denver	11	606	1976
44	Does Anybody Really Know What Time It Is? - Chicago	12	612	1971
45	I'll Meet You Halfway - Partridge Family	10	613	1971
46	Sugar Daddy - Jackson 5	12	614	1972
47	O-O-H Child - Five Stairsteps	13	623	1970
48	I Am...I Said - Neil Diamond	11	626	1971
49	An Old Fashioned Love Song - Three Dog Night	13	627	1971
50	The Letter - Joe Cocker	13	636	1970
51	Only You - Ringo Starr	12	637	1975
52	Saturday In The Park - Chicago	12	644	1972
53	Peace Train - Cat Stevens	13	646	1971
54	25 Or 6 To 4 – Chicago	13	653	1970
55	The Bitch Is Back - Elton John	11	658	1974
56	Jet - Paul McCartney & Wings	12	659	1974
57	Don't Cry Daddy - Elvis Presley	13	667	1970
58	Don't Expect Me To Be Your Friend - Lobo	12	677	1973
59	Earache My Eye (Featuring Alice Bowie) - Cheech & Chong	12	679	1974
60	Proud Mary - Ike & Tina Turner	13	688	1971
61	Psychedelic Shack - Temptations	12	690	1970
62	The Twelfth Of Never - Donny Osmond	13	705	1973
63	Another Day - Paul McCartney	11	715	1971
64	Everything I Own - Bread	13	720	1972
65	Without Love (There Is Nothing) - Tom Jones	10	730	1970
66	Never Been To Spain - Three Dog Night	11	731	1972
67	For All We Know - Carpenters	13	743	1971
68	Little Bitty Pretty One - Jackson 5	10	754	1972
69	My Little Town - Simon & Garfunkel	13	760	1975
70	Vehicle - Ides of March	13	763	1970
71	Heat Wave - Linda Ronstadt	12	767	1975
72	Some Kind Of Wonderful - Grand Funk Railroad	13	769	1975
73	Day Dreaming - Aretha Franklin	11	773	1972
74	Travelin' Band - Creedence Clearwater Revival	11	785	1970
75	I'll Never Fall In Love Again - Dionne Warwick	11	794	1970
76	Jingle Jangle - Archies	13	795	1970
77	Ma Belle Amie - Tee Set	13	797	1970
78	If - Bread	13	801	1971
79	Oh My My - Ringo Starr	13	803	1974

	Title - Act	Wks	Rank	Peak Year
80	**Sweet Hitch-Hiker** - *Creedence Clearwater Revival*	10	810	1971
81	**Wildwood Weed** - *Jim Stafford*	13	814	1974
82	**Love Or Let Me Be Lonely** - *Friends Of Distinction*	13	822	1970
83	**Where Is The Love** - *Roberta Flack & Donny Hathaway*	13	824	1972
84	**What Is Life** - *George Harrison*	11	825	1971
85	**Helen Wheels** - *Paul McCartney & Wings*	12	827	1974
86	**Share The Land** - *Guess Who*	12	828	1970
87	**How Sweet It Is (To Be Loved By You)** - *James Taylor*	13	829	1975
88	**Reeling In The Years** - *Steely Dan*	13	839	1973
89	**Another Saturday Night** - *Cat Stevens*	13	843	1974
90	**Use Me** - *Bill Withers*	13	849	1972
91	**Immigrant Song** - *Led Zeppelin*	13	855	1971
92	**Don't Knock My Love - Pt. I** - *Wilson Pickett*	13	860	1971
93	**Feelin' Stronger Every Day** - *Chicago*	13	863	1973
94	**Evil Ways** - *Santana*	12	869	1970
95	**Love Her Madly** - *Doors*	12	872	1971
96	**Rock Steady** - *Aretha Franklin*	10	890	1971
97	**Saturday Night's Alright For Fighting** - *Elton John*	12	891	1973
98	**See Me, Feel Me** - *Who*	13	895	1970
99	**I Woke Up In Love This Morning** - *Partridge Family*	12	907	1971
100	**She's Not Just Another Woman** - *8th Day*	13	908	1971
101	**China Grove** - *Doobie Brothers*	12	913	1973
102	**I Just Want To Celebrate** - *Rare Earth*	12	914	1971
103	**I Wanna Be Where You Are** - *Michael Jackson*	12	920	1972
104	**Gimme Dat Ding** - *Pipkins*	13	937	1970
105	**Goodbye To Love** - *Carpenters*	12	939	1972
106	**It's Only Make Believe** - *Glen Campbell*	13	942	1970
107	**Liar** - *Three Dog Night*	13	947	1971
108	**Old Days** - *Chicago*	11	953	1975
109	**Only Yesterday** - *Carpenters*	12	955	1975
110	**Ventura Highway** - *America*	13	957	1972
111	**For The Love Of Money** - *O'Jays*	13	959	1974
112	**I'm Just A Singer (In A Rock And Roll Band)** - *Moody Blues*	13	960	1973
113	**Take It Easy** - *Eagles*	13	961	1972
114	**I'll Have To Say I Love You In A Song** - *Jim Croce*	13	962	1974
115	**Hot Rod Lincoln** - *Commander Cody And His Lost Planet Airmen*	13	963	1972
116	**Two Divided By Love** - *Grass Roots*	11	974	1971
117	**Once You Get Started** - *Rufus Featuring Chaka Khan*	13	975	1975
118	**Sweet Seasons** - *Carole King*	11	976	1972
119	**Love On A Two-Way Street** - *Moments*	13	982	1970
120	**Masterpiece** - *Temptations*	13	983	1973
121	**I Won't Last A Day Without You** - *Carpenters*	12	990	1974
122	**Keeper Of The Castle** - *Four Tops*	13	997	1973
123	**Inner City Blues (Make Me Wanna Holler)** - *Marvin Gaye*	11	998	1971

Year	Number	Year	Number
1970	27	1975	14
1971	34	1976	1
1972	20	1977	0
1973	14	1978	0
1974	13	1979	0

Highest Entries

Records entering the chart at No. 50 or higher. Average entry of records across the decade is in the 80s.

Rank	Title - Act	Entry No.	Peak
1	Heartache Tonight - *Eagles*	23	10-Nov-79
2	Too Much Heaven - *Bee Gees*	27	30-Dec-78
3	I'll Be There - *Jackson 5*	28	24-Oct-70
4	Never Can Say Goodbye - *Jackson 5*	29	29-May-71
5	Tusk - *Fleetwood Mac*	31	3-Nov-79
6	Let It Be – *Beatles*	32	28-Mar-70
6	Tragedy - *Bee Gees*	32	17-Mar-79
8	Someone Saved My Life Tonight - *Elton John*	33	16-Aug-75
9	Without Love (There Is Nothing) - *Tom Jones*	34	7-Feb-70
10	My Sweet Lord - *George Harrison*	37	19-Dec-70
11	The Long And Winding Road - *Beatles*	38	13-Jun-70
11	Mama's Pearl - *Jackson 5*	38	6-Mar-71
13	I'll Never Fall In Love Again - *Dionne Warwick*	39	7-Feb-70
13	Love You Inside Out - *Bee Gees*	39	9-Jun-79
15	Goodnight Tonight – *Wings*	41	19-May-79
16	Lookin' Out My Back Door - *Creedence Clearwater Revival*	42	3-Oct-70
17	ABC - *Jackson 5*	43	25-Apr-70
17	Don't Look Back - *Boston*	43	30-Sep-78
17	Alive Again - *Chicago*	43	9-Dec-78
20	Psychedelic Shack - *Temptations*	44	7-Mar-70
21	Kentucky Rain - *Elvis Presley*	45	14-Mar-70
21	Travelin' Band - *Creedence Clearwater Revival*	45	14-Mar-70
21	Doesn't Somebody Want To Be Wanted - *Partridge Family*	45	3-Apr-71
24	What Is Life - *George Harrison*	46	10-Apr-71
24	Rock Steady - *Aretha Franklin*	46	11-Dec-71
24	Island Girl - *Elton John*	46	8-Nov-75
24	I Wish - *Stevie Wonder*	46	29-Jan-77
28	Blowing Away - *5th Dimension*	47	31-Jan-70
28	You're All I Need To Get By - *Aretha Franklin*	47	27-Mar-71
28	Bridge Over Troubled Water - *Aretha Franklin*	47	29-May-71
28	Maybe Tomorrow - *Jackson 5*	47	14-Aug-71
28	Little Bitty Pretty One - *Jackson 5*	47	3-Jun-72
28	Don't Go Breaking My Heart - *Elton John And Kiki Dee*	47	7-Aug-76
28	Da Ya Think I'm Sexy? - *Rod Stewart*	47	3-Feb-79
35	For All We Know - *Carpenters*	48	20-Mar-71
35	Another Day - *Paul McCartney*	48	1-May-71
35	Down By The Lazy River - *Osmonds*	48	4-Mar-72
35	Do You Feel Like We Do - *Peter Frampton*	48	20-Nov-76
35	Hot Stuff - *Donna Summer*	48	2-Jun-79
35	Don't Bring Me Down - *Electric Light Orchestra*	48	22-Sep-79
41	Up Around The Bend - *Creedence Clearwater Revival*	49	30-May-70
41	Hi-De-Ho - *Blood, Sweat & Tears*	49	5-Sep-70
41	Oye Como Va - *Santana*	49	3-Apr-71
41	The Drum - *Bobby Sherman*	49	29-May-71
41	The Bitch Is Back - *Elton John*	49	26-Oct-74
41	Sorry Seems To Be The Hardest Word - *Elton John*	49	1-Jan-77
41	Ego - *Elton John*	49	20-May-78
41	Stay//The Load-Out** - *Jackson Browne*	49	12-Aug-78
41	Shine A Little Love - *Electric Light Orchestra*	49	21-Jul-79
41	Babe - *Styx*	49	24-Nov-79
41	Send One Your Love - *Stevie Wonder*	49	22-Dec-79
52	Honey Come Back - *Glen Campbell*	50	21-Feb-70
52	My World - *Bee Gees*	50	4-Mar-72
52	Philadelphia Freedom - *Elton John Band*	50	12-Apr-75

**Single sides of charted Two-Sided Winners [TSW] not included.

Highest Exits

Records leaving the chart at No. 30 or higher. Average exit point for records achieving the Top 40 changed from about No. 40 in the early '70s to about No. 90 by the end of the decade.

Rank	Title - Act	Exit No.	Peak
1	Hey Lawdy Mama - *Steppenwolf*	21	16-May-70
2	Gotta Hold On To This Feeling - *Jr. Walker & The All Stars*	22	4-Apr-70
2	Mercy Mercy Me (The Ecology) - *Marvin Gaye*	22	28-Aug-71
4	Give Me Just A Little More Time - *Chairmen Of The Board*	23	14-Mar-70
4	Vincent - *Don McLean*	23	13-May-72
4	I Saw The Light - *Todd Rundgren*	23	17-Jun-72
7	Jingle Jangle - *Archies*	24	24-Jan-70
7	Want Ads - *Honey Cone*	24	5-Jun-71
7	Nathan Jones - *Supremes*	24	26-Jun-71
7	Stand By Me - *John Lennon*	24	26-Apr-75
11	Don't Cry Daddy - *Elvis Presley*	25	24-Jan-70
11	Who'll Stop The Rain - *Creedence Clearwater Revival*	25	7-Mar-70
11	Never Can Say Goodbye - *Jackson 5*	25	29-May-71
11	Theme From "Summer Of '42" - *Peter Nero*	25	8-Jan-72
11	Make Me The Woman That You Go Home To - *Gladys Knight & The Pips*	25	29-Jan-72
11	All The King's Horses - *Aretha Franklin*	25	15-Jul-72
11	Pinball Wizard/See Me, Feel Me - *New Seekers*	25	5-May-73
18	Dream Baby (How Long Must I Dream) - *Glen Campbell*	26	17-Apr-71
18	Joy To The World - *Three Dog Night*	26	17-Apr-71
18	Battle Hymn Of Lt. Calley - *C Company Featuring Terry Nelson*	26	15-May-71
18	I Don't Know How To Love Him - *Helen Reddy*	26	12-Jun-71
18	Do You Know What I Mean - *Lee Michaels*	26	23-Oct-71
18	Convention '72 - *Delegates*	26	25-Nov-72
18	Uneasy Rider - *Charlie Daniels*	26	1-Sep-73
18	Thank God I'm A Country Boy - *John Denver*	26	14-Jun-75
26	Holly Holy - *Neil Diamond*	27	3-Jan-70
26	Jam Up Jelly Tight - *Tommy Roe*	27	10-Jan-70
26	Without Love (There Is Nothing) - *Tom Jones*	27	7-Feb-70
26	I'll Meet You Halfway - *Partridge Family*	27	19-Jun-71
26	Don't Knock My Love - Pt. I - *Wilson Pickett*	27	3-Jul-71
26	How Can You Mend A Broken Heart - *Bee Gees*	27	14-Aug-71
26	Rain Dance - *Guess Who*	27	9-Oct-71
26	You Could Have Been A Lady - *April Wine*	27	20-May-72
26	Ask Me What You Want - *Millie Jackson*	27	17-Jun-72
26	Diary - *Bread*	27	24-Jun-72
26	Nice To Be With You - *Gallery*	27	24-Jun-72
26	I'm Coming Home - *Stories*	27	5-Aug-72
26	You Haven't Done Nothin' - *Stevie Wonder*	27	2-Nov-74
39	Evil Woman Don't Play Your Games With Me - *Crow*	28	10-Jan-70
39	Baby Take Me In Your Arms - *Jefferson*	28	14-Feb-70
39	He Ain't Heavy, He's My Brother - *Hollies*	28	14-Mar-70
39	Rainy Night In Georgia - *Brook Benton*	28	14-Mar-70
39	Bridge Over Troubled Water - *Aretha Franklin*	28	29-May-71
39	Don't Pull Your Love - *Hamilton, Joe Frank & Reynolds*	28	31-Jul-71
39	The Day I Found Myself - *Honey Cone*	28	22-Apr-72
39	Old Man - *Neil Young*	28	10-Jun-72
39	Thunder And Lightning - *Chi Coltrane*	28	11-Nov-72
39	Looking Through The Eyes Of Love - *Partridge Family*	28	27-Jan-73
39	Smoke On The Water - *Deep Purple*	28	28-Jul-73
39	Where Peaceful Waters Flow - *Gladys Knight & The Pips*	28	11-Aug-73
39	Get It Together - *Jackson 5*	28	20-Oct-73
39	Basketball Jones Featuring Tyrone Shoelaces - *Cheech & Chong*	28	3-Nov-73
53	Celebrate - *Three Dog Night*	29	28-Mar-70
53	Look What They've Done To My Song Ma - *New Seekers*	29	24-Oct-70
53	Power To The People - *John Lennon/Plastic Ono Band*	29	8-May-71
53	Cry Baby - *Janis Joplin*	29	19-Jun-71
53	Walk Away - *The James Gang*	29	17-Jul-71
53	The Story In Your Eyes - *Moody Blues*	29	25-Sep-71
53	Never Been To Spain - *Three Dog Night*	29	12-Feb-72
53	Heart Of Gold - *Neil Young*	29	18-Mar-72
53	Amazing Grace - *Royal Scots Dragoon Guards*	29	1-Jul-72
53	I Need You - *America*	29	8-Jul-72
53	Go All The Way - *Raspberries*	29	14-Oct-72
53	Keeper Of The Castle - *Four Tops*	29	20-Jan-73
53	"Cherry Cherry" From Hot August Night - *Neil Diamond*	29	12-May-73
53	Junior's Farm - *Paul McCartney & Wings*	29	4-Jan-75
53	Before The Next Teardrop Falls - *Freddy Fender*	29	7-Jun-75
68	Let's Work Together (Part 1) - *Wilbert Harrison*	30	21-Feb-70
68	New World Coming - *Mama Cass Elliot*	30	28-Feb-70
68	Come Running - *Van Morrison*	30	2-May-70
68	Brother Rapp (Part 1) & (Part 2) - *James Brown*	30	30-May-70
68	Big Yellow Taxi - *Neighborhood*	30	22-Aug-70
68	That's Where I Went Wrong - *Poppy Family*	30	17-Oct-70
68	Silver Moon - *Michael Nesmith & The First National Band*	30	9-Jan-71
68	Blue Money - *Van Morrison*	30	10-Apr-71

Rank	Title - Act	Exit No.	Peak
68	**Cool Aid** - *Paul Humphrey & His Cool Aid Chemists*	30	12-Jun-71
68	**Signs** - *Five Man Electrical Band*	30	4-Sep-71
68	**Rock And Roll Lullaby** - *B.J. Thomas*	30	1-Apr-72
68	**Isn't Life Strange** - *Moody Blues*	30	17-Jun-72
68	**Sylvia's Mother** *Dr. Hook And The Medicine Show*	30	17-Jun-72
68	**Peaceful** - *Helen Reddy*	30	5-May-73

Rank	Title - Act	Exit No.	Peak
68	**I Can Understand It** - *New Birth*	30	19-May-73
68	**It's Only Rock 'N Roll (But I Like It)** *Rolling Stones*	30	21-Sep-74
68	**The Bitch Is Back** - *Elton John*	30	26-Oct-74
68	**Roll On Down The Highway** *Bachman-Turner Overdrive*	30	8-Mar-75
68	**Poetry Man** - *Phoebe Snow*	30	12-Apr-75

The Top 150 One-Hit Wonders

For this list, a "hit" is defined as appearance on the *Cash Box* Top 100. Some one-hit wonders in *Cash Box* may have had second "hits" in other magazines or other decades.

Rank	Act - Title
1	**Anita Ward** - *Ring My Bell*
2	**Marvin Hamlisch** - *The Entertainer*
3	**"Deliverance" Soundtrack** - *Dueling Banjos*
4	**Mungo Jerry** - *In The Summertime*
5	**Clint Holmes** - *Playground In My Mind*
6	**M** - *Pop Muzik*
7	**Byron Mac Gregor** - *Americans*
8	**Floaters** - *Float On*
9	**Alicia Bridges** - *I Love The Nightlife (Disco 'Round)*
10	**David Naughton** - *Makin' It*
11	**Barry DeVorzon and Perry Botkin, Jr.** - *Nadia's Theme (The Young And The Restless)*
12	**Sister Janet Mead** - *The Lord's Prayer*
13	**Pratt & McClain** - *Happy Days*
14	**Mike Oldfield** - *Tubular Bells*
15	**Suzi Quatro And Chris Norman** - *Stumblin' In*
16	**Pipkins** - *Gimme Dat Ding*
17	**J.D. Souther** - *Only The Lonely*
18	**Godspell** - *Day By Day*
19	**Gwen McCrae** - *Rockin' Chair*
20	**Peter McCann** - *Do You Wanna Make Love*
21	**David Dundas** - *Jeans On*
22	**Beginning Of The End** - *Funky Nassau-Part I*
23	**Mocedades** - *Eres Tu (Touch The Wind)*
24	**Tom Clay** - *What The World Needs Now Is Love/ Abraham, Martin And John*
25	**Reunion** - *Life Is A Rock (But The Radio Rolled Me)*
26	**Keith Carradine** - *I'm Easy*
27	**Shirley (And Company)** - *Shame, Shame, Shame*
28	**Danny O'Keefe** - *Good Time Charlie's Got The Blues*
29	**Freddie Hart** - *Easy Loving*
30	**Bazuka** - *Dynomite-Part 1*
31	**McFadden & Whitehead** - *Ain't No Stoppin' Us Now*
32	**Brighter Side Of Darkness** - *Love Jones*
33	**Sanford/Townsend Band** - *Smoke From A Distant Fire*
34	**Nick Lowe** - *Cruel To Be Kind*
35	**Loudon Wainwright III** - *Dead Skunk*
36	**Ram Jam** - *Black Betty*
37	**Chi Coltrane** - *Thunder And Lightning*
38	**Silver** - *Wham Bam*
39	**Miguel Rios** - *Song Of Joy (Himno A La Alegria)*
40	**Dean Friedman** – *Ariel*
41	**Pete Wingfield** - *Eighteen With A Bullet*
42	**Patti Smith Group** - *Because The Night*
43	**Malo** – *Suavecito*
44	**Brass Construction** - *Movin'*
45	**Santa Esmeralda** - *Don't Let Me Be Misunderstood*
46	**Ace Frehley** - *New York Groove*
47	**Matthews' Southern Comfort** - *Woodstock*
48	**Les Crane** – *Desiderata*
49	**Pipes And Drums And The Military Band Of The Royal Scots Dragoon Guards** - *Amazing Grace*
50	**Black Oak Arkansas** - *Jim Dandy*
51	**Roger Whittaker** - *The Last Farewell*
52	**Wing And A Prayer Fife And Drum Corps.** - *Baby Face*
53	**Ernie (Jim Henson)** - *Rubber Duckie*
54	**Patrick Hernandez** - *Born To Be Alive*
55	**Michael Parks** - *Long Lonesome Highway*
56	**Bell & James** - *Livin' It Up (Friday Night)*
57	**Sniff 'n' The Tears** - *Driver's Seat*
58	**Larry Groce** - *Junk Food Junkie*
59	**Mac And Katie Kissoon** - *Chirpy Chirpy Cheep Cheep*
60	**Sailcat** - *Motorcycle Mama*
61	**Gene Redding** - *This Heart*
62	**Paul Stookey** - *Wedding Song (There Is Love)*
63	**Richie Havens** - *Here Comes The Sun*
64	**Roger Voudouris** - *Get Used To It*
65	**Eruption** - *I Can't Stand The Rain*
66	**Polly Brown** - *Up In A Puff Of Smoke*
67	**Johnny Wakelin And The Kinshasa Band** - *Black Superman – "Muhammad Ali"*
68	**Wilton Place Street Band** - *Disco Lucy (I Love Lucy Theme)*
69	**Cledus Maggard** - *The White Knight*
70	**Chris Thompson** - *Hot Summer Nights*
71	**Crabby Appleton** - *Go Back*
72	**France Joli** - *Come To Me*
73	**Chanson** - *Don't Hold Back*
74	**Gunhill Road** - *Back When My Hair Was Short*
75	**Cliff DeYoung** - *My Sweet Lady*
76	**Cyndi Grecco** - *Making Our Dreams Come True*
77	**Ronnie McDowell** - *The King Is Gone*
78	**Hotlegs** - *Neanderthal Man*
79	**Delegates** - *Convention '72*
80	**Sweet Sensation** - *Sad Sweet Dreamer*
81	**Lou Reed** - *Walk On The Wild Side*
82	**Cross Country** - *In The Midnight Hour*
83	**Street People** - *Jennifer Tomkins*
84	**Peter Nero** - *Theme From "Summer of '42"*
85	**Mashmakhan** - *As The Years Go By*
86	**Jeanne Pruett** - *Satin Sheets*
87	**Dwight Twilley Band** - *I'm On Fire*
88	**Michael Zager Band** - *Let's All Chant*
89	**Tycoon** - *Such A Woman*
90	**Barbara Fairchild** - *Teddy Bear Song*
91	**Meri Wilson** - *Telephone Man*
92	**Sweathog** – *Hallelujah*
93	**Jake Holmes** - *So Close*
94	**Instant Funk** - *I Got My Mind Made Up (You Can Get It Girl)*
95	**Shirley Brown** - *Woman To Woman*

Rank	Act - Title
96	**Natural Four** - Can This Be Real
97	**Manu Dibango** - Soul Makossa
98	**Dave And Ansil Collins** - Double Barrel
99	**Ian Thomas** - Painted Ladies
100	**Stargard** - Theme Song From "Which Way Is Up"
101	**Q** - Dancin' Man
102	**Flash** - Small Beginnings
103	**Justin Hayward** - Forever Autumn
104	**John Phillips** - Mississippi
105	**Elephant's Memory** - Mongoose
106	**Neighborhood** - Big Yellow Taxi
107	**Chee-Chee and Peppy** - I Know I'm In Love
108	**McGuinness Flint** - When I'm Dead And Gone
109	**Pickettywitch** – That Same Old Feeling
110	**Alan Parsons** – I Wouldn't Want To Be Like You
111	**Maynard Ferguson** - Gonna Fly Now (Theme From "Rocky")
112	**5000 Volts** - I'm On Fire
113	**Bloodrock** - D.O.A.
114	**Liz Damon's Orient Express** - 1900 Yesterday
115	**Vincent Bell** - Airport Love Theme (Gwen and Vern)
116	**Emitt Rhodes** - Fresh As A Daisy
117	**Jo Jo Gunne** - Run Run Run
118	**Stillwater** - Mindbender
119	**Ian Gomm** - Hold On
120	**Hagood Hardy** - The Homecoming
121	**Lost Generation** - The Sly, The Slick, The Wicked
122	**John Handy** - Hard Work
123	**Clean Living** - In Heaven There Is No Beer
124	**Bill Amesbury** - Virginia (Touch Me Like You Do)
125	**Original Caste** - One Tin Soldier
126	**Sounds Of Sunshine** - Love Means (You Never Have To Say You're Sorry)
127	**Joe Stampley** - Soul Song
128	**Lady Flash** - Street Singin'
129	**Herbie Hancock** - Chameleon
130	**Johnny Cash & June Carter** - If I Were A Carpenter
131	**Diana Ross & Michael Jackson** - Ease On Down The Road
132	**Robin Gibb** - Oh! Darling
133	**Mama Cass Elliot** - New World Coming
134	**Boomer Castleman** - Judy Mae
135	**Frankie Avalon** - Venus
136	**Jones Girls** - You Gonna Make Me Love Somebody Else
137	**Road Apples** - Let's Live Together
138	**Lauren Wood** - Please Don't Leave
139	**Ashton, Gardner & Dyke** - Resurrection Shuffle
140	**Joneses** - Sugar Pie Guy (Pt. 1)
141	**Chuck Brown & The Soul Searchers** - Bustin' Loose (Part 1)
142	**Les Emmerson** - Control Of Me
143	**Rubicon** - I'm Gonna Take Care Of Everything
144	**Red Sovine** - Teddy Bear
145	**Celebration featuring Mike Love** - Almost Summer
146	**Rubettes** - Sugar Baby Love
147	**Boys In The Band** - (How Bout A Little Hand For) The Boys In The Band
148	**Benny Bell** - Shaving Cream
149	**Mass Production** - Firecracker
150	**Gary's Gang** - Keep On Dancin'

The Act Intensity Index

Includes all acts with at least 5 charted hits. Average ranks are calculated by dividing total earned natural points by total weeks on the chart, then expressing that score on a rank basis.

	Act	Chart Wks.	Avg. Points	Avg. Rank		Act	Chart Wks.	Avg. Points	Avg. Rank
1	Beatles	55	271.9	8.17	46	R. Dean Taylor	31	148.5	15.83
2	Andy Gibb	115	264.8	8.39	47	Terry Jacks	39	145.5	15.98
3	Bee Gees	332	251.5	8.82	48	Billy Preston	112	145.4	15.98
4	Chic	97	244.5	9.05	49	Carly Simon	159	142.4	16.52
5	Simon & Garfunkel	55	233.4	9.44	50	Fleetwood Mac	146	142.3	16.53
6	Michael Jackson	103	228.0	9.62	51	Neil Sedaka	107	141.9	16.63
7	Roberta Flack	103	222.9	9.80	52	Gloria Gaynor	61	141.6	16.67
8	Donna Summer	199	213.2	10.14	53	Carole King	123	141.6	16.68
9	Jackson 5	276	208.3	10.32	54	John Denver	253	141.3	16.73
10	Don McLean	50	207.8	10.34	55	Cornelius Brothers & Sister Rose	69	140.5	16.90
11	Partridge Family	94	200.2	10.62	56	Steve Miller Band	86	139.7	17.07
12	Gilbert O'Sullivan	84	200.2	10.62	57	Lynn Anderson	45	139.1	17.17
13	Paul McCartney & Wings / Wings	282	197.4	10.73	58	Badfinger	59	137.6	17.48
14	Stevie Wonder	248	197.2	10.73	59	David Cassidy	46	136.7	17.67
15	Creedence Clearwater Revival	86	192.8	10.90	60	Barbra Streisand	169	134.8	18.05
16	Three Dog Night	207	192.1	10.92	61	Gordon Lightfoot	106	134.6	18.08
17	Ringo Starr	127	191.0	10.96	62	Bread	156	133.9	18.21
18	Robert John	61	189.1	11.14	63	Rita Coolidge	86	133.9	18.22
19	Frankie Valli	91	188.0	11.34	64	Raiders	59	133.3	18.35
20	Elton John	309	186.8	11.53	65	Donny Osmond	146	131.2	18.75
21	John Lennon/Plastic Ono Band	54	185.6	11.74	66	Bo Donaldson And The Heywoods	49	130.7	18.85
22	Paul Simon	118	185.3	11.79	67	Sylvers	87	130.2	18.96
23	Carpenters	289	180.4	12.60	68	Helen Reddy	245	130.2	18.96
24	Rod Stewart	211	180.1	12.65	69	Joe Tex	48	129.6	19.08
25	KC & The Sunshine Band	193	174.2	13.64	70	Diana Ross	209	129.1	19.17
26	Captain & Tennille	157	173.5	13.75	71	America	145	127.3	19.54
27	Osmonds	122	166.7	14.88	72	James Taylor	151	126.8	19.63
28	Edwin Starr	40	165.4	15.03	73	Temptations	190	126.5	19.71
29	Eagles	224	163.8	15.11	74	Stories	50	126.3	19.73
30	George Harrison	118	162.4	15.17	75	Hollies	78	125.5	19.91
31	Marvin Gaye	151	161.4	15.22	76	Spinners	197	124.8	20.01
32	Leo Sayer	104	161.3	15.22	77	Tom Jones	114	123.7	20.05
33	Sly & The Family Stone	98	161.1	15.23	78	Neil Young	59	123.4	20.06
34	Olivia Newton-John	225	157.3	15.42	79	Melanie	111	123.1	20.08
35	Barry Manilow	254	156.1	15.47	80	Barry White	149	122.7	20.09
36	Honey Cone	55	155.3	15.51	81	B.J. Thomas	156	122.7	20.09
37	Tony Orlando And Dawn	225	154.4	15.55	82	Dr. Hook	173	121.5	20.14
38	Al Green	206	154.0	15.57	83	Foreigner	119	120.8	20.17
39	Cher	143	153.6	15.59	84	Average White Band / AWB	67	120.8	20.17
40	Hamilton, Joe Frank & Reynolds	70	153.4	15.60	85	Chicago	314	120.7	20.17
41	Gerry Rafferty	81	152.3	15.65	86	Bay City Rollers	114	120.6	20.18
42	Commodores	209	152.1	15.66	87	Love Unlimited Orchestra	47	120.4	20.18
43	Jim Croce	124	150.6	15.73	88	Isaac Hayes	80	120.3	20.19
44	Village People	76	148.9	15.81	89	Linda Ronstadt	220	119.4	20.22
45	Rolling Stones	181	148.6	15.83					

#	Act	Chart Wks.	Avg. Points	Avg. Rank	#	Act	Chart Wks.	Avg. Points	Avg. Rank
92	O'Jays	181	118.5	20.26	141	Orleans	74	99.7	21.10
93	Gladys Knight & The Pips	246	118.3	20.27	142	Little River Band	121	99.6	21.12
94	Eric Clapton	125	118.2	20.27	143	Three Degrees	46	99.6	21.13
95	Freda Payne	61	118.1	20.27	144	Jim Stafford	79	99.5	21.16
96	Al Wilson	57	117.9	20.28	145	Supertramp	80	98.7	21.42
97	Wayne Newton	49	117.6	20.30	146	Abba	200	98.3	21.57
98	Led Zeppelin	85	117.1	20.32	147	5th Dimension	178	98.0	21.65
99	Bill Withers	111	116.8	20.33	148	Earth, Wind & Fire	237	98.0	21.68
100	Boz Scaggs	79	116.6	20.34	149	Chi-Lites	95	97.7	21.75
101	George McCrae	41	116.5	20.34	150	Stylistics	186	96.0	22.33
102	Ozark Mountain Daredevils	52	116.4	20.34	151	Bad Company	101	95.9	22.38
103	Andy Kim	58	115.4	20.38	152	Henry Gross	41	95.5	22.50
104	Smokey Robinson & The Miracles	75	114.8	20.41	153	Anne Murray	176	95.2	22.60
105	Staple Singers	128	114.6	20.42	154	Bachman-TurnerOverdrive	118	94.9	22.71
106	Undisputed Truth	41	114.2	20.43	155	Electric Light Orchestra	228	94.9	22.71
107	Freddy Fender	75	114.0	20.44	156	England Dan & John Ford Coley	115	94.8	22.74
108	Hot Chocolate	95	113.5	20.46	157	10cc	96	94.7	22.78
109	Glen Campbell	174	113.1	20.48	158	Tommy James	80	94.5	22.85
110	Yvonne Elliman	86	112.9	20.49	159	Dionne Warwick	82	93.8	23.07
111	Ray Stevens	107	112.7	20.49	160	Mac Davis	104	93.7	23.11
112	Grand Funk Railroad	166	111.7	20.53	161	Charlie Daniels Band	45	93.6	23.15
113	Billy Joel	148	111.0	20.56	162	Jefferson Starship	126	93.5	23.15
114	War	179	109.8	20.61	163	Luther Ingram	70	93.4	23.20
115	Sweet	115	109.4	20.62	164	Kansas	99	93.4	23.21
116	Moody Blues	78	109.4	20.63	165	Ohio Players	154	93.3	23.22
117	Queen	131	109.3	20.63	166	Eddie Kendricks	146	92.6	23.48
118	Doobie Brothers	219	109.3	20.63	167	Kenny Rogers	111	91.9	23.68
119	Ambrosia	55	109.2	20.63	168	Harry Chapin	74	91.7	23.77
120	Daryl Hall & John Oates	136	109.1	20.63	169	Lobo	143	90.8	24.05
121	Eric Carmen	92	109.0	20.64	170	Raspberries	74	89.5	24.50
122	Neil Diamond	278	108.6	20.66	171	Natalie Cole	101	89.0	24.68
123	Aretha Franklin	208	107.7	20.69	172	Steely Dan	150	88.7	24.75
124	Manhattans	84	106.5	20.74	173	Alice Cooper (Solo)	89	88.3	24.90
125	Bobby Sherman	87	106.4	20.74	174	Kool & The Gang	135	87.8	25.07
126	Nilsson	99	105.9	20.76	175	Clarence Carter	66	87.5	25.17
127	Deep Purple	32	104.7	20.81	176	Supremes	95	87.5	25.18
128	Rufus Featuring Chaka Khan	118	104.2	20.83	177	Johnnie Taylor	138	87.1	25.31
129	Emotions	72	104.0	20.84	178	Starbuck	68	84.9	26.05
130	Santana	92	103.7	20.85	179	Bob Seger	127	84.7	26.09
131	Guess Who	173	102.7	20.89	180	Bob Welch	67	84.7	26.11
132	Dickie Goodman	44	102.2	20.91	181	Elvis Presley	294	84.4	26.20
133	Pointer Sisters	98	102.1	20.92	182	David Bowie	120	83.6	26.47
134	Joan Baez	45	102.0	20.92	183	Harold Melvin And The Blue Notes	106	83.2	26.60
135	Rose Royce	77	101.8	20.93	184	Tommy Roe	60	83.1	26.63
136	Paul Anka	115	101.4	20.94	185	Johnny Rivers	101	82.9	26.70
137	Styx	150	101.1	20.95	186	Doors	42	81.7	27.10
138	Boston	84	100.8	20.97	187	Charlie Rich	124	81.2	27.26
139	Johnny Nash	71	100.6	20.97	188	Bobby Vinton	91	81.1	27.31
140	Pablo Cruise	97	100.1	20.99	189	Cat Stevens	147	80.7	27.42

#	Act	Chart Wks.	Avg. Points	Avg. Rank	#	Act	Chart Wks.	Avg. Points	Avg. Rank
190	Todd Rundgren	91	80.3	27.58	240	Andy Williams	35	58.4	42.63
191	Joe Cocker	113	80.2	27.61	241	Tavares	136	58.4	42.63
192	Curtis Mayfield	86	80.0	27.67	242	Bob Dylan	93	58.2	42.85
193	Loggins & Messina	74	79.9	27.71	243	Ike & Tina Turner	68	58.1	42.88
194	Who	140	79.3	27.91	244	Charles Wright And The Watts 103rd Street Rhythm Band	49	58.0	43.04
195	Babys	56	79.1	27.95					
196	Lynyrd Skynyrd	84	78.4	28.20	245	Blood, Sweat & Tears	52	57.7	43.33
197	Cheech & Chong	67	77.8	28.39	246	James Brown	240	57.6	43.38
198	Four Tops	154	77.7	28.42	247	Bobby Goldsboro	52	57.5	43.48
199	Firefall	105	77.6	28.46	248	The Isley Brothers	197	57.5	43.49
200	Main Ingredient	111	77.2	28.59	249	Joe Simon	164	57.2	43.84
201	B.T. Express	61	76.6	28.80	250	Stephen Stills	45	56.7	44.27
202	Wilson Pickett	95	75.1	29.32	251	Steppenwolf	59	56.7	44.27
203	Brownsville Station	75	74.7	29.44	252	Ronnie Dyson	58	56.0	45.02
204	Kiss	157	74.5	29.49	253	Marshall Tucker Band	52	55.4	45.63
205	Jackson Browne	82	74.5	29.51	254	Kinks	58	53.7	47.28
206	Grass Roots	105	73.7	29.76	255	Bobby Womack	106	53.3	47.67
207	Seals & Crofts	152	73.7	29.76	256	Johnny Cash	42	53.3	47.71
208	Aerosmith	116	73.6	29.80	257	Moments	59	53.3	47.75
209	Albert Hammond	72	73.3	29.89	258	Judy Collins	65	53.2	47.85
210	Donny And Marie Osmond	94	72.4	30.21	259	Cars	65	53.0	48.97
211	George Benson	74	72.3	30.23	260	Flaming Ember	36	53.0	48.00
212	Lou Rawls	74	71.9	30.36	261	Persuaders	45	52.1	48.89
213	Art Garfunkel	74	71.7	30.45	262	Denise LaSalle	44	51.3	49.66
214	Bloodstone	65	71.6	30.45	263	Jr. Walker & The All Stars	44	50.8	50.23
215	Donna Fargo	73	70.3	30.89	264	Tyrone Davis	120	50.8	50.25
216	Alice Cooper (Group)	92	70.2	30.95	265	Jackie Moore	43	50.6	50.37
217	Eddie Money	78	69.4	31.60	266	Wet Willie	68	48.4	52.57
218	Chairmen Of The Board	58	69.4	31.62	267	Van Morrison	69	48.3	52.72
219	Melissa Manchester	84	69.0	32.02	268	Foghat	66	47.9	53.06
220	Joni Mitchell	74	68.5	32.46	269	ZZ Top	54	47.8	53.20
221	Robert Palmer	55	67.5	33.49	270	Beach Boys	85	47.4	53.61
222	Atlanta Rhythm Section	141	67.4	33.65	271	Addrisi Brothers	55	47.2	53.80
223	Engelbert Humperdinck	99	65.9	35.11	272	J. Geils Band	80	47.2	53.81
224	Heart	136	65.4	35.63	273	Dave Mason	59	46.4	54.58
225	Mark Lindsay	58	64.9	36.07	274	Tower Of Power	50	46.4	54.64
226	Jerry Reed	64	64.9	36.09	275	Poco	72	46.3	54.69
227	Five Man Electrical Band	56	63.9	37.13	276	Gene Cotton	60	46.2	54.78
228	Bette Midler	71	63.0	38.97	277	Ronnie Milsap	49	45.1	55.88
229	Jimmy Buffett	79	62.7	38.34	278	Candi Staton	97	44.6	56.44
230	Dolly Parton	77	62.1	38.92	279	Brenda & The Tabulations	34	44.4	56.65
231	Paul Davis	129	61.9	39.14	280	Nitty Gritty Dirt Band	60	43.3	57.67
232	Leon Russell	49	61.5	39.49	281	Ray Price	48	43.3	57.71
233	Betty Wright	57	61.0	40.00	282	Millie Jackson	84	42.8	58.15
234	Jethro Tull	51	61.0	40.04	283	Impressions	70	42.7	58.33
235	David Gates	68	60.6	40.35	284	First Choice	44	42.6	58.36
236	The New Seekers	61	59.6	41.43	285	Rufus Thomas	50	41.4	59.60
237	Maureen McGovern	64	58.7	42.28	286	Band	51	41.2	59.76
238	Dramatics	112	58.6	42.39	287	Delfonics	67	41.0	60.03
239	Leif Garrett	61	58.6	42.44	288	New Birth	49	39.8	61.18

	Act	Chart Wks.	Avg. Points	Avg. Rank		Act	Chart Wks.	Avg. Points	Avg. Rank
289	Detroit Emeralds	57	39.5	61.51	303	Crusaders	42	31.2	69.76
290	Independents	44	39.3	61.73	304	Emerson, Lake & Palmer	26	31.2	69.85
291	B.B. King	121	38.5	62.49	305	Smokey Robinson	91	28.9	72.07
292	Al Martino	57	36.9	64.05	306	Dennis Yost And The Classics IV	32	28.7	72.31
293	Conway Twitty	43	36.7	64.28	307	Intruders	38	28.4	72.63
294	James Gang	39	36.4	64.62	308	Tanya Tucker	29	27.4	73.59
295	Dells	78	35.9	65.13	309	Suzi Quatro	35	24.9	76.14
296	Starz	34	35.4	65.62	310	Bobby Bland	43	23.2	77.79
297	Funkadelic	44	35.3	65.70	311	Jerry Butler	55	21.5	79.51
298	Kris Kristofferson	56	35.2	65.82	312	Tim Moore	34	17.9	83.09
299	Waylon Jennings	39	33.2	67.82	313	Jackie DeShannon	25	17.8	83.16
300	Merle Haggard	33	32.6	68.42	314	Chilliwack	23	17.0	83.96
301	Ray Charles	66	32.2	68.82	315	Buddy Miles	26	16.9	84.12
302	Quincy Jones	46	31.9	69.11					

Acts Appearing on 50 or More Weekly Charts

Multiple entries in a week count once.

#	Act	Wks On	Pct. of '70s
1	Chicago	292	55.9%
2	Elton John	289	55.4%
3	Carpenters	284	54.4%
4	Jackson 5	262	50.2%
5	Elvis Presley	261	50.0%
6	Bee Gees	258	49.4%
7	Paul McCartney & Wings / Wings	248	47.5%
8	John Denver	240	46.0%
9	Helen Reddy	240	46.0%
10	Neil Diamond	240	46.0%
11	Stevie Wonder	236	45.2%
12	Earth, Wind & Fire	231	44.3%
13	Tony Orlando And Dawn	224	42.9%
14	Olivia Newton-John	224	42.9%
15	James Brown	223	42.7%
16	Gladys Knight & The Pips	219	42.0%
17	Barry Manilow	218	41.8%
18	Doobie Brothers	212	40.6%
19	Diana Ross	207	39.7%
20	Electric Light Orchestra	207	39.7%
21	Eagles	204	39.1%
22	Aretha Franklin	204	39.1%
23	Three Dog Night	199	38.1%
24	Al Green	198	37.9%
25	Isley Brothers	197	37.7%
26	Spinners	193	37.0%
27	Linda Ronstadt	191	36.6%
28	Abba	189	36.2%
29	Rod Stewart	188	36.0%
30	Temptations	188	36.0%
31	Stylistics	183	35.1%
32	War	177	33.9%
33	O'Jays	175	33.5%
34	Anne Murray	175	33.5%
35	KC & The Sunshine Band	174	33.3%
36	Commodores	172	33.0%
37	5th Dimension	171	32.8%
38	Glen Campbell	171	32.8%
39	Dr. Hook	169	32.4%
40	Grand Funk Railroad	166	31.8%
41	Rolling Stones	160	30.7%
42	Guess Who	160	30.7%
43	Donna Summer	159	30.5%
44	Barbra Streisand	159	30.5%
45	Joe Simon	159	30.5%
46	Carly Simon	158	30.3%
47	Bread	155	29.7%
48	Seals & Crofts	152	29.1%
49	Ohio Players	151	28.9%
50	Marvin Gaye	150	28.7%
51	Four Tops	149	28.5%
52	Barry White	148	28.4%
53	Cat Stevens	147	28.2%
54	Eddie Kendricks	146	28.0%
55	B.J. Thomas	146	28.0%
56	America	144	27.6%
57	James Taylor	143	27.4%
58	Captain & Tennille	142	27.2%
59	Kiss	141	27.0%
60	Steely Dan	141	27.0%
61	Cher	140	26.8%
62	Who	140	26.8%
63	Lobo	139	26.6%
64	Styx	137	26.2%
65	Johnnie Taylor	137	26.2%
66	Tavares	133	25.5%
67	Atlanta Rhythm Section	133	25.5%
68	Donny Osmond	133	25.5%
69	Paul Davis	129	24.7%
70	Staple Singers	128	24.5%
71	Fleetwood Mac	127	24.3%
72	Heart	127	24.3%
73	Queen	127	24.3%
74	Kool & The Gang	123	23.6%
75	Billy Joel	122	23.4%
76	Osmonds	122	23.4%
77	Daryl Hall & John Oates	120	23.0%
78	Little River Band	120	23.0%
79	Tyrone Davis	120	23.0%
80	David Bowie	120	23.0%
81	B.B. King	120	23.0%
82	Ringo Starr	119	22.8%
83	Eric Clapton	119	22.8%
84	Bob Seger	116	22.2%
85	Aerosmith	116	22.2%
86	Carole King	116	22.2%
87	Bachman-Turner Overdrive	115	22.0%
88	Paul Anka	115	22.0%
89	Sweet	113	21.6%
90	Billy Preston	112	21.5%
91	Dramatics	112	21.5%
92	Rufus Featuring Chaka Khan	110	21.1%
93	Main Ingredient	110	21.1%
94	Kenny Rogers	109	20.9%
95	Tom Jones	109	20.9%
96	Paul Simon	109	20.9%
97	Jim Croce	109	20.9%
98	Joe Cocker	109	20.9%
99	Charlie Rich	108	20.7%
100	England Dan & John Ford Coley	108	20.7%
101	Bill Withers	108	20.7%
102	Ray Stevens	107	20.5%
103	Gordon Lightfoot	106	20.3%
104	Harold Melvin And The Blue Notes	106	20.3%
105	Bobby Womack	106	20.3%
106	Grass Roots	105	20.1%
107	Bay City Rollers	104	19.9%
108	Mac Davis	104	19.9%
109	George Harrison	104	19.9%
110	Neil Sedaka	103	19.7%
111	Jefferson Starship	103	19.7%
112	Foreigner	102	19.5%
113	Johnny Rivers	100	19.2%
114	Firefall	100	19.2%
115	Natalie Cole	100	19.2%
116	Michael Jackson	99	19.0%
117	Bad Company	99	19.0%
118	Candi Staton	97	18.6%
119	Leo Sayer	96	18.4%
120	Peter Frampton	96	18.4%
121	Roberta Flack	96	18.4%
122	Melanie	96	18.4%
123	Andy Gibb	95	18.2%
124	Supremes	95	18.2%
125	Chi-Lites	95	18.2%
126	Wilson Pickett	95	18.2%
127	Partridge Family	94	18.0%
128	Kansas	94	18.0%
129	Hot Chocolate	94	18.0%
130	10cc	94	18.0%
131	Donny And Marie Osmond	94	18.0%
132	Engelbert Humperdinck	94	18.0%
133	Nilsson	93	17.8%
134	Bob Dylan	93	17.8%
135	Pointer Sisters	92	17.6%
136	Alice Cooper (Group)	92	17.6%
137	Santana	92	17.6%
138	Frankie Valli	91	17.4%
139	Todd Rundgren	91	17.4%
140	Bobby Vinton	91	17.4%
141	Smokey Robinson	91	17.4%
142	Eric Carmen	90	17.2%
143	Pablo Cruise	89	17.0%
144	Alice Cooper (Solo)	89	17.0%
145	Sly & The Family Stone	87	16.7%
146	Chic	86	16.5%
147	Rare Earth	86	16.5%

Act	Wks On	Pct. of '70s
148 Sylvers	86	16.5%
149 Yvonne Elliman	85	16.3%
150 Gilbert O'Sullivan	84	16.1%
151 Manhattans	84	16.1%
152 Millie Jackson	84	16.1%
153 Jackson Browne	82	15.7%
154 Melissa Manchester	81	15.5%
155 Lynyrd Skynyrd	81	15.5%
156 Curtis Mayfield	81	15.5%
157 Dionne Warwick	81	15.5%
158 Tommy James	80	15.3%
159 J. Geils Band	80	15.3%
160 Rita Coolidge	79	15.1%
161 Bobby Sherman	79	15.1%
162 Jim Stafford	79	15.1%
163 Jimmy Buffett	79	15.1%
164 Boston	78	14.9%
165 Led Zeppelin	78	14.9%
166 Moody Blues	78	14.9%
167 Dells	78	14.9%
168 Steve Miller Band	77	14.8%
169 Boz Scaggs	77	14.8%
170 Dolly Parton	76	14.6%
171 Crystal Gayle	76	14.6%
172 Hollies	76	14.6%
173 Beach Boys	75	14.4%
174 Brownsville Station	75	14.4%
175 Eddie Money	74	14.2%
176 Raspberries	74	14.2%
177 Orleans	74	14.2%
178 Harry Chapin	74	14.2%
179 Joni Mitchell	74	14.2%
180 Loggins & Messina	74	14.2%
181 Art Garfunkel	74	14.2%
182 Donna Fargo	73	14.0%
183 Isaac Hayes	73	14.0%
184 Emotions	72	13.8%
185 Albert Hammond	72	13.8%
186 Creedence Clearwater Revival	72	13.8%
187 Gerry Rafferty	71	13.6%
188 Poco	71	13.6%
189 Lou Rawls	71	13.6%
190 George Benson	71	13.6%
191 Bette Midler	71	13.6%
192 Smokey Robinson & The Miracles	71	13.6%
193 Trammps	70	13.4%
194 Luther Ingram	70	13.4%
195 Impressions	70	13.4%
196 Cornelius Brothers & Sister Rose	69	13.2%
197 Hamilton, Joe Frank & Reynolds	69	13.2%
198 Van Morrison	69	13.2%
199 Rose Royce	68	13.0%
200 David Gates	68	13.0%
201 Wet Willie	68	13.0%
202 Ike & Tina Turner	68	13.0%
203 Supertramp	67	12.8%
204 Delfonics	67	12.8%
205 Average White Band / AWB	66	12.6%
206 Cheech & Chong	66	12.6%
207 Foghat	66	12.6%
208 Clarence Carter	66	12.6%
209 Ray Charles	66	12.6%
210 Bloodstone	65	12.5%
211 Judy Collins	65	12.5%
212 Starbuck	64	12.3%
213 Jerry Reed	64	12.3%
214 Cars	64	12.3%
215 Johnny Nash	64	12.3%
216 Maureen McGovern	64	12.3%
217 Freddy Fender	63	12.1%
218 Bob Welch	63	12.1%
219 Stephen Bishop	63	12.1%
220 L.T.D.	63	12.1%
221 Village People	62	11.9%
222 Heatwave	61	11.7%
223 Robert John	61	11.7%
224 Freda Payne	61	11.7%
225 Gloria Gaynor	61	11.7%
226 New Seekers	61	11.7%
227 Maxine Nightingale	60	11.5%
228 Nitty Gritty Dirt Band	60	11.5%
229 Gene Cotton	60	11.5%
230 B.T. Express	59	11.3%
231 Raiders	59	11.3%
232 Leif Garrett	59	11.3%
233 Badfinger	59	11.3%
234 Moments	59	11.3%
235 Player	58	11.1%
236 Andy Kim	58	11.1%
237 Dave Mason	58	11.1%
238 Kinks	58	11.1%
239 Ronnie Dyson	58	11.1%
240 Chairmen Of The Board	58	11.1%
241 Steppenwolf	58	11.1%
242 Neil Young	57	10.9%
243 Detroit Emeralds	57	10.9%
244 Betty Wright	57	10.9%
245 Marilyn McCoo & Billy Davis Jr.	56	10.7%
246 Al Wilson	56	10.7%
247 Redbone	56	10.7%
248 Five Man Electrical Band	56	10.7%
249 Kris Kristofferson	56	10.7%
250 Al Stewart	55	10.5%
251 Ambrosia	55	10.5%
252 Robert Palmer	55	10.5%
253 Addrisi Brothers	55	10.5%
254 Honey Cone	55	10.5%
255 Jerry Butler	55	10.5%
256 Babys	54	10.3%
257 Gallery	54	10.3%
258 ZZ Top	54	10.3%
259 Miracles	53	10.2%
260 Tommy Roe	53	10.2%
261 Mark Lindsay	53	10.2%
262 Jennifer Warnes	52	10.0%
263 Marshall Tucker Band	52	10.0%
264 Ozark Mountain Daredevils	52	10.0%
265 Shaun Cassidy	51	9.8%
266 John Travolta	51	9.8%
267 Journey	51	9.8%
268 Simon & Garfunkel	51	9.8%
269 Blood, Sweat & Tears	51	9.8%
270 Jethro Tull	51	9.8%
271 Bobby Goldsboro	51	9.8%
272 Steve Miller	50	9.6%
273 Michael Johnson	50	9.6%
274 Stories	50	9.6%
275 Raydio	50	9.6%
276 Andrew Gold	50	9.6%
277 Michael Murphey	50	9.6%
278 Al Martino	50	9.6%
279 Rufus Thomas	50	9.6%
280 Tower Of Power	50	9.6%

Acts with 50 or More Consecutive Chart Weeks

A general late '70s increase in a song's chart stay coupled with fewer song entries relative to the early '70s gives an advantage to acts from late in the decade.

	Act	Hits in Streak	Streak Weeks	Streak Began:	Streak Ended:
1	Andy Gibb	5	95	23-Apr-77	10-Feb-79
2	Al Green	8	92	31-Jul-71	28-Apr-73
3	Donna Summer	6	86	13-May-78	29-Dec-79+
4	Billy Joel	7	86	12-Nov-77	30-Jun-79
5	Gladys Knight & The Pips	8	82	20-Jan-73	10-Aug-74
6	Abba	5	81	21-Feb-76	3-Sep-77
7	Daryl Hall & John Oates	6	80	14-Feb-76	20-Aug-77
8	Captain & Tennille	5	72	26-Apr-75	4-Sep-76
9	Kiss	7	63	28-Aug-76	5-Nov-77
10	Heatwave	3	61	9-Jul-77	2-Sep-78
11	Barry Manilow	5	59	4-Feb-78	17-Mar-79
12	Leo Sayer	4	59	16-Oct-76	26-Nov-77
13	Kenny Rogers	3	59	18-Nov-78	29-Dec-79+
14	Village People	4	56	24-Jun-78	14-Jul-79
15	Fleetwood Mac	4	55	8-Jan-77	21-Jan-78
16	Chic	3	54	28-Oct-78	3-Nov-79
17	James Brown	9	53	26-Dec-70	25-Dec-71
18	Barry Manilow*	3	53	18-Sep-76	17-Sep-77
19	Steely Dan	4	52	26-Nov-77	18-Nov-78
20	Eagles	3	51	31-May-75	15-May-76
21	Steve Miller (Solo)	3	50	8-May-76	16-Apr-77

Notes:

Donna Summer and Kenny Rogers (+) had streaks in progress at decade's end. Summer's streak extended 18 weeks into 1980, and Rogers' 12 weeks into 1980.

Barry Manilow (*) put together two streaks for this list.

Andy Gibb, Heatwave and Steve Miller strung all their charted records as one streak.

If not for one off week, Leo Sayer's streak would have been 71.

No. 1s by Act

Act	No. 1s	Wks No. 1
Bee Gees	8	25
Stevie Wonder	8	9
Paul McCartney & Wings / Wings	7	13
Elton John	7	9
Jackson 5	7	9
Three Dog Night	5	11
Carpenters	5	6
John Denver	5	5
KC & The Sunshine Band	4	7
Tony Orlando And Dawn	4	7
Helen Reddy	4	5
Diana Ross	4	4
Ringo Starr	4	4
Rod Stewart	3	13
Andy Gibb	3	10
Donna Summer	3	9
Roberta Flack	3	8
Commodores	3	6
Olivia Newton-John	3	4
Billy Preston	3	3
Eagles	3	3
Marvin Gaye	3	3
Michael Jackson	3	3
Temptations	3	3
Chic	2	8
Beatles	2	6
George Harrison	2	6
Carole King	2	5
Simon & Garfunkel	2	5
Sly & The Family Stone	2	5
Barbra Streisand	2	4
Leo Sayer	2	4
Partridge Family	2	4
Paul Simon	2	4
Al Green	2	3
B.J. Thomas	2	3
Captain & Tennille	2	3
Cher	2	3
Neil Sedaka	2	3
Rolling Stones	2	3
Staple Singers	2	3
Barry Manilow	2	2
Barry White	2	2
Chicago	2	2
Eddie Kendricks	2	2
Fleetwood Mac	2	2
Frankie Valli	2	2
Gladys Knight & The Pips	2	2
Glen Campbell	2	2
Gordon Lightfoot	2	2
Grand Funk Railroad	2	2
Hamilton, Joe Frank & Reynolds	2	2
Jim Croce	2	2
Linda Ronstadt	2	2
Neil Diamond	2	2
O'Jays	2	2
Ray Stevens	2	2
Silver Convention	2	2
Spinners	2	2
Debby Boone	1	8
The Knack	1	6
Don McLean	1	4
Osmonds	1	4
Peaches & Herb	1	4
Starland Vocal Band	1	4
A Taste Of Honey	1	3
America	1	3
Anita Ward	1	3
Barbra & Neil	1	3
C.W. McCall	1	3
Elton John and Kiki Dee	1	3
Emotions	1	3
Gilbert O'Sullivan	1	3
Mary MacGregor	1	3
Nick Gilder	1	3
Rupert Holmes	1	3
Shocking Blue	1	3
Styx	1	3
Bill Withers	1	2
Billy Paul	1	2
Carly Simon	1	2
Charlie Rich	1	2
Chuck Berry	1	2
Crystal Gayle	1	2
Daryl Hall & John Oates	1	2
Doobie Brothers	1	2
Edwin Starr	1	2
Elton John Band	1	2
Exile	1	2
Gerry Rafferty	1	2
Guess Who	1	2
Herb Alpert	1	2
Honey Cone	1	2
Isaac Hayes	1	2
John Sebastian	1	2
Johnnie Taylor	1	2
Manhattans	1	2
Marilyn McCoo & Billy Davis Jr.	1	2
Meco	1	2
Melanie	1	2
MFSB	1	2
Nilsson	1	2
Norman Greenbaum	1	2
Ozark Mountain Daredevils	1	2
Player	1	2
Rick Dees & His Cast Of Idiots	1	2
Robert John	1	2
Rose Royce	1	2
Shaun Cassidy	1	2
Terry Jacks	1	2
Wild Cherry	1	2
"Deliverance" Soundtrack	1	1
Abba	1	1
Ace	1	1
Al Wilson	1	1
Alan O'Day	1	1
Allman Brothers Band	1	1
Amii Stewart	1	1
Andy Kim	1	1
Aretha Franklin	1	1
Average White Band / AWB	1	1
Bachman-Turner Overdrive	1	1
Bad Company	1	1
Barbra Streisand/Donna Summer	1	1
Bay City Rollers	1	1
Bellamy Brothers	1	1
Bill Conti	1	1
Billy Swan	1	1
Blondie	1	1
Blue Swede	1	1
Bo Donaldson And The Heywoods	1	1
Boz Scaggs	1	1
Bread	1	1
Byron Mac Gregor	1	1
Carl Douglas	1	1
Chi-Lites	1	1
Clarence Carter	1	1
Climax	1	1
Cornelius Brothers & Sister Rose	1	1
Creedence Clearwater Revival	1	1
David Bowie	1	1
David Essex	1	1
David Geddes	1	1
David Soul	1	1
DeFranco Family	1	1
Dickie Goodman	1	1
Dionne Warwicke & Spinners	1	1
Donny Osmond	1	1
Dr. Hook	1	1
Earth, Wind & Fire	1	1
Edgar Winter Group	1	1
Elvis Presley	1	1
Eric Burdon And War	1	1
Eric Carmen	1	1
Eric Clapton	1	1
Four Seasons	1	1
Four Tops	1	1

Act	No. 1s	Wks No. 1
Freddy Fender	1	1
Gallery	1	1
Gary Wright	1	1
George McCrae	1	1
Gloria Gaynor	1	1
Harry Chapin	1	1
Hollies	1	1
Hues Corporation	1	1
Hurricane Smith	1	1
James Taylor	1	1
Janis Ian	1	1
John Lennon/Plastic Ono Band	1	1
Johnny Nash	1	1
Labelle	1	1
Lobo	1	1
Looking Glass	1	1
Love Unlimited Orchestra	1	1
Lynn Anderson	1	1
Mac Davis	1	1
Main Ingredient	1	1
Manfred Mann's Earth Band	1	1
Marvin Hamlisch	1	1
Maxine Nightingale	1	1
Minnie Riperton	1	1
Miracles	1	1
Moody Blues	1	1
Neil Young	1	1
Ohio Players	1	1
Paper Lace	1	1
Paul & Linda McCartney	1	1
Paul Anka	1	1
Peter Frampton	1	1
R. Dean Taylor	1	1
Raiders	1	1
Randy Newman	1	1
Rhythm Heritage	1	1
Rita Coolidge	1	1
Rufus Featuring Chaka Khan	1	1
Samantha Sang	1	1
Sammy Davis, Jr.	1	1
Smokey Robinson & The Miracles	1	1
Steve Miller	1	1
Steve Miller Band	1	1
Stories	1	1
Stylistics	1	1
Sylvers	1	1
Three Degrees	1	1
Tom Jones	1	1
Undisputed Truth	1	1
Van McCoy	1	1
Vicki Lawrence	1	1
Walter Murphy And The Big Apple Band	1	1
Wayne Newton	1	1
Yvonne Elliman	1	1

Two-Sided Winners

Here you will find two lists, the first consisting of sixty-nine records whose A and B sides charted independently of each other, arranged chronologically by Peak Date. The second, shorter list consists of seven records whose two sides charted in any one of three combinations: 1) A/B, 2) A/B and A alongside B, 3) A/B and A *without* B.

Independently Charting A and B Sides

Act	A	Peak Rank	Peak Date	B	Peak Rank	Peak Date
Sly & The Family Stone	Thank You (Falettinme Be Mice Elf Agin)	1	21-Feb-70	Everybody Is A Star	40	7-Feb-70
5th Dimension	The Declaration	66	28-Feb-70	A Change Is Gonna Come/ People Gotta Be Free	84	14-Mar-70
Creedence Clearwater Revival	Travelin' Band	5	14-Mar-70	Who'll Stop The Rain	13	7-Mar-70
Doors	You Make Me Real	40	9-May-70	Roadhouse Blues	76	16-May-70
Guess Who	American Woman	1	16-May-70	No Sugar Tonight	39	18-Apr-70
Creedence Clearwater Revival	Up Around The Bend	2	30-May-70	Run Through The Jungle	48	2-May-70
Beatles	The Long And Winding Road	1	13-Jun-70	For You Blue	71	23-May-70
Wilson Pickett	Sugar Sugar	16	27-Jun-70	Cole, Cooke And Redding	61	18-Apr-70
Elvis Presley	The Wonder Of You	10	4-Jul-70	Mama Liked The Roses	65	16-May-70
Five Stairsteps	O-o-h Child	4	1-Aug-70	Dear Prudence	69	18-Apr-70
Crow	Cottage Cheese	66	15-Aug-70	Slow Down	94	4-Apr-70
Elvis Presley	I've Lost You	18	5-Sep-70	The Next Step Is Love	30	19-Sep-70
Creedence Clearwater Revival	Lookin' Out My Back Door	1	3-Oct-70	Long As I Can See The Light	57	22-Aug-70
Temptations	Ungena Za Ulimwengu (Unite The World)	30	24-Oct-70	Hum Along And Dance	88	7-Nov-70
George Harrison	My Sweet Lord	1	19-Dec-70	Isn't It A Pity	46	12-Dec-70
Linda Ronstadt	The Long Way Around	74	23-Jan-71	(She's A) Very Lovely Woman	94	13-Feb-71
Elvis Presley	I Really Don't Want To Know	13	6-Feb-71	There Goes My Everything	57	2-Jan-71
Elvis Presley	Where Did They Go, Lord	34	10-Apr-71	Rags To Riches	45	27-Mar-71
Neil Diamond	I Am...I Said	4	24-Apr-71	Done Too Soon	69	12-Jun-71
Paul McCartney	Another Day	6	1-May-71	Oh Woman Oh Why	55	13-Mar-71
Aretha Franklin	Bridge Over Troubled Water	2	29-May-71	Brand New Me	72	26-Jun-71
Guess Who	Albert Flasher	35	26-Jun-71	Broken	77	24-Apr-71
Tom Jones	Puppet Man	14	26-Jun-71	Resurrection Shuffle	40	24-Jul-71
Joe Cocker	High Time We Went	29	3-Jul-71	Black-Eyed Blues	100	17-Jul-71
Lobo	She Didn't Do Magic	44	7-Aug-71	I'm The Only One	76	26-Jun-71
Chicago	Beginnings	11	21-Aug-71	Colour My World	75	17-Jul-71
Poppy Family	Where Evil Grows	50	2-Oct-71	I Was Wondering	90	10-Apr-71
Rod Stewart	Maggie May	1	9-Oct-71	Reason To Believe	80	4-Sep-71
Chicago	Questions 67 And 68	13	27-Nov-71	I'm A Man	67	30-Oct-71
Aretha Franklin	Rock Steady	7	11-Dec-71	Oh Me Oh My (I'm A Fool For You Baby)	70	29-Jan-72
Donny Osmond	Hey Girl	9	1-Jan-72	I Knew You When	83	4-Dec-71
Isaac Hayes	Let's Stay Together	45	15-Apr-72	Soulsville	94	6-May-72
Luther Ingram	You Were Made For Me	57	29-Apr-72	Missing You	72	19-Feb-72
Billy Preston	Outa-Space	1	8-Jul-72	I Wrote A Simple Song	96	12-Feb-72
Jackie Deshannon	Vanilla Olay	95	15-Jul-72	Only Love Can Break A Heart	96	2-Sep-72
Wings	Mary Had A Little lamb	48	15-Jul-72	Little Woman Love	95	22-Jul-72
Rolling Stones	Happy	14	26-Aug-72	All Down The Line	77	29-Jul-72

Act	A	Peak Rank	Peak Date	B	Peak Rank	Peak Date
Joe Cocker	Midnight Rider	31	21-Oct-72	Woman To Woman	52	13-Jan-73
Spinners	I'll Be Around	1	25-Nov-72	How Could I Let You Get Away	89	26-Aug-72
Joe Simon	Trouble In My Home	69	23-Dec-72	I Found My Dad	74	11-Nov-72
Rita Coolidge	My Crew	87	13-Jan-73	Fever	90	27-Jan-73
Bobby Womack & Peace	Harry Hippie	25	17-Feb-73	Sweet Caroline	42	14-Oct-72
Elvis Presley	Steamroller Blues	10	2-Jun-73	Fool	79	19-May-73
Clarence Carter	Sixty Minute Man	51	25-Aug-73	Mother-In-Law	66	23-Jun-73
Carole King	Believe In Humanity	24	1-Sep-73	You Light Up My Life	62	4-Aug-73
Donny Osmond	A Million To One	28	22-Sep-73	Young Love	41	18-Aug-73
Donny Osmond	Are You Lonesome Tonight	16	26-Jan-74	When I Fall In Love	73	15-Dec-73
Elvis Presley	I've Got A Thing About You Baby	30	16-Mar-74	Take Good Care Of Her	63	16-Feb-74
James Brown	Coldblooded	78	28-Dec-74	Funky President (People It's Bad)	87	16-Nov-74
Paul McCartney & Wings	Junior's Farm	4	4-Jan-75	Sally G	49	15-Feb-75
Guess Who	Dancin' Fool	24	11-Jan-75	Seems Like I Can't Live With You, But I Can't Live Without You	88	24-May-75
George McCrae	I Get Lifted	54	8-Mar-75	I Can't Leave You Alone	58	16-Nov-74
Odia Coates	Showdown	62	5-Apr-75	Don't Leave Me In The Morning	80	10-May-75
Bobby Vinton	Beer Barrel Polka	45	26-Apr-75	Dick And Jane	87	1-Mar-75
Linda Ronstadt	When Will I Be Loved	1	21-Jun-75	It Doesn't Matter Anymore	80	16-Aug-75
Jessi Colter	You Ain't Never Been Loved (Like I'm Gonna Love You)	56	27-Sep-75	What's Happened To Blue Eyes	78	8-Nov-75
John Denver	I'm Sorry	1	11-Oct-75	Calypso	26	22-Nov-75
B.T. Express	Peace Pipe	40	15-Nov-75	Give It What You Got	46	13-Sep-75
Linda Ronstadt	Heat Wave	4	15-Nov-75	Love Is A Rose	70	20-Sep-75
Olivia Newton-John	Let It Shine	28	17-Jan-76	He Ain't Heavy…He's My Brother	80	29-Nov-75
Conway Twitty	Don't Cry Joni	51	17-Jan-76	Touch The Hand	75	12-Jul-75
Elton John	Grow Some Funk Of Your Own	9	28-Feb-76	I Feel Like A Bullet (In The Gun Of Robert Ford)	18	6-Mar-76
Rolling Stones	Fool To Cry	9	12-Jun-76	Hot Stuff	60	21-Aug-76
Helen Reddy	I Can't Hear You No More	41	4-Sep-76	Music Is My Life	75	28-Aug-76
Klaatu	Sub-Rosa Subway	57	30-Apr-77	Calling Occupants	91	2-Apr-77
KC & The Sunshine Band	I'm Your Boogie Man	1	4-Jun-77	Wrap Your Arms Around Me	80	24-Dec-77
Lenny Le Blanc	Hound Dog Man (Play It Again)	56	1-Oct-77	Sharing The Night Together	99	12-Jun-76
Eric Clapton	Promises	11	13-Jan-79	Watch Out For Lucy	45	31-Mar-79
Styx	Renegade	18	26-May-79	Sing For The Day	41	17-Feb-79

Notes:

Don't Cry Now/Rubberneckin' by Elvis Presley would have qualified but Rubberneckin' peaked outside the '70s.

Assigning points for these sides for their ranking in Section 1 is described in "The Scoring System Explained."

Records Charting as A/B Only (3) or as A/B and Independent Sides (4)

A/B Only is indicated by two DNC (Did Not Chart); A/B + Independent is indicated by 0 or 1 DNC. Titles are ordered chronologically by Peak Date.

Act	A/B	Peak Rank	Peak Date	A	Peak Rank	Peak Date	B	Peak Rank	Peak Date
Five Stairsteps	Because I Love You// America/Standing	71	24-Oct-70	DNC			DNC		
Kiss	Detroit Rock City// Beth	25	25-Sep-76	Beth	7	13-Nov-76	Detroit Rock City	94	28-Aug-76
Wings	Girls' School// Mull Of Kintyre	31	31-Dec-77	Girls' School	38	17-Dec-77	DNC		
Elvis Costello	Watching The Detectives//Alison	61	8-Apr-78	DNC			DNC		
Jackson Browne	Stay// The Loadout	22	12-Aug-78	Stay	58	24-Jun-78	DNC		
Queen	Bicycle Race// Fat Bottomed Girls	18	30-Dec-78	DNC			DNC		
Abba	Voulez-Vous// Angeleyes	85	8-Sep-79	Voulez-Vous	86	1-Sep-79	Angeleyes	76	13-Oct-79

Record Labels of the '70s
Labels with Four or More Charting Singles

Label	Count	Label	Count	Label	Count
Columbia	372	Janus	20	Neighborhood	7
Capitol	267	Sussex	20	Paramount	7
Atlantic	219	T.K.	20	Philips	7
A&M	200	Hot Wax	19	Roadshow	7
Warner Bros.	196	Invictus	19	Scotti Brothers	7
RCA Victor	180	Rocket/MCA	19	Vanguard	7
Epic	144	Bearsville	18	Dunhill/ABC	6
United Artists	124	Brunswick	18	Evolution	6
ABC	119	De-Lite	18	Glades	6
Elektra	107	Shelter	18	Jet	6
Mercury	107	Volt	17	Lifesong	6
MCA	101	Cotillion	16	Mega	6
Motown	101	Island	16	Parachute	6
Arista	82	Metromedia	16	People	6
Polydor	82	Barnaby	15	Polydor/Kolob	6
Bell	80	Fame	15	Roxbury	6
Asylum	77	Rare Earth	15	Threshold	6
MGM	77	Dakar	14	20th Century Fox	5
Tamla	76	Kirshner	14	ABC/Blue Thumb	5
Atco	70	Liberty	14	Amherst	5
Dunhill	69	Rolling Stones	14	Avco Embassy	5
Big Tree	64	Mushroom	13	Cleveland Int'l/Epic	5
20th Century	62	Cadet	12	Lionel	5
Casablanca	60	Colossus	12	MGM South	5
Apple	59	King	12	Rocky Road	5
Buddah	58	Mums	12	Salsoul	5
Reprise	58	Philly Groove	12	Sound Stage	5
RSO	58	Sire	12	Top & Bottom	5
RCA	48	ABC/Dot	11	Track/MCA	5
Stax	47	Dot	11	UK	5
Philadelphia Int'l	46	Enterprise	11	Amaret	4
Private Stock	41	Infinity	11	ARC	4
Gordy	37	Kapp	11	Blue Sky	4
London	34	KoKo	11	Chess	4
Uni	30	Stang	11	Chimneyville	4
Parrot	29	Swan Song	11	Dark Horse	4
Capricorn	28	Alston	10	Dial	4
Ariola America	27	Blue Thumb	10	Drive	4
Chrysalis	27	EMI America	10	Duke	4
Decca	27	Grunt	10	Entrance	4
Spring	27	Midland Int'l	10	Event	4
Kama Sutra	26	Deram	9	GSF	4
Roulette	26	GRC	9	Imperial	4
Fantasy	25	Harvest	9	Kudu	4
Westbound	25	MAM	9	Lizard	4
Avco	24	Monument	9	Mainstream	4
Hi	24	Portrait	9	Mankind	4
Ode	24	Playboy	8	Musicor	4
Scepter	24	Steed	8	Planet	4
T-Neck	24	Wand	8	Plantation	4
Bang	23	ABC/TRC	7	Pye	4
Curtom	23	Brother/Reprise	7	Rainy Wednesday	4
Chelsea	21	EMI	7	Sunflower	4
Soul	21	Gamble	7	Tangerine	4
Warner/Curb	21	Haven	7	Whitfield	4
		Millennium	7	Windsong	4

About The Authors

DANN ISBELL has been fascinated by the charting of pop music and its ties to popular culture for more than fifty years. Born and raised in Southern California, Dann has spent his past thirty-five years in Taiwan where he teaches in the Department of English at National Central University. He is the author of the book, *Ranking the '60s: A Comprehensive Listing of the Top Songs and Acts from Pop's Golden Decade*.

BILL CARROLL is Adjunct Professor of Chemistry at Indiana University, Bloomington, IN, and a past president and past Board chair of the American Chemical Society. Thirty-six years after his doctorate and an industrial career that included numerous scientific publications, he returned to his first love: popular music, the charts and Top 40 radio, using physical science data handling techniques to create music chart analytics.

www.ingramcontent.com/pod-product-compliance
Lightning Source LLC
Chambersburg PA
CBHW082104230426
43671CB00015B/2606